Fowler's

Concise Dictionary of Modern English Usage

THIRD EDITION

T0058351

Jeremy Butterfield is a freelance lexicographer, language expert and writer, and an OUP author. For many years he worked in senior editorial positions in Collins English and Bilingual Dictionaries. He is also the author of the popular book on the English language, *Damp Squid: The English Language Laid Bare* (2009), as well as the *Oxford A–Z of English Usage* (2013). Jeremy is the editor of the fourth edition of the renowned *Fowlers Dictionary of Modern English Usage* (2015).

The most authoritative and up-to-date reference books for both students and the general reader.

Many of these titles are also available online at www.oxfordreference.com

Fowler's

Concise
Dictionary
of Modern
English Usage

THIRD EDITION

Edited by JEREMY BUTTERFIELD

OXFORD
UNIVERSITY PRESS

OXFORD
UNIVERSITY PRESS

Great Clarendon Street, Oxford, OX2 6DP,
United Kingdom

Oxford University Press is a department of the University of Oxford.
It furthers the University's objective of excellence in research, scholarship,
and education by publishing worldwide. Oxford is a registered trade mark of
Oxford University Press in the UK and in certain other countries

© Oxford University Press 1999, 2008, 2016

The moral rights of the author have been asserted

First published 1999
First published as an Oxford University Press paperback 2002
Second edition published 2008
Third edition published 2016

Published in the United States of America by Oxford University Press
198 Madison Avenue, New York, NY 10016, United States of America

British Library Cataloguing in Publication Data
Data available

Library of Congress Control Number: 2014945276

ISBN 978-0-19-966631-7
ebook ISBN 978-0-19-106230-8

Printed in Great Britain by
Clays Ltd, Elcograf S. p. A

Preface to the Third Edition

Fowler's Concise Dictionary of Modern English Usage gives readers accessible guidance on the best use of today's English. It offers over 4,500 succinct, reasoned entries with detailed explanations and clear recommendations that help you to express yourself in a way that is both up to date and correct. An abridged version of the most celebrated book ever published on English usage, *Fowler's Modern English Usage*, it condenses the wealth of information in that book for the benefit of readers who need speedy access to authoritative guidance.

Fowler's Concise Dictionary answers the whole range of queries posed by people striving to write correct, current English. It includes guidance on tricky points of grammar (whether to use *which* or *that*, *everyone* followed by plural pronouns), spelling (*co-, fulfil, idiosyncrasy*), punctuation (*semicolon, comma*), syntax (*bored with* or *by, data*, singular or plural), style (*clichés, iconic*), and appropriate word choice (*classic / classical, confusable words*).

Hundreds of authentic examples drawn from the unique resources available to Oxford University Press illustrate the points under discussion. Chief among those resources is the *Oxford English Corpus* (abbreviated in the text to *OEC*), a database of written and spoken twenty-first century English from all over the world. It contains two and a half billion words of texts, and covers the whole gamut of English writing styles from literary novels and specialist journals to everyday newspapers and magazines, blogs, emails, and social media. Downloaded largely from Internet websites, these texts provide comprehensive evidence about how English is used (and misused) at all levels of formality throughout the English-speaking world.

When crucial information can be presented most clearly in table form, entries are given a special layout. These entries are of several kinds. Some provide information on interesting aspects of English, such as *American English, dialect, misquotations*; some summarize and list points that recur throughout the book, such as *gender-neutrality* or *Latin plurals;* others, such as *mute e* and *-able, -ible*, provide general rules to help unravel the complexities of English spelling.

This book is an updated version of Robert Allen's 2008 *Pocket Fowler's Modern English Usage*, which was a cut-down of *Fowler's Modern English Usage*. The present text adds around 200 new entries to the *Pocket*. All existing entries were reviewed, and those that required bringing up to date or further clarification were edited accordingly. A few entries seemed no longer relevant and have been dropped. In their place are the new entries, among which the reader will find words reflecting changes in communication since 2008, such as *hashtag, phablet, selfie, tweet, unfriend, unfollow, viral,* and *wilfing*.

Several new entries discuss mistakes which, though themselves not new, have become more widespread: *obtuse* used to mean *abstruse*, 🞩 *alot* spelt as one word, 🞩 *baited breath* for *bated breath*, 🞩 *eminent danger* for *imminent danger*. (The 🞩 symbol throughout the book indicates an incorrect or unacceptable use.) Other new entries discuss the clichés and euphemisms that continue to thrive in certain kinds of discourse, e.g. *address* (verb), *best practice, challenging, collateral damage, community, defining moment, steep learning curve*.

Vogue words come and go, and those added to this volume include *achingly, angsty, best practice, closure, reference* (verb), and *passionate*. Retained from the earlier text is *iconic*, which Robert Allen described as 'a word that appears to have become all of a sudden as indispensable as it is meaningless in practically every paragraph of popular journalism'.

Apart from checking in the *Oxford English Corpus*, and also in American corpora (*corpora* is the standard plural of *corpus*), I have also benefited from being able to consult the *Oxford English Dictionary* (*OED*), now constantly edited in electronic form, and

Oxford Dictionaries Online, as well as the invaluable *Oxford Dictionary for Writers and Editors*. I have used such sources to review and revise the rulings on preferred spellings (as an example, *fetus* now predominates almost universally over *foetus*).

Donald Watt and Penny Trumble copy-edited and proofread my changes, and through their efforts considerably improved the text, for which I am most grateful. My thanks go also to the commissioning team of Rebecca Lane and Joanna Harris, and to Clare Jones and Cornelia Haase in the production team, who dealt with the publication of this book with their usual cheerfulness and efficiency.

JEREMY BUTTERFIELD

Dunblane 2015

Abbreviations

Abbreviations, other than the standard ones, have been restricted to a handful of frequently occurring items:

AmE	American English
AusE	Australian English
BrE	British English
c	century (19c = 19th century, and so on)
CanE	Canadian English
IndE	Indian English
IrishE	Irish English
ME	Middle English (from 1150 to 1500)
NewZE	New Zealand English
OE	Old English (up to 1150)
SAfrE	South African English

The following bibliographical references are used:

COD	*Concise Oxford Dictionary*, usually the eleventh edition (2006)
Fowler (1926)	H.W. Fowler, *A Dictionary of Modern English Usage* (1926)
Fowlers (1906)	H.W. and F.G. Fowler, *The King's English* (1906; a second edition was published in 1907 and a third in 1931)
Gowers (1965)	Sir Ernest Gowers, *A Dictionary of Modern English Usage* (second edition, 1965)
MWCDEU	*Merriam-Webster Concise Dictionary of English Usage* (2002)
NODWE	*New Oxford Dictionary for Writers and Editors* (2005)
ODO	*Oxford Dictionary Online*
OEC	*Oxford English Corpus*
OED	*Oxford English Dictionary*
OED2	*Oxford English Dictionary*, second edition (1989)
SOED	*Shorter Oxford English Dictionary*, usually the sixth edition (2007)

The symbol ✖ is used to show uses that are regarded as incorrect or unacceptable.

Within an entry, an asterisk in front of a word cross-refers the reader to other headwords that contain helpful supplementary information: **can** *verb*. the verb *can* is classed among the *modal verbs . . .

Phonetic transcriptions

The letters used to indicate pronunciations are those of the ordinary English alphabet with their normal values. The following special cases should be mentioned:

uh	the indeterminate sound as in *garden* and *porter*
ah	as in *dark*
aw	as in *awful* and *born*
dh	as in *this*
iy	as in *ice*
oh	as in *bone*
oo	as in *boot*
oo-uh	as in *sure*
ow	as in *cow*
uu	as in *book*
kh	as in *loch*
zh	as in *measure*

Primary stress is indicated by bold type, e.g. the noun *project* is given as **proj**-ekt, and the verb as pruh-**jekt**.

Glossary

The principal grammatical terms used in this book are as follows. Further information on some of them, and on other terms, can be found in the main text:

active voice   the form of a verb in which the subject performs the action and the object (if there is one) is affected by the action (*The house **stands** on a corner* / *France **beat** Brazil in the final*). See also PASSIVE VOICE

adjective   a word that describes another word, usually a noun or pronoun (*the **green** door* / *The weather was **pleasant*** / *She is **French***)

adverb   a word that qualifies a verb (*She speaks **softly***), an adjective (***rather** nice*), or another adverb (***very** quickly*)

attributive   denoting an adjective or noun that is put before another word, normally a noun, to qualify or describe it in some way (***brown** shoes* / ***table** lamp*)

clause   a group of words normally containing a verb and its subject. A main clause makes sense by itself and can constitute an entire sentence, e.g. *The train arrives at 6 o'clock.* A subordinate clause is one that qualifies a main clause, e.g. *The train arrives at 6 o'clock **if it is running on time***

conjunction   a word used to join words, phrases, and sentences, such as *and*, *but*, and *if*

countable nouns   nouns that form plurals, e.g. *ship*, *crisis*, *fellow-traveller*, *kindness* (= a kind act). See also MASS NOUNS and UNCOUNTABLE NOUNS

determiner   a word that goes before a noun and determines its status in some way, such as *a*, *the*, *this*, *all*, and *such*

diphthong   a vowel in which the sound changes within a syllable, as in *coin*, *day*, *deer*, *loud*, *pain*, *wear*, etc.

infinitive   the simplest uninflected form of a verb (*come*, *make*, *try*, etc.), and the form that appears as the headword in dictionaries. A *to*-infinitive is this form preceded by *to*: *I want **to go** to the library*

inflection   the change in the form of a word to indicate a change in its grammatical role, e.g. from singular to plural in nouns (*book* / *books*, *church* / *churches*) and from present tense to past tense in verbs (*want* / *wanted*, *make* / *made*)

interjection   an exclamation such as *ah*, *gosh*, and *whoops* (often printed with an exclamation mark)

intransitive   denoting a verb that does not take an object (*We **arrived** at noon*)

main clause   *see* CLAUSE

mass nouns   nouns which form plurals with the meaning 'a type of ...' or 'a quantity of ...', e.g. *bread*, *medicine*, *wine*. See also COUNTABLE NOUNS and UNCOUNTABLE NOUNS

modifier   a word that modifies or qualifies the meaning of another word. Modifiers are usually attributive nouns (***table** lamp* / ***expiry** date*) and adjectives (*a **large** cake* / *the **English** language*), or adverbs (*We're **almost** ready*)

noun a word that names a person or thing, including common nouns (*bridge, girl, sugar, unhappiness*) and proper nouns (which name specific persons or things, e.g. *Asia, Concorde, Dickens*)

passive voice the form of a verb in which the object of the active verb (*see* ACTIVE VOICE above) becomes the subject and the subject of the active verb is optionally expressed as an agent introduced by the preposition *by*. The passive voice is illustrated by the sentences *Brazil **were beaten** in the final* and *Brazil **were beaten** by France in the final*

predicative denoting a word, especially an adjective, that is used after a linking verb (*The food was **terrible** / They are becoming **angry***)

preposition a word that stands before a noun or pronoun (or later in a sentence, referring back to a noun or pronoun) and establishes its relation to what goes before, such as *after, on, for,* and *with* (*They came **after** dinner / the man **on** the platform / What did you do it **for**?*)

pronoun a word used instead of a noun or noun phrase that has already been mentioned or is known, including the personal pronouns *I, you, she, us*, etc., the relative pronouns *that, which, who*, etc., the interrogative pronouns, *who, what*, etc., and the demonstrative pronouns *this, that, those*, etc.

subordinate clause *see* CLAUSE

tense the form of a verb in relation to time, e.g. present tense (*makes*), past tense (*made / has made*) and future tense (*will make / is going to make*)

that*-clause** a subordinate clause introduced by the conjunction *that* (*I know **that it is true)

***to*-infinitive** *see* INFINITIVE

transitive denoting a verb that takes an object, i.e. has a following word or phrase which the action of the verb affects (*They **lit** a fire*)

uncountable nouns nouns which do not form plurals, e.g. *adolescence, heating, richness, warfare.* See also MASS NOUNS and COUNTABLE NOUNS

verb a word that describes an action or state and is normally an essential element in a clause or sentence: *She **locked** the door / We **were** lucky*

a, an, called the indefinite article (or, by some grammarians, determiner). In origin, *a* and its by-form *an* are versions of the Old English *an* meaning 'one'.

1 Before all normal words or diphthongs *an* is required (*an actor, an eagle, an illness, an Old Master, an uncle*). Before a syllable beginning in its written form with a vowel but pronounced with a consonantal sound, *a* is used (*a eulogy, a unit, a use; a one, a once-only*). Before all consonants except silent *h, a* is usual: *a book, a history, a home, a household name, a memorial service, a puddle, a young man;* but, with silent *h, an hour, an honour.*

2 In most circumstances *a* is pronounced with an unstressed indeterminate sound uh or uhn, but it is sometimes emphasized as ay or an in slow diction or to emphasize singleness (*I said a piece, not several*). Practice differs with *h*-words in which the first syllable is unstressed: *a* (or *an*) *habitual criminal; a* (or *an*) *hotel.* There is evidence, especially in written English, for the continued use of *an* before *habitual, historian, historic(al), horrific,* and *horrendous,* but the choice of form remains open. However, *an hotel* now sounds dated (1930s) and *a hotel* is more usual.

3 With single letters and groups of letters that are pronounced as individual letters, be guided by the pronunciation: *a B road, a TUC leader;* but *an A road, an FA Cup match, an SAS unit* (assuming the abbreviations are not mentally expanded to their full forms, which would alter the choice).

4 *A* and *an* normally precede the word or words they determine (*a popular person, an ugly building*), but it follows the adjectives *many, such,* and *what* (*many a year, such a family, what an awful nuisance!*). It also follows any adjective preceded by *as* or *how* (*Iris Murdoch is as good a writer as Virginia Woolf* / *He did not realize how tiresome a person he could be*) and often an adjective preceded by *so* (*So bold a move deserved success*), although *such* is now more usual (*Such a bold move deserved success*). In some circumstances the positioning is optional: either before or after an adjective preceded by *too* (*too strict a regime* or *a too strict regime*) and before or after the adverbs *quite* and *rather* (*at quite an early hour* or *at a quite early hour; it's rather a hard puzzle* or *it's a rather hard puzzle*). With *few* and *lot,* however, the only possible order is *quite a few* and *quite a lot. A good few* is now commonly used.

5 *A* and *an* are also used to distinguish a particular person or artistic or literary creation: *Do you know a Lucy Smith?* / *They own a Van Gogh* / *She plays a Broadwood* [piano]; and to denote a standard quantity of something that is normally uncountable: *Do you want a beer?* / *I've been trying a new cheese.* Note also the following uses in time measurement: *once a fortnight, £20,000 a year, half an hour, 50 miles an hour.*

abacus. The plural is *abacuses,* when referring to a counting device. In its architectural meaning the plural of *abacus* is *abaci,* **ab**-uh-sy.

abbreviations. There are several kinds of abbreviations: shortenings, contractions, initialisms, and acronyms.

1 *Shortenings* of words, though formerly condemned by literary figures such as Addison and Pope (18c), are now a common convention, with varying degrees of formality (*ad* = advertisement, *bike* = bicycle, *pub* = public house, *rhino* = rhinoceros, *telly* = television). Some are the usual forms, with the original forms now regarded as formal or technical (*bus* = omnibus, *fridge* = refrigerator, *gym* = gymnasium, *turps* = turpentine, *zoo* = zoological garden).

2 *Contractions* are a type of shortening in which letters from the middle of the word are omitted (*Dr* = doctor, *St* = saint) and are sometimes marked as omitted by use of an apostrophe (*can't* = cannot, *we've* = we have).

3 *Initialisms* are abbreviations consisting of a sequence of the initial letters of words that are pronounced as separate letters: *a.m.*, *BBC*, *DfES* [= Department for Education and Skills, in the UK], *HIV*, *MP*, *UN*. Practice varies as to including full points between the letters; the style recommended here is not to include them when all the initials are capitals and in some other cases. When the form has a plural, this is formed by adding an *-s*, now normally without an apostrophe (e.g. *MPs* rather than *MP's*). Possessives are formed in the usual way (e.g. *MP's* singular, *MPs'* plural).

4 *Acronyms* are initialisms that have gone one stage further and acquired the status of words, being pronounced and treated grammatically as such (*Aids*, *laser*, *NATO*, *PIN* [= personal identification number], *radar*). In some cases the original expansions have become irrelevant, as with *laser* and *radar*. (*See more fully at* ACRONYM.)

abdomen. Stress is normally on the first syllable.

abduction (18c) is the forcible leading away of a minor (with or without the minor's consent) for marriage or seduction or the breaking of a legal custodial arrangement for the children of divorced parents. Although there is some overlap in meaning with *kidnap* (late 17c), kidnapping is not restricted to minors and is usually done for the purpose of demanding a ransom from the victim's family or employers. The more recent *hijacking* (20c, of unknown origin) applies specifically to vehicles, especially aircraft. All three words have applied to the seizure and detention of political hostages in the Middle East since the 1980s and particularly in the first decade of the 21c. *Carjacking* is an urban development of the 1990s and still features widely in news reports, where *carjack* appears as a verb and a noun (*Police said the violence used was the worst they had come across in the 30 carjack incidents in the area since the start of the year*—Times, 1994 / *Three axe-wielding thieves robbed a cash van, crashed a stolen car into a bus and carjacked a woman in Timperley yesterday morning*—Manchester Evening News, 2007).

abductor is spelt *-or*, not *-er*.

abettor, abetter. *Abettor* is the standard spelling in legal terminology. *Abetter* is occasionally found, describing a person who merely encourages someone in an activity: *A warrant for his arrest as an abetter of the prince was issued.*

abide is now limited to two main meanings, and has lost many others over seven centuries of use along with several redundant inflections, including *abode*. The principal meaning 'to bear, tolerate' is now only used in negative contexts, usually with a modal auxiliary verb (*Those ordinary Aryan Australian girls whose coarse complexions and lumpy features he could not abide*—H. Jacobsen, 1986). Its other main meaning in current use is with *by*, meaning 'to stand firm by' (*We must abide by our decision*). In its other meanings, it tends to be used mostly in the present tense, most famously as an imperative in a hymn (*Abide with me; fast falls the eventide*—H. F. Lyte, 19c), or as a participial adjective (*I accept this award with an abiding faith in America*—Martin Luther King, 1964, accepting the Nobel Peace Prize).

abjure, adjure. *Abjure* means 'to renounce on oath' (*He had abjured, he thought, all superstitions*—Iris Murdoch, 1985) and to abjure one's country (or realm) is to swear to abandon it for ever. It is also used in the weakened sense 'to renounce' (*Are faculty members willing to abjure e-mail in communicating with their students and colleagues?*—*The Nation*, 2002 [*OEC*]). By contrast, *adjure* means 'to request earnestly' with or (now) more frequently without an oath (*They were all talking at once, adjuring each other to have fresh cups of tea*). Neither word is in everyday use, but they are found in literature and can cause confusion when wrongly used.

-able, -ible. *See box overleaf.*

able-bodied, abled. It is best to avoid using *able-bodied* to mean 'not having a physical disability', since many people with disabilities object to its use in this way. A better word choice is *nondisabled*. *Abled*, meaning 'not disabled', is a revival of an obsolete 16c word, and is first recorded in print in the US in the 1980s. It is now occasionally used in the phrases *differently abled* and *less abled* as a more positive alternative to *disabled*: *They were gentle . . . kids, who took endless pains to guard against what they referred to as 'the exploitation of the differently abled'*—A. Maupin, 1992. / *Getting about for less abled residents isn't easy*—*Bolton Evening News*, 2003 [*OEC*].

ableism, meaning 'discrimination in favour of the abled' (i.e. against people with disabilities), is first recorded in the

US from the early 1980s. There is a corresponding adjective and noun *ableist*: *The cover design appears to be rather male-dominated, white, ableist*—*Rouge*, 1990. So far, the spelling with *-le-* is much more common, with little evidence for the less satisfactory spellings *ablism* and *ablist*. *See* -ISM.

able to. The construction *to be able to* (do something), with an active *to*-infinitive, is a natural part of the language, extending to inanimate as well as animate subjects (*By his proceeding to the beach . . . the next phase of the attack was able to proceed*—*New Yorker*, 1986). It plays a useful role in compensating for the deficiencies of *can* in the future and perfect tenses (*will be able to* / *have not been able to*), with modal verbs such as *might* (*I might be able to*), and with verbs such as *become*, *appear*, and *seem* (*They don't seem to be able to do it*). When the infinitive is passive, however, it is better to use *can* or *could*, and to avoid *able to*, which sounds too forced (*No evidence that an air rifle was able to be fired*—*Times* (heading of Law Report), 1988).

abode. In the meaning 'a dwelling place', *abode* is falling into disuse except in the fixed expressions: *(of) no fixed abode*, used of someone without a permanent address; *place of abode*, meaning where someone lives; and *right of abode*, especially as applied to citizens of Hong Kong who sought the right to settle in Britain after 1997. It has not entirely gone from literature in its ordinary use (*The house, standing at the edge of a fair-sized tract of woodland and once, perhaps, the abode of gamekeepers*—Kingsley Amis, 1974), and is often used humorously or ironically, preceded by a possessive such as *my* and an adjective, especially in the combination *humble abode* (*I will be hosting a soiree at my humble abode on the night in question*—weblog, 2004 [*OEC*]).

-ABLE, -IBLE.

1 general. These two suffixes are derived from Latin endings *-abilis* and *-ibilis*, either directly or through Old French. Of the two, *-able* is an active suffix that can be freely added to the stems of transitive verbs, whereas the set of *-ible* words is a closed one with meanings that are less susceptible to analysis. A few words exist in both forms (e.g. *collectable* and *collectible*); others appear to but differ in meaning (e.g. *passable, passible*). Most words are formed from verbs, but some are formed from nouns (e.g. *comfortable, peaceable*).

2 meaning. The primary meaning these suffixes convey is 'able to be -ed' or 'capable of being -ed', e.g. *bearable, curable, manageable*. Some meanings, however, are active rather than passive, e.g. *agreeable* = willing to agree, *changeable* = apt to change, *comfortable* = able to give comfort, *viable* = able to live. Others, such as *reliable*, are formed somewhat in defiance of syntax (here, *on* is suppressed). Many words acquire special meanings, e.g. *actionable, appreciable, biddable, creditable, disposable, forgettable, incredible, noticeable, passable, remarkable, reprehensible, tolerable, unspeakable*.

3 spelling problems. The spelling of the source word changes under certain conditions, since *-able* and *-ible* both begin with a vowel. The most important are:

a Words in *-y* (preceded by a consonant) change *y* to *i*: *dutiable, rectifiable, undeniable*. But note *employable, enjoyable*.

b With some exceptions, words in silent *-e* lose the *e* when *-able* is added: *adorable, excusable, lovable, losable, removable, usable*. But note the preferred forms *giveable, hireable, likeable, nameable, rateable, saleable*.

c Words in *-ce* and *-ge* normally retain the *e*: *bridgeable, changeable, chargeable, noticeable, peaceable*.

d Words of more than two syllables ending in *-ate* lose this ending when *-able* is added: *alienable* (not *alienatable*), *appreciable* (has special meaning), *calculable, demonstrable, estimable* (has special meaning), *inestimable* (has special meaning), *penetrable, tolerable*. However, words of two syllables would not be viable without the ending and therefore retain it: *creatable, debatable, dictatable, locatable, translatable*.

e A final consonant is normally doubled when it is doubled in ordinary inflection: *biddable, forgettable, regrettable*.

f Words of more than one syllable ending in *-fer* double the *r* when the stress is on the final syllable, but do not when the stress is earlier in the word: *conferrable, deferrable, offerable, preferable, profferable, insufferable* (but in *transferable* the stress is variable on the first two syllables). *Infer* makes *inferable* and *inferrable*, and *refer* makes *referable* and *referrable*.

The following table shows the principal forms in *-able* and *-ible,* and also shows forms that are liable to be confused (e.g. *impassable* and *impassible*)

words ending in -able

abominable	deferable	impassable (= *unable*
acceptable	definable	*to be crossed; see also*
actionable	demonstrable	impassible)
adaptable	deniable	impeccable
adjustable	deplorable	imperturbable
adorable	desirable	implacable
advisable	despicable	impressionable
agreeable	detachable	improvable
alienable	developable	indefatigable
allowable	dilatable	indescribable
amenable	dispensable	indispensable
amiable	disposable	indubitable
analysable	dissolvable	inflatable
appreciable	drivable	inimitable
arguable	durable	insufferable
ascribable	dutiable	irreconcilable
assessable	eatable	irreplaceable
available	educable (= *able to*	justifiable
bearable	*be educated; also*	knowledgeable
believable	educible)	laughable
blameable	endorsable	leviable
bribable	equable	likeable
bridgeable	equitable	liveable
calculable	evadable	losable
capable	excisable	lovable
changeable	excitable	machinable
chargeable	excusable	malleable
clubbable	expandable (*also*	manageable
collectable	expansible)	manoeuvrable
comfortable	expendable	marriageable
conceivable	extendable (*also*	measurable
conferrable	extendible,	mistakable
confinable	extensible)	movable
confusable	extractable (*also*	mutable
consolable	extractible)	nameable
contractable (*of a*	feeable	noticeable
disease; also	finable	objectionable
contractible)	foreseeable	obtainable
copiable	forgettable	operable
creatable	forgivable	palatable
creditable	frameable	payable
curable	gettable	peaceable
datable	giveable	penetrable
debatable	hireable	perishable
declinable	imaginable	permeable
defendable (*in literal*	immovable	persuadable (*also*
meanings; also	immutable	persuasible)
defensible)	impalpable	pleasurable

preferable	reputable	tradable
prescribable	retractable	transferable
preventable	saleable	tuneable
pronounceable	scalable	unconscionable
provable	serviceable	undeniable
rateable	sizeable	unexceptionable
readable	solvable	unget-at-able
receivable	statutable	unknowable
reconcilable	storable	unmistakable
rectifiable	suitable	unscalable
registrable	superannuable	unshakeable
regrettable	timeable	usable
reliable	tolerable	
removable	traceable	

words ending in -ible

accessible	divisible	invisible
adducible	educible (= *able to be*	irascible
admissible (*also*	*educed*; *also*	irreducible
admittable)	educable)	irrepressible
audible	eligible	irresponsible
avertible	exhaustible	irresistible
collapsible	expansible	irreversible
comprehensible	expressible	legible
contemptible	extendible (*also*	negligible
contractible (= *able to*	extendable, extensible)	ostensible
be shrunk; *also*	feasible	perceptible
contractable)	flexible	perfectible
convertible	gullible	permissible
credible	impassible	persuasible (*also*
deducible	(= *unfeeling*; *see also*	persuadable)
deductible	impassable)	plausible
defensible (*of an*	inaudible	reducible
argument etc.; *also*	incorrigible	reprehensible
defendable)	incredible	reproducible
destructible	indelible	resistible
diffusible	indigestible	responsible
digestible	indivisible	reversible
dirigible	infallible	risible
discernible	inflexible	suggestible
discussible	intangible	suppressible
dismissible	invincible	susceptible

abolishment, abolition. Both words date from the 16c and have been used principally about concepts and institutions such as authority, laws, beliefs, feelings, and sins. In the 18c and 19c, *abolition* took on special meanings relating to the slave trade and capital punishment, which caused *abolishment* to be restricted to more neutral and ad hoc uses emphasizing the process rather than the result (*The deregulation of financial markets and abolishment of fixed commission rates—Institutional Investor* (NEXIS), 1989 / *It's a negation of him, an abolishment of him, like ripping a medal off his chest*—Margaret Atwood in *New Yorker*, 1990). There are roughly 30 times as many instances of *abolition* in the *OEC* as there are of *abolishment*.

aborigines. This Latinate word has been applied since the 16c to the original inhabitants of a country *ab origine* (from the beginning). For the singular, the etymologically criticized form *Aborigine* has become firmly established in Australia (early 19c). Both *Aborigine(s)* and *Aboriginal(s)* are always written with a capital letter *A* in Australian contexts. In Australian sources, *Aboriginal* is used more often than *Aborigine* as an adjective, but less often as a noun. But Australian Aborigines prefer to be known as *Indigenous Australians*, and this phrase is becoming more and more standard. *Aboriginal* is the term used by the Australian government, but is disliked by Indigenous Australians themselves. The abbreviated form *Abo* is nowadays considered offensive.

abortive, aborted. The central meaning of *abortive* since the time of Shakespeare has been 'coming to nought, fruitless, useless, unsuccessful'. It can be applied to attempts, efforts, missions, coups, and rebellions, negotiations, proposals, etc., and to any action that proves to be unsuccessful, even the most trivial (*An abortive attempt to do the Times crossword*—A. N. Wilson, 1982). *Aborted* is not, despite the protestations of the American writer William Safire, a better alternative, since it denotes actual failure whereas *abortive* can be used of failure that is merely imminent or potential.

abound can have as its subject things that are plentiful or (followed by *in* or *with*) the place where things are plentiful: *Mulberry trees abound in Oxford*—[note that *in* goes with *Oxford*, not abound!]—Jan Morris, 1978 / *A few years since this country abounded in wild animals*—A. Moorehead, 1963 / *The text, written in Yinglish and American, abounds in euphemisms*—Observer, 1974. The word is also common intransitively with no complementation: *When the idea of a university of the air was first floated, sceptics abounded.*—Listener, 1984. / *Internet cafes abound*—New Humanist (magazine), 2005 [*OEC*].

about. **1 as a preposition.** In the meaning 'roughly, approximately' (e.g. *It took about ten minutes*), *about* is the usual BrE word; *around* is also used, and is much more common in AmE. *Round about* is more informal, and is largely confined to BrE.

2 meaning 'concerning'. In this meaning, *about* is either a preposition or a conjunction (followed by *which, how,* etc.): (preposition) *The quarrels were about money* / (conjunction) *There was a great deal of discussion about which versions should be used.* Since the 1930s, the phrase *to be about* (something) has developed a special meaning 'to be primarily concerned with' and even 'to have as its aim', as in *Love and war were about winning, not fair play*—A. Price, 1982. When precision is important, it is better to use a less ambiguous phrase, e.g. *Love and war had winning as their purpose, and did not involve fair play.*

The phrase *what it's all about* is a cliché, and should be restricted to less formal contexts: *They like the feeling that they have had to fight other men for possession. That is what it is all about, really.*—Anita Brookner, 1984.

3 used instead of of. In informal language, *about* is tending to replace *of* in uses such as *We're more aware about it / The Vietnamese are disdainful about Chinese cooking / The issue about how such things are monitored.*

4 be about to. In affirmative contexts, *to be about to* denotes intention: *I am about to go shopping.* The more idiomatic negative use, *not be about to,* indicating determination not to do something, should only be used informally: *I'm not about to foist something on the general public just for the sake of releasing something*—Record Mirror, 1982. In more formal usage, it is better to use one of several alternatives such as *do not intend to* (or, more emphatically, *have no intention of*), *am not likely to,* etc.

abridgement, abridgment. The first is the preferred British form, and is given first in dictionaries. In the US *abridgment* is given first in dictionaries, but the spelling *abridgement* is as frequently used in practice.

abrogate, arrogate. *Abrogate* means 'to repeal, annul, or cancel' such things as laws, rules, treaties, and other formal agreements (*The Cabinet clung stubbornly to the belief that the mere signing of the agreement itself abrogated imperial preferential tariffs*—D. Aitchison, 1969 / *He abrogated at once the Penal Code*—W. H. Auden, 1969); *arrogate* means 'to lay claim to without justification' (*That sort of writing which has arrogated to itself the epithet 'creative'*—D. J. Enright, 1966 / *The illegal but effective authority which the Assembly of the United Nations seemed now to have arrogated to itself*—H. Macmillan, 1971).

absolutely. This word has a string of important meanings in the broad area 'in an absolute position, manner, or degree', and can be applied to many domains of physical and conceptual activity including language and politics. It has also come to be used as a mere intensive comparable to *completely* or *utterly,* even in non-gradable contexts (*absolutely awful, absolutely delightful, absolutely essential, absolutely necessary, absolutely nothing, absolutely out of the question*). In conversation, *absolutely* is used 'absolutely' (i.e. without a grammatical complement) as a strong affirmative reply: *'Think you can do that?' 'Absolutely!' Dusty replied turning to her computer*—Kristin Goode, 2003 [*OEC*].

It is no exaggeration to say that, at least in Britain, and apparently also in the US, it has altogether ousted 'yes' from the speech of middle-class media persons and pundits. In any interview it is sure to crop up, usually several times. It is undergoing, or has already undergone, the same erosion of meaning that has reduced 'awesome' to the status of 'nice'; such erosion is a natural feature of language. With *no* and *not,* it is often used in speech as an emphatic refusal or denial: *'Because your mother insisted.' 'Absolutely not.'*—B. Neil, 1993. / *There's absolutely no point in saving for a pension on my current wages*—BBC News, 2004 [*OEC*].

absolve. 1 Pronunciation is now normally with -z-, not -s-.

2 The usual construction is with a direct object, or in the passive, followed by *of* or *from*: *It absolved him of all responsibility*—L. A. G. Strong, 1948 / *Absolve me from all spot of sin*—James Agee, 1950 / *Kant regarded himself as absolved from this promise by the monarch's death*—R. Scruton, 2001 / *First he tries to absolve himself of any blame*—weblog, 2005 [*OEC*].

abstract nouns. 1 Abstract nouns denote ideas, qualities, or states rather than concrete objects. They are words such as *difference, equality, justice, love, quality, size,* and *truth.*

2 Many usage writers warn against the overuse of abstract nouns, and Gowers (1965) coined the term 'abstractitis' as a label for it. There are many subject areas, such as philosophy, about which it would be impossible to write without using abstract nouns. However, unnecessary use of abstract nouns instead of the verbs from which they come often leads to needlessly dense writing, particularly by business people, academics, civil servants, and others in public service. Gowers gave the example of: *Participation by the men in the control of the industry is non-existent* [rewrite as *The men have no part in controlling the industry*]. A more recent example from a Scottish government organization runs as follows: *Specific considerations will need to be given to what assistance minority groups will require to fully participate and contribute to the design, development and delivery of policies and services.* Drastic surgery seems called for, starting with removing several abstract nouns: *considerations* (we'll pass over the fact that it is plural), *design, development,* and *delivery.* Rewriting it as follows makes the message more direct and forceful, not to say shorter: *We need to think about how we can help minority groups play their full part in designing, developing and delivering policies and services.*

abstruse, obtuse are confused surprisingly often, usually with *obtuse* replacing *abstruse.* Topics, subjects, theories, etc. which are *abstruse* (from Latin *abstrusus* 'concealed, hidden') are obscure or difficult to understand, e.g. *an abstruse philosophical inquiry.* Someone who is *obtuse* is annoyingly insensitive or slow in understanding, e.g. *He wondered if the doctor was being deliberately obtuse.* Using *obtuse* to mean

'obscure, difficult', though often done, is not recommended, since some people will consider it a rank mistake, despite its being recognized in some dictionaries. Examples: (abstruse) *lectures on a series of abstruse topics, not excluding Roman laxatives and prophylactics*—Daily Telegraph, 2007 / *The language is abstruse and esoteric, almost incomprehensible*—www.freeindia.com, 2004 / (obtuse) *There is a crispness to Imelda Staunton that has the positive snap of a headmistress dealing with some rather obtuse children*—Scotland on Sunday, 2004 / *Henry III was equally politically obtuse in his dealings with Henry of Navarre*—Canadian Journal of History, 2000 / (obtuse used dubiously) *While many academics shelter themselves beneath obtuse writing and inaccessible subject matter, Gould had the confidence to address the world with clarity and common sense*—Human Nature Review, 2002.

abuse *noun.* This has developed a sinister violent meaning, 'maltreatment or (especially sexual) assault of a person', and is now widely familiar in the specific context of *child abuse*, of which various aspects include *physical abuse, domestic abuse, ritual abuse, sexual abuse,* and even *satanic abuse.* At the same time its older meaning, 'misuse or improper use', has been greatly extended in explicit combinations such as *alcohol abuse, drug abuse, heroin abuse, solvent abuse, steroid abuse, substance abuse,* etc., all associated with harmful or narcotic substances.

abysmal, abyssal. The frequency of these two words is the reverse of that of the parent words: *abysmal*, with its figurative meaning 'very bad' and a literal meaning relating to gorges, outer space, etc., is common, whereas *abyssal* is limited to technical usage in oceanography, 'belonging to one of the deepest levels of the ocean' (e.g. in the term *abyssal floor*) and geology, where it has a meaning, similar to *plutonic*, relating to igneous rock (as in *abyssal hills*). By contrast, *abyss* is still used (usually in figurative uses denoting disaster, e.g. *They are staring into the abyss*), whereas *abysm* (under 20 in the *OEC*) is not. Examples of *abysmal*: (figurative) *The day was hot, the organisation ... excellent, and the cricket of generally abysmal quality—Wisden Cricket Monthly*, 1992 / *Video ads have been tried many times before and, each time, have been abysmal failures—Aardvark Daily*, NewZE 2004 [*OEC*] / *The US is not alone in its abysmal ignorance of the democratic processes of countries it considers its staunchest allies—Cherwell Magazine Online*, 2005 [*OEC*] / (literal) *Far, far beneath in the abysmal sea—P*. Allardice, 1990.

academic. The central meanings of this word ('of or belonging to an academy or institution for higher learning') survive, but a little more than a century ago it developed a depreciatory range of meanings 'merely theoretical, having no practical applications': *All the discussion, Sirs, is—academic. The war has begun already—H*. G. Wells, 1929 / *The strike ... was dismissed as 'largely academic' by Merseyside Health Authority—Times*, 1990 / *We do not yet know how many of these attacks are attributable to al Qaeda, but that is a pretty academic question*—weblog, AmE 2002 [*OEC*].

accent. 1 The noun is stressed on the first syllable and the verb (meaning 'to lay stress on, to emphasize' in various senses) on the second.

2 In general use, an accent is 'individual, local, or national mode of pronunciation', as in *a Scottish accent, a slight accent*, etc.: *She had ... the accent of a good finishing school*—John Braine, 1957 / *'Crème de framboises,' she read in her governessy accent*—S. Hill, 1969 / *She*

resembled Jackie Kennedy, but—surprisingly—had a strong Scottish accent—J. Bow, 1991. It is also used to mean the position of the stress in a word, and a sign put on a word in writing to mark a feature of its pronunciation: *You must pronounce this all as one word with the accent on the first syllable*—C. S. Lewis, 1955. There are other special meanings in art and music. The meaning relating to pronunciation is the earliest one, and has given rise to extended uses, in which accent means 'a distinctive feature or emphasis': *After 1926 the accent was to lie on the development of technical education*—R. Pethybridge, 1990 / *The early autumn of 1992 produced no less than four major auctions with an accent on matters aeronautical*—FlyPast, 1992. This use is common in advertising and marketing: *Accent is on comfort when you step in for a relaxing drink*—promotional material in British National Corpus, 1990s.

3 As a verb, *accent* means 'to place an accent on (a word or syllable)'. In figurative meanings, *accentuate* is generally used, but *accent* is not uncommon in discussions of fashion, design, or decoration: *I observed a severe grey skirt, the waist accentuated by a leather belt*—William Golding, 1967 / *Collingwood also has a rather learned look, accentuated by steel spectacles*—R. Cobb, 1985 / *Economic globalization can accentuate existing differences in societies*—Baylis & Smith, 2001 / *warm beige walls accented by graceful tiles with leafy patterns and dark-wood tables*—Boston Globe, 2011.

accept, except. There is little danger of confusion in spoken contexts, since all they have in common is their similar pronunciation in conversation, but their spelling is open to confusion. David Crystal reported in his book *Who Cares About English Usage?* (1984) that several of 20 English undergraduates asked to choose between *Shall we accept / except his invitation to dinner* chose *except*.

access, accession. 1 as nouns. Fowler distinguished between these two in detail in order to prevent their being confused. There is, however, no evidence in the *OEC* that they are ever confused.

2 as verbs. Since the 1890s, *to accession* has meant 'to enter as a new book in a library' (*The new books have been promptly accessioned*—G. M. Jones, 1892). More recently, *access* has taken on a verbal meaning 'to gain access to (data held in a computer)', e.g. *Design engineers can now access the computer directly through terminals in their offices*—*Scientific American*, 1977 / *One easily notices that consumers accessing pornography are mostly male*—AmE source, 2002 [*OEC*]. This use is part of the everyday vocabulary of the field and bothers nobody. Closely related to this use is the metaphor of the brain as computer in the meaning 'bring to mind', as in *when the speaker is temporarily unable to access the word in Spanish*—*American Speech*, 1987.

The relatively recent meaning (1978) that some people dislike (on the grounds that it is an example of 'verbing') is 'to approach or enter a place' in more generalized contexts such as *The kitchen may be accessed from the dining room*. There are synonyms aplenty (*reach, approach, enter*, etc.). Alternatively, rephrasing is always an option.

accessory, accessary. These two words come by different routes from the same Latin source of our word *accede*. In AmE, *accessory* is dominant both as a noun and as an adjective, and it has fast become so now in BrE, although *accessary* is still used occasionally (where before it was used invariably) as a term in law in both varieties. But -*ory* is

preferable in all meanings: *As the one person who knew of their illegalities I felt I was becoming an accessory after the fact*—S. Unwin, 1960 / *If he buried the captain, as he says, he's an accessory*—R. Macdonald, 1971 / *Accessory ideas associated with the principal idea*—M. Cohen, 1977 / *An accessory role is played by another cellular enzyme*—Health news release, AmE 2005 [*OEC*].

As a noun, *accessory* has become widely used in the 20c to refer to smaller articles of dress (gloves, handbag, etc.) or the extras in a motor vehicle (foglights, radio, etc.). *Accessories ... may be considered essential to an outfit.*—Alison Lurie, 1981 / *Since September 11th, the emphasis has changed from using the flag as a fashion accessory to using it to show solidarity as a country*—weblog, AmE 2003 [*OEC*].

accommodate, accommodation. These are among the most commonly misspelt words in English: there are two *c*s and two *m*s. The verb *accommodate* is followed by *to* when it means 'adapt' and by *with* when (less usually) it means 'to equip, supply, oblige': e.g. *His eyes quickly accommodated to the gloom / Major Kent was accommodated with a hammock chair*—G. A. Birmingham, 1908 / *The principles of natural justice have to be accommodated to the nature of the body deciding it*—High Court transcripts, AusE 2005 [*OEC*].

accompanist is now the standard form of the word for 'a person who plays a musical accompaniment'. The secondary form *accompanyist*, used by Dickens, is now occasionally encountered in AmE. Some classical musicians dislike the term (preferring *pianist*) when applied to the piano part in chamber music for two instruments or for piano and voice (and indeed some composers gave priority to the piano in the titles of their pieces, e.g. 'sonata for piano and violin').

accomplice, accomplish. The standard pronunciation of both words is now -kum-, not -kom-.

according. **1** *according as.* This is now well established as a subordinating conjunction meaning 'depending on whether, to the extent to which', despite Fowler's long warning (1926) against its use: e.g. *Llanaba Castle presents two quite different aspects, according as you approach it from the Bangor or the coast road*—Evelyn Waugh, 1928 / *Glass plates of equal thickness behave quite differently, according as they contain lead or not*—Laura Otis, 2002.

2 *according to.* This is used as a complex preposition, and means (a) in a manner that is consistent with (something), e.g. *His schemes are not going according to plan,* (b) as stated by (a person or authority), e.g. *According to our records, the account is in credit* / *I have acted according to my conscience*—Anthony Blunt, 1979 / (with an element of uncertainty or disbelief) *According to them, we're supposed to stay at home,* (c) in a manner or degree that is in proportion to (something), e.g. *Arrange the blocks according to size and colour* / *My price varied from twenty to fifty pounds according to the neighbourhood and the customer*—Graham Greene, 1966.

account. The phrase *on account of* is a slightly formal preposition meaning 'because of' (*He remained miserable and ashamed, largely on account of his appetite which continued to torment him*—Anita Brookner, 1988). Its use (with or without *of*) as a conjunction is nonstandard: e.g. *Account of you think you're tough you're going up to State Prison where you'll have to prove it*—E. Leonard, AmE 1994 / *It took us until dinner, twelve hours to crank out six-two pizzas, on account we couldn't get the ingredients right the first few times*—Trinkah, AmE 2005 [*OEC*].

accumulative *see* CUMULATIVE.

accusative is a grammatical term denoting a noun or pronoun that is governed by a verb or preposition, e.g. *house* in *Then we saw the house* and *They stood in front of the house*. In English it is only certain pronouns that change their form in the accusative (e.g. *him, them, us*): *see* CASES.

accused. *The accused,* meaning a person who has been accused in law, is an everyday use. *The* or *an accused man, person, banker,* etc., in which the individuals are only generically identified, are also routinely acceptable. It is inadvisable, however, to use expressions such as *the accused thief* or *the accused rapist,* which specify the type of criminal, since identification with the crime is in question by the very use of the term *accused. Alleged* would be a better word here.

Achilles heel, Achilles tendon. Whether you insert the apostrophe in either expression is matter of convention and style, rather than of correctness. *The New Oxford Dictionary for Writers and Editors* leaves it out of both.

achingly. *Achingly* means literally 'in an aching manner; so as to cause continuous dull pain' (e.g. *My eyes—dry now, achingly dry—flashing a wretched hostility back into his*—R. Broughton, 1873). Its use modifying an adjective and meaning 'acutely, intensely' is not new: *It is too achingly brilliant—it wants repose*—New Monthly Magazine, 1883. Nowadays, it is quite widely used, particularly in arts journalism, to modify adjectives such as *sad, poignant, tender, melancholic,* even *beautiful,* where it retains a link with its literal meaning: *It is* *hysterically funny and achingly sad, but without a hint of sentimentality—Scotland on Sunday, 2005 / The chief narrator, Rosamond, is an achingly lonely old woman, who lost her one great love when she was in her twenties—ABC Radio,* AusE 2008.

To use it to intensify words such as *hip, trendy, fashionable,* is a mannerism of a certain superficial and gushy style of journalistic writing. It seems to be following the pattern of *awfully, dreadfully, terribly,* etc. as an intensifier, with no reference whatsoever to its literal meaning.

acid test. When Fowler was preparing the first edition of *Modern English Usage,* he remarked that *acid test* was undoubtedly the popularized technical term 'most in vogue at the moment of writing (1920)'. In scientific use it meant the use of nitric acid to test for gold; in transferred use (typically as *the acid test*) it had acquired the broad sense 'a critical or conclusive test', a use that was popularized by Woodrow Wilson two years before Fowler was writing (*The treatment accorded Russia by her sister nations in the months to come will be the acid test of their good will—Times,* 1918). The term is also used with *an* (*Fallujah is an acid test for the way the US deals with entrenched military resistance—*news transcript, AusE 2004 [*OEC*]) and is occasionally qualified in some way (*It's a better time to put Kesey to the moral acid test—*website, AmE 2004 [*OEC*]). For other extensions of technical terms *see the table at* POPULARIZED TECHNICALITIES.

acknowledgement. This spelling is preferred in BrE, although *acknowledgment* is more usual in AmE.

acoustic. 1 Earlier in the 20c two pronunciations were competing with each other: one with -ow- and the other with -oo-. The second has prevailed, despite

Fowler's prediction that 'if the word came into popular use, it would probably be with -ow-', based on traditional assumptions about the English pronunciation of Greek.

2 The noun *acoustics* is construed as singular when used to mean 'the science of sound' (e.g. *Acoustics is a branch of physics*), and as plural when used to mean 'the acoustic properties of a building' (e.g. *The dire acoustics don't do the band any favours / There are brilliant acoustics in there*).

acronym. 1 This term, which was first used in the 1940s, denotes a type of abbreviation made up of a set of initials that are pronounced as a single word, as *Nato* is (as distinct from *BBC*). An *acronym* is generally treated as a word in its own right in other ways, for example in the formation of plurals when appropriate. Examples of familiar acronyms include: *Aids* (acquired immune deficiency syndrome), *ASH* (Action on Smoking and Health), *PIN* (personal identification number), *SIM card* (subscribed identification module), *Unesco* (United Nations Educational, Scientific, and Cultural Organization), and *WASP* (White Anglo-Saxon Protestant). Some of these, especially the names of organizations, start off as ordinary abbreviations (often with full stops) and develop into acronyms; others (e.g. *ASH*) are deliberately contrived so as to lend themselves to pronunciation as words and hence acquire acronym status artificially.

2 Examples of acronyms that form ordinary nouns are *laser* (light amplification by stimulated emission of radiation), *radar* (radio detection and ranging), and *SWOT* (strengths, weaknesses, opportunities, threats: used in business assessments).

3 In everyday use, *acronym* is sometimes applied to abbreviations that are properly initialisms, since they are pronounced as separate letters (e.g. *EU* = European Union, *DVD* = digital versatile disc).

act, action. 1 The distinction between the two words in their general meanings is not always clear: we are judged by our acts or by our actions. In general, however, *action* has more of the notion of performance, and extends to inanimate things (we can speak only of the *action*, not of the *act*, of a machine), whereas *act* connotes more strongly the fact of something done and also implies responsibility rather more necessarily than *action* does (hence the *Acts of the Apostles*, not the *Actions*, which Fowler (1926) suggested as the logical preference). *Action* is also used attributively in expressions such as *action committee, painting, replay*, etc., whereas *act* is not. The *actions* of a person are usually viewed as occupying some time, and (in the plural) denote the habitual or ordinary deeds of a person, the sum of which make up his or her conduct. *Act*, by contrast, normally means something brought about rapidly or over a short period, especially in phrases with *of* (*an act of God, an act of madness*).

2 Both words have special meanings which are exclusive to each (an *act* of a play, an *act* in a variety show, military *action*, etc.), and in fixed expressions (*to put on an act, caught in the act, to clean up one's act, to get one's act together, to take action, actions speak louder than words, where the action is, a piece of the action*, etc.).

3 *Action*, in its modern use as a transitive verb meaning 'to take action on (a decision or request, etc.)' is best left to the evasive and inflated language of business and HR (*Dismissal will be actioned when the balance of probabilities suggests that an employee has committed a criminal act—Daily Telegraph*, 1981).

activate, actuate. *Activate* (17c) originally meant 'to make active' (as in *activate the lungs*). It fell out of use for a time at the end of the 19c, and was marked as obsolete in the first *OED*. New uses in physics, chemistry, and other branches of science have brought it back into prominence and *actuate* (also 17c in current meanings), once dominant, is now in decline (under 500 in the *OEC*). *Activate* (over 10,000 in the *OEC*) is the normal word in mechanical contexts such as burglar alarms, traffic lights, flight plans, and also occasionally in the context of human behaviour, where the choice is perhaps influenced by *motivate* (e.g. *Are they activated by concern for public morality?*). *Actuate*, which has a much higher proportion of passive uses with *by* than does *activate*, is less common in physical and mechanical contexts, and is generally restricted to less appealing abstract qualities such as anger, greed, jealousy, malice, etc. (*His opposition was actuated by a different and more compelling motive than that of her other relatives*—David Cecil, 1948 / *the real objects that actuate our sentiments and passions*—BrE source, 2000 [*OEC*].

active. The active voice of verbs is illustrated by the sentence *Italy beat France in the final*, in which the subject of the verb (*Italy*) performs the action and the object (*France*) is affected by the action. The passive equivalent is *France were beaten by Italy in the final*, in which the grammatical roles of the two participants in the action are reversed. *See* PASSIVE.

actual is often used redundantly in ways that add nothing to the meaning: *Mr Healey said the press did not print Labour's actual policies. 'Not a sausage.'—Times*, 1981. Examples of legitimate use are: *He gathered there were few actual artists in the room* [as distinct

from would-be artists]—Beryl Bainbridge, 1980 / *The actual total* [as distinct
from the provisional total] *was surely
higher*—Scientific American, 1980.

actually is one of a number of words,
like *definitely, really, surely*, etc., which
are used freely as emphasizers, either in
relation to words or phrases (*Often it
wasn't actually a railway station but a
special stopping place in the middle of
nowhere*—New Yorker, 1987) or as sentence adverbs qualifying a complete
statement (*I'd like to see those scrap
books again, actually*—Lee Smith, 1983 /
*'I told you, I've got problems at work.'
'Actually, you didn't.'* Such uses are
more common in speech, where they
help with continuity and sentence balance. It is clearly a useful if somewhat
overused word.

actuate *see* ACTIVATE.

acumen. The 19c pronunciation as
recorded in the original *OED* was with
the stress on the second syllable. This is
still the dominant pronunciation in
AmE, but in BrE stress on the first syllable is now standard.

ad, advert are frequent shortened
forms of *advertisement*, both dating from
the middle of the 19c and now very
widespread (*If you examine the adverts
for personal computers . . . you'll find that
almost nowhere do the ads promise you
any kind of concrete benefit*—Your Computer, 1984). *Ad* is the most common of
the three forms, followed by *advertisement*, while *advert* is little used in North
American English.

AD should be placed—in recognition of
what it stands for (*anno Domini*, in the
year of Our Lord)—before the numerals
it relates to, i.e. AD 44 (not 44 AD). It is
customary for convenience, however,
to write 'the third century AD' to correspond to 'the third century BC'. In print,

AD is often put in small capitals. Note
that the alternative CE (for 'Common
Era') is often used (following the date)
as a culturally neutral alternative, along
with BCE ('before Common Era'). This
device seems to satisfy the demands of
political correctness despite the fact that
it is merely a disguised continuation of
the same system.

adagio has the plural form *adagios*.

adamant. Its use as an adjective
meaning 'stubbornly unshakeable or inflexible' is first recorded in an example of
1816; as a noun meaning a hard rock or
mineral it goes back to the time of King
Alfred, originally as a vague term often
imbued with fabulous associations, and
later as a synonym for 'diamond'. In
modern use the noun is 'only a poetical
or rhetorical name for the embodiment
of surpassing hardness', and the adjective is the principal use (*His appointment had met with the adamant
opposition of almost all the Fellows*—
Tom Sharpe, 1974), also giving rise to an
adverb *adamantly* (*When she mentions
him at all in her diary, it is in adamantly
negative terms*—S. Quinn, 1988).

adapter, adaptor. The spelling with
-er is more than three times as common
as that with *-or* in both meanings of the
word, although it is useful to restrict
adaptor to the device and *adapter* to the
(much less used) meaning 'a person who
adapts (something or to something)'.

addenda is a plural form meaning
'a list of additional items'; if there is
only one, *addendum* is the word to use.
Addenda should be treated as plural,
not (except informally, like *agenda*)
as singular when the meaning is 'a set of
addenda' (as in *a new edition with an
invaluable addenda*).

addle, addled. The usual word now is
addled, and is applied (a) to eggs, and

(b) figuratively, to brains (i.e. the mind). Originally, *addle* was a noun meaning 'stinking urine or other liquid filth', although its associations have usually been with eggs and heads, both seen as capable of 'addling', hence *addle-brain(ed), addle-head(ed)*, etc.

address *verb*. Although it seems at first glance to promise forceful action, *address* as a verb can justifiably be criticized for being overused. Moreover, when someone undertakes to *address an issue*, it is often unclear to what exactly they are committing. Will they merely note it as something to be dealt with at an unspecified future date, analyse it in depth, or actually resolve it as soon as humanly possible? To avoid what some people regard as a bit of a woolly cliché, it may be better to specify the exact measures you intend taking. Or else use *resolve, deal with*, or *sort out* instead.

addresses. It is now customary to use as little punctuation as possible in addresses, omitting commas at the ends of lines and before street names. Personal titles are also becoming less usual, especially when addressing a woman (to avoid having to choose between the alternatives *Miss, Mrs*, and *Ms*), e.g.:
Jane Smith
44 High Street
Newtown
(A postal code can be put on the same line as the town or below it.)

-ade. Nearly all words of two or more syllables ending in *-ade* are derived from French, although some are originally from other Romance languages. Most of these are now pronounced -ayd, not -ahd: *accolade, arcade, balustrade, barricade, blockade, brigade, brocade, cascade, cavalcade, colonnade, crusade, decade, escapade, lemonade, marmalade, masquerade, palisade, parade, serenade, tirade*. A small group vary

between the two pronunciations, including: *fanfaronnade, fusillade, glissade, pomade, promenade, rodomontade*; and a few are always pronounced -ahd: *aubade, ballade, facade*.

adequate. 1 In its meaning 'proportionate to the requirements', sufficient, *adequate* is most commonly used without a complement (*There is an adequate supply of food in the flooded area*). When it has one, this is either *for* or *to* (*Their earnings are adequate for/to their needs*). It is also used idiomatically to mean 'barely sufficient': *The standard rapidly sinks to a level which is, at best, adequate but at worst incompetent*.

2 Arguments that *adequate* is an absolute are as invalid and contrary to usage as similar arguments for *unique*. Language is rarely as absolute as purists would like, and it is natural to find *adequacy* graded by adverbs and in terms of comparatives and superlatives (*We are seeking a more adequate return on our investments / The work done is fairly adequate / The most adequate description yet released of the horror of the hijacking*).

adherence, adhesion. Both words were adopted from French in the 17c, and come from the Latin verb which also gives us our verb *adhere*. *Adherence* is now mostly used in figurative senses relating to beliefs, loyalties, laws and regulations, etc., whereas *adhesion* has tended more and more to imply physical contact between surfaces, e.g. the grip of wheels on road or rail, the sticking or gluing together of two surfaces, etc. Contrary uses are also found, especially of *adhesion* in figurative meanings, but these no longer sound natural (*Others . . . fell under his control through the adhesion to France of their ruler, the Prince-Bishop of Liège*—Winston Churchill, 1957 / *his blind adhesion to the failed ideology of socialism*—weblog, NewZE 2005 [*OEC*]).

ad hoc (Latin, 'to this') has been used in English since the 17c, principally as a quasi-adjective meaning 'designated for a specific purpose' as in an *ad hoc committee* or an *ad hoc appointment*. It should be printed in roman, as two separate words without a hyphen. When it has connotations of lack of planning or system, it may be modified by an adverb (e.g. *The arrangement seems extremely ad hoc to them*). Only one derivative has achieved a tenuous foothold in the lexicon: *adhocracy*, meaning bureaucracy devoid of planning or forethought. The use of ad hoc measures with no long-term strategy is labelled *adhocism*, but the word is rarely used.

adieu This rather literary word for 'goodbye' is pronounced **adyoo**. The plural can be either *adieus* or, less frequently, *adieux*, both pronounced with final -ooz.

adjacent, adjoining. These two words do not mean the same, but they share a meaning, so they should be used with care in order to create statements that cannot be misinterpreted. *Adjacent* can mean either 'near' or 'touching', whereas *adjoining* invariably denotes immediate contact (as its link with 'join' suggests). *Adjacent angles* in a triangle are separated by the length of one side of the triangle, and *adjacent tables* are next to each other, but with a space between. However, while an *adjacent parcel of land* sometimes describes one that is merely nearby, it often refers to one which is joined. Similarly, an *adjacent room* may be, for example, across a corridor, or it may share a common wall or walls. That is where the ambiguity arises, and in many cases it would be clearer to use *adjoining*. Unambiguous examples: *With no time to reconsider, I slipped into the adjoining bathroom to disrobe*— www.travelintelligence.net / *Within a*

few minutes the runaway animal, which had broken loose from a field adjoining the railway line, was taken back home— Stamford Mercury, 2007. Ambiguous examples: *The accommodation is completed by two adjacent rooms which are off a corridor to the right of the hall*— Sunday Business Post, 2003 / *a country immediately adjacent to their own*— Contemporary Review, 2002. Are the rooms and countries mentioned merely near each other, or joined in some way?

adjective. 1 general. The term *adjective* was itself an adjective for a hundred years before it became used as a noun for one of the parts of speech. Joseph Priestley, in *The Rudiments of English Grammar* (1761), was perhaps the first English grammarian to recognize the adjective as a separate part of speech, although some earlier writers had used the term in this way. An alternative term, first used in the mid-19c, is *modifier*, which also covers the grey area of attributive nouns, for example *city* in *city council* and *table* in *table lamp*. For a more detailed analysis of types of adjective, the reader is referred to a standard grammar such as Greenbaum's *Oxford English Grammar* (1996), 134–41.

An adjective has three forms, traditionally called a positive (or absolute), e.g. *hot, splendid*, a comparative, e.g. *hotter, more splendid*, and a superlative, e.g. *hottest, most splendid*.

2 attributive and predicative. Most adjectives can be used in two positions: either before the noun (attributively, as in *a black cat, a gloomy outlook*) or after it, normally separated by a verb of state (predicatively, as in *the cat is black, the outlook seemed gloomy*). A few adjectives, usually denoting status, exceptionally stand immediately after the noun (postpositive, as in *the body politic, the president elect*).

Some adjectives are normally restricted to predicative position (e.g. *afraid, aware*), and others are restricted to attributive position, either always (e.g. *main* as in *the main reason* / ☒ *this reason is main*) or in certain meanings (e.g. *big* as in *He is a big eater* / ☒ *As an eater he is big, mere* as in *This is mere repetition* / ☒ *The repetition is mere*, and *whole* as in *Have you told the whole truth* / ☒ *The truth I have told is whole*). In these examples, predicative status has to be achieved by repetition of the noun or by the use of *one* (*The truth I have told is the whole truth* / *This reason is the main one*).

Other adjectives that have been restricted in the past are now becoming more mobile; for example, *aware* and *ill* are increasingly heard (often modified by an adverb) in attributive position, as in *a highly aware person* and *an ill woman*.

3 comparison. Adjectives of one or two syllables normally form their comparative and superlative forms by adding *-er* and *-est*, sometimes with modification of the stem (*soft, softer, softest; happy, happier, happiest*). Adjectives of more than two syllables are normally preceded by *more* or *most* instead of inflecting (*more frightening; most remarkable*). For special effect, however, a polysyllabic adjective will sometimes be inflected (*'Curiouser and curiouser!' cried Alice*—L. Carroll, 1865 / *One of the generousest creatures alive*—Thackeray, 1847/8 / *The winningest coach in Southwest Conference basketball history*—Chicago Tribune, 1990). *See also* -ER AND -EST FORMS OF ADJECTIVES. Conversely, *more* and *most* are sometimes used, for emphasis or special effect, when inflected forms are available: *This was never more true than at present* / *That was the most cruel thing you could have said.*

4 'absolute' adjectives. Some adjectives, because of their meaning and function, are called *absolute* or *non-gradable*. They are not normally used in comparative or superlative forms and cannot be qualified by adverbs such as *fairly, largely, more, rather,* or *very* that intensify or moderate along a notional range. Non-gradable adjectives comprise classifying adjectives such as *dead, rectangular, scientific,* or descriptive adjectives with a meaning that does not permit gradability, such as *equal, impossible, supreme, total, unique*. There are exceptions to this rule, but these are normally obvious special cases: *All animals are equal but some animals are more equal than others*—George Orwell, 1945 / *His profile is ... most utterly perfect*—Jane Gardam, 1985. Absolute adjectives can be regularly qualified by adverbs that denote an extreme or completeness, such as *absolutely, completely,* and *utterly,* since these are consistent with the non-gradable function of the adjectives concerned: *The ... ghosts ... made the place absolutely impossible*—Harper's Magazine, 1884. In this sentence, *absolutely impossible* is acceptable, and so is *completely* or *utterly impossible,* but *fairly* or *rather impossible* would not be.

5 position of adjectives. In numerous fixed expressions denoting status, an adjective is placed immediately after the noun it governs: e.g. *attorney-general, body politic, court martial, fee simple, heir apparent, notary public, poet laureate, postmaster-general, president elect, situations vacant, vice-chancellor designate, the village proper*. In other cases, an adjective can follow a noun for syntactic reasons, i.e. as a matter of sentence structure rather than peculiarity of expression (*The waiter ... picked up our dirty glasses in his fingertips, his eyes impassive*—Encounter, 1987), or for rhetorical effect (*Before the loving hands of the Almighty cradled him in bliss eternal*—Nigel Williams, 1992).

6 hyphenation. There is no need to insert a hyphen between a combination of adverb in *-ly* and adjective qualified by it, even when it stands in attributive position: *a highly competitive market / abundant recently published material / lawfully elected prime ministers / fully qualified lawyers.* When the adverb does not end in *-ly*, however, a hyphen is normally required to reinforce its status: *a well-known woman / an ill-defined topic.*

7 compound adjectives. These have proliferated in the 20c, and are formed from combinations of noun + adjective (*accident-prone, acid-free, child-proof, computer-literate, machine-readable, user-friendly, water-insoluble*) noun + past participle (*computer-aided, custom-built, hand-operated*), noun + -ing participle (*data-handling, pressure-reducing, stress-relieving*). Some formations are based on longer phrases (*back-to-basics, in-your-face*) and some of the more informal compounds give rise to adverbial derivatives (*balls-achingly, mind-blowingly*).

A new kind of compound adjective emerging in technical and scientific work is the type *landscape ecological principles* (= the principles of landscape ecology), in which the second element of the name of the subject (*landscape ecology*) has been turned into an adjective. Another example is *physical geographical studies*, where it would be better to say *studies in physical geography.*

8 adjectives used as adverbs. Some adjectives have corresponding adverbs that are identical, e.g. *fast, late, straight,* and the type *monthly, weekly,* etc. So you can say *He left in the late afternoon* or *He left late in the afternoon.* Adverbs without *-ly* and those in *-ly* often occur in close proximity (*'I play straight, I choose wisely, Harry,' he assured me*—John Le Carré, 1989). In other cases, adjectives are used as adverbs only informally,

often in fixed expressions such as *come clean* and *hold tight.* To these may be added *real* and *sure,* which in the UK are often taken to be tokens of informal North American speech (*That was real nice / I sure liked seeing you*).

9 adjectives used as nouns. A typical extension in the use of some descriptive adjectives is with the, forming plural (or occasionally singular) nouns meaning 'those who are . . . ', e.g. *the beautiful, the deaf, the poor, the sublime, the unemployed, the unusual.*

Other adjectives stand as countable nouns: *the ancients, the classics, collectables, explosives, submersibles.*

10 transferred epithets. A curiosity of English is the ways in which an adjective can be made to operate obliquely, qualifying a person or thing other than the word it relates to grammatically. This is a further extension of the standard use of adjectives to classify things in relation to their human associations; a *female toilet* means a toilet for women and a *gay bar* means a bar frequented by homosexuals: *'It's not your stupid place,' she says. 'It's anyone's place.'*—Penelope Lively, 1987 [the person addressed, not the place, is stupid] / *I will be sitting quietly at the kitchen table stirring an absent-minded cup of coffee*—Chicago Tribune, 1989 [the person, not the coffee, is absent-minded]. The traditional name for this phenomenon is *transferred epithet* or *hypallage.*

adjudicator is spelt *-or.*

adjure *see* ABJURE.

adjust. Three new uses of this verb entered the language in the 20c:

1 Intransitive, with or without *to*: to adapt oneself to something (*She seemed to have adjusted to her new status with little difficulty*—L. Niven, 1983 / *She needs time to adjust*—S. King, 1979).

2 Intransitive, standing for passive: to become adjusted or be capable of being adjusted. *The lights were too bright and it took my eyes a long time to adjust—Southern Ocean Review, NewZE 2004 [OEC].*

3 Transitive, with *for*, in the presentation of statistical information (*Lenders vary as to when they adjust your repayments for tax relief—What Mortgage, 1986*).

administer, administrate. For many centuries, the normal word corresponding to *administration* and meaning 'to manage (affairs)' has been *administer* (*The Rezzoris were minor Austrian gentry administering the outposts of empire—London Review of Books, 1990*). In recent years, however, the longer form *administrate* (first recorded in the 17c) has increasingly been used as if it were a newly invented back-formation, and is now awkwardly challenging *administer* in its traditional meanings: *The machinery of such aid is still primed by administrators eager to go out and administrate—Times, 1981 / They* [speed cameras] *are very expensive to install, maintain, administrate and police—Yorkshire Post, 2006. Administer* is, on the other hand, routinely used to mean 'to give (medicine) to a patient' (*I was brimming with alcohol—administered to loosen my tongue—A. Price, 1982*) and is also being increasingly used in two other meanings:

1 to inflict (punishment, blows, etc.) on someone (*Two others held her feet while the headmaster administered the cane—B. Emecheta, 1974*).

2 in medical contexts *administer* is used instead of *minister to* (an injured person, etc.): *The fact that Ranjit is still alive today is a tribute to the ambulance attendants who administered to him at the scene—Oxford Times, 1977 / American doctors, being vastly rich, have better things to do with their leisure time than administer to patients at weekends—Times, 1994.*

admission, admittance. Like many word pairs, these two have competed with each other for several centuries (*admission* first recorded in Middle English, *admittance* in 1589) without ever establishing totally independent territories. In the meaning corresponding to *admit* = 'to acknowledge or accept as true', *admission* is the word to use, not *admittance*. Where they get in each other's way is in meanings related to 'the action of admitting, letting in, to a place'. *Admission* is the dominant word of the two: it alone has a countable use (*There are more admissions in the sciences this year*), and it is the only one to have developed attributive uses (*admission charge, fee, money, officer, policy, process, ticket*). *Admittance* hangs on determinedly, especially as the word used on notices on entrances (e.g. *No admittance except on official business*) but also as an erroneous alternative in meanings where *admission* is required (*The DTI's lack of admittance of negligence in this affair is a travesty of justice—Times, 1988*).

admit. 1 *Admit of* is now only used in the meaning 'to allow as possible, leave room for' (always with an abstract object: *The circumstances will not admit of delay / It seems to admit of so many interpretations*), and even here the construction seems old-fashioned. In its other meanings, *admit* is transitive (*He admitted the injustice of it*, not ✖ *He admitted of the injustice of it*), and takes a *that*-clause (or clause without *that*) as a common construction (*He admitted [that] it was unjust*).

2 The phrase *admit to*, meaning 'to confess to, to acknowledge', a relatively recent addition to the language, is especially common in journalism (*Many of these are returns from disappointed customers who admit to having been sucked in by the hype—Express, 2007*).

adopted, adoptive. The correct use of each word is as follows: a child is *adopted* and its parents are *adoptive*. The distinction has become eroded in recent usage, especially in extended uses with reference to countries, homes, etc.

adult. 1 It is usually pronounced with stress on the first syllable in BrE and on the second syllable in AmE, but there is variation among speakers throughout the English-speaking world, and the AmE pronunciation is gaining ground in the UK too.

2 Since the 1950s, changing social attitudes have caused the word *adult* to be used euphemistically with the meaning 'sexually explicit', applied to certain categories of films, magazines, etc.

advance. 1 *advance, advanced*. The meanings are different, *advance* being a noun used attributively or as a modifier to mean 'placed in advance; going before', as in *advance copy, advance guard, advance payment*, etc., whereas *advanced* means 'far on in development' as in *an advanced degree, an advanced age, an advanced young woman*, etc. The two are sometimes confused, however, as is illustrated by a sign informing road users about impending roadworks entitled ⊠ *advanced notice*, even though the simple metal panel looked anything but technologically sophisticated. Although ⊠ *advanced notice* seems to be the most common collision of the two words, confusion also occasionally travels in the other direction, with e.g. ⊠ *advance cell technology* for *advanced cell technology*.

2 *advance, advancement*. *Advance* is much the commoner word of the two in the general sense of 'progress, going before' (*the advance of knowledge / an advance of £100 / the advance of old age / seats booked in advance*, etc.). *Advancement* is far from extinct (*1985/6 was another year of great advancement for Glaxo Inc. / The structure of the department allows for speedy advancement*) but has a different meaning, 'raising to a higher position; promotion' and should not be used in the general sense that *advance* has. *The advance of new ideas* means their increasing effect, whereas *the advancement of new ideas* means the process of encouraging and supporting them.

adverb. 1 general. The term *adverb* covers a wide variety of words, and is the least satisfactory of the conventional word categories applied to English. The principal adverb uses answer the question 'how?' or 'in what manner?', many of these being formed by the addition of the suffix -*ly* to adjectives (e.g. *carefully, quickly, steadily, well*), 'when?' or 'how often?' (e.g. *soon, regularly, yesterday*), 'where?' (e.g. *downstairs, here, outside*), and 'to what extent?' (e.g. *extremely, hardly, somewhat*). For a more detailed analysis of types of adverb, and for further terminology, the reader is referred to a standard grammar such as Greenbaum's *Oxford English Grammar* (1996), 141–52.

2 formation of adverbs. The most common formation is achieved by adding -*ly* to adjectives, as in *regularly, steadily*, and *quickly*. Other adverbs are identical with adjectives (*fast, well*), and members of a third type are formed by adding other elements such as -*ward(s)*, -*ways* and -*wise* to nouns, as in *edgeways, homewards*, and *clockwise* (some of these are also adjectives). In the 20c the range of adverbs ending in -*wise* increased enormously, with many new ad hoc (and often criticized) formations, such as *anthem-wise* and *hind-foot-wise*. Use of these should be confined to occasions when a humorous or other special effect is called for.

3 position of adverbs.

a Adverbs that qualify single words such as adjectives, nouns, and other adverbs generally precede them as closely as possible (*often late / very large / quite a while / too modestly*).

b The position of adverbs in phrases and clauses follows fairly clear rules, i.e. between an auxiliary verb and a main verb (e.g. *Roosevelt's financial policy was roundly criticized in 1933 / He had inadvertently joined a lonely-hearts club*), except for emphasis or when the adverb belongs closely to what follows the main verb (*There is little chance that the student will function effectively after he returns to China*), between one auxiliary verb and the next when there is more than one (e.g. *A car dealer who could certainly have afforded to hire someone*), and not between a verb and its object (*Gradually the Chinese communists abandoned the Soviet methods / He dutifully observes all its quaint rules / They aim to set each subject briefly into context / Did he hear her correctly? See also* ONLY; SPLIT INFINITIVE.

4 sentence adverbs.
Some adverbs (such as *clearly, happily, hopefully, thankfully, unhappily*) refer to a whole statement, and form a comment associated more closely with the speaker or writer than with what is said. This can be seen by comparing the use of *unhappily* as an ordinary adverb of manner (*She went unhappily to bed*) with its use as a sentence adverb (*She was, unhappily, too ill to leave the house*). In this use, the adverb often stands at the beginning of the sentence: *Clearly, we will have to think again*.

Use of sentence adverbs is well established in English, and the only one that has given rise to controversy is *hopefully*, which has developed this role in the mid-20c (*see* HOPEFULLY).

5 adverbial use of nouns of time.
The adverbial use of days of the week (singular and plural) and similar words, familiar in AmE and some other varieties, is not common in current BrE: *From now on gentlemen, Tuesdays and Thursdays you're going to learn to think like white men*—V. O'Sullivan, 1985 (New Zealand) / *Tuesday night, the board approved the addition of a new subsection*—Chicago Tribune, 1987 / *I was to be offered an option of taking her with me summers*—Saul Bellow, AmE 1987.

6 comparison of adverbs. *See* -ER AND -EST.

adversary is stressed on the first syllable.

adverse, averse. These two words both come from the Latin word *vertere* 'to turn', but *averse* (= turning away) means 'opposed to' and is typically used in negative contexts of people, whereas *adverse* (= turning towards, hostilely) is used of things and means 'opposing one's interests; unfavourable' (*adverse circumstances, adverse weather conditions*) or even 'harmful' (*the adverse effects of drugs*): *The creation of a large source of illegal income has serious adverse consequences*—Mirror, 2007 / *This proud, but humiliated, most complicated of politicians was not averse to flattery*—M. Almond, 1992.

advert *see* AD.

advertise is spelt *-ise*, not *-ize*.

advertisement is pronounced with the main stress on the second syllable in RP, but often on the third syllable (ad-vuh-**tiyz**-muhnt) in many regional varieties of English.

advertising, language of. In a study of the use of language to influence and persuade people, the American scholar Dwight Bolinger (*Language, the Loaded Weapon*, 1980) describes several techniques which advertisers share with other persuaders in manipulating language to their own ends. These may be summarized as (1) literalism, in which an assertion is made that is literally true but will normally be understood in special ways that the advertiser intends (e.g. *Dentists recommend Colgate* suggests that all dentists recommend it whereas only two need be found to justify the statement made), (2) euphemism, in which less favourable aspects are made to sound more appealing (e.g. something that is *average* may be described as *standard* and a small quantity of a product may be described as *handy version* or *fun size*), and uninteresting concepts are made to sound more interesting (e.g. *crafted* instead of *made, ultra-pure* instead of *clean* or *fresh*), (3) use of jaunty vocabulary and slogans (e.g. *Drinka pinta milka day, Every picture tells a story*), and (4) the use of special syntax to associate the customer with a product (e.g. *Aren't you glad you use Dial?* and *Put a tiger in your tank*), both of which make an assumption to flatter and reassure the customer. *See also* EUPHEMISM; SLOGAN.

advice, advise. 1 *Advice* is a noun ('an opinion given about future action') and *advise* a verb ('to give advice to'), in both BrE and AmE: *The hardest thing is knowing where to go to get help, to get the advice and information you need*—The Face, 1990 / *It may make sense to take professional advice on the wording of an appropriate letter*—M. Edwards, 1991 / *We're advising all our clients to sit tight, at the moment, and neither to buy nor to sell*—A. Davidson, 1989 / *I would advise anyone thinking of a relationship with her now to stay well clear*—Daily Record, 2007.

2 The verb *advise* can never be spelt *-ize*.

3 Both words are used in a special sense in commercial and related uses:

advice here is countable and is used to mean 'piece of information' (usually in the plural) or 'a document giving information' (*Now we're looking to encourage our customers to send remittance advices electronically*—Accountancy, 1993), and *advise* means 'to notify, to give information to', typically followed by *of* or a *that*-clause (*The student will be advised of the name and address of the tutor*—Tutors' Handbook 1991 / *She has advised us that a letter is in the process of being submitted*—Northern Echo, 2007).

advisedly. It should be pronounced as four syllables.

adviser, advisor. Both forms occur throughout the English-speaking world, and *advisor* is recognized as a variant by many dictionaries. Despite impressions that *-er* is predominantly BrE and *-or* AmE, in the *OEC*, the *-er* form is nearly three times as common, and so the traditional spelling still predominates. *Advisor* is probably influenced by the existence of *advisory*; but *adviser* is preferable: *The Service would never forgive me a mucky divorce, dear*—not its legal adviser—John Le Carré, 1989 / *The goose . . . shuffled off to see if she could find some advisors*—Jeanette Winterson, 1985.

advocate *verb.* **1** In a letter written in 1798 Benjamin Franklin asked Noah Webster, the lexicographer of American English, to use his authority to 'reprobate' this word, which was then new in the meaning 'to recommend or plead in favour of', although the verb had been in use for at least a century and a half with the meaning 'to act as advocate'.

2 Fowler's view (1926) that 'unlike *recommend, propose, urge*, and other verbs, *advocate* is not idiomatically followed by a *that*-clause, but only by an ordinary noun or a verbal noun' has proved to be unsound. All three constructions are found and are acceptable:

(noun) *He had been expelled by the National Executive for continuing to advocate a political alliance with Communists*—George Brown, 1971 / (verbal noun) *I would advocate the keeping of animals at school*—A. S. Neill, 1915 / (that-clause) *We would always advocate that people don't get involved in a new relationship early in recovery because it creates dependency*—Sunday Star, 2007.

-ae, -as, as plurals of nouns in *-a*. Most English nouns in *-a* are from Latin (or Latinized Greek) feminine singular nouns in the nominative case, which in Latin forms the plural ending *-ae*. But some have a different Latin origin: e.g. *subpoena* is not nominative, *comma* and *drama* are neuter forms, and *addenda*, *data*, and *stamina* are plurals, and so with these words plural in *-ae* is not possible. Other words are not from Latin at all: e.g. *sofa* is from Arabic and *swastika* is from Sanskrit.

Of those words that are genuinely able to have plurals in *-ae*, some more technical ones do so (*algae*, *larvae*), whereas those in general use form English plurals in *-as* (*areas*, *ideas*, *villas*) and those in both technical and general use have both forms depending on the domain of use (*antennae* or *antennas*, *formulae* or *formulas*, *nebulae* or *nebulas*).

ae-, e-. There is a tendency to simplify spellings with *ae-* in BrE to *e-* in AmE, e.g. *esthetic* for *aesthetic* and *anemic* for *anaemic*, but both types are used.

aeon, meaning 'a long period of time', is more often spelt with initial *ae-* in BrE but elsewhere, especially in AmE, and in scientific writing, as *eon*. The pronunciation for both spellings is **ee**-on. *See also* EPOCH.

aerie, aery (nest of a bird of prey) *see* EYRIE.

aesthete, aesthetic are spelt with initial *ae-* in BrE and pronounced **ees**-theet and ees-**thet**-ik. In AmE they are pronounced **es**-theet and es-**thet**-ik. The recognized US variant spellings *esthete* and *esthetic* are rarely used in practice. *See also* ASCETIC.

affect, effect. 1 These two words are often confused. It may be useful to remember that *effect* is most common as a noun meaning 'a result or consequence' (*In England, at any rate, education produces no effect whatsoever*—Oscar Wilde), and that *affect* is most common as a verb meaning 'to make a difference to' (*Bodily exercise indirectly affects all the organs of the body / These measures chiefly affect* [i.e. are directed at] *drug-pushers / It will not affect* [i.e. have a bearing on] *his chances of promotion*). As a noun, *affect* survives only as a technical term in psychology. As a verb, *effect* means 'to bring about, to cause, to have as a result' (*to effect changes, to effect a cure, to effect a rescue*).

2 *Affect* also means 'to assume (a character); to pretend to have or feel or do something, etc.' (*As he reached the pick-up point, he should affect to slow down as if hunting for a car*—John Le Carré, 1989). This is a different word although it is ultimately related to the one above.

affix is a grammatical term for word elements added at the beginnings or ends of words (e.g. *anti-, post-, re-, -able, -ness, -tion*). It is also used for elements put in the middle of words (infixes) such as Eliza Doolittle's *abso-blooming-lutely*.

afflict *see* INFLICT.

aficionado borrowed from Spanish ('supporter, enthusiast'), this word has the plural *aficionados*, not *-oes*, and is spelt with only one letter *f*, not two. It can be pronounced uh-fis-yuh-**nah**-doh or uh-fish-yuh-**nah**-doh, but not uh-fix-yuh-**nah**-doh. The final -*o* shows that it is masculine in Spanish; feminine *aficionada* can be used in English to refer to a woman.

African American (both without and with a hyphen) as a noun and adjective is currently the most neutral term in the US to refer to Americans of African origin, though *black* (or *Black*) is also still widely used. *African American* has eclipsed *Afro-American*, which was first recorded in the 19c and became widespread in the 1960s and 1970s, but is now mostly used in anthropological and cultural contexts.

aftermath. The original sense in agriculture (a second or later mowing or the crop of grass which springs up after the first mowing) is 16c (along with *aftercrop* and *aftergrass*) and the figurative sense is 17c. In its figurative meaning, *aftermath* usually denotes something unpleasant or unwelcome in itself, or something that follows on an unpleasant or unwelcome event (such as war or disease), but these unfavourable connotations are not present in the literal meaning. Examples: *Depression is sometimes an immediate aftermath of completing a piece of work*— A. Storr, 1979 / *In total, nine ambulances, four paramedics, a rapid response car and a rapid response doctor were needed to deal with the aftermath of the violence*—*Birmingham Post*, 2007. The phrase 'in the aftermath of' is a useful staple of news reporting, (e.g. *in the aftermath of Hurricane Sandy*), to the extent that it tends to be overused: it fits somewhat awkwardly in contexts where the event preceding the aftermath can hardly be considered unpleasant or unwelcome, e.g. *an odd mix of visuals Kahlua aimed at audiences in the United States in the aftermath of the brand's celebrity-driven launch*—*Art Bulletin*, 2000.

afterward, afterwards. *Afterward* is used chiefly in North America (*Afterward, he had a long and satisfying career with the city Welfare Department*—*New Yorker*, 1987 / *Afterward they were enormously and finally sick of each other*— Alice Munro, 1987 (Canada). Even in North America, however, despite American dictionaries giving preference to *afterward*, it is still less frequent than *afterwards*, which is much more often used throughout the Anglosphere.

age. There is an idiomatic use that differs between BrE and AmE: BrE has *at the age of* . . ., and AmE has *at age* . . . (*It all started when he got diphtheria, at age eighteen*—*New Yorker*, 1991).

aged is pronounced as one syllable in (e.g.) *The house has aged well*, and as two syllables in (e.g.) *an aged man*.

ageing, aging. The great Atlantic divide between AmE and BrE spelling here manifests itself unexpectedly. US dictionaries give preference to *aging*, with *ageing* as an alternative; British dictionaries do the reverse. The *OEC* data shows that in the US and Canada *aging* is massively more frequent, although *ageing* is occasionally used. In Britain the opposite is true, and elsewhere the forms compete on more equal terms, *ageing* being the commoner.

ageism, agism. The first appearance in the *OED* of *ageism*, meaning 'prejudice or discrimination on the grounds of a person's age', and of its related adjective *ageist*, dates from 1969. According to the *OEC* data, *ageism* is more common, but not hugely so, than its near synonym *age discrimination*. The spelling *ageism* is much more often used than *agism*, although the second is recognized as a variant in US dictionaries. Spelling the word *ageism* with an *e* has the advantage of visually preserving the link with *age*,

a

and of avoiding the *ag-* being read the way it is in *aggro*.

agenda. 1 The essential plurality of this word (= things to be done) has been worn to extinction by usage. Its dominant sense now is 'a list of items of business to be considered at a meeting, etc.' and it is often used in extended or figurative meanings (*Mrs Walton said she hadn't a spare moment. She had a busy agenda*—Beryl Bainbridge, 1975 / *There is a feeling that we have got to draw up a new agenda now*—Marxism Today, 1986). It has even produced a plural in *-as*: *Iraqi Shias, Sunnis and Kurds are united in being able to use the Americans' presence to pursue separate and often conflicting political agendas*—Guardian 2007. The singular *agendum* is purely notional, although it is occasionally used, e.g. in the context of academic bodies: *The Estates Bursar was called on to introduce Agenda Item 3. They mean Agendum 3, thought Jake*—Kingsley Amis, 1978.

2 The phrase *hidden agenda* (first recorded in 1971) has powerful and sometimes sinister connotations (*Sex was the hidden agenda at these discussions*—Margaret Atwood, 1987 / *The hidden agenda could easily appear to be that 'our drama is the least important thing in the school'*—B. Woolland, 1993).

aggravate. The meaning 'to annoy or exasperate' has existed in good sources since the early 17c; despite this, Fowler (1926) snobbishly recommended that it 'should be left to the uneducated'. The dominance of the current sense has not put paid to the original meaning, 'to increase the gravity of', and the two meanings now stand side by side. Examples: (older sense) *These misfortunes were greatly aggravated by the policies of the English Government*—Winston Churchill, 1958 / (later sense) *Do not aggravate them, be quiet, smile nicely*—Peter Carey, 1982 / *Jane Fairfax*

aggravates her in all sorts of ways—T. Tanner, 1986. The later meaning has given rise to a common participial adjective *aggravating* (like *annoying*): e.g. *It was aggravating that he had to do so many little jobs himself*—Mary Wesley, 1983. In law, *aggravating* factors or circumstances make an offence (such as *aggravated assault*) more serious and the word in this sense is therefore the opposite of *mitigating*.

aggression. Note that it has two gs.

aggressive. 1 Note that it has two gs.

2 The modern commercial world has added the meanings 'self-assertive; energetic, enterprising' to the word when it is applied to the techniques of marketing and salesmanship or to selling goods or services: *We are seeking an aggressive senior level manager with excellent business acumen*—advertisement in The Times, 1985.

aggressor. Note that it has two gs and is spelt *-or* not *-er*.

agism *see* AGEISM, AGISM.

agitator is spelt *-or*, not *-er*.

ago, since. *Ago* is followed by *that*, not *since*, in constructions of the type *It is 10 years ago that* [not *since*] *he died. Since* is used without *ago*: e.g. *It is 10 years since he died.*

agreement. 1 definition. Grammatical agreement (also called *concord*) is the correct relation to each other of different parts of a sentence, so that (for example) the form of the verb corresponds to its subject (*The house was small, and its walls were painted white*), and the gender and number (singular or plural) of a pronoun conforms to that of the person or thing it refers to (*He had never been close enough to a girl to consider making her his wife*). As English has lost many inflections over centuries of use, agreement is more closely restricted to particular aspects of sentence structure than it is in some other languages (e.g. German).

2 two typical problems. Lengthy sentences in which the verb is separated from its singular subject by intervening words in the plural can cause the speaker or writer to put the verb in the plural, but this is incorrect: *The consequence of long periods of inactivity or situations in which patients cannot look after themselves* ✖ *are often quite severe and long-lasting.* Here there are three options: change *consequence* to *consequences*, change *are* to *is*, or (probably best) recast the sentence more simply, e.g. *Long periods of inactivity . . . can often have quite severe and long-lasting consequences.*

In shorter sentences, the verb is also often forced out of agreement with its subject when a significant plural noun intervenes (note the mischief played by the word *of* here as elsewhere): ✖ *Copyright of Vivienne's papers are in the keeping of the Haigh-Wood family—Literary Review,* 1985 / ✖ *The spread of nuclear weapons and technology are likely to make the true picture very different—Dædalus,* 1991 / ✖ *At least one in two churches are likely to be burgled next year—Times,* 1992. Care should be taken to ensure proper agreement in such cases.

Difficulties also occur when the form of the subject is not so obviously singular or plural, for example when it is a phrase (e.g. *fish and chips / more than one*), when it includes an indefinite such as *each, every, any,* or *none,* when it has a parenthetic addition whose grammatical status is unclear (e.g. *My brother, together with a whole lot of his friends, . . .*), when it is a single word of doubtful number (e.g. *agenda* or *data*), or when it is a collective noun (e.g. *the government, a group of people*).

3 two nouns joined by *and*. These normally form a plural subject and require a plural verb: *Speed and accuracy are what is needed / Fish and chips are served in the evening.* But when the noun phrase is regarded as a singular unit, it can take a singular verb: *Fish and chips is my favourite meal / Romeo and Juliet is showing at the local cinema.* This can extend to concepts that are distinct in themselves but are regarded as a single item in a particular sentence: *A certain cynicism and resignation comes along with the poverty of Italian comedy.* The convention is very old, with evidence dating back to Old and Middle English. Clearly there will be borderline cases, and then it is what sounds natural that matters: *The hurt and disbelief of parents' friends and families is/are already quite real / The extent and severity of drug use in the United States has/have been a shock to the medical director.*

4 indefinite pronouns. In many cases, these (*each, either, every, everybody, neither, none, no one,* etc.) govern a singular verb, but sometimes the context calls for a plural, especially when the sense is of collectiveness rather than individuality: (singular) *Neither of these figures illuminates the case against Trident—*David Steel, 1985 / *None of her features is particularly striking—*David Lodge, 1962 / (plural) *Neither the government nor the tribunal, surely, want to bear responsibility—Daily Telegraph,* 1987 / *None of our fundamental problems have been solved—London Review of Books,* 1987. *See also* EACH; EITHER; EVERY; NEITHER; NONE.

In the case of *one of those who,* the verb can be either singular or plural depending on whether *one* or *those* is regarded as the antecedent of *who*: (singular) *Perhaps you were one of those fellows who sees tricks everywhere—*Peter Carey, 1985 / *I am one of those people who wants others to do what I think they* *should*—Joan Bakewell, 1988 / (plural) *Lily had … been one of those numerous people who are simply famous for being famous* [note that *numerous* plays a part in emphasizing plurality]—Iris Murdoch, 1987 / *That's one of those propositions that become harder to sustain the further they're explored*—Kingsley Amis, 1988.

5 subjects separated by *as well as*, *together with*, etc. Nouns joined by other linking words or quasi-coordinators (e.g. *accompanied by, as well as, not to mention, together with*, etc.) are followed by a singular verb if the first noun or noun phrase is singular, because the addition is not regarded as part of the grammatical subject (as is shown by its being enclosed between commas): *A very profitable company such as British Telecom, along with many other companies in the UK, is not prepared to pay a reasonable amount* / *Daddy had on the hairy tweed jacket with leather elbow patches which, together with his pipe, was his trade mark.*

6 words like *agenda* and *data*. These are plural in form but are usually singular in sense and govern a singular verb: in *The agenda is on the table*, the reference is to a single item. The process can be discerned more clearly in the older word *news*, which has long been construed as a singular noun despite its plural form: *Is there any news?* See AGENDA; DATA.

7 collective nouns. These are, by contrast, words such as *committee, government, group*, which refer to a group of people, animals, or objects but are singular in form. In BrE, the practice is well established of construing such words either with a singular verb (when unity or collectivity is being emphasized) or with a plural verb (when individuality or corporateness is being emphasized). Examples: (singular) *Each succeeding generation of gallery visitors finds it easier to recognize Cubist subject-matter* / *A*

group of four young men, in denim overalls, was standing close to him / (plural) *The jury retired at five minutes past five o'clock to consider their verdict* / *Let us hope that the Ministry of Defence are on your side this time.* It is important to avoid a mixed style, as in ⊠ *The government has decided to postpone their decision.*

In AmE it is customary for a singular verb to be used with collective nouns: *The government routinely imposes differential taxes on hotels, bars … and the like*—Bulletin of the American Academy, 1987. But in both BrE and AmE collective nouns of the type *a* + noun + *of* + plural noun can govern a singular or plural verb: *A fleet of helicopters was flying low*—New Yorker, 1986 / *A handful of bathers were bobbing about in the waves*—Philip Roth, 1987 / *A rich and detailed picture of a world in which a multitude of elements were intertwined*—New York Review of Books, 1989.

8 other plural forms treated as singular. (1) Titles of books, plays, films, etc. (because the words 'the book etc. known as …' are implicit): *Great Expectations is an account of development of identity* / *Star Wars has diverted some six billion dollars from the federal treasury.* (2) Names of illnesses (because the words 'the illness known as …' are implicit): *Mumps often occurs in adults* / *Measles is normally a childhood disease.*

9 clash of agreement. Sometimes there is a clash of agreement within a sentence, for example when the speaker or writer wants to avoid 'his' or 'his or her', and recourse to the plural is an old device: *Everyone was in their shirtsleeves*—F. Tuohy, 1984 / *No one in their senses wants to create instability*—Denis Healey, 1985 / *I really resent it when I call somebody who's not home and they don't have an answering machine*—Chicago Tribune, 1988 / *Each parent has a duty to do the best for their own child*—Independent, 1996.

10 subject–complement agreement. When a subject and a complement of different number are separated by the verb *to be* (or verbs such as *become, seem*, etc.), the verb should agree with the number of the subject: (singular) *The only traffic is ox-carts and bicycles / The problem is the windows / The view it obscured was pipes, fire escapes, a sooty-walled well /* (plural) *The socials were a big deal to her / The house and garden were a powerful cauldron of heat and light / The March events in Poland were a natural stage in the evolution of communism.* There are some exceptions, depending on the sense in particular cases: *More nurses [i.e. the subject of more nurses] is the next item on the agenda.*

See also COLLECTIVE NOUN; EITHER; GENDER-NEUTRALITY; MANY; NEITHER; THERE IS.

ahead of. This prepositional phrase has been in use since the 18c in the physical sense 'in front of' and from the following century in the figurative sense 'better than, superior to (in quality, performance, etc)'. Its meaning in relation to time dates from the beginning of the 20c with a use by George Bernard Shaw in *The Devil's Disciple* (III.78: *We are some minutes ahead of you already*). Shaw is also credited with an early use (in 1934) of the cliché *ahead of its* (or *one's*) *time* (*On the Rocks* I.219: *Women and men who are ahead of their time. They alone can lead the present into the future. They are ghosts from the future*).

In a development dating from the 1980s, *ahead of*, referring to time, has come to mean 'before', often, but not always, with the idea of 'in preparation for' or 'taking account of' (*Seismic imaging of far-side solar activity allows us to anticipate the appearance of large active regions more than a week ahead of their arrival on the eastern solar limb—Internet website*, 2002 [OEC] / *Some ISPs such as Wanadoo are investing in LLU but decline to reveal any significant detail because they don't want to give the game away ahead of a commercial launch—The Register*, 2005).

This use, which originated in AmE, has a resounding ring of newspaper or TV reporting and is awkward and jargonistic in general usage, where, let us hope, it is unlikely to find much favour.

-aholic. This suffix, derived from *alcoholic*, meaning 'someone addicted to alcohol' (late 19c), forms words that mean kinds of addiction, and has moved into common use in the last three or four decades, principally in *workaholic* (1968), *chocoholic* (1961), and *shopaholic* (1984). The suffix appears as *-holic* in words of two syllables ending in an *-er* sound, e.g. *sugarholic* (1965), *computerholic* (1977). It has proved to be a useful and productive word element, whose progress in the language is to some extent a reflection of social preoccupations: witness the more recent *blogaholic* and *rageaholic*.

aid. The noun dates from 1940 in its meanings 'material help given by one country to another' (*Christian aid, foreign aid, Marshall aid*, etc.), and took on a further use as the second element in the names of occasions organized to raise money for charitable causes (*Band Aid, Fashion Aid, School Aid, Live Aid*, etc.). The use was triggered by Band Aid, the name of a rock group formed by Bob Geldof in 1984 to raise money for the relief of famine in Ethiopia.

aid, aide. An *aid* is someone who helps (in various ways), whereas an *aide* denotes one of three more specific functions: (1) an assistant to an important person, especially a political leader (*presidential aides, a former aide to Mr Brown*), (2) short for *aide-de-camp*, a high-ranking officer in the armed services (*Brigadier Monson summoned his* *five closest aides for a working lunch*—N. Barber, 1984), (3) a person employed as an assistant or ancillary worker, especially in a hospital or as a visitor to the home of an ill or elderly person (*Just before he died a nurse's aide brought his dinner tray into the room*—E. L. Doctorow, 1989).

Aids, an acronym derived from *acquired immune deficiency syndrome*. The spelling as a word with an initial capital has superseded the older form *AIDS*, a preference intensified by the occurrence of several combinations such as *Aids-related, Aids vaccine*, and *Aids awareness*.

aim. The verb has two principal constructions in its abstract meaning: you can *aim at* something (analogous with aiming at a target in the physical meaning) or *at doing* something, or you can *aim to do* something (*The directive aims at ensuring open passage through the borders*—Financial Times, 1984 / *We should aim to re-cycle half our household waste within 10 years*.—Independent, 1989). The construction with *to*, for long the more common option in AmE, has excellent credentials, and is modelled on the analogy of similar verbs such as *intend, mean, plan*, etc. There is also a natural preference for the *to* construction when the progressive form of *aim* (*is* or *are aiming*) is used (*Today, our orchestras are aiming to provide every child with a live performance during their time at school*—Times, 2007). In the passive, however, the *at* construction is obligatory (*The technology in question is aimed at improving the quality of life of the inhabitants*—N. Woodall, c.1991).

ain't. 1 *Ain't* is one of the most controversial words in current English, arousing passions that one would never have dreamt of from such a seemingly inoffensive word. '*Do you hear? Don't say "ain't" or "dang" or*

"*son of a buck*" ... *You're not a pair of hicks!*' scolds a mother in a *New Yorker* short story. In 1942 Eric Partridge could hardly bear to include it ('I blush to record it') in *Usage and Abusage*, and *Webster's Third New International Dictionary* of 1961 included it solely on grounds of currency, earning widespread condemnation for not castigating it more strongly. Because social disapproval is so strong, no dictionary of current English will admit it to the ranks of standard English. The reasons for this lie in the word's history.

2 *Ain't* has been an undisputed element in Cockney speech at least since the time of Dickens ('*You seems to have a good sister.' 'She ain't half bad.*'—Our Mutual Friend, 1865). It also features widely in the language of comic strips and modern rap music (of US origin). The *OED* used to note that 'the contraction is also found as a (somewhat outmoded) upper-class colloquialism'. It has also been espoused in intellectual circles as an affectation, which tends to confuse the issue (*I've not the spirit to pack up and go without him. Ain't I a craven*—Virginia Woolf, 1938 / *Still working the Cape Cod and Florida cycle. And it ain't too bad*—Yale Alumni Magazine).

3 The formation of *ain't* is irregular, which in part accounts for the stigma attached to it. It is an 18c word, attested earlier in the form *an't* (e.g. in Fielding). Unlike other contractions, such as *isn't, aren't*, and *haven't, ain't* is not a reduced form of any logical ancestor. Note, by the way, that *aren't* also is exceptional in being used in tag questions for *am I not* as well as *are they not, are you not*, and so on (*I'm coming too, aren't I?*). The logical contraction *amn't*, is not in use, presumably because it would be too awkward to articulate (and might be shortened to *an't* or *ain't?*).

4 It is unlikely that *ain't* will be admitted to standard English in the foreseeable future, if ever. For now, it stands at the door, out on the pavement, not yet part of the language household except as an affectation or in catch-phrases, at best handled with tweezers and at worst regarded as the clearest single token of illiteracy.

air *verb*. Meanings to do with exposing to the air in various senses date from the time of Shakespeare, and the now familiar use with opinions, grievances, etc. as objects date from the late 19c. The meaning 'to broadcast' (first recorded in the mid-20c) draws on the sense of the noun 'a medium for transmission of radio waves'; this originated in AmE (*It aired a heartwarming TV commercial on the importance of savings institutions—Wall Street Journal*, 1989) and has become common also in BrE in transitive and intransitive uses (*The obligation to keep records of all programmes aired—Economist*, 1981 / *the controversial docudrama Bloody Sunday, which caused a storm when it aired on British TV last year—*film review, BrE 2004 [*OEC*]).

aitch *see* H.

à la. When used in English to mean 'in the style or manner of', despite being feminine in French, *à la* does not vary according to the sex of the person mentioned (*There were giant landscape photocollages à la David Hockney / Afternoon talk shows à la Oprah*).

à la carte in its culinary meaning refers to dishes that can be ordered as separate items, not as part of a set meal, e.g. *an à la carte menu, eating à la carte*. *À la carte* is also a metaphor for choosing parts of something that is sold as a package, particularly in the entertainment industry (e.g. *Everyone understands where the music industry will end up some years down the line: selling songs à la carte to consumers with few or no*

restrictions). It is also used more abstractly for selecting particular aspects of a belief system, policy, etc. that is usually considered as a whole (e.g. *It is not possible to be in favour of the death penalty à la carte. The state either claims the right to impose this doom or it does not*). This phrase can work as an elegant shorthand, and often the context, as in the previous example, clarifies its exact meaning. But you may also risk being discourteous to readers and listeners not as familiar as you with the niceties of fine dining.

albeit (15c) is not an uncommon word, despite its possibly quaint look and the fact that it includes a subjunctive verb (*all be it that*). It is generally used with a following adjective, adverb, or non-finite clause: *It is an unwelcome, albeit necessary, restraint—A. Storr, 1972 / Some physical contact, albeit simply a touch, was needed—R. Stone, 2002.*

   It can also introduce a finite clause, without *that*, or (particularly in BrE) with it: *Their voices, too, albeit the accent was provincial, were soft and musical—1878 / In most EU countries the central bank plays a role here, albeit that the supervision is often entrusted to another agency—BrE, 2000 [OEC].*

albino has the plural form *albinos*.

alga is normally used in its plural form *algae*, pronounced **al**-jee, or occasionally **al**-gee.

alibi is originally a legal term meaning 'a plea that when an alleged act took place one was elsewhere'. The earliest use of *alibi* (18c) corresponded to that of the Latin adverb meaning 'elsewhere': those under suspicion had to prove that they were *alibi* (elsewhere). From this use it rapidly hardened into a noun: an *alibi* was 'an instance of being alibi' (*Since you think I murdered him, I had better produce my alibi—S. Brett, 1979*).

In the 20c it has developed a colloquial weakened meaning 'an excuse; a plea of innocence' (*I have an alibi because I'm going to have a baby*—L. P. Hartley, 1951 / *So far delivery has not lived up to expectations raised by the bold, soaring rhetoric, and the alibis are running out*—*Independent*, 2002). This colloquial use is first recorded in American sports writing and then in detective fiction (naturally, or surprisingly, enough). The corresponding sense of 'a person providing an alibi' has followed suit (*Tom and Maureen are my alibis*—C. Hare, 1949) and there is even a verb, although its inflections make it too awkward for widespread use (*She's alibi-ed by Mrs. Fitch*—J. Cannan, 1958 / *There's got to be someone to alibi us*—L. Duncan, 1978).

alien. From the 14c to the 19c inclusive, *alien* as an adjective meaning 'of nature or character different from' was followed by *from* (*This uncouth style, so alien from genuine English*—H. Reed, 1855). About the end of the 19c, this construction gave way to one with *to*, by analogy with words like *adverse*, *repugnant*, and *opposed*, rather than *different*. The construction with *to* is now routine (*Thinking, and certainly brooding, were quite alien to his character*—J. C. Oates, 1980 / *The implied snobbery of the remark was quite alien to the whole way in which she had been brought up*—A. N. Wilson, 1982). The construction with *from* still occurs from time to time (*A reflection upon how far man has come to feel himself alien from the animal kingdom of which he is a member*—A. Storr, 1968).

all. 1 *all* or *all of.* *All* can be used before singular or plural nouns, and *of* is not needed except before pronouns standing alone (*all human life* / *all the time* / *all children* / *all tickets* / *all of them* / *all you people*). The construction with *of* is comparatively recent (first recorded *c.*1800) and is probably due to association with *none of, some of, little of, much of,* etc. (*He will have to be all of these things*—Anita Brookner, 1986 / *All of the company's profits had been used to salary him*—B. Ripley, 1987 / *At each stop, all of us visitors were greeted by a hail of celebratory statistics*—*New Yorker*, 1989). There is also a common idiomatic use with quantities (*It must have been all of fifteen minutes of . . . dull, homesick silence*—Mark Twain, 1883 / *Even I, all of eight years old, couldn't stand another second of his shrieking*—*Me Three Magazine*, AmE 1944).

2 When *all* is the subject of the verb *to be* followed by a plural complement, the linking verb is expressed in the singular: *All I saw was fields*—Nigel Williams, 1985 / *In some sense, all we have is the scores*—*incomplete and corrupted as they often are*—*New Yorker*, 1989.

3 See also ALL RIGHT; ALL THAT; ALL TOGETHER; ALL TOLD; ALREADY; for *all but*, see BUT 7.

all-around is an optional AmE variant of *all-round* (*The best all-around American school* / *A good all-around player*).

allay has inflections *allays, allayed, allaying.*

alleged, allegedly. 1 *Alleged* is pronounced as two syllables, and *allegedly* as four.

2 Their role is to distinguish an unproven accusation (i.e., an allegation) from a proven fact or event (*the victim of the alleged fraud* / *their alleged attackers*). The disclaiming qualification they provide is not needed in sentences in which the context already makes the situation clear: *An Iraqi prisoner has described how he was [allegedly] subjected to vicious beatings*—*Independent*, 2004. The disclaimer would be needed were we to make the sentence a direct statement not attributed to the victim:

An Iraqi prisoner was allegedly subjected to vicious beatings.

allegory, fable, parable. 1 All three words denote a narrative or story the characters and events in which symbolize other persons and events. *Allegory* flourished in medieval literature and later (Spenser's *Faerie Queene*, 1590–6; Bunyan's *Pilgrim's Progress*, 1678–84, in which the journey of the hero Christian stands for the life of the human soul; Dryden's *Absalom and Achitophel*, 1681), and allegorical elements are present in much modern writing, e.g. Virginia Woolf's *Between the Acts* (1941), which by means of a village pageant presents 'a communal image of rural England, past and present', or Orwell's *Animal Farm* (1945).

2 A *parable* is a special kind of allegory, especially in the New Testament, in which a moral point is made from an everyday story. A *fable* also makes a moral point, but is couched in terms of fictional characters who are often made to do impossible things (e.g. animals speak).

allegro has the plural form *allegros*.

allergy dates from the early 20c in its medical meaning 'sensitiveness to pollen, certain foods, antibiotics, etc.' It is attested earlier in German (*Allergie*) and is derived from the Greek words *allos* 'other, different' and *ergon* 'work'. Its extended meaning, involving antipathy to all sorts of things, dates from the 1940s; an early instance is a famous one by Auden: *Before the Diet of Sugar he was using razor blades And excited soon after with an allergy to maidenheads—For the Time Being*, 1944. *Allergic* in its medical meaning dates from about the same time as *allergy*, and it was used metaphorically slightly earlier than *allergy* was (1937 in the *OED*). In current use, allergies and being allergic can be applied to anything or anyone you dislike or have an aversion to, such as change, the number 13, debt, opera on television, or negotiating with terrorists. Though disliked by Gowers in his edition of *Modern English Usage*, it is now standard, if somewhat hyperbolic.

alley has the plural form *alleys*.

allot *verb* has inflected forms *allots, allotted, allotting*, but note *allotment* (one *t*).

allow. 1 This verb matches *admit* in having a wide range of common uses, transitive and intransitive, with *that-*clauses, and with an infinitive complement. For several centuries it has alternated in many meanings with the phrasal verb *allow of*. Some of these meanings are now obsolete, but one has survived, presumably to avoid ambiguity with *allow* = 'permit, authorize', although it sounds old-fashioned (e.g. *Jortin is willing to allow of* [= *accept as valid*] *other miracles*—J. R. Lowell, 1849).

2 In the meanings 'to acknowledge, concede', *allow* followed by a clause has been in continuous use since the 17c (e.g. *I suppose it will be allowed us that marriage is a human society*—Milton, 1643 / *'You know best, Captain,' Hugh Macroon allowed with grave courtesy*—Compton Mackenzie, 1947 / *Kerry never allowed that perhaps the greatest failure has been that of Nato countries to provide the peacekeepers they had promised*—weblog, BrE 2002 [*OEC*]).

3 The construction *allow as how*, meaning 'to state as an opinion, have to admit that' is restricted to AmE and dialect uses (*She allowed as how my old friend J. J. was flying on Monday morning*—N. Thornburg, 1976 / *He allowed as how she was faithful*—T. Morrison, 1981).

allowedly is pronounced as four syllables.

all right As the *Oxford Dictionary On-line* puts it, 'There is no logical reason for insisting that *all right* should be written as two words rather than as *alright*'. Nevertheless, dozens of usage guides, before and after Fowler (1926), have insisted and insist still that *all right* is preferable. It is therefore wise to avoid the spelling *alright* in any kind of formal writing, despite its much higher frequency. There are, in fact, various arguments in its favour, especially: (1) the need to distinguish it from the use in which *all* is a pronoun and not an adverb, as in *He finished the crossword and got it all right*, (2) the analogy of *altogether, already*, etc., which were once written as two words before becoming single words and similarly need to be distinguished from two-word forms having other meanings, and (3) its pronunciation as a single word. Nonetheless, *all right* should be used for the time being, not *alright*. Examples: (all right) *One advantage of the permissive society is that it's all right to live together before marriage*—Woman's Own, 1971 / *It's all right for you ... You won't have to do the post-mortem with these guys*—Len Deighton, 1974 / *'Oh, all right', she said, 'go and be damned.'*—Graham Greene, 1980 / (alright) *They've been bloody inscrutable alright*—P. Cave, 1979 / *You'll be alright, love*—Chinua Achebe, 1987 / *If you've got the ears to know what sounds good you're going to be pretty much alright*—Guitarist, 1992. *See also* ALREADY; ALL TOGETHER.

all-round *see* ALL-AROUND.

all that, as in *not all that good*, is common as a colloquial intensifier (*I looked around the stock. It wasn't all that brilliant, I must admit*—J. Leasor, 1969 / *I'm just not all that happy right now*—weblog, AmE 2004 [*OEC*]. Gowers (1965) judged that the use was 'well on its way to literary status', and it is indeed now a standard construction, though still with the faintest tang of the conversational about it.

all together, altogether. These are often confused, because their meanings encroach on one another. *All together* means 'everyone together', and the word *all* is usually removable without damaging the syntax or affecting the meaning: *One victim and five suspects, all together in a sealed room*—A. Morice, 1971. *Altogether* is adverbial and can mean (1) 'entirely; in every way': *The idea of counselling in schools is not altogether new*—Times, 1970 / *Martinez was not altogether unknown. But the antagonism of people in Chicago is insignificant. He has another ball game in mind altogether*—Saul Bellow, 1982, (2) 'in all, in total': *You owe me £400 altogether*, and (3) 'considering everything', *The weather was bad and the hotel overcrowded. Altogether, it was a disappointing holiday.*

It is much more common for *all together* to be wrongly written for *altogether* than the other way round. Examples of wrong spelling: (should be *altogether*) *The federal government doesn't seem all together that bothered*—CNN transcripts, 2007 / (should be *all together*) *It's really interesting how altogether we can feel like a human race, not any more any single country*—CNN transcripts, 2007.

all told. This phrase, meaning 'when all are counted or included', is first recorded in 1850. Originally used in contexts that included numbers (e.g. *There are 12 all told*), it has now spread to unquantified contexts (e.g. *All told, I enjoyed life in the army*). This use is standard in informal speech. If you wish to avoid it in formal writing, *all in all* and *all things considered* are perfectly good substitutes.

allude, allusion. 1 It has been claimed by some critics that to *allude* to someone or something can only properly mean to mention them 'indirectly or covertly', i.e. without mentioning their name, unlike *refer*, which means to mention them directly, i.e. by name. So, according to this view, if you *refer* to Julius Caesar you name him, whereas if you *allude* to him you identify him without naming him, e.g. 'the Roman dictator assassinated in 44 BC'. In practice, *allude* is often used to mean 'refer' (e.g. *He had star quality, an element often alluded to in Arlene's circle of show-biz friends*—Gore Vidal, 1978 / *She tabled a letter alluding to fraud that caused alarm amongst her fellow councillors*—AusE source, 2003 [*OEC*]).

2 *Allusion* and *reference* should follow the same principle, *allusion* involving indirect mention and *reference* involving direct mention by name, but again in practice the distinction blurs at the edges: *She came across allusions to her family in the papers*—Vita Sackville-West, 1931 / *Midway in the questioning . . . he'd begun to notice the number of allusions to a particular November weekend*—Truman Capote, 1966 / *There were hints and allusions about his troubles to his friends*—D. Halberstam, 1979 / *She was . . . annoyed that he could make her feel so uncomfortable by his veiled allusion to last night*—A. Murray, 1993. The use of both words in the way described is well established and perfectly acceptable.

3 Beware of confusion between *allusion* and *illusion*, which means 'a deception or misapprehension about the true state of affairs'.

ally. 1 This is now normally stressed on the first syllable as a noun. As a verb, the first syllable is normally stressed in BrE, the second in AmE.

2 The verb has four typical constructions: (1) transitive, (2) intransitive, (3) reflexive (*Since Siegfried alone has the strength to win the Valkyrie for Gunther, they must ally themselves with him*—A.

Huth, 1985), (4) passive (*We hear she's currently allied with a very flakey anarchist guy*—John Le Carré, 1983).

3 *Allied* is used as a general adjective meaning 'relating to or belonging to allies (whether or not identified)' (*The man . . . made his astonishing parachute jump into allied territory*—*Times*, 1970 / *The Vice President also wants to know just what allied or U.S. initiatives Europeans would welcome to get the stalemated talks . . . going once again*—*Times*, 1977). By convention, the noun *Allies* and the adjective *Allied* are spelt with a capital letter when they refer to Britain and her allies in the First and Second World Wars (*In the air, Allied losses fell from an average of 5% per raid to 1.5%*—*Sunday Times*, 2004).

almanac is now spelt -*ac* except in traditional titles including *The Oxford Almanack* and *Whitaker's Almanack*.

almost. *During the next week Morel's temper was almost unbearable*—D. H. Lawrence, 1913. *Almost* has a special role in diluting or 'downgrading' adjectives and adverbs that express an extreme, as if the user wants to keep the notion at arm's length or to allow some means of defence against a challenge; in this use the role of *almost* is closer to that of 'somewhat' than to its own normal meaning 'nearly'. A correspondent to *The Times* in 2003 noted a use that was positively counter-intuitive: *In response to Jack Straw's apparent condemnation of the foundation hospitals plan there was 'an almost audible gasp'*. How did he know? He knew because the gasp was almost inaudible or barely audible; *almost* and *barely* (or alternatives such as *hardly* or *scarcely*) have subtly complementary roles in avoiding uses that tip unwittingly into the absurd.

alongside. *Alongside* is both an adverb (*Kevin came quickly alongside*) and a preposition (*the two vehicles were* *alongside each other / learning to read begins very early indeed, alongside learning to talk*). It has been used as a preposition with or without *of* for some two centuries and both constructions are still available; use with *of* is now less usual in BrE although it still occurs (*Margaret turned round to walk along-side of the girl in her feeble progress homeward*—L. Otis, 2002). It is more common in AmE (*Certain plants thrive alongside of each other*—website, AmE 2004 [*OEC*]).

alot. This single-word spelling of *a lot* is now not uncommon. It goes without saying that it is non-standard, and to be avoided. Nevertheless, it illustrates rather strikingly how arbitrary the convention of spelling certain pairs of words together or separately can be. Examples: ⊠ *My parents have been out alot the past 2 weeks* / ⊠ *The recession has affected the advertising business alot* / ⊠ *We still had alot of fun, just a different kind of fun.* Compare AWHILE.

already. 1 As an adverb (*I have already paid*), *already* is spelt as one word, and is not to be confused with the two separate words *all ready* (*We are all ready to start now*).

2 *Already* is sometimes used in AmE and other varieties, and informally in BrE too, to mean 'yet, still' or even (in its weakened use) 'now', as in the following examples: *Give me the watermelon already*—D. Greenburg, AmE 1964 / *I called you up but you weren't there already*—J. Platt, SAfr 1984. This use is non-standard, and should be avoided except in informal contexts.

alright *see* ALL RIGHT.

also. 1 *Also* should be used as an adverb (*Besides being an astronomer and mathematician, Grassi was also an architect*), and not a conjunction equivalent to *and* or *as well as* (*Remember your passport and money; also the tickets / He has made a good impression. He writes well and keeps to deadlines. Also, he's an agreeable person*).

2 The normal position is before the main verb and after auxiliary or modal verbs (*It was also held to be the cause of the milder form of the illness known as AIDS-related complex*—New York Review of Books, 1986 / *Both wines also come in sweeter demi-sec version*—Which?, 1984 / *He also believes that a garden shouldn't be too manicured*—Sunday Times, 2004). In most circumstances, it is pedantic and against natural usage to insist on positioning *also* to clarify the part of the sentence it refers to, as in *My brother also is coming* [i.e. as well as my sister], to distinguish from *My brother is also coming* [i.e. as well as telephoning].

alternate, alternative. 1 Both words are adjectives and nouns and come from Latin *alternus* meaning 'every second' and have had closely related meanings over several centuries of usage. Now however, there is a clear distinction which needs to be observed. *Alternate* as an adjective means '(of two things) each following and followed by the other', as in *alternate days. Alternative* means 'available or usable instead of another', as in *an alternative solution to the problem*. In other words, *an alternative thing* replaces something else, whereas *an alternate thing* exists as well as something else. In current AmE, *alternate*, with stress on the first syllable, has usurped the territory of *alternative* in its ordinary meaning (*I would have no fear about being able to make a safe landing at an alternate airport*—USA Today, 2004).

2 Since the late 1960s the adjective has increasingly been used to mean 'purporting or claiming to represent an acceptable or preferable alternative to that in traditional use', as in *alternative medicine* (mainly homoeopathic or holistic), *alternative energy* (non-nuclear and not using fossil fuels), *alternative fuel* (and *alternative-fuel vehicles, AFVs*), *alternative birthing* (avoiding artificial methods), *alternative society* (rejecting traditional values), *alternative technology* (conserving resources), *alternative theatre* (using non-traditional techniques).

3 *Alternative* as a noun means something that is available or usable instead of something else. The traditional view that an *alternative* must be one of two possibilities, because the source word, Latin *alter*, means 'other of two' is not sustainable, and *alternative* has been regularly used since the mid-19c with reference to any number of possibilities (*The aim of counselling is to open up the personal world of experience in which the person feels 'stuck' so that he or she may find alternative ways of coping with the world of events which confronts him or her*—Counselling, 1983 / *Write to everyone who is providing you with goods or services confirming the details some weeks before the wedding so that you have time to make alternative arrangements if you have to*—York Evening Press, 2004). The traditional use is still found, and lies at the heart of the word, most often as *the alternative* (*The alternative of 'public limited company' is the abbreviation 'p.l.c.'*—Companies Act, 1980).

4 *Alternate* as a noun is much less common. In AmE it is often used with the meaning 'an alternative', a reserve (player), a variant, in which case it is stressed on the first syllable, **awl-tuh-nuht** (*I was fourth alternate in the Miss Teenage South Carolina pageant*—William Boyd, 1984 / *The twelve jurors and six alternates in Room 318 of the United States Courthouse*—New Yorker, 1986). In BrE this meaning is not so commonly found, although it is related to one that was in use in the 18c.

5 *Alternate* is also a verb (pronounced -neit in the final syllable), meaning '(of

two or more things) to succeed one another in turns': *In a democratic system political parties expect to alternate in office*—P. Richards, 1988.

although, though. *Though* can always be used instead of *although*, but the reverse is not true.

1 Both words can be used as a conjunction introducing a subordinate clause (*He did well, although he did not win an outright majority*—Economist, 1981 / *Though there was a tendency for students to factionalize, there were always students good about diplomacy*—Christian Science Monitor, 1982 / *Although the defendant had undoubtedly committed an offence of failing to give full particulars, that was not an arrestable offence*—Times, 1984). Where they are interchangeable, however, *although* generally has a stronger concessive force, and is somewhat more usual in initial position in a sentence.

2 In the following uses, *though* alone is possible: (1) as an adverb in medial or final position (*It is true though that one misses out on one's husband's early years of struggle*—Times, 1985), (2) in inverted constructions (*Young though he is, he doesn't look it*), (3) in the fixed expressions *as though* and *even though* (*Anderson is a borderline New Waver who looks as though she has been out in the rain upside down*—Washington Post, 1982 / *He was by no means a dry, boring theoretician even though he wrote extraordinarily advanced books on dance*—Margot Fonteyn, 1980).

alto has the plural form *altos*.

altogether *see* ALL TOGETHER.

aluminium. The BrE spelling accords well with other element names such as magnesium, potassium, sodium, etc., whereas the AmE spelling *aluminum* (stressed on the second syllable) is the one adopted by its discoverer, Sir H. Davy, in about 1812.

alumnus (stressed on the second syllable) means a former student or pupil, and comes from a Latin word meaning 'nursling'. It is more common in AmE than in BrE. The plural form is *alumni* (pronounced -niy) and the female form is *alumna* (plural *alumnae*, pronounced -nee). Rival views on the pronunciation of Latin words in English mean that the masculine and feminine plural pronunciations are sometimes reversed.

a.m. As an abbreviation of Latin *ante meridiem* 'before noon', *a.m.* is pronounced as two letters and written in the form *8.15 a.m.* (in AmE *8:15 a.m.*). Note that *12.00 a.m.* is midnight and *12 p.m.* is midday; because of the uncertainty these designations cause, the explicit forms *12.00 midnight* or *12.00 midday* are often to be preferred. The abbreviation is sometimes used informally as a noun: *I arrived here this a.m.*

amateur. The standard pronunciation is now **am-uh-tuh**.

ambidextrous. Note the spelling -*trous*, not -*terous*.

ambience, meaning 'the character and atmosphere of a place', is derived from French *ambiance* (a form which is also occasionally used in English). It is firmly established in the language after a century or so of use. Both spellings are in use, although *ambiance* differs in having a non-naturalized nasal pronunciation of the final syllable. The corresponding adjective *ambient* has developed a special meaning relating to instrumental electronic 'New Age' music: *Ambient music looks to have a future in this country as the official artform of the cyberpunks*—Face, 1995.

ambiguity. 1 *Ambiguity* in language denotes the possibility of more than one meaning being understood from what is heard or read. Intentional ambiguity can be effective, for example as a literary device or in advertising. Our concern here is with unintentional and misleading ambiguity that occurs in ordinary speech and writing, most often as a result of poor word order. The Fowlers (1906) devoted several pages to ambiguities of this kind, but their (mostly literary) examples now seem contrived and unreal, as do many of the examples given in grammar books.

2 Typical ambiguities in everyday language usually involve the association of a word or phrase with the wrong part of the sentence (*The council plans to notify parents whose children are affected by post*, where *by post* should be placed after *parents*), or the unclear application of a negative (*They did not go out to water the plants*, which can mean either they did not go out at all, or they did go out but not to water the plants; similarly with the type *We did not go to the shops because we were expecting visitors*: see BECAUSE 2).

3 Ambiguity also arises from words that have more than one meaning or function, as in *Visiting friends can be tiresome* / the famous line *The peasants are revolting* / *The Minister appealed to her supporters*, and from false or unclear reference, as in *If the children don't like their toys, get rid of them* / *We only have two first editions* (and no other books?).

In speech, ambiguity is nearly always eliminated by intonation; in writing, attention to these relatively few problem areas will be enough to avoid the ambiguities that matter.

ambivalent, ambiguous. The terms *ambivalent* and *ambivalence* are first recorded in about 1916 in the context of psychology, and in particular the Jungian notion of 'the coexistence in one person of contradictory emotions or attitudes towards a person or thing'

(*OED*). C. S. Lewis distanced himself somewhat from using *ambivalent* when he said that 'Death is . . . what some modern people would call "ambivalent". It is Satan's great weapon and God's great weapon'. *Ambivalent* applies to feelings and attitudes, whereas *ambiguous* refers to more concrete things such as statements and events and their meanings: (ambivalent) *Women can be extremely ambivalent about their own ambition and aggression at work*—*She*, 1989 / *Examination of what is entailed and what is expected have* [sic] *produced ambivalent conclusions*—*State of Prisons*, 1991 / (ambiguous) *This remark may in isolation be ambiguous*—law report, BrE 2003 [*OEC*] / *Reform is an ambiguous word*—*Business Week Magazine*, 2003. In the following sentence, *ambivalent* would be the better choice: *Booksellers are feeling ambiguous about marking or commemorating the anniversary of the attacks of September 11*—weblog, AmE 2002 [*OEC*].

   Ambivalently is also found, often where *ambiguously* would be more suitable: e.g. *The people who inhabit Gormenghast, ambivalently described as 'figures' and 'shapes', are poised between the two meanings*—M. H. Short et al., 1987.

ameba *see* AMOEBA.

amen is pronounced both **ah**-men and **ay**-men.

amend, emend. 1 *Amend* is the more common word, used of making adjustments to a document or formal proposal (such as a parliamentary act). Its etymological meaning is 'free from fault' (from Latin *mendum* or *menda* 'fault, blemish'), and there is always a notion of correction or improvement in its meaning.

   2 *Emend* and *emendation* are used mainly to refer to the activity of textual scholars in proposing changes in the reading of texts and manuscripts so as

to make them more intelligible or to remove errors.

America. To English speakers outside North America, the term *America* means first and foremost the USA, and *North America* is used to denote a larger geographical area including also Canada and Mexico. The terms *American* and *North American* are used correspondingly as adjectives and nouns. *Central America* refers to the countries in the narrow strip of land to the south of Mexico (including Guatemala, Nicaragua, and Panama), and *South America* to the region to the south of the Panama Canal, including Argentina, Brazil, Chile, Colombia, etc.

American English. *See box overleaf.*

American Indian, as a term for an aboriginal inhabitant of North America and parts of the Caribbean, is less offensive than *Red Indian*, but *Native American* (*see* NATIVE) is even more acceptable. *Indian* is an ethnically erroneous name which is due to a mistaken identification of the area by European explorers in the 15c and 16c. Whenever possible, however, specify the name of the particular people, such as *Apache, Comanche,* or *Sioux*.

amid, amidst. *Amid*, recorded as a preposition and adverb before the Norman Conquest, developed two secondary forms, *amides* (cf. *always*) and *amidst* (cf. *against, amongst*). *Amides* has dropped out of use, and *amid* and *amidst* have survived only as prepositions. In the 1880s the *OED* noted that 'there is a tendency to use *amidst* more distributively than *amid*, e.g. of things scattered about, or a thing moving, in the midst of others'. It is difficult to discern this distinction maintained in current use. Both words have an air of formality, especially *amidst*, which is much less common (less than a quarter as many

AMERICAN ENGLISH.

1 general. Fowler in *Modern English Usage* (1926) did not include an entry on American English and said little on the subject, although he cast occasional aspersions on so-called 'undesirable aliens' (such as *belittle*). Since then attitudes to American English have hardened, and the prevailing view among some who seek (or claim) to preserve standards in English is often hostile. However, it is linguistically misconceived and historically unjustified to regard the American influence on English as necessarily harmful; both varieties have been enriched by contact with each other and with other varieties, including Australian English and South African English. It should also be remembered that Canadian English (influenced by French) is a valid variety, and the boundaries between the Englishes of Canada and the USA are becoming much harder to draw precisely.

American English differs from British English in several important ways, in matters of vocabulary, spelling and inflection, idiom, grammar, pronunciation, and punctuation. Some of the more significant differences are due to uses that disappeared in BrE but survived in AmE (such as the use of *gotten* as a past participle of *get*, and the use of *theater* and other spellings in -*er*), and others are due to developments in AmE after it went its own way.

2 vocabulary. AmE has long been a copious source of new vocabulary in BrE, and many items are now used with little or no awareness of their origin (e.g. *belittle*, *commuter*, *OK*, *to snoop*, *to fly off the handle*). Recently imported Americanisms tend to cause the most disapproval (e.g. the sentence adverb *hopefully*, verbal forms of nouns such as *hospitalize*, cultural 'media' terms such as *gameshow*, phrase-based words such as *downsizing* and *ongoing*, and slang vocabulary such as *cop-out* and *hacking*), and whole areas of vocabulary development such as the political correctness movement (which has given us *intellectually challenged, vertically challenged*, and other euphemisms in which a 'positive' word *challenged* has replaced a 'negative' word *handicapped*). There are significant loans in the other direction: *central heating, gay* (meaning homosexual), *miniskirt*, and *kiss of life* are all British in origin and are now widely used in North America. Some terms are known only on one side of the Atlantic because the institutions they denote are confined to one side, e.g. *duplex* (in the US) and *giro* (in the UK). The table shows some of the more important differences of core vocabulary between the two varieties.

British	American
aeroplane	airplane
aluminium	aluminum
aubergine	eggplant
autumn	fall
banknote	bill
biscuit (dry)	cracker
biscuit (sweet)	cookie
bonnet (of car)	hood
braces	suspenders
brooch	pin
bumper (of car)	fender

chemist's	drugstore
chips (food)	French fries
cinema	movie theater
coffin	casket
courgettes	zucchini
crisps	potato chips
curtains	drapes
drawing pin	thumbtack
driving licence	driver's license
dustbin	garbage can
estate agent	realtor
first floor	second floor
flat	apartment
frying pan	skillet
ground floor	first floor
handbag	purse
icing	frosting
kerb	curb
lavatory	washroom
lift	elevator
lorry	truck
main road	highway
motorway	expressway
nappy	diaper
pavement	sidewalk
petrol	gasoline or gas
potato chips	French fries
pram	baby carriage
queue	line
railway	railroad
rise (in salary)	raise
roundabout (in road system)	rotary
rowing-boat	rowboat
rubbish (domestic)	trash
shoelace	shoestring
sweets	candy
tap (for water)	faucet
tart	pie
traffic jam	gridlock
tram	streetcar
trolley (at supermarket or airport)	cart
trousers	pants
underground	subway
undertaker	mortician
veranda	porch
vest	undershirt
waistcoat	vest
wallet	billfold
windscreen	windshield
zip	zipper

a

3 spelling and inflection. Some spelling differences concern particular words and are not applied systematically (e.g. AmE *aluminum, maneuver, pajamas*); these need to be verified in a dictionary that records both spellings (such as the *Concise Oxford Dictionary*). The principal systematic differences in BrE and AmE spelling are:

a Simplification of the digraph vowels *-ae-* and *-oe-* to *-e-* (as in *ameba* and *estrogen*; but initial *ae-*, as in *aesthetic*, still tends to dominate in AmE as well as BrE). This is beginning to make an impact on British spelling, for example *encyclopedia* (much deprecated largely on grounds of intellectual snobbery). *See also* FOETUS.

b Use of *-ense* instead of *-ence* as a noun ending (as in *defense* and *pretense*; *see also* LICENCE).

c Use of *-er* instead of *-re* as a noun ending in many words (as in *center* and *theater*); but note *acre, massacre, mediocre,* and *ogre* in both varieties.

d Use of *-or* instead of *-our* as a noun ending (as in *color* and *harbor*).

e Reduction of *-ou-* to *-o-* (as in *mold*).

f Use of *-l-* instead of *-ll-* in verbal inflection (as in *instal, rivaled, traveler*) and converse use of *-ll-* instead of *-l-* (as in *installment, skillful*).

g Suppression of a final mute *-e* in inflection (as in *milage* and *salable*), but not after a soft *c* or *g* (as in *changeable*).

h Reduction of final *-ogue* to *-og* (as in *analog* and *catalog*).

i Exclusive use of *-ize* instead of *-ise* in verbs that allow both spellings in BrE, and variant use of *-ize* in verbs that are only spelt *-ise* in BrE (as in *civilize, privatize,* and *advertize*).

j Use of *-z-* occasionally instead of *-s-* (as in *analyze* and *cozy*).

4 idiom. There are occasional differences in shared idioms. Examples are: BrE *man on the street* / AmE *man in the street* / BrE *a new lease of life* / AmE *a new lease on life* / BrE *leave well alone* / AmE *leave well enough alone*.

5 grammar. Most of the more important grammatical differences concern use of auxiliary and modal verbs (*do, have, shall, will,* and others such as *dare*):

a AmE favours the type *Did you go?* rather than *Have you been?*, *I don't have* rather than *I haven't got*, *They just left* rather than *They've just left*, *I didn't use* (or *used*) *to* rather than *I used not to*, and *Let's not* rather than *Don't let's* (as in *Let's not argue*). These preferences are also found to a lesser degree in BrE.

b Some BrE constructions are not available in AmE, e.g. BrE *We weren't to know* (BrE/AmE *We couldn't know* or *couldn't have known*), BrE *meant to* (= BrE/AmE *supposed to*) as in *The food here is meant to be very good*.

c There are differences in the way prepositions are used. For example, AmE has *out the window* and *off of the floor* where BrE has *out of the window* and *off the floor*.

d AmE has retained *gotten*, an older form of the past participle of *get* which has fallen out of use in BrE. It is used in AmE as well as got. *See* GOTTEN.

e AmE differs in the use of *shall* and *should*: *see* SHALL AND WILL; SHOULD AND WOULD.

f For differences in the use of *dare* and *need*, *see* DARE; NEED.

g *See also* MAY, MIGHT; OUGHT.

6 pronunciation. As with spelling, there are particular differences and systematic differences. Examples of the first are *schedule* (sk- in AmE, sh- in BrE) and *tomato* (tuh-**may**-toh in AmE, tuh-**mah**-toh in BrE). It is beyond the scope of this book to explore the pronunciation systems of both varieties in detail, but a few special differences might be mentioned:

a The letter *r* is pronounced or partly pronounced when it occurs in the middle of a word whether or not it is followed by a vowel, whereas typically it is not in BrE received pronunciation, as in *hard* and *rare*.

b The vowel *a* is pronounced a as in *had*, not ah as in *hard* in words such as *after, can't, dance,* and *path*.

c Pronunciation of short o as in *box* is closer to ah as in *barks*.

d Pronunciation of yoo as in *tube* is closer to oo as in *boob*.

e Pronunciation of *er* in words such as *clerk* rhymes with *murk*, not with *mark* as in BrE.

f Pronunciation of final syllables in -*ile* (as in *fertile* and *hostile*) is -uhl, not -iyl as in BrE.

g Pronunciation of *t* following *n* and followed by an unstressed syllable is much less marked in AmE than in BrE (as in *mental* and *twenty*).

7 punctuation. American practice differs in the use of quotation marks and associated punctuation (*see* QUOTATION MARKS) and uses a different style in dates (*see* DATES). Other points are noted in individual entries on punctuation marks.

examples in the *OEC* as *amid*). Typical examples: (amid) *I . . . have often stood by the Frome at Woolbridge, enjoying the mellow manor house amid its water-meadows*—Times, 1987 / *Victor was packed off to boarding school amid angry disputes over money*—History Today, 2002 / (amidst) *This woman, sitting with such modest dignity amidst my students and colleagues*—Michael Frayn, 1989 / *She took her bows on stage amidst baskets of flowers*—ballet website, BrE 2004 [*OEC*]. In general use, *amid* and *amidst* have tended to be replaced by *among* or *in the midst of.*

Amish. Usually *the Amish*, the members of a strict Mennonite sect now living mainly in Pennsylvania and Ohio. The first syllable can be pronounced as in *ham, farm,* or *fame*.

amoeba The standard spelling in both the UK and the US is *amoeba; ameba* is an accepted, but not common, variant in the US. The plural generally used in technical scientific writing is *amoebae; amoebas* is less common in scientific language, but widely used elsewhere. The spelling of the related adjective is much more often *amoebic* than *amebic*.

amok, amuck. The word is normally used in the phrase *to run amok/amuck*, which means, in its literal sense, 'to run about wildly in a violent rage', and is an extension of a particular meaning in Malay anthropology (*Edward now wore the manic look of some animal transferred into the wrong environment, as though he might run amok, or bite*—Penelope Lively, 1990). It is just as often used metaphorically, i.e. not involving physical action (*With Thatcher running amok through the welfare state, lobby groups are preoccupied defending what was once thought unassailable*—New Scientist, 1991 / *It wasn't his fault that* *her feelings seemed to be running amok*—E. Rees, 1992). Occasional unidiomatic uses occur (*The place was amok with running kids with running noses*—weblog, BrE 2005 [*OEC*]). The spelling *amok*, which is closer to the original Malay *amoq* meaning 'attacking in frenzy', is more common (five times more in the *OEC*) and is preferable.

among, amongst. 1 *Among* is now roughly ten times more common than *amongst*. It is the oldest form, which gave rise to the by-forms *amonges* (14c, no longer in use) and *among(e)st* (16c). There is no demonstrable difference of meaning between the two forms, and the distribution is unclear except that *amongst* seems to be less common in AmE than in BrE. An older view, which Fowler (1926) followed, that *amongst* is commoner before a word beginning with a vowel, is not borne out by the evidence (the most common word following *amongst*, as with *among*, is in fact *the*). Examples: (among) *The giants war among themselves*—J. M. Coetzee, 1977 / *There were a lot of young people among the temporary staff*—Penelope Fitzgerald, 1980 / *Britain also has the lowest level of welfare expenditure among the countries of the European Community*—*Times*, 1985 / (amongst) *They stood on the edges of the lamplight amongst the wattles by the creek*—Peter Carey, 1988 / *If a settled view is formed amongst voters that the additional money on the NHS has been wasted progressive politics will be in trouble for decades*—*Independent*, 2007.

2 *Among* is much more often used than *amongst* in the expression *among other things*. This expression is strictly illogical, since *among* is inclusive and *other* is exclusive, but it is well established and usually causes no adverse comment. Perhaps it gets by on the coat-tails of the Latin equivalent *inter alia*, also self-contradictory but which few would venture to challenge.

3 For choice of *among* and *between*, *see* BETWEEN 2.

amoral *see* IMMORAL.

amount, number. *Amount* is normally used with uncountable nouns (i.e. nouns which have no plural) to mean 'quantity' (e.g. a *reasonable amount* of *forgiveness, glue, resistance, straw*, etc.), and *number* with plural nouns (e.g. a *certain number* of *boys, houses, jobs*, etc.). *Amount*, however, is fast invading the territory of *number*, especially when the following plural noun is regarded as an aggregate or collection. Examples: *Fame had magnified the amount of the forces*—1849 in *OED* / *I have any amount of letters for you*—George Bernard Shaw, 1893 / *I expect you get a fair amount of road accidents on these winding roads*—Rachel Billington, 1988 / *Billy's had a tremendous amount of problems*—T. McGuane, AmE 1989 / *Booksellers have less and less space for the amount of books that are being published*—*The Author*, 1990 / *The amount of bulbs she would find between the stones next spring*—A. Huth, 1991. Note that *quantity* can be used with all types of nouns (*a large quantity of parcels* / *a small quantity of sugar*).

ampersand is the name of the symbol & used as a short form of 'and'. It was used extensively by H. W. Fowler, both in print and in writing, and is most common in handwritten work, although the more cursive plus sign + is tending to oust it. It also occurs frequently, often for stylistic purposes, in company names, as in *Marks & Spencer*. The word itself is a contraction of '& per se (= by itself) and', which was the way that printers once referred to the character; the form of the symbol is perhaps a stylized version of Latin *et* 'and'.

amphitheatre (*amphi-*, not *ampi-*) is a word for a type of ancient Roman arena that forms a complete circle, like the Colosseum in Rome. It was used mainly for gladiatorial spectacles. It is not an alternative word for an ancient theatre used for drama (such as the one at Epidaurus in southern Greece), which was typically open at one end.

ample. Fowler (1926) wrote that *ample* was 'legitimate only with nouns denoting immaterial or abstract things' such as *opportunity, praise, provision*, and *time*. He did not accept that it could be properly used in attributive position before nouns like *butter, coal, oil*, and *water* that denote substances of indefinite quantity, although it was acceptable to place it predicatively with such words, as in *The coal is ample*. The logic was uncharacteristically opaque, and the argument untenable. Although *ample* is still most often used with words such as *evidence, opportunity, proof, provision, reason, room, scope, time, warning*, etc., there is ample evidence of its use with material substances, and among the words it most frequently modifies are *breast, bosom*, and *cleavage*. Other examples: *It was also to be a station for the motor-car age, situated on ample land with large car-parks*—J. Richards et al., 1988 / *The River Lea forming the eastern boundary of the metropolis provided good communication, ample supplies of water, and motive power for the mills*—J. Marriott, 1991 / *A leaf has ample stores of chlorophyll*—chemistry website, AmE 2004 [*OEC*].

amuck *see* AMOK.

an (indefinite article) *see* A, AN.

anaemia, anaemic are spelt -*ae*- in BrE and -*e*- or -*ae*- in AmE.

anaesthetic is spelt -*ae*- in BrE and -*e*- in AmE.

analogous is pronounced with a hard *g*. It should properly be used in contexts involving definite comparisons that justify the notion of analogy (*Terrorism is more analogous to a virulent, malignant illness, a plague that needs to be exposed, contained and then, yes, eradicated with the most precise surgical and other means*—The Nation, 2001). In practice, however, it does not always manage to keep its distance from the more general word *similar*. Originally confined largely to technical language, the word has spread rapidly into general usage (complemented by *to* or *with*): *Some have suggested that the effort needed to defeat the terrorists is analogous to the cold war*—Commonweal, 2001 [*OEC*].

analogy. 1 In the study of language, *analogy* is the name given to the process by which the use of words follows precedents set by other words without going through all the stages that produced those precedents. This is a fundamental aspect of the way languages develop, and applies to all aspects of usage, including word-formation, spelling, inflection, meaning, collocation, and pronunciation. For example, the noun *starvation* (18c) was formed on the analogy of other words such as *vexation* (15c); the dialect and AmE past form *dove* (from *dive*) was formed on the analogy of *strove* (from *strive*); the pronunciation of *controversy* on the first or second syllable is by analogy with types represented respectively by *matrimony* and *monotony*. The formation *seascape* (and later *skyscape* and *waterscape*) was modelled on *landscape, workaholic* on *alcoholic*, and *sexist* (and later *ageist* and others) on *racist*. *Software* (in computing) was formed on the analogy of *hardware*, and later *shareware*; more recently we have seen the invention of terms for more intrusive and sinister phenomena such as *adware* and *malware*.

2 Sometimes false analogies come into play, leading to uses that either appear erroneous (as sometimes in the speech of children) or prevail despite the falseness of the analogy (as with *alright*, modelled on *altogether*). More often, the role of analogy is overlooked by those who criticize aspects of usage (such as the sentence adverb *hopefully*) in isolation.

analyse is spelt *-yse* in BrE and *-yze* in AmE.

analysis has the plural form *analyses* (pronounced -seez).

anathema. 1 The meaning has changed over several centuries of use. Originally a Greek word meaning 'a thing dedicated' it then came to mean 'a thing dedicated to evil; an accursed thing' and then, in the context of the Christian Church, 'the act or formula of consigning to damnation', in which use it is still found with historical reference; the plural is *anathemas* (e.g. *The pope had ended the Council with two final anathemas which were intimately connected with Anselm's situation*—R. W. Southern, 1990).
 2 Its use as a quasi-adjective meaning 'accursed' and in weakened senses 'intolerable', often followed by *to*, dates from the 18c. It is used in predicative position only (after a verb) and is arguably a kind of uncountable noun (similar to *pleasure*): *The policy they embraced was however anathema to many Conservatives, who rightly saw in it the beginning of the end of British rule in India*—Roy Jenkins, 1988 / *This leads very quickly to the 'hoping something turns up' syndrome which is anathema to most managers*—J. Harvey-Jones, 1988 / *Waif look is anathema to fashion house*—headline in *Times*, 2007.

anchovy. The pronunciation stressing the first syllable **an**-chuh-vee is commoner than the older pronunciation, stressing the second, an-**choh**-vee.

ancillary derives ultimately from the Latin noun *ancilla*, 'handmaid'. Its main modern meaning of 'providing necessary support to the essential operations of a central organization, especially a hospital', and its use as a noun, both date from the mid-20c. The standard pronunciation is an-**si**-luh-ri, but there is a tendency for people to pronounce an *i* after the double *l*, resulting in the five syllables of an-**si**-lee-uh-ri. As a result, the word is often wrongly spelt ✖ *ancilliary*.

and. 1 The simplest-looking words are often among the most complicated in use, and *and* is no exception. The normal function of *and* is to join words, phrases, and sentences: *John and Mary are brother and sister* / *They dealt with the matter quickly and efficiently* / *an acute and wary sense of the ordinary*. In some cases it links parallel words that form a fixed expression that cannot normally be reversed (*fish and chips*, ✖ *chips and fish; first and foremost,* ✖ *foremost and first; Romeo and Juliet,* ✖ *Juliet and Romeo*).
 2 For guidance on grammatical agreement in sentences with subjects containing and (e.g. *Fish and chips is/are my favourite meal*), see AGREEMENT.
 3 *And* is often omitted for contextual effects of various kinds, especially between sequences of descriptive adjectives which can be separated by commas or simply by spaces (*The teeming jerry-built dun-coloured traffic-ridden deafening city*—Penelope Lively, 1987).
 4 There is a persistent belief that it is wrong to begin a sentence with *And*, but the practice will be found in literature from Anglo-Saxon times onwards, especially as an aid to continuity in narrative and dialogue. The *OED* provides examples from the 9c to the 19c, including one from Shakespeare's *King John*: *Arthur. Must you with hot Irons, burne out both mine eyes? Hubert. Young boy, I must. Arthur. And will you? Hubert. And I will.* It is also used for other rhetorical

purposes, especially to denote surprise (*O John! and you have seen him! And are you really going?*—1884 in *OED*) and sometimes just to introduce an improvised afterthought (*I'm going to swim. And don't you dare watch*—G. Butler, 1983). It is however poor style to separate short statements into separate sentences when no special effect is needed: *I opened the door and I looked into the room* / ✻ *I opened the door. And I looked into the room.*

5 *And all* is a well-established tag added to the end of a statement, as in *Isn't it amazing? He has a Ph.D. and all*—J. Shute, 1992. With the nominal meaning 'also, besides, in addition', the use has origins in dialect, as can be seen from the material from many regions given in the *English Dialect Dictionary* (often written in special ways, e.g. *ano', an'-all, an' a'*). In many of the examples it seems to lack any perceptible lexical meaning and to be just a rhythmical device to eke out a sentence.

6 *And also* has special uses, to show progression (*faster and faster*), cause and effect (*do that and I'll send you to bed*), duration (*they ran and ran*), a large number or quantity (*miles and miles*), and addition (*four and four are eight*), purpose (where *and* replaces *to*: *Try and come tomorrow*). See also TRY AND.

7 Another special use, recorded in the *OED* from the 16c, is to express 'a difference of quality between things of the same name or class', as in W. S. Gilbert's lines from *The Gondoliers* (1889): *Well, as to that, of course there are kings and kings. When I say I detest kings I mean I detest bad kings*. To this we may add some modern examples: *There are ways to steal and there are ways to steal*—New Yorker, 1988 / *There is homelessness and homelessness. . . . The sort of homelessness which means despair is quite different from the sort that means adventure*—Times, 1991.

8 For discussion of the received wisdom that you must never put a comma before *and*, see COMMA.

and/or is a formula indicating that the items connected by it can be taken either together or as alternatives. Its principal uses are in legal and other formal documents (*These ratios indicated that the changes in the order of crystallinity were similar to those with the water content and/or dehydration and temperature for gelatinization among and/or within cultivars*—Annals of Botany, BrE 2001), and in logic (*The best philosophy . . . embodies a picture of the world and/or a set of values*—E. Craig, 2002). In general use the effect can be ungainly: *Stalin, characteristically insensitive to Western public opinion and/or relying on the political ambiguity of these phrases in the existing context, signed it*—The Oxford Companion to United States History, 2001. A more comfortable way of expressing the same idea is to use 'X or Y or both', and in some cases 'or' by itself will do.

anemone. Note that the sequence of consonants is *n-m-n*, not (as is sometimes heard) *n-n-m*. The words comes from Greek *anemos* 'wind' and is therefore akin to the English word *animated* and related words.

angle *noun*. This word had been used since the 1870s in the meaning 'the aspect from which a matter is considered' (*The old stagers . . . the men who knew all the angles, who had great experience*—Nevil Shute, 1944), often with a defining word: the *OED* gives examples of statistical angles, selling angles, and propaganda angles. Examples: *For US television . . . competition for the same audience within the same time-slot drives producers and planners to look for the new exploitation angle which will differentiate their product within the market*—Screen, 1991 / *He is always on the alert for a new angle, always individual in* *expression—Art Newspaper*, 1992. To avoid any possible connotations of underhandedness in the word, you might wish to use any of its synonyms, namely *perspective, point of view, position, standpoint,* or *viewpoint.*

Anglo-. People in Scotland and Wales understandably view this combining form (as in *Anglo-French, Anglo-Irish,* etc.) with some distaste, but it continues to be used as the standard term. The alternative term *Brito-* has not acquired any general currency, and is restricted to certain special cases, e.g. *Brito-Arctic* (relating to British territory in the Arctic) and *Britocentric* and related words.

angst, angsty. The Victorian novelist George Eliot is the first person, according to the *OED*, to have used the German word *Angst* ('fear') in English, albeit in inverted commas, in a letter of August 1849. It is now part of general language with the meaning 'a feeling of deep anxiety or dread, typically an unfocused one about the human condition or the state of the world in general', or, more trivially, as a synonym for any kind of anxiety. Examples: *Full of existential angst and loneliness, her paintings are able to evoke an empathetic response from the viewer—Art in America,* 2004 / *A collective wail of middle-class angst went up from mainstream party leaders: what have we done?—Daily Telegraph,* 2009.

Angst's offspring *angsty* first appeared in 1956, and now seems set to follow its sire into literary, or pseudo-literary, use: *Rare is the teen who doesn't have at least one journal filled with shame-inducing pseudo-profundity, or a private collection of angsty song lyrics—Montreal Mirror,* 2005 / *In the midst of all my angsty rambling last week, a ray of sunlight shone through the gloom—*weblog, BrE 2005.

annex, annexe. In BrE and AmE the verb is *annex*. In AmE the noun is usually also spelt *annex*. In BrE both spellings are correct, but *annexe* is somewhat more frequent. In legal and administrative writing, *annex*, denoting an addition to a document, with no final *e*, is the accepted convention.

anniversaries. The normal practice is to refer to the 10th, 20th, 30th, etc. anniversary of an event, but special names have come to be associated with the more significant anniversaries. The principal names for wedding anniversaries are *silver* (25 years), *pearl* (30), *ruby* (40), *golden* (50), and *diamond* (60, sometimes 75). For public events the following terms are used: *centenary* or (AmE) *centennial* (100), *sesquicentenary* (150 years), *bicentenary* (200), *tercentenary* (300), *quatercentenary* (400: NB not *quarter-*), *quincentenary* (500), *sexcentenary* (600), *septcentenary* (700), *octocentenary* (800), *millenary* (1,000). In AmE, the compounds end in *-centennial* rather than *-centenary*. *See* CENTENARY.

annual *see* PERENNIAL.

annul is spelt with one *l*, and has inflected forms *annulled, annulling*. The corresponding noun is *annulment*.

anonymous *She sits in an anonymous hotel lobby in central London having fled Russia to seek political asylum in Britain—Independent,* 2007. *Anonymous* is so widely used in its extended meaning 'having no distinguishing or remarkable features', making it a synonym of *nondescript* or *characterless* rather than of *nameless*, that the primary meaning 'having no name' can be compromised. Obviously, in the example above, the hotel lobby, or the hotel at least, has a name, and so the intended meaning is clear, but this may not always be the case: *Luckily I was in the company of a* *celebrity, drunk on gin and an anonymous beauty, drunk on celebrity*—*Fresh Yarn*, AmE 2005. Did the writer know the beauty's name?

anorak, a word of Greenland Eskimo origin, has taken on a new meaning from its association with people waiting around in cold weather (in anoraks, supposedly) to watch trains and aeroplanes or do other things the rest of the world can sneer at. Hence an *anorak* is 'a boring, studious, or socially inept person with unfashionable and solitary interests'. Its most common application is in the field of computing, as one might expect: *'Cyberspace' is no longer the preserve of techno-nerds and anoraks*—*Guardian*, 1994. Derivatives such as *anorakish* and *anoraksia* so far have little currency.

anorexic, anorectic. Both words, adjectives derived from *anorexia* meaning 'obsessive loss of appetite', are in use, but *anorexic* is far more common, while *anorectic* is confined to technical medical writing. *Anorexic* is also used absolutely as a quasi-noun. Examples: *He became listless, anorexic, and increasingly sleepy, refusing to eat or crawl*—*Lancet*, 1961 / *Contrary to the popular image of the disturbed teenager, the anorexic is not typically a product of a 'broken home'*—S. Macleod, 1989 / *Do they think I'm anorexic, or just plain thin?*—J. Dawson, 1990.

another. For *one another* see EACH 3.

ante-, anti-. 1 These two prefixes need to be distinguished, if only to ensure correct spelling. The first means 'before, preceding' and forms words such as *antenatal* ('before birth') and *antechamber* ('a room leading to another'). The second, which is much more common, means 'opposite, opposed to, against', and forms words such as *anti-*

aircraft, anti-American, and *anti-hero* ('the opposite of a hero').

2 When creating new words on this model, BrE tends to use the hyphen much more than does AmE, e.g. *anti-war sentiments* as opposed to *antiwar sentiments*. Both BrE and AmE keep the hyphen when the second element begins with a capital letter, e.g. *anti-American*, *anti-Semitic*.

3 The *OED* points out that the model for all these words is *Antichrist* and its derivative *anti-Christian*, which, along with *antipope*, were the only examples in use before 1600. There are no *anti-*combinations in Shakespeare.

antenna has the plural form *antennae* (relating to the sensory organs of insects) and *antennas* (relating to radio aerials).

Anthony. In standard English it is pronounced with a *t* not *th*. But the pronunciation with *th* is common in US English, and heard more and more often in British English, another victim of the 'speak-as-you-spell' school of thought.

anticipate. 1 Here lies another of the great usage battlegrounds, where the conflict is all the more fraught for overlapping meanings that confuse the issue. The two primary and undisputed meanings are (1) to be aware of (a thing) in advance and act accordingly (e.g. *Lecky has anticipated what the animal liberationists are now saying*—*Listener*, 1983) and (2) to forestall (a person) and take action before they do (e.g. *I'm sorry*—*do go on, I did not mean to anticipate you*—John Le Carré).

2 Fowler scornfully rejected a third meaning, to expect or foresee (e.g. *Wing mirrors were selling better than they had ever anticipated*—Margaret Drabble, 1987 / *They have every right to be there, and we do not anticipate any change in that status*—*USA Today*, 1988 / *One would not expect Cleopatra to have suffered such a fate, nor did she herself* *anticipate it*—A. Fraser, 1988). This meaning was formerly classed as 'disputed' in successive editions of the *Concise Oxford Dictionary* but in the current (2006) edition, and in the larger *Oxford Dictionary of English* (2003), it is placed first without any comment as (comfortably) the dominant sense, with the definition 'to regard as probable'. Like *expect*, it can be followed either by a noun or noun phrase (*She anticipated scorn on her return to the theatre*) or by a *that*-clause (*It was anticipated that the rains would slow the military campaign*). Despite its wide currency, however, it can still irritate more traditional readers (and listeners), perhaps because it is an ugly word compared with the more elegant and straightforward alternative *expect*.

antisocial *see* UNSOCIABLE, UNSOCIAL.

anxious. It is as well to be aware that using anxious to mean 'eager' or 'keen' (e.g. *She's very anxious that you should like her*—A. N. Wilson, 1982) may displease some people, especially in the US. There, this use has been criticized by several usage authorities since the early 20c. The objection is based on the axiom that *anxious* (1623) should be restricted to meaning 'worried, nervous'; in other words, it should reflect a state of *anxiety*, 'uneasiness or trouble of mind' (first recorded in a work of *c.*1525 by Sir Thomas More). However, the contested meaning dates back to the 18c, when *anxious* came to mean 'full of desire and endeavour' and was constructed with *to*; the phrase *anxious to please* appeared in Robert Blair's poem *The Grave* (1743), and Lord Nelson declared in 1794 that '*The General seems as anxious as any of us to expedite the fall of the place*'. Some examples suggest both eagerness and anxiety (e.g. *Punch was always anxious to oblige everybody*—Kipling, 1888). Many, however, suggest only eagerness,

as in the following: *No one seemed very anxious to come up with the spondulicks*—Private Eye, 1980 / *There are a number of men only too anxious to buy themselves a knighthood who might be most attracted to a project that catches the public sympathy*—Claire Rayner, 1991.

The best that can be said is that for certain audiences it is wise to avoid using *anxious* to mean 'eager', despite the fact that it is historically well attested, was described by Fowler (1926) as a 'natural development', and is absolutely standard.

any. 1 use with singular or plural nouns. *Any* can be used with a singular or plural noun, or with an uncountable noun such as *homework* and *happiness*, to denote choice from three or more people or things (for choice from two, *either* is used): *The most basic of data security precautions for any individual or company employing microcomputers is the making of back-ups*—Times, 1985 / *This letter is addressed to you and is not being copied to any other party*—Daily Telegraph, 1986 / *At any moment a change in voltage can wipe out what one has written*—Listener, 1985 / *Any food found in passengers' luggage will be confiscated* / *Neither government was behind it, nor were there any sponsors, angels, captains of commerce or industry*—Los Angeles Times, 1986. When used with a singular countable noun (i.e. one that has a plural, such as *book* or *person*) it is always assertive in meaning: *I did not want any book* (= I wanted a particular book) as distinct from *I did not want any books* (normally = I wanted none) and *I did not want any sugar* (normally = I wanted no sugar).

2 as a pronoun. *Any* functions as a pronoun as well as a determiner: *A caller can use any of eight different long distance companies*—New York Times, 1985 / *If you keep ferrets don't let any* *escape / It's as good an excuse as any to buy a new car.*

3 with comparatives and superlatives. It is better to use a comparative with *any other* than a superlative with *any*: not ⊠ *the most brutal piece of legislation of any passed by this government* but *a more brutal piece of legislation than any other passed by this government.* An alternative is to use *all* instead of *any*: *the most brutal piece of legislation of all those passed by this government.*

4 *any one* and *anyone*. As one word, *anyone* means the same as *anybody* and is interchangeable with it (*Anyone could do that / Anybody could do that*). As two words, it means 'any single person or thing', as in *You can have any one you like* (*any you like* would include the possibility of more than one). Examples: *The virtual photon rematerializes into any one of a very large number of possible combinations of new particles*—Scientific American, 1978 / *If you think you could help in any one of the areas, please talk to the Parish Priest*—Sligo Weekender, 2004.

5 other one-word and two-word forms. *Any more* is used chiefly after a negative and is usually written as two words in BrE (*He is not lying there any more*—Penelope Lively, 1987), although it is found more often as one word in other varieties and increasingly also in BrE (*He wasn't a schoolkid anymore*—M. du Plessis, SAfr 1983 / *That's not happening anymore because they're all finding better conditions abroad*—Evening News (Edinburgh), 2007). Perhaps it is needless to point out that when *more* modifies a following adjective *any* has to be a separate word (*It doesn't get any more real than when the acrid smoke from a pile of green logs in a circular stone-flanked hearth doesn't escape from an Iron Age roundhouse*—Birmingham Post, 2007).

Anyhow is only written as one word and is a (usually more informal) alternative for *anyway* (*Anyhow I'm carving out a career there teaching the boss's daughter to read novels*—Thomas Keneally, 1985 / *Home is not the place for charm anyway*—London Review of Books, 1987). Note that *any way* is spelt as two words to retain their separate meaning, as in *Is there any way I can help?* and *Do it any way you like.*

Any place and *any time* are also often spelt as single words in AmE: *She said she would vote for him anytime*—New Yorker, 1987 / *I wouldn't have wanted to know her as a child, but once a man, anytime*—M. Doane, 1988 / *Content is available anytime, anyplace, and on whatever device the owner desires*—Business Week Magazine, AmE 2002.

The archaic adverbial form *any ways* survives in the Book of Common Prayer (*All those who are any ways afflicted . . . in mind, body, or estate*) and in the Authorized Version of the Bible (*And if the people of the land doe any wayes hide their eyes from the men*). Otherwise it is restricted to informal AmE: *So who promised this guy anything anyways?*

6 as an adverb. *Any* is correctly used as an adverb to emphasize a comparative adjective or adverb (*They are not treated like schoolgirls any longer / He can't play any better / She refuses to go any further*). In informal AmE, and occasionally in BrE, it can stand alone with the meaning 'at all': *We're used to responsibility. Doesn't worry us any*—Agatha Christie, 1937 / *It's not going to help any with my exams*—New Yorker, 1988.

apart from, aside from. *Apart from* has been standard in BrE from the early 17c (e.g. *There are few exciting and visitable relics of [Mesolithic] human life apart from caves*—R. Muir, 1983 / *The raven, who apart from anything else was*

much stronger in the air than the dove—
Julian Barnes, 1989); *aside from,* an
equivalent expression used alongside
apart from in AmE since the early 19c
(*Cutler believes that, aside from voyeur-
istic entertainment, the show will influence the presidential election year*—
Philadelphia Weekly, 2004) is now found
from time to time in BrE contexts (*Aside
from abolition of exchange controls by
the other major economies, the Government insists that Britain's inflation rate
be brought more in line with that of her
trading partners*—Guardian, 1989 /
*Aside from his corporate profile, however,
little is known of Lord Browne the man*—
Herald (Glasgow), 2007).

apartheid There are several ways of
pronouncing this Afrikaans word denoting a now—fortunately—defunct form of
institutional white supremacism. The
pronunciation uh-**part**-hayt comes closest to the Afrikaans; but other pronunciations, with the -*h*- pronounced or silent,
uh-**part**-hyd/-hyt, uh-**par**-tyd/-tyt, are
also heard. No one pronunciation can be
said to be more correct than any other.

apex. In scientific writing, such as botany and anatomy, the standard plural
form is *apices* **ay**-pi-seez. In other contexts *apexes* tends to be more used (e.g.
*Kurdistan is one of the major apexes for
military operations against the Iraq
army*—BBC press release, 2003).

apiece, meaning 'for each one', is normally placed immediately after a direct
object (*After buying his brothers a pint
apiece* [he] *had to be content with a half
for himself*—Melvyn Bragg, 1969 / *The
actresses have one beautiful costume
apiece*—New Yorker, 1987). It should
always be written as one word, although
its underlying meaning explains
mistakes such as ⊠ *We thought we'd
charge $25 a piece*—Raw Vision, 2005.
Conversely, the informal, originally AmE
adverbial phrase *a piece,* meaning 'a

short distance' is written as two words (*If
you're in the area, check out the Mau
Mau bar down the road a piece as well*—
weblog, BrE 2004). It is occasionally
found written as one, e.g. ⊠ *so we
headed to another one down the road
apiece*—Urban Scrawl, NewZE 2004
[*OEC*].

a posteriori, a Latin term meaning
'from what comes after', is pronounced
with the initial *a* as in *hate* and the final -*i*
as in *eye.* It is used to characterize reasoning or arguing from known facts to
probable causes, as in the proposition
'The prisoners have weals on their backs,
so they must have been whipped'. The
opposite concept is **a priori.*

apostrophe. Fowler (1926) gave no
information on this punctuation mark at
the letter A except a cross-reference to
an entry called 'possessive puzzles',
which sounds rather more entertaining.
He concentrated on a number of difficulties arising from use of the apostrophe, and the same tactic is adopted here
in a place where the user will be more
likely to look. Each problem is headed by
a typical example that illustrates it.
    In general, it should be borne in mind
that the apostrophe denotes either (1) a
possessive, or (2) omitted letters.

    1 *girl's, girls'* **as possessive.** The first
is singular (one girl), and the second is
plural (two or more girls).

    2 *women's* and *children's* **as
possessive.** When the plural ends in a
letter other than *s,* the possessive is
formed by adding '*s*: *the children's
games, the men's boots, the oxen's hoofs,
the women's cars,* etc.

    3 *video's for rent.* This is the so-
called 'grocers' apostrophe', an apostrophe misapplied to an ordinary plural,
particularly in words ending in -*o* but
also in quite harmless words such as
apple's and *pear's* (e.g. *pear's 30p a*

pound). It is, needless to say, illiterate in ordinary usage.

4 who's and whose. These are sometimes confused (e.g. *Who's turn is it?*): *see* WHO's.

5 possessive of names ending in -s. Add *'s* to names that end in *s* when you would pronounce them with an extra *s* in speech (e.g. *Charles's, Frances's, Thomas's, The Times's, Zacharias's*); but omit *'s* when the name is normally pronounced without the extra *s*, particularly if the last syllable of the name is pronounced *-iz* (e.g. *Bridges', Connors', Moses'*). Classical names ending in *s* conventionally add no *s*: (e.g. *Mars', Herodotus', Xerxes'*). With French names ending in (silent) *-s* or *-x*, add *'s* (e.g. *Dumas's, le Roux's*) and pronounce the modified word with a final *-z*.

6 hers, its, ours, etc. An apostrophe should not be used in pronouns of this type (e.g. *a book of hers*). Note that *its* is normally used in attributive position, i.e. before a noun (*Give the cat its dinner*) and should be distinguished from *it's* = 'it is': *see* ITS, IT'S.

7 MPs, the 1990s, etc. The apostrophe is no longer normally used in the plural of abbreviated forms (e.g. *Several MPs were standing around*), although it is of course used in the possessive (e.g. *The BBC's decision to go ahead with the broadcast*). It is used in plurals when clarity calls for it, e.g. *Dot your i's and cross your t's*.

8 I'll, they've, you're, etc. The apostrophe is used to form these regular contractions with pronouns, and occasionally with nouns (e.g. *The joke's on them*): *see* ABBREVIATIONS 2.

9 cello, flu, etc. The apostrophe is no longer needed in words that are originally contractions but are now treated as words in their own right, e.g. *cello, flu, phone, plane*. Other words retain them in their spelling, usually in the middle of

the word rather than at the beginning, e.g. *fo'c'sle, ne'er-do-well, o'er, rock 'n' roll*.

10 Barclays Bank, etc. The apostrophe is rapidly disappearing in company names and other commercial uses, e.g. *Barclays Bank, Citizens Advice Bureau*. Though occasionally disapproved of, the practice can be justified as an attributive rather than possessive use of the noun (i.e. *Barclays Bank* is attributive, implying association with *Barclays*, whereas *Barclays' Bank* is possessive, implying ownership by people called *Barclay*).

appal is the correct BrE spelling (AmE *appall*), with inflections *appalled, appalling*.

apparatus is normally pronounced with *-rat-* as in *rate* (not as in *part*). The plural is *apparatuses*.

apparent is normally pronounced with short *a* (as in *bat*); pronunciation as in *parent*, though once dominant, is only occasionally heard.

appeal. The transitive use as a legal term is AmE (e.g. *The US government plans to appeal the cotton ruling, and it could be years before any penalties kick in*—Reason (magazine), 2004). The standard equivalent in BrE is *appeal against*, although the transitive use is becoming more common (*Mr Marshall's legal representatives had submitted papers appealing against a decision made by judges two weeks ago*—York Evening Press, 2004 [*OEC*]).

appear, appeared. For phrases of the type *She appeared to have encouraged him, see* PERFECT INFINITIVE.

appeasement, meaning 'the process of satisfying a potential aggressor', has had unfavourable overtones since its use in the 1930s in connection with Nazi Germany, and now always carries the implication of making shameful or inadvisable concessions. As late as the 1920s, it was used more neutrally, as in Winston Churchill's statement in relation to Turkey, *Here again I counsel prudence and appeasement.*

appendix has the plural form *appendices* when referring to parts of books and documents, and *appendixes* in anatomical contexts.

applicable. The traditional pronunciation, stressing the first syllable, **ap**-plik-uh-b'l, has largely been replaced in BrE by second-syllable stress, ap-**plik**-uh-b'l, which is the pronunciation the current *OED* puts first. US dictionaries tend to put the traditional pronunciation first.

apposition. 1 *Apposition* is the placing of a noun or noun phrase beside another noun and noun phrase, where it shares the same grammatical function, as in *A portrait of Benjamin Disraeli, the famous statesman*, in which *the famous statesman* is in apposition to *Benjamin Disraeli*. Words in apposition are called *appositives*. In this example, the appositive gives additional information, and is called *non-restrictive*; in other cases, the appositive is an essential part of the expression and is called *restrictive*, e.g. *William the Conqueror, the author Penelope Lively.*
2 Note that the appositive element can stand first when it is a descriptive title or identifier preceding a name, e.g. *Chancellor Merkel of Germany, civil rights campaigner Martin Luther King.* Originating in AmE, this practice is rapidly spreading to BrE, especially in newspapers.
3 For a more detailed treatment of apposition, *see* Greenbaum, *Oxford English Grammar* (1996), 230–33.

appraise, apprise. Like many near-sounding words with some relation of meaning, these are often confused.

Appraise means 'to assess the value of (something or someone)' (e.g. *When a man is stripped of all worldly insignia, one can appraise him for what he is truly worth*—Charles Chaplin, 1964 / *It was an interval at least long enough for him to appraise the situation*—Antonia Fraser, 1988). *Apprise* is a rather formal or bureaucratic word and means 'to inform, to give notice to' and is normally constructed with a personal object followed by *of* (e.g. *He was annoyed that I had not bothered to apprise him of the upsetting news sooner*—P. Bailey, 1986). It is common in the constructions *be apprised* and *keep someone apprised* (*In truth she did make a mistake—there is no denying it—and she was speedily apprised of it by her brother*—J. Sutherland, 2000).

appreciate. Its normal meaning 'to acknowledge with gratitude', especially in business correspondence (e.g. *I appreciate everything that you have done to help us*) and to form polite requests (e.g. *It would be appreciated if you would reply by return of post*) is uncontroversial. More controversial is its use with *how* or a *that* clause (e.g. *I appreciate that you are disappointed by the outcome*). Gowers (1965) discouraged this use, proposing *realize* instead, which is sometimes the better word although in some contexts the notion of *sympathize* is also needed.

apprehend, comprehend. In the meanings in which they overlap, these two words denote slightly different aspects of understanding. *Apprehend* means to grasp or perceive a general idea or concept, whereas *comprehend* means to understand an argument or statement. Both can be followed by a simple object or by a *that*-clause. Examples: (apprehend) *She drew a breath, long enough to apprehend that he was about to step from one world into* *another*—Iris Murdoch, 1962 / *As the mind apprehends and tries to make sense of the world, it develops ever-richer and more sophisticated concepts*—J. Wolff, 2003 / (comprehend) *Speak more slowly so that we can comprehend everything you say*—Bernard Malamud, 1966 / *Some people find it hard to comprehend how we can love and adore a being whom we also 'fear' at the very same time*—Evangelical Times, 2005.

apprise is spelt *-ise* not *-ize*. For its meaning, *see* APPRAISE.

a priori, a Latin term meaning 'from what is before', is pronounced with *a* as in *hate* and with both *i*s as in *eye*. It is used to characterize reasoning or arguing from causes to effects, as in the proposition 'Because they were wearing handcuffs it was obvious that they had been taken into custody'. The opposite concept is **a posteriori*.

apropos is pronounced with stress on the first syllable and the last syllable as in *so*. Despite its French origin (17c), it is always written in English as one word without an accent. Its main uses are as a preposition, with or without a linking *of* (*Her voice, as has been mentioned apropos that of Boudicca, was not harsh*—Antonia Fraser, 1988 / *And then I thought, apropos of my last blog entry, about gender roles*—weblog, AmE 2004). *Apropos of nothing* (and informal variants such as *apropos of bugger all*) has become a cliché that means little more than 'unexpectedly, out of the blue' (*Apropos of nothing she declared that love must be wonderful*—G. Clare, 1981).

apt, liable, prone. 1 Used with *to*, *prone* is by far the most common statistically, *liable* comes second, and *apt*, perhaps surprisingly, trails in third place.

2 *Apt to* and *liable to*, followed by an infinitive, are virtually interchangeable, except that *liable* carries a greater notion of responsibility for the result, which is generally implied to be undesirable. Examples: *Pick up any 'documentation' ...and you are apt to be... bombarded by gibberish*—New York Times, 1982 / *Given that it's the exam season, I'm apt to be distracted by just about anything*—weblog, BrE 2005 [*OEC*]. In this use, *apt to* is tending to force out the alternative *prone to*, although this is still used in relation to habits and continual actions: *The one unquestionable advantage of the multiflora stock is the fact that it is less prone to throw up suckers than any of the others*—N. Young, 1971.

3 *Liable to* and *prone to*, unlike *apt to*, can be followed by a simple object, and in this use *liable to* also has the meaning 'subject to (a penalty)': *The affected children themselves are liable to behavioural problems such as temper tantrums*—Journal of the Royal Society of Medicine, 1980 / *Anyone convicted of giving away examination papers to candidates will be liable to two years in jail*—Daily Telegraph, 1982. Both words can usefully be followed by a verbal noun in *-ing* (*EB ...makes her skin as fragile as a butterfly's wing and prone to blistering*—Manchester Evening News, 2003).

4 *Likely to*, followed by an infinitive, is more neutral than the other words in fitting well into favourable as well as unfavourable contexts. It is also far more common than the other three put together: *A plan to help young homebuyers is likely to be announced within the next week*—Times, 1973 / *For the parents of teenagers who are likely to have encounters with the police, the teenage years can be a nightmare*—BBC Parenting, 2004.

aquarium has plurals *aquariums* (general use) or *aquaria* (technical use).

Arab, Arabian, Arabic. 1 These three terms refer to different aspects of Arabia and its people: *Arab* means a member of the Semitic people now inhabiting large parts of the Middle East and North Africa, and is also used as a quasi-adjective before a noun (*the Arab people* / *Arab hopes* / *Arab philosophy*); *Arabian* is an adjective having geographical reference to Arabia (*the Arabian peninsula* / *an Arabian camel* / *Arabian fauna*); and *Arabic* is a noun and adjective denoting a language (*Do you speak Arabic?* / *Arabic literature*).

2 *Arabic* is written with a capital initial in the expression Arabic numerals (the numbers 1, 2, 3, etc., as distinct from the Roman numerals I, II, III, etc.). It is written with a small initial in *gum arabic*, a type of gum exuded by African acacia trees.

3 The expression *street Arab*, first recorded in 1853, and for about a century commonly applied to a homeless child or other vagrant living on the streets, is now pretty much obsolete, and if used could be regarded as offensive.

arbiter, arbitrator. *Arbiter*, a more literary word (16c), is now restricted to the meaning 'a judge or authority' as in *an arbiter of taste*. For the meaning 'a person appointed to settle a dispute', the slightly older form *arbitrator* (15c) is now the correct word to use, although the meanings overlap and *arbiter* is still often found in this meaning. Examples: (arbiter) *She was not so much an arbiter of fashion as she was fashion itself*—D. Halberstam, 1979 / *The great nineteenth-century critic and arbiter of taste, John Ruskin*—L. Hudson, 1985 / *Harley then insisted that the tournament director, who is the ultimate arbiter at professional tournaments, be summoned*—M. Hamer, 1991 / (arbitrator) *Either party may apply to have the dispute referred to arbitration by the judge or by an outside arbitrator*—R. C. A. White, 1985 / *Edward insisted on intervening in the succession dispute . . . not as an impartial*

arbitrator, but as feudal overlord of Scotland—Oxford Companion to British History, 2002.

arc *verb*, meaning 'to produce a luminous electrical discharge' is inflected *arced, arcing*, with the *c* hard despite being followed by an *e* and *i* respectively.

archaeology is the BrE spelling, and the more common spelling everywhere; *archeology* is an AmE variant, itself less common in the US than the *-aeo-* spelling.

archaism. 1 Archaisms are words and phrases that have fallen out of general use but are used for special effect, normally in literature. These vary in effect from the gently old-fashioned or playful (e.g. *erstwhile, gentlewoman, goodly, hence, lest, methinks, perchance, quoth*) to the unnatural or even unusable (e.g. *peradventure, whilom*).

2 Archaisms are most commonly found in allusive use in literature, e.g. *If Mimi's cup runneth over, it runneth over with decency rather than with anything more vital*—Anita Brookner, 1985 (an Old Testament allusion to *Psalms* 23:5) / *The whole creation groaneth and travaileth in pain together*—Iris Murdoch, 1987 (a New Testament allusion to *Romans* 8:22). Archaic word forms also occur in titles, as in *The Compleat Girl* (by Mary McCarthy, 1963, in allusion to Isaak Walton's *The Compleat Angler*), *Whitaker's Almanack* (which preserves an older spelling of *almanac*), and in fixed expressions such as *olde worlde* and many new formations modelled on *a-changing*, e.g. *a-basking, a-brewing, a-wasting*.

3 *See also* the separate entries for ALBEIT; NAY; UNBEKNOWN.

ardour is spelt *-our* in BrE and as *ardor* in AmE.

are, is *see* AGREEMENT.

aren't I *see* BE 4.

argot is a term for the jargon of a special group or class of people. *See* JARGON.

arguably is first recorded only in 1890, and did not appear in the original *OED*, but now it seems indispensable. It is used as a sentence adverb (qualifying a whole statement). Examples: *Arguably, this is another kind of corruption, but it was in general a very long-range bribery, and it was invariably offered in the guise of friendship*—R. M. Sunter, 1986 / *It is arguably one of our most successful companies*—Sunday Times, 2004. *Arguably* is most appropriate in contexts that are open to genuine argument and disagreement. In general use, however, it implies little or no argument. In principle, a way of investing the opinion expressed with greater authority, it is often hardly more forceful in effect than 'possibly' or 'perhaps'. As such, it is a useful safety net for those who are unsure of their facts or lack the courage of their convictions: *Meet the man with the surname everyone knows, Giorgio Armani, who arguably adorns more bodies worldwide than any other living designer*—Clothes Show, 1991.

arise. The meaning of *arise* 'to get out of bed' has now given way to *rise*, except in literary use, and its principal current meaning in ordinary speech and writing is 'to come into existence or be noticed'; usually with reference to abstract concepts such as questions, issues, difficulties, complications, doubts, thoughts, opportunities, etc. *See also* AROUSE.

aristocrat, aristocratic. There are two ways of pronouncing *aristocrat*, a word derived from French *aristocrate*, coined during the French Revolution in 1789, and first mentioned in that form in English in the same year. You can emphasize either the first syllable **a**-ris-tuh-krat or the second a-**ris**-tuh-krat. The

first is still the standard one in British English. The second is the standard American pronunciation, but is fast gaining ground in Britain too, particularly among transatlantic academics and pundits. Interestingly, it was once the standard in Britain, so it could be viewed as a revival rather than an intrusion. *Aristocratic* is normally pronounced emphasizing the fourth syllable in British English, a-ris-tuh-**kra**-tik, and emphasizing the second in American English, a-**ris**-tuh-kra-tik.

armadillo has the plural form *armadillos*.

armour is spelt *-our* in BrE and as *armor* in AmE.

aroma. 1 *Aroma* now denotes any pleasant smell, as befits a word that originally meant 'spice' (13c to 18c), and has given rise to *aromatherapy*, 'massage or other treatment using extracts and essential oils', which likewise befits the special meaning of *aroma* 'the distinctive fragrance exhaled by a spice, plant, etc.'
　2 The plural is *aromas*.

around, round. 1 In general, BrE prefers *round* and AmE prefers *around*, both as an adverb and as a preposition, except in certain more or less fixed expressions or restricted collocations. In BrE it is usual to say *Winter comes round, The wheels go round, Send the book round, Show me round*, whereas in all these cases AmE would normally use *around*.
　2 *Around* is obligatory in fixed expressions such as *fool around, mess around, sit around*, etc, *all around* (as in *All around there are signs of decay*), and *to have been around*. In some of these, *about* is also possible, but not *round*.
　3 BrE still tends to prefer *about* as a preposition meaning 'approximately', although *around* is also used (e.g. *There*

are about/around 100 in all / Come about/around 4 o'clock), whereas AmE generally prefers *around. See* ABOUT.

4 However, the distribution of *around* and *round* is subject to considerable variation in practice, as the following examples show: (*around* as preposition) *Jesse . . . moped around the house all day—*Lee Smith, AmE 1983 / *The area around Waterloo—*R. Elms, BrE 1988 / *They stood grouped around their luggage—*M. Bracewell, BrE 1989 / (*round* as preposition) / *A map rolled up round a broom handle—*Jeanette Winterson, BrE 1985 / *He looked round the table as if daring anyone to smile—*David Lodge, 1988 / (*around* as adverb) *Stay around till she gets back—New Yorker,* AmE 1989 / *Hartmann's sunny . . . attitude was marvellous to have around—*Anita Brookner, BrE 1988 / *The devices have been around a while—USA Today,* AmE 1988 / *I went around to the front door—New Yorker,* AmE 1989 / (*round* as adverb) *In the end she talked me round—*Nina Bawden, BrE 1987 / *The news had gotten round pretty fast—New Yorker,* AmE 1998.

arouse. *Rouse* is almost always preferred in the literal sense with a person or animal as object. *Arouse* is chiefly used to mean 'to call into being' with reference to feelings and emotions. Generally, if you *rouse* someone you wake them or stir them into activity; if you *arouse* them, you excite them or make them angry or suspicious: *The word 'theory' has always aroused suspicion amongst the English, who see themselves as practical people and sound empiricists—*B. Bergonzi, 1990 / *About five o'clock we were roused by the distant thudding of an engine—*S. Stewart, 1991.

arrogate *see* ABROGATE.

artefact, 'a product of human art or workmanship', is the more common

spelling in BrE; in AmE *artifact,* corresponding to pronunciation rather than etymology (Latin *arte factum,* 'made by [human] art'), is dominant. That spelling may well be considered wrong by some readers in Britain.

artiste rhymes with *feast* and means 'a professional performer, especially a singer or dancer', It is a separate borrowing from French and not, as some people seem to think, a feminine form of *artist,* which has the distinct meaning of someone who works in one of the fine arts. As a blog on www.dailyartist.com puts it, *An artiste is something you don't want to be, that is, if you consider yourself an artist. Artiste,* which conveys no judgement that the performance is in fact artistic, is now regarded as at best an affectation and at worst an insult; usually a word such as *performer* would do just as well. Examples: *Distinguished people make a practice of visiting the opera, and pull rank so as to meet the artistes, especially attractive females—*R. Butters, 1991 / *Bollywood might soon be a viable ticket to superstardom for these artistes—The Week* (India), 2004.

as. 1 problems with *as . . . as . . .* In this common construction, the first *as* is an adverb, and the second is either a preposition or a conjunction.

a When no verb follows, e.g. *as good as we* / *as good as us,* you are faced with a choice between pronouns. Your alternatives are the subject pronoun *as . . . as I/we/he/she/they* and the object pronoun *as . . . as me/us/ him/her/them.* (The issue does not arise with *it* and *you* or with nouns) In normal conversational English the second pattern is more usual, and the first is only used in more formal contexts or in an effort to avoid criticism from purists. It should be added that both patterns are grammatically sound, since *as* can function as a preposition (as it does in *as good as us*) and as a conjunction (as it does in *as good as we / as good as we are*). In these cases, the first *as* is classified as an adverb (as *good as . . .*).

b Note that choosing the appropriate pronoun can avoid ambiguity, as in *I don't like George as much as them* [= I don't like George as much as I like them] / *I don't like George as much as they* [= I don't like George as much as they like him]. This facility is not available with nouns (e.g. *I don't like George as much as Henry*), and ambiguity must then be clarified either by intonation (in speech) or by rephrasing (in writing, e.g. *I don't like George as much as I like Henry*, or better, *I prefer Henry to George*).

c Note also that in negative constructions the first (adverbial) *as* can be replaced by *so*: *not so good as us*. With *so*, it is unusual to use the *I/we/he/she/they* option.

2 *as* = 'in the capacity of'. In this use, *as* is a preposition, and it is used to show the role or function of a person or thing: *I hear you are employed as a teacher / It is as a cellist that she is best known*. Care must be taken to avoid false links with the *as* clause, as in the following examples, which at best show poor style and at worst are downright ambiguous: *As a medical student his call-up was deferred*—Penelope Fitzgerald, 1986 / *As a 32-year-old law enforcement professional, you know that I do not like being forced to release prisoners from jail*—Chicago Tribune, 1988 [Who then is the professional?].

3 omission of *as*. *The board appointed him (as) CEO.* There is a group of verbs to do with selecting, classifying, or viewing people and things in certain ways, e.g. *appoint, deem, describe, elect*, which take an object (*him*) and an object complement (*CEO*). Whether to insert *as* between object and complement depends on which of three groups the verb falls into. (a) usually without *as*: *consider, declare, proclaim, pronounce, reckon*; (b) *as* is obligatory: *accept, acknowledge, characterize, choose, class, count, define, describe, designate, label, nominate, regard*; (c) both constructions are possible: *appoint, elect, nominate, proclaim, pronounce, rate, reckon*. Note that *consider* and *regard*, although having much the same meaning, differ in the matter of *as*: *We regard you as a model pupil / We consider you a model pupil*.

The adverb *as* is sometimes casually omitted in spoken English in comparisons: *She used to come regular as clockwork / It was soft as butter / They were good as gold*. This is not good practice in more formal or written English.

4 *as* = 'because'. Fowler (1926) rejected the use of *as* = 'because' when it followed the main clause, as in *I gave it up, as he only laughed at my arguments*; but he permitted it when the *as* clause came first, as in *As he only laughed at my arguments, I gave it up*. This objection now sounds as dated as the examples chosen, and the position of the clause is determined not by spurious principles of syntax but by the degree of emphasis needed for each part of the sentence.

5 *as* = 'though'. *As* is used in the same way as *though* in concessive clauses such as *much as I like them* and *good as they may seem*, in which a contrary statement follows: *good as they may seem, I have known much better ones*. In AmE, and increasingly in BrE, an initial *as* is also used in the manner of a comparison. These two examples show the difference: *As poor as they are, the fashion sense here blows my mind*—Independent, 2008. / *There was a call waiting from Yordan. Late as it was, I reached him in Madrid*—B. Gordon, 1999.

6 _as_, relative pronoun. Its use as a relative pronoun is now largely confined to the constructions _same as_ or _such as_: _We can expect the same number to turn up as came last year_ / _Such repairs as have been made to the house are most acceptable_. These constructions are less common in everyday spoken English. Other constructions with _as_ as a relative pronoun occur only in non-standard or regional English, both in BrE and AmE: _It's only baronets as cares about far-things_—Thackeray, 1847/8 / _This is him as had a nasty cut over the eye_—Dickens, 1865 / _I don't know as I expected to take part in this debate_—_Harper's Magazine_, 1888 / _There's plenty as would like this nice little flat, Mr. E_—Anthony Burgess, 1963.

7 _as and when_. This now common phrase meaning 'whensoever', introducing a future event whose occurrence remains in doubt, is surprisingly recent, not being recorded in the _OED_ before 1945. It is also used elliptically in informal (especially spoken) language to mean 'when possible, in due course'. Examples: _He would . . . snatch pub meals as and when he could_—P. McCutchan, 1975 / _All bream . . . will devour a small fish as and when the opportunity arises and they have the inclination to do so_—G. Marsden, 1987 / (elliptical) _They confirmed the existing main roads as future traffic arteries to be widened 'as and when'_—_Listener_, 1965 / _She can redo them and we just micro-wave them as and when_—spoken material in British National Corpus, 1992.

8 _as from_, _as of_. The formula _as from_ is used in contracts and agreements to indicate the date from which certain items or clauses are to take effect. This use is reasonable when the date is retrospective: _The rate of payment is increased as from the 1st September last_. For present and future dates the _as_ is superfluous: _Your redundancy takes effect from today_ [not _as from today_].

Phrases of the type _as of now_, _as of today_, etc., first recorded in the work of Mark Twain in 1900, are now well established in standard English in the UK and elsewhere. Examples: _I'm resigning from the committee as of now_—D. Karp, 1957 / _As of today, I do not believe Tebbit has enough votes to win_—J. Critchley, 1990.

9 _as if_, _as though_. **a** These two conjunctions are virtually interchangeable, except that _as if_ is somewhat more natural in exclamations (_As if I would!_).

b When the conjunction introduces a possibility or likelihood (often after a verb like _appear_, _look_, _seem_, or _sound_) the normal tense is used: _He speaks as though even the rules which we freely invent are somehow suggested to us in virtue of their being right_—M. Warnock, 1965 / _When the left wing of the Labour Party looks as if it is going to lose, it is described as bananas_—_Times_, 1980 / _It is as if he has given up on America and in so doing he has given up on grappling with the complexity of his position and allegiances_—_Times Literary Supplement_, 1986.

c When the conjunction introduces a comparison based on a hypothetical or impossible proposition, either the past tense or the subjunctive is used, which coincide in form except that the third person singular subjunctive of _to be_ is _were_, not _was_. It is impossible to draw a meaningful distinction in current usage between these two alternatives, which only exist in this case, except that the subjunctive _were_ theoretically denotes a stronger element of hypothesis or supposition than does the past tense _was_: _Most of them had been out of touch with him for many years, but he spoke to them as if it was only yesterday_—David Lodge, 1980 / _As if India were not already finding batting hard enough, the crowd_

started . . . *performing what is apparently
called the 'human wave'*—Times, 1986 /
*His body felt as though he were trembling,
but he was not*—B. Moore, 1987 / *He
devoured all, exhausted, as though his
life was in danger*—A. S. Byatt, 1987.
An elliptical construction, with the verb
to be omitted, is also possible: *The tan-
pura player . . . strummed the strings as if
in a mesmerised state*—Anita Desai,
1980.

10 as per. This preposition, meaning
'in accordance with', is more or less
restricted to business correspondence
and to such publications as DIY manuals
(e.g. *as per specification*). In general use
it occurs most frequently in the colloquialism *as per usual* and humorous
variants of it: *So I took her up a cup of
tea . . . as per usual on her headache
days*—Katherine Mansfield, 1923 / *I'll
stay in a pub . . . As per usual*—J. Bingham, 1970 / *Same old jolly camp-fire life
went on as per usual*—Julian Barnes,
1989 / *She knew better, didn't she. As per
always*—P. Bailey, 1986.

11 as such. *As such*, meaning 'in this
capacity' or 'accordingly', is an established and valid expression, but it tends
to be over-used in contexts where it adds
little meaning: (useful) *Euro-MPs are
not against the Euro-quango as such*—
English Today, 1985 / (redundant)
*Today, computers do little computing as
such outside of specific areas. They are
more concerned with manipulative tasks
such as word processing*—New Scientist,
1987. In many cases, an expression such
as *in principle* would serve better: instead of *There is no objection to the sale of
houses as such*, write *There is no objection
in principle to the sale of houses.*

12 as to. *As to* is called a complex
preposition, and has a useful role to
play when a simple preposition like *of* or
about is not available or has another
meaning. It means 'concerning' or 'with
regard to': *It is correct as to colour and

shape / The rates of postage vary both as
to distance and weight.*
   When a simple preposition is available, as it often is after a noun, it is better
to use it: ☒ '*Vladimir telephoned the
Circus at lunch-time today, sir,*' Mostyn
began, leaving some unclarity as to [use
about or *regarding*] *which 'sir' he was
addressing*—John Le Carré, 1980 / *The
setting and languages leave no doubt as
to* [use *about or concerning*] *its African-
ness*—English World-wide, 1980 / *Western newspapers have been full of
speculation as to whether China was
playing a 'Soviet card' against the United
States*—Christian Science Monitor, 1982.

13 For *as long as*, see LONG. For *such
as*, see SUCH.

**as bad or worse than . . . / as good
or better than . . .** are examples of
what are known as 'mixed constructions
in which an element, in this case the
second *as* (*as bad as, as good as*) has
been omitted. It is common, especially
in spoken English, and does not obscure
meaning, but it has been subject to criticism since the 18c. To avoid it in writing,
there are three options. If we take as our
model the sentence *We're sure they can
judge a novel just as well if not better than
us* (*London Review of Books*, 1987), they
are, in increasing order of the editing
involved (1) add the *as*, and introduce
commas, i.e. *just as well as, if not better
than, us*; (2) add the *as* and place the
comparative after the term of comparison, i.e. *just as well as us, if not better*; (3)
insert the construction *at least as* before
the relevant adjective or adverb and remove the comparative, *i.e. at least as well
as us*. This last option may subtly change
the meaning, and so cannot be applied
indiscriminately.

ascendancy, ascendant. 1 The
recommended spellings are *-ancy, -ant*,
although *ascendency* and *ascendent* are
still sometimes found in print, but are

about ten times less common in the *OEC* data.

2 *Have/establish/ gain ascendancy over* and *be in the ascendant* are the normal phrases, and refer to a position of power achieved, not of power being gained. *Even when the Gestapo system was in the ascendant over much of Europe, . . . Churchill had faith that it would one day be possible to defeat Nazism altogether—BBC History*, 2004. *Ascendant* here means 'supreme' or 'dominant', not 'ascending'.

However, by a natural association of the word with the corresponding verb *ascend* 'to rise', it is often used in a progressive or upward sense, to mean 'in the process of gaining control', and this meaning is recognized by the *Oxford Dictionary Online*, among others.

3 Although *in the ascendant* is the standard and traditional form of the phrase, the *OEC* data shows that *in the ascendancy* is used rather more often. Some people will no doubt continue to regard it as a mistake, but for others the distinction has already clearly been lost. Examples: unquestionable uses (ascendancy) *But even if the moderates regain the ascendancy, it may not be enough to persuade many of the protesters to return home—Daily Telegraph*, 2012 / (ascendant) *Pragmatism is in the ascendant. Letwin has suffered from his failure to sound an early alarm about the danger posed by the NHS reforms—New Statesman*, 2011 / questionable uses (in the ascendancy) *Up to 1947 the left was in the ascendancy—Socialist Worker Online*, 2005.

ascetic. Presumably because its *-etic* ending is the same as in *aesthetic*, *ascetic* is sometimes wrongly used for it, despite its very different origins and meanings. *Ascetic* comes ultimately from the Greek word for a Christian monk or hermit, and as an adjective originally described self-discipline in abstaining from all

forms of indulgence for religious reasons (e.g. *The old Ascetick Christians found a Paradise in a Desert—*Sir T. Browne, 1682). Nowadays it is still often used in this strictly religious sense, and also more generally, to denote a way of life free from self-indulgence: *Senior advisers describe an ascetic lifestyle: one meal a day, working through lunch, and in the evenings on official papers—Guardian*, 2008.

Aesthetic comes from an Ancient Greek verb meaning 'to perceive'. It applies to the perception, appreciation, or criticism of what is beautiful, and is often applied to values, experiences, qualities, and pleasures. Examples: *Henry's good-natured wit is an additional joy in an elegant body of work already delivering ample esthetic pleasure—Art in America*, 2005 / *If you love the aesthetic qualities of black-and-white photography, you'll fall head-over-heels with what Criterion's achieved here—DVD Verdict*, 2004. *See also* AESTHETE, AESTHETIC.

ascribe *see* SUBSCRIBE.

as far as *see* FAR.

Asian, Asiatic. 1 Both words can be pronounced with *-zh-* as in *measure* or as *-sh-*. In AmE the first is far more common, and it is becoming the standard in BrE too.

2 Since the second half of the 20c *Asian* (a slightly older word) has replaced *Asiatic*, as noun and adjective, when the reference is ethnic, because *Asiatic* is thought to have disparaging overtones. In BrE *Asian* is also used to denote people from Asia, especially the Indian subcontinent, or their descendants, living in Britain. In North America it refers to people from China, Japan, and other countries of East Asia.

3 *Asiatic* is standard in scientific and technical use, for example, in biological and anthropological classifications, e.g. *Asiatic lion / lily / Greeks / peoples*.

Asian American is the standard word in the US to refer to people of Asian, particularly East Asian, descent.

aside, a side. Written as one word, *aside* is an adverb meaning 'to or on one side', as in *to put aside, to take aside*, etc., or a noun meaning words in a play spoken to the audience out of hearing of the other characters. In the meaning 'on each side' it must be written as two words, as in *They are playing five a side* and *a five-a-side team*.

aside from *see* APART FROM.

as per *see* AS 10.

assassinate, assassination. 1 The traditional meaning of *assassinate* 'to kill an important person for political reasons' has been extended in recent times to include any person regarded by his or her killers as a political or sectarian target, including journalists, students, and civilians on the streets, and the corresponding noun *assassination* has followed this tendency. Examples: *Students at the University of Altantico in Antioquia were assassinated in front of a classroom in which they were being taught*—Z Magazine, AmE 2003 / *About 65 or 70 or so government officials and security forces had been targeted for assassination and random violence and killings*—ABC news transcript, AusE 2004.

2 An older figurative meaning of *assassinate*, meaning 'to destroy (someone's reputation)' has also been revived: *Those around Bush, many of whom came of age during Vietnam and almost none of whom served, have attempted to assassinate the character and insult the patriotism of anyone who disagrees with them*—Whiskey Bar, AmE 2004. The noun is especially common in the expression *character assassination*: *The important thing is to end your character assassination of the manager with some*

magnanimity—Observer Sport Magazine, 2004.

assignment, assignation. An *assignment* is a task or piece of work allotted to a person, in a meaning originating in AmE. In law it is also a legal transfer of a right or property, or the document that effects the transfer. The main current meaning of *assignation*, which is pronounced with a hard g, is now 'an appointment to meet, especially between lovers'. Its original meaning 'the act of assigning, apportionment' is still in use, especially in technical or semi-technical contexts: *Marriage plays an important role in this by the assignation of children to membership of particular groups*—weblog, BrE 2004 [OEC].

The normal word for the act of assigning something is, however, *assignment* (*The assignment of responsibility is a major issue here*).

assimilation is the process by which the formation of words is influenced by existing words, and the spelling and pronunciation of word-elements are affected by the elements that follow or come before. The word *cockroach*, from Spanish *cucaracha*, developed its modern spelling by being assimilated in the 18c to the English words *cock* and *roach*. In spelling, *in-* is assimilated to *il-* in words such as *illumination* and to *im-* in words such as *impossible*. In phonetics, an initial *s* can be assimilated to *sh-* when preceded by a word ending in *sh* or *ch*, as for example in *lunch score*.

assist has the same meaning as *help*, and shares the same grammatical constructions. In many contexts the two words are interchangeable, but *help* is usually preferable, *assist* being, in Fowler's term (1926), a 'genteelism' to be avoided. However, *assist* has connotations of formality that are sometimes needed, as in *A young man who assisted*

him with the management of the farm—
Truman Capote, 1966: *who helped him*
would have seemed too casual.

assume, presume. 1 Both words can
mean 'suppose' and are often interchangeable in this meaning. Fowler
(1926) maintained that there is a stronger element of postulation or hypothesis
in *assume* and of a belief held on the
basis of external evidence in *presume*,
but in practice the uses are not always
that distinct. Both words can be followed
by a *that*-clause (or one with *that* omitted), by an object followed by a *to*-infin-
itive, or by a simple object: (assume)
*Throughout the book . . . the authors as-
sume the validity of neo-classical economics as taught in the United States—*
Times Literary Supplement, 1974 / *When
you're young you assume everybody old
knows what they're doing—*Martin Amis,
1987 / *This is assumed to refer to some
sort of demonstration similar to April's
Peking riot—Daily Telegraph*, 1976 /
(presume) *I often hear the ungrammatical term 'one pence'. I presume this is
because the occurrence of a single penny
is becoming a thing of the past—Daily
Telegraph*, 1974 / *The Able Criminal . . .
may be presumed . . . to be emotionally
stable and 'well-adjusted'—*Eric Ambler,
1977.
    2 *Assume* and *presume* also coincide
in a range of meaning that may be summarized as 'to take on oneself', although
you generally assume roles and identi-
ties but presume attitudes and bearings.
The intransitive use with a *to* infinitive is
available only with *presume*. Examples:
*He was writing 'Gerontion', a dramatic
monologue in which he assumes the persona of the 'little old man'—*Peter Ackroyd, 1984 / *He looked surprised—almost
annoyed—as if a servant had presumed
too great a familiarity—*P. P. Read, 1981 /
*It is a reckless ambassador who would
presume to preempt his chiefs—*Henry
Kissinger, 1979.

assuming (that) is used to mean 'on
the assumption that', and since *assuming* is the participle of the verb *to assume*,
it is open to the objection that the subject of the sentence has to be capable of
assuming things, whereas of course the
conceptual subject of the phrase is the
people involved. It can be followed by a
noun (or noun phrase) or by a *that*-
clause: *Assuming an average of three feet
per step, this equates to patients walking
around an extra three quarters of a mile
each day—Medical News Today*, AmE
2005 [*OEC*] / *Assuming that the museum
is open on Monday, the car will pick us up
at 10 a.m.* There is no doubt at all about
the intended meanings here.

assure, assurance. *Assure* has never
found public acceptance in the meaning
of 'to secure the future payment of an
amount with insurance'. It is used by
some insurance offices and agents, especially when death is the event insured
against (*the life assured*). Outside those
circles, you *insure* your life and take out
life assurance (or *insurance*)

assure, ensure, insure. These three
words overlap in meaning, and all have
to do with aspects of certainty or security. *Assure* means 'to make (a person)
sure, to convince', and can be followed
by *of* or a *that*-clause (*She had to leave,
but we were assured of future visits / I
solemnly assured him I would say nothing to any one*). It also has special uses in
to rest assured ('to be comfortably certain') and as an adjective *assured*,
meaning 'self-confident'. *Ensure* means
to 'make certain, guarantee', and is followed either by a simple object or (more
commonly) by a *that*-clause (*an important decision which ensures personal
freedom for all American women / The
purpose of the scheme was to ensure
that claims when made were paid within
thirty days*). *Insure* is restricted to
the meaning 'protect by insurance'

(*The policy insures them against personal liability claims / You can't insure against drought / It was up to the individual to insure his own property*). It is also sometimes used, especially in AmE, where *ensure* is the standard spelling (*There are a few techniques marketers use to insure greater success with letters / Also, insure that none of your close family members or friends have the same problem*).

assuredly is pronounced as four syllables, uh-**shaw**-rid-li.

asterisk. (*). This has many special uses, the most common of which is as a marker in a text to draw attention to a footnote, or in a handwritten document to signal an addition. It is also used, especially in older writing, to stand for letters omitted from coarse slang words, e.g. *c**t, f**k*. In linguistic usage, it denotes (1) a hypothetical form of a word, and (2) an incorrect or impossible usage, e.g. **They promised us to go.*

asthma is pronounced **ass**-muh in BrE, and **az**-muh in AmE. The *-th-* is not normally pronounced in either variety.

asthmatic. To describe people affected by asthma, it is desirable to avoid using *asthmatic* as a noun, e.g. ☒ *In 1999, the auto maker found that asthmatics in Madison County visited the hospital far more often than others—BusinessWeek*, 2002. This is because the humanness of the people concerned should not, as it should not with other disabilities, be reduced to a single medical condition ('the disability is not the person'). The preferred formulation for the plural is 'people with asthma': '*Sometimes people with asthma will have difficulty controlling their health problems if there's mould in the building*', says Patry—*Montreal Mirror*, 2001 [OEC].

astronaut is first recorded, with hypothetical reference, in 1928. It is now the standard term for a person trained to travel in a spacecraft. A Russian space traveller, however, is usually called a *cosmonaut*.

as well as. 1 A verb following a subject that includes *as well as* should agree with the noun or pronoun that precedes *as well as*: *He believes that tutor as well as pupil benefits from the arrangement—Oxford Today*, 1990. So the verb here is in the singular. This is because the phrase *as well as pupil* is regarded as a parenthesis, and not as part of the main sentence, which is grammatically complete without it. In contrast, if *as well as* were replaced by *and* the sentence would read *He believes that tutor and pupil benefit from the arrangement.* See also AGREEMENT 3.

2 *As well as* is used both as a conjunction, in which case a following pronoun agrees with a preceding noun or pronoun (*It was obvious that he had been consulted as well as I—Graham Greene*, 1965) and, more commonly, as a preposition (in which case the last example would read . . . *as well as me*). It may also be followed by a verbal noun, ending in *-ing* especially when it is put at the beginning of a sentence: *As well as being highly collectable . . . they make surprisingly roomy containers for all sorts of items—Daily Telegraph*, 1980. Here usage has largely overtaken Fowler's preference in principle for a form of the verb that matches the verb used earlier in the sentence (e.g. *His death leaves a gap as well as creates a by-election*). This construction still occurs, typically when an auxiliary or modal verb such as *have* or *will* precedes (*I'm sure the children will learn a lot from the project as well as enjoy themselves getting stuck in to the mud and planting the bulbs—Bolton Evening News*, 2003).

-asy. There are only four nouns in common use that end in -asy as distinct from -acy. These are *apostasy, ecstasy, fantasy,* and *idiosyncrasy*. In all these cases the ending is not a distinct suffix but corresponds via French and Latin to Greek nouns ending in -asia or -asis. Ecstasy is made up of words meaning 'standing outside oneself' (and therefore subscribes to the same notion as the idiom *be beside oneself*), and *idiosyncrasy* means literally a 'personal mixture', from Greek roots *idios* 'personal' and *krasis* 'mixture'.

asylum. 1 The word is no longer used, except with historical reference, of a psychiatric hospital, which is now typically called *clinic, psychiatric unit,* or simply *hospital* or by its name. The principal use of *asylum* now is to denote the status (in full, *political asylum*) sought by political refugees or *asylum seekers*.

2 The plural *asylums* is only used in the older meaning.

at. 1 *at about*. The *OED* illustrates this use (e.g. *at about seven o'clock in the evening*) with examples from 1843 onward, and occasional objections can now safely be ignored.

2 *at all*. In Standard BrE, this prepositional phrase meaning 'in every way, in any way' is restricted to negative constructions, questions, and conditional statements: *I did not speak at all / Did you speak at all? / If you spoke at all*. Its earlier use meaning 'of all, altogether' survives in Ireland and in some BrE and AmE dialects (e.g. *John Cusack is the finest dancer at all*—P. W. Joyce, 1910).

3 *at or in*. It is more usual to use *in* when permanent location or continued habitation is involved, and is required when the place is a country or region rather than a place such as a town or city: *Timbuktu is in Mali / He lives in Helsinki / The festival takes place in Salzburg in August / She grew up in Switzerland*.

At is more usual with reference to more transitory association, and is much more common with specific places: *The plane landed at Nadi in Fiji / There is a railway station at Leuchars*. A further distinction is demonstrated by the sentences *They are at St Andrews* [= a member of the University] and *They are in St Andrews* [living in or visiting St Andrews].

4 *where it's at*. This colloquial expression, meaning 'the fashionable scene or area of activity', swept into AmE in the 1960s and is now common in BrE and other varieties. It should be avoided in more formal English.

ate is normally pronounced to rhyme with *bet*, although pronunciation to rhyme with *bait* is also common.

-athon, -thon. The popularity of this suffix illustrates how English nonchalantly plays fast and loose with etymology. The *-athon* element has no meaning in the Greek from which it comes, but is merely part of the place name Marathon, where a decisive battle was fought in antiquity. Using the suffix in this way has been described as 'barbarous', but no matter. It combines with verbs or nouns to denote an activity, especially a sporting one, carried out for an unusually prolonged time, very often as a fundraising event, for example a *skipathon* by children to raise funds for their primary school. Some words created by adding *-thon* disappear no sooner than the event so described has happened, e.g. a *blogathon*, but others become established and are recognized by dictionaries, such as *walkathon*, and (with reduction to *-thon*) *telethon*. Words created using *-(a)thon* do not require hyphens, and their plural is *-ons*. The word *'thon* is occasionally found as an informal shortening of *marathon* meaning a long-distance race.

-ati. This plural suffix, used to create nouns denoting prominent groups of people associated with what is specified by the stem word, was introduced into English in 1599. However, the several modern words containing the suffix take their inspiration from the slightly later *literati* (1620), the *-ati* part of which seems to be an amalgam of the Latin and Italian masculine plural past participle *-ati*. In modern *-ati* words the suffix can be added at will to stems which come from neither Latin nor Italian, two topical examples being *bloggerati* and *twitterati*. This useful suffix has generated words that have become established, such as *technorati* and *digerati* (the elite of, or people who are very knowledgeable about, the digital technology world). Others that have not become fully established include, at one end of the social spectrum, *lagerati* ('lager louts') and *blazerati* ('blazer-wearing sports officials') at the other.

atrium. Once confined to Roman archaeology and architecture (referring to the open-roofed hall or central courtyard of a Roman house), this word is now more likely to be encountered in its modern architectural meaning of 'a central hall in a modern building, typically rising through several stories and having a glazed roof'. For both these meanings, the more common plural is *atria*, not *atriums*, and in the medical meaning it is also the norm. *See* LATIN PLURALS.

attitude. One might say that this is now a word with attitude, in its 20c meaning 'aggressive or uncooperative behaviour', which represents a special application of one kind of characteristic attitude (in the established meaning 'a person's settled opinion or behaviour'): *If I'm out there for months with everybody yelling at me, I'm going to cop an attitude—New York Times*, 1985. The word is still moving on, and now has a positive connotation, 'assertiveness, style, panache': *In this job, you've gotta have attitude, hang loose, ready for anything—Police Review*, 1990. It should only be used in this way informally; more formally the word needs explicit clarification: for the first meaning use *uncooperative attitude* or even simply *poor* (or *bad*) *attitude*, and for the second meaning *strong* (or *positive*) *attitude*.

attributive. 1 In grammar, *attributive* denotes a word, normally an adjective or noun, that is put before another word, normally a noun, to qualify or describe it in some way (eg. *brown* in *brown shoes* and *table* in *table lamp*). *See further at* ADJECTIVE 2.
2 English allows several nouns to be placed in succession, as in *a museum conservation department*, and this practice is especially common in newspaper headlines, which aim at concision: *sex cinema blaze man pleads guilty—Independent*, 1995 / *expenses row councillor forced out—Evening News* (Edinburgh), 1995.

aubretia, aubrietia, aubrieta. Horticulture provides fertile ground for misspelling, there being no good reason why experts in the art and science of growing things should be equally skilled at spelling. *Aubretia* is named after a French botanist called Claude Aubriet, and the original spelling was *aubrieta*, which is the plant's genus name. In nontechnical use, however, the forms *aubretia* and *aubrietia* are now more usual.

audit *verb.* British readers of American books and newspapers might be puzzled by the use of *audit* to mean 'to attend (a class) informally' without working for a particular qualification: *She audited his undergraduate lectures; she waylaid* *him in the department office*—Alison Lurie, 1974.

auger, augur. *Auger* is an Old English word for a tool for boring holes. *Augur*, from the Latin word for soothsayer, is used occasionally to mean a prophet, but is more usual as a verb in the expressions *augur well* and *augur ill*, meaning 'to portend, to suggest a specific outcome'. Examples: *Everything augured badly—they weren't meant to be together*—E. J. Howard, 1965 / *The novel augured well for a successful career in fiction-writing*—J. Pope Hennessy.

aught is an Old English word that survives only in the fixed expressions *for aught I know* and *for aught I care*, and as such is restricted to literary or archaic use.

augur *see* AUGER.

aural, oral. *Aural* means 'to do with the ear' (from Latin *auris* ear) and *oral* means 'to do with the mouth' (from Latin *os, oris* mouth). An *oral examination* is one done by speaking rather than by writing; an *aural examination* is a medical examination of the ear. Both words are pronounced the same way, with the first syllable as in *or*, adding to the confusion. *See also* VERBAL.

Australian English. 1 Most of the distinctive features of Australian English concern pronunciation, vocabulary, and idiom; there are few differences in the written or literary language.

2 pronunciation. The sound of Australian English is characterized principally by its vowels, which differ from those of BrE in several ways: the vowels of *fleece, face, price, goose, goat, mouth* all begin with rather open, slack sounds not unlike those used in Cockney speech; the vowels of *dress, strut, start, dance, nurse* have a much closer and tighter sound than in BrE. In unstressed syllables, Australian *-es* and *-ed* (as in *boxes* and *studded*) have a sound like *e* in *garden*, so that *boxes* sounds much the same as *boxers*, whereas BrE has the sound of *i* as in *pin*; Australian final *-y* and *-ie-* (as in *study* and *studied*) has a longer sound more like *beat* than *bit*. Australian English is closer to AmE in its lighter pronunciation of *t* and *l* when occurring between vowels (as in *butter* and *hollow*).

3 vocabulary and idiom. The main differences arise from the local landscape, natural history, and way of life, and can be seen in geographical names (e.g. *bush, creek, paddock, scrub*; conversely BrE *brook, dale, field, forest* are rare in Australian), and in names of plants and animals, some of Aboriginal origin and borrowed further in BrE (e.g. *budgerigar, wallaby*). Word formations peculiar to Australian English include a productive colloquial suffix *-o* in words such as *commo* = communist and *smoko* = tea-break. Relatively few items of general vocabulary, whether neutral or informal in register, have come into BrE (e.g. *barrack, crook* = 'ill, unwell', *dinkum, ropeable* = 'angry', *walkabout*), and still fewer idioms (the best known probably being *she'll be right* = 'all will be well').

authentic, genuine. 1 Fowler (1926) tried to establish a distinction in meaning between these two words, reserving *authentic* for the truthfulness of (for example) a book's contents or a picture's subject and *genuine* for the status of its alleged creator. In the sentence *The Holbein Henry VIII is both authentic and genuine*, the implication is that the portrait really is of Henry VIII (and therefore *authentic*) and is really by Holbein (and therefore *genuine*). This distinction is difficult to maintain in practice, and items such as documents, antique furniture, signatures, and many others are regularly described as *authentic* or *genuine* without any identifiable distinction in meaning.

2 An especially important domain in which *authentic* has been used in recent years is that of 'early' music (i.e. before about 1700), where *authentic instruments* are those made and played according to the principles of the period in which the music was written; and so a violin (for example) can be an *authentic* baroque one, although it may be of modern manufacture and therefore not *genuine* or *original*. An increasingly common alternative is *period instruments*, first recorded in the 1920s but not widely used until the 1970s.

author. 1 *noun*. An *author* is a male or a female writer; *authoress* is widely regarded as depreciatory or even offensive when used by men, although women writers still use it occasionally of themselves (*The authoress would like to dedicate this story to her father*—website, AmE 2004 [*OEC*]).

2 *verb*. The verb is 16c, some two centuries later than the noun, and has been used both transitively and intransitively, although in current use it is typically transitive: *Whenever the students thought they were evaluating the work of a man, they assessed it as far more impressive than when they thought it was authored by a woman*—M. Ross, 1989 / *During his professional career, he has authored more than 250 technical and marketing publications*—*Apply Magazine*, AmE 2003. Since the mid-20c this use of *author* has been greatly extended in AmE and BrE to areas of activity outside the arts, such as sport and the cinema, and even crime (*Pinochet's life over the past three years has been a miserable story of unending flight—from legions of prosecutors the world over determined to bring him to book for crimes he is alleged to have authored*—*Time Magazine*, 2004). *Co-author*, meaning to share authorship, is now common.

3 *Authoring* is a recent addition to the language of computing, and means 'the process of creating multimedia documents for electronic publishing': *In order to profit from the possibilities of hypertext, teachers have to be provided with powerful authoring environments which allow them to create complex hypertexts.*—*Literary and Linguistic Computing*, 1992.

authoritarian, authoritative.
These two words should be carefully distinguished as their implications are quite different. *Authoritarian* is generally used of people or their actions and has the unfavourable meaning 'favouring or encouraging strict obedience to authority' (with overtones of excess); typical collocates include *regime, ruler, government, personality*, and *leadership*. *Authoritative* is generally used of things that people say or write, or the manner of their saying them (*voice* is a common collocate), and has the favourable meaning 'recognized as true or dependable'. Examples: (authoritarian) *The West was happy to bolster authoritarian governments that were not controlled by the Soviet Union to prevent them from turning communist*—*Foreign Affairs* (magazine), 2004 / (authoritative) *He was cool, authoritative, and well spoken / a very authoritative article which looks at whether the Queen or the Governor General is Australia's head of State*—J. Ray, 2003.

automaton has the plural forms *automata* and *automatons*, the first being preferred in scientific writing. *See* LATIN PLURALS.

automobile. This word, together with *car*, is the standard term in AmE, but in BrE it is used little apart from in the name *Automobile Association*.

autumn *see* FALL.

auxiliary verbs. An auxiliary verb is one that is used before another verb to form a particular tense or mood, for example *be* in *We were going, have* in *They have gone,* and *do* in *Do you mind?* Sometimes more than one auxiliary verb is used to form a tense, as in *We will be going* and *You have been warned.* Some verbs, such as *can, may,* and *would,* are called modal (or modal auxiliary) verbs, and others (notably *dare* and *need*), though less obviously auxiliary in function, are called semi-modal verbs because they behave in similar ways (for example, you can say *dare not* and *need not,* which is characteristic of auxiliary verbs). *See also* BE; CAN; DO; HAVE; MAY, MIGHT; MODAL VERB; OUGHT; SHALL AND WILL.

avail. 1 The noun is used frequently in the somewhat literary phrases *of no avail* and *to little/no avail,* meaning 'having little or no use or effective result', and poses no problems.

2 There are also straightforward verb uses that are also slightly formal or literary in flavour, as in *Words avail very little with him* and *His good works availed him nothing,* and the reflexive use *avail oneself of* as in *to avail oneself of opportunities.* The reflexive construction is also found in the passive, especially in AmE: *Individual contracts may not be availed of to defeat or delay the procedure*—*Legal Times,* 1982. In BrE this use should be avoided in favour of words such as *use, exploit, employ,* and *utilize.*

3 The construction which is most often criticized and should be avoided is *avail of* used without the reflexive pronoun (*myself, yourself,* etc.) as in ☒ *I want to encourage other people within the police service who are also retiring under the severance scheme to avail of the opportunities for training*—*Guardian,* 2009.

avant-garde is a 15c word originally meaning 'the front part of an army' (now

expressed by *vanguard*). It was revived in the 20c to mean 'pioneers or innovators', especially in the arts; its main uses are in the expression *the avant-garde,* in attributive uses such as *the avant-garde cinema* and *avant-garde design,* and with a qualifying word such as *the international avant-garde.* It retains a French pronunciation with a nasalized second syllable in *avant,* and is written with a hyphen.

avenge, revenge. The principal differences to bear in mind are (1) that you *avenge* a person (including *yourself*) or an act but *revenge* only an act or *yourself* (usually *on* someone), and (2) that *avenge* is only a verb but *revenge* is a noun as well (in fact more commonly so). Differences in meaning, though proposed from time to time, are too subtle to have any practical use as guidance. Examples: (avenge) *The ferocity and guile with which Absalom had avenged the rape of his sister*—D. Jacobson, 1970 / *That brave god will leap down from his steed when he has to avenge his father's death*—K. Crossley-Holland, 1980 / *Through characterization the novelist has the means to avenge himself on his enemies*—P. D. James, 1993 / (revenge) *It wasn't just that I could never revenge myself upon him*—S. Mason, 1990 / *If I were to revenge myself upon you . . . that would be an act of despair*—Iris Murdoch, 1993 / *He revenged the French attack on the Sussex coast in autumn 1515 by retaliating effectively in a series of devastating raids on Normandy*—*Oxford Dictionary of National Biography,* 2008.

averse. 1 *averse, aversion.* Both words are followed by *to,* despite arguments (notably by Dr Johnson, challenged at some length in the *OED*) that *from* should be used. Examples: *Nor was he averse to being reminded of Calcutta*—Anita Desai, 1988 / *Vic wasn't averse to* *keeping Everthorpe guessing whether he and Robyn Penrose were having an affair*—David Lodge, 1988 / *Dr Mainwaring's prescription had not cured her aversion from the prospect of becoming hopelessly senile in the company of people who knew her*—Kingsley Amis, 1974 / *He had a lifelong aversion to British officialdom*—John Le Carré, 1989.

2 averse, adverse. *See* ADVERSE.

avid, meaning 'eager or greedy', is used either attributively (before a noun, commonly an agent noun such as *collector* or *reader*) or predicatively followed by *for* (or, now rarely, *of*): *Since getting the equipment two years ago, I've become an avid collector of compact discs*—CD Review, 1992 / *He was avid for news of how it was all going, and regretting that he couldn't be part of it*—J. Spottiswoode, 1991.

avoid, avert, evade. *Avoid* and *evade* overlap in meaning, but *evade* has a stronger sense of guile or trickery in escaping from an obligation (such as paying income tax). *Avert* means 'to turn aside' (which is its literal meaning in *averting one's gaze*, etc.), and so 'to take action to prevent (something unwelcome, such as danger)'. Examples: *Measles vaccine should be avoided by children who are receiving steroids*—D. J. Rapp, 1970 / *These rules could be evaded, but their evasion was preferable to a reign of snoopery and an encouragement of informers*—A. Paton, 1981 / *If governments act . . . it will be possible to curb man-made emissions of greenhouse gases over the coming decades, and so avert the worst predictions of climate scientists*—Independent, 2007. There is a corresponding difference in meaning between the nouns *avoidance* and *evasion*.

avouch, avow, vouch. *Avouch*, meaning 'to assure, guarantee, acknowledge' and overlapping with *avow*, can be found in the Bible (AV), Spenser, Marlowe, Milton, Byron, and Thackeray, but despite these fine credentials is no longer in general use. *Avow* is still in use and means 'to declare (a belief, one's faith, an intention, etc.)'. *Vouch* is restricted to the phrase *to vouch for* (somebody or something), as in *I can vouch for them* and *I can vouch for their honesty.*

await, wait. *Await* is a transitive verb meaning 'to wait for', and cannot usually be used without an object: *We will await the outcome* is equivalent to *We will wait for the outcome* (but has a stronger element of suspenseful expectation). The phrase *we will await and see* is generally considered ungrammatical because in it *await* is being used intransitively. Similarly, some people dislike the not uncommon use with an implied but not expressed object, e.g. *a warm welcome awaits* (i.e. you / us / them). *Wait* is generally intransitive (and transitivized by *for*), but has a limited number of collocates in transitive use, as in *Wait your turn* and *Don't wait tea.*

awake, awaken, wake, waken.

1 forms. Although the history of these words, and in particular of the various forms of past tense and past participle, is highly complex (see the *OED* entry), in current use *awake* and *wake* can be paired as strong verbs having a change of vowel, and *awaken* and *waken* can be paired as weak verbs. For the first pair, the past forms are *awoke* and *woke*, and the participial forms are *awoken* and *woken*. The second pair are regular, with past and participial forms *awakened* and *wakened.*

2 meanings. All four verbs can be used transitively or intransitively, but *wake, awaken,* and *waken* are more formal or literary in effect. *Wake* is the only one to be followed optionally by *up*. Examples will clarify all these points:

(awake) *I awoke from a deep sleep / She awoke to the sound of driving rain / She awoke her sleeping child / The accident awoke old fears /* (awaken) *They awakened at dawn / There was enough noise to awaken the dead / There is a need to awaken motorists to the dangers of speeding in foggy conditions / The episode awakened her interest in impressionist painting /* (wake) *When do you usually wake in the morning? / I usually wake up at seven / Will you wake me up when it's time to go? / We woke up early this morning / I woke her up when it became light / I was woken by the wind in the night /* (waken) *They wakened at dawn / We were wakened by the storm / When she fell asleep nothing would waken her.*

aware. 1 *Aware* is generally predicative in use, i.e. it stands after a noun or as a complement after a verb such as *be, become, grow, seem,* etc. It can be followed by *of* or a *that*-clause: *I had to be aware of . . . the balance between committed pro-marketeers and committed anti-marketeers*—Harold Wilson, 1976 / *The young people are well aware that they are being ripped off by these parasites*—Frendz, 1971.

2 In the 20c, uses of *aware* either alone or attributively (before a noun) have become more common in the generalized meanings 'well-informed' and 'alert to circumstances' which do not refer to particular items of knowledge: *Revolutionarily aware people can't be fooled by these kinds of people*—Frendz, 1971 / *The painfully aware state that seems to have succeeded her earlier calm*—Anita Brookner, 1985 / *The people concerned are caring, concerned and aware—and you haven't the faintest idea what they're talking about.*—Times, 1986. Use with a qualifying adverb, as in *environmentally aware,* is also well attested, both attributively and predicatively.

3 The noun *awareness* has developed a corresponding generalized meaning: *Lord Scarman recognises that the awareness campaign needs forcefully to target the government*—City Limits, 1986.

awesome has followed the route of words like *fantastic, tremendous,* etc., in acquiring, especially in AmE, a favourable meaning 'very good or impressive', and this meaning has spread into BrE alongside its traditional meaning 'inspiring awe'. Examples: *The roadside drinkers stare open-mouthed at the sight of the awesome Ford GT40*—Today, 1992 / *If the English performances in Paris and Edinburgh had been executed by New Zealand they would be proclaimed as awesome and unstoppable*—Rugby World and Post, 1992. In the slang of a certain age group *awesome* has a generalized favourable sense (like *cool* and *wicked*): *Reading week was awesome: instead of doing any work I went on holidays*—weblog, 2004 [*OEC*].

awful. 1 There are two main stages in the development of this word from its primary meaning (which goes back to the time of King Alfred) of 'inspiring awe'. First, from about 1800 it came to mean 'very bad' (as in *awful weather, an awful time*); then gradually it was reduced further in force to take on the role of a catch-all intensifier deriving its sense from the context (with positive connotations in some cases, notably *an awful lot*). It has also served as an adverb meaning the same as *awfully,* i.e. little more than 'very' (*It is an awful lovely place*—Dickens, 1844), but this use is non-standard in current BrE, and markedly informal in AmE.

2 The corresponding adverb *awfully* has followed the same route, and now means little more than 'very' (as in *awfully kind of you*). It is best restricted to spoken or casual written English and should be avoided in more formal contexts.

awhile, a while. Both expressions have the same origin in the word *while*, but *awhile* is strictly adverbial whereas *a while* is a noun phrase (very often preceded by *for*): *When he reached the street-sign he stopped awhile and stood beneath it*—Colin Dexter, 1983 / *I'm going away for a while*—B. Neil, 1993. The tendency to write *a while* as one word is encouraged because *a while*, although a noun phrase, can also have a semi-adverbial function: *We had to wait a long while* [= for a long while].

axe is the standard spelling in BrE and other varieties apart from AmE, which favours *ax*. In BrE the verb has inflected forms *axes, axed, axing*.

axis has the plural form *axes*, pronounced **ak**-seez.

aye. 1 The *OED* notes that the word meaning 'yes' appears suddenly about 1575 and is common about 1600, but its origin is un-known. Its principal uses now are in some northern British varieties (especially Scottish), as a parliamentary term (*The ayes have it*), and in nautical language (*Aye aye, sir*). It is pronounced as in *eye*.

2 The word meaning 'ever', as in *for aye*, is a different word first recorded about 1200. It is pronounced as in *hay*.

3 Both words are also spelt *ay*.

B

bacillus is pronounced with a soft *c*. The plural is *bacilli*, with the final *-i* pronounced like *eye*.

back. A use that is chiefly AmE but familiar in the UK and likely to become BrE eventually is *back of*, meaning 'behind, in the back of' (*His computer . . . locates a spare space back of the plane—Keyboard Player*, 1986). But *in back* and *in back of* are unlikely to make the transition, being markedly AmE and un-British: (in back) '*What luck,' she muses, sliding back in* [*the car*]. '*Get in back, Herman.*'—B. Ripley, 1987 / (in back of) *Should I or should I not go out to the swimming pool in back of my sister's condominium?*—A. Beattie, 1980.

back-formation. 1 A *back-formation* is a word (often a verb) formed from a longer word (often a noun) which appears to be a derivative of the newer word; for example, *burgle* (19c) is a back-formation from *burglar* (which is six centuries older) and *sculpt* (19c) from *sculptor* (17c). Some words are revived as back-formations, such as *conject* (which occurs in Chaucer and Shakespeare); *see also* ADMINISTER, ADMINISTRATE.

2 Many established back-formations cause little comment; examples are *diagnose* (from *diagnosis*), *donate* (from *donation*), *laze* (from *lazy*), *legislate* (from *legislation*), and *televise* (from *television*), whereas others are sometimes still resisted; the chief targets are *enthuse* (from *enthusiasm*) and *liaise* (from *liaison*), which can be avoided by using phrases such as *be enthusiastic* and *form a liaison* (and *interact* will often do instead). Both, however, are now common.

backlog. The current figurative meaning 'arrears of uncompleted work' is an Americanism from the 1930s which passed rapidly into British use. The original physical meaning 'a log placed at the back of a fire' dates from the 17c; in between is an earlier meaning 'a reserve supply', which extended in use to abstract things (for example, goodwill) and gave rise to the current meaning. In this meaning it is often used with a preceding noun, e.g. *capacity backlog, orders backlog*: *Jordan temporarily closes its border with Iraq to ease the refugee backlog*—Keesings, 1990 / *Extra staff brought in to clear the backlog should be kept on until a thorough review is made*—J. King et al., 1993

backslang is a type of slang in which words are pronounced backwards and take on a special (often derogatory) meaning, such as *yob* for 'boy'.

back to basics is a 1990s British political slogan redolent of John Major's years in office, invoking a return to fundamental principles of honesty and decency, which is likely to recur from time to time. When used adjectivally, it should be hyphened (*a back-to-basics campaign*).

backward, backwards. 1 For the adverb, both forms are in use, although *backward* is somewhat more common in

AmE and *backwards* in BrE: *Talk ran backward from the events of the morning*—A. Munro, CanE 1987 / *I walked backward to look at her in the sun*—E. L. Doctorow, AmE 1989 / *Not knowing where he was, and trying to work his way backwards*—R. Cobb, BrE 1985. In the fixed expressions *bend* (or *lean*) *over backwards, backwards and forwards,* and *to know backwards, backward* is only found occasionally outside AmE: *He'll bend over backwards to please a client*—M. Bail, AusE 1975 / *An eclectic collector . . . , he knows the showrooms backwards.*—*Financial Times*, 1983 / *The door kept swinging backwards and forwards*—Anita Brookner, 1984 / *They move backward and forward between denial and anger and depression, unable to break out of the circle of despair*—G. Carmichael, 1991.

2 For the adjective, the correct form in standard English is *backward*: *He watched her walking away without a backward glance.*—R. Sutcliff, 1954 / *Getting involved with the blind in any way seemed like a backward step*—Ved Mehta, 1987.

3 In addition to the directional meanings, *backward* has developed the sense 'slow to learn',' (applied to children). This is now often considered offensive and should be replaced by more neutral and considerate terms such as *having learning difficulties,* cumbersome though these tend to be.

bacterium is a singular noun and its plural is *bacteria*. Erroneous uses of *bacteria* as a singular noun are regrettably common in newspapers: *A common gut bacteria may be a major cause of rheumatoid arthritis*—*Independent,* 1991.

bad, badly. 1 After the verb *feel, bad* is an adjective complement (meaning either 'guilty, ashamed' or 'unwell') rather than an adverb: *To be absolutely honest, what I feel really bad about is that I don't feel worse*—Michael Frayn, 1965. After *to be* and most other verbs, *badly* is required: *Things started to go badly for them / They sank seventeen ships and badly damaged eight more / Russia badly needed Finish products / We are not too badly off.* In these cases, *bad* is used only informally or in dialect: *I only came cause she's so bad off*—L. Hellman, 1934.

2 In a slang (principally youth slang) use originating in US Black English, *bad* means the very opposite of its traditional meaning, i.e. 'excellent, very good', and in this meaning even has special degrees of comparison *badder, baddest*: *She said that part of the problem was that they often wanted to distinguish themselves by being badder than their rivals. Badder? Surely the comparative of bad is worse? But then worse has connotations of being less good at doing something.*—*Spectator,* 1993. This is a good example of how one of the most basic words can be twisted and pulled in all directions, rather as *wicked* and *mean* have been in the past.

bade, the past tense of *bid,* can be pronounced bad or bayd.

baggage. 1 *Baggage* and *luggage* overlap in use, although *baggage* generally connotes something heavier and bulkier and less easily transportable by hand. Some collocations are more or less fixed, e.g. *excess baggage, baggage claim, baggage handler*; and a few British rail stations still have *left-luggage* offices (rarely, though occasionally, *left-baggage*). In the US a person who looks after the baggage of passengers on a train or at a hotel is called a *baggageman*. At air terminals *hand baggage* and *hand luggage* seem to be freely used in both BrE and AmE.

2 In figurative uses, *baggage* is always used: *She was not an intellectual; her philosophical baggage was comparatively light.*—K. O. Morgan, 1990 / *He was* *loudly proclaiming the need for a 'new' left that had the courage to throw off the ideological baggage of the past*—Logos Journal, 2004.

bail, bale. 1 The spelling *bail* (ultimately from Old French *bailler* 'to take charge of') is always used with reference to securing the release of a person with an undertaking to return to court on an appointed day. Figuratively, too, a person or organization may be *bailed out*, or released, from a debt or other difficulty (*a desperate junkie who keeps getting bailed out of trouble by his mother*).

2 In the meaning 'to scoop water out of a boat', or 'to make an emergency parachute jump from an aircraft' the spelling *bale* (*out*) is now usual, as if the action were that of letting a *bale* (i.e. bundle, as in *bale of hay*) through a trapdoor, even though the word is of different origin from the noun *bale* (from Old French *baille*, 'bucket'). *Bale out* also has the figurative sense 'escape abruptly from a difficult situation' (*I won't be offended if you want to bale out early*) and because this comes close to the corresponding (transitive) use of *bail out* (in 1 above) it can sometimes intrude on it; but the distinction between the two words is a useful one and is best preserved.

baited. For the misspelling *with baited breath, see* BATED.

balance. 1 The noun is about four centuries older than the verb, and has derived several figurative uses from its primary meaning of 'an apparatus for weighing', as for example in accounting (where the notion of balancing the books is ever-present) and in more abstract uses such as *the fragile balance between peace and war*. Two centuries ago, the word branched out from the accounting sense in the US and came to mean 'something (other than money) left over' (*I'll bring the balance of our things / *

The balance of the penalty still has to be paid). Some critics consider that this use is not good style, and simpler words such as *rest* or *remainder* should be used.

2 The word occurs in a number of fixed or semi-fixed expressions such as *balance of nature, balance of power, balance of probabilities, in the balance, on balance, to maintain a balance, to redress the balance, to strike a balance, to tip the balance, and to upset the balance.* These are all established and acceptable uses.

bald-faced *see* BAREFACED.

baleful, baneful. These two somewhat literary words are little used in everyday language; *baleful* is slightly better known perhaps than *baneful*. Since they overlap in meaning, they tend to be confused. *Baleful* (from *bale*, 'misery') means 'having an evil influence' or 'menacing', and is used in particular of people's presence or appearance, whereas *baneful* (from *bane*, poison) developed from its earlier meaning 'poisonous' to 'causing harm or ruin'. Examples: (baleful) *The baleful presence of his father in the house was like a constant reproach*—R. Hayman, 1981 / *Foghorns boom in still longer and lower choruses of baleful warning*—Iain Banks, 1986 / (baneful) *The baneful memory of that night haunted her, sometimes tormented her*—Iris Murdoch, 1987. *Baleful* is the more likely to be needed, especially with reference to looks and glances.

bale out *see* BAIL.

balk *see* BAULK.

ball game, ballpark. 1 *Ball game,* an American name for baseball, is the core of several informal idioms in which it means 'a state of affairs', as in *a whole new ball game*. It seems to fit naturally into BrE and to be understood perfectly well in other countries where baseball is hardly known: *It was a different ball-game in those days and you bloody well know it*—W. J. Burley, 1991.

2 *Ballpark*, though even more remote culturally, has also entered BrE in the idioms *in the right ballpark*, meaning 'approximately correct', *in the same ballpark*, meaning 'of the same kind' or 'similar' (*It is encouraging to see that the recent total is in the same ballpark*—financial website, BrE 2003 [*OEC*]), and *ballpark figure*, meaning one that is approximate. Colourful though it is in casual conversation, it is best avoided in more formal contexts.

ballot *verb*. The inflected forms are *balloted* and *balloting*. See DOUBLING OF FINAL CONSONANTS IN INFLECTIONS.

balmy, barmy. These two words come from two roots, although the lines of descent have become intertwined: *balmy* (meaning 'deliciously fragrant') comes from *balm* and *barmy* (as now used colloquially, meaning 'stupid') comes from *barm*, meaning 'froth'. However, *barmy* is an altered form of *balmy*, which also had the colloquial meaning in the 19c and early 20c. Consequently they may be regarded as spelling variants; but current usage favours the distinction given above. Since the 1980s the expression *barmy army* has been used informally to describe groups of political fanatics and, by extension, jingoistic sports supporters (especially of the English cricket team) and others: *We've had what feels like 900 years of Blair's barmy army now so we know how the system works*—weblog, NewZE 2005 [*OEC*].

banal, pronounced buh-**nahl** and meaning 'trite, feeble, commonplace', is a loanword that has survived, despite Fowler's diatribe ('imported from France by a class of writers whose jaded taste relishes novel or imposing jargon'),

because no other word in English provides the same touch of venom: *Books are filled with pictures rather than text, and with trivial content and banal style, to make them 'easier to read'.*—*New Scientist*, 1991. Alternatives listed by Fowler, including *commonplace* and *trite*, simply won't do, and nowadays we relish words of French origin rather more than him. For other words of this type, *see* LOANWORD.

baneful *see* BALEFUL.

banjo. The recommended plural is *banjos*, although *banjoes* is also found.

Bantu (plural the same or *Bantus*), referring to a large group of indigenous peoples of Central and northern Africa, is now offensive both as a noun and an adjective, because of its irredeemable associations with the apartheid era in South Africa.

bar, barring. 1 *Bar*, used as a slightly formal preposition meaning 'except', has been in use since the 18c. In current use it is often followed by a number (or *none*): *My sister-in-law for whom I probably care more than I care for anyone in the world bar one other*—Penelope Lively, 1983 / *The best detection expert I know, bar none*—Ruth Rendell, 1983. It is also used in the idiom *all over bar the shouting*, when an outcome is all but assured; and in giving the odds in racing (e.g. *33-1 bar the rest*).

2 *Barring*, which is attested much earlier (15c), is also still used in the general meanings, and collocates regularly with words expressing misfortune or reversal: *Barring accidents, we should win another Grand Slam*—*Rugby World and Post*, 1991 / *The young working-class man in industrial employment could expect his income to reach its peak in early manhood and stay constant thereafter, barring disasters such as unemployment.*—J. Weeks, 1992. Notable among

the few positive collocates of *barring* are miracles and similar manifestations: *Barring a miracle or divine intervention, Sligo Rovers' season will be bereft of cups or league accolades*—Sligo Weekender, 2004.

barbarian, barbaric, barbarous.
1 These words had their origins in people's ideas about foreign languages. The Greek word *barbaros*, 'barbarian', which is the ultimate source of all these words, meant someone who spoke words sounding like *ba ba*. To the Greeks, the *barbarians* were foreigners, and principally the Persians, but the word carried no depreciatory overtones in itself. Over the centuries the non-Hellenic, non-Roman, or non-Christian peoples became regarded as enemies who violated and plundered the civilized world, and this gave rise to the unfavourable connotations of the term *barbarian* and associated words. By an understandable process of sense-development, in the 16c to 17c the word came to be applied to any person or group regarded as uncivilized or uncultivated, and in current use has many extended meanings, although a major area of use is still historical: *Enlightenment man has undoubtedly been a man of power, but he has also been a barbarian*—A. Walker, 1988 / *Many survived the depredation of the barbarian incursion of the late third century from which Britain was spared*—G. Webster, 1991 / *She would not have minded if he had hired the Albert Hall to denounce her as a barbarian and certainly cared nothing for his kitchen sulks and drawing-room sarcasm*—A. T. Ellis, 1993.
2 Since the 15c, *barbaric* has been applied to foreign customs, language, and culture that are regarded as backward or uncivilized: *The noble savage . . . turns out to be a barbaric creature with a club and a scalping knife*—H. J. Laski, 1920 / *Some of the subsidiary*

practices [in fox-hunting] such as the 'blooding' of children are little short of barbaric—Independent, 1998. Another (17c) use of the word, to describe exotic objects brought from abroad, has been confined to literary contexts such as Lawrence of Arabia's description of Arab costume as *splendid and barbaric*. In modern use, it is applied to brutal or wicked physical treatment of people, and is somewhat stronger and more specific than *barbarous*, which has a more general reference and is softened by its use in aesthetic as well as physical contexts: *Formulating his phrases carefully in the barbarous French prose these people used*—D. Bagley, 1966 / *No doubt they are also the victims of a gross and barbarous fallacy*—Enoch Powell, 1991.

barbarism, barbarity. *Barbarism* has the widest scope of reference, being applied to matters of taste as well as human behaviour, and it has a special meaning in relation to language (*see* BARBARISMS). *Barbarity* (and occasionally *barbarousness*, although this is not normally needed) always refer to savage cruelty or extremely uncivilized behaviour. Examples: *It has taken a woman to remind us all that there are people out there who are determined that Northern Ireland will not be dragged down to the level of barbarity displayed by the terrorists*—Ulster Newsletter, 1991 / *He took up a new job in Berlin on the very day in 1930 when the Reichstag election heralded unprecedented barbarism in Europe*—New Scientist, 1991 / *I do not believe urban barbarism is about to engulf us*—East Anglian Daily Times, 1993.

barbarisms are words that are judged to be ill-formed for various reasons, usually because they are derived from a mixture of Latin and Greek roots (e.g. *television*) or a mixture of Latin/Greek and English roots (e.g. *breathalyser*). The objection is pedantic and irrational and is largely disregarded in the blizzard of present-day word creation. *See also* LOST CAUSES.

barbecue is a noun and a verb (and has inflected forms *barbecues, barbecued, barbecuing*). It is sometimes written in facetious respellings such as *Bar-B-Q* (and hence *barbeque*), which are not standard.

barefaced. *Barefaced liars* and *barefaced lies* are shameless and undisguised. This image or metaphor has been around since the 18c, and developed from the literal meaning of *barefaced*, 'without a mask or face covering', and then 'undisguised'. People have found the metaphor puzzling, and have therefore replaced *barefaced* with *baldfaced*. This form is well established in AmE in this meaning, and recognized in dictionaries. In BrE, however, it may well be regarded as a mistake, and the *OED* does not currently recognize that it has this meaning. *Bold-faced* is also used to replace *barefaced*, particularly in AmE.

barely, like *hardly* (see HARDLY 1) and *scarcely*, should normally be followed by *when*, not *than*, if a clause follows: *Chance had barely begun to sip his drink when dinner was announced—* J. Kosinski, 1983.

barman, barmaid are the BrE names for a man and woman respectively who serve drinks at a bar. The AmE equivalents are *barkeeper* (or *barkeep*) and *bartender*, although the gender distinction is less clear-cut. In BrE the gender-neutral form *barperson* is available, but is rarely used outside the anodyne and politically correct world of job advertisements.

barmy *see* BALMY.

baroque 1 The term is applied to certain forms of European art, architecture, and music of the late Renaissance and 18c. It is normally spelt with a small initial, as is *rococo*, which refers to a slightly later period of art and music (e.g. Watteau and Mozart rather than Rubens and Handel), although the two terms tend to overlap in some uses.

2 More recently, the word has come to be applied outside the artistic sphere with rather negative connotations as an elegant way of describing anything viewed as excessively complicated or convoluted: *The difficulty is that in practice it has led to an increasingly baroque system of a state retirement pension—* OEC, 2002 / *The film cuts out some of the (rather baroque) complications of the novel—*OEC, 2004.

barring *see* BAR.

basalt is pronounced **bas**-awlt.

base, basis. The two words overlap in meaning, but broadly *base* is physical (the *base of a column*, a poison with an *arsenic base*), while *basis* is figurative with a primary meaning 'that on which something depends', as in a *basis for action*, the *basis of an argument*, or doing things on a *friendly basis*. *Base* is occasionally found in figurative meanings too, especially in semi-fixed collocations such as *customer* (or *client*) *base* and *base of support*. In language, it has the special meaning of a philological root (*The word* cairn *is derived from a Celtic base*).

based. 1 *based on.* To base one thing on another is to use the second as the basis for the first, and it is frequently used in the passive, as in *arguments based on statistics*. Avoid using *based on* as an unattached participle without a clear antecedent (☒ *The Prime Minister will be judged based on these events*: better . . . *will be judged on criteria based on these events*, or . . . *will be judged according to these events*). Avoid it especially in initial position: *Based upon the*

US Democratic Party's new policy, I'd appeal to the world via the UN to assist us in withdrawing troops from Iraq—Independent, 2007. In recent usage based around is often illogically used, and should be avoided: ⊠ The article is based around a concept which occurred to him as he lay on a Scilly Isles beach in 2000—news reports, BrE 2003 [OEC].

2 -based. In the 20c, the participle based is commonly used in combination with a noun, meaning 'based on . . .', as in community-based, land-based, program-based (in computing), research-based, rule-based, science-based, technology-based, etc.

basically has developed in the 20c from a specific meaning 'essentially, fundamentally', to a more or less meaningless sentence filler comparable to actually and really: Basically, I feel great, except for fatigue—M. Ali, 1987 / Basically I see myself as a frank individual—Saul Bellow, 1988 / I think it basically comes down to the language barrier—Observer Sport Magazine, 2004. This should be avoided in written English that aims to be precise and succinct.

basis The plural form is bases, pronounced **bay**-seez, while the plural of base is pronounced **bay**-siz. Expressions such as on a regular basis, on a daily basis, and on a voluntary basis are sometimes frowned on when simpler adverbs (regularly, daily, voluntarily) are available, but the longer forms often make the point more effectively, can produce a better sentence balance, and are well established. See also BASE.

bated breath. The idiom with bated breath, meaning 'in great suspense' (e.g. he waited for a reply to his offer with bated breath), is often misspelt ⊠ with baited breath. Bated comes from the

obsolete verb bate, a shortened form of abate, and 'to bate one's breath' originally meant to restrain one's breathing, and make it soft and gentle. Since neither bated nor bate appears elsewhere, it is not surprising that people replace the unknown bate with the more familiar bait—although it is hard to imagine what baited breath might be, other than distinctly fetid. The fishy spelling is, for the time being at least, incorrect. See also FOLK ETYMOLOGY.

bath, bathe verbs. In BrE to bath is to have a bath (i.e. wash oneself immersed in a domestic bath), and to bathe is to go into the sea or a river to swim (although usage in this meaning is now dated) or (transitively) to wipe or soothe a wound with liquid. In AmE, bathe is used much more commonly in the washing sense. In both varieties, have or take a bath is a common alternative.

bathroom in BrE means a place for washing and taking a bath, and may or may not include a lavatory; in AmE it is first and foremost a lavatory: The man . . . grew up . . . in a town where he was unable to use the same bathroom as white residents—Chicago Tribune, 1987.

baulk, balk. 1 pronunciation. It should be pronounced bawlk (with l).

2 spelling. The usual BrE spelling is baulk, although balk is more common in AmE. The primary use is as a verb meaning (1) followed by at: 'to hesitate, refuse to go on', as in For one thing, the government may baulk at giving the financial guarantee—New Scientist, 1991, (2) followed by of: 'to thwart', as in I gave her the number and hung up feeling baulked of my escape—L. R. Banks, 1987 / Fenella had the feeling that they were simply mustering their strength again; they had been baulked of their prey and they had retired—B. Wood, 1993. There are a few technical noun meanings, including a line in billiards and snooker and a length of sawn timber; the same spelling rules apply.

BC should be placed after the numerals to which it relates, as in 55 BC. When a range of dates is given, the second date should be put in full, as in 55–53 BC (since 55–3 BC has another meaning). In printing style, BC is normally put in small capitals. The culturally neutral BCE ('before Common Era') is also used: see the comment on this at AD.

be. 1 linking singular and plural. Very often the subject of the verb *be* is singular and the complement plural, or vice versa, and in these cases the verb should agree with the subject: *Gustave is other animals as well*—Julian Barnes, 1984 / *These huge biographies are usually a mistake nowadays*—N. Stone, 1985. But when the subject is a collective noun, the verb may be in the plural, following the usual pattern with such nouns: *Its prey are other small animals*—David Attenborough, 1987. When the subject is the relative pronoun *what*, the verb is singular: *What I'm really interested in . . . is the objects in this house*—New Yorker, 1986.

2 subjunctive forms. The verb *be* has two residual subjunctive forms, *be* and *were*. These subjunctive forms are rapidly disappearing from use, but are still quite often found in the following types of clause:

a replacing *if* or *whether*, at the head of a clause, with inversion of subject and verb: *We would much prefer to support specific projects, be they in management schools or in university laboratories*—Journal of the Royal Society of Arts, 1986 / *Were this to happen, it would have a massive adverse impact on U.S. security, with America losing her hegemony in the Asia Pacific region*—Contemporary Review, 2001.

b after *if* in hypothetical conditions: *If the truth be told, I never wanted to fly away with the sky-gods*—J. M. Coetzee, 1977 / *If I were obliged to rough out a blueprint of the Church of the future, I would start with the need for good popular theology*—Gerald Priestland, 1982. However, the past indicative form *was* is often used instead of *were*, especially in conversational style: *I wouldn't tell the police if I was you*—R. Hopcott, 2002 [*OEC*].

c in dependent clauses after verbs of advising and instructing such as *demand, insist, suggest*, etc: *The Admiralty insisted that the case be clarified*—P. Wright, 1987 / *In order to broaden the 'target audience' of your newsletter . . . I might suggest that such material be written at a lower level of readability.*—Underground Grammarian, 1982; also after nouns and phrases of equivalent meaning: *It is important in today's vote that the principle itself be accepted*—Times, 1985 / *She demanded that they be clean and well-behaved*—online essay, AmE 2005 [*OEC*].

d in certain fixed expressions such as *be that as it may, far be it from me, the powers that be*, etc.

3 the case of the complement after be: *it's me/him/us* etc. versus *it's I/he/ we*. The monks of Rheims, as quoted by the grammarian Dean Alford in 1864, cried out when they saw the anathematised jackdaw: 'That's him!' and not 'That's he!'. In both speech and writing, the type *it's me/him/her/us/them* is now virtually universal, except when a relative pronoun follows, as in *It was he who would be waiting on the tow-path*—P. D. James, 1986. See further at CASES 2.

4 *reduced forms*. *Am, is*, and *were* are reduced to *'m, 's*, and *'re* respectively after pronouns and nouns (*I'm over here* / *She's just coming* / *We're late, are we?*), except when the noun ends in a sibilant sound (✗ *The church's just up the road*). *Aren't*, used for *am not* in the question form *aren't I* as well as *are you/they not*, is irregular; *ain't* is irregular and widely deplored (*see* AIN'T).

5 ellipsis of *be*. *Be* is often omitted, especially in informal contexts, in cases such as *They are sorry for what they did and anxious to make amends / We're leaving now and catching the 9.00 train*. When *be* is used as an auxiliary verb and as a linking verb in the same sentence, it must be repeated because its role is different: *The bill was overtaken by the 1964 election and its postponement was welcome*.

beat is largely defunct as a participial form, except in the phrase *dead-beat*. Otherwise it is confined to (especially AmE) dialect and non-standard uses: *You hear on television nowadays about little children getting beat up or treated nasty*—New Yorker, 1988.

because. 1 because, as, since, for. *Because* is a conjunction that normally introduces a dependent clause and answers the question 'why?' (or, sometimes, 'how?'). It can relate directly to the statement made, as in *I came because I wanted to see you*, which answers the (real or notional) question 'Why did you come?', or (like *for*) it can relate to the status of the proposition, as in *I know he committed suicide, because his wife told me*, which effectively answers the question 'How do you know he committed suicide?' and not the question 'Why did he commit suicide?'; in this sentence, the comma has an important structural function.

Because can also stand first in the sentence, as in *Because we missed the train, we had to wait a long time*. It is also in order to use *because* after an introductory *it is, it's, that's, this is*, etc.: *It is because these Christian values are*

apparently being cast off by the present leadership of the Conservative Party . . . that many Christians are turning to the Alliance.—Church Times, 1985.

As and *since* are often used at the beginning of a sentence, and (unlike *because*) tend to emphasize the main statement rather than the reason. *For* can only follow the main statement, and is a coordinating conjunction, whereas *because* is a subordinating conjunction.

2 after negatives. Using *because* after a negative statement (e.g. *I do not play cards because I enjoy good company*, i.e. one containing a word such as *not* or *never* or including a word in *un-* etc.) can technically cause ambiguity because it is not clear whether the reason given is an invalid one for a positive statement (i.e. *I do play cards, but not because . . .*), or a valid one for a negative statement (i.e. *I do not play cards, and the reason is . . .*). However, the context will often make the meaning clear: *Very many people . . . do not attend church because they are bored by ritualistic services*—Lancashire Life, 1977 / *Her twin was told she was unlikely to have children because of her husband's low sperm count.*—Daily Telegraph, 1979. When necessary, a comma will usually remove any ambiguity: *The graphic equalizer is not for every hi-fi customer, because it does require some skill, time and patience in usage*—Gramophone, 1976.

3 the reason is . . . because. . . . *The reason for this was because I was the only one who could sign it, because the account was in my name*—Ben Elton, 1991. This construction is often rejected on grounds of style in favour of *the reason is . . . that . . .*, since *because* is logically redundant after *reason*. But redundancy is a regular component of idiom, and given that both constructions are common it is becoming harder to insist on the point. In the following example, it would weaken the statement considerably to replace *because* with *that*: *The minipill was developed for one reason alone: because it was believed to provide safe contraception*—*New Scientist*, 1970. However, *because of* should be avoided in this kind of construction: ☒ *The reason we have no light is because of a broken fuse* should read *The reason we have no light is that the fuse is broken.*

4 because of. With the reservation given in the last paragraph, *because of* is a legitimate use in many positions in a sentence: *Because of the deterioration of the sugar in the blood it was decided, after consultation, to carry out an exchange blood transfusion*—*Glasgow Herald*, 1970 / *He'd have to watch his step . . . not to make a hash of things, because of over-anxiety*—J. Wainwright, 1976.

5 at the head of a dependent clause governing a main clause, as in *Because we don't explicitly ask these questions doesn't mean they aren't answered*—*New Yorker*, 1986. This kind of construction, though common in speech, is awkward in written English because the main clause is uncomfortably delayed, and the sentence should be recast, e.g. *These questions are still answered even though we don't explicitly ask them.*

bedevil. In BrE the final letter *l* is doubled to give *bedevilled, bedevilling*, but in AmE it is not: *bedeviled, bedeviling*. *See also* DOUBLING OF FINAL CONSONANTS IN INFLECTIONS.

been and (gone and) – appears in popular speech in Dickens (*Pickwick Papers*, 1836), and is still common in casual and jocular contexts, although it now sounds somewhat dated (*And what's more, he's been and gone and got it printed*—P. Bailey, 1986).

begin *see* COMMENCE.

begrudge, grudge. These two words overlap in meaning, but not completely. To *begrudge someone something* (such as success or a reward) is to envy them for having it, whereas to *grudge something* is to resent the giving (by yourself or someone else) of something that you think you have a right to. Both words are commonly used in negative contexts. Examples best clarify the distinction, although the meanings overlap in practice: *I imagine you won't grudge me a glass of brandy first*—Penelope Fitzgerald, 1988 / *Considering the responsible job they do, we should not begrudge them a good income*—*Daily Mail*, 2007.

beg the question means, strictly speaking, to question an unproved assumption that is used as the basis for an argument. For example, to ask 'why do you listen to that rubbish?' begs the question when the quality of the music is the point at issue. In general use, *beg the question* has come to mean (1) 'bring a question to mind' (e.g. *I am not saying these drivers should be prosecuted, but if the new rules are not enforced, it begs the question what is the point of it?*— *Northern Echo*, 2007) and (2) 'avoid a straightforward answer' (e.g. *He simply begged the question by saying that the decisions he disapproved invented new rights*—*New York Review of Books*, 1987). These weakened meanings should be avoided in precise English; available alternatives are, for (1) *raise* (or *suggest* or *invite*) *the question*, and for (2) *evade* (or *avoid*) *the question*.

behalf is now used in BrE only in the phrase *on behalf of* (AmE *in behalf of*), which means (1) 'in the interests of', and (2) 'as a representative of' (*He used to make payments and pick up money on behalf of Mafia mobsters*—*Times*, 1982). It should not be used to mean 'on the part of', as in *The detail may be trivial but it betrays an astounding lack of*

appreciation on behalf of the author—
Times, 1994.

behove. Now most often used in formal writing with *it* as a dummy subject to
mean 'it is necessary for someone to do
something' (e.g. *What books does it be-*
hove me to read? / It behoves us to know
as much as possible about local govern-
ment). In BrE the second syllable rhymes
with *grove*. In AmE the word is generally
spelt *behoove* and the second syllable
rhymes with *move*.

being as should only be used in casual
conversation: *Being as how you can't be*
married, you'd better have him chris-
tened—G. V. Higgins, 1979.

belabour. Spelt *belabor* in AmE, can
mean (1) to thrash, to assail physically
and (2) to assail with words. Examples:
I got very mad as expected, and tried to
belabour both of them—A. Burgess, 1971 /
It was in vain that the fiery little George
Augustus, and his wife, belaboured Wal-
pole with their arguments—C. Chenevix
Trench, 1973. Since the last century,
these two meanings have been joined by
another, especially in AmE: *belabor* is
used in the combination *to belabor a*
point, a question, a theme, etc. Some
dictionaries accept this use, but the *OED*
has not yet entered it, and many British
speakers would consider it at best a
novelty, at worst a mistake for *to labour*
the point.

belittle is, to the surprise of many, an
Americanism, disapproved of by Fowler
(1926) as an 'undesirable alien', at
least in its meaning 'decry, depreciate'.
(*Never belittle anything that your patients*
earnestly believe—*Oxford Companion to*
US History, 2001). This objection is a lost
cause (*see* LOST CAUSES); the verb is now
standard in BrE and has produced a
quasi-adjective, *belittling*. The physical
meaning 'to dwarf by contrast', which
Fowler accepted, is no longer used.

belly is a standard word for the front
part of the human body below the
breast, despite marked fluctuations in
acceptability over many centuries of use;
alternatives are *abdomen* (more technical and formal), *stomach* (more specific)
and *tummy* (more colloquial, especially
in children's use). There are many
transferred uses, e.g. the underside of an
animal, the underside of an aeroplane,
the front part of a cello, etc.

beloved traditionally has two pronunciations, each determined by the word's
role in the phrase. As a past participle
(*beloved by all, was much beloved*), it has
two syllables: bi-**luvd**. As an adjective
(*dearly beloved brethren; the beloved wife*
of), or as a noun (*my beloved*), it normally has three: bi-**lu**-vid. This distinction is, sadly, in danger of being
forgotten, even by those, such as the
clergy, who should know better. *See also*
AGED; BLESSED.

below, beneath, under. These
three words appear to be synonymous,
but many contexts call for one in preference to another. *Beneath* is somewhat
more literary in use. *Under* in its physical
sense is rather more literal than the
other two: *under the bridge* means directly underneath it, whereas *beneath*
the bridge suggests a wider area, and
below the bridge can also mean down-
stream from it. It is customary to say
below par, below the belt, to go below (in
a ship), *the information below, the tem-*
perature is below 20 degrees; conversely
a man under 40, under one's breath,
incomes under £10,000, under the sun,
under the circumstances, under one's
thumb, under sentence of death, and
beneath contempt, be beneath one.

benchmark. This is a busy word with
an interesting history and some recent
developments. In its original physical
meaning it referred to a wedge-shaped
incision made by surveyors in a vertical

surface so that a bracket could be inserted to form a *bench* or support for surveying equipment at a fixed and reproducible height. By the 1880s it had developed a figurative meaning, 'a point of reference, a standard'; more recently, the rapid growth in the use of personal computers has led to the development of *benchmark* software designed to perform comparative tests on different models. This meaning has also spawned a verb used in IT and, much more often, in general contexts, meaning to 'evaluate (something) by comparison with a standard' (e.g. *We are benchmarking our performance against external criteria*). In this meaning the preposition most often used before the standard mentioned is *against*.

benefit has inflected forms *benefited*, *benefiting*, with one *t* not two.

benign is principally used in medicine to mean 'not life- threatening'; its opposite is *malignant*. The word *benignant*, meaning 'kindly' or 'beneficial', has largely fallen out of use.

bereaved, bereft. The verb *bereave*, meaning 'to deprive (someone)', is normally used in the passive. When the meaning refers in general ways to possessions, feelings, etc., the past participle is *bereft*: *Without her, he felt bereft as a child at a boarding school*—A. N. Wilson, 1982. Strictly, there should be a sense of being deprived; *bereft of* should not be used as a synonym for *lacking* or *without* (as in *bereft of manners*). In the context of death the form is *bereaved* (*If it is your own mother who is bereaved, the fact that you are grieving too will probably help you both a good deal*—E. Deeping, 1979), and this is frequently used adjectivally (*It needs to be remembered that bereaved people stay at home*—J. Pardoe, 1991).

berk is a BrE slang term for a fool. It is not usually regarded as strongly

offensive, despite its association, via rhyming slang *Berkshire Hunt* (pronounced as in AmE), with *cunt*.

berserk, meaning 'wild, frenzied', is now mostly confined to the expression *to go berserk*. It is in origin a Norse word for a warrior who fought with wild fury. *Berserk* may be pronounced either buh-**zerk** or buh-**serk**, although the first is now more common.

beseech has alternative forms for the past tense and past participle, *beseeched* and *besought*. They are about equally common, and have respectable literary pedigrees. Examples: *Why had he not wept, screamed, fallen to his knees, beseeched, raged, seized Jean by the throat?* —Iris Murdoch, 1987 / *The Lord is praised and besought and worshipped*— Penelope Lively, 1987.

beside, besides. *Beside* is only used as a preposition meaning 'next to' (*He heard Lee come up beside him*—A. Hassall, 1989), whereas *besides* is both an adverb meaning 'also, moreover' (*Besides, it was not the first disappointment*—S. Studd, 1981) and a preposition meaning 'as well as' (*Besides newsstands and supermarket checkouts, books are pumped out through mail-order clubs*— *Economist*, 1993 / *They have nothing in common besides being terribly sexy*—*Eye Weekly* (Toronto), 2003). *Beside* also occurs in fixed expressions, e.g. *to be beside oneself, beside the point*, but it should not be used in a general way, as in ☒ *Beside their homework, they have letters to write*, when *besides* is needed.

besiege like *siege*, is spelt *-ie-*.

best practice. This phrase belongs to the babble of business jargon. It started life meaning a practice 'which is accepted by consensus or prescribed by regulation as correct' and therefore had some connection with recognized, objective standards, or even with legal requirements. Since then it has come to be wildly overused to mean merely a method that delivers better results than other similar methods. So overused is it that *Forbes* magazine included it in its 2012 list of the 32 most annoying 'pearls' of business gobbledygook.

bet has past and past participle forms *bet* and *betted*; both are correct although *bet* is preferable, and is more common in BrE and (even more) in AmE. But *betted* is also found (*I'd have betted you wouldn't be much good at taking somebody out*—Kingsley Amis, 1988). When a sum of money is specified, only *bet* is possible (*He bet me £50 he would win*).

bête noire is always written with the final *e* on *noire*. The plural is *bêtes noires*, with both *s*'s silent.

better. 1 had better. This common idiom is used in the form *We had better go home* or *We'd better go home*; the negative form is *We'd better not go home* and the interrogative *Hadn't we better go home?*. Informally (but not in more formal contexts), the word *had* is sometimes omitted: *We better go home*; and in the second person (as an imperative) the preceding pronoun is omitted too: *When you're feeling censorious, better ask yourself which you'd choose*—P. D. James, 1986.

2 better, bettor. In the meaning 'one who bets', *bettor* is more common in AmE, and *better* in BrE. *Bettor* has the advantage of being distinct from the comparative of *good*, although their distinct uses keep them out of each other's way.

between. 1 general. *Between* is an adverb (*houses with spaces between*) and a preposition (*houses with spaces between them*). We are concerned here with *between* as a preposition.

2 between and among. Many people, and usage guides, cling to the idea (probably influenced by the use of *between* in relation to physical distance between points), that *between* is used when two people or things are involved and *among* must be invoked when more than two are involved. But this line is supported neither by the explanations of the *OED* nor by usage, which constantly refer to two or more parties: *Does he sigh between the chimes of the clock?*—J. M. Coetzee, 1977 / *Things that had happened a long time since*—*between Isaac and myself*—Nigel Williams, 1985. *The death of his sister had changed things between Marcus, Ruth and Jacqueline*—A. S. Byatt, 1985 / *The programme is delivered through partnerships between all levels of government*—*Northern Rivers Echo News*, AusE 2004.

There are, however, cases where *among* is the better word to use, normally when the underlying notion is of collectivity rather than separation: *There were a lot of very young people among the temporary staff*—Penelope Fitzgerald, 1980 / *The UN . . . does have machinery designed to . . . keep the peace among nations*—*Christian Science Monitor*, 1987. Conversely, *between* and not *among* is used when there are only two people or things (as in the first 1985 example in the preceding paragraph), and when the people or things (of whatever number) are specified (as in the second 1985 example). Before reflexive pronouns (*ourselves*, *themselves*, etc) *among* and *between* are used interchangeably.

3 between . . . and . . . . *Between* should be followed by *and*, not other words such as *or*, as in the following examples: ✖ [*This*] *leaves Britain with the choice between being ruined by runaway inflation or by a series of disastrous* *strikes—Daily Telegraph*, 1970 ☒ *My feet got so sensitive I could sense the difference between tarvia, gravel, or concrete immediately—Islander* (Victoria, BC), 1972. Similarly, it is important to say *between 1914 and 1918*, or *from 1914 to 1918* (also expressed as *1914–18*), not *between 1914–18*. See also FROM.

4 between each, between every. Constructions such as *22 yards between each telegraph pole* and *pause between every mouthful* are often deplored on the grounds that logical grammar calls for the addition of *and the next* to each group of words. Informally, however, this construction is typical and unremarkable, although it is best avoided in more formal contexts. Examples: *The 30-minute headway between each bus reduced to a 50-minute headway—Courier-Mail* (Brisbane), 1970. The construction *between every two* is ambiguous as to 'between two' and 'between two pairs', and is best avoided.

5 between you and I, though found in Shakespeare (but so is *between you and him*, not *he*), is an example of hypercorrection, influenced perhaps by the purist insistence on sentences of the type *'Who's going?' 'Anne and I.'* (in which *Anne and me* is also possible). Since *between* governs both pronouns, the correct construction is *between you and me, between you and us*, etc.: *Tiny bit boring, between you and me*—Penelope Mortimer, 1962.

6 repeated between. In long sentences, there is always a temptation to insert a second *between* as a *reminder* of what the statement is about: *You need to decide between voting for a party which, against all advice, introduced the poll tax, a form of tax first used in the 14th century, and one that dislikes the rates system but has no alternative to offer*. Putting a second *between* before *one that dislikes* is tempting because of the length of the

sentence but it would be ungrammatical, and the sentence would be better recast.

bevel. In BrE the final letter *l* is doubled to give *bevelled, bevelling*; in AmE it is not: *beveled, beveling*. See DOUBLING OF FINAL CONSONANTS IN INFLECTIONS.

beware is of Old English origin, and except for a period from about 1600 to the late 19c has lacked inflected forms, being used chiefly in the imperative (*Beware of the dog!*) or after a modal auxiliary such as *do* and *must* (*Do beware of the dog / We must beware of impostors*). Use with a direct object is found in Shakespeare (*Since I am a dog, beware my phangs—The Merchant of Venice* III.iii.7 / *Beware the Ides of March—Julius Caesar* I.ii.20) and other poetic writing, but is not a feature of ordinary speech or writing, except allusively. In current English, *of* is used as a link word: *Beware of flying elephants and risk-free bonds—Sunday Times*, 2005.

bi-. This prefix denoting 'two' or 'twice' causes much confusion in words such as *biweekly, bimonthly*, etc., because it is used to mean (for example) 'twice a week' as well as 'every two weeks'. Rules do not help because they are not universally followed; it is best to avoid the problem by using terms such as *twice a week* and *twice-weekly* on the one hand, and *every two weeks* and *fortnightly* on the other. *Bi* (without the hyphen) is a recent informal shortening of *bisexual.*: *There are no gay or lesbian or bi or tranny bookstores in Lisbon—Curve* (magazine), AmE 2002 [*OEC*].

biannual (19c) normally means 'twice a year', as distinct from *biennial* (17c), which means 'every two years' or 'lasting two years'. Since usage is not consistent on this point, it is sometimes better to use alternatives such as *half-yearly* or *twice-yearly* instead of *biannual* and *two-yearly* for *biennial*.

bias. The verb has inflected forms *biased, biasing,* although -ss- is also found. The plural of the noun is *biases*.

Bible. Use a capital initial when it refers to the scriptures collectively (*Read your Bible*), but a small initial when it refers to a copy of the book (*three bibles*) or is allusive (*Wisden is the cricketer's bible*).

bicentenary, a noun meaning 'two-hundredth anniversary' and also a corresponding adjective, is pronounced -teen- more usually than -ten-. It is the usual term in BrE, whereas *bicentennial* is more usual in AmE and elsewhere.

biceps is spelt the same in the plural.

bid has past tenses *bade* (in general meanings: *We bade them farewell*) and *bid* (in card games and the auction room: *We bid successfully for the portrait*). The corresponding past participle forms are *bidden* and *bid*.

biennial see BIANNUAL.

billion now means 'a thousand million' in BrE as it always has in AmE, and its old BrE meaning of 'a million million' has been superseded. When preceded by a numeral, the plural is *billion* (unchanged: *three billion people*), but *billions* is used when it is followed by of (*billions of people*).

bimonthly see BI-.

bin, short for *waste-bin*, has given rise in BrE to a transitive verb *to bin*, meaning 'to throw away' or (figuratively) 'to reject': *Who remembers the kind of middle-class good behaviour, thrift and modesty that have been binned along with Bromo, the Church Times and meals for one?—Independent on Sunday*, 1990. The inflections are *binned, binning*.

biopic. This informal word for a film biography (pronounced **biy**-oh-pik) originated in America in the 1950s and belongs to the same stable as the slightly later *docudrama, although its tone is somewhat more condescending: It has most of the classic attributes of the antifascist biopic—predictability, smugness and 20-20 hindsight—Listener*, 1984.

bipolar disorder, a term that came into use in medical circles in the 1970s, is now preferred to *manic depression* to signify 'a form of mental illness characterized by one or more episodes of mania typically accompanied by one or more episodes of major depression' (*OED*).

bivouac *verb* has inflected forms *bivouacked, bivouacking*.

biweekly *see* BI-.

black. As a consequence of the civil rights and Black Power movements of the 1960s, *black* became the most widely used and accepted term in the 1960s and 1970s, replacing *Negro*. Adopted by Americans of African heritage to signify a sense of racial pride, it remains the most widely used and generally accepted term also in Britain today. In AmE the term *African American* is also used. *Colo(u)red people,* common in the early part of the 20th century, is now regarded as offensive, both in the US and Britain. In Britain, *black* is inappropriately used to refer to people of South Asian as well as African origin, and this use is offensive. For a time it was thought appropriate to spell *black* with a capital initial as a racial term, but the normal preference now is for a small initial. *Black* is used in certain fixed collocations such as *black music* and *Black English*.

Black English is the form of English spoken by many black people, especially as an urban dialect of the United States.

The name (apart from a chance occurrence recorded in 1734) and the recognition of Black English as a distinctive and describable form of AmE date from the time of the civil-rights movement in the 1960s. It has many distinct grammatical features (e.g. uninflected plurals and double negatives) and items of vocabulary which are not imperfections but are characteristic of a creolized form of English.

blame *verb*. **1** Two constructions are now standard: *to blame someone for something* and *to blame something on someone*. Gowers (1965) described the second as a needless variant, but such strictures are futile in the face of incontrovertible evidence of usage. Examples: *I blame women for acquiescing to a system that requires dependence and compliance—Mothering Magazine*, AmE 2003 / *Telewest blamed a large part of the loss on foreign exchange fluctuations—The Register*, 2004 / *Not all the problems can be blamed on Philip—*history website, BrE 2005.

2 The derivative in *-able* retains the final *e*: *blameable*.

blanch, blench. *Blanch* means first and foremost 'to make (something) white' (especially vegetables by dipping them in boiling water) and (intransitively) 'to become pale' (from fear, shock, embarrassment, etc.); a by-form *blench* is also used in this sense. Confusingly, there is another (Old English) word *blench*, which overlaps slightly with *blanch/blench* in its meaning 'to quail, flinch', as in *Strong men blenched and broke into a sweat of embarrassment when made to dance 'Ring-a-ring o' roses' in public outside Guildhall—Times*, 1974.

blatant, flagrant. 1 *Blatant* was invented by the 16c poet Spenser to describe a thousand-tongued monster in *The Faerie Queene*. It now means

'glaringly conspicuous', and overlaps in meaning with *flagrant* but has rather less of *flagrant*'s implications of offensiveness: *It was a blatant lie* means that the lie was obvious; *It was a flagrant lie* means that (when discovered) it was outrageous. *Blatant* typically modifies words such as *attempt, discrimination, disregard, disrespect, hypocrisy, intrigue, lie, mischief, racism, rip-off,* and *violation; flagrant* also modifies *disregard* and *violation*, as well as *abuse, breach, denial, dishonesty, example, foul, impropriety, incompetence,* and *violator*.

2 The adverbial form *blatantly* (unlike *flagrantly*) has developed a weakened meaning, especially in youth slang, as a stock form of intensifier like *absolutely* and *extremely*.

blend *noun*. For the linguistic term, *see* PORTMANTEAU WORDS.

blessed, blest. As an attributive adjective (i.e. used before a noun), *blessed* is pronounced as two syllables: *The Blessed Sacrament / every blessed night*. When used as the past tense and past participle of the verb *to bless*, it is pronounced blest (one syllable): *The bishop (had) blessed his wife and children before he died / I'm blessed if I know*. The spelling *blest* is now mostly confined to use in poetry and hymns.

blind. As with other words designating disabilities, such as *deaf*, it is better to avoid using the formulation *the* + nominalized adjective, i.e. *the blind*, to refer to groups of people in society with sight problems. Such use is quite rightly perceived as diminishing and limiting people's individuality. Instead, use *blind people*, which is the wording now adopted by the British Royal National Institute of Blind People (RNIB) in its name.

bloc is a 20c loanword from French, meaning 'a combination of parties, governments, groups, etc. sharing a common purpose'. The phrase *bloc vote* is now being increasingly used instead of the traditional *block vote. See also* EN BLOC.

blog, a diary or set of personal comments published on the Internet, is a word rather like *cello*. The full form is *weblog*, but this, like *violoncello*, is the preserve of formal documents and manuals (and bibliographical citations in this book). For interest, in the *OEC* there are six times as many instances of *blog* in its various forms as there are of *weblog*. *Blog* has already given rise to an agent noun *blogger*, a verb *to blog*, and a verbal noun *blogging*. Not surprisingly, *blogger* outnumbers the seldom heard *weblogger* by 30 to 1. Remember to double the g!

blond, blonde. These two forms retain a trace of the grammatical gender they have in French, since *blonde* is normally used (as a noun and an adjective) of a woman. With *blond*, however, the distinction is less clear-cut: a *blond*, or a *blond* person, can be a woman or a man, and *blond* hair can belong to either sex. Examples (BrE unless otherwise specified): *Crews of tall, blond men who hardly ever spoke*—T. Findley, CanE 1984 / *His blond eye-lashes gave him a bemused look*—Penelope Fitzgerald, 1988 / *Her blonde plaits reaching halfway down her bony back*—Colin Dexter, 1989 / *The little girls whispered to each other, their blond heads shining in the rather dark room*—New Yorker, AmE 1990 / *Lugging that doll of hers, a thing with blonde shiny hair*—A. Duff, NewZE 1990.

bloody. 1 *Bloody* developed its meaning in BrE as 'a vague epithet expressing anger, resentment, etc.' in the 18c, and rapidly became a mere intensifier, especially in negative contexts (*not a bloody one*). The *OED* called it 'foul language',

and as recently as 1995 the *Concise Oxford Dictionary* called it 'coarse slang'; but since then, it has seemed increasingly tame, and other words having taken on its former mantle of offensiveness: *You want to use your bloody loaf, Stubbs, or we'll never win this war the way you're carrying on*—Brian Aldiss, 1971.

2 As an adverb *bloody* has been used conversationally as an intensifier since the later 17c in combinations such as *bloody drunk, bloody angry*, and *bloody ill*. G. B. Shaw was entitled to expect a sharp reaction from the audience when in 1914 he caused Eliza Doolittle to exclaim 'Walk! Not bloody likely.' As with the adjective, however, this use weakened considerably in effect during the 20c, and formed a regular part of the language of television dramas in expressions such as *serves you bloody right* and *you bloody well do it or else*.

3 These uses are recorded in American dictionaries, but are not properly part of AmE. It is a pleasing myth that Australians use them more freely and vigorously than in other parts of the English-speaking world, and the colourful entry in the *Australian National Dictionary* (1988) appears to support it, with examples of use steeped in the language of pioneering adversity and 'ranging in force from mildly irritating to execrable': *You must think yourself a damned clever bushman, talking about tracking a bloody dingo over bloody ground where a bloody regiment of newly-shod horses would scarcely leave a bloody track*—M. J. O'Reilly, 1944.

blue-sky meaning 'creative or visionary', as in *blue-sky thinking*, has become something of a cliché and is best used sparingly. It was once a vogue phrase, but its popularity—some would say fortunately—seems to have waned somewhat, probably because of the ridicule often heaped on it. In the meaning mentioned it is surprisingly long in the tooth, having its origins in AmE in the 1950s, and being recorded in the British *Economist* as long ago as 1967: . . . *this is blue-sky stuff.*

bluish is preferred, not *blueish.*

boat. A *boat* is a 'small vessel propelled on water' by various means, and includes vessels used for fishing, for cargo, or to carry passengers. A *ship* is a large sea-going vessel, especially when part of a navy. A submarine, however, despite its designation HMS, is referred to as a *boat* rather than a *ship* (if the choice has to be made between these two).

boatswain is now generally pronounced **boh**-suhn regardless of whether it is spelt this way or as *bosun.*

bogey, bogie, bogy. The latest editions of the Oxford dictionaries prefer *bogey* for the golfing term and the mischievous spirit, and *bogie* for the railway term. *Bogy* is classed as a variant of *bogey* in the second meaning. From the mid-19c in AusE *bogey* has had the informal meaning 'a spell of bathing or swimming'.

boggle, boggling *verb. Boggle*, originally used of frightened horses, is used with and without an object: the mind can *boggle* at something and something can *boggle* the mind (or the imagination etc.). The expression *mind-boggling*, first recorded in *Punch* in 1964, predates the regular transitive use, and has been joined since the 1970s by the more colloquial reduced form *boggling*: *Serious damage can mean even more boggling bills*—Which?, 1990 / *It's just boggling that they didn't decide to at least do one of these songs for the live album*—music website, AmE 2005 [*OEC*].

bog-standard is one of those informal but likeable expressions that seem older than the dictionaries suggest. In 2006 it

was added to the online version of the *OED*, with evidence from 1968. Its derogatory connotations wrongly lead many people to think that it is somehow connected to *bog*, the colloquial British word for a toilet. The most likely explanation, however, is that it is an alteration through mishearing of *box-standard* meaning 'basic, standard'. The noun *box standard* was known in the 1880s, and the adjective *box-standard* is first recorded as being used in early 1983 by the British inventor Sir Clive Sinclair. The expression is usually spelt with a hyphen: *Most UK adults have a bog-standard, old-fashioned bank account that pays 0.1% interest on credit balances*—business website, 2004.

bold-faced *see* BAREFACED.

bona fide, bona fides. 1 *Bona fide* is an adjectival and (now rarely) adverbial phrase meaning 'in good faith' and hence 'genuine(ly)' (*a bona fide tourist*). *Bona fides* is a noun phrase meaning 'good faith' and hence 'honest intention'. *Bona fides* is singular in Latin, and when it means 'good faith' is correctly treated as a singular (uncountable) noun in English: *His bona fides has been questioned*. However, it has also developed the meaning of 'documentary evidence showing that a person is what they claim to be; credentials' and in this use it is plural: *All strangers whose bona fides . . . are not completely verified must be immediately reported to your superior officer.* **2** The pronunciation is **boh**-nuh **fiy**-deez.

bored is normally construed with *by* or *with*: *How bored she was with that face!*—D. Devine, 1970 / *He got bored with working in the scout hut*—L. Henderson, 1976 / *Very many people . . . do not attend church because they are bored by ritualistic services*—Lancashire Life, 1977. Use with *of*, sometimes heard conversationally and on Internet blogs, is non-standard (despite the analogy of *tired of*): *I think people might get bored of seeing me*—ballet website, BrE 2004 [OEC].

born, borne. It is sometimes forgotten that *born*, relating to birth, is a past participle of the verb *to bear*, and that *I was born on a Friday* means 'My mother bore me on a Friday'. *Born* is also used in figurative expressions such as *an indifference born of long familiarity*. In all other meanings, the past participle of *bear* is *borne* (*I have borne with this too long* / *He was borne along by the wind*), and this form is used with reference to birth when the construction is active, or when it is passive followed by *by* (the mother): *She has borne no children* / *Of all the children borne by her only one survived*.

Borstal is a former name for British institutions for reforming young offenders. It is still found in print in allusive use, but the correct terms to use now are *detention centre* and *youth custody centre*.

botanic, botanical. Both forms have been in use since the 17c. *Botanical* is more common in general use, although *botanic* is obligatory in traditional names such as the *Botanic Garden* in Oxford and the *Botanic Gardens* in Edinburgh.

both. 1 general. *Both*, when modifying a single item, refers to two things or persons (*both houses* / *both women*); when, as *both . . . and . . .*, it couples two items, each of these may be singular (*both the woman and the man*) or plural (*both the women and the men*), although care must be taken to avoid misunderstanding if the first item is plural, as in the example just given.

2 position. *Both* is a mobile word and can be linked to particular pairs of sentence elements: *They work both by day and by night* / *He both loves and hates his brother* / *The work is both rewarding and enjoyable* / *I hope to be both a writer and a musician*. When there are more than two items involved, the word *both* should be omitted: *I want to be a writer, a musician, and a painter*.

3 awkward constructions. Because *both* is so flexible in use, its intended meaning can sometimes be unclear:

a *We both won a prize* can mean either (1) 'we've won one prize between the two of us', or (2) 'we won a prize each'. It is better to use *each* or to rephrase with a word such as *joint*, as appropriate: *We each won a prize* / *We won a joint prize*.

b *You will see a tree at both ends of the road* is not so much ambiguous as counter-intuitive, since the tree can only be in one place. Rephrase as *You will see a tree* [or *trees*] *at each end of the road*.

c *Books are useful both for pleasure as well as for learning* is a sequence to be avoided: *both* should always be paired with *and*: *Books are useful both for pleasure and for learning*. Note also the repetition of *for*: see the next item.

d *Her speech was both detrimental to understanding and to peace* needs to be rephrased so that the two elements governed by *both* match each other: *Her speech was detrimental to both understanding and peace* or *Her speech was detrimental both to understanding and to peace*; compare *Her speech was both detrimental to understanding and damaging to peace*. This applies especially to use of the definite or indefinite article: *Both the man and woman* should be corrected to *Both the man and the woman*.

e *He was acting on both our behalfs* is better expressed as *He was acting on behalf of us both*.

f *We find them both equally responsible* is a common construction in speech, but *both* is strictly redundant, and should be omitted in more formal writing: *We find them equally responsible*.

bottleneck, meaning a holdup or constriction in traffic, dates from the late 19c, and is now used more widely of obstructions in processes of various kinds. Care should be taken to avoid unsuitable elaboration of the image, as in *curing* or *ironing out a bottleneck*, and strictly speaking a *bottleneck* cannot be *big* or *extensive* or even *major* without producing a counter-intuitive effect: *A Parcel Force van . . . had stopped to deliver to the shops, completely blocking the street, creating a huge bottleneck that no one could get out of*—news website, BrE 2005 [*OEC*].

bottom line is an accounting term for the line in a profit-and-loss account that shows the final figure. It has developed a figurative meaning 'the decisive factor or objective', which is still somewhat informal, and rather overused: *The bottom line is that we all love music and want to play it*—New Musical Express, 1992. In financial contexts it can be unclear whether the meaning is literal or not: *The bottom line could eventually mean demands for higher council tax bills*—television broadcast, 1993. In such cases it is better to use alternatives such as *consequence, crux, issue, upshot*.

bowsprit is pronounced with *bow-* as in *low*.

brackets. The term is used generally of the punctuation marks (), [], {}, <>, although the first set is properly called *parentheses*, the second *square brackets*, the third *curly brackets* or *hooked brackets*, and the fourth *angle brackets*. The mark resembling a curly bracket, used to link items on more than one line, is called a *brace*.

In editing or describing documents it may be confusing if you use the general word when you mean a specific type of bracket. In particular, it is useful to remember that in AmE *brackets* often means 'square brackets'.

brainstorm, brainstorming. An attendee on a course once rebuked me for using the word *brainstorming*. I should, so I was instructed, have used the phrase *thought shower*. This is an urban myth, much like the idea that Eskimos have dozens of words for 'snow'. The myth flourishes in the mistaken idea that *brainstorm(ing)* is offensive to people affected by epilepsy, but no organization in the field of epilepsy has a policy banning these words. You can therefore use them whenever you wish without the burden of being thought politically incorrect, or having to use the ridiculous *thought shower*.

brand-new is the correct spelling, not *bran-new*. The term originally meant 'fresh like a *brand* [= burning torch] from a furnace'.

breach, breech. The spelling of these two words is often confused. *Breach* is a noun and verb meaning 'a break' or 'to break' (as in *a breach of contract, to breach the enemy's defences*), whereas *breech* means 'the back or lower part of something', and is applied principally to part of a rifle, the buttocks (now only in *breech birth*, when a baby is born bottom first), and (in the plural *breeches*, pronounced **brich**-iz or **breech**-iz), to a type of trousers.

breakdown can mean, in addition to its meaning in relation to machines, human health, and aspects of human behaviour, 'an analysis of statistics or information': *The breakdown of expenses . . . is relatively detailed in some cases but not in others*—J. Greenwood et al., 1989. Care should be taken to avoid possible confusion when the word might be understood in more than one way: *The suggestions called for a breakdown of Post Office performance*—weblog, BrE 2005 [*OEC*].

breakthrough, originally a military word and formerly a vogue word in its figurative use, is now commonplace. It is spelt as one word, is commonly qualified (especially in journalism) by words such as *new* and *major*, and is regularly followed by *in*, as in *a breakthrough in cancer research*.

breech *see* BREACH.

briar, brier. Both spellings apply to two distinct words, meaning a prickly bush and a type of wood (or a pipe made from it). The preferred spelling for both words is *briar*.

bring, take. The essential difference between these two words corresponds to that between *come* and *go*, and is intuitive to a native speaker: *bring* implies movement towards, and *take* movement away from, the person speaking: *Take your bike and bring me a newspaper*. When the standpoint of the speaker is unstable, there is a choice: *Shall I bring the camera?* is spoken in terms of the destination and *Shall I take the camera?* in terms of the starting point. In other varieties of English, and in some dialects, the pattern differs.

Brit is a colloquial term (early 20c) for a British person, especially when abroad. Its use is more typically affectionate than hostile or offensive.

Britain, Great Britain, the British Isles, England, etc. 1 Use of these terms causes confusion, at home and abroad. *Great Britain* refers to the largest island in the group, which is divided between England, Scotland, and Wales. Politically, it means these three countries (since the Act of Union of 1707), and excludes Northern Ireland, the Isle of Man, and the Channel Islands. *Britain* is an informal term with no official status; it often means the same as *Great Britain* but can also include Northern Ireland.

2 *The British Isles* is a geographical term for the group of islands including Great Britain and Ireland and also the smaller islands around them, such as the Isle of Man and the Scottish islands. Nowadays the phrase *Britain and Ireland* is often preferred.

3 *The United Kingdom* is a political term, in full *the United Kingdom of Great Britain and Northern Ireland*, and includes these countries but not usually the Isle of Man or the Channel Islands.

4 *England* strictly refers to a single political division of Great Britain, but it is commonly substituted for (*Great*) *Britain*, especially in AmE. This causes some offence in Scotland and Wales, and should be avoided in BrE. The same is true of *English* used instead of *British*.

5 There is, surprisingly, no convenient general term for a citizen of the United Kingdom: *Briton* is normally confined to historical (or jocular) reference, and *Britisher* is AmE.

Briticism is the term for a language feature that is peculiar to BrE, not *Britishism*.

Brito- *see* ANGLO-.

broadcast *verb*, by analogy with *cast*, is unchanged in its past form and past participle: *The programme will be broadcast on Saturdays*.

broccoli is spelt with two *c*s and, despite its plural origin in Italian, is treated (like *spaghetti*) as a singular mass noun in English: *Let it simmer until the broccoli is soft*.

brochure, pamphlet. The two words used to be more or less synonymous, but have gone separate ways: a *brochure* is a glossy leaflet used in advertising, whereas a *pamphlet* is a small unbound printed booklet, normally meant to be informative rather than promotional.

Brochure is stressed on the first syllable in BrE and on the second in AmE.

broker, as a Stock Exchange term, was replaced in the UK in 1986 by *broker-dealer* (which reflects increased responsibilities), although *broker* will still be found in informal use.

brother-in-law means (1) one's wife's or husband's brother, (2) one's sister's husband, (3) one's sister-in-law's husband. The plural is *brothers-in-law*.

browse. The meaning 'to scan the Internet, a website, or data files' can be transitive or intransitive: (transitive) *Internet cafés aren't just places to buy coffee and browse the Web, they're a place to meet friends and communicate new ideas in a dynamic setting*—Flak Magazine, AmE 2004 / (intransitive, with *through*) *Michael continued to browse through the files*—D. P. LaSelle, AmE 2004. A *browser* is a computer program with a graphical display for reading files on the Internet.

brunette is the standard form in BrE, and is invariably used of a woman. In AmE *brunet* is occasionally found, with the same restriction in use.

bruschetta. First recorded in print (in English) in 1954, by the pioneering foodie writer Elizabeth David, this 'toasted Italian bread drenched in olive oil and served typically with garlic or tomatoes' is in origin a peasantry dish. If you wish to say the word *all'italiana*, pronounce it broo-**sket**-ta, with a short pause before the second *t* sound. However, since most people pronounce it broo-**she**-tuh, this pronunciation seems likely to win, and is already recognized as an alternative in most dictionaries. Remember, though, to spell the word with *-sch-* not *-sh-*.

brusque. English first borrowed this word from French—which had already borrowed it from Italian—in the 17c.

In the 18c the spelling was sometimes anglicized to *brusk*, which occasionally occurs nowadays, and which, although 'logical', has to be considered non-standard. Pronunciation is a matter of personal whim: the options are to rhyme it with *tusk*, which is also the recommended US pronunciation; to pronounce the *-us-* as in *roost*, which is closest to the original French; or rhyming with the vowel in *foot*.

buck naked, butt naked. To refer informally to someone in a state of complete undress, which is the original version, and which is more correct? Those two questions are often asked about this AmE phrase, which is now also used elsewhere in the English-speaking world. The short answer is that nobody knows for sure, but *buck naked* is found in sources earlier than *butt naked*. It is possible that the *buck* part refers to the colour of *buckskin*, (*in the buff*, derived, from buff leather, provides a parallel with that image). It has also been suggested that the *buck* part is a shortening of the slang term *bucket*, meaning 'buttocks'. Since the phrase is informal in any case, it should only be used in appropriate contexts. And since the *butt* in *butt naked* could be considered slightly vulgar, *buck naked* avoids the risk of giving offence.

buffalo has the plural form *buffaloes*.

buffet, meaning refreshments, is pronounced **buu**-fay or (especially in *buffet car*) **buf**-ay. In AmE the stress is on the second syllable, pronounced the same way.

bug, virus. In their biochemical meanings the distinction between these two words is clear enough, but in the domain of computing and the Internet they are sometimes confused. A *bug* is a fault—usually occurring through error—in a file or program that causes it not to work properly, whereas a virus is a malicious piece of software introduced, typically over the Internet or via email, in order to cause damage to the system it invades. *Trojans* and *worms* are particular kinds of virus.

bugger is more acceptable as a swear word than it used to be, at least in BrE. Uses such as *bugger me, bugger-all,* and *I'll be buggered* (*if*), are all commonly heard on radio and television, although they remain highly informal and should not normally be used outside the domain of casual conversation. The word remains somewhat more offensive in AmE.

bulk, as a noun preceded by *the* and denoting size is used with *of* and singular or collective nouns, as in *the bulk of the book* / *the bulk of his land* / *the bulk of the clergy.* Some people object to *bulk* being used with a countable noun in the plural to mean 'most': *the bulk of policemen, the bulk of brewers,* etc. But this usage has a long pedigree, including Addison and Hume, is well established, and is generally uncontentious in modern English: *As far as basic analog technology goes, the bulk of our clients want to keep it that way—Mix* (magazine), *AmE 2003* / *The bulk of the forces were tied down on the front south of Rome—history website, BrE 2003 [OEC].*

bullet points. People are often unsure how to write and punctuate bullet points. As bullet points are relatively recent, it is hardly surprising that there are no hard-and-fast rules. Also, much depends on:

- the writer's visual sensibility;
- the medium in which bullet points are being used (e.g. White Paper vs Powerpoint); and
- the intended audience (e.g. designers vs lexicographers).

The following advice is merely a rule of thumb.

1 For bullet points that are not complete sentences, you:

- need not begin with a capital letter
- can leave out any punctuation at the end of each bullet

But if you prefer to have punctuation:

- you can finish each bullet with a semicolon;
- you can add 'and', if you wish, after the last-but-one bullet, as in this list; and
- you can put a full stop after your last bullet point.

It is important to make sure that the structure of your points is parallel, as in the previous two lists. The second one would not be parallel if it were

- finish each bullet with a semi-colon;
- you can add 'and', if you wish, after the last-but-one bullet, as in this list; and
- put a full stop after your last bullet point.

because the first and last points would be commands, while the middle one would not.

2 When your bullet points are complete sentences:

- It is generally advisable to finish each one with a full stop.
- You can leave full stops out if you want your text to have a very clean, uncluttered look.
- Even then, it is advisable to put a full stop after the last one.

You should bear in mind that in onscreen presentations with few complete sentences, punctuation at the end of bullet points may clutter the look. In other written material you should consider the overall look of the document, the number of bullet points, and their length. If you find your bullet points are getting rather long, you should assess them to see whether they are actually making more than one point. Finally, whichever style you choose, aim to be consistent.

bulwark is pronounced with stress on the first syllable, **buul**-wuhk. The second syllable is pronounced with the unstressed sound of the *-ock* in *haddock*, not like *war*.

bunch as a collective noun in abstract senses (*a bunch of people* / *a bunch of questions*) varies widely in its degree of informality from simple metaphor (*A bunch of weary runners crossed the line at last*) to near-slang, often affected by the word it collocates with (*The police were behaving like a bunch of thugs*).

bur, burr. *Bur* is recommended for 'a clinging seed-vessel or catkin' and *burr* for 'a rough edge' and associated meanings.

bureau has the plural form *bureaux* (pronounced -z) in BrE, although *bureaus* is more common in AmE.

burgle, burglarize. *Burgle* is a BrE back-formation from *burglar*, and was originally condemned. *Burglarize*, although the regular word in AmE, is treated with the same disapproval on the British side of the Atlantic as *burgle* once was.

Burma. The military authorities in *Burma* have promoted the name *Myanmar* as the official name for their state since 1989; *Burma* is often preferred by people who oppose military government and support the re-establishment of democracy.

burnt, burned. These two forms for the past tense and past participle of burn are largely interchangeable, but *burned* is more common as the active past (*She burned her hand on the kettle* / *She has burned her hand*); in the passive, *burnt* is more adjectival (emphasizing the result), and *burned* more verbal (emphasizing the action): *The cottage was burnt down last week* / *The cottage was burned down by vandals*.

bus is now spelt without an apostrophe. As a noun it has the plural form *buses*, and as a verb it has inflected forms *buses*, *bused*, *busing*.

business, busyness. *Business* means 'one's affairs or concern' and associated meanings. For a noun meaning 'a busy state, busy activity', use *busyness*: *Despite his normal frantic busyness, Williams met them all with that same gentle smile—Context* (magazine), AmE 2002 [*OEC*].

but. 1 general. *But* is a preposition and conjunction, and is used contrastively: (preposition) *Everyone seems to know but me* / (conjunction) *Everyone seems to know but I don't*. In more modern usage, as the *OED* and Fowler (1926) have both recognized, the roles of *but* as a conjunction and preposition have become inextricably confused, and this fact gives rise to some vexed problems of usage. These are described in the following paragraphs, each headed by a typical example of the problem.

2 *Everyone but she* [or *her?*] *can see the answer.* Fowler explored this problem in some depth, and concluded that *but* in this meaning is more a conjunction than a preposition, and therefore the case of a following pronoun is variable. When the phrase introduced by *but* is associated with the subject of the sentence, the pronoun should be treated as subjective (i.e. *No one saw him but I*) and when the phrase is associated with the object, the pronoun should be treated as objective (i.e. *I saw no one but him*). When the association is not as clear-cut as this, the case of the pronoun is determined by the position of the *but*-phrase in the sentence: when the *but*-phrase is in the subject area, the

b

pronoun should be treated as subjective (i.e. *Everyone but she can see the answer*) and when the *but*-phrase is in the object area it should be treated as objective (i.e. *Everyone can see the answer but her*). Usage is unstable when the verb is intransitive: *Everyone knows but her* is somewhat more natural than *Everyone knows but she*).

3 *I disagree. But what do you think?* The widespread public belief that *but* should not begin a sentence seems to be unshakeable. But it has no foundation in grammar or idiom, and examples are frequent in good literature: *All animals have sense. But a dog is an animal.*—Locke, 1690 / *But this rough magic I here abjure*—Shakespeare, *Tempest*, 1610 / *Of course they loved her, the two remaining ones, they hugged her, they had mingled their tears. But they could not converse with her*—Iris Murdoch, 1993. The initial position of *but*, as with *and*, is a matter not of grammar but of style.

4 *Who knows but that the whole course of history might [or might not?] have been different?* When this construction is used with a negative or (especially) in a question, there is always a temptation to make the second part of the sentence negative. It is usually better to rephrase: *Who knows: the whole course of history might have been different?*

5 *But your answer, moreover, is unacceptable.* A further contrasting word, such as *however, nonetheless, moreover,* etc., should not be used in a clause introduced by *but*. If the second word is needed (i.e. if *moreover* is the right word to use), omit *but*: *Your answer, moreover, is unacceptable.* Note, however, that *but still* is a standard idiom, especially informally: *It's late but still you did want me to stay.*

6 *He is not upset but he is relieved.* The repetition of *he is*, when this is the same person as at the first mention, is normally redundant: *He is not upset but*

relieved. However, it is often added in conversation, with rhetorical emphasis on the second *is*.

7 idioms. *But* is used in a number of fixed idioms:

a *all but*. *By the end of the war this attitude had all but disappeared*—P. Wright, 1987.

b *cannot (help) but*. The insertion of *help* is not attested before the late 19c but is now common: *The frailty of man without thee cannot but fall*—Book of Common Prayer, 1549 / *She could not help but plague the lad*—H. Caine, 1894 / *She could not help but follow him into the big department store*—B. Rubens, 1987.

c *but what*. *It's no telling but what I might have gone on to school like my own children have*—Lee Smith, 1983 (US). This use is now old-fashioned, and limited to informal and non-standard uses.

d *rhetorical use*. *Ah, but who built it, that we tiny creatures can walk in its arcades?*—Margaret Drabble, 1987. This use is not normally found in everyday English.

butt naked *see* BUCK NAKED, BUTT NAKED.

buy *verb*. The originally American meaning 'to believe', first noted in 1926, is now well established in everyday speech (e.g. *He says he's heard it all before, and he doesn't buy it*) but is best avoided in more formal writing in the UK.

buy-in meaning 'agreement with, or acceptance of, a policy or suggestion' is another word so often bandied about in the business world that it has ended up nauseating even some of that world's less verbally challenged inhabitants. As a result, *Forbes* magazine included it in its 2012 list of the 32 most annoying items of business jargon. If you wish to avoid the jargon, why not try using *support,* *agreement*, or, if that's what you really mean, *acquiescence*.

buzzword *see* JARGON; VOGUE WORDS.

by *prep.* *By* has so many functions that care should be taken to avoid ambiguity of the kind typified by the sentence, more hilarious than truly ambiguous, *He was knocked down by the town hall*. It is better to use another preposition such as *close to* or *in front of*. Fowler warned against the use of too many *by*s (in different senses) in one sentence, as in (not his example): *Send stories by reporters by fax by the end of Friday*. Such sequences are more likely to occur in more hurried forms of spoken English.

by, by-, bye. These three forms have different functions. *By* is a preposition or adverb (*Come by / By the river*); *by-* is a prefix meaning 'secondary, subordinate' (forming words such as *byroad* and *bypass*. Hyphenation practice varies: *byline* (a line in a newspaper column giving the writer's name) and *byname*, and the two mentioned above, tend to be written as one word whereas *by-law*, and longer forms such as *by-election* and *by-product*, are hyphenated. In some cases, a variant spelling *bye-* is also found (e.g. *bye-law*), but this is best avoided; and *bye* is a noun meaning 'something additional or left aside' (e.g. in cricket and golf). The idiom *by the by* (in which the second *by* is a variant of *bye*) means 'by the way, incidentally'.

by far and away *see* FAR AND AWAY.

Byzantine is spelt with a capital initial when the reference is historical or cultural (*the Byzantine Empire*) and with a small initial when the meaning is 'intricate, complicated' (*byzantine intrigues*). There are several pronunciations in use; those recommended are **biz**-uhn-tiyn and biz-**an**-tiyn.

cable has until recently been a mainly countable noun (*a cable* / *this cable*) meaning a length of thick rope or wire, or a telegram. With the arrival of *cable television*, its use as an uncountable noun (AmE, now also BrE) has been reinforced: *I'm watching a movie on cable*—L. Block, 1982.

cacao is a seed pod (or its tree) from which cocoa and chocolate are made, and should not be confused with the word *cocoa* itself. *Cacao* comes from a Nahuatl (Native Central American) word.

cache, cachet. People sometimes confuse these two words, wrongly using *cachet* when *cache* is required. Despite having five letters in common, and coming ultimately from the same French verb (*cacher*), in English they are completely unrelated. A *cache* of something is a 'collection of items of the same type stored in a hidden place' such as an *arms cache* or *a cache of gold* and rhymes with *cash*. *Cachet* is 'prestige, high status; the quality of being respected or admired' and is pronounced **ka**-shay. Examples (correct use): *Several inmates seized a cache of grenades and other weapons and killed six security officers, including a high-ranking counterterrorism official*—OEC, 2011 / *The department stores knew they had to offer something different, something perceived to have more cachet*, N.Y. Times, 2004; / (*cachet* wrongly used for *cache*) ☒ *Egyptian excavators this week chanced upon a cachet of limestone reliefs*—OEC, 2005.

cachou is a lozenge for sweetening the breath, and should be distinguished from the nut (and tree) *cashew*, especially as they are both pronounced **kash**-oo.

cactus. In general use the plural is *cactuses*, in botany it is often (but not always) *cacti*.

caddie, caddy. *Caddie* (originally Scottish) is a golf-attendant; *caddy* is a container for tea.

cadre means (1) a group of servicemen (pronounced **kah**-duh), (2) a group of political activists (often pronounced **kay**-duh).

Caesarean, Caesarian. The first spelling is now more usual, and the initial *c* is sometimes written small.

caesura, meaning 'a cut or division', is a term in prosody, both Classical and Old English, and refers to the division of a metrical foot between two words. In Old English (e.g. *Beowulf*) it is marked in print by an extra space between the words. In later English verse it is chiefly noticeable in long metres such as that of Tennyson's *Locksley Hall*: *Till the war-drum throbb'd no longer, // and the battle-flags were furl'd.*

cafe is such a familiar word that it can be spelt without an accent. It should still be pronounced **kaf**-ay in BrE, however, not (except humorously) kaff or kayf. In AmE the word also means 'a bar or nightclub', and is generally pronounced kaf-**ay**. In recent years the word has started a new life in communications technology, in terms such as *Internet cafe* and *cybercafe*.

cagey is more recent than people realize (first recorded 1909) and is an Americanism. This is a better spelling than its variant *cagy*.

calculate. 1 The meaning 'to suppose or reckon', without any reference to working something out, is regional American in origin (19c, eg. *I calculate it's pretty difficult to git edication down at Charleston*) and is not standard in any variety of English. None the less it does occur: *Many executives . . . calculate that their best interests lie in not conforming to factory regulations*—S. Box, 1992. *See also* RECKON.
   2 The corresponding adjective is *calculable*.

calculus. The plural for the medical meaning ('a hard mass formed by minerals within the body, especially in the kidney or gall bladder') is usually *calculi*, the last vowel rhyming with *lie* or *tea*. The plural of the mathematical meaning is *calculuses*.

calendar, meaning a list of days and months, is spelt this way. *Calender* (with -*er*) is a press for paper or cloth, and **colander* is a strainer.

calends, the first month of the ancient Roman calendar, is spelt with a *c*- not a *k*-.

calf. Both words (the animal and the part of the leg) have the plural form *calves*.

calibre is pronounced **kal**-i-buh. The American spelling is *caliber*.

caliph is pronounced **kay**-lif and is spelt with a *c*-. Other spellings have fallen out of use.

callus means 'a hard thick area of skin or tissue', and should be distinguished from *callous*, which is related to it but now much more often means 'unfeeling, insensitive'.

calorie, originally a unit of heat (from Latin *calor*, 'heat'), in the 20c has stepped out of the physics laboratory into general use as a measure of the energy value of food. The general public have adopted what physicists call the *large calorie* (i.e. the amount needed to raise the temperature of 1 kilogram of water through 1°C).

cambric, meaning a fine white linen, is pronounced **kam**-brik, or sometimes **kaym**-brik.

camellia is spelt with two *l*'s, despite its pronunciation kuh-**mee-li**-uh.

cameo has the plural form *cameos*. In its meaning 'a small character part in a play or film', it is used mainly attributively, as in *cameo part, cameo role*, etc.: *Rather than play these zonking great parts . . . I will try to find some dazzling little cameo roles*—*Times*, 1976.

campanile, a bell-tower, is Italian, and is pronounced kam-puh-**nee**-lee.

can *noun. Can* is the word generally used in BrE for the container when the contents are liquid (*a can of beer / a can of soup*). When the contents are solid, *tin* is more usual (*a tin of beans / a tin of peaches*) but *can* is used for this too in AmE.

can *verb.* The verb *can* is classed among the **modal verbs, and has a wide range of uses, expressing (1) possibility, (2) ability, (3) permission (where it overlaps with *may*).
   Examples: (1) **possibility** *Anyone can make a mistake / Manned spacecraft can now link up with other spacecraft in outer space / He can be very trying.*

(2) **ability** *His four-year-old son can already ride a bicycle / Murray could read more than forty languages.*

(3) **permission** *No one can play the organ without the consent of the vicar / Can I speak to your supervisor, please?* In more formal or polite contexts, *may* is preferable and more usual, e.g. *May I have another sandwich, please?*. However, in the past tense, *could* has largely replaced *might*, e.g. *At that time only rectors could* [= were entitled to] *receive tithes.* In some cases, a distinction between *can* and *may* needs to be preserved, e.g. *I'll drop in tomorrow, if I can* [= if I am able, if I have the time, etc.] and *I'll drop in tomorrow, if I may* [= if you will permit me, if that is convenient for you, etc.].

canard means 'an unfounded rumour or story' and is pronounced either **kan**-ahd or kan-**ahd**.

candelabrum, because of its Latin origin, has the plural form *candelabra*, but *candelabra* has taken on a new life as the more common singular form for the word meaning 'a large branched candlestick or lamp-holder', and has its own plural *candelabras*: *four silver candelabras*—Walter Scott, *Ivanhoe.*

cannon. 1 This word for a large gun is now confined, apart from its historical reference, to a shell-firing gun in aircraft (a use first recorded in 1919). Historically the word is used both as an ordinary noun (with plural *cannons*), and as a collective (as in Tennyson's *Cannon to the right of them, Cannon to the left of them*, etc.).

2 *Cannon* should be carefully distinguished in spelling from *canon*, meaning (1) 'a rule' and (2) 'a member of a cathedral chapter'; confusion can be unfortunate.

cannot is usually written as one word, although *can not* occurs from time to time in letters, examination scripts, etc. The contraction *can't* is fairly recent (around 1800) and does not occur (for example) in Shakespeare. *Can't* is often articulated even when *cannot* is written.

canoe *verb* has inflected forms *canoes, canoed, canoeing.*

canon see CANNON.

cant now usually means 'insincere pious or moral talk': *shameful surrender to the prevalent cant and humbug of the age—Daily Telegraph*, 1992. Its older (18c-19c) and often derogatory meaning, 'the secret language or jargon used by certain classes or professions', is confined to historical novels and scholarly discussion of language.

can't see CANNOT.

canto, a division of a long poem, has the plural form *cantos* (recommended) or *cantoes.*

canvas, canvass. 1 *Canvas* with one *s* means 'coarse cloth'. The plural is *canvases* and as a verb ('to cover or line with canvas') it has inflected forms *canvases, canvassed, canvassing.*

2 *Canvass* with two *s*'s is a verb meaning 'to solicit votes' and a noun meaning 'the soliciting of votes'. Its inflections retain the double *s* (*canvasses, canvassed*, etc.).

capercaillie is a Scottish Gaelic word for a wood-grouse. This is now the normal spelling (formerly also *capercailzie*, the *z* representing *y* in older Scots orthography), and the pronunciation is cap-uh-**kay**-li.

capita, caput see PER CAPITA.

capital, capitol. *Capital*, the most important town or city of a country or region, is to be distinguished from *Capitol*, which is (1) the hill in Rome where the geese saved the day, and (2) the

American legislative building in Washington DC (and other similar buildings in the USA).

capitalist is now normally stressed on the first syllable, although you still occasionally hear it stressed on the second.

capitals. Capital letters are used to signal special uses of words, either (1) to mark a significant point in written or printed matter (especially the beginning of a sentence), or (2) to distinguish names that identify particular people or things from those that describe any number of them. Practice varies when people and things do not always fit neatly into one or other of these two categories. This article deals with the elementary uses first, and then with the less straightforward ones.

1 basic uses. Capital letters are used almost invariably (1) to begin a new sentence (or a quotation within a sentence), (2) as the first letters of proper names and personal names (*New York* / *John Smith*), (3) in certain special cases by convention, e.g. the personal pronoun *I*. These elementary rules cause little difficulty, but beyond them practice and usage become unstable, and different publishing houses have varying sets of rules about them.

2 other uses. a Prefixes and titles forming part of names referring to one person: *the Duke of Wellington, Sir Bob Geldof, Her Majesty the Queen, Queen Elizabeth the Queen Mother, His Excellency the American Ambassador*. When the reference is general, i.e. to many such people, a capital is not used: *every king of England from William I to Richard II* (where *king* is a common noun like *monarch* or *sovereign*).

b Titles of office-holders when these refer to a particular holder: *I have an appointment with the Mayor* / *He was appointed Bishop of Durham*; but not when the reference is general or

descriptive: *He wanted to be a dean* / *When I become king*.

c Recognized and official place-names: *Northern Ireland* (but *northern England*, which is simply descriptive), *Western Australia, South Africa, New England, the Straits of Gibraltar, Plymouth Sound, London Road* (when it is an address; but *Take the London road*, i.e. the road to London, which is descriptive).

d Names of events and periods of time: *the Bronze Age* (and, e.g., *Bronze-Age Crete*), *the Middle Ages, the Renaissance, the First World War* (but *the 1914–18 war* is generally regarded as descriptive). Archaeological and geological eras are now generally often written with a small initial: *chalcolithic, palaeolithic*.

e Names of institutions, when these are regarded as identifying rather than describing: *Christianity, Buddhism, Islam, Marxism, the (Roman) Catholic Church, the House of Lords*. The word *State* has a capital initial when it is meant to refer to the institution as a whole, so as to distinguish it from the ordinary use of the word; similarly *Church* is an institution (*disestablishment of the Church*) whereas *church* is a building or local body (*go to church* / *the church down the road*).

f Abbreviations and initialisms are usually spelt with capitals, whether they refer to institutions or are more generic (*BBC, MPs*); but acronyms, which are pronounced like words and behave like words, often become wholly or partly lower-case (*Nato, radar, Aids*).

g Names of ships and vehicles: *The Cutty Sark, HMS Dreadnought, the US bomber Enola Gay*. Note also *a Boeing, a Renault, a Spitfire*, which are trademarks: see next section.

h Proprietary and brand names (trademarks): *Anadin, Cow & Gate, Kleenex, Persil*. A capital initial should strictly also be used when the reference is generic (e.g. *can you lend me a Biro*), but in practice this is more common in the regulated world of published print than in general writing. Brand and company names also generally begin with a capital letter, e.g. *J Sainsbury, Tesco,* except those where the company itself has chosen otherwise, e.g. *eBay,* with the second letter in upper case, and the now defunct *bmi,* all lower case.

i Words derived from proper names: *Christian* (noun and adjective), *Machiavellian, Shakespearian.* But a small initial is used when the reference is remote or conventional, or merely allusive: *arabic letters, french windows, mackintosh, wellington boot;* and when the sense is an attribute or quality suggested by the proper name: *chauvinistic, herculean, titanic.* Verbs follow the same rule: *bowdlerize, galvanize, pasteurize.* The guide in this area is the extent to which the name on which the word is based is present in the meaning used, as it clearly is with *Shakespearian* but not with *titanic* (which is undoubtedly used by many who are unaware of the mythological Titans).

j Medial capitals. The uses we have discussed so far all concern the first letters of words. Use of capitals within words is confined exclusively to commercial usage, and has no other purpose or effect than to highlight or distinguish the name: *CinemaScope, InterLink.*

caption. Fowler called this 'rare in British use, and might well be rarer'. Despite this disapproval (*see* LOST CAUSES), it is now a common word on both sides of the Atlantic, meaning (1) a title below an illustration and (2) a heading to a newspaper article or book chapter. Despite this meaning, it comes from Latin *capio* 'to take', and has no direct connection with Latin *caput,* 'head'.

carat, caret. *Carat* (AmE *karat*) is a measure of the purity of gold; *caret* is a mark (Λ) for showing an insertion in printing or writing.

caravanserai is pronounced with stress on -van- and the final syllable rhyming with *eye.* It means an inn for travelling merchants or pilgrims in the Middle East (first noted by the geographer Hakluyt in 1599), and is of Persian origin. Several other spellings are now thankfully extinct.

carburettor. This is the standard spelling in BrE, as distinct from AmE *carburetor* (with one *t*).

carcass, the dead body of an animal, is the preferred form (rather than *carcase*) and has the plural form *carcasses.*

care. The modern colloquial expression *I couldn't care less* dates from the 1940s (*OED*: the first example is of a book title). More recent is the AmE expression *I could care less,* which has more or less the same meaning (*My ordeal was over and I could care less what he did now*). The stress pattern is different: normally on *couldn't* in the first and on the pronoun *I* in the second, which suggests an awareness of the switch and in some measure accounts for the synonymy of two apparently opposite constructions.

careen is originally a nautical word (recorded by the geographer Hakluyt in 1600) referring to the tilting or turning over of a ship, either at sea or in dock for repairs. In AmE *careen* has developed the meaning 'hurtle or rush headlong': *A lot of Russians careening along the road on liberated bicycles*—H. Roosenburg, 1957 / *The van careened across the road, almost running into the ditch*—B. Moore, 1987. In this use it has been influenced by the similar-sounding but unrelated word *career,* which is the standard word for this meaning in BrE.

caret *see* CARAT.

cargo has the plural form *cargoes.*

Caribbean is spelt with one *r* and two *b*s. In BrE the main stress is on the third syllable; in AmE and in the Caribbean itself, it falls either on the second or the third syllable.

caries is pronounced **kair**-eez (two syllables).

carillon, meaning a set of bells, has various pronunciations in the *OED* and its derivative dictionaries. The dominant one is probably kuh-**ril**-yuhn, although **kar**-il-yuhn is also given. A French pronunciation, more common in the 19c, is now hardly heard.

carousal, carousel. 1 *Carousal* is pronounced kuh-**rou**-zuhl and means a good time with drinking.

2 *Carousel* is pronounced ka-ruh-**sel**, and means (1) a merry-go-round, (2) a moving (and usually circular) conveyor-belt system for delivering passengers' luggage at airports, and (3), in historical contexts, a tournament.

carrel is a private cubicle for study in a library (20c) and is a revival of a much earlier use denoting a small enclosure or study in a monastery in medieval England, a meaning which died out with the dissolution of the monasteries in the 16c.

cartel in its modern use referring to a price-fixing business arrangement is pronounced kah-**tel**, influenced by the German word *Kartell*. In its earlier use referring to the exchange of prisoners, its stress was on the first syllable.

Carver, carver. These are two words meaning types of chair. A *Carver* (with capital *C*) is in AmE a chair with arms, a rush seat, and a back having horizontal and vertical spindles. It is named after J. Carver, the 17c governor of Plymouth Colony. A *carver* (small *c*) is in BrE the principal chair of a set of dining chairs, intended for the person who carves.

case. 1 There are two distinct nouns:

a The one meaning 'an example of an occurrence': *In this case they are wrong.* From this use there have developed several idiomatic phrases (*in case, in any case, in some cases, in the case of*) as well as several more concrete meanings, notably in law (*the case for the prosecution*) and medicine (*seven cases of cholera*). There is also the grammatical meaning, which seems to have little to do with the others but is connected etymologically. The word dates from the 13c in English and is derived ultimately from Latin *casus*, 'falling', hence 'occurrence'.

b The one meaning 'receptacle or container etc.': *Put the cases in the car.* The origin of this word is Latin *capsa* (with the same meaning), and it also dates from the 13c in English. Although this word has given rise to several technical meanings, e.g. in masonry and printing, it has been far less productive of idioms.

2 Most people use these words without difficulty and probably without any awareness that there are two separate words. Usually they do not get in each other's way, but beware of using a phrase with *case*, especially *in the case of*, when it is not needed: *In every case except that of France the increase has been more rapid than in the case of the U.K.* [where *In every country except France the increase has been more rapid than in the U.K.* is preferable]. Fowler gave many examples as evidence of what he called 'flabby writing', but such a strong reaction is less justified today when the idiom seems dated and in decline.

3 The idiom *in case* is also a conjunction: *Take your umbrella in case it rains.* In AmE, it can also mean 'if' (i.e. it is a shortening of the phrase *in the case that*): *In case it rains I can't go* [= If it rains I can't go]. Coming at the beginning of a sentence, this use can cause initial confusion to speakers of BrE.

cases. 1 Cases are the functions of nouns, pronouns, and adjectives in sentences, as reflected in their endings or some other aspect of their form. The chief cases we are concerned with are:

subjective (or nominative): the function of subject of a verb or sentence (e.g. *house* in *The house was on fire*).

objective (or accusative): the function of object, after a transitive verb or preposition (e.g. *book* in *Give me the book* and *Look in the book*). Of less concern in English are:

genitive (or possessive): the function of possession or ownership (e.g. *Jane's* and *my* in *Jane's umbrella is in my car*).

dative: the function of reference or relation (e.g. *me* in *Give me the book*).

Most English speakers now think of cases chiefly in connection with other, more inflected, languages such as Latin and German. In English, case-endings and case-forms, which were once a feature of nouns (*stan, stanes, stane* meaning 'stone'), have become restricted over many centuries to plurals and possessives of nouns (*books, children, boy's, girls'*, etc.) and to the pronouns (*me, whom, ours*, etc.). One consequence of this disappearance of cases is that English speakers may have partially lost an instinctive power to recognize case distinctions. Another way of looking at it is that the reduction process is continuing.

2 The concept of case helps to clarify certain problems of English usage:

a what happens after the verb *be*. Since the subject and the complement of *be* are historically in the same case (i.e. *be* does not take an object), *it is I* and *it is he* (or *she*) are grammatically sounder than *it is me* and *it is him* (or *her*). However, usage is changing and it is becoming more and more difficult to sustain *It is I* (and still worse, *It is only we*) in speech without risking affectation. In writing, greater care is often needed.

Many writers prefer the subjective forms, especially when the pronoun is followed by a relative clause beginning with *who* or *that*: *If I were he, I should keep an eye on that young man*—C. P. Snow, 1979 / *This time it was I who took the initiative*—R. Cobb, 1985 / *That might very well be he at this moment, causing the doorbell to chime*—Kingsley Amis, 1988. But notice the difference in reported, especially informal, speech: *Too much of a bloody infidel, that's me*—Thomas Keneally, 1980 / *'So . . .' says Jasper. 'That's him, the old fraud.'*—Penelope Lively, 1987 / *Can this be me? Driving a car?*—New Yorker, 1988.

verdict: In less formal English the objective (*It is me*) is acceptable and often preferable (*Can this be I?* offends euphony and even common sense). In more formal English the subjective is preferable except where this produces awkwardness.

b what happens after *as* and *than*. A problem arises because these function partly as prepositions and partly as conjunctions, and their roles are not clear-cut. In broad terms when *as* or *than* are felt to be prepositions the objective case is used (*as lucky as me*), and when they are felt to be conjunctions the subjective case is used (*as lucky as I*, with *am* understood). Examples: *He was as apprehensive as I about our meeting*—J. Frame, 1985 / *I hope you have a more cheerful Christmas than we*—Evelyn Waugh, 1955 / *He was eight years older than I*—Lord Hailsham, 1990 / *He seems to be as lonely as me, and to mind it more*—David Lodge, 1991 / *I wanted you to be wiser than me, better than me*—P. Hillmore, 1987.

verdict: There is a marked tendency towards using the objective case in more recent writing, with the subjective sounding more formal and often decidedly old-fashioned (as in the Waugh and Hailsham examples). *See also* AS 1; THAN 1.

c what happens after *but*. The objective form is preferable, though in practice both types occur: (subjective) *No one understands it, no one but I—* J. M. Coetzee, 1977 (objective) *'Who knows about this?' 'Nobody but me and a couple of guys here on the platform know for sure.'*—M. Machlin, 1976. *See also* BUT 2.

d what happens after *not*. Since this is more common in speech, the objective case is common: *'Who did this thing?' 'Not me.'* In writing, the subjective occurs more frequently: *It must be he who is made of india-rubber, not I*—Angela Carter, 1984. (This is an extended example of the use after *be* discussed in 2a above.)

e *who* and *whom*. This is one of the most contentious pronoun issues of our age. *Whom* seems to be on the decline; but it is incorrectly used as much as *who* (hyper-correction again): ⊠ *Do you know whom it was that came last night?* (where *whom* is the complement of *was* and not the object of *know*). The issue is more fully discussed in the article **who and whom*.

f case-switching. Change of case in pronouns within the same sentence is a common feature of English, and often goes unnoticed. Examples: *Me, I don't trust cats*—Garrison Keillor, 1989 / *Me thinking I'd probably got some filthy fever in spite of the jabs*—Julian Barnes, 1989 / *We sat down on either side of the radiogram, she with her tea, me with a pad and pencil*—Jeanette Winterson, 1985.

cashew *see* CACHOU.

casino has the plural form *casinos*.

casket. In America and some other English-speaking countries outside Britain, *casket* is used as an alternative for *coffin*. In BrE, a *casket* is a container for funerary ashes.

cast *verb*. This Old Norse word has competed for centuries with Anglo-Saxon *throw*, and its credentials include an array of 83 meanings in the *OED*. In current usage, however, it often sounds archaic or rhetorical, influenced by the New Testament *He that is without sin among you, let him first cast a stone—* John 8:7, and is largely restricted to a range of familiar phrases and idioms, such as *cast an eye over*, *cast lots*, and *cast aside*. In ordinary contexts, *throw* is the more natural word.

cast *noun*, **caste**. **1** The noun *cast* is derived from the verb and has a number of special meanings, including the actors of a play or film, an object made in metal, and its use as in *a person of a moral cast*, plus a host of curious technical meanings (e.g. in hawking).

2 *Caste*, referring to class divisions in India, is now the established spelling, although *cast* is much more common before 1800. It is derived from Spanish and Portuguese *casta*, 'race, lineage', and is related to *chaste*.

caster, castor. The two forms represent several words and overlap in usage: *caster* is the only spelling for a few technical meanings; *castor* (a different word) is the only spelling for the oil; and both are used for the sugar (which is named after the type of pot it was put in) and for the small swivelling wheel on the feet of furniture. Although you are never wrong if you use *castor* for the principal meanings, *caster* is recommended for the sugar, and *castor* for the small wheel.

casualty. The main current meaning is now 'a person killed or injured in a war or accident'. The historically earlier meaning of the mishap itself is less common, although the two are sometimes interwoven, e.g. *All wars have caused casualties among civilians.*

catachresis means 'against usage' and is a grammatical term referring to the improper use of words. Typical examples in everyday language are the use of *infer* to mean *imply* (but *see* INFER, IMPLY) and the use of *refute* to mean *repudiate*. Examples of literary (and therefore acceptable) catachresis include Dylan Thomas's phrase *once below a time*.

catacomb. Now pronounced **kat**-uh-koom; but **kat**-uh-kohm is heard in AmE.

catchphrase is a term (mid-19c) for a phrase that catches on quickly and that is often used without direct allusion to its first occurrence (when this is known). Examples are: *Not tonight, Josephine* (associated with Napoleon but more likely a Victorian music hall invention), *for my next trick* (from magicians' patter), and *have a nice day* (1970s, originally AmE, exact origin disputed). Many more examples are given in Eric Partridge's *Dictionary of Catch Phrases* (1977). More recent catchphrases, many of them disseminated by radio and television, include *economical with the truth* (1986, used by the Cabinet Secretary, Sir Richard Armstrong), *get a life* (early 1990s), *level playing field* (1980s, originally AmE), and *move the goalposts* (1980s). *See also* CLICHÉS.

catch-22, from the title of a novel by Joseph Heller (1961), is used mainly in the phrase *a catch-22 situation*, which strictly does not mean any dilemma or difficulty but one 'from which there is no escape because of mutually conflicting or dependent conditions'.

cater *verb*. There are two typical constructions, with *for* (which is more usual), and with *to* (perhaps influenced by *pander*, and more common in AmE). There is no real distinction in meaning between the two, except that use of *to* with a personal object seems less natural, at least in BrE: *The following suggested items can be obtained from shops which cater for local Chinese communities*—China Now, 1978 / *Gingerbread caters for all categories of single parents*—Times, 1980 / *He feels cheated because society does not cater to his irrational wishes*—Bruno Bettelheim, 1960 / *I saw the town of Mystic, . . . today a town largely catering to tourists and day trippers from New York*—weblog, AusE 2004 [OEC].

catholic is a word of Greek origin meaning 'universal' and 'of universal human interest', and retains this meaning in English when spelt with a small initial (as in *catholic styles, tastes*, etc). When spelt with a capital initial it refers to the Roman Catholic Church, although historically its range of reference is wider than this, embracing all Churches claiming to be descended from the ancient Christian Church. Although the meaning is clear in (for example) *Catholics and Protestants*, use *Roman Catholic* when there is any room for uncertainty.

Caucasian. The normal word, as noun and adjective, in American English (and increasingly elsewhere) for a white person (as distinct from an African-American, a Japanese person, etc.). It avoids referring to skin colour or racial group, and is therefore politically less sensitive than alternatives. It is also, as adjective and noun, the normal word used in all English-speaking countries for the people, language, etc., of the Caucasus.

cavalcade is derived from Latin *caballus* 'horse', and was brought into English via French with meanings associated with marches or processions on horseback. The association with horses was rapidly discarded, and in the 17c any procession came to be called a cavalcade. Noel Coward used the word as the title of a play in 1931, and claimed to have revived it in the process. The final element -*cade* forms the (irregular) basis of the word *motorcade*, used for a procession in motor vehicles and first recorded in AmE in 1913.

caveat is pronounced **kav**-i-at, and means 'a warning or reservation': *Any discussion of legal action must be preceded by a caveat on costs*—M. Binney et al., 1991 / *Bearing in mind some caveats below, it is possible to predict the relative difficulty of a writing task*—*National Curriculum*, 1989. In more formal and technical writing, *caveats* are *added*, *entered*, *issued*, *offered*, *placed*, *put in*, etc.: *Catherine Destivelle issued a similar caveat from the floor about the situation in the Alps*—*Climber and Hill Walker*, 1991 / *The doctor was invited . . . to place a caveat in his report stating that it was based on very limited information*—*Manchester Evening News*, 2004.

cease. This 14c loanword from French is slowly yielding to *stop* (as *cast* has to *throw*) except in a few set phrases (notably *ceasefire* and *without cease*) and where 'we substitute it for *stop* when we want our language to be dignified' (Fowler, 1926). Fowler thought that *cease* ought to be allowed to go into honourable retirement, but it appears to have plenty of active life left for special uses. It is also capable of being followed by a *to*-infinitive, often producing a better effect, whereas *stop to* do something has its own special meaning ('pause to' or 'make a special effort to'). We could not, for example, substitute *stop* for *cease* in sentences of the following type, with a personal subject, without effectively reversing the sense: *Sherlock Holmes never ceased to analyse and respect the brilliance of his enemy, Moriarty*—*Observer*, 2004.

ceiling 1 *Ceiling* has been used by government departments and administrators since the 1930s to mean 'an upper limit' (as in *a ceiling on prices*), and is sometimes contrasted with *floor*, which is a lower limit. As with *target*, care needs to be taken not to use it in contexts that are incongruous: a *ceiling* can be *reached*, for example, or *raised* or *lowered* or *adjusted*, or can be *high* or *low* or *unrealistic*, but it cannot (without absurd effect) be *extended* or *exceeded* or *increased*. It is also unwise to associate it with words that are also associated with it in its literal use, such as *suspend*.

2 A *glass ceiling* has been used since the 1980s, originally in AmE and increasingly in BrE, to symbolize a notional barrier to professional advancement, especially affecting women and members of minorities: *For most top amateurs there is a glass ceiling on the professional circuit, and it does not take them long to hit it*—*Economist*, 1995.

celeb. Few words are more indicative of our modern obsession with fame than this truncated form of *celebrity*. Andy Warhol predicted that one day everyone would be world-famous for fifteen minutes; nowadays, being in the spotlight for even less time can guarantee immortality in our *celeb culture*. As an abbreviation of *celebrity*, *celeb* is still markedly informal, and so should be avoided in formal writing.

celibate. Traditionally celibate refers to people permanently abstaining from sexual relations for religious reasons: *Religious dress and grave goods were used to differentiate celibate priests and monks from ordinary secular men*—*OEC*, 2005.

Recently, speakers have started to use *celibate* to mean abstaining from sexual intercourse, not indefinitely, but for a limited period: *I'd just as soon be alone and celibate than to [sic] be out in the clubs and the bars trying to 'hook up'*—*OEC*, 2008.

Purists consider this extended use incorrect, but it usefully expresses with a single word what would otherwise be a whole clause, i.e. in the last example above 'not have sex'.

cello is the normal word for *violoncello*, and it is spelt without an initial apostrophe. The plural is *cellos*. If the full form has to be used, note the (Italian) spelling *violon-*.

Celsius is a particular scale of temperature based on a hundred degrees from freezing to boiling, and is named (like *Fahrenheit*) after an 18c scientist. Note that *centigrade* is a generic term for any such scale, and has been displaced by the more exact *Celsius* in weather reports and general usage.

Celt, Celtic are pronounced with initial k-, except for the name of the Glasgow football club, which is pronounced s-.

censer, censor, censure. 1 A *censer* (from an Anglo-French root related to *incense*) is a vessel for burning incense; a *censor* (from a Latin word meaning 'to assess') is an official who decides on the suitability of films, plays, etc. for public performance.
 2 As a verb, *censor* 'to act as censor of', should be distinguished from *censure* 'to criticize harshly'.

centenary is pronounced sen-**teen**-uh-ri. It is the usual term in BrE (as both noun and adjective) to denote a hundredth anniversary. In AmE and elsewhere, *centennial* is more usual. For forms based on *centenary* denoting longer periods (*bicentenary, sesquicentenary,* etc.) *see* ANNIVERSARIES.

centigrade *see* CELSIUS.

centre around, centre round, influenced by verbs of motion such as *gather* and *move*, is now a common construction for the meaning 'to have (something) as a centre; to be mainly concerned with', criticism on the

grounds of illogicality notwithstanding. Examples: *That strange figure around whom this account properly centres*— W. Sansom, 1950 / *There is the added enticement of a plot centred around a real historical event*—Listener, 1983. To be completely safe, use *centre on, base on,* or *revolve (a)round.*

centrifugal, centripetal are both generally stressed on their third syllable, respectively sen-tri-**fyoo**-guhl and sen-tri-**pee**-tuhl. Their meanings are complementary: *centrifugal* relates to movement away from a centre and *centripetal* to movement towards a centre. *Centrifugal* occurs more often, and this may account for the change in stress, which was formerly also (somewhat awkwardly) on the second syllable.

century. 1 The start of a new millennium makes everyone aware of the difficulty of reckoning when a century (let alone a millennium) truly begins and ends. In arithmetical terms, the 21st century should be reckoned as having begun on 1 January 2001, since 2000 was strictly the last year of the 20th century (and 2nd millennium). But who waited until the end of the year 2000 before celebrating the millennium? In popular usage, a new century begins on 1 Jan. of the year ending in -00, and this is unlikely to change however loudly purists may protest.
 2 Nonetheless, in formal reckoning each century (*the 5th, the 16th,* etc.) contains only one year (500, 1600) beginning with the number that names it, and ninety-nine (401–99, 1501–99) beginning with a number lower by one.

ceremonial, ceremonious. 1 *Ceremonial,* meaning 'with or concerning ritual or ceremony', is a neutral descriptive adjective (as in *ceremonial occasions / ceremonial dress / for ceremonial reasons*). *Ceremonious,* meaning 'having or showing a fondness for ceremony', is a more evaluative and judgemental word. The difference can be seen by contrasting *ceremonial entry* with *ceremonious entry*: the first is an entry (in the abstract sense) marked by normal ceremony, whereas the second is an affectedly elaborate or grand entry (in the physical sense). Examples: *Lord Mackan has had a busy programme of special ceremonial events on top of his normal Household chores*—Sunday Express, 1981 / *On the far side of the hearth the headman was sitting with his legs crossed, his back very straight, ceremoniously smoking a hookah*—M. Connell, 1991.

2 *Ceremonial* is also used as a noun, meaning 'proper formalities': *He had had to fight for everything he had done, fight the people who wanted to wrap him up safely and wheel him out for a bit of ribbon-cutting and ceremonial*—P. Junor, 1991.

certainty, certitude. Leaving aside special meanings in philosophy, both words imply the absence of doubt about the truth of something, but *certitude* is a more subjective feeling whereas *certainty* is, strictly speaking, verifiable. In practice, however, *certitude* is falling out of use (and has almost no countable usage, as in *a certitude* and *certitudes*), and *certainty* is taking over its functions. Examples: (certainty) *He was filled with certainty, a deep, sure, clean conviction that engulfed him like a flood*—R. P. Warren, 1939 / *He never had the absolute certainty that one day he'd get the boat*—R. Ingalis, 1987 / (certitude) *An obsession with statistics as the sole ground of certitude in a changing world*—Encounter, 1964 / *We craved certitude and order, and Oxford gave us both*—Ved Mehta, 1993.

cervical means 'relating to the neck' (as in *cervical vertebrae*) or 'relating to the cervix (or neck of the womb)'. The

term has emerged from the domain of laboratories with the advent of nation-wide cervical screening and cervical smears. Its pronunciation in general use, **serv**-i-kuhl, is being influenced by the preference in medical circles for serv-**viy**-kuhl.

chagrin. The dominant standard pronunciation of the noun in BrE is **shag**-rin, and in AmE shuh-**grin**. The adjective derived from it is spelt *chagrined*, pronounced the same way with the addition of a final -d.

chairman, chairwoman, chairperson, chair. The term *chairman*, which combines connotations of power with grammatical gender bias, has been a keyword in feminist sensitivities about language. *Chairwoman* dates from the 17c, but (as the *OED* notes) it was hardly a recognized name until the 19c, and even then it did not solve the problem of how to refer neutrally to a chairman/chairwoman when the gender was unknown or irrelevant. Two gender-neutral alternatives emerged in the 20c: *chairperson* and *chair*, both first attested in the 1970s, although *chair* was already in use to mean 'the authority invested in a chairman': *I was recently challenged for using 'chairman' to describe my position. My accuser went on to assert that I was being insensitive to the work of the Equal Opportunities Commission by not using 'chairwoman', 'chairperson', or 'chair'.*—Ann Scully, Times, 1988. *Chair* seems to be more popular than *chairperson*, partly because it seems less contrived and partly because it is more malleable in meaning, whereas *chairperson* requires the impossibly cumbersome derivative *chairpersonship*. Although it could once be claimed that *chairperson* tended to be used as an alternative for *chairwoman* rather than for *chairman or chairwoman* (that is to say, that a chairperson was usually a woman) this is increasingly less the case as usage evens out. *See also* -PERSON.

chaise longue. The plural form of this word, meaning 'a sofa with a backrest at only one end', is *chaises longues*, pronounced **shayz** long, like the singular. The unfamiliar-looking spelling of *chaise longue* ('long chair' in French) has led many people to interpret it as *chaise lounge*. This is regarded as a mistake in British English but is a common and accepted variant in US English.

challenged established itself in the 1980s and 1990s as a combining element forming politically correct alternatives to potentially sensitive or offensive descriptions of people, as in *cerebrally challenged* (= stupid), *intellectually challenged* (= backward), *financially challenged* (= poor), *grammatically challenged* (= illiterate, inarticulate), *physically challenged* (= disabled), and *vertically challenged* (= shorter than average). Most of these, however, are used either humorously or as a self-conscious form of political correctness, and alternatives are often available that are less depleted of semantic relevance (e.g. *children with special needs* for *educationally subnormal* and *backward*).

challenging *adjective*. This vogue, positive word, is a bit of a cliché. Like *issue*, it seems to be ousting its synonyms (especially *difficult*) from the linguistic stage, presumably because they are not dynamic enough. *Challenging* is a paradoxical word. On the one hand, it evokes notions of difficulty, e.g. *a challenging time / a challenging year*; on the other, it suggests excitement and mental or physical stimulation, e.g. *challenging work / a challenging job*. Its combination of meanings makes it useful when both aspects are indeed involved. Problems can arise, however, when they are not. Responding to nearly 500 complaints about a depiction of extreme violence, a

BBC statement included the wording 'We acknowledge that certain scenes may have been challenging.' This sounds like a euphemism for 'upset many viewers'. A good thesaurus will help any writer find replacements for this overused word.

chamois is pronounced **sham**-wah, with plural spelt the same and pronounced **sham**-wahz. When it means *chamois leather*, it is normally pronounced **sham**-i and **sham**-iz.

champagne should strictly speaking be used only of a sparkling white wine from the Champagne area of France, although it is loosely used of other similar wines.

changeable is spelt with an *e* in the middle to preserve the soft sound of the *g*.

chap, meaning 'man, boy', is a 16c shortening of *chapman* meaning 'pedlar'. It originally meant 'a buyer, customer', and only acquired its present-day colloquial meaning in the 19c. It tends to be used affectionately and is often qualified by positive descriptive words such as *clever, decent, nice, lovely, old, young,* etc. In modern use it can sound somewhat dated.

chaperone, meaning 'someone who accompanies and looks after another person or group of people', is the recommended spelling, not *chaperon*. It is pronounced **shap**-uh-rohn.

char is short for *charlady* and *charwoman*, and as a verb has inflected forms *charred, charring*. Other terms such as *cleaner* (in offices) and *daily help* (in private houses) are now more usual, and *char* has a decidedly period flavour about it.

character. Fowler (1926) argued that *character* should not be used (1) as an alternative to forming abstract nouns in

-ness, -ity, etc., e.g. *Every housing site has its own unique character—Country Life*, 1972 [instead of *uniqueness* or . . . *is unique*], and (2) in the construction *of a . . . character* (with an adjective before *character*), e.g. *These zones were to be of a different character from typical streets, with traffic levels that would vary according to their functions—Architecture Weekly*, 2004 [instead of simply *different* or . . . *were to differ from* . . .]. These economies should be kept in mind in more formal written contexts, although *character* is well established in more general usage as an alternative for *quality* or *nature*.

charge *noun. In charge of* has two constructions: A can be *in charge of* B, and B can be *in the charge of* A (with an inserted *the* now usual) or in A's charge (in which case *the* is implicit). In all cases, A is given authority over B. Examples: *She didn't think it unreasonable to put Sebastian in Rex's charge on the journey—Evelyn Waugh*, 1945 / *Until they are 12 months old, the hound puppies are in the charge of the walkers who keep them at their homes—Leicester Mercury*, 1984 / *I was recently . . . put in charge of six other copywriters, two of them men—New York Times*, 1980. However, the construction *in charge of* will be found with the meaning 'in the charge of' (as distinguished above) in writing of the earlier part of the 20c, and in these cases only the context can prevent ambiguity: *The young prince was doing lessons at Ludlow in charge of the Queen's brother, Lord Rivers—Josephine Tey*, 1951.

charisma. 1 This is originally a Greek word meaning 'gift of grace'. It acquired its current meaning 'a gift or power of leadership or authority' when the sociologist Max Weber used it in this way (in German) in 1922. It has been used widely in association with major political figures, including J. F. Kennedy, Mikhail Gorbachev, and Nelson Mandela, and is now used as a synonym for 'influence' or 'authority' or even 'attraction' or 'charm' in various contexts, impersonal as well as personal: *Spacecraft sent there in recent years have dispelled legends and added reams of sound, ordered data, yet the charisma of Mars remains—San Francisco Examiner*, 1976 / *She presents well, has charm, charisma and vitality, but comes across as severely intellectual—Business*, 1991.
2 The adjective *charismatic*, in addition to its religious meanings (as in *the charismatic movement*), has developed in line with *charisma* and can be used of a person, an achievement such as *performance*, or an abstraction such as *leadership, personality, presence*, or *quality*. There is also an adverb *charismatically*: *He had a charismatic quality about him that had long made him one of Europe's most eligible bachelors—A. MacNeill*, 1989 / *She blossomed from a precocious teenager . . . into a charismatically attractive woman with towering talent.—S. Stone*, 1989.

charlatan, meaning 'a person falsely claiming special knowledge', is pronounced **shah**-luh-tuhn.

chastise is spelt -*ise*, not -*ize*.

chateau, a large French country house or castle, is now spelt in English-language contexts without the circumflex on the *a* that it has in French. The preferred plural is *chateaux*, pronounced with a final -z.

chattering classes, the. This phrase was coined in 1980 by a right-leaning British political commentator to ridicule journalists, whose job is to comment on events, as well as liberal intellectuals, who merely like talking about them. It is now well established in Britain with negative connotations: *A battle between*

Middle England—the sensible heart of the British middle classes—and Islington Person, the politically correct voice of the chattering classes—Daily Mail, 1994. It, or its variant, *the chattering class*, has since then become part of World English, usually with clearly political overtones: (CanE) *The Toronto chattering classes are abuzz with word of a new CBC show this fall—Frank Magazine*, 2004. In some contexts it is merely a shorthand for the influential people in a particular group: (AmE) *Six weeks from now, much of Hollywood's chattering class will descend on Toronto for the annual 10 days' orgy of new product—OEC*, 2005. Given its toxic connotations, it is best avoided when no venom is intended.

chauvinism is still used in its original meaning, associated with the eponymous Napoleonic veteran Nicolas Chauvin, of 'exaggerated or aggressive patriotism'. In English (though not in French) it has developed a range of extended uses signifying other kinds of excessive loyalty or prejudice, including *cultural chauvinism, economic chauvinism, ethnic* (and *racial*) *chauvinism, religious chauvinism, white chauvinism, female chauvinism*, and, most famously, *male chauvinism* (first recorded in 1940). *Male chauvinism* and *male chauvinist* are so well established now that they are often used in the simple forms *chauvinism* and *chauvinist*, usually without any danger of ambiguity because the context is all.

chav, like *spiv*, is a British invention, and equally ingenious in matching its sound with the implied attitude. It is used pejoratively to refer to a young lower-class person who behaves badly and wears designer clothes (usually fake). The word first appears in print in the 1990s although its origins are obscure: it may be derived from a theatrical slang word *chavy* meaning 'child' or from Romany *chavi* meaning 'woman', either of which is more likely than a connection with the name *Chatham* (in Kent) which has also been proposed.

cheap, cheaply adverbs. *Cheap*, used as an adverb, has one meaning, 'at a low price', and regularly follows the verb as closely as possible: *Picture-books seem to end up by being sold off cheap as remaindered volumes—Country Life*, 1981. *Cheaply* has this meaning and also means 'in low esteem': *The small Renault is underpowered and rather cheaply built—M. Harris*, 1980. A regular idiom is *to come cheap* (or occasionally *cheaply*): *A gondolier doesn't come cheap—but punting down the canals is the very best way to explore—Best*, 1991 / *The brothers enjoyed the hedonistic pleasures of the big city's pleasures that did not come cheaply—R. Long*, 1990.

check, cheque are the AmE and BrE spellings respectively for an order written on a bank account. In AmE, *check* is also the word for BrE *bill* (in a restaurant).

checkers is the AmE name for the game in BrE called *draughts*.

cheerful, cheery. For the ordinary meanings 'full of cheer, cheering, gladdening', *cheerful* is the usual word, and can be applied to a person or a person's appearance or disposition, as well as to utterances and activities (e.g. *cheerful banter / cheerful cries / a cheerful greeting / a cheerful time*) and occasionally places (*a cheerful room*). It also occurs in the informal fixed expression *cheap and cheerful*, meaning 'simple but practical', and is used more generally with the notion of tolerant good humour (e.g. *a cheerful acceptance of the inevitable*). *Cheery*, which Dr Johnson called 'a ludicrous word', is more colloquial, is suggestive of high spirits, and is used to describe a person, mood, demeanour, voice, etc.

cheers, long established as a salutation used before drinking, has developed a meaning in BrE noted by the *Times* columnist Philip Howard: *By a remarkable transition from the pub to the sober world at large outside cheers has become the colloquial synonym in British English for 'thanks'.* In a sense halfway between these two, *cheers* also means 'goodbye'.

cheque is the standard BrE spelling for the word in its banking sense. *See also* CHECK, CHEQUE.

chequered is the standard BrE spelling for the word in its literal meaning 'having a pattern of alternately coloured squares' and in its figurative meaning 'uneven, of varied fortune', as in *a chequered career.*

cherub has a plural *cherubim*, pronounced **cher**-uh-bim when referring to angelic beings, and *cherubs* when referring to adorable children. The adjective *cherubic* is pronounced chi-**roo**-bik.

Chicano (feminine *Chicana*) refers to Americans of Mexican descent. Deriving from the Spanish word *mejicano* ('Mexican'), the word became current in the early 1960s, used by politically active groups. It is still in frequent use but has become less politicized. However, Mexican-Americans with less militant political views might find the words offensive. *Hispanic* is a more generic word denoting people in the US of Latin-American or Spanish descent.

chide, meaning 'scold', in current usage has a past tense and past participle *chided*, although these forms have been unstable (with *chid*, *chode*, and *chidden* also recorded) over the word's thousand years of history.

childish, childlike. Both words are now used to describe the behaviour of adolescents and adults rather than children. *Childish* has developed a generally depreciatory meaning 'having the immature characteristics of a child', whereas *childlike* has the favourable meaning 'having the good qualities (such as innocence) associated with a child'. Examples: *His childlike curiosity about life was held in check by childish timidity*—M. Holroyd, 1974 / *John observing his daughter, saw her now as more grown-up, less childish*—Iris Murdoch, 1976 / *He captures the artist's childlike earnestness and charm, but is not always so successful with the moments of stormy intensity*—New Zealand Listener, 2004.

chimera, a word for a mythological fire-breathing female monster, has (in addition to two biological meanings) a figurative meaning 'a forlorn or illusory hope'. *Chimera* is the recommended spelling, not *chimaera*, and it is pronounced kiy-**mee**-ruh. The adjective *chimerical* (with stress on the second syllable) means 'illusory': *This fed the chimerical belief that it was possible to spend less on government programs that were already suffering from chronic underinvestment, and then expect them to yield better results*—J. Hari, 2004 [OED].

Chinese, Chinaman. *Chinese* is the standard word, both as a noun (with plural the same) and an adjective, for people and things relating to China. *Chinaman*, the form recommended by Fowler (1926), has developed unfavourable overtones and is no longer in ordinary use.

chock-full is now the dominant form, having triumphed over variants such as *choke-full* and *chuck-full*. These spelling difficulties have been aggravated by uncertainty as to the origin of the element *chock*, which also occurs in *chock-a-block* (with the same meaning).

cholesterol. This crucial word in modern healthcare is often misspelt. The most common misspelling seems to be *cholostorol*, with *-orol* instead of *-erol*; nearly as common, by a process of reversing the position of letters (known as *metathesis*), are spellings beginning with *chlo-*, e.g. *chloresterol*, *chlorestorol*.

chorale is derived from German *Choral-(gesang)* and means a stately hymn tune. In AmE it also means a choir or choral society. The final e was added to reinforce the pronunciation with stress on the second syllable (kuh-**rahl**); compare *locale* and *morale*.

chord, cord. 1 Although we are dealing here with three English words, their histories are very much intertwined, and their ultimate origin is in the Latin word *chorda* which has several meanings. To begin with, there are two distinct words spelt *chord*: (1) in music, a group of notes sounded together to form the basis of harmony (this is a shortening of *accord* respelt with an initial *ch-*), and (2) a technical word in mathematics and engineering, meaning a straight line joining the ends of an arc, the wings of an aeroplane, etc. (this is a 16c refashioning of *cord* after the initial *ch* of the Latin source). The idiom *to strike a chord* relates, somewhat surprisingly, to the second of these meanings.

2 The word *cord* = string, rope, etc., and in *spinal cord, umbilical cord, vocal cord*, etc., is descended, via Middle English and Old French *corde*, from Latin *chorda* in its meaning 'a string of a musical instrument'. The anatomical sense is sometimes spelt *chord*, but this spelling is not recommended. *Cords* (plural) is an informal—and more convenient—word for *corduroy trousers*.

chorizo is a word borrowed from Spanish to denote a kind of highly spiced pork sausage. British and American dictionaries suggest the pronunciation chuh-**ree**-zoh as the standard. You can also pronounce the *z* as an *s*: chuh-**ree**-soh. Some people, including famous cooks, pronounce the *z* as in *pizza*, chuh-**rit**-soh, a pronunciation which is not recommended.

Christian name. In a multicultural society such as Britain and the USA have become, this term should be avoided in favour of the culturally neutral *first name* or *forename*. In AmE *given name* is also used.

chronic is used of a disease that is long-lasting (as opposed to *acute*), and has the same implication of continuing severity when used of other circumstances. An *acute* problem is intense but brief, whereas a *chronic* problem is severe and likely to persist: *Richard Wallace . . . bought no furniture, not wishing, perhaps, to add to the already acute problems of storage space*—D. Mallett, 1979 / *Traffic congestion has become so chronic in Britain's cities that vehicles travel at an average speed of just 8 mph*—Back Street Heroes, 1988. The word is also used colloquially as a term of mild disapproval, especially in the phrase *something chronic*.

chrysalis has a plural *chrysalises* in general use or *chrysalides* (four syllables with stress on the second) in technical usage.

chuffed. This BrE word has the general colloquial meaning 'pleased, delighted': *You were pleased at the time. Chuffed in fact.*—Paul Scott, 1977. In some local uses in the UK the word also means the exact opposite, 'displeased, disgruntled': *Don't let on they're after you, see, or she'll be dead chuffed, see?*—C. Dale, 1964. The explanation seems to be that the two meanings reflect different uses of the dialect word *chuff*, which means 'proud, conceited' in some parts of the country and 'ill-tempered, surly' in others.

chute is the standard spelling in the meanings (1) a sloping channel or slide, and (2) a parachute.

cicada is pronounced si-**kah**-duh, although si-**kay**-duh is also heard.

cigarette is normally stressed on the third syllable in BrE and on the first syllable in AmE. Even in BrE, however, the stress can fall on the first syllable when the rhythm of the sentence seems to prefer this (as in *Cigarettes are dear*).

cinema. Today, in BrE one can still say that one is going to the *cinema* to see a *film*; in AmE one goes to *the movies* or to a *theater* to see a *movie*. In Australia and New Zealand, one goes to *the pictures* or a *picture theatre* to see a *film*. However, *movie* is spreading fast into BrE and other varieties, and will undoubtedly take over in the end (*In many ways this movie heralded a new dawn in gritty British film-making*—Radio Times, 1998). *Motion pictures*, or the *motion-picture industry*, is used of the business world of film-making in all varieties of English.

cipher is the recommended spelling, not *cypher*.

circumcise is spelt *-ise*, not *-ize*.

circumstance. The debate about the merits of *in the circumstances* and *under the circumstances* continued for most of the 20c. The pedantic view is that since circumstances are, etymologically speaking, around (*circum*) us, we must be *in* them and not *under* them; but Fowler rightly rejected this argument as puerile and observed that *under the circumstances* 'is neither illogical nor of recent invention (1665 in *OED*)'. The *OED* further noted that 'mere situation is expressed by *in the circumstances*, action affected is performed *under the circumstances*', a subtle distinction that is useful as a general guide but no more: *Never, under any circumstances, solder connections to the tags with them already on the cartridge*—Hi-Fi Sound, 1971 / *As a writer, and collector of unusual information, I would be interested to hear from people who have seen the 'little people' or any strange, apparently non-human beings, under any circumstances whatever*—Stornoway Gazette, 1973 / *We understand that in normal circumstances we wouldn't be entitled to any money*—radio transcript, AusE 2001 [*OEC*]. Choice is also affected by the presence of an adjective or other qualifier for *circumstances*: *in present circumstances, in exceptional circumstances, under these circumstances, under no circumstances*, etc., are all idiomatic constructions.

city is applied in many English-speaking countries to any large town, and the official use of the term varies from country to country. In Britain it is properly used of a town that is declared to be a city by royal charter and has a cathedral. As a result cities vary greatly in size and population: Edinburgh (population 450,000), Oxford (population 135,000) and Wells (population 10,000) are all cities, as is the City of London, which is the business centre of the capital although no more than one square mile in area and having a resident population of a little over 7,000.

civil partnership is 'a legally recognized union of a same-sex couple, with rights similar to those of marriage' (*COD*, 2006). In the UK, a form of civil union was brought into force by the Civil Partnership Act of 2004. In official use, however, the word *marriage* is not used in this context.

clad *see* CLOTHE.

claim *verb*. There are three areas of difficulty with this word. The first concerns *claim + that*, and the second *claim + to*. The third concerns the expression *to claim responsibility*.

1 claim + that. In this construction, *claim* should not be used as a mere synonym for *allege, assert, declare, maintain, say*, etc., but should contain an element of argued contention: *He claimed that adding VAT to domestic fuel and power would help create a greener and cleaner world by stimulating the use of more energy efficiency measures—Environment Digest, 1990* / ✸ *The Sun claims that the Stonebridge council estate in north London 'is Britain's tinderbox where Los Angeles-style riots could explode at any time'—New Statesman, 1992.*

2 claim + to. Fowler objected to the use of this construction when the subject of *claim* is not the same as the subject of the infinitive; so *I claim to be honest* is acceptable but ✸ *I claim this to be honest* is not. Passive constructions such as ✸ *This central Asian wine was claimed to be drinkable for up to 10 years—Oxford Companion to Wine, 2000* would also be rejected on the same principle. The weight of current usage, however, has all but overturned this rule, and it is principally on grounds of style that alternative constructions using *assert, contend, maintain*, etc., might be preferred.

3 claim responsibility for. In news reports, it is often said that a particular group *claimed responsibility* for (an attack, bombing, etc.). The objection is that the use of *claim* implies something laudable or desirable, whereas a terrorist attack is neither. Alternative expressions such as *accept or admit responsibility* or *declare that* (they were responsible) avoid these sensitivities, but *claim* is likely to remain by far the commonest verb used in this connection in the mass media.

clandestine. The recommended pronunciation in BrE and AmE stresses the second syllable, and has a short *i* in the third, klan-**des**-tin. Alternatively, the first syllable can be stressed: **klan**-des-tin. In AmE pronouncing the last syllable to rhyme with *tine* and *teen* is acceptable, but to British ears sounds odd.

classic, classical. 1 *Classical* is the customary word when reference is to the arts and literature of ancient Greece and Rome (*a classical scholar / classical Greek / architecture of classical proportions*), to traditional forms of dance (*classical ballet*), and to serious or conventional music, i.e. that of Bach, Mozart, Beethoven, Brahms, etc. (although it applies more strictly to the 18th century, after the Baroque period and before the age of Romanticism). *Classical* has come to be widely used in marketing circles to denote anything made in a supposedly traditional style: *Classical designs of branded clothing are on show—Shanghai Star, 2003.*

2 *Classic* means 'of acknowledged excellence' (*the classic textbook on the subject*) or 'remarkably typical' (*a classic example of money wasting*) and in some uses combines the two (*Chefs learn the classic sauces in their first years of training—Times, 2004*). In general use, it has come to mean little more than 'significant, or noteworthy': *Most home workers are women ... a classic case of powerless employees—Guardian, 1973* / *It was never classic snooker but at least it kept the sell-out crowd on the edge of their seats—York Evening Press, 2003.* The *Classic races* in Britain are the five main flat races, namely the Two Thousand and the One Thousand Guineas, the Derby, the Oaks, and the St Leger.

clauses. 1 A clause is a group of words normally containing a verb and its subject. A main clause makes sense by itself and can constitute an entire sentence,

cleft

e.g. *The train arrived at 6 o'clock*. Alternatively, a sentence can be made up of more than one main clause linked by a conjunction, e.g. *The train arrived at 6 o'clock and the passengers got out*. A subordinate clause is one that qualifies a main clause, e.g. *The train arrived at 6 o'clock **when it was already dark*** or *The train arrived at 6 o'clock **in order to let the passengers out***. A clause can have the status of another part of speech; for example it can be an adverb (as in the sentence just given), an adjective (*The train **which left Tokyo this morning** arrived at 6 o'clock*), or a noun (The train arrived at ***what we thought was 6 o'clock***). A relative clause is one beginning with *who, which,* or *that* that gives extra information, as in the second example above. Relative clauses can be restrictive (or defining), as in the same example ('Which train? The one from Tokyo') or non-restrictive, as in *The train, **which left Tokyo this morning**, arrived at 6 o'clock* (in which the fact of leaving Tokyo is incidental information and not essential to the meaning).

2 There are various ways of analysing clauses and sentences. The most important abbreviations used are S (subject), V (verb), O (object), C (complement), and A (adverbial), as in *My son* [S] *considers* [V] *the price* [O] *quite reasonable* [C] *in the circumstances* [A]. For a fuller description, and more complex examples of notations, see Greenbaum, *Oxford English Grammar*, 311–55.

clean, cleanly. *Clean* has been an adverb meaning 'completely, outright' since Old English and is still used as one, as in *The bullet went clean through his shoulder-blade*. *Cleanly* is an adverb of manner, and is often used figuratively: *Cut branches off cleanly, nearly flush with the trunk, without leaving a stump to die back and become diseased—Express,* 2006. Note also the adjective *cleanly* (pronounced **klen**-li), which means

'habitually clean': *persons of refined and cleanly habits and decent language— Spartacus International,* 2003. This meaning will probably be more familiar in its derivative noun form *cleanliness,* which is proverbially next to *godliness.*

clear, clearly. The grammatical situation is similar to that in the preceding entry, with *clear* available as an adverb in two principal meanings, (1) 'completely' (*They got clear away*), (2) 'in a clear manner, with clear effect' (*They spoke out loud and clear*). In this last use, it should be pointed out that *clear,* like *loud,* is used as a semi-adjective; but it is usually reckoned to be an adverb, as it is in a number of fixed expressions such as *keep clear, stand clear, stay clear,* and *steer clear. Clearly* is an adverb of manner, and can sometimes be used instead of *clear* in meaning (2): *They spoke out loudly and clearly / The author writes clearly and concisely.* It is also used figuratively, often as a sentence adverb: *These people clearly have a more pressing problem—R. Leggatt,* 2001.

cleave. There are two words, both from Old English, with this spelling. One is a mostly literary word for 'cut', and has inflected forms (past) *cleaved, clove,* or *cleft,* and (past participle) *cleaved* or *cloven.* The adjective is *cloven* in *cloven-footed* and *cloven hoof,* and *cleft* in *cleft palate* and *in a cleft stick.* It is chiefly in these fixed expressions that the word is generally known. The other word means 'to stick, adhere', and inflects more regularly (past) *cleaved,* (past participle) *cleaved.* It occurs chiefly in the Authorized Version of the Bible (where a past form *clave* is also found): *The nobles held their peace, and their tongue cleaved to the roof of their mouth—Job* 29:10.

cleft see CLEAVE.

cleft lip is the standard accepted term and should be used instead of *harelip*, which is likely to cause offence.

clematis. The standard pronunciation in BrE stresses the first syllable, **kle-muh-tis**, but the main stress is often put on the second syllable, especially in other varieties of English. *Clematis* is the form usually used to denote the plural, with no change (e.g. *In fact clematis come in a variety of guises*). Alternatively, you can use the plural *clematises*. The form *clematii*, though not infrequently encountered, is completely wrong.

clench, clinch. *Clinch* is a 16c variant spelling of *clench*, and has since been regarded as a separate word. We *clench* our teeth, fingers, and fists; and we *clinch* an argument, bargain, or deal. Lovers *clinch* when they embrace closely, and so do boxers and wrestlers when they embrace too closely. A remark or statement that decides an argument is (informally) a *clincher*. Usually nails are *clinched* (not *clenched*) to make a *clinker-built* (or *clincher-built*) boat.

clever *see* LOST CAUSES.

clew *see* CLUE.

clichés. 1 A cliché is a phrase that has become meaningless with overuse; for example, it is now meaningless to wish someone *a nice day* because a once sincere intention has become an empty cliché. The French word *cliché* means a stereotype printing block, which produced the same page over and over again.

2 Fowler's entry in this topic (1926) was less than six lines long, and quoted only two examples: *a minus quantity* (as in *Clothing among them was a minus quantity*) and *the order of the day* (as in *Engine troubles were the order of the day*). Since then, the list of fixed expressions that are commonly regarded as

clichés has grown, and everyone has their own favourites from those they condemn in the usage of other people. Anthony Burgess mocked clichés in *Inside Mr Enderby* (1963): *He was, however, on the whole, taking all things into consideration, by and large, not to put too fine a point on it, reasonably self-sufficient.* The list can be extended with the following, among others: *at the end of the day, at the tender age of* (anything up to about 30 depending on the context), *at this moment in time, conspicuous by one's* (or *its*) *absence, the elephant in the room* (something obvious but too awkward to mention), *explore every avenue, in this day and age, keep a low profile, leave no stone unturned, the light at the end of the tunnel, move the goalposts, on the back burner, over the moon, put your money where your mouth is, ruffle feathers, sick as a parrot, situation* (as in *crisis situation*), *level playing-field, not my cup of tea, take on board, until such time as, you name it.*

3 Despite a vigorous defence by Nicholas Bagnall (*A Defence of Clichés*, 1985), they are normally condemned or ridiculed on grounds of style. Christopher Ricks wisely observed (1980) that 'the only way to speak of a cliché is with a cliché'.

client has extended its range of use dramatically in recent years. It means, essentially, 'someone who buys the services of a professional person', such as a lawyer or accountant; and a prostitute traditionally has *clients*. Someone who buys something from a shop is a *customer*, doctors have *patients*, and hotels and restaurants have *patrons* (but takeaways are regarded as shops and have *customers*). In the more competitive world of privatized public transport, *passengers* are often referred to as *customers* or sometimes *clients*; this usage is entirely contrived. There is some shift of usage in the social services, in the interests of neutral description: a social worker, for example, will now have *clients* rather than the more judgemental *cases* or *patients*.

climactic, climatic, climacteric.

Climactic means 'forming a climax' and is a favourite word of sports reporters and theatre critics (*I pleasurably recall the climactic, closing minutes of the first act—Evening Standard*, 2006); *climatic* means 'relating to climate' and typically modifies words such as *conditions, factors, fluctuations, change, variation,* and so on (*He takes a look at what climatic change could mean for the flora and fauna of the British mainland—New Statesman*, 1992); and *climacteric* is a noun meaning 'the period of life when fertility and sexual activity are in decline'.

climate developed its figurative meaning 'the prevailing trend of opinion or public feeling' as early as the 17c, despite its modern ring. Examples: *The whole climate of thought will be different—* George Orwell, 1949 / *We must . . . take account of the intellectual climate of the time—*David Crystal, 1971 / *A real attempt had now to be made to change the political climate under which the Roman way of life could be accepted—* G. Webster, 1991.

cling, after a period of instability, has now rejected the past form *clang,* and has settled for *clung* as both the past tense and past participle.

clitoris. This word comes via New Latin from Greek. The standard plural is *clitorises*; *clitorides* replicates the Greek plural, and is also used, but is rather technical. *Clitori* is wrong.

clone is derived from Greek *klōn* 'twig, slip', and came into use at the beginning of the 20c as a technical term in botany and biology. In addition to its now generally familiar original use, it has developed into what Fowler would have called a 'popularized technicality' denoting close resemblances of various kinds between people and things, especially in the domain of electronic equipment: *Amstrad [is] leading the cut price clones attacking IBM personal computers on price—Marketing*, 1986 / *These days you don't have to be Led Zeppelin for some bunch of clones to reproduce your music onstage—Times,* 2007. As a verb, *clone* has developed corresponding transitive senses: to *clone* a person or thing is to make a close copy. It is also worth bearing in mind that the noun was adopted in gay culture in the 1970s to refer to a homosexual man who adopted an ubermale or -macho appearance and manner.

close, closely. The adjective *close* merges into an adverb in uses such as *come close, lie close, run close, stick close,* etc., especially in figurative uses: *Opera and large gatherings ran each other close for first place among her dislikes—* J. Aiken, 1977 / *By this time his work had come close to complete abstraction—* I. Chilvers, 2000. The adverb *closely* dates from the 16c and is used as an adverb of manner or degree, often in non-physical contexts: *The only language closely related to Sinhalese is Maldivian—Language*, 1972 / *We recognize that we will be closely scrutinized by the government—*CNN news transcripts, 2004 [*OEC*].

close, shut *verbs.* *Close* has a greater implication of formality and politeness than does *shut,* which often sounds merely peremptory. *Close the door* suggests an invitation and can have undertones of intimacy, whereas *Shut the door* is a more straightforward and business-like command. *Closed* is also used in a number of fixed expressions: *a closed* *book, a closed shop, behind closed doors, a closed society*.

closure. How times change. The *closure* Fowler included in his 1926 edition is a parliamentary term which he was at pains to distinguish from other ways of bringing a debate to an end. Much more relevant to most people nowadays is the meaning derived from psychoanalysis, namely 'a sense of personal resolution; a feeling that an emotionally difficult experience has been conclusively settled or accepted'. This formerly technical term has become part of general language in phrases such as *to achieve closure / bring closure / find closure / get closure*: *His death will bring closure to all those traumatized no matter if they believe he is guilty or not*—OEC, 2002.

It is in danger of becoming a rather woolly cliché.

clothe has two past and participial forms: *clothed* (the normal word) and *clad*. *Clothed* is suitable for most contexts (except when the less formal word *dressed* is called for), whereas *clad* is reserved for special uses: (1) as a literary word, and (2) with a qualifying word as in *ill-clad, insufficiently clad*, etc., and in figurative uses such as *ice-clad, ivy-clad*, etc. These uses also have a strong literary flavour.

clue is the normal spelling in the group of meanings to do with signs or evidence. *Clew*, which is a variant of the same word, is now principally used as a nautical term meaning 'the lower or after corner of a sail'.

co-. *See box opposite*.

coastal *see* LOST CAUSES.

coccyx, meaning a bone at the base of the spine, is pronounced **kok**-siks. The plural is *coccyxes* or (more rarely) *coccyges* (**kok**-si-jeez).

cocoa *see* CACAO.

coffin *see* CASKET.

cogent. To be *cogent*, an argument has to persuade or convince; to be *coherent* it only has to make sense.

cognoscenti is the plural form of the originally Italian word *cognoscente* 'one who knows a subject thoroughly; a connoisseur'. It can be pronounced kog-nuh-**shen**-tee, the first syllable rhyming with *cog*, or, more rarely, kon-yuh-**shen**-tee. The singular is hardly ever used, but is sometimes mistakenly written for the plural, as in: ⊠ *the giant table and chair plonked in a public place that has drawn high praise from the art cognoscente*—OEC.

coherent, cohesive. Both words come from a Latin root related to our word *cohere*, but their meanings are different. *Coherent* means 'logical and consistent' and is applied to speakers and their arguments. *See also* COGENT. *Cohesive* means 'tending to stick together' and is generally used either physically (as with liquid mixtures, for example) or in abstract contexts. To illustrate the difference in the abstract use of the two words, a *coherent* approach to an issue is one which is consistent and well considered; a *cohesive* approach is one which aims to promote greater unity among the people involved. Examples: *The company lacks a coherent strategy for future success in online music sales*—OEC, 2004 / *I'm still waiting to hear a coherent argument against gay marriage*—OEC, 2005 / *He was not able to show that they acted together as a cohesive political force*—T. Harris, 1993 / *The fate of the cohesive gel implant rests in the results of studies in the years ahead*—Cosmetic Surgery Times, 2003. / *Living and travelling together in cohesive groups is a feature of nomadic peoples*—OEC, 2002.

CO-.

Co- is a prefix of Latin origin, and is used to form words that include the meaning 'together, in common'. Spelling practice varies with regard to use of a hyphen: some words (especially when the second element begins with a vowel) include it, whereas others are written as one word. The diaeresis (ö) that formerly punctuated words as in *coöperate*, is now largely disused. Recommended spellings are as follows:

coagulate	cofactor	co-opt
coalition	cogeneration	coordinate
co-author (noun	cohabit	co-parent
and verb)	cohere	co-partner
coaxial	co-host	co-pilot
co-determination	coincide	co-respondent (in
co-driver	coition	divorce case)
co-education	co-latitude	co-signatory (to an
coefficient	co-occur	agreement etc.)
coequal	co-occurrence	co-star
coeval	co-op	co-worker
coexist	cooperate	uncooperative
coexistent	cooperation	uncoordinated
coextensive	cooperative	

cohort. A *cohort* (*cohors*) of the Roman army was an infantry unit equivalent to one-tenth of a legion, and typically consisted of about 500 soldiers. In the plural it has often been used as a literary word for 'army', as in Byron's reference to Sennacherib (1815): *And his cohorts were gleaming in purple and gold.* As well as a technical meaning in demography, in the 20c the word developed a meaning (originally AmE) 'an assistant, colleague, accomplice', probably influenced by the coincidence of the first element with the prefix *co-*: *Mr Stratton consented . . . to partake together with his cohort of a sandwich and a glass of milk*—A. Cross, 1967 / *The impending trial of Bobby Seale, chairman of the Black Panther movement, and his eight cohorts in New Haven*—Sunday Times, 1970 / *Brock and Emma had one wall, Bob, Johnny and their cohorts the other wall and centre aisle*—John Le Carré, 1979. The incongruity of this use is masked by its frequent appearance in the plural, and the singular even appears to be a kind of back-formation.

coinages are words and meanings used for the first time. Words created for the physical sciences (such as *gas* and *radar*) are often publicly coined (for example, in a journal), so that the moment and sources of their creation are recorded; but this is rarely the case with more general vocabulary unless this too is invented for a special purpose (as with *charisma* and *robot*) and still less so with slang and colloquial English, even when these are phrase-based. Coinages are often based on analogy with existing words (e.g. *software* from *hardware*, and then *shareware* and *malware* and others from *software*), on compounding (e.g.

lunatic fringe, smart card, double whammy), on blending words (e.g. *motel* from *motor* and *hotel, edutainment* from *education* and *entertainment, podcast* from *iPod* [personal audio player] and *broadcast*), on use of prefixes and suffixes (e.g. *reflagging, deskill, productize*), on phrases, real or notional (e.g. *gobsmacked, me-too, plugged-in*). *See also* NEW WORDS.

colander, meaning 'a kitchen strainer', is spelt this way, although *cullender* will be found in older writing. *See also* CALENDAR.

Cold War, for the years of suppressed hostility between the USSR and the West after 1945, is spelt with initial capitals, *the Cold War*. The concept disappeared with the collapse of communism in Eastern Europe from about 1989, but it is still referred to historically. The phrase survives, however, in the weakened sense of 'a state of rivalry and tension between two rival factions, persons, etc', in which meaning lower case is appropriate: *Ultimately, however, the police could at best lower the temperature of the cold war between ghetto and suburb, not remove the sources of conflict—OEC*, 2000.

coleslaw is spelt *cole-*, not *cold-*. This element is from Dutch *kool* 'cabbage'.

colic has a derivative adjective *colicky* (with *k* to harden the sound).

coliseum, colosseum. Both are variants of the same word, derived from the ancient name (*colosseum*) of the Flavian amphitheatre in Rome, which in turn was named after a large statue (or *colossus*) of Nero which stood nearby. The form *Coliseum* is used of theatres and music halls and, especially in America, of theatres and large buildings used for sport or exhibitions.

collaborate, collaborator. The primary meaning of the verb, 'to work in conjunction with someone else', can still be used despite the sinister overtones it acquired when used of cooperation with the enemy during the second World War. This is true also of the agent noun *collaborator*: *I wanted to work with a group of dancers and artistic collaborators over a sustained period of time—* dance website, 2002 [*OEC*].

collapsible is spelt *-ible*, not *-able. See* -ABLE, -IBLE.

collateral damage is a heavily disguised technical term, in effect a euphemism, used by the military and by politicians for civilian casualties in war. It is based on a sense of *collateral* (itself derived from Latin *latus* 'side') dating from Chaucer, 'lying aside from the main subject, line of action, issue, purpose, etc.' (*OED*). In ordinary use it conveys a sense of evasion that can verge on the offensive.

colleague, comrade. A *colleague* (etymologically 'one chosen along with another') is a fellow worker, typically a white-collar worker. The *OED* noted that the word was 'not applied to partners in trade or manufacture', i.e. blue-collar workers, but this is no longer true. A *comrade* was originally a 'room-mate' (via French from Spanish *camarada*). Members of the armed forces are *comrades* and not *colleagues*; and so formerly were (and to a limited extent still are) members of trade unions and of communist parties (who used 'Comrade' as a personal title in order to avoid bourgeois designations such as 'Mr').

collectable, collectible. Fowler (1926) said that the first is better, and this is still true. *See* -ABLE, -IBLE.

collective noun. 1 A collective noun is one that is singular in form and denotes a number of individuals, for example *audience, choir, committee, flock,* *multitude.* Apart from the names of individual animals, birds, etc. (*deer, grouse, sheep, trout*) and names for groups of them (*a pride of lions, a gaggle of geese,* etc.), and names of institutions, firms, and teams (*CNN, Ernst and Young, Real Madrid,* etc.), there are some 200 collective nouns in common use in English.

2 The principal question of usage with collective nouns is whether they should be treated as singular or plural. In BrE, the practice is well established of construing them either with a singular verb to emphasize unity or with a plural verb to emphasize individuality. For a fuller discussion of the point, see AGREEMENT 3. It is particularly important to maintain consistency within a statement, avoiding, for example, a singular verb with a plural pronoun following, as in ⊠ *A family displaced by fighting prepares* [singular] *to return to their* [plural] *village—Independent,* 2006.

3 When a collective noun is followed by *of* + plural noun or pronoun (as in *a number of people*), there is a general preference for a plural construction: *A large number of conductors want to hear the great artists—Dædalus,* 1986 / *A handful of their members have been agents of Moscow—London Review of Books,* 1987; but again a singular is used when collectivity rather than individuality is the main point: *A decade ago there was only a handful of bioethicists in the country—British Medical Journal,* 1978. *See also* NUMBER OF.

4 Names of institutions and political entities, e.g. *the United States, the United Nations, the Vatican, the Commons, Congress,* are always treated as singular whether the form of the name is singular or plural (e.g. *The United States has demanded a more open Japan—Dædalus,* 1987 / *The CEGB finds it 25 per cent cheaper to buy in French electricity—Daily Telegraph,* 1987).

5 Names of animals, birds, and fish that are the same in the singular and plural are treated as singular or plural (or as a singular mass noun) accordingly: *Five bison were grazing in a shaded part of the valley / Trout will for some time still be a premium fish, selling at about £1 each.*

6 For collective nouns of the type *a pride of lions* etc., *see* PROPER TERMS.

college has many long-established meanings: (1) a body of officials, membership of which is a privilege or honour, e.g. *College of Cardinals, College of Arms, College of Physicians,* etc., (2) an establishment for further education, normally part of a university as at Oxford, Cambridge, London, and elsewhere. In wider educational circles, *college* has been traditionally used in the names of some of the ancient public schools (notably Eton and Winchester). As the provision of secondary, tertiary and professional education in Britain has increased and changed in recent years, the word applies to a much broader group of educational and professional institutions: *business colleges, teacher-training colleges, sixth-form colleges, secretarial colleges, military* and *naval colleges, colleges of agriculture,* etc. One consequence is that a general phrase such as *at college* has become somewhat elastic: it can mean at a university, pursuing a specific profession at any of the many different kinds of institution listed above, or merely doing post-GCSE (or, in Scotland, post-Standard Grade) work. Depending on the situation, it is often helpful to use a more specific phrase.

collide, collision. There is no basis for the assertion sometimes made that these two words should be restricted to circumstances involving an impact between two *moving* objects. A vehicle can be said to *collide* with a tree, a bollard, or any other fixed object as well as with another vehicle, whether moving or not. In factual reporting, however, *hit* is often a more straightforward choice: [*They*] *died when their car hit a tree between Penzance and Land's End yesterday—Times*, 1990.

collocation is a term in descriptive linguistics for the customary association of words with other words. A *bystander* is usually said to be *innocent, consequences* are often *far-reaching,* and *politicians* are *cautiously optimistic.* For some reason, Catholics are described as *devout* whereas Protestants are *staunch.* Other aspects of collocation include the function words needed to complete the sense of other words (e.g *agree + with* or *to* or *on*) and the typical order of words, as in *fish and chips* and *spick and span,* neither of which can normally be reversed.

colloquial is a term used in dictionaries and books on language to describe the less formal vocabulary and grammar of everyday speech. In some dictionaries, *informal* is used instead (as being less judgemental), although the implications for usage are the same. *Slang* denotes a greater degree of informality, and typically involves a stronger element of metaphor or imagery. *See* SLANG.

collude, collusion. Both words involve a notion of fraud or dishonesty. It is correct to speak of dealers *colluding,* or acting *in collusion,* in insider dealing on the stock exchange; but it would not be correct to refer to authors *colluding* to write a book (the correct word would be *collaborating*).

colon. 1 The colon is the punctuation mark that is least used and least well understood in ordinary writing (as distinct from printing). The principal difference between it and the semicolon lies in the relation of what precedes and follows each in the sentence.

A semicolon links two balanced or complementary statements, whereas a colon leads from the first statement to the second, typically from general or introductory statement to example, from cause to effect, or from premiss to conclusion.

2 The respective roles of semicolon and colon are shown by the following example punctuated in two ways: *It was a beautiful day; we played cricket on the green / It was a beautiful day: we played cricket on the green.* In the first version, the two statements about the weather and playing cricket are equally balanced and might alternatively be separated by *and* or written as two distinct sentences separated by a full stop. In the second version, the colon makes the second statement much more explicitly a consequence of the first.

3 A colon is also used to introduce a list: *The following will be needed: a pen, pencil, rubber, and ruler.* Note that the colon should not be followed by a dash, although this practice is more common in older printing.

4 In AmE, a colon follows the initial greeting in a letter (*Dear Ms Jones:*), but in BrE a comma is customary. A colon also separates hours and minutes in notation of time in AmE (*10:30 a.m.*).

colossal. In its physical sense 'of immense size', *colossal* dates from the early 18c, and was not listed by Dr Johnson (1755). The first use in its figurative meaning 'remarkable, splendid' is attributed to Mark Twain: *I do not suppose that any other statesman ever had such a colossal sense of humour, combined with the ability to totally conceal it—American Claimant,* 1892. This use, which verges on the colloquial, should be used sparingly: *This astonishing journey took a colossal amount of determination—* B. Taylor, 2002.

colosseum *see* COLISEUM.

colour. In BrE the customary spellings of words related to *colour* are *colourable* (= specious, counterfeit), *colourant* (= colouring substance), *colourful*, *colourist* (= a painter in colour), and *colourless*, but *coloration* (= a colour scheme), *colorific* (= producing colour), *colorimeter* (= a measuring instrument), and *decolorize* (= remove the colour from). In AmE all have *-or-*, not *-our-*.

coloured, written with a capital C, in South Africa denotes a person of mixed descent, and in the plural denotes a racial group as officially defined under the former apartheid laws. Use of this term by white people in Britain and elsewhere to refer to non-white people is offensive but less common than formerly.

columnist, meaning a writer of a newspaper column, is pronounced with the *n* expressed.

combat is normally pronounced with stress on the first syllable as both noun and verb. The same applies to the derivatives *combatant* and *combative*. The verbal inflections are *combated, combating*.

combining forms. This term, which may well have been used first by the *OED* editors, denotes a word form that is only used in combination with other elements. The normal linking vowel is *-o* (e.g. *Anglo-*, *electro-*) or *-i* (*alti-*, *horti-*). Combining forms can also occur at the ends of words (e.g. *-imeter*, *-ology*).

come is one of several verbs (others include *go* and *try*) which can be followed by *and* instead of *to* (*Come and see*). It can also be followed by a participle in *-ing* (*Will you come swimming tomorrow?*). Occasionally, and usually for rhetorical effect, it is followed by an infinitive without *to*: *We can sell this house, you can come live with us*—Lee Smith, AmE 1983 / *Come let us say a prayer together*—Jane Gardam, BrE 1985.

comedian. In Shakespeare's *Twelfth Night* (1601), Olivia asks the disguised Viola, who has come to woo her on behalf of Orsino with a lover's speech ready to deliver, 'Are you a comedian?', meaning 'Are you a comic actor?'. At a slightly earlier date (1581), the word is recorded in the meaning 'writer of comic plays'; together these constitute the earliest records of the word. Its current meaning, applied to both men and women, is 'a humorous entertainer on stage, television, etc.' A French-derived feminine form, *comédienne*, is recorded from about 1860. It is nowadays either restricted to historical reference, or used only in conjunction with the performer's name, or where her sex is otherwise relevant. It is spelt without an accent. In the meaning 'writer of comedies', *comedian* is mostly used of the ancient writers Aristophanes, Menander, Plautus, and Terence, to distinguish them from the tragedians Aeschylus, Sophocles, and Euripides.

comic, comical. These two words overlap in meaning, but *comic* is the more common of the two and is the only one with the purely descriptive meaning 'relating to or in the nature of comedy', as in *comic actor* and *comic opera*. *Comical* is a more evaluative word, meaning 'funny, causing laughter', as in *comical appearance* and *a comical situation*; *comic* can also have this meaning but is often taken to imply intention rather than effect. The following examples demonstrate the different perspectives of these words in this meaning: *Both brothers laughed out loud at the deliberately comic delivery of his English phrases as they shook hands*—A. Grey, 1983 / *In reality, the relationship was a strained and sometimes comical mismatch, a 50-year-long saga of crossed purposes—Daily Telegraph*, 1992 / *He wiped his head, looking almost comical in his shorts and sandals*—N. Barber, 1992 / *Simply* *said, this anthology is too long. None of it lacks literary charm, that is certain; but much of it lacks any actual comic element*—First Things (magazine), 2005.

comity, pronounced **kom**-i-ti, means 'considerate behaviour towards others'. It has a special meaning in international law, occurring often in the semi-fixed expression *comity of nations* (or *peoples*, etc.), of 'the mutual recognition by nations of the laws and customs of others': *. . . should be borne in mind that these are matters which affect the comity of nations*—Weekly Law Reports, 1992. It should not be used in the weaker meaning 'a group of nations that are well disposed to one another', although this is often found in print, e.g. *There were voices which spoke for Russia in the comity of civilised people other than those of ministers and Tsars*—Peter Ustinov, 1983.

comma. There is much variation in the use of the comma in print and in everyday writing. Essentially, its role is to give detail to the structure of sentences, especially longer ones, and to make their meaning clear by marking off words that either do or do not belong together. It usually represents the natural breaks and pauses that occur in speech. The principal uses are as follows:

1 To separate adjectives coming before a noun: *a cold, damp, badly heated room* / *a ruthless, manipulative person*. The comma can be replaced by *and* between a pair of adjectives to make a stronger effect: *a ruthless and manipulative person*. The comma is omitted when the last adjective has a closer relation to the noun: *a distinguished foreign politician* / *a dear little baby*.

2 To separate the main clauses of a compound sentence when they are not sufficiently close in meaning or content to form a continuous unpunctuated sentence, and are not distinct enough to

warrant a semicolon. A conjunction such as *and, but, yet*, etc., is normally used: *The road runs close to the coast, and the railway line follows it closely*. It is incorrect to join the clauses of a compound sentence without a conjunction (the so-called 'comma splice'): ☒ *I like swimming very much, I go to the pool every day*. (In this sentence, the comma should either be replaced by a semicolon, or retained and followed by *and*.) It is also incorrect to separate a subject from its verb with a comma: ☒ *Those with the lowest incomes and no other means, should get the most support*. (Remove the comma.)

3 A comma also separates complementary parts of a sentence, and can introduce direct speech: *Parliament is not dissolved, only prorogued* / *The question is, can this be done?* / *He then asked, 'Do you want to come?'*

4 An important function of the comma is to prevent ambiguity or momentary misunderstanding: *In the valley below, the houses look very small* (The valley is not below the houses) / *Mr Hogg said that he had shot, himself, as a small boy* (Mr Hogg shot things other than himself).

5 Commas are used in pairs to separate elements in a sentence that are not part of the main statement: *There is no sense, as far as I can see, in this suggestion* / *It appears, however, that we were wrong* / *There were, to be sure, at least four pubs in the village*. They are also used to separate a relative clause from what it refers back to when the clause is not a restrictive or identifying one (*see* CLAUSES): *The book, which was on the table, was a gift*. (Without the comma, the relative clause would identify the book in question rather than give extra information about it: *The book which/that was on the table was a gift*). A single comma usually follows adverbs (such as *already, however, moreover*) in initial position in a sentence: *Already, the sun was* *shining / Moreover, you were late home from school.*

6 Commas are used to separate items in a list or sequence. Usage varies as to the inclusion of a comma before *and* in the last item; the style recommended here is to include it (the so-called 'Oxford comma'): *We ordered tea, scones, and cake.* Other practice is to include it only to avoid ambiguity: *We ordered tea, bread and butter, and cake.*

7 Omit the comma between nouns in apposition, e.g. *my friend judge Leonard / her daughter Mary*; but keep it when the noun is a parenthesis e.g. *His father, Humphrey V. Roe, was not so fortunate.*

8 Commas are used in numbers of four or more figures, to separate each group of three consecutive figures starting from the right, e.g. *14,236,681.* Omit the comma when giving house numbers in addresses (*44 High Street*), and in dates (*27 July 2001*).

commando has the plural form *commandos.*

commence, begin, start. 1 *Commence* is a more formal Latinate word for *begin* or *start.* Fowler's advice (1926) was to use *begin* and its derivatives except when these seem incongruous (which is in fact rare); occasions when *commence* is more appropriate include official announcements, statements of historical importance, and suchlike. It is therefore a sound rule to use *begin* in all ordinary contexts unless *start* is customary (e.g. *The engine started at once / They usually start work at 9.30 / The game started on time*), and to reserve *commence* for more formal occasions, such as the law (*to commence an action*), warfare (*Hostilities commenced on 4 August*), and the domain of ceremonial (*The procession will commence at 2 p.m.*).

2 Constructions available to *commence* are more limited than to *begin*; in particular *begin* can more readily be

followed by a *to*-infinitive, whereas a verbal noun is now more natural after *commence*: *They began to eat* or *They began eating* but *They commenced eating.* However, *commence + to* will be found in older writing. Definitely to be avoided is a mixed style of *to + verbal noun*: ✷ *Then he commenced to coming by our place*—M. Golden, 1989.

commentate is an unsurprising back-formation from the noun *commentator.* It is first recorded as a rare word from the late 18c in the general sense 'to comment', and was revived in its current use in sports broadcasting in the 1950s, when a more definite word than *comment* was needed (*During his career he commentated on 202 classic races*—BBC Sport, 2005).

commercialese is the special language of business correspondence. Much of the more arcane terminology, such as *ult.* (= *ultimo*, last month), *prox.* (= *proximo*, next month), and *duly to hand* (= received) has disappeared, although one or two phrases still linger in the correspondence of more conservative business circles.

commiserate was a transitive verb for about three centuries: *She did not exult in her rival's fall, but, on the contrary, commiserated her*—H. Ainsworth, 1871; but under the influence of *condole with* and *sympathize with*, it is now construed with *with* (despite the disapproval of Fowler, modified somewhat by Gowers): *We often commiserate with ourselves, feeling that no one has to go through what we are called to endure, and that no one understands*—Evangelical Times, 2005.

commissionaire, meaning a uniformed door-attendant, is spelt with two *m*s, two *s*'s, and one *n.*

committee can take a singular or plural verb, pronoun, etc., depending on the meaning. If the emphasis is on the relevant committee's collective nature, or unity, it is treated as singular; if the emphasis is on the individuality of its members, it is treated as plural. Examples: *The committee proposes an Official Information Act to cover leakage of information*—Times, 1972 / *The local party's General Management Committee will vote for their choice next Monday evening*—Wandsworth Borough News, 1977 / *An international committee on viral names has been looking into the problem*—Capital Gay, 1986. When the verb is in the past or constructed with an auxiliary verb such as *will* or *may*, it is unclear whether it is singular or plural. In order to make it clear that individuality is being emphasized, expressions such as *the members of the committee* are used: *I was also pleased to hear that two members of the committee will be visiting Australia to see what has happened there*—Bolton Evening News, 2003. See AGREEMENT 3.

common see MUTUAL.

commonality. Once restricted to technical writing (*Commonality can be increased when subjects are asked to predict common normative responses*—Journal of General Psychology, 1971) it has, especially in the US, become a staple of writing styles which value portentousness for its own sake: *As a meditation on the commonality of death and sex and of the impotent struggle of goodness and taste against the wars that mankind seems addicted to, The White Countess has much to offer*—Film Inside Out, 2005.

Those wanting to keep their prose closer to the ground might wish to replace it with *common ground, common features, connection, link*, or any of a dozen other, less high-falutin' words which can replace it in most contexts.

communal is traditionally pronounced with stress on the first syllable in BrE, but is often nowadays stressed on the second syllable, in line with the dominant AmE pronunciation.

commune is stressed on the first syllable as a noun, and on the second as a verb, as in *to commune with nature*.

community in the sense of 'a place considered together with its inhabitants' has given rise to attributive uses such as *community police officer, community care* (long-term care for the ill and elderly), *community service* (unpaid work to be done by offenders instead of imprisonment), and *community home* (a home for young offenders). Used absolutely, *community* is often shorthand for 'the black community' (in an area), and the term *community leaders* tends to be used in the same racial context.

compact is stressed on the second syllable as a verb (e.g. *trampling on the lawn will also compact the soil*) and predicative adjective (e.g. *the new roadster is extremely compact*). As a noun (meaning 'an agreement' or 'a case for face-powder') and as an attributive adjective, the stress is normally on the first syllable, except that it is variable in *compact disc*.

comparable is pronounced with main stress on the first syllable. Its uses with *to* and *with* correspond to the meanings given at *compare, with a marked preference in current usage for *to*: *This heroin is comparable in quality to that being sniffed by U.S. troops in Vietnam*—R. Parkes, 1973.

comparatively, like *relatively*, has been used since at least the early 19c as a 'downtoning' adverb, even where actual comparison is not involved: *He had had comparatively little to do with women*—P. Newton, 1972 / *It was a comparatively* *shabby office*—G. Markstein, 1981. These uses are justified on the ground that there is usually implicit comparison of some kind, even if it is as vague as 'compared with others'. Fowler (1926) restricted his comment to the use of *a comparatively few* (with indefinite article), but Gowers (1965) extended the disapproval to the type *Casualties were comparatively few*, arguing that no comparison, not even an implicit one, is made. This distinction, however, is impossible to sustain, since *few* behaves like an ordinary descriptive adjective in being gradable: if one allows *very few* the objection to *comparatively few* falls.

comparatives *see* ADJECTIVE 3; -ER AND -EST FORMS.

compare with, compare to. 1 In general usage, these two constructions are used interchangeably; AmE generally prefers *to* when there is a choice, whereas in BrE the choice is more evenly divided. A broad distinction in principle should be kept in mind, namely that *compare to* is used to liken two things whereas *compare with* is used to weigh or balance one thing against another. When Shakespeare in his famous line asks *Shall I compare thee to a Summers day?*, he is likening, even though in the end he shows his beloved to be *more lovely* than a summer's day.

2 This broad distinction can be seen in the following modern examples, although the use of *to* in the 1976 example violates it: *American Opinion . . . compared the familiar peace symbol to an anti-Christian 'broken cross'*—*Time*, 1970 (likening) / *He did not individually compare other women with her, but because she was the first, she was equal in his memory to the sum of all the others*—J. Berger, 1972 (balancing) / *Compared to war-reporting of the Spanish war . . . Journey to a War is superficial and uninformative*—S. Hynes, 1976 (balancing) /

Salim's flight to London can be compared . . . to the Romeward journey in Virgil—*London Review of Books*, 1979 (likening) / *The company produced a creditable performance, particularly when compared with the results of many of its competitors*—*Daily Telegraph*, 1992 (balancing).

3 When a subordinate clause or phrase is introduced by the participial form *compared*, the preposition is either *to* or *with*, although here usage is moving in favour of *to*: *The church looked dimly mysterious compared with the glare of the passage*—P. D. James, 1986. *This was a modest sum compared to what other people spent*—Tom Wolfe, 1987 / *Compared to physics and astronomy, cosmology is a young science*—*Science Show* (ABC Radio), AusE 2003 [*OEC*].

4 In BrE *with* is obligatory when *compare* is used intransitively, because the balancing rather than the likening notion predominates: *His achievements do not compare with those of A. J. Ayer*—*Sunday Times*, 1988. In AmE, however, *compare to* is possible here: *None of those birds compare to L.A. pigeons*—*LA Weekly*, 2004. *See also* COMPARABLE; COMPARISON 2.

comparison. 1 For *comparison of adjectives*, *see* ADJECTIVE 3.
2 *Comparison* as the noun equivalent of *compare* is normally followed by *with*, not *to*, and this applies also to the expression *by* or *in comparison*: *By comparison with some of the 20 million tons a year North Sea finds it is a drop in the ocean*—*Daily Telegraph*, 1974 / *It doesn't bear comparison with the contact you can get with a live theatre audience*—S. Brett, 1977.

compass points. Use capital initials for *north, south, east*, and *west* when these are part of recognized names, e.g. *North London / South America / the East*

End. The same applies to *northern, southern*, etc., when these have specific geographical reference, as in *Western Australia* and *Northern mythology*. In general reference, use small initials: *an easterly wind / southern parts of the country*. See CAPITALS 2C.

compelling, compulsive. Both words involve a sense of strong urging and are derived from Latin *compellere* meaning 'to drive on'. An activity or habit that is *compulsive* affects an individual in a way they cannot control (a near synonym is *addictive*): *Franklin was . . . a compulsive composer of lists and instructions—New York Metro*, 2004. *Compelling* is used of arguments and information that is convincing or effective (the synonym here is *persuasive*). So when a newspaper television review described a historical programme as being *on the receiving end of the BBC's compulsive docudrama treatment*, the word needed was *compelling*, since the programme was presumably well-presented and persuasive rather than addictive.

compendium has plurals *compendiums* (preferred) and *compendia*.

competence, competency. 1 Fowler (1926) remarked that 'neither has any sense in which the other cannot be used', and noted that the first form is gaining ground. This assertion remains generally valid, and in the meantime *competence* has won out in the currency battle over *competency*. *Competency* has a stronger role as a countable noun in the sense 'a competent skill or feature', and is found in the plural, especially in AmE: *Here they . . . write a monthly action plan and determine what skills and competencies will be required to achieve their goals—Apply Magazine*, 2002.
    2 *Competence* was given a special meaning in language learning by Noam Chomsky in 1962: *competence* for him

means what a speaker of a language knows implicitly, as distinct from *performance*, which is what the same person actually uses in language production.

complacent, complaisant have the same pronunciation apart from -s- in the first and -z- in the second. Both are derived from the Latin word *complacere* 'to please'. *Complacent* means 'calmly confident' and normally has unfavourable connotations, i.e. 'too easily satisfied; smugly self-confident': *A quarter of a century later, the conventional wisdom of British mandarins looks complacent, self-serving, ill-informed, and outmoded—Independent*, 1989. *Complaisant* means 'politely deferential' or 'too willing to please': *He went north to join his apparently complaisant wife for Christmas and Liza went to Cornwall—P. Street*, 1990. It is no longer much used in ordinary speech and writing: *obliging* and *acquiescent* are more common alternatives.

complected, complexioned. *Complected*, meaning 'having a specified complexion', was first recorded in 1806 in the US and is still more common there than elsewhere. *Complexioned* is more common in all varieties of English, including American, and to many British ears *complected* will sound jarringly American. Examples: *They told me the man they meant wasn't dark complected—W. Faulkner*, 1932 / *She was a good-looking, dark-complected lesbian—way out in the open about that—M. Chabon*, 1990.

complement is a term in grammar for a word or phrase added to a verb to complete the predicate of a sentence. (In the examples that follow, the complement is in bold type.) The most common form of complement is the type that follows a verb of state such as *be, look, seem*, etc.: *I am **his brother** / She looked **lovely** / You seem **to be unhappy** / They remained **out of reach***. A complement can also relate to the object of a sentence rather than its subject (*He called his mother a fool*), and the term is sometimes extended to include words and phrases that complete the sense of other words, e.g. adjectives (*fond of chocolate*) and prepositions (*over the moon*).

complement, compliment, complementary, complimentary.

1 *Complement* and *compliment* each function as noun and verb, and are pronounced exactly the same. As nouns they are pronounced **kom**-pli-muhnt with a *schwa (an indistinct unstressed vowel sound) in the final syllable. The verbs are pronounced **kom**-pli-ment with a fully pronounced final syllable. Both words are derived from Latin *complere* 'to fill up'; *complement* means 'something that completes' and should be distinguished from *supplement* which means 'something that adds to'. A *compliment* is 'a spoken or written expression of praise'.

2 The derivative adjectives have corresponding meanings. *Complimentary* means 'expressing a compliment' and has the additional meaning 'given free of charge' (e.g. *complimentary tickets*). *Complementary* means 'completing' or 'forming a complement': *Chelsea Theatre is a small yet dynamic new writing theatre enriched by a complementary programme of arts activities*—theatre reviews website, 2004 [*OEC*], and has a special use in the context of medical therapy that falls outside the scope of scientific medicine but supports it (e.g. acupuncture and osteopathy).

complete *adjective*. For discussion of whether it is appropriate to qualify *complete* with words such as *very, more, rather*, etc. (submodifiers), see UNIQUE.

complex. 1 The noun is familiar as a term in psychology meaning 'a group of repressed feelings or thoughts which cause abnormal behaviour or mental states', usually with some qualifying

word, e.g. *inferiority complex, Oedipus complex*, and *persecution complex*. This use has permeated everyday language in non-technical meanings. Examples: *Both of them had a complex about economy and living within a budget*—Mary McCarthy, 1954 / *The roadmen went and got into a muddle with their flags . . . One of them . . . apparently gets a power complex every time anyone puts a red flag into his hand*—C. Aird, 1973.

2 But by far the most common use of *complex* as a noun is in the sense 'a group or network of buildings or systems', typically qualified by adjectives or nouns such as *housing, industrial, leisure, shopping, sports*, etc., that pinpoint the activities involved. A *power complex* is more likely to be describing either an energy installation or the structure of political decision-making than an obsession with influence and authority.

complexion is spelt *-xion*, not *-ction*.

complexioned *see* COMPLECTED, COMPLEXIONED.

complex prepositions. *Complex* (or *compound*) *prepositions* consist of two or more words together having the function of a preposition, e.g. *according to, apart from, in accordance with, with regard to*. Fowler (1926) objected to their overuse in journalism, 'stuffing up the newspaper columns with a compost of nouny abstractions'. He had a point, but they cause little trouble today and should only be avoided, as a matter of clear style, when something more simple is available: e.g. *about* or *concerning* will often do in place of *with regard to*. Others, such as *away from* and *out of*, are straightforward and necessary, since *away* and *out* (unlike *in*) do not function as prepositions by themselves.

compliment, complimentary *see* COMPLEMENT, COMPLIMENT, COMPLIMENTARY, COMPLEMENTARY.

comply, conform. The two verbs share the notion of acting in accordance with a wish, command, rule, or guideline. The typical patterns are *comply with* and *conform to*. Both are also used absolutely, with a difference of implication: one *complies* by observing a specific order or instruction, and *conforms* by behaving according to a social convention. Examples: *The NHS is obliged to comply with the provisions of Community law even before they have been fully incorporated into English law*—J. Montgomery, 2002 / *What I am addressing is that the conditions for the early Earth described in the Bible over 2,000 years ago conform to the conditions we now know to be the case*—weblog, 2004 [*OEC*] / (absolute) *Henry coveted Anne Boleyn, who would not comply without the assurance of marriage*—J. Guy, 2000 / *Girls who play flute want to conform, want to fit in, which often stems from insecurity*—weblog, 2003 [*OEC*].

compose *see* COMPRISE.

composite is now pronounced **kom**-puh-zit, not -ziyt in BrE but kuhm-**po**-zit in AmE.

compound is pronounced with stress on the first syllable as a noun and on the second as a verb. Technically, to *compound a felony* in law is to condone it in exchange for some consideration, and does not mean 'to make (it) worse'. But to use the phrase in the latter meaning is nowadays standard. *Compound* meaning 'a large enclosure' is an entirely distinct word derived via Portuguese and Dutch from Malay *kampong*.

compound prepositions *see* COMPLEX PREPOSITIONS.

comprehend *see* APPREHEND.

comprise. 1 *Comprise* is often confused with *compose, consist,* and *constitute*. All four words are used to describe how parts make up a whole, but they start from different ends of the equation. *Comprise* has the whole as its subject and its parts as the object, e.g. *The top floor comprises three bedrooms and a bathroom*. *Consist of* takes the same perspective, and one could equally say *The top floor consists of three bedrooms and a bathroom*, although it is more usual to use *consist of* when referring to ideas and concepts rather than physical things. Reversing the construction with *comprise* in the form *Three bedrooms and a bathroom comprise the top floor* is sometimes criticized. Alternatives here are *compose, constitute,* or (more informally) *make up*. See also INCLUDE.

2 Also often criticized are the hybrid construction *comprise of* and the passive *be comprised of* (both instead of *consist of*). Examples of correct uses: *Love comprises among other things a desire for the well-being and spiritual freedom of the one who is loved*—Muriel Spark, 1984 / *Our opposing team comprised school friends Arnie, 27, a teacher, and Danny, 26, a film director*—Evening Standard, 2007. Examples of criticized uses: *The league comprises of eight teams*—OEC, 2004 / *Rivers in this area are mainly comprised of domestic and industrial effluent, and many have been fishless in living memory*—K. Hawkins, 1993 / *As this team of scientists was comprised entirely of men the experiment necessarily involved letting the male subjects design computerised images of their ideal women*—Observer, 2007.

computerate is a word to which Fowler could well have objected, on the grounds that it is a 'hybrid' of the English word *computer* and the suffix *-ate*, which is not now generally used to create new words. Despite his hypothetical objections, it is usefully shorter than *computer-literate*, which is an alternative that can be used to avoid upsetting purists.

computerese. 1 The language of computer terminology has become familiar to the English-speaking world in the last twenty years or so as the technological revolution has impinged on the lives of most people both at work and in their homes. Since much of the development in this field has been led by North American organizations, English has become the electronic lingua franca much as it has been the international medium of communication in air travel and other domains. Most recently, the rapid expansion in use of the *Internet* (or *World Wide Web*) has produced a vocabulary of its own, both at technical level and in everyday slang. Much of the technical jargon is based on initialisms of three or more letters, such as *http* (= *hypertext transfer protocol*), *ISP* (= *Internet service provider*), *www* (= *World Wide Web*, used in website *addresses*), *Wi-Fi* (= *Wireless Fidelity*, for transmission of data over wireless networks), and *VOIP* (*voice over Internet protocol*, a technology for making telephone calls over the Internet).

2 Other terminology is based on or adapted from words that belong to the basic core of English: people buy *hardware* and install *software* on it, and occasionally *freeware* (but they need to beware of *adware* and *malware*); their desk becomes a *workstation*; many computer programs are manipulated by using a *mouse* to make choices from a *menu*; computer symbols are *icons*; a location on the *Internet* is a *site*, which is *accessed* by means of a *home page*, and the data is explored by *browsing* or *surfing* (usually with a *browser*). People communicate by *email* (= *electronic mail*) as distinct from *snail mail* (= the ordinary postal service), send aggressive messages by *flaming* (a revival of an old meaning), and break into other people's systems by *hacking*. Medical analogy is invoked to alert users to the dangers of computer *bugs* and *viruses*, some

of which may be *macro-borne* (= communicated by copying an infected macro program). What is most interesting from the point of view of language is how little of this vocabulary has developed extended meanings in other contexts, leaving the world of computer jargon a closed environment, borrowing words from everyday language and signally failing to return them.

concave means 'having an outline or surface like the *interior* of a circle or sphere', whereas *convex* means 'having an outline or surface like the *exterior* of a circle or sphere'.

concensus is incorrect; the correct spelling is *consensus*.

concept. The technical meaning of the word in philosophy is 'an idea or mental image which corresponds to some distinct entity or class of entities, or to its essential features'. In non-philosophical circles, it is widely used in the weakened sense of 'an abstract idea', especially in marketing and design: *He was the man who invented the concept of a weekly news magazine*—D. Halberstam, 1979.

Although some people consider this extended meaning overused, there is room for both sets of uses. In many contexts, however, what is described as a *concept* can more modestly be called an *idea*.

concern *noun*. In the meaning 'anxiety, worry', *concern* is normally followed by *about*, *at*, or *over*, or by a *that*-clause: *Concern has been expressed at the manner in which the whole operation has been put together and actioned*—Rescue News, 1985 / *'Big-band' Mozart; smooth, rich, warm, mellow and played with love and fastidious concern over the tiniest detail*—CD Review, 1992 / *There was also concern about the spread of the fire to other flats and the supermarket itself*—news website, BrE 2005 [OEC] / *The*

French political establishment publicly expressed concern that one of the country's largest financial institutions might come under Italian control—Business, 2007. When purpose is involved, a to-infinitive is usual (These [approaches] shared a concern to develop the full psychological potential of individual learners—Concise Oxford Companion to the English Language, 2000), and when the meaning is 'personal interest or involvement', it is more often followed by for (It is only a shame that this outcome will have been brought about by market forces and legislation rather than by any innate concern for dog welfare—She, 1989).

concerned. The idiomatic expression as far as . . . is/are concerned is well established and normally harmless, but Gowers (1965) suggested that it was often unnecessary, and could be replaced by a simple preposition. For example, The punishment does not seem to have any effect so far as the prisoners are concerned would be better expressed as The punishment does not seem to have any effect on the prisoners. Such economies are worth bearing in mind.

concessive. A concessive clause or phrase is one that is typically introduced by a conjunction such as although, but, or though, or by a preposition such as despite or in spite of, and expresses a sense that is contrary to what is expected in the rest of the statement: Two letters in Portuguese were sent me to translate, although I knew no Portuguese—Graham Greene, 1980 / His poems . . . though self-absorbed . . . are not self-admiring— J. Carey, 1981 / There were strong arguments in favour of nuclear energy, despite concerns about the disposal of radioactive waste—Birmingham Post, 2007.

concord see AGREEMENT.

concur, meaning 'to express agreement', has inflected forms concurred, concurring. It is normally used absolutely, or followed by with (a person, idea, conclusion, etc.) and/or in (a matter), or followed by a that-clause: If the doctor desires to treat the patient, he is often in a strong position to persuade such a relative to concur—I. Kennedy, 1988 / A later internal annual review of Birmingham's Partnership concurred with some of these findings—P. Lawless, 1989 / Modern biblical scholars concur that the letter ascribed to Jude is of too late a date to have been written by any contemporary of Jesus—R. Leigh, 1992 / Simpson concurs that 'Leonidas made the right decision, and for the right reasons'—History Today, 2002 / Everyone who knows Brown concurs in one thing—that his formative influence was his background, and in particular his late father John— Guardian Unlimited, 2004.

condemn has a silent final -n, but this is pronounced in its derivatives condemnable, condemnation, and condemnatory.

condole see CONSOLE.

conduct is pronounced with stress on the first syllable as a noun and on the second syllable as a verb.

confederacy, confederation see FEDERATION.

confer has inflected forms conferred, conferring. In the meaning 'consult' it is normally followed by with (a person) and/or about or over (a matter). The derivative adjective is spelt conferrable.

confidant, confidante, stressed on the first syllable or (in the case of confidante) on the first or last syllable, mean 'a close friend in whom one confides', and refer respectively to a male or female and a female. They are alterations of an earlier form confident (stressed on the first syllable), and were probably attempts to imitate the French pronunciation of the final syllable *-ent, -ente*.

confine is pronounced with stress on the first syllable as a noun and on the second as a verb.

conflict is pronounced with stress on the first syllable as a noun and on the second as a verb.

confusable words. *See box overleaf.*

congeries, pronounced kon-**jeer**-iz and derived from Latin *congerere* 'to heap together', is a collective name for any disorderly collection of people or things. It is singular despite its plural-looking form: *The Galaxy is nothing else than a congeries of innumerable stars distributed in clusters*—*Natural History* (magazine), AmE 2003. It is only rarely encountered and practically never needed in ordinary discourse (there are under 100 examples in the *OEC*). The plural is also *congeries*.

conjoined twins. This more accurate and correct term has supplanted the older term *Siamese twins* in all contexts other than informal conversation.

conjugal, meaning 'relating to marriage', is pronounced with stress on the first syllable.

conjunction. A conjunction is a word such as *and, because, but, for, if, or,* and *when* which is used to connect words, phrases, clauses, and sentences. Coordinating conjunctions join like with like: *The room is large **and** bright* / *She would have to go back **and** look for it* / *You can come in **but** you cannot stay long* / *Would you like tea **or** coffee?* Subordinating conjunctions join a subordinate clause to a main clause: *I shan't go **if** you won't come with me* / ***As** we're early let's have a drink* / *I was late **because** I missed the train.* Pairs of conjunctions such as

either . . . or . . . and *neither . . . nor . . .* are called correlative conjunctions: *He must be **either** drunk **or** mad* / *I **neither** know **nor** care.* Some conjunctions are much more common in BrE than in AmE; these are *whilst* (*I would like to thank many friends and colleagues for their encouragement whilst I was writing this book*— R. Jackson, 1981), *now* (*Now the tourist season's starting it's better to have someone there, like a caretaker*—Iris Murdoch, 1980), *and nor* (*Nobody in the dying Constituent Assembly believed it, and nor did the royal family*—W. Doyle, 2003), and *but nor* (*I don't need any cosseting but nor am I too independent*— *Saga Magazine*, 2004). The more important conjunctions are treated in separate articles: *see* AND; BECAUSE; BUT; FOR; etc.

conjure is pronounced **kun**-juh in the meaning 'to perform magical tricks' and kuhn-**joo**-uh in the meaning 'to beseech'.

conjuror is the recommended spelling, not *conjurer*.

connection is now the dominant spelling, although *connexion* (preferred by Fowler) will be found in older printing styles. Fowler also wrote at length against what he regarded as the excessive use of *in connection with*, which he castigated as 'a formula that every one who prefers vigorous to flabby English will have as little to do with as he can'. Certainly, when a simple preposition such as *by* or *about* or *into* will do instead, it should be used: *inquiries in connection with the vandalizing of a local school* would be better expressed as *inquiries into the vandalizing of a local school*.

connote, denote. Both words mean broadly 'to signify' but that is where the correspondence ends. A word *denotes* its primary meaning; it *connotes* attributes

CONFUSABLE WORDS.

1 Pairs of words are most often confused because they are similar in form (or spelling) and share some aspect of meaning, as with *fortunate* and *fortuitous*, or *prevaricate* and *procrastinate*.

(a) Some pairs are confused only in writing, although the meanings and even the parts of speech differ (e.g. the verb *forbear* and the noun *forebear*).

(b) In some cases, the confusion is in one direction only: *infer* is used controversially to mean *imply* but the same is not true the other way round.

(c) In other cases, the differences in meaning and use are so subtle that it is virtually impossible to choose between them, as with *sensual* and *sensuous*.

(d) Some pairs have a long history of interaction and meaning overlap (e.g. *admission* and *admittance*), whereas in other cases a later word encroaches on an earlier word that, despite being originally distinct, is close to it in form and meaning (e.g. *biennial* on *biannual*; *childlike* on *childish*).

(e) Some pairs consist of words that originally had the same meaning but diverged with time (e.g. *continual* and *continuous*; *ensure* and *insure*), whereas others consist of words whose relation in meaning has often changed historically (e.g. *disinterested* and *uninterested*).

2 Confusing these pairs is a matter both of language production and of language understanding. In some cases the writer/speaker will be unsure which word to use, thereby causing ambiguity or doubt from the outset; in others it will be the reader/hearer who is uncertain, either because of ignorance or because the context allows more than one interpretation. The following table shows pairs of words that are commonly confused or used in place of each other, and a brief summary of the main modern meaning. Also shown is the date the word entered English in the part of speech, though not necessarily in the precise meaning, at issue. (ME stands for Middle English, i.e. before about 1470; and OE for Old English, i.e. before 1150.) The selection is representative but by no means exhaustive, and you will find other pairs in this book.

For further information on the words listed, see the individual entries.

word	date	meaning	word 2	date	meaning
adherence	ME	(to belief etc.)	adhesion	15c	sticking
admission	ME	(general meanings)	admittance	16c	right to be admitted
adverse	ME	unfavourable	averse	16c	opposed
affect	ME	cause change in	effect	16c	bring about
allusion	16c	indirect reference	illusion	ME	deceptive appearance
alternate	16c	one after another	alternative	16c	available instead
altogether	OE	entirely	all together	ME	everyone together
ambiguous	16c	(statements etc.)	ambivalent	20c	(feelings etc.)
amend	ME	change	emend	ME	alter (text etc.)
appraise	ME	assess value of	apprise	17c	inform

avoid	ME	keep away from	evade	15c	avoid by guile
baleful	OE	menacing	baneful	16c	causing harm
baluster	17c	(in balustrade)	banister	17c	(in staircase)
biannual	19c	twice a year	biennial	17c	every two years
censor	16c	act as censor of	censure	16c	criticize harshly
childish	OE	(immature qualities)	childlike	16c	(good qualities)
coherent	16c	logical and clear	cohesive	18c	sticking
complacent	17c	too confident	complaisant	17c	too willing to please
condole	16c	express sympathy	console	17c	give comfort to
continual	ME	repeated	continuous	17c	going on without a break
council	OE	administrative body	counsel	ME	advice etc.
credible	ME	believable	credulous	16c	too ready to believe
decided	18c	unquestionable	decisive	17c	conclusive
decry	17c	belittle	descry	ME	catch sight of
definite	16c	clear and distinct	definitive	ME	decisive, authoritative
deprecate	17c	disapprove of	depreciate	ME	lower in value
discomfit	ME	disconcert	discomfort	ME	make uneasy
discreet	ME	circumspect	discrete	ME	distinct
disinterested	17c	impartial	uninterested	17c	not interested
draft	16c	preliminary sketch etc.	draught	ME	air current etc.
elusive	18c	difficult to find	illusory	16c	deceptive in appearance etc.
enormity	ME	(act of) wickedness	enormousness	17c	large size
ensure	ME	make sure	insure	ME	take out insurance on
euphemism	16c	milder term	euphuism	16c	affected style of writing
evince	16c	make evident	evoke	17c	draw forth (feelings)
exceptionable	17c	open to objection	exceptional	19c	unusually good
flaunt	16c	display ostentatiously	flout	16c	disregard (rules etc.)
forbear (verb)	OE	desist from	forebear (noun)	15c	ancestor
forego	OE	go before	forgo	OE	go without
forever	18c	continually	for ever	ME	eternally
gourmand	ME	glutton	gourmet	19c	food connoisseur
homogeneous	17c	of the same kind, uniform	homogenous	19c	of common descent
illegal	17c	against the law	illicit	16c	not allowed

imply	ME	strongly suggest	infer	15c	deduce, conclude
impracticable	17c	not able to be done	impractical	19c	not practical
inapt	17c	not suitable	inept	16c	clumsy, unskilful
incredible	ME	not believable	incredulous	16c	unwilling to believe
ingenious	ME	well thought out	ingenuous	16c	innocent, honest
interment	ME	burial	internment	19c	being interned
its	16c	(possessive pronoun)	it's	17c	= it is
luxuriant	16c	lush	luxurious	ME	comfortable and rich
masterful	ME	domineering	masterly	16c	highly skilful
militate	16c	have force (against)	mitigate	ME	make less severe
observance	ME	keeping a law or custom etc.	observation	ME	perception, remark
occupant	16c	person in a vehicle etc.	occupier	ME	person living in a property
official	ME	having authorized status etc.	officious	15c	aggressive in performing duty
perquisite	ME	extra privilege etc.	prerequisite	17c	something needed in advance
perspicacious	17c	having insight, perceptive	perspicuous	15c	clearly expressed
pitiable	ME	deserving pity	pitiful	ME	causing pity, contemptible
precipitate	17c	headlong	precipitous	17c	abruptly steep
prevaricate	16c	act evasively	procrastinate	16c	defer action
purposely	15c	intentionally	purposefully	19c	resolutely
refute	16c	prove to be false	repudiate	ME	reject, disown
regrettable	17c	causing regret, undesirable	regretful	17c	feeling regret
sensual	ME	gratifying the body	sensuous	17c	gratifying the senses
slither	ME	slip or slide	sliver	ME	long thin piece
titillate	17c	excite pleasantly	titivate	19c	adorn, smarten
tortuous	ME	twisting, devious	torturous	15c	causing torture, tormenting

associated with the broad primary meaning. So the word *spring* denotes the first season of the year, but connotes fresh growth, renewal, young love, and so on.

consensus. Note the spelling, not *concensus*. It means 'general agreement', and is often used (1) in collocations with *of*: *consensus of authority, evidence, opinion*, etc. (although *consensus of* *opinion* is strictly tautological), and (2) in more recent usage, in attributive uses such as *consensus view, consensus politics*, etc.

conscientious is spelt *-tious*, not *-scious*.

consequent, consequential.

   1 *Consequent* is used either attributively or with *on* or *upon* and means 'resulting, following in time', with an element of causation that is not present in the purely temporal word *subsequent*: *He does not mention the decline in . . . control consequent upon self-employment—Times*, 1973 / *Australian ratings terms have been revised to incorporate the introduction of colour TV and consequent multi-set use in many homes—TV Times* (Brisbane), 1977.

   2 *Consequential* has two principal meanings: (1) 'of the nature of a consequence or sequel' (*All identity systems carry consequential dangers as well as potential benefits—*weblog, 2003 [*OEC*]) and (2, despite Fowler's objections) 'of consequence, significant'. In this second meaning, *consequential* belongs more naturally in predicative position (after a verb or after one implied): *Time passes, none of it consequential—*weblog, BrE 2003 [*OEC*]; it is less convincing in attributive position (before a noun), although this occurs, especially in AmE: *opening a crucial phase of what the distinguished writer Elizabeth Drew this week rightly called America's 'most consequential election in decades'—Guardian*, 2004.

conservative, in the meaning 'moderate, cautious, low', as in *a conservative estimate*, is one of Fowler's *lost causes. He regarded it as a ridiculous 'slipshod extension' and rejected it outright. But it is now well established in the language and is entirely acceptable.

consider, in the meaning 'to regard as being', occurs in three typical constructions, two that are accepted and a third that is disputed: (1) with a noun or adjective complement in apposition to the object: *I consider them friends / I consider them friendly*, (2) with *to be* inserted between the object and its complement: *I consider them to be friends / I consider them to be friendly*, and (3) more controversially, influenced by words such as *regard* and *treat*, with *consider* followed by *as*: *I consider them as friends / I consider them as friendly*. *See* further at AS 3. Construction (2) is especially common in reflexive use when an adjective (rather than a noun) follows (*I consider myself to be well-informed*) and in passive constructions (*medicines that are considered to be safe during pregnancy*), and (3) is the least common. Examples: *The patient . . . could not be considered as cured—*M. Balint, 1968 / *The baby was considered to be at high risk—Lancet*, 1977 / *The village boys considered it a privilege to enjoy a stroll with him in the evenings—*M. Das, 1987 / *She . . . does not consider herself a photojournalist in any conventional sense—*website, AmE 2004. Note, however, that *as* can have a different syntactic function, associated with the object and not with *consider*, and these uses are acceptable: *Cologne Opera and San Francisco Ballet have both inspected the theatre and are considering it as* [= in its capacity of] *a venue—Times*, 1980. *See also* CONSIDERING.

considerable, meaning 'much; a lot of' is used in BrE only of abstract things, such as *attention, concern, delay, difficulty, distance, doubt, evidence, expense, experience, improvement, influence, interest, pain, pleasure, progress, sums of money, talent, thought, time, variation*, and *work*. In AmE it is used in this meaning of concrete things as well, especially mass nouns such as *grain, salt*, etc. BrE achieves this by using a formula such as *a considerable amount* (or *quantity) of: We used a considerable amount of water before the fire was brought under control*—Bolton Evening News, 2003.

considering has been used for centuries as a preposition and conjunction meaning 'taking into account (that)'. Like *given and *granted, it is grammatically independent of the subject: *It's odd that one boasts considering that no one is ever taken in by it*—Virginia Woolf, 1921 / *He looks round his palace of a house with sniffly and quite unfair resentment, considering its comfort*—New Yorker, 1974. There is also an absolute use, which should only be used informally: *These were years of disappointment . . . for Nash, in what was, considering, a remarkably successful career in writing*—New York Times Book Review, 1990. *See also* PARTICIPLES 3, 4.

consist is followed by *of* or *in*. *Consist of* means 'to have as its parts or elements' (in physical and abstract contexts): *Testing consists of checking that the students can carry out the task by the criteria detailed in the objectives*—Teaching Clinical Nursing, 1986 / *Otherwise her wardrobe consisted only of three or four shabby black skirts and four or five shapeless black sweaters*—Angela Carter, 1993; *see* further at COMPRISE. *Consist in* means 'to have as its essential features': *This defence consists in establishing . . . that the derogatory words—or at least their sting—were true*—Journal of the Royal Society of Arts, 1977. The two meanings can easily overlap, as can the notion of a thing's constituents and its characteristics: *Kim's Game consists in enumerating as many as possible of a miscellaneous assemblage of objects briefly glimpsed shortly before*—Michael Innes, 1972.

console. 1 *Console* is pronounced with stress on the first syllable as a noun (= panel, cabinet, etc.), and on the second syllable as a verb (= 'to comfort'). The words have different origins: the noun from Latin *solidus* 'solid' (cf. *consolidate*) and the verb from Latin *solari* 'to soothe'.

2 The verb *console* means 'to comfort' and takes an object or can be used absolutely: *David has us to console him*—A. Price, 1976 / *Always ready to comfort and console*—N. Grainger, 2004. It should not be confused with the less common word *condole*, which means 'to express sympathy', and is followed by *with*: *The priest came to condole with Madeleine*—Michele Roberts, 1993.

consort is pronounced with stress on the first syllable as a noun, and on the second as a verb.

consortium has the plural *consortia* in writing more often than *consortiums*, but in speech it might sound somewhat pompous.

conspicuous. The phrase *conspicuous by its* (or *one's*) *absence* is a cliché. *See* CLICHÉS.

constable should be pronounced kun-, not kon-.

construct, construe are related words (from Latin *struere* 'to build') which are both used to denote grammatical function. A word is *construed* or *constructed* with (e.g.) *on* when *on* is its regular complement, e.g. *insist on* and *rely on* (the *OED* abbreviates this to 'const. *on*'). You can also *construe* (but not *construct*) a sentence when you analyse its grammar in order to determine its meaning; this sense also has a more general application equivalent to 'interpret': *Henceforth, religion was construed as a private matter*—First Things (magazine), 2004.

constructive in general use means 'helpful, positive', as in *constructive criticism*. In this meaning it is the opposite of *destructive*. In legal language it is often applied to 'what in the eye of the law amounts to the act or condition specified' (*OED*), and is current in the phrase *constructive dismissal*, whereby an employer alters an employee's conditions in such a way that continued employment becomes impossible.

construe *see* CONSTRUCT.

consummate is pronounced **kon**-syuu-mayt, with the stress on the first syllable, as a verb and kuhn-**sum**-uht, with the stress on the second syllable, as an adjective (meaning 'complete, perfect').

consumption, in the meaning 'a disease causing wasting of the tissues', has been replaced in the 20c by more specific clinical names, especially by *tuberculosis* or *TB*.

contact *verb*. The meaning 'get in touch with' originated in the US in the early 1920s and was greeted with open hostility by purists for several decades, but it is now well established in AmE and BrE. The stress pattern is unstable; most often the stress is on the first syllable, but the normal pattern of stress on the second syllable for the verb (and first for the noun) is beginning to establish itself.

contagious. A contagious disease is one transmitted by physical contact, as distinct from an infectious disease, which is transmitted by micro-organisms in the air or in water. In figurative use, *contagious* and *infectious* overlap in modifying positive or welcome things (e.g. *delight, enthusiasm, laughter, sense of fun,* and *vigour*), whereas *contagious* (but not typically *infectious*) is also extended to things that are unwelcome or unpleasant (e.g. *corruption, folly, greed, guilt, panic,* and *suffering*).

contemporary, contemporane-ous. 1 *Contemporary* has two main meanings: (1) 'living or occurring at the same time', both as an adjective (often followed with *with*) and as a noun (often followed by *of*): *Austen Layard, a contemporary of Wallace who had discovered the ancient city of Nineveh*—L. Blair, 1988 / *The finest novelists contemporary with him, particularly George Eliot and Hardy, are drawn to describe similar interiors for related, although slightly different, reasons*—P. Tristam, 1989, and (2) 'existing or done at the present time' (as in *contemporary literature*) and hence 'up-to-date, modern' (as in *contemporary ideas* / *contemporary furnishings*). The logic of this sense, which appears at first sight to be inconsistent with the first, is that it is elliptical for 'contemporary with the present'. The risk of ambiguity is largely theoretical, although it might occur in a sentence such as *music performed on contemporary instruments*, where it is not clear whether *contemporary* refers to the time of the music or the time of the performance.

2 *Contemporaneous* (17c) is an adjective restricted to the first meaning, and is available when all risk of misunderstanding needs to be eliminated. It is found surprisingly often, especially in historical contexts: *Built in the thirteenth and fourteenth centuries, they are contemporaneous with many of the great Gothic cathedrals of Europe*—S. Stewart, 1991 / *Workers . . . experienced an absence of light and air that made conditions even in contemporaneous London and Paris seem favourable*—S. Lash, 1990.

contemptible, contemptuous.
Contemptible in current use means 'deserving contempt' (*His defiant and sulky defence of his right to pat bottoms and hump secretaries, or pin women to the wall in sexual passes, is contemptible*—Independent, 2006), whereas *contemptuous* means 'showing contempt' (*He has a fine independence of outlook and*

a contemptuous disregard for whatever is smart or fashionable among opinion-formers—Private Eye, 1977).

content. 1 *Content* is pronounced with stress on the second syllable as a verb (see 2), adjective, and noun (meaning 'a contented state': see 3), and on the first syllable as a noun (meaning 'what is contained': see 4).

2 *Content oneself with* (not *by*) is the right form of the phrase that means 'not go beyond (some course of action)', when followed by a verbal noun: *Fans of classic Japanese cinema have had to content themselves with reading about, rather than seeing, films like Drunken Angel*—film website, 2000 [*OEC*].

3 *Content* and *contentment* both mean 'a contented state', but *contentment* is the more usual word, with *content* found chiefly as a poetical variant in the expression *to one's heart's content*.

4 *Content* and *contents* both mean 'what is contained' in physical and abstract senses. There is little difference in meaning; *content* is the more usual choice when the thing in question is a mass noun (and obligatory when preceded by a defining word, e.g. *protein content*), and *contents* is the more usual choice when a number of countable items is involved, but exceptions are not hard to find: *Questions like the protein content of bacon butties . . . and the vitamin rating of corned beef sarnies*—Times, 1980 / *The whisky bottle was still in play, though its contents . . . had not shrunk catastrophically*—M. Hatfield, 1981 / *In a sideline to the main argument for God's existence, Descartes considers the content of a number of different ideas he has*—T. Sorell, 2000.

contest is pronounced with stress on the first syllable as a noun and on the second syllable as a verb.

continual, continuous. 1 *Continual* is the older word (14c), and once had

all the meanings it now (since the mid-19c) shares with *continuous* (17c). Fowler (1926) expressed the current distinction somewhat cryptically as follows: 'That is *-al* which either is always going on or occurs at short intervals and never comes (or is regarded as never coming) to an end. That is *-ous* in which no break occurs between the beginning and the (not necessarily or even presumably long-deferred) end.'

2 *Continuous* is used in physical contexts (such as lines, roads, etc.) and is preferred in technical contexts (e.g. *continuous assessment / continuous playback / continuous stationery*). The other principal use is when referring to time: *continuous* here means 'going on uninterrupted' whereas *continual* means 'constantly or frequently recurring'. The following examples show how difficult it is to keep the two meanings apart: *The correspondence between the two men was continuous throughout the next few months*—V. Brome, 1978 / *The 1840s were years of continuous self-education for Philip Henry Gosse*—A. Thwaite, 1984 / *The house and garden had seen their best days, and the decline was now continual, from season to season*—R. Frame, 1986 / *His son was a continual source of amusement and delight to him*—E. Blair, 1990 / *He singled out two big issues that should be addressed: 'The first is the continual underfunding of road and rail infrastructure.'*—Lloyd's List, 2006. Note that other words are sometimes preferable, e.g. (in place of *continual*) *constant, habitual, intermittent, recurrent, repeated*, and (in place of *continuous*) *ceaseless, constant, incessant, unbroken, uninterrupted*. Note also that *constant* can be used to mean both *continual* and *continuous*.

3 Of the corresponding adverbs, *continually* (14c) is older by far than *continuously* (17c). Here, for some reason, the current distinction is clearer to see; *continually* can be defined as 'repeatedly; again and again' and *continuously* as 'without interruption': *This lost energy must be continuously supplied by the engines*—C. E. Dole, 1971 / *He said that the business of the court . . . was being continually held up by irrelevancies*—J. B. Morton, 1974 / *The black coat had lost its warmth and he shivered continually*—J. M. Coetzee, 1983 / *Clinical governance requires that the quality of medical care be continuously monitored*—*Bath Chronicle*, 2001. In the following example, *continuously* seems to be wrongly used for *continually*: *The Chinese officials also continuously stated that they could put a stop to inflation at any time*—P. Lowe, 1989.

continuance, continuation, continuity. 1 *Continuance* (14c) is much less common than *continuation* (also 14c). It is used when the context requires the meaning 'a state of continuing in existence or operation' (i.e. a fact) rather than 'the act or an instance of continuing' (i.e. a process), which calls for *continuation*. Examples: *The step-up in the air war might even jeopardize the continuation of the talks themselves*—*Newsweek*, 1972 / *Tiering [of dresses] is a continuation of the peasant theme that has been with us for what seems like a long, long time*—*Detroit Free Press*, 1978 / *Confusion has arisen about their desperate continuance of the struggle which was manifestly lost*—Antonia Fraser, 1988 / *The continuance of hunting is the bastion for the defence of every other legitimate country sport*—*Bristol Evening Post*, 2003.

2 *Continuity* means 'the state of being continuous' or (more concretely) 'an unbroken succession (of a set of events)': *Each shipment of wood parts will have a continuity of quality*—*House and Garden*, 1972 / *The Homewood is the only substantial prewar modernist house with continuity of occupation and contents*—*Guardian*, 2003. It has a special meaning

in the cinema and broadcasting, denoting the process whereby separate shots or recordings are linked together to form a continuous sequence with consistent details.

continue should not be followed by *on* (adverb), although this is sometimes found in informal writing: *I continued on down the street*—A. Bergman, 1975. Use either *continue* (without *on*) or a verb of motion (such as *go, move*, etc.) with *on*. This use of the adverb should be distinguished from the preposition *on*, which has a linking role and is quite acceptable: *I fear that, if we continue on our present path, we are going to fail*—*Modern Age*, 2003.

continuous, continuously *see* CONTINUAL, CONTINUOUS.

continuous tenses are tenses (or more strictly, aspects of tense) of the types *I am staying, they were going*, etc., as contrasted with the simple tenses *I stay, they went*, etc. They are also known as *progressive tenses*.

contract is pronounced with the stress on the first syllable as a noun and on the second syllable as a verb, except that in the phrasal verb *contract in* (or *out*) the stress is more variable.

contractable, contractible *see* -ABLE, -IBLE.

contractions *see* ABBREVIATIONS 2.

contractual is the correct adjective form to refer to contracts, as in *contractual obligations*. *Contractural*, which is sometimes mistakenly used (on the analogy of *procedural, structural*, etc.), is a medical term, relating to persistent contractions.

contralto has a plural *contraltos*, not (as in Italian) *contralti*.

contrary. 1 The position of the main stress has fluctuated over the centuries, and the *OED* notes that poets from Chaucer to Spenser and Shakespeare placed it on both the first and the second syllable according to need. In current English, the stress is now placed on the first syllable for the adjective and the noun, except in the meaning 'perverse, obstinately self-willed', in which the stress is on the second syllable, probably under the influence of the nursery rhyme beginning *Mary, Mary, quite contrary*.

2 The phrase *on the contrary* is properly used only in a statement intensifying a denial of what has just been stated or implied: *Experience in beekeeping is not necessary—on the contrary a beginner's input can be extremely useful—Gloucester Citizen*, 1999. *On the other hand* denotes a differing (not necessarily opposite) point of view, and is often paired with *on the one hand*.

3 The phrase *to the contrary* is used in AmE in the meaning of *on the contrary* (see 2), but in BrE is used only as a mid-sentence or end-of-sentence adverbial as in *There is plenty of evidence to the contrary*.

contrast. 1 *Contrast* is pronounced with stress on the first syllable as a noun and on the second syllable as a verb.

2 In current use, the verb is normally constructed with *with* or *and*, and is used transitively and intransitively: *Data is sometimes contrasted with information, which is said to result from the processing of data—J.* Chandor, 1970 / *Some anthropologists have sought to contrast the 'guilt cultures' of Western Europe with 'shame cultures'—A.* Giddens, 1977. *Last night's crisis at the BBC contrasted with the sense of heartfelt relief inside No 10—Guardian Unlimited*, 2004 [*OEC*].

3 The noun can be followed by *to, with*, or *between*, and is also used in the fixed expressions *by contrast* and *in*

contrast (*to* or *with*): *Gloria would have been able to detect few noteworthy points of contrast between sexual arousal and rabies—Martin Amis*, 1973 / *In contrast, the heaviest elements of the same groups . . . are metallic or semimetallic—D. M. Adams*, 1974 / *Marx, by contrast, has a single-cause theory: all the evils of society arise from private property—P.* Johnson, 1977 / *Expenditure on the justice system presents a stark contrast with the swingeing cutbacks of other areas in the public sector—M.* Brake, 1992 / *In contrast to alcohol, smoking is more likely to be toxic in any dose—Daily Mail*, 2007.

contribute. The standard pronunciation is with the main stress on the second syllable, although (as with *distribute*) pronunciation with stress on the first syllable is increasingly heard.

control freak is a convenient and colourful informal derogatory term for a person who is obsessive about exercising control over others (*Her father . . . was a twisted control freak and a brutal thug—Daily Mail*, 2007). Like many such uses it becomes difficult to avoid using it, but less informal alternatives for more formal contexts include *authoritarian* (adjective and noun), *disciplinarian*, and (in a more extreme sense) *martinet*.

controversy. The stress is always placed on the first syllable in AmE and normally in BrE too, although a variant with stress on the second syllable is becoming increasingly common, despite the strictures of purists. Early stress on words of more than three syllables is unusual in English (*excellency, matrimony*, and *presidency* are others), and so the shift is not surprising. The argument sometimes heard that a link vowel should not be stressed is confounded by words such as *archaeology* and *helicopter*.

conundrum is a 16c word of unknown origin, perhaps a facetious invention. It has a plural *conundrums*.

converse is pronounced with stress on the first syllable as an adjective and noun (= the opposite), and on the second syllable as a verb (= to have a conversation).

convert is pronounced with stress on the first syllable as a noun and on the second syllable as a verb.

convertible is spelt *-ible*, not *-able*. See -ABLE, -IBLE.

convex *see* CONCAVE.

convict is pronounced with stress on the first syllable as a noun and on the second syllable as a verb.

convince. The use followed by a *to*-infinitive, on the analogy of *persuade, induce, encourage,* and other words, is recorded from the 1950s and is still disapproved of by many, although it is now common, especially informally: *He wants to convince me to become his disciple*—B. Aldiss, 1993.

cookie, not *cooky*, is the established spelling in its various meanings: in AmE 'a biscuit' and (slang) a person (as in *tough cookie*), in Scottish 'a plain bun'. Since the 1980s *cookie* has become more familiar in all forms of English as a computing term for a set of data sent by the server of an Internet website to a user's browser to identify and track the user's future access to a that website.

cool, a wide-ranging term of approval that defies conventional definition but means roughly 'fashionably impressive and acceptable' or simply 'okay, fine', is one of the best known words that was once part of youth slang: *He had seen Devon in the street and hid from him, unable to smile in his face and say that everything was cool*—G. Joseph, 2001. Flourishing in the 1950s, its use declined after the following decade, and then achieved a revival at the end of the 20c. It is now used by people of any age, in conversation or texting, especially in the meaning 'OK, fine', but should be avoided in any kind of more formal writing. As applied to music (especially jazz) *cool* denotes a style that is restrained and relaxed. Then in the 1990s *Cool Britannia* (a play on 'Rule Britannia' and derived from the title of a 1967 song) came to symbolize Britain perceived as a stylish and fashionable place and an international centre of contemporary art, popular music, film, and fashion.

coomb is the usual form (rather than *combe*) in Britain for a valley or hollow on the side of a hill or a short valley running up from the coast. In place-names, however, *-combe* is more usual, as in *Ilfracombe, Winchcombe,* etc.

cooperate is now the preferred spelling, without a hyphen and without a diaeresis on the second *o*. See CO-.

cope. The traditional construction followed by *with* has been in common use since the 16c: *Like many religious professionals, I cope with festivals, but I can't really enjoy them*—L. Blue, 1985. Absolute uses without *with* have been recorded since the 1930s: *It wasn't as if Marcia was an invalid or unable to cope, even if she was a bit eccentric*—Barbara Pym, 1977.

copula in grammar is a verb, such as *be, become, feel, get,* etc., that links the subject and complement of a sentence, as in *He **is** a pilot / She **felt** annoyed / They **look** hungry / Will it **turn** cold?* Such a verb is also called a *copular verb*.

cord *see* CHORD.

co-respondent, meaning 'a person named in a divorce case', should be distinguished from *correspondent*. See CO-.

corn means 'wheat or oats' in BrE, and 'maize' in AmE.

corporal, corporeal. Both words are now largely restricted to particular uses. *Corporal* means 'relating to the human body' and is found chiefly in the expression *corporal punishment* (beating, spanking, etc., now effectively banned in schools in the European Union). In other uses, *bodily* or *personal* is more usual. *Corporeal* means 'bodily, physical, material, as distinct from spiritual': *Apart ...from his existence as a corporeal omnipotent first cause, all else about God was a matter of faith*—R. S. Woodhouse, 1988.

Avoid writing *corporeal punishment* by mistake for *corporal punishment*.

corps, corpse. *Corps*, meaning 'body of people', is pronounced like *core* in the singular and like *cores* in the plural. It should be distinguished from *corpse*, meaning 'dead body', which is pronounced kawps.

corpus, meaning 'a collection of writings', has a plural *corpora*, although *corpuses* is increasingly found. In the domain of language and linguistics it is used to refer to a collection of texts of all kinds, written and spoken, which are read and analysed by a computer program designed to produce statistics and sort the material into accessible forms, usually as a screen concordance of consecutive lines with the word being studied (the *keyword*) in the centre of each line. The best known corpora in current use are the British National Corpus, the Cobuild Corpus (Collins-Birmingham University International Language Database), now called the Bank of English, the Survey of English Usage (at University College London), and the Oxford English Corpus on which the present work extensively draws.

corpus delicti means literally 'the body of a crime', and refers to all the facts and circumstances that together constitute a breach of the law. In lay use, it means the concrete evidence of a crime, especially the body of a murdered person. *'Well, where is the corpus delicti, old chap?' The ritual began*—W. J. Burley, 1991.

This phrase is often misspelt as *corpus delecti*, or less commonly as *corpus dilecti*, which respectively would translate from Latin as 'the body of the chosen [male] one' and 'the body of the loved [male] one'.

corrector, meaning 'a person who points out faults', is spelt *-or*, not *-er*.

correlative is each of a pair of words used to link corresponding parts of a sentence, e.g. *both...and..., either... or..., neither...nor....* Correlatives that involve a subordinate clause include *hardly...when...* and *if...then....*

correspond. If one thing is similar or analogous to another, or related closely to it, it is said to correspond *to* it: *Gandhi's concept of Religion corresponds to his concept of Truth*—G. Richards, 1991. If one thing is in harmony or agreement with another, it is said to correspond *with* or *to* it: *There were two bedrooms to correspond with the rooms downstairs*—D. H. Lawrence, 1921 / *The broadcasting service should be conducted by a public corporation...and its status and duties should correspond with those of a public service*—R. Negrine, 1992. If two people exchange letters, they are said to correspond *with* one another: *Though it is not known how the two friends met, they were corresponding with each other by 1945*—F. Spalding, 1991. In all these meanings, *correspond* can also be used absolutely, without *to* or *with*: *My broth-er Michael . . . and I corresponded about socialism and religion*—Tony Benn, 1979. It is also common as a participial adjective *corresponding*: *For the corre-sponding period in the previous year 818 men had been accommodated, plus 22 women and one child*—B. Cashman, 1988.

corrigendum, meaning 'something that should be corrected', is normally used in its plural form *corrigenda*.

corrupter, meaning 'a person or thing that corrupts', is spelt *-er*, but *corruptor* is a common variant in AmE.

corset, meaning 'a closely-fitting undergarment worn by women', has the derivative forms *corseted* (one *t*).

cortège, meaning 'a funeral proces-sion', is printed in roman type with a grave accent on the *e*. It is pronounced kaw-**tayzh**.

cortex, meaning 'the outer part of a bodily organ' (as in *cerebral cortex*, re-ferring to the brain), has the plural form *cortices*.

coruscate, excoriate. Confusion of these two somewhat literary words—caused by the coincidence of the syllable *-cor-* and the ending *-ate*—is a common malapropism. To *coruscate* (from Latin *coruscare*) is to glitter or give off flashes of light, and it can be used figuratively: *a coruscating blend of the searingly honest . . . and the completely deluded.* However, to *excoriate* someone is to criticize them harshly, literally 'to remove their skin', the physical meaning of the word, derived from Latin *corium* 'skin'. A typical misuse follows: ⊠ *The government's response to the tax credits fiasco, which will cost taxpayers unfore-seen amounts, is still inadequate, a cor-uscating report from MPs warns*—*Scotsman*, 2007. Here, the word

intended is *excoriating*, but it might have been better to avoid the minefield alto-gether and use a more straightforward but equally satisfactory word such as *withering* or *blistering*. The same goes for *coruscating* in its correct sense: less troublesome alternatives include *glitter-ing, glowing, shimmering, dazzling*, and *gleaming*, and people are more likely to know what these mean.

'cos is a reduced form of *because*, first recorded in 1828 and only used to rep-resent very casual speech: *'They'll be good if I tell them, Mister.' 'Then why aren't they?' ''Cos I tell 'em to be bad.'*—Evelyn Waugh, 1942 / *They wouldn't take me 'cos I'd had a touch of TB*—M. Butterworth, 1974. The initial apostro-phe is often omitted in the most informal contexts, but it is better to keep it: *She wept cos she knew she'd never feel that way again*—weblog, AmE 2002 [*OEC*].

cosmonaut *see* ASTRONAUT.

cosset, meaning 'to pamper', has inflected forms *cosseted, cosseting*.

cosy, as an adjective meaning 'com-fortable' and a noun meaning 'a cover for a teapot', is spelt *cosy* in BrE and in other varieties except AmE, which pre-fers *cozy*. To *cosy up to* someone mean-ing 'to ingratiate oneself (with)', is originally AmE, and is informal.

cot. There are two words with this spelling. The word meaning 'a small bed for a child' is Anglo-Indian; *cot death* is a term dating from the 1970s for the unexplained death of a baby while asleep (the AmE form is usually *crib death*). The (mainly literary) word meaning 'a small shelter; a cottage' is Old English, and is used in combinations such as *sheep-cot*.

cote, pronounced like *coat*, is another form of the Old English word *cot* given in the preceding entry. It is most commonly used in *dovecote*, meaning 'a shelter for doves', and also occurs occasionally in other forms such as *sheep-cote* and *swine-cote* (these being hyphenated).

couch, meaning 'an upholstered piece of furniture' differs from a *sofa* in having only one raised end and in being designed for lying on as well as sitting on. It also has special (and often evocative) uses as in *psychiatrist's couch*, on which the recumbent patient tells all. It is also a poetic word for a bed, but in ordinary use is essentially different from a bed: *I've made a bed up for you on the couch*—Martin Amis, 1973.

couch, a type of grass, is pronounced either like the item of furniture, or as kooch.

could *modal auxiliary*. **1** *See* CAN. It functions as (1) the past tense of *can*, as in *We could see for miles*, (2) as a conditional equivalent to *would be able to*, as in *I could take you in the car if you like*, and (3) as a more tentative form of *can* in questions seeking permission: *Could I see you tomorrow?* The negative form is *could not*.

2 could of. This is an illiterate alteration of *could've* = could have, and occurs in the writing of children and some adults.

council, counsel. 1 These are now distinct words and are only distantly related. A *council* is an administrative body or meeting, and its members are *councillors*. *Counsel* is advice given formally and often professionally; *counsel* or *a counsel* is a barrister or other legal adviser. A *counsellor* is someone who gives professional advice, especially on personal and social matters; in AmE *counselor* is also a courtroom lawyer.

2 Note that in Britain a member of the *Privy Council*, the body of advisers appointed by the Queen, is a *Privy Counsellor*.

3 Only *counsel* can be used as a verb, meaning 'to give advice to'; it has inflected forms *counselled*, *counselling*.

countable nouns, also called *count nouns*, are nouns that form plurals, e.g. *ship, crisis, fellow-traveller, kindness* (= a kind act). They differ from *uncountable* (or *non-count* or *uncount*) nouns, which do not form plurals, e.g. *adolescence, heating, richness, warfare*; and from *mass* nouns, which form plurals only in the sense of 'a type of...' or 'a quantity of...', e.g. *bread, medicine, wine*. Some words are countable in one meaning and uncountable in another, e.g. *ice, iron, paper*.

counterpart means 'the equivalent of a person or thing in another place or system'. It can refer to many aspects of similarity but principally has to do with function and behaviour, and is typically preceded by a possessive word: *Southern schools are now more integrated than their northern counterparts*—Times, 1974 / *With the same power at his elbow as his Continental counterpart the British car assembly worker produces only half as much output per shift*—M. Edwardes, 1983.

counterproductive is familiar enough now to be spelt as one word. It is a modern word (first recorded in 1959) which has mushroomed in use to describe any action or series of actions having the opposite of the desired effect: *Security measures will be counterproductive if they provoke resentment*—Independent, 2006.

count nouns *see* COUNTABLE NOUNS.

countrified, countrify, meaning 'rural' and 'to make rural', should be spelt this way, not *countryfied, countryfy*.

coup, meaning 'a sudden and successful move', or 'an illegal seizure of power' (in full *coup d'état*), is pronounced koo. The plural is *coups*, pronounced kooz.

couple. 1 *Couple*, as in '*a couple of* . . . ', needs to be used and understood with care, as it retains its original meaning of 'two' alongside its more informal meaning 'a few'. *A couple of friends* will usually mean two friends, no more or less, whereas *a couple of hours* may mean two hours or three hours or an indeterminate period of time.

2 *Couple* is a singular noun that can be used with a singular or plural verb. A plural construction is usual when *couple* means 'two married people or partners' or when it is followed by *of* and a plural noun (*see* COLLECTIVE NOUN): *Palimony, the term for sharing money after an unmarried couple have split up*—*Time*, 1980 / *There are a couple of expressions you should listen out for when visiting this side of the world*—*Aberdeen Evening Express*, 2005.

3 *Couple* has developed attributive uses in the constructions (1) *a couple more* (+ plural noun): '*How's your work?' 'Nearly done. A couple more days.'*—Maurice Gee, NewZE 1992, and (2) more controversially, and principally in AmE, *couple* (+ plural noun): *In the next couple months we got to know each other like real buddies*—Garrison Keillor, 1989. This last use sounds decidedly alien to British ears, at least for now.

coupon should be pronounced **koo**-pon, not with a quasi-French nasalized second syllable.

course *see* OF COURSE.

courteous, courtesy are pronounced with initial **kert-**.

courtesan is pronounced kor-ti-**zan**, with stress on the last syllable.

courtesy is pronounced **ker**-tuhsi. It is widely used attributively, qualifying nouns describing services that are (if only supposedly) provided as a courtesy to the clients or would-be clients of an organization, e.g. a *courtesy car* is one provided in place of a customer's existing car when this is unavailable for some reason. A *courtesy visit* is one made unbidden and—most notoriously of all—a *courtesy* (*telephone*) *call* is an unsolicited sales or marketing call that is at best only nominally courteous. This usage is a typical instance of euphemistic labelling by the world of advertising and marketing of activities that would be more immediately rejected if they were given names that were more appropriate.

courtier is pronounced with initial **kort-**.

court martial is spelt as two words as a noun, and the recommended plural is *courts martial*, though *court martials* is also used. As a verb it is spelt with a hyphen, and it has inflected forms *court-martialled*, *court-martialling*, in BrE, and *court-martialed*, *court-martialing* in AmE.

covert, meaning 'secret, disguised', is pronounced like *cover*, although the American English pronunciation as in *over* is gaining ground in Britain and elsewhere.

cozy *see* COSY.

crabbed, meaning 'irritable' or 'hard to decipher', should be pronounced as two syllables.

craft *verb* has been revived as a verb in the language of advertising (*bungalows of locally crafted brick and tile*) and in literary and other criticism (*He had by then perfected the swagger of the Identikit newspaper tycoon and had crafted his performance beautifully*—*Independent on Sunday*, 2005).

crape, crêpe. *Crape* is used for a band of black silk or ornamental silk worn as a sign of mourning, and *crêpe*, with an accent, but in roman type, is used for other gauze-like fabrics having a wrinkled surface and in *crêpe paper* (crinkled paper used in making decorations).

crash. Since the 1950s, *crash* has been used attributively (before a noun) to denote something such as a course or programme that is done or undertaken urgently or quickly, e.g. *a crash course in Russian* or *a crash diet*. In this use, *crash* seems to be unaffected by possible associations of collision and violence (or indeed of computer failure), though *a crash course in driving skills* might come dangerously close to suggesting them.

crayfish, a 16c alteration of an earlier word *crevis* (or *crevisse*), is the usual word in Britain for a small lobster-like freshwater crustacean. Americans call them *crawfish*, and Australians and New Zealanders often abbreviate the word to *cray* (as in *cray-fishing* and *cray-pot*).

cred *see* CREDENCE, CREDIT, CREDIBILITY 4.

credence, credit, credibility. 1 In general use, *credence* means 'belief, trustful acceptance', and is used mainly in the expression *to give* (or *lend*) *credence to*, which means 'believe, trust': *The radicality of these changes . . . had lent credence to the set of beliefs described above*—*Dædalus*, 1979.

2 The phrase *to give credit to* once meant much the same as *to give credence to*, i.e. 'to believe', but in current use it is more likely to be used in the form *to give a person credit (for* something), meaning to ascribe some good quality to them: (also used with a layer of irony): *You chaps do tend to give the rest of us credit for perceptions about your work that we don't . . . always have*—John Wain, 1953 / *They search for ages for the wrong word which, to give them credit, they eventually find*—East Anglian, 1993.

3 *Credibility* shares some of the meaning of both *credence* and *credit* in

that belief lies at the heart of its meaning, but it is used rather to mean 'the condition of being credible or believable': *The empirical basis of theory is fundamental to its reliability and its validity and, in the end, its credibility*—P. H. Mann, 1985. This meaning, now largely confined to special domains such as religion and philosophy, has been overshadowed by an extended meaning 'reputation, status': *It was clear to the [American] President that his credibility was on the line with the leaders in Hanoi*—*Guardian*, 1970 / *By then, however, the fatal damage to the Prime Minister's credibility will have been done*—*Today*, 1992. Such credibility is regularly *enhanced, established, gained, lost, maintained*, and so on.

The overlap between the older and the newer meaning can be seen in uses such as the following: *A major French archaeological discovery that was declared fraudulent by many prehistorians in the 1920's has now regained credibility as a result of dating studies conducted at three independent laboratories*—*Scientific American*, 1975.

4 Two special uses of *credibility* that have arisen recently are *credibility gap*, meaning 'an apparent difference between what is said and what is true' (*Official American statements are no longer taken on trust. . . . The phenomenon . . . is called the 'credibility gap'*— *Guardian*, 1966) and, chiefly in BrE, *street credibility* (often reduced informally to *street cred*), meaning 'acceptability among fashionable young urban people' (*Motor enthusiast David George has seen his Ford Granada gain street credibility with its very own TV career*— *Bolton Evening News*, 2005).

credible, creditable, credulous. *Credible* means 'able to be believed', when referring to people or statements: *I stand on the balcony, apparently musing on this very credible story, but really wondering how soon we can step back* inside—R. James, 1989 / *Was it credible that Elise should have a car accident that involved no other vehicle, no jay-walking pedestrian, no treacherous roads?*—K. Kingston, 1993. It also has an extended meaning 'convincing, having substance', comparable to that of *credibility*: *He fought a remarkable re-election campaign . . . , recovering his popularity not least through his total control of the media, as well as the lack of a credible challenger*—J. Palmowski, 2003. *Creditable* means 'bringing credit; deserving praise': *The company produced a creditable performance, particularly when compared with the results of many of its competitors*—*Daily Telegraph*, 1992. *Credulous* means 'too ready to believe, gullible': *It could be argued that the very incomprehensibility of the modern world has made us even more credulous*—J. Empson, 1989.

crêpe *see* CRAPE.

crescendo. 1 A *crescendo*, which in Italian means 'growing' (from *crescere* 'to grow'), is originally a musical term for a gradual increase in loudness or force, or a passage played in this way. From this developed an extended meaning referring to other cumulative increases in force or effect: *His second-in-command at the Embassy . . . was unrattled by the crescendo of disaster to the allied cause*—J. Colville, 1976. In the 1920s, and apparently first in AmE, it developed further to mean the result rather than the process of increasing, and has been widely used as a synonym for *peak* or *climax*, notably in phrases such as *reach* (or *rise to) a crescendo*: *In the past week, as the date approached for the annual review of her detention order, international pressure reached a crescendo*—*Independent*, 2007. This newer use is disputed, but is likely to prevail because it is the more commonly required meaning. Alternatives available include:

apogee, climax, culmination, peak, pinnacle, and *summit*.

2 The plural is *crescendos. Crescendo* is occasionally used as a verb meaning 'to increase in loudness or intensity', and has inflected forms *crescendoes, crescendoed, crescendoing.*

cretin is now pronounced **kret**-in in BrE, but was previously pronounced **kree**-tin, which is the standard pronunciation in AmE. It was originally used to mean (in current terminology) 'a person who is deformed and mentally retarded as the result of a thyroid deficiency' and is etymologically related to the word *Christian*. Its dominant meaning in general use now (first recorded in the 1930s) is 'a fool, one who behaves stupidly'. This use is widely regarded as offensive.

crevasse, crevice are both derived from a Latin root *crepare* meaning 'to break with a crash'. A *crevasse* is a deep open crack or fissure in a glacier; in AmE it is also used to mean a breach in a river embankment. A *crevice* is a narrow cleft or opening, usually one in the surface of anything solid such as rock or a building.

crick, rick. Both words are commonly used of strains or sprains of the neck, back, joints, etc. *Crick* appeared earlier (15c as a noun, though not until 19c as a verb); *rick* is apparently of dialect origin and is first recorded as a verb in about 1800 and as a noun in the mid-19c. A variant form *wrick* has now fallen out of use.

cringe, meaning 'to shrink back in fear', has inflected forms *cringed, cringing.*

cripple, meaning 'a person who is permanently lame' is now regarded as offensive. Use *disabled person* instead.

crisis. 1 The plural is *crises,* pronounced **kriy**-seez, not ✘ *crisises.*

2 The word is derived via Latin from a Greek root meaning 'turning point', and should strictly refer to a moment rather than a continuing process, so that uses such as *a prolonged crisis* are strictly speaking self-contradictory. However, a word as useful as *crisis* will not allow itself to be strait-jacketed in this way, and many examples of the disputed use will be found: *The continuing and ever occurring crisis in the inner-cities, where large numbers of people are trapped in a cycle of poverty—Black Panther*, 1973 / *The fact that today we are in deep and continuing crisis is evident from other sources than the Morning Star—Morning Star*, 2002. Some element of change should be present in the meaning (*The death of his father . . . triggers off a crisis for him too, producing a temporary breakdown, dismissal from his job, separation from his wife, the lot—Times*, 1970); and the word should not be used as an enfeebled synonym of words such as *difficulty, dilemma, problem*, and *quandary* (*Scott Lithgow . . . were desperate for staff throughout the crisis—Economist*, 1975 / *To make matters worse a crisis in the Council came to a head—*W. Green, 1988 / *Down came the rain again. Faced with the crisis of surrendering the proudest record in rugby, Munster dug deep again—Observer*, 2007).
3 *Crisis* is often used with a defining word, either an adjective or an attributive noun as in *economic crisis, energy crisis, financial crisis, food crisis, hostage crisis, identity crisis, midlife crisis, refugee crisis*, etc. It has also come to be used with the redundant addition of *situation*, a use that should be avoided: ⊠ *When a crisis situation with a pupil arises, exclusion follows too rapidly—Guardian*, 2003.

criterion, meaning 'a principle or standard by which something is judged', has a plural *criteria*. This plural form is often taken to be singular, a use that is not standard: *A report . . . will tell councillors that the bidding criteria has significantly changed since the previous bid—Rochdale Observer*, 2002. The following examples illustrate correct uses of the singular and plural: *The Ottoman Empire . . . was a multi-national state, . . . the criterion of differentiation among its subjects was religion and not nationality—*A. Mango, 1971 / *Some possible criteria for this area of work are listed below—*J. Thorpe, 1989 / *Thus stated, Hume's criterion is quite vague—*J. Losee, 2001. In order to render *criteria* effectively singular, a collective such as *set* can be used: *However, we may wish to use a different set of criteria—*A. Lawton et al., 1991 / *The study's findings would be measured against a group of criteria—Lloyd's List*, 1994.

criticism in everyday use means 'finding fault', although strictly *criticism* can be favourable as well as unfavourable. The sense is more neutral in terms such as *literary criticism* and *textual criticism*.

critique is pronounced with stress on the second syllable, and means 'a critical essay or analysis'. Fowler (1926) said of the noun that 'there is some hope of it dying out', and offered the alternatives *review, criticism*, and *notice*. Nonetheless, *critique* remains in use, albeit often in contexts that justify Fowler's implied accusation of pretentiousness: *This melange of stroboscopic graphics, jingles and one-liner critiques—Art Line*, 1989 / *Drawing on earlier feminist critiques of male-centred approaches to research . . . —Times Higher Education Supplement*, 2007.

Some critics object to *critique* as a verb on the grounds that it is a modern extension of a noun use, but the verb's antiquity invalidates this argument. As with the noun, it seems legitimate to use the word in contexts suggesting detailed analysis has happened, such as: *Instead time should be spent critiquing the research design and the methodology section before accepting the research results—OEC, 2001.*

Criticism is more valid, however, when the verb is used to mean more generally 'to judge critically (an action, person, etc.), not necessarily in writing': *By the end of the Keating era, no-one could critique Aboriginal policy without being labelled racist—OEC, 2004 / And yes, I like to critique the Times coverage of foreign affairs from time to time—OEC, 2003.*

crochet, meaning a type of handicraft, is pronounced **kroh**-shay as a noun and a verb. The verb has inflected forms *crocheted, crocheting,* with the *t* remaining silent in both.

crocus, the flower, has plural forms *crocuses* (several flowers) and *crocus* (used collectively). *Croci* is limited to technical contexts.

crotch, crutch. It's as well not to confuse these two words. *Crotch* is the part of the human body between the legs at their junction with the torso; a *crutch* (although it is occasionally used as a variant of *crotch*) is a support (both physical, typically a long stick used to support the body, and figurative, e.g. *it has been said by some that God is just a crutch*).

crow *verb*, meaning 'to make the sound of a cock' and 'to boast', has past forms *crowed* (more usual) and *crew* (only in the first meaning, often in allusion to the cock in the New Testament account of Christ's betrayal). The past participle is always *crowed.*

crown. When *the Crown* is used to mean 'the office of the monarch', it should be treated as grammatically neuter and not as the gender of the king

or queen: *The Crown can only act on the advice of its* [not *her* or *his*] *Ministers.*

crucial. 1 *Crucial* means 'decisive, critical', and is often used as a more effective and more expressive alternative for *important* or *significant: There are four crucial stages in cheesemaking—* J. G. Davis, 1976 / *I understand that you must edit letters, but the crucial point on avoiding sexist language was omitted—Today's Horse,* 1991.

2 The same thing has happened to the adverb *crucially,* which is sometimes used as a synonym of 'importantly', and even of 'very' or 'extremely': *At this juncture, two crucially fundamental questions now emerge—Guardian,* 1989 / *Crucially, he promised to undertake an immediate and fundamental review of the tax—Parliamentary Affairs,* 1991.

cruel has the forms *crueller, cruellest* in BrE and *crueler, cruelest* in AmE.

crumby, crummy. When the reference is to actual crumbs, as in a *crumby loaf* or a *crumby tablecloth,* use *crumby.* When the meaning is 'dirty, squalid; inferior, worthless', use *crummy.*

-ction *see* -XION.

cubic, cubical. *Cubical* means only 'shaped like a cube' (*a case that's roughly cubical in shape*) whereas *cubic* has other meanings as well, as in *cubic equation, cubic measure, cubic metre,* etc., and also the meaning 'cube-shaped' in technical applications such as *cubic alum.*

cui bono? This Latin phrase, printed in italics, literally means 'to whom (is it) a benefit?', i.e. in English 'who stands to gain (from an act or circumstance)?', with the implication that this person is responsible for it. As Fowler (1926) pointed out, it does not mean 'to what purpose?' or 'what is the good?'.

cul-de-sac is pronounced **kul**-duh-sak and should be printed in roman type.

cullender *see* COLANDER.

cult. 1 In the meaning 'a particular form or system of religious worship', especially when referring to ritual and ceremony, *cult* dates from the 17c. In the 19c, archaeologists applied the term to primitive practices which they did not think worthy of the name *religion*; hence *cult* acquired unfavourable connotations and is objected to by many whose activities are now described by it.

2 *Cult* has also developed extended meanings: (1) 'a devotion or homage to a person or thing', as in *the cult of beauty* and *the Wordsworth cult*, (2) in the 20c, 'a popular fashion followed by a specific section of society': *The eastern cult for junk food may be having a remarkable effect on the health and appearance of Japan's youngsters*—*Times*, 1986. In a further extension, *cult* is commonly used attributively (before a noun) to denote something that has a special following, as in *cult classic, cult figure, cult film, cult status*, etc.

cultivable, cultivatable are both used in the meaning 'capable of being cultivated'; the first is more comfortable and was preferred by Fowler (1926). Neither word is particularly common in everyday usage, being recorded with a combined total of about 240 in the *OEC*, but within this tiny statistic *cultivable* leads by about six to one.

cultivated, cultured are both used to mean 'having refined tastes and manners and a good education', but they part company in other meanings. *Cultivated* distinguishes a crop raised in a garden from one growing wild; and *cultured* is used of pearls (also called *culture pearls*) formed under controlled conditions.

culture. 1 Here is a word that had mixed fortunes in the 20c, and means all things to all people. It is one of the 1,000 most commonly used English words, and there are well over 300,000 examples of it (including the plural form and compounds such as *culture-bound*) in the current Oxford English Corpus in diverse meanings generally related to the *OED*'s definition 'the civilization, customs, artistic achievements, etc., of a people, especially at a certain stage of its development or history'. In many of these examples *culture* is used generically and not in relation to any particular people or time: *For him spiritual and political ideas were becoming more and more inseparable in his concern with 'culture' as a whole*—R. Crawford, 1990. In others it has very specific reference, and is often preceded by a defining adjective or noun: *Unofficial sources report that the two organisations aimed to research and develop Mongol culture*—*Amnesty*, 1992.

2 The word has also developed more limited reference within a broader 'culture', as in *consumer culture, corporate culture, drugs culture, political culture, pop culture, yob culture, youth culture*, etc.: *The miners' strike revealed the range of new movements and organisations which have been arenas . . . for the development of working-class culture and working-class consciousness*—T. Lovett, 1988 / *It was, nonetheless, a film that tried to solicit an understanding of the emerging drug culture*—J. Parker, 1991 / *Pop music and its link with youth culture should be an important field of study in media education*—*Action*, 1991.

3 Since as long ago as 1940, the previously mentioned meaning has been used in a more restricted way to refer to 'the philosophy, practices, and attitudes of an institution, business, or other organization' as in *corporate* or *organizational culture*: *Managers see their role as creating a culture in which the team can* make a sound contribution to agreed goals—*Management Accounting*, 1991. This meaning is now a standard part of the language, even though it has been something of a vogue word, and can at times be used rather vaguely.

4 Significant 20c combinations of the word include *culture shock*, meaning 'the feeling of disorientation experienced by a person suddenly subjected to an unfamiliar culture or way of life'; *culture clash*, meaning 'a failure of one culture to understand another with which it comes into contact'; and *culture vulture*, meaning 'a person eager to acquire culture'. They were joined in the 1990s by *culture jamming*, 'the subversion of advertising and other mass-media output (by parody, alteration, etc.) as a form of protest against consumerism, corporate culture, and the power of the media': *Beginning with spoof advertisements, culture-jamming has grown to encompass defacing billboards to alter their message and campaigns such as TV Turnoff Week and Buy Nothing Day—Times*, 2006.

cum. This Latin preposition meaning 'with', apart from its use in Latin loanphrases such as *cum grano salis* ('with a grain of salt'), has been used for several centuries in place-names such as *Horton-cum-Studley*. Its main use since the 19c has been as a combining word used to indicate a dual nature or function, as in *kitchen-cum-dining-room*. Hyphens are nowadays optional. Examples: *'Do you work there?' 'Yes, as a sort of administrator cum priest.'*—J. Higgins, 1985 / *Young designers get a pick-me-up from Vienna's coffee house cum design store—Metropolis* (magazine), 2003.

cumulative, accumulative are both used in the meaning 'formed or increasing by successive additions', although *cumulative* is now more usual (as in *cumulative arguments, effect, evidence,*

force, etc.). *Accumulative* is however still found (there are around 100 examples in the *OEC*), and by virtue of its form has stronger associations with the process of *accumulating*: *Explanations of whatever kind are not universal answers, merely part of a progressive and accumulative act of learning and knowing*—G. Watson, 1991.

cuneiform, meaning 'ancient wedge-shaped writing', is now normally pronounced as three syllables in BrE, i.e. **kyoo**-ni-fawm, and as four in AmE, i.e. kyoo-**nay**-i-fawm.

cupful. In the plural, care should be taken to distinguish *cupfuls* from *cups full*. A *cupful* is a measure, and so *three cupfuls* is a quantity regarded in terms of a cup; *three cups full* denotes the actual cups, as in *three cups full of water*.

cupola, meaning 'a rounded dome on a roof', is pronounced **kyoo**-puh-luh. The plural is *cupolas*.

curb, kerb. In BrE, *curb* is a noun meaning 'a check or restraint' and a verb meaning 'to restrain'. As a noun it also means 'a strap fastened to a bit on a horse', and 'a fender round a hearth'. In AmE, *curb* has these meanings and is also 'a stone edging to a pavement (*sidewalk*)', which in BrE is spelt *kerb*.

curio is a 19c familiar abbreviation of *curiosity*, and means 'a rare or unusual object or person'. The plural is *curios*.

curriculum, meaning 'a course of study', has a plural *curricula*. A *curriculum vitae* (abbreviated to *CV* or *c.v.*) is a brief account of a person's education and professional experience. The plural is *curricula vitae* (*curricula vitarum* is impossibly pedantic), although *CVs* gets round this awkwardness.

curtsy, meaning a woman's or girl's formal greeting, is spelt *curtsy* in preference to *curtsey*. Its plural is *curtsies* (in similar preference to *curtseys*), and as a verb it has inflected forms *curtsies, curtsied, curtsying*.

cute started out in the 18c as a shortened form of *acute* in the meaning 'quick-witted, clever'; for a while it was often written with an apostrophe, and will be found that way in Dickens. This meaning has died out in BrE but is still a feature of AmE. In AmE, beginning in the 1830s, a new informal meaning emerged, 'attractive, charming, pretty (often in a mannered or amusing way)'. It is now very common in AmE as a general term of approval rather similar to *nice*, and can refer to activities and practically anything else as well as people and things: *Yes, Lisa runs a little gym in the West Palm. We all go there to work out. Isn't that cute?*—P. Booth, 1986. In BrE, this use is often more self-conscious, and is generally limited to babies and other small things with quaintly attractive characteristics, or to sexual attractiveness and desirability.

cutting. The *cutting edge*, based on the notion of a tool doing effective work, is a modern idiom meaning 'the pioneering aspect of an enterprise'. It is derived from a figurative meaning that dates from the 1850s, and to be *at the cutting edge* is to belong to the forefront of progress or fashion: *No one of these people ... would ever have considered themselves an educational pioneer, but the work they did was always at the cutting-edge of program development*—W. M. Cruickshank, 1958 / *The original Korova, a cutting-edge bar and gig venue, is very different to glamorous, converted church Alma de Cuba*—Guardian, 2007.

cyber-. A by-product of the word *cybernetics* is the use of its first element *cyber-* in a wide range of computer terms: *cybercafe* (a cafe equipped with terminals to access the Internet), *cybercrime* (criminal activity conducted over the Internet, such as identity fraud), *cybersex* (sexual arousal from computer images), and, the most commonly used derivative of all, *cyberspace*, referring to the notional environment within which electronic communication via the Internet occurs.

cybernetics. The term was introduced in 1948 by Norbert Wiener, meaning 'the theory or study of communication and control in living organisms or machines'. The word was derived from the Greek word *kubernētēs* 'steersman'. It spread rapidly to refer to organisms treated as if they were machines, to observed similarities between neural activity and the electronic devices of modern communications, and so on.

Cyclops, a mythological one-eyed giant, is pronounced **siy**-klops, and its plural is *Cyclopes*, pronounced **siy**-kloh-peez.

Cymric, meaning Welsh, is pronounced **kim**-rik.

cynic, cynical. *Cynical* is the adjective form used in the meaning 'doubting human sincerity or integrity' and has developed a further meaning 'disregarding normal rules or standards', as in *a cynical foul, a cynical tackle*, etc. *Cynic* is used with direct reference to the Greek philosophers who bore this name.

cynosure, meaning 'a centre of attraction or admiration', is pronounced **sin**-uh-zyoo-uh or **siy**-uh-zyoo-uh. Its earlier meaning 'guiding star' related to its use as the name of a constellation, and the current meaning is immortalized by Milton's phrase *The Cynosure of neighbouring Eyes* in 'L'Allegro' (1632).

cypher *see* CIPHER.

czar *see* TSAR.

dado, meaning the lower part of the wall of a room, or the plinth of a column, has the plural *dados*.

dais, meaning 'a low platform', is pronounced as two syllables, **day**-is.

dampen was once regarded as an Americanism, but is now established as a variant of *damp* (verb) in BrE, especially in figurative uses: *Everyone ignored the snow that had failed to dampen the impact of John F. Kennedy's brilliant oratory*—Jeffrey Archer, 1979 / *In that way, she argued, speculation about the marriage would be dampened rather than intensified*—Today, 1992 / (literal) *Most weights of watercolour paper are dampened and stretched before painting*—The Artist, 1993.

dangling participles *see* PARTICIPLES 3.

dare *verb*. **1** *Dare* is an example of a so-called semi-modal auxiliary verb, because, like the modal verbs *can, may, should*, etc., it is used in certain special ways, but unlike these fully modal verbs it can also behave like an ordinary verb. Its special characteristics are (1) use with a so-called 'bare' infinitive without *to* (*I'm not sure that I dare answer*), (2) use in the negative and in questions without *do* (*I dare not answer / Dare I answer?*), although in practice interrogative forms are normally confined to *how dare you, he, they*, etc., as discussed in 6 below, (3) a third person singular form *dare* without addition of *s* (*He says he dare not*

answer). Note that in all these uses *dare* is an auxiliary verb followed by an infinitive without *to*.

2 *Dare* is also used as an ordinary verb, with or without a following *to*-infinitive, forming negatives and questions with *do*, and having a third person singular form *dares*: *They would not dare to come / Do you dare to contradict me? / I don't dare to answer / He dares to answer / Tell me if you dare.* In practice, not all these options are used, and some constructions sound more natural than others. For example, *I don't dare to answer* is perfectly grammatical, but *I dare not answer* is more idiomatic, at least in everyday English. In the present tense, *dare* behaves as a modal verb much more often than as an ordinary verb.

3 As a modal verb, *dare* is sometimes used in the past without inflection. Though formerly condemned (by the *OED* among others) as 'careless', the practice is common in writing as well as speech: *'Yes, yes,' she stuttered, then 'thank you', as an afterthought. She dare not look at his face*—M. Duckworth, 1960.

4 It is also noticeable that *dare* occurs more frequently in negative constructions and in questions, or preceded by *if*. As we have seen, the negative form can be *dare not* or *do* (etc.) *not dare*; and *dare not* is contracted to *daren't* in informal use (*I daren't answer*). The past *dared not* is rarely if ever contracted to *darednt*.

5 Further examples follow of *dare* used as a modal verb and as an auxiliary verb: (modal) *He hates only because he* *dare not love*—J. M. Coetzee, 1977 / *I dare not speak these dreams to any person*—Garrison Keillor, 1986 / *No one dared defy the group by going out at the last moment*—Ian McEwan, 1986 / (ordinary) *Marcus wouldn't dare to tell a lie like that unless it was true*—R. Hill, 1970 / *I did not dare to look down*—B. Rubens, 1985 / *How do they dare to be different?*—*New Yorker*, 1987 (This construction is needed to avoid the special meaning of *how dare they . . . ?*) / *She no longer dared to go into these shadowy apartments*—Anita Brookner, 1988.

6 There are two other special uses of *dare*: (1) in the phrases *how dare you* (etc.) *. . . ?* and *don't (you) dare . . .* , both normally followed by a bare infinitive (*How dare you come in without knocking?*—R. Dahl, 1984 / *Now you sit down there and don't you dare even look at anybody till I get back*—Kingsley Amis, 1988 / *How dare someone walk up my path and take my property?*—*Gloucestershire Echo*, 2007), and (2) in the phrase *I dare say* (or *I daresay*, as one word), meaning 'it is probable', normally followed by a *that*-clause (often with omission of *that*) (*I daresay I'll come back to it, in the fullness of time*—Penelope Lively, 1987).

7 Finally, there is the use of *dare* with an object, meaning 'to challenge or defy someone (to do something)', followed by a *to*-infinitive: *He looked round the table as if daring anyone to smile*—David Lodge, 1988.

dash. 1 There are, in formal printing at least, two types of dash: the en-rule (-) and the em-rule (—). An en-rule is twice the length of a hyphen, and an em-rule is twice the length of an en-rule. Most word-processing programs are able to distinguish the two lengths of rule, but in ordinary writing no distinction is usually made (and many people are not even aware that one exists).

2 The shorter en-rule has two principal uses: (1) to separate a range of numbers or dates, as in *pages 34–6* and *the 1939–45 war*, and (2) to join the names of joint authors and suchlike, as in *the Temple–Hardcastle project* and *Lloyd-Jones, 1939* (as a citation; *Lloyd-Jones*, with a hyphen, would be a single double-barrelled name).

3 The longer em-rule is the more familiar in everyday use, and corresponds to what most people understand by the term *dash*. Its principal uses are: (1) a single dash used to introduce an explanation or expansion of what comes before it (*It is a kind of irony of history that I should write about the French Revolution in the very country where it has had the least impact*—*I mean England, of course*—*Encounter*, 1990), and (2) a pair of dashes used to indicate asides and parentheses, forming a more distinct break than commas would (*Helen has only seen her father once in her adult life and*—*until her flight from Grassdale*—*her brother is a virtual stranger to her*—J. Sutherland, 1996). The use of a dash to stand for a coarse word (e.g. *f-*) in reported speech is much less common than it used to be, because public acceptance of these words being spelt out is that much greater.

data. 1 Fowler, writing before the computer age, declared uncompromisingly that '*data* is plural only', and pointed to the singular *datum*, which he conceded even then to be comparatively rare. For much of the time, *data* is used in contexts in which a conscious choice between singular and plural is not necessary: *Written sources provide systematic periodic data that can show trends and provide other relevant facts*—J. Waters et al., 1989. In some technical contexts (such as *sense-data* in philosophy), in which the information is regarded as several items, the plural is still usual; but in general use there is a marked tendency towards the singular after about 1970, under the influence of computing (see below), and most examples of the plural have to be sought from an earlier date: *It is no wonder if some authors have gone so far as to think that the sense-data have no spatial worth at all*—William James, 1890 / *Most of the data concerning shock and vibration on airplanes are classified*—Macduff and Curreri, 1958 / *The data come from fairly high doses of radiation*—Scientific American, 1972.

2 After about 1970, the primary meaning of *data* passed to the domain of computing, in which the information concerned is normally regarded as a unit, so that *data* is treated as singular and used with words such as *its*, *this*, and *much*, rather than *their*, *these*, and *many* (which now sound pedantic and even precious in this connection). This tendency has had a major influence on more general use. If the sentence in the quotations of 1958 and 1972 above were written today, the verbs would almost certainly be *is* and *comes* rather than *are* and *come*. Examples of singular use: *They have done little to analyse and interpret this data*—Computer Weekly, 1971 / *Data is stored on a disk . . . as minute patches of magnetism*—P. Laurie, 1985 / *Everything that is happening to Mount St Helens is a 'classroom' experience for geologists and scientists scrambling to gather as much data as they can*—New Scientist, 1980 / *This data is open to a variety of interpretations*—T. Harris, 1993. The plural, however, also continues to be used to emphasize the plural implications of the word *data*: *The data . . . are mapped so that each class has, as far as possible, an equal number of countries*—P. M. Mather, 1991.

datable is spelt this way, not *dateable*. *See* -ABLE, -IBLE.

dates. 1 The recommended style for BrE is *5 June 2007*, with no comma between the month and year. However, many newspapers, as well as American practice generally, prefer the style *June 5 2007* or *June 5, 2007*. In numerical notation, there is an important difference of practice on the two sides of the Atlantic: *5/6/07* means 5 June 2007 in Britain and 6 May 2007 in North America. The use of zeros to fill out single-figure days and months has been encouraged by the prevalence of machine-readable forms in which every box or blank space has to be filled in.

2 Since 11 September 2001, dates in abbreviated notational form have come to stand for major incidents, typically terrorist attacks, associated with a particular day: 9/11 (using the American sequence of month and day) is the attack on New York which demolished the World Trade Center and killed thousands of its occupants in 2001, and 7/7 (which by chance is the same in both BrE and AmE) stands for a series of coordinated attacks that took place on public transport in London on 7 July 2005.

daughter-in-law means one's son's wife. The plural is *daughters-in-law*.

day, month, week, year are singular in expressions such as *a three-day week* and *a two-month term*.

day and age. The phrase *in this day and age* is a cliché. It slid into the language in the 1940s, although a film called *This Day and Age*, released in 1933, is not certainly the source. It should be avoided in favour of more straightforward terms such as *nowadays* or *at the present time*.

de- is a highly active prefix in current English, forming verbs and their derivatives. Notable 20c examples (with date of first record indicated) include: *debrief* (1942), *decaffeinate* (1927), *decertify*

(1918), *decommunize* (1980), *de-emphasize* (1938), *de-escalate* (1964), *denet* (1962), *deregulate* (1964, with *deregulation* 1963). Note that a hyphen is usual when the second element begins with an *e*; in other cases it is optional.

dead letter, in general use, is properly a rule or regulation that is no longer observed; for example, capital punishment is a dead letter when it remains on the statute book although it is not used. The term should not be applied to aspects of life that have simply passed out of fashion, or to proposals that have been dropped without achieving any currency (*The leader of Glasgow council . . . has conceded that redrawing the boundaries is now a 'dead letter'*—*Sunday Times*, 2001). In AmE a *dead letter* is also an undelivered or unclaimed item of post, and on both sides of the Atlantic a *dead letter box* is a place where messages can be left and collected anonymously.

deaf mute is now regarded as derogatory because it implies an incapacity to communicate. It is more appropriate to use neutral terms such as *profoundly deaf*.

deal *noun*. The phrase *a deal*, used for *a good deal* or *a great deal*, is now mainly confined to informal or dialectal use (*The decision saved him a deal of trouble*). *A great deal* and *a good deal* should not be used to mean 'a large number' of countable things (✻ *A great deal of people have complained*); in these cases use *a great many*.

Dear, as part of a formal greeting at the beginning of a letter, was introduced in the 15c in various formulas. *Dear Sir* and *Dear Madam* have become the most formal types, with *Dear Mr Jones* and *Dear Mrs/Miss/Ms Jones* serving as more socially neutral alternatives. Increasingly people are using the full name as in *Dear John Smith* or *Dear Jane Smith*, or (especially in circular letters) a descriptive name as in *Dear Customer* or *Dear Colleague*, in order to avoid the need for a title, which is a welcome tendency.

dear, dearly. You *love* someone *dearly* (i.e. very much), whereas you *buy* or *sell* something, or something *costs* you, *dear* or *dearly*.

debacle, pronounced day-**bah**-kuhl, has lost its accents in recent usage, although they are still sometimes retained in more conservative printing and writing practice.

debar, disbar. *Debar* means 'to exclude from admission or a right', as in *They were debarred from entering*, whereas *disbar* has the more specific meaning 'to deprive (a barrister) from the right to practise'. Both words double the *r* in inflection.

debatable is spelt this way, not *debateable*. See -ABLE, -IBLE.

debouch is pronounced di-**bowch** to rhyme with *pouch*.

debrief *verb* means 'to obtain information from (a person) on the completion of a mission or after a journey'. It started life in military circles but has since infiltrated other spheres of activity in all varieties of English. People are sometimes confused about who is the subject and who the object of *debriefing*, in other words, who *debriefs* whom: it is the person responsible for and in charge of the task, mission, report, etc., who debriefs others: *Marine Corporal Wassef Ali Hassoun is safe in Germany this afternoon after being debriefed by his superior officers*—*OEC*, 2004. The use of the passive is common, as in the example just given.

debris is usually spelt without an accent, and is pronounced **deb**-ri, although duh-**bree** is normal in AmE.

debut is usually spelt without an accent, and is pronounced **day**-byoo.

debutant, debutante are pronounced **deb-** or **dayb-**, and are normally spelt without accents. A *debutant* is a male performer, and a *debutante* a female performer, appearing in public for the first time. The other meaning of *debutante*, a young woman making her social debut, is passing into history.

deca-, deci-. In the metric system, *deca-* means multiplied by 10, so that a *decalitre* is 10 litres, and *deci-* means divided by 10, so that a *decilitre* is a tenth of a litre or 100 ml.

decade. The preferred pronunciation is **dek**-ayd, although di-**kayd**, sounding like *decayed*, is increasingly heard.

decade names. To write decade names, you can use either words, i.e. *the sixties, the nineteen sixties*, or figures, *the 1960s*. If using figures, you should give them in full, as just shown, rather than *the 60s*, even though this is how you would say it. You do not need to put an apostrophe before the letter *s*, e.g. *the 1950s, the 1970s, the 1870s*. When you use the name of the decade to define and sum up a historical or cultural period, you should write it in words, and may use an initial capital letter, e.g. *Paris in the Twenties*. The numerical form simply indicates a time span, e.g. *the oyster blight of the 1920s*.

deceptively. 1 *His voice was deceptively innocent, and she was led right into the trap*—E. Rees, 1992. Was his voice innocent or not? The answer seems to be that the appearance was of innocence whereas the reality was of something more sinister, and *deceptively* is therefore being used in the same way as *apparently* or *misleadingly*. This balance of meanings is more obvious when *deceptively* is used with words such as *appear*,

seem, etc.: *Bill, who rarely played more than five minutes in any game because of a heart condition, was one of that rare breed who made the art of football look deceptively simple*—M. Gist, 1993.

2 But *deceptively* does not readily accompany an adjective that denotes something unfavourable or unwelcome, in the way that the more neutral word *apparently* does. When the appearance is unfavourable and the reality is favourable *deceptively* still seems to accompany the favourable adjective, as in the following example which is an echo of familiar estate agents' jargon: *Manoeuvring down the narrow steps into the boat, and turning into the airy and deceptively spacious lounge, Birbeck was greeted by Branson and Al Clark*— M. Brown, 1989. In this case, the lounge is claimed to be spacious (favourable) but appears not to be (unfavourable, i.e. the reverse of the balance found in the earlier examples), but it is understandable that no one in these circumstances would want to say that the room is (for example) *deceptively cramped*. Here, the analogy is with *surprisingly* (which strengthens the meaning of the adjective) rather than with *apparently* (which reduces it). This second type of use is idiomatic rather than suspect, but for those who prefer a stronger element of logic in their language an alternative word such as *surprisingly* or *unexpectedly* might be preferable.

decided, decisive. 1 Both words relate to decision and decision-making, and their meanings overlap; but there are clear differences. Used of people, *decided* means 'having clear opinions' and *decisive* means 'able to decide quickly'; used of circumstances, *decided* means 'definite, unquestionable' and *decisive* means 'deciding an issue, conclusive'. In some contexts either word can be used, but with different implications: a *decided victory* is one that is overwhelming, whereas a *decisive victory* is one that (whether overwhelming or not) has a definite effect on the course of a war. Managers are *decided* when they have a definite opinion on a subject, and *decisive* when they make decisions promptly and effectively.

2 The corresponding adverbs are *decidedly* (= unquestionably, undeniably) and *decisively* (= with conclusive effect). The first typically associates with adjectives, e.g. *decidedly different / decidedly odd / decidedly uncomfortable*, the second with verbs, e.g. *act decisively / win decisively / respond decisively*.

decimate has changed its meaning because the old one is no longer needed. Historically, *decimate* means 'to kill one person in ten', and had its origin in military punishments. As the need for this meaning diminished, a new one emerged, the now familiar one 'to kill or destroy a large number or proportion of (people or things)': *In killing Moss, they'd used sufficient ammunition to decimate a small army*—R. Perry, 1979 / *The forest has largely gone, decimated by a forest industry that is just now assaulting the final remains*—*Dædalus*, 1988 / *The populations of dolphins and porpoises in the Black Sea have been decimated*—M. Donoghue et al., 1990.

decor is usually spelt without an accent, and is pronounced **dek**-aw.

decoy is pronounced with stress on the first syllable as a noun and with variable stress as a verb.

decrease is pronounced with stress on the first syllable as a noun and on the second syllable as a verb.

decry, descry are related in origin but now have widely different meanings. To *decry* something is to disparage or deplore it (*She decries the spread of tower blocks and the failure to turn derelict sites into green spaces*—*Evening Standard*, 2007); to *descry* is a somewhat literary word meaning to catch sight of a person or thing in the distance (*Her thoughts were brought to an abrupt end, as she descried two figures on their way up the path*—J. Ashe, 1993).

deduction, induction. *Deduction* is the inferring of particular instances from known or observed evidence; *induction* is the inferring of a general rule from particular instances.

deem is a fairly formal word, often used in legal contexts, for 'judge, consider', and is followed either by a complement without *as* or by a *to*-infinitive: *He was a senior policeman, and as such deemed to be unflappable*—B. Mather, 1973 / *In Ireland what a man said was deemed more important than what he did*—*Times Literary Supplement*, 1980 / *Many in the cyber-security world . . . were deemed to have a vested interest in exaggeration*—*Daily Telegraph*, 2007.

It is non-standard to insert *as* between *deem* and its complement, as in: ⊠ *It is important because many deem bikers as the missing link between early apes and modern humans*—OEC, 2004.

deep, deeply. *Deep* is used as an adverb both in physical senses (*With the horses provided you could trek deep into the forest*—*Drive*, 1972 / *Johnny was standing with his back to the window, his hands thrust deep into his pockets*—E. Nash, 1993) and figuratively (*He was soon deep in studies of . . . the biology of unicellular organisms*—*Microscopy*, 1973) *Deeply* is normally used only as an intensifying adverb in combinations such as *deeply aware, deeply satisfying*, etc., and when the meaning is 'profoundly, thoroughly': *Powell himself was said to be deeply bothered by that*—*New Yorker*, 1977 / *They had kissed and caressed, but it was deeply frustrating*—D. M. Thomas, 1990 / *This closely* *observed, deeply moving documentary follows a year in the life of a small French village primary school in the Auvergne—Observer*, 2005.

defect should be pronounced with stress on the first syllable as a noun (= fault, imperfection) and on the second syllable as a verb (= to go over to an enemy or rival).

defective, deficient. *Defective* means 'having a defect (= fault)', whereas *deficient* means 'having a deficiency (or lack)'. So *eyesight, components, goods, logic, mechanisms, products, workmanship*, etc., can all be *defective* if they are not working or done properly; and *courage, diet, funds, protein, the water supply*, etc., can all be *deficient* if there is not enough of them. Neither word is used any longer in professional contexts relating to mental abnormality, but *defective gene* is a standard term in genetics.

defence is the spelling in BrE, *defense* in AmE.

defer has the inflections *deferred, deferring*, and the derived forms *deference* (= respect, with stress on the first syllable), *deferral*, and *deferment* (postponement, both with stress on the second syllable).

deficient *see* DEFECTIVE.

defining moment dates from the 1970s and denotes an event or occasion considered with hindsight as epitomizing or determining subsequent events or circumstances. Nothing much is ever really 'defined' in any sense of that word, and the expression is often no more than a pseudo-rhetorical synonym for *turning point*, a modern cliché devoid of genuine meaning: *But did this London Fashion Week live up to its promise? Was it a defining moment in fashion history or a*

parade of fashion dinosaurs?—Daily Telegraph, 2007.

definite, definitely have useful roles as emphasizing words, and should not be dismissed too readily as superfluous: *His expression was bland, unreadable, but there was a definite glint in his eye that made her pulse begin to race—* E. Richmond, 1991 / *And pickled onions had definitely been a bad idea—* S. Shepherd, 1988. Since the 1930s, *definitely* has come into widespread use informally as a strong affirmative reply meaning 'certainly, indeed': *'Would they recommend that the experiment is repeated another year?' 'Oh, definitely.'—Sunday Times*, 1959. See also ABSOLUTELY.

definite, definitive both refer to things that are said or written. *Definite* means 'clear and distinct', as in *definite advantage, improvement, possibility*, etc., whereas *definitive* means 'decisive, unconditional, final' as in *definitive answer, statement, diagnosis, conclusion*, etc. A *definitive version, work, study, account, guide*, etc., is a printed work that is regarded as the best authority on its subject and likely to remain so. Only *definitive* has connotations of authority and conclusiveness: a *definite answer* is one that is clear and specific, whereas a *definitive answer* is authoritative and dependable.

definite article *see* THE.

defriend *see* UNFRIEND.

defuse, diffuse. The only thing that distinguishes *defuse* from *diffuse* in speaking is that its first vowel is a long *i*, rhyming with *tea*, as opposed to the short *i* of *diffuse*. Given that, it is perhaps not surprising how often *diffuse* (correctly = to disperse) is used for *defuse* in its figurative meaning 'to remove tension or potential danger from (a crisis, etc.)'.

Examples of this wrong use are: ⊠ *An early cut in base rates, which would… diffuse the dispute between the Chancellor and the Prime Minister—Times*, 1988 / ⊠ *The Scott report is a time-bomb stealthy politicians and officials are trying to diffuse—Guardian*, 1995 / ⊠ *She is coping because she has learned that forgiveness is the only way to diffuse ire and hatred—Birmingham Evening Mail*, 2007. Since this mistake is especially common in newspapers, we might suspect that close writing deadlines are the culprit.

degree. In Sheridan's *The Rivals* (1775), we find the assertion *Assuredly, sir, your father is wrath to a degree*, meaning 'your father is extremely cross'. The use survived in more florid English into the 20c and was accepted by Fowler (1926) 'however illogical it seems'. But this meaning is now dated, and in current use *to a degree* means 'to some extent' rather than 'to a great extent' and this is what will be understood if the word *degree* is not qualified: *W. J. Bryan was to a degree exceptional even in the USA—P. Wiles*, 1969. To avoid any doubt, qualify the word *degree* in some way, as in *to a large degree / to a certain degree / to some degree / to an amazing degree* etc. The informal phrase *to the nth degree* (taken from mathematics) means 'to a very great degree' or 'indefinitely'.

deify, deity. The pronunciations preferred now in the *COD* (2006 edition) are **day**- rather than the traditional **dee**-, although the latter persists in more conservative circles. *The Deity* (= God), is spelt with a capital initial.

déjà vu, meaning in French 'already seen' and hence 'an illusory feeling of having experienced a situation before', is recorded first (1903) in the language of psychology and spread rapidly and widely in general use. The parallel phrases relating to other senses, *déjà entendu* (= heard, 1965) and *déjà lu* (= read, 1960) still sound somewhat affected.

deliberative now means only (1) 'appointed for the purpose of deliberation or debate', (*The political bureau was now to consist of 400 members and would be a deliberative rather than an executive body—Keesings*, 1990), and (2) 'using deliberation' (*Some problem-solving will take the form of a deliberative weighing of consequences—M. Leahy*, 1991).

delimit *see* LIMIT.

deliver. In addition to its established meanings to do with bringing and providing physical things, *deliver* has developed a vogue intransitive use (without an object) equivalent to 'provide what is agreed or expected': *Mrs. Gandhi could not deliver on her promises—Scientific American*, 1976 / *The foregoing is proof that local government is delivering at the regional level—Herald* (Glasgow), 2003. It is elliptical for *deliver the goods*, a phrase used in the same sense from the mid-19c. The elliptical use is common in journalism because it encapsulates so much in a single word; for similar reasons it also features prominently in the language of business and management. In everyday language it tends to sound contrived or even slick.

delusion, illusion overlap in meaning because both are to do with things wrongly believed or thought for various reasons. There is, however, a distinguishing principle: a *delusion* is a wrong belief regarded from the point of view of the person holding it (and has special uses in psychiatry, as in *delusions of grandeur*), whereas an *illusion* is a wrong belief or impression regarded externally. *Delusion*, unlike *illusion*, has a corresponding verb, *delude*, and the action of this verb is sometimes implicit in the choice between *delusion* and *illusion*. The following examples will help to clarify these points: (delusion) *He suffered from the delusion that everything smelled of cats*—Arthur Koestler, 1947 / *That was the way delusions started, thinking there was anti-Jewish feeling when there wasn't*—P. H. Newby, 1968 / *Amorous delusions concerning . . . a lecherously attentive neighbour and her kindly but pre-occupied husband*—*Daily Telegraph*, 1970 / *Ed continues to labour under the delusion that I'm a Liverpool fan*—*Guardian Unlimited*, 2003 / (illusion) *In the world as we know it . . . freedom is largely an illusion*—J. M. Roberts, 1975 / *The illusion must be maintained that this was a purely Polish debate with no intrusion being made by the Soviet Union*—J. A. Mitchener, 1983 / *Alfred Crowther loved his first-born child, but he had no illusions about him*—B. T. Bradford, 1986.

de luxe is written as two words in BrE and pronounced duh **luks** or (less often), duh **looks**. In AmE it tends to be written as one word, and variously pronounced.

demand. You demand something *from* or (less commonly) *of* someone (*demanded an apology from* or *of him*), and you make a demand *on* someone *for* something (*kept putting more demands on the overworked staff for their time*).

demi- is a less productive prefix than it used to be, being overshadowed by *semi-* and *half-* (and occasionally *hemi-* for words of Greek origin). It survives in a number of English words, some of them loanwords from French, e.g. *demigod, demi-monde, demi-pension, demi-sec, demisemiquaver, demitasse. Demijohn* (a size of bottle) is probably a corruption of French *dame-jeanne* (= Lady Jane).

demo is an informal shortening of *demonstration* in two meanings, (1) 'a

public march or gathering in support of some cause', and (2) 'a practical explanation of something, e.g. a machine works'. In its common computing application, *demo* is often used attributively (before a noun) to mean 'demonstrating the capabilities of', as in *demo software / demo disc / demo tape.*

demur, meaning 'to raise scruples or objections' has inflected forms *demurred, demurring.* It is normally used in negative contexts and without a complement (*When asked they did not demur*), although it is occasionally followed by *at* or *to* (*did not demur at my suggestion*). As a noun it is confined to the expression *without demur* meaning 'willingly, unhesitatingly' (*expected them to obey without demur*).

denote *see* CONNOTE.

denouement, meaning 'the final unravelling of a plot in a story, etc.', is usually printed in roman type without an accent. It is quite often misspelt *denoument.*

dentures was originally a genteelism (first recorded in 1874) for *false teeth*, but is now standard in more formal use.

depart is now used intransitively (without an object) either without any complement or followed by *from* (a point of departure) or *for* (a destination). Its use with an object is restricted to the formal or literary phrase *depart this life*, meaning 'to die', (with occasional variants such as *depart the stage*), but in AmE is more common in general use (*They would depart the house at eight each morning*), being recorded in uses by J. K. Galbraith, Robert Craft, and others.

depend. 1 *Depend* in its main meaning is followed by *on* or *upon*: *It was quite wrong to come to depend too much upon one's children*—Penelope

Fitzgerald, 1979 / *As grandfather grew older... he seemed to depend increasingly on my company*—J. Simms, 1982. It is also commonly used in the informal expression *you can depend on it/that* etc.: *I'll have a damn good try... You can depend on that*—A. Price, 1982.

2 The slightly archaic meaning 'to hang down', which is the word's etymological meaning, is still used in some literary contexts (*From a beam crossing the low ceiling depended a mobile, the property of Parker*—Elizabeth Bowen, 1968), but it is not a feature of normal usage.

dependant, dependent. Until recently the only correct spelling of the noun meaning 'a person who relies on another for financial support' in British English was *dependant*, as in *a single man with no dependants*. However, the variant *dependent* is also now standard, and indeed is as common as *dependant* in the *OEC*. In AmE *dependent* is the standard form for the noun. The adjective meaning 'depending or conditional on something or someone else' should always be spelled -*ent*, not -*ant*, as in *we are dependent on his goodwill*.

dependence, dependency. *Dependence* is 'a state of depending'; *dependency* can also mean this but is more usually 'something, especially a country or province, that is dependent on another'. The distinction was somewhat blurred by the emergence in British politics in the 1980s of the term *dependency culture*, meaning 'a way of life determined by being dependent on state benefits'.

depositary, depository. A *depositary* is a person or authority to whom something is entrusted, a trustee. A *depository* is (1) a storage place for furniture, books, etc., and (2) a source (normally a book or suchlike, occasionally a person) of wisdom or knowledge.

depot, pronounced **dep**-oh, is printed in roman type with no accents.

deprecate, depreciate. 1 The two words are similar in form and in current use overlap somewhat in meaning, but their origin is different. *Deprecate* is from Latin *deprecari* 'to prevent by prayer' and its primary current meaning is 'to express disapproval of (a person or thing)': *When news of this 'record' multiple birth emerged last weekend, few dared to deprecate it*—Sunday Times, 1987. *Depreciate* is from Latin *depretiare* 'to lower in value' and currently means (1) without an object, 'to become lower in value or price' (*Experience has shown me that their cars are more reliable and depreciate less*—Mail on Sunday, 1985), and (2) with an object, 'to undervalue, to disparage' (*Before this Wilde depreciated pity as a motive in art; now he embraced it*—R. Ellmann, 1969). It is in this last meaning that the overlap in meaning occurs, the intruder normally being *deprecate* in place of *depreciate*: *Dealers have felt a need to deprecate their own firms' values, to disassociate themselves from them*—A. Davidson, 1989 / *A talent that results in giving exquisite pleasure to collectors of memorabilia is to be admired, not deprecated*—M. J. Staples, 1992. As a result *depreciate* is being more and more confined to its financial meaning in relation to currencies, share values, etc.

2 This intrusion on the part of *deprecate* is reflected in the derivative adjectives *self-deprecating* and *self-deprecatory* meaning 'disparaging oneself', and the noun *self-deprecation*, where the meanings are closer to *depreciate* than *deprecate*: *Barton... smiled, and then his face changed again, the old, self-deprecating expression over it*—Susan Hill, 1971 / *Sadly he declined, saying in a charmingly self-deprecatory way that he doubted he had any views worth hearing*—L. Kennedy, 1990 / *She* *may arguably be the most successful female chef in Britain, but her modesty and self-deprecation is more akin to that of a fish-and-chip shop-owner*—Scotsman, 2007. These forms and uses are now fully established, although *self-depreciation* is also occasionally found: *She [George Eliot] wrote of her 'isolation' or 'excommunication' from the world and she was prone to morbid self-depreciation*—Times, 1996.

deprivation, meaning 'depriving or being deprived (of something)', is pronounced dep-ri-**vay**-shuhn, with stress on the third syllable. It should be distinguished from *privation*, which means 'lack of the comforts or necessities of life'.

de rigueur is pronounced duh ri-**ger** and is printed in roman. It is occasionally misspelt as *de rigeur*, with the first *u* lacking.

derisive, derisory. Although their meanings have coincided since their first appearance in the 17c, in current use they are for the most part kept separate, *derisive* meaning 'scoffing, scornful' as in *derisive laughter* and *derisive remarks* and *derisory* meaning 'ridiculously small or insignificant' as in *a derisory pay offer* and *a derisory contribution*. *Derisive* is occasionally found used mistakenly for *derisory* (☒ *a derisive offer of a purse split at 90 per cent to 10 per cent in favour of the world champion*—Evening Standard, 1992).

descendant, descendent. In BrE *descendant* is the noun and *descendent* is the adjective, but in AmE each may be spelt *-ant* or *-ent*.

description. Fowler (1926) discouraged the use of *description* as an alternative to *kind* and *sort* in expressions such as *crimes of this description*, but the use has become well established

and often seems appropriate if sometimes a little old-fashioned: *If you sell pottery or trinkets of any description, why would you pay rent for a shop or a market stall . . . when you can market your wares worldwide for a small fee?*—Observer, 2005.

descriptive. As applied to language, the term denotes a concept of grammar as describing actual practice rather than laying down theoretical rules. *See* PRESCRIPTIVE.

desert, dessert. There are two unrelated words spelt *desert*: one, with stress on the first syllable, is the barren area of land, and the other, with stress on the second syllable, is what one deserves, as in *get one's just deserts*. The verb *desert*, meaning 'to abandon' and stressed on the second syllable, is related to the first of these words. Finally *dessert*, with two *s*'s and stressed on the second syllable, is a word for 'the sweet course of a meal'.

deserter is spelt *-er*, not *-or*.

deservedly is pronounced as four syllables.

desiccated, from Latin *siccus* meaning 'dry', is spelt in this way, not *dessicated*.

desideratum meaning 'something lacking or needed', is pronounced -**ah**-tuhm or -**ay**-tuhm and has the plural form *desiderata*.

designer has been since the 1960s a vogue word first used in the fashion world to describe articles bearing the name of a famous designer and therefore prestigious and expensive. In this use *designer* is used attributively (before a noun), as in *designer dress, jeans, shoes*, etc. The word then spread into much wider use to signify anything regarded as fashionable or specially made, with all sorts of figurative applications: *He* *remembered thinking to himself; so it's finally happened—designer industrial action*—David Lodge, 1988. A *designer drug* is a synthetic compound made to simulate an existing illegal 'recreational' drug, *designer stubble* is the 'short, bristly growth on a man's unshaven face . . . purposely cultivated for a supposedly rugged and masculine appearance or to suggest a fashionably casual dishevelment' (*OED*), and a *designer baby* is one whose genetic make-up has been artificially selected by genetic engineering combined with in vitro fertilization. All three combinations date from the 1980s.

despatch *see* DISPATCH.

desperado is pronounced des-puh-**rah**-doh, and has the plural form *desperadoes*.

despicable. Pundits and usage gurus since Fowler (1926) have been urging us to pronounce *despicable* with the stress on the first syllable, but unsurprisingly usage has swung in favour of a more comfortable pattern with the stress on the second syllable.

despise must be spelt *-ise*, not *-ize*. *See* -ISE.

despite, in spite of These two prepositions are largely interchangeable and both can be followed by nouns or noun phrases or by constructions introduced by a participle (a verb ending in *-ing*): *played despite an ankle sprain / had a restless night, despite cuddling for hours / stayed in Munich in spite of Wagner's seduction of his wife / were not admitted in spite of having higher grades.* In all these examples, *despite* could be replaced by *in spite of* and vice versa. If a clause with a verb has to follow, this must be linked with *the fact that* and not simply *that*: *He earned more than her despite* [or *in spite of*] *the fact that she*

worked longer hours. But note that *although* or *even though* can often replace the unwieldy sequence 'despite the fact that' without any loss of meaning.

dessert *see* DESERT.

destruct. 1 This is a back-formation from *destruction*, formed as a specific alternative to *destroy* to denote a calculated action, originally with reference to malfunctioning space missiles, then in other military or related contexts, and later in figurative uses. The normal past tense is *destructed*. Like all so-called 'ergative' verbs, it can be used transitively (with an object) and intransitively (without an object): *At this point it was destroyed (or 'destructed' as the official explanation puts it) by remote control*—*Times*, 1958 / *This was the prevalent left view until Thatcher's third term destructed, and Labour triumphalism had one last go*—*New Statesman*, 1992. It is also used as a noun, normally in attributive position (before another noun), as in *destruct system*.

2 The reflexive form *self-destruct* appeared in the late 1960s, in North America, and follows the same grammatical functions of *destruct*. Its figurative uses have developed on both sides of the Atlantic to such an extent that this is now by far the most common use of the word, occurring typically in sports reports (defeated teams, failing managers, and so on) and political commentary: *His country's presidency in the EU has self-destructed and yet we are expected to see him steer EU policy for the next six months*—*Times*, 2003.

destructible is spelt *-ible*, not *-able*. *See* -ABLE, -IBLE.

détente should be spelt with an accent and printed in roman.

deter has inflected forms *deterred*, *deterring*, and also doubles the *r* in the derivative forms *deterrence* and *deterrent* (both pronounced with *-ter-* as in *ten*).

deteriorate should be pronounced with all five syllables articulated. Pronunciation as if it were *deteriate* is often heard but should be avoided. A similar problem occurs with *temporary* and other words.

determiner. A determiner is a word that goes before a noun and determines its status in some way, such as *a, the, this, all*, and *such*. A *predeterminer* occurs before another determiner (*all* the time) and a *postdeterminer* occurs after another determiner (*The only* one).

detract, distract. Both words are used transitively (with an object) followed by *from*; but their meanings are different. *Detract*, which (more than *distract*) means 'to take away (a part of something), to diminish' and is generally used without an object (i.e. intransitively): *If anything even remotely detracts from my life in a rugby sense it gets binned*—Irish Examiner, 2003. *Distract* means 'to divert the attention of' with a person, the mind, etc. as the object: *This speculation should not distract us from the real issues*—Daily Record, 2006. *Detract* sometimes encroaches on *distract*, especially in the expression *detract attention from*, which was an accepted usage in the early 19c but should now be avoided in favour of *distract attention from*.

devil's advocate is someone who argues against a proposition or belief in order to test it. It should not be used to mean someone who supports a bad or wicked cause. Its origin lies in the Roman Catholic official (in Latin *advocatus diaboli*) who tests the case for canonization of a candidate for sainthood by preparing and arguing the case against it.

devise must be spelt *-ise*, not *-ize*. *See* -ISE.

devoid, meaning 'lacking', is followed by *of* and is predicative in position, i.e. it comes after the word it refers to, with a linking verb: *Many of the pieces for middle-aged women in Welsh drama are devoid of humour*—Daily Post (Liverpool), 2007. It should not be followed by *from*, nor should it be used absolutely, i.e. without a complement, as in: ☒ *I think of the times that we live in as culturally and artistically devoid*—OEC, 2004.

devolve is a verb of reviving fortunes in the age of political devolution. Its three principal uses are as follows: (1) you devolve powers, authority, etc., *on* or *upon* someone, (2) power, authority, etc., devolves *on* or *upon* someone, and (3) a right, benefit, etc., devolves *to* (or occasionally *on*) someone. The word appears frequently in the form *devolved* to refer to a body or its powers when these have been devolved by a national government (as has happened in the UK in Scotland, Wales, and Northern Ireland): *Our increasing dependence on tourism calls for highly devolved decision-making*—Glasgow Herald, 1986 / *This is a devolved issue and is the responsibility of the Welsh Assembly Government*—Times, 2007. The back-formed verb *devolute*, found occasionally in the 19c, is now virtually extinct.

dexterous is preferable to *dextrous*. Both are pronounced **dek**-struhs.

diabolic, diabolical. *Diabolic* is used primarily with direct reference to the devil (as in Byron's *Satan . . . merely bent his diabolic brow an instant*, 1822), whereas *diabolical* is used overwhelmingly in its extended meanings 'bad, disgraceful, awful', describing such things as the weather, road traffic, the performance of a football team, communications, and 'liberties': *Asked our postman about communications between Tunisia and England. He said they were 'diabolical'*—S. Townsend, 1982 / *Then, all of sudden, the gendarmes burst in and nabbed the first two blokes they saw who looked like English toffs, which was a diabolical liberty*—*Daily Telegraph*, 2004. However, *diabolical* is sometimes used in the original 'devilish' sense, especially when the rhythm of the sentence is improved by it (*demonology, the study of devilish phenomena in general and the crime of diabolical witchcraft in particular*—*Canadian Journal of History*, 2001).

diagnose is properly used to mean 'to make a diagnosis of' with the disease or problem as the object; passive uses predominate. Now, however, it is increasingly used with a person as object, usually followed by *as* with a verb participle: *He was diagnosed as having an anxiety neurosis*—*British Medical Journal*, 1984 / *Tens of thousands of people are being incorrectly diagnosed with hayfever, asthma and even epilepsy*—*Bristol Evening Post*, 2004. At present, however, this use does not extend to things: you can diagnose clutch trouble in a car but you cannot yet diagnose a car as having clutch trouble.

diagnosis has the plural form *diagnoses* (pronounced **-gnoh**-seez).

diagram *verb*, meaning 'to represent by means of a diagram' (*the outline is diagrammed on the cover*), has the forms *diagrammed, diagramming, diagrammatic*. In AmE the verbal forms are often *diagramed, diagraming*.

dial *verb* has inflected forms *dialled, dialling* in BrE and *dialed, dialing* in AmE.

dialect. *See box opposite.*

dialogue is a conversation between two or more people. The first element has nothing to do with *di-* meaning 'two', but is derived from Greek *dia-* meaning 'through, across'. It is now often used of the talking process involved in negotiations and discussions, for example between one country and another or between trade unions and management. In AmE it is frequently spelt *dialog*.

diarrhoea is spelt in this way in BrE and *diarrhea* in AmE.

dice is in origin the plural of *die* (as in *the die is cast*, meaning 'the decisive step has been taken'). *Dice* are also the small cubes bearing 1 to 6 spots on each face, used in games of chance; this form is also used for the singular (*He had a dice in his pocket*).

dichotomy means 'a division into two' (from Greek *dicho-* meaning 'apart' and *-tomos* meaning 'cutting'). The word has long-established meanings in technical domains such as logic, astronomy, and the life sciences; in the 20c it moved into general use to mean 'a difference or split' (e.g. *a dichotomy of opinion*) and often implies a contrast or a paradoxical circumstance: *By a dichotomy familiar to us all, a woman requires her own baby to be perfectly normal, and at the same time superior to all other babies*—John Wyndham, 1957 / *The coffee-table featured a couple of Shakespeare texts and a copy of Time Out—an intriguing dichotomy*—Martin Amis, 1973.

dictate is pronounced with the stress on the first syllable as a noun (as in *the dictates of conscience*) and with the stress on the second syllable as a verb (as in *dictate a letter*).

didn't ought may be the result of a collision of the strange behaviour patterns of two modal verbs, *do* and *ought*,

DIALECT.

Dialect is the language form of a region, and varies from the standard language in matters of vocabulary, grammar, and pronunciation. Some dialects are also related to social class and ethnic origin. The dialects of the United Kingdom are recorded in Joseph Wright's magnificent but now dated *English Dialect Dictionary* (1896–1905) and in *A Survey of English Dialects* (1962–8) edited by Harold Orton and others. There is also a *Linguistic Atlas of England* (1978), edited by Orton and others, and numerous monographs and glossaries published by local dialect societies. Although words and uses that are grammatical within a dialect do not normally enter the standard language, there are some common words and phrases that had their origins in dialect, as is shown in the table below. Care should be taken to avoid confusing a dialect with a variety: Scottish English, for example, is a variety and not a dialect.

Some common words and idioms of dialect or local origin:

word	date	original meaning or source
beach	16c	shingle, pebbles
binge	19c	(as verb) = to soak
bleak	16c	pale, colourless
cack-handed	19c	cack = excrement
clever	16c	nimble-handed, adroit
cosh	19c	Romany *koshter* = stick
elevenses	18c	elevens = morning meal
feisty	19c	ficety (US) = aggressive
old-fashioned (as in *an old-fashioned look*)	20c	knowing, precocious
pal	17c	Romany = brother
poke (as in *a pig in a poke*)	ME	bag, sack
tab	ME	short broad strap etc.
wilt	17c	become limp, droop

Bleak and *clever* are recorded at an earlier date in meanings that are historically unconnected to the later ones. ME = Middle English

but its origins are in dialect and it features in literature only as a (sometimes stereotypical) representation of rustic or poorly educated speech: *And I hope none here will say I did anything I didn't ought. For I have only done my duty*—Michael Innes, 1942 / *You didn't ought to have let that fire out*—William Golding, 1954.

die *noun see* DICE.

die *verb.* When used with a complement, the normal uses are to die *of* a disease, old age, etc., to die *from* (or occasionally *of*) a wound, neglect, etc., and to die *for* (a cause). The originally AmE idiom *to die for*, meaning 'outstandingly good', is informal only. When used before a noun (attributively), it is hyphenated: *Excellent Vietnamese fare, including to-die-for softshell crabs—Post* (Denver), 1995 / *Blonde and elegant, Lisa has bounced back from having babies to sport a figure to die for—Mirror,* 2007.

dietitian, meaning an authority on diet, is the recommended spelling, not *dietician.*

differ is widely used without any complement: *While their aims and activities differ slightly, all are clubs in the sense of recruiting members—R. Brown, 1993.* It can be followed by *from* in the meaning 'to be unlike': *These languages . . . differ from the Polish dialects discussed above—Language,* 1975 / *Most British school and college mathematics classrooms do not differ much from those of a hundred years ago—D. Pimm,* 1988. When it means 'to disagree (with someone)' it is either used independently (*We agreed to differ*) or followed by *with,* but this use is becoming much less common as *disagree* takes over from it: *Dissanayake . . . had subsequently differed with the President on such issues as the handling of the withdrawal of Indian troops from Sri Lanka—Keesings,* 1990.

different. 1 Fowler wrote in 1926 that insistence 'that *different* can only be followed by *from* and not by *to* is a superstition'. It is in fact a 20c superstition that refuses to go away, despite copious evidence for the use of *to* and *than* dating back to well before 1700. First of all we should recognize that for much of the time *different,* when used predicatively (after a verb) is used without any complement at all: *But tonight would have been different—A. Wells,* 1993. We may then put *than* aside for a moment and concentrate on *different from* and *different to.* The argument in favour of *from* is based on the relation

of *different* to *differ* (which is followed by *from* in this meaning); but this is an artificial construction based on the principles of Latin and not English grammar, and is contradicted by the varying practice of *accord* (*with*) and *according* (*to*). English works by analogy, and here the influence comes from words that have the same function, such as *comparable, equivalent,* and *similar.*

2 There are indeed occasions when *from* is inelegant and *to* is more natural, especially when *different* is separated from its complement (e.g. by an adverbial phrase), as will be seen from following examples which illustrate both uses: (from) *Casual shacking up was quite different from holy matrimony—* M. Underwood, 1980 / *The Anglo-American approach to copyright was thought to be different from the approach taken by France and other European countries—New Yorker,* 1987 / *He's no different from my brother, in the end—* Nadine Gordimer, 1988 / *What makes chenille different from other carpets is that it's the product of two distinct processes—E. Blair,* 1990 / (to) *He looked no different at first to other boys Margaret had known—M. Leland,* 1986 / *I found that a meadow seen against the light was an entirely different tone of green to the same meadow facing the light—* Scots Magazine, 1986 / *They don't seem to be any different to us—Chicago Tribune,* 1989 / *Sound waves are very different to water waves but the length of a sound wave changes with its frequency in the same way—J. Downer,* 1989.

3 *Different than* is a more complex issue. It is better established in AmE than in BrE, especially when *different* is followed by a clause: *It used to be they'd play at different times than on the U.S. stations, but not any more—Globe & Mail* (Toronto), 1977 / *This discrepancy is intriguing because most scallops have a* *very different mode of life than other species*—Bulletin of the American Academy of Arts & Sciences, 1987 / *It was in so many ways entirely different than he could ever have imagined*—Internet website, AmE 2004 [*OEC*]. BrE looks more strongly askance at this construction than it does on *different to*, and the objection can be better justified on grounds of style than the objection to *to* can be justified on grounds of grammar. It is natural to want to avoid an awkward relative construction such as we find in Joyce Cary's much discussed sentence *I was a very different man in 1935 from what I was in 1916*; for some the answer is *I was a very different man in 1935 than I was in 1916*, but a little lateral thinking might steer us right round the problem by suggesting an alternative: *I was not the same man in 1935 as I had been in 1916*. One should not presume to rewrite Joyce Cary, but this kind of solution might do better for those who simply want to stay clear of linguistic mantraps.

4 The case for *to* and *than* is more compelling, as occasional alternatives to *from*, when *different* is used in an adverbial phrase such as *in a different sense*, and when they follow the adverb *differently*, where *from* can become uncomfortably cumbersome: *Sebastian was a drunkard in quite a different sense to myself*—Evelyn Waugh, 1945 / *A false sense of security which makes drivers behave quite differently on motorways than on ordinary roads*—Daily Telegraph, 1971 / *The lepidopteran proboscis is very differently constructed from that of the Diptera*—Proctor & Yeo, 1973 / *Perhaps our minds work differently to the physical world around us*—G. Hartnell, 2004.

5 Note that *different* is commonly found in everyday use as a convenient synonym for more austere words such as *distinct, separate, various*, etc.: *Children's perceptions of their sexual roles are*

built up from many different sources—N. Tucker, 1981 / *After four or five different activities have been described, you read the list of activities*—R. McCall, 1992 / *For sociology graduates there are career opportunities in many different areas*—Edinburgh undergraduate prospectus, 1993. If the exact meanings of the other words given above are needed, use them; otherwise this use of *different* is a useful one.

differential is a noun and adjective with several technical and general meanings. As an adjective it is used principally in combinations such as *differential rates of interest*, which are not just different rates of interest but rates based on quantifiable differences (such as the type of investment). In the same way, a *differential* is a determining factor based on some difference, and is not the difference itself. Examples: (noun) *Differentials do exist between blue- and white-collar workers, but they appear to be narrower than in most Western companies*—B. Eccleston, 1989 / (adjective) *As a result the effects of differential mortality rates for men and women are exacerbated*—C. Ungerson, 1991 / *CDs are cheaper in Asia, because the music industry deploys differential pricing*—The Register, 2004. It should not be used to mean simply 'distinguishing' or 'making a difference', as in ⊠ *A small event like mother-in-law coming to stay can have a differential impact on newly marrieds*—J. Mattinson et al., 1989.

differently abled is a politically correct alternative for *disabled*. See POLITICAL CORRECTNESS.

diffuse *see* DEFUSE.

diffusible is spelt *-ible*, not *-able*. See -ABLE, -IBLE.

digest is pronounced with stress on the first syllable as a noun (meaning 'a summary') and with stress on the second syllable as a verb (meaning 'to absorb (food) in the body').

digraph is a combination of two letters which together represent a single speech sound, e.g. *dg* in *judge* and *ea* in *head*. Certain digraphs are printed as ligatures, in which the two letters are joined, e.g. *æ*.

dike see DYKE.

dilatation, dilation mean 'making or becoming wider' (from Latin *latus* meaning 'wide'). *Dilatation* is the normal word in medical contexts, whereas *dilation* is more usual in general use. The verb is *dilate*.

dilatory, meaning 'given to or causing delay', is pronounced **dil**-uh-tri. The same stress pattern applies, rather more awkwardly, to the derivative forms *dilatorily* and *dilatoriness*.

dilemma is now usually pronounced with the first syllable rhyming with *die*. The correct meaning is 'a choice between two undesirable alternatives' and has its origin in rhetoric and logic, where it relates to a special kind of argument involving two unfavourable choices. It should not be used as a mere synonym of *difficulty*, *problem*, and similar words, although overlap in meanings will often blur the distinction. Examples: (correct) *The dilemma is logically insoluble: we cannot sacrifice either freedom or the organization needed for its defence*—Isaiah Berlin, 1949 / *It is possible to raise only one cheer for user charges as a means of avoiding the dilemma of cutting public services or increasing taxes*—Times, 1976 / (questionable) *He was caught in a dilemma, a choice between doing a show or going on a much-needed vacation*—

D. Halberstam, 1979 / *Three corridors: one to the left, one ahead, one to the right . . . 'Dilemma. Left, right or centre?'*—Dirk Bogarde, 1980 / *Mr Salmond has a dilemma: if he cancels the trams, he is thwarting the will of parliament, but if he allows it to go ahead he will be going against the will of his party*—Scotsman, 2007.

A *moral dilemma* is a choice between two morally questionable courses of action: *He would tell children a story with a moral dilemma. He would ask them to tell him 'who is naughtier': a boy who accidentally broke fifteen cups or a boy who breaks one cup trying to reach a jam jar when his mother is not around*—Self-help Magazine, 2004 / *Ashanti has a moral dilemma. Should she tell her best friend Trina that her boyfriend is sleeping with new girl on the block Donna?*—Guardian, 2005 (a genuine dilemma since both telling and not telling involve moral difficulties). In many cases, the context does not enable us to judge whether the usage is strictly correct, because not enough details are given for this: *That a rising young officer with an eye for suspicious behaviour might have moral dilemmas is tantalisingly never explored*—Sunday Times, 2005. As a working rule, however, *moral dilemma* should not be used where clearly only a single moral difficulty is involved.

dilettante, meaning 'someone with superficial or affected knowledge of a subject', is spelt with a double *tt* in the middle, and only a single *l*, and has plural forms *dilettanti* or *dilettantes*. It comes from Italian, and is pronounced di-li-**tan**-ti, similarly to *vigilante*, not like French debutante.

dingo, a wild Australian dog, has the plural form *dingoes*.

diocese is pronounced **diy**-uh-sis, and the plural *dioceses* is pronounced either

diy-uh-seez or, less commonly, **diy**-uh-si-siz.

diphtheria, the bacterial disease, is spelt with -*ph*- and should be pronounced dif-, not dip-.

diphthong, meaning a speech sound in which the articulation changes from one vowel to another, as in *coin, loud, pain, spoke,* etc., is spelt with -*ph*- and should be pronounced dif-, not dip-. Diphthongs are a common feature of English pronunciation.

direct, directly. Because *direct* is an adverb as well as an adjective, it gets in the way of *directly*, which is an adverb only. *Directly* is used (1) before an adjective in senses corresponding to those of *direct* (*They were directly responsible for the accident*), and (2) to mean 'immediately', both of time and position (*I'll come directly / Directly after this, he was taken away / The house is directly opposite*). *Direct* is usual when it means 'by a direct route' or 'without any intermediary' (*Some flights go direct from Heathrow to Los Angeles / You can buy them direct from the manufacturer*). In informal contexts, *directly* can be used as a conjunction meaning 'as soon as, the moment after' (*She came directly I called*).

direct object. In grammar, a direct object is the noun or pronoun or phrase that is directly affected by the action of a transitive verb. In the sentence *They bought a new house, a new house* is the direct object of the verb *bought*. See also INDIRECT OBJECT; INTRANSITIVE AND TRANSITIVE VERBS.

dirigible, meaning 'capable of being guided', is spelt -*ible* not -*able*. It is also used as a noun, meaning 'a dirigible machine'. See -ABLE, -IBLE.

dis- is a prefix which actively continues to form nouns, adjectives, adverbs, and verbs with the meaning 'not' or 'the reverse of' the meaning of the word it is attached to. Relatively modern formations include *disarmingly* (1901), *disincentive* (1946), *disinformation* (1955), *disempowerment* (1971). Note that *disfunctional* is a variant of *dysfunctional* (formed on the prefix *dys*- meaning 'bad, badly') and is not connected with this prefix *dis*-.

disability, the language of. The language now generally considered suitable to describe and refer to people with different kinds of physical or mental disabilities is very different from what it was only a couple of decades ago. The changes are due partly to the activity of organizations promoting the interests of particular groups with disabilities, and partly to increased public sensitivity to language that might perpetuate stereotypes and prejudices, a sensitivity honed by the phenomenal popularity of the 2012 Paralympic Games in London. Just as most people of goodwill studiously avoid previously established sexist or racist uses of language, so they are more sensitive to the appropriate way in which to talk about people with disabilities.

If you want to use appropriate language, you need not only to avoid words which have been or are being superseded, such as *mongolism* or *backward*, and which are listed below with their more neutral equivalents. You should also try to:

1 avoid using *the* + an adjective to refer to the whole group, as in *the blind, the deaf*. The reasoning behind this is twofold: the humanity of people with a disability should not be circumscribed by the disability itself ('the disability is not the person'); talking about people with a given disability as a group diminishes their individuality. The preferred formulation these days is 'a person with ...' or 'people with...', as in *people with sight problems, people with asthma,* or *people with disabilities.*

2 avoid using words such as *victim, suffer from,* and *wheelchair-bound* which suggest that the person concerned is the helpless object of the disability. Suitable alternatives to *suffer from* are *have, experience,* and *be diagnosed with.* Instead of talking about *victims* you can talk about people who have a particular disability; and instead of *wheelchair-bound* you can say *who use(s) a wheelchair.*

3 eschew words which once related to disabilities and which have now become colloquial, especially as insults, such as *mongoloid, mong, spastic, psycho,* or *schizo.*

Some of the terms below are better established than others, and some groups with disabilities favour specific words over others. These lists are offered only as a general guide.

disabled. The word *disabled* has been used since the 1960s as the standard term to refer to people with physical or mental disabilities, and remains the most generally accepted term in both BrE and AmE today. It superseded words that are, to a greater or lesser degree, offensive, such as *crippled, defective,* and *handicapped,* and has not yet been overtaken itself by newer coinages such as *differently abled* or *physically challenged.* Although the usage is very widespread, some people regard using the adjective as a plural noun (as in *the needs of the disabled*) as dehumanizing, because it tends to treat people with disabilities as an undifferentiated group, defined merely by their capabilities. To avoid offence, a more acceptable term would be 'people with disabilities'.

disassemble *see* DISSEMBLE.

disassociate *see* DISSOCIATE.

disastrous should be pronounced as three syllables (di-**zah**-struhs), not as four (di-**zah**-stuh-ruhs).

Older Term	Neutral Term
able-bodied	non-disabled
asthmatic (noun)	person with asthma
backward	having learning difficulties, having a learning disability
blind	partially sighted, visually impaired
cripple	person with a disability, person with mobility problems
deaf aid	hearing aid
deaf-and-dumb	deaf without speech
deaf-mute	deaf without speech
diabetic (noun)	person with diabetes
disabled	having a disability
handicapped	having a disability
harelip	cleft lip
to help	to support
invalid	person with a disability
mongol	person with Down's syndrome
spastic	person with cerebral palsy
stone-deaf	profoundly deaf

disbar *see* DEBAR.

disc, disk. The normal spelling in BrE changed from *disk* at the time of the original *OED* (1896) to *disc* by the time of *OED2* (1989); in AmE it has remained *disk*. In computer terminology, however, the American spelling is dominant everywhere (as in *hard disk, disk drive*, etc.), but in other technical applications, including *compact disc* and *disc camera*, it is spelt with a *c*, not *k*.

discernible is spelt *-ible*, not *-able*. *See* -ABLE, -IBLE.

disciplinary is pronounced with stress on the first or third syllable, depending partly on its position in a sentence.

disco is a shortened (and now standard) form of *discothèque*, meaning 'a club or party with recorded pop music for dancing'. The plural form is *discos*, and as a verb, meaning 'to dance at a disco', it has the forms *discoes, discoed, discoing*.

discomfit, discomfort. *Discomfit* in current English means 'to thwart the plans of' (its original meaning) or 'to embarrass or disconcert'. In its weaker second meaning, in which it occurs most often in the form *discomfited*, it overlaps with the unrelated word *discomfort*, which means 'to make uneasy', and in the normal flow of speech it is not always possible—for speaker or hearer—to distinguish them. Examples: (discomfit) *I should have corrected her, but, discomfited, missed the right moment*—Alison Lurie, 1969 / *Widger was not wholly without Schadenfreude at seeing his informative colleague discomfited for once*—Edmund Crispin, 1977 / *He turned away from her, discomfited at her glance*—L. Appignanesi, 1992 / (discomfort) *His Section's Mediterranean operations, where his cheerful courage discomforted the Germans and Italians,*

are dealt with in later chapters—J. Ladd, 1979 / *The show, entitled 'Banality', was eerie, discomforting, and seemed to offend nearly everyone*—The Face, 1990.

discontent, meaning 'lack of contentment', is pronounced with the stress on the last syllable. Shakespeare's famous opening lines from *Richard III*, *Now is the winter of our discontent Made glorious summer by this sun of York*, have provided one of the most prolific of modern political clichés, *winter of discontent*, first used with reference to industrial unrest in Britain in 1978–9.

discount is pronounced with stress on the first syllable as a noun, and with stress on the second syllable as a verb.

discourse is pronounced with stress on the first syllable as a noun, and with stress on the second syllable as a verb.

discover, invent. To *discover* something is to find something that was hidden or not known; to *invent* something is to devise it by human effort: Halley *discovered* a comet and Galileo *invented* a telescope. Information as well as physical things can be *discovered*, and in this case a *that*-clause is common: *They discovered that they had been underpaid for months*. Similarly, excuses, stories, etc., can be *invented*, although a *that*-clause is not permissible.

discreet, discrete have the same origin in the Latin verb *discernere* meaning 'to sift', but their meanings are very different. *Discreet* means 'circumspect in speech or action', can be used of people or things, and is common as an adverb *discreetly*: *A public telephone stood in one corner of the discreetly lit foyer*—R. Busby, 1971 / *I noticed a few discreet establishments that looked as unauthentic, or as authentic according to your viewpoint, as New York's massage parlours*—Times, 1972. *Discrete* means 'distinct, separate': *It's a single flowing movement of eight discrete monumental pieces in steel . . . created by the American sculptor Richard Serra*—Times, 2005.

discriminating, discriminatory.

Both words are related to the noun discrimination in two very different senses, and it is important to choose the right one. *Discriminating*, when used as an adjective, is appreciatory and means 'showing good taste or judgement' (*will appeal to the discriminating buyer*) whereas discriminatory is unfavourable and means 'showing discrimination or prejudice' (as in *discriminatory attitudes, behaviour, legislation, practices*, etc.).

discus has the plural form *discuses*.

discussible is spelt *-ible*, not *-able*. See -ABLE, -IBLE.

disenfranchise, disfranchise,

meaning 'to deprive of a vote', have both been in the language for several centuries. At present *disenfranchise* is the more common of the two. Both verbs should be spelt *-ise*, not *-ize*. See -ISE.

disguise *verb* is spelt *-ise*, not *-ize*. See -ISE.

dishevelled (spelt *disheveled* in AmE). Pronounced di-**she**-vuhld, i.e. the first syllable rhymes with *dish*, not dis-**he**-vuhld. It is also one of that delightfully quirky group of words containing negative prefixes that have no opposites: there is no *hevelled*, just as there is no *kempt*. See also DISGRUNTLED.

disinformation, a more sinister equivalent of *propaganda*, is first attested in 1939 in relation to a German 'Disinformation Service'. Since then it has usually been applied to the activities of various intelligence and political groups during the Cold War and after: *One technique of the Central Intelligence Agency . . . is dis-information . . . The Agency has expensive facilities for producing fake documents and other means for misleading foreigners*—New Republic, 1975 / *When Saddam was captured in the 'spider hole' outside his hometown of Tikrit, his briefcase yielded important paperwork about the Iraqi resistance although it also showed that . . . he was being fed disinformation by some of the minders around him*—Daily Mail, 2004.

disingenuous, meaning 'insincere, having secret motives', is the opposite of *ingenuous* meaning 'innocent, honest', and is applied to people and their actions: *The somewhat disingenuous slogan of 'ban the bomb'*—Harold Macmillan, 1971 / *I should be disingenuous if I pretended not to be flattered*—William Golding, 1982 / *Every feminist critic has encountered the archly disingenuous question: 'What exactly is feminist criticism?'*—B. Bergonzi, 1990 / *'I thought Amy wasn't here much,' said Theodora disingenuously*—D. M. Greenwood, 1991.

disinterest is 17c and has two current meanings corresponding to those of the more commonly used word **disinterested*. These are (1) impartiality, (2) lack of interest. A third meaning, 'something contrary to one's advantage', is now virtually obsolete. The first meaning is found in earlier writing (*We here see Morris working, with entire disinterest, at his work*—Saturday Review, 1896), but the second is now far more common, despite the controversy attached to the corresponding meaning of *disinterested* (*The general reaction . . . was a mixture of curiosity, disinterest, fear, and embarrassment*—M. Morse, 1965 / *He misread my quietude . . . as either agreement or disagreement. It was neither. Pure, unadulterated disinterest*—Chinua Achebe, 1987 / *Despite British radio's disinterest in new music, and the reduced influence of the music press, I believe real talent will *eventually get through*—N. York, 1991). At present the best course is to avoid using the word in this meaning, either by replacing it with the more explicit phrase *lack of interest* or by rephrasing. (A form *uninterest* is occasionally found, predominantly in North America, but is not in wide use: *She had no idea . . . whether all men went through periods of uninterest*—Sebastian Faulks, 1989 / *That was largely due to the frustration with the sound quality at the club, and seeming uninterest from the audience*—*Eye Weekly* (Toronto), 2003.)

disinterested. 1 The use of *disinterested* to mean 'uninterested', although not a problem to Fowler (1926), is a keyword in current debates about correct usage. Those who rage most furiously are not always aware, however, that the word has changed its principal meaning several times during the nearly four centuries of its existence. It began by meaning 'not interested', then about 1650 developed the meaning 'impartial, unbiased', and has more recently tended to revert to its older meaning. These meanings reflect the different meanings of *interest*, as differently used in *They showed no interest in the idea* and *They have an interest in the business*.

2 The alternative word *uninterested* has had an opposite history, originally meaning 'impartial' and later meaning 'not interested', although it shows no sign of returning to its earlier meaning. The problem then lies with *disinterested*. Informed opinion is divided into those who believe that a useful distinction, between *disinterested* = impartial and *uninterested* = not interested, is being eroded, and those who are content to let *disinterested* serve as a synonym of *uninterested* as long as other words are available for the other meaning (*impartial, neutral, objective, unbiased, unprejudiced*).

3 The following examples of *disinterested* show the strong presence of both meanings in current usage: (= impartial) *Many competent and disinterested experts on world poverty often stress the sterility of the East–West confrontation*—*Encounter*, 1981 / *She could imagine the coroner's disinterested voice*—J. Bedford, 1984 / *But of course none of the observers of twelfth-century England was disinterested*—Antonia Fraser, 1988 / *The doctor ran her hands round again, with the same disinterested precision*—Sara Maitland, 1990 / *American foreign policy has rarely been disinterestedly philanthropic*—*Scotland on Sunday*, 2002 / (= not interested: note that in this meaning *disinterested* is often followed by *in*, on the analogy of *uninterested*) *Washington ensured that he would appear to be what in fact he was, a republican gentleman disinterested in power*—*Times Literary Supplement*, 1988 / *She remains stubbornly neat and unadorned, disinterested in fashion*—S. Johnson, 1990 (Australia) / *Those disinterested in oriental delicacies lounge on sofas, drinking glasses of potent Leffe beer*—*Sunday Herald* (Glasgow), 1999.

4 The recommendation must be to restrict *disinterested* to the meaning 'impartial' and to use alternative words when necessary to avoid possible misunderstanding. *Uninterested* remains the standard and recommended form in the meaning 'lacking interest': *I wouldn't say that—he was totally uninterested in both of us*—Graham Greene, 1980 / *He gave . . . a certain impression of being uninterested in people except at an agreeably superficial level*—D. Fraser, 1982 / *To viewers who are uninterested in politics, it was worse than the World Cup*—*Observer*, 1990.

disk *see* DISC.

dislike *verb*. The normal construction is with an object, which can be a noun

(*We dislike modern art*) or a verbal noun (*They dislike being absent*). It is non-standard to follow *dislike* with a *to*-infinitive, although this is sometimes found: ☒ *She was hounded by a fear of imminent poverty that made her dislike to spend any money at all*—B. Guest, 1985.

dismissible is spelt *-ible*, not *-able*. See -ABLE, -IBLE.

disorient, disorientate. Both verbs have a long history (*disorient* being first recorded in 1655, *disorientate* in 1704) and both are still in use meaning 'to confuse (someone) as to whereabouts'. In most contexts *disorient*, being shorter, is preferable, and it is about three times as frequent in the *OEC* data. Curiously, to judge by the same data, BrE shows a marked preference for *disorientate*. The noun is *disorientation*.

dispatch is the preferred form, not *despatch* (which was first recorded, probably in error, by Dr Johnson).

dispel means 'to drive away in different directions, to disperse', and is used literally with reference to fog, mist, clouds, and so on and (more commonly) with generalized abstract nouns (*dispel fear / dispel myths / dispel notions / dispel suspicions*). It is less idiomatic to use *dispel* with a singular countable entity that cannot be regarded as divisible, such as an accusation or rumour; in these cases alternatives such as *rebut, refute*, etc. are often preferable.

dispensable is spelt *-able*, not *-ible*. See -ABLE, -IBLE.

dispenser is spelt *-er*, not *-or*.

dispersal, dispersion are both used to mean 'dispersing, spreading', but in non-technical meanings *dispersal* refers more to the process and *dispersion* to the result. The following examples show the difference of emphasis: *More efficient dispersal of sulphur dioxide at source cannot be regarded as an acceptable long term solution*—I. M. Campbell, 1977 / *Unlike the dispersals of the teacher-training college libraries, . . . those from the older Universities are frequently discussed and the causes and problems are widely realised*—W. J. West, 1992 / *In Yugoslavia, . . . there is a wide dispersion of incomes between different regions.*—H. Lydall, 1989 / *It is wrong . . . to poison the sea with materials whose dispersion is difficult to control*—*Economist*, 1993. *Dispersal* is the more common word with reference to groups of people, as in *crowd dispersal*.

disposable is spelt *-able*, not *-ible*. See -ABLE, -IBLE.

disposal, disposition. In general, *disposal* is the noun corresponding to *dispose of* (= get rid of) and *disposition* corresponds to *dispose* (= arrange). So *the disposition of the furniture* refers to the way the furniture is laid out, whereas *the disposal of the furniture* refers to its removal. *Disposal* also occurs in the fixed expression *at some one's disposal*, and *disposition* has the special meaning 'temperament, natural tendency'.

disputable is now normally pronounced with the stress on the second syllable.

dispute is pronounced with the stress on the second syllable both as a noun and as a verb, but the tendency to stress the noun on the first syllable has become increasingly common, especially in the context of industrial relations.

dissatisfied, unsatisfied. There is a subtle but significant difference in the use of these two denials of satisfaction, and this corresponds to the differing force of the prefixes *dis-* and *un-*. To be *dissatisfied* is to feel or show positive rejection of satisfaction: synonyms are therefore *discontented, displeased, unhappy*, etc. Whereas *unsatisfied* describes a situation rather than a feeling, and a situation that might change at that. In sum, *dissatisfied* (and *dissatisfaction*) are emotional words, whereas *unsatisfied* (*unsatisfaction* has no modern currency) is a factual one. Examples: (dissatisfied) *Many investors are still dissatisfied with independent financial advisers—Times*, 1989 / *Despite being a dissatisfied customer, you tolerated their excuses—Inc.* (magazine), AmE 2004 / (unsatisfied) *His appetite for life was sated, even if ambition remained unsatisfied—Independent*, 1994 / *What the response here suggests is a very strong and as yet unsatisfied demand amongst Scots for non-religious funerals—Scotsman*, 2005.

dissect is often mistakenly used instead of *bisect*, as when an acquaintance told me that he had crossed Wales on roads that 'dissected it'. *Dissect* means 'to cut into pieces', not 'to cut into two'; in other words, it is formed on the prefix *dis-*, not *di-*. The pronunciation should therefore technically be di-**sekt**, not diy-**sekt**, although the second is often heard, probably under the influence of *bisect*.

dissemble means 'to pretend; to disguise or conceal'. *One of nature's innocents. He couldn't dissemble if he tried—* P. O'Donnell, 1971. It should not be used to mean 'to take apart' as if it were a shorter form of *disassemble*.

dissimilar. Followed by *to*, much less frequently by *from*: (to) *He underwent a revelation not dissimilar to St Paul's on the road to Damascus—*Godfrey Smith, 1984; / (from) *It is not dissimilar from the situation you have here—OEC*, 2002.

dissociate, meaning 'to end an association with', is first recorded in 1623, slightly later than its variant *disassociate*,

and is now the more favoured form. It is followed by *from* and is often used reflexively (with *oneself* etc.): *The mother immediately dissociated herself from this conversation—*V. Glendinning, 1989 / *He is at pains to dissociate Reagan's party from the one he helped steer to victory in 1968—New York Review of Books*, 1990. *Disassociate* was passed over by Fowler (1926) but was described by Gowers (1965) as a needless variant. Nonetheless it is almost as common in current usage as the shorter form and is often preferred when the reversal of *associate* is emphatic: *Any other woman would have disassociated herself, gone where she wasn't known, changed her name—* A. L. Barker, 1987 / *M. Sarkozy has gone to great pains to disassociate himself from both M. Chirac's record and his style of government—Independent*, 2007.

dissoluble, dissolvable are both pronounced with the stress on their second syllables. *Dissoluble* is the general word meaning 'capable of being separated into elements or atoms' and *dissolvable* is normally restricted to its meaning 'able to be dissolved in liquid'.

distensible means 'capable of being distended or stretched'; the alternative form *distendible* is now obsolete.

distil is now spelt with one *l* in BrE and with two *l* s in AmE. The inflections in both varieties are *distilled, distilling*, and the noun derivatives are *distillation, distiller*, and *distillery*.

distinct, distinctive. 1 Both words are related to the verb *distinguish*, but *distinct* means essentially 'separate, different' (*The word has several distinct meanings*) or 'unmistakable, decided' (*She has a distinct impression of being watched*), and is closer to *distinguishable*, whereas *distinctive* means 'characteristic, identifying' (*The bird has distinctive black and white wing* markings) and is closer to *distinguishing*. *Distinct* is often followed by *from* (*Holiness is distinct from goodness*), and this construction is common in the prepositional phrase *as distinct from*.

2 Examples of both words: (distinct) *Scrambling, as distinct from fell walking and rock climbing, is a Cinderella of a sport*—Guardian Weekly, 1978 / *It was a comparatively shabby office . . . Euram Marketing gave a distinct impression of watching the pennies*—G. Markstein, 1981 / *Software designers have used two distinct methods in their attempt to provide the perfect package*—Micro Software Magazine, 1982 / *I can still hear her distinct, rather emphatic, very self-assured speech*—R. Cobb, 1983 / (distinctive) *Everyone who knew the Temple School will remember the distinctive smell of Freddie's office*—Penelope Fitzgerald, 1982 / *Her main 'discovery' . . . was the distinctive way in which Marx had challenged all previous political traditions*—D. May, 1986 / *We currently have a number of distinctive looking dogs in kennels that have not been reported missing*—Cornishman, 2007.

distinctly, used to qualify an adjective as in *distinctly interesting*, belongs to the outer realms of Fowler's *lost causes. It was a 1920s vogue word that he much despised, less on linguistic grounds than because of the condescending attitude it revealed in the user, especially when used in combination with an otherwise complimentary word such as *fine* or *majestic*. Fowler had a point, and he would probably find confirmation of his opinion in more recent use, which often coyly distances the user from what is being said: *That night the singing was distinctly husky and out of tune*—J. B. Morton, 1974 / *Religious references . . . to the Virgin Mary behaving in a way that is distinctly vampirish have been glossed over*—N. Tucker, 1981 / *Young has distinctly craggy features*—Herald (Glasgow), 2007.

distribute should be pronounced with the stress on the second syllable, although (as with *contribute*) pronunciation with stress on the first syllable is increasingly heard.

distributive in grammar means 'referring to each individual of a number or class'. Distributive adjectives and pronouns are words such as *each, every, either, neither*. A distributive plural is one that corresponds to individuals separately rather than jointly, as in *They wear gowns on formal occasions*, meaning each person wears one gown. In such contexts a singular noun is often idiomatic, and one could equally say *They wear a gown on formal occasions*.

distributor is spelt *-or* in all its meanings, not *-er*.

distrust, mistrust are largely interchangeable both as nouns and as verbs, although *distrust* is more common. Examples: (distrust) *He was labelled as a diehard and a bigot, when he actually distrusted the diehards and was himself distrusted by the bigots*—J. Ramsden, 1978 / *Just as quickly came the deep bitter distrust of all white people*—M. Darke, 1989 / (mistrust) *He didn't mistrust her exactly, there was just something he couldn't get to the bottom of*—Ann Pilling, 1987 / *Pornography and a fear of rape play a huge part in girls' mistrust of their own bodies*—J. Dawson, 1990.

diurnal is not an ordinary synonym of *daily* but has special technical meanings (especially in medicine and the life sciences) opposed to *nocturnal*: *During the last two hundred years, the European continent has seen a period of intensifying persecution of the diurnal birds of prey*—M. Bijleveld, 1974. In general contexts, *diurnal* has a quasi-humorous effect, as with many technical words used in this way: *For at least 10,000 years the human race has, at regular and officially* *sanctioned intervals, abandoned the hard diurnal grind of work and taken to the streets—Guardian, 2007.*

dive *verb*. In BrE the standard past tense is *dived*: *I dived into bed fully clothed and slept for five hours—weblog, 2001 [OEC]*. In the 19c *dove* occurred in British and American dialect use and it remains a regular use alongside *dived* in northern parts of America and in Canada: *The plane ducked and dove, the lights went out—New Yorker, 1989*. It appears to have been first used in print by Longfellow (1855): *Straight into the river Kwasind Plunged as if he were an otter, Dove as if he were a beaver.*

diverse, divers. Both words once shared the meaning now confined to *diverse*, i.e. 'varied, unalike', qualifying singular and plural nouns, as in *Why is it so diverse, so varied in its character?—J. Houston, 1990 / Can a single author cover the diverse techniques of physical biochemistry?—New Scientist, 1991. Divers*, which is marked 'archaic or literary' in the *ODO*, now means 'several, sundry' without the notion of variety: *Evelyn Underhill (author of divers fat books on mysticism)—D. Davie, 1991.*

divest has traditionally been used as a rather formal word meaning 'to undress' and, in the reflexive form *divest oneself of*, 'to dispossess oneself of'. In this second meaning it typically refers to rights, powers, etc., or is used as a humorous alternative to 'get rid of': *By about 1900, . . . you were generally well-advised to divest yourself of a regional accent if you wanted to rise and get on in the world—Daily Mail, 2004)*. To these uses were added in the 1950s, first in AmE and then elsewhere, the financial meanings 'to sell off (a subsidiary company)' and 'to cease to hold (an investment)': *We are continually evaluating our asset base to divest assets that are not required for future operations—Lloyd's*

List, 2004. The corresponding noun is *divestment*.

divisible is the current word meaning 'able to be divided', not normally *dividable*.

divorcee is the established word in either gender for someone who has been divorced. The French forms *divorcé* and *divorcée* are also used for a man and a woman respectively, especially in AmE, and are useful when a gender-specific term is needed.

do *verb*. **1 general.** *Do* is one of the most productive and complex verbs in English, although a great deal of its use comes naturally to speakers of English as a first language. Essentially, *do* has two functions: (1) as an ordinary verb (*I am doing my work*), and (2) as an auxiliary verb forming tenses and aspects of other verbs (*I do like swimming / What do you think?*).

2 as an ordinary verb. *Do* is used as an ordinary verb, with or without an object, in a vast range of meanings connected with activity of all kinds. The following examples are typical but not comprehensive: *I'll see what the children are doing* (= carry out, perform) / *Shall we do a casserole?* (= make) / *She did chemistry at university* (= studied) / *The garden needs doing* (= deal with, attend to) / *Have you done your teeth?* (= clean) / *Do as I do* (= behave, act) / *The school is doing Macbeth this year* (= perform) / *We did 100 m.p.h.* (= reach, achieve). There are also many colloquial uses which are best kept for informal conversation, e.g.: *We'll do the art gallery tomorrow* (= visit) / *They were done for shoplifting* (= prosecuted); and idiomatic expressions (*It'll do no harm / A hat does nothing for me / This will do us fine* etc.).

3 as an auxiliary verb. In this role, *do* serves several key functions in relation to other verbs:

a Forming negative statements (either as *do not* or as *don't*) and questions in which the main verb is a plain infinitive without *to*: *They do not want to come* / *I don't like it much* / *Do they want to come?* / *Don't you like it much?* / *Do they not want to come?*

b Forming stronger or more emphatic positive statements: *I do like your garden* / *If you do come, you can stay with us* / *We did enjoy ourselves* / *Do remember the shops are closed tomorrow.*

c Forming constructions in which the subject follows the verb (inversion): *Never did he want to try that again* / *Only after a long wait did he get to see the doctor* / *So angry did this make him that he had to leave the room.*

d In so-called 'tag questions': *They don't like dancing, do they?* / *We met at the party, didn't we?*

e In constructions in which *do* (or *do so*) stands for a main verb to avoid having to repeat it (called a *substitutive* function): *My wife likes travelling much more than I do* / *We said we'd buy one if you did too* / *We get on well and have done* [so] *for years* / *'He said I could doss down here.' 'He couldn't have done.'* Note that uses of *do* following another auxiliary verb, as in the last example, are less common in AmE (which prefers *We get on well and have for years*).

f There is also the emphatic construction, not recorded before the 18c, in which *do* (normally *does* or *did*) stands at the head of a subordinate phrase: *She likes the old books, Dickens and Jane Austen, does my old lady*—Kingsley Amis, 1988 / *He does have a sense of humour does Mr Marr*—Nigel Williams, 1992. This use is clearly conversational and should not be used in more formal contexts.

4 don't have = haven't got. *Don't have* and *do you have* (with past forms *didn't have* and *did you have*) are more usual in AmE than the corresponding BrE *haven't got* and *have you got*, (with past forms *hadn't got* and *had you got*), as in the following pairs of examples: (AmE) *I don't have any money* / (BrE) *I haven't got any money* / (AmE) *Do you have the time?* (BrE) *Have you got the time?* / (AmE) *I didn't have my passport* / (BrE) *I hadn't got my passport. Don't have* is spreading into other varieties of English but still retains its American flavour: *We don't have any beer. Just red wine.*—*New Yorker*, AmE 1986 / *But you don't have a car*—M. Duckworth, NewZE 1986 / *We don't have that kind of thing in my house, man*—A. Brink, SAfrE 1988 / *'Don't you have central heating?' Clare asked*—F. King, BrE 1988 / *She didn't have a pen or paper on her*—*News of the World*, BrE 2005.

Question: Have you got a room for the night? Answer: Yes, we do. This apparently illogical use of *do*, replacing *have* as the auxiliary verb, arises because the question implicitly answered is *Do you have a room for the night?* It is a common pattern in AmE, and causes less surprise to British speakers now than formerly, since it has also become a feature of BrE. Note, finally, that Fowler's argument (1926) for rejecting *do have* and *don't have* in uses referring to particular instances (i.e. ✶ *Do you have a newspaper?* [at this moment] as opposed to *Do you have sugar* [habitually]?) was one of his weaker propositions and ignored the force of American usage.

5 contracted forms. The contracted forms *don't* (= do not), *didn't* (= did not), and *doesn't* (= does not), though not recorded in print before the 17c, are now customary in the representation of speech, and are gradually spreading into less formal business English, although it is best to avoid them in descriptive prose and in any writing intended for recipients not known to the writer.

6 I don't think. This is so idiomatic that its slight illogicality, once the cause of disapproval, now goes unnoticed. When you say *I don't think I've ever met anyone like you*, you mean to say *I think I've never met anyone like you*; but the second alternative, though possible, is far less natural in ordinary conversation.

7 non-standard uses. There are three non-standard uses of *do* which should be mentioned:

a *done = did*. This is common in regional and uneducated speech in Britain and elsewhere: *I think it done him good*—Mark Twain, 1873 / *I never done anybody any harm*—*Listener*, 1969.

b *don't = doesn't*: *He don't do much work*. This is generally regarded as illiterate.

c *done* (= have already) is confined to American dialect: *I don't know what you need with another boy. You done got four*—E. T. Wallace, 1945.

do *noun*. The plural form is *dos*. *See* DOS AND DON'TS.

do (the musical note). Use **doh*.

dock in BrE is an artificially enclosed body of water for the loading, unloading, and repair of ships; in the plural it means 'a dockyard'. In AmE, however, a *dock* is a ship's berth or wharf.

docudrama is a word first recorded in AmE in 1961 for a dramatized documentary film. It has since spread into BrE along with *docusoap* (1990), a documentary dealing with a particular group of people or location over a period of time. *See also* INFOTAINMENT.

dodo has the plural form *dodos*.

dogged is pronounced as one syllable when the meaning is 'continually troubled or harassed' as in *He was dogged by misfortune* and as two syllables (**dog**-id) when the meaning is 'tenacious and determined' as in *a dogged fighter*.

doh is the preferred spelling for the musical note, not *do*.

doily, meaning 'a napkin', is spelt like this, not *doiley* or *doyly*. (despite the word's origin: it is named after a 17c London draper called Doiley). The plural is *doilies*.

doll's house is the normal form in BrE, but *dollhouse* is more usual in AmE.

Domesday, or in full *Domesday Book*, is the record of the lands of England made on the orders of William I in 1086. It is pronounced with the first syllable as in *doom*, and is a Middle English variant of the word *doomsday* meaning 'the day of the Last Judgement' (because the book was regarded as a final authority).

dominate, domineer. *Dominate* means primarily 'to exercise control or influence over' and is used transitively (with an object). *Domineer* is a more judgemental word meaning 'to behave in an arrogant and overbearing way' and is often used with *over* or in the adjectival form *domineering*: *The term ballbuster . . . is a graphic, forceful expletive, typically applied to a domineering female*—*Verbatim*, 1975 / *The low and degrading disposition of those who unfortunately domineer over us*—*Times*, 1997 / *You should also try to keep the lid on the personalities that might have a tendency to domineer*—*Guardian*, 2006. Transitive use of *domineer* (with an object) is occasionally found but is ungrammatical: ▣ *Not infrequently you may have a successful businessman, who is used to being powerful in the boardroom, who domineers and abuses his wife at home*—*Newcastle Journal*, 1997.

domino has the plural form *dominoes*.

donate, meaning 'to give (money etc.) voluntarily', is a back-formation from *donation* and spread rapidly from

American to British usage: *She could donate certain organs to assist in research or spare-part surgery*—Barbara Pym, 1977 / *Some [parks] were royal hunting grounds before they were donated by monarchs*—Sunday Times, 2003.

doomsday *see* DOOMSDAY.

dos and don'ts. You do not need to use an apostrophe to form the plural of words not usually used as nouns, such as *do*. It is therefore not necessary to insert an apostrophe in the word *dos* in the phrase *dos and don'ts*, but one is required before the letter *t* in *don'ts*. Similarly, *fair dos* should be written without an apostrophe.

dossier is pronounced **do**-see-uh and **do**-see-ay with about equal frequency. Both pronunciations are acceptable.

double entendre means 'a word or phrase open to two interpretations, one usually *risqué* or indelicate'. The equivalent term in French is *double entente*, which exists with the same meaning in English, but is practically never used.

double negative. 1 *He never did no harm to no one*—The Archers (radio broadcast), 1987. This, and other double negative constructions, can easily be found in all varieties of English used throughout the world. It is commonly associated with poorly educated East London English and Black English spoken in the US: *I don't take no money from no white folks*—Chicago Tribune, 1990.

2 It surprises many people, for whom double negatives are self-evidently wrong, to know that they were once an integral feature of standard English, and are to be found in Chaucer, Shakespeare, and other writers up to the 17c. For reasons that are no longer discoverable, the logic then changed: instead of compounding each other, a sequence of negatives came to be regarded as self-

cancelling; in other words, an arithmetical argument replaced a linguistic one. Thereafter, playwrights put double negatives into the conversation of vulgar speakers, and 18c grammarians roundly condemned them.

3 In current English, a type of double negative is used with intentional cancelling effect, as a kind of figure of speech as in *It has not gone unnoticed* (i.e. It has been noticed) and *This was a not unwelcome development* (i.e. It was very welcome). On the other hand, double negatives used to reinforce each other are taken as sure signs of a poor education and are rarely tolerated in normal speech. However, since attitudes have changed remarkably in the past on this issue, they may well change again.

4 Double negatives also occur, especially in speech, in uses of the type *You can't not go* (i.e. you cannot consider not going, you have to go), in which *not go* is effectively a unified concept expressed in a verb phrase.

double passive *see* PASSIVE 2B.

double possessive. This is a construction such as *a friend of my father's* and *an admirer of hers*, in which the possessive state is indicated by *of* and the possessive form of the noun *father* or pronoun *hers*. It is well established in English alongside the simpler form (*a friend of my father*), and is useful in avoiding ambiguity by distinguishing between (for example) *a picture of the king* (= an actual portrait of the king) and *a picture of the king's* (= a picture owned by the king). Use of the double possessive is normally limited to nouns and pronouns denoting people, and so you would not normally say (for example) *an admirer of the British Museum's*. The use is also less idiomatic with nouns, as distinct from pronouns, when the relationship implied by *of* is not fully possessive, as in *an admirer of my mother*

(= someone who admires my mother) as compared with *an admirer of my mother's* (= an admirer my mother has). But you would always say *an admirer of hers* and not *an admirer of her*.

double subject. This is a name for a construction in which a noun subject is followed by a supporting pronoun, as in Longfellow's *The skipper he stood beside the helm*. The *OED* describes this use as 'common in ballad style and now in illiterate speech'. Examples: *From time to time I clean. Mrs Pollypot she don't like cleaning.*—Mary Wesley, 1983 / *My cousin he didn't go to college*—Jessica Williams (citing a second-language learner), 1987.

double whammy. The first record of the word *whammy* in the *OED* dates from 1940, but it was popularized from 1951 onwards through the American cartoon strip L'il Abner. *Whammy* means 'an evil influence or hex' and so a *double whammy* means 'a twofold blow or setback': *And high exchange rates create the double whammy of less revenue from exports and more competition from cheaper imports*—OEC, 2004.

By a strange reversal of meaning, *double whammy* is also sometimes used to mean the polar opposite, i.e. a double stroke of luck, as in: *the double whammy of Best Film and Outstanding British Film*—OEC, 2011.

doubling of final consonants in inflection. *See box overleaf.*

doubt *verb*. **1** *I doubt whether he'll come* and *I doubt if he'll come* are the standard constructions when *doubt* is used in the affirmative to mean 'think it unlikely'. When *doubt* is used in the negative to mean 'think it likely', a *that*-clause is normal: *I don't doubt that he'll come*. The logic behind this difference is that when *doubt* is in the affirmative it implies uncertainty in the following

clause (which is consistent with use of *whether* or *if*), whereas when it is used in the negative it implies probability in the following clause (which is more consistent with *that*).

2 This rationale lies behind the objection many people have to the increasing use of *doubt* in the affirmative followed by a *that*-clause or by an object clause without a conjunction. This is commonly regarded as an Americanism, but it is attested in BrE use at the end of the 19c. Examples: (with *that*) *Schiller doubted that a poetic measure could be formed capable of holding Goethe's plan*—B. Taylor, 1871 / *I doubt that the White House is responsible for this rash of tittle-tattle*—Alistair Cooke, 1981 / *I doubt that the okapi which died ... would agree with Mark Twain that 'Wagner is not as bad as he sounds'*—Independent, 1994 / (with object clause) *He doubted Ferrari would sue him*—New Yorker, 1986 / *I doubt there was anything really wrong with him*—Anita Brookner, 1992.

doubtful, dubious. 1 The constructions that follow *doubtful* correspond to the pattern outlined for *doubt*, with *whether* and *if* still dominant but a *that*-clause now increasingly common: *It is doubtful that in the right-to-life controversy the rights of the unborn child will be inviolate*—A. E. Wilkerson, 1973 / *It is doubtful whether the Peloponnesian detachment was dispatched during the actual celebration of the Olympic games*—Classical Quarterly, 1976 / *Murray was doubtful as to whether this would be enough*—N. Tranter, 1987 / *Even if Amelia McLean had made more ambitious claims, it is doubtful whether anyone would have listened to her*—S. Reynolds, 1989 / *It was doubtful if Midge would ever again sleep in their old bedroom*—D. Rutherford, 1990 / *It seems doubtful that such an item would have been produced much after c.1550*—J. Litten, 1991.

DOUBLING OF FINAL CONSONANTS IN INFLECTION.

The table below explains the differing practice in English shown by the forms *hotter, enrolled, offered, targeted*, in which the root word (*hot, enrol, offer, target*) ends in a single consonant. Practice can also differ with the same word in BrE (e.g. *traveller*) and AmE (e.g. *traveler*). A key factor is the position of the stress in each case, and it is therefore useful to distinguish between words of one syllable and words of more than one syllable. The inflections and suffixes which affect the spelling in these ways are: *-ed* and *-ing* (in verbs); *-er* and *-est* (in adjectives); *-er* (forming agent nouns such as *traveller*); and *-y* (forming adjectives such as *rickety* or adverbs such as *initially*).

1 words of one syllable. Words ending in a single consonant double the consonant when adding any of the suffixes given above:

verbs

beg	begged	begging	beggar
clap	clapped	clapping	
dab	dabbed	dabbing	
squat	squatted	squatting	squatter
throb	throbbed	throbbing	
rub	rubbed	rubbing	

An exception is *bus* (verb = take people by *bus*), which has forms *bused, busing*.

adjectives

fat	fatter	fattest	fatty
glad	gladder	gladdest	
wet	wetter	wettest	

When the final consonant is *w, x,* or *y* this is not doubled:

verbs

tow	towed	towing
vex	vexed	vexing
toy	toyed	toying

When the final consonant is preceded by more than one vowel (other than *u* in *qu*), the consonant is not normally doubled:

verbs

boil	boiled	boiling	boiler
clean	cleaned	cleaning	cleaner
squeal	squealed	squealing	squealer

adjectives

clean	cleaner	cleanest	cleanly
loud	louder	loudest	loudly

2 words of more than one syllable. Words ending in a single consonant double the consonant when the stress is placed on the final syllable:

verbs

allot	allotted	allotting	
begin		beginning	beginner
occur	occurred	occurring	occurrence
prefer	preferred	preferring	preference [*sic*]

Note the change of stress in *preference*, which affects the spelling. But the same exception as above applies to *w*, *x*, and *y*:

verbs

guffaw	guffawed	guffawing
relax	relaxed	relaxing
array	arrayed	arraying

Words that are not stressed on the final syllable do not double the consonant unless it is an *l*:

verbs

audit	audited	auditing	auditor
ballot	balloted	balloting	
benefit	benefited	benefiting	
bias	biased	biasing	
bigot	bigoted		
blanket	blanketed	blanketing	
budget	budgeted	budgeting	
carpet	carpeted	carpeting	
chirrup	chirruped	chirruping	
cosset	cosseted	cosseting	
crochet	crocheted	crocheting	
ferret	ferreted	ferreting	
fillet	filleted	filleting	
focus	focused	focusing	
gallop	galloped	galloping	
gossip	gossiped	gossiping	
hiccup	hiccuped	hiccuping	
leaflet	leafleted	leafleting	
market	marketed	marketing	
offer	offered	offering	
picket	picketed	picketing	
plummet	plummeted	plummeting	
profit	profited	profiting	
ricochet	ricocheted	ricocheting	
rivet	riveted	riveting	
rocket	rocketed	rocketing	
target	targeted	targeting	

thicken	thickened	thickening	
trumpet	trumpeted	trumpeting	
visit	visited	visiting	visitor
vomit	vomited	vomiting	

Exceptions in BrE:

input		inputting	
output		outputting	
kidnap	kidnapped	kidnapping	kidnapper
worship	worshipped	worshipping	worshipper

In AmE the forms are usually *kidnaped, worshiping*, etc.

In BrE words ending in *t* in the above list are the ones most likely to appear with a doubled consonant (under the influence of *fitted, fitting*), i.e. *budgetted, leafletting*, etc. *Focus* also sometimes inflects *focussed, focussing*. However, it is best to keep to the basic rule in these cases too.

Words ending in -*l* normally double the *l* regardless of where the stress is placed in the word:

verbs

annul	annulled	annulling	
appal	appalled	appalling	
cancel	cancelled	cancelling	
channel	channelled	channelling	
chisel	chiselled	chiselling	
counsel	counselled	counselling	counsellor
dial	dialled	dialling	
dishevel	dishevelled	dishevelling	
enrol	enrolled	enrolling	
extol	extolled	extolling	
fulfil	fulfilled	fulfilling	
grovel	grovelled	grovelling	groveller
impel	impelled	impelling	
initial	initialled	initialling	
instil	instilled	instilling	
label	labelled	labelling	
level	levelled	levelling	leveller
libel	libelled	libelling	
marshal	marshalled	marshalling	
model	modelled	modelling	
panel	panelled	panelling	
quarrel	quarrelled	quarrelling	
revel	revelled	revelling	reveller
rival	rivalled	rivalling	
shovel	shovelled	shovelling	
travel	travelled	travelling	traveller
tunnel	tunnelled	tunnelling	

adjectives		
cruel	crueller	cruellest

Exceptions:

verbs		
appeal	appealed	appealing
conceal	concealed	concealing
reveal	revealed	revealing
parallel	paralleled	paralleling

In AmE the final *-l* is not usually doubled:

	BrE (always)	AmE (usually)
cancel	cancelled	canceled
	cancelling	canceling
cruel	crueller	crueler
	cruelly	cruelly [*sic*]
dial	dialled	dialed
	dialling	dialing
duel	duelling	dueling
jewel	jeweller	jeweler
	jewellery	jewelry [*sic*]
label	labelled	labeled
	labelling	labeling
marvel	marvelled	marveled
	marvelling	marveling
travel	travelled	traveled
	travelling	traveling
	traveller	traveler

2 *Doubtful* and *dubious* overlap in meaning but they should not be confused. *Doubtful* implies uncertainty about facts, whereas *dubious* implies suspicion about the value or genuineness of something or someone. Both words can be used of people or situations, but *dubious* is not normally followed by any of the constructions described above in relation to *doubt* and *doubtful*. The following examples (in addition to those already given) will clarify the differences between *doubtful* and *dubious*: (doubtful) *We're always a little doubtful about statements that have to be forced out of witnesses by revealing*

the extent of our prior information—
R. Hill, 1987 / 'Are you sure?' she said
doubtfully—T. Pratchett, 1990 / If your
tap water is of doubtful quality then you
must be prepared to remedy the situation
or use rain water instead—Practical
Fishkeeping, 1992 / Then meeting Sophie's anxious gaze, she said briskly,
'Now don't look so doubtful.'—M. Bowring, 1993 / (dubious) We still had the
dubious privilege of representing two
'resting' actors—M. Babson, 1971 /
Dreaming of luxury, of the quick buck
dubiously acquired—R. Barnard, 1980 /
Christine was a little dubious about Judith using brown eyeshadow, worrying
that her eyes might end up looking
bloodshot—She, 1989 / The right of people to know the human cost was over-
ruled on the dubious grounds that this
information could help the enemy—
Action, 1991 / Voters are already
dubious about the point of a deputy
prime minister—Times, 2007.

**doubtless, no doubt, undoubt-
edly, doubtlessly. 1** Fowler (1926)
rightly noted that doubtless and no
doubt, used adverbially, convey probability rather than certainty about what
follows, so that They are doubtless [or no
doubt] guilty and No doubt he [or He
doubtless] meant well connote no more
than strong belief and reassurance respectively. If real conviction is intended,
it is important to use undoubtedly or
without (a or any) doubt, as is shown by
substituting them in the example already
given: They are undoubtedly [or without
doubt] guilty.

2 Doubtlessly, for long made unnecessary by the adverbial role of doubtless,
is making a strong comeback, first in the
US and then in Britain: The current argument . . . doubtlessly offers a cogent and
easily understood explanation for the
current deadlock in East–West relations—Washington Post, 1984 / The
overall effect is of a sobriety that can . . .

make even Britten's doubtlessly 'greater'
War Requiem sound a mite theatrical—
Independent, 1994.

dour, meaning 'severe, stern', is pronounced in BrE to rhyme with tour and
not with sour, although the second pronunciation is common in AmE and AusE.

douse, dowse. Three verbs are involved here: (1) douse, pronounced like
the noun house, meaning 'to doff (a hat
etc.)', (2) douse, pronounced like the first
one and possibly related to it, meaning
'to plunge into water', and (3) dowse,
pronounced like the verb house, meaning 'to use a divining rod to search for
underground water or minerals'.

dove see DIVE.

down- as a prefix produced many 20c
verbs, e.g. downgrade (1930), download
(in computing, 1980), downplay (1968),
downscale (1945), downsize (1975),
downturn (1909; also as a noun, 1926).
Many of these are reversals of existing
phrasal verbs (e.g. play down, scale
down), but by no means all of them are
(e.g. there is no form size down and turn
down normally has a different meaning).

downmarket, an adjective and adverb denoting the inferior end of the
market, is so well established that it is
surprising to find that its first record in
the OED dates from no earlier than 1970.
See also UPMARKET.

downsize, meaning 'to reduce in size
or scale', is first recorded in the 1970s
with reference to the manufacture of
smaller and more economical motor
cars. In the US in the early 1980s it rapidly acquired its now primary meaning,
in the euphemistic jargon of business
management, of reducing the personnel
of an organization by redundancies and
other drastic measures: Decline in demand for certain products and other factors 'make it imperative to downsize the

business'—*Washington Post*, 1983. It behaves like a so-called ergative verb in being used as an intransitive with the object made the subject: *New York hospitals 'will downsize'*—*New York Times*, 1986. Its meaning has also been extended (1) to refer to moving from where one lives to somewhere smaller: *I do like the house, but there comes a time when you have to move on and downsize*—*Hull Daily Mail*, 2007; (2) mainly in American English, as a rather bitter euphemism for making someone redundant: (AmE) *When John Young was downsized from his job last year, he didn't throw a pity party*—*OEC*, 2004; (3) again largely in AmE, as a synonym for 'reduce' in phrases such as: *Russia must now downsize its ambitions in Latin America because its pockets are no longer so deep*—*OEC*, 2008. These last two uses are not recommended in British English.

Down's syndrome. Named after J. L. H. Down, an English physician (1828-96), the earliest example of *Down's syndrome* in the *OED* is from 1961. This term has now become standard in medical and lay use as a replacement for the offensive older term *mongolism*, now, thankfully, consigned to the linguistic dustbin. To refer to someone who has *Down's syndrome*, the appropriate phrase is *a person with Down's syndrome / baby with Down's syndrome*, etc.

downstairs. *Downstairs* is the normal form for both the adjective (*the downstairs lavatory*) and the adverb (*go downstairs*). *Downstair* (formerly used occasionally as an adjective) is now virtually obsolete.

down to, up to. 1 When referring to people and their actions, *down to* suggests obligation or responsibility whereas *up to* suggests opportunity. If you say *It is up to them* you imply that they have a choice about how to act, whereas if you say *It is down to them* you imply that

they are responsible for acting or having acted in some way. Examples: *The boom in Gucci and Pucci and . . . Lacoste 'names' on clothes, bags and other ornamentation is all down to the Yuppies*—*Sunday Telegraph*, 1985 / *Poor ethos in a school may be down to one person, good ethos is down to everyone*—*Times Educational Supplement*, 1999. The origin of this use is possibly connected with the phrase *come* (or *be put*) *down to*, which has a similar meaning: *My remarks . . . should be put down to my own lack of sympathy with the scientistic vision which Thomas upholds*—*Times Literary Supplement*, 1980 / *One of the biggest fears is not being believed. It nearly always comes down to one person's word against another's*—*Sunday Mercury*, 1998.

2 *Down to* and *up to* are used interchangeably in the meaning 'until' (*up to the 19th century* or *down to the 19th century*), except that the viewpoint is slightly different, *up to* being essentially forward-looking and *down to* backward-looking.

downward, downwards. The only form for the adjective is *downward* (*in a downward direction*), but *downward* and *downwards* are both used for the adverb, with a preference for *downwards* in BrE: *She ferreted in her bag; then held it up mouth downwards*—Virginia Woolf, 1922 / *Every time he looked downward he grew dizzy*—J. M. Coetzee, 1983 / *It would be unacceptable if the quality of life went downwards*—*Aberdeen Evening Express*, 2004.

dowse *see* DOUSE.

dozen is a collective noun used in two ways, (1) as *dozen*, preceded by a numeral, meaning a unit of twelve (*two dozen eggs*), and (2) as *dozens*, in informal use, meaning 'very many' (*We made dozens of mistakes*).

drachm is a British unit of weight or measure formerly used in pharmacy, equivalent to one-eighth of an ounce (60 grains), or one eighth of a fluid ounce (60 minims) in liquid measure. The abbreviation is *dr*. *See also* DRAM.

drachma, a silver coin of ancient Greece (and the monetary unit of modern Greece before the introduction of the euro in 2002), has the plural form *drachmas*.

draft, draught. *Draft*, originally a phonetic respelling of *draught*, is used for (1) a preliminary sketch or version (*She made a first draft of her speech*), (2) a written order for payment by a bank, (3) a military detachment. A *draftsman* is someone who drafts documents. *Draught* is used in all other common meanings (game of *draughts*, a current of air, a ships' displacement, beer on *draught*, a dose of liquid medicine, a *draught*-horse). In AmE, *draft* is used for all these meanings and the game of *draughts* is called *checkers*.

dram is (1) a small drink of spirits, and (2) another spelling of *drachm.

drank *see* DRINK.

drawing should not be pronounced with an intrusive -*r*- as if it were spelt *drawring*.

dream. For the past tense and past participle *dreamt* and *dreamed* are both used: *dreamed* is pronounced dreemd (and occasionally dremt) and *dreamt* is pronounced dremt. *Dreamt* is used in both BrE and AmE, and *dreamed* tends to be used more for emphasis and in poetry: *Ever since he was little, he dreamed of distinguishing himself in life*—website, AmE 2004 [*OEC*]

drier *noun see* DRYER.

drier, driest, drily are the comparative (= more dry) and superlative

(= most dry) forms, and an adverb form, of *dry*. *See also* DRYLY.

drink. Notwithstanding a great deal of change over centuries of use, the standard forms in current use are *drank* for the past tense (*They drank tea*) and *drunk* for the past participle (*They had drunk tea*). *See also* DRUNK, DRUNKEN.

drink-driving is the form in BrE for the legal offence of driving a vehicle with an excess of alcohol in the blood; in AmE it is *drunk driving* (usually as two unhyphened words). The corresponding forms for the offender are *drink-driver* and (again mostly without hyphen in AmE) *drunk driver*.

driving licence is the form in BrE, and *driver's license* is the form in AmE.

drunk, drunken. In general *drunk* is used predicatively (after a verb: *He arrived drunk*) and *drunken* is used attributively (before a noun: *We have a drunken landlord*). There is sometimes a slight difference in meaning, *drunk* referring to a particular occasion and *drunken* suggesting habit. *Drunken* also qualifies nouns for circumstances and events as well as people (*A drunken brawl ensued*). *Drunk* is used as a noun, meaning 'a person who is drunk'.

dry *see* DRIER, DRIEST, DRILY.

dryer is the preferred spelling for the noun meaning 'a machine or device that dries clothes, hair, etc.', not *drier*, but both are correct.

dryly. As the adverb formed from *dry*, this spelling is nowadays more common than *drily* throughout the English-speaking world. The spelling *drily* conforms to the rule that words ending in –*y* change it to –*i* before a suffix. Some people prefer it for that reason, especially in BrE, where it is still slightly more frequent than *dryly*.

dual heritage is a relatively recent and more positive way than *mixed race* of referring to the fact that someone has parents of different ethnic origins from each other. It is used as a noun on its own, or else to modify another noun: *Amar is proud of his dual heritage: 'I am proud to be African and proud to be European'*—OEC, 2010 / *A new charity for people with dual-heritage children*—OEC, 2002.

due to. 1 The use of *due to* is one of the key topics of discussion in debates about correct usage, along with *infer/ imply* and the split infinitive. As an adjective meaning 'owing, payable, attributable, (of an event etc.) intended to happen or arrive' and so on, *due* + (optional) *to* causes little difficulty, and the following examples are unexceptionable: *Pay Caesar what is due to Caesar, and pay God what is due to God*—New English Bible, 1961 / *Incorrect speed is generally due to a worn idler wheel*—Reader's Digest Repair Manual, 1972 / *It was due to start at four o'clock, but didn't begin until twenty past*—William Trevor, 1976 / *Part of her happiness, her unaltered sense of her own superiority, was due to a sense of virginity preserved*—Anita Brookner, 1988. In all these uses, *due* is an adjective with a complement formed by the preposition *to* or by a *to*-infinitive, and they are compositional rather than idiomatic.

2 A problem arises when *due to* is used as a fixed prepositional phrase, on the analogy of *owing to* (which no one objects to in this way, for some reason), in which there is no noun or pronoun antecedent that can be regarded as qualifying and no linking verb such as *be* or *become*. The purist view of the matter is that *There was a delay due to bad weather* is acceptable because *due* qualifies *delay*, whereas ✖ *The train was delayed due to bad weather* is

unacceptable because *due* is grammatically unattached. (In some cases, it should be noted, the sentence can be construed either way, underlining the weakness of basing judgements about usage on close grammatical analysis: *Out in the countryside, two million people are at risk of starvation, due to the failure of the harvest*—Independent, 1996.) At present it is prudent to avoid this use of *due to* and to use alternatives such as *owing to, because of*, or *on account of*. However, *due to* is in strong pursuit of *owing to* and will undoubtedly become standard during the 21c, if only because analogy is a powerful force and *due to* has the considerable advantage of convenience over its more awkward rival.

3 Examples of the disputed use: *Due to the incidence of Christmas and New Year statutory holidays it has been necessary to rearrange certain collection days*—Alyn and Deeside Observer, 1976 / *Michael . . . hated mathematics at school, mainly due to the teacher*—Times Educational Supplement, 1987 / *In the past 25 years the population has trebled due to the building program*—East Yorkshire Village Book, 1991 / *This kind of lucrative deal went downward in recent years due to the world economic situation*—Evening Standard, 2004.

4 due to the fact that. In this expression *the fact that* is used to turn a prepositional phrase into a conjunction. It can be awkward in use, and is often avoided by substituting *because*: *That this slippage is so slight is due to the fact that* [substitute *because*] *the other Enterprise staff have worked a great deal of extra time*—Annual Report, 1993. In some cases, however, this substitution does not work well, especially when there is a strong link between *due* and an antecedent noun, as in the following examples: *The success of the tampon is partly due to the fact that it is hidden*—

Germaine Greer, 1970 / *Part of this fris-son... is undoubtedly due to the fact that woman as a whole has been seen as a pacifying influence throughout their his-tory*—Antonia Fraser, 1988.

dumb. 1 *Dumb* now has such strong connotations of stupidity and low intel-ligence that its original meaning, 'not able to speak', is often regarded as of-fensive. It is more appropriate to use neutral terms such as *speech-impaired*.

2 The ailing fortunes of *dumb* as a verb were revived in the late 1990s by the emergence of a new phrasal verb *dumb down*, meaning 'to make more simple or less intellectually demanding' in depre-ciatory senses. It tends to be used primarily in the context of education, the arts, and broadcasting, and has an irresistible immediacy of meaning and nuance: *Successive education ministers have preferred to dumb down exams and glory in vacuous statistics than to deliver real education progress*—Express, 2005. The expression is also used intransitively (without an object): *I've never believed in this whole idea that you have to dumb down to get an audience*—Scotsman, 2002.

dumbfound, dumbfounded, meaning 'to nonplus' and 'nonplussed', are formed on *dumb* and *confound* and should be spelt with a -*b*-.

dunno, a phonetic representation of *I don't know*, is first recorded in 1842 and is widely used in fiction and drama in illiterate or highly informal speech: *'Now it's back the way it used to be.' 'Why?...' 'Dunno, sweet. Do not know.'*—New Yorker, 1986.

dustbin is the normal word in BrE for a rubbish bin, although the shorter form *bin* is widely used informally (and *wheelie bins*, tall bins on wheels, have been in use since the 1980s: the term is Australian in origin). *Dustman* has largely been replaced by *refuse collector*.

In AmE *dustbin* is largely restricted to figurative use (e.g. *consigned to the dustbin of history*), and the normal term is *garbage can* or *trash can*.

Dutch *see* NETHERLANDS, LOW COUN-TRIES, HOLLAND, DUTCH.

duteous, dutiful. Both words mean 'observing one's duty' and date from the 16c; Shakespeare used both, though with a preference for *duteous*. *Dutiful* is now standard.

dutiable *see* -ABLE, -IBLE.

dwarf. The traditional plural in BrE is *dwarfs*, although *dwarves* is increasingly found, perhaps under the influence of J. R. R. Tolkien, who used it regularly. To use *dwarf* to mean simply a very short person is, of course, offensive. To de-scribe people who have dwarfism, terms suggested on the websites of support groups include the following: *little people, people of restricted growth, people of short stature*, and *people having dwarfism*.

dwell in the meaning 'live, reside', is mainly used in literary contexts or for special effect. The past and past partici-ple is *dwelt*, not *dwelled*.

dye *verb* meaning 'to colour with dye', has the forms *dyes, dyed, dyeing*, to avoid confusion with the forms of *die* (*dies, died, dying*).

dyke, dike. In the meaning 'embank-ment', *dyke* is the preferred form. This is also true of the different (slang) word *dyke*, meaning 'a lesbian'.

dynamo has the plural form *dynamos*.

dynast, dynasty are pronounced din- in BrE and **diyn-** in AmE.

dysentery is pronounced in BrE as three syllables, and in AmE as four syl-lables, with stress on the first in both cases.

e- is a modern prefix based on the term *electronic*, and is applied to various products and facilities available through the Internet: an *e-book* is an author's work downloaded in machine-readable form, an *e-ticket* is an authorization to travel by train or air replacing the conventional printed ticket, and *e-voting* is a system of recording a vote in an election on the Internet or by other electronic means instead of marking a ballot paper. Its most familiar use, however, is in the now universal term **email* (which is familiar enough to dispense with the hyphen).

each. 1 singular or plural. *Each* is treated as singular when it stands by itself as a pronoun, when it comes before a singular noun (*each house*), and when it is followed by *of* and a plural noun (*each of the houses*): *Each group is responsible for its own quality control*—A. Francis, 1986 / *Each of the two key fobs has its own snap fastening*—Sunday Express, 1981 / *Almost all accidents start with a simple error on the part of the pilot that leads to a chain of events, each of which makes the situation worse*—D. Piggott, 1991 / *What the treaty did not do was to make the two kingdoms of France and England one; they were to remain separate, each with its own legal and administrative identity*—C. Allmand, 1991. When *each* follows and qualifies a plural noun or pronoun, it is treated as a plural since it is the noun or pronoun and not *each* that determines the singular or plural status of the sentence:

They each carry several newspapers, a whole crop of the day's papers and the Sundays—Tom Stoppard, 1976 / *In the last four beats of the third bar . . . the voices each have slight differences in note-lengths and the placing of syllables*—R. Brindle Smith, 1986.

2 each and every. This is regarded as a cliché and is best reserved for special effect as in Sylvia Plath's allegory of the fig-tree representing life: *I wanted each and every one of them, but choosing one meant losing all the rest*—The Bell Jar, 1963.

3 each other. The belief that *each other* refers to two people or things and *one another* to more than two is a superstition already rejected by Fowler (1926). Historical usage shows that there is no basis for such a restriction, and many contrary examples can be found from good writers: (*each other* referring to more than two) *We took off in a motorcade traveling at a speed of close to 100 miles per hour with cars tailgating each other*—Henry Kissinger, 1982 / *Everybody knew each other or about each other*—Anita Brookner, 1983 / *I sit in one of the smaller theatres at the Young Vic and watch Brecht's characters driving each other into action through the coherence and confidence of their belief and argument*—Observer, 2007 / (*one another* referring to two) *He and Gussy were evidently very fond of one another*—A. N. Wilson, 1978 / *There is no such thing as complete harmony between two people, however much they profess to love one* *another*—Anita Brookner, 1984 / *We saw one another at weekends but this put a strain on the relationship*—*Sun*, 2007.

4 For the differences between *each* and *every*, see EVERY.

early on is first recorded in BrE in 1928 and only later in AmE. It is a kind of back-formation from *earlier on*, itself modelled on *later on* (first recorded 1882). *Early on* and *earlier on* are both now common in both BrE and AmE: *The BBC recognised early on that there was money to be made from selling archive programmes on video*—*New Scientist*, 1983 / *Early on, he puts a coin in a newspaper vending-machine*—*New Yorker*, 1987 / *Earlier on, religion had supplied a drug which most of the clergy were quite ready to administer*—V. G. Kiernan, 1990.

earn has a past and past participle form *earned* (*They earned £200 a week / earned income*), although *earnt* is found from time to time in newspapers, reflecting its pronunciation and by analogy with *learnt*: *Ray and Alan Mitchell once worked gruelling hours and earnt good money as contract plumbers in London*—*Independent*, 1992 / *Its pretax profits are tipped to be just above the £40.3m earnt at the same time last year*—*Business & Money*, 2007.

earth is spelt with a capital initial (*Earth*) when it is regarded as a planet of the solar system. Like *Mars, Venus*, etc., it is then used without *the* (but note *the planet Earth*).

earthen, earthly, earthy. *Earthen* is used only in the physical sense 'made of earth' (either soil, or clay as in *earthenware*): *No city or government wants to build earthen structures or allow them to be built*—*New Scientist*, 1971. *Earthly* has two meanings, (1) denoting the earth or human life on earth, as distinct from *heavenly* (*They set themselves the*

difficult task of disentangling this cosmic dust from the earthly sort*—*Economist*, 1991) and (2) as an intensifying word in informal use in negative contexts (*A trainee is no earthly use in here at all*—M. Frayn, 1969). *Earthy* means (1) 'of or like the earth or soil', (2) figuratively, 'somewhat coarse or crude': *My friend Lindsey said I was consumed with earthy desires and unable to reach the higher planes*—S. Rowbotham, 1985 / *In one direction only a little earthy bank separates me from the edge of the ocean*—R. Sale et al., 1991 / *Ian McEwan is our only real native rival in telling the earthy, inside story of contemporary life*—*Express*, 2007.

east, eastern, easterly *adjectives*. What is said here applies equally to *north, south*, and *west*, and their corresponding forms. *East* denotes physical position (*on the east side of town*) and is spelt with an initial capital (*East*) when forming part of a recognized name (*New York's East Side*), whereas *eastern* denotes regional and cultural association (*eastern forms of art*). *Easterly* is used chiefly of a wind blowing from the east (*an easterly wind / from an easterly direction*), and also of movement towards the east or a position achieved by this movement (*We took an easterly course / the most easterly part of the constellation*).

eastward, eastwards. The only form for the adjective is *eastward* (*in an eastward direction*), but *eastward* and *eastwards* are both used for the adverb, with a very marked preference for *eastwards* in BrE, and for *eastward* in AmE: *Traffic snarled eastwards along Brompton Road at a snail's pace*—G. F. Newman, 1970.

easy is established as an adverb in fixed expressions such as *take it easy, have it easy, go easy on, easy does it*, and *stand easy*. Otherwise its use as an adverb is non-standard, though common informally in BrE as well as AmE, especially when followed by a comparison with *as: We'd get a confession out of him easy as blinking*—R. Rankin, 1993. The main use of *easily* is in the meanings 'by far, by a wide margin', as in *The home team won easily*, and 'very probably' (*It could easily rain*).

eatable, edible. *Eatable* means 'fit to be eaten' and is normally applied to food, whereas *edible* means 'suitable for eating' and is often contrasted with what is poisonous or harmful (e.g. *edible mushrooms / edible snails*).

eBay. The online retailing company name is spelt with a lower case *e* followed by an upper case letter *b*, and all as one word. At the beginning of a sentence, or in headlines, the *e* looks better capitalized, *Ebay*, with lower-case *b*, but that spelling is not approved by the company.

ebullient is pronounced with the second syllable as in *bulb*, not as in *bull*.

echelon is written without an accent over the first letter *e*, and is pronounced **e**-shuh-lon, or **ay**-shuh-lon. Gowers (1965) regarded the meaning 'a level or rank in an organization or in society' as a slipshod extension of the original English meaning 'a military formation of parallel rows' (*The rear echelons of the army mutinied and seized the crossings over the Rhine*—M. Howard, 2003). Both meanings are in use, but the extended meaning is by far the more common: *You could easily picture the upper echelons of the Royal Family sat behind the wheel of one of these*—Fyne Times, 2004. The word is derived from French (ultimately from *échelle* meaning 'ladder'), and it has developed in the same way in that language too.

echo has the plural form *echoes*. As a verb, it has inflected forms *echoes, echoed, echoing*.

ecology has spread rapidly in the 20c from technical to general use to mean 'the study of the interaction of people with their natural environment'. An earlier spelling *oecology*, reflecting its origin in the Greek word *oikos* meaning 'house' (the same root as in *economy*), is hardly ever used. *Ecology* has also produced the prolific prefix *eco-*, as in *eco-catastrophe* (1969), *eco-correct* (1994), *ecodoom* (1973), *eco-friendly* (1989), *eco-label* and *-labelling* (1989), *ecopolitics* (1973), *eco-terrorist* (1988), *eco-warrior* (1987), etc.

economic, economical. 1 These are both adjectives answering to the word *economy*: *economic* in the meanings 'relating to economics' and 'frugal, characterized by good economy', and *economical* in the meaning 'sparing in the use of resources'. An *economic cost* is one that is practical and makes good business sense, whereas an *economical cost* is one that is modest and not excessive.

2 The phrase *economical with the truth*, meaning 'saying just as much as is needed or relevant', is a political cliché of our times, recalling earlier notions of Burke and others that 'in the exercise of all virtues, there is an economy of truth'. In its present form it alludes to events of 1986, when the British Cabinet Secretary Sir Robert Armstrong, giving evidence during the 'Spycatcher' trial (in which the British government sought to prevent the publication of a book of that name by a former MI5 employee), referred to a former statement in the following way: *It contains a misleading impression, not a lie. It was being economical with the truth*. Phrases such as this are not easily forgotten, and allusive references abound, e.g.: *Contrast Lord Butler's forensic exposure of intelligence* *failures this week with the smoothly arrogant evidence in defence of the Iraq dossier presented to the Hutton report last year, and you have a picture, if not of deception, then of men who were being severely economical with the truth—* Scotland on Sunday, 2004.

ecstasy is spelt *-asy*, not *-acy*. The drugs meaning is first recorded in the US in 1985 and is often spelt with an initial capital (*Ecstasy*).

ecumenical, meaning 'relating to the whole Christian world', is spelt *ecu-* and not (as formerly) *oecu-*. The root is Greek *oikoumenē* 'the inhabited world'. The first syllable is pronounced either **ek-** or **eek-**.

-ed and -'d. The adjectival form *-'d* is sometimes added instead of the more usual *-ed* when the root word ends in a fully pronounced vowel, e.g. *subpoena'd, shanghai'd*. Practice varies, however, and forms such as *antennaed, concertinaed, shampooed*, and *subpoenaed* are preferred in modern styles. The exceptions are initialisms used as verbs, such as *KO'd* and *OD'd*.

-ed *see* -T AND -ED.

edgy. The older meaning, 'peevish and irritable', is derived from the idiom *have one's nerves on edge*. Since the 1970s, however, a new, still informal, meaning 'at the forefront of ideas, trendy' has come to the fore, based on another idiom built on the notion of the edge: *at the cutting edge* (*see* CUTTING). *Show Euro-cool by dolloping on some good and edgy and far more grown-up crème fraîche instead* — Nigella Lawson, 1998.

-edly. 1 The suffix occurs in a number of familiar words such as *advisedly, allegedly, assuredly, deservedly*, and *unreservedly*, of which some date back to the 14c but most date from the 17c to 19c. In

a lengthy article, Fowler (1926) listed these along with many highly abstruse and idiosyncratic forms that were unlikely to survive, such as *admiredly, ascertainedly, harassedly, incensedly*, and *statedly*, some of which were not even entered in the *OED*. There are also a few 20c forms, including *painedly, unashamedly*, and (not mentioned by Fowler) *reportedly*.

2 Normally *-edly* is pronounced as two additional syllables, even when the *-ed* element is not separately pronounced in the root words; this is true of all the words listed in the first sentence of the previous paragraph. That is to say, *advisedly, assuredly*, and *deservedly* are pronounced as four syllables, and *fixedly* and *markedly* as three. Adverbs from adjectives follow this rule when *-ed* is pronounced as a separate syllable in the adjective, e.g. *cold-blooded* and *high-handed* generate *cold-bloodedly* and *high-handedly*, both with four syllables, but *shamefaced*, in which the *-ed* is not pronounced, generates *shamefacedly* which can have three or four syllables.

3 A few awkward cases remain. One wonders how Browning would have pronounced *starchedly* in his *Red Cotton Night-Cap Country* (1873); and how D. H. Lawrence would have pronounced *painedly* in his *England, My England* (1921); and indeed how the *OED* editors articulated to themselves the forms *admiredly, depressedly, labouredly*, and *veiledly* when they set them down as part of the language. All, however, are spoken too rarely to cause any real problem.

-ee is an active suffix originally drawn from Old French words denoting the recipient of a grant or the like, as in *lessee* and *patentee*. In more recent formations, *-ee* denotes (1) the recipient of an action, often corresponding to an agent-noun in *-er* or *-or* (*addressee, amputee, employee, trainee*; more recently *shortlistee* 'a person who has been shortlisted'), (2) in a few cases, a person who performs an action or is associated with it (*attendee* = a participant at a conference or meeting, *escapee*, *refugee*, *standee* = a standing passenger). A *conferee*, as well as being 'a person on whom something is conferred', is another word for a participant at a conference; the formation is impeccable in the first sense but less secure (perhaps 'a person who confers [with others]') in the second. A few are mainly confined to AmE, e.g. *enrollee* and *retiree*. The *-ee* in *bootee* and a few other words is a separate suffix of obscure origin; that in *goatee*, *jamboree*, *marquee*, and *settee*, is yet another (or possibly more than one).

-eer is a suffix first recorded in the 17c, replacing an earlier (French) form *-ier*. One of its first occurrences is in *mountaineer* (first used in Shakespeare's *The Tempest*, 1610, in the meaning 'one who lives in the mountains'). In more recent use, it has taken on disparaging connotations, as in *pamphleteer* (1642), *profiteer* (1912), *racketeer* (1928), and *marketeer* (originally 1832 in a neutral sense, now a person engaged in marketing in the sense of 'product promotion'). There are many derivatives in *-eering*, e.g. *buccaneering* (1758), *electioneering* (1760), *privateering* (1664), and associated verbs, some of them independently formed (e.g. *electioneer*, 1789) and others as back-formations (e.g. *mountaineer*, 1892). It is interesting to note that the *-eer* suffix in *domineer* ('to behave overbearingly') and *commandeer* ('to take official possession of') has a different origin as these words are derived from Dutch.

effect *noun* and *verb see* AFFECT.

effective, effectual, efficacious, efficient. 1 All these words mean 'having an effect' of some kind, but with different applications and shades of meaning. *Effective* means 'having a

definite or desired effect' that is actual rather than theoretical: *The toothbrush is undoubtedly the most effective weapon in the fight against bacterial plaque*— Daily Telegraph, 1971 / *She is most effective as a live performer of her own material*—New Yorker, 1975 / *Referring fracture patients for a DXA scan has been effective in helping prevent further breaks*—Scotsman, 2007. *Cost-effective* means 'productive in terms of cost'. *Effectual* means 'capable of producing the required result or effect', independent of a personal agent, and is often more theoretical than actual: *The rich ought to have an effectual barrier in the constitution against being robbed, plundered, and murdered, as well as the poor*— A. Arblaster, 1987 / *The rim of my hat, while effectually shading my eyes, did not obstruct my vision*—J. Davidson, 1991. A person cannot be described as *effectual* although he or she can be described as *ineffectual*, i.e. 'lacking the ability to produce results': *The Rangers' problems stemmed from the habit that . . . the team's general manager . . . had of hiring ineffectual cronies to coach the club*—New York Times, 1979.

2 *Efficacious* applies only to things, and means 'producing or sure to produce the required effect': *It is perhaps dubious to argue that a prayer or worship becomes more efficacious if more people join in*—S. Lamont, 1989 / *How can I persuade them, when they go to the bar, that a Perrier or a tonic water might be just as efficacious as alcoholic liquor?*— S. J. Carne, 1990. *Efficient* refers to a person's or thing's capacity to do work and produce results with minimum effort and cost: *You police spies don't seem to be a very efficient bunch, letting an old man be drowned while you are supposed to be keeping a watch on him*—G. Sims, 1973 / *Older systems can be improved with modern, efficient components and controls can be added to improve fuel economy*—Ideal Home, 1991. In recent use, *efficient* is sometimes preceded by an attributive noun that defines the scope of the efficiency, notably in relation to *energy*: *Flights can be 'offset', which means you work out your carbon emissions and then send money to fund tree planting or energy efficient technologies*—*Daily Mail*, 2007.

effete is a 17c word originally meaning 'worn out by bearing offspring' (from Latin *fetus*) with reference to animals. It rapidly developed the transferred meaning '(of a material substance) that has lost its special quality or virtue', and by the late 18c was being applied to persons or systems that had lost their effectiveness. In the 20c it has come to be applied to effeminate men, though not, despite its etymology, to women who are or look as if they are past child-bearing age: *'Do you mind if I sit down?' asked the young man in effete, accented English*—R. Kee, 1991. It is still commonly used of ineffective institutions: *Mollycoddled, pampered by modern mores, man is becoming effete, though not totally emasculated*—*Herald* (Glasgow), 2001.

e.g. is short for Latin *exempli gratia* and means 'for example'. It should be distinguished from *i.e.*, from Latin *id est*, which means 'that is to say'. To non-Latinists, in other words to most people, the two are a source of endless confusion, to avoid which, both should be confined to footnotes or to bracketed information. In running text *e.g.* can be replaced with 'for example' or 'such as', and *i.e.* by 'that is (to say)' or 'namely'. Both should always be printed lower case roman with two points and no spaces.

ego has the plural form *egos*.

egoism, egotism. 1 Both are 18c words for 'preoccupation with oneself' in various ways. There is no etymological difference to affect their meanings, and the intrusive -*t*- in *egotism* is unexplained. When Fowler wrote about these words (1926), *egotism* was the more popular form, and his prediction that *egoism* would oust it has not been fulfilled. It is useful to maintain a distinction: *egotism* is the general word for excessive self-centredness, whereas *egoism* is a more technical word in ethics and metaphysics for theories which treat the self as the basis of morality and sense-perception. In an extended meaning, *egotism* also means self-seeking conceit, whereas *egoism* is a more straightforward preoccupation with the self and an excessive use of *I*. The meanings are however so close that they will not stay apart in ordinary usage, nor will those of the corresponding personal designations *egoist* and *egotist* (although strictly an *egoist* is someone who subscribes to a type of morality based on the importance of the self and an *egotist* is a self-seeker) and of the adjectival forms *egoistic / egoistical* and *egotistic / egotistical*.

2 Some examples follow: (*egoism* and its derivatives) *I have never gone out of my way for man, woman, or child. I am the complete egoist*—Vita Sackville-West, 1931 / *He can retain his insights into another person, and use them in choices of means, without abandoning his long-term egoistic ends for the altruistic goals to which he briefly felt himself drawn*—A. C. Graham, 1985 / *He* [i.e. C. S. Lewis] *writes about it in unforgettably dramatic terms and with the sublime egoism (to use the word purely, with no pejorative sense) of a man alone with God*—A. N. Wilson, 1990 / (*egotism* and its derivatives) *Nothing so confirms an egotism as thinking well of oneself*—Aldous Huxley, 1939 / *He was continually talking about himself and his relation to the world about him, a quality which created the unfortunate impression that he was simply a blatant egotist*—H. Miller, 1957 / *I* *had always thought him to be egotistical and attention-seeking*—D. M. Thomas, 1990 / *It amazed her that she'd ever believed herself in love with him, that she'd deluded herself into seeing his arrogance and his egotism as positive qualities*—S. Marton, 1993.

egregious. Of its two opposed meanings, 'remarkably good, distinguished' (as in Marlowe's *egregious viceroys of these eastern parts* in *Tamburlaine*) and 'remarkably bad', only the second is now in use, although it is also used to mean 'exceptional, unusual' more neutrally. The word comes from Latin *grex* meaning 'flock', and originally meant 'towering above the flock', i.e. 'prominent'. Modern examples: (with bad overtones) *It may well be the case that an egregious idiocy has formed the basis of a political tradition*—*Twentieth Century British History*, 1991 / *I have waited a long time to catch The Economist out on an egregious factual error*—*Economist*, 1993 / *While the most egregious excesses of the Internet bubble were to be found in America, rather than here, it is certainly not safe to assume that our markets are immune from the same problems*—*Independent*, 2005 / (neutral) *The inside is unified and austere, apart from an egregious baroque reredos, with a barrel vault, [etc.]*—J. Sturrock, 1988 / *He was truly egregious but a kind man and a good skipper*—*Dictionary of National Biography*, 1993.

eighties. This information is put here because *eighties* occurs first alphabetically, but it applies equally to *nineties*, *twenties*, *thirties*, and so on. These words, whether denoting decades or the years of a person's life, are spelt without an initial apostrophe, i.e. *eighties*, not '*eighties*. The years from 2000 to 2009 are sometimes informally called the *noughties* (based on the noughts on which the numbers are formed).

either. **1 pronunciation.** The pronunciations **iy**-dhuh and **ee**-dhuh are about equally common.

2 parts of speech. *Either* functions in two ways: as an adjective or pronoun, and as an adverb or conjunction. In all these uses, it means essentially 'one or other of two'; when more than two alternatives are involved an alternative word (such as *any*) or construction is often needed, at least in more formal contexts. (This aspect is discussed further in section 3 below.)

a adjective and pronoun. *Either* means 'one or the other of two' (*Either book will serve the purpose* / *Either of you can go*) or 'each of two' (*We sat down on either side of the table*).

b adverb and conjunction. The basic meaning is 'as one possibility or alternative', and is normally balanced by *or* (*You may have either tea or coffee* / *Either come in or go out, but don't just stand there*). The position of *either* and *or* should be such that the grammatical structures are correctly balanced, as in *Either I will go with John or I will stay here with you* but not in ⊠ *Either I will go with John or stay here with you*. It is also used with a negative, normally at the end of a clause or sentence (*She didn't want to come, either* / *There is no time to lose either*).

3 *either* with more than two. The essential duality of *either* is shown by the following example: *We either rely on our children to translate for us or we can try to catch up*—*Illustrated London News*, 1980. If the number of alternatives is extended to more than two, opinion is divided about the elegance and even the acceptability of the results; in general a greater tolerance is necessary in conversational English, but in formal English it is advisable to restrict *either* to contexts in which there are only two possibilities. In the case of the adjective and pronoun use, *either* should be replaced by *any* when a choice from more than two is involved (*Any of the books will serve the purpose*). It should be noted, however, that *any* can mean one or more than one, and so *any one* should be used when this is the meaning (*Answer any one of the following three questions*).

4 singular or plural after *either*. Normally *either* governs a singular verb (*Has either of you seen my pen?* / *Either John or Peter has got it*), but with the type *either of* (+ plural) a plural construction is sometimes used to emphasize the plurality of the statement as a whole, especially in inverted questions when the verb comes first (*Have either of you two ladies received an anonymous letter?*—A. E. W. Mason, 1924). Notional and grammatical agreement are in conflict in informal uses such as *Either John or Jane avert their eyes when I try to take their photograph*. When one of the alternatives is singular and the other plural, normal usage is to make the verb agree with the one closer to it (*Either the twins or their mother is responsible for this*). See also NEITHER.

ejector is spelt *-or*, not *-er*.

eke out. Fowler (1926) wanted to limit the use of this phrasal verb to refer to things that can be made to last longer or go further, i.e. a supply: 'you can eke out your income or a scanty subsistence with odd jobs or by fishing, but you cannot eke out a living or a miserable existence.' The meaning to which he referred is shown in: *Her mother . . . edited 'Aunt Judy's Magazine' to eke out the clerical income*—H. Carpenter, 1985 / *With its hints on how to eke out rations, homilies on cod liver oil, and recipes for eggless pasta, this was regarded as a vital part of the war effort at a critical point in the nation's fortunes*—OEC, 2001.

The use which Fowler rejected has nonetheless been standard since the 19c, and in current use the most commonly

found verb objects are *living, livelihood, existence*, and *subsistence*. So it is futile to object to it: *Some runaway slaves . . . contrived to eke out a subsistence*—Darwin, 1845 / *He lived with his parents until their death, and thereafter eked out a marginal living as a messenger*—Oliver Sacks, 1985 / *Eliza . . . declared she was skint and on the dole and was desperately trying to eke out a living as a musician*—Express, 2006.

elder, eldest, older, oldest. 1 *Elder* and *eldest* mean the same as *older* and *oldest* but they are much narrower in their range of use, being applicable only to people and only as nouns or attributive adjectives (before nouns). You can say *his elder brother* / *her sister is the eldest* / *John is my eldest son* / but you cannot say ⊠ *John is elder than Paul* / ⊠ *Which one is eldest?* / ⊠ *Who has the elder car?* In these cases, *older* or *oldest* has to be used, as it can also in the cases where *elder* and *eldest* are legitimate.

2 *Elder* has special uses in *elder hand* (in cards), *elder* (= senior) *partner*, and *elder statesman*, and (as a noun) is the title of lay officers of the Presbyterian Church.

elector is spelt *-or* not *-er*.

electric, electrical. In most contexts *electric* is the natural choice, especially to describe a device that works by electricity (*electric blanket* / *electric kettle*). *Electrical* is reserved for contexts in which the meaning is, more generally, 'relating to or concerned with electricity', as in *electrical engineering*.

electrocute. This portmanteau word, first recorded in 1889, contains the combining form *electro-* + *-cute* modelled on *execute* (verb). There seems to be an important difference in usage and meaning between BrE and AmE. In the US, where the word was coined to refer to the process of execution by electric current, if you are *electrocuted*, you die. As a result, phrases such as *to be electrocuted to death, to be fatally electrocuted*, etc., are considered a tautology there. In BrE, you can suffer an electric shock and refer to the event as being *electrocuted*, and it can also mean, in context, dying from or being executed by electric shock.

elegant variation is the name Fowler (1926) gave to a celebrated article, nearly six columns long, on misguided avoidance of repetition which leads the user into stylistic traps that are anything but elegant, such as using *women* and *ladies*, *cases* and *instances*, or *have, possess*, and *own* in parallel uses in the same sentence, for example *The total number of farming properties is 250,000; of these only 800 **have** more than 600 acres; 1,600 **possess** between 300 and 600 acres, while 116,000 **own** less than eight acres apiece.* Another kind of variation is represented by the sentence *We much **regret** to say that there were very **regrettable** incidents at both the mills.* Although he found fault with Thackeray (*careering during the season from one great dinner of twenty **covers** to another of eighteen **guests***), Fowler's main targets were 'minor novelists and reporters'. A modern type of elegant (or not so elegant) variation occurs frequently in journalism, and involves the substitution of a general description for a specific name, for example: ***Mr Hume** and his wife Pat were guests at a birthday party in New York, organised by the SDLP, at which **the Nobel peace prize winner** was presented with a framed tribute from President Clinton—Irish News, 2007.*

elegy, eulogy. An *elegy* was originally a lament for the dead, of which literary examples are Milton's *Lycidas* (1637) and Shelley's *Adonais* (1821). In the course of time, it came to mean any sorrowful poem or one written in the

metre associated with elegies, as in Gray's *Elegy Written in a Country Churchyard* (1751). A *eulogy* was originally a speech honouring a dead person, and has come to mean more generally anything formally written or spoken as a personal tribute.

elemental, elementary. *Elemental* refers primarily to the forces of nature and in particular to the ancient belief in the 'four elements' of earth, water, air, and fire, as in *elemental fire / elemental forces / elemental spirits / etc. Elementary*, on the other hand, means 'rudimentary, introductory', as in *elementary school / elementary mathematics / etc.* In modern physics, elementary means 'not able to be decomposed', as in *elementary particle.*

elephant. This noble animal has given rise to a number of phrases and idioms, such as *white elephant* and *see the elephant* (mainly AmE, meaning 'to gain experience of the world'). More recently, the presence of an *elephant in the room* signals 'a big problem or controversial issue which is obviously present but ignored or avoided as a subject for discussion, usually because it is more comfortable to do so' (*OED*). The phrase originates in North America and has spread rapidly to British use: *By the mid 1990s Martha's personal behaviour was the elephant in the room that nobody wanted to discuss. The elephant got bigger—Daily Telegraph, 2003.*

elevator is the word used in AmE and sometimes elsewhere for what in BrE is called *lift*. However, Americans as well as Britons use the word *ski-lift* for the device that carries skiers up a slope.

elicit, illicit. Confusion arises occasionally because both words are pronounced the same way (i-**lis**-it). *Elicit* is a verb meaning 'to draw out or evoke (an answer, admission, etc.)' whereas *illicit* is an adjective meaning 'unlawful, forbidden'. Examples of mistaken use: ⊠ *Whenever I publish a piece such as this it often illicits more questions than it provides answers—OEC*, 2004 (read *elicits*) / ⊠ *Whitfield, the local minister with whom Addie had an elicit affair, arrives at the house to direct her funeral—OEC*, 2002 (read *illicit*).

eligible. *Eligible* means 'fit or entitled to be chosen' (*eligible for a pension*) or 'desirable, suitable' (*an eligible bachelor*).

It ends in *-ible*, not *-able*, as is sometimes found.

ellipsis. 1 meaning. Ellipsis is the omission from a sentence of words which are normally needed to complete the grammatical construction or meaning. It occurs most often in everyday speech, in expressions such as *Told you so* (= I told you so) and *Sounds fine to me* (= It *or* that sounds fine to me), and also occurs regularly in all kinds of spoken and written English.

2 idiomatic ellipsis. Ordinary English grammar normally calls for the omission of certain elements, especially when they might otherwise be repeated from a previous occurrence in the same sentence. Examples are the definite article (*He heard the whirr and ⋏ click of machinery*), the infinitive marker *to* (*I was forced to leave and ⋏ give up my work at the hospital*), the subject of a verb (*I just pick up wood in a leisurely way, ⋏ stack it and ⋏ slowly rake the bark into heaps*), and the verb itself after *to* (*Knowledge didn't really advance, it only seemed to ⋏*) or after an auxiliary verb (*We must ⋏ and will rectify the situation*). More complex forms of ellipsis occur in literature, often for special effect: *Henriques knew they would eat his tongue for wisdom, ⋏ his heart for courage and for fertility ⋏ make their women chew his genitals—N. Shakespeare*, 1989. Other examples are

given by S. Greenbaum, *Oxford English Grammar* (1996), 77–8.

3 unacceptable types. The extent to which English allows words to be omitted in these ways is determined by what can reasonably be supplied by the hearer or reader from the rest of the sentence, without causing ambiguity or confusion. Ellipsis is not possible when the omitted word is not identical in form and function to its role where it is present, as in ⊠ *No state has ⋏ or can adopt such measures*, in which the word to be supplied is *adopted*, not *adopt*. Nor is it permitted when there is a change from active to passive in an omitted verb, as in *Our officials ought to manage things better than they have been*, in which the word to be supplied is *managed*, not *manage*; nor again when the construction changes, as in *The paintings of Monet are as good ⋏ or better than those of van Gogh*, which should read *. . . are as good as or better than those of van Gogh*. Less obviously wrong, but best avoided, are cases where number (singular / plural) changes, as in Fowler's characteristically gruesome example *The ring-leader was hanged and his followers ⋏ imprisoned* (with ellipsis of *were*).

4 omission of *that* in relative clauses. *See* THAT 3B.

5 ellipsis in non-standard speech. Ellipsis of auxiliary verbs such as *can, do,* and *have* is a feature of non-standard speech in AmE: *Well how you expect to get anywhere, how you expect to learn anything?—E. L. Doctorow*, 1989 / *I haven't seen you all summer, where you been at?—M. A. Dante*, 2004.

6 punctuation mark. *Ellipsis* is also used to mean a punctuation mark consisting of (usually) three full points to mark either a pause or the intentional omission of words (for example in quoting).

else. 1 The usual possessive forms are *anybody else's*, *someone else's*, etc., and not (for example) *anybody's else*, although this was used until the mid-19c: *They look to me like someone else's, to be frank*—Penelope Lively, 1987 / *We would like to think our service is better than anyone else's*—Daily Record, 2007.

2 In questions, *else* invariably follows an interrogative pronoun, as in *What else did he say?* Postponement of *else* to the end of the sentence, as in *What did he say else?*, although possible up to the early part of the 20c, is no longer grammatical.

3 Thus use of *else* as a conjunction to mean 'otherwise, if not', which has been common in literature since the Middle Ages, now seems archaic but is still found in informal speech: *Fortunately it* [i.e. a staircase] *was not spiral, else I would have succumbed to vertigo*—B. Rubens, 1985.

elusive, illusive, illusory. *Elusive* is the adjective corresponding to *elude*, and means 'difficult to grasp (physically or mentally)'. *Illusory* is the adjective corresponding to *illusion*, and means 'deceptive, not real or actual'. Examples of each: *Preparations are now complete and they set off in a few days' time to try and capture that elusive denizen of the deep*—the Loch Ness Monster—Stornoway Gazette, 1971 / *The notion that Britain has suddenly been rendered entirely 'safe' or 'secure' is illusory*—Times, 2005.

The word *illusive* means the same as *illusory*, but is very rarely used in that way. Instead, nine times out of ten it is a mistake for *elusive*: ✘ *Sharks up to forty feet are quite common, although when Helen was there they proved to be illusive*—OEC, 2005.

email, short for *electronic mail*, is a term that has become familiar enough to be spelt as one word, without a hyphen. Its grammatical behaviour follows that of *mail*, i.e. it is a noun and a verb; you can send an *email* and you can *email* messages and people. *See* E-.

emails. 1 Writing and receiving emails is now so much a part of everyday personal and business life that it warrants guidance comparable to that for writing letters (*see* LETTER FORMS). Generally speaking, emails tend to combine the immediacy of conversation with the formality or semi-formality of letter writing, a situation that sometimes makes people uncertain about the appropriate way to express themselves. The main areas of uncertainty concern the opening greeting, signing off, and the style and level of formality in the message.

2 opening greeting. Using *Dear*— makes an email somewhat formal. It is appropriate in business, when emailing a new contact, or an established contact, relations with whom you wish to keep on a formal footing. Whether and at what point you switch to a less formal opening is for you to judge, depending on how your relations with the other person are developing. In other contexts, email's affinity with conversation encourages much more casual greetings such as *Hello*— and *Hi*—, as in a hastily written message or in text messaging (*see* TEXT MESSAGE).

3 signing off. Similarly, to sign off nowadays with *Yours* or *Yours sincerely* is extremely formal in an email, though normal, of course, in a letter. (If you feel the need to write *Yours faithfully* you should be writing a conventional letter with a proper letterhead.) It is quite legitimate to close the email with a simple statement of your name, without any sign-off, but this may strike some people as rather cold. The most commonly used sign-offs nowadays are the informal conversational ones such as *Best wishes*, *All the best*, and *Best regards*. If you are not comfortable with any of those, *Thanks* is unlikely to go amiss, particularly if the email is a request of some kind.

4 level of formality. In a professional context, the normal conventions of spelling, grammar, and punctuation should govern what you write. Resist the temptation to be too informal, or to ignore punctuation and capitalization in the way that you might when texting, or to use abbreviations such as *u*, *gr8*, and so forth (*i dont want to go to france this year do u*). A professional email is decidedly not a text message, though, of course, in personal emails, if you know someone well enough to know they will not be offended, or baffled, by using text conventions, feel free. It goes without saying that you should not write in capital letters, which, by convention, is SHOUTING.

5 other issues.

a As with any piece of writing destined to be read by someone else, you should read through what you have written to check for grammar and spelling.

The best way to do this is to print out before you send, since even spellcheckers will not detect every glitch.

b Your subject line should ideally tell the recipient at a glance what your message is about, and whether it requires any action by them. At the same time, it should be as concise as possible. For example, *Linguistics from Oxford— Available on Inspection* informs the recipient in just six words what the topic is and what action they can take, i.e. order an inspection copy.

c Emails should ideally be short, so that the content can be read in one screen, without scrolling down. Bullet points and lines between paragraphs help make the information easier to process. If you find that your email is turning into a lengthy e-missive, it is

likely that another way of presenting the information would be better, such as an attached text file, chart, etc. Alternatively, a separate email per topic may be a solution.

d There are many other points to consider when composing an email, for example, not writing something you would be embarrassed if people other than the recipient saw, since emails can be forwarded and forwarded again, ad infinitum, and their contents come back to haunt you. However, the previous advice falls outside the scope of what is strictly language-related, and there are any number of websites you can consult for detailed information about how to make your emails effective, interesting, appealing, and so forth.

emanate. The standard pronunciation of this word is **e**-muh-nayt with a short initial *e*, rather than **ee**-muh-nayt.

embargo. The noun has the plural form *embargoes* and the verb the inflections *embargoes*, *embargoed*, *embargoing*.

embarrass, embarrassment are spelt with two *r*s and two *s*'s.

embed can be spelt *em* or *im*-. *Embed* is the more common form, and is recommended, since many people would consider *imbed* a mistake.

emigrant, immigrant, migrant.
1 An *emigrant* is someone who leaves his or her home country to live in another country; and an *immigrant* is one who comes to live in a country from abroad. The same person is therefore an *emigrant* on going through the exit gate at a port or airport and is an *immigrant* when given permission to take up residence in the country of arrival. The corresponding verbs are *emigrate* and *immigrate*. (Note one *m* in *emigrant* etc. and two *m*s in *immigrant* etc.)

2 A *migrant* is (a) a migrating animal or bird, (b) in Australia and New Zealand, an immigrant, or (c, in full *economic migrant*) someone who travels from one country or area to another to find work or an improved standard of living. An *émigré* (French = having emigrated) is a political emigrant, originally one from France during the French Revolution.

eminent. Some people write *eminent danger* when what they presumably mean is *imminent danger*. It is possible they do this because they pronounce the *e-* and the *i-* at the beginning of the two words similarly. If it means anything at all, 'eminent danger' would be great danger. Something *imminent* is of course something about to happen, so *imminent danger* is a danger that is very close at hand.

emote is a back-formation meaning 'to express emotion'. It is first recorded in America in 1917, and although it was once largely restricted to the language of ballet and theatre critics and to photography it has expanded more recently into general usage, but usually with more than a soupçon of sarcasm or humour: *The female sitter had to emote in some way, either by dressing up or by gazing with drooping head into a bowl of flowers*—Amateur Photographer, 1970 / *How are you going to get up and emote in front of an audience?*—L. S. Schwartz, 1989 / *She settles in her seat, accepts coffee, flirts with the ticket-collector, cuts up rough about the price of a first-class upgrade, gets distraught at the sight of someone narrowly missing their train, and generally emotes all over the place*—Independent, 2002.

emoticon. The word is a blend of *emotion* and *icon* and denotes a representation often formed by means of standard word-processing keystrokes of a person's face (normally the writer's) expressing a particular emotion such as

anger, fear, frustration, surprise, delight, etc. It is a common feature of emails and text messaging, and is pronounced i-**moh**-ti-kon, with the stress on the second syllable.

emotional, emotive. *Emotional* and *emotive* both mean 'connected with or appealing to the emotions', but *emotional* is the word more often used in the neutral sense 'relating to emotions' whereas *emotive* has a stronger sense of 'causing emotion': *In this oppressive society women need the care and emotional support of other women*— A. Wilson, 1988 / *The whole subject of removing children from their parents was no less emotive for them than for other members of the community*—R. Black, 1992. *Emotional*, but not *emotive*, also means 'easily affected by emotion' with reference to people *(All of us get elated and emotional as we stroll through a pine grove on a hot summer day when the old trees fill the air with their pungent fragrance*—P. Heselton, 1991). *Emotive* is more commonly used of words or behaviour that tends to arouse emotions, and often qualifies words such as *issue, language, topic*, etc. *(He was just firing a smokescreen of emotive words and phrases*—Gavin Lyall, 1982), whereas *emotional* describes feeling and actions that involve emotion in themselves *(From a good script will emerge a film in which every scene carries an emotional charge*—J. Park, 1990). However, the considerable overlap in meaning is shown by the fact that the two words could be exchanged in the last two examples without making any major difference to the way they are understood.

empathy. 1 This is originally a term used in psychology and aesthetics meaning 'the power of identifying oneself mentally with (and so fully comprehending) a person or object of contemplation'. In general use it tends to replace *sympathy* or *feeling for* when these words are sometimes more appropriate; *sympathy* can be felt without the element of personal experience that is implied by *empathy*: *Seeing our sadness, our empathy with the pain she was surely suffering, she said, 'What's wrong with you all?'*—A. Davis, 1975 / *It was a hard life, and Byron recounts it with empathy and gusto*—Anthony Burgess, 1986. It also gained some currency from educationists who established a fashion for teaching history by getting pupils to feel *empathy* for (or *empathizing* with) people of other ages, as an antidote to preoccupation with political history. But all that has changed again.

2 The corresponding adjective is either *empathic* or *empathetic* (the more usual form in the *OEC*, although neither is of particularly high frequency).

employee has long since replaced *employé* (feminine *employée*) as the dominant form in BrE for someone who is employed. In AmE the alternative form is *employe*, pronounced as three syllables and usually stressed on the second.

emporium is a formal word for a large retail store or a centre of commerce. The principal plural form is *emporia*, although *emporiums* is almost equally common.

empower, empowerment. *Empower* is a 17c verb meaning 'to give power or authority to'. In the 1970s it acquired a new meaning, 'to make (someone) able to do something', implying the freedom to adopt moral values and principles of one's choice as advocated by members of the New Age movement and others. A person who is *self-empowered* is able to act independently of the constraints imposed by conventional values: *These self-empowered individuals are motivated by teamwork and developing broader skills rather than just achieving*

conventional status—*Independent*, 1995. The corresponding nouns are *empowerment* and *self-empowerment*.

-en adjectives. The practice of adding *-en* to nouns denoting a substance, as in *golden*, *silken*, and *woollen*, dates from Old English. From the earliest time, however, and especially from the 16c, there has been a tendency to use the corresponding noun before another noun (i.e. attributively), as in *a gold* [*not golden*] *brooch* and *silk* [*not silken*] *curtains*. By this process, forms in *-en* have been enabled to develop figurative meanings, so that we are now much more likely to encounter *brazen impudence* than *brazen rods*, *leaden skies* rather than *a leaden roof*, and *a silken touch* rather than *silken curtains*.

enamel has the forms *enamelled*, *enamelling* in BrE and *enameled*, *enameling* in AmE.

enamour is commonly used in the form *be enamoured of*, or sometimes *be enamoured with*, usually in negative or ironic contexts: *I am not so much enamoured of the first and third subjects*—Dickens, 1866 / *Not all feminists were so enamoured with such tactics*—F. Mort, 1987 / *He was also not enamoured of the music, although he later found it much more enjoyable*—M. Hodkinson, 1990. The US spelling is *enamor*.

en bloc, meaning 'as a whole', was adopted into English in the later 19c, and is now normally regarded as naturalized and, therefore, printed in ordinary roman type.

enclose is the recommended form for the word meaning 'to close in, include, etc.', not *inclose*.

encomium, meaning 'a formal expression of praise', has the plural form *encomiums* or, rather less often, *encomia*.

encrust, meaning 'to cover or decorate something with a crust', is preferable to *incrust*.

encyclopaedia, encyclopedia. This word is first recorded in English in the 16c, and was adopted from a late Latin word which in turn was based on a supposedly corrupted form of a Greek term meaning 'general education' in the arts and sciences. The standard AmE form *encyclopedia* is now also very common in British book titles, especially of books of general information as distinct from books on special areas of knowledge, where the older form *encyclopaedia* is still holding its own.

endear. To *endear* someone to someone else means 'to make someone popular with or liked by someone'. The meaning is easy to grasp, but some people use it with unconventional grammar. You can *endear yourself* to other people: *she endeared herself to all who worked with her*. Alternatively, a quality someone has, or an action on their part, can *endear* them to other people: *Flora's spirit and character endeared her to everyone who met her*. But to say *his cooperative attitude endeared me to him*, when you mean 'made *me* like *him*', is to describe who likes whom the wrong way round; it should be *his cooperative attitude endeared him to me*.

endeavour is the spelling for the noun and verb in BrE, *endeavor* in AmE. *See* FORMAL WORDS.

ended, ending. *Figures for the period ending / ended 31 December*. In referring to periods of time, *ended* is used to denote the terminal date when the time is in the past, and *ending* when the time is in the future or (in current use) in the past; so *ending* is never wrong. The word used of the initial date is always *beginning*, never *begun*.

endemic, epidemic. An *endemic* disease is one that is regularly or only found among a particular people or in a particular region, whereas an *epidemic* disease is a temporary but widespread outbreak of a disease. *Epidemic*, but not *endemic*, also functions (more usually) as a noun. Both words have extended meanings in relation to things other than diseases: *It is among managerial and professional workers that sponging, skiving and malingering is epidemic—New Society*, 1975 / *Recurrent energy crises are endemic in African agricultural societies*—G. T. Nurse, 1985 / *Action must be taken to tackle the endemic problem of begging in the city centre—Belfast Telegraph*, 2007.

end of the day. *At the end of the day* is one of the less attractive 20c clichés. It is first recorded in 1974 and means no more than 'when all's said and done': *But, at the end of the day, it is an amateur sport and everyone is free to put as much or as little into the game as he chooses—*B. Beaumont, 1982.

endorse. It is interesting to reflect that this word's modern marketing meaning 'to give one's approval to (a product)' was labelled by the *Concise Oxford Dictionary* in 1914 as 'vulgar in advertisements'. Its original meaning is 'to write on the back of (a document)', from Latin *dorsum* 'back', with various applications in law and commerce. In the 19c it came to mean 'to support (an opinion)', from which the use in advertising developed.

end product, end result. Both have been criticized for containing an element of redundancy, since both a product and a result must necessarily come at the end, but they are well established. *End product* was first used in chemistry by Rutherford to describe 'a stable, non-radioactive nuclide that is the final product of a radioactive series'.

enforce is the correct spelling, not *inforce* (which however survives in *reinforce*). Its typical grammatical objects are such things as a law or rule, a ban, a policy, a person's wish, etc. The derived adjective is *enforceable*.

England, English *see* BRITAIN, GREAT BRITAIN, THE BRITISH ISLES, ENGLAND, ETC.

English worldwide. English is used as a first language by an estimated 375 million people, and as a second language by over 400 million people (estimates vary widely). There are many varieties and styles of English in different parts of the world; see AMERICAN ENGLISH; AUSTRALIAN ENGLISH; BLACK ENGLISH; DIALECT; ESTUARY ENGLISH; STANDARD ENGLISH. The diversity of English is reflected in the titles of recent books on English worldwide, such as Tom McArthur, *The English Languages* (1998), Jennifer Jenkins, *World Englishes: A Resource Book for Students* (2003), and Braj Kachru et al., *The Handbook of World Englishes* (2006).

enhance means 'to improve or intensify (something already good)' and is used typically with reference to achievements, reputations, values, effectiveness, efficiency, performance, capability, etc. It is not used with a person as object; *The book enhanced her reputation* is correct, but *The publication of her book enhanced her* is not.

enjoin. 1 *Enjoin* has meanings connected with commanding and issuing instructions, and is typically used in three constructions: (1) you enjoin a person *to* do something, (2) you enjoin something *on* a person, and (3) you enjoin *that* something should happen. Fowler (1926) wrote that the first of these 'is not recommended', but his reasons were not convincing even then and this construction is now too common and

useful to be objected to: *The church had enjoined the faithful to say an Ave Maria*—Barry Unsworth, 1985 / *I was particularly enjoined to keep away from the dogs, and never to give any of them my hands*—Liverpool Daily Post, 2003 / *He not only enjoins us to eat bread, ... but he asks that we 'empathise' with the yeast as it goes about its leavening work*—Sunday Times, 2006.

2 In an almost opposite meaning, in use in legal language since the 16c, *enjoin* means 'to prohibit or forbid' (an action); in this meaning it can refer to a person or thing, and is typically followed by *from*: *The Al-Fayed brothers ... sought to enjoin the Observer from publishing the results of its continuing enquiries*—Observer, 1986 / *Metropolitan Life ... has filed a suit to enjoin the takeover*—Times, 1988.

enjoy continues to be used with reference to things that are the complete opposite of enjoyable (such as ill health or a poor reputation), despite its identification as a 'catachrestic' (incorrect) use in the *OED*: *Despite the jokey reputation that middle-class British hotels enjoy, they compare very well indeed for comfort with their European and US counterparts*—Homes & Gardens, 1970 / *As a child he enjoyed poor health (one of those phrases loaded with unintended irony that so amused him in later life)*—Independent, 1996. This use is no more than an apparently illogical development of meaning characteristic of all languages, and it is well established.

enormity, enormousness. 1 Both words are derived from Latin *e norma* meaning 'out of the ordinary', and both originally had meanings associated with wicked and criminal aspects of abnormality. *Enormity* (15c) is older than *enormousness* (17c), and its first recorded meanings are 'a breach of the law, a crime'. Both words have also been used unexceptionably at different times to mean what *enormousness* now means, 'very great size', but by the end of the 19c *enormity* was confined again to its special meaning, 'great wickedness', as in *The enormity of the crime shocked everyone*, and to its concrete use as in *The regime inflicted many enormities on its opponents*. This distinction continues to be defended by many advocates of careful usage in most contexts.

2 Because *enormousness* is such an awkward word, and alternatives such as *hugeness* and *immensity* are not much better, *enormity* is beginning to compete with it again in contexts that have nothing to do with wickedness, depravity, and suchlike, but these uses are likely to attract disapproval: ☒ *A wide-angle lens captures the enormity of the Barbican Centre, London's new arts complex—Times*, 1982 / ☒ *The enormity of such open spaces momentarily alarms her—*Susan Johnson, AusE 1990 / ☒ *He didn't have much time to think about the enormity of what he was taking on—Express*, 2007.

3 In the examples that follow, *enormity* is used correctly according to the criterion given above: *Hanging would seem quite a lenient sentence considering the enormity of his crime in those harsh old days—*R. Long, 1990 / *I did not know then that one frequently fails to live up to the enormity of death—*Anita Brookner, 1990 / *The word arrogance is almost too small to contain the enormity of the offence here—Scotsman*, 2007. There is a practical point to be made, that generalized use of *enormity*, given its special meaning, can lead to ambiguity in contexts such as *We all recognize the enormity of their achievement*, when the achievement in question might anyway be open to different interpretations. However, meanings legitimately overlap in sentences such as the following: *She tried to be a strength for her daughter, but was overwhelmed by the enormity of what was happening to them all—*R. Black, 1992.

enough, sufficient, sufficiently.
1 *Enough* functions as both an adjective and an adverb, whereas *sufficient* requires modification as *sufficiently*. As an adjective (or modifier), *enough* will normally serve, but *sufficient* is more idiomatic when a more qualitative point is being made. For example, in the sentence *There will inevitably be concerns that the courts' powers are not sufficient for worthwhile penalties to be imposed—Bristol Evening Post*, 2007, *sufficient* implies the inadequacy more harshly than if *enough* had been used. *Enough* also has two grammatical characteristics that are not shared by *sufficient*: (1) *enough* cannot be used with mass nouns denoting quantity, such as *number, supply*, etc., preceded by the indefinite article; you can say *a sufficient number* but not ☒ *an enough number,* and (2) *enough* can be placed postpositively (after the word it qualifies), as in *They have money enough for a holiday* and *They do not have a large enough house*, which places a greater emphasis on the commodity or attribute in question.

2 Choice between *enough* and *sufficiently* when they are used as adverbs is normally determined by the degree of formality needed, *sufficiently* being the more formal. The main grammatical difference between them is that *enough* is placed after the word it qualifies when this is an adjective or another adverb: *He was not firm enough* and *She did not sing well enough* but *He was not sufficiently firm* and *She did not sing sufficiently well*. There is no difference in use when they qualify verbs or clauses: *They are not working enough* and *They are not working sufficiently*.

enquire, enquiry, inquire, inquiry.
The forms in *en-* and *in-* have long been

largely interchangeable. At present the *in-* forms are dominant in all meanings in AmE, whereas in BrE there is a tendency to prefer the *in-* forms for official or formal types of investigation and (to a lesser extent) the *en-* forms for routine or general types of information-seeking. The differences in BrE are seen in these typical collocations: (formal investigation) *inquiry agency / judicial inquiry / public inquiry / a committee to inquire into the allegations /* (general information-seeking) *enquired after her health / several enquiries about the job / directory enquiries / door-to-door enquiries.*

enrol is spelt with one *l* and is inflected with two *l*s in *enrolled, enrolling, enroller,* but there is only one *l* in *enrolment.* In AmE, there are two *l*s in all these forms, including *enroll* itself.

en route. This phrase from French (*en* = in, *route* = road) has been in use since the 18c. It is printed in roman, not italics, and is correctly written as two words, not as one, which commonly happens, especially in AmE. The spellings *on route* and *onroute* are also both mistakes. They are presumably caused because the phrase is pronounced nowadays in an anglicized way as **on root**, whereas it used to be pronounced in a French fashion.

ensure *see* ASSURE.

enter. Neither Fowler nor Gowers, nor even Burchfield in 1998, included an entry on *enter*, which is surprising given its range of collocation and usage. It is both transitive (i.e. takes an object) and intransitive: you can *enter a place* or simply *enter.* A person who enters a building may well be doing so illegally (as in *breaking and entering*). Joining a profession such as the church or the law is also described as a form of *entering.* You can enter *on* or *upon* a property or, in non-physical senses, a legal

agreement or contract. If you enter *into* something you become involved in it (a use that the *OED* traces back to Coverdale in the 16c) or begin to discuss it. *Entering* information in a register makes a record of it there, and the same can be said of data stored electronically, which is also *entered* into a computer file.

enterprise is spelt *-ise*, not *-ize*.

enthral is spelt with one *l* and is inflected with two *l*s in *enthralled, enthralling,* but there is only one *l* in *enthralment.* In AmE, there are two *l*s in all these forms, including *enthrall* itself; and there is a variant *inthrall.*

enthuse is a 19c back-formation meaning 'to show enthusiasm' or 'cause enthusiasm in', and is used with and without an object; you can enthuse people, enthuse *over* or *about* something, or simply enthuse (typically with direct speech): *As we talk he is enthusing over the result of the recent devolution referendum—Scotsman,* 1997 / *London's biggest challenge is to enthuse younger generations with the Olympic ideals—Guardian,* 2007 / *'The sheer scale, height, glam, glitz is just going to be mind-blowing,' enthused Donovan—Daily Telegraph,* 2007. Although regarded with disfavour by those for whom verb back-formations are second-class words, it is here to stay, and serves a useful purpose.

entrench, meaning 'to establish firmly', is spelt *en-*, not *in-*.

envelop, envelope. *Envelop* (with stress on the second syllable) is the form for the verb, meaning 'to wrap up, surround, etc.', and it inflects *envelops, enveloped, enveloping. Envelope* (with stress on the first syllable, now normally pronounced **en-** rather than **on-**) is the form for the noun, meaning 'a container for a letter, etc.'.

-en verbs from adjectives. *See box overleaf.*

environs, meaning 'the surrounding area of a place', is a plural noun and should be pronounced in-**viy**-ruhnz, with the same pattern as in *environment.*

envisage, envision. 1 *Envisage* is an early 19c loanword from French, meaning at first 'to look in the face of' and then (its current meaning) 'to have a mental picture of (something yet to happen)'. Fowler (1926) dismissed it as an 'undesirable Gallicism' and recommended as alternatives the words *face, confront, contemplate, recognize, realize, view,* and *regard.* Gowers (1965) added *imagine, intend,* and *visualize* to the list of words for which *envisage* was 'a pretentious substitute'. None of these will always quite serve, however, and only some of them can be substituted for *envisage* in its common construction followed by a verbal noun (*We do not envisage leaving just yet*).

2 Neither Fowler not Gowers noticed the arrival, first in Britain (1921) and then more assertively in America, of the closely synonymous word *envision,* meaning 'to see or foresee as in a vision'. The evidence of current use shows that *envision* is strongly favoured in AmE and *envisage* in BrE, but the division is not absolute and *envision* is becoming more common in BrE. Examples: (envisage) *The best scenario . . . that we can envisage is one in which all those who want to do formal work will have an opportunity of doing two or three days a week—Journal of the Royal Society of Arts,* 1980 / *So mother envisaged us all here, gathered round staring down in this ghastly way—* Penelope Lively, 1989 / *Smith does not envisage bringing in a replacement—Times,* 2006 / *I did not envisage it would get as bad as this—Independent,* 2006 / (envision) *His blackest hypochondria had never envisioned quite so miserable a*

*Catastrophe—*Lytton Strachey, 1921 / *They envision themselves wearing berets . . . and crawling about the rubble, throwing Molotov cocktails—Melody Maker,* 1968 / *It may be only the stuff of newspaper editorials, of course, to envision a strategy in which the United Nations takes decisive action—Sunday Times,* 1990 / *The Hubble was working as envisioned—*weblog, CanE 2005.

eon is an American spelling of **aeon.*

ephemeral. Derived from a Greek word meaning 'living only a day; short-lived', and first introduced into English in the 16c, *ephemeral* is traditionally pronounced i-**fem**-(uh)-r(a)l, with a short second *e,* although the pronunciation with a long *e* is also valid. Possibly its most famous appearance is in Auden's *Lullaby: Time and fevers burn away Individual beauty from Thoughtful children, and the grave Proves the child ephemeral.*

epic. 1 *Epic* is a term traditionally applied (first as an adjective, later as a noun) to narrative poems that celebrate the achievements of the heroes of history or legend, such as the *Iliad,* the *Odyssey,* Virgil's *Aeneid,* Milton's *Paradise Lost,* the *Chanson de Roland,* the Old English elegiac poem *Beowulf,* and the Hindu *Mahābhārata* and *Rāmāyana.* The name normally applied to Old Norse narrative poems of this kind is *saga.*

2 The word has been extended in more recent usage to refer to any major literary work, theatrical performance, or (especially) film, which has some claim to be regarded as exceptional in length, subject matter, or scale of treatment: *I want very much to see the Birth of a Nation, which is said to be a really great film, an epic in pictures—*Aldous Huxley, 1916 / *Talking of films, Meier is still working on his wild, underground epic, Snowball, as well as producing a new Hollywood movie called MM—Face,*

-EN VERBS FROM ADJECTIVES.

1 There are about fifty verbs ending in -en (e.g. cheapen, harden) which have been formed from adjectives. The table given below shows that this process of verb formation was at its most productive in Middle English and in the early modern period up to about 1700. There is only one possible pair before the Norman Conquest (11c), namely the Old English antecedents of fast and fasten, but the relation of these two words to one another is not at all straightforward. The table also shows representative examples of (1) adjectives (such as blind) which function as verbs without adding -en, (2) adjectives which have two verb forms in current use (such as smooth), (3) adjectives (such as hot, long, and strong) which resort to cognates (heat, lengthen, and strengthen), and (4) adjectives (such as cold) which have no corresponding verb form at all. Dates refer to forms in the preceding columns, and are of the formation of the word, whether or not in the meaning(s) now current.

2 Other verbs, such as enfeeble, enlarge, and enrich (all ME), were formed by adding the prefix en- rather than the suffix -en.

3 Nearly all the -en verbs which came into existence in the 16c and 17c joined or replaced words that were spelt in the same way as the adjective. For example, deep already existed as a verb in the Anglo-Saxon period, and deepen did not join it and compete with it until the 16c.

4 By 1700 the productive power of the suffix had largely disappeared. The 18c produced only broaden, madden, and tighten; the 19c only coarsen, quieten, smarten, and tauten; and the most recent is neaten (1898).

adjective	verb 1	date	verb 2	date	verb 3	date
black	black	ME	blacken	ME		
bright			brighten	OE		
broad			broaden	18c		
cheap			cheapen	16c		
coarse			coarsen	19c		
cold						
damp	damp	ME	dampen	16c		
dark			darken	ME		
dead			deaden	17c		
deaf			deafen	16c		
deep			deepen	16c		
fast			fasten	OE		
fat			fatten	16c		
flat	flat	16c	flatten	17c		
foul	foul	OE				
fresh			freshen	17c		
glad			gladden	ME		
good						
hard			harden	ME		
hot	hot	OE			heat	OE
lame	lame	ME				
less			lessen	ME		

light (= not heavy)			lighten	ME		
light (shining)	light	OE	lighten	ME		
like			liken	ME		
long					lengthen	ME
loose	loose	ME	loosen	ME		
mad			madden	18c		
moist			moisten	16c		
neat			neaten	19c		
quick			quicken	ME		
quiet	quiet	ME	quieten	19c		
red			redden	17c		
ripe			ripen	ME		
rough	rough	15c	roughen	16c		
sad			sadden	ME		
sharp			sharpen	ME		
short			shorten	ME		
sick			sicken	ME		
slack			slacken	16c		
smart			smarten	19c		
smooth	smooth	ME	smoothen	17c		
soft			soften	ME		
stiff			stiffen	15c		
still	still	OE				
stout			stouten	19c		
straight			straighten	16c		
strong					strengthen	ME
sweet			sweeten	ME		
taut			tauten	19c		
thick			thicken	ME		
tight			tighten	18c		
tough			toughen	16c		
weak			weaken	ME		
wet	wet	OE				
white			whiten	ME		
wide			widen	17c		
worse			worsen	ME		

1992. It has also gone full circle in acquiring a new adjectival meaning 'great, heroic' variously used before a noun (attributively): *The Communists' Red Army had just completed its epic Long March from the Southeast to its new headquarters at Yenan*—Time, 1977 / *In his epic landscape of Jerusalem executed in April of 1830, Roberts draws the Holy City in silhouette*—R. Fisk, 1991 / *It was from fear of his intellect sinking into torpor that he finally took up the battle against drink. It was an epic struggle, marked by his terrible and yet frequently comic accounts of failure after failure*—Independent, 2000.

epicentre (AmE **epicenter**). Some pundits insist that *epicentre* has only a technical meaning, namely 'the point on the earth's surface vertically above the focus of an earthquake'. One writer cautions: 'Do not use it as a fancy word for "centre", which too many pretentious writers do.' So, should non-seismologists avoid it at all costs? It depends. In what seems like a legitimate extension of its core meaning, it denotes the central point of something, typically a difficult or unpleasant situation, e.g. *the two farms treated as the epicentre of the outbreak of the bird flu.* To object to its use in that way seems a trifle pedantic. More debatable, however, is its use to heighten descriptions of creative, cultural or political movements, which seems to be largely a mannerism of British journalism, e.g. *I want to be at the epicentre of youth culture for as long as I care to continue working—Guardian,* 2003.

Replacing *epicentre* with *centre of* or *right at the centre of* would not change the meaning and would be less pompous.

epidemic *see* ENDEMIC.

epigram, epigraph. Both words come from the same Greek roots meaning 'to write (or written) on'. *Epigram* is slightly earlier (16c) and has two principal meanings in current use, (1) a short poem with a witty or ingenious ending, and (2) a terse or pungent saying. A third meaning, a dedicatory or explanatory inscription on a building, tomb, coin, etc., is now obsolete and is supplied by *epigraph*, which also means a short quotation or pithy sentence put at the beginning of a book, chapter, etc., as a foretaste of the leading idea or sentiment to be found in the work.

episcopalian means 'belonging or referring to an episcopal church', i.e. a church founded on the principle of government by bishops. It refers primarily to the Anglican Church in Scotland and the US, which has elected bishops; in this context it is spelt with a capital initial, *Episcopalian.*

epistle refers primarily to the letters of the New Testament, e.g. the Epistle of St Paul the Apostle to the Romans. It is sometimes used ironically or whimsically to mean a letter of any kind: *When mischievous gossip columnists were prompted to discuss her age, she put them down with a peremptory epistle to The Times—Evening Standard,* 2003.

epithet. An *epithet* is an adjective indicating some quality or attribute (good or bad) which the speaker or writer (or the verdict of history) regards as characteristic of a person or thing, e.g. *Charles the Bold, Ethelred the Unready, Philip the Good, William the Silent,* and many figures (*Alexander, Alfred, Peter, Pompey,* etc.) called *the Great.* An *epithet* can also be a noun used as a significant title or appellation, e.g. *William the Conqueror, Vlad the Impaler.* In more casual use, *epithet* simply means 'description' or 'name': *This is a character who is quite happy to be known by the epithet 'Dopey', having been born with big ears and not much hair—Independent on Sunday,* 2005.

epitome, pronounced as four syllables (i-**pit**-uh-mi), is derived from a Greek word literally meaning 'to cut into'. It has two main meanings in English, (1) a person or thing typically representing a quality or class (*Little did he dream when he designed the polka dot that one day it would become the epitome of fashion—New Yorker,* 1970), and (2) a summary or shorter version of something written (*The book . . . is not intended to be popular. No doubt a lively epitome will one day be made for general reading—* Evelyn Waugh, 1956).

epoch. 1 An *epoch* is the beginning of a distinctive period in the history of something or someone, whereas an *era* is a period of history characterized by particular circumstances or by a particular series of events. A *period* is a more general term for a distinct portion of time in relation to a person's life or to human history and an *aeon* is an immeasurable length of time often used in more rhetorical contexts. In geology, the three terms *epoch*, *era*, and *period* have special meanings: *era* denotes the largest unit of time, a *period* is a division of this, and an *epoch* is a subdivision of a *period*.

2 The adjective *epoch-making* is first recorded in the 19c (Coleridge had used *epoch-forming* in 1816), and is now widely used as a rather exaggerated way of saying 'remarkable, significant' as well as (more appropriately) 'historic': *This was an epoch-making moment in the history of Egypt, like the day a dam bursts*—N. Barber, 1984 / *There were a large number of epoch-making events whose 40th anniversaries were celebrated towards the end of last year, as readers will undoubtedly recall*—*Times Educational Supplement*, 2004.

eponym, eponymous. 1 An *eponym* is a person after whom something is named, such as a building, an institution, an organization, a machine, a product, or a process. Examples include: *Alzheimer's disease*, from Alois *Alzheimer*, 1864–1915, German neurologist; *Braille*, from Louis *Braille*, 1809–52, French inventor; *buckminsterfullerene*, from the American designer and architect Richard *Buckminster Fuller*; *diesel*, from Rudolf *Diesel*, 1858–1913, German engineer; *mackintosh*, from Charles *Macintosh*, 1766–1843 (with a change of spelling); *Morse code*, from S. F. B. *Morse*, 1791–1872, American inventor; *sandwich*, from the 4th Earl of *Sandwich*, 1718–92.

2 The adjective *eponymous* is used in the following way: *Beowulf* is the *eponymous* hero of the Old English poem of that name; *Emma* is the *eponymous* heroine of the novel *Emma* by Jane Austen; and *Robinson Crusoe* is the *eponymous* hero of *The Life and Strange and Surprising Adventures of Robinson Crusoe* by Daniel Defoe.

equable, equitable. Both words come from Latin *aequus* meaning 'equal', but their meanings are different. *Equable* means 'even and moderate, regular' and is typically used with words such as *climate, disposition*, and *temperament*. It denotes avoidance of extremes as well as avoidance of change. *Equitable* means 'just, fair' (usually with reference to several parties involved), and is typically used with words such as *agreement, distribution, principle, remedy, settlement*, and *solution*.

equal. 1 As a verb, *equal* has inflected forms *equalled, equalling* in BrE and *equaled, equaling* in AmE.

2 As an adjective, *equal* is followed by *to* (*The square on the hypotenuse is equal to the sum of the squares on the other two sides*), whereas the verb takes a direct object without *to* (*The square on the hypotenuse equals the sum of the squares on the other two sides*). *Equal to* also has the meaning 'fit for, able to deal with' (*I hope I shall be equal to the challenge*— P. Street, 1990); when it is followed by a verb this should be a verbal noun ending in *-ing*, not an infinitive (*They are not equal to performing* [✘ *to perform*] *the task*).

3 Ellipsis (omission) of *to* should be avoided in phrases such as *equal to* or *greater than*, as in *Their budget must be equal to or greater than the minimum total cost of supplying the expected output*—B. C. Smith, 1988. *See* ELLIPSIS.

e

4 *Equal* is often regarded as an absolute that cannot be qualified by words such as *very, more, rather,* etc. However, this rule does not apply to all its meanings, and it is legitimate to say, for example, *They wanted a more equal allocation of resources,* in which *equal* means 'fair' as much as 'divided equally'. There is also George Orwell's famous line *All animals are equal but some animals are more equal than others—Animal Farm,* 1945, which is often recalled allusively in uses such as the following: *All victims are equal. None are more equal than others.—*John Le Carré, 1989 / *The embryo has rights. Are all human beings equal, or are some more equal than others?—Sun,* 2005.

equally. Fowler (1926) condemned the use of *equally as* (*They are equally as good*) as an 'illiterate tautology', preferring either *They are equally good* or *They are as good.* Another possibility, which goes some way to providing the sentence balance that *equally* gives, is *They are just as good.*

equilibrium is pronounced with the first syllable either ek- or eek-. The recommended plural form (not often needed) is *equilibria,* though *equilibriums* is occasionally found.

equip has inflected forms *equipped, equipping.* The noun form is *equipment.*

era see EPOCH.

-er and -est forms of adjectives and adverbs. *See box opposite.*

-er and -or. These suffixes form 'agent nouns' denoting either a person or a thing that performs the action denoted by the word's stem; this is sometimes a word in its own right and sometimes not, e.g. *dispenser, farmer, maker, porter, sailor, suitor.* In theory, -er can be added to any English verb to form an agent noun; but in practice both -er and -or forms are used, sometimes as active English suffixes and sometimes as elements borrowed with the word as a whole (e.g. *doctor* from Old French *doctour* from Latin *doctor*). Choice between the two suffixes is purely historical and does not have any principled distinction. Note however that some agent nouns exist in two forms, e.g. *adviser* and *advisor* (the second probably influenced by *advisory*).

When -er is added to verbs ending in a consonant + -y, the y is normally changed to i, as in *carrier, occupier,* etc. Exceptions are *flyer,* which is now more usual than *flier,* and *drier,* which alternates with *dryer.*

-er and -re (noun and verb endings, e.g. *center / centre, theatre / theater*) *see* -RE AND -ER.

eraser is spelt -er, not -or. See -ER AND -OR.

ere, pronounced like *air* and meaning 'before', has been in continuous use as a preposition and conjunction from the Old English period. Now it is only used for archaic effect or in poetry, but it refuses to disappear altogether: *And time seemed finished ere the ship passed by—*Edwin Muir, 1925 / *I would give you a gift ere we go, at your own choosing—*J. R. R. Tolkien, 1954 / *In that cluster of villages, London by name, Ere slabs are too tall and we Cockneys too few—*John Betjeman, 1958 / *No thriftful scrutiny was drawn When, ere creation's mighty dawn, Thou plannedst man's abode—*P. Falvury, 1968.

erotica, meaning 'erotic literature and art' is in origin a plural noun, but nowadays it is usually treated as a singular mass noun, with the following verb in the singular: *None of Minton's erotic drawings have resurfaced, even today*

-ER AND -EST FORMS OF ADJECTIVES AND ADVERBS.

1 general. This article deals with the forms of the comparative and superlative of adjectives and adverbs, either by inflection (*larger, largest; happier, happiest*) or by using *more* and *most* (*more usual; most unfortunately*). It also deals in outline with the rules for using the various forms available. *See also* ADJECTIVE; ADVERB.

2 adjectives that have -er and -est forms. The adjectives that take *-er* and *-est* in preference to (or as well as) *more* and *most* are:

a words of one syllable (*fast, hard, rich, wise*, etc.).

b words of two syllables ending in *-y* and *-ly* (*angry, early, happy, holy, lazy, likely, lively, tacky*, etc.) and corresponding negative forms in *un-* when these exist (*unhappy, unlikely*, etc.). Words ending in *-y* change the *y* to *i* (*angrier, earliest*, etc.). In some cases only the *-est* form is used (e.g. *unholiest* but *more unholy*).

c words of two syllables ending in *-le* (*able, humble, noble, simple*, etc.).

d words of two syllables ending in *-ow* (*mellow, narrow, shallow*, etc.).

e some words of two syllables ending in *-er* (*bitter, clever, slender, tender*, etc., but not *eager*). In some cases only the *-est* form is used (e.g. *bitterest* but *more bitter*).

f some words of two syllables pronounced with the stress on the second syllable (*polite, profound*, etc., but not *antique, bizarre, secure*, etc.).

g other words of two syllables that do not belong to any classifiable group (e.g. *common, cruel, pleasant, quiet*); some words can take *-er* and *-est* although the forms sound somewhat less natural (e.g. *awkward, crooked*).

Adjectives of three or more syllables need to use forms with *more* and *most* (*more beautiful, most interesting*, etc.).

3 adverbs that have -er and -est forms. The adverbs that take *-er* and *-est* in preference to (or as well as) *more* and *most* are:

a adverbs that are not formed with *-ly* but are identical in form to corresponding adjectives (e.g. *runs faster, hits hardest, hold it tighter*).

b some independent adverbs (e.g. *often* and *soon*).

Adverbs in *-ly* formed from adjectives (e.g. *richly, softly, wisely*) generally do not have forms in *-er* and *-est* but appear as *more softly, most wisely*, etc. The phrase *easier said than done* is a special case, in that there is no equivalent use as an adverb of the simple form *easy*.

4 choice of forms. With adjectives and adverbs of one syllable it is usually less natural to use *more* and *most* when forms in *-er* and *-est* are available, although there are exceptions that are not readily explained: *The job was harder than they thought* sounds less idiomatic in the form *The job was more hard than they thought*, whereas *John had never been gladder to be on Arabella's side* sounds slightly more idiomatic as *John had never been more glad to be on Arabella's side*. With adjectives of two syllables it is often possible to form comparatives and superlatives both by *-er* and *-est* forms and with *more* and *most*. For example, the sentences *He was most unhappy when he was on his own* and *He was unhappiest when he was on his own* are both idiomatic, although the first but not the second can mean 'extremely unhappy' as well as 'most unhappy (of all)', in accordance with the different meanings of *most*.

5 superlatives in comparison of two. The comparative forms are meant to compare two persons or things and superlative forms more than two, and it is normally ungrammatical to use the superlative in the role of the comparative, as in *The largest of the two*, although this is commonly found in spoken and written English. Use of the superlative is however idiomatic in certain fixed expressions, such as *Put your best foot forward / May the best man win / Mother knows best*, in which the comparison may effectively be of two but the idiom is sufficiently generalized to weaken strict duality.

6 literary uses. Some unconventional and ungrammatical formations are found as stylistic devices in literature, e.g. Shakespeare's *easiliest, freelier, proudlier, wiselier*, Charles Lamb's *harshlier, kindlier, proudlier*, Tennyson's *darklier, gladlier, looselier, plainlier*, George Eliot's *neatliest*, and Lewis Carroll's *curiouser. See also* ADJECTIVE 3. Other formations are occasionally used for comic effect, e.g. *admirablest, loathsomer, peacefulest, wholesomer*. Such devices belong to the category of special usage that makes exceptions to normal grammatical rules.

---

when erotica has become much sought after—F. Spalding, 1991.

To use it with a plural verb sounds more than a tad pedantic, e.g. *Erotica are much in evidence in the world of videos*.

In many uses number is not explicit: *That part of Rasputin which saved so many female souls went on display in 2004, in St Petersburg's first museum of erotica*—*Independent*, 2007.

err, meaning 'to do wrong', is pronounced as in *her*. *Errant*, meaning 'doing wrong', is pronounced with the first syllable as in *merry*.

erratum, meaning 'an error (in printed matter)' is pronounced e-**rah**-tuhm. It is a singular noun, with a plural *errata*. *Errata* should not be used as a singular noun on the analogy of *agenda*, as in ✖ *It was not intended to print an errata*. If a singular noun referring to several *errata* is needed, a phrase such as *list of errata* is preferable.

ersatz is a German loanword meaning 'a substitute or imitation' and is first recorded in English in 1875. It is still used, often in attributive position (before a noun, e.g. *ersatz coffee / an ersatz culture*), and is pronounced in a naturalized manner as **er**-satz or **air**-satz.

erstwhile is a word that dates from Old English, and is still occasionally found, mainly as an adjective meaning 'of old, former' and typically with reference to the recent past: *While he may be less popular than he was, he is still held in more esteem than his erstwhile colleagues*—*Morning Star*, 2007.

escalate is a 1920s back-formation from *escalator* (first recorded in 1900), and has burst the bounds of meaning that a word for a moving staircase might be expected to impose. Not surprisingly, *escalate* is now rarely used in its first meaning 'to travel on an escalator'. By the 1950s, it had come into regular use to mean 'to increase or develop rapidly by stages', chiefly in the context of military and political conflict. Typical examples from that time (the first intransitive, the second transitive, i.e. with an object) are: *The possibility of local wars 'escalating into all-out atomic wars'—Manchester Guardian*, 1959 / *Using tactical nuclear weapons which would be likely to escalate hostilities into a global nuclear war—Economist*, 1961. In more recent use, *escalate* continues to be used in such contexts but has extended beyond them: *The police more often came under physical attack and began to respond with a steadily escalating counter-violence—Liberty and Legislation*, 1989 / *Her previous calm gave way to terror that escalated until it threatened to overwhelm her—E. Blair*, 1990 / *Motoring organisations yesterday urged drivers involved in a road rage encounter to try to keep calm and not to react in a way which could escalate the situation—Herald* (Glasgow), 2000.

To *escalate* has latterly gained a novel, transitive meaning, which is 'to refer an issue to a manager or superior', e.g. *In the event that you need to escalate an issue, our technical staff are ready to help.* It is part of the jargon of IT and of call centres, and best avoided outside those rarefied environments.

escape *verb and noun*. There are three significant 20c uses, the first two of the verb and the third of the noun:

1 In intransitive use (without an object), to describe astronauts overcoming gravity and leaving the earth's atmosphere: *A spaceship will escape from Earth at 11.2 kilometres a second—Journal of the British Interplanetary Society*, 1949.

2 In transitive use (with an object), to mean 'to escape from (a place)', both of astronauts as in the previous paragraph and in other contexts, such as escape from a convent in the following example: *It transpires she may have escaped Santa Clara to look for a well-known terrorist—N. Shakespeare*, 1989. This is a revival of an older use and shows an obvious relation to more standard transitive uses as in escaping *danger, arrest, criticism, suspicion*, and other unwelcome circumstances. Note that to *escape prison* usually means 'to avoid a custodial sentence' (*A former lollipop lady who stabbed her husband in a row over debts has escaped prison—South Wales Evening Post*, 2007); if an escape from a state of imprisonment is meant it is better to say *escape from prison*.

3 In computing, *escape* is a noun denoting a function (and keyboard key) that ends an operation or affects a following sequence of commands in some way. For anyone who has fallen into any of the engulfing traps that computer technology can lay for the unwary, the notion of *escape* provides a potent image.

escapee is first recorded in use by Walt Whitman, who refers to *southern escapees* in a memoir (1875–6) of his experiences as a hospital visitor during the American Civil War. It has come in for much adverse criticism from those who think that *escaper* (on the analogy of *deserter*) is the form called for, but the word is established and is supported by other forms such as *refugee*. It also accords well with the active use of the past participle (which is passive in form), as in *an escaped prisoner*. See -EE.

escort is pronounced with the stress on the first syllable as a noun and on the second as a verb.

Eskimo has the plural form *Eskimos*, but *Eskimo* also is used as a collective in archaeological and anthropological contexts to refer to the people as a whole and their languages. The term *Inuit* (the plural of *inuk* meaning 'person'), however, is the correct term to use specifically of the peoples inhabiting the regions from north-west Canada to western Greenland, because it is preferred by these peoples themselves.

especial, especially, special, specially. 1 There is no longer any great difficulty with *especial* because *special* has all but driven it out, although it is still used occasionally to refer principally to exceptional personal qualities or attributes as in *your especial charm.* The adverbs *specially* and *especially* present a much bigger problem, because each continues to usurp the role of the other quite extensively. Essentially, the difference is this: *especially* means 'chiefly, much more than in other cases' and can qualify adjectives and adverbs as well as verbs, whereas *specially* means 'for a special or specific purpose' and qualifies verbs, participial adjectives formed from verbs (as in *specially made*), and occasionally (when it encroaches on *especially,* as described at 3 below) adjectives.

2 The following examples show this distinction: (especially) *The sumo wrestlers are not especially tall, but they are especially big*—C. James, 1978 / *Ancient woods . . . are especially important for wildlife*—*Times,* 1982 / *Insist on listening to some music, preferably piano music that shows up wow and flutter especially well*—*Listener,* 1982 / *The transfer of Britain's most sophisticated technologies (especially in laser and micro-computing) . . . will have appalling effects on the British economy*—*City Limits,* 1986 / (specially) *This fine piano was made specially for us*—*Chicago Tribune,* 1977 / *I gathered these specially in bud, because I thought it would be nice to see them open out in the warmth of the house*—D. Madden, 1988 / *If it's suitable for your job, try using a plaster repair product as it's specially formulated to be easier to apply and smooth out than conventional plaster*—*Evening Gazette,* 2007.

3 The meanings of the two words come closest when qualifying an immediately following adjective, as in the following examples in which each word is virtually interchangeable for the other, although *especially* is still the more correct: *It's a pretty anonymous mark. Not one I'm specially proud of, either*—Penelope Lively, 1991 / *The function of the criminal law, as we see it, is . . . to provide sufficient safeguards against exploitation or corruption of others, particularly those who are specially vulnerable because they are young, weak in body or mind or inexperienced*—T. Newburn, 1992. *Specially* more usually encroaches on *especially,* but sometimes *especially* is the offender: ☒ *The fiddler plunged his hot face into a pot of porter, especially provided for that purpose*—Dickens, 1843 / ☒ *These Pakistani garments are created especially for the wearer by a joint effort of the women of the family*—A. Wilson, 1988.

espresso, a name for strong black Italian coffee (from a word meaning 'pressed out'), is correctly spelt with initial *es-* not *ex-,* a variant influenced by English *express* which was standard in the 1950s and 1960s.

Esq. This abbreviation is a 16c shortening, as a written form of address, of *esquire,* which originally denoted 'a young aspirant to knighthood who attended and served a knight', and was later extended to refer to other classes of men including peers, lawyers, and so on. By the mid-20c *Esq.* had become a courtesy designation, principally in correspondence, with no significance as to rank. When *Esq.* is used, it follows the name and replaces any prefixed title (*Mr, Dr, Capt,* etc.) that would otherwise be used. With one exception (US lawyers addressing themselves), its use is restricted to Britain, and even here it has largely died out as other conventions have come into use.

-esque is a suffix forming adjectives, and corresponds to French *-esque* or Italian *-esco* (from the medieval Latin ending *-iscus*). In English it occurs in words derived from Italian and French, e.g. *grotesque, picaresque, picturesque*, and is an active suffix added to personal names to form adjectives meaning 'in the style of...', e.g. *Audenesque, Disneyesque, Schumannesque, Turneresque*. (It will be noticed that such words would only awkwardly make alternative forms in *-ian*).

-ess. 1 This suffix forms nouns denoting female persons or animals, and was adopted in Middle English from the Old French form *-esse* (from late Latin *-issa*). The first wave of *-ess* words in English (*countess, duchess, empress, hostess, mistress, princess*, etc.) were all imported in their entirety from French. From this beginning, *-ess* rapidly became an active suffix added to words that already existed in English, e.g. *Jewess* (14c, Wyclif), *patroness* (15c), *poetess* (16c, Tyndale); and it supplanted the older native female suffix *-ster*, which now survives only in *spinster*. These words were formed by substituting *-ess* for *-er* in words such as *adulterer / adulteress*, or by adding *-ess* to the stem of words such as *author / authoress*. In some cases, a feminine form predated a corresponding masculine form; for example, *sorceress* (14c, Chaucer) is attested before *sorcerer* (1526, Tyndale). Some words required modification or refinement, producing (for example) *governess* in place of the earlier *governeresse* and *ambassadress* instead of the (unrecorded) alternative *ambassadoress*.

2 The *OED* records over 100 words in *-ess* formed from Middle English to about 1850, some merely fanciful or now obsolete (e.g. *entertainess,*

farmeress, vicaress) but others still in regular use (e.g. *ambassadress, heiress, mayoress*).

3 In the 20c, the feminist and politically correct movements have had a devastating effect on the fortunes of many *-ess* words, and have effectively brought the life of *-ess* as an active suffix to an end. Those regarded as especially offensive are (on racial grounds) *Jewess* and *Negress*, and (on gender grounds) occupational terms such as *actress, air hostess, authoress, manageress, poetess, proprietress, stewardess, waitress*, all of which have yielded to gender-neutral alternatives, either the traditional masculine forms (*actor, author, manager, poet, proprietor, waiter*) or specially devised forms (*flight attendant, waitperson*). Other words continue unchallenged, among them *abbess, adulteress, adventuress, ambassadress, duchess, goddess, governess, heiress, murderess, postmistress, princess, songstress*. Some of these are unalterable titles, others are not simply female equivalents of the masculine form (e.g. an *ambassadress* is the wife of an *ambassador*; a *mayoress* is the wife of a *mayor*, and in both cases a female office-holder would be called by the *-or* forms), and others are encountered too rarely (or only in special contexts such as fiction) to cause disquiet.

4 A further limitation on the use of many *-ess* forms is that they cannot be followed by *of* to identify them in relation to a work or achievement; instead of *the authoress of Persuasion* you have to say *the author of Persuasion*. It is possible, however, to say *the goddess of love*, in which *of* plays a somewhat different role.

Essex. This name of one of the English Home Counties conjures up an image originating in the 1980s of the brash, amoral, self-made right-wing young businessman lacking all refinement and cultural interest, and his promiscuous, materialistic girlfriend: *An alarming tale of Essex girl jokes and sexual innuendo—Independent on Sunday*, 1995 / *Funny, finely-tuned and flashier than an Essex boy on a night out in Romford—Sun*, 2007.

-est (forming superlatives of adjectives and adverbs) *see* -ER AND -EST FORMS.

Establishment. *The Establishment* (with a capital *E*) means 'the group in society exercising authority or influence, and seen as resisting change' and, by extension (with a small *e*), 'any influential or controlling group' as in *the literary establishment, the military establishment, the media establishment*, and so on.

estate. 1 The meaning of *estate* in the term *three estates of the realm* is a historical one, 'an order or class forming part of the body politic'. The *three estates* are the Lords Spiritual (i.e. the heads of the Church), the Lords Temporal (i.e. the peerage), and the Commons. The term dates from the 15c, and has been used of similar institutions in other countries. A misuse, noted by the *OED*, which identifies the three elements as the Crown, the House of Lords, and the House of Commons, is first recorded as early as 1559. A *fourth estate*, the newspaper press, was added (possibly by Edmund Burke) in the early 19c.

2 *Estate* meaning 'a landed property' is first recorded in the late 18c. In the 20c this was supplemented by a meaning noted by C. S. Lewis in his *Studies in Words* (1960): *When I was a boy estate had as its dominant meaning 'land belonging to a large landowner', but the meaning 'land covered with small houses' is dominant now.*

3 *Estate car* is a general term in BrE for a kind of car that has the internal accommodation extended into the rear

with a door at the back; it differs in shape from a *hatchback*. The equivalent term in AmE is *station wagon*.

esthete, esthetic are less common American spellings than **aesthete, aesthetic.*

estimable means 'worthy of esteem, admirable'. *Estimatable* is the form required for the meaning 'capable of being estimated', although it is only rarely used.

estimate. How you pronounce *estimate* depends on whether you are using it as a noun or a verb. As a noun, e.g. *our first estimates were too low*, it is pronounced **e**-sti-muht. As a verb it is pronounced **e**-sti-mayt, with the final vowel given its full value. Quite often you hear the verb pronounced **e**-sti-muht, like the noun, but this is incorrect.

estimation. 1 Fowler described the use of *estimation* in the phrase *in my estimation* (= in my opinion) as 'illiterate', a verdict which is negated by several centuries of use in this meaning: *The dearest of men in my estimation*—E. W. Lane, 1841 / *It was about this time that Martin took a great slump in Maria's estimation*—J. London, 1909 / *Get it right, and you go up in everyone's estimation. Get it wrong, and you're a clot and a failure*—Scotsman, 2007.

2 *Estimation*, in addition to the meaning just discussed, is the process of forming a judgement or calculation, as distinct from *estimate* (noun), which is the result of the process, i.e. (1) an approximate decision about cost, size, value, etc., or (2) the cost or size itself, as in—*The total estimate comes to £500*.

estrogen, estrus. The standard AmE spellings of BrE *oestrogen, oestrus*.

Estuary English is the name for a variety of informal and allegedly classless English spoken in the area of the

Thames Estuary, i.e. London and parts of the Home Counties (notably Essex). The term was coined in 1984 by a London scholar named David Rosewarne. As well as peculiarities of vocabulary (such as *cheers* for *thank you* and *mate* for *friend*), the most recognizable features of Estuary English are phonetic: the replacement of *t* by a glottal stop in words such as *butter* and *water*, the replacement of *l* by a sound like *w* in words such as *full* and *ball-game*, and other features described more fully in books such as Paul Coggle's *Do You Speak Estuary?* (1993).

et al. is an abbreviation of Latin *et alii* (= and other people) or *et alia* (= and other things), and is used to avoid listing a long sequence of names, only the first or the first few being given, as in *Smith, Jones, et al.* It is regularly used in bibliographical citation for works having several authors, and is printed in roman or italic type according to the particular style in use. It is appropriately used for references to people; for other categories *etc.* is preferable.

etc. 1 This is an abbreviation of the Latin phrase *et cetera* meaning 'and other things of the same kind', and is pronounced et **set**-uh-ruh or et **set**-ruh, despite the temptation to articulate the first syllable ek on the analogy of words such as *ecstasy* and *excellence*.

2 It means 'and so on' or 'and the rest', and can refer to people or things or both. Practice varies regarding the punctuation that precedes and follows *etc.*, but in general it is best to treat it as if it were 'and so on', i.e. precede it by a comma when it comes after two or more items already separated by commas (*We need pencils, paper, etc.*), but not when it comes after a single item or two items without a comma (*We need paper etc.* / *We need some pencil and paper etc.*). It should be

followed by a comma when a comma would be used in the case of 'and so on' (*We need pencils, paper, etc., as well as a desk to work on*).

3 Since *etc.* includes 'and' in its element *et*, it is illiterate to write *and etc.* (or *& etc.*). The form *&c*, though once common (and used by Fowler in ordinary writing), is now out of fashion.

ethics, morals. 1 Both terms are concerned with the practice of right and wrong. The *Concise Oxford Dictionary* (1995) defines *ethics* as 'the science of morals in human conduct'; what this means is that morals forms the basis of abstract principles whereas ethics are the application of these principles in human activity, especially in specific areas of activity such as law and medicine (*professional ethics*).

2 Of the corresponding adjectives, *ethical* describes what is right or wrong in terms of an accepted code of behaviour, whereas *moral* describes what is right or wrong in principle, as affecting human behaviour generally: *The various moral systems of the world may include many of the same moral ideas*—G. A. & A. G. Theodorson, 1970 / *They believe in the moral superiority of primitive over civilised man*—Daily Telegraph, 1972 / *It is neither easy nor ethical to perch with notebook or video camera over spontaneous scenes of human mating or aggression*—New Scientist, 1983 / *If you want your bank to have an ethical lending policy, then write to them and say so, or switch to a bank that does have one*—Express, 2007. *Moral* also occurs in a few fixed expressions such as *moral certainty* (= strong probability), *moral courage*, *moral majority*, and *moral support*, and here means 'having a psychological effect associated with confidence in a right action'.

ethnic is now principally used to denote a section of a community having

e

distinct racial, cultural, religious, or linguistic characteristics not shared by the rest of the community. *Ethnic* is typically used to describe clothing, dance, music, and other customs that distinguish such people: *The Radio Authority has helpfully decreed that classical music, light orchestra and non-amplified jazz, folk, country and ethnic music aren't pop—Times Educational Supplement*, 1991 / *Vegetarian dishes in various ethnic cuisines—Mexican, Thai, Indian, Italian, Japanese, Middle Eastern, etc.—New Musical Express*, 1991. An *ethnic minority* (first recorded in 1945) is a section of a community that forms a minority within a larger community, for example Sikhs, Muslims, and West Indian people in Britain. In a further development of the term, people are described as being (for example) *ethnic Turks* when they are of Turkish origin but living in a country other than Turkey; in recent times we have heard a great deal about *ethnic Vietnamese* in Cambodia and *ethnic Albanians* in Serbia: *The ethnic Albanian ministers had been tendering their resignations one by one since late March—Keesings*, 1990.

ethnic cleansing. This unfortunate euphemism, highly reminiscent of the *final solution* and other expressions to do with the suppression of peoples, is first recorded in 1991 in connection with events in the former Yugoslavia that continued through the 1990s. It means 'the mass expulsion or extermination of people from a minority ethnic or religious group within a certain area': *The area has a large number of towns and villages, many emptied of Muslims and Croats in three years of ethnic cleansing—Times*, 1995. The term has since been extended in use to other contexts, some retrospectively (such as the treatment of peoples in Palestine after 1948, and of the Ugandan Asians in the 1970s).

ethnic names and stereotypes.
1 slang names for people. These range from the neutral or affectionate (*Brit* = someone British, *Mick* = an Irishman) via the category of often though not always derogatory (*Limey* (in America) = someone British, *Yank* (in Britain) = an American) to the invariably offensive (*dago* = Spaniard, *Yid* = Jew). Across this range much depends on the relationship between the user of the term and the hearer. Most offensive of all in current use are *Nigger* for a black-skinned person (so offensive that it is illegal to use it under laws in New York and pressure groups in the US want to see it removed from dictionaries) and *Paki* for a person from Pakistan or the Indian subcontinent generally. The origin of some terms is obscured or forgotten; many have to do with trivialized conceptions of supposed habits (*Frog* = Frenchman, from the practice of eating frog's legs in France, *Kraut* = German, from the eating of sauerkraut in Germany, etc.), others are fanciful formations (*Pommy* (in Australia) = English immigrant, from *pomegranate* as a word-play on *immigrant*), and others again develop folk etymologies (e.g. *wog* = foreigner, supposedly an acronym of *westernized* (or *wily*) *oriental gentleman* but more likely a shortening of *golliwog*). Some are of unknown origin (e.g. *kike*, AmE = Jew). A fuller account of this topic will be found in the *Oxford Companion to the English Language* (1992), 381–4, from which much of this material is drawn.

2 stereotypes. Ethnic stereotypes have long featured as a component of idiom in many languages, and these often have more to do with popular conception than historical truth. Increased sensitivity to unfavourable ethnic description in the 20c has led to a strong disapproval of many terms, such as *street Arab* and *young Turk*. Most notorious of all has been the use of *Jew* as an opprobrious term for 'a mean or grasping person', a historical use which arose from the association of Jews with medieval money-lending and was duly recorded in successive editions of the *Concise Oxford Dictionary* but dropped (on grounds of lack of currency) from the ninth edition (1995).

-ette is a suffix corresponding to an Old French form *-ette* and is found in English (mostly from the 19c) in four types of noun, either as an active suffix or as part of a word adopted from French:

  1 diminutive words, e.g. *chemisette* (= a small chemise, 1807), *cigarette* (= small cigar, 1842), *novelette* (= a short novel, 1820), *pipette* (= a small pipe, 1839), *statuette* (= a small statue, 1843). Formations of the 20c include *kitchenette* (= a small kitchen, 1910), *launderette* (which is not just a diminutive but means a special kind of self-service laundry, 1949), *diskette* (= a small computer disk), *superette* (= a small supermarket, chiefly AmE and Australian, 1938). In some words, such as *launderette* and *serviette* (originally Scottish, and reintroduced into standard English in the 19c: *see* U AND NON-U), *-ette* is not strictly a diminutive, but is best considered in this category.

  2 feminine words, a usage launched in a spectacular way with the word *suffragette* (1906), a female supporter of, and active campaigner for, women's right to vote. No word of this kind coined since has had the same resonance. The American scholar H. L. Mencken (writing in 1921) noted the appearance of a string of ephemeral formations including *conductorette* and *farmerette*, but the only one to attain any permanent currency was *usherette* (1925): *What the hell are you holding that torch for as if you were a bloody usherette?*—A. N. Wilson, 1990. This, together with *undergraduette*

(1919, and see below) and *majorette* (AmE, in *drum majorette*, 1938), represent a distinct anticlimax after a promising start. A trickle of trivial words continued in the post-war years, until the suffix was taken up by male chauvinist magazine writers in the 1980s to form depreciatory and often hostile terms for women such as *bimbette, hackette, snoopette, undergraduette* (a revival of the 1919 word), *whizzette*, and even *womanette*. None of these has achieved any continuing currency. Only *ladette* from the 1990s ('a young woman who behaves in a boisterously assertive or crude manner'—*COD* 2006) looks likely to survive in real usage.

  3 names of fabrics, some but not all imitations of something else, e.g. *muslinette* (1787, the first recorded), *leatherette* (1880), *flannelette* (1882), *stockingette* (1824, now more usually written as *stockinet*), and *winceyette* (1922, a lightweight cotton fabric for nightclothes, from wincey, itself an alteration of woolsey in linsey-woolsey).

  4 names of commercial foods. Trade names such as *Clubettes* (small crackers), *Creamettes* (a type of pasta), *Croutettes* (a stuffing mix), and *Toastettes* (a kind of tart)—all possibly modelled on *croquette*, a term of French origin for a fried roll of potato or meat—were popular in America in the 1990s but now sound dated.

etymology. 1 *Etymology* is the study of the history and derivation of words, and *an etymology* is the history of a particular word. Most dictionaries of concise size and larger give detailed accounts of a word's sources, which can be from other English words (e.g. newspaper) or from other languages (e.g. *kiosk* via French from Persian). Some words borrowed from other languages have been assimilated to English-looking forms; for example Spanish *cucaracha* has given us *cockroach* by assimilation with the English words *cock* and *roach* (*see* ASSIMILATION).

2 The vast majority of English words (apart from those made from existing English words) are derived from Old English (Anglo-Saxon), from Norse languages, or from a late form of Latin via French words that came into English after the Norman Conquest in 1066. A succinct account of the main sources of English words is given in the *Concise Oxford Dictionary* (1995), ix–xii, to which the reader is referred for further information. It is disappointing for many people that the origins of some quite familiar and important words remain obscure or unknown. The histories of *boy* and *girl* are unknown before Middle English, *dog* has no identified Germanic cognates, many informal or slang words, such as *bamboozle, caboodle, cagey, clobber, gimmick, jiff*, and *posh*, have no verified origins, despite spurious claims made for some of them (such as the supposed 'port outward starboard home' origin of *posh*), and some words that appear to be made up of distinctive elements, for example *contraption* and *theodolite*, are also doubtful or unknown in origin.

3 Certain words, possibly including some of those in the last paragraph, are onomatopoeic, i.e. they represent a sound with which their meanings are associated, such as *clang, plonk*, and *thwack*; and a few words that are less obviously connected with sounds, such as *blizzard* and *jumble*, also belong to this class.

4 The word *etymology* itself comes from a Greek word *etymon* meaning 'true'. However, the etymology of a word represents its original meaning rather than its true meaning in any judgemental sense. Appeals to etymology to defend the use of words against change in meaning (as for example with **decimate*), though commonly made, are usually futile, since few words in the core vocabulary of English now mean what they used to mean, as the complex history of *nice* demonstrates.

eulogy *see* ELEGY.

euphemism. *See box opposite.*

euphuism (not to be confused with **euphemism*) is an affected or high-flown style of writing or speaking, originally applied to work of the late 16c and early 17c written in imitation of John Lyly's *Euphues* (pronounced **yoo**-fyoo-eez 1578–80). The name is derived from Greek *euphuēs* meaning 'well-endowed by nature'.

Eurasian is a term (noun and adjective) first used in the 19c for a person of mixed European and Asian (especially Indian) parentage. In modern use, however, it is more often used to refer to a person of mixed white American and SE Asian parentage: *He strolls away with the Eurasian beauty clinging to his arm*— OEC, 2004.

Euro-. 1 *Euro-*, shortened to *Eur-* before certain vowels, is one of the more productive combining forms of the 20c, as a linguistic reflection of far-reaching political and economic developments across Europe. The form is first used in the 1950s in hyphenated combinations such as *Euro-African* and *Euro-American*, and in the institutional names *Eurovision* (1951, a network of European broadcasting organizations) and *Euratom* (1956, = European Atomic Energy Community). The first generalized words are *Euro-dollar* (1960, a dollar held outside the US, though not necessarily in Europe), the disparaging *Eurocrat* (= European bureaucrat, 1961), and the not much more favourable *Eurocentric* (= regarded in European terms, 1963). The first uses related to Europe (or Western Europe) generally, and this

EUPHEMISM.

Euphemism is the use of a milder or vaguer word or phrase in place of one that might seem too harsh or direct in a particular context, and a *euphemism* is such a word or phrase. The most productive subjects for euphemism are bodily functions, sexual activity, death, politics, and violence. Euphemisms in these and other areas of language use are given in the table below.

word or phrase	common euphemisms
lavatory	bog (slang), comfort station, convenience, little boys' room, little house, loo, restroom (AmE), washroom (AmE), water closet (WC)
urinate	have a tinkle (slang), pass water, relieve oneself, spend a penny, take a leak (slang)
have sexual intercourse with	make love to, sleep with
prostitute	call girl, fallen woman, streetwalker
die	depart this life, give up the ghost, kick the bucket (slang), pass away, pass on
kill	do away with, remove, take out, terminate
redundancy	downsizing, rationalizing, restructuring, slimming down

Examples of phrasal euphemism are *collateral damage* (= accidental destruction of non-military areas), *ethnic cleansing* (= mass expulsion or extermination of ethnic minorities), *final solution* (= Nazi extermination of European Jews), *friendly fire* (= killing of soldiers on one's own side), *helping the police with their inquiries* (= under interrogation and imminent arrest), *pacification* (= evacuation and destruction of villages in war), *regime change* (= forcible overthrow of a hostile foreign government), and (facetiously) *tired and emotional* (= drunk).

meaning continues in formations such as *Euromissile* (1979) and *Eurostrategic* (1977), whereas many terms that arose in the 1960s and since refer more specifically to the European Community (now Union) in relation to the UK's potential and later actual membership, especially the notorious *Eurosceptic* (1986) and its antonym *Europhile*, both used as adjectives and nouns, and other irreverent formations including *Eurobabble* (1986, in a US source) and *Eurojargon*.

2 Like many prolific combining forms, *Euro-* has succeeded in detaching itself and forming a word in its own right: *The Euro terrorists announced ... that they had set up a 'Western European Revolutionary offensive'—Evening Standard*, 1987 / *The name Britannia had been dropped from the deal because its nationalistic connotations could have obvious drawbacks in a pan-Euro venture—European Investor*, 1990. It has also become the informal name of several European-based sports championships, notably in golf and football. With a lower-case initial *e-* it has been since 1995 the official name of the common currency adopted by some members of the EU, with coins and notes going into circulation in 2002.

evade see AVOID.

evasion, evasiveness. *Evasiveness* is the quality a person has of being *evasive*, whereas *evasion* is the process or result of this quality, or an instance of it: *He has been in the trenches too long not to be a master at mixing sincerity with eva-siveness—Rolling Stone*, 1977 / *Their failure to take any action to put a stop to the racism on this show is an evasion of their responsibilities—Mirror*, 2007. *Eva-sion* has a special meaning in relation to legal obligations, and differs from *avoidance* in denoting illegality: *He'd been had up for offering bribes to council employees: the whole story had been ri-diculous, tales of . . . call girls and twen-ty-pound notes, of tax evasion and porno-movies—Margaret Drabble*, 1977. *See* also AVOID.

eve means 'the evening or day before' (as in *Christmas Eve*) and, in figurative use, also means 'the time just before an event' (as in *the eve of the election*). In the following examples, *eve* is literal in the first two phrases, is figurative in the third, and may be either in the last two: *On Christmas Eve / on the Eve of St Agnes / on the eve of great developments / on the eve of the battle / on the eve of departure.* The meaning in particular cases is often clear from the context.

even is normally placed immediately before the word or phrase that it qual-ifies: *Doctors must pursue costly and even dangerous investigations / She is talking even more loudly / He even enrolled in a business studies course.* In some cases *even* qualifies an entire subordinate clause: *Even if my watch is right we shall be late.* When *even* qualifies a verb formed with an auxiliary or modal verb (*can, do, have, might,* etc.), it is placed between the auxiliary verb and the

infinitive (*He had even managed to laugh at it / I did not even bother to read it*) and this is also the case when *even* qualifies the complement of the verb *It might even cost £100.* In informal contexts involving negatives, *even* sometimes comes at the end of a sentence: *They didn't want anything to eat, or a drink even.*

evenness is spelt with two *n*s.

event. 1 *In the event of* is a somewhat awkward prepositional phrase used to mean 'if such-and-such (should hap-pen)'. It is followed by a noun or verbal noun: *The 12 members of the Basle cen-tral bankers' club have made reciprocal arrangements to make short-term loans to each other in the event of any currency coming under severe pressure—Times,* 1968 / *Every manned space flight . . . has a back-up crew, to replace the prime crew in the event of illness or death—R.* Turn-ill, 1970 / *In the event of a strike, it will not be able to fulfil its contract obliga-tions—Birmingham Post,* 2007. The ex-pression has picked up some bad vibes from its extended form *in the unlikely event,* familiar to air travellers from its euphemistic reference to danger: *In the unlikely event of a landing on water . . .* It has also been criticized as long-winded, because it means no more than 'if'. It is formal in tone, and is best avoided outside formal contexts, since it can sound pompous.

2 In the language of law and business in both AmE and BrE, the phrase *in the event (that)* is used as a conjunction: *A metal tubular structure over the cockpit which protects the driver in the event the car overturns—Publications of the American Dialect Society,* 1964 / *Parties should consider at the outset the payment of their advisers' fees in the event that the transaction aborts—D. J. Cooke,* 1993.

eventuality, eventuate. Both words date from the 18c and have had their fair share of criticism. *Eventuate* was derided by De Quincy (1834) as 'Yankeeish' and by Dean Alford (1864) as 'another horrible word', and Fowler (1926) castigated both as 'flabby journalese', leaving a string of 'characteristic specimens' to speak for themselves. It is undeniable that *result* or *come about*, or sometimes simply *happen*, are often preferable alternatives: *It had been intended to have educated Saudi women dealing with the public at the exhibition, but... this had not eventuated—Times,* 1986 / *I hope a sensible result eventuates—Express,* 2002. *Eventuality* has been less fiercely attacked, although it is often a mere synonym for circumstance, event, or possibility: *Although he had been ordered not to destroy it, Harmel was prepared for the eventuality—*C. Ryan, 1974 / *It is essential you cover every eventuality—Daily Mail,* 2007.

ever. 1 as intensifier. In informal conversation *ever* is sometimes used as an intensifier immediately after an interrogative word such as *who, what, why,* etc.: *Who ever can that be? / What ever did you say to him? / Why ever should you think that?* These uses should be distinguished from the one-word forms *whoever, whatever,* etc., which are relative pronouns: *I'll do whatever you want.* See WHATEVER, WHAT EVER; WHOEVER, WHO EVER.

2 did you ever? This expression is informal only, and has a distinct Victorian ring: *'And where is she now?' 'In a studio.'... 'Did you ever!' said Mrs. Fanshaw—Peel City Guardian,* 1892.

3 ever so. An older use after *if* or *though* with the meaning 'at all, in any degree' now sounds archaic and has almost disappeared: *Though Sir Peter's ill humour may vex me ever so, it never shall provoke me—*Sheridan, 1777. It is now overshadowed by the same phrase used (since the mid-19c) in positive contexts

as an intensive meaning 'extremely, immensely': *It's the greatest idea, and I'm ever so grateful—*J. Leland, 1987 / *Broken bones sounded ever so unpleasant—*O. Drake, 2001. This use is largely restricted to conversational English.

every. 1 differences between *each* and *every*. Both words denote all the people or things in a group, and both normally govern a singular verb (for some exceptions *see* EACH). But *each* is a pronoun (as in *I'll take three of each*) as well as an adjective (or determiner), whereas *every* is only an adjective (or determiner); you cannot say ⊠ *I'll take three of every,* although you can say *I'll take three of every kind. Each* can refer to two or more items, whereas *every* can only refer to three or more. The meaning is also slightly different in that *each* regards the people or things concerned separately, whereas *every* regards them collectively.

2 typical uses of *every*. *Every* is used (1) with singular countable nouns to denote three or more (*It would be quite impossible to prosecute every motorist / The new version is better in every way / The company has a training day for every new employee / They have every right to be here*), (2) with some abstract uncountable nouns referring to a feeling or attitude (*We have every sympathy for their case / I have every confidence in you*), (3) with nouns of time to form adverbial phrases denoting frequency (*She comes every day / We get an extra day off every three weeks / We see them in town every now and then*), (4) with numbers to denote distribution (*They investigate one case in every ten / The police were stopping every third car*). When a possessive pronoun precedes a noun, *every* comes between them: *She'll look after your every need.*

3 every single, every other. *Single* serves as an intensifier after every (*I was* *able to hear every single word*), and *other* denotes alternate items in a group (*Every other house had a garage*).

4 *every one.* As two words, *every one* can refer to people or things, and each word retains its distinct meaning (*When we cut up the apples, every one of them was rotten*). Written as one word, *everyone* refers only to people: *see* EVERYONE.

everybody has been written as one word since the 19c, and alternates with *everyone* with no difference in meaning. Both words take a singular verb, but pronouns in the continuation of the sentence are often plural to denote neutrality of gender. This is a perfectly natural and acceptable part of English, with a very long historical pedigree, even though many usage writers have objected to it: *Everybody seems to recover their spirits*—Ruskin, 1866 / *Everybody has a right to describe their own party machine as they choose*—Winston Churchill, 1954 / *'There's a bus waiting outside the terminal to take everybody to their hotels,' said Linda*—David Lodge, 1991. *See* AGREEMENT 4.

everyday is written as one word when it is used as an adjective before a noun (i.e. in attributive position): *They were wearing everyday clothes.* As an adverbial phrase, *every day* is written as two words: *He meets her nearly every day.*

everyone, as an indefinite pronoun meaning the same as *everybody*, is now regularly spelt as one word. This convention is surprisingly recent (20c); the *OED* (in 1894) preferred *every one* (two words), while Fowler (1926) presented a spirited argument in favour of the linked form *everyone.* As with *everybody*, *everyone* takes a singular verb but can be followed by a plural pronoun or possessive in the continuation of the sentence to denote neutrality of gender: *Everyone then looked about them silently, in*

suspense and expectation—W. H. Mallock, 1877 / *Everyone was absorbed in their own business*—A. Motion, 1989 / *The classical allegories look like surreal school outings in which everyone got to take their clothes off, and then was sorry*—M. Vaizey, 1991. *See* AGREEMENT 4. Unlike *every one* written as two words (*see* EVERY 4), *everyone* refers only to people.

everyplace is a modern AmE synonym of *everywhere*: *Although, like everyplace else, the White Elephant had engaged a corps of college students*—Saturday Review, 1976 / *She sets them on the floor because everyplace else is taken*—Internet website, AmE 2003 [*OEC*].

every time, used as an adverbial phrase and conjunction, should be written as two words: *It happens every time / Every time they come, there's an argument.* It is increasingly found as one word, both in BrE and AmE, but this is still incorrect: ✖ *Everytime I see a new line on my face, I'm also hysterically thinking it's all over*—The Face, 1990 / *It felt like he was reciting a poem everytime he opened his mouth*—Internet website, 2005 [*OEC*].

evidence *verb.* The word is decidedly awkward as a verb, whether meaning 'to serve as evidence of, to attest' (*The closer links with the London company were evidenced by the acquisition of LGOC-type buses and equipment*—K. Warren, 1980) or, more loosely, 'to indicate' (*Everything he was and did evidenced distinction*—Nadine Gordimer, 1990). It is not needed in everyday use, and can sound pretentious because other more straightforward words are available (e.g. *attest, demonstrate, exhibit, indicate, show*) and are sometimes, but not invariably, preferable.

evilly, the adverb from *evil*, is spelt with two *l*s.

evince is used mainly in formal English (or, as Fowler put it, by 'those who like a full-dress word better than a plain one') to mean 'to show or make evident (a quality or feeling)'. One might add that it is usually found in the company of other full-dress words: *They constantly evince a smug hermeticism that is graceless and slight—Times*, 1987.

ex-, used as a prefix meaning 'former', causes no difficulty when it is attached to single words (*ex-convict / ex-president / ex-lover*). Fowler's objection to its use with noun phrases (*ex-Lord Mayor / ex-Prime Minister*) as 'patent yet prevalent absurdities', is uncharacteristically pedantic, and the eye easily accommodates most expression of this kind. In more awkward cases, especially where further hyphenation is involved, *former* is always available (*a former trade-union leader*). *Ex-* has a special use in *ex-directory*, meaning 'not listed in a (telephone) directory', in *ex-dividend*, meaning 'before payment of a dividend', and in *ex-VAT*, meaning 'before VAT has been added'.

exact is the correct verb to use with the noun *revenge*, to convey the meaning of inflicting it. You *exact* revenge *on* someone *for* something. Because *exact* is a verb on the fringes of most people's active vocabulary, they often change the phrase to *extract revenge* or *enact revenge*. Until universal usage or dictionaries dictate otherwise, these variants are likely to be regarded as incorrect. Examples (*exact* correctly used): *Nick, the leader, exacts revenge on Morgan by smashing his bicycle in front of the entire school—DVD Verdict*, 2001 / *Robert Carlyle played a terrifying psychopath who exacted revenge for the Hillsborough soccer disaster—Yorkshire Post Today*, 2005 / (*extract* wrongly used) ✖ *Simply by staying, you extract a revenge of sorts: for so long as you are still in the company,* *your CEO is not going to be able to forget the embarrassing incident—Financial Times*, 2009 / (*enact* wrongly used) ✖ *A swift and bloody revenge is enacted by a pair of gamine young women—Guardian* (Film), 2009.

exalt, exult. Though unrelated and having different meanings, these two words are sometimes confused because they look and sound similar. *Exalt* (pronounced ig-**zawlt**) means 'to praise highly', and is often used in the participial form *exalted*, meaning 'grand, noble', with reference to status, ideals, etc.: *No member of your Government should consider his position to be more important and exalted than that of the Paramount Chief—Rand Daily Mail*, 1917. *Exult* (pronounced ig-**zult**) means 'to feel great joy or triumph', and is common in its adjectival form *exultant*: *Alice could hardly prevent herself from openly exulting—Doris Lessing*, 1986 / *As the camera pulled back on the last shot and credits were shown on the screen, the tension in the studio relaxed, replaced by an exultant mood—S. Conran*, 1992. The meanings come very close in the corresponding nouns, *exaltation* = expression of praise, and *exultation* = expression of joy.

exceedingly, excessively. Both words came into use in the late 15c. *Exceedingly* (16c in its current meaning) means 'very, extremely', and is now used only with adjectives and adverbs (most often *well*): *His room was exceedingly cold—P. Fitzgerald*, 1982 / *Judd was doing exceedingly well as an air cadet—C. Lorrimer*, 1993. *Excessively* has a much stronger meaning 'too, by too much', and is used with verbs as well as adjectives and adverbs: *She may exercise excessively, spending hours each day in the gymnasium—Abraham & Llewellyn-Jones*, 1984 / *In Enid Blyton's work, this excessively simple world* *picture is carried to extremes*—N. Tucker, 1981.

except. 1 Use as a conjunction is now archaic, as in the famous passage in Psalms (AV, 127:1): *Except the Lord build the house, they labour in vaine that build it* (in more modern translations this is rendered *Unless the Lord builds the house . . .*).

2 *Except* should not normally be used by itself to mean 'except that' or 'but', although this is common informally and in conversation: *The day he turned 18, Trojan moved into his own council flat in Caledonian Road. Except he didn't like it*—The Face, 1987.

3 *Except for*, as in *They all came except for James*, is also somewhat informal, and is best avoided when *except* alone will do: *They all came except James*. At the beginning of a sentence, however, *except for* is needed: *Except for James, everyone brought a gift with them.*

excepting is correctly used as a preposition instead of *except* when it follows *not* (or another negative) or *always*: *His comprehensive knowledge of the Lakes stood above that of all the men of his time, not excepting Wordsworth*—J. Sloss et al., 1984. An alternative, though less usual, construction is . . . *Wordsworth not excepted*. Examples of uses in which *except* would be preferable are: ✗ *Faith had left all her jewellery, excepting mother's pearl and ruby eternity ring, to Dorothea Shottery*—Susan Hill, 1969 / ✗ *More than other governments, excepting that of the Soviet Union, they developed cultural policies designed to defend culture and French culture in particular*—R. Gildea, 2002. Worse still is to use *excepting* in this way followed by a *that*-clause: ✗ *I cannot describe it excepting that it was one of the most wonderful things I ever saw or heard in my life*—history website, BrE 2003 [*OEC*].

exception. The proverb *the exception proves the rule* means 'the existence of an exception shows that a rule exists in those cases that are not exceptions'. It should not be used to mean 'the exception becomes the rule', although this is often found.

exceptional, exceptionable. These adjectives relate to different meanings of *exception. Exceptional* means 'unusual, not typical', i.e. 'forming an exception' in a favourable sense: *Schizophrenes are often held to be people of exceptional charm*—D. Cory, 1977 / *You could get an exceptional trade-in price for your old car*—Sunday Express, 1980. *Exceptionable* means 'to which exception may be taken', i.e. 'open to objection': *There is nothing intrinsically wrong with, or legally exceptionable about that*—England and Wales High Court (Commercial Court) Decisions, 2004. It is not a common word (there are only a few examples in the *OEC*), and it is more often used in the negative form *unexceptionable*, meaning 'not open to objection, perfectly satisfactory'. All the more surprising, then, that *exceptionable* is occasionally found used by mistake for *exceptional*: ✗ *The establishment Whigs . . . came to argue that resistance was only allowable in exceptionable circumstances, such as those of 1688*—T. Harris, 1993.

excessively *see* EXCEEDINGLY.

exchangeable is spelt with three *e*s.

excise is spelt *-ise*, not *-ize*. As a noun and verb in the 'tax' meaning, it is pronounced with the stress on the first syllable, **ek**-size; as a verb meaning 'to remove by cutting' it is pronounced with stress on the second syllable, ik-**size**.

excitable is spelt without an *e* in the middle.

exclamation mark. In ordinary writing, the exclamation mark (!) should be used sparingly, and in particular should not be used to add a spurious sense of drama or sensation to writing that is otherwise undramatic or unsensational, or to signal the humorous intent of a comment whose humour might otherwise go unrecognized. There are a number of established uses:

1 To mark a command or warning: *Go to your room!* / *Be careful!*

2 To indicate the expression of a strong feeling of absurdity, surprise, approval, dislike, regret, etc., especially after *how* or *what*: *What a suggestion!* / *How awful!* / *Aren't they odd!* / *What a good idea!* / *They are revolting!* / *I hate you!*

3 To express a wish or a feeling of regret: *I'd love to come!* / *If only I had known!*

4 To indicate someone calling out or shouting: *Outside Edith's house, someone knocked. 'Edith!'* / *'You're only shielding her.' 'Shielding her!' His voice rose to a shriek.*

Many literary uses can be found in the *Oxford Dictionary of Quotations*. The following are a few representative examples: *I weep for Adonais—he is dead! O, weep for Adonais!*—Shelley, 1821 / *Yet still the blood is strong, the heart is Highland, And we in dreams behold the Hebrides!*—J. Galt, 1829 (translated in Blackwood's Magazine) / *Nearer, my God, to Thee, Nearer to Thee!*—S. F. Adams, 1841 / *Oh, to be in England Now that April's there . . . While the chaffinch sings in the orchard bough In England—now!*—Robert Browning, 1845 / *Fools! For I also had my hour; One far fierce hour and sweet*—G. K. Chesterton, 1900 / *What a queer thing Life is! So unlike anything else, don't you know, if you see what I mean*—P. G. Wodehouse, 1919 / *Six days of the week it* [i.e. *work*] *soils With its sickening poison—Just for paying a*

few bills! That's out of proportion—Philip Larkin, 1955.

exclusion has become the officially used word in education for what used to be called, rather more dramatically and with stronger physical implications, *expulsion*. Similarly, a school pupil is said to be *excluded* rather than (as formerly) *expelled*. But the term is no freer than its predecessor from unwelcome overtones, since *exclusion order*, 'an order issued under any of various Acts of Parliament excluding a person from a particular location, esp. as a means of preventing the commission of certain criminal acts' (*OED*), has occupied this ground as a term in UK law since the 1940s (originally with reference to Palestine).

excusable is spelt without an *e* in the middle.

executive in general use denotes one of three branches of government of which the other two are the *legislative* and the *judicial*. In the UK, it also denotes a rank of civil servant above *administrative* and *clerical*, and in the UK and US it means a high officer with important duties in a business organization. In attributive use (before a noun) *executive* has developed a meaning used in marketing to describe anything promoted as suitable for use by executives, i.e. luxurious or exclusive: *You can quaff from 'executive bars' . . . in 'executive suites' and top up from 'executive ice machines' on 'executive floors' . . . We have . . . luxuriated over 'executive menus' (smoked salmon is an extra with the 'executive breakfast'), and I once gratefully pocketed my 'complimentary executive gifts'.*—Lucinda Lambton, *Listener*, 1989.

executor, meaning an official appointed to carry out the terms of a will, is pronounced with the stress on the second syllable. It should be distinguished from *executioner*, an official who carries out a sentence of death.

exercise, both as a noun and a verb, is spelt *-ise*, not *-ize*, and has only one *c*.

exhaustible is spelt *-ible*, not *-able*. See -ABLE, -IBLE.

exhaustive, exhausting. Both words are derived from the verb *exhaust*, but relate to different meanings. *Exhaustive* relates to the meaning 'use up the whole of' (as in *exhausting a supply*) and means 'thorough or comprehensive': *We have all read the Steering Committee's exhaustive report*—D. Meiring, 1979 / *Now, after exhaustive research covering more than 2,500 Premiership matches, it has been proved: referees are 'homers'*—*Times*, 2006. *Exhausting* relates to the meaning 'to tire (a person)' and means 'extremely tiring' or 'draining of strength': *He's known as the studio's resident Romeo, with a social life and a string of girlfriends which must be exhausting rather than exhilarating*—*Leicester Chronicle*, 1976. Beware of using *exhaustive* when you mean *exhausting*: ☒ *All of this may have been down to tiredness after an exhaustive season in lifting the Heineken Cup in May*—*Mirror*, 2006.

exigent, exiguous. Neither word is common in ordinary usage and both are formal. Both are related to Latin *exigere* in its two meanings 'to enforce payment of' and 'to weigh exactly'. *Exigent* corresponds to the first of these and means 'exacting' or 'urgent': *He was a man whose personal life, though occasionally exigent, never became a siren song*—A. S. Byatt, 1988 / *It was . . . very much the brainchild of its two editors who ensured that its range and quality of content was up to their own exigent standards*—*Independent*, 1999. *Exiguous* corresponds to the second meaning and

means 'very small, sparse, scanty': *She gulped it down, paid the exiguous dispensing fee, and left the premises*—E. R. Taylor, 1991 / *For an octogenarian who has led an extraordinarily rich life, a mere two sparse pages of chronology is just about as biographically exiguous as you can get*—*Times Higher Education Supplement*, 2002.

exit. In stage directions the correct style is *Exit Macbeth* (when one person leaves the stage) and *Exeunt Banquo and Fleance* (when more than one person leaves). The two forms are the third person singular and third person plural present tense of the Latin verb *exire* 'to go out'.

-ex, -ix. See box opposite.

ex officio is a Latin phrase meaning 'by virtue of one's office or status' (*The principal is ex officio a member of the board of governors*). It is printed in italics, and should not be spelt with a hyphen when used attributively (before a noun), as in *an ex officio member of the committee*, although people often insert an unnecessary hyphen.

exorcize, meaning 'to expel (an evil spirit or influence)' is preferably spelt *-ize*, although *-ise* is common.

exoteric, exotic. Both words are derived ultimately from Greek *exō* meaning 'outside'. *Exoteric* is the opposite of *esoteric*, and means 'intended for people generally'; *exotic* means 'coming from or associated with a foreign country', often with connotations of the remarkable or bizarre, as in *exotic dances, exotic animals*, and *exotic locales*.

expandable, expansible are two forms of the derivative of *expand*. See -ABLE, -IBLE.

expect was the object of much criticism during the 19c when it was used to

-EX, -IX.

Naturalized Latin nouns ending in -*ex* and -*ix* vary in their plural forms, sometimes (as English words) adding -*es* and sometimes (as Latin words) changing the ending to -*ices*. The following table lists the most important words and their plural forms.

singular	principal meaning	plural
apex	highest point (technical)	apexes apices
appendix	supplement in book (medical)	appendices appendixes
codex	manuscript in book form	codices
cortex	outer part of an organ	cortices
duplex	apartment on two floors (AmE)	duplexes
helix	spiral curve	helices
ilex	tree or shrub	ilexes
index	list in book (technical)	indexes indices
matrix	mould, grid structure, etc.	matrices *or* matrixes
murex	mollusc	murices
radix	number or symbol	radices
silex	quartz or flint	*no plural*
simplex	thing in its simplest form	simplexes
vertex	highest point	vertices *or* vertexes
vortex	mass of whirling fluid	vortices *or* vortexes

mean 'to suppose, surmise', as in *I expect you'd like a drink*. Fowler, however, regarded it as a natural extension of meaning and wrote (1926) that 'it seems needless purism to resist it'. This view has been supported by the weight of usage, especially in spoken English. *An Asda checkout worker was celebrating after she and her partner scooped a £12.8m Lotto win. . . . A colleague at Asda said: . . . 'I don't expect she'll be coming back here.'—Liverpool Daily Post*, 2005.

expedience, expediency. Both forms are in use in the meaning 'fitness, suitability, advantage', although *expediency* is roughly ten times more common, according to the evidence of the *OEC*. The rhythm of the sentence often

determines which is used: *The present mentality on the island emphasises short cuts, expedience and disdain for professional standard—New Scientist*, 1991 / *At the time there was a case to be made for the new policy satisfying the demands both of expediency and humanity—K. Tidrick*, 1992.

expiry, expiration. The main meaning of *expiry* is 'the end of the validity or duration of something', as in *on expiry of the lease at the end of the month*. It is also a rather formal or euphemistic word for 'death'. *Expiration* is the standard word in American English for the first meaning, as in the *expiration date* on a food product. *Expiration* can also mean 'the act of breathing out', and one's dying breath. Both words are derived from Latin *expirare* meaning 'to breathe out'.

expletive is an adjective and a noun: both are pronounced ik-**splee**-tiv, with the stress on the second syllable. The primary meaning is 'filling out a sentence, line of verse, etc.', and the noun denotes a word that does this, typically in verse, without adding any meaning. In more recent use *expletive* as a noun will be familiar in the extended sense 'an oath or swear word', a use that goes back to Sir Walter Scott (*We omit here various execrations with which these honest gentlemen garnished their discourse, retaining only such of their expletives as are least offensive—Guy Mannering*, 1815).

exploit is pronounced with the stress on the first syllable as a noun (meaning 'a bold or daring feat') and with the stress on the second syllable as a verb (meaning 'to take selfish advantage of'), **eks**-ployt and iks-**ployt** respectively.

export is pronounced with the stress on the first syllable as a noun and with the stress on the second syllable as a verb.

exposé, meaning 'a revealing of something discreditable', is pronounced as three syllables and is printed in roman type with an accent on the final *e*. The accent is sometimes omitted in AmE.

exposition is sharply distinguished in meaning from *exposé*. Its main meanings are (1) a comprehensive description and explanation of an idea or theory, (2) in music, the part of a movement, especially in sonata form, in which the principal themes are first presented, and (3) a public exhibition, usually referring to one of the great 19c exhibitions, and only occasionally to a modern one.

ex post facto is a legal phrase meaning 'with retrospective action or force', as in *increasing its guilt* ex post facto / ex post facto *laws*. Strictly speaking, as Fowler (1926) noted, the spelling should be *ex postfacto* (meaning 'on the basis of the later enactment'), but the phrase has been written as three words since the 17c. It is printed in italics.

expressible is spelt *-ible*, not *-able*. See -ABLE, -IBLE.

expresso *see* ESPRESSO.

exquisite. The position of the stress has been moving over the last two centuries from the first syllable (**eks**-kwi-zit), which used to be the rule, to the second (iks-**kwi**-zit), which is now very common. Neither Fowler (1926) nor Gowers (1965) made any comment, but there are many who continue to prefer the older stress pattern despite its awkwardness.

extant previously used to mean just 'existing', so that heresy, fashion, roads, etc., could all be *extant*. Now, it means 'continuing to exist, surviving', i.e. having withstood the ravages of time, so that ancient texts, fossils, species, literature, organisms, old churches, etc., are the kinds of thing now described as *extant*. It is generally pronounced ek-**stant** but can also be **ek**-stuhnt.

extemporaneous, extemporaneously *see* EXTEMPORE.

extempore, pronounced as four syllables, means 'spoken or done without preparation', and can be used as an adverb or an adjective. On the grounds of brevity it is, arguably, preferable to the cumbersome alternatives *extemporaneous / extemporaneously*, but they are much more common, and rather less formal. *Impromptu*, which is much more frequent than any of them, means much the same and is a generally understood word.

extend. Fowler (1926) and others have castigated the use of *extend* to mean 'to give, to offer' in expressions such as *extend a welcome*. Fowler wrote that '*extend* in this sense has done its development in America, and has come to us full-grown via the newspapers—a bad record'. Few would object to its use today, which is common: *Sincere thanks were extended to all those who contributed to the success of the exhibition—Middlesbrough Catholic Voice, 1992 / An open invitation has been extended to interested people to come along to Eastside recreation ground and discuss ideas on Saturday, June 16 from noon, whatever the weather—Sussex Express, 2007.*

extendable, extendible, extensible are all acceptable spellings, the least frequent being *extendible*. *Extendable* is more frequent, is used in general contexts, and is the form recommended in *Garner's Dictionary of Legal Usage*. The most commonly used of the three is *extensible*, largely in computing contexts, because of its appearing in *Extensible Markup Language* (XML) and its offshoots.

extenuate means 'to lessen or reduce the seriousness of (guilt or an offence)' and usually occurs in the participial form *extenuating*: *Poverty and desperation are extenuating factors in Bangladesh, but not in the United States—New Yorker, 1973 / The law itself, framed as it is in terms of strict liability, is not concerned with any niceties which might be provoked by extenuating circumstances—K. Hawkins, 1993.*

exterior, external, extraneous, extrinsic. 1 The four words are related, and all have meanings based on *outside*. *Exterior* and *external* both refer to the outside of things in contrast to the inside (*Most manufacturers describe their exterior wall paints as masonry paint—Do It Yourself* (magazine), 1991),

and medicine is for *external use* when it is applied to the outside of the body; but *exterior* is generally physical only, whereas *external* is also applied in abstract or figurative meanings (*Changes in staff, changes in curriculum and increasing external demands making planning a chancy business—M. Sullivan, 1991); the *external world* is the world beyond one's perception. As a noun, however, *exterior* has the abstract meaning 'the outward or apparent behaviour or demeanour of a person': *How about your pal Ivan? Does he have sensitive feelings under that Neanderthal exterior?—D. Ramsay, 1973 / Bob, who hides a sparky humour behind a grizzled exterior, said tenants who were taking his beers were doing it on a 'belligerent, sod-the-brewer basis'—What's brewing?, 1991. External* is used as a noun generally in the plural to mean 'the outward aspects or circumstances': *The place has all the appropriate externals, chimneys choked with ivy, windows with jasmine, worm-eaten shutters, mossy thatch—P. Tristam, 1989 / Eventually he found all forms of religion involving 'externals' and ordinances unsatisfying—Dictionary of National Biography, 1993 / Add to that his inability to nail the externals of his characters' lives and his failure to conjure the campus mood (never mind the national zeitgeist), and the result is a disappointingly empty novel—weblog, IndE 2004.*

2 Something that is *extraneous* is introduced or added from outside and is foreign to the object or entity in which it finds itself. Uses are both physical and abstract: *Several other insects attach extraneous objects or material to themselves, but for very different reasons—M. & T. Birkhead, 1989 / A moment later any extraneous thoughts were driven from his mind—I. Watson, 1993. Extraneous* points are irrelevant matters brought into a discussion from which they have been excluded or to which they do not properly belong: *We were properly prevented by the law from making any extraneous comment beyond what we had agreed with Ian and his lawyers—Liverpool Daily Echo, 2005.* Something that is *extrinsic* is not an essential and inherent part of the thing in question, and is often contrasted with *intrinsic: Motivation may be considered as either intrinsic or extrinsic; intrinsic motives include those of exploration and curiosity, and extrinsic those of status and social approval—B. O'Connell, 1973 / Your personal belongings may be frugal and of little extrinsic value, but when they are lost or stolen, the cost of replacement can be surprisingly high—S. Meredeen, 1988.*

extol, meaning 'to praise enthusiastically', is spelt *-ol* in BrE and has inflected forms *extols, extolled, extolling.* In AmE *extoll* is an allowable variant, but *extol* (with the same inflections as in BrE) is much more common.

extraordinary in British English is normally pronounced ik-**straw**-di-nuh-ri as five syllables, not six, the *a* being merged into the following *or* to form one syllable.

extraterritorial, meaning 'situated or having force outside a country's territory', has ousted the variant form *exterritorial,* which is nowadays almost nonexistent.

extravert *see* EXTROVERT.

extrinsic *see* EXTERIOR.

extrovert, meaning 'outgoing and sociable' (also used as a noun to denote such a person), is now usually spelt *extro-* (on the analogy of *introvert* and *controvert*), although *extra-* is the better (and slightly earlier) formation, and the one used by Jung when writing in English.

exult *see* EXALT.

-ey and -y in adjectives. The normal suffix used to form adjectives from nouns is *-y*, as in *dusty, earthy, messy.* Nouns ending in a single consonant preceded by a single vowel normally double the consonant: *fatty, funny, nutty.* Some adjectives are formed from verbs rather than nouns: *chewy, fiddly, runny.* When the root ends in *-e* this is normally suppressed: *bony, chancy, crazy, hasty, nosy, shady,* etc. Some adjectives, however, are formed with *-ey*:

1 Those formed from nouns ending in *-y: clayey, skyey.* Note that *cagey* (also *cagy*) and *phoney* (also *phony*) are both of unknown etymology, and do not belong to this category. *Fiddly* is formed on the verb *fiddle,* not the noun.

2 Those formed from nouns ending in *-ue: bluey, gluey.*

3 *Holey,* meaning 'full of holes', is spelt *-ey* to distinguish it from the adjective *holy* = sacred.

eye *verb* has inflected forms *eyes, eyed, eyeing.*

eyrie, meaning 'nest of a bird of prey', is the preferred spelling in BrE, while in AmE it is *aerie.* The word is probably derived via medieval Latin from an Old French word *aire* meaning 'a lair of wild animals'.

fabulous originally meant 'mythical, legendary', but already in the 17c its meaning was extended to refer to anything astonishing or incredible, whether or not it belonged to fable or legend. The word enjoyed a revival in America and Britain in the 50s and 60s in the weakened sense 'marvellous, wonderful', and spawned a shortened form *fab*. *Fab* now sounds dated, but *fabulous* is still very much in use in this meaning: *Miss Mitchell, looking, one must admit, fabulous, played down her frenzy*—*Cambridge Review*, 1959 / *She stretched her stockinged toes towards the blazing logs. 'Daddy, this fire's simply fab.'*—*Times*, 1963 / *Trueman puffed at a cigarette and said he looked fabulous*—A. Ross, 1963 / *That's a fab idea. I think I will*—B. T. Bradford, 1983 / *He thought she looked fabulous, just like a dream*—R. Ingalis, 1987 / *True love does not mean squirming while he or she has a fab time*—*Express*, 2007.

facade, meaning the outward aspect of something (both physical and abstract), is fully naturalized and has lost its cedilla in English. It can also be written *façade*, but that spelling is nowadays in a minority.

face up to, meaning 'to confront, accept bravely' (normally with a non-personal object), was first noted in America and Britain in the early 1920s, and at first provoked great criticism, Eric Partridge (1942) objecting to it as 'a needless expression, the result of the tendency to add false props to words that

can stand by themselves'. The fury has long subsided, and the expression is listed in the *Oxford Dictionary of English* (2003) without any label limiting usage. Examples of recent use: *He won't face up, can't face up, to them being gone*—K. Hulme, 1984 / *Why don't you simply face up to the past?*—Kazuo Ishiguro, 1986 / *These are problems which it is a major responsibility of government to face up to*—*Parliamentary Affairs*, 1991.

facile pronounced **fas**-iyl in BrE and **fas**-uhl in AmE, means 'easy, smooth, effortless' with reference to people or what they do, and there is always a derogatory implication of something too easily achieved and of little value. A *facile speaker* is one for whom speaking comes easily and who therefore speaks glibly (rather than persuasively), and a *facile task* is one that is easily done but hardly worthwhile. If these connotations are not intended, a more neutral or positive synonym such as (with reference to people) *able, accomplished, fluent*, etc. or (with reference to achievements) *effortless, fluent, natural*, etc., should be used instead. However, in sports writing in particular *facile* is used with no negative connotations to refer to wins and winners, and means simply 'easy': *Charlestown under-14 girls under the management of Tom and Grainne McLoughlin began the season with a facile victory over Aughamore*—*Western Nationalist*, 2004.

facilitator, though dating from as far back as the 1920s, has a modern ring as a vogue word for a person responsible for the day-to-day management of people and processes when the word is aimed at a specific objective; it combines the meanings of *manager, mediator,* and *coordinator.* The grammar can be somewhat forced when the word is used in job titles: a *community facilitator* is an official who promotes community relations, a *workshop facilitator* organizes the resources for a business discussion, and a *marriage facilitator* provides counselling to those intending to be married. Some may baulk at the jargon-like effect of statements such as the following: *Teachers today are facilitators helping children to use their own computer skills to access information*—*Guardian,* 2007.

facility, faculty. 1 *Facility* (from Latin *facilis* meaning 'easy') means 'ease or ready ability to do something, aptitude': *Firstborn children have greater verbal facility, and there is evidence that they have more successful relationships with their teachers*—*Journal of Genetic Psychology,* 1973. It also has a concrete meaning which has proliferated greatly in the 20c, of 'something that provides an amenity or service', used in the singular or plural and referring either to the provision of an amenity or to the amenity itself: *Other recreational facilities include two lighted tennis courts, a swimming pool and a jogging trail*—*Philadelphia Inquirer,* 1976 / *You don't need a generously proportioned tub to fit a spa or whirlpool bath facility*—*Do It Yourself,* 1990 / *Solihull Council . . . has set out plans to build a 'large' casino at the NEC, although the facility could be built anywhere in the borough*—*Birmingham Post,* 2007. A common use is in finance and banking, to denote an arrangement such as a loan or overdraft: *If you want credit, a bank facility is usually better value than even a good dealer can offer*—*Opera Now,* 1990.

2 *Faculty* means 'an aptitude or ability to do something' in the sense of an inborn or inherent power rather than a proficiency developed (for example) by practice. The *faculty of language* is the natural ability of humans to speak, whereas a *facility for language* is an individual's particular skill in speaking.

fact. 1 The expression *the fact that* has long had an important function in enabling clauses to behave like nouns: *Some studies give attention to the fact that non-smokers cannot avoid inhaling smoke when breathing smoky air*—G. Richardson, 1971 / *The fact that I am gay is written down in black and white*—*Gay News,* 1978 / *Ethnic minorities will hopefully be tempted into the force by the fact that a black and female PC is given a starring role in the film*—*Guardian,* 1984 / *The fact that Nixon was willing to make his chastisement public suggests . . . that the President at least understands 'the parameters of the problem'*—*Time,* 1970. When standing at the head of a sentence (as in the second and fourth examples), the words *the fact* can sometimes be omitted without harming grammatical integrity, but a degree of emphasis or focusing is lost. Sentences made to depend on *the fact that* can often be recast to their advantage in other ways: *A small group of western European politicians and activists were in Moscow, drawing public attention to the fact that the mayor of Moscow has banned* [read *drawing public attention to a ban by the mayor of Moscow on*] *any Gay Pride march*—*Independent,* 2007. Verbs that can be complemented by a *that*-clause do not need to be linked by *the fact that,* so that the sentence ▣ *We acknowledge the fact that mistakes have been made* can be rephrased as *We acknowledge that mistakes have been made,* and ▣ *They convinced him of the fact that it was right* can be rephrased as *They convinced him that it was right.* The phrases *owing to the fact* *that* and *despite the fact that* can normally be replaced by *because* and *although* respectively, thereby producing a more economical and clearer structure. For *due to the fact that see* DUE TO 4.

2 *Fact* is used in a number of idioms: *in fact, as a matter of fact, in point of fact, the fact is*, etc. These often serve to assist the rhythm and continuity of speech, but can easily become overused and redundant in written material.

factious, fractious. *Factious* is a rather rare word meaning 'characterized by faction or dissension', as in *factious quarrelling. Fractious* has nothing to do with *factious,* but is sometimes confused with it; it means 'irritable, peevish', as in *a fractious child.* In the following sentence *factious* is presumably the word intended: *In this chapter we have traced the fractious history of relations between ethnic groups in America and the larger 'races' which encompass these*—R. Singh, 2003.

factor, aside from its technical senses, means 'a fact or circumstance that contributes to a result', and the notion of cause lies at the heart of its use, as in Gladstone's sentence (1878) *The first factor in the making of a nation is its religion.* A modern example of its proper use is: *Other factors can alter the Earth's climate from millennium to millennium and decade to decade*—C. Tudge, 1991. In recent years, however, *factor* has become widely used in a weakened meaning 'consideration, aspect, feature' with little or no notion of causality: *A very important factor in the teaching of tennis is the value of practice once the lesson is over*—*Tennis World*, 1991. A newish use dating from the 1980s (originally *the Falklands factor*) involves adding a preceding proper noun to specify an event, person, or even brand considered to have a significant effect on people's voting patterns, buying habits, etc.: *The*

continuation of the Iraq factor, uncertainty over the general economic situation and shaky stock markets all play their part—*Birmingham Post*, 2003. The *feel-good factor* is a feeling of material security in society, which occasionally yields to the *feel-bad factor.*

The flagging fortunes of *factor* as a verb have been boosted with the evolution of the phrasal verb *factor in,* meaning 'to include (a factor) in an assessment, plan, etc.': *All the political and military variables should be factored in before Israel decides on a response*—*Los Angeles Times*, 1991. It originated in business talk in AmE and has spread rapidly to British use, even achieving some general currency; *factor out* is also occasionally found: *Busy lifestyles have created buildings which have factored out healthy living*—*Guardian*, 2005.

faculty *see* FACILITY.

faeces, meaning 'excrement', is pronounced *fee*-seez and is spelt with *-ae*- in BrE but *-e-* in AmE. The corresponding adjectival forms are *faecal* and *fecal* (pronounced with a hard *c*).

fag, faggot. In BrE a *fag* is a colloquial word for (1) a piece of drudgery or a wearisome or unwelcome task, (2) a cigarette, and (3) a junior pupil at a public school who runs errands for a senior. In BrE a *faggot* is a ball or roll of seasoned chopped meat that is baked or fried, and in BrE and AmE it is a bundle of sticks or twigs bound together as fuel. In AmE both *fag* and *faggot* are offensive words for a male homosexual.

faint, feint. Both words come from the same Old French root *feindre* 'to feign'. *Faint* is used as an adjective meaning 'indistinct, pale' or 'feeling dizzy', as a noun meaning 'a loss of consciousness', and as a verb meaning 'to lose consciousness'. *Feint* is used as a noun meaning 'a sham attack or blow as a diversion', as a verb meaning 'to make a feint', and (since the 19c) as an adjective denoting faint lines on ruled paper.

fair, fairly *adverbs. Fair* is used in its ordinary meaning 'in a fair manner' in several fixed expressions, e.g. *to bid fair, to play fair, fair between the eyes.* In dialect use and in some non-British varieties it is used to mean 'completely, fully, really', as in *It fair gets me down.* It should be remembered that *fairly* has several meanings: (1) in a fair manner (*He treated me fairly*); (2) moderately, to a noticeable degree (*The path is fairly narrow / a fairly good translation*); (3) utterly, completely (*He was fairly beside himself*). In some contexts it is difficult to know (as with *quite*) whether the meaning is 2 or 3, although in speech intonation can clarify which is meant.

fait accompli, pronounced fayt uh-kom-**plee**, means 'a settled arrangement or circumstance that cannot be altered'. It is now usually printed in roman type. The plural is spelt *faits accomplis.*

faithfully. For *Yours faithfully, see* LETTER FORMS.

fall and *autumn* are used on both sides of the Atlantic as the name for the third season of the year, although in everyday use *autumn* is standard in BrE and *fall* in AmE. *Fall* is a shortening of the phrase *fall of the year* or *fall of the leaf,* and was in British use from the 16c until about 1800. The word *autumn* dates from the 14c, and comes from Latin *autumnus,* but the ultimate origin is obscure.

false analogy *see* ANALOGY.

falsehood, falseness, falsity. The three words, all to do with departure from the truth or what is true, have a considerable overlap in meaning and are sometimes interchangeable. *Falsehood* is the intentional telling of an untruth,

and a *falsehood* is a lie or untruth. In *OEC* data, *falsehood* is twice as frequent as *falsity,* itself four times more frequent than *falseness. Falsity* typically associates with *beliefs, claims, propositions,* and *statements,* while *falseness* is often applied to what is perceived as empty or insincere. Examples: *A half-truth was a falsehood, and it remained a falsehood even when you'd told it in the belief that it was the whole truth*—Aldous Huxley, 1939 / *As it had always been, truth and falsehood were inextricably intertwined in that statement*—S. Naipaul, 1980 / *The engagement had probably not been a complete falsity, a piece of acting*—Humphrey Carpenter, 1982 / *The biggest danger in diplomacy is falseness, dishonesty and lack of credibility*—D. Freemantle, 1988 / *The title track from his last album . . . is a typically excoriating Pop lyric—a diatribe at the falsity and emptiness of modern life*—Independent, 2002.

famed is an originally literary word meaning 'made famous', and is found (for example) in Shakespeare and Byron, often followed by *for* (the cause of the fame): *The English, for example, were famed for their assumptions of innate superiority*—J. Wormald, 1991 / *Once famed as 'Baghdad by the Bay' in the days when such an appellation was a compliment, San Francisco has gone the way of many major U.S. cities*—Daily Telegraph, 1992 / *We're a small club from a small town that's probably more famed for marriages than football*—Daily Record, 2007. It is not a mere synonym of *famous,* although it is often found with that meaning, especially in newspaper writing. *Renowned* and *celebrated* could often replace it, and would be less trite: *In the cemetery where tens of thousands of soldiers lay, he [Abraham Lincoln] delivered his famed address championing 'government of the people, by the people, for the people'*—Observer, 2004.

fan, fanatic, fanatical. *Fanatic* is common as a noun meaning 'a person having excessive or misguided enthusiasm for something'; as an adjective it is rather less used than *fanatical*, but still occurs: *He was a fanatical worker, often doing thirteen or fourteen hours a day*—A. Thwaite, 1984 / *Apple creates almost fanatic identification, almost entirely through a narrative that started with a single Superbowl ad in 1984*—*OEC*, 2006. The abbreviated form *fan*, meaning 'a keen supporter', occurs in an isolated use in AmE as early as 1682, though not again until the late 19c when it became part of the ritual language of baseball, and then passed into general use in AmE, BrE, and elsewhere in the 20c in the senses 'a supporter, an admirer' (of a person or thing). *Fan mail* is first recorded in 1924, *fan letter* in 1932, and *fan club* in 1941, and other combinations are in use, including *fanzine* (= fan magazine), first recorded in 1951.

fantastic. 1 *Fantastic* is one of the most popular colloquial terms for 'excellent, very enjoyable'. It is first recorded with this meaning in the 1930s and is now used in all sorts of contexts: *Oh, Val, isn't it fantastic? . . . It's amazing, isn't it?*—Margery Allingham, 1938 / *Then suddenly I get a call saying, 'We are going on the road,' so I was in and it was fantastic*—*Guitarist*, 1992. The adverb *fantastically* is also common as a general intensifier: *He's fantastically good-looking*—Iris Murdoch, 1989 / *I felt my badminton was going to suffer and I wasn't doing fantastically at uni either*—*Herald* (Glasgow), 2007.

2 Both *fantastic* and *fantastically* meanwhile continue to be used in their more literal meanings connected with fantasy and imagination, albeit somewhat compromised by the newer meanings: *We gazed in wonderment at the fantastic shape of the small island of Tindholmur as we passed*—B. Tulloch, 1991 / *De Quincey frequently dreamt of a fantastically elaborate and labyrinthine building*—R. Castleden, 1993.

fantasy, phantasy. 1 The *OED*, echoed by Fowler (1926), tried to assert a distinction between these two spellings, the first reflecting the Greek spelling and the second the more immediate French source of the word, 'the predominant sense of the former being "caprice, whim, fanciful invention", while that of the latter is "imagination, visionary notion"'. In modern use there is no such distinction, and *fantasy* prevails in all meanings.

2 The use of *fantasy* in attributive position (before a noun) is relatively recent. *Fantasy world* dates from 1920, and Michael Innes (J. I. M. Stewart) appears to have been the first to use *fantasy life*, followed by C. Day Lewis (but their hyphen is not now usual): *They have their tenure in remaining—remote, jewelled and magical—a focus for the fantasy-life of thousands*—Hamlet, Revenge!, 1937 / *It is said that an only child develops a particularly vivid fantasy-life*—Buried Day, 1960. In the 1980s came a new development with the invention, first in America and then in Britain, of a game called *fantasy football*, in which participants choose an imaginary team made up of real-life players; the actual performance of these players determines the fortunes of the fantasy team and ultimately the winner of the game. Other combinations in the same language domain include *fantasy league* and *fantasy baseball*.

far. 1 *far from* **+ noun.** This is a common way of expressing denial or rejection of a proposition: *The American dream seems as far from reality as my Communist dream*—Guardian, 1986. Its function as metaphor is more strongly evident in the variant form *far removed* from: *The trial will seem far removed from the red-light districts and suburbs where Sutcliffe struck—Observer*, 1981.

2 (so) far from —ing. This construction, first recorded in the 17c, is used to reject or deny one proposition and assert another. The use of *so* was still current in 1926, when Fowler cited the example *So far from 'running' the Conciliation Bill, the Suffragettes only reluctantly consented to it. So* is still very occasionally used for emphasis, but in general use it has tended to drop out of the construction: *Far from there being any noticeable improvement in the quality of relationships as practised among freaks, I would say there has been a distinct deterioration—Ink*, 1971 / *Far from wanting to hug any hoodies, he described rioting youths two years ago as 'scum' and wants to create a ministry of immigration and identity—Business*, 2007.

3 far-flung. This quite modern word (first recorded in 1895) calls to mind Kipling's *Recessional* (1897): *God of our fathers, known of old, Lord of our far-flung battle-line.* Fowler (1926) wrote of 'its emotional value . . . as a vogue-word. The lands are distant; they are not far-flung; but what matter? *Far-flung* is a signal that our blood is to be stirred.' The *far-flung Empire* has been replaced by less stirring concepts, but the adjective is still widely used as way of suggesting remoteness and inaccessibility: *We have a number of inhouse petroleum engineers to help us evaluate deals that involve assets in far-flung corners of the world—Herald* (Glasgow), 2007.

4 as far as / so far as. In adverbial clauses of the type *as far as . . . is concerned* or *as far as . . . goes* (in which *so* is still an occasional variant), the verbs *is* (or *are*) *concerned* and *goes* (or *go*) is preferably retained: *The old pals act will operate as far as the press is concerned—*T. Heald, 1975 / *As far as foreign money is concerned, Russia is safe—Sunday*

Telegraph, 2003 / *There are always buyers of liability insurance . . . who punch above their weight so far as their knowledge of the subject goes—Lloyd's List*, 2007.

The shortened version *as far as* with no verb is, however, not uncommon: *Our drivers must be extra careful as far as driving—OEC*, 2001. The expression *as far as I am concerned* is commonly used as a kind of emotional disclaimer: *I started out with some idea of serving the community and bunk like that, and now the community can get on with it as far as I'm concerned—*J. Bingham, 1975 / *To just dump 12,000 books in skips and then cart them off for recycling is completely wrong as far as I'm concerned—Bristol Evening Post*, 2007. *See also* IN SO FAR AS.

farrago, meaning 'a confused mess or muddle', comes from a Latin word meaning 'mixed fodder' (from *far* = corn), and is normally used in abstract senses. In journalistic use it is often reduced to a general term for anything disapproved of, a pejorative alternative to 'show' or 'spectacle': *The director can't resist staging the entire farrago as a coarse pantomime-romp commentary on the composer's notorious love of money—Sunday Times*, 2003. The plural form is *farragos* in BrE and *farragoes* in AmE.

farther, further. 1 general. *Further* is the older form, being recorded in Old English and probably related to our word *forth*, while *farther* is a Middle English variant of *further;* from this stage the two words came to be used as the comparative of *far*, and by the 17c had entirely replaced the other Middle English forms *farrer* and *ferrer. Farther* is related only coincidentally in form to *far*, although this coincidence seems to have influenced its use. It is never wrong to use *further* and *furthest*, whereas *farther* and *farthest* are restricted in use, and in cases where there is a choice *further* and *furthest* still tend to be more common.

2 use of *farther*, *farthest*. The principal role of *farther* is in expressing physical distance, corresponding more closely to the notion of 'more far' and 'most far': *The gulls rose in front of him and floated out and settled again a little farther on*—Virginia Woolf, 1922 / *And now the prince is scouring the farthest reaches of the globe for his bride*—J. M. Coetzee, SAfrE 1977 / *Most DIY owners find that five to ten miles is the farthest they want to travel*—Today's Horse, 1991. This apparent preference may be carried over into uses that represent degree rather than physical distance, but within the context of a wider distance metaphor: *'Why, Lord, no honey!' I told her. 'It's the farthest thing from my mind.'*—Lee Smith, AmE 1983 / *Kasparov simply saw farther, 'much, much farther', than the machine*—New York Times Magazine, 1990.

3 use of *further*, *furthest*. *Further* and *furthest* are more usual when the meaning is one of degree rather than physical distance: *He . . . found English currency confusing and the driver sought to confuse him further*—Evelyn Waugh, 1961 / *It seeks the furthest extension of the educationally valuable among the masses*—Encounter, 1987 / *In the case of her friendship with Flaubert she went one decade further and became a mother-substitute*—Economist, 1993.

4 other evidence. The following examples show that the pattern is not totally consistent, with *further* (in particular) being used in ways associated with *farther* and (less so) vice versa: *This was the lower fountain, furthest from the house*—A. S. Byatt, 1987 / *'You get a lot farther using your nose than your palate,' Patty says about wine-tasting*—New Yorker, 1987 / *The New Delhi station which did appear, somewhat further away, was a functional monstrosity in concrete and steel*—J. Richards et al., 1988 / *One, Lewis Holt, actually worked in Fleming's laboratory, and took the purification a stage farther than any of the previous workers*—M. Weatherall, 1990 / *The ferryman pointed to a thatched, low-roofed timbered hut further along the shoreline*—P. C. Doherty, 1991. Overall, the evidence shows a somewhat stronger presence of *farther* and *farthest* in AmE, but American usage guides do not normally reflect this tendency in their guidance.

5 special uses. There are some uses that are exclusive to *further*:

a When used as a sentence adverb: *Further, shameful as it might be to admit it, the idea of the play had started to interest him rather*—Kingsley Amis, 1958 / *Further, he was not given particulars of the grounds for the committee's decision*—P. Leyland et al, 2002.

b When it is an adjective meaning 'additional' or an adverb meaning 'additionally' or 'also': *He wrote for booklets containing further particulars of almost every device he saw advertised*—Elizabeth Bowen, 1949 / *Dundee's modern shopping precinct has now been further decorated with paint-sprayed gang slogans*—Scotsman, 1973 / *The apartment was further defended by a police lock*—J. Aiken, 1975 / *Hobbs has three further days to find another Triumph Hurdle winner*—Times, 2004.

c In certain fixed expressions in which *further* is an adjective, e.g. *further education*.

d In the formal expressions (1) *further to*, used especially in business correspondence to refer to matters raised previously: *Further to our letter of 20 August . . .*, and (2) *until further notice*.

e In the compound adverb *furthermore*.

f As a verb meaning 'to favour or promote (an idea, scheme, etc.)': *No city has done more than Coventry since the* *war to further the cause of international-ism—Times*, 1973 / *There has been greater emphasis by unions upon legislative enactment to further their general objectives—R. Bean*, 1992.

fascination. People are sometimes puzzled by which preposition to put after *fascination*, since *with*, *for*, and *of* are all used. The choice depends to an extent on which meaning of *fascination* is being invoked, for it can mean either (1) 'the state of being fascinated' or (2) 'the power to fascinate someone; the quality of being fascinating'. When it means (1), *with* is the most appropriate and frequent: *In recent years, the public's fascination with architecture has grown at an exponential rate—Art Business News*, 2001 / *From an early age I was always frustrated as my fascination with other languages was doused by drills in sentences one would never use—Language Log*, 2003.

When it means (2), the preposition *for* is used in front of the person who is fascinated, while *of* precedes the thing that possesses the quality of being fascinating: *the architecture of Rome and the Mediterranean coastline hold a special fascination for him—Apollo* (magazine), 2005 / *But the perpetual fascination of the human face remains—Royal Academy Magazine*, 2005.

Sometimes *for* is used instead of *with* in meaning (1), but for some people this seems unidiomatic: *But nevertheless his sincerity and passion, and his fascination for all aspects of the human condition, good and bad, shine through—At the Movies*, 2005.

fascism, fascist. 1 When Fowler wrote in 1926, Mussolini had not long been established in power, and the future of these words, and their Italian counterparts *fascismo* and *fascista*, was uncertain. Fowler suspended judgement on their anglicization 'till we know

whether the things are to be temporary or permanent in England'. The concepts are still very much with us: the English words are now generally written with small initial letters (except sometimes with specific historical reference) but are still pronounced in an Italian manner with the central consonant as *sh* (**fash**-izm / **fash**-ist), and the Italian forms are not used at all except in the special contexts of Italian history.

2 As the *OED* notes, *fascist* has been watered down in meaning to provide a convenient, emotive, and somewhat imprecise way of branding anyone 'who advocates a particular viewpoint or practice in a manner perceived as intolerant or authoritarian'. (*Fascism* has undergone the same process.) Both are usually modified by a preceding noun used attributively, and the *OED* has entered *body fascist* (1978) as well as *eco-fascist* (1987) and *health fascist* (1980). *Islamic, Christian, religious, gay*, and *cultural fascists* feature in the *OEC* data, but the word is capable of infinite extension. *She doesn't eat sugar and does yoga at dawn, but not to lose weight. Earl Dittman hears how Gwyneth Paltrow is fighting the body fascists—Big Issue*, 2002 / *It'll be fun to see what happens when the tobacco fascists run headlong into the human rights fascists—Canadian Lawyer*, 1997.

fatal, fateful. Both words have to do with the workings of fate, and their complex histories, fully explored by the *OED*, have often intertwined. Fowler (1926) wrote a fond defence of the special meaning of *fateful*, 'having far-reaching consequences', which (unlike *fatal*) might be good or neutral as well as bad: *In summing up 1934 we can see, in the light of what was to come, that it was a fateful year—J. F. Kennedy*, 1940 / *The fateful sequence of events had started with a malfunction in the main pumps supplying cooling water to the reactor's* core—C. Aubrey, 1991. *Fatal* means 'causing death' (as in *fatal accident*), and can refer to inanimate things and situations as well as to those able to suffer actual death: *Even when your trump suit is solid, it may still be fatal to touch it too early*—Country Life, 1976 / *The existence of these private but non-fee-paying schools will have a deeply depressing, if not fatal, effect on other schools in the area*—M. Warnock, 1989. The closest synonyms to *fatal* in this meaning are *catastrophic, disastrous, ruinous*. The collocation *fatal flaw*, which originates as a term in literary criticism for the decisive weakness in character that leads to tragedy, is often used hyperbolically to add significance to the notion of a serious weakness or objection, making it often little more than a cliché: *Until he faces up to his own fatal flaws, he has no hope of conquering them*—Today, 1992 / *The fatal flaw in the ban-smacking brigade's thinking is their inability to recognise the difference between a parental smack and violence*—South Wales Evening Post, 2004.

father-in-law means one's wife's or husband's father. The plural is *fathers-in-law*.

fathom, a unit of measurement of depth, is sometimes left unchanged in the plural when preceded by a number, i.e. *six fathom deep* but the plural is nowadays more usual, i.e. *six fathoms deep*, and *several fathoms deep*.

fatwa. A *fatwa* (from Arabic *fatā* 'to instruct by a legal decision') is a legal ruling given by an Islamic religious leader. It came dramatically to western attention in 1989 when by such a ruling Iran's Ayatollah Khomeini called for the death of the writer Salman Rushdie for publishing *The Satanic Verses* (1988), which many Muslims considered blasphemous. (The ruling was effectively withdrawn by 1998.) *Fatwa* is already

undergoing extensions of meaning, and is erroneously used to mean 'sentence of death' (which, in the case of Rushdie, it meant only in effect). The plural in English contexts is *fatwas*, and the use of a verb form is also recorded: *Unlike many writers and artists, Chahine hadn't been fatwaed, but he felt threatened nevertheless*—New Yorker, 1995.

faucet is a late Middle English word meaning 'a tap for drawing liquor from a barrel or cask'. In BrE it survives in technical uses (often combined with *spigot*), but in domestic use it has given way entirely to *tap*. In AmE, *faucet* is in widespread use for an ordinary water tap, but its distribution is uneven, with *spigot* in use in the south and *cock* and *tap* also in use.

fault verb. To *fault*, meaning 'to blame, find fault with', has been criticized as an awkward verbalization by some modern usage guides, especially in America, though not by Fowler (1926), nor by Gowers (1965) who declared supportively that it was enjoying a revival. The use dates from the 16c and is now fully established: *Martita wasn't too keen on Fay Compton I gathered (though she couldn't fault her perfect diction)*—Alec Guinness, 1985.

fauna, flora, meaning respectively the animal life and plant life of a particular time or region, are derived from the names of Roman goddesses and are singular (uncountable) nouns, which means that the verbs following them are in the singular, as are any qualifying words preceding them, e.g. *this fauna is . . .*, not *these fauna are . . .*. The plural forms, though rarely needed, are *faunas* and *floras* (occasionally *faunae* and *florae*).

faux pas, meaning 'a minor blunder or indiscretion', is pronounced foh **pah** and is now fully naturalized in English and printed in roman type. The plural form is the same, pronounced foh **pahz**.

favour, favourable, favourite are the normal BrE spellings, as distinct from *favor, favorable, favorite* in AmE.

fax is first recorded in 1948 as a shortened form of *facsimile* (*process*, etc.) and quickly established itself in the standard language as a noun and verb during the 1980s when *fax machines* came into widespread use. The word has been accepted much more readily than *pix* (= pictures) and *sox* (= socks), presumably because no comfortable alternative exists, *facsimile transmission* being too technical and awkward for ordinary use.

fay, fey. *Fay* is a literary word for *fairy*. Used attributively (before a noun), it has the meaning 'fairy-like': *When she made formal use of figures in her landscapes, they were somewhat mannered, almost fay children*—Listener, 1962. *Fey* is an unrelated word of great antiquity originally meaning 'fated to die soon', a meaning it still has in Scottish English. In due course it came to denote a kind of frenzied excitement associated with impending death, and in extended use it means 'strange, other-worldly; elfin, whimsical': *She's got that fey look as though she's had breakfast with a leprechaun*—D. Burnham, 1969 / *Scraggy hair, fey smile, dress like a wet dishcloth. Another example of why being too thin really isn't sexy*—Times, 2007. In this last meaning it makes close contact with *fay*, and in speech, of course, they are indistinguishable. That explains why *fay* is sometimes used where *fey* is meant: *There's something a bit fay about it* [*tennis*]. *It's for middle-class kids who can afford to have their kit cleaned once a day—by Nanny*—BBC Sport, 2004.

faze means 'to disconcert, disturb' and is used informally in mainly negative contexts: *It is a pretty daunting prospect going on stage for forty minutes but it does not seem to have fazed her*—S. Stone, 1989 / *The one thing I am not going to do is look remotely fazed or ruffled*—E. Galford, 1993. It is in origin a 19c AmE variant of the ancient verb *feeze* 'to drive off, to frighten away' and has nothing to do with the ordinary verb *phase*, although this spelling is sometimes mistakenly used.

fearful, fearsome. 1 *Fearful* means 'full of fear; frightened, apprehensive', usually referring to something specific, and is normally followed by *of* or by a clause introduced by *that* or *lest*: *Eisenhower's official policy was to remain aloof, fearful that any direct intervention would make Castro a martyr*—N. Miller, 1989 / *He became very fearful of cars, buses and stairs, eventually shutting himself in his room, with the curtains drawn, for 14 months*—Guardian, 1989 / *She stood outside looking up at a creamy moon, fearful lest some bat might fly into her hair*—Julian Barnes, 1990. It is also used of feelings and circumstances that are characterized by great fear: *His mother had brought him up to hold priests in fearful reverence*—G. McCaughrean, 1987, and, like *dreadful*, in the weakened meaning 'very great', of things and situations: *In fact it had been very hard bought, some of the winnings, taking fearful tolls of nerve, straining every atom of him*—Nicolas Freeling, 1972 / *When I approached the lower door I heard some fearful screams, groans and noises of struggling*—Northern Echo, 2007.

2 *Fearsome* means 'appalling or frightening, especially in appearance', and is often applied to reputations: *Ichiro continued to regard me with the most fearsome look*—Kazuo Ishiguro, 1986 / *Rhododendrons . . . have become a fearsome forest weed, preventing the growth of other plants*—Outdoor Action, 1989 / *Why do swans have this fearsome* *reputation? A friend who had a flock of them on his lake says they're gentle creatures—Daily Mail*, 2005.

They are occasionally confused, with *fearful* being dubiously used for *fearsome*: *He was an enforcer for Arthur Thompson Sr, the Glasgow crime boss, and developed a fearful reputation before they parted company in the 1980s—Sunday Times*, 1985 / ⊠ *He claimed that it* [i.e. Antarctica] *was cut off from the rest of the world by a region of fire and some others went on to say that fearful monsters inhabited it—*John Long, 2001.

feasible. The key to the use of this word, and the problems associated with it, lies in its relation to the different meanings of *possible*. *Feasible* has three main uses, two unremarkable and one controversial, all associated with different aspects of possibility:

1 With reference to ideas, projects, etc., 'capable of being done or carried out': *Changes became feasible over a period of time—*Harold Wilson, 1976 / *There was no question that a tunnel was technically feasible, but I wanted to know what the economics would be—*N. Fowler, 1991 / *Clearly, it is not feasible to have cameras covering the whole of the track—Hansard*, 1992.

2 With reference to people and things generally, 'capable of being used or dealt with successfully': *The sixties should see them* [i.e. labour-saving devices] *put into commercial production in sufficient quantity to make them financially feasible—Sunday Times*, 1960 / *The new semi-automated test could at last make massive screening programmes for cervical cancer economically feasible—New Scientist*, 1991.

These first two meanings are often hard to distinguish, although essentially the first refers to actions and processes whereas the second refers to what is being dealt with or considered; they are given separately in the *OED* but are combined in the *Concise Oxford Dictionary* ('possible to do easily or conveniently'). Perhaps only compilers of dictionaries attempt to see a difference.

3 With reference to a theory, proposition, etc., 'able or likely to be the case': *Even if we dropped the price range we looked at, it was quite feasible it would eventually go beyond our budget—Belfast Telegraph*, 2007. This third, and controversial, meaning comes closest to being a synonym of *possible* (in its meaning 'able to be the case' rather than 'able to be done') or *probable*, and Fowler urged strongly that when these words can be substituted without affecting the meaning they should be. The examples he gave, unattributed but probably from newspapers, were: *Witness said it was quite feasible* [better *possible*] *that if he had had night binoculars he would have seen the iceberg earlier* and *We ourselves believe that this is the most feasible* [better *probable*] *explanation of the tradition*.

Each case must be treated on its merits, but when the context requires the sense of likelihood or probability (as in the 2007 example above) rather than practicality it is prudent to test first whether *possible* or *probable* might not be the more satisfactory word (this will occur most often in constructions of the type *It is feasible that . . .*), and to use *feasible* only if both the other words seem unnatural or unidiomatic.

feature *verb.* Fowler (1926) warned against the extension of the meaning 'to give special prominence to' which he identified as originating in cinema announcements. He cited an unattributed example of 1924: *Boys' school and college outfits, men's footwear and undergarments, as well as . . .*, *are also featured*, and urged the use of *display* or *exhibit* instead. But his words went unheeded, and the verb *feature* is now standard both with an object, as in the example just given, or without, often being further diluted to mean merely 'include' or 'be included', as in Fowler's original example: *I was to have my name featured for the first time at the top of the bill*—Charlie Chaplin, 1964 / *Libraries and the youth service feature prominently in many of the local authority cuts*—*Times*, 1976 / *A brutal day in the Alps, featuring five climbs, the longest of which covers over 5,400 ft in 12 miles*—*Sunday Times*, 2007.

February should be pronounced with both *r*s fully articulated. It is now common, especially in AmE, to hear the word pronounced as if it were *Febuary* (and it is occasionally spelt that way too, which is a great deal worse).

federation, confederation, confederacy. *Federation* and *confederation* are the more precise constitutional terms, a *federation* being a union of federal states and a *confederation* being a union of states in alliance. *Confederacy* is a looser term for an organization of states such as the southern states of the US which seceded from the Union in 1860-1, thus precipitating the American Civil War.

feedback developed its meaning in general use, 'information about something from the people that have used it or been involved in it, as a basis for improving it', in the 1960s: *They would like feedback from the last issue, articles from individuals and groups giving a socialist-feminist analysis of activities*—*Women's Report*, 1976 / *The aim of marking is ... to give constructive feedback so that the students' work steadily improves*—*Electronic Publishing*, 1991. Earlier technical uses in electronics and biology date from earlier in the 20c. It is worth bearing in mind that this 'popularized technicality' is for many people a bête noire; less potentially irritating alternatives include *comment*, *criticism*,

evaluation, or just plain, old-fashioned *response*.

feel *verb*. **1** *Feel* is followed by an adjective to denote the nature of a feeling, whether physical or emotional: *I'm feeling cold* / *They began to feel afraid*. For *to feel bad*, see BAD 1.

2 Occasional, but misguided, opposition has been expressed to the use of *feel* in the intuitive meaning 'to think, believe, consider' or, as the *OED* puts it, 'to apprehend or recognize the truth of (something) on grounds not distinctly perceived; to have an emotional conviction of (a fact)'. The use goes back to Shakespeare (*Garlands ... which I feel I am not worthy yet to wear*—*Henry VIII* IV.ii.91), and has been current ever since in standard use. Modern examples: *But perhaps it was a little flat somehow, Elizabeth felt. And really she would like to go*—Virginia Woolf, 1925 / *If Pascal had been a novelist, we feel, this is the method and the tone he would have used*—Graham Greene, 1969 / *Many gays either were in therapy or felt they should be*—E. White, 1980.

feel-good, feel-bad. We have had the *feel-good factor* and *feelgoodism* since 1977, when the *New York Times* reported that *the latest aberration in the American pursuit of happiness is the feelgood movement*. The word had been used earlier in *Dr Feelgood*, a term for a physician who provided short-term palliatives rather than effective cures. In the 1990s, the term *feel-good factor* came increasingly to be associated with material prosperity as a political and social factor. The antidote to all this is the *feel-bad factor*, which dates from the early 1990s: *We're all so insecure about our short-term contracts and our feel-bad factors that we're terrified of appearing keen to leave the office*—*Guardian*, 1995. It is still with us: *It is ironic that our nurses could be the first arm of the public* *sector to suffer the full brunt of the so-called feel-bad factor, the term used by economists to describe the creeping whiff of impending gloom—Sunday Times,* 2007.

feint *see* FAINT.

fellow, in its meaning 'belonging to the same class or activity' used attributively (before a noun), is sometimes hyphenated and sometimes written as a separate word: *fellow citizen* or *fellow-citizen.* The modern tendency is to spell such combinations as two words even when the second element is an agent noun (as in *fellow traveller*) and to add a hyphen to avoid any ambiguity, notably when the combination is an *-ing* form: *He has no qualms about saying . . . that Oppenheimer was 'a fellow-travelling humanist', and that he behaved with deplorable disloyalty to some of his colleagues—Times Higher Education Supplement,* 2004 / *He had copied and pasted the words from a fellow blogger who was expressing his alarm at the actions of the Royal Society—Guardian,* 2006. But the *-ing* form needs its freedom when it belongs with the following word: *Hatch's lost boy, 28-year-old Kit, sets out to be a cool, round-the-world backpacker and ends up caught uneasily between fellow travelling companions Carlos and Dominique—Scotsman,* 2001 / *The answer gradually emerges as he quizzes the two fellow travelling salesmen he has invited to meet him—Times,* 2004.

female, feminine. 1 general.
Female is used as an adjective, contrasting with the etymologically unrelated word *male*, to designate the sex of humans and animals that can bear offspring and to designate plants that are fruit-bearing. *Feminine* is used only of humans and has two additional meanings: (1) denoting characteristics or qualities associated with women, and (2) contrasted with *masculine* and

neuter, denoting a class of grammatical gender. Both words also have technical meanings in various domains. In broad terms *female* is used principally to indicate the sex of a person, animal or plant, whereas *feminine* is used of characteristics regarded as typical of women, i.e. beauty, gentleness, delicacy, softness, etc. *See also* WOMANLY, WOMANISH.

2 *female* as a noun. *Female* has a long history in the meaning 'a female person'; 'a woman or girl', but despite this several 19c usage guides advised against the use on the grounds that it was unsuitable to apply the same term to animals and human beings. The *OED* (in 1895) said of *female* used as a synonym for *woman* that 'the simple use is now commonly avoided by good writers, except with contemptuous implication'. This observation holds good in our gender-sensitive age, and it would be difficult to contemplate *female* being used in this way without some degree of disparagement being intended or understood: *He had no option now but to speak to his landlady in the morning about letting this homeless female have his bed for the night—M. J. Staples,* 1992. The use is best reserved for use in natural history and for occasions when a general or neutral term is needed (for example, in medical or other technical writing) to include both *woman* and *girl*, or to avoid the social distinctions still sometimes inherent in *woman* and *lady*: *More than 55 females, from babies to elderly women, have been killed during the first year of the Uprising—Spare Rib,* 1989 / *We have found that females with male twins are significantly disadvantaged compared to those with female twins or compared to males with male twins—Daily Mail,* 2007.

feminine designations. For most agent nouns and nouns indicating occupation no distinction is made between masculine and feminine: *clerk,* *cook, councillor, counsellor, cyclist, doctor, lecturer, martyr, motorist, nurse, oculist, palmist, president, pupil, secretary, singer, teacher, typist,* etc. A few, such as *actress, hostess, manageress,* and *usherette,* exist in feminine forms, but those in *-mistress* corresponding to the masculine *-master* (e.g. *postmistress, schoolmistress*) have fallen out of use. There is still an expectation, often subconscious, that some occupations will be held by a man (e.g. *chef*) and that others will be held by a woman (e.g. *secretary*), but these barriers are falling fast. In practice, if there is a need to be specific about the gender of an occupational or agent noun, a feminine noun such as *woman, lady,* or *girl* is sometimes used (*woman driver, lady doctor,* etc.), although this too can offend sensitivities because corresponding male designations are only occasionally used in contexts in which the occupation has strong female associations (*male nurse, male typist,* etc.). The circumstances of these uses illustrate well the tensions between linguistic convention and social progress. *See also* -ESS; -ETTE; GENDER NEUTRALITY; -MAN; -PERSON; -WOMAN.

feminineness, feminism, femininity. These are the only survivors from a whole host of 19c formations which also included *feminacy, feminality, feminility,* and *femininitude* (the last a nonce-word used in 1878). *Feminineness* and *femininity* have much the same meaning, 'the fact or quality of being feminine', but *feminineness* is an unusual word choice. *Feminism* rapidly developed a special meaning 'advocacy of the rights of women on the grounds of equality of the sexes', a meaning which it retained with increased force in the later part of the 20c.

feral, ferial. Both words are usually pronounced with the first syllable as in *ferret* rather than *fear,* although the

second form is occasionally heard. *Feral* means 'wild' (from Latin *ferus* 'wild') and is applied (a) to animals in a wild state after escape from captivity and (b) to institutions and people compared to them (*This week, the Prime Minister attacked the British media as 'a feral beast', reserving special criticism for this newspaper—Independent,* 2007). *Ferial* (from Latin *feriae* 'holiday') is an ecclesiastical term denoting a day not appointed for a festival or feast.

ferment, foment. 1 *Ferment* is pronounced with the stress on the first syllable as a noun and with the stress on the second syllable as a verb.

2 As verbs, *ferment* and *foment* are often confused because they are pronounced approximately the same way and their uses overlap in their figurative meanings. To *ferment* means literally 'to effervesce or cause to effervesce' (from Latin *fervēre* meaning 'to boil') and figuratively 'to excite or become excited'; and so it can be transitive (with an object) or intransitive: you can *ferment* trouble or trouble can *ferment. Foment* means literally 'to bathe with warm or medicated liquid' (from Latin *fomentum* meaning 'poultice') and figuratively 'to instigate or stir up' (especially trouble). *Foment* is only transitive: you can *foment* trouble but trouble cannot *foment.* Examples: *Gladstone's complaint in 1874 that the opposition fomented by the Daily News had been 'one main cause' of the weakness of his late government was, of course, a simplism—Times Literary Supplement,* 1977 / *He hosted the meetings where the rebellion was fomented which ousted Mrs Thatcher from power—Today,* 1992 / *What are the TUC on about? Why are they fermenting trouble at this of all moments?—People,* 2002 / *They funded courses in car mechanics and carpentry as a chance to own a business for unemployed young men* *whose frustration was fermenting dangerously—Sunday Times, 2007.*

ferrule, ferule. *Ferrule*, also spelt *ferrel*, is the ring or cup used to strengthen the end of a walking-stick or umbrella, and is derived from Latin *ferrum* meaning 'iron'. A *ferule*, also spelt *ferula*, is a flat implement formerly used for beating schoolchildren, and is derived from Latin *ferula* meaning 'giant fennel'.

fertile. The standard pronunciation now is -tiyl in BrE and -tuhl in AmE.

fervent, fervid. Both words mean 'ardent, intense' with reference to speech, feelings, etc. There are two significant differences in their use: (1) *fervent* but not *fervid* is also used of people, with nouns such as *admirer, advocate, believer, follower, opponent*, and *supporter* among the typical collocates, and (2) *fervent* has positive connotations whereas *fervid* can sound negative, rather like the difference between *warm* and *feverish* as applied to feelings. Examples: (fervent) *Every available wall space was covered with graffiti and fervent slogans*—T. Strong, 1990 / *I make those criticisms as a fervent admirer of the army*—Sunday Times, 2005 / *I'm 45 and was hoping fervently that the Government might make menopause illegal before it engulfed me*—Express, 2007 / (fervid) *While a fervid interest in sex overpowered other girls, she listened to their confidences unmoved*—C. Brayfield, 1990 / *I'm afraid your rather fervid imagination is running away with you*—E. Rees, 1992. *Fervidly* is not typical but is occasionally found (*those within America who are fervidly anti-Bush*—weblog, AmE 2004).

fervour is spelt -*our* in BrE and *fervor* in AmE.

-fest is a new suffix derived from the German word *Fest* meaning 'festival, celebration'. It occurred first in AmE in the late 19c in the word *gabfest* meaning 'a gathering for talking' and spread rapidly to produce other words such as *talk fest, shooting fest, liquor fest*, etc. It has also spread to BrE in formations such as *discofest, filmfest, funfest, rockfest*, etc.

festal, festive. Both words are derived from the Latin words *festum* meaning 'feast' and *festus* meaning 'joyful', and mean 'in the nature of a feast or festival'. *Festive* is much the more common, and is the one generally chosen when the meaning is 'cheerful, joyous, celebratory': *A room can look festive and jolly without being overwhelmed by lots of gaudy decorations*—Ideal Home, 1991. *Festal* lies somewhat closer to its etymological connection with festivals: *It was eaten with a spoon and served on festal days as part of the main course*—Good Food, 1992. The *festive season* is a way of describing Christmas, and *festive* also occurs with words such as *air, atmosphere, mood*, and *occasion*.

fete, an outdoor public function to raise money for charity, has largely lost its circumflex accent in English.

fetid, meaning 'stinking', is normally pronounced **fet**-id, occasionally **feet**-id. The spelling *fet*-, rather than *foet*-, is now the majority spelling.

fetish. 1 *Fetish*, meaning 'a thing evoking special respect' (and more precise meanings in anthropology and psychology), is now pronounced **fet**-ish. The word is a 17c adoption of French *fétiche*, and was originally an African object or amulet having magical power, although the word itself is not of African origin.

    2 Fowler (1926) extended the use of *fetish* as a term for 'current literary rules misapplied or unduly revered'. These included the *split infinitive, insistence on *from* after **different*, aversion to putting a *preposition at the end of a sentence, and the idea that two consecutive metaphors are necessarily 'mixed' (*see* METAPHOR AND SIMILE 2). To these may now be added the use of **hopefully* as a *sentence adverb, insistence that **none* is always singular, and insistence that **agenda*, **data*, and other such words are always plural.

fetus, foetus. Medical usage in Britain and the US favours *fetus*, following the word's origin in Latin *fetus* 'offspring'. In AmE this spelling is preferred generally, but *foetus* is still common in non-medical use in BrE, largely because of the misconception that the *-e-* spelling is some kind of Americanism; but *fetus* is gradually taking over. The corresponding adjective is *fetal* in AmE and medical usage, with *foetal* becoming less common in BrE even in general use.

few. 1 *Few* may be used with or without preceding *a*, although the sense is slightly different. *There were few seats left* means there were not many (and is negative in implication), whereas *There were a few seats left* means that some were still left (and is positive in implication).

2 For *comparatively few*, see COMPARATIVELY.

fewer, less. As a general guide, *fewer* is used with plural nouns (*fewer books*, *fewer people*) and indicates number, whereas *less* is used with singular nouns and indicates amount (*less money* / *less happiness*). However, there is an extensive no man's land between these two positions. To begin with, *less* can be used idiomatically with *than* followed by plural nouns when these denote something closer to an amount than a numerical quantity, as with distances, periods of time, ages, and sums of money: *less than*

5 miles to go / *less than six weeks* / *children less than three years old* / *less than £100*. Supermarket checkouts are correct when the signs they display read *5 items or less* (which refers to a total amount), and are misguidedly pedantic when they read *5 items or fewer* (which emphasizes individuality, surely not the intention). Examiners often invite candidates to write a summary of a passage of prose in *fifty words or less*. In some borderline cases it is more idiomatic to use *less* when *fewer* would put an unwelcome emphasis on the numerical quantity rather than the cumulative effect of the total: ... *unashamedly rejoiced in having had in his house at one time no less than five Nobel Prize Winners*—Margaret Drabble, 1987. But *less* should be avoided when it comes before an otherwise unqualified plural noun: ▣ *I shall care about less things*—Penelope Fitzgerald, 1980 / ▣ *There is not enough money being spent on rehabilitation and, if we spend more, we could save a lot of money with less people reoffending*—Bury Free Press, 2007. See also LESS 3.

fey see FAY.

fiancé, fiancée. The first is masculine and the second is feminine. Both words are pronounced fi-**on**-say.

fiasco has the plural form *fiascos*.

fiat. The legal term, meaning 'an authorization or order', is pronounced **fee**-at or **fiy**-at. The make of car (*Fiat*) is pronounced **fee**-at.

fibre is the spelling in BrE and *fiber* in AmE.

fictional, fictitious. *Fictional* means 'occurring in fiction', i.e. in a piece of literature, whereas *fictitious* means 'invented, unreal; not genuine'. So *Oliver Twist* is a *fictional* name when it refers to Dickens's character, and a *fictitious* name when someone uses it as a false or assumed name instead of their own. Similarly, events are *fictional* when described in a work of fiction, and *fictitious* when invented in ordinary life.

fidget as a verb has inflections *fidgeted, fidgeting*.

field. In the meaning 'an area of operation or activity, a subject of study', *field* tends to be overused, and it is advisable to be aware of available synonyms. The most commonly needed are (for fields of study) *sphere, subject, area, discipline, domain,* (for areas of operation or responsibility) *area, province, department, line, speciality, responsibility,* (sometimes) *territory*. These also need to be used with care, for fear of avoiding the hackneyed only to adopt an alternative that is precious or stilted, as can happen with *department* and *territory*, or still worse *métier*, for example. It is also true that *in the field of* is often merely a verbose way of saying *in*, and could be avoided in, for example, *there is much talk about new discoveries in the field of genetics*.

fifties *see* EIGHTIES.

figure. 1 Both the noun and the verb are pronounced **fig**-uh in BrE but **fig**-yuh in AmE. The derivative forms *figural, figuration,* and *figurine* have the -y- sound in both BrE and AmE; but *figurative* (**fig**uh-ruh-tiv) lacks it in BrE.

2 As a verb, *figure* is used informally, especially in AmE and often with *out*, to mean 'work out, calculate, think'. To *figure on* something is to plan it or take it for granted, and in AmE something *figures* when it makes sense or seems likely.

figure of speech is any of several recognized linguistic devices used to make language lively or more colourful, such as *metaphor and *simile.

fillers are words such as *actually, you know, in fact, really,* and *I mean,* and pause markers such as *er* and *um,* that have little or no meaning and are merely used to help maintain a flow, and sometimes improve sentence balance, in conversational English. Their routine use is quite legitimate, and everyday conversation would be unnatural without them.

finable *see* FINEABLE.

final clause, in grammar, is a clause that states a purpose, especially when introduced by a formula such as *to, in order to, in order that, so as to, in the hope that,* etc.: *He turned on the plane's radio, in order to hear the traffic controller*—New Yorker, 1972 / *The Labour administration massaged the basis of the calculation of the exchange rate . . . so as to make the situation appear better*—Daily Telegraph, 1982 / *In order to fully understand an alarm reaction it is useful to think back many thousands of years to the time of the caveman*—S. Enright et al., 1990 / *Just dozing off willy-nilly for a few months, in the hope that the world will be a less loony place when you wake up: not an option*—Scotsman, 2007.

finale, meaning the last part of something, is pronounced as three syllables (fi-**nah**-li), not as two.

finalize, as a synonym of *complete* or *finish*, came into use in the 1920s in Australia and New Zealand, then in the US and, in the 1930s, in Britain. It was widely denounced by usage pundits such as Partridge and Gowers as an unnecessary addition; but it often has a stronger sense of effective conclusion than is conveyed by *complete* or *finish*: *Arrangements have also been finalized for the establishment of a ranching scheme at Jaldesa*—Inside Kenya Today, 1971 / *The two companies now have 120 days to finalize an implementation* *agreement under the terms of the letter of intent—Lloyd's List*, 1995.

fineable, meaning 'liable to a fine', is more often spelt this way, not *finable*. This spelling contradicts the general rule that words ending in silent -*e* (*fine*) lose it when -*able* is added, but makes the link with the noun *fine* clearer, and avoids possible misreading as **fin**-uhbl.

fine toothcomb *see* TOOTHCOMB.

fiord *see* FJORD.

fire *verb*, meaning 'to dismiss from a job', has its origins in AmE in the 1880s, when it was also used as a phrasal verb to *fire out*. Fowler (1926) entered both forms without much comment apart from mentioning their American origin; by the time Gowers wrote (1965), only the simple verb *fire* was used, and he noted that it was 'still an American colloquialism, though making headway among us at the expense of the verb to *sack*'. As it turns out, *fire* stands alongside *sack* as one of two words used regularly and unproblematically in informal English.

firing line, line of fire. To be in *the line of fire* is literally to be within range of a gun or missile, and metaphorically to be likely to be criticized. *Ranger Peter Jones, who fired the fatal bullet, told the hearing he was unaware that Ranger Maguire was in the line of fire—Daily Telegraph*, 2013 / *Civil servants in the line of fire have been getting their excuses in early—Daily Telegraph*, 2012.

To be *in the firing line* originally meant the front line of troops armed with guns and facing the enemy in battle; as the front line they would be the most exposed to enemy bullets. From this developed the meaning of being in a situation where one is likely to be blamed or criticized. So this metaphorical use describes the same situation as

the metaphorical use of *line of fire*. *In the firing line is the museum's director, a former Financial Times journalist appointed in 2001—ODO / It is a great shame that once again, council staff are in the firing line over sickness levels—ODO*.

Some people insist that only *to be in the line of fire* can express the metaphor. This is the worst kind of pedantry, because idiom is based on customary usage and not on the hypercorrect interpretation of an original phrase whose meaning people have modified.

firm *adverb* is used mainly in two fixed expressions, to *stand firm* and to *hold firm to*. In all other contexts the natural adverbial form is *firmly*: *The bracket was firmly fixed to the wall*.

first. 1 When used with a number, *first* (like *last*) normally precedes it, as in *the first three cars*. This practice dates from the 16c, when *first* came to be regarded more as an adjective than as a noun; before that time, it was common to say *the two* (or *three, etc.*) *first . . .* . In current use, the order *the three first cars* would suggest three cars that came first in three races, and not the three cars that came first, second, and third in the same race.

2 In listing a sequence of points or topics, some people insist that the first item is introduced by *first*, not *firstly*, although the continuation can be *secondly, thirdly, fourthly*, etc. The reason for this is that *first* early on had a role as an adverb, and the use of *firstly*, though established by the 17c, was felt to be an unnecessary affectation. Today this rule seems little more than a superstition, and various sequences are in use: *first . . ., secondly . . ., thirdly*; *firstly . . ., secondly . . ., thirdly . . .* ; *firstly . . ., second . . ., third . . .* Of these, the first two options are both acceptable, but the third is inconsistent.

first name *see* CHRISTIAN NAME.

fish. The plural form is normally *fish* (*nets full of fish / They caught seven fish yesterday*); but *fishes* is sometimes used to emphasize a plural rather than a collective concept and to denote kinds of fish: *feed the fishes / food fishes like cod and flounder*. In biblical allusions, *fishes* is used rather than *fish*: *five loaves and two small fishes*.

fit *verb*. In BrE the past tense and past participle are *fitted* in all meanings: *The dress fitted well / The dress fitted her well / We've fitted a new lock to the front door*. In some parts of the US, *fit* also is used in intransitive uses: *His head fit snugly into his collar like a shell into a canister*—D. Pinckney, 1992 / *Many questions were put; none fit*— *Bulletin of the American Academy*, 1994.

fix. The meanings of the verb, which is first recorded in the 15c, and the noun, not recorded until the early 19c, do not correspond very well.

1 *noun*. **a** The earliest meaning of the noun is 'a difficulty, predicament, dilemma', which is originally AmE but was soon used in BrE as well, for example in a letter written by Charlotte Brontë in 1839: *It so happens that I can get no conveyance . . . so I am in a fix*. This meaning remains common in BrE, although it still has a slight American flavour: *Since she had vowed to remain celibate, she was in rather a fix when her father planned to marry her to the King of Sicily*—B. Cottle, 1983 / *The patient will indeed be in a fix from which he may find it hard to extricate himself*—C. Rycroft, 1985.

b From the 1930s in the US, a dose of a narcotic drug came to be called a *fix-up* and then a *fix*, and this use (only *fix*) spread into BrE in the 1950s with the increased circulation of hard drugs such as heroin: *A weird scene where the dope peddlers gather to beat up Johnny, who gets more into debt with each 'fix'*—

Oxford Mail, 1958 / *He needed her as a drug addict needs his fix*—Iris Murdoch, 1985. From this drugs meaning other figurative meanings soon developed: *Many people seem addicted to exercise and get depressed if they don't get their daily fix*—*Company*, 1985 / *What food can't you live without? A weekly fix of my mum's Sunday roast*—*South Wales Echo*, 2007.

c A *quick* (or *cheap*) *fix* is a hasty remedy that deals with a difficulty in the short term; the expression is recorded first in a hyphenated adjectival form from the 1950s, a use which remains common: *Quick-fix reflectors and diffusers, heavy duty bi-pin lampholders*—*Architectural Review*, 1959 / *The most recent 'quick-fix', suggests the committee, is desalting*—*New Scientist*, 1966 / *For them conventional war has been lived through and they think nuclear weapons are a cheap fix to deter it*—*Green Magazine*, 1990 / *If anyone thinks it will be easy, I would urge them to think again about these quick-fix training gimmicks*—*Stoke Sentinel*, 2007.

2 *verb*. There are three uses of the verb that call for comment, all American in origin and one still exclusively so.

a (Also to *fix up*.) 'To prepare (food or drink).' *You must fix me a drink*, Fanny Trollope said in her *Domestic Manners of the Americans* (1839); and Bret Harte, an American writer, wrote in a work of 1891, *Mother'll fix you suthin' hot*. The use is familiar in BrE, but still has a faint American feel to it: *When I am quite exhausted, go and cook a meal, fix a drink*—Nina Bawden, 1981 / *There would be waiters who'd fix you a drink and there would be a little buffet and people would go swimming in the nude in the pool*—*Scotsman*, 2006.

b (Also to *fix up*.) 'To mend or repair (something broken or not working).' This meaning is first recorded in AmE in the late 18c, and has spread to other varieties of English: *Other men would have fixed that fuse in a few seconds—News of the World*, 1990.

c The informal American expression *to be fixing to* (do something), meaning 'to be about to or preparing to' (do it), first recorded in 1716, is still hardly ever encountered outside the US: *If you're after Lily, she come in here while ago and tole me she was fixin' to git married—*E. Welty, *c.*1980 / *Mr Bush produced a Pittsburgh couple who, he said, were 'fixing to get married', and explained that they would pay an additional $996 . . . under current tax rules 'when they say "I do"'—Times*, 2000.

fixation was used from the 17c with the general meaning 'the action of fixing'. Its current meaning of 'obsession, fixed idea' is a legacy of the use in Freudian psychosexual theory: *Don has this very definite fixation that I am going to bang up our . . . new car—*E. J. Barr, 1973 / *He adds his voice to those condemning the modern fixation on fitness at the expense of honing cricket skills—Wisden Cricket Monthly*, 1992 / *The former Northern Ireland Ombudsman also warned that a fixation with past conflicts could threaten the delicate political arrangements established to strengthen reconciliation there—Daily Mail*, 2007. It also has technical uses in chemistry and medicine.

fixedly is pronounced as three syllables. *See* -EDLY.

fixedness, fixity. Both are 17c words with a range of meanings to do with abstract senses of fixing and being fixed, but *fixedness* is now used much less often than *fixity*: *Beaten into a fixity of revolutionary purpose, the peasants will have no more of it—Times Literary Supplement*, 1984 / *A film that seemed able to contemplate death ends up by denying even the fixedness of character—*

Independent, 1990 / *What distinguishes perversion is its quality of desperation and fixity—New York Times*, 1991. *Fixity* is the more common choice in combination with *purpose*: *News must provoke restlessness, unease, mild anxiety, curiosity, hunger for more. For politicians, it is the enemy of fixity of purpose—Observer*, 2000.

fjord is the recommended and more frequent spelling for the Norwegian sea inlet, not *fiord*, but both are correct.

flaccid can be pronounced **flak**-sid or **flas**-id, which is probably more frequently heard.

flagrant *see* BLATANT.

flair, meaning 'an instinct for what is excellent, a talent', was adopted into English from French in the late 19c. It should be distinguished from the unrelated noun and verb *flare* meaning 'a dazzling flame of light' etc., which is 16c and of unknown origin.

flamingo has plural forms *flamingos* (preferred) or *flamingoes*.

flammable, meaning 'easily set on fire', was revived in modern use (in BrE by the British Standards Institution) and used together with the noun *flammability* in place of *inflammable* and *inflammability* (which have the same meaning) in order to avoid people interpreting the *in-* forms as having the negative meaning 'not easily set on fire'. The negative forms now recommended are *non-flammable* and *non-flammability*.

flannel has inflected forms *flannelled, flannelling* in BrE and *flaneled flaneling* in AmE. *Flannelette*, a napped cotton fabric imitating flannel, is spelt *-l-* in both varieties.

flare *see* FLAIR.

flat, flatly. The dominant adverbial form *flatly* is always used figuratively with words of denial and rejection such as *contradict, deny, oppose, refuse,* and *reject. Flat* is used in fixed expressions such as *flat broke* and *turn something down flat*, and to mean 'exactly and no more' as in *two minutes flat. Flat* is only semi-adverbial, and mainly adjectival, in uses such as *The ladder was standing flat against the wall*.

flaunt, flout. The two words are unrelated. To *flaunt* means 'to display ostentatiously': *Women should have it both ways—they should be able to flaunt their sexuality and be taken seriously—* E. Wurtzel, 1998. To *flout* means 'to show contempt for (a rule, the law, etc.)': *Countries engage in covert activities because they do not want to flout the rules openly—Encounter*, 1987. The confusion, apart from the similarities of sound, may be due to the notion of conspicuousness common to both actions, and it is noteworthy that *flaunt* is used mistakenly to mean *flout* but the reverse does not occur: ☒ *By flaunting these rules, Hong Kong and Shanghai have challenged the Bank's authority—Daily Telegraph*, 1981 / ☒ *The fact that a shop so close to the scene of the tragic crash is still flaunting licensing laws will no doubt cause more outrage—Hastings Observer*, 2007.

flautist, flutist. *Flutist* is the older term (17c) for a player of the flute, and is still preferred in AmE. *Flautist* was adapted from the Italian word *flautista* in 1860, and is now the more usual form in BrE.

flavour is spelt *-our* in BrE and *flavor* in AmE. In BrE the derivatives (*flavouring, flavoursome,* etc.) are also spelt *-our* except *flavorous*.

fledgling is the recommended spelling, not *fledgeling*, for a bird that has just fledged, and when used as a modifier, as in *fledgling democracy*. This is despite the word's derivation via the verb *fledge* (as in *fully fledged*) from an obsolete adjective *fledge* meaning 'ready to fly'.

flee, meaning 'to run away, escape', is most often used in its past tense *fled. Flee* has a somewhat literary or romantic flavour: *The fourteenth Dalai Lama . . . has lived in exile in the Indian Himalayas since 1959, when Khamba rebels persuaded him to flee from Lhasa—Times*, 1973.

fleshy, fleshly. The distinction in current use is as follows. *Fleshy* relates to flesh in its physical sense and means primarily 'plump, fat' (e.g. *fleshy hands / fleshy fruit*), whereas *fleshly* relates to the allusive senses of flesh, and means 'carnal, sensual, sexual' (e.g. *fleshly desires / fleshly thoughts*).

fleur-de-lis, a heraldic lily, is spelt this way for preference rather than *fleur-de-lys* or *flower-de-luce* (which occurs in AmE). It is pronounced fler-duh-**lee**, and the plural is *fleurs-de-lis*, pronounced the same way.

flier *see* FLYER.

floatation *see* FLOTATION.

flora *see* FAUNA.

floruit, pronounced **flor**-oo-it, is a Latin third-person singular verb in the past tense meaning 'he or she flourished'. In English it is used with a following designation of date to indicate when a writer, painter, etc., is believed to have been alive and working, e.g. *floruit 1750*.

flotation is now the dominant spelling for the word meaning 'the process of launching or financing a business or commercial enterprise'. It has replaced the earlier form *floatation*, on the analogy of words such as *flotilla, flotsam,* etc.

flotsam and jetsam. The traditional distinction between goods found afloat at sea (*flotsam*) and goods found on land after being cast ashore (*jetsam*) is not historically straightforward, and is now largely theoretical since the words are often used together. *Jetsam* (late 16c) is recorded slightly earlier than *flotsam* (early 17c), and is a form of *jettison* meaning 'to throw overboard'. *Flotsam* is derived from an Anglo-French word related to *float*. In combination or on its own each word can refer metaphorically to objects or people viewed as of little value. *There are cell phones, TVs, toys, gadgets, trinkets, clothes, and appliances—all the flotsam and jetsam upon which America's standard of living now rests—Financial Sense Online*, AmE 2005 / *Disney's live-action division has a history of releasing cinematic flotsam, but this is one occasion when they have unearthed a rare gem—ReelViews*, AmE 2002 / *All in all, it's a standard picture of urban despair. Except that this collection of human jetsam contains several specimens of an altogether better-heeled class of lush—Businessweek*, AmE 2001.

flounder, founder. These two words are easily confused because they are similar in both form and meaning. The physical meaning of *flounder* is 'to struggle in mud or while wading' and hence 'to stumble or move clumsily'. From these meanings developed two abstract senses: 'to show or feel great confusion; to be out of one's depth' and 'to be in great difficulty'. To *founder* physically refers to a ship filling with water and sinking, and in the abstract to a plan, scheme, intention, etc., coming to nothing or failing. Typically, things like economies, careers, and negotiations *flounder*, as can people, while things like marriages and relationships *founder*, often *on* something. It is usually *flounder* which is used instead of

founder, as in the last two examples below. The following examples are intended to illustrate and clarify the differences: (*flounder* = struggle as if in mud) *The family physician bucks the case to a psychosomaticist, who flounders in jargon—Time*, 1971 / (= show confusion) *'You'll feel better later on,' he floundered—H. Forrester*, 1990 / (= be in difficulty) *Despite a financially secure face put forth by executive director Gray Montague, the company was floundering in $800,000 of accumulated red ink—Dance Magazine*, 2005 / *In 1979 he left The New York Times under controversial circumstances, and his career floundered in the 1980s—Columbia Journalism Review*, 2005 / (*founder* = sink) *I wanted to leave England . . . I did not intend to be aboard when that particular Titanic finally foundered in a sea of bureaucracy—K. Hagenbach*, 1980 / (= fail) *Without . . . help, the marriage may founder, thus providing . . . another dire example to romantic young people that 'arranged marriages are best'—P. Caplan*, 1985 / *There are concerns that Irish demands for its own commissioner could founder on opposition from Germany and the Benelux countries—Guardian*, 2005 / (= come to nothing) *Alfred's quest to obtain a vital set of aerial photographs has foundered in a Kafkaesque comedy of setbacks and misunderstandings—Times*, 2006 / (*flounder* used for *founder*) *Creativity, once a hallmark of primary education, floundered on the exams altar—Times Educational Supplement*, 2007 / *Bit by bit, season by season, he is removing the remnants of those anguished days when a promising career floundered on the rocks—Scotland on Sunday*, 2005.

flu, a 19c shortening of *influenza*, is used (with or without *the*) as often as the full form, except in more formal contexts. The older form *'flu* (with initial apostrophe) has dropped out of use.

flunkey, a (usually derogatory) term for a liveried servant or (in extended use) a toady, is the preferred spelling, not *flunky*. The plural is *flunkeys*.

flutist *see* FLAUTIST.

fly. 1 The noun is used as a collective in special names for various small flies or aphids that trouble gardeners, such as *fruit fly* and *greenfly*. These accordingly function as singular nouns (with plural *-flies*) and collective plurals: *It is easy to see that would-be DIY funeral undertakers would be as welcome as a swarm of greenfly at the Chelsea flower show*—J. Spottiswoode, 1991.

2 In literary usage, the perfect form of the verb can be *is* (or *are*) *flown* as well as *has* (or *have*) *flown* when the meaning is 'escape', although this may now sound dated and in present-day use the notion of prisoners having or being flown is more likely to be in the context of their transportation.

flyer, flier. *Flyer* is the preferred spelling in all varieties of English for all meanings of this agent noun formed from the verb *fly*, i.e. meaning an aviator or a handbill, and in the phrase *to get off to a flyer*, meaning to get a flying start. In BrE it is the recommended form. In AmE *flyer* and *flier* are roughly as frequent one as the other, but in the phrase *to take a flier / flyer on* something, meaning to indulge in a speculative venture, *flier* is more common.

fob off. There are two ways of using this phrasal verb. You can fob someone off *with* something (or just fob someone off, with no further complement stated), or you can fob something off *on* someone; in both cases someone is deceived into accepting something inferior or unwelcome. The first construction seems to be more common: *She tried to fob him off tactfully at first, but then he became brutal*—D. M. Thomas, 1990 /

Do not allow yourself to be fobbed off without getting the information you need—G. Brandreth et al., 1992 / *There is no 'mass audience' of uncritical couch potatoes ready to be fobbed off with any old rubbish*—East Anglian Daily Times, 1993 / *We all know when we return we have to take a drop in salary and pay higher taxation but these agencies were fobbing me off with junior positions*—Sunday Times, 2000 / (*on* construction) *Aghast at the roll-call of drunks, adulterers and pederasts that Central Office had fobbed off upon him,* [etc.]—J. Paxman, 1990 / *We no longer hear much about one of the worst wines ever fobbed off on us by the French*—Sun, 2006. The act of deceit is a *fobbing-off*, with the occasional plural *fobbings-off*: *We are also aware of other children in the borough in a similar position, and have had first-hand accounts of delays, fobbings-off, and 'dumping' in unsuitable nurseries*—Guardian, 1997.

fo'c'sle is a much reduced form of *forecastle*, the forward part of a ship where the crew has its quarters. In both spellings the word is pronounced **fohk**-suhl.

focus. The noun has plural forms *focuses* in general use and *foci* (**foh**-siy) in technical use, and the verb has inflected forms *focuses, focused, focusing*, although some printing styles prefer forms with *-ss-*.

foetal, foetus *see* FETUS.

foetid *see* FETID.

fogey, fogy. This occurs mainly in the expressions *old* (and now also *young*) *fogey*. *Fogy* was formerly the dominant spelling; Thackeray and Charles Kingsley, for example, wrote about *old fogies*, implying a singular form *fogy*. But with the more recent arrival of the *young fogey* ('a young person with conservative tastes and attitudes'), the spelling with -*ey* is now more common in the singular, although the plural *fogies* is more common, rather than *fogeys*, corresponding to the singular *fogey*.

foist. If you *foist* something *on* or *upon* someone, you pass it off as genuine or superior when it isn't (*inferior articles foisted on the general public at exorbitant prices*); if you *foist* something or someone *on* or *upon* someone, you force them to accept an unnecessary or unwelcome thing or person (*she had no desire to have an elderly relative foisted on her*). The most frequently used preposition is *on*, followed by *upon*, and occasionally *onto*. The phrasal verb *foist off* is standard in American English, but is unusual in BrE, e.g. *whose woeful activities smack of the same mentality that foisted McCarthyism off on an unwary public*—OEC AmE, 2002. Note that you can foist something *on* someone but you cannot foist someone (off) *with* something: *I can't go around the house badgering my family about this sort of stuff, so I have to foist it on the public instead*—*Sunday Express*, 2001.

An older use with a person or thing as object followed by *in* or *into*, meaning 'to introduce surreptitiously or unwarrantably', is now found only rarely: *Dylan writes that he detested being foisted into the role as a spokesman for the protest generation and took every opportunity to sabotage that status*—OEC AmE, 2004.

folio has the plural form *folios*.

folk as an ordinary word for people in general is tending to fall out of use in BrE, except in northern parts of England, and in Scotland, where it is standard, and occasionally elsewhere to denote a greater degree of affection than the word *people* does: *Even folk who know little about Scotland have probably heard of the Trossachs*—*Scottish World*, 1989 /

What Ursula brought home every week made all the difference to the old folk—David Lodge, 1991. It also survives strongly in certain specific uses:

1 As the last element of compounds and fixed expressions, or qualified by an adjective, as in *menfolk, north-country folk, townsfolk, womenfolk*. In general use, however, even these are beginning to sound somewhat jokey or precious.

2 In the plural (usually *folks*) to mean 'one's parents or relatives': *That really messes us up if my folks try to get hold of me*—L. Duncan, 1978 / *The folks wouldn't like it too much*—R. J. Conley, 1986. *Folks* is also used as a light-hearted form of address to an audience by public entertainers, and this is sometimes imitated (in the second and third persons) for special effect by journalists and writers: *Yes, folks, in 1990, 2,245 people were murdered in the city of New York*—Bernard Levin, 1991 / *Most folks don't really care that the music they download is in violation of copyright*—website, AmE 2003.

3 In the singular as an elliptical form of the term *folk music* (see 4 below).

4 In attributive combinations in which *folk* is joined to a second word, some of the combinations being loan translations from German, e.g. *folk dance, folk dancing, folk memory, folk music, folk singer, folk song, folk tale, folkways*; and especially in *folklore*.

folk etymology is 'a popular modifying of the form of a word or phrase in order to make it seem to be derived from a more familiar word'. Examples are *cockroach* (from Spanish *cucaracha*), *sparrow-grass* (a dialect and colloquial name for *asparagus*), and *hiccough* (a later spelling of *hiccup* under the mistaken impression that the second syllable was related to *cough*). The term is also applied more generally to any popular but mistaken account of the origin of a word or phrase, such as

Amazon (explained by the Greeks as derived from *amazos* 'breastless', as if from *a-* 'without' + *mazos* 'breast', referring to a fable that the Amazons cut off the right breast so as to draw a bow more easily) and *posh* (that it is formed from the initials of *port out starboard home*, referring to the more comfortable accommodation on ships formerly sailing between England and India).

following has long been used as a participial adjective either qualifying a noun, as in *for the following reasons*, or by itself as a quasi-noun, as in *The following are my reasons*. From this has developed a use of *following* as a quasi-preposition independent of any noun: *Used car prices are going up, following the Budget*—*Observer*, 1968. This use was not a problem for Fowler (1926) but Gowers (1965) condemned it in cases where the connection between the two events is 'merely temporal' and the preposition *after* would serve. In the example just given, there is a strong element of consequence, and so the use of *following* is perhaps justified, but this is not so in the example that follows, in which *after* could have been used with no loss of meaning: *Following the meeting it was decided a group of five or six representatives from Acklam will regularly meet with council officers to discuss the issues and the way forward*—*Evening Gazette*, 2007. In some cases there is even a possibility of ambiguity with other meanings of *following*: *Police have arrested a man following extensive inquiries.*

font *see* FOUNT.

foot. The normal plural form *feet* alternates with *foot* when used as a unit of measurement: *She is six feet / foot tall / a plank ten feet / foot long*. When such a phrase is used attributively (before a noun), a hyphen is normally placed between the numeral and *foot*, as in *a*

12-foot dinghy. When the number of inches is also given, *foot* is more common than *feet*: *He is six foot eight.*

footprint. First recorded in the 16c, *footprint* has for several centuries been largely confined to its literal meaning, with only occasional figurative uses (as in Longfellow's *'We can make our lives sublime, and, departing, leave behind us Footprints on the sands of time'*—*A Psalm of Life*, 1838). Then in the 1980s it developed a special meaning which is redolent of the times we live in: 'an environmental consequence of human activity in terms of pollution, damage to ecosystems, and depletion of natural resources' (*OED*). A *carbon footprint* is a measure of the carbon emissions of a particular individual, organization, or community. Other frequent compounds with *footprint* include *ecological footprint* and *environmental footprint*, which both refer to a measure of the impact of a person, community, or organization on the environment in terms of resource use, especially expressed as the area of land in hectares required to sustain a prevailing pattern of production and consumption.

for. 1 As a coordinating conjunction introducing a clause that gives a reason or explanation, *for* has two features of use not shared by *because* and *since*: (1) it cannot come at the beginning of a sentence but must follow a main clause: *He picked his way down carefully, step by step, for the steps were narrow*—G. Greene, 1988, and (2) it is normally preceded by a comma, except occasionally when the sentence is short: *It was gloomy and damp, for the sun could hardly shine through the tops of the trees*—*New Yorker*, 1989 / *I wanted a setting for my own little life, for I did not think that I should know too many people*—Anita Brookner, 1990 / (comma omitted) *He did not cry any more for it* *did not help*—D. Matthee, 1986. In most uses, *for* is rather more formal in effect than either *because* or *since*.

2 In AmE *for* is used to introduce a subordinate clause after certain verbs: *I didn't intend for you to find out*— J. McInerney, 1985 / *I can't afford for that bike to break down*—*New Yorker*, 1986. In BrE other constructions would be used instead; for example *intend* would be followed by a *that*-clause or more likely a *to*-infinitive (*I didn't intend you to find out*).

for- and fore-. The prefix *for-* occurs in a number of words formed in Old English, such as *forbid*, *forgive*, and *forsake*. It is not an active prefix in the sense of being used to form new words. *Fore-*, on the other hand, is a prefix native to English and is widely used to form verbs and nouns from existing words in the general meanings 'before, in front' with regard both to space and to time, e.g. *forearm, foreshorten, foretell*. Special care should be taken to distinguish between words that exist in both *for-* and *fore-* forms; *see* FORBEAR, FOREBEAR; FORGO, FOREGO.

forbear, forebear. 1 *Forbear* is a verb (pronounced with the stress on the second syllable) meaning 'to abstain from, go without' and is usually followed by *to* + infinitive or *from* + verb in *-ing*: *He did not enquire after their progress and Nutty forbore to mention it*—K. M. Peyton, 1988 / *Naturally he couldn't forbear from upsetting me*—Will Self, 1993. Its past form is *forbore* and its past participle is *forborn*.

2 *Forebear* is a noun (pronounced with the stress on the first syllable) meaning 'an ancestor': *Henry Carew had chosen the Church as some of his forebears had done*—T. Hayden, 1991 / *An early forebear went to Chicago and made a fortune in the grain business*—*Daily Mail*, 2007. *Forebear* is also used

figuratively: *Writing with what at times seems near-compulsive erudition, he details the philosophical and political forebears and descendants of just about every significant thinker whose work has any relevance to science or policy*—*Times Higher Education Supplement*, 2000. The situation is complicated somewhat by the fact that most dictionaries allow *forbear* as a variant of *forebear*, but the advice here is to maintain the distinction.

forbid. 1 The past tense is *forbade*, although *forbad* is occasionally used and cannot be said to be wrong. The pronunciation of *forbade* is fuh-**bayd** or (as if it were *forbad*) fuh-**bad**.

2 *Forbid* can be followed by a noun (often a verbal noun): *Cars are forbidden on the beach / The law forbids smoking in public places altogether*. When *forbid* has a personal object it is normally followed by *to* + infinitive: *I forbid you to go / We were forbidden to go*. A construction with object + *from* + verb in *-ing* is also found, on the analogy of *prevent* and *prohibit*: *He overcame the barrier known as the 'colour line' which effectively forbade blacks from boxing whites*—E. Cashmore, 1982 / *Current laws forbid a company from operating a reactor even after it has been built*—*New Scientist*, 1991. Fowler (1926) regarded this construction as 'unidiomatic' but it has been in use since the 16c and is likely to remain so since the analogies are powerful. This construction is occasionally used with omission of *from* (*The petition asked the king to forbid villeins sending their children to school*—S. J. Curtis, 1948 / *Remember though that Google's Adsense terms strictly forbid you designing web sites purely with the intention of earning Adsense income*—www.articlealley.com, 2005.), but this can be regarded as nonstandard.

forceful, forcible. 1 The principal use of *forceful* is in the meaning 'vigorous, powerful', whereas *forcible* means primarily 'done by or using force'. *Forceful* can be used of people as well as actions, whereas *forcible* is used only of actions. Fowler (1926) identified the difference in meaning as follows, and the definition is useful: 'while *forcible* conveys that force rather than something else is present, *forceful* conveys that much as opposed to little force is used or shown; compare *forcible ejection* with *a forceful personality*.' In practice, the two words are generally kept apart, but occasionally swap places.

2 Examples: (forceful) *It might be easier to . . . start again from scratch, crystallizing a lifetime's experience into a hundred forceful pages?*—Iris Murdoch, 1976 / *He was strong and his resources of stamina enabled him to play just as forcefully in the final ten minutes of a game as in the first ten*—S. Studd, 1981 / *There will probably be one or two forceful characters who will try to dominate the proceedings*—Times, 2001 / (forcible) *He favoured the forcible sterilization of criminals, diseased and insane persons, and 'worthless race-types'*—J. R. Baker, 1971 / *Section 47 of the National Assistance Act 1948 allows for the forcible removal from their own homes of elderly people who are not mentally ill*—O. Stevenson et al., 1990 / *She was lightly mugged and forcibly deprived of some expensive clip-on ear-rings*—Independent, 2002. Either word can be used wrongly for the other, but it is *forceful(ly)* that usually ousts *forcible* or *forcibly*: ☒ *Vaughan has spoken forcibly about the confusion caused by split captains*—Daily Telegraph, 2007 / ☒ *the contention of the mothers that forceful removal can have both significant short-term and long-lasting harm, particularly for younger children*—NY Times, 2008.

forceps. The form ending in -*s* is both singular and plural. Some people

mistake it for a plural, and create the non-existent ☒ *forcep*.

forebear *see* FORBEAR.

forecast is pronounced with the stress on the first syllable both as a noun and as a verb. As a past form and past participle, *forecast* (identical to the form of the present tense) has more or less ousted *forecasted*.

forecastle *see* FO'C'SLE.

foregather *see* FORGATHER.

forego *see* FORGO.

foregoing means 'preceding, previously mentioned' and is used as an adjective corresponding to the verb *forego* = to precede, especially in writing to refer to points made in earlier parts of the text: *If the foregoing representation of Jesus Christ can be accepted, it would be the end of the mysticism surrounding him*—W. E. Gale, 1988 / *The foregoing is proof that local government is delivering at the regional level*—Herald (Glasgow), 2003. It is sometimes wrongly spelt as *forgoing*: ☒ *for the forgoing reasons, the application is dismissed*—Ontario Superior Court Decisions, 2004.

foregone means 'previous, completed' and is used mainly in the expression *foregone conclusion*, meaning 'an easily foreseen or predictable result': *Given the anecdotal evidence—just ask that taxi driver, won't you?—the outcome of such an investigation was a foregone conclusion*—Times, 2001.

forehead. The pronunciation **faw**-hed, reflecting the word's spelling, is now much more usual than **fo**-rid, which was once favoured and is still recommended by some dictionaries.

foreign words and phrases.
1 Fowler (1926), in an article entitled

'foreign danger', warned that 'those who use words or phrases belonging to languages with which they have little or no acquaintance do so at their peril'. He was thinking primarily of so-called 'non-naturalized' expressions that are customarily put in italics in printed matter so as to alert the reader to the presence of something unusual. Some of these expressions tend to retain the grammatical behaviour of the languages from which they were borrowed, notably in the formations of plural forms, so that the plural of *curriculum vitae* (see CURRICULUM), for example, can cause some initial difficulty (it has to be *curricula vitae*, unless one resorts to *CVs*). Further difficulty is caused by uncertainty as to whether a word is naturalized or not; **referendum* has the plural form *referenda* if it is not naturalized and *referendums* if it is (and for those in doubt about this one, naturalized forms ultimately, and rightly, prevail). Problems also occur when the meaning in English changes from that in the source language, or when mistaken meanings are applied, as with **cui bono?*

2 Foreign words and phrases tend to be printed in italic type when they are considered to be less familiar to ordinary English readers, but the category of those that are regarded as fully naturalized and therefore to be printed in ordinary roman type is rapidly growing. For examples, see the separate entries including BÊTE NOIRE; CORPUS DELICTI; DE RIGUEUR; DÉTENTE; DOUBLE ENTENDRE; EX OFFICIO; FAIT ACCOMPLI; FAUX PAS; IBID.; INGÉNUE; INTER ALIA; JEU D'ESPRIT; LAISSEZ-FAIRE; MATERIEL; MODUS OPERANDI; MODUS VIVENDI; PETITIO PRINCIPII; PIÈCE DE RÉSISTANCE; PIED-À-TERRE; PIETÀ; PIS ALLER; POST HOC, ERGO PROPTER HOC; RAISON D'ÊTRE; REDUCTIO AD ABSURDUM; SINE QUA NON; ULTRA VIRES.

forename see CHRISTIAN NAME.

forensic means 'connected with courts of law' (from Latin *forum* meaning 'public square' where among other things judicial business was done), and should not be used as a general word for 'technical, scientific'. *Forensic evidence* means 'evidence presented in connection with a legal trial' and is usually, though not necessarily, medical or technical evidence; a *forensic scientist* is a scientist employed by a police department. Informally, *forensic* is also used elliptically to mean 'a forensic department or unit': *Perhaps the boys at forensic had made a gaff*—M. Maguire, 1976.

for ever, forever. This is generally written as two separate words in BrE (but generally as one word in AmE) when the meaning is 'for all future time' (*He said he would love her for ever*) and as one word when the meaning is 'always, continually' (*They are forever complaining*).

foreword, preface. *Preface* is the traditional word (first recorded in the 14c) for the author's introductory remarks at the beginning of a book, normally dealing with the practicalities of the book's development and making due acknowledgements rather than introducing its content (which in some cases is done by an *Introduction*). *Foreword* is a 19c word (originally used as a term in philology) for an introductory section of a literary work, and practice has varied between use of this term and *Preface*. More recently, publishers have sometimes favoured the inclusion of both a *Foreword* (usually written by a distinguished or authoritative person other than the author) as well as a *Preface* written by the author. In such cases, the *Foreword* is placed first.

for free, for real. These two phrases, originally Americanisms, are regularly used informally in BrE, and are now well established, despite occasional objections. In many case *free* on its own would

work: *Two pilots have in fact done the job
'for real'—both Sqn Ldr Marshall and Flt
Lt Dave Fischer have put Harriers down
on the deck of HMS Bulwark*—RAF News,
1977 / *I'd love a research assistant, but
you have to pay for them. And most
people want me to do things for free!*—
C. Tickell, 1991 / *I think the James
Bond themed music encouraged people to
relax and gamble in the happy knowledge
the money was not for real*—Hull Daily
Mail, 2002 / *The days have gone when
you could park for free across the road
from the theatre*—Birmingham Post,
2007.

forgather is the recommended spelling for this word meaning 'to assemble,
meet together', rather than *foregather*,
which is also found by association with
the prefix *fore-* (*see* FOR- AND FORE-). It is
a 16c Scottish loanword from Dutch
vergaderen used in the same sense; the
fore- element does not mean 'in
advance'.

forge has a derivative form *forgeable*,
with an *e* in the middle.

forget has the inflected form *forgetting*
and the derivative form *forgettable*,
both with *-tt-*.

forgive has a derivative form *forgiv-
able*, without an *e* in the middle.

forgo, forego. Both words are pronounced with the stress on the second
syllable. *Forgo* means 'to go without,
abstain from'; *forego* means 'to go
before, precede' and occurs principally
in the forms *foregoing* and *foregone*
(*see also* FOR- AND FORE-).

forgot, as a past participle used instead
of *forgotten*, is limited to archaic and
dialect language, and to use in some
forms of AmE.

forlorn hope now means only 'a faint
hope, an enterprise which has little hope
of success', but its form has nothing to
do with the English word *hope*. It was a
16c adaptation of Dutch *verloren hoop*,
literally meaning 'lost troop', and in
English originally meant 'a picked body
of men detached to lead an attack'. The
current figurative use, first recorded in
1641, has driven out all memory of the
original meaning.

formal words. Fowler (1926) aptly
identified words 'that are not the plain
English for what is meant' and characterized choice between different words
for the same thing in terms of the clothes
we choose: 'we tell our thoughts, like our
children, to put on their hats and coats
before they go out.' The examples he
gave now sound dated ('We think of our
soldiers as *plucky fellows*, but call them
in the bulletins *valiant troops*'), but the
message is as vivid as ever. *Peruse* is
more formal than *read, purchase* than
buy, alight than *get off, luncheon* than
lunch, endeavour than *try, evince* than
show; and *purloin* is more formal (or,
often, more humorous) than *steal*. Other
words are formal because they are restricted to special domains of technical
usage, for example *aperture* (for *opening*), *edifice* (for *building*, when it is large
and imposing), and *neonate* (for *newborn baby*). As is the case with most of
these, formal words can be turned on
their heads and made to look silly in
trivial or jokey use. Different modes of
writing and speaking call for different
levels of vocabulary. At one extreme
there is the language of legal documents,
business, and academic monographs; at
the other there is the language of everyday conversation, with a broad range
of styles in between. The language of
broadcasting and journalism, in particular, has become a great deal less formal
in recent years, to such an extent as to
cause unease among those who mistakenly identify formality, or the lack of it,
with standards of English.

format is pronounced **faw**-mat, and as a verb has inflected forms *formatted, formatting*. The verb dates from the 1960s and is mostly used in the context of computing.

former, latter. 1 These two words are used individually or contrastively (as *the former* and *the latter*) to refer to the first and second respectively of two people or things previously mentioned; in this role they are used attributively (before a noun) or, more usually, absolutely (with no noun following): *He had to be either a woman or a cross-dresser. His money was on the former*—J. Leavell, 2004 / *My aunt advised me to steer clear of street scenes and go for parish churches or country houses. As a keen enthusiast of architecture, I went for the latter category*—*Derby Evening Telegraph*, 2005.

2 For the meaning of *former* contrasted with *latter*, there are several points of usage to consider:

a In their contrastive uses, *former* and *latter* are more often used without a following noun: *The relationship between capitalist and non-capitalist modes is one of exploitation, in which the former creams off the surplus from the latter*—T. Cubitt, 1988. They are occasionally used attributively (*No one mentioned the latter point and only four teachers the former*—D. Pimm, 1988), but care needs to be taken in these cases to avoid possible ambiguity with the 'having been previously' meaning of *former*: the sentence *I am sure the former view will prevail* needs its context to clarify whether it is an earlier view or the first of two views that is intended.

b *Former* (in particular) and *latter* should only be used in writing when they are close to their antecedents, so that the reader is not forced to search back over earlier passages in order to establish the identity of the persons or things referred to.

c When more than two people or things are involved, *former* and *latter* should not be used; either *first* and *last* should be used, or the sentence should be rephrased: ⊠ *Though her bibliography includes Hecht, Snyder, and Daiches, she omits the latter's first name* [correct to . . . *Daiches' first name*]—*Modern Language Notes*, 1957.

d When *former* and *latter* refer to something in the plural, they are regarded as plural in turn: *The former describe events which are possible if not mundane, while the latter are metaphors*—J. Empson, 1989.

3 Each word also has a meaning not shared correspondingly by the other. *Former* means 'having been previously but no longer' (as in *her former partner, the former president*, etc.); when another adjective or qualifier is present, *former* normally comes after it to ensure association with the noun: *The Lockerbie bomber has revealed his despair at being jailed for mass murder in letters to a famous former inmate*—*Mirror*, 2002. *Latter* denotes the last or most recent part of a process or period of time (*He was relieved to be posted back to . . . the High Commission in Singapore during the latter stages of the Malayan Emergency*—*Times*, 2007)

formidable. The standard pronunciation is with the stress on the first syllable, although the word is often heard with the stress on the second syllable.

formula. The traditional distinction as regards the plural form is that *formulas* is used in general writing, and in chemistry and mathematics it is *formulae*, pronounced -lee. The *OEC* data shows, however, that formulas is the predominant form in all kinds of writing, while *formulae* is more common in general use in AmE than in BrE.

for real *see* FOR FREE, FOR REAL.

forsake, meaning 'to give up, go without', is spelt *for-* not *fore-*, and has inflected forms *forsook, forsaken. See* FOR- AND FORE-.

forte. There are two distinct, though related, words with this spelling. One comes via French from Latin *fortis* ('strong') and means 'a person's strong point'. It is generally pronounced **faw**-tay or **faw**-ti, although the older pronunciation is **fawt**, and some people insist that it is the only correct one. The plural, if needed, is *fortes*. The other word comes via Italian *forte* and is an instruction in music to play a passage loudly or strongly. It is pronounced **faw**-ti in an anglicized way, or **faw**-tay in a more Italian manner. It is also used as a noun meaning such a passage, and the plural is again *fortes*.

forth. The phrase *and so forth* is a less common and somewhat more literary alternative for *and so on*, used after the enumeration of items that could be continued further. There is no difference in meaning, despite the associations of assertiveness that *forth* has in expressions such as *go forth* and *set forth*.

forties *see* EIGHTIES.

fortuitous, fortuitously. 1 The *OED* shows *fortuitous* to be a word with only one meaning, 'caused by chance, accidental'. Addison wrote in the *Spectator* in 1712 that *the highest Degree of* [*wisdom*] *which Man can possess, is by no means equal to fortuitous Events*. It is first recorded in the 17c, and was used for nearly three centuries without difficulty. But about 1920 it started to get in the way of the older (Middle English) word *fortunate*, which is also connected with the working of chance and more specifically with the good effects of chance. (Whether this confusion was due to a double association with *fortunate* and *propitious* cannot now be determined;

but *propitious* is sometimes the word called for rather than *fortunate*.) In an example given by Fowler (1926), the word required is *fortunate* but the word used is *fortuitous*: *I must say I should not have expected so fortuitous a termination of a somewhat daring experiment*. This encroachment is restricted to events and circumstances; with reference to people, *fortunate* remains unthreatened so far: *I was fortunate in being on the spot to take this photograph—Country Life*, 1971.

2 Modern examples of *fortuitous* wrongly used to mean 'fortunate' or 'fortunately coincidental' and of *fortuitously* in corresponding adverb senses are: ☒ *Ellen Orford in the poem is a middle-aged woman and it was fortuitous for me that I was about the right age* [*to sing the role*]—Joan Cross, 1983 / ☒ *King successfully persuaded them to lend the collection for the exhibition . . . A move which proved fortuitous for the future of the national music collection—Independent*, 1995 / ☒ *She called for help—to her party's health spokesman, . . . with whom, most fortuitously, she had been dining minutes earlier—Guardian*, 2007. An unwelcome effect of this confusion is that it is not always possible to know which meaning is intended in a particular use of *fortuitous*, since in many cases an event can happen equally by plain chance or by good chance: *I had already made up my mind to join the South African tour when it happened, so it was fortuitous in a way—Today*, 1992 / *He returns to St Petersburg to claim a fortuitous inheritance—Times*, 2003 / *The dossier was fortuitously found by a Labour staffer—Independent*, 2007. *Fortuitous* is too useful in its primary meaning for this uncertainty to be acceptable, and care should be taken not to use it when *fortunate* or a similar word such as *propitious* is the word intended. In the following examples, *fortuitous* is used in its proper sense: *His presence was not fortuitous. He has a role to play; and you* *will see him again*—A. Brink, 1979 / *Quite fortuitously, Morse lights upon a set of college rooms which he had no original intention of visiting*—Colin Dexter, 1983 / *In some instances death is caused fortuitously*—M. Jefferson, 1992 / *Things come to a head when they all go to the country together. Is it a fortuitous accident or a cunning plot?*—*Sunday Times*, 2005.

forum has two possible plural forms *forums* and *fora*, the second reflecting the word's Latin origin. The first is several times more frequent in *OEC* data, and is preferable for all meanings other than 'a public square in an ancient Roman town or city'. However, *fora* is quite often used as the plural, especially in technical or formal, especially legal, writing. When used of 'an Internet site where users can post comments about an issue', it creates a piquant discord between the modern and the ancient.

forward, forwards. 1 For the adjective, the only form in standard English is *forward*: *It has four forward gears and reverse controlled by a speed-sensing governor*—*Daily Telegraph*, 1971 / *Already clouds of steam were rising, obscuring the forward view*—D. Rutherford, 1990 / *The aggressor's own forward momentum even strengthens the force of the counter-blow against him*—P. Lewis, 1991. In addition to its directional meanings, *forward* has the meaning 'bold in manner, precocious': *Any child who requested a book by title he at once designated as 'forward' or 'lippy'*—R. Roberts, 1971.

2 For the adverb, *forward* is now the preferred form by a very wide margin in all varieties of English. In many fixed expressions *forward* is obligatory: *bring forward* (= move; propose), *come forward* (= volunteer), *look forward to, put forward* (= propose). In other meanings also there is a marked preference for

forward: 'to the front, into prominence' (*Hugh stepped forward. 'It's me, don't be frightened.'*—Mary Wesley, 1983 / *Her mind refused to bring any such memory forward*—E. Jolley, AusE 1985 / *Then Nigel Carew drew his sabre and thrust it into the hand of his youthful son and pushed him forward*—T. Hayden, 1991 / *A dozen parties came forward, but the best deal was from a consortium*—*Sunday Times*, 2004), 'in advance, ahead' (*Civilian volunteers from the town carried sacks of grenades forward to the men in action*—J. Ladd, 1979), 'onward so as to make progress' (*Rossi expressed surprise that the Commission was 'apparently no further forward than in 1984'*—C. Rose, 1990 / *He had continually to be looking at his watch and calculating whether they were forward enough*—G. E. Evans, 1993), 'towards the future, continuously onwards' (*The overall feeling is that the Jockey Club is genuinely concerned with helping the industry move forward*—*Independent*, 1989).

3 The set expression *backwards and forwards* is preferred in all varieties of English to *backward and forward*, except in AmE, where the two versions are equally frequent: *the door kept swinging backwards and forwards*—A. Brookner, 1984 / *Roll your shoulders, backward and forward, 10 times*—*American Fitness*, 2004. Otherwise, the remaining strongholds of *forwards* are BrE and Irish English, and its most common use is to denote straightforward movement towards the front: *Certain single-celled organisms are propelled forwards in the water*—*New Scientist*, 1971 / *Then he leaned forwards and touched Colin's forearm*—Ian McEwan, 1981 / *It was Amelia who came forwards*—K. Newman, 1990 / *The opponent sees the opening and moves forwards to sweep or punch you*—D. Mitchell, 1991. In all these examples, however, *forward* would be at least as natural (except in the 1990 example, in which the use of *forwards* describes physical movement, whereas *come forward* would be interpreted in the metaphorical meaning of 'volunteer').

foul, foully. The normal adverb from *foul* is *foully* (pronounced with both *l*s): *Jerome had done foully, but not so foully as he himself and all here believed*—Ellis Peters, 1993. The older form *foul* survives in the expressions *foul-mouthed* and *to fall foul of*.

fount, font. These are the traditional British and American spellings respectively of the term meaning 'a set of printing type of one size or face'. *Font* is now also used in BrE, and is rapidly ousting *fount*. Both words are only remotely connected with *fount* meaning 'fountain, source' (*see* FOUNT, FOUNTAIN) and *font* meaning 'a basin for water in a church'.

fount, fountain. *Fount* is a shortening of *fountain* (compare *mount* and *mountain*) and is mainly used in poetry and for special effect. It also occurs with the meaning 'source, origin' in phrases such as the *fount of* (*all*) *wisdom, knowledge*, etc. *Font* is increasingly being used in such phrases, but many people will judge it to be incorrect.

fowl. The collective use of the singular form is now largely restricted to compounds such as *guineafowl* and *wildfowl*.

foyer, meaning 'the entrance hall in a theatre, etc.', is pronounced **foy**-ay in BrE and foy-uhr in AmE.

frac, fracking. 1 Particularly in AmE *fracking* and *frackin'* are used as euphemisms for the F-word, which is unfortunate for proponents of the much-disputed technology. Anti-fracking protesters holding placards reading 'frack off' are punning on this well-established use: *And the design that was replaced was pretty fracking lovely already*—weblog, NewZE 2003 / *Honestly, wherever I go in my nightmares, Hello frackin' Kitty is there, waiting*—OEC, Am 2007.

2 The verb *frack* and the verbal noun *fracking* are derived from the *frac-* part of *fracturing* in the earlier (1948) term *hydraulic fracturing*. They refer to 'the process of fracturing subterranean rock by the injection of water into existing fissures at high pressure, usually in order to facilitate the passage of some fluid (especially oil or gas) through an otherwise impermeable barrier': *We've also drilled and cased our first Utica Shale well, which is below the Marcellus, and plan on fracking it in about a month*—OEC, 2010 / *This is no time to lift the fracking ban; it's time to make it permanent*—New York Times, 2011.

fracas, meaning 'a noisy disturbance', is pronounced **frak**-ah in BrE and **fray**-kuhs in AmE. Its plural form is also *fracas*, pronounced **frak**-ahz and **fray**-kuhs respectively.

fraction in general use means 'a very small part': *Teaching loads at white schools often are only a fraction the size of those at black schools*—Saturday Review, AmE 1971. This use is idiomatic despite the pedantic objection occasionally heard that a fraction can be nine-tenths as much as one-tenth. In some cases, however, the point is reinforced by an adjective such as *small* or *tiny*: *A desperate recruitment campaign has begun to woo British workers back—but only on a tiny fraction of their original salaries*—Daily Star, 2006. See also PERCENTAGE.

fractious *see* FACTIOUS.

fragile, frail. 1 *Fragile* is pronounced **fraj**-iyl in BrE and **fraj**-uhl in AmE.

2 *Fragile* is normally used of things being easily broken, whereas *frail* is normally used of people being infirm or in poor physical condition: *The lectern at* the Guildhall is a classic example of one that looks beautiful but is too small and fragile to use—H. Thomas & L. Gill, 1989 / After Charlotte's death in 1943, the villagers all noticed how extraordinarily frail and sunken Shaw looked—National Trust Magazine, 1990. There is an overlap in meaning created by the figurative use of both words in the sense 'weak, easily overturned': OPEC last week managed to preserve its fragile unity—Observer, 1985 / The drinking, drug-taking and the high-pitched battles soon toppled the frail structure of their romance—J. Rose, 1990 / The fragile peace that has held in the holy city since June was shattered by deadly fighting that began late on Wednesday—Guardian, 2004. In general, fragile tends to be used more often than frail in this meaning, whereas frail alone has the meaning 'morally weak, easily yielding to temptation'.

fragmentary should be pronounced stressing the first syllable, but is often pronounced stressing the second syllable.

framework. Sir Ernest Gowers (1965) was greatly offended by what he saw as the overuse of the expression within (or in) the framework of, meaning broadly 'in the context of'. Presumably he grew tired of reading it in successions of official Civil Service memos and reports, and he devoted a lengthy article to discouraging its use; but his judgement that 'it has become so trite that the very sight of it may nauseate the sensitive reader' is personal rather than objective. It is also listed among the 'clichés and modish and inflated diction' in the Oxford Guide to English Usage (1994). It is true that effective images like this one can lose power through constant use, but it is difficult to find evidence of excessive use in the case under review, and it is hard to fault examples such as the following: The

exercise of justice is only possible within the framework of established institutions which command respect—Roger Scruton, 1980 / Sound and colour go together naturally . . . and have enormous potential for healing and raising energy levels, especially when used within the framework of gentle, deep silence and inner stillness—Cornishman, 2004.

Frankenstein, in Mary Shelley's Gothic tale (1818) of the same name. Frankenstein is a scientist who creates and brings to life a manlike monster which eventually turns on him and destroys him. So, Frankenstein is the name of the creator of a monster and not of the monster itself, which has no name. Since at least 1838, however, the name has been used to suggest 'something that becomes terrifying or destructive to its maker', as if it referred to the monster and not its creator. This use is recognized in dictionaries and is so much part of the language that to criticize it or try to correct it, as some do, is as pointless as insisting that 'blood, sweat, and tears' should be corrected to Churchill's original 'blood, toil, tears and sweat'. Its laboratories in Brittany . . . have invented a way of messing around with the bacteriological process in order to produce a Frankenstein of cheeses—Independent, 2002.

The phrase Frankenstein's monster is quite widely used, in addition to Frankenstein on its own: Did the EU effectively create a Frankenstein's monster when it stitched a handful of moribund legacy currencies to the Deutschmark to create the euro?—Sunday Business Post, 2004.

Frankenstein food, a semi-humorous informal way of describing genetically modified food, dates from the late 1980s. Use of Frankenstein in this way has led to Franken- being used as a prefix, particularly in Frankenfoods, but also with other words, to suggest danger or terror, e.g. Frankenfish for the snakehead. Early

*Danish studies suggest these effects will turn out to be beneficial and that GM crops actually boost numbers of local wild birds and insects. So much for Frankenstein foods—Observer, 2003 / Europeans have never liked genetically modified organisms, or GMOs. The products—nicknamed 'Frankenfoods'—have been banned in Europe for the past five years—*www.inthesetimes.com, 2003.

frantically is the correct form of the adverb from *frantic*, not *franticly*.

-free is a suffix used in dozens of common words such as *acid-free* (paper), *alcohol-free, duty-free, fat-free, hands-free, interest-free, smoke-free, tax-free*. A hyphen should separate it from the word it is joined to, i.e. *alcohol-free* not ☒ *alcohol free* or ☒ *alcoholfree, hands-free* rather than ☒ *handsfree* or ☒ *hands free*, etc.

free gift is recorded from 1899 and has persisted in use in advertising and marketing circles, despite its evident tautology.

freeman, free man. A *free man* is a man who is free in general senses (literally or metaphorically). A *freeman* is (1) a person who is granted the freedom of a city, or (2) in historical uses, a person who is not a slave or serf.

free rein, meaning 'unrestricted scope for action', should be spelt this way, not *free reign* (as if it were connected with *reign* in the sense 'rule'). The following examples should be corrected accordingly: ☒ *If they are given free reign to invest and produce they will grow—New Yorker, 1987* / ☒ *Those offenders would have been arrested and brought to justice far sooner, rather than having a free reign to reoffend—Express, 2007.*

French words and phrases used in English. *See box overleaf.*

frequentative. Frequentative verbs express repeated or continuous action and are formed with certain suffixes, in English principally *-er* and *-le*. Examples are *chatter, clamber, flicker, flitter, glitter, slumber, crackle, dazzle, paddle, sparkle, wriggle*.

fresco, meaning a type of wall-painting, has plural forms *frescoes* (preferred and more usual) and *frescos*.

friar, monk. A *friar* is a member of a mendicant (i.e. living on alms) or originally mendicant religious order of men, especially the Augustinians, Carmelites, Dominicans, and Franciscans, who live among the people and do good works. A *monk* can include these, but properly denotes a member of a religious community living apart under vows of poverty, chastity, and obedience.

Friday (and other days of the week). *Friday*, being the first day of the week alphabetically, is chosen to make this point, which also applies to the other six. The suppression of *on* in adverbial references to days of the week (*See you Friday / He normally eats fish Fridays*) has spread to BrE from America, but the use remains informal in Britain, especially in the singular. Only an American would say or write that something 'happened Tuesday' instead of 'happened last Tuesday', or to give a real example: *When Goosen took his family to dinner here Tuesday night, not a single person asked for an autograph—Houston Chronicle, AmE 2005 [OEC].*

friendlily is available as an adverb from *friendly* but because of its awkwardness it is rarely used: *The women . . . still addressed him friendlily—William Trevor, 1980 / The nuisance on the train still friendlily smiles, but he's looking for more than a chat and a drinking companion now—Independent, 1995.* There are well under a hundred examples on

FRENCH WORDS AND PHRASES USED IN ENGLISH.

1 English has been receptive to words and phrases from French for several centuries. The process has been continuous although there are two periods of special importance: the years after the Norman Conquest (11c), and the time of the French Enlightenment (18c) when movements in science and philosophy exposed gaps in the vocabulary of English (much as the French computing industry and media are absorbing English words at the moment). Many words from these periods have now been fully assimilated into English and behave like English words with no hint of foreignness (e.g. *button, glory, ounce, place, prime, uncle*, etc.). In the 19c, people's moral and other sensitivities were protected by the euphemistic use of French in expressions such as *affaire de cœur* (first recorded in English in 1809), *crime passionnel* (1910), and *ménage à trois* (1891), and in the domains of art, literature, food, and wine French was felt to have an appropriacy corresponding to perceived national stereotypes.

2 The process of assimilation into English is illustrated by the noun *abandon*, meaning 'surrender to natural impulses', which entered the language early in the 19c. It was first printed in italics as a foreign word and pronounced in the French manner with a nasalized final syllable. By the early 20c it was printed in ordinary roman type as an English word (in James Joyce's *Ulysses*, for example), and about the same time, or a little later (after Daniel Jones's *English Pronouncing Dictionary* of 1917), it acquired the anglicized pronunciation that is now familiar, aided by the pre-existence of the fully assimilated verb. Hundreds of French loanwords had a similar history between the time of their adoption into English and their complete assimilation, and others are in the process of doing so. In the assimilation process, accents have tended to constitute the most important feature of the original language when these are present, but in more recent usage the most familiar words, such as *cafe* and *facade*, have lost their accents as no longer being necessary orthographic supports for a partly French pronunciation. Nonetheless, pronunciation remains the element in a word's assimilation that is slowest to change.

3 The table below lists a selection of French words and phrases to illustrate four levels of adoption into English: A = printed in italic type and pronounced in a French manner (with some modification, e.g. in the articulation of *r*, the introduction of the indeterminate schwa sound, whose phonetic symbol is /ə/, shown in this book as uh, for unaccented vowels, and the elimination of nasalized sounds); B = Gallicisms mainly confined to literary or scholarly use; C = printed in roman type but retaining some features of the French pronunciation; D = fully anglicized and printed in roman type.

word / phrase	approximate meaning	date	category
affaire de cœur	love affair	19c	A
à merveille	wonderfully	18c	B
arrière-pensée	ulterior motive	19c	B
au fond	basically	18c	B
au pied de la lettre	literally	18c	B
baroque	of 17c and 18c art	18c	D

billet-doux	love letter	17c	C
bizarre	strange	17c	D
blasé	indifferent	19c	D
brunette	brown	16c	D
cachet	sign of prestige	17c	D
cafe	coffee house	19c	C
camembert	cheese	19c	C
cartel	association of manufacturers	16c	D
charlatan	sham, fraud	17c	D
clairvoyant	one who foresees	17c	D
crime passionnel	crime of passion	20c	A
déjà vu	already seen	20c	C
eclair	cake	19c	D
enfant terrible	unconventional person	19c	A
escargot	edible snail	19c	C
esprit de corps	team spirit	18c	A
esprit de l'escalier	inspiration too late	20c	B
facade	outward appearance	17c	C
gigolo	paid escort or lover	20c	D
laissez-faire	non-interference	19c	C
mayonnaise	thick sauce	19c	D
ménage à trois	household of three	19c	A
nom de guerre	name assumed in war	17c	A
nom de plume	pen-name	19c	C
pièce de résistance	most remarkable item	18c	A
point d'appui	strategic point	19c	B
sobriquet	nickname	17c	C
soi-disant	so-called	18c	B
son et lumière	sound and light effects	20c	C
touché	word used to concede a point	20c	C
tour de force	feat of skill	19c	C
tournedos	cut of beef	19c	C

the *OEC*; the phrasal alternative *in a friendly way* (or *manner*) often serves better.

frier *see* FRYER.

frock was originally a male garment, especially the mantle of a monk or priest. Discarded by men, the word came back into favour in the 19c as a synonym of *gown* or *dress* for women or girls. Fowler described it as a vogue-word used 'especially for a dress regarded from the decorative point of view'. It is still in use but can have a distinct period flavour or it can be disparaging or facetious.

An advertisement for a sports car in the 1990s showed the car with a supermodel in an elegant designer dress standing beside it. The caption read 'our latest model . . . and Claudia Schiffer in a frock'. The phrase *posh frock* seems to be particularly BrE.

frolic *verb* has inflected forms *frolicked, frolicking*.

from. Avoid the mixture of styles shown in the type *He was chairman of the board from 1999–2003*. This should be expressed either as *He was chairman of the board 1999–2003* or as *He was* *chairman of the board from 1999 to 2003. See also* BETWEEN 3.

from whence, from hence. 1 Although widely disapproved of on the grounds that *from* is redundant, *from whence* has a long and distinguished history of use in questions (*From whence these Murmurs, and this change of mind*—Dryden, 1697) and in indirect questions or as a conjunction introducing a relative clause (*No man can say from whence the greater danger to order arises*—F. Harrison, 1867). The phrase with *from* continues to be used in modern writing: *When they show the captive a picture of the City of London, that he may know from whence they come, he displays no interest*—Penelope Lively, 1991 / *Dark clouds had gathered over the hills to the north, from whence came the lucky changeling folk in times long past*—S. Koea, NewZE 1994 / *It should go back as close as possible to the spot from whence it came*—Daily Telegraph, 2007. The modern uses have mostly to do with people's origins and can be justified stylistically as archaisms (cf. *Thys felowe, we knowe not from whence he ys*—Tyndale, 1526). In general use, if *whence* has to be used, it is best used without *from*; but of course the problem can be avoided altogether by rephrasing in a way that is in any case more natural in modern English: . . . *so that he can know where they come from* / . . . *to the spot it came from*, and so on.

2 The *OED* gives numerous examples, dating from the 14c to the 19c, of the use of *from hence*. A typical 19c example is *From hence I was conducted up a staircase to a suite of apartments*—W. Irving, 1820. In current English this use is effectively dead, except as a stylistic device in writing that needs to sound old-fashioned, e.g. historical novels.

front *verb*. The word has existed as a verb since the 16c in the straightforward sense 'to have its front in a specified direction', i.e. 'to face'. Typical subjects of the verb include buildings, rooms, or prospects. A parallel strand of meaning involves confrontations of various kinds between people, as when Sir Andrew Aguecheek in Shakespeare's *Twelfth Night* (I.iii.54) misunderstands the instruction to 'accost' Olivia's companion Maria, thinking 'Accost' is her name and is told by Sir Toby '"Accost" is front her, board her, woo her, assail her'. A modern use developed remotely from this meaning is 'to present or be the host of (a television or radio programme)'; this has all but replaced the verb *compère*, which now has a decidedly old-fashioned ring.

fruition has only an indirect connection with *fruit*, but the false association led it astray in the 19c. Its current meaning 'fulfilment, the realization of aims' (especially in the phrase *come to fruition*) dates from then; before that it meant 'enjoyment' (from the Latin deponent verb *frui* 'to enjoy'), a meaning which is still listed in dictionaries of current English though hardly much used.

fryer is the preferred spelling for the agent noun meaning 'a person or thing that fries', not *frier*.

-fs, -ves. *See box opposite.*

fuchsia, the plant, is correctly spelt this way (after the 16c German botanist Leonhard *Fuchs*), not *fuschia*, although this is sometimes wrongly used (and encouraged by the word's pronunciation, **fyoo**-shuh).

fuel *verb* has inflected forms *fuelled, fuelling* in BrE and *fueled, fueling* in AmE.

-ful is a suffix forming nouns that denote amounts, as in *cupful, handful, mouthful*, etc. In many cases these nouns develop meanings that are remote from the word that forms the first element; for example, a *handful* means 'a

-FS, -VES.

Nouns ending in -*f* and -*fe* have plural forms as shown in the table below:

noun	-fs plural	-ves plural	verb form
beef	beefs (= kinds of beef)	beeves (= oxen)	
belief	beliefs		
calf		calves	calve, calved
dwarf	dwarfs	dwarves (*see* DWARF)	dwarf, dwarfed
elf		elves	
half		halves	halve, halved
handkerchief	handkerchiefs		
hoof	hoofs	hooves (*see* HOOF)	hoof, hoofed
knife		knives	knife, knifed
leaf		leaves	leaf, leafed
life		lives	live, lived
loaf		loaves	loaf, loafed
oaf	oafs		
proof	proofs		prove, proved
roof	roofs	rooves (*see* ROOF)	roof, roofed
scarf	scarfs	scarves (*see* SCARF)	
self		selves	
sheaf		sheaves	sheave, sheaved
shelf		shelves	shelve, shelved
staff	staffs	staves (music)	staff, staffed
thief		thieves	thieve, thieved
turf	turfs	turves (*see* TURF)	turf, turfed
wharf	wharfs	wharves	
wife		wives	
wolf		wolves	wolf, wolfed

small number' as well as 'an amount that can be held in the hand'. The plurals of these words are *cupfuls, handfuls, mouthfuls*, etc.

fulcrum is pronounced **fuul**-kruhm or **ful**-kruhm and has most often the plural form *fulcra*, particularly in technical or scientific writing, but *fulcrums* in its metaphorical meaning of 'a thing that plays a central or essential role': *And, as he was one of the fulcrums of the Maori cultural renaissance of the early 1970s,*

his place in our history is the same—New Zealand Listener, 2004.

fulfil is the BrE spelling; in AmE it alternates with *fulfill*. The inflections in both varieties are *fulfilled, fulfilling*. The corresponding noun is *fulfilment* in BrE and either *fulfillment* or *fulfilment* in AmE.

full survives as an adverb only in the phrases *full well* (as in *You know full well what I mean*) and *full in the face* (as in

The ball hit him full in the face). Other uses (e.g. *full early, full fain*) are now somewhat literary or archaic; in Shakespeare's *Full fathom five thy Father lies* (*Tempest* I.ii.399), the meaning is 'fully, quite' and refers to the number.

fullness is spelt with two *l*s, but the form *fulness* occurs in 19c and earlier printed works.

full stop. 1 The principal use of the full stop (also called *point, full point,* and *period*) is to mark the end of a sentence that is a statement (as in this sentence). This applies to sentences when they are not complete statements or contain ellipsis (*see* SENTENCE), as in the opening of Dickens's *Bleak House* (1852–3): *London. Michaelmas term lately over, and the Lord Chancellor sitting in Lincoln's Hall. Implacable November weather*. If the sentence is a question or exclamation, the mark used is the **question mark* or **exclamation mark*, which include a full stop in their forms.

2 The full stop is also used to mark abbreviations and contractions, although this use is diminishing, partly as a matter of printing style and partly because many abbreviations have become more familiar and no longer need identification. The distinction between abbreviations (e.g. *I.o.W.* = Isle of Wight) and contractions (e.g. *Dr* = Doctor), though arguably a useful one, has been rapidly eroded by this process, so that shortenings of various kinds are printed and written without full stops, e.g. *BBC, etc, ie, IoW, Mr, Ms, pm* (= post meridiem), *St* (= Saint or Street), etc. The style recommended here involves dropping full stops in initialisms that are all capital letters (e.g. *BBC, NNW* = north-north-west, *TUC*), in many contractions (*Dr, Mr,* etc.), and in acronyms that are pronounced as words (e.g. *Anzac, Nato*), but retaining them in lower-case initialisms such as *a.m., e.g.,* and *i.e.* and in

shortened words such as *Oct.* (= October), *Tues.* (= Tuesday), and *Visc.* (= Viscount). In mixed styles the tendency now is to omit points, as in *DPhil, MLitt,* and *GeV* (= gigaelectronvolt). The important point, however, is to achieve consistency within a particular piece of writing or printing. Some shortenings have a greater need of full stops to avoid possible ambiguity with other words in some contexts, e.g. *a.m.* (= ante meridiem), *no.* (= number).

3 If an abbreviation with a full stop comes at the end of a sentence, another full stop is not added when the full stop of the abbreviation is the last character: *Bring your own pens, pencils, rulers, etc.* but *Bring your own things (pens, pencils, rulers, etc.)*.

4 Full stops are routinely used between units of money (£11.99, $27.50), before decimals (10.5%), and between hours and minutes (10.30 a.m.; AmE 10:30 a.m.).

fulsome. 1 The first meaning of *fulsome* was 'copious, abundant', but it had lost this along with other meanings by the 16c and acquired an unfavourable sense 'excessive, cloying', especially with reference to praise or flattery. This meaning remained the dominant one until the second half of the 20c, when *fulsome* began to be used in favourable meanings, so that *fulsome praise* meant high or lavish praise rather than excessive or nauseating praise. This new use, more common in AmE but increasingly found in BrE too, should be avoided, because the adverse meaning is still much in use and there is a danger of unfortunate misunderstanding. Examples of dubious and correct uses follow: ☒ *Critics, who insist the Pope has not gone far enough in apologising, will be expecting him to express fulsome remorse—Irish News,* 2006 / *I walk sure-footedly through the minefield that* *separates fulsome idolatry from condescending anecdotal chit-chat—Times Literary Supplement*, 1977. Useful alternatives to *fulsome* in the controversial 'favourable' sense include *lavish, generous, enthusiastic, effusive, exuberant, copious, glowing*, and *extravagant*.

2 *Fulsome* is also occasionally used to mean 'full-figured', with reference to a woman's figure, by fashion writers who analyse the word as consisting of *full* + *-some* as in *handsome, wholesome*, etc.: *The craze for the fulsome figure . . . may come to an end sometime in the next couple of decades, say those in the know—Sunday Times*, 1998.

fun, first recorded in 1700 and stigmatized by Dr Johnson as a 'low cant word' (i.e. ephemeral jargon), has long hovered on the brink of adjectival status (*It was really fun*) and more recently has taken a step further in informal attributive uses such as *We had a fun time* or *That would be a fun thing to do*. It still has a way to go, however, since it cannot yet be qualified by intensifying adverbs such as *very* or *extremely* (use of *great* instead gives away the noun's disguise). It also lacks the comparative and superlative inflections that a single-syllable adjective normally has, although *more fun* as in *This sounds more fun* is legitimate; *funner* and *funnest* have appeared in youth slang in AmE and are now found in BrE too, albeit usually in a jocular form: *She is also looking forward to the camaraderie of her country's locker room. 'Teams,' she said, 'are so much funner.'—Guardian*, 2004.

function. 1 The noun has a number of technical meanings in mathematics and information technology, and has acquired general meanings that caused Fowler (1926) to categorize it as a *popularized technicality. As a noun, it is often used somewhat pretentiously in meanings for which other words would serve as well: (1) *role, duty*, or

responsibility (*This function is now discharged by departmental select committees—H. Calvert, 1985*), (2) *use* or *purpose* (*Identify the main functions of a hedge before deciding its composition—Gardeners' World*, 1991), (3) *action, activity*, or *performance* (*He was embarrassed about the nature of his illness and reluctant to discuss his bowel function with anyone—J. Merchant et al., 1989*), (4) *capacity, facility*, or *operation* (especially with a preceding word: *How will the trade and investment function be carried out with such a reduction in resources—Times*, 2005), or (5) *party* or *gathering* (*It was not the kind of function to which Nat was accustomed to go, but his father's employer . . . pressed a ticket on him—Frederic Raphael, 1960*).

2 As a verb, *function* often substitutes unnecessarily for more workaday words such as *act, operate, think*, or *work*: *Excessive heat may make us feel 'stupid'—and unable to function mentally—U. Markham*, 1991 / *Workers had to leave offices, while restaurants and bars were unable to function—many being forced to turn away customers from their half-eaten meals—Express*, 2007. The phrase *to be a function of* is a direct borrowing from mathematics, and usually means little more than *to be caused by: This suggests that, in part, the housewife's dissatisfaction with her work is a function of downward social mobility—A. Oakley*, 1990.

3 There is a place for *function* as a formal and technical word, but in general use the alternatives suggested above are usually worth considering.

functional. In addition to its special meanings in medicine and psychology, the primary meanings of *functional* are (1) 'designed or intended to be practical rather than attractive', a synonym of *utilitarian*, and (2) 'having a function, working'. Since the 1990s the word has been used in the second meaning to describe a type of food, originated in Japan, that contains health-promoting additives instead of the conventionally harmful ones: *Functional foods are sometimes wrongly referred to in the media as 'miracle foods', implying they are something of a panacea, negating the need for a healthy diet—Grocer,* 1996.

funerary, funeral, funereal. *Funerary* is the standard adjective in the neutral meaning 'of or used at a funeral or funerals', as in *funerary ashes, funerary urn,* etc. It dates from the late 17c and has replaced *funeral,* which was originally an adjective but became predominantly a noun from the 16c onwards (in uses such as *funeral expenses* and *funeral rites* it is a noun used attributively and not an adjective). *Funereal,* which is first recorded in 1725, has a special judgemental meaning 'appropriate to a funeral', either 'deadly slow' (like a funeral procession) or 'gloomy, dreary, dismal': *Her mother and brother had departed to the kitchen from where Wexford could hear their muted whisperings and the funereally careful clink of cups*—Ruth Rendell, 1981 / *Even with Donald there, Aileen thought, the place had a funereal silence about it*—C. F. Roe, 1992 / *Outside the traffic is creeping through the city centre at a funereal pace*—Mirror, 2005.

fungus has the plural form *fungi,* pronounced **fung**-giy or **fun**-jiy, although *funguses* is sometimes used, especially to mean 'types of fungus'. The most frequent adjectival form is *fungal, fungous* and *fungoid* being rather rare. *Fungus* itself is sometimes used attributively before a noun, as in *a fungus infection.*

funnel *verb* has inflected forms *funnelled, funnelling* in BrE and *funneled, funneling* in AmE.

funny. In some contexts it can be unclear whether the meaning intended is: (1) amusing, comical (as in *a funny joke*), (2) strange, hard to explain (as in *a funny look*). Since the 1930s, as first recorded in a novel by Ian Hay, the first meaning has come to be called *funny-ha-ha* and the second meaning *funny-peculiar* when they need to be distinguished.

furore, meaning 'an uproar, an outbreak of fury', is pronounced as three syllables, fyoo-**raw**-ri, or fyoo-**raw**-ray. The word is spelt *furor* in AmE and pronounced **fyoo**-raw.

further, furthest *see* FARTHER.

fuse. There are two distinct words: (1) the one meaning 'a device for igniting a bomb' is 17c from Latin *fusus* 'spindle', and (2) the one meaning 'a device or component for protecting an electric circuit' is 19c, derived from the earlier verb meaning 'to melt'. The first of these words, but not the second, is usually spelt *fuze* in AmE.

-fy. This suffix forming English verbs corresponds to French *-fier* and Latin *-ficare.* It occurs from the 15c onwards in words either borrowed whole from French or modelled on French forms (e.g. *beautify, classify, horrify, pacify*), and is also an active suffix occasionally forming new (often somewhat jocular) words such as *bullify* (18c = to make into a bully), *Frenchify* (16c), and *ladify* (17c). These words have inflections in *-ifies, -ified, -ifying.* When there is a choice of spelling between *-ify* and *-yfy* (as with *countrify/-yfy* and *ladify/-yfy*) the spelling in *-ify* is preferable. A small group of words end in *-efy* (e.g *liquefy, stupefy*) and inflect *-efies, -efied, -efying.*

gabardine. This is the recommended spelling for the word meaning 'a smooth durable cloth' or a raincoat made from it. The form *gaberdine* is used with historical reference to the smock worn by almsmen and beggars, and by Jews on the Elizabethan stage, as in Shakespeare's *Merchant of Venice* I.iii.111 (Shylock): *You call me misbeliever, cut-throat, dog, And spit upon my Jewish gaberdine.*

Gaelic, pronounced **gal**-ik or **gay**-lik, denotes any of the modern Celtic languages spoken in Ireland (Irish Gaelic), Scotland (Scottish Gaelic), and the Isle of Man (Manx). There are two main varieties that were ancestors of these languages: Brythonic (or *P-Celtic*), also the indigenous language of Wales and Cornwall and taken by Britons to Brittany, and Goidelic (or *Q-Celtic*), which spread from Ireland into the Isle of Man and Scotland.

gala is normally pronounced **gah**-luh but the traditional pronunciation, as recorded in the *OED* (1899) and as used in the Durham Miners' Gala, is **gay**-luh. Both pronunciations are in use in AmE. The plural form is *galas.*

gallant is pronounced **gal**-uhnt in the ordinary meaning 'brave', and guh-**lant** in the special meaning 'attentive to women, amorous' and the related noun 'lover or paramour'. Fowler thought that these two uses were, even then (1926), 'perhaps moribund', but they persist,

usually in fictional or romantic contexts rather than in everyday language.

galley has the plural form *galleys.*

Gallicisms. Fowler (1926) used this term to describe what he called 'borrowings of various kinds from French in which the borrower stops short of using French words without disguise'. That is to say, they are words that have been assimilated in various ways, or in some cases translated, into English. While acknowledging their established contribution to English vocabulary, he gave a warning not to use them as a kind of affectation derived from their foreignness. There are three principal types of Gallicisms; Fowler was thinking especially of the third:

1 French words which have been adapted to suit the ordinary conventions of English by dropping accents or substituting English endings, e.g. *actuality* (from French *actualité*) and redaction (from French *rédaction*). See *also* FRENCH WORDS AND PHRASES USED IN ENGLISH.

2 Mismatches, i.e. words that do not mean in English what they mean in French; for example, *papier mâché* is literally 'chewed paper' and does not exist in this meaning in French (the equivalent is *carton-pâte*), *duvet* in English means 'a continental quilt' but in French means 'a sleeping-bag', and *cagoule*, which in English means 'a windproof outdoor garment with a hood', in French means a monk's hood or 'a child's balaclava'. Some food terms have different meanings in the two languages: *fromage frais*, which is now widely seen in British supermarkets, is what in French is called *fromage blanc*, *fromage frais* being a fresh unmatured type of cheese.

3 Loan translations, i.e. expressions adopted from French in a more or less literally translated form, e.g. *gilded youth* (from French *jeunesse dorée*), *jump* (or *leap*) *to the eyes* (French *sauter aux yeux*), *marriage of convenience* (French *mariage de convenance*), and *that goes without saying* (French *cela va sans dire*).

gallop meaning 'to go at a fast pace', has inflected forms *galloped, galloping*.

gallows has been treated since the 16c as a singular noun, with a (rarely used) plural *gallowses*. *Gallows humour* means 'grim and ironical humour'.

galore, meaning 'in plenty', comes after the word it qualifies (*bargains galore in our spring sale*). It is derived from Irish *go leór* meaning 'to sufficiency, enough'.

galosh, meaning 'a waterproof overshoe', is normally used in the plural *galoshes*. This spelling is preferred to the variant *golosh*.

gambit, in its generalized meaning 'an opening move in a conversation, meeting, set of negotiations, etc.', is a technical term taken from chess (*see* POPULARIZED TECHNICALITIES), where the meaning is 'an opening in which a player sacrifices a piece or pawn to secure an advantage'. In the extension of meaning, the notion of sacrifice has largely disappeared: *Liza was attractive and her response to some of his occasional conversational gambits on the way home had been interesting and unusual*— P. Street, 1990 / *These questions are often opening gambits for a negotiation of some sort*—P. Davies, 1991.

Beware of confusing gambit with gamut: ☒ *The acting was excellent, the cast portraying the whole gambit of emotions with great conviction.*

gambol, meaning 'to skip or frolic playfully', has inflected forms *gambolled, gambolling*. In AmE the forms *gamboled, gamboling* are also used.

gamut. In music, *gamut* properly means 'the note G at the pitch now indicated by the lowest line of the bass staff'. (The word is formed from medieval Latin *gamma* (= the note G) + *ut*, the first of six arbitrary names forming the hexachord (*ut, re, mi, fa, sol, la*); these were said to be taken from the initial letters of a sequence of Latin words in the office hymn for St John the Baptist's day.) It was later extended to mean 'the whole series of notes used in medieval or modern music', and this has given rise to the generalized meaning 'the whole series or range or scope of anything' which chiefly occurs in the expression *run* (or *go through*) *the* (*whole / full*) *gamut* (= experience the whole range of): *Both men were put through the full gamut of emotions*—*Irish News*, 2003. Beware of confusing *gamut* with *gauntlet*: ☒ *No need to run the gamut of residents parking until next January*— *Times*, 2007.

gantry is spelt in this way when it refers to any of various structures supporting a crane, set of railway signals, space rocket, etc. In the meaning 'a wooden stand for barrels', it is also spelt *gauntry* and pronounced **gawn**-tri.

gaol, gaoler, *see* JAIL, JAILER.

gap 1 The word is widely used as the second element of expressions denoting 'a divergence in views, sympathies, development, etc.' Those recorded in the *OED* include *age gap* (1963), *credibility gap* (first recorded in 1962), *export gap*

(1952), *gender gap* (1969), *generation gap* (1962), and *technology gap* (1967).

2 Since the 1980s the practice of students taking a break from full-time education in order to travel and gain experience of the world between school and university has been institutionalized in the term *gap year*.

garage. The standard pronunciation in BrE is **ga**-rahzh, although some speakers say **ga**-rij or (with the stress on the second syllable) guh-**rahzh**. The dominant pronunciations in AmE are guh-**rahzh** and guh-**rahj**.

garrotte is the customary spelling for the word (verb and noun) to do with killing by strangulation. In AmE the dominant spelling is *garrote* (with inflections *garroted, garroting*), although other forms are also found.

gas. The plural of the noun is *gases*, but the verb has inflected forms *gasses, gassed, gassing*. *Gas*, short for *gasoline*, is the most usual word in AmE for BrE *petrol*, and permeates BrE in colloquial expressions such as *step on the gas*.

gaseous. The dominant pronunciation in standard English is **gas**-i-uhs; **gay**-si-uhs is now only rarely heard. In AmE the variant **gash**-uhs is sometimes heard.

gasoline is the AmE term for what in BrE is called *petrol*, a volatile liquid obtained from petroleum. This spelling is preferred to *gasolene*, but the word is normally used in its shortened form *gas*. See GAS.

-gate is a suffix taken from the name *Watergate*, a building in Washington, DC containing the headquarters of the Democratic Party, which was the centre of a break-in and political scandal in 1972. The suffix is used in potentially limitless combinations to denote an actual or alleged scandal that is in some way comparable. Some are likely to be ephemeral and soon forgotten; examples that possibly still have some resonance are *Dianagate* (1989, referring to secretly recorded conversations between the Princess of Wales and her friend James Gilbey) and *Monicagate* (1998, referring to a sexual scandal involving Monica Lewinsky and President Bill Clinton). While most formations add *-gate* to a proper name of a person or place, it can also be attached to other nouns, e.g. in Britain *pastygate* (2012, referring to the outcry at the Chancellor's decision to impose 20% VAT on hot pasties) and *piegate* in Australia (2012, when a government minister swore at the shop owner selling him a pie). These formations are a godsend to journalists wishing to instil the breath of scandal into short, eye-catching headlines.

gateau, a loanword from French meaning 'a rich cake', has the plural form *gateaux*, or occasionally *gateaus*, both endings being pronounced -ohz. The circumflex accent of the original French *gâteau* is no longer used in English.

gauge is spelt in this way, not *guage*.

gauntlet. There are two distinct words here: (1) 'a stout glove' used in the expression *throw down the gauntlet* (= accept a challenge), from an Old French diminutive of *gant* meaning 'glove', and (2) used in the phrase *run the gauntlet* (= undergo a punishment or ordeal), assimilated from an earlier form *gantlope*, of Swedish origin. The second word is sometimes spelt *gantlet* in AmE.

gay. 1 *There is no historical case for homosexual ownership of 'gay'. So can we have our word back, please.*—Paul Johnson, 1995. This typifies the reaction of many people to this major change, occurring from the mid-20c but with occasional earlier evidence, in the use of an English word that was already on the wane. At this time, the homosexual community made it clear that they wanted to be called *gay* instead of *homosexual* or any of the other derogatory names including *fag, faggot, fairy, homo, pansy,* and *queer.* The first substantial evidence is from the 1950s: *In a way it was an odd threesome. It occurred to me that Esther rather hung round our two gay boys*—E. Lambert, 1951. The historical basis for this use of *gay* is sometimes sought in earlier meanings: (17c) 'addicted to social pleasures and dissipations' (as in *gay dog* and *gay Lothario*) and (19c) '(said of a woman) leading an immoral life, living by prostitution'. But these older and hardly favourable meanings constitute dubious precedents, and in all probability the connection was impressionistic rather than analytical. Whatever the case, the new meaning looks here to stay, and dictionaries of current English tend to list it first of the several meanings of *gay.* There are a number of points to be made in defence of the new meaning: it is useful to have a word that is not offensive; the traditional meaning of *gay* was in any case acquiring something of a period flavour; and there are plenty of synonyms available: *merry, jolly, cheerful, happy, high-spirited, lively,* and others that can be found in a good thesaurus.

2 *Gay* is also used in the meaning 'intended for, used by, or associated with homosexuals' (as in *gay bar* and *gay politics*), and as a noun: *What about gays, one asks, and will there be facilities for them to relate significantly to each other?*—*Sunday Telegraph*, 1985. Unlike the adjectival use, however, the noun *gay* usually denotes male homosexuals only, and the phrase *lesbians and gays* (or the other way round) is used to show clearly that both sexes are meant: *One end result has been an increase in the extent to which gays and lesbians have been subjected to physical violence*—J. Dollimore, 1991 / *Mariela continues much of her mother's work through the national centre for sex education, of which she is director, an organisation that campaigns for the rights of lesbians, gays and transsexuals*—*Guardian*, 2007. The *gay gene* is a slang term for DNA sequences which can supposedly predispose an individual to homosexuality.

3 It should be mentioned that, despite all the inhibitions reviewed above, the traditional meaning of *gay* is still alive and well for some writers: *She had lived a very gay life in London, when she was on the stage*—Nina Bawden, 1991 / *But she disobeyed him, brought the baby out, and he had never found her so gay, so welcoming*—Marina Warner, 1992.

gazebo, pronounced guh-**zee**-boh and meaning 'a small building, especially one in the garden of a house, that gives a wide view of the surrounding area', has the plural form *gazebos*. The word is 18c, and is thought to be a fanciful formation on *gaze*, as if it were a Latin future verb (*gaze* + *-ebo*) meaning 'I will gaze (at the view)'.

geezer is a (now somewhat dated) slang term for a person, usually a man. It is a late-19c adaptation of *guiser* meaning 'mummer', reflecting a dialect pronunciation.

gelatin, gelatine. *Gelatin* (pronounced **jel**-uh-tin) is the usual form in chemical use, and in AmE in all uses, but *gelatine* (pronounced **jel**-uh-teen) is common in BrE in contexts to do with the preparation of food.

gender. 1 Since the 14c the word has been primarily a grammatical term denoting groups of nouns in terms of their being masculine, feminine, or neuter. In the earliest form of English (Old English or Anglo-Saxon, *c.* 740 to

1066), nouns fell into three classes, masculine, feminine, and neuter: *stān* (stone) was masculine, *giefu* (gift) was feminine, and *scip* (ship) was neuter. The definite article and most adjectives varied to accord with the gender of the accompanying noun, as they still do in other languages. By the end of the 11c, this system was lost. In modern English grammatical gender exists only in the singular personal pronouns *he, she, it, his, hers, its*, etc., and in some feminine endings such as *-ess, -ette* (imported from French), and *-ine*.

2 Although nouns associated with female and male persons and animals are generally feminine or masculine as appropriate, grammatical gender and sexual gender do not have a complete correspondence in any language, which accounts for some of the anomalies that can cause offence in our modern gender-sensitive age (e.g. in referring to vehicles as *she*).

3 The evidence in the *OED* shows that the term *gender* was also used as a term meaning 'the sex of a person', although the *OED* editors (1899) marked this as 'now only jocular'. Since the 1960s this meaning has come back into regular use, especially among feminists, to emphasize 'the social and cultural, as opposed to the biological, distinctions between the sexes' (*OED2*, 1989). This revival, which is a useful one, has given rise to many new compound expressions, including *gender bias, gender difference, gender discrimination, gender equality, gender gap, gender imbalance, gender identity, gender model, gender politics, gender role, gender-specific*, and *gender stereotype*; and academic disciplines now include the field of *gender studies*.

gender-neutrality. 1 In English, explicit grammatical gender is chiefly confined to the third-person singular personal pronouns and determiners, *he, she, it, his, hers, its*, etc. From earliest times until about the 1960s it was unquestionably acceptable to use the pronoun *he* (and *him, himself, his*) with indefinite reference to denote a person of either sex, especially after indefinite pronouns and determiners such as *anybody, anyone, each, every*, etc., after gender-neutral nouns such as *person, individual*, and *speaker*, and in fixed expressions such as *every man for himself* and *one man one vote*. The feminist movement has greatly intensified sensitivities in this area, and alternative devices often have to be found. When a gender-neutral pronoun or determiner (i.e. one that is free of grammatical gender) is needed, the options usually adopted are *he or she* (or *his or her*, etc.), or the plural forms *they, their, themselves*, etc.: *Each client should take the advice of their estate agent, who will take into account the style of the property,* [*etc.*]—*Real Property Guide* (Edinburgh), 1995 / *Anyone who involves themselves in such issues does so for their own salvation*—*Big Issue*, 1998. This use of plural pronouns is not new, but a revival of a practice dating from the 16c and common in 19c literature (*Whenever a person says to you that they are as innocent as can be in all concerning money, look well after your own money, for they are dead certain to collar it, if they can*—Dickens, 1853). Insistence on differentiation can lead to awkwardness in a sentence in which the problem recurs, typically causing the writer to resort finally to convenience at the expense of inconsistency: *I cannot urge this bargain version too strongly on anyone who loves this work, even if he or she already has another performance in their collection*—*Gramophone*, 1995. There is also a danger that plurality will run away with the sentence: ✖ *Ultimately someone will lose their lives over this*—*Edinburgh Herald & Post*, 2002. An alternative strategy is to rephrase the sentence, for example by couching the whole thing in the plural; by this device the last example but one above becomes . . . *on all those who love this work, even if they already have another performance in their collection*, although the loss of singular focus can sometimes blur the sense.

2 Artificial devices, including the use of composite forms such as *s/he, hesh, wself*, etc., have not found general currency, partly because they are difficult to articulate and are only possible in writing. A reflexive pronoun *themself* is occasionally found and is likely to become more common, but at present it is non-standard: *It is not an actor pretending to be Reagan or Thatcher, it is, in grotesque form, the person themselves*—I. Hislop, 1984 / *Someone in a neutral mood can devote themself solely to problem solving*—*Independent*, 1995.

genealogy, meaning '(the study of) a person's line of descent', is derived from a Greek word *genea* meaning 'race, generation'. The existence of so many words ending in *-ology* (*archaeology, psychology, sociology*, etc.) and the influence of its own derivative word enealogical (with a stressed *-o-*), traps some people into pronouncing *genealogy* as if it too ended in *-ology*, and even into spelling it that way.

generator is spelt *-or* in all its meanings, not *-er*.

genius. 1 This generally has the plural form *geniuses*; *genii* is only used in mythology to refer to certain spirits.

2 *Genius* is one of those nouns like *fun, magic*, and *rubbish*, which are rapidly spreading their wings as adjectives of a sort. *Genius* doesn't have all the qualities of a standard adjective—you can't modify it with *very, more*, etc., although you can use *most*—but it often appears in informal writing in the phrases *genius idea* / *genius move* / *genius touch*, etc. This seems to be a further extension of its use to modify nouns denoting professions and vocations, as in *genius artist, genius inventor*, etc. Some people wince at this new use, so for the time being it is best confined to informal writing, despite being a colourful addition to the lexicon of English. Examples: *the extraordinary documentary on genius artist Moebius*—undated, [*OEC*] / *Then, out of nowhere this genius idea flashed through my head*—2008, BrE [*OEC*].

gent (= gentleman). Apart from its use in commercial circles (e.g. *gents' outfitters*) and (in the UK) the colloquial euphemism the Gents, meaning a men's lavatory, this shortening is mainly used to indicate sociability, courtesy, etc., e.g. *He's a perfect gent*.

genteel. Its primary meaning is 'affectedly or ostentatiously refined or stylish', but it is often used ironically to mean 'of or appropriate to the upper classes'.

genteelism. Fowler (1926) described *genteelism* as 'the substituting, for the ordinary natural word that first suggests itself to the mind, of a synonym that is thought to be less soiled by the lips of the common herd, less familiar, less plebeian, less vulgar, less improper'. It is euphemism taken a stage further by virtue of the inappropriate social context into which the substitute word is placed. Fowler's list included items that would now be considered normal or even preferable, such as *assist* for *help, close* for *shut, mirror* for *looking-glass*, and *stomach* for *belly*. Others, such as *anent* for *about* and *domestic* for *servant*, have fallen out of use or are no longer socially relevant. A few might be thought valid as genteelisms: e.g. *carafe* for *water-bottle, edifice* for *building, endeavour* for *try, expectorate* for *spit, inquire* for *ask, lingerie* for *underclothing, peruse* for *read, perspire* for *sweat*, and *sufficient* for *enough*. To these may be added *dentures* for *false teeth, desire* for *want, hard of hearing* for *deaf, lounge* for *sitting-room,* and *retire for the night* for *go to bed.* See *also* U AND NON-U.

genteelly, the adverb from *genteel,* is spelt and pronounced with two *l*s.

gentle. The phrase *the gentle art,* which was used with clever irony by the American painter James McNeill Whistler in his title *The Gentle Art of Making Enemies* (1890), had already become a cliché by the time Fowler wrote (1926). As well as being used allusively in titles, e.g. *The Gentle Art of Singing* (1927), it occurs in general contexts: *Grant took full advantage of the lunchtime lull in traffic, and in dere-stricted areas excelled himself in the gentle art of speed with safety*—Josephine Tey, 1936 / *Hype is an American word for the gentle art of getting a tune into the pop charts without actually selling any records*—Sunday Times, 1968. / *There's a gentle art to Indian cooking but it doesn't have to be labour-intensive*—Observer, 2006. *The gentle art* is also an affectionate name for the sport of angling.

gentleman. The word *gentleman,* formerly a term indicating social class, has largely fallen out of use in this meaning with the gradual erosion of class distinctions. It survives as a form of address (usually as *ladies and gentlemen*), in the phrase *gentleman's agreement* (an informal agreement not binding in law) and as a term of general polite reference, especially in public (*I have a question from the gentleman in the second row*). The designation *gentlemen* is still occasionally seen on signs for public lavatories, but *men* is more usual. The feminine form *gentlewoman,* meaning 'a woman of good birth or breeding' has almost entirely fallen out of use except as an archaism or for special effect (*Underwear, as anyone au fait with the night-time antics of the Hilton/*

Spears/Lohan *generation will attest, is an unnecessary part of a young gentlewoman's wardrobe in the modern age*—Sunday Review, 2007).

genuflection, meaning 'a bending of the knee', is the preferred spelling, although *genuflexion* is also in use.

genuine is pronounced **jen**-yoo-in in standard BrE. In AmE the pronunciation **jen**-yoo-iyn is widespread (sometimes for humorous effect) but non-standard, as it also is in BrE.

genus, the term for a taxonomic grouping in biology, is pronounced **jee**-nuhs. The plural is *genera,* pronounced **jen**-uh-ruh.

geo- has been an active prefix from the 19c, forming words to do with the earth in its various aspects. It has taken on a new lease of life in relation to present-day concerns about the environment and the effects human behaviour is having on it, with words from around 1900 or later such as *geopolitics, geostrategic* ('relating to the strategy required in dealing with geopolitical problems'—*COD*), and *geothermal* ('relating to or produced by the internal heat of the sun'). A *Geopark* is an area of special geological interest and outstanding natural beauty set aside for travellers to visit, each being part of a European organization of 35 such places worldwide endorsed by UNESCO.

geographic, geographical. Both forms have a long history, *geographic* being first recorded in 1630 and *geographical* in 1559. Throughout the English-speaking world, the two forms are roughly equal. The longer form predominates in BrE, but *geographic* greatly outnumbers it in AmE.

geometric, geometrical. As with *geographic, geographical,* the longer form is about a century older than the shorter one (1552 and 1630 respectively). In this case, the shorter form is more common in a 3:1 ratio throughout the English-speaking world as a whole. In BrE it is somewhat more frequent than *geometrical*, but massively so in North American usage, both in fixed collocations and in general contexts. The only fixed phrase in which *geometric* is almost invariable is *geometric mean*. OEC data suggests that *geometric* is by far the preferred choice when the meaning is 'characterized by or decorated with regular lines and shapes', e.g. *geometric design / motif / pattern / shape*.

geriatric is the normal, semi-official term used in Britain and the US when referring to the health care of old people (*a geriatric ward*; *geriatric patients*). Outside such contexts, it typically carries overtones of being worn out and decrepit and can therefore be offensive if used to refer to people, as in *the photographer's bemused, bright-colour studies of the geriatric residents of San City*. In fact, it may be seen as insulting to old people if used of anything else other than them, e.g. *the US is full of geriatric coal-fired power stations*. See also ELDER.

German words used in English. *See box opposite.*

gerrymander meaning 'to manipulate election districts unfairly', is originally a US word formed from the name of Elbridge Gerry, governor of Massachusetts in 1812. His name was pronounced with a hard initial *g*, and the word was at first pronounced likewise, but pronunciation with a soft *g* (j-) is now standard in both AmE and BrE.

gerund *see* VERBAL NOUN.

gesticulation, gesture. 1 *Gesture* is a somewhat older word (15c) than *gesticulation* (16c), and both are related to Latin *gestus* meaning 'action'. In

current use they overlap in their meanings to do with movement of the body or parts of the body as a mode of expression, and it is the degree of animation that governs the choice, *gesticulation* indicating a much more theatrical movement of the arms or body. The extended meaning of *gesture*, 'a friendly action intended to evoke a positive response', first came into English as recently as the early 20c: *The gift of your Medal of Honour to a British comrade in arms . . . is a gesture of friendly sympathy and good will which we will not forget*—*Times*, 1921 / *Flowers didn't occur to Sneed until he had arrived at the hospital, and there the gesture was pointless*—G. F. Newman, 1970.

2 A neologism from the end of the 20c that has extended this use is *gesture politics*, defined as 'political action which concentrates primarily on publicity value and influencing public opinion'. It is normally used with connotations of disapproval: *There is no room for gesture politics. If we want to open debate about the future and our constitution, that is fine*—*Daily Mail*, 1995.

get. 1 range of use. *Get* is one of the most frequently used and most productive words in English. Often it has virtually no meaning in itself and draws its meaning almost entirely from its context, especially in idiomatic uses such as *get to bed, get dressed, get home, get the flu, get a letter, get a new hat, get going, get rich, get one's feet wet, get a train*, and so on. It will be seen from these examples as an all-purpose substitute for a whole range of verbs including *arrive, become, buy, catch, collect, obtain, receive*, etc. *Get* also has a highly productive role in forming idiomatic phrasal verbs such as *get along, get at, get away, get away with, get back, get by, get down to, get on, get out, get over, get through, get together*, etc.

2 supposed overuse. The view that *get* is an overused word and should be

GERMAN WORDS USED IN ENGLISH.

English has been steadily adopting words from German for several centuries, although there are fewer loans of phrases than there are from French. There are sometimes changes of form (e.g. *kaput*) or changes of meaning (e.g. *spiel*). The table below shows the more important loans, with their dates of first appearance in print and their meaning, together with an indication of whether they have been naturalized in English (i.e. are printed in roman type and regarded as English words) or non-naturalized:

word	meaning	date	naturalized
angst	guilty anxiety	1922	yes
blitz	sudden attack	1940	yes
echt	authentic	1916	no
edelweiss	Alpine plant	1862	yes
ersatz	artificial, imitation	1875	yes
kaput	broken, not working	1895	yes
kindergarten	children's nursery	1852	yes
kitsch	garish or gaudy art	1926	yes
poltergeist	mischievous ghost	1848	yes
quartz	mineral	1676	yes
rucksack	type of bag	1853	yes
Schadenfreude	enjoyment of another's misfortune	1867	no
spiel	glib talk	1896	yes
ur-	original, earliest	1889	yes
waltz	dance	1781	yes

avoided in good English is a superstition. It was not a problem for either Fowler (1926) or Gowers (1965), whose entries on this word dealt with different aspects of its use. There are some uses that should be recognized as informal, e.g. *We got along fine* might be better expressed as *We were on good terms* in more formal contexts and *What are you getting at?* as *What are you suggesting [or implying]?*, but there is no advantage in *I received a letter this morning* over *I got a letter this morning* nor in *She's gone to collect her post* over *She's gone to get her post*. Many idiomatic phrases involving *get*, such as *get away with*, *get down to*, and *get to* (= have an opportunity to: *The problem with giving money to projects like these is that the general public never gets to see the results*—Birmingham Post, 2000) are effectively neutral in terms of register and can be used in virtually any context.

3 *have got* = possess. This was one of the issues that Fowler and Gowers dealt with, as mentioned above. Fowler wrote that '*have got* for *possess* or *have* is good colloquial English but not good literary English', and Gowers suggested that 'the intrusion of *got* into a construction in which *have* alone is enough originated in our habit of eliding *have*. *I have it* and *he has it* are clear statements, but if we elide we must insert *got* to avoid the absurdity of *I've it* and the even greater absurdity of *he's it.*' In negative contexts and questions, BrE *have* (or *had*) *not got* and *have* (or *had*) *you got?* is as common as (and somewhat less formal than) *do* (or *did*) *not have*, and *do* (or *did*) *you have?*, but the second alternative is the usual form in AmE.

4 The neologism *get a life*, meaning 'to start living a fuller or more interesting existence', is informal only: *The aristocracy is having to make some hard decisions: whether to pretend that the twentieth century never happened or to jump ship, join the middle class and get a life—Tatler*, 1993.

5 *See also* GOT, GOTTEN.

get-at-able, meaning 'accessible, attainable', is recorded from the late 18c, and is now more common than the older form COME-AT-ABLE.

geyser. The pronunciation in both its main meanings ('hot spring' and 'heating apparatus') is now **gee**-zuh, although **giy**-zuh is also used for the 'hot spring' meaning. In America and New Zealand, where the 'heater' meaning is not used, the pronunciation is uniformly **giy**-zuh.

ghastlily, the adverb from *ghastly*, is best avoided as being too awkward to say.

ghetto has the plural form *ghettos*.

ghoul, ghoulish. *Ghoul*, meaning (1) 'an evil spirit' and (2) 'a person morbidly interested in death', is pronounced gool. *Ghoulish* similarly rhymes with *foolish*.

gibber, gibberish are pronounced **jib**-uh-.

gibbous, meaning 'convex, protuberant', especially with reference to the moon, is pronounced **gib**-uhs.

gibe, jibe. The second spelling is the recommended one both for the verb meaning 'to jeer, mock', and for the

noun 'an insulting or mocking remark; a taunt': *It wouldn't be responsible to make promises I can't keep. That's Nick Clegg's job', he jibes—Daily Telegraph*, 2011 / *Spalding, whose time in Glasgow was stormy, directs a few jibes at Scotland's cultural shibboleths—Scotland on Sunday*, 2002. See also (the sailing term) GYBE; JIBE, GIBE, GYBE.

gigolo, meaning 'a woman's paid escort or lover', is pronounced **zhig**-uh-loh or **jig**-uh-loh, and has the plural form *gigolos*.

gild, meaning 'to cover thinly with gold', has a past participle *gilded* (*The porcelain is gilded by a magma of gold*), but the adjectival form is either *gilt* (*gilt tooling / gilt-edged securities*) or *gilded* (*gilded youth*). This word should be distinguished from the noun *guild* (with *u*), meaning 'a medieval association of craftsmen or merchants'.

gild the lily, meaning 'to try to improve what is already as beautiful as it can be', is a not quite accurate quotation from Shakespeare, King John IV.ii.11: *To gilde refined Gold, to paint the Lilly; To throw a perfume on the Violet,* [etc.].

gill. The word for 'the respiratory organ in fishes' is pronounced gil, and the word for 'a unit of liquid measure' is pronounced jil.

gimmick, a word of unknown origin meaning 'a trick or device, especially to attract publicity or trade', entered AmE in the 1920s, appearing first in glossaries and then in writers such as James Thurber (1948). Few other words passed so quickly from being a slang word to being a part of normal English.

gingerly. Unlike hundreds of adjectives ending in *-ly* (*beggarly, fatherly, friendly*, etc.) *gingerly* works as an adjective and adverb. It does so without changing form, which causes confusion about which part of speech constitutes its essence. In fact, it nearly always functions as an adverb (= in a careful or cautious manner) and very, very rarely as an adjective (= showing great care or caution). Examples (adverb): *He descends gingerly from the cab—New Yorker*, 1990 / *and they start gingerly to shift timbers and bricks—* P. Lively, 1991; (*adjective*) *Decision-makers must now, therefore, treat with* [sic] *this evidently explosive situation in a gingerly fashion—Guardian* (Trinidad), 2005.

gipsy *see* GYPSY.

gird. The normal past tense and past participle of the verb meaning 'to encircle or secure with a band or belt' is *girded*, but *girt* has been in use as recently as the 19c and is still used as an archaism, especially in adjectival compounds such as *sea-girt.*

girl is still used with reference to younger adult women, despite pressure from the feminist movement, especially when contrasted with corresponding male terms such as *boy, lad,* or *guy.* Its wider application has however diminished with the disappearance of those social institutions with which the word has been associated historically, for example the employment of female domestic servants (who were called *girls* whatever their age). *Girl* instead of *woman* remains accepted usage in several contexts: in referring to a regular female companion as a *girl* or *girlfriend*; in titles of books and films (e.g. Kingsley Amis's *Take a Girl Like You,* 1960, Helen Gurley Brown's *Sex and the Single Girl,* 1962, and Mary Wesley's *Not That Sort of Girl,* 1987), in the lyrics of popular songs (e.g. *Diamonds are a girl's best friend,* Leo Robin, 1949; *Thank you girl,* Lennon & McCartney, 1964), in the expressions *glamour girl, cover girl, page three girl, it girl* (a young woman socialite), etc., and

in the plural use of *the girls* to refer to a group of young women friends, analogous to *the boys.* In general use, however, *woman* or *young woman* are to be preferred, especially when contrasted with *man. See* LADY, WOMAN.

girly is the more common spelling by far, but *girlie* is also used and is not wrong.

girt *see* GIRD.

given, given that. *Given* is used as a preposition, and both it and *given that* as a conjunction (introducing a subordinate clause) with the meaning 'granted or assuming (that)'. The history of their use shows them to be free of the need to be attached to a particular subject, and so they are not so-called 'unattached participles' (*see* PARTICIPLES 3, 4). In the following modern examples, *given* is grammatically free of the subject of the main clause in each case: (preposition) *He didn't think that, given her ambitions and temperament, she would enjoy it—* A. West, 1984 / *There are doubts over the quality of the player he will be able to attract, given the uncertainty hanging over the north London club—Daily Telegraph,* 2007 / (conjunction) *Given how busy the Spanish monarchs were in the 1480s, it's a wonder they gave Columbus any notice at all—Chicago Tribune,* 1988 / *The sectors which are now almost wholly dependent on crude . . . will be forced to contract. Given that climate change caused by burning oil is cooking the planet, this might appear to be a good thing—Guardian,* 2003.

A *given* (as a noun) is a term from philosophy evidently first used by William James in 1879 (*If the philosopher fails to find a satisfactory formula of exorcism for his datum, the only thing he can do is to . . . assume the Given as his necessary ultimate*) and now used more generally in the sense 'a known or established fact or situation'.

g

given name *see* CHRISTIAN NAME.

glacial, glacier. The standard pronunciations in BrE are **glay**-see-uhl and **glas**-i-uh respectively; in AmE they are **glay**-shuhl and **glay**-shuhr.

gladiolus is pronounced gla-di-**oh**-luhs, and the plural form is *gladioli*, pronounced gla-di-**oh**-liy.

glamorous. Some people mistakenly suppose that to drop the *u* before the *r* in *glamorous* is an American only spelling, and they therefore spell the adjective ✖ *glamourous*. In fact, *glamorous* is the correct spelling on both sides of the pond and everywhere else, while *glamourous* is universally a mistake

glamour is spelt *-our* in BrE and either *-our* or *-or* in AmE. The word is originally Scottish, and was brought into general literary use by Walter Scott about 1830. It is an alteration of the word *grammar* (or more precisely, of the old form *gramarye*) with the meaning 'occult learning, magic, necromancy'. It then passed into standard English and meant 'a delusive or alluring charm'; nearly a century later, in the 1930s, it acquired its main current meaning, first in AmE and then in BrE and elsewhere, relating to the charm or physical allure of a person (usually a woman).

glance, glimpse. A *glance* (which can be followed by *at, into, over,* or *through*) is a brief look (*He cast a doting glance at his wife*—M. Underwood, 1973 / *There were glances of frustration as balls went astray and half-chances failed to be converted*—Independent, 1999), whereas a *glimpse* (which is usually followed by *of*) is what is seen by taking a glance rather than the glance itself (*The automatic roof light gave me a quick glimpse of two men, then the driver reached up to switch it off*—A. Ross, 1970 / *Here's a possible glimpse of the future: It's the year 2030,*

our landfill rubbish dumps are full, there are tight restrictions on shipping our junk to Third World countries, and we are producing more rubbish than ever—Leicester Mercury, 2004). There is a corresponding difference in the use of the verbs, and *glimpse* can be transitive (take a direct object) whereas *glance* requires a linking preposition: *He glanced down at the face of his gold Rolex*—W. Wager, 1970 / *I wanted to glimpse the buildings, monuments and streets from which the nightmares of the past century had been unleashed*—Daily Telegraph, 2004.

glass ceiling *see* CEILING.

glasses is the usual term in both BrE and AmE for what are also called in BrE (though not in AmE) *spectacles*. In AmE *eyeglasses* is often used in the same meaning, but this has long fallen out of use in Britain.

glassful. In the plural, care should be taken to distinguish *glassfuls* from *glasses full*. A *glassful* is an amount contained in a glass, and *three glassfuls* (e.g. of water) means three times this amount, though not necessarily held in three glasses. *Three glasses full* (of water) means three different glasses each full of water. Note that there is no form *glassesful*. *See also* CUPFUL.

glimpse *see* GLANCE.

-glish *see* SPANGLISH.

global has developed its meaning from the original simple meaning 'spherical, round' to 'all-inclusive' in abstract senses (19c) and, more recently, 'world-wide, involving the whole world', as in *global warfare* and the *global village* (coined by Marshall McLuhan in 1960 to denote the effective shrinking of the world by virtue of advanced communications), and especially in *global warming*, a term that became established in the 1980s to refer to the increase in the temperature of the earth's atmosphere caused by carbon emissions and other factors. *Globalism* and *globalization*, terms that date from about 1960, refer to the global, i.e. international, scale on which commerce, politics, and other aspects of human activity have tended to operate in recent years. In computer technology from the 1960s onwards, *global* means 'operating on the whole of a file or program', so that a *global change* made to an item is one that affects every occurrence of that item.

glue *verb* has inflections *glues, glued, gluing*; the adjective is *gluey*.

glycerine is spelt *-ine* in BrE and *-in* in AmE. In technical writing *glycerol* (same meaning) is used.

gn-. English words beginning in *gn-* are pronounced with the initial *g* silent, i.e. *gnat* and *gnostic* are pronounced nat and **nos**-tik respectively. Exceptions are the food-term *gnocchi* (a 19c loanword from Italian), which is pronounced **nyo**-ki, and the animal name *gnu* (from a South African language), which is sometimes pronounced nyoo as well as noo.

go. 1 The noun has the plural form *goes*.
 2 There are six uses of the verb that call for comment (these apply also to the current past form *went*, a form of the verb *wend* which replaced the cognate past forms of *go* from about 1500):
 a *it goes without saying.* This is a naturalized Gallicism (*see* GALLICISMS), from French *cela va sans dire*. Native English equivalents are *needless to say, of course*, and others, which some people prefer.
 b *go* + **bare infinitive.** The construction *go* + infinitive without *to* was the primary construction until the 17c, occurring many times in Shakespeare (e.g. *He is walked up to the top of the hill.*

I'll go seek him—1 Henry IV II.ii.10). Although this construction survives in AmE (e.g. *I'll go put your lovely flowers in water*—John Updike, 1986), in BrE it is now confined to a few fixed expressions such as *let him go hang* (*for all I care*). In BrE the current constructions are *go* + *and* + infinitive or *go* + *to*-infinitive: *Let's go and see that film at the local*—K. Benton, 1976 / *She . . . said she would go and turn the sprinkler off herself*—New Yorker, 1986 / *I went to buy some milk and a group began chanting my name while they banged some tins together*—People, 2005.
 c *go* + *and.* The combination *go* + *and* + infinitive often has special meanings, e.g. (1) 'to be so foolish, unreasonable, or unlucky as to': *You herd cattle all day, you come to despise them, and pretty soon . . . you have gone and shot one*—Garrison Keillor, 1990, and (2) as an instruction in the imperative: *It's late, child . . . Go and get some sleep*—J. M. Coetzee, SAfrE 1977.
 d *go* = **say.** The use in question here is illustrated by the following example: *Butch and I were discussing this problem, and Butch goes, 'But you promised you'd do it.' Then I go, 'Well, I changed my mind.'*—Chicago Tribune, 1989. *Go* is always used in this way with past reference (though very often in the present tense, as here). It may be regarded as an extension of the meaning that refers to a thing making a sound, as in cows going moo and bells going dong, and a transitional stage between names of sounds and reported speech can be discerned in the evidence given by the *OED*: *He was roused by a loud shouting of the post-boy on the leader. 'Yo-yo-yo-yo-yoe,' went the first boy. 'Yo-yo-yo-yoe,' went the second*—Dickens, 1836 / *She was a dear little dickey bird, 'Chip, chip, chip,' she went*—Illustrated Victorian Songbook, 1895. The extended use in reported speech is especially common in school and

youth language, and is also heard in conversational adult use.

e *go for it*. In 1987, the (American) cox of the Oxford boat in the University Boat Race wore a shirt with the slogan *Go for it* displayed on the back, thereby signalling the arrival in Britain of this popular American phrase of the 1980s: *I told her about Scott* [i.e. a boyfriend]. *Eileen said, 'Go for it, Andrea!'—New Yorker*, 1986. It may be seen as an extension of the meaning of *go* illustrated by uses such as *go for someone* (or *something*) *in a big way*, i.e. 'be enthusiastic about, be enamoured of': *He* [*Prometheus*] *had defied the established order, so people like Blake, Byron and Shelley went for him in a big way—Scotsman*, 2005.

f *don't go there* is a forceful or even aggressive warning to the person addressed to avoid a subject. The idiom, first recorded in the 1990s, is vivid but highly informal: *Don't talk about my childhood. Don't even go there. You know nothing!*—fiction website, AmE 2004 [*OEC*].

gobbledegook. 1 The term, though not the concept, was unknown to Fowler (1926); Gowers (1965) knew it, but like Fowler put his material in an entry called *jargon. Gobbledegook* (or *gobbledygook*, the commoner spelling in AmE) is the extensive use of unintelligible jargon in printed information that is intended for a general readership. Jargon within particular fields of study, such as computing or linguistics, is quite legitimate; it becomes *gobbledegook* when ordinary people not experienced in those domains are expected to understand it. The term is first recorded in America in 1944, and was probably coined as a representation of a turkey-cock's gobble.

2 The following passage from an American policy document about transport plans (as reported in a Chicago newspaper of 1995) shows gobbledegook in its most potent form: *While EPA* [*the Environmental Protection Agency*] *will solicit comments on other options, the supplemental notice of proposed rulemaking on transportation conformity will propose to require conformity determinations only in the metropolitan planning areas* (*the urbanized area and the contiguous area(s) likely to become urbanized within 20 years*) *or attainment areas which have exceeded 85 percent of the ozone, CO, NO2, PM-10 annual, or PM-10 24-hour NAAQS within the last three, two, one, three, and three years respectively*. Doubtless the statement made good sense to members of the EPA, and its accuracy is not in question. The fault lies in its inability to make any more than laborious sense to the general public to whom it was addressed.

3 Dr James Le Fanu, medical correspondent of the *Daily Telegraph*, reported (in 1995) a much more worrying case of the result of a cervical smear test sent to a patient in the following form: *The results of your test showed early cell changes* (*mild dyskaryosis suggesting CIN I*) *and wart virus changes*. The patient was advised to have a repeat test in six months, but no further explanation was offered. She turned to Dr Le Fanu, and he translated it for her as follows: *There are some funny-looking cells* (*'dyskaryosis'*) *which may or may not indicate the very earliest signs of precancerous change* (*'suggesting CIN I'*) *which almost always returns to normal with no treatment. However, when associated with evidence of infection with the wart virus, it is slightly more likely to progress up through grades CIN II and III—at which point something may need to be done, hence the need for a further test in six months' time*. Dr Le Fanu concluded that until those responsible for sending such reports to women include a translation of what they mean, 'tens of thousands of women every year . . . will continue to be unduly and unforgivably frightened'.

4 Other areas of information that are vulnerable to gobbledegook include law, social services, welfare, taxation, banking, local government, and technical subjects (including art and literary criticism). In some domains, especially law, complex language arises from a need to achieve detailed precision and to avoid the ambiguity or uncertainty that can result from using everyday language. Efforts are being made to improve the clarity of public documentation, and have been furthered by the work of writers such as George Orwell, Sir Ernest Gowers (*The Complete Plain Words*, 1954 and later editions), and others, by writers of several manuals entitled *Plain English for Lawyers*, and by the work of the Plain English Commission (see M. Cutts, *The Oxford Guide to Plain English*, 2nd edition, 2004). The following from the arts pages of a modern newspaper shows that gobbledegook is not confined to the world of officialdom: *In some ways, the notion of longevity has become eccentric, or proposed as simply an example of historical signage: the breadth of Proust's fiction, for example, or the gravitas of Henry Moore's sculpture. Culturally we tend to be more focused on the neurasthenic effects of the short-term, than the vista of the long term. Within an increasingly secular and fragmentic [sic] society, the notion of sacred or civic art has been replaced by a culture of commentary and reaction to a culture, in fact, which is more linked to topicality than to longevity*—*Independent*, 2003. The newspaper's own chief copy-editor commented a few days later: 'I won't try to translate that into plain English. Anyone who thinks that they can is cordially invited to have a go.' It appears that no one ever did.

5 *See also* JARGON; OFFICIALESE; PLAIN ENGLISH.

god, God. Whether or not one believes in a divine supreme being, it is conventional to capitalize *God* when it refers to 'the creator and ruler of the universe and source of all moral authority' in monotheistic religions—Christianity, Islam, Judaism, etc., and in phrases associated with that meaning: *God the Father, God forbid, God's gift to women, to play God*, etc. When the word refers to a deity, an image of a deity, or in its metaphorical meanings, it is written with a lower case initial *g*. Thus, *the Hindu god Shiva, wooden gods from the Congo, don't make money your god, the fashion victims for whom he is a god*, etc. Most style guides recommend that pronouns and adjectives referring to the monotheistic God should be written in lower case (i.e. *he* not *He*) as in the Bible and the *Book of Common Prayer: And God called the light Day, and the darkness he called Night.*

gold, golden. Of these adjectives, *gold* is used more often to denote something made of gold (*gold ring / gold watch*), whereas *golden* is used of colours and in abstract and figurative meanings referring to wealth generally (*golden hair / golden retriever / golden goose / golden handshake*).

good survives as an adverb only in nonstandard AmE, e.g.: *I'm looking after the place good*—Maurice Gee, 1994. The use in *feel good* (which is current in BrE and AmE) is adjectival, not adverbial: *I didn't feel too good the next day*—S. Wall, 1991.

goodbye is spelt as one word and (as a noun) has the plural form *goodbyes*. The AmE variant *good-by* has the plural form *good-bys*.

good will, goodwill. The more frequent spelling is the single word *goodwill*, both for the meaning 'the intention and hope that good will result' and for 'the established reputation of a business regarded as a quantifiable asset'. *Good will* as two words is an option for the first meaning, but not the second.

The hyphenated form *good-will* should only ever be used in front of another noun, e.g. *good-will ambassador / good-will gesture*, but *goodwill* is more frequent in that position.

google. Here is one of the key words of our age (in more than one sense of the word *key*), rising within the space of less than ten years (the first record in the *OED* is of 1999) from nowhere to almost total familiarity, even to those who are not computer-literate. *Google*, it hardly needs to be said, is the proprietary name of an Internet search engine, ranked by its supporters alongside inventions such as the wheel and the microchip in its usefulness. To *google* is to search for information on the Internet using a search engine, and like other verbs based on everyday activities derived from proprietary terms (*hoover, xerox*, etc.) it has a small initial letter when used in this way, because a verb cannot be registered as a trademark. For this reason, most modern dictionaries include the word as a verb only, which is both intransitive and transitive: one can *google* something sought (*Met this woman last night at a party and I came right home and googled her*—New York Times, 2001) or one can simply *google*. No doubt in time the word will give rise to extended and figurative uses as well.

gossip has inflections *gossiped, gossiping*; the adjective is *gossipy*.

got. The past and past participle of *get* is as productive as the verb as a whole. Some noteworthy uses are informal and verge on the non-standard:

a Use with *to*-infinitive, meaning 'to have an opportunity to': *This was considered a bonus for me, because I got to sit in the front*—F. Kidman, NewZE 1988 /

Mark and his mother had moved to Holland when he was just four months old, meaning he never got to meet his dad—Mirror, 2004.

b Elliptical for *have got* = possess: *What you got in that jar, Alvie?*—M. Eldridge, AusE 1984 / *I can't get my head around it, Sharon. Suddenly I got three fathers*—Times, 1987 / *Right now, we got nine cops in the Miami police department being tried for murder*—The Face, AmE 1987.

c *Got to*, elliptical for *have got to* = must: *We just got to live. Isn't that so?*—A. Fugard, SAfrE 1980 / *'We got to help these people,' he says, 'any way we can.'*—Newsweek, 1990.

d Use of *got to be* to mean 'came round to being': *It got to be 11 p.m. We left the way we had come*—New Yorker, 1989.

gotten. 1 Few language traits mark someone as American more readily than their natural use of *gotten* instead of *got* as an alternative past participle of *get*. (These uses are also spreading to Australia and New Zealand, as some of the examples given below will show.) Although it was once in regular use, *gotten* had been extinct in standard language in southern Britain (except in *ill-gotten*), but *gotten* seems to be coming into use here also. In AmE, it is used particularly when the meaning is 'have (or has) obtained or acquired', i.e. when it denotes coming into possession; when it denotes the fact of possession now, *got* is used. The difference can be seen by comparing the two sentences *We have gotten an apartment in Manhattan*, which means we have recently acquired it, and *We have got an apartment in Manhattan*, which means we have one available to us (as well as a house in Boston, for example). BrE uses *got* in both cases, with consequent ambiguity in some cases. Examples: *An army friend . . . had gotten us tickets for a Tchaikovsky extravaganza*—Philip Roth,

1979 / *Have you gotten your paper the last couple of Sundays?—New Yorker*, 1986 / *I'd only gotten about 4 hours of sleep the night before*—weblog, CanE 2005 [*OEC*].

2 *Gotten* is also used when the meaning is 'have (or has) become, come, developed, etc.', i.e. when a notion of progression is involved: *Has my reputation in town gotten that bad?*—T. Winton, AusE 1985 / *This last year and a half I've gotten to fill out a lot of forms*—John Updike, 1986 / *People in the USA have gotten much healthier in the past 30 years—USA Today*, 1988 / *Many shipping companies have gotten rid of their nautical inspectors—Lloyd's List*, 2001 (German speaker) / *It's strange that I still haven't gotten used to it over the past fifteen years*—fiction website, AmE 2004.

gourmand, gourmet. The older of these two historically unrelated loanwords from French is *gourmand*, which came into English in the 15c, first as an adjective meaning 'greedy, fond of eating' and later as a noun denoting such a person, which remains its primary meaning. In the 18c it developed the meaning that *gourmet* (early 19c) was to have, i.e. 'a connoisseur of good eating'. Conservatives prefer to confine *gourmand* to its original meaning, but very often people use it as a synonym for *gourmet* with no connotation of gluttony. *Gourmet*, unlike *gourmand*, is also used attributively (before a noun), as in *gourmet food* and *gourmet meal*.

government, governance. Note the *n* in the middle of *government* (based on the word *govern* with the noun suffix *-ment*), and that it should be pronounced as well as written. *Government* is the workaday word for the system by which a state or community is governed, and also denotes the process of governing and the particular group that is allegedly doing the governing. Particularly in AmE, *governance* can be used as a synonym for *government* to refer to the process of governing (e.g. *Beijing's monolithic city governance is also vastly different to that of Shanghai, where smaller district councils are entrusted with much more authority —OEC*, AusE 2005). *Governance* can also refer to the manner in which something is administered or managed, particularly a business or organization. Of Middle English origin (and therefore two centuries older than *government*), it was at one time somewhat recherché, but has become something of a vogue word as a result of various flagrant examples of political and financial mismanagement: *By contrast, study of the governance of companies, large or small, is only beginning*—S. Ackroyd, BrE 2002 / *It must be hoped earnestly that succeeding prime ministers will retrieve the principles of good governance—Times*, 2007.

Governor-General. The recommended plural form is *Governors-General*, although *Governor-Generals* is also found.

graceful, gracious. Both words are derived from Latin *gratia* meaning 'the quality of being pleasing', but their meanings are different. *Graceful* means 'having or showing grace or elegance' and is generally used of physical appearance and movement (*a graceful bow / graceful dances / a graceful gesture / graceful lines / a graceful movement*). *Gracious* means 'showing grace, kindly, courteous' and refers to things that people say and do rather than their physical attributes (*gracious acknowledgement / gracious hospitality / a gracious response*). It also has the meaning 'characterized by elegance and wealth' (*gracious living / gracious wealth*). Occasionally *graceful* is used where *gracious* would be appropriate, as in ⊠ *The unsuccessful candidates were graceful in defeat.* The adverb *graciously* occurs often in the meaning 'courteously, kindly': *'Oh, aye,' said Jock graciously, 'he's magic with that mashie.'—Scotsman*, 1976.

gradable adjectives are adjectives that can vary in the intensity of their meaning, have comparative and superlative forms, and can be qualified by adverbs such as *very*, *too*, *fairly*, etc. *Greedy, large, patient*, and *rich* are all gradable, whereas *dead, female, married*, and *rectangular* are non-gradable or absolute adjectives. *See* ADJECTIVE 4; UNIQUE.

graduate *verb*. There is no problem with the ordinary intransitive meaning (without an object), as in *He graduated from Yale in 1994* and *She graduated last year*. The newer AmE use with the name of the university or college as a kind of adverbial with *from* omitted (*He graduated Yale in 1994*, compare *He teaches school*, in which *at* is omitted) is more controversial, and is not standard in BrE. Note that in AmE *graduate* can refer to completion of a high-school course as well as of a university degree.

graffiti is in origin a plural word, but its use has developed rapidly. Before the 1960s it was mainly used by art historians and archaeologists to refer to drawings or writing scratched on the walls of ancient buildings (notably at Pompeii). Spray-can daubings since the 1960s have brought the word dramatically into general use, with the result that *graffiti* is generally accepted as a mass noun like *confetti* or *spaghetti*: *That haunting graffiti inscribed on the approaches to Paddington station—Times*, 1980 / *'I don't need drugs,' the T-shirt graffiti proclaims—Observer*, 1981 / *There was little or no hooliganism in those days, and what graffiti there was would be written largely in Latin, with*

here and there the odd something of Greek—*Independent on Sunday*, 1998 / *The main concern was the impression graffiti creates of the district*—news website, BrE 2004 [OEC]. The *COD* since its 10th edition of 1999 has marked the word as 'treated as sing[ular] or pl[ural]', and the singular *graffito* is now rarely used except in technical contexts or by way of pedantry.

gram, gramme. The shorter form is now usual for the metric unit of mass. The abbreviation is *g* (without full point).

grammar is the system by which words are used together to form meaningful utterances. It denotes both the system as it is found to exist in the use of a language (also called *descriptive grammar*) and the set of rules which form the basis of the standard language, i.e. the variety of a language that is regarded as most socially acceptable at a given time (also called *prescriptive grammar*). *See* STANDARD ENGLISH.

grammatical agreement, concord *see* AGREEMENT.

grammatical gender *see* GENDER.

grand **compounds.** *See box opposite.*

grande dame, a highly resonant term for an influential woman within a particular sphere, was borrowed from French in the 18c and is now sufficiently naturalized to be printed in ordinary roman type. The term is often used in a possessive structure (*grande dame + of + noun*) as in *Germaine Greer—the nearest thing we have to an iconic grande dame of feminism—Scotsman*, 1995 / *A ... hugely acclaimed portrayal of feminism's grande dame, Virginia Woolf—Sunday Express*, 2004.

granny, an affectionate name for *grandmother*, is spelt *-y*, not *-ie*, although

GRAND COMPOUNDS.

Grand, which is derived via French from Latin grandis meaning 'full-grown', is used in combination with other words to form words denoting (1) rank (*grand duke*), (2) family relationships involving a gap of more than one generation (*grandmother*), and other items involving large size or status (*grand slam*). Most of these compounds are now spelt either as one word (especially the relationships) or as two, although some of the relationship terms are also written with a hyphen. The following table shows the principal items:

ranks	grandma	grand master (chess)
grand duchy	grandmother	Grand National
grand duchess	grand nephew	grand opera
grand duke	grand niece	grand piano
	grandpa	Grand Prix
family relationships	grandparent	grand slam (sport, bridge)
grand aunt	grandson	grandstand
grandchild	grand uncle	grand total
grandad		grand tour
granddaughter	*miscellaneous*	grand unified theory (physics)
grandfather	grand jury	

Terms denoting family relationships are spelt with a capital initial (e.g. *Grandma*) when used as a form of address in letters etc.

the choice is more open in Scotland. It is spelt with a capital initial (*Granny*) when used as a form of address in letters etc. The plural form is *grannies*.

granted. 1 Like *considering and *given*, *granted* can be used as a preposition and (as *granted that*) conjunction that is grammatically free of the subject: *And, granted the initial assumptions . . . I think it stands the test*—A. White, 1965 / *Granted that Americans are not interested in Atlantic union, the emotional value to them of European union is enormous*—Listener, 1961. It can also function as a sentence adverb, but this should only be used in informal language: *Granted, it was not hard to interest a security man, who apart from a regular soldier had the most boring job on earth*—Thomas Keneally, 1985 / *I somehow don't see life in an ordinary manner, not even this sere and monotonous existence in Africa; granted, it browns me off sometimes, but I do pretty well on the whole*—I. Young, 1990. See also PARTICIPLES 3, 4.

2 The common expression *take for granted* is constructed with a simple object or by a *that*-clause (often with a preceding *it*, informally with omission of *that*): *It was taken for granted that the astronauts would be brought down in the Bermuda 'recovery area' at 12.22 a.m.*—Listener, 1965 / *He took it all for granted, and would never have a clue just how blessed he was*—F. Cooper, 1991 / *If she missed his letters for a few days, she would probably stop taking him for granted*—F. Pitt-Kethley, 1991 / *As a* *teenager, I took it for granted I would never get a boyfriend and was severely bullied—Express*, 2007.

gratis. In BrE and AmE most often pronounced **grat**-is, with **grah**-tis as an option in BrE and **gray**-tis in AmE.

gratuity is a rather grand word for 'tip', and is often found on restaurant menus and bills. In BrE, it also refers (without the same pretension) to a special payment awarded to employees on retirement or to members of the armed forces, police, etc., on discharge.

gray is a common AmE variant of *grey*.

greasy is pronounced **gree**-si in its literal meaning 'smeared with grease' and **gree**-si or **gree**-zi when applied to an unctuous or smarmy person.

Great Britain *see* BRITAIN, GREAT BRITAIN, THE BRITISH ISLES, ENGLAND, ETC.

Grecian. The adjective *Grecian* has steadily retreated before the word *Greek*, and is now idiomatically restricted to describing architecture (*Grecian columns*), facial outline (especially *Grecian nose*) and a soft low-cut slipper. Otherwise *Greek* is the natural word (*Greek alphabet / Greek history / Greek language*). A third form, *Greekish*, was largely obsolete by the end of the 19c. *Grecian* is no longer used as a noun, except in the old joke involving the line *How much does a Grecian urn?*.

Greek plurals *see* LATIN (AND GREEK) PLURALS.

greenhouse effect. This important but often misunderstood term is defined by the *Concise Oxford Dictionary* (2006) as 'the trapping of the sun's warmth in a planet's lower atmosphere, due to the greater transparency of the atmosphere to visible radiation from the sun than to infrared radiation emitted from the planet's surface'. Despite the broadening of this definition since earlier editions, the almost exclusive focus of attention of this term is the Earth. A *greenhouse gas* is a gas, primarily carbon dioxide, that contributes to the *greenhouse effect*. For *global warming*, *see* GLOBAL.

greenness, the quality of being green, is spelt with two *n*s.

grey is the dominant form in BrE, although *gray* is also used in AmE. In an unusually long note the *OED* (1901) recorded that 'an enquiry by Dr. Murray in Nov. 1893 elicited a large number of replies, from which it appeared that in Great Britain the form *grey* is the more frequent in use, notwithstanding the authority of Johnson and later English lexicographers who have all given the preference to *gray*'.

grievous, meaning 'severe, causing grief or suffering' (as in *grievous bodily harm*), is sometimes wrongly pronounced as if it were *grievious*, and also spelt this way.

griffin, griffon, gryphon. A *griffin* (also spelt many other ways, e.g. *griffon* and, e.g. by Lewis Carroll, *gryphon*) is 'a mythical creature with an eagle's head and wings and a lion's body'. A *griffon* is (1) a small dog like a terrier, and (2) a large vulture. All three uses represent variants of the same word, which is derived from Greek *gryps* referring to the mythical creature.

grill, grille. A *grill* is a device for cooking food, and the food itself. A *grille* is a metal grid, for example, protecting the radiator of a motor vehicle, or separating staff from customers in a bank. This is sometimes wrongly spelt *grill*.

grimace, meaning 'a distortion of the face' or 'to make a grimace', is most commonly stressed as **grim**-uhs. The second syllable can also be stressed, as gri-**mays**.

grimy, meaning 'covered in grime, dirty', is spelt *grimy*, not *grimey*. The comparative and superlative forms are *grimier* and *grimiest*, and the occasionally needed derivative forms are *grimily* and *griminess*.

groin, groyne. The *groin* is the part of the body between the belly and thigh; a *groyne* (AmE *groin*) is a low wall or timber framework built out from a sea-shore to prevent beach erosion.

grotto has the plural form *grottoes*.

ground, grounds. Both the singular and the plural are used in the expressions *on the ground* (or *grounds*) *that*, and *grounds* is more common in the expression *grounds for* (complaint etc.): *Occupations that various insurance companies consider to be grounds for rejection of applications for auto insurance . . . included . . . paperhangers, . . . sports coaches and assistants, travelling salesmen, . . . and doctors—New Yorker,* 1975 / *The Post Office tried to register the name Viewdata for its product but this was refused on the ground that it was too all-embracing a title—Guardian,* 1979 / *Fundamentalist Jews are limbering up to oppose the plan on the grounds that it will depict scenes from the New Testament as well as the Old—Daily Telegraph,* 1985 / *If you think you have grounds for complaint, you must first write to the firm that sold the policy—Sunday Times,* 2004.

group names of animals (e.g. *a pride of lions*) *see* PROPER TERMS.

grovel, meaning 'to behave obsequiously', has inflected forms *grovelled*, *grovelling*, and in AmE also *groveled*, *groveling*.

groyne *see* GROIN.

gruelling, meaning 'extremely arduous or demanding', is spelt with two *l*s in BrE and also as *grueling* in AmE.

gryphon *see* GRIFFIN.

guano, meaning 'bird dung used as a fertilizer', is pronounced **gwah**-noh, and has the plural form *guanos* (in the sense 'types of guano').

guarantee, guaranty. The two words have close meanings relating to the fulfilment of a legal obligation. *Guarantee* is used for the verb, and also for the noun when the obligation relates to the quality of a product or service, whereas *guaranty* is a noun only (plural *guaranties*), is mostly restricted to legal and commercial contexts, and refers primarily to undertakings to pay a debt if the person or party primarily responsible defaults.

guerrilla is the recommended spelling in English for the word meaning 'a member of an independent fighting force', not the common variant *guerilla*. The spelling *guerrila* with a single *l* is recognized by the *OED* but is not recommended. The word is pronounced guh-**ril**-uh, like *gorilla* (the animal). Because of that identical pronunciation, the marketing technique known as *guerrilla marketing*, which uses innovative, low-cost techniques to create a marketing buzz, is sometimes misspelt ☒ *gorilla marketing*.

guess. The informal use of *I guess* meaning 'I think it likely, I suppose' developed in America in the late 18c from the standard use of the phrase meaning 'it is my opinion or hypothesis (that)'. The Americanness of the informal use was marked and commented on throughout the 19c and much of the 20c, and it still has the flavour of an Americanism, but it is now widespread throughout the English-speaking world:

No, I guess I don't look at him very much—Gore Vidal, 1955 / *Martha. You remember them now? George. Yes, I guess so, Martha*—Edward Albee, 1962 / *I guess it takes a long time to grow up*—M. Sarton, 1978 / *I guess you're supposed to think to yourself that you're in a garden*—R. Ingalls, 1985 / *I guess this is my bed and I have to lie on it. Wash the sheets, plump up the pillows and try to make the best of it*—weblog, BrE 2005 [*OEC*]. Use of *I guess* as a tag at the end of a statement is characteristic of AmE: *He would have been watching the returns in the Senate elections I guess*—A. Broinowski, 1973 / *It's about a meter and a bit under water—about three or four feet, I guess?*—weblog, CanE 2005 [*OEC*].

guesstimate. This popular little portmanteau word (*guess* + *-timate*, from *estimate*) usefully suggests a figure based on a mixture of guesswork and reasoning, and adds dignity, if not credibility, to what might otherwise be dismissed as 'back of an envelope' calculations. Like other words still considered informal, it is older than one might suspect, being first recorded from 1936 in the US. The verb arrived in 1942, also in the US. Both noun and verb follow the pronunciation of *estimate*, i.e. **ges**-ti-muht and **ges**-ti-mate respectively. The spelling with two *s*'s is rather more common than *guestimate*, but both are correct.

guest has developed a wide range of uses in which payment may or may not be involved (as it is with *paying guests* and *guest workers*). The development of attributive uses (before a noun) that go well beyond the core meaning of *guest* may be seen in *guest beer, guest blogger, guest editor, guest speaker, guest star, guest worker, guest writer*, and others. Some people object to the common use in the entertainment industry of the

word as a verb, e.g. *He guested on the show two weeks ago*. This originally AmE meaning has been around for at least 70 years, and seems a useful shorthand for 'appear as a guest'.

guild *see* GILD.

guillemot, the name of a bird, is pronounced **gil**-i-mot.

gullible, meaning 'easily fooled or cheated', is spelt *-ible* not *-able.*

gunwale, meaning 'the upper edge of a ship's side', is pronounced **gun**-uhl.

gusseted, meaning 'having gussets' (in meanings connected with clothing and architecture), is spelt with one *t*, not two.

guts, meaning 'courage or determination', is more forceful and less neutral than either of these words. It is now only slightly informal, although it is more so in idiomatic expressions such as *hate a person's guts* and *work one's guts out* (in which *guts* has a more literal meaning within a broader metaphor).

guttural is a non-technical term denoting a consonant produced in the throat or by the back of the tongue and the soft palate, for example k and hard g. It is often applied to accents and languages, particularly German.

guy, in informal use, means primarily 'a male person' in BrE and (especially in the phrase *you guys*) 'a person (of either sex)' in AmE. In BrE it is fast replacing *chap*, which now sounds dated, and plural use relating to either sex is increasing. The use of *guy* to mean 'a male person' established itself in North America towards the end of the 19c and has made steady progress in Britain and other parts of the English-speaking world, especially Australia and New Zealand. Examples: *You guys all belong*

in the same ballpark—Observer, 1970 /
*I'm just as romantic as the next guy, and
always was*—John Lennon, 1980 / *She
was a regular guy, a good sport and a fine
actress*—quoted in American Speech,
1983 / *I could see John by the bar talking
to some guys*—New Yorker, 1989.

gybe *noun and verb.* This sailing term
is spelt *gybe* in BrE and *jibe* in AmE.
See also GIBE, JIBE; JIBE, GIBE, GYBE.

gymnasium. The preferred plural
form is *gymnasiums*, although *gymnasia* is
widely used. In Germany and Scandinavia
the word (pronounced ghim-**nah**-zi-
uum) also means 'a school that prepares
pupils for university entrance'.

gynaecology, meaning 'the physio-
logical study of women', is pronounced
with a hard initial g. The spelling is *-ae-*
in BrE and *-e-* (*gynecology*) in AmE.

Gypsy, Gipsy. The term has both
ethnic and general reference: either to
a member of a dark-skinned nomadic
people of Hindu origin and associated
with Egypt (hence the name) or a person
who adopts the same mode of life. The
OED gave priority to *gipsy*, but this
spelling is far less usual now, and the
form recommended here is *Gypsy*
(capitalized) when the reference is to
the people, and *gypsy* (with small initial
letter) in the generalized meaning
'a free spirit'.

h. 1 The sound of *h* (aitch) at the beginning of words such as *have* and *house* and in the middle of words such as *ahead* and *behave* is known technically as a voiceless glottal fricative. In Britain, the presence or absence of this sound in speech is one of the key factors in the social evaluation of an individual's use of language or, as the *OED* expressed it, it 'has come to be regarded as a kind of shibboleth of social position'. Dropping initial *h*, in particular, is associated with the working-class and poorly educated speech of East London, so that there is no difference between the sounds of (for example) *hedge* and *edge*, *hill* and *ill*, and *high* and *eye*.

2 Dropping one's aitches may be a sign of uneducated speech, but standard speakers do not always notice that certain function words (e.g. *has, have, had*), pronouns, and possessives tend to lose their initial h sounds when these occur in unstressed positions in rapid speech, e.g. *She shoved him into her car*, in which *him* is articulated as *im* and *her* as *er*. Until the beginning of the 20c, words containing the letters *wh* (e.g. *what, whistle, nowhere*) were regularly pronounced with the h sound intact by most RP (received pronunciation) speakers in England as well as other parts of Britain and America. But the *Concise Oxford Dictionary* and most other dictionaries of current English, when they give a pronunciation at all, give an unaspirated w sound in their phonetics for all this class of words, reflecting the fact that the aspiration of

wh has largely disappeared from spoken standard English in England, so that there is no audible difference between the sounds of (for example) *whales* and *Wales*, *where* and *wear*, and *whit* and *wit*.

3 The use of *an* instead of *a* as the form of the indefinite article before words beginning with an unstressed but lightly aspirated *h* (e.g. *an habitual complaint / an historic occasion*) is in decline: *see* A, AN 2.

habitué, meaning 'a habitual visitor or resident', is now printed in roman type and pronounced in an anglicized manner as huh-**bit**-yoo-ay. The plural is *habitués*, pronounced huh-**bit**-yoo-ayz. In writing the determiner *an* instead of *a* is still widely used before this word.

hackneyed, meaning 'made commonplace or trite by overuse', is spelt *-eyed*. For *hackneyed phrases*, see CLICHÉS.

had. 1 *had better*. See BETTER 1.

2 *had have*. This occurs with unreal (or unfulfilled) propositions in the past, constructed either with *if* (or an equivalent construction) as in the sentence *If I had have known, I would have said something* or with a verb expressing an unfulfilled intention, such as wish: *I wish you'd have kept quiet*. Though now associated with dialect and informal usage, the construction can be traced back in print to the 15c, e.g. *Had not he have be* [= *been*], *we shold never have* *retorned*—Malory, 1470–85. In a discussion of this issue in the journal *English Today* (1986), Professor Frank Palmer commented that 'there is a problem with past unreal, because it needs to mark past tense twice, once for time and once for unreality'. Another correspondent pointed out the type *had* + *a-* + verb as shown in the first part of a sentence in Galsworthy's *Strife* (1909): *If we'd a-known that before, we'd not a-started out with you so early*, which is distinct from the substitution of *of* for *have* in American regional use: *It was four o'clock in the morning then, and if we'd of raised the blinds we'd of seen daylight.*—Scott Fitzgerald, 1925. The upshot is that constructions of this type, of which *had have* is the most common in BrE, should be avoided in more formal speech.

3 had rather. The type *I had rather* is as idiomatic as, though much less common than, *I would rather*, and in its contracted form *I'd rather* is indistinguishable. In historical terms it was formed on the analogy of the now archaic type *I had liefer* meaning 'I should hold it dearer': *I had rather err with Plato than be right with Horace*—Shelley, 1819 / *I had rather gaze on a new ice age than these familiar things*—Jeanette Winterson, 1985.

haemo-, hemo-. This combining form derived from Greek *haima* meaning 'blood' occurs in words such as (BrE) *haemoglobin, haemophilia, haemorrhage*, etc. In AmE they are written *hemo-*. Note the two *r*s in *haemorrhage*.

hair-brained is an incorrect variant (first recorded in 1581 and still often found) of *hare-brained*, meaning 'rash, wild'.

hairdo, meaning 'the style or styling of a woman's hair', is informal only. The plural form is *hairdos*.

hale is the spelling in the expression *hale and hearty*. It comes from an Old English word *hāl* meaning (and related to) 'whole'.

half. 1 When *half* is followed by a singular noun (with or without *of* in between), the verb is also singular, and when the noun is plural the verb is plural: *Half of the country is employed in agriculture / Half the people like the idea / Half that amount is enough*. Occasionally, by the principle of 'notional agreement', the structure half (of) + collective noun can correctly be used with a plural noun: *Nearly half (of) the population lose at least half their teeth before they reach the age of 40*.
2 In some phrases concerned with quantities, measures of time, etc., the position of *half* can come before or after *a* or *an*, e.g. *I'll have half a pint* (no hyphen) or *I'll have a half-pint* (with a hyphen). In most cases, however, the order *half a year, half a million dollars*, etc., is more usual. Repetition of the article, as in ✗ *It took a half an hour*, is non-standard.

hallo *see* HELLO.

Halloween is nowadays much more often spelt without an apostrophe than with (*Hallowe'en*) and pronounced hal-oh-**een**.

halo has the plural form *haloes*.

handful has the plural form *handfuls*. *See* -FUL.

handicap as a verb has inflected forms *handicapped, handicapping*.

handicapped is first recorded in the early 20c referring to a person's mental or physical disabilities. In BrE it was the standard term until relatively recently. It has now been largely superseded by *disabled*, or, when referring to mental disability, *having learning* *difficulties* or *learning-disabled*. In AmE, however, *handicapped* remains acceptable. Its figurative use seems uncontentious: *The acting is handicapped by Gibson's need to show religious rapture—OEC*, BrE 2004.

handkerchief. The recommended plural is *handkerchiefs*, not *handkerchieves*.

handsome is applied equally to men and women who are, as Dr Johnson put it, 'beautiful with dignity'. In current use there is a tendency to use the term of women only when they are middle-aged or elderly.

hangar, hanger. A *hangar* is a large shed for housing aircraft; a *hanger* (in full *coat-hanger*) is a light frame with a hook for hanging clothes. Both are pronounced **hang**-uh, without the middle *g* being sounded twice, unlike *finger*.

hanged, hung. In standard usage, the past tense and past participle of *hang* is *hanged* with reference to capital punishment and *hung* in other meanings. So curtains and pictures are *hung* but a convicted murderer is (or was) *hanged*. The distinction can be traced back ultimately to the existence of two separate words, one Old English and the other Old Norse. *Hung* is occasionally used in the meaning of *hanged*, especially in regional and dialect use, and is not wrong, just less usual. Many, however, will regard it as an outright mistake.

hanger-on, meaning 'an unwelcome follower or dependant', has the plural form *hangers-on*.

hara-kiri, meaning 'Japanese ritual suicide', is spelt with a hyphen, and as shown, which corresponds most closely to the original Japanese, although the variant *hari-kari* is old-established and quite often still used.

harass. There are two pitfalls with this word meaning 'to trouble or annoy repeatedly' and its derivatives *harassing*, *harassment*, etc. One is the spelling, with only one *r* (unlike *embarrass*); the other is the pronunciation, which in Britain was traditionally **ha**-ruhs with the stress on the first syllable. The pronunciation huh-**ras** with second-syllable stress has spread rapidly from AmE to BrE and now seems to be the dominant one.

harbinger is pronounced **har**-bin-juh not **har**-bing-uh. In both its meanings, i.e. 'a person or thing that announces or signals the approach of another' (e.g. *witch hazels are the harbingers of spring*) and 'a forerunner of something' (e.g. *these works were not yet opera but they were the most important harbinger of opera*), it is standardly followed by *of*: Occasionally *for* is incorrectly used: ✖ *For Bartram, the performance tonight was a harbinger for future success— OEC*, AusE 2004.

harbour is spelt *-our* in BrE and *harbor* in AmE.

hardly. 1 *hardly . . . when . . .* and *hardly . . . than . . .* The standard construction is *hardly . . . when . . .* : *Hardly had the two children been freed when they* [i.e. a rescue team] *were on the spot, having covered the ground in a snow-tractor—Country Life*, 1971. The construction with *than*, though increasingly common and perhaps suggested by the analogy of *no sooner . . . than . . .* , is disapproved of by some people: ✖ *Hardly had the chalky jet stream dissipated above the horizon than it was time for another jetaway get-away to points west—American Square Dance*, 1991.

2 *can't hardly.* Since *hardly* already has a negative or restricting force, use of another negative (as in *I can't hardly believe it*) is non-standard, but is often used informally: ✖ *Mom just loaded us* *with fried chicken and I can't hardly walk*—New Yorker, 1988 / ⊠ *No, Swedon can't write anything. He can't hardly write his own pawn-tickets*—Penelope Fitzgerald, 1990.

hard words. *See box overleaf.*

hare-brained, meaning 'rash, wild', is more commonly spelt *hare-*, not *hair-*.

harelip *see* CLEFT LIP.

harem, an Arabic word denoting the women living separately in a Muslim household, is spelt this way in English. It is usually pronounced **hah**-reem, although pronunciation with the second-syllable stress is also heard. In AmE the stress is on the first syllable, which is pronounced either as in *hair* or as in *hat*.

hashtag. As a noun, it refers to the use of the hash symbol (#) in front of a word or phrase on social media sites such as Twitter to identify and group messages on a specific topic. When used as a verb, the inflections are *hashtagging, hashtagged*: *Kim posted a close-up on Instagram of the towering white Giuseppe Zanotti heels she wore today during their outing, hashtagging the designer, Kanye and 'CruelSummer'*—OEC, 2013.

have. 1 For the type ⊠ *No state has ⁄ or can adopt such measures, see* ELLIPSIS 3.

2 In a sentence of the type *Some Labour MPs would have preferred to have wound up the Session before rising,* the present infinitive is preferable, i.e. *Some Labour MPs would have preferred to wind up the Session before rising,* although the perfect infinitive is sometimes found when the past nature of the unperformed action is being emphasized. Examples: *'I would have preferred to do this my own way,' he said*—New York Times, 2006 / *If I had my choice of a dream job, I would have liked to have*

been the next Walt Disney or Hanna-Barbera—Black Enterprise, 2005.

3 have to and have got to. In the meaning 'must', *have to* normally denotes habitual or continuing necessity (*I have to wear contact lenses*) whereas *have got to* denotes immediate or temporary necessity (*I've got to catch a train in half an hour*). In the past tense, *had to* is much more usual than *had got to*: *In addition to his normal day's work in the library, he had to care for a complete invalid, shop on the way home, . . . and then translate demanding tomes until one or two o'clock in the morning*—D. Murphy, 1979 / *He knew . . . that in order not to lose control irretrievably of his life he had to hold on to his job*—William Boyd, 1981. The only available perfect and pluperfect forms are *have had to* and *had had to*: *They like the feeling that they have had to fight other men for possession. That is what it is all about, really*—Anita Brookner, 1984 / *Turning the other cheek was for girls who hadn't had to give blow jobs to tramps in exchange for a few pieces of candy*—P. Booth, 1986 / *Since Sara had not had to show I.D. at the motel she'd given them a different alias*—D. P. La Selle, 2004.

4 For *don't have* = *haven't got* and *do you have* = *have you got, see* DO 4.

5 For *had have, see* HAD 2.

haver, meaning 'to hesitate', is originally Scottish. This meaning spread south of the border in the 20c, but in its other meanings 'to talk foolishly' and (as a plural noun *havers*) 'nonsense' it is still anchored in the north.

he. 1 For *he* or *him* after the verb *be, see* CASES 2A.

2 For the expression *he or she, see* GENDER-NEUTRALITY.

heading for, headed for. In BrE the expression meaning 'to be going in a particular direction' is *to be heading for*

HARD WORDS.

Hard words is a semi-technical term for what it immediately suggests, long and difficult words that are often derived from Latinate rather than English sources, such as *rebarbative* (= repellent) and *nugatory* (= futile, trifling). The first English dictionaries devoted much space to hard words, explaining words of foreign origin in terms of native English words. The following list is drawn from Robert Cawdrey's Table *Alphabeticall* of 1604:

agnition	acknowledgement	Latin *gnoscere* 'to know'
carminate	to card wool	Latin *carmen* 'a card for wool'
combure	to burn up	Latin *comburere* 'to burn up, consume'
deambulation	a walking abroad	Latin *ambulare* 'to walk'
enarration	exposition or commentary	Latin *narrare* 'to relate'

All these words are now obsolete. The following, from the *Shorter Oxford English Dictionary* (6th edition, 2007), are still in use:

claustration	enclosure, confinement	Latin *claustrum* 'enclosed space'
coriaceous	like leather	Latin *corium* 'leather'
edulcorate	purify	Latin *dulcis* 'sweet'
evasible	able to be evaded	Latin *evadere* 'to evade'
idoneous	apt, suitable	Latin *idoneus* 'apt'
infraction	act of breaking an agreement	Latin *frangere* 'to break'
straticulate	arranged in thin layers	Latin *stratum* 'laid down'
tergiversation	equivocation, betrayal	Latin *tergum* 'back' and *vertere* 'to turn'
velleity	a mere wish	Latin *velle* 'to wish'

(in physical and figurative contexts, e.g. *heading for trouble*). In AmE *to be headed for* is also common and this form is becoming commoner in BrE and other varieties of English: *You're bloody cheerful . . . for a bloke that's headed for a number one reaming* [= *reprimand*] *from the CO*—J. Charlton, 1976 / *They were headed for the perilous North Channel . . . if they survived the wolfpacks*—D. Grant, 1980 / *Deng Xiaoping barreled on down the capitalist road last week—but he might be headed for a collision*—*Bulletin* (Sydney), 1984 / *They were all headed for Ralph's house*—*New Yorker*, 1991.

headline language *see* JOURNALESE.

headquarters can legitimately be used either as a singular (*a large headquarters in Paris*) or as a plural (*The firm's headquarters are in Paris*). The singular more often denotes the physical premises and the plural the institution in its broader sense.

head up. This phrasal verb has passed rapidly from AmE to British use, and means 'to take charge of (an enterprise or group of people)'. There is not a great deal of difference in meaning between *head up* and the simple verb *head*, except that *head up* has stronger implications of *taking* charge as distinct from *being* in charge.

healthful, healthy. It may be useful for British English speakers to know that some Americans insist that the correct word to convey the meaning 'conducive to health' is *healthful*, and that *healthy* can never be so used. One should therefore, they claim, speak of *healthful eating / food / diets / lifestyles*, etc.: *When healthful living and moral character were equated, good sexual hygiene meant abstaining from all sexual activities—Oxford Companion to the Body*, BrE 2001.

The supposed distinction is a completely artificial one, invented in America in the 19c. Tenaciously upheld by a few, it has never made significant inroads in Britain, and defies actual usage everywhere. The *OEC* data shows that throughout the English-speaking world *healthy* is roughly 70 times more common than *healthful*, and 40 times more frequent even in the latter's North American heartland. It occasionally appears in BrE, as in the example shown.

heaps. *There was heaps of time*—Mary Wesley, 1983 represents the normal colloquial idiom when the word following *heaps of* is a singular or mass noun (and the same is true of *loads of, lots of, masses of*, and similar expressions). But when the following noun is plural the verb should be plural too: *Heaps of bands are doing this stuff—X-Press Online*, AusE 2004. Note that *heaps* is plural whenever it is used literally rather than idiomatically: *Great heaps of cumulo-nimbus cloud were boiling up*—Dick Francis, 1970 / *Massive heaps of junk were collected in the harbor—Environmental History*, AmE 2004 [OEC].

heave. The past tense and past participle is *heaved* in its ordinary meanings 'to lift, haul, throw, etc.' and 'to utter (a sigh)', and *hove* (1) when the meaning is 'come into view' (*She hove around the Minister's flank with the effect of an apparition*—Thomas Keneally, 1980), and (2) in nautical usage (*The ship hove to / The anchor was hove up*). Some people make the mistake of thinking that there is a verb form *hove*, and thus write incorrect phrases such as ✖ *He had seen 60 hove into sight, and assumed that must mean he was no longer up to it—Scotland on Sunday*, 2002.

hectic. 1 The meaning that is now the dominant one, 'busy and confused', is fairly recent (early 20c) and has developed in the same way as the figurative meaning of *feverish*. *Hectic* was originally an adjective or noun referring to the kind of fever that accompanied consumption (*For like the hectic in my blood he rages*—Shakespeare, *Hamlet* iv.iii.80); its physical use declined with the decline in occurrence of the disease itself, but fevers are still with us. An early figurative use occurs in Kipling: *Didn't I say we never met in pup-pup-puris naturalibus, if I may so put it, without a remarkably hectic day ahead of us?—Traffics & Discoveries*, 1904. Modern examples follow (note that *hectic* often comes before a period of time): *At times, though, in these hectic weeks of organization, ... it seemed we should never make our deadline for packing all our gear ready to go to India*—Chris Bonington, 1971 / *After the hectic activity of summer, I look forward to doing more relaxed boating and fishing trips in early autumn*—B. Tulloch, 1991 / *Back at work after a hectic, but highly enjoyable, long weekend*—weblog, BrE 2004 [OEC].

2 The adverb from *hectic* is *hectically*: *Hectically she scrabbled for something constructive to say*—R. Ash, 1993. Note also that *hectic* is still occasionally used in its medical sense: *The hectic face on the thin neck rose too sharply out of the* *collar of a silk blouse*—Anita Brookner, 1990.

hegemony, meaning 'political leadership of a group of states', is pronounced hi-**jem**-uh-ni or hi-**gem**-uh-ni, with the *g* either hard or soft and with the stress on the second syllable.

Hegira, the term denoting Muhammad's departure from Mecca in AD 622 and used for dates in the Muslim era, is pronounced **hej**-i-ruh in BrE and in AmE more commonly huh-**jiy**-ruh. The spelling *Hejira* is occasionally found.

heifer, meaning 'a cow that has not borne a calf', is spelt this way.

heinous, meaning 'extremely wicked', is pronounced **hee**-nuhs.

heir. An *heir apparent* is an heir whose claim cannot be set aside by the birth of another heir. An *heir presumptive* is an heir whose claim may be set aside if another heir with a stronger claim is born. *Heir apparent* is often used now of a person regarded as likely to succeed to the position held by the head of a political party, business organization, etc.

helix, pronounced **hee**-liks and meaning 'a spiral or coiled curve', has the plural form *helices*, pronounced **hel**-i-seez, or occasionally *helixes*.

Hellene, Hellenic are the noun and adjective respectively referring to the people and culture of Greece, ancient and modern. They are normally used in the context of the history, literature, and archaeology of Greek lands. *Hellene* is pronounced **hel**-een and *Hellenic* is pronounced he-**len**-ik or he-**lee**-nik.

hello, hallo, hullo. *Hello* is by far the most usual spelling in the *OEC* data, the other two being in a tiny minority. *Hallo* is more common in AusE than

elsewhere, and *hullo* more common in BrE and now the least usual, despite being the first recorded (in 1857). The plural form is *-os*.

helmeted, meaning 'wearing a helmet', is spelt *-eted*.

help *verb*. *Help* is one of the oldest words in English, going back to the time of King Alfred (9c). It has two principal meanings in current English: 'to assist' (*Can I help you?*) and 'to prevent' (*I can't help it*). These two apparently unrelated meanings are connected by the use of *help* to refer to dealing with disease and misfortune, in which the interrelation between providing help and preventing suffering is clearer. There are three issues to explore with *help*, the first two connected with the 'prevent' meaning and the third with the 'assist' meaning:

1 *cannot help but.* This use is illustrated by the example *She could not help but notice that all the passengers on the bus were pensioners*—S. Mackay, 1984. The construction used here is common, and is a fusion of two other typical constructions: *She could not but notice . . .* and *She could not help noticing . . . .* It is preferable to use either of these constructions in more formal contexts, although the fused construction is common informally and is likely to become more so.

2 *more than* [or *as little* etc. as] *I can help.* This idiom is illustrated by the examples *Don't sneeze more than you can help* and *Sneeze as little as you can help.* Fowler, in an uncharacteristically weak and rambling article (1926), found this construction indefensible and corrected the examples to *Don't sneeze more than you must* and *Sneeze as little as you can.* These emendations are unexceptionable in themselves, but correcting idiom on the grounds of logic is a futile exercise.

3 help + to-infinitive. The construction *help someone to do something* (as in *He helped me to dig out my driveway*) has been shortened since the time of Shakespeare to *help someone do something* (*He helped me dig out my driveway*). Shakespeare used both constructions, omitting *to* when *help* is itself preceded by *to*: *The day will come that thou shalt wish for me To help thee curse this poisonous bunch-backed toad—Richard III* I.iii.247. The reluctance to repeat *to* accounts for some but not all of the following modern examples, which are taken from several varieties of English: (*to* omitted) *The purpose is as much to help the actors discover their roles as to work out cinematically-effective moves—Daily Telegraph*, 1970 / *I had helped her carry it to her bedroom—*Garrison Keillor, AmE 1986 / *Mandy helped him choose something for Claire—*C. K. Stead, NewZE 1986 / *When he is done he instructs Ria to help him pull the wire tight—*S. Johnson, AusE 1990 / *Twice she had asked him to help her attach her stockings to her garter straps while she combed her hair or did her nails—*fiction website, AmE 2005 [*OEC*] / (*to* included) *The levees were helping to aggravate the problem they were meant to solve—New Yorker*, 1987 / *His words helped me to laugh and feel very pretty—*fiction website, AmE 2003 [*OEC*] / (*to* repeated) *If a male employee asks for time off to stay at home with his sick wife to help to look after her and the kids, the affiliative manager agrees—Harvard Business Review*, 1976 / *She allowed Pearl to help her to stack up her hair—*Iris Murdoch, 1983 / *This scheme aims to help us to continue working later in our lives by eliminating age discrimination—*business website, BrE 2003 [*OEC*]. There does not seem to be any distinction in preferences between AmE and BrE or the other major varieties of English.

hence. For the use of *from hence, see* FROM WHENCE, FROM HENCE.

hendiadys, pronounced hen-**diy**-uh-dis, is derived from a Greek phrase meaning 'one by means of two'. It is a figure of speech in which a single complex idea is expressed by two words connected by a conjunction (usually *and*), for example *nice and easy, good and ready*.

he or she *see* GENDER-NEUTRALITY.

her should not be used as part of the coordinated (i.e. multiple) subject of a clause in standard English, although the use is found in some regional and dialect usage: ☒ *Her and Kitty didn't have much to do with each other anymore—*N. Virtue, 1990.

here. The type *this here friend of mine* and *these here bicycles* is confined to uneducated speech, but *here* placed after the noun is standard: *your friend here / these bicycles here.*

hereby, herewith. These two formal words are the strongest survivors of a group of words that also includes *herein, hereof, hereto, heretofore,* and *hereunder,* and even they are restricted to the contexts of legal and business correspondence or to humorous imitations of them: *I hereby promise never to smoke again / Herewith I enclose a cheque to cover my subscription.* The other words are mainly confined to legal language and are rapidly being forced out in the interests of *plain English.

here is, here are. The normal agreement rules apply in most cases, i.e. *Here is* [or *Here's*] *my ticket* and *Here are my tickets.* However, in spontaneous speech a sentence such as *Here's some flowers for you* is idiomatic and acceptable.

hero has the plural form *heroes.*

heroin, heroine. Both words are pronounced the same way, **her**-oh-in. The first is the drug and the second is the principal woman in a novel, play, etc. Despite their closeness of form and pronunciation, they generally manage to stay out of each other's way, but occasionally *heroine* is wrongly used for *heroin*, as in the unintentionally comical *The aim is to help heroine addicts break their habit.*

hers. This possessive pronoun, as used in *The blame is not hers but mine*, is written without an apostrophe. *Hers* is wrongly used in the following example and should be replaced by *her*: ☒ *I was checking both hers and my email.* (The error is obvious if the sentence is simplified by the removal of *and my*.)

herself, himself, itself. These pronouns have two primary roles, (1) as reflexives (*He was talking about himself* / *Mary was looking at herself in the mirror* / *He made himself a cup of coffee*), and (2) to emphasize a person (or animal) denoted by a noun or pronoun (*The supervisor herself called* / *The lock itself is still working*). *Himself* is still used as a pronoun applying to everyone, i.e. to both sexes, despite the weakening of this role with the simple pronoun *he*. This is probably because the alternative *himself or herself* is rather cumbersome, while the gender-neutral *themself* is not widely accepted: *None of us was willing to commit himself to a clear-cut opinion*—R. Linder, 1955 / *In this way the casual viewer . . . is liable to come away with the impression that here is an anti-Semite attempting to denazify himself*—*Daily Telegraph*, 1970 / *This problem faced by the teacher who sees himself as deliverer of prepacked information is admirably expressed by Caldwell Cook*—H. Pluckrose, 1987 / *The investigator himself may not know whether these effects have occurred*—A. Ashworth, 1992.

hesitance, hesitancy, hesitation. All three words are first recorded in English in the early 17c, and the story

since then has been one of advancement for *hesitation* and of sharp retreat for the other two, especially for *hesitance* although this occurs occasionally. There is a residual distinction between *hesitancy* and *hesitation*; the first denotes a tendency, whereas the second denotes a fact or action (and occurs in the plural): (hesitancy, hesitance) *He understood the hesitancy of many landlords to rent to male rather than female students*—*Daily Colonist* (Victoria, B.C.), 1973 / *An examination of the client's hesitance, however, indicates that he is not at all sure about the terminology and that he may simply be echoing the wording of the charge*—J. Citron, 1989 / *He was reluctant to begin and his hesitancy made her look questioningly at him*—T. Hayden, 1991 / (hesitation) *He had driven the Deputy Director . . . half mad with his hesitation, his recycled arguments for accepting and not accepting*—D. Bloodworth, 1978 / *Women have trouble communicating in a 'male' language and the result is hesitations, false starts, and so on*—D. Cameron, 1992. *Hesitation* but not *hesitancy* is used in the idiomatic phrases *not have a moment's hesitation* and *without hesitation*: *When Granpa asked me what I wanted for my fifteenth birthday I replied without a moment's hesitation, 'My own barrow.'*—Jeffrey Archer, 1991 / *When in 1974 I was flattered by an invitation to make a T V appearance as the Dimbleby lecturer, I accepted without hesitation*—A. Goodman, 1993 / *He answered clearly and without hesitation*—business website, 2004 [*OEC*].

hew has the past form *hewed* and alternative past participles *hewn* or *hewed*. In its literary meaning 'to chop or cut' *hewn* is much commoner in BrE and AmE, especially in passive constructions and when used adjectivally (e.g. *roughly hewn*). In the largely American phrase *hew to* (= adhere to), *hewed* is the preferred form for both perfect and passive. Examples: (hewn) *The planks, or 'chynes', were cut to size for me, so I can't claim to have hewn the wood myself* —Robert Leggatt, BrE 2005 / *By the end there is a rickety, roughly hewn bridge between them*— *Guardian*, BrE 2004 / (hewed) *After the tree had been chopped down the part to be hewed was cleared of limbs and also peeled*—OEC, undated / *But in the general election, McCain has hewed closer to Penn's advice*—*Time Magazine*, 2008.

hiccup has inflected forms *hiccuped, hiccuping*. The spelling *hiccough*, formed by false association with *cough*, has nothing to recommend it.

hierarchic, hierarchical. *Hierarchical* is 40 times more common, while *hierarchic* is a rather rare, self-conscious choice.

hike, meaning 'an increase (in prices, wages, etc.)', was first recorded in 1931 in the US and has long since spread to become a staple of the informal language of British journalism. It is worth remembering, however, that some newspapers' style guides proscribe it absolutely: *The oil industry is still accommodating itself to its new size following the* 1979 *price hike*—D. Hedley, 1986 / *An announcement by Argentina's President Carlos Menem rescinding a planned threefold hike in the duties on paper imported for book production was greeted with delight by hundreds of publishers*—*Bookseller*, 1993 / *He warned that back-to-back hikes in May and June were a 'very real possibility', particularly if consumer price inflation comes in at 3 per cent or above in April*—*Irish News*, 2007.

him should not be used as part of the coordinated (i.e. multiple) subject of a clause in standard English, although the use is found in some regional and dialect usage: ✗ *Him and Carol lived too high, kept buying stuff they couldn't nohow afford*—Truman Capote, 1965.

him or her *see* GENDER-NEUTRALITY.

himself *see* HERSELF.

hindsight. At first used to mean 'the backsight of a rifle', since the later part of the 19c it has been used in an abstract sense 'wisdom or knowledge after the event', especially in the phrase *in* (or *with*) *hindsight*: *With hindsight, it was probably the best thing that could have happened to him, otherwise he would no doubt have ended up as a Bomber Pilot*— J. Beech, 1989 / *In hindsight, if I had been aware of the exact nature of the Foreign Legion, . . . I would have been much more hesitant about joining*—C. Jennings, 1990.

hinge. The present participle is better spelt *hingeing* to make explicit the sound of the soft g, but the *OEC* data shows that *hinging* is much more often used, despite its slightly odd look.

hippo, hippopotamus. The respective plural forms are *hippos* and *hippopotamuses*.

his. For *his or her see* GENDER-NEUTRALITY. For the use of *his* to refer back to *one, see* ONE.

Hispanic. In the US *Hispanic* is the standard accepted term, as adjective and noun, to refer to Spanish-speaking people living there. Other, more specific, terms such as *Latino* and *Chicano* are also used where occasion demands: *For some students, especially Hispanic females, perceived gender roles affect career choice*—OEC, AmE 2004 / *About 20 percent of the Bay Area market is composed of Hispanics*—OEC, AmE 2000. *See also* CHICANO.

hisself is non-standard for *himself*, and arises from the tendency to regard *self* as a noun and to place possessive pronouns and adjectives in front of it (e.g. *his very self*).

historic, historical. Both words are used to mean 'of or concerning history, belonging to the past rather than the present', but *historical* is the more objective word denoting something that happened in the past, whereas *historic* describes not simply what belongs to the past but what has an important role in the past, i.e. it means 'famous or important with regard to history'. A *historical* treaty is one that took place (as opposed to one that is fictitious); a *historic* treaty is one that is of great importance in history (as opposed to one that is insignificant). *Historic* is often used with reference to buildings and monuments: *The president of the Historic Houses Association . . . plays down too much euphoria over the Chancellor's proposed substitution of inheritance tax for capital transfer tax—Daily Telegraph*, 1986 / *After visiting the Hayward Gallery I spent a half-hour just gazing along the river line, the historic buildings sharp in the clear, cold, sunny air—*D. M. Thomas, 1990. When the meanings are confused, it is usually *historic* that is used when *historical* would be more appropriate: *Extinct volcanoes are those that have not erupted in historic time, whereas active volcanoes have been seen to erupt—*M. A. Summerfield, 1991 / *It may involve the use of relevant historic documents—*R. Brooks, 1993.

historic present is the technical term to denote narrative that is put in the present tense for dramatic effect, although it is describing events in the past. It is a device beloved of presenters of radio or TV history programmes. For example: *She had no notion of how welcome she would be. But Raymond **opens** the door before she can touch the bell, and he **hugs** her around the shoulders and **kisses** her twice—*A. Munro, 1989.

hither, meaning 'to or toward this place', is an ancient word that existed in Old English. In current English it is restricted, except for formal or archaic uses, to a number of fixed phrases: *hither and thither* or *hither and yon* (= in various directions), and *come-hither*, used adjectivally to mean 'enticing, flirtatious', as in *a come-hither look*.

HIV. Since the abbreviation stands for 'human immunodeficiency *virus*', the word *virus* is strictly redundant in the phrase *HIV virus*, although this is now established usage.

hoard, horde. A *hoard* is a large stock or store of money or accumulated objects (in archaeology, for example); a *horde* is a large collection of people or animals, and is used in the singular or plural, often disparagingly: *A horde of football fans attempt to lure into their bedrooms a pair of tarts by arrangement with the pimpish day porter—Daily Telegraph*, 1976 / *I am happy for there to be a zillion blurry images of me doing my Tesco shopping, among the hordes of fellow citizens, if it helps catch terrorists or shoplifters—Times*, 2007.

When the two words are confused, it is usually *hoard* that is incorrectly used: ⊠ *At night they hog the road dropping off hoards of tourists at the go-go bars—Pattaya Mail*, 2000.

hoe *verb* has inflected forms *hoes, hoed, hoeing*.

hoi polloi. The normal construction is *the hoi polloi*, meaning 'the masses, the common people'. The fact that *hoi* in the original Greek expression (literally 'the many') already means 'the' is therefore ignored; objection to this now seems pedantic, is countered by the weight of usage (Dryden, Byron, and others, not to mention W. S. Gilbert), and itself ignores the need for naturalness in

English, since omission of *the* would usually be awkward. Examples: (with *the*) *Nothing like a yacht to ensure your privacy and not having to mix with the hoi polloi*—Jeffrey Archer, 1991 / (without *the*) *Seat-holders were let in through side doors while hoi polloi had to come in through the front in the hope of getting what they could*—J. Munson, 1991 / *We learn . . . that by appearing for a photo call and chat with hacks in a local pub, the second in line to the throne is in touch with hoi polloi*—*Sunday Herald*, 2007.

hoist, meaning 'to raise or haul up', has past and past participle forms *hoisted*. Historically *hoist* is a participial form of an earlier verb *hoise* (with the same meaning), and it survives in this form in the expression *hoist with one's own petard*, meaning literally 'blown up by one's own bomb' and hence 'adversely affected by one's own bad schemes for others'.

holey, meaning 'full of holes', is spelt *-ey* to distinguish it in writing and print from the adjective *holy* meaning 'sacred'.

Holland *see* NETHERLANDS, LOW COUNTRIES, HOLLAND, DUTCH.

holy grail. In Arthurian legend the *holy grail*, the cup from which Christ is said to have drunk at the Last Supper, is the object of long quests by dedicated knights. In allusive use it should stand for something of great value that is sought with great difficulty (and usually not found). It should not be used as an alternative for much more mundane notions such as everyday targets and objectives: ⊠ *So what are the benefits and how does a company achieve the Holy Grail?*—*Lloyd's List*, 2007.

home. 1 As an adverb, *home* has many idiomatic uses as in *come home* and *go*

home, see someone home, drive a nail (or *point*) *home*, etc. When the meaning is 'in his or her home' the British preference is to use *at home* (*He stayed at home* / *Are they at home?*) whereas AmE prefers *home* by itself (*He stayed home* / *Are they home?*).

2 As a noun, *home* means 'the place where one lives', and when referring to the building is distinguished from *house* in designating residential function as well as physical existence: *The well secured home probably includes an entryphone, grilles, . . . and an alarm*—*Financial Times*, 1982. It is usual to say *in the privacy of one's own home* rather than *one's own house*, and estate agents tend to prefer *home* as having a more personal sound. In AmE, *home* is used much more freely than in BrE *house* would be used: *In Beverly Hills and Bel Air, we saw the homes* (*never called houses*) *of Jane Withers, Greer Garson, and Barbra Streisand*—*Guardian*, 1973.

home in on, hone in on. Which of these alternatives is correct? *A teaching style which homes in on/ hones in on what is important for each pupil*? Where you live will affect your view. US Editors and readers may well think *home in* a mistake, while the opposite applies in Britain. Who is right? *Home in* is a metaphor, from *home* used as a verb to describe how a missile or aircraft is directed to a target (e.g. *The other helicopter located the dinghy by homing in on the bleeping of the emergency distress call*). To *hone* means 'to sharpen a knife with a whetstone', or 'to improve a skill or talent'. Across the English-speaking world, *home in* is about 70% more frequent than *hone in*. In AmE, *home in* makes up just over half of occurrences, but in BrE the picture is different. Of the total BrE pie, 85% is *home in*. *ODO* calls *hone* a mistake. The *OED*, however, does not. On the other side of the pond,

MWCDEU suggests that it 'seems to have become established in American usage'. The *hone in* variant has been around for nearly half a century and is used in many parts of the English-speaking world. Some dictionaries list it without comment; others warn against it. If you use it, you should bear in mind that some people will consider it a mistake; others will reach the same conclusion if you use *home in*. To avoid the problem, you could use *focus on, concentrate on, zero in on*, or any other synonym that suits your context.

homely. The connotations of this word as applied to a person (usually a woman) are favourable in BrE, in which it means 'simple, unpretentious' and disparaging in AmE, in which it means 'unattractive, dowdy': *Homely and welcoming, owners Doug and Karen Richards have gone out of their way to ensure visitors are immediately put at their ease—Cornish Guardian, 2005 / A homely woman with an apron on answers the door—A. Drai, AmE 2002.*

homepage, home page. 'The initial page displayed to a visitor of a website or intranet site, typically containing introductory information and links to other parts of the site'. There is no consensus about writing this as two words or one. The *OED, ODO*, and *NODWE* give it as two, as does Merriam-Webster online and the AP stylebook. But many people write it as one, as does the *Guardian* style guide, and the *OEC* data shows use in practice is evenly split. If you are not bound by specific editorial guidelines or house style, you can please yourself, but perhaps writing it as two words is the safer option for the time being.

homo-, homoeo-. These two prefixes are derived from the Greek words *homos* meaning 'same' and *homoios* meaning 'of the same kind', and this difference in meaning is reflected in the English

words formed on them, e.g. *homosexuality* denotes sexual attraction towards the *same sex* and *homoeopathy* denotes treatment of disease by using small doses of drugs that have the *same kind* of effect as the disease itself. Words in *homo-* are pronounced either hom- or hohm-, whereas words in *homoeo-* are more usually pronounced hom-. In AmE, *homeo-* is the more usual spelling.

homogeneity, meaning 'being of the same kind', is traditionally pronounced -ji-**nee**-i-ti rather than -ji-**nay**-i-ti, i.e. with the stressed syllable having the sound of *bee*, not *bay*.

homogeneous, homogenous. *Homogeneous* is pronounced with the stress on the third syllable and means 'of the same kind': *The most common way of grouping was to sort the children by ability . . . and to make the groups as homogeneous as possible—R. Alexander, 1992.* The word *homogenous* (stressed on the second syllable) was formerly used in biology to mean 'having a common descent', but has been largely superseded by *homogenetic*, so as to become a loose cannon colliding frequently with *homogeneous*: ⊠ *The community was not homogenous, but made up of a multitude of different groups with different attitudes and beliefs—Guardian, 1989. Homogeneous* is still the better word to use, but many dictionaries now recognize *homogenous* as a legitimate variant spelling of the same meaning.

homograph, homonym, homophone. *Homonym* is a generic term for a word having the same spelling or sound as another word but a different meaning. Homonyms are either *homographs*, words written the same way (e.g. *bat* denoting either an implement or an animal and *entrance* meaning either 'a way into a place' or 'to beguile') or *homophones*, words pronounced the same way but (usually) not spelt the same way (e.g. *pair* and *pear*, *hoard* and *horde*, *right* and *write*).

homosexual, pronounced either hom- or hohm-, is still the term often used in more formal contexts, although *gay* has become the usual, non-judgemental word in everyday language, and far outnumbers it in the *OEC* data.

Hon. is an abbreviation of (1) *honourable*, especially in parliamentary contexts (*The Hon. Member for Lincoln*) and as a courtesy title given to sons and daughters of members of the nobility and to civic dignitaries such as the Lord Mayor of London (the correct form is with the first name in full, e.g. *The Hon. James Brown*), and (2) *honorary*, as in *The Hon. Secretary*. For full details see *Debrett's Correct Form* or other manuals dealing with forms of address.

hone in on *see* HOME IN ON, HONE IN ON.

honeyed is recommended in preference to *honied* for both literal meanings (*honeyed figs*) and figurative meanings (*spoke in honeyed tones*).

honorarium, a voluntary payment made for professional services that are provided nominally without charge, is pronounced with the third syllable as in *air*. The plural form is more usually *honoraria* than *honorariums*, because the word itself is rather formal, but both forms are correct.

honour, honourable are spelt *-our* in BrE and *honor, honorable* in AmE.

hoof has a plural from *hooves* (more usual) or *hoofs*.

hope. Apart from the expression *to live in hopes*, the use of the plural noun in phrases such as *to be in hopes, in the*

hopes that, etc., is more characteristic of AmE than of BrE: *He never said a kind word to them, and they worked like dogs in hopes of hearing one*—Garrison Keillor, 1989. The normal BrE equivalent is *in the hope of* (or *in the hope that*): *Clerks double-book their barristers in the hope that one of the cases will be settled before getting to court*—*Economist*, 1983.

hopefully. 1 This has been used since the 17c as a straightforward adverb of manner: *As lovers do, as lovers will, they travelled hopefully to Paris*—Maurice Gee, 1985 / *Out on the corridor, Nurse Bodkin was hovering hopefully near a suspended piece of mistletoe*—E. McGrath, 1990. According to the evidence of the *OED*, after an isolated use in 1932, the controversial use of *hopefully* as a sentence adverb mushroomed in the 1960s, first in AmE and almost immediately afterwards in BrE: *We asked her when she expected to move into her new apartment, and she answered, 'Hopefully on Tuesday.'*—*New Yorker*, 1965 / *I want a bigger range to choose from and hopefully this role will help me*—S. Stone, 1989 / *He is buried with his mammy and hopefully they are together*—*Sunday Mirror*, 2007.

2 In its controversial use, *hopefully* is what is known as a 'sentence adverb'. Sentence adverbs express the speaker's attitude to what they are saying or writing, and comment on the whole clause or sentence, not on a specific word. Like *thankfully*, *hopefully* stands apart from other sentence adverbs such as *clearly, frankly, honestly, sadly, unfortunately*, etc. They can be resolved grammatically into phrases such as *it is clear / sad / unfortunate that* or *to speak frankly / honestly, to be frank / honest with you*. *Hopefully* cannot be resolved in the same way, and so it is viewed as anomalous and irregular. It is also accused of being ambiguous: allegedly the Robert Louis Stevenson quotation

'It is a better thing to travel hopefully than to arrive' is now ambiguous because of the modern use of *hopefully*. The argument based on ambiguity, however, is less than compelling; sentences of the type *They are working hopefully towards a solution of the problem* will normally be clear enough either from intonation (in speech), from where *hopefully* is placed in the sentence, or from context. For more on this issue, *see* SENTENCE ADVERBS.

3 These uses of *hopefully* and *thankfully* are well established and are here to stay but strong rearguard actions continue to be fought over them. Bear in mind that *hopefully*, in particular, can produce irritation and disgruntlement in readers.

horde *see* HOARD.

horrid. *Horrid* may be seen as the least emphatic in a series of adjectives meaning 'disagreeable' which proceed with increasing severity to *horrible* and *horrifying*. *Horrendous* and *horrific*, once stronger still than any of these, have lost much of their power through overuse in popular fiction, film, and broadcasting. In older literature, references to *horrid spears, mountain peaks, thickets*, etc., reflect a now obsolete meaning 'bristling, shaggy, rough'.

hospitable. The traditional pronunciation, still shown in the *OED*, with the stress on the first syllable, has given way to second-syllable stress.

hospitalize, meaning 'to send or admit (a patient) to hospital', first recorded in 1901, is regarded with some suspicion by many editors, especially in BrE, but is standard in AmE.

host *verb*. This is first recorded in the 15c, and is not, as many think, a modern back-formation from the noun. For this reason, objection to the use of *host* in its

more modern meanings of (1) 'to act as host or compère of (a television show)' and (2) 'to organize an event to which others are invited and make all the arrangements for them' is somewhat misconceived. It may nevertheless be prudent in some quarters to use the readily available alternatives such as *present / introduce* and *stage / organize*, and others which a decent thesaurus can suggest. *See also* FRONT.

Hottentot, the origin of which is not known for certain, is first recorded in the late 17c as a name applied by white Europeans to the Khoikhoi group of peoples of South Africa and Namibia. It is now regarded as offensive when referring to people and should always be avoided in favour of *Khoikhoi* or the names of the particular peoples, such as the *Nama*. The only acceptable modern use for *Hottentot* is in the names of animals and plants, such as the *Hottentot cherry*.

house *see* HOME.

how come? This colloquial, originally American, phrase, meaning 'how is it (or did it happen) that?', first noted in the mid-19c, has long since become international: *'How come you're still thin?' she asked with amusement*—A. Munro, 1989.

however. 1 When *ever* is being used as an intensive after the interrogative adverb *how*, as in *How ever did you do it?*, the two words should always be written separately.

2 *However*, in the meaning 'nevertheless', has many possible positions in a clause. If it is put at the beginning, it should be followed by a comma: *I should be angry if the situation were not so farcical. However, I had a certain delight in some of the talk*—William Golding, 1980. This use should be distinguished from *however* used at the beginning of a sentence as an ordinary adverb meaning 'no matter how', which is not followed by a comma: *However confident he may be that he has outgeneralled a woman, a man likes to have reassurance on the point from a knowledgeable third party*—P. G. Wodehouse, 1973. In mid-sentence, *however* is preceded and followed by commas. The choice of position depends on the word being emphasized, which is normally the one that comes immediately before *however*: *Even with the stimulatory measures, however, the deficit does not seem likely to be excessive in the years to come*—*Times*, 1981 / *That, however, is not the point of this essay*—weblog, BrE 2005 [*OEC*]. It is preceded by a comma when it occurs at the end of a sentence: *The presence of a girl in a group of tipsy young men keeps them in check, however*—*Lancashire Life*, 1978 / *None of this is quite as complicated as it sounds, however*—computing website, AmE 2005.

3 There are two erroneous uses to guard against: (1) *however* as a simple substitute for *but*: ✖ *They came for dinner, however they left before ten* and (2) a sentence allowed to run on when *however* should have a capital letter and start a new sentence: ✖ *Resources for doing so are not available, however, the matter will be reviewed at a later date.*

hullo *see* HELLO.

human, humane, humanitarian.
1 The notion that *human* should only be used as an adjective and that *human being* should be used for the noun is found in some older usage books (though not Fowler, 1926) but is not supported by the weight of usage. Many examples of *human* as a noun will be found in *OED*2, to which may be added: *There rose before his inward sight the picture of a human at once heroic and sick*—William Golding, 1954 / *The*

human got in and, still holding the box with exaggerated care, placed it on its knees—T. Pratchett, 1992 / *Sorry, dear, I forgot that you humans need to eat every day*—J. Slater, 2003.

2 As an adjective, *human* is used predominantly as a classifying word in non-judgemental contexts, qualifying words such as *body, eye, life, mind, nature, race, rights*, and *voice*. The difference between *human* and *humane* in their judgemental meanings is that *human* denotes a generalized quality that distinguishes (actual or ideal) human behaviour from that of non-humans, whereas *humane* denotes a quality as it affects treatment of other people: (human) *When he pushed the postern closed behind him she stepped back into the gateway, eyeing him with very human caution*—J. Byrne, 1993 / *To highlight his human qualities, Kong was given more expressive features than a normal gorilla*—*Times*, 2004 / (humane) *This is only a temporary solution and there have been many attempts to organise more humane working systems*—W. T. Singleton, 1989 / *We must ... seek a more humane way to deal with asylumseekers that keeps families together*—*Morning Star*, 2007. Note, however, that *humane* is used with reference to animals as well as people: *There is a range of attitudes including the position of those who can accept whaling in principle if it can be made more humane in practice*—*Animal Welfare*, 1992 / *A dog's ear infection was so severe that the only humane option was for him to be put to sleep, a court heard*—*South Wales Echo*, 2007.

3 *Humanitarian* is a 19c word and was originally a noun used in theological contexts. From the 1850s it has had the adjectival meaning 'practising humanity or humane action', and it is a common word in modern contexts of international aid and support: *Reports from Jordan indicated that Iraqi businessmen fearful* *of incurring penalties were no longer prepared even to transport food and essential humanitarian supplies to Iraq—* Keesings, 1990. In more recent use it has developed a wider meaning relating to wars and catastrophes, as in *humanitarian crisis, disaster*, etc., where the sense is 'requiring humanitarian action', in effect the opposite of the original meaning. Usage is stretched too far if it is treated virtually as equivalent to *humane*: ✖ *A legal war is not necessarily a humanitarian war.*

humankind. First recorded in the 17c as an occasional variant of *mankind*, *humankind* has gathered strength in the 20c, largely because it serves well as a gender-neutral term for the human race: *One single species—humankind—is putting the Earth at risk—BBC Wildlife*, 1990.

humour is spelt -*our* in BrE and *humor* in AmE, and the same distinction applies to the derivative *humourless / humorless*. *Humorous* and *humorist*, however, are spelt the same way in both varieties.

hyaena *see* HYENA.

hybrid formations are words made up of elements belonging to different languages. They vary widely in the degree of irregularity they represent, from the routine addition of English prefixes and suffixes to stems from French (*bemuse, besiege, genuineness*) or vice versa (*breakage, disbelieve, readable*) to the merging of major word elements with different origins, as with *bureaucracy* (18c, from French *bureau* and Greek -*kratia* 'rule'), *coastal* (19c, from English *coast* and the Latin-derived suffix -*al*: *see* LOST CAUSES), *gullible* (19c, from English *gull* 'to deceive' and the Latin-derived suffix -*ible*), *speedometer* (20c, from English *speed* and the Greek-derived combining form -*ometer*), and *television* (20c, from Greek *tēle-* 'far' and *vision*, a

word of Latin origin). Some so-called blends and portmanteau words are in effect hybrids, e.g. *breathalyser* (20c, from English *breath* and Greek-derived *analyse*) and *workaholic* (20c, from English *work* and *alcoholic*, a word derived via French from Arabic). In a language as eclectic in its origins as modern English the formation of such hybrids is natural and inevitable, and it is difficult to discern a sustainable principle behind the occasional objections that are made in the letter columns of the broadsheet newspapers to formations of this kind.

hyena is generally spelt -*e*-, but -*ae*- is still correct, if old-fashioned. The plural is *hy(a)enas*.

hygiene, hygienic are spelt -*ie*- and pronounced respectively **hiy**-jeen and hiy-**jee**-nik in BrE, but usually hiy-**je**-nik in AmE. The Greek word from which these words are ultimately derived is the first word (an adjective) of *hugieinē technē*; 'art of health'.

hyper-, hypo-. These prefixes are derived from Greek prepositions *huper* and *hupo* meaning 'over, above' and 'under, below' respectively. In English, *hyperthermia* means 'abnormally high body temperature' and *hypothermia* means 'abnormally low body temperature'; *hypertension* means 'abnormally high blood pressure' and *hypotension* means 'abnormally low blood pressure'. Both prefixes are usually pronounced in the same way (**hiy**-puh), and the meaning may have to be clarified by the context in which they are used. In other words the prefix does not correspond so closely to sense; for example, *hypochondria* means 'excessive anxiety about one's health' (suggesting *hyper-* rather than *hypo-*) and is derived from a Greek word meaning 'the soft parts of the body below the ribs', where such feelings were thought to arise. *Hypercritical* duly means 'excessively critical', but *hypocritical* and *hypocrisy* (pronounced hip-, not hiyp-) are derived from a Greek word *hupokrisis* meaning 'acting a part, pretence'.

hyperbola, hyperbole. The second, pronounced hiy-**per**-buh-li, is a figure of speech involving an exaggerated statement that is not meant to be taken literally, e.g. *a thousand apologies*. It should not be confused with *hyperbola*, pronounced hiy-**per**-buh-luh, a term in geometry, the plural of which is generally *hyperbolas*, though *hyperbolae* is also found. *Hyperbolae* is occasionally used by mistake for *hyperbole*, e.g. ✖ *Classical academics who are not generally prone to hyperbolae referred to him as 'undoubtedly the greatest general of his race and probably of antiquity'*—weblog, 2005.

hypercorrection is a modern (20c) term for the application of a grammatical rule, especially in sensitive areas of usage, in a case where it is not appropriate. Examples are (1) the use of a pronoun form *I, he,* etc., instead of *me, him,* etc., e.g. ✖ *It is time for you and I to have a talk* on the analogy of *It is time you and I had a talk*, and (2) use of *as* instead of *like* as a preposition, e.g. ✖ *He talks as a fool*, influenced by the preference for *as* when used as a conjunction: *He talks as a fool talks*.

hyphen. In print, a hyphen is half the length of a dash; unlike the dash, it has the purpose of linking words and word elements rather than separating them. Beyond this apparently simple rule, in the world of real usage, lies chaos (Fowler's word, 1926), especially when use of the hyphen is governed by contextual discretion rather than clear-cut rules. The following paragraphs describe the main uses of the hyphen, beginning with the more routine and ending with the least straightforward:

1 To join two or more words so as to form a single expression, e.g. *co-worker, dry-clean, get-at-able*, and words having a grammatical relationship which form a compound, e.g. *load-bearing, punch-drunk*. The routine use of the hyphen to connect two nouns to form a compound word is diminishing in favour of one-word forms, especially when the elements are of one syllable and present no problems of form or pronunciation, as in *birdsong, eardrum*, and *playgroup*, and in some longer formations such as *figurehead, nationwide*, and even (despite the clash of vowels) *radioisotope*, which is entered in this form in the *OED*. However, a hyphen is often necessary to avoid a pile-up of consonant or vowel sounds in a word, e.g. *co-opt, fast-talk, pile-up, take-off*. In the area of choice between spelling as one word with hyphen and as two words, the second option is now widely favoured, especially when the first noun acts as a straightforward modifier of the second, as in *filling station* and *house plant*. Different house styles in publishing and journalism have different preferences in many of these cases.

2 To clarify the meaning of a compound that is normally spelt as separate words, when it is used attributively (before a noun): *an up-to-date record / the well-known man*; but *the record is up to date / The man is well known*; also (with no ambiguity) *prettily furnished rooms*.

3 To join a prefix to a name or designation, e.g. *anti-Christian, ex-husband*. There is no satisfactory way of dealing with the type *ex-Prime Minister*, in which the second element is itself a compound, except to rely on the tendency of readers to use their knowledge of the world to choose the natural meaning, i.e. 'former Prime Minister' (which makes sense) rather than 'Minister who was once Prime' (which is nonsense). A second hyphen, e.g. *ex-Prime-Minister*, is not recommended.

h

4 To avoid ambiguity by separating a prefix from the main word, e.g. to distinguish *re-cover* (= provide with a new cover) from *recover* and *re-sign* (= sign again) from *resign*.

5 To represent a common second element in all but the last word of a list, e.g. *two-, three-, or fourfold*.

6 To clarify meanings in groups of words when the associations are not clear or when several possible associations may be inferred. This is the area of usage that involves the greatest initiative and discretion on the part of the writer, and it is also the area to which Fowler devoted most of his attention. The best way of offering guidance is to give examples in which careful hyphenation prevents misunderstanding: *The library is reducing its purchase of hard-covered books* / *Twenty-odd people came to the meeting* / *The group was warned about the dangers of extra-marital sex* / *There will be special classes for French-speaking children*.

7 The hyphen is also used in printing to divide a word that comes at the end of a line and is too long to fit completely. The principle here is a different one, because the hyphen does not form a permanent part of the spelling. Printers have sets of rules about where to divide words; for example, between consonants as in *splen-dour* and between vowels as in *appreci-ate*, and words of one syllable should not be divided at all, even quite long ones such as *queues* and *rhythm*.

hypo- *see* HYPER-, HYPO-.

hypocritical, hypercritical *see* HYPER-, HYPO-.

hyponym, hypernym. In linguistics, a *hyponym* of a given term is a more specific term in the same domain; e.g. *spaniel* is a hyponym of *dog*, and *bag*, *box*, and *cup* are hyponyms of *container*. A *hypernym* is a more general term, so that *dog* is the hypernym of *spaniel*, and *container* of *bag*, *box*, and *cup*. Because the two words can sound the same in speech, the alternative term *superordinate* is often used instead of *hypernym*.

hypothecate, hypothesize. The better word for 'to form a hypothesis' is *hypothesize*, and it is used with or without an object or with a *that*-clause: *Quick to learn, quick to grasp concepts and to hypothesize, they need the best minds to provide appropriate support and challenge*—J. Spink, 1989 / *It was then decided to hypothesize a particular market situation for a single product line*—C. Tomkins, 1991 / *I hypothesise that if I move and turn the lamp in a particular way I will get the result I want*—W. T. Singleton, 1989. *Hypothecate*, which is sometimes used in this meaning, primarily means 'to give as a pledge or security' (from Greek *hupothēkē*; 'deposit') especially in the context of taxation in which the money raised is used for a special purpose: *An alternative scheme for financing the NHS involves the removing of finance from general taxation and the introduction of a health stamp or hypothecated tax*—P. Hardy, 1991. Use of *hypothecate* to mean 'hypothesize' is recognized by dictionaries, but may confuse some readers.

hypothesis, meaning 'something proposed as a basis for reasoning', has the plural form hypotheses, pronounced -seez.

I. 1 *I*, the first person pronoun representing the speaker (or writer), is a shortening of earlier forms *ic, ich, ik*, etc., and has been written as a capital letter at least since the development of printing imposed uniformity in the 15c.

2 Popular preoccupation with the correctness (or hypercorrectness) of *'John and I'* (rather than *'John and me'*) as an answer to questions such as *Who do you mean?* has led to an absurd proliferation of the use of *I* where *me* is correct because the pronoun is governed by a verb or preposition. The best known case, *between you and I*, is discussed at the entry for **between* (section 5). Other types are shown by the following examples: ⊠ *I think she disapproved of Beth and I, just quietly*—S. Johnson, AusE 1990 / ⊠ *'What is it?' asked Lemprière. 'Part of you and I,' said Septimus*—L. Norfolk, 1991 / ⊠ *...after seeing you and I lingering over a late breakfast*—*Chicago Tribune*, 1991. The fallacy of these uses can readily be seen by isolating the pronoun and removing the noun it is paired with in each sentence, e.g. ⊠ *I think she disapproved of I, just quietly*.

i before e. The traditional spelling rule '*i* before *e* except after *c*' should be extended to include the statement 'when the combination is pronounced -ee-', as in *believe, brief, fiend, hygiene, priest, siege*, and in *ceiling, deceive, conceit, receipt, receive*, etc. The extension to the rule is necessary in order to take account of words such as *beige, freight, neighbour, sleigh, veil, vein, weigh* (all pronounced -ay-), *eiderdown, feisty, height,* *heist, kaleidoscope, sleight* (all pronounced -iy-), and words in which the *i* and *e* are pronounced as separate vowels, e.g. *holier, occupier*. This leaves *caffeine, protein*, and *seize* as the most important exceptions to the rule as qualified.

ibid. is a shortening of Latin *ibidem* 'in the same place' and is used principally in printed matter to indicate a reference to a source already mentioned.

-ible *see* -ABLE, -IBLE.

-ic, -ical adjectives. 1 There are three main categories: (1) only an adjective ending in -*ic* is currently used (e.g. *alcoholic, basic, dramatic, linguistic, patriotic, public*), (2) only an adjective ending in -*ical* is currently used (e.g. *chemical, practical, radical*), and (3) adjective ending in -*ic* and -*ical* are both used, often with a difference in meaning (e.g. *classic / classical, comic / comical, economic / economical, historic / historical*) but sometimes with no difference in meaning (e.g. *geographic / geographical, problematic / problematical*). Pairs that represent a difference in meaning are discussed as separate entries. When there is no difference in meaning, choice is often determined by considerations of idiom and sentence rhythm. Assertions relating to regional distinctions (e.g. that -*ic* forms are more common in AmE) lack adequate statistical support.

2 With one exception, all these adjectives, whether they end in -*ic* or -*ical* or both, form adverbs in -*ically* (*basically, dramatically, geometrically, practically*, etc.). The exception is *public*, which has an adverb form *publicly*.

icon, iconic. 1 The original meaning of *icon*, 'a devotional painting on wood of Christ or a saint in Byzantine Christian art', has been all but obscured—except in specialist use or as a vague memory—by modern uses first in the language of media and marketing and then in computing. From the 1950s in America and soon after in Britain, *icon* has acquired an extended meaning of 'a person or thing regarded as a representative symbol, or as worthy of admiration or respect'. The word is often qualified in a way that specifies the relevant domain: in 2000, for example, the press referred to *Hollywood's female gay icons Jodie Foster, Susan Sarandon and Jamie Lee Curtis—Sunday Mail*. Other frequently occurring phrases are *American / cultural / fashion / feminist / rock / and style icon*. This transfer of meaning is analogous to that of *symbol*, which is often still the better word. In computing, an *icon* is familiar in a more physical transfer of meaning as a symbol or graphic representation on a VDU screen of a program or function.

2 As with *symbol* and *symbolic*, the increased use of *icon* has been matched by *iconic*. Previously a word of limited currency in the sense 'relating to or of the nature of an icon', it denoted in particular the conventional style of victorious athletes as depicted in ancient Greek statuary. From the 1970s it has come to be applied predominantly to a person or institution considered to be important or influential in a particular social or cultural context, and collocates with words such as *brand, building, figure, image*, and *status*. It is widely criticized as being overused, particularly in the language of marketing and journalism, and overuse has quickly robbed it of its original impact. A *Guardian* columnist even suggested that '"iconic" has become a synonym for "vaguely familiar if you're particularly interested in that sort of thing"'. Beware therefore of redundant uses in which *iconic* is a meaningless 'filler' that tells the reader nothing because the thing described is familiar enough already (or in need of rather more explanation for the benefit of the ignorant than a vogue word will achieve): *A passenger ferry collided with a pleasure boat under Sydney's iconic harbour bridge yesterday—Independent*, 2007. Even worse is the unintentional absurdity produced by the common phrase *iconic image*, in which the writer seems blithely unaware of what an *icon* originally is: *The opening scene of Ingmar Bergman's 1957 masterpiece is one of the most iconic images in cinema history—Empire*, 2002. An 'iconic image' is equivalent to a 'symbolic symbol' and no one would, in all seriousness, write such a thing. It is not pedantic to insist on this kind of awareness, but respectful of the ways in which precise and graphic old meanings underlie more generalized modern usage.

3 The spelling *ikon* is occasionally used when the meaning is religious (the ikon of Our Lady of Tsarskoe Selo is a sentimental painting of the Virgin with Christ).

-ics. 1 There are a few names of arts or of branches of study that end in -*ic*, of which the most important in general use are *logic, magic, music*, and *rhetoric*. Otherwise the normal ending for terms of this kind is -*ics*: *acoustics, classics, economics, ethics, mathematics, obstetrics, physics*, and many others. (In some cases a singular noun exists with a different meaning: a *classic* is something of acknowledged fame or quality, an *ethic* is a set of moral principles, and a *statistic* is an item of statistical data.) Although these are plural forms, they take singular verbs when they are the name of a subject and a plural verb when they are used generally: compare *Economics is her main interest* and *The economics of the foreign aid are extremely complex.*

2 Another class of nouns in *-ics* corresponds to adjectives in *-ic* or *-ical*, e.g. *heroics, hysterics, tactics*, and these are treated as regular plurals, e.g. *Heroics are out of place.*

idea. *Idea* is followed by *of* + noun (or verbal noun) when the meaning is 'notion, concept' (*It's not my idea of having a good time*) and by a *to*-infinitive when after a construction with the verb *be* (*The idea is to get the ball in the hole*).

idiom in the context of language has two principal meanings: (1) the manner of expression that characterizes a language, and (2) a group of words that has a meaning not deducible from the individual words. The first can therefore be seen as the sum total of all the instances of the second. Examples of idioms in the concrete second meaning are *over the moon, under the weather, might as well*, and *hard put to it.* The adjective *idiomatic* draws on both these meanings in denoting what is natural and customary in the use of a language; as Fowler recognized (1926), 'grammar and idiom are separate categories', so that a mode of expression can be idiomatic or grammatical or both or neither. Fowler's various examples are still valid and useful: *It was not me* and *There is heaps of material* are idiomatic but ungrammatical, *The distinction leaps to the eyes* and *a hardly earned income* are grammatical but unidiomatic, *He was promoted captain* and *She all but capsized* are both grammatical and idiomatic, and *You would not go for to do it* is neither.

idiosyncrasy, meaning 'an individual's particular habit or mode of behaviour', is derived from the Greek words

idio- 'own, peculiar', *sun* 'together', and *krasis* 'mixture' and so its etymological meaning is 'a peculiar mixing together'. It is wrong to spell it *-cracy*, as if it were connected with words such as *democracy* and *autocracy.*

i.e. is short for Latin *id est* and means 'that is to say'. It should be distinguished from *e.g.*, from Latin *exempli gratia*, which means 'for example'. In other words, *i.e.* explains whereas *e.g.* illustrates. *See also* E.G.

-ie, -y. 1 These suffixes are used in pet-names and diminutives. There is often a free choice between *-ie* and *-y*, except that *-y* is always used in the pet-names *baby, daddy, ducky, granny, hubby, mummy*, and *sonny*, and in the diminutives *bunny, fatty, kitty, nappy*, and *teddy*, and *-ie* is always used in the diminutives *bookie, girlie*, and *goalie*, and is the preferred form in a number of words associated with Scotland (*beastie, kiltie, laddie, lassie*, etc.). In other cases (*dearie / deary, goalie / goaly, nightie / nighty*, etc.), it is largely a matter of individual preference or of a particular printing style. Spellings of individual words will be found in the current edition of the *Concise Oxford Dictionary*. The plural forms of all these words end in *-ies.*

2 Spelling of personal names (*Jamie, Katie, Molly, Sally, Willie*, etc.) is not a matter of choice but of the form favoured by the bearer of a particular name.

if. 1 *If* is followed by the subjunctive form *were* (instead of *was*) when the condition it introduces is hypothetical or impossible to fulfil, as in *If I were younger, I'd travel the world. Was* is used (1) informally in such cases (*If I was younger, I'd travel the world*), and (2) to indicate past tense in which the condition is capable of fulfilment (*If I was younger, I wasn't any wiser*). Use of the subjunctive form *be* (instead of *am, is*, or *are*) is now decidedly old-fashioned: *If this be true, all is not lost. See* SUBJUNCTIVE MOOD.

2 *If* and *whether* are both used to introduce noun clauses as in *Tell me if / whether you can come*, but *whether* is regarded as somewhat more formal and is preferable in avoiding possible ambiguity (in the sentence just given, a possible interpretation, though not the natural one, when *if* is used is 'If you can come, tell me (some other thing)'.

3 *If* and *though* are both possible in constructions of the type *a cheap, if / though risky method*, although again there is sometimes a small risk of ambiguity in the use of *if*.

4 *If* is sometimes used in a clause without any continuation, either as a way of making a strong assertion or as a polite request. This use is normally limited to conversation: *Well, if that isn't the best thing I've heard since I was home*—Compton Mackenzie, 1919 / *'There's your tea. Drink it.' . . . 'If I could have another lump of sugar.'*—Graham Greene, 1988 / *Natasha, if I could see you for a minute, please*—fiction website, AmE 2004 [*OEC*].

if and when. *If and when the law catches up with them, I hope it has it in for them*—*Punch*, 1967. This phrase (along with *as and when* and *unless and until*) almost belongs to the category of the Fowlers' *lost causes, but not quite. They wrote of it in *The King's English* (1906), 'this formula has enjoyed more popularity than it deserves; either "when" or "if" by itself would almost always give the meaning', and gave several examples to support their case, making an exception of the following quotation from Gladstone: *If and when it was done, it was done so to speak judicially*, in which the force of both *if* and *when* is needed. Significantly, this was their only example in the past tense; all the other examples referred to future

time. While it is true that *if* alone (when there is doubt) or *when* alone (when there is no doubt) would often serve, there are contexts in which a point needs to be made about both the likelihood of the event happening and its timing: *Many drugs will be given if and when needed, probably with no obvious rhythm*—J. M. Waterhouse et al., 1990. The expression is especially popular with lawyers because at the very least it makes the same point doubly effective.

ignoramus, meaning 'an ignorant person', has the plural form *ignoramuses*. It was originally a law term from the Latin word meaning 'we do not know', and the ending has nothing to do with Latin nouns in -*us*.

ikon *see* ICON, ICONIC.

-ile. Many nouns and adjectives ending in -*ile* (*docile, domicile, facile, fertile, fragile, missile, mobile, sterile, virile*, etc.) are pronounced -iyl in BrE and -uhl in AmE. The main exceptions are *automobile* and *imbecile*, which are usually pronounced -eel in both varieties, and *profile*, which is pronounced -iyl in both varieties, as (with some variation) are the statistical terms *decile, percentile*, and *quartile*.

ilk is a word that can arouse passions when it is used to mean 'kind or sort': *Fifteen years a faithful husband, that was his ilk*—Saul Bellow, 1987. *Ilk* arrived at this meaning by a strange route: originally it meant 'same' (Old English *ilca*), but was pushed aside in this role by the arrival in the Middle English period of *same* (from Old Norse). In Scotland from the 15c, the phrase *of that ilk* emerged with the meaning 'of the same place, territorial designation, or name', to denote the names of landed families, e.g. *Guthrie of that Ilk* = Guthrie of (a place also called) Guthrie. The Scottish use was rapidly misunderstood south of the border and by the 18c the word *ilk* had acquired the meaning 'family, class' and hence 'kind or sort', and we are back at the point where we started. Although there is much evidence of the spread of the popular use, it should be borne in mind that it can sound highly questionable to anyone (not necessarily Scottish) who is familiar with the word's historical usage. Examples: *Her husband's employment was not of the ilk of the typical man on the job on the coast*—A. Kennedy, NewZE 1986 / *I'm being flippant. Irresponsible in the well-known propensity of my ilk*—Kingsley Amis, 1988 / *Circumscription of any ilk is dangerous*— American Atheist Mag., 2004.

ill, sick. *Ill* and *sick* share responsibilities in peculiar ways, and are not always interchangeable. To begin with, *ill* is more usually predicative (placed after a verb, as in *She was ill*), whereas *sick* occurs naturally in attributive position (before a noun, as in *She was a sick woman*) as well as predicatively (as in *She was sick*), and in compounds such as *sick leave* and *sick room*). *Ill* is used attributively only in the broader sense 'out of health' (*He was an ill man when I last saw him*), in the extended meanings 'faulty, unskilful' (*ill judgement / ill management*), in idioms and proverbs (*do an ill turn to / It's an ill wind that blows nobody any good*). It also occurs adverbially in compounds (*ill-behaved / ill-considered*). In BrE, *to be sick* and *to feel sick* have the special meanings 'to vomit' and 'to be inclined to vomit', and to underline the anomalies of the two words a person can *look ill* and then *report* (or *go*) *sick*. In varieties of English other than BrE, the overlaps in meaning and usage vary considerably, and in some varieties there is little difference other than the more formal nature of the word *ill*. In AmE, the meaning 'vomiting' is normally supplied by the phrase *sick to* (or *at*) *one's stomach*.

illegal, illegitimate, illicit, unlawful. The different meanings of these words correspond to the meanings of *legal, legitimate, licit* (now rarely used), and *lawful*. Something is *illegal* when it is in all circumstances against the law, *illicit* when it is in some circumstances against the law or prohibited in some way, and *illegitimate* when it is contrary to custom or common justice as well as (or instead of) contrary to the law. *Unlawful* is a somewhat old-fashioned word for *illegal* and refers to divine as well as human law. *See further at* LEGAL, LAWFUL.

illegible, unreadable. In current use what is *illegible* is not clear enough to be decipherable (as in *illegible handwriting*), and what is *unreadable* can be physically read but is too dull to be worth reading or too difficult to be understood.

illicit *see* ELICIT, ILLICIT; ILLEGAL, ILLEGITIMATE, ILLICIT, UNLAWFUL.

illiteracies. This was a term used by Fowler (1926) to denote examples of 'a kind of offence against the literary idiom that is not easily named' and he identified its chief habitat as the correspondence columns of the newspapers. The instances he gave included *aggravating* (= annoying), *between . . . or . . .* instead of *between . . . and . . .*, *however* for *how ever* in the type ⊠ *However did you find out?*, *like* used as a conjunction (⊠ *If I could think like you do*), frequent use of split infinitives (⊠ *Am ready to categorically affirm*), *think to* (= remember to, as in ⊠ *I did not think to tell them,*), and *individual* to mean 'person'. In 1965 Gowers added three more instances: *between you and I*, *likewise* used as a conjunction (⊠ *Its tendency to wobble . . . likewise its limited powers of execution*), and *neither* with a plural verb (⊠ *For two reasons neither of* *which are noticed by Plato*). Some of these illiteracies may still be so called, notably, as explained elsewhere, *between you and I* (*see* BETWEEN 5) and *however* for *how ever*. In other cases, time has moved on, and the *Concise Oxford Dictionary* lists many of the castigated uses with the label 'informal' or without any restriction.

illiterate, innumerate. *Illiterate* (16c) means 'unable to read or write' or 'poorly educated'; *innumerate* (20c) means 'having no knowledge of or aptitude for the principles of mathematics'. The corresponding positive forms *literate* and *numerate* date from about the same times, although *numerate* is attested much earlier (15c) in a now obsolete meaning 'numbered, counted'.

illusion *see* DELUSION.

illusive, illusory *see* ELUSIVE.

image is an old word (13c) derived from Latin *imago* meaning 'copy, likeness, picture' and in all its meanings suggests a real or mental picture. Since the late 1950s it has been used by marketeers, advertisers, and political spin doctors to mean 'a concept or impression created in the minds of the public about a particular person, product, institution, etc.': *The first task of the public relations man, on taking over a business client, is to 're-engineer' his image to include something besides the production of goods*—J. K. Galbraith, 1958 / *In contrast to the image of police work as exciting and dangerous . . . , patrolling was invariably boring and somewhat aimless*—I. Marsh, 1992 / *Mounted police charges and mass arrests kept the demonstrators out of the embassy, but the image of the building was darkened for good*—*Guardian*, 2002.

imaginable, meaning 'able to be imagined', is spelt without an *e* in the middle.

imaginary, imaginative. *Imaginary* means 'existing only in the imagination, not real', whereas *imaginative* means 'having or showing a high degree of imagination'. Both words can be applied to people as well as things; an *imaginary* person is one who does not really exist (e.g. is fictitious), whereas an *imaginative* person is one who is creative or inventive.

imbalance is a surprisingly recent word (19c), first used as a technical term in ophthalmology and now used generally in many contexts: *The imbalance in the world's financial system has become grotesque*—*Times*, 1969 / *The marked increase in the average salary reflects both the imbalance of supply and demand for health workers*—*Scientific American*, 1973 / *Teaching implies an imbalance of knowledge, otherwise it would not be necessary*—B. Bergonzi, 1990.

imbroglio, an originally Italian word meaning 'a confused or complicated situation', has the plural form *imbroglios*.

imbue *see* INFUSE.

imitate has a derivative form *imitable* meaning 'able to be imitated'.

immanent *see* IMMINENT.

immediately has been used informally since the early 19c, especially in BrE, as a conjunction equivalent to *immediately after*: It appears not to have caught on in AmE, and some US commentators consider it wrong. *I starting writing 'Jill' immediately I left Oxford*—Philip Larkin, 1983 / *Immediately I heard the front door I switched off his computer*—Nigel Williams, 1992.

immigrant *see* EMIGRANT.

imminent, immanent. The more common word *imminent*, derived from the Latin word *minēre* 'to threaten', means 'about to happen' and has connotations of threat or danger. *Immanent*, derived from the Latin word *manēre* 'to remain', means 'indwelling, inherent' and is chiefly used in theology to denote the divine presence throughout the universe.

immoral, amoral. Both words are applied to people, to people's actions, and to standards of behaviour. *Immoral* means 'morally wrong, wicked', whereas *amoral* means 'having no morals', i.e. 'outside the scope of morality' and is strictly neutral in meaning, although in practice both words are used judgementally. Examples: (amoral) *Children are first amoral . . . then enter a pre-moral stage, when social and authoritarian factors are the main restraints*—M. E. Wood, 1973 / *For someone who appeared so gleefully wicked and amoral, Cleo seemed surprisingly dim when it came to character judgment*—C. Storm, 1993 / (immoral) *This view takes into account the general view that crime is or ought to be those actions which are considered so immoral or damaging that they should be subject to punishment*—J. D. Rogers, 1987 / *Simon criticised Jesus for allowing such an immoral woman to touch him*—R. Cooper, 1990.

immovable is spelt without an *e* in the middle, and the usual meaning is 'unyielding, unwilling to change one's mind'.

immune is followed by *to* or *from*. When the reference is to disease or some other form of harm or danger, *to* is more usual, and when *from* is used it is more often in the context of legal liabilities, but these distinctions are far from clear-cut and both constructions are found

regardless of context, with *to* somewhat more common than *from*: (to) *Each country will be concerned to maintain the invulnerability of its submarine-based strategic missiles, which are essentially immune to attack from land-based weapons*—Scientific American, 1972 / *A situation could arise where harmful bacteria, having become immune to disinfectants, survive to cause illness which cannot be treated by antibiotics*—R. North, 1985 / *Anywhere that remains immune to fashion is to be lauded*—Times, 2004 / (from) *Those who have a commitment to the Christian faith are not thereby immune from depression*—M. Batchelor, 1988 / *The laws affecting the common land were supervised by Down Drivers, themselves not immune from prosecution*—M. Lister, 1988 / *Real diamonds have a quite distinctive, soapy texture to the surface and are immune from water*—Frederick Forsyth, 1989 / *Royal grants may also explain why some churches . . . enjoyed unusually extensive rights of sanctuary which developed into privileged zones immune from secular authority*—W. Davies, 2003.

immunity, impunity. In non-medical contexts *immunity* means 'freedom or exemption from an obligation, penalty, or unfavourable circumstance' and like *immune* can be followed by *to* or *from*: *Balder was a son of the most senior god, Odin, and one version of the legend says he was blessed with the gift of immunity from harm*—H. Hauxwell et al., 1989 / *Immunity to rubella does not protect a person from measles, or vice versa*—medical website, AmE 2004 [OEC]. *Impunity* has the more limited meaning 'exemption from punishment or from the injurious consequences of an action', is not followed by *to* or *from*, and is used chiefly in the phrase *with impunity*: *In our dreams we can do with impunity things we would like to do in real life but cannot*—make love with a

Hollywood sex symbol or murder our boss—J. Grant, 1990.

impact. The literal meaning of the noun is 'the action of one body coming forcibly into contact with another', and refers to physical collision. The figurative meaning 'strong effect or influence' is justifiable when there is a corresponding figurative notion of a collision (*the impact of Christianity on social justice*), but it is questionable when the meaning is no more than 'effect, impression' (*the impact of new policing methods on the crime figures*). The verb, which is pronounced with the stress on the second syllable, is older than the noun in its physical meaning ('press closely into or in something'). Intransitive uses began to appear in the 20c, and in 1962 it was reported in a work called *Basic Astronautics* that a Soviet space rocket *had impacted onto the Moon's surface*. About the same time figurative uses began to proliferate, corresponding to the figurative meaning of the noun, and these remain common, especially in journalism: *The Magazine . . . is not the place for consideration of national or international events except in so far as they impact on Oxford*—Oxford Magazine, 1956 / *Radiographers are a dedicated and highly professional group of workers and regret any action which impacts on patient care*—Manchester Evening News, 2004. There has been continued opposition to these uses, both in Britain and in America. When there is so much hostility, it is prudent to use more familiar synonyms, such as *effect*, *influence*, and *impression* for the noun and *affect*, *influence*, or *have an effect on* (or, more specifically, *endanger*, *threaten*, *risk*, etc., when the consequences are unfavourable) for the verb.

impactful is a word often derided for its overuse in marketing and related fields, even moving someone to say online 'I could never love someone who uses the word impactful.' Those who bridle at the verb *to impact* will find this adjective doubly repellent. But a case exists for its usefulness. Its *ODO* definition as 'having a major impact or effect' shows that it really has two meanings. One is synonymous with *effective* which could replace it in contexts such as: *I think the FM radio ads are the most impactful. Or at least amusing*—weblog, 2005.

To express the meaning 'having a major impact', in contrast, it is arguably a useful shorthand for the whole clause which would have to be used instead in examples such as: *'Laura Mackie has produced some of BBC Drama's most impactful serials over the past year,' says Jane Tranter*—BBC press release, 2004. Use it if you wish, but be aware of the health warning it comes with.

impassable, impassible. *Impassable* means 'that cannot be traversed' and refers to roads, stretches of countryside, etc. *Impassible* means 'incapable of feeling emotion' or 'incapable of suffering injury', and is pronounced with the second syllable as in *passive* rather than as in *pass*. It is a rare and learned word, but its spelling is sometimes mistakenly used for *impassable*, e.g. ☒ *dirt roads, which become nearly impassible during wet weather*—OEC, 2005.

impasse, meaning 'a deadlock, or position from which progress is impossible', is pronounced many different ways, but the recommended pronunciations in BrE are am-**pahs** and **am**-pahs, and in AmE **im**-pahs and im-**pahs**.

impeach in BrE means 'to charge with a crime against the State, especially treason', and in AmE means 'to charge (the holder of a public office) with misconduct'. It does not mean 'to dismiss from office' in either variety.

impel has inflected forms *impelled*, *impelling*.

imperial, imperious. In its original meaning, *imperial* relates to an empire or emperor (*Britain's imperial past*; *Nero and the imperial family*). From this, it developed the meaning of 'magnificent' or 'commanding'. In contrast, *imperious* is a more judgemental word, meaning 'overbearing, domineering': *It's implied in an imperious tone that the Egyptians have a duty to the entire world to protect their museums*—Spiked (magazine), 2011 / *He could be fierce and domineering , but behind the imperious manner was a shy man who did not easily establish personal relationships*—Oxford Dictionary of National Biography, 2001. (*Imperial* is sometimes used as an approximate synonym of *imperious* (e.g. *I faced the dark form beside me and used my best imperial voice*), which has led to the distinction between the two becoming weaker.) In sports journalism in particular, *imperious* is used to mean something like 'commanding' or 'effortlessly superior', but this use is not recommended: ⊠ *Johansson was in imperious form in the first set as he overpowered Wang with thundering groundstrokes*—Taipei Times, 2005.

imperialism. This word is first attested in the 19c, when it reflected the British politics of the time and denoted what was seen as the benevolent spirit or principle of empire. In the 20c, it came to be used disparagingly, first by the Communist bloc with reference to the US and the Western powers generally, and then conversely to refer to the imperial system or policies of the USSR in the countries over which it held sway. Imperialism is now a largely historical concept, although the word is still used in political writing of the continuing or potential imperial policies of certain countries, predominantly the US but also the West generally in the context of Middle Eastern politics. *Cultural imperialism* is the attempt to impose social or cultural characteristics, such as language, on other nations, typically to further the political and commercial interests of the imposer: *A list in which Anglo-American films so outnumber the rest of the world is, in my opinion, a list based on arrogant cultural imperialism: believing English-language culture far superior to all others is the real elitism*—Guardian, 2007.

imperil, meaning 'to put at risk, to endanger', has inflected forms *imperilled*, *imperilling* in BrE and *imperiled*, *imperiling* in AmE.

impersonal verb. In current English this term is restricted to verbs used in the third person singular with indefinite *it* as subject, e.g. *it is snowing, when it rains, it makes no difference*.

impinge, meaning 'to have an effect (on)', has a present participle *impinging*, with no *e*.

implement, as a verb, is a useful word used first in Scotland in the sense 'to put (a treaty, agreement, etc.) into effect', a meaning it still has in general usage. In the 20c its use has been greatly extended to cover any kind of idea, policy, proposal, suggestion, etc., as a general synonym for *carry out*, *effect*, *fulfil*, and other words. Although objections are sometimes raised to this use, it is well established and is often a better word than any of these synonyms might at first seem to be. It also has the advantage of a ready noun form *implementation*.

imply *see* INFER.

import. The noun is pronounced with the stress on the first syllable, and the verb with the stress on the second syllable.

important, importantly. Both words have a special elliptical use dating from the 1930s, in which one or other stands by itself (or qualified by *more, most*, etc.) as a kind of sentence adverb: *Perhaps more importantly, income not applied to exclusively charitable purposes is not exempt from taxation—Times*, 1972 / *But, more important, a linked policy can be encashed—surrendered—before maturity date—Daily Telegraph*, 1973 / *But most important of all, we begin by giving you the training you need—Scientific American*, 1973 / *More important, Mr Deng gave China a new revolutionary vision in the decade of reform from 1978—Economist*, 1991 / *In Nigeria he is at the more liberal end of the Christian spectrum. More importantly, he is in the front line of relations between Christianity and Islam—Times*, 2007. The use of (*more* etc.) *importantly* is sometimes criticized on the grounds that (*more* etc.) *important* (elliptical for *what is more important*) is adequate, but both words are commonly used in this way and *importantly* conforms more closely than *important* does to the regular type of sentence adverb.

impostor is the recommended spelling, not *imposter*.

impracticable, impractical. These two words have related meanings to do with the impossibility of doing something, and correspond to the positive forms **practicable, practical. Impractical* is a relatively recent (19c) word and means the same as *unpractical*, i.e. 'not practical or realistic'; it can also be used of a person, with the meaning 'lacking the ability to do practical things', and usually has a general application. *Impracticable* means 'not able to be carried out, not feasible', and is more usually applied to particular cases. In practice, however, the two words are close enough in meaning to run the frequent

risk of getting in each other's way: *As his arms were full of books it would have been impracticable for him to wave—J. I. M. Stewart*, 1974 / *I have always been ridiculously impractical...I cannot repair a fuse—F. Howerd*, 1974 / *Her plans were so impractical that someone like me was necessary to point this out—Anita Brookner*, 1987 / *It would be impracticable to provide full-time security in cemeteries—Birmingham Post*, 2003 / *If she lost her licence it would have a catastrophic effect....It would be totally impractical for her to use public transport—Essex Chronicle*, 2007.

impresario, meaning 'an organizer of public entertainments', has the plural form *impresarios*.

imprint is pronounced with the stress on the first syllable as a noun (e.g. the *imprint page* of a book) and on the second syllable as a verb (e.g. *He'd always have this ghastly image imprinted on his mind*).

impromptu, as a noun meaning 'an extempore speech or performance' or 'a short piece of instrumental music', has the plural form *impromptus*.

improvable, meaning 'able to be improved', is spelt without an *e* in the middle.

improvise is spelt *-ise*, not *-ize*.

impunity *see* IMMUNITY.

in. 1 Use of *in* instead of *for* with reference to past time (*We have not spoken in more than a year*) has spread from AmE to BrE. It is used in contexts that are explicitly or implicitly negative, and as such is a revival of an older English use: *To Westminster Hall, where I have not been...in some months—Samuel Pepys*, 1669. More recent examples are: *Mark had never been near his house in a year—Compton Mackenzie*, 1924 / *The first* *bridge across the Bosphorus in 2,300 years . . . is now being built—Daily Telegraph, 1971 / The ostensible reason for their first trip to London in several years was a new album—Evening Standard, 2003.*

2 In meanings to do with place, in certain contexts AmE uses *on* or *at* where BrE uses *in*: *a store on Fifth Avenue / They are all in school now.*

3 See also the separate entries for INASMUCH AS; IN ORDER THAT; IN SO FAR AS; IN THAT.

in- and un-. **1** Both prefixes are used to make negative forms of adjectives and nouns; *in-* is Latin in origin and is no longer active in making new words, whereas *un-* is English in origin and is a living prefix. Historically, some words have existed in both *in-* and *un-* forms, but one or other of them normally drops out in the end, so that (for example) *unability* gave way to *inability* in the 18c, although *unable* and not *inable* is the corresponding adjective. Other mismatches occur with the pairs *imbalance / unbalanced, uncomprehending / incomprehensible, indigestible / undigested, indisputable / undisputed, indistinguishable / undistinguished, unseparated / inseparable, instability / unstable,* and others.

2 Choice between *un-* and *in-* forms is not normally a problem for native speakers of English, with occasional exceptions such as *inadvisable / unadvisable* (both in use), *inarguable / unarguable* (both in use), *incommunicative / uncommunicative* (both in use), *inconsolable / unconsolable* (the first now preferred), *indecipherable / undecipherable* (both in use), *inhuman* (= brutal, unfeeling) / *unhuman* (not human), *insupportable* (= intolerable) / *unsupportable* (= indefensible), and others.

3 Note that *in-* is not used to form negative forms of verbs, whereas *un-* is (*undo, unmask, unsettle,* etc.).

inapt, inept. These two words overlap to an extent in their basic meanings 'inappropriate, unsuitable' and 'unskilful' respectively. *Inapt* tends to mean rather the first of these, and applies only to actions and circumstances, whereas *inept* means rather the second, is much more common, and applies to people as well as actions: *In this respect, the oft-quoted cathedral metaphor is not inapt—* J. Richards et al., 1988 / *She believes it would be politically inept to cut such training programmes at a time when the jobless total is rising fast—Today,* 1992 / *Nicholas was inept at all forms of promiscuity except gossip—Esquire,* 1992 / *His inapt use of the colloquial 'just for kicks' undermines his claim—Guardian,* 2007. So if you say that a person's reply is *inapt* and *inept*, you mean that it was both inappropriate and clumsily expressed. The noun derivative of *inept* is *ineptitude*: *displays of astounding political ineptitude by Byers—Scotland on Sunday,* 2002. Occasionally *inaptitude* is inappropriately used to express this meaning: *to cover up their inaptitude, unwillingness and jealousy of others—OEC,* 2002.

inartistic *see* UNARTISTIC.

inasmuch as is a rather formal and awkward expression meaning 'to the extent that, in so far as' or more simply 'in view of the fact that, since'. The preferred style is two words (as here) rather than four, since this underlines the unity of the expression. Examples: (first meaning) *Inasmuch as she could be pleased, the idea of this marriage pleased her—*C. Blackwood, 1977 / *These provisions apply only inasmuch as trade between Member States is affected—*D. I. Bainbridge, 1993 / (second meaning) *Inasmuch as Gray was Perdita's father, he was to be treated with a reasonable degree of respect—*B. Guest, 1985 /

Inasmuch as the work involved would be mainly done in the spring, summer and autumn, there are many benefits to be enjoyed—fresh air, exercise, recreation, relaxation and a sense of pride in having achieved something of beauty which others may share—Cornishman, 2004.

in back of *see* BACK.

inchoate means 'undeveloped' or 'just begun' and is derived from the Latin word *choare* 'to begin': *It was obviously necessary that we should continue our still inchoate discussion over a drink—D. M. Davin, 1975 / She is not allowed to express her real, if inchoate, feelings for Robert Marlin—T. Tanner, 1986.* It should be distinguished from *incoherent*, which means 'lacking logic or consistency' (✖ *The rest of his inchoate speech was devoted to—[etc.]—Independent,* 2001), and *chaotic*, which means 'having no order, utterly disorganized or confused' (✖ *The protesters at Genoa, inchoate and unfocused though they may be, . . . can be considered the heroes of today's society—Scotland on Sunday,* 2001).

incidence. The *incidence* of a disease or crime is how often it happens, e.g. *an increased incidence of cancer.* It is quite distinct from *incident*, but confusions between the two words do happen. (1) *Incidence* is not a sophisticated synonym for *incident*, and should not be so used, as in ✖ *In another incidence, this time while at High Greave, he is alleged to have 'fixed it' for him to extend a car park—Yorkshire Post,* 2005. (2) It is sometimes wrongly used when *instance* would be correct. In this quote by Baroness Neville-Jones, the mistake presumably belongs to the journalist transcribing rather than the noble Lady: ✖ *This is another incidence of the failure of the Government to safeguard sensitive information and yet another example of a lapse in discipline—Daily Telegraph,*

2008. (3) The plural *incidents* seems to be sometimes used by mistake for *incidence*: ✖ *a number of articles about increasing incidents of accidental deaths in the public hospital system in the state of New South Wales—World Socialist,* 2004.

incident, incidental *adjectives.* *Incident* has been almost entirely replaced as an adjective by *incidental*, so that a sentence such as *Those in the highest station have their incident cares and troubles* now sounds decidedly dated. This freeing of *incident* from its older role as an adjective has coincided with its greatly increased use as a noun with the meaning 'a particular episode or distinct event receiving general attention', a use in which it can refer to a wide range of events from the most important (terrorist attacks, leakages of radiation from nuclear power stations, and so on) to the most minor or trivial (domestic arguments, demonstrations at meetings, traffic mishaps, etc.). In police use it has a special application reflected in the compound forms *incident book, incident room,* etc., in which *incident* is not an adjective but the noun used attributively.

incidentally is spelt this way and not (as the pronunciation in rapid speech might suggest) *incidently.* Its usual role is as a sentence adverb marking a new stage in speech (or sometimes writing). It is used both to make a remark apparently unconnected with the topic, as in the first example, or to add information, as in the second: *Incidentally, thanks to Tommy Hands, I nearly became a landlord myself—A. J. P. Taylor, 1983 / Words commonly used in the Dales just two generations ago were now a mystery to many young people. Attercop, which, incidentally, translates as 'spider', and blashy, which means 'wet weather', have evidently long gone—Independent,* 2007.

incise, meaning 'to cut into, engrave', is spelt *-ise*, not *-ize*. The noun derivative is *incisor* (usually meaning a front tooth), not *-er*.

incline is pronounced with the stress on the first syllable as a noun (meaning 'a slope') and with the stress on the second syllable as a verb (as in *be inclined to*).

inclose is not the correct form: *see* ENCLOSE.

include, comprise. Like *comprise*, *include* has the whole as its subject and its parts as the object. The difference is that *comprise* generally denotes the whole set of parts whereas *include* can be selective, so that if a house *comprises* two living rooms, two bedrooms, a kitchen, and a bathroom, there are six rooms in all, whereas if the house *includes* these rooms there may be others as well. *Include* is often used to single out a particular item or subset, in which case *comprise* is again inappropriate: *The study . . . found that women preferred to use text or email to communicate. The survey did not include work calls but did count conversations with banks or insurance companies*—*Express*, 2007. *See also* COMPRISE.

including. There is evidence, both in BrE and in AmE, of *including* used with a prepositional phrase introduced by a word such as *by, in, to*, etc.: *Copies of this notice are being distributed on a wide scale including to overseas establishments*—radio broadcast, 1990 / *We find free speech under assault throughout the United States, including on some college campuses*—*International Herald Tribune*, 1991 / *Holme . . . set off from Poole intending to preach at 30 ports, including in Northern Ireland, the Isle of Man, the Outer Hebrides, Orkney and Shetland*—*Western Daily Press*, 2007.

incognito, when used as a noun meaning either 'a secret identity' or 'a person with a secret identity', has the plural form *incognitos*.

incommunicado, meaning 'having no communication with others', is spelt with two *m*s.

incomparable, meaning 'matchless, without an equal', is pronounced with the stress on the second syllable.

in connection with *see* CONNECTION.

inconsolable is now preferred to *unconsolable*. *See* IN- AND UN-.

increase is pronounced with the stress on the first syllable as a noun, and with the stress on the second syllable as a verb.

incrust *see* ENCRUST, which is the preferred form.

incubator, meaning 'a device for keeping a baby at a constant temperature', is spelt *-or* not *-er*.

incubus, meaning 'a male demon believed to have sexual intercourse with sleeping women' and hence 'a nightmare', generally has the plural form *incubi* (**ing**-kyoo-by), but *incubuses* is also occasionally used and is correct.

inculcate means 'to urge or impress (an idea, fact, etc.) on someone' and is derived from the Latin word *inculcare* 'to stamp with the heel' (Latin *calx*). It has the fact or idea as its object, optionally followed by *in, into, on*, or *upon*: *I have tried to inculcate in my pupils an attitude of intelligent laziness*—*Guardian*, 1989 / *He faced an uphill struggle to inculcate some road sense into some of the wildest learner-drivers on the planet*—*Independent*, 2005. Use with the person as object, on the analogy of *indoctrinate*, is also found but is not generally considered standard: ☒ *They will also try to* *inculcate you with a spurious respect for a 'culture' which not only fails to distinguish between what is good and what is profitable [etc.]*—*Punch*, 1992.

incur, meaning 'to suffer or experience', has inflected forms *incurred, incurring*.

indecipherable *see* IN- AND UN-.

indefinite article *see* A, AN.

indent is pronounced with the stress on the first syllable as a noun and with the stress on the second syllable as a verb.

index. In general use the plural is normally *indexes*, but in mathematical and scientific contexts it is *indices*.

Indian. In BrE an *Indian* is first and foremost a native or national of India. In the American context its use arose from the mistaken belief of Columbus and other voyagers who reached the east coast of America in the 15c and 16c that they had reached India by a new route. *Indian* and *Red Indian* are now regarded as old-fashioned and inappropriate, and more reminiscent of stereotypical images of the Wild West than of contemporary America. *American Indian*, or preferably *Native American*, should be used instead.

indict, meaning 'to accuse formally', is pronounced in-**diyt**, and the same pronunciation applies to its derivatives *indictable* and *indictment*.

Indigenous Australians *see* ABORIGINES.

indigestible is spelt *in-*.

indirect object. 1 In grammar, an indirect object is a person or thing named as the recipient of the direct object of a transitive (or more strictly, 'ditransitive') verb. In the sentences *I gave my sister a book* and *I gave her a book, my sister* and *her* are the indirect objects. It will be seen that in this type the indirect object usually precedes the direct object. When both direct and indirect objects are pronouns, the reverse order is sometimes found (*I gave it her back*).

2 An alternative to this ditransitive construction is to use a preposition (usually *to* or *for*) before the indirect object with the indirect object then following the direct object (*I gave a book to my sister* / *I handed the book to her* / *I handed it to her*).

3 Verbs other than those of giving can have indirect objects, e.g. *Tell me the truth* (in which *me* is the indirect object) / *He cooks his wife a hot meal every evening* (in which *his wife* is the indirect object). *See also* DIRECT OBJECT; INTRANSITIVE AND TRANSITIVE VERBS.

indirect question. In grammar, an indirect question reports what someone has asked, as opposed to a direct question, which uses the person's exact words, often in inverted commas, and using the word order typical of questions. For example, '*What do they want to do?*' is a direct question while its indirect form is *I asked them what they wanted to do*. As in the previous example, indirect questions consist of a 'reporting' verb, usually *ask*, or more formally *enquire*, followed by a clause reporting the question. That clause uses the word order used in statements, and does not use the auxiliary 'do / does / did' etc. The tense of the verb in a direct question often needs to change in the indirect question, and the pronouns may need to as well: '*How long have you been waiting?*' becomes *I asked him / her / them how long he / she / they had been waiting*; and '*When will you go, Mary?*' becomes *I asked Mary when she would go*. When the direct question calls for an answer 'yes' or 'no', the indirect form is introduced by *if* or *whether*: (direct) *Do* *you want to go for a walk?* / (indirect) *I'll ask them whether they want to go for walk.* Since indirect questions follow the word order of statements, they are not followed by a question mark; it is non-standard to write, for example, ✺ *I asked them what did they want to do?* or ✺ *Tell me how old are you?*

indirect speech *see* REPORTED SPEECH.

indispensable is spelt *-able*, not *-ible*. *See* -ABLE, -IBLE.

indisputable is pronounced with the stress on the third syllable. *See also* IN- AND UN-.

indissoluble, meaning 'unable to be dissolved', is pronounced with the stress on the third syllable.

indistinguishable is spelt *-able*, not *-ible*.

individual. When used as a noun, *individual* should denote a single person in contrast with a group of people or with society as a whole: *the role of the individual in the community* / *She continues to treat them as individuals.* It is less satisfactory, and can often sound quaint or affected, when used simply as a synonym for *person*, and in this use it is normally restricted to humorous or disparaging contexts: *There was an odd individual standing by the door* / *Individuals arrived in their own cars.*

indivisible, meaning 'unable to be divided', is spelt *-ible*, not *-able*. *See* -ABLE, -IBLE.

indoor, indoors. The adjective is *indoor* (*indoor games*) and is a shortening of an earlier form *within-door*. *Indoors* is an adverb (*Let's go indoors now*) and represents an earlier form *within doors*.

induction *see* DEDUCTION.

industrial action is an established term (first recorded as recently as 1971 in the *OED*) denoting various kinds of industrial protest including strikes, working to rule, overtime bans, etc. The word *action*, paradoxical though it may seem, refers to the activity of protest and has a precedent in the term *political action* (late 19c).

inedible, uneatable. *Inedible* has two aspects: it refers to plants, animals etc. that cannot be eaten, either because they are inherently poisonous or harmful, or because they have been made so; it also refers to food that is disagreeable or impossible to eat because of the way it has been prepared or cooked. *Uneatable* in nearly all cases has only this second meaning, and is several times less frequent than *inedible*. The dividing line between the two words is best illustrated by examples: (inedible) *Arnolds rules out overpicking and forest management practices, because both edible and inedible mushrooms have declined and all types of mature forests show similar drops*—www.Realclimate.org, 2005 / *Mulching also assures that light does not reach the tubers; potatoes exposed to light turn green and produce a toxin that renders them inedible*—Mother Earth News, 2003 / *I assumed this was a peace offering, probably one of her inedible fruit cakes that had been the cause of the W.I.'s unpleasant altercation with Trading Standards*—weblog, 2005. / (uneatable) *It was a typically minimalist 'gourmet' spread of undercooked steak and uneatable entrée*—weblog, 2004.

ineffective, ineffectual. *Ineffective* means 'not producing any effect' and normally refers to actions or processes. *Ineffectual* often refers to people, and means 'lacking the ability to produce results'. The distinctions are more fully discussed at *effective.

inequity, iniquity. These two words are related in form, meaning, and derivation. *Inequity* is the opposite of *equity* and means 'inequality, unfairness, injustice': *He believes that politicians need to tackle the inequities that divide society—Times Educational Supplement*, 2007. *Iniquity* means 'grossly immoral or unjust behaviour': *It is easy for a well-fed English woman like myself to ... protest about the iniquity of racial prejudice—* M. & L. Hoy, 1991. Confusion happens in both directions. Sometimes *iniquity* is used when *inequity* is meant: ⊠ *I suggest this iniquity be removed as soon as possible—Daily Telegraph*, 1992. The set phrase *a den of iniquity* sometimes becomes ⊠ *a den of inequity*: ⊠ *The notion that Dublin is a den of inequity and there are no drugs anywhere else is not true—Carlow Nationalist*, 2005.

infamous *see* NOTORIOUS.

infectious *see* CONTAGIOUS.

infer, imply. 1 The only point noted by Fowler (1926) was that the inflected forms of *infer* are *inferred* and *inferring*, and this is thankfully still true (but note *inferable* or *inferrable*, with one *r* or two, and *inference* with only one *r*). Fowler made no comment on the meaning of *infer*, and it was left to Gowers (1965) to add a short note to the effect that 'the use of *infer* for *imply* is sadly common—so common that some dictionaries give *imply* as one of the definitions of *infer* without comment'. The *Concise Oxford Dictionary* (2006) warns against this meaning and distinguishes the primary meanings of the two words: (*infer*) 'to deduce or conclude from facts or reasoning', (*imply*) 'to suggest the truth or existence of (something not expressly asserted), to insinuate or hint'. The problem lies in the fact that deduction and suggestion can often be seen as part of the same process. It is nearly always *infer* that encroaches on *imply* (but see paragraph 3 below for

clarification of 'nearly'), and the *OED* puts the issue in its historical context by giving examples dating from the 16c onwards.

2 The following examples show in four groups the correct meanings of both words and then the disputed or unclear usage of *infer*: (*imply* correctly used) *Vast stretches of abandoned concrete underfoot imply that someone once had plans for this land—New Yorker*, 1986 / *It is a shocking departure from the procedures of good governance apparently designed to skirt Cabinet approval and the oversight that implies—Daily Mail*, 2007 / (*infer* correctly used) *One might infer, from Judy's appearance, that her business rather lay with the thorns than the flowers—Dickens*, 1853 / *You would have been able to infer from the room alone the nature of those who lived in it—* D. M. Davin, 1979 / *No reference to any living person is intended or should be inferred—Saul Bellow*, 1987 / *One of the things I inferred from the article was that the author felt that de Beauvoir was somehow living the open relationship because it was what Sartre wanted—* weblog, AmE 2005 [*OEC*] / (*infer* used for *imply*) *I can't stand fellas who infer things about good clean-living Australian sheilas—Private Eye*, 1970 / *These were the ones who had made a slightly sulky entrance (inferring rebellion), and had then proceeded to sit on the floor—*M. Bracewell, 1989 / (*infer* ambiguously used) *Many good reasons exist in favor of private executions, without inferring or saying 'governments are ashamed of the death penalty'—*B. R. Hall, AmE 1846 / *She was 'flabbergasted' when complaints were made that she had taken financial advantage of him by inferring they had an 'exclusive relationship'—Express*, 2004.

3 The only domain in which *imply* is used where *infer* might be expected is in legal language, in which the inference and the conclusion are regarded as part of the same process, as the following extract shows: *When a possessory interest in property is conveyed, a court may imply from the circumstances that the parties also intended to grant or reserve an easement as well despite their failure to say so in the deed.* Otherwise, it is *infer* that has broken the bounds of logic and is on the loose in the arena of idiom.

inferable *see* INFER 1.

inferior is not a true comparative (like *lower*, for example) and is followed by *to*, not *than*: *When we are together there's no competition; neither of us feels better than or inferior to the other*—J. Dawson, 1990. When used attributively (before a noun), it means 'of poor quality' rather than 'less good'. *I have had to put up with inferior accommodation, lousy food and paltry pocket money*—M. & L. Hoy, 1991 / *We pay them to grow inferior tobacco crops so bad that they are exported—at profit to those farmers—to Africa to boost smoking there*—Sunday Mercury, 2007.

inferno has the plural form *infernos*.

infinite, infinitely are derived from the Latin word *infinitus* meaning 'without limit' (Latin *finis* 'end'), and this is the proper meaning of these words in English. In practice, however, they tend to be used in the weaker senses 'very great' and 'very much'; this use is standard in English but can often be replaced by alternatives such as *extensive, vast, substantial, considerable, immense, enormous,* or in some cases even simply *great* or *huge* (or their adverbial equivalents). Examples: *The infinite variety of Chinese food, with classic dishes such as Peking duck and shark's fin soup*—Country Life, 1973 / *Embassy Court, a crumbling, rust-streaked, 11-storey apartment block on the Brighton seafront, looks infinitely better now you can see less of it*—Guardian, 2004. When smallness of size or number is meant,

infinitesimal and *infinitesimally* are the words to use: *She worked crouching down, and the infinitesimal pace of her labours made her feel like an ant, toiling away earnestly at a microscopic task*— J. Rogers, 1990 / *'String theory' explains this by postulating that all matter is aligned in infinitely long strings, of infinitesimally small width, which vibrate like the strings of a cello*—Times, 2002.

infinitive. The infinitive of a verb is its simplest uninflected form, and the form that appears as the headword in dictionaries. When used in sentences, there are two basic kinds of infinitive: (1) the bare infinitive, identical to the form just mentioned, which is used with auxiliary verbs such as *can, may, shall, should, will, would,* etc., with the so-called semi-modal verbs *dare, help,* and *need,* and after idiomatic expressions such as *had better* (*I had better **wait**), (2) the *to*-infinitive, in which the base form is preceded by the particle *to*, which is used with verbs such as *expect, have, hope, want,* etc., in expressions of purpose (***To call** attention, ring the bell*), in idiomatic expressions such as *to be honest, to put it mildly, so to speak,* etc., and to form noun phrases which can be the subjects of other verbs (***To err** is human*). When a second infinitive follows a *to*-infinitive, this is often expressed as a bare infinitive without another *to*: *I want **to go** to the library and **get** a book.*

inflammable, inflammatory. *Inflammable* has the same meaning, i.e. 'easily set on fire', as *flammable*, which is now preferred in official advisory contexts: *see* FLAMMABLE. *Inflammatory* means 'tending to cause inflammation (of the body)' and figuratively (especially in the context of speeches, leaflets, etc.) 'tending to cause anger'.

inflatable, which since the 1950s has been used as a noun as well as an adjective, is spelt without an *e* in the middle.

inflection. 1 *Inflection* is the process by which words change their form by the addition of suffixes or other means in accordance with their grammatical role. Inflection of nouns usually involves the addition of *-s* or *-es* to form plurals (*book / books*, *church / churches*); of verbs, the addition of *-s* or *-es*, *-ed*, and *-ing* to form third-person present-tense forms (*want / wants*), past tenses (*wanted*), past participles (*wanted*), and present participles (*wanting*); and of adjectives, to form comparative and superlative forms, the addition of *-er* and *-est*, sometimes with modification of the stem as in *happier*, *happiest*.

2 In the context of phonetics, *inflection* means 'modulation (i.e. adjusting the tone or pitch) of the voice'.

3 The alternative spelling *inflexion* applies to both meanings, but it is considered old-fashioned and Oxford style prefers *inflection*.

inflexible is spelt *-ible*, not *-able*. *See* -ABLE, -IBLE.

inflict, afflict. Both words are concerned with the suffering of unpleasant circumstances, but they have different constructions. *Inflict* has the unpleasantness as object, and *afflict* has the victim: *He knew also that the greater part of the ills which had afflicted him were due, indirectly, in chief measure to the influence of Christian teaching*—S. Butler, 1903 / *It was he who had inflicted an appendectomy of doubtful necessity on Harry forty-two years ago*—R. Goddard, 1990 / *For rain in summer is the mortal enemy of the serious punter, a plague as bad as any of those which afflicted ancient Egypt*—Scotland on Sunday, 2007. *Afflict* is often used in the passive, followed by *with* or *by*: *Most commanders would have been afflicted with convenient deafness at that moment, but*

Davout rounded on the speaker at once—R. Butters, 1991 / *Campbell recalls never having heard his boss afflicted by such 'long pauses and gabbling' before or since*—Sunday Times, 2007.

inform is a formal equivalent of *tell* and is generally limited to official contexts. It is followed by *of* or a *that*-clause (*The police informed them of their rights / An announcement informed us that the train was about to arrive*), but (unlike *tell*) does not have the instructional meaning followed by *to* (⊠ *Please inform them to wait outside*).

informant, informer. An *informant* is a neutral term for someone who gives information, especially about language, culture, etc. to a linguist or anthropologist. An *informer* is someone who gives information against another person to the authorities, and it has sinister or unfavourable overtones.

infotainment, first recorded in the US in the 1980s, means 'broadcast material that seeks to inform and entertain'. It belongs to a group of media-related portmanteau words of the late 20c: *see* also DOCUDRAMA.

infringe, meaning 'to violate (a rule or law)', has inflected forms *infringed*, *infringing*. In current use it is used both transitively (with an object, e.g. *The players were penalized for infringing the off-side rule*) and intransitively followed by *on* or *upon*, with the more general meaning 'encroach on, threaten': *The measure threatens to infringe upon and restrict our right to travel in certain countries.*

infuse. When using the word in its physical meaning, you can *infuse* (a plant, herb, etc.) in a liquid in order to extract its properties, or (by a linguistic process that Fowler called 'object-shuffling') you can *infuse* (a liquid) by inserting something in it. The figurative meanings of *infuse* behave in corresponding ways: you can *infuse* (a quality or attribute) *into* a person or thing or you can *infuse* (a person or thing) *with* a quality or attribute. Examples: *Joanna Trollope's latest delicious novel . . . focuses on two men, lifelong friends of sixty-something, whose younger women infuse them both with seemingly eternal vigour*—She, 1989 / *He did his best to infuse good humour into his voice*—H. Forrester, 1990. *Imbue* could be used in the second construction with the same meaning: *A girl imbued with such qualities would be very special and extremely dangerous*—R. Hamilton, 1993.

ingenious, ingenuous. These two words are distantly related and both have undergone a major shift in meaning. *Ingenious* came into English via French from a Latin source derived from *ingenium* 'cleverness'; it originally meant 'intellectual, talented', but the meaning gradually weakened and its current sense is less complimentary and even depreciatory, '(of a person) clever, showing aptitude for devising curious devices' and '(of a device or idea) cleverly contrived': *There were the ingenious hand-made toys, the shadow-puppets manipulated on sticks*—H. Trevelyan, 1971 / *I see . . . that some ingenious person . . . has videotaped my television series*—Brian Aldiss, 1980 / *The score ingeniously employs reeds, brass, percussion and lower strings, instruments that can be associated with power and oppressive darkness*—MV Daily, AmE 2003 [*OEC*]. *Ingenuous*, by contrast, is derived from Latin *ingenuus* 'freeborn' and originally meant 'befitting a free man, noble in character', eventually weakening in sense to mean 'open, frank, candid': *Getty arrived half an hour late with the ingenuous excuse that he had miscalculated how long it would take*

him to walk from the Ritz to Boodles Club in St James's Street—Art Newspaper, 1992 / *She smiled ingenuously and the openness of her face seemed to ease his bad temper a little*—S. Wood, 1993 / *Akimov speaks with ingenuous enthusiasm about his commitment to unifying the company*—Guardian, 2001. The noun *ingenuity* was originally a derivative of *ingenuous* but was usurped by *ingenious* in the 16c, so that in current use *ingenuity* corresponds to *ingenious*, and *ingenuousness* corresponds to *ingenuous*. See also DISINGENUOUS.

ingénue, meaning 'an innocent or unsophisticated young woman', is first recorded in English in Thackeray's *Vanity Fair* (1848). It is not now printed in italics, is best written with the accent (though that is sometimes left off), and is pronounced in a quasi-French way ã-zhuh-noo.

-ing forms. The suffix *-ing* is added to verbs to form *verbal nouns (***Smoking** in enclosed public places is now illegal*) and *participles (*The house had a **smoking** chimney*).

ingrained is the normal spelling for the word meaning 'deeply rooted, inveterate' or (in physical senses) 'deeply embedded'.

ingratiate, a 17c Latinate loanword, is now normally used reflexively (with *oneself* etc.) in the meaning 'to render oneself agreeable to someone, to bring oneself into favour with someone': *The child glared at me so fiercely that I tried to ingratiate myself by asking who was her favourite composer*—M. Dibdin, 1991. The non-reflexive use is not standard: ☒ *He was going to pretend that his limp was cured, and that would ingratiate him with Matta, help him set his trap*—R. Campbell, 1993 / ☒ *Her first records with John Lennon didn't exactly ingratiate her to Beatle fans with their feedback-drenched,* *primal scream freak-outs*—music reviews website, AmE 2004 [*OEC*]. (Better alternatives in these examples would be *commend him to* and *endear her to*.) *Ingratiate* occurs frequently in the adjectival form *ingratiating*: *He was a typical British Council smoothie, with a fatuous grin and an ingratiating manner*—James Kirkup, 1991.

inherent is pronounced with the second syllable as in either *heron* or *here*, with a preference for the first of these.

inheritor, meaning 'a person who inherits', is spelt *-or*, not *-er*. It can be used of both a man and a woman.

inhuman, inhumane. The difference in meaning between these two words corresponds to that between *human* and *humane* (*see* HUMAN, HUMANE). *Inhuman* means 'lacking the qualities proper to human behaviour; cruel, brutal', whereas *inhumane* denotes a lack of feeling or compassion as it affects treatment of other people. Both words can be used of people, actions, or attitudes. Examples: (inhuman) *An Ankara MP... who called for an inquiry in parliament yesterday, described the incident as 'inhuman torture'*—*Guardian*, 1989 / *Claudia could see that locking up a Masai for a crime he did not understand was cruel and inhuman*—J. Cartwright, 1993 / (inhumane) *They have, after all, been traditionally concerned with restricting the use of weapons which are considered indiscriminate or inhumane*—J. Dewar et al., 1986 / *He was by no means an inhumane individual; he was a loving father, he was faithful to his wife for many years and to his mistress until death*—E. Acton, 1992 / *He must reverse judges' rulings that 24-hour control orders are inhumane*—*Sun*, 2007.

iniquity *see* INEQUITY, INIQUITY.

initial, as a verb meaning 'to mark or sign with one's initials', has inflected forms *initialled, initialling* in BrE and *initialed, initialing* in AmE.

initialisms *see* ABBREVIATIONS 3.

initiate, in the sense 'to instruct (a person) in some piece of knowledge', has the person as object and not the item of knowledge. You can *initiate* someone *in* or *into* something but you cannot *initiate* something *in* or *into* someone. The correct word for the second construction is *instil*. Examples of each: *Parsons is so smitten with Hubbard that he almost immediately initiates him into the highest levels of his occult church and uses him as an assistant in various rituals*—*LA Weekly*, AmE 2004 / *While I have managed to instil these ideals into my kids, many of those they encounter in the streets or parks have not been taught one jot of respect for anyone*—*Liverpool Daily Post*, 2007.

-in-law is added to the name of a relation to denote relationship by marriage (*mother-in-law, son-in-law*, etc.). Plurals are formed by adding *-s* to the main element, e.g. *mothers-in-law*. *In-laws* is used colloquially to refer to such relations generally; it is only idiomatic in the plural.

innings. In cricket, *innings* is both singular (*the first innings*) and plural (*the best of his three innings*). In AmE, the word used in baseball has a singular form *inning* and a plural form *innings*.

innuendo, meaning 'an indirectly disparaging hint or remark', has plural forms *innuendoes* and *innuendos*. The word is derived from a Latin gerund (verbal noun) meaning 'by nodding at', i.e. 'by pointing to, by meaning'. In English it was originally used in legal contexts to introduce an explanatory aside or comment, rather like *i.e.*, meaning 'that is to say'; then it came to be used as a noun denoting the aside itself, from which the current meaning developed.

innumerate *see* ILLITERATE, INNUMERATE.

inoculate, meaning 'to inject with a vaccine', is spelt with one *n*.

in order for. This allows a looser construction than **in order that* and avoids attendant problems with the mood and type of the following verb: *In order for this to work, the change from symmetry to broken symmetry must have taken place very slowly inside the bubble*—Stephen Hawking, 1988. This construction should be distinguished from the expression *in order* meaning 'acceptable, allowable as a procedure', which can be followed by *for: Is it in order for us to ring up your father and ask him to dine?*—Ngaio Marsh, 1977.

in order that. 1 Historically, *in order that* has been rather more restricted in the grammatical construction that follows it than has the less formal alternative *so that*. Fowler, writing in 1926, regarded use of the subjunctive (*in order that nothing be forgotten*) as archaic, use of the modal verbs *may* and *might* as the regular construction (*in order that nothing might be forgotten*), the use of *shall* and *should* as permissible in some contexts (*in order that nothing should be forgotten*), and the use of *can, could, will,* and *would* as 'undoubtedly wrong' (*in order that nothing can be forgotten* / *in order that nothing would be forgotten* / etc.). It is doubtful whether Fowler was correct about usage even in his own day. Today, with electronic language data available to check our intuitions about language, the facts are (1) that the subjunctive is increasingly used and is therefore by no means archaic, and (2) the modal verbs, including *can* and

could, shall and *should* (though rarely *will* and *would*), as well as *may* and *might*, are freely used when the context calls for them, although the *could, should,* and *would* forms are more common in each pair, and (3) that in order to avoid these problems many people are resorting to the alternative *in order for . . . to . . .* (see 4 below).

2 Examples of usage over the last ninety years or so will illustrate the grammatical range of this construction:

(may, might) *Stabilisation of wages is an urgent necessity in order that the industry might enjoy continued peace*—World's Paper Trade Review, 1922 / *A suitable block-and-tackle is essential in order that the boat may be hauled far enough up the shore to be safe from 'rafting' ice*—Discovery, 1935 / *He always insisted upon a certain reserve in order that the artist might give 'full measure' on the stage*—Dancing Times, 1990 / *The staff is committed to developing a genuine curiosity and love of learning in order that every child may be able to stretch and build upon their talents*—Croydon Guardian, 2004.

(can, could) *The motor should be wound up fully for each record played, in order that the turntable can rotate at its normal and even speed*—P. A. Scholes, 1921 / *The Telematics Programme . . . looks at users' needs and requirements in order that entire networks can talk to each other ready for 1992*—Practical Computing, 1990 / *Poor old cockerel . . . was also going to be 'cut' later that day in order that an offering could be made once more to Muniapa, God of the forest*—fishing website, BrE 2002 [OEC].

(shall, should) *In order that he shall be said to make a moral judgement, his attitude must be 'universalisable'*—A. E. Duncan-Jones, 1952 / *He faces obstinately towards the future rather than the past, resolving to unmask the worst in order that it should not come to pass*—C. Welch, 2001 / *A new trial of*

Mooney should be had in order that no possible mistake shall be made in a case where a human life is at stake—history website, BrE 2003 [*OEC*].

(do) *I can only hope that such methodology will be adopted by teachers new to media work in order that learning about the media does not become a bookcover here and a story-board there with little attempt at a coherent conceptual context*—*Times Educational Supplement*, 1990.

(subjunctive) *It is necessary to overcome this stability in order that a chemical reaction take place*—*Chemical Reviews*, 1952 / *In order that he be regularly scared by Authority, he should present himself every six months to the Service's Legal Adviser*—J. Le Carré, 1989 / *Another recent development in fouling is where the opposition is fouled well away from the scoring zone and each subsequent foul is perpetrated by a different player in order that yellow cards be avoided*—news website, IrishE 2003 [*OEC*].

3 Use of the subjunctive is often awkward in negative constructions because the modal verb *do* is not available, but negative examples are found, mostly in AmE but occasionally also in BrE: *Paulin vacillates in his claims in order that he not have to meet the responsibilities of arguing any of them out*—*London Review of Books*, 1990 / *We asked him to remove the pictures that violated trademark, in order that we not be sued*—weblog, AmE 2005.

4 When the subject of the purpose clause is the same as that of the main clause, the alternative and simpler expression *in order to* is available (*see* IN ORDER TO). When it is not the same (as in most of the examples given above), the looser construction *in order for . . . to . . .* has become much more common (*see* IN ORDER FOR).

in order to. This expression of purpose, which is in origin a complex preposition, has been in use since the 16c. In current use it is formed with a *to*-infinitive to mean 'with the purpose of (doing), with a view to': *Rozanov . . . had taken a sharp right-hand turn in order to avoid going along the road*—Iris Murdoch, 1983 / *The High Court lawsuit highlights the lengths insurance firms are willing to go to in order to protect their reputation and their clients*—*Daily Telegraph*, 2007. Use of the simpler preposition *to* instead of *in order to* is often preferred when the rhythm and emphasis of the sentence allow it, and this is sometimes less formal in effect: *The path takes an unscheduled turn to miss a big tree*—C. K. Stead, 1986 / *I went there to find the largest rose in the world*—*Western Mail*, 2007. The presence of *to* in a different role in the vicinity, especially another *to*-infinitive (as in the first 2007 example) is sometimes a factor in preferring the longer form *in order to*.

input, now pronounced with the stress on the first syllable both as a noun and as a verb, has defied the linguistic obsolescence that might have been apparent to the *OED* editors and assumed a new life in the domains of statistics, psychology, electronics, and (especially, since the late 1940s) computing. In all these, the essential meaning is (for the noun) 'information or data put into a system' and (for the verb) 'to enter (information or data) in a system'. The past and past participle forms of the verb are either *input* or *inputted*, and the present participle is *inputting*.

inquire, inquiry *see* ENQUIRE, ENQUIRY, INQUIRE, INQUIRY.

insanitary, unsanitary. Both words mean 'so dirty or germ-ridden as to be a danger to health' and were coined in the 1870s as a by-product of the Victorians' drive for better health. *Unsanitary* is much more common in all varieties of

English; *insanitary*, when used at all, occurs mainly in BrE.

inside of, meaning 'in less than (a period of time)' as in *It'll be finished inside of three days*, is a colloquial expression first recorded in AmE in the 1830s. It has made its way into other varieties of English, and is now heard informally in BrE, though its Americanness is still apparent. A related though now dated expression found in BrE is *for the inside of*, which has the somewhat different meaning 'for the most part of': *At first Isabel had only meant to stay away for the inside of a week*—L. P. Hartley, 1955.

insidious, invidious. Both words suggest harmful results, but despite their similarity tend not to be confused, except in one specific phrase. *Insidious* (from Latin *insidiae* 'ambush') means 'proceeding in a gradual, subtle way but with very harmful effects' (*An insidious form of sexism pervades most biographies of famous women, a tendency to treat women's work as peripheral to their lives*—Ms, 1973), whereas *invidious* (from Latin *invidia* 'envy') means 'likely to excite resentment or indignation' (*I hope it is not invidious . . . to single out here the museums for mention*—Oxford University Gazette, 1984). So *insidious* has more to do with the process and *invidious* more to do with its effect. *Invidious* also refers to comparisons that are unfair or that discriminate unjustly (*This decrees that a company cannot make fraudulent claims or invidious comparisons with another product*—British Medical Journal, 2004). It is in this meaning that *insidious* is sometimes wrongly used: ✖ *That plays right into the hands of those Christian anti-Semites . . . who make insidious comparisons between a 'loving' Christianity and a 'cruel' Judaism*—First Things (magazine), 2003.

insightful, meaning 'showing insight or understanding', is first recorded in a work by John Galsworthy in 1907. Since then it has become an omnipresent word of catch-all praise in many kinds of writing in which the writer probably has no precise idea of the compliment being paid: *She created a film which was memorable, intriguing and moving, a warm and insightful reconstruction of a vanished age*—Listener, 1982 / *It was a wonderful insightful exhibition*—Modern Painters, 1988 / *Sales people must be emotionally literate, pick up signals from clients and be insightful about their own emotions*—Daily Telegraph, 2007. The problem with this overused word (there are several thousand examples in the *OEC*) is that it depends so heavily on *insight*, which fails to support it with any corresponding force of meaning.

insignia, meaning 'badges or distinguishing marks of office', is in origin a plural of Latin *insigne*, although *insigne* is rarely used in English, and would be rather pretentious. *Insignia* may be used either as a plural noun or as a singular (mass) noun, e.g. either *Their insignia were worn on their coats* or *Their insignia was worn on their coats*. In BrE it is not generally accepted as a countable noun, i.e. preceded by *an* or used in the plural, e.g. *They wore an insignia on their coats* / *They wore insignias on their coats*, but this use is standard in AmE and accepted by AmE dictionaries.

insist takes several constructions in current English in the meaning 'to assert as a demand': you can *insist on* something (or *on doing* something), you can *insist that* something *be* done (subjunctive, with *that* optionally omitted, or with *should* as an alternative), or you can simply *insist* (with no complement). Examples: *Tony insisted that she accompany him to a meeting of the Literary Society*—A. S. Byatt, 1985 / *And I,* *maliciously, insisted he take the most comfortable chair*—Penelope Lively, 1987 / *Henry had not wanted to bring Louisa on the expedition but she had cried to go, and the adults insisted that she not be left behind*—L. Clarke, 1989 / *The family received me very warmly and Signora Ugolotti insisted that I should have something to eat*—W. Newby, 1991 / *They insisted on spending ages there wandering around choosing a book each*—*Yorkshire Post*, 2002 / *Keep it sexual by insisting that she leave her underwear at home*—fashion website, AmE 2004. When *insist* means 'assert as a fact or truth', it is followed by a *that*-clause with an ordinary indicative (i.e. not subjunctive) verb: *He insisted that the government was incapable of resolving the structural crisis of the country*—*Socialist Worker Online*, 2003.

in so far as, meaning 'to the extent that', can be written as four words, and is shown in this form in the *OED*, but *insofar as* is about twice as frequent. In both forms the *as* is kept detached: *The exercise of reviewing his life was proving monstrous in so far as it revealed the places in which it had gone irredeemably wrong*—Anita Brookner, 1988 / *Insofar as I had thought at all about what Italians did on vacation, I imagined the inhabitants of the cities joyfully rushing towards the provinces for the whole of August*—*Times*, 2004. It is a rather formal phrase, and can often be replaced by *so far as*, *as far as*, or, when it does not really express the idea of 'to the extent that', recast with little loss of meaning in a simpler construction with *since* or *because*.

insoluble, unsolvable. *Insoluble* relates to the meanings of *dissolve* as well as *solve*, and therefore refers to difficulties, questions, and problems that cannot be answered as well as to substances that cannot be absorbed in liquid. *Unsolvable* is more limited in range, corresponding only to the first of these meanings. In the *OEC* data, it is as common as *insoluble* when associated with *problem*(s).

inspector is spelt *-or*, not *-er*.

install is spelt with two *l*s and has inflected forms *installed, installing*. The noun is *instalment* in BrE and *installment* in AmE.

instantly, instantaneously. *Instantly* means 'immediately' and refers to the point at which something happens, whereas *instantaneously* means 'in an instant' and refers to the (imperceptibly short) period of time that something takes: *He pressed the override switch and the computer came instantly to life*—A. Haig, 1974 / *Her throat had been slashed viciously, and she must have died almost instantaneously*—R. Long, 1990. The result can often be the same, but the difference of emphasis is worth bearing in mind.

instigate properly means 'to bring about by excitement or persuasion, to foment or provoke', and usually refers to an antisocial or discreditable action, such as violence, wars, revolts, riots, acts of terrorism, or political coups: . . . *a radical association that . . . instigated campus riots that succeeded in closing down a number of universities over a period of months in 1969*—*New Yorker*, 1975. Because of its similarity of form to *institute*, it has been increasingly used in the more neutral meaning 'to start or set up', with reference to formal activities such as inquiries, legal proceedings, reviews, and searches: *The objective of this new phase is to . . . instigate legal, policy and institutional reforms at the country level*—*Lloyd's List*, 2007. Passive uses are common: *The scam has already been the subject of a Welsh television* *documentary, instigated by Richard's early research*—news website, BrE 2003 [*OEC*]. With so many synonyms available (*institute, initiate, launch, establish, inaugurate*, etc.), it is a pity that *instigate* cannot be reserved to its special and useful meaning, but to insist on this now is to support a *lost cause, further undermined by the more casual use of the derivative noun *instigation*, idiomatically in the phrase *at the instigation of* (*At Houston's instigation, local jazzmen would play for the youngsters at assemblies and school dances*—*Guardian*, 2007). We might however continue to fight a rearguard action against the use of *instigate* with a personal object in place of more suitable words such as *encourage* and *incite*: ☒ *Another group drove civilian vehicles and distributed weapons to the people, instigating them to kill the American troops*—weblog, AmE 2004 [*OEC*].

instil, instill. *Instil* is spelt with one *l* in BrE and as *instill* in AmE. The inflected forms are *instilled, instilling* in both varieties. The non-physical meaning is 'to introduce (a feeling, idea, etc.) into a person's mind': *They believed, quite wrongly, that to instil a sense of guilt into me would ultimately be for my good*—R. Hitchcock, 1989 / *Many noted the significance the new Prime Minister has given in recent days to the values and morals that were instilled in him while he was growing up in Fife*—*Scotsman*, 2007. Some people object to its being used with the person as object, tempting though this sometimes is in passive use: ☒ *During the war my mother and brother and I went to Norfolk, and there I was instilled with a love of the countryside*—*Sunday Express*, 1986. In this construction, the alternatives *imbue, infuse*, and *inspire* are available. *See* INFUSE.

instinct *see* INTUITION.

instinctive, instinctual. The normal adjective from *instinct* in everyday use is *instinctive*, which can refer to people and animals or to their behaviour and actions. *Instinctual* is used mainly in technical contexts such as psychology and psycholinguistics, and is modelled on other forms such as *conceptual* and *habitual*, which seem to afford it an extra authority not shared by the more generalized word *instinctive*. If used outside a technical field, *instinctual* can easily be tarred with the brush of pretentiousness: *'I'm trying to make the personal-networks group ebb and flow into other parts of Motorola like an amoeba, so that I don't know where their people end and mine start,' she says. 'It's not instinctual in a high-testosterone culture'*—*Fast Company* (magazine), 2000.

institute, institution. Both words are used with reference to organizations and societies set up to pursue some specific literary, scientific, legal, or social purpose, and choice usually depends on the form already used for a particular name. The earliest *institute* mentioned in the *OED* is the *Mechanics' Institute* (established in 1823), and the earliest institution is the *Royal Masonic Benevolent Institution* (founded in 1798). Famous recent examples include the Women's Institute (first established in Canada in 1897 and then extended to other countries in the early 20c) and the *British Standards Institution* (the UK national body on standards, established in the 20c). In the generalized meaning 'something established by law or custom', as applied for example in the UK to the monarchy, the Grand National, the last night of the Proms, etc. (though no longer to capital punishment and the Workhouse, which featured in Fowler's 1926 list), *institution* is the only word used.

instructor is spelt *-or*, not *-er*.

insubstantial is much more frequent than *unsubstantial* for the word meaning 'lacking substance or solidity'.

insufficient is a useful word because *enough* has no corresponding negative form, but *not enough* is often more natural and usually less formal-sounding. Another alternative in some contexts is *inadequate*, which can refer to quantity as well as quality.

insupportable, unsupportable *see* IN- AND UN-.

insurance *see* ASSURE, ASSURANCE.

insure *see* ASSURE, ENSURE.

intaglio, an originally Italian word meaning 'an engraved design or gem', is pronounced in-**ta**-li-oh or in-**tal**-yoh and has the plural form *intaglios*.

integral is both a noun (used in mathematics) and an adjective (meaning 'forming a whole' or 'necessary to the completeness of a whole'). As a noun it is pronounced with the stress on the first syllable; as an adjective it may be pronounced with the stress on the first or the second syllable, although the first is often preferred.

integrate essentially means 'to make whole' and is widely used of bringing separate or disparate elements together to form a unity. Since the late 1940s it has been used to refer to the social absorption of distinct groups, especially ethnically or culturally different peoples or disadvantaged elements. In this meaning it is used both transitively (with an object) and (less often) intransitively: *Those children who came knowing some English integrated well*—New Statesman, 1966 / *Old people, sick people and isolated people need access to a telephone if they are to be fully integrated with the rest of society*—Nature, 1972 / *From these beginnings developed the startling and*

revolutionary notion that in residential areas traffic and people should not be segregated but instead should be integrated—R. Rolley, 1990. The noun *integration* has developed a corresponding meaning, and those who favour it are known as *integrationists*: *In the work of black authors who are integrationists a tacitly separatist or ethnically independent element appears frequently*—Black Scholar, 1971. It is also used adjectivally: *Ashcroft initially honored the moderate, integrationist legacy of his mentor and predecessor*—Nation, AmE 2001.

intelligent design is a disarmingly reassuring term for the belief that life should be explained as the creation of an intelligent agent (i.e. God) rather than as the result of a process of natural selection. Dating from the mid-19c in America, it intentionally disguises the element of faith and belief that is involved in such a view, and represents an aggressive attempt to rationalize the irrational as a reaction to the scientific arguments of evolutionists. Many see the term as a dishonest evasion, and it should be used with great care, as it comes with a great deal of emotive and political baggage.

intelligentsia is a singular noun meaning 'the class of intellectuals regarded as possessing culture and political initiative'. The form of the word is Russian, and it was originally applied disparagingly in pre-revolutionary Russia. In a weakened sense, it also means 'people doing intellectual work'. It can have both singular and plural concord, like other collective nouns, i.e.: *But the intelligentsia also bears some responsibility, since it privileges its own experience over that of the common people*—History Today, 2003 / *Not only did the left-wing intelligentsia dislike uppity lower-middle-class arrivistes: they positively discouraged the most deprived*

*working-class people from rejecting
their 'roots'—City Journal* (New York),
2002.

intend. *Intend* is followed in standard
usage by a *to*-infinitive (*We intend to go /
We intended you to go*), by a verbal noun
(*We intend going*), or by a *that*-clause
(*We intended that you should go*). In the
passive, it is followed by *for* in the
meaning 'be meant or designed for'
(*These are intended for children*). Non-
standard constructions include the type
⊠ *He didn't intend for Wales to lose,*
which should be expressed as *He didn't
intend that Wales should lose,* and the
informal AmE type *Don't pick up a
magazine unless you intend on buying it,*
which should be expressed as *Don't pick
up a magazine unless you intend buying
[or intend to buy] it.*

intense, intensive. In the broad
meaning 'existing in a high degree, extreme' as applied to feelings and qualities, *intense* is the word to use. (It also
applies to people, in the sense 'apt to feel
strong emotion'.) *Intensive,* which used
to share aspects of the non-personal
meaning of *intense,* is now reserved for
the special meaning 'directed to a single
point or objective, thorough, vigorous':
*The country has suffered from intensive
over-planning—Times,* 1977. Special applications include the terms *intensive
care* (of medical treatment, in this form
from the 1960s) and *labour-intensive*
('needing a large workforce', 1950s).

intensifier in grammar is a class of
adverbs that amplify or add emphasis to
a gradable adjective (i.e. an adjective
with a meaning capable of a range of
force), such as *extremely, greatly, highly,*
and *very.* Some adjectives are also
classed as intensifiers, for example *complete* as in *a **complete** fool, single* as in
*not a **single** word, sure* as in *a **sure** sign,*
and *whole* as in *a **whole** month.*

intensive *see* INTENSE. It is also an
older term for **intensifier.*

intention is followed either by
of + verbal noun or by a *to*-infinitive,
the first of these being somewhat more
common and the second influenced by
the verb *intend: I have no intention—no
present intention—of standing for Parliament—*Harold Macmillan, 1979 /
*He went to Cambridge to read Natural
Science, with the intention of becoming
a geologist—*H. Carpenter, 1981 / *He has
given notice of his intention to turn up
this evening—*Kingsley Amis, 1980 / *It
was never the intention to start the second
battle of Maldon—*Essex Chronicle, 2004.

inter, intern. *Inter* (with the stress on
the second syllable) means 'to bury (a
corpse)' and has inflected forms *interred,
interring. Intern* means 'to arrest and
confine (an alien) in time of war'. *See
also* INTERMENT, INTERNMENT.

inter-, intra-. *Inter-* is a combining
form meaning 'between, among' (*inter-
city / interlinear*) or 'mutually, recipro-
cally' (*interbreed / intermix*), whereas
intra- forms adjectives and means
'on the inside, within' (*intramural /
intravenous*).

inter alia is Latin for 'among other
things'. Since *alia* is neuter plural it does
not normally refer to people. The Latin
equivalent would be *inter alios,* but this
is never used. The English alternative
among others does not have this restriction and is preferable in general use.

interceptor, meaning 'a person or
thing (especially an aircraft) that inter-
cepts', is spelt *-or,* not *-er.*

interchange is pronounced with the
stress on the first syllable as a noun and
with the stress on the third syllable as a
verb.

interchangeable is spelt with an *e* in the middle to preserve the soft sound of the *g*.

intercourse. The use of this word as short for *sexual intercourse* (first recorded in 1798 but not common before the 20c) has made it difficult to use it in its general meaning 'communication or dealings between individuals, nations, etc.', and a claim such as that of Maria Eliza Rundell (1745–1828) in her *New System of Domestic Cookery* that a wife's role was to provide 'the sweet refuge of a husband fatigued by intercourse with a jarring world' might now be seriously misunderstood. Even the phrase *social intercourse*, unambiguous though it is in print, can cause uncertainty when heard in the run of ordinary conversation.

interdependence, interdependency. Both forms are in use with no difference in meaning, but *interdependence* is much more common.

interest is now normally pronounced **in**-trist or **in**-trest, with the first *e* unpronounced. The same applies to the derivative words *interested, interesting*, etc.

interestingly is recorded as a *sentence adverb from the 1960s, and is now common: *Interestingly, what exercises Lord Chalfont is not the existence of nuclear weapons, an existence which, he says, cannot be repealed*—Martin Amis, 1987.

interface. The use of this word was transformed between the publication of the original *OED* entry in 1901 and that of the updated entry in *OED*2 in 1989. To the earlier editors it meant simply 'a surface lying between two portions of matter or space, and forming their common boundary'. In the 1960s, two disciplines adopted it for their own special use and effectively rivalled each other in their efforts to propel it into vogue use: the computer industry and that special branch of sociology known as communications theory, represented especially by the Canadian critic and theorist Marshall McLuhan (*The Gutenberg Galaxy*, 1962). Now, an *interface* was, on the one hand, 'an apparatus designed to connect two scientific instruments, devices, etc., so that they can be operated jointly' and, on the other, 'a point where interaction occurs between two systems, processes, subjects, etc'. Its vogue status was assured when it was applied ever more widely to the relations between business development and marketing systems, lecturers and students, unions and management, and other areas of public life: *The issue of insanity as a defense in criminal cases . . . is at the interface of medicine, law and ethics*—*Scientific American*, 1972. McLuhan was also responsible for the first use of *interface* as a verb, meaning 'to come into interaction with', first recorded in 1967, and a corresponding use in computing and electronic technology soon followed. There are signs that the onslaught from this word has abated somewhat, leaving it to be used more effectively in technical domains. This is fortunate, when more familiar (and usually more precise) alternatives, such as (for the noun) *boundary, contact, link, liaison, meeting point, interaction*, and (for the verb) *communicate, have contact with, interact*, are readily available to cater for the general meanings. The popular press, however, still embraces the word when writing about gadgets: *The principle might work well on the current generation of 'smart' mobile phones, but interfacing with the interface is much easier when you're walking down the street than flying down the motorway*—*Hull Daily Mail*, 2007.

interior, internal. The differences in meaning and usage between these two words correspond to those between *exterior* and *external* (*see* EXTERIOR, EXTERNAL). *Interior* is a noun as well as an adjective and refers in physical senses to the inside of things in contrast to the outside, whereas *internal* is primarily an adjective and is also applied in abstract or figurative meanings: *Politicisation of religion means the internal transformation of the faith itself—Listener*, 1978 / *Beset by internal dissent and external opposition, the community discontinued complex marriage in 1879 and formally dissolved in 1881—Oxford Companion to United States History*, 2001. An *internal investigation* is one conducted by an organization into its own affairs, and an *internal phone call* is one made from one member of staff to another in the same building or office. With reference to the body, *internal injuries* are those sustained by the inside organs, and medicine for *internal use* is meant to be swallowed. The word is also used occasionally as a noun in the plural to mean 'intrinsic qualities' and in various technical applications.

interlocutor, meaning 'a person who takes part in a dialogue or conversation', is spelt *-or*, not *-er*, and is pronounced with the stress on the third syllable.

interment, internment. *Interment* means 'the burial of a corpse', whereas *internment* means 'the confinement of aliens in time of war'. *See also* INTER, INTERN.

intermezzo, as used in the contexts of music and drama, has the plural forms *intermezzos* and *intermezzi*, which are equally frequent.

intermission, meaning 'an interval between parts of a play, film, etc.', is American in origin but is now as widely used in BrE as the traditional word *interval*.

intermittent, meaning 'occurring at intervals', is spelt *-ent*.

in terms of. *Let's face it—in terms of artistic talent, Emin isn't fit to wipe Monet's backside—Cherwell Mag. Online*, 2005. In 1993, the Oxford philosopher Michael Dummett had awarded this complex preposition the distinction of being 'the lowest point so far in the present degradation of the English language', when used as an all-purpose connector as in the example just given. Extreme though this opinion may be, and contrary to usage (there are thousands of occurrences in the *OEC*), the use it condemns is a far departure from the original (18c) use of the phrase as an expression of a precise mathematical relation. In its now predominant generalized use, *in terms of* is used most appositely when it states a particular specifying relation: *The impact of Ibsen . . . did much to revitalize the degenerate English theatre and force it to think in terms of living ideas and contemporary realities—* J. Mulgan & D. M. Davin, 1947 / *Justifying space in terms of material wealth is as ridiculous as saying that man went to the Moon merely to be able to return with velcro zips and non-stick frying-pans—New Scientist*, 1991. When the meaning intended is as vague as 'in relation to', 'concerning', or 'as regards' (as in the example given at the beginning), these expressions are preferable.

intern is pronounced with the stress on the second syllable as a verb (*see* INTER, INTERN) and with the stress on the first syllable as a noun (also spelt *interne*, meaning 'a recent graduate in medicine' or 'a person working as an apprentice in one of the professions', principally American use).

international community. This expression has found favour in recent years with politicians and journalists, and one can see why. It is a convenient catch-all phrase invoked when international support for a policy or action is needed (or, more often, presumed), much as 'public opinion' is invoked in domestic politics. In neither case is any specific attribution or verification possible; yet both empty phrases sound impressive. The earliest evidence in the *OED* dates from the late 1950s and shows the expression to have originated in legal language: *Could the papacy ... be properly regarded as a member of the international community of the law of nations?*—R. A. Graham, 1959. Recent examples: *Pretoria sees the Eminent Persons Group as a useful channel of communication with the ANC and the international community*—*Financial Times*, 1986 / *The way in which Saddam Hussein still behaves is unacceptable to us, to the United Nations and to the international community, and we shall continue to keep pressure on him*—*Hansard*, 1992 / *China's rising status on the world stage leads the international community to ask what road China will pursue to achieve its development*—*Morning Star*, 2007.

internecine. Dr Johnson had a hand in changing the use of this word, which its Latin origin shows to mean 'characterized by great slaughter'. He mistakenly understood the prefix *inter-* to denote reciprocal or mutual action and defined *internecine* as 'endeavouring mutual destruction', thereby setting the word on the way to its primary current meaning. Despite the objections of the more fervent purists, who invoke the word's pre-Johnsonian credentials, it is used in its later meaning with reference to physical war and killing and has developed an extended or trivialized meaning applied to the battles of the boardroom and other areas of business and public life: *The electorate ... finally gagged on their traditional roughage of internecine strife*—*Times*, 1974 / *He was on edge, engaged in flaming rows, head-blasting music mayhem and internecine squabbling with his garage band compadres Crazy Horse*—*New Musical Express*, 1991 / *That gives you some idea of the internal rivalry and internecine squabbling that went on*—*BBC History*, 2004.

Internet has a capital *I*.

internment *see* INTERMENT, INTERNMENT.

interpersonal, once the preserve of psychologists, has embedded itself in the language of the curriculum vitae, in which no applicant's credentials are adequate without an endorsement of his or her *interpersonal skills*, i.e. the ability to deal effectively with other people. It is also widely used by sociologists to refer to the ways in which people treat each other in everyday life: *The social workers in their study appeared to be more aware than the psychiatrists of the relevance of interpersonal and family problems*—K. Hawton et al., 1990.

interpretative, interpretive. The preferred form for this word meaning 'serving to interpret or explain' is *interpretative*, on the analogy of *authoritative*, *qualitative*, and *quantitative*: *You may be wondering why I am rabbiting on about interpretative processes when the theme of this article is how to build a bracket clock*—*Practical Woodworking*, 1990. However, *interpretive* is about twice as common, perhaps reinforced by the natural tendency to articulate both words in this way in rapid speech: *Chinese culture has undergone major interpretive phases in recent decades*—*Dædalus*, 1991.

interregnum, meaning 'an interval when normal government is suspended', has the plural form *interregnums* and *interregna*, the first being more frequent.

intestinal, meaning 'relating to the intestines', is pronounced with the stress on the second syllable (in-**tes**-ti-nuhl) or on the third syllable (in-tes-**tiy**-nuhl, increasingly in BrE).

in that, which is difficult to analyse grammatically, is effectively a conjunction, but it is not easy to find in dictionaries. Shakespeare used it: *Let him die, in that he is a Fox—2 Henry VI* III.i.257. Fowler (1926) regarded it as obsolescent (becoming obsolete) and warned against the misuse that idiomatic expressions are liable to on their way out of the language. But Fowler's judgement was at fault, and the examples he gave were not typical of usage, and so he was tilting at windmills. The expression still has a place at the core of everyday usage and means rather more than is conveyed by *because*: *They work like disks in that they can be partially erased—Management Computing*, 1990 / *The vessels . . . are unusual in that they have no engine room—Ships Monthly*, 1991 / *We have some similarities, in that we both make fun of rock, while loving it, intensely—*film reviews website, BrE 2004 [*OEC*].

in the circumstances *see* CIRCUMSTANCE.

into, in to. 1 *Into* is written as one word when the meaning is unified in expressing motion towards or to within a destination (*He walked into a tree* / *She put her hand into his*). However, when *in* and *to* retain their separate roles, it is important to write them as separate words, usually when *to* is not connected with *in* but is part of a following *to*-infinitive or refers forward to a noun or phrase: *People dropped in to see them* / *He accompanied her in to dinner* / *They were listening in to our conversation*.

2 The modern use of *into* meaning 'involved in or knowledgeable about' (usually as a transitory interest), is informal only: *First I was into Zen, then I*

was into peace, then I was into love, then I was into freedom, then I was into religion. Now I'm into money—New Yorker, 1971.

intra- *see* INTER-.

intransitive and transitive verbs. A verb is transitive when it 'takes an object', i.e. it has a following word or phrase which the action of the verb affects (*They **lit** a fire*), and is intransitive when it does not take an object (*We **arrived** at noon*). Some verbs are always or predominantly transitive (*assure, bury, deny, put*); others are always or predominantly intransitive (especially verbs of motion such as *arrive, come, go*, etc.); and others are sometimes transitive and sometimes intransitive (for example, *move* is transitive in the sentence *Go and **move** the car* and intransitive in the sentence *The car **moved** down the road*, and *cook* is respectively intransitive and transitive in the sentences *I like to cook* and *I'm going to cook the breakfast*). Some verbs appear to have two objects, which in traditional grammar are called *direct* and *indirect*: in the sentence *They **gave** her an apple*, *apple* is the direct object (= what they gave) and *her* is the indirect object (= the person who got the apple). *See also* DIRECT OBJECT; INDIRECT OBJECT.

intransitive past participles. Most past participles are of transitive verbs and, when used as adjectives, denote an action performed on the noun or phrase they qualify; for example, the phrase *a **polished** table* denotes the state of the table as having been polished. However, some verbs that are intransitive nonetheless form past participles which are used as adjectives, as in *an **escaped** prisoner* (= a prisoner who has escaped), *a **failed** writer* (= a writer who has failed), ***fallen** leaves* (= leaves that have fallen), and *a **grown** man* (= a man who has grown up, *not* a man who has been grown). In these cases the nouns or phrases they qualify are the subjects rather than the objects of the corresponding verbs. *See* PARTICIPLES.

intrigue *verb*. **1** The inflected forms are *intrigued, intriguing*.

2 The predominant current meaning is 'to arouse the curiosity of; to fascinate'. When Fowler wrote (1926) this was a fairly new sense (first attested in the 1890s) and the need for what he regarded as an affected Gallicism puzzled him when an apparent wealth of synonyms, including *fascinate, mystify, interest*, and *puzzle, perplex* (he could also have mentioned *absorb, captivate, enchant*, and *enthral*), was already available. But none of these has quite the same element of the mildly sinister or elusive that *intrigue* draws from its other meanings, past and present (principally the still current one 'to carry on an underhand plot'). Like some of the synonyms mentioned, *intrigue* is commonly used in its participial form *intriguing*. Examples: *Even more intriguing than the sociology of fashion is its psychology*—Observer, 1974 / *We are in turn sympathetic, intrigued, shocked, entertained—but oh the yearning for the world she magically conjured*—A. Huth, 1992.

intrinsic means 'inherent, essential, belonging naturally' and is the opposite of *extrinsic*: *The study of portraits on coins is . . . as much about the political factors that influenced them as about their intrinsic or moral interest*—A. Burnett, 1991. *See* EXTERIOR 2. The corresponding adverb is *intrinsically*.

intrusive r is the insertion of the sound of an unwritten *r* between one vowel sound and another, as in *draw-r-ing* for *drawing* and *umbrella-r-organization* for *umbrella organization*. Though much criticized, it is common even in received pronunciation and follows the pattern of linking *r* in words ending in an *r* that is only pronounced when a vowel follows, as in *far away* (*see* LINKING R).

intuit, an 18c back-formation from *intuition*, means 'to know or deduce intuitively', and is a mainly literary or technical word: *Maud decided she intuited something terrible about Cropper's imagination from all this*—A. S. Byatt, 1990 / *It is never easy to intuit an Asian cafe's specialty on a first visit*—LA Weekly, 2004.

intuition, instinct. The two words overlap in meaning, and the *OED* indeed uses *intuition* in one of its definitions of *instinct*. Both refer to intellectual activity and both denote processes in which knowledge is apprehended without using any process of reasoning. An important difference, however, is that *intuition* is confined to humans whereas *instinct* is attributable to the animal world at large. In extended meanings, *intuition* means 'immediate insight' into a fact or feeling (as in the notorious phrase *a woman's intuition*), and *instinct* means 'unconscious skill' (*an instinct for getting the best deal*); these meanings too refuse to stay apart. Examples: (intuition) *A student's intuition moves far more swiftly than can an instruction manual, and I believe that self-tuition is the finest form of education*—R. Brindle Smith, 1986 / *Whatever that small voice of intuition was telling her about her destiny, common-sense decreed that the Prince already had a full hand of potential suitors*—A. Morton, 1993 / (instinct) *Blythswood Square, once home of the infamous poisoner Madaleine Smith, and latterly, numerous other ladies with hearts of loose change and the instincts of a blushing tarantula*—E. Chisnall, 1989 / *Running out was totally unprofessional, but she had acted purely on instinct*—J. Evans, 1993.

Inuit *see* ESKIMO.

inured means 'accustomed to something' and that something is usually unpleasant. One can also become inured to a person: *It's clear that she's not inured to Walter at all—Flak Mag.*, 2004. It is not a synonym for 'immune', and *inure* is not a synonym for 'protect': ✷ *In this unfolding economic scenario, complacency is the order of the day. We are all inured against headlines—Financial Sense Online*, 2005. / ✷ *Does he think by injecting religion into a piece it inures it from criticism?—Classical Net Reviews*, 2004.

invalid is pronounced with the stress on the second syllable as an adjective (meaning 'not valid') and with the stress on the first syllable as a noun (meaning 'a person affected by disease or injury').

inveigle. The recommended pronunciation of this verb meaning 'to entice or persuade by guile' is in-**vay**-guhl rather than the alternative in-**vee**-guhl.

inventor is spelt -*or*, not -*er*.

inventory, meaning 'an official list of goods etc.', is pronounced **in**-v(uh)n-t (uh)-ri in BrE and **in**-vuhn-taw-ri in AmE, and by BrE speakers who don't know any better.

inversion. In grammar, *inversion* is the process by which the normal order of words, with the subject followed by the verb and then by the object or complement (if any) as in *We play football on Saturdays* is broken by putting the subject after the verb (as in questions: *Do you play football on Saturdays?*) or by putting the complement (or part of it) first in the sentence, often for emphasis (*On Saturdays, we play football*). Other regular forms of inversion, usually requiring little conscious effort by native speakers, occur as follows:

1 In direct speech, the subject and the verb (*say, cry, shout*, etc.) that identify the spoken words are optionally inverted: *'Hey!' shouted Mrs. House, who sat inside with her jumpsuit around her knees—New Yorker*, 1992.

2 After negatives placed in initial position for emphasis, the subject and verb are routinely inverted: *Yet never before had I seen anything so scarlet and so black—J. M. Coetzee*, 1990.

3 After initially placed *so* followed by an adjective, the subject and verb are inverted: *He had hardly been aware, so nervous was he, of what he had been saying—Peter Carey*, 1988.

4 In a sentence in which a statement is followed by a reinforcing form of *do*: *She enjoyed a laugh, did Lilian—Margaret Drabble*, 1987.

5 In declarations beginning with an adverb, when the subject of a following intransitive verb is a noun: *Here comes the train* but *Here they come*.

6 In condition clauses with omission of *if* or *whether*: *Were this done, we would retain a separate Bar with skill—Times*, 1986 / *Statistically, afterworlds—be they Christian, Greek, Pharaonic—must be populated almost entirely by children—Penelope Lively*, 1987.

7 In certain types of comparison involving a statement after *than*: *Poland's power structure included neither more nor fewer Jews than did the power structure in Rumania or in Hungary—Dædalus*, 1987.

8 Words are placed first for special effect in poetry and rhetorical writing: ***His soul** proud science never taught to stray—Pope* / ***Trusting** she had been, she who had been reared in the bosom of suspicion—Margaret Drabble*, 1987. This has spilled over into more informal usage, in which the effect is awkward rather than striking and should be avoided except in conversation: ***Great literature** it's not, but . . . it's short, pithy—The Face*, 1987.

inverted commas *see* QUOTATION MARKS.

investigative. In BrE this is normally stressed on the second syllable, in-**ves**-ti-guh-tiv, with the fourth syllable pronounced indistinctly as a schwa. In AmE it is pronounced with a secondary stress as -*gative*, rhyming with *native*. This looks like another word whose British pronunciation is giving way to an American one, like *resource* and *research*.

investigator is spelt -*or*, not -*er*.

investor is spelt -*or*, not -*er*.

invidious *see* INSIDIOUS, INVIDIOUS.

invincible, meaning 'that cannot be defeated', is spelt -*ible*, not -*able*. *See* -ABLE, -IBLE.

invisible is spelt -*ible*, not -*able*. *See* -ABLE, -IBLE.

invite *noun* (with the stress on the first syllable). This is a good example of a word that has been in more or less continuous use since the 17c but has not attained the acceptability afforded to its rival, *invitation*. Dr Johnson must have known it but did not include it in his Dictionary (1755), nor did Charles Richardson in 1863. It was admitted with a 'colloquial' label to the *OED* (1901) and its failure to gain respectability was noted by Fowler (1926), who commented that 'it is less recognized as an English word than *bike*'. Seventy years on, things have hardly changed, and the general consensus seems to be that as a noun *invite* belongs to the informal or even comic realms of language use: *The four detectives didn't await an invite into the house*—G. F. Newman, 1970 / *He scoffs, indicating the dodgier invites entreating his attendance at this or that launch*—Sunday Express Magazine, 1987 / *He knows a particularly good printer who did the invites for his cousin's wedding*—Precision Marketing, 1989 / *We got an invite to Emerald's birthday party*—K. Lighter, AmE 2004.

involve. 1 This heavily used word has extended its meaning from the notion of envelopment or entanglement (it is derived from the Latin word *involvere* meaning 'to enwrap') to less precise forms of connection, as in *What does the work involve?* and *No other vehicle was involved* (in police descriptions of one-vehicle accidents). Resistance to this natural development in meaning belongs to the domain of *lost causes.

2 The participial form *involving* used as a quasi-preposition is often better replaced by a simpler word: *A collision took place involving a private motor vehicle and a lorry* (use *between*) / *There was no reduction last year in the number of cases involving cruelty to horses* (use *of*).

inward, inwards. The only form for the adjective is *inward* (*the inward route*), but *inward* and *inwards* are both used for the adverb, with a preference for *inwards* in BrE: *Our instructor starts us on snowplough turns* (*with the tips of the skis pointing inwards*)—Observer, 1978 / *The casements can all be opened inwards*—P. Steadman, 2001.

iodine, the chemical element and the antiseptic made from it, is pronounced either **iy**-uh-deen or **iy**-uh-din. In AmE it is also pronounced **iy**-uh-diyn.

-ion, -ment, -ness. These three suffixes are all used to form nouns; -*ion* and -*ment* represent Latin elements via Old French and are normally added to verbs to form nouns of action (*abridgement, excision*) or state (*contentment, vexation*), whereas -*ness* is an Old English form, is normally added to adjectives to form nouns of state (*bitterness, happiness*) or instances of a state or quality (*a kindness*), and is the most active suffix in forming new words. Regarding -*ion* and -*ment*, the choice is largely determined by the forms already existing in Old French, although some nouns were formed on existing English verbs (e.g. *acknowledgement, amazement, ful-filment*). Some verbs have given rise to more than one form, usually with a difference in meaning (e.g. *commission* and *commitment* from *commit, excitation* and *excitement* from *excite*).

Iranian is pronounced i-**ray**-ni-uhn in BrE, and i-**ray**-ni-uhn, i-**rah**-ni-uhn, or iy-**ray**-ni-uhn in AmE.

irascible, meaning 'irritable, hot-tempered', is spelt -*ible*, not -*able*. *See* -ABLE, -IBLE.

iridescent, meaning 'showing gleaming colours, rainbow-like', is spelt with one *r*, being derived from the Latin word *iris* (stem *irid-*) meaning 'rainbow'.

iron curtain. The phrase had its origin in the 18c with reference to a safety device lowered in theatres between the stage and the auditorium. Its figurative use referring to any impenetrable barrier evolved in the early 19c and it acquired its classic meaning in the 20c when used of the East-European sphere of influence exercised in the postwar years by the Soviet Union. The locus classicus (though not the first use, which was in 1920) was a speech given by Winston Churchill in the US in 1946: *From Stettin, in the Baltic, to Trieste, in the Adriatic, an iron curtain has descended across the Continent.* Although the term has developed various allusive uses (*I don't want the United States to appear like an 'Iron Curtain' to the Vietnamese—Freedomways*, 1967), the dismantling of the Berlin Wall in 1989 and the collapse of the Soviet Union caused it to lose its potency except as a vivid historical reminder.

ironic, ironical, ironically. For the adjective, choice between *ironic* and *ironical* seems to be determined largely by sentence rhythm, and by the fact that *ironic* is massively more frequent than

ironical. Both words properly mean 'of the nature of irony', i.e. implying the opposite of what is literally or normally meant by a word, look, etc.: *She gave an ironical laugh as she looked at Guy—*Olivia Manning, 1977. In this sentence, *ironical* shows that the laugh was marking something other than the usual humour. Both words, however, are now increasingly used to mean simply 'odd, strange, paradoxical', and the same is true of the corresponding adverb *ironically*: *It is paradoxical, 'ironical' as people say today, that the constitution should bestow this power on someone who laments constitutionitis in others—Observer,* 1987 / *It is ironic that such a beautiful orderly house should be the setting of our messy little farce—*S. Mason, 1990 / *Ironically the bombing of London was a blessing to the youthful generations that followed—*I. &. P. Opie, 1969 / *Ironically, many modern writers have been nihilistic toward modern culture—Dissent,* AmE 2004. These uses, which are well established despite frequent criticism of them, perhaps contain an echo of the concept of *dramatic irony*, in which an audience is made aware of an act or circumstance that affects the action on stage (or screen) in a way that is unknown to one or more of the participants in the drama.

iron out is a common phrasal verb, American in origin and used informally to mean 'to remove (difficulties etc.)'. As the physical image is still fairly near the surface, it is prudent to avoid contexts that might sound incongruous. Gowers (1965) pointed out the absurdity of ironing out bottlenecks, and to this may be added the following from the age of the Internet: *I'm still ironing out a couple of bugs over at my Back Pages, which is my new blog—*weblog, AusE 2003.

irony. In the ordinary use of language *irony* means primarily 'an expression of meaning by use of words that have an opposite literal meaning or tendency'. When we look out of the window at the pouring rain and exclaim 'What a lovely day!', we are using a trivial form of irony. Literary forms of irony include (1) *dramatic irony*, in which an audience is taken into the writer's confidence and is made aware of more than the participating characters know, and (2) so-called *Socratic irony* (after the Greek philosopher Socrates, who used it), in which a participant in a discussion falsely purports to be ignorant of a matter in order to elicit a particular response from the other participants. A fuller historical account of irony in language will be found in the *Oxford Companion to the English Language* (1992), p. 532.

irreducible, meaning 'that cannot be reduced', is spelt *-ible*, not *-able*. *See* -ABLE, -IBLE.

irrefutable, meaning 'that cannot be refuted', should be pronounced with the stress on the second syllable, although pronunciation with stress on the third syllable is gaining ground.

irregardless is in origin probably a blend of *irrespective* and *regardless*. It is sometimes found in humorous contexts and is non-standard.

irrelevance, irrelevancy. Both words are in use and there is no distinction in their meaning, but *irrelevance* is more common.

irreparable, irrepairable. *Irreparable* refers to what cannot be recovered or made good and is pronounced with the stress on the second syllable. It typically qualifies words such as *damage, loss, harm, injury*, and *prejudice*. The word to describe physical objects, machines, etc., that cannot be repaired is *unrepairable*, pronounced with the stress on the third syllable as in *repair*; but *irreparable damage* is the normal expression whether or not the damage is physical:

These people were supposed to be making us fit and instead they were doing irreparable damage to my heart and lungs— J. Herriott, 1977 / *The strikers had defied a decree... to end the strike, which he said was causing irreparable damage to the economy—Keesings, 1990 / It is an irreparable loss easily understood by all who have had the privilege of knowing him—Boston Globe, 2011.*

Irrepairable is in the *OED* with both the meanings described above, but both are marked obsolete. In sentences such as the following, therefore, *irreparable* should be used instead: ✖ *If it turns out that the allegations are indeed unfounded, irrepairable damage to the reputation of those involved has been done—weblog AmE, 2006.*

irreplaceable, meaning 'that cannot be replaced', is spelt *-able* and with an *e* in the middle to preserve the soft sound of the *c*. *See* -ABLE, -IBLE.

irrepressible, meaning 'that cannot be restrained', is spelt *-ible*, not *-able*. *See* -ABLE, -IBLE.

irresistible, meaning 'that cannot be resisted', is spelt *-ible*, not *-able*. *See* -ABLE, -IBLE.

irrespective of. This expression is variously regarded by grammarians as an adjective plus a preposition, an adverbial phrase (alternative to *irrespectively of*, which is also found though much less often), or a complex preposition. The difficulty of classification arises because of the detached way in which the expression is used, undermining the status of *irrespective* as an adjective: *People sometimes judge actions to be right irrespective of their consequences—* A. J. Ayer, 1972 / *The beginner in chess, who tries to follow his plans irrespective of his partner's countermoves, will soon go down in defeat—Bruno Bettelheim, 1987 / A great deal of time and energy is given to ensuring that opportunities are* *given to all boys irrespective of sporting ability*—Croydon Guardian, 2004.

irresponsible is spelt *-ible*, not *-able*. See -ABLE, -IBLE.

irreversible, meaning 'that cannot be changed or undone', is spelt *-ible*, not *-able. See* -ABLE, -IBLE.

irrevocable, meaning 'that cannot be changed or recalled', is pronounced with the stress on the second syllable.

irridescent is a spelling mistake for *iridescent.

is. 1 For general points of usage *see* BE. Some common and interesting idiomatic uses of *is* are given here.

2 For *is* after a compound subject, as in *Fish and chips is my favourite meal, see* AGREEMENT 3. For problems of agreement between subject and complement when one is singular and the other is plural, as in *More nurses is the next item on the agenda, see* AGREEMENT 5.

3 ...is what...or...is how...following a statement. *One never knows with these lefties, is what I always say*—A. Brink, 1988 /*You step up to him and you cart him all over the park, is what you do*— S. Fry, 1990. This use, as the contexts of these examples show, is highly informal.

4 is nothing to do with. This construction, as an alternative to *has nothing to do with*, was defended by Fowler (1926) as the more natural choice in everyday speech 'when we...are not in the mood for weighing words in the scales of grammar', is found in the 19c (*This is nothing to do with your life*—H. S. Merriman, 1896), but is less common than the construction with *have* in current use to judge by the evidence in the British National Corpus and in the *OED*.

5 —is —. *Let anyone repeat, as often as he pleases, that 'the will is the will'*— Locke, 1690 /*A man's a man for a' that*— Burns, 1790 /*Home is home though it is*

never so homely—Charles Lamb, 1823. These older literary uses are echoed in 20c occurrences: *A job's a job, that was the thing*—Maurice Gee, 1985 / *She worried about Colin's wrist in the cast but a trip out was a trip out, and the day mustn't be spoiled*—N. Virtue, 1990. Occasionally the word *is* is repeated (echoing Gertrude Stein's *Rose is a rose is a rose is a rose, is a rose... —Sacred Emily*, 1913): *There is only one art form common to all sorts and conditions of people: the poster...A hoarding is a hoarding is a hoarding*—Guardian, 1970.

6 postponed and repeated *is*. This somewhat informal use dates from the early 19c: *He's a sad pickle, is Sam!*— M. Mitford, 1828 / *Yes, he is true to type, is Mr Heard*—Ronald Knox, 1932.

7 ...is all. *No one's interested, is all*— M. Doane, 1988. This idiomatic expression, used for emphasis at the end of a sentence, sounds dialectal but is found in standard (especially American) works of fiction.

-ise as a verbal ending is sometimes optional as an alternative to *-ize* (*baptise, prioritise*) and is sometimes obligatory because of a word's origin (*advertise, compromise, exercise*). See more fully at -IZE, -ISE IN VERBS.

island, isle. The two words are etymologically unconnected. *Island* is derived from an Old English word *īgland*, which is a combination of *īg* (itself meaning 'island') and *land*; *isle* is a reduced form of *insula*, the Latin word for 'island'.

-ism and -ity. These noun-forming suffixes are derived via Old French from the Latin noun endings *-ismus* and *-itas*. The suffix *-ism* forms nouns based on verbs, adjectives, or nouns (*baptism, criticism, heroism*), and has a number of special meanings: (1) a political or religious movement or system of thought (*atheism, Buddhism, realism*), (2) a pathological condition (*alcoholism,*

Parkinsonism), (3) a special feature or peculiarity of language (*Americanism, Gallicism*), (4) a basis of prejudice or discrimination (a 20c development first apparent in *racism*, and more recently in *sexism, ageism, speciesism*, etc.). The suffix *-ity* has the special role of forming abstract nouns from comparative forms (*inferiority, majority*) but in general has the more limited meaning 'a quality or condition, or an instance of it' (*authority, humility, purity*). Some words have produced nouns (with different meanings) in both *-ism* and *-ity* (*liberalism / liberality, modernism / modernity, realism / reality*, etc.).

issue *verb*. The use reflected in the sentences *They issued the people with passports* and (perhaps more typically) *The people were issued with passports* is military in origin and in its general application (on the analogy of *provide* and *supply*) was disapproved of by Fowler (1926), who advocated the type issue + direct object (*They issued passports to the people*). It has nonetheless become well established during the 20c, at least in BrE although it occurs less often in AmE (*People in Russia's second city . . . are issued with coupons which entitle them to basic foodstuffs at subsidized state prices*—Chicago Tribune, 1991).

-ist is a suffix forming nouns and adjectives corresponding to various kinds of noun in *-ism* (*atheist, Buddhist, evangelist, racist, sexist*) and nouns denoting a person engaged in some activity or pursuit (*archaeologist, balloonist, cyclist, economist*). Some words have an alternative form in *-alist* (*agriculturalist / agriculturist, educationalist / educationist*) and in these cases both forms are correct.

italics. Italics are *a style of sloping type, like this*, and are used for a number of special purposes, principally:

titles of books, films, works of art, etc.: *David Copperfield, Gone with the Wind, Mona Lisa.*

titles of long poems: *Paradise Lost.*

names of newspapers etc.: *Daily Express, Radio Times.*

names of ships and vehicles: *Ark Royal, Concorde.*

foreign words and phrases: *amour propre, ne plus ultra* (*see* FOREIGN WORDS AND PHRASES).

for emphasis: 'Oh, come on, it can't be *that* bad.'

For other uses see *New Hart's Rules*, 121–5. In writing, italics are shown by underlining.

itch *verb*. *Itch* is recorded with the transitive meaning 'to cause to itch' from the 16c, but in BrE is now usually informal only, although it is still standard in AmE. Some examples are poetic: *The thick super-salty water of the Mediterranean, which tires and itches the naked eye*—R. Campbell, 1951 / *The dice already itch me in my pocket*—Louis MacNeice, 1951. Another transitive meaning, mainly down-market AmE, is 'to scratch (a part of the body)', as in *Don't itch your leg*—Chicago Tribune, 1991.

-ite. The adjectival ending is derived chiefly from Latin past participles in *-itus*. The length of the Latin *i* varied, but no longer directly influences the pronunciation in English (*definite* with short *i* and *recondite* with long *i* were not so in Latin, for example). The *-ite* in *anthracite, dynamite, Jacobite*, etc., is a different form, and is always pronounced with a long *i*.

it is I, it is me *see* CASES 2A.

its, it's. *Its* is the possessive form of *it* (*The cat licked its paws*) and *it's* is a shortened form of *it is* (*It's raining again*) or occasionally *it has* (*I don't know if it's come*).

itself *see* HERSELF.

-ize, -ise in verbs. *See box opposite.*

-IZE, -ISE IN VERBS.

1 spelling. The primary rule is that all words of the type *authorize/authorise*, *civilize/civilise*, *legalize/legalise*, where there is a choice of ending, may be legitimately spelt with either *-ize* or *-ise* throughout the English-speaking world (except in America, where *-ize* is always used). Oxford University Press and other publishing houses (including *The Times* until recently) prefer *-ize*; Cambridge University Press and others prefer *-ise*.

The reason there is a choice is that the *-ize* ending, which corresponds to the Greek verbal ending *-izo* (whether or not the particular verb existed in Greek in the same form), has come to English in many cases via Latin and French sources, and in French the spelling has been adapted to *-ise*. A key word showing the line of descent is *baptize*, which answers to Greek βαπτίζω, which transliterates into Latin and Latin script as *baptizo*; the French have opted for *baptiser*, and a large proportion of English writers and publishers have followed suit by writing the word as *baptise*. People are generally aware of the choice, but often mistakenly regard the *-ize* ending as an Americanism; and they find it especially hard to countenance in words which do not have corresponding nouns in *-ation* but other forms in which the letter *s* features, such as *criticize* (*criticism*), *hypnotize* (*hypnosis*), and *emphasize* (*emphasis*).

It is important to note that there are some words in which there is no choice: they have to be spelt with *-ise* because they come from words in which the relevant elements are *-cise*, *-mise*, *-prise*, *-vise*, or other forms unconnected with *-izo/-iso*. The most important of these words are given in the table below:

verbs that must be spelt with -ise		
advertise	despise	improvise
advise	devise	incise
apprise	dis(en)franchise	merchandise
arise	disguise	prise (open)
chastise	enfranchise	revise
circumcise	enterprise	supervise
comprise	excise	surmise
compromise	exercise	surprise
demise	franchise	televise

The AmE spelling of *analyse*, *catalyse*, etc., as *analyze*, *catalyze*, etc., is also a separate matter: *see* -YSE, -YZE.

2 status of such verbs. The oldest English verb in *-ize* is *baptize* (13c), mentioned above. Other examples over the centuries are *authorize* (14c), *characterize* (16c), *civilize* (17c), *fossilize* (18c), and *terrorize* (19c). Apart from the spelling question, there is a widespread belief that there are too many new verbs of this kind. Objections have been raised to *finalize, prioritize, hospitalize* and (with more reason) *permanentize*. Forms not attested before 1950 include, in addition to those given in the table below, a whole lot of forms beginning with *re-* including *resensitize* and *retribalize*, and noun derivatives such as *institutionalization* and *privatization*. However, these words represent a small proportion of new words and meanings in English, even among verbs, and it is significant that fewer than ten words in *-ization* or *-ize* are entered in each of the two editions (1991 and 1997) of the *Oxford Dictionary of New Words*, out of a vocabulary total of 2000 items in each. There are many opportunities for ad hoc or nonce formations, and some examples are given in the table. All have their uses on occasions and will come and go as needed without becoming part of the permanent stock of language.

Words in -ize, -ization, *or* -izer *recorded after 1950.*
Nonce and ad hoc forms are marked with an asterisk

word	comment or source
annualize	
capsulize	
computerize	
condomize*	*Newsweek*, 1987
containerize	
decontextualize	
denuclearize	
disasterize*	
funeralize*	recorded as obsolete in the 17c and now revived
incentivize	
invisibleize*	Iris Murdoch, 1991
liquidizer	a machine
marketization	
modularize	
operationalize	
packetize	
peripheralization*	
privatize	
psychedelicize*	2 citations in the OED
rehospitalization	
remobilize	
ruggedize	'to make rugged'
securitize	'to convert (a loan) into marketable securities'
technologize	
texturize	
transistorize	common in the 50s and 60s
trivializer	a person
weaponization	

3 verdict. English has always been highly productive in forming new verbs to represent actions and processes related to social and material developments. Many of these have used suffixes such as *-ize* and *-ify*. Some of the 20c newcomers will drop by the wayside; others will survive through the 21c and beyond, despite the occasional creasing of brows. Together they provide significant linguistic insights into social change.

jacket *verb*, meaning 'to cover with a jacket', has inflected forms *jacketed*, *jacketing*, with one *t*.

jail, jailer are now the more common forms than *gaol*, *gaoler* in BrE and are the dominant spellings in AmE. They are the preferred spellings, except in historical contexts in which the *gaol-* forms might be more appropriate.

jargon. 1 history of the term. The *OED* gives several meanings for *jargon*, all except one mostly derogatory in connotation. The prevailing current senses of the word are (1) 'words or expressions used by a particular group or profession', and (2) 'incomprehensible talk, gibberish', with the second regarded as arising conceptually out of the first, although this is not how the meanings evolved historically. The exception just mentioned is the meaning 'the inarticulate utterance of birds', which is the oldest sense, is found in Chaucer, and as the *OED* notes 'has been revived in modern [i.e. 19c] literature', e.g. by Longfellow: *With beast and bird the forest rings, Each in his jargon cries or sings—Return of Spring* 6. Both meanings described above developed (apart from an isolated Middle English use of the second) in the 17c; there is a good example in the notice 'Bookseller to Reader' published with Swift's *Tale of a Tub* (1704): *If I should go about to tell the reader, by what accident I became master of these papers, it would, in this unbelieving age, pass for little more than the cant or jargon of the trade.*

2 jargon in the right place. Every profession and sphere of activity develops its own jargon to enable its members or participants to communicate effectively with one another; medicine, law, gastronomy, sociology, and (most recently) computing are well-known examples. The following example is drawn from a work of literary criticism: *The view of the text . . . has been seriously challenged in recent years, mainly by structuralist and semiological schools of criticism. According to these, the text has no within, beneath or behind where hidden meanings might be secreted. Attention is instead focused exclusively on the processes and structures of the text and on the ways in which these produce meanings, positions of intelligibility for the reader or the specific effects of realism, defamiliarisation or whatever*—T. Bennett, 1982. This example shows that jargon consists of ordinary words used in special ways as well as specially devised words (such as *defamiliarisation*). Jargon often arises from a need for precision, when terms that would be acceptable in general contexts are not precise enough in specialized use, combined with a need for concision in order not to repeat lengthy expressions that are likely to recur in a piece of specialist or academic writing.

3 jargon in the wrong place. Examples are given in the entry for **gobbledegook* of jargon misused, when it is intended to be intelligible to the public at large or to people who are not members of the profession or activity concerned. In the *Oxford Guide to Plain English* (2004), 154–6, Martin Cutts quotes the following example of jargon used by a housing association in letters to its tenants explaining why modernization work has been delayed: *Find attached a draft programme for the anticipated commencement date on your property and we anticipate that the work will take three or four days to complete. Your next contact will be by the contractor . . . who will contact you individually about a week prior to the start at your house. If you anticipate any problems with access arrangements or require any further information, please do not hesitate to call . . . [etc.].* Cutts rewrites this section of the letter as follows, removing the jargon and simplifying the structure to produce a version that is not only much clearer but more reassuring to the reader, given that the letter is intended to be reassuring: *I attach a programme which shows the likely starting date for work on your property. We expect the work will take three or four days to complete. You will hear next from the contractor . . . who will contact you about a week before work at your house begins. Please call . . . if you think the contractor will have any problems with access to your house, or if you need any more information.*

jejune is pronounced ji-**joon**. It properly means 'meagre, scanty; dull or uninteresting' and is used primarily of ideas or arguments. It is derived from the Latin word *jejunus* meaning 'fasting', and originally meant 'without food' in English. The writer Kingsley Amis famously defended the traditional meaning of *jejune* against users of a newer meaning 'puerile, childish, naive', which first appeared in a play by George Bernard Shaw (*His jejune credulity as to the absolute value of his concepts—*

Arms and the Man, 1989). This meaning may have arisen by a false association with *juvenile*, and it is now a very common one: *Mother seemed jejune, at times, with her enthusiasms and her sense of mission*—M. Howard, 1982 / *There's no passion in your jejune little world, is there?*—weblog, BrE 2005. Despite its currency, this is an awkward and cumbersome usage which can usually be avoided by using readily available and unambiguous alternatives such as *childish*, *infantile*, or *juvenile*, and *innocent*, *guileless*, *ingenuous*, or *naive*. In some cases, it is impossible to tell which meaning is intended: *Perhaps your superiors realized that your rhetoric is sloppy, tendentious, jejune and banal*—weblog, AmE 2003.

je ne sais quoi. This French expression, meaning literally 'I don't know what', is first recorded in one of the earliest English dictionaries, in 1656. Since then it has become a standard, if somewhat highfalutin, part of English, to refer to an indefinable quality, and is nowadays generally written in roman, rather than in italic.

jetsam see FLOTSAM AND JETSAM.

jettison in current use is a verb meaning 'to discard' and refers to physical things as well as abstractions (e.g. ideas). Its origins are as a noun in maritime law, meaning 'the action of throwing goods overboard, especially to lighten a ship in distress'. Its verb inflections are *jettisoned*, *jettisoning*.

jeu d'esprit, meaning 'a witty or humorous trifle', is pronounced zher des-**pree** and is printed in italics. It has the plural form *jeux d'esprit* (pronounced the same).

jewel has inflected forms *jewelled*, *jewelling*, and the derivative form *jeweller*. In AmE the usual forms are *jeweled*, *jeweling*, and *jeweler*.

jewellery should be pronounced **joo**-uhl-ri, not **joo**-luh-ri (as in *foolery*). The form *jewelry* is usual in AmE and is sometimes used in BrE.

Jewess, though in use since the 14c, now has derogatory overtones (for racial reasons and because of gender sensitivity) and should be avoided, although Jewish people are said to use it among themselves.

jibe, gibe, gybe. Spelling and meaning are in a pretty pickle here, because all three words are pronounced identically. The largely AmE meaning 'agree' has one spelling only, namely *jibe*; but the meaning 'taunt' as a noun or verb is spelt both *jibe* and *gibe*, while the sailing term ('change course by swinging the sail across a following wind') is *gybe* or *jibe*, according to whether you are British or American. Matching meaning to spelling: (1) ('taunt') both *jibe* and *gibe* are correct, the first being far commoner, although most historical *OED* quotations show *gibe*: (*'It wouldn't be responsible to make promises I can't keep. That's Nick Clegg's job,' he jibes—Daily Telegraph*, 2011 / *Spalding, whose time in Glasgow was stormy, directs a few jibes at Scotland's cultural shibboleths—Scotland on Sunday*, 2002 / *Where be your gibes now? your gambols? your songs?—Hamlet*),

(2) the sailing term *gybe* is the preferred form in BrE and *jibe* in AmE (*But halfway through a slightly wobbly but adequate gybe, my instructor Beth called out from behind me—OEC*, BrE 2005 / *I'll have to jibe, a far riskier maneuver that puts the stern of the boat through the wind—New York Times*, 2011),

(3) ('agree, be in accord') the standard spelling is *jibe*. *Webster's* recognizes *gibe* as an alternative, but people may well see it as a mistake: (*On the whole, the*

remix is cleaner than the original, jibing well with the other compositions—www. pitchfork.com, AmE 2004).

See also GYBE.

jiu-jitsu *see* JU-JITSU.

jockey has the plural form *jockeys* as a noun, and as a verb (used especially in the expression *jockey for position*) has inflected forms *jockeys, jockeyed, jockeying*.

joined-up. The original meaning referring to handwriting with linked characters has been applied as a metaphor in BrE since the 1980s to suggest coherence and consistency of thought and action. The most common areas of usage are administration and government, where it was at one time an overused journalistic cliché. More recently, it has become less popular. *The gladiatorial style of debate may give way to what one new woman MP described as 'joined-up thinking'—Observer*, 1997 / *To dumb down the assessment of doctors is not joined-up Government—Daily Telegraph*, 2007.

joke *verb*. The archaic sense 'to poke fun at' has surfaced again in recent very informal uses such as *don't joke me* = don't kid me. This use is appealing but non-standard.

journalese. Some words and uses are peculiar to the language of newspaper articles and, more especially, newspaper headlines. Examples are *probe* for 'investigation' or 'investigate' (*Hong Kong missing millions probe*), *quiz* for 'interrogate' (*Police quiz councillors over expenses fraud*), *package* for 'deal' (*Steel bosses offer new pay package*), and *swap* for 'transplant' in the medical sense (*Baby heart swap drama*). Combinations of nouns in headlines (as in the last example), use of the present tense, and use of a *to*-infinitive to denote future time, are common features: *Councillor planning action over go-go girl affair claim— Evening News* (Edinburgh), 1994 / *Sex cinema blaze man pleads guilty— Independent*, 1995 / *Premier to defy unions over £3.60 minimum wage— Daily Mail*, 1998. Puns, as the most concise form of written humour, feature prominently in headlines, e.g. *Hirst's sheep give Britain art failure—Independent*, 1998 (reporting an opinion poll which found that the 'pickled sheep' art of Damien Hirst was among least liked by British visitors to art galleries).

journey has the plural form *journeys*.

judgement, judgment. Throughout the English-speaking world, both spellings are in use, and both are correct, but overall *judgment* is the commoner of the two by a ratio of roughly 4:1. *Judgement* is somewhat more usual in general use in BrE, but *judgment* is dominant in legal contexts.

judging by, judging from. Both forms are used with the meaning 'if we are to judge by...' at the head of a clause and only loosely connected grammatically to the main clause. If you are worried that by using them you will lay yourself open to the charge of using a 'dangling participle', you could use *if we are to judge by* instead: *Judging from her voice, she had been crying*—M. Nabb, 1989 / *Fen for the most part seemed absorbed in his own thoughts, which, judging by his expression, did not please him*—A. Murray, 1993 / *Lots of people have been enjoying the Simon vibe all over again judging by the big crowds which have been turning up for their recent shows*—*Waterford News and Star*, 2003.

judicial, judicious. These two words, both derived from the Latin word *judex* meaning 'judge', are easily confused although their current meanings are distinct. *Judicial* means 'relating to

judges or legal processes' (*a judicial inquiry / a judicial review / judicial proceedings / a judicial separation*), whereas *judicious* means 'sensible, prudent; sound in judgement' in general contexts (*judicious use of time / a judicious assessment / a judicious selection*). A *judicial* decision made by a judge is one in accordance with the law, whereas a *judicious* decision (whether made by a judge or some other person) is one that is wise and discerning when all factors are taken into account.

ju-jitsu, the Japanese system of unarmed combat and physical training, is preferably spelt this way, not *jiu-jitsu*.

jumbo has the plural form *jumbos*.

juncture. *Juncture*, which occurs principally in the expression *at this juncture*, strictly speaking denotes a 'coincidence of events producing a critical or dramatic moment'. In practice it is often used to mean simply 'at this moment, now'. Unless you wish to stress that the situation being discussed is critical or dramatic, you run the risk of sounding longwinded and pompous by using *at this juncture*: *The United States came to Vietnam at a critical juncture of Vietnamese history*—F. Fitzgerald, 1972 / *Liz hoped that at this juncture Shirley would go to bed*—Margaret Drabble, 1987 / *It is vital, at this juncture, that the government does not give in to bullying by arms companies*—*Morning Star*, 2007.

junta, a Spanish loanword meaning 'a political or military clique taking power after a coup or revolution', is now generally pronounced in an anglicized way as **jun**-tuh in BrE. In AmE the more Spanish-sounding **hun**-tuh is standard. The plural form is *juntas*.

jurist A *jurist* in BrE is an eminent expert in law, but in AmE the word is often applied to any lawyer or judge.

juror, a member of a jury, is spelt *-or*. The term *juryman* is fast disappearing, and *jurywoman* is almost extinct except in occasional historical references.

just *adverb*. **1** When it means 'a little time ago', *just* is used differently in BrE and AmE. In BrE the usual construction is with a perfect tense formed with *have*: *I have just arrived home*, but in AmE the verb is normally a simple past form: *I just arrived home*. Care needs to be taken to avoid misunderstanding, since *just* can also mean 'only, simply' as in *They are just good friends*. So a sentence such as BrE *I have just seen my brother* and, even more, AmE *I just saw my brother* can mean either 'I have recently seen my brother' or 'I have seen my brother and no one else' (or, perhaps, 'I have seen my brother and have done nothing else'). In speech, intonation will usually clarify the meaning, but in written English the difficulty may need to be resolved by rephrasing.

2 The phrase *just now* has several meanings, and the primary meaning can change from one part of the English-speaking world to another. The principal possibilities are (1) with past reference, 'a short time ago' (*What was it you were saying just now, child?*—E. Jolley, 1985 / *When I returned to the house just now I sensed that something unusual had occurred*—S. Craven, 1993), (2) with a present continuous tense, 'at this moment' (*Just now I'm going with a Catholic, who lives down in Armagh*—F. Kippax, 1993), (3) with a simple present, 'for the time being, right now', common generally with a negative (*She cannot afford to think about her mother just now*—J. Neale, 1993) but characteristically Scottish in positive use (*I have my home in Britain just now*—*Express* (Scottish edition), 2007), (4) with a future tense in South African and Indian English, 'very shortly, in a little while' (*The men on cell duty will do that just now*—A. Sachs, SAfrE 1966).

juvenile has a neutral meaning 'relating to or associated with young people' (*juvenile crime*) and a derogatory meaning 'immature' (*Behaving in a juvenile way*).

Kaffir. The word *Kaffir* is first recorded in the 16th century (as *Caffre*) and was originally simply an innocuous descriptive term for a particular ethnic group. Although it survives in the names of a few plants, such as the *Kaffir lily*, it is always a racially abusive and offensive term when used of people, and in South Africa its use is actionable.

keep. The construction *keep* + object + *from* + *-ing* verb is idiomatic in current English: *His hands held flat over his ears as if to keep his whole head from flying apart*—Martin Amis, 1978. The intransitive use of *keep* + *from* + *-ing* verb is recorded in the *OED* from the 19C but is now common in AmE, and is also used in BrE: *Maria cut the wheel to the left, to keep from hitting the cans*—T. Wolfe, 1987 / *'How do I get to buy food and keep from starving?' he once said*—*OEC*, 2009.

kerb is the standard BrE spelling of the word for a stone edging to a pavement or raised path. In AmE it is spelt *curb*: *see* CURB.

Khoikhoi. To refer to the indigenous peoples of Namibia and parts of South Africa, *Khoikhoi* should be used in preference to *Hottentot*, since the latter is likely to cause offence: *see also* HOTTENTOT.

kid, in its informal meaning 'child' (*He's only a kid* / *He came with his wife and kids*), has a long history, being first recorded in the 17c, but is still only suitable for more informal use. The verb *to kid*, meaning 'to trick or tease', is

early 19c and possibly derived from this noun; it has the same level of informality.

kidnap has inflected forms *kidnapped*, *kidnapping* in BrE; in AmE the forms *kidnaped*, *kidnaping* are also used.

kidnapping *see* ABDUCTION.

kidney has the plural form *kidneys*.

kilo has the plural form *kilos*.

kilometre is spelt *-metre* in BrE and *-meter* in AmE. The word is better pronounced with the stress on the first syllable, in line with other words for measures such as *kilogram* and *millimetre*, although pronunciation with the stress on the second syllable, on the (less secure) analogy of words such as *barometer* and *speedometer*, is increasingly common and is standard in AmE and other non-British varieties.

kimono, meaning 'long loose Japanese robe', has the plural form *kimonos*, or occasionally (as in Japanese) *kimono*.

kin is now a rather old-fashioned term for one's relatives or family. It is mostly used in the fixed expressions *next of kin* and *kith and kin*.

kind. *Of its kind* is too often used as a meaningless hedge: *Then the Harrogate Crime Writing Festival was launched, which has grown to become the most successful of its kind in the UK*—*Independent on Sunday*, 2007. Here, the kind of festival in question has already been identified. Or are we being invited to believe that there are different kinds of book festival devoted to crime writing? More likely, the reporter has not felt able to bestow unqualified praise and falls back on 'of its kind' as a subconscious defence mechanism, or 'downtoner', rather like *almost. The effect may be to produce disappointment or even confusion in the reader. In such cases, it is better just to leave the phrase out altogether.

kinda *see* KIND OF.

kindly, as used to introduce a formal request (*You are kindly requested to refrain from smoking / Kindly refrain from smoking*), now has a dated sound to it, and it is never quite clear who it is who is being *kind* (a point Fowler noticed in 1926). A modern alternative, often seen for example on notices in restaurants and taxis, uses the style *Thank you for not smoking*, which straightforwardly assumes that the request has already been complied with.

kind of, sort of. 1 These expressions mean much the same, and share the same grammatical problem. Difficulties can arise with *this, that, these,* and *those*. When followed by a singular noun, the correct form is (e.g.) *this kind* [*or sort*] *of house*, not *this kind* [*or sort*] *of a house*. When they are followed by a plural noun, many purists insist on making *kind* or *sort* plural as well, e.g. *these kinds* [*or sorts*] *of houses*. To say *this kind* [*or sort*] *of houses* is ungrammatical, but an alternative style *these kind* [*or sort*] *of houses* has been in use since the 14c. Although this too is ungrammatical on a normal interpretation, its rationale lies in regarding *kind of* as an adjectival phrase qualifying the following noun (in this case, *houses*), with the demonstrative pronoun *these* or *those* also qualifying *houses* rather than qualifying *kind* (or

sort). This structure is now very common in colloquial contexts: *She was used to these kind of smells in the night-time bedclothes*—M. Duckworth, 1960 / *We can't let these sort of people get away with it*—Birmingham Post, 2007. Alternatives are *these kinds* (or *sorts*) *of*— and —*of this kind* (or *sort*): *The pressure here is to consider the . . . circumstances which do, in fact, coerce people in these sorts of ways*—M. Whitford et al., 1989 / *Conservatives can be every bit as ideologically lethal as liberals when ballots of this kind are placed in their hands*—White House Studies, 2003. The second of these alternatives suits a context in which another modifying word is present (*future* in the following example): *The decline of letter-writing makes future books of this sort unlikely*—New Zealand Listener, 2003.

2 In AmE, *kind of a* is often used informally where in BrE it would be *a kind of*: *We're kind of a middle-aged Sonny and Cher*—Washington Post, 1973.

3 *Kind of* and *sort of* also occur as adverbial phrases in informal contexts, especially in AmE: *All these rich bastards driving up the property values have kind of made it impossible for everyone else*—New Yorker, 1987 / *He just sort of glanced at the photos and then carried on talking*—N. Watts, 1990.

4 The uses shown in paragraphs 2 and 3 are characteristically American and should not be used in more formal speech or writing. An even more informal written form is *kinda*, which represents the sound of *kind of* in rapid speech: *There was this real weirdo in here, rifling about the desks, wearing some kinda disguise*—S. James, 1993 / *I feel kinda bad for not being as excited as I should be about Audrey getting into NYU*—fiction website, AmE 2004 [*OEC*]. Again this use is chiefly AmE, and although it is non-standard it is extremely common, with around 20,000 examples in the *OEC*.

knee-jerk is a popularized technicality taken from the physical meaning 'a sudden involuntary kick caused by a blow on the tendon just below the knee when the leg is hanging loose'. It is now popular among politicians, broadcasters, etc., especially in the phrase *knee-jerk reaction*, as an adjective meaning 'instant and barely considered': *The [motor] industry's . . . knee-jerk support for road construction and its opposition to tighter air pollution standards have not endeared it to the public—Times,* 1991 / *The Braer disaster produced a knee-jerk reaction among many hoping to improve safety standards at sea—East Anglian,* 1993 / *That is what's so damning about the knee-jerk opposition of so many anti-war liberals, it's based in animus, not logic—weblog, AmE 2003.*

kneel. The past and past participle form *knelt* is now more common than *kneeled* in all varieties of English: *Some of the recruits knelt to pray before retiring, presumably for strength—Anthony Burgess, 1987.*

knife. The plural form of the noun is *knives,* but the inflected forms of the verb are *knifes, knifed, knifing.*

knit. The past tense and past participle form of the verb in its main meaning is *knitted* (*a knitted scarf*). In figurative meanings, *knitted* and *knit* are both used (*She knit/knitted her brows*) but in figurative phrases such as *closely / close, tightly / tight knit* only *knit* is possible.

knock up. Care needs to be taken with this phrasal verb, which in BrE means 'to wake by knocking on the door' and in AmE (and increasingly in BrE too) means 'to make pregnant'. In intransitive use, to *knock up* is to practise tennis strokes before the start of formal play, and a *knock-up* is a period of practice.

know. The expression *you know,* inserted as an aside in a sentence in speech, sometimes has real meaning, e.g. in introducing extra information that the hearer is likely to know already, but generally it is a meaningless sentence filler like *I mean: People get the wrong idea, thinking we might be, you know, glamorous or brilliant or something— Sunday Times,* 1974.

know-how, meaning 'technical expertness or practical knowledge', is first recorded in print in AmE in 1838, but did not come into widespread use until about a century later. It is now established in both Britain and America, and is acceptable in all but the most formal contexts.

knowledgeable is spelt with an *e* after the *g.*

Koran, the sacred book of Islam, is normally spelt this way in English contexts. However, the forms *Quran* or *Qur'an,* a closer transliteration of the Arabic original (meaning 'recitation'), are also used, the first quite often, the second rather rarely.

kosher, meaning 'fulfilling the requirements of Jewish law', is pronounced **koh**-shuh.

kowtow, meaning 'to act obsequiously', is pronounced with each syllable rhyming with *cow,* and is no longer spelt *ko-tow.*

kudos, meaning 'glory, renown' (usually in connection with a particular event or achievement), is a (19c) singular noun derived from a Greek noun with the same meaning. Its occasional use in the 20c as if it were plural, with even a singular back-formation *kudo,* is non-standard verging on the illiterate: ✷ *This did not win Mr. Eisenhower many kudos in the press—Wall Street Journal,* 1963 / ✷ *With every kudo its writers achieve, more visitors flock to the site—weblog, IrishE 2004.*

label *verb* has inflected forms *labelled*, *labelling* in BrE and *labeled*, *labeling* in AmE.

laboratory is pronounced in BrE with the stress on the second syllable and in AmE with the stress on the first syllable (and the final syllable like *Tory*).

labour is the standard spelling in BrE, whereas *labor* is the standard form in AmE.

lack *verb*. The use with *for* meaning 'to be short of something' in negative contexts seems to have originated in the 19c: *If you are inclined to undertake the search, I have so provided that you will not lack for means*—Rider Haggard, 1887 / *Here's hoping he'll never lack for friends*—Mark Twain, 1892 / *You get a lower standard of trim, but you don't lack for much in the way of essential equipment*—Which? Car Buying Guide, 1987 / *'I can see by those here present that Samuel did not lack for friends,' said the priest who now filled the place of Father Michael*—P. Bryers, 1993.

lackey, meaning 'an obsequious parasite', has the plural form *lackeys*.

lady, woman. The division of usage between these two words is complex and is caught up in issues of social class. In George Meredith's *Evan Harrington* (1861), the heroine, Rose Jocelyn, is rhetorically asked, *Would you rather be called a true English lady than a true English woman, Rose?*, and it is still the case that *lady* denotes social standing

and refinement and is the female equivalent of *gentleman*, whereas *woman* is the normal word that is generally neutral in tone but in some contexts can sound over-direct or discourteous (*Which of you women is Mrs Jones?*). The more affectionate connotations of *lady* also make it characteristic of children's language. As well as its use as a title, *lady* is used in certain fixed expressions, such as *lady of the house, the Ladies* (or *Ladies'*, a women's public lavatory), a *lady's man*, and others, and in the form of address *ladies and gentlemen*. In AmE, though less in BrE, *lady* has developed an informal meaning rather like *dame*, both as a form of address (*Where are you going, lady?*) and in third-person reference (*She's some lady*). In designations of profession, *lady* now sounds impossibly condescending (as in *lady doctor*), and has given way to *woman* (as in *woman doctor*) although this too is now considered sexist in implying that doctors are typically male and exceptionally female (*see also* FEMININE DESIGNATIONS). As a general rule, *lady* comes across as being socially and historically loaded, and the more neutral *woman* is preferable despite its occasional bluntness of tone.

laid, lain. *Laid* is the past and past participle of *lay*, whereas *lain* is the past participle of *lie. See* LAY, LIE.

laissez-faire, laissez-passer. The first means 'abstention by people in authority from interference in the actions of individuals', and the second 'a pass or permit'. Both are normally printed in roman. Beware of writing *laisser* instead of the correct *laissez*.

lama, llama. The form with one *l* is the Tibetan or Mongolian Buddhist monk, whereas the form with two *l*s is the South American animal.

lamentable, meaning 'deplorable, regrettable', is correctly pronounced with the stress on the first syllable, not the second (though either is acceptable in AmE).

Lapp. Although this term is still widely used and is the most familiar to laypeople, the indigenous people widely known by this name consider it somewhat offensive and prefer *Sami*. The name *Samiland* for the area they inhabit is not yet fully established.

largesse, largess. The first is now the more frequent spelling for this word meaning 'generosity' or 'money given freely', not *largess* as recommended by Fowler in 1926. *Largess*, however, is also still used, especially in AmE, and is correct, though infrequent in other kinds of English.

larva has the plural form *larvae*, pronounced **lah**-vee.

lasso is pronounced la-**soo** in BrE and **las**-oh in AmE. The plural form of the noun is *lassos* and the verb has inflected forms *lassoes, lassoed, lassoing*.

last. 1 When used with a number, *last* (like *first*) normally precedes it, as in *the last three cars. See* FIRST 1.

2 In listing a sequence of points or topics, *lastly* (or *finally*) is preferable to *last*, especially when the preceding items are introduced with numbers ending in -*ly*: *first* (or *firstly*) . . . , *secondly* . . . , *thirdly* . . . , *lastly* . . . For the choice between *first* and *firstly, see* FIRST 2.

3 *among the last, one of the last*. In a sentence such as the following, *last* in its context means no more than *few* and

should be replaced by that word: *This week the forest, among the last* [read: *few*] *remaining of its type in Europe, faces the sternest test yet of its survival—Independent*, 2007.

last but not least. When Antony in Shakespeare's *Julius Caesar* (III.i.190) greets Caesar's assassins, he takes their hands in the order Brutus, Cinna, Casca, and Trebonius, and says to Trebonius: *Though last, not least in love, yours, good Trebonius*. Though used here (and elsewhere in Shakespeare) to good effect, this phrase is now a cliché and should be avoided except in the few cases when it has real meaning.

late, former, one-time, sometime. All these words are used occasionally (the first two a little more than that) to describe the earlier status of a person or thing. A *late husband* is one that is no longer alive, whereas a *former husband* (or *ex-husband*) is one that is no longer a husband (but is more likely than not still alive). *Sometime* is used more of the official function a person or thing has had, for example a building may be the *sometime* headquarters of the KGB; *former* and *one-time* are also possible here and would be more usual in everyday language. *See also* ERSTWHILE; FORMER, LATTER.

later on *see* EARLY ON.

Latin (and Greek) plurals. *See box opposite.*

latter is used in the phrase *the latter*, which contrasts with *the former* to refer to the second of two previously mentioned items so as to avoid lengthy repetition. *See* FORMER, LATTER.

laudable, laudatory. The essential difference is that *laudable* means 'deserving praise' whereas *laudatory* means 'expressing praise'. So an

LATIN (AND GREEK) PLURALS.

Plurals of Latin words used in English are formed according to the rules either of the source language (*apex/apices, stratum/strata*) or of the borrowing language (*gymnasium/gymnasiums, arena/arenas*). In some cases more than one form is in use, sometimes with a usage distinction (*appendix/appendices/ appendixes, formula/formulae/formulas*) and sometimes with no clear distinction (*cactus/cacti/cactuses*). Words ending in *-is* usually follow the original Latin form (*basis/bases, crisis/crises*) for reasons of euphony, and the same rule operates in other cases (*nucleus/nuclei*). A more alien form is the originally Greek plural *-mata* of words ending in *-ma* in the singular (*lemma/ lemmata, stigma/stigmata*). There are occasional surprises; for example we might expect the plural of *crux* to be (Latin) *cruces* but it is in fact more often (English) *cruxes*. There is a trap for the unwary with Latinate nouns ending in *-us* or *-um* which cannot form plurals in *-i* or *-a* for formal grammatical reasons: *hiatus* (a fourth-declension noun in Latin with a plural *hiatus*), *ignoramus* (a first-person plural verb in Latin, not a noun), *octopus* (a Romanized form of a Greek word *octopous*), *vademecum* (*cum* being a preposition meaning 'with'). The table below shows the types of plural that the more commonly used Latin words have in English; when there is more than one both are shown:

singular form	Latin-type plural	English plural
addendum	addenda	
alga	algae	
atrium	atria	atriums
apex	apices	apexes
appendix	appendices	appendixes
aquarium	aquaria	aquariums
arena		arenas
automaton	automata	automatons
basis	bases	
cactus	cacti	cactuses
codex	codices	
compendium	compendia	compendiums
corpus	corpora	corpuses
corrigendum	corrigenda	
cortex	cortices	cortexes
crematorium	crematoria	crematoriums
crisis	crises	
crux	cruces	cruxes
desideratum	desiderata	
encomium	encomia	encomiums
focus	foci	focuses
formula	formulae	formulas
forum	fora	forums
genus	genera	
gymnasium	gymnasia	gymnasiums
helix	helices	helixes

index	indices	indexes
lemma	lemmata	lemmas
matrix	matrices	matrixes
maximum	maxima	maximums
memorandum	memoranda	memorandums
miasma	miasmata	
minimum	minima	minimums
momentum	momenta	momentums
moratorium		moratoriums
nucleus	nuclei	
oasis	oases	
radix	radices	
referendum	referenda	referendums
stigma	stigmata	stigmas
stratum	strata	
thesis	theses	
vortex	vortices	vortexes

Further information will be found in the separate entries for some of these words.

action or attitude that is *laudable* calls for a *laudatory* response. The two are rarely confused, but confusion does occasionally happen: ⊠ *so they can help the federal government in its ongoing, highly laudatory* [read: *laudable*] *attempts to reach 100 percent compliance*—www.futurepundit. com, 2005.

lavatory, the standard word in the early part of the 20c for a receptacle for urination and defecation (and the room containing it), has tended to give way to alternatives such as *loo* (the usual middle-class word) and *toilet* (still non-U but the word mostly used in official contexts, on notices, etc.). See also TOILET; U AND NON-U.

lawful see LEGAL.

lay, lie. These two words cause confusion even to native speakers of English because their meanings are related and their forms overlap. *Lay* is a transitive verb, i.e. it takes an object, and means 'to place on a surface, to cause to rest on something'; its past form and past

participle are both *laid* (examples: *Please lay it on the floor / The teacher laid the book on the desk / They had laid it on the floor / Babies should be laid down to sleep on their backs*). *Lie* is intransitive, and means 'to rest or be positioned on a surface'; its past form is *lay* (i.e. identical with the present form of the other verb), its present participle is *lying*, and its past participle is *lain* (examples: *Go and lie on the bed / She went and lay on the bed / He is lying on the bed / The body had lain in the field for several days*). The principal mistakes in the use of these verbs are using *lay* for *lie*, *laid* for *lay* (past of *lie*), and *lain* for *laid*: ⊠ *We are going to lay* [read: *lie*] *under the stars by the sea*— Sun, 1990 / ⊠ *Standing in a semicircle, we had lain* [read: *laid*] *all our uniforms and possessions at our feet*—C. Jennings, 1990 / ⊠ *It was very uncomfortable and painful especially when I laid* [read: *lay*] *down to sleep*—Mirror, 2003.

layman, layperson. In accordance with the trend towards replacing words ending in -*man* to avoid the charge of sexism, intentional or otherwise, *layperson* (1972), plural *laypeople* or (less often) *laypersons,* is widely used, to denote both non-clergy and non-experts: *in layperson's terms; scholars and educated laypeople alike.* This trend is particularly evident in American English. Nevertheless, even there, the traditional *layman* is still the more frequent term. *See* SEXIST LANGUAGE; *see also* CHAIRMAN, CHAIRWOMAN, etc.

lb., an abbreviation for *pound* (weight), is derived from Latin *libra* 'pound'. The plural form is *lb.* or *lbs.*

LCD. Strictly speaking, to talk about an *LCD display* is a pleonasm, since the *D* already stands for *display:* *l*iquid *c*rystal *d*isplay. However, this classic case of tautology misleads nobody.

leach, leech. Because they sound the same, this pair are easily confused. *Leeches* are bloodsucking worms, of the kind that Humphrey Bogart famously found himself covered with in *The African Queen.* Someone described as a *leech* sponges off others (*they are leeches feeding off the hard-working majority*) and this use has a related verb (*he's leeching off the abilities of others*). To *leach* means to remove a substance from soil by the action of water (*the nutrient is quickly leached away*), and has an intransitive use (*pesticides and fertilizers that leach into rivers*). Examples of confusion: ☒ *I didn't want it to leech into my own work*—www.bookslut.com, 2004; ☒ *what your small business computer consulting company can do to protect itself against freeloaders and other time and financial leaches*—*Article Alley,* 2005.

lead, led. *Lead* is the present tense of the verb meaning 'to go in front', 'to take charge of', etc., and its past form is *led.* A common mistake is to use *lead* for the past form and pronounce it led in speech, probably on the false analogy of *read:* ☒ *His idea was the one that lead to*

the solution of the mascara mystery—*Chicago Sun-Times,* 1990.

There are several hundred examples of the phrase *has* (or *have*) *lead to* in the *OEC,* including this one: *At times undemocratic practices have lead to a breakdown in trust*—current affairs weblog, BrE 2004.

leadership. The established meanings 'the position of a leader' and 'the ability to lead' were joined in the 20c by the meaning 'group of leaders'. The use of the suffix *-ship* to refer to a group of people, as in *membership* and *readership,* has been criticized but is standard and useful: *A dinner for the heads of the Senate Committees and the Leadership on both sides and their wives*—Mrs L. B. Johnson, 1964 / *Following an LDP conference, the party leadership announced on Sept. 19 that it planned to break away from the coalition which had backed Aquino*—Keesings, 1990 / *This leadership had got on fairly well with the Labour Ealingites*—*Times,* 2007.

leading question. In law, a *leading question* is one which suggests to a witness the answer he or she is expected to make, and the use of such questions is strictly controlled by Judges' Rules. In general use the term is often extended to mean a 'loaded' or 'searching' question, as indicated by the response 'that's a leading question'. The phrase also seems to be incorrectly used of urgent or pressing questions, as in the last example below: *The applicant's barrister may not 'lead' by asking questions which suggest a certain answer. If a barrister does ask leading questions, the respondent's barrister may interrupt and object*—*Sunday Business Post,* 2003 / *Begin your exchange with an 'I' message: 'I'm concerned', 'I'm confused', or 'I'm frustrated'. Also acceptable as a leading question: 'What the heck is going on?'*—*Selfhelp Magazine,* 2004 / *Following the end of the First World*

War, the leading question in the mining industry was whether or not the state would return the coal mines to their pre-war owners—K. Laybourn, 1990.

leaf. The noun has the plural form *leaves*, and the verb has inflected forms *leafs, leafed, leafing* (*He was leafing through a book*).

-leafed, -leaved. Both forms are in use in combinations such as *broad-leafed/-leaved* and *four-leafed/-leaved*, but there is a preference for *-leaved* in current use.

leaflet. As a verb, meaning 'to distribute leaflets to', *leaflet* has inflected forms *leafleted, leafleting*.

lean *verb*. The past form and past participle can be either *leaned* (pronounced leend or lent) or *leant* (pronounced lent). The first is the preferred form in all varieties of English, while *leant* is used more in BrE than it is elsewhere. Examples: *Georgia Rose . . . leaned forward and blew out every one of her candles*—Lee Smith, AmE 1983 / *Syl smiled back at me and leaned across and took my hand*—A. T. Ellis, 1987 / *His tone was weary, and he leant his head down on one hand*—Iris Murdoch, 1993 / *Ben just leaned over and kissed me*—fiction website, NewZE 2003 [*OEC*] / *Felix leant forward in his chair and leant his elbows on the table*—fiction website, AmE 2004 [*OEC*].

leap *verb*. The past form and past participle can be either *leaped* (pronounced leept or lept) or *leapt* (pronounced lept). The second is the preferred form in all varieties of English. Examples: *I can't say that wretch I leaped in after was much of a loss to the human race*—P. Bailey, 1986 / *She had leapt on board the boat like a boy*—New Yorker, 1994 / *The dad-of-two suffered a near fatal motorcycle accident when a deer leapt on to his bike*—Mirror,

2007 / *A man was recovering in hospital yesterday after he leaped into a bog to save a blind horse from drowning*—Liverpool Daily Post, 2007.

learn *verb*. **1** The past form and past participle are in BrE either *learned* (pronounced lernd or lernt) or *learnt* (pronounced lernt); *learned* is more usual as the past form and, in AmE, as both past form and past participle. Examples: *So, what was learned from this experience?*—Essays & Studies, 1987 / *A point that none of my bright young officers seem to have learnt at school*—B. L. Barder, 1987 / *Ideally, you should treat each child as an individual, with his own list of words to be learnt*—M. Torbe, 1988 / *She learned that the vessel had come, and was glad, for she said that the young man would speak for her*—Dorothy Dunnett, 1989 / *The Ministry of Defence and the Treasury will agree to finance equipment projects worth more than £30 billion this week, . . . The Times has learnt*—Times, 2007.

2 The use of *learn* to mean 'to teach', though standard for writers of earlier ages such as Caxton, Spenser, Bunyan, and Johnson (1755), fell into disfavour around 1800 and appears in non-standard contexts in 19c and modern literature: *If she knows her letters it's the most she does—and them I learned her*—Dickens, 1865.

learned is pronounced as one syllable when it is the past and past participle of *learn*, and as two syllables (**ler**-nid) when it is an adjective meaning 'having or showing much knowledge'.

learning difficulties. This term became common in the 1980s to describe a wide range of abnormalities including Down's syndrome, dyslexia, and the complaint known as *attention deficit disorder*. In emphasizing the difficulty experienced rather than any perceived deficiency, it is less demeaning than *mental handicap* and related terms are, and is the standard term in official contexts in the UK.

lease of life. In BrE the idiom is *a new lease of life*, whereas in AmE it is generally *a new lease on life*. In all other varieties of English both forms are used indifferently.

least. 1 *Least of all* means 'especially not' and should only be used in negative contexts: *I am not going to try to play the role of prophet, least of all Jeremiah*—Listener, 1973.

2 Use *less*, not *least*, when contrasting two things: *The latter aircraft was the less pleasant to fly*—E. Brown, 1983 (an example that is exemplary with regard both to *less* and to *latter*).

leave, let. *Leave* is well on its way to forcing out *let* in certain idiomatic uses, especially in *leave / let be* (*Will you leave / let me be? I'm trying to work*), *leave / let go* (*Please leave / let go of the handle*), and above all in *leave / let alone* when it means 'to refrain from disturbing, not interfere with' (*I'll leave / let you alone to get on with it now*). *Leave alone* is the only possibility when the meaning is 'not to have dealings with' (*I wish you'd leave the matter alone*), and *let alone* is still dominant in the meaning 'still less, not to mention' (*They never buy a newspaper, let alone read one*).

leech *see* LEACH, LEECH.

leftward, leftwards. The only form of the adjective is *leftward* (*a leftward glance*). For the adverb, *leftward* and *leftwards* are used both in BrE and AmE (*turn leftward / leftwards*). As with many other words having alternative endings in *-ward* / *-wards* (*backward / backwards, upward / upwards*, etc.) the form in *-ward* is much more frequent in BrE, and the reverse is true in AmE.

legal, lawful, legitimate, licit.
1 All four words share the basic meaning 'conforming to the law'. Something is *legal* when it is authorized by the law of the land, *legitimate* when it conforms to custom or common justice, and *lawful* (a more old-fashioned word) when it conforms to moral or divine law. *Legal* is the only choice in the neutral descriptive meaning 'relating to the law' (as in *legal language*), and *legitimate* alone has the meaning 'born of married parents'. *Licit*, which means much the same as *lawful*, is the least used of all these words, although *illicit* is somewhat more common. *See also* ILLEGAL.

2 For *legitimate* as a verb, *see* LEGITIMATE, LEGITIMIZE.

legalese is a fairly recent term (first recorded in 1914) for the complicated technical language used in legal documents. Legal language has become complex and difficult for the layperson to understand because of a need to be both precise and comprehensive in the points made; nonetheless, there is now a vigorous campaign in progress, led (in the UK) by the Plain English Campaign and (in the US) by the Plain English Forum and others, to simplify legal language in everyone's interests. These intentions are hardly new. Nearly 200 years ago, Thomas Jefferson, third president of the US, railed against statutes 'which from verbosity, their endless tautologies, their involutions of case within case, and parenthesis within parenthesis, and their multiplied efforts at certainty, by saids and aforesaids, by ors and ands, to make them more plain, are really rendered more perplexed and incomprehensible, not only to common readers, but to the lawyers themselves' (quoted in D. Mellinkoff, *The Language of the Law*, 1963). Tom McArthur, a well-known writer on language, reported in the *Oxford Companion to the English Language* (1992), 595, that 'in 1983, an

English court ordered a law firm to pay £93,000 damages for unintentionally misleading a client by using "obscure" legal language in a letter of advice'. Martin Cutts, in the *Oxford Guide to Plain English* (2004), devotes a chapter to lucid legal language, and gives examples of complex language rewritten in a simpler form. As well as indicating complexities of grammatical structure, he points to words and phrases that notoriously cause difficulty to those not versed in the law: *aforesaid, be empowered to, failure to comply with, forthwith, heretofore, in the event of, pursuant to, the said—, thereto*, and many others.

legendary. *Legendary* (unlike *mythical*) means much more than 'belonging to legend (or myth)', it speaks of greatness and romance: *Many tales arose out of this legendary mountain—The Times,* 2002. It is best kept for people and achievements that belong to the past or are strongly associated with it, where legend is rooted. To use *legendary* in the context of the present or the recent past invites anticlimax: ☒ *Jahangir Khan, the legendary Pakistani player who is now President of the World Squash Federation*—sport website, 2004 [*OEC*] / ☒ *We will hear his legendary recording of 1985*—BBC radio broadcast, 2005. These uses have become popular since the extension of the parent word *legend* to refer to contemporary celebrities such as film stars and pop 'idols' (another such word, now giving way to ICON). These uses of *legendary* raise our hopes only to dash them in mild absurdity. When it is used in contexts that are specifically centred on history and not legend the effect can be laughably incongruous: ☒ *Oliver Stone's biopic of the legendary leader* [Alexander the Great] *who ruled faraway lands more than 300 years before the birth of Christ—Independent,* 2004. Use it sparingly.

legible, readable. In current use *legible* means 'clear enough to be read' (as in *legible handwriting*); *readable* can also have this sense but more often means 'well written and interesting to read': *She writes unassuming, quietly readable novels—Scotsman,* 2006. Both words are used in the first meaning in the following combinations: *barely, clearly, easily legible / readable.*

legitimate, legitimize. 1 As a verb, *legitimate* is pronounced with the last syllable as -ayt and means 'to make legitimate or legal'. *Legitimize*, which is the only form used in the meaning 'to make (a child) legitimate', is much more frequently used in all varieties of English: *My companion had up his sleeve something that would legitimate his employing my Christian name—*J. I. M. Stewart, 1974 / *You . . . forget the very people who legitimize your authority—*Chinua Achebe, 1987 / *This exhibition helps legitimize the last quarter century's most incontrovertible cultural phenomenon—Sunday Herald,* 2000 / *Citizens of the New World sought to legitimate young democratic nations by recalling a grander, classical past—*C. Freeland, 2003 / *She raised the present action* [in 1827] *that the defender, having been born a bastard in England, where the . . . subsequent marriage of the parents does not legitimize offspring, therefore should be held to be a bastard still—Times,* 2007.

2 For *legitimate* as an adjective, *see* LEGAL.

leisure is pronounced **lezh**-uh in BrE and **leezh**-uh in AmE.

lend. 1 *see* LOAN. Use of *lend* for *borrow* (*Can I lend your pen?*) occurs in some British dialects but is non-standard.

2 Use of *lend* as a noun occurs in British dialect use and colloquially in New Zealand, but is non-standard: *Could you give me the lend of a bob?—* Frank Sargeson, NewZE 1946 / *Just* *ringing this feller to ask if I could have a lend of his gun*—J. Howker, BrE 1985.

lengthways, lengthwise. For the adjective only *lengthwise* is used: *The driver was sleeping in a doubled-up lengthwise position.* For the adverb both forms are available: *a hollow tube split lengthways/lengthwise.* AmE prefers the second, BrE the first.

lese-majesty, originally meaning 'treason' or 'an insult to a sovereign or ruler', is pronounced leez **maj**-is-ti and is printed in roman. The French form *lèse majesté* is also used in English, and its pronunciation is closer to the French. The term no longer has any legal force in English, having been replaced by *treason*. Nowadays, the term is generally used to describe any action that can be viewed as undermining the dignity or reputation of a public figure: *In the days when Montagu Norman or Lord Cromer governed the Bank of England it would have been lese-majesty for the press to give them nicknames*—Scotland on Sunday, 2002 / *They do for gardening, he says, risking the ultimate lese-majesty, what Delia Smith's How To Cook did for cooking*—Sunday Herald, 2002.

less. 1 For *less* and *fewer*, see FEWER, LESS.

2 For *much less*, see MUCH MORE, MUCH LESS.

3 *less* and *lesser.* *Less* is a comparative form of *little*, and is used with singular mass nouns to mean the opposite of *more*: *less butter / less noise.* It cannot be used with plural nouns (in which case **fewer* is used), nor with a preceding *a* or *an* (in which case an alternative such as *lower* or *smaller* is used: *I want to pay less rent* but *I want to pay a lower rent*) *Less*, however, and not *fewer* is idiomatic after *one* in a phrase such as *one less thing to worry about. Lesser* is a so-called double comparative and means 'not so

great (i.e. important or significant) as the other or others'; it is preceded by *a* or *the* (*a lesser man than him / the lesser evil*). It is not used to refer to physical size or number; in these cases use *smaller, lower*, etc. (*a smaller car / a lower price*).

-less. 1 This suffix dates back to Old English and is used to form adjectives from nouns (*doubtless, endless, power-less*). It has also been added to verbs with the meaning 'not affected by the action of the verb', although few of this type survive (*countless, dauntless, numberless* (possibly from the noun), *tireless*). As a living suffix it can now only be added to nouns.

2 A hyphen is used when the suffix is added to a noun ending in *-ll* (*wall-less, will-less*), but not when added to one ending in a single *l* (*soulless, tailless*).

lessee, lessor. The *lessee* is the person who holds a property by lease, and the *lessor* is the person who lets a property by lease.

lesser see LESS 3.

lest, despite its slightly archaic flavour, lives on in the language and is one of the mainstays of the subjunctive in English: *I shall say nothing about alcohol lest I be pilloried by publicans*—Julian Critchley, 1987 / *The site also contains a convenient link to PayPal lest anyone want to donate money*—weblog, AmE 2002. An alternative construction, especially after verbs of fearing or apprehension, is with *should: I can see you're in a fever lest slick Ben and his moll should get back . . . before you make your getaway*—Ngaio Marsh, 1962 / *And she also felt slightly nervous lest the large house should suddenly disgorge many other hidden residents*—Margaret Drabble, 1988. Use of the indicative is already evident, and often sounds perfectly natural (the subjunctive is identifiable only in the third person singular anyway):

He would never have repeated the story lest it weakened our war effort—A. N. Wilson, 1977 / *Mr. Howard had better do some research, lest he wants to be a party to a huge white elephant rapid-transit line*—news website, CanE 2004.

let. 1 It is obvious that any pronoun following *let* and preceding an infinitive, e.g. *let me go*, should be in the objective case (*me, him, her*, etc.) and not the subjective (*I, he, she*, etc.), since it is the object of *let*. However, mistakes can occur when there are two pronouns joined by *and* or when the pronoun is followed by a clause with *who*: ✖ *Let you and I say a few words about this unfortunate affair* (read *Let you and me*…) / *Let he who did this be severely punished* (read *Let him who*…).

2 The type *let us* (or *let's*) + infinitive is well established in English (*Let's hold more chat*—Shakespeare, 1588). More colloquial forms occur, especially in AmE: *Let's you and me duck out of here*— J. Macdonald, 1950, but these are considered non-standard. When *let* is used to introduce a firm request, rather than a casual suggestion, the two words should be written separately: *Let us try once more*.

3 The negative form of *let's* is *let's not* or (in BrE) *don't let's*. In AmE, *let's don't* is used informally.

letter forms. 1 Many of the more formal formulas for writing letters that were noted by Fowler (*Your obedient servant, Yours respectfully*, etc.) have disappeared even from business letters and the letter pages of the more traditional newspapers. So too has the practice of addressing colleagues by their surnames only (*Dear Jones*). The standard forms of opening are: (1) to individuals in a company or organization who are known to you or whose names you know *Dear Mr Smith / Mrs Jones / Ms Brown*, or (more informally) *Dear John / Jane*. The corresponding conclusion is normally *Yours sincerely* (with capital Y), or, in the case of people you know well, *With kind regards, With best wishes*, or some variant or combination of these; (2) in personal correspondence more intimate forms such as *My dear John, My dearest Jane, My darling Jim*, etc., are used, with an appropriate conclusion such as *Yours ever, All love*, etc.; (2) in business and other more formal contexts, the inclusive *Dear Sir or Madam* is recommended; otherwise, if they correspond to the sex of the recipient(s), *Dear Sirs / Sir / Madam*, with the conclusion *Yours faithfully* or (somewhat less formally) *Yours truly*. See also EMAILS.

2 For forms of address in special cases such as bishops or members of the nobility, readers should consult the latest edition of a work such as *Debrett's Correct Form*.

leukaemia is the spelling for the disease in BrE, and *leukemia* in AmE.

level. 1 The phrase *at — level* is well established and has a useful role to play: *No work is at present supported at international level on oil seeds such as sunflower, safflower and rapeseed*—Nature, 1974 / *The Treasury took the lead in setting up official inter-departmental committees, some at permanent-secretary level*—Harold Wilson, 1976 / *If you are looking for a vice-chancellor, ideally you want to appoint a candidate who knows how the system works at national level*— Times Higher Educational Supplement, 2006.

2 *Level playing field*, describing a situation in which all have a fair and equal chance of success, was a vogue phrase in the 1980s and 1990s. It rapidly achieved the status of cliché, and lends itself to verbal play particularly among journalists: *That is not a level playing field. It is not even just a home-field advantage. It is* *like asking their competitors to play ball in a swamp—Washington Journalism Review*, 1990 / *One of several suggestions was that BSkyB might be broken up to level the playing field—Business & Money*, 2007.

3 For the verb, the inflected forms are *levelled, levelling* in BrE and *leveled, leveling* in AmE.

leverage. 1 The first syllable is pronounced **leev** in BrE and **lev** in AmE.

2 The *OED* records the verb first from 1937 in a physical sense, and from 1971 in its financial sense of 'to use borrowed capital for (an investment), expecting the profits made to be greater than the interest payable' as in a *leveraged buyout*. Many editors detest as pretentious jargon the use of the verb to mean 'to use something to maximum advantage', widespread in AmE (less so elsewhere), particularly in business, computing, and military speak (e.g. *Google also understands the capacity of the Web to leverage expertise—Fast Company* (magazine), 2003 / *So we're leveraging our strong regional relationships to build national ties—Brandweek*, 2000). It has even figured in *Forbes* magazine's list of 'jargon madness'. Hostility to the word has multiple causes: it is an example of verbing; it is perceived as being overused; it is jargonistic; it can also be somewhat vague. In short, a term to be used with extreme caution.

liable, likely *see* APT.

liaise, liaison. The noun *liaison*, pronounced li-**ay**-zon in BrE and in various ways in AmE, became fully anglicized early in the 20c, replacing its nasalized final syllable with -uhn or -on. Since the early 19c, it has had the meaning 'an illicit sexual relationship', but is now more likely to be used in the meaning 'close communication or cooperation'. The verb *liaise* has not developed the

sexual meaning but is used instead in military and business contexts and is a key word in management jargon in the sense 'cooperate or have direct dealings' (though not widely used in North American English): *The coordinating nurse on each shift 'liaises' with the admissions office regarding bed availability—Professional Nurse*, 1992 / *We liaise with all appropriate law enforcement authorities and provide information and analytical techniques relating to the recognition and detection of counterfeit products—Scotland on Sunday*, 2007. The following sentence may help you remember that both words require a letter *i* before and after the letter *a*: You must li*ai*se with colleagues in *I*reland and *I*taly.

libel, slander. 1 *Libel* is a published false statement that is damaging to a person's reputation, whereas *slander* is a malicious false statement that is spoken about a person. In popular usage the terms are sometimes used interchangeably, but the difference should always be borne in mind. The legal issue has become more complicated in recent years now that uncertainty exists about how far the word *published* can be extended to cover email, Internet websites, and other forms of electronic (as distinct from print) media of communication.

2 As a verb, *libel* has inflected forms *libelled, libelling* in BrE and usually *libeled, libeling* in AmE.

licence, license. In BrE, the noun is spelt *licence* and the verb *license* (and so *licensed premises, licensing hours*, etc., although *licenced* is occasionally seen and can be justified on the ground that it is formed from the noun rather than the verb). In AmE, both the noun and the verb are spelt *license*.

lichee *see* LYCHEE.

lichen. The dominant pronunciation of the plant name is **liy**-kuhn (as *liken*), although **lich**-uhn is also heard in BrE (but not in AmE).

lichgate *see* LYCHGATE.

licorice *see* LIQUORICE.

lie *see* LAY, LIE.

lie, = tell an untruth, has inflected forms *lies, lied, lying*.

lien, meaning 'a right over another's property to protect a debt charged on that property', is pronounced leen or **lee**-uhn.

lieutenant is pronounced lef-**ten**-uhnt in BrE (but with the -f- sound usually omitted when referring to the navy) and loo-**ten**-uhnt in AmE. The -f- sound in BrE may be due to a (pre-19c) reading of Old French *lieu* as *liev* or *lief*.

life. The plural is *lives* except that the art term *still life* has the plural form *still lifes*.

life cycle. The term is first recorded in 1855 in its biological meaning 'the series of changes in the life of an organism'. During the 20c, however, it developed different extended meanings, and in the 1940s the anthropologist Margaret Mead could write of the modern man: *Here he is, only in middle age, and his life is over . . . no new fields to conquer . . . So while he is not out of a job . . . the very nature of the life-cycle in America is such that he feels like an old man—Male and Female*, 1949. The term is now used of other human activities involving origin, development, change, and eventual decline and death, such as business and economics: *In principle the task of the project manager is to plan, organize and lead a group of people to complete a project life cycle*—S. A. Bergen, 1990 / *We provide a fully integrated service covering all assurance and advisory needs to the entrepreneur at every stage of the business life cycle*—Birmingham Post, 2007. This is a natural development of meaning when a cycle of events is involved, but it can sound portentous to use the term when the simple word *life* or another word such as *process* would do equally well, e.g. *You can change the look at any time and know that the long hair has a limited life cycle.*

life insurance *see* ASSURE, ASSURANCE.

lifelong, livelong. *Lifelong* (19c) is a combination of *life* and *long*, and means 'lasting or continuing for a lifetime' (*his lifelong companion*). *Livelong*, pronounced **liv**-long, is a much older word (15c) and is a combination of *lief*, meaning 'dear, beloved', and *long*. It is a literary word used as an intensive or emotional form of *long* in describing periods of time (e.g. *the livelong day*).

lifestyle. The term will be familiar to modern readers in the meaning given in the *Concise Oxford Dictionary* (2006): 'the way in which a person lives', although it has a much older, specialized meaning introduced to the language of psychology by the neurologist Alfred Adler in the 1920s. In recent years it has been absorbed into marketing jargon to refer to 'the way in which one lives (or chooses to live) one's life, especially with regard to quality of life', and has developed an attributive use (i.e. coming before a noun): *The latest lifestyle choice for the vibrant elderly is the 'retirement village'*—Independent, 1995. In some contexts, *way of life*, or even just *life*, seems preferable to a word that has become so bogged down in promotional hype. The derivative word *lifestyler*, meaning 'someone with a special lifestyle', has an ephemeral ring but is now common, often linked with the word *alternative* to denote people who lead unconventional lives: *The centre is built on a hilltop amid a broadleaf wood and is home to a community of proselytising alternative life-stylers—Holiday Which?, 1991 / The recent influx of new voters from Boston into southern New Hampshire and alternative lifestylers into neighbouring Maine had boosted the Democratic vote—Independent, 2000.*

ligature, in printing, is a pair of letters printed in a joined form, e.g. *æ. See* DIGRAPH.

light. 1 The phrase *in the light of*, meaning 'having regard to, considering', is more often heard in the form *in light of* in AmE: *In light of what you've told us, we have decided to leave earlier.*

2 In BrE the past tense and past participle of the verb are usually both *lit* (*We lit the fire when it grew dark / He had already lit his pipe / The streets are all well lit*), but *lighted* is also used adjectivally when there is no qualifying adverb (*She had a lighted cigarette in her hand*). In AmE, *lighted* is often used in contexts where *lit* would be normal in BrE: *She lighted a candle and turned off the lamp—New Yorker, 1987.*

lightning, lightening. *Lightning* is the spelling for electrical flashes in the sky (*thunder and lightning*), whereas *lightening* is a form of the verb *lighten* (*I welcome the lightening of this burden that's imposed on councils—Birmingham Post, 2006 / a key step in lightening the balance sheet—Times, 2007*). *Lightning* is originally a contracted form of *lightening*.

like. 1 *like* **as a conjunction.** *Like* is used as a preposition in the sentence *Please try to write like me* and as a conjunction in the sentence *Please try to write like I do*. In the second sentence, *like* is used instead of *as*, and this use seems still to be one of the cardinal

issues by which a person's awareness of what is correct or incorrect grammar is judged. Fowler (1926) wrote that 'every illiterate person uses this construction daily; it is the established way of putting the thing among all who have not been taught to avoid it'; and Evelyn Waugh wrote of his close friend and fellow writer Henry Green in the 1940s that 'only one thing disconcerted me . . . The proletarian grammar—the "likes" for "ases", the "bikes" for "bicycles"'.

Nonetheless, there is plenty of good evidence for this use. The *OED* gives examples from Shakespeare, Southey, William Morris, and other good writers. In more recent usage, *like* is often used as a conjunction in three principal ways; (1) with the verb repeated or a form of *do* replacing it (*They didn't talk like other people talked—Martin Amis, 1981 / I'm afraid it might happen to my baby like it happened to Jefferson—New Yorker, 1987 / The retsina flowed like the Arno did when it overflowed in 1966—Spectator, 1987*), (2) in AmE and Australian English, though less in BrE, to mean 'as if' or 'as though' (*I wanted him born and now it feels like I don't want him—E. Jolley, 1985 (Australia) / She acts like she can't help it—Lee Smith, AmE 1987*), (3) replacing *as* in fixed or semi-fixed expressions such as *as I said* (*Like you say, you're a dead woman—Mary Wesley, 1983 / Like I said, I haven't seen Rudi for weeks—Thomas Keneally, 1985*).

Clearly, *like* continues to assert its right to be regarded as a conjunction, and there is little doubt that this right will be recognized in time. For the present, the advice has to be: when *as* (or *as if* or *as though*) can be substituted for *like*, use these alternatives, which are absolutely safe: *They didn't talk as other people talked / Now it feels as if I didn't want him.*

2 use of *like* as a filler. In this use, *like* is added parenthetically to a statement. This is conversational only, and even then is often disapproved of as non-standard: *Hayley was pleased. 'That's him. He's, like, got her hypno-tized.'*—Maurice Gee, 1990. It is now a regular feature of the informal language of young people, and can occur several times in a single sentence.

3 *like* in idiomatic phrases. This category includes phrases such as *like anything, like mad, like blazes*. These again belong only in informal conversational style: *The horse . . . went like blazes*—De Quincey, 1853 / *They wept like anything to see Such quantities of sand*—Lewis Carroll, 1872 / *It's like my home show really, so I've been training like mad*—*Evening Gazette*, 2007.

like verb. *I should like* is normal in BrE and *I would like* in other varieties, although in practice the contracted form *I'd like* is common, especially in speech. These forms are followed either by a *to*-infinitive (*I should like to come too*) or by an object followed by a *to*-infinitive (*They would like us to come too*). The past form is *should* (or *would*) *have liked to*, and in this case the normal *to*-infinitive should follow, e.g. *I should have liked to come too*, not ⊠ *I should have liked to have come too* (but *I should like to have come too is also possible*). The construction *like* + *for* + object + *to*-infinitive is largely confined to AmE: *I'd like very much for you to meet him*—*New Yorker*, 1988.

-like. In occasional or less familiar formations, and when the first part ends in *-l*, a hyphen is used (*cat-like, eel-like*), but more established combinations are spelt as one word (*childlike, lifelike, statesmanlike*).

likeable is the preferred form everywhere except the US, where *likable* is standard.

likely. 1 As an adverb, *likely* needs the support of a qualifying or intensifying word such as *more, quite*, or *very* (*They've quite likely left by now* / *It's more likely a toadstool*), whereas in AmE it often stands alone: *It is possible to predict that within a few years the microfiche likely will move into the study and home*—*Publishers' Weekly*, 1971 / *While the population has likely increased in the past couple of decades, many researchers point out that the animals are still in jeopardy*—*Defenders of Wildlife*, 2004 [*OEC*].

2 For use of *apt, liable*, and *likely*, *see* APT.

likewise, like *also*, is used as an adverb and not a conjunction in standard English: *Go and do likewise* / *They likewise prefer reading*. In uses where it might be a conjunction, it normally needs the support of a genuine conjunction such as *and*: *A heated window, and likewise rear wipers, are essential*. It is however permissible for *likewise* to stand at the head of a sentence, where its role is still mainly adverbial: *Two feet of air space separate the inner and outer walls. Likewise, there is a basement under Jackson Hall, and a 'technical attic' at the ceiling*—*Architecture Week*, AmE 2002.

-lily. Few adjectives in *-ly* form adverbs in *-lily* because they are too awkward to use. As Fowler noted (1926), 'it is always possible to say *in a masterly manner, at a timely moment*, and the like, instead of *masterlily, timelily*'. Some adjectives in *-ly* retain the same form for the corresponding adverb, e.g. *kindly*. A few forms in *-lily* are in occasional use, most but not all adjectives in which *-ly* is part of the stem rather than an adjectival ending. The most common is *friendlily*, followed by *sillily, jollily*, and *uglily*, all found in newspaper writing despite being ungainly: *One of his superior* *officers, who was friendlily disposed to him—Times*, 1992 / *Tomlinson's French is uglily distorted—Evening Standard*, 1999 / *To see how sillily they did it—Observer*, 2004 / *I chose people who treated me rather jollily really—Herald* (Glasgow), 2005. Others, such as *livelily*, *surlily*, and *wilily*, are virtually non-existent.

limey, limy. *Limey* is the adjective corresponding to the fruit called *lime*, whereas *limy* relates to the caustic alkaline substance. *Limey* (with a capital initial letter) is an AmE slang term for a person from Britain, and arose from the enforced consumption of lime juice in the British navy.

linchpin, originally a pin put through the end of an axle to keep the wheel in position, is mostly used in its figurative sense 'an indispensable person or thing'. It is spelt *linch-* in preference to *lynch-*, and as one word.

line. In Fanny Burney's *Cecilia* (1782) the question is asked *Where, then, do you draw the line?*, meaning how far can a person expect to be independent. The image of drawing lines has fed English idiom for several centuries, extending to the more explicit notion of (1) a line drawn *under* something (by which a difficult or embarrassing period of events is regarded as resolved or finished: *The eviction of a similar number of British diplomats from Moscow will be taken as a signal that Russia wishes to draw a line under the whole affair—Daily Telegraph*, 2007) and (2) *a line drawn in the sand* (suggesting a limit to movement or action much as a line in the sand marks a physical limit: *He had crossed a line in the sand etched by decades of sectarian division—Sunday Mail*, 2004). The second form of the phrase tends to be used in the same way as the first, however, even to the extent of producing absurdities such as the following: *All further*

discussion is redundant, so let's draw a line in the sand under the entire episode—Morning Star, 2004.

lingo, a colloquial word for a language or the special vocabulary of a language, has the plural form *lingos*.

linking r is the sounding of a normally silent written letter *r* when a vowel sound follows, as in *in a pair of gloves* and *pour out the tea*. This is quite correct, but *see* INTRUSIVE R.

liquefy, meaning 'to make liquid', is spelt *-efy*, not *-ify*. Its inflected forms are *liquefies, liquefied, liquefying*.

liqueur, the strong usually sweet alcoholic spirit, is spelt with two *u*s.

liquorice is the BrE spelling, and *licorice* the AmE spelling, of the word denoting a black root extract used as a sweet.

lira, the chief monetary unit of Italy before the introduction of the euro in 2002 and still that of Turkey, has the plural form *lire*, which in English is pronounced in the same way as the singular.

lit *see* LIGHT.

litany, liturgy. A *litany* (from Greek *litē* 'prayer') is in its literal sense a prayer couched in the form of a sequence of petitions. It has a figurative use in expressions such as a *litany of curses* or *woes*. A *liturgy* (from Greek *leitourgia* 'public service, public worship') is a prescribed form of worship, embracing many individual prayers and petitions. *Litany* is also used figuratively to mean 'a tedious recital or repetitive series' seen as resembling a form of religious ritual (e.g. *a litany of complaints, failures, lies, problems, woes*). Occasionally *liturgy* is mistakenly used in this sense: ☒ *Heidegger was by no means the only twentieth-century intellectual to subscribe* *to an inexhaustible liturgy of anxieties about modernity and the perils of city life—Times Literary Supplement*, 2011.

litchi *see* LYCHEE.

lite was first used in advertising in the 1960s to describe a product, especially beer, lower in weight, calorie content, etc., than the standard ones. Since then this simplified spelling variant of *light*, often placed after the noun it qualifies, has become a usefully humorous or dismissive way of characterizing more abstract notions as superficial or lacking in seriousness: *I am the happy feminist, the feminist who likes men, the feminist lite—Playboy*, 1992 / *That is why the worldwide ascendancy of lite anti-Americanism is a dangerous trend. And not only for Americans—New Perspectives Quarterly*, 2003.

literally. Few words have the capacity to cause such mirth: *My grandfather, King George VI, who had literally been catapulted onto the throne—*Prince Edward as quoted in *Private Eye*, 1998. There will always be occasions when this type of hilarity is best avoided; on the other hand, a little linguistic reflection will reveal a logical rigour behind a much derided use.

1 The literal (16c) meaning of *literally* is 'in a literal sense': *This was a china warehouse indeed, truly and literally to be called so—*Daniel Defoe, 1719. It is still used in this way, with reference to the meaning of individual words (with the word *mean* often explicitly present) and to the broader sense in which phrases and sentences are to be understood: *He . . . was literally too tired to move—*J. Gores, 1972 / *The cracker in Georgia cracker literally means a person who still cracks corn—*S. B. Flexner, 1982.

2 In the course of time, *literally* became caught up in the language of metaphor, in which English abounds, and

we find this type of use: *Every day with me is literally another yesterday for it is exactly the same—*Pope, 1708. From this it is a short step for the word to become an intensifier contained wholly within metaphor: *For the last four years . . . I literally coined money—*F. A. Kemble, 1863. In other examples we can see the word half in and half out of the realm of metaphor: *Crabs and lobsters are literally to be found crawling round the floor waiting for an order—Good Food Guide*, 1973 (the creatures are physically crawling around the floor but are, we may assume, only metaphorically waiting for an order).

3 This historical development explains how the word has apparently reversed its meaning; in fact it has done no such thing but has been absorbed into the metaphor; once understood as part of the verbal image and not as external to it, the use makes good linguistic sense. It is doubtful though whether this rationale will satisfy those who see the developed meaning of *literally* as sloppy and inappropriate (which it rarely is) or as ludicrous (which it sometimes appears to be): *Most of the buildings on the corniche have literally been face-lifted—Blitz*, 1989 / *They* [supermarkets] *can literally play God, even to the point of sending food back to the genetic drawing board for a redesign—Guardian*, 1995.

4 In another very common type, *literally* introduces a fixed expression or cliché that has some particular (often punning) relevance to the context: *We have lived in a wonderful variety of houses, including . . . a leaking gothic horror of a Victorian rectory in deepest Sussex that was literally falling to pieces—Medau News*, 1980 / *There is a catastrophic 'implosion' . . . followed by a shock-wave which literally blows the star apart in what is called a supernova outburst—*Patrick Moore, 1990 / *Today, Cerezo's letter to the villagers is literally carved in stone; a six-foot-high marble* *and stone replica stands opposite 13 rough wooden crosses, marking the spots where the villagers fell—New Statesman, 1992 / Smith's hundreds of bookshops literally spread the word—Independent on Sunday, 1998.*

5 To be avoided is the use of *literally* in a trite semi-apologetic way that seemingly seeks to overcome a fear in the writer that the reader will not believe what is said, carrying a 'please believe me' or 'I'm not kidding you' tag: *Thus the Prime Minister, the chief executive of the British Government, had literally no idea that he lacked the means to do what he wanted* [here *literally* adds nothing to the sense and is redundant]— *Independent, 2006 / I suspect that many wine-drinkers are sailing through their lives not realising there are literally hundreds of interesting wines produced in the land of the free—Scotland on Sunday, 2007.*

6 The conclusion is: avoid using *literally* when the effect might be distracting or comic; but it can be used to good effect in cases where it reinforces a strong verbal image.

litotes, pronounced liy-**toh**-teez or li-**toh**-teez, is a figure of speech in which an assertion is made by means of understatement or denial of an opposite, as when St Paul declared that he was 'a citizen of *no mean* city' (Acts 21:39). Typical modern examples include *not bad* (= very good), *not uncommon* (= quite frequent), and *it was nothing* (as a statement dismissing one's own achievement). *Litotes* is therefore the opposite of *hyperbole* or overstatement.

litre is the BrE spelling for the metric unit, and *liter* the AmE spelling.

liturgy *see* LITANY.

liveable is the preferred form in BrE, and *livable* in AmE and CanE.

-lived *see* LONG-LIVED; SHORT-LIVED.

livid. The meaning that is more familiar today, 'furiously angry', is a recent one not recorded before the 20c. The earlier (17c) meaning, still in use, is 'of a bluish leaden colour; discoloured by bruising': *A huge, livid, recently healed scar ran along the right side of his face—P. Abrahams, 1985.*

llama *see* LAMA.

-l-, -ll-. *See box overleaf.*

Lloyd's, Lloyds. The name of the London society of underwriters is spelt *Lloyd's* (also *Lloyd's List, Lloyd's Register*), whereas the name of the bank is *Lloyds Bank* (no apostrophe).

loadstar, loadstone *see* LODESTAR, LODESTONE.

loaf. The plural form of the noun is *loaves*; the third person singular of the verb is *loafs*.

loan *verb*. In 19c British English, *loan* was a standard alternative for *lend*, but by the time Fowler wrote (1926) *loan* had been largely driven out by *lend*, although it has continued in use in AmE. In current use *loan* is much more often used in non-British varieties of English than in BrE, but it is also used in BrE in the literal meaning of 'grant someone something temporarily on the understanding that it will be returned': *Delaney told him he could loan him $50 a week—Thomas Keneally, AusE 1985 / The problem was how to stretch the small amount of money he had been loaned by Herr Pfuehl—Anita Desai (IndE 1988) / Don't loan those jeans to your younger and svelter sister—Metropolis (magazine), AmE 2003 / The Penrith-based scheme . . . provides farming families with a computer loaned free-of-charge for six months—www.thisisthelakedistrict.co.uk, BrE 2003.* It is also used in BrE too in

-L-, -LL-.

Much confusion is caused by differing spelling practice in BrE and AmE in verbs of two syllables pronounced with the stress on the second syllable, e.g. *enthrall/enthral* and *fulfil/fulfill*. Practice varies even within each variety of English; the following table lists the recommended spellings:

BrE	AmE
annul	annul
appal	appall
befall	befall
distil	distill
enrol	enroll
enthral	enthrall
extol	extol
fulfil	fulfill
install	install
instil	instill

The recommended spellings for nouns in *-ment* are:

BrE	AmE
annulment	annulment
enrolment	enrollment
enthralment	enthrallment
extolment	extolment
fulfilment	fulfillment
instalment	installment
instilment	instillment

For the spelling of inflected forms of verbs in *-l* (*appal, appalled, appalling, etc.*) *see* DOUBLING OF FINAL CONSONANTS IN INFLECTION.

the context of making something valuable (such as a work of art) available by a formal arrangement to an institution for a period: *The painting has been loaned annually to the National Gallery for two-month periods since 2002—Times,* 2007. (An alternative, more pleasing to some, is *on loan* (*from*).) In normal contexts, however, *loan* is a so-called 'needless variant' of *lend*.

loanword is a word adopted, normally with little change in form, from another language. Examples in English are *blitz* (from German), **locale* (from French), and *kiosk* (from Turkish). A *loan translation* is a word used in translation from another language: *loanword* itself is a loan translation of German *Lehnwort*.

loath, meaning 'averse, reluctant', as in *loath to comment*, is spelt *loath* much more often than *loth*, but the latter is perfectly correct. Technically it should be pronounced like *both*, but is often pronounced exactly the same as the verb *loathe* meaning 'to hate', which rhymes with *clothe*. As a result the two words are

quite often confused: (*loathe* used
for *loath*) ✖ *The young seventies family
man . . . was loathe to purchase the same
car that his fifty-five-year-old father
might own*—B. Elton, 1991; (*loath* used
for *loathe*) ✖ *I loath reading a review
that tells me more about the critic than
what they are critiquing*—David Poland,
2003. The adjective *loathsome*, meaning
'hateful, repulsive', is derived from
loathe and the first part is pronounced
like the verb.

locale, meaning 'a scene or locality,
especially with reference to an event or
occurrence taking place there', was
adopted in the 18c from French in the
form *local* and respelt in the 19c by
writers such as Walter Scott to indicate
that the stress lay on the second syllable
(loh-**kahl**).

locate is an 18c Americanism that
in some people's view still has a
transatlantic flavour, especially in its
intransitive use (without an object) as
in *Numerous industries have located
in the area*. In BrE, this meaning is
more commonly expressed as *relocate*,
also originally an Americanism (19c):
*I am advising your colleague . . . to
relocate*—Robert McCrum, 1991. In
all varieties of English, *to be located*
is a synonym for 'to be situated'
(*The supermarket is located in the
northern outskirts of the city*). It has
been criticized as unnecessary, since
the sentence just quoted would mean
the same without it, but the use is too
well established to cause most people
any qualms.

lodestar, lodestone are the preferred spellings, not *load-*.

loggia, a word of Italian origin meaning 'an open-sided gallery or arcade', is
pronounced **lo**-juh in BrE and **loh**-juh in
AmE, and has the plural form *loggias*.

logically, especially when placed at
the beginning of a sentence as an adverb
qualifying the whole of it, often has little
to do with the application of logic and
simply prepares us for (or beguiles us
into accepting) the writer's different
point of view: *Logically, it is the Europeans who are out of step [with respect to
time] and not us*—Croydon Guardian,
2004.

long. The conjunction *as* (or *so*) *long as*
has two main meanings: (1) 'during the
whole time that' (*You can stay as long as
you like*), and (2) 'provided that, only if'
(*You can stay as long as you help me*). In
some contexts the two meanings overlap
in a way that can produce ambiguity. *So
long as* tends to have the second meaning (*That's okay, so long as we understand each other*) but it occurs in the
first, especially in AmE (*He would cooperate only so long as it served his purpose*). In the second meaning, it is more
likely to be preceded by a comma (*You
can stay, as long as you help me*), and the
shortened form *long as* is occasionally
found in informal reported conversation:
*'It's all right,' he said, 'long as you are
here'*—Graham Greene, 1938.

longevity, meaning 'long life', is pronounced lon-**jev**-i-ti, not long-**gev**-i-ti.

longitude. The recommended pronunciation is **lon**-ji-tyood rather than
long-gi-tyood. Beware of pronouncing it,
let alone spelling it, *longtitude*.

long-lived is pronounced long-**livd** in
BrE and long-**liyvd** in AmE.

look. 1 non-standard uses. Various
idiomatic uses of *look* are confined to
particular parts of the English-
speaking world and are not part of
standard English: for example *look you*
as a way of attracting attention,
found in Shakespeare (*Why, look you,
how you storm!*—The Merchant of

Venice I.iii.140) and still used in Wales, *looky here* (an AmE variant of *look here*), and the colloquial AmE (20c) form *lookit* used with the meaning 'Look!' or 'Listen!'.

2 look + to-infinitive. *I shall hereafter look to be treated as a person of respectability*—T. Huxley, 1900. This type, meaning 'to expect', has been in continuous use since the 16c but is beginning to sound dated and is falling into disuse. Still in regular use is a form of this in which the continuous tense is often used (*am looking*, etc.) and the sense is more of hope or intention than of expectation: *The home team will be looking to get a result against the visitors next Saturday*—*Times*, 1988 / *The council had been looking to take ownership of the historic Moat for a number of years*—*Kildare Nationalist*, 2003. In a third type, *look + to*-infinitive means 'to look as if, to appear': *The owl looked to be encircled by six cloaked hitmen*—J. E. Maslow, 1982. Although there is a theoretical risk of ambiguity here, this does not seem to occur in practice.

3 look + adverbs and adjectives. The meaning we are concerned with here is 'appear, seem'. Uses with an adverb complement (as in Shakespeare's *The skies looke grimly*) are now virtually extinct. Uses with adjectives are normal, as in *to look black, blue, cold, elderly, foolish, small, stupid*, etc.

4 look like + clause *You look to me . . . like you was made out of old wichetty grubs*—Patrick White, AusE 1961 / *Looks like your child's birthday is news again this year*—*Guardian*, 1973 / *Katherine now looked like she wanted to throw her plate at Sammy*—fiction website, AmE 2003. For comments on this construction, *see* LIKE 1.

loose, loosen. Both words involve removal of restraints, physical or otherwise. The difference is that *loose* releases or sets free whereas *loosen* only makes more loose (or less tight). To *loose* a prisoner from his bonds is to set him free; to *loosen* his bonds is to make them less tight although he remains a captive. Unwelcome things are *loosed on* people when people have to endure them: *Mere anarchy is loosed upon the world*—*Daily Mail*, 2003.

Lord's, the name of the London cricket ground, is spelt with an apostrophe.

lose. The verb *lose* is occasionally written as *loose*, especially by writers in a hurry. The verb *loose* has a quite different meaning, and has enough problems of its own (*see* LOOSE, LOOSEN).

lose out, meaning 'to be unsuccessful', is recorded in AmE from the mid-19c and is now common in BrE as well. It has various shades of meaning, and is not simply a synonym for *lose*. Followed by *on*, it means 'not to get a fair chance in': *Like most birds she didn't want to lose out on a nosh-up*—A. Draper, 1970. Followed by *to*, it means 'be defeated or worsted by': *The popular press, thrown off balance and uncertain of its role, lost out to the heavies and the provincials*—*Author*, 1971 / *Sales will go down and all parties lose out*—*Ideas Factory*, BrE 2004 [*OEC*].

lost causes. Each generation has its own preoccupations about language, and the transitory nature of some of these tends to be overlooked. Some issues of current concern are listed at the entry for **fetish*; these include the split infinitive, the ending of a sentence with a preposition, use of the sentence adverb *hopefully*, and the use of *from* after *different*. None of these concerns has any firm basis in grammar or language structure; the split infinitive, for example, is a 19c superstition. In the 18c, Dr Johnson disliked words that he classified as 'low words' (he did not use the term 'slang') such as *bogus, coax, joke, flog, prim, rogue, snob*, and *spree*; all these are now accepted items of general vocabulary. Among Fowler's strictures that we may now regard as lost causes are: *agenda* (use *agendum* for the singular), *belittle* (= disparage, an undesirable alien), *cachet* (should be 'expelled as an alien'), *data* (plural only), *caption* (in the sense 'title or heading': 'rare and might well be rarer'), *category* (use *class*), *clever* (= well-read or studious, 'much misused, especially in feminine conversation'), *coastal* and *tidal* (badly formed barbarisms), *conservative* (= moderate, cautious in estimating), *distinctly* (as in *distinctly interesting*), *malnutrition* ('a word to be avoided'), *negotiate* (= tackle successfully, an 'improper' sense), and *suchlike* (= the like, 'now usually left to the uneducated'). *See also* IF AND WHEN. More recently, strictures on the use of *decimate, echelon, instigate*, and *involve*, on the pronunciation of multi-syllable words such as *controversy* and *formidable*, on the formation of words of mixed origin (such as *television*), and on the use of *graffiti* as a singular mass noun, have all joined the band of lost causes. To regard them in this way is a recognition of the force of language change, rather than a concession to declining standards. *See also* SUPERSTITIONS.

lot. The phrases *a lot of* and *lots of* (*a lot of time* / *lots of people*) are common and highly versatile, being used freely with singular (uncount) nouns and plural nouns. In positive contexts, *a lot of* is idiomatic (*There is a lot of time*) and *lots of* is informal; in negative contexts, *much* or *many* or *a great deal of* are usually better alternatives in more formal contexts (*We do not have much time*).

loud, loudly. *Loud* is occasionally used as an adverb, especially in semi-fixed expressions such as *loud and clear* (*I can hear you loud and clear*: *loudly* and *clearly* could also be used here, but would sound less natural). In other contexts it is used informally, but *loudly* is the better choice when it comes to writing: *She spoke loud* [read: *loudly*] *enough for the whole class to hear*.

louvre, meaning '(one of) a set of overlapping slats for ventilation', is spelt in this way in BrE and *louver* in AmE.

lovable is the preferred spelling everywhere, not *loveable*, though the latter is also correct, and slightly more often used in BrE than *lovable*.

love. In literature of the 16c to 19c, the expression *to make love to* means 'to court, to be amorous towards' (*'Who's had the impudence to make love to my sister!' cried Harry*—George Meredith, 1861), whereas in modern literature it means 'to have sexual intercourse with'. This more specific meaning arose during the 20c, and has driven out the older meaning much as the sexual sense of *intercourse* has driven out, or at least compromised, all its other uses. If you come across the expression in print, a check of the date of publication will help avoid misreading the meaning.

lovey, an informal way of addressing a loved one or (in more recent use) a theatrical colleague, is spelt in this way, not *lovy*. The plural is *loveys*. An alternative spelling is *luvvy*, plural *luvvies*.

low, lowly. *Low* can function as an adjective (*a low ceiling* / *low wages*) and as an adverb with a wide range of verbs (*to aim low* / *fly low* / *hang low* / *lie low*). *Lowly* is an adjective meaning 'humble, modest' (*of lowly station*); its use as an adverb is now largely confined to poetry or to the phrase *lowly paid* used instead of *low paid*.

low hanging fruit. Sometimes ridiculed as an overripe outgrowth of business and management speak, this phrase is not particularly common outside those spheres. It can be defended as an exceptionally vivid, immediately graspable metaphor, whose freshness has not yet withered on the vine. That said, it is still likely to figure high on many people's list of rancid management talk, and what precisely it means is often rather vague. Examples: *Discovering and developing new drugs is getting more difficult and expensive. The low-hanging fruit has been plucked*—www.motleyfool.co.uk, 2003 / *I see us going forward by addressing three key areas. We must continue to cultivate our low-hanging fruit such as properties like Harry Potter*—*Black Enterprise*, 2002.

lunge, meaning 'to make a sudden movement forward', has the participial form *lunging*, not *lungeing*, which means 'exercising a horse with a long rope (or *lunge*)'.

luxuriant, luxurious. These two words, both connected with the word *luxury* (in turn derived from the Latin word *luxus* meaning 'abundance'), have got in each other's way since the 17c. Nonetheless, their meanings are distinct, as R. M. Ballantyne recognized in his *Coral Island* (1858): *The trees and bushes were very luxuriant / Altogether this was the most luxurious supper we had enjoyed for many a day*. Essentially, *luxurious*, the more general word, means 'rich or abundant in luxuries or comforts' whereas *luxuriant* has the specific meaning 'rich or abundant in foliage or vegetation'.

-ly forms adverbs (*boldly, quickly*; *see* ADVERB 2) and adjectives (*goodly,* *kindly*). Some adjectives form adverbs in -*ly* in addition to being used as adverbs themselves, always with distinctions in meaning (e.g. *dear / dearly, direct / directly, hard / hardly, right / rightly, tight / tightly*). See the entries for these words, and for other aspects, *see* -EDLY; -LILY.

lychee (pronounced **liy**-chee), the name of a Chinese fruit, is most often spelt this way, then as *lichee*, and rarely as *litchi*. All three forms are pronounced **lee**-chee in AmE.

lychgate, meaning 'a roofed gateway to a churchyard', should be spelt *lych-* and as one word, in preference to *lich-*, although the latter is still accepted as a variant. The word is derived from the Old English word *līc* meaning 'corpse' + *gate* because the gateway was formerly used at burials for sheltering a coffin until the clergyman's arrival.

lyric, lyrical. *Lyric* is the adjective to use when referring to a type of poetry that expresses the poet's feelings in set forms such as an ode or sonnet (*lyric poet / lyric poet / lyric verses*). A *lyric* is a poem of this kind, and since the middle of the 20c *lyrics* (plural) has denoted the words of a popular song. *Lyrical* is occasionally used in the same meaning as *lyric* (as in Wordsworth's title *Lyrical Ballads*, 1798), but mainly means 'expressing the writer's, musician's, artist's, etc., feelings in an expressive and beautiful way' (e.g. *the intensely lyrical violin concerto*). It is also widely used in the expression *wax lyrical*, meaning 'to talk enthusiastically about something'.

M

Mac-, Mc-. In British dictionaries and lists of names, it is usual to order all names spelt with these prefixes as if they were spelt *Mac-*, so that a user who is unsure of the spelling does not have a lengthy search. A typical sequence is therefore *Maccabees, McCarthyism, mace, McNaughten rules, macramé*. In American practice, however, it is more usual to place names beginning with *Mc-* at their literal place in the sequence, i.e. after words in *mac-* and any in *mb-*, so that *McCarthy* might appear more than twenty pages further on than *Macdonald*.

macabre is pronounced muh-**kah**-bruh, although it tends to sound like muh-**kah**-buh, with the last *r* lost, in rapid speech.

Machiavellian, a noun and adjective denoting a politically devious schemer, is spelt with a capital initial letter and two *l*s.

machinations, meaning 'scheming, laying plots', is pronounced mak-i-**nay**-shuhnz or mash-i-**nay**-shuhnz.

machismo, meaning 'assertive or aggressive masculinity', is still not completely naturalized into English and its pronunciation varies between muh-**chiz**-moh and muh-**kiz**-moh. The first is in line with its pronunciation in Spanish, the language from which English has borrowed it.

macho, pronounced **match**-oh, is mostly used as an adjective meaning

'assertively or aggressively masculine'. The pronunciation **ma**-ko is occasionally heard but is not recommended.

mackintosh, the waterproof coat, is spelt with a *k*, although the inventor's name was Charles *Macintosh*. But the full form is hardly ever used, *mac* being used instead.

madam, madame. The English form *madam* is a now somewhat formal or affectedly courteous form of address to a woman (*Dear Madam / Madam Chairman / Can I help you, madam?*), and is also a term (should one be needed) for a woman brothel-keeper. When addressing royalty, the shorter form *ma'am* is used. *Madame*, pronounced muh-**dahm**, is the right form of address to a woman from any foreign nation (not necessarily French).

maelstrom, an originally Dutch word meaning 'a state of great confusion', is pronounced **mayl**-struhm.

maestro, meaning 'a distinguished musician or artist', is pronounced **miy**-stroh, and has plural forms *maestros* or, much less frequently, the Italian plural *maestri* (**miy**-stri).

Mafia, pronounced **maf**-i-uh, is spelt with a capital initial when it refers to the organized international body of criminals in Sicily, southern Italy, and the US; a member of the Mafia is a *Mafioso* (maf-i-**oh**-zoh), plural *Mafiosi* (maf-i-**oh**-zi). The form *mafia*, with small initial, is used in the extended meaning 'any group exerting a sinister hidden influence' (as in *the literary mafia*).

Magdalen, Magdalene. The names of the colleges in Oxford (*Magdalen*) and Cambridge (*Magdalene*) are pronounced **maw**-dlin. In the full biblical name *Mary Magdalene* (= of Magdala in Galilee), *Magdalene* is pronounced **mag**-duh-lin or mag-duh-**lee**-ni. The form *magdalen*, pronounced **mag**-duh-lin, was formerly used to mean 'a reformed prostitute' or 'a home for reformed prostitutes'.

Magi, as in *the three Magi*, is pronounced **may**-jiy. It is the plural of *magus* (**may**-guhs), which denotes a member of a priestly caste in ancient Persia.

magic, magical. The two words compete with one another in all the main senses, 'relating to magic', 'produced by or as if by magic', and 'wonderful', although in certain fixed expressions such as *magic lantern* and *magic square* only *magic* is used. When used in its descriptive role, *magic* still behaves more like a noun than an adjective; otherwise, *magic* and *magical* are largely interchangeable, however close or remote the connection with magic and related phenomena: *. . . In the evenings, when the afterglow makes the whole valley magic*—J. Ashe, 1993 / *She had not been kissed for over two years and it was magical*—P. Wilson, 1993. In the second half of the 20c, *magic* came to be used informally both in attributive position (before a noun) and by itself as a term of enthusiastic approval (*We had a magic time* / *It's magic!*).

magma, meaning 'fluid material under the earth's surface', has the plural form *magmas* (no longer *magmata*).

Magna Carta is the usual spelling now for the famous English charter of 1215, although *Magna Charta*, once the dominant form, is still occasionally found, especially in AmE. *Charta* and *Carta* are both valid forms in Latin. The phrase can be used with or without the definite article *the* / *The*, but there is a slight preference nowadays to drop it.

magneto, a shortened form of *magneto-electric machine*, has the plural form *magnetos*.

magnum opus, from the Latin neuter of *magnus* 'great' + *opus* 'work', refers to a work of art, music, or literature that is regarded as the most important or best that its creator has produced. The *OED* attributes its first use to Boswell: *My Magnum Opus, the Life of Dr. Johnson . . . is to be published on Monday, 16th May*—letter of 19 April, 1791. *Opus* can be pronounced with a short or long *o*, and the plural is more often the hybrid Latin-English *magnum opuses* than the strictly correct Latin *magna opera*. It is also used in the form *opus magnum*.

magus *see* MAGI.

major is commonly used, especially in journalism, to mean 'important, significant', without any notion of comparison inherent in the word's origins. A political leader invariably gives a *major* speech, a reference book is published in a *major* new edition, broadcasters produce a *major* new series, and *major* accidents occur regularly on main roads and motorways. This use is too well established for it to be condemned, but *major* is better used when the element of comparison is present, so that a *major* work is important relative to other lesser works, a *major* road is contrasted with a minor one, and so on.

major-general has the plural form *major-generals*.

majority. There are two issues relating to this word:

1 *majority* = 'the greater number or part'. *An informed minority of the 'public' was opposed to escalation, while the majority was rather malleable in its opinion*—Canadian Journal of History, 2000 / *The vast majority have now come to terms with their destiny*—Encounter, 1987. As these examples show, when the word is used in this meaning the verb can be either singular or plural, depending on whether the people or things concerned are thought of as a group or as individuals. *Majority* is routinely used in the plural in this meaning, particularly when modified: *Majorities in various countries are, of course, critical of American foreign policies*—weblog, AmE 2004 [OEC] / *Enmity between Hindus and Muslims led the British to partition British India, creating East and West Pakistan, where there were Muslim majorities*—OEC, 2004.

2 *majority of* + noun. *Majority* in this use means 'the greater number' of people or things, and the noun following *of*, together with its related verb, is generally plural: *A majority of them come from the Scheduled Castes*—Times of India, 1972 / *The majority of school buildings are dilapidated and decaying*—Encounter, 1987 / *I fully accept that the vast majority of kids in South Woodham are good*—news website, BrE 2004 [OEC]. Uses with uncount nouns (*the majority of the work* / *the majority of the time*) are disliked by critics who insist that only plural nouns or collective nouns such as *group, population, public,* etc., which denote a collection of individuals, can be used: *Gillray, in common with the vast majority of his public, did not want to take the Jacobin side*—M. Billig, 1991 / *They are simply out of touch with the majority of the electorate and have been for many years*—Bolton Evening News, 2003.

However, the use with uncount nouns is widespread and must be considered standard grammatically, even if undesirable stylistically. In many cases the simpler *most of* can easily replace it, e.g. *He spent the majority of* [read: *most of*] *his working life as a schoolteacher*—television news, 1996.

Similarly, the standard phrase *the vast majority of* has been criticized as overused, wordy, and easily replaceable by *most*, e.g. *The vast majority of music* [read: *most music*] *is execrable in quality*—arts website, 2004.

majorly The originally American use of *majorly* as an intensifier meaning nothing more than 'really, very' (e.g. *It was a real bachelor pad, majorly slimy*—Montreal Gazette, 1995) is informal. It is widely disliked by many people and should be avoided in any kind of serious or academic writing. The following examples show the kind of informal journalistic style to which it is suited: *However, there are some majorly cool bits here and there*—www.bit-tech.net, BrE 2005 / *'People majorly screwed up' she says of the treatment she received when she was diagnosed with stage 4 ovarian cancer in 1994*—The Advocate, AmE 2001.

malapropisms. Fowler (1926) was right to point out that malapropisms, or 'the use of a word in mistake for one sounding similar', occur occasionally, as 'single spies, not in battalions, one in an article, perhaps, instead of four in a sentence', unlike the utterances of the eponymous Mrs Malaprop in Sheridan's *The Rivals* of 1775 in which they come thick and fast. Two modern examples: *One, a head of English, could not explain the function of an intransigent* [instead of *intransitive*] *verb and advised me to 'forget it'*—letter in Sunday Times, 1988 / *When she heard our Gloucester house was haunted, she uttered the immortal*

line, *'You'll have to get the vicar in
to circumcise* [instead of *exorcise*] *it—*
J. Cooper, 1991.

male, masculine, manly. 1 Both
male and *masculine* entered the language from Old French in the 14c and
rapidly took on distinct roles. *Male* is
used as an adjective and noun, contrasting with the unrelated word *female*,
to designate the sex of humans, animals,
and plants that can beget offspring by
insemination or fertilization. *Masculine*
is used only of humans and has two
additional meanings: (1) denoting
characteristics or qualities associated
with men, and (2) contrasted with
feminine and *neuter*, denoting a class of
grammatical gender. Both words also
have technical meanings in various
domains. In broad terms *male* is used
principally to indicate the sex of a
person, animal or plant, whereas *masculine* is used of characteristics (once,
and to some extent still) regarded as
characteristic of men, especially physical
strength, vigour, competitive assertiveness, etc. *Manly* (13c, originally referring
to humans generally but now only to
men) also has this meaning but is more
positive and complimentary than *masculine*. As a noun, *male* does not carry
the unfavourable implications of *female*,
and used before another noun denoting
a profession is the standard way of
specifying someone's sex, e.g. *male
nurse / male doctor*, etc. *See* FEMALE,
FEMININE.

2 Two 20c uses of *male*, both largely
promoted by the feminist movement, are
in the terms *male chauvinist* (first
recorded in 1970), meaning 'a man who
is prejudiced against women', and *male
menopause* (1949), meaning 'a crisis of
potency, confidence, etc., said to afflict
men in middle life'.

**malicious, malign, malignant,
malevolent. 1** All four words are

connected with doing harm or evil (from
Latin *malus*), but there are important
differences. *Malicious* means 'intending
to do harm' and is associated with people (or occasionally animals) and their
actions: *The dog that destroys Gabriel
Oak's sheep is over-enthusiastic, not
malicious*—Margaret Drabble, 1976.
Malignant is used principally in medical
contexts of life-threatening diseases and
tumours; its more general meaning,
'feeling or showing intense ill will', is still
found (*He would have a sensation of
something malignant about to crush
him*—G. Watson, 1991) but is now overshadowed by the technical use. The
shorter form *malign* is used mostly of
things that are evil in their nature or
effects (*She was no longer the victim of
chance, of a malign fate*—W. J. Burely,
1989); it has also been used in the medical sense as an opposite of *benign* but
has largely given way to *malignant*.
Malevolent means 'wishing harm to
others' and refers rather to general
disposition than to particular actions or
conduct: *Trees were brooding presences,
soughing incantations. Every bush hid
an invisible force, frequently malevolent*—
W. McIlvanney, 1975. *Malevolent* is often
used of looks and sounds: *He had a nervous twitch which jerked at a muscle at
the corner of his thin-lipped mouth and a
malevolent stare*—A. Granger, 1991.

2 The corresponding nouns are *mali-
ciousness, malignancy,* and *malevolence*.
The noun *malignity* is derived from *malign* and has enjoyed substantial usage
over several centuries in the meaning
'wicked ill will or hatred', which it still
has although it is used much less than
formerly: *He seems spiritually empty, just
golden-haired and glitteringly superficial,
yet with flashes of satanic malignity and
suppressed fears*—ABC Magazine, 2007.

mall, in the meanings 'a sheltered walk
or promenade' and 'an enclosed shopping precinct', is increasingly heard in

Britain in the form mawl (already familiar in America, Australia, and elsewhere), rather than mal. But mal is still obligatory in the London place-names *The Mall*, *Chiswick Mall*, and *Pall Mall*.

malnutrition belongs firmly to the list of Fowlerian *lost causes. 'A word to be avoided,' wrote Fowler in 1926, 'as often as *underfeeding* will do the work.' Alas for Fowler, *underfeeding* has not done its work, although the related form *underfed* is still going strong as an alternative for *malnourished*. It is interesting, though, that we are so ready to use the technical term in general contexts.

man has been used for centuries in the generalized meaning 'a human being (regardless of sex)', and is embedded deep in idiom and verbal imagery: *Man cannot live by bread alone / Every man for himself / Be one's own man / as good as the next man / a man for all seasons /* etc. It is no use protesting that in Old English the word referred not only to an adult human male, but also to a human being irrespective of sex and that there is no necessary implication of male supremacism in the use of the word. The word's ambiguity is its downfall, and because of changing social attitudes, some men as well as women see it as an unacceptable outward sign of male dominance. There are alternatives available, though none of them is completely without awkwardness: *person* or *one* for *man* in the countable sense (*One cannot live by bread alone / as good as the next person*), and *humanity* or *humankind* for *man* in the collective sense (*Humankind cannot live by bread alone*). As these examples suggest, however, such substitutions can sound rather contrived, and it will take some time for them to sound completely natural. But in everyday language there is every reason to respect gender sensitivities in language, unless one can be sure (and how could

one?) that nobody will be offended by the generic use of *man*. *See also* HUMANKIND; SEXIST LANGUAGE.

-man, as a suffix in occupational words such as *chairman* and *craftsman*, is normally restricted now to male contexts in accordance with changing attitudes to the word *man. When the person concerned is a woman, forms in *-woman* or *-person*, or some other gender-neutral term such as *police officer* for *policeman* and *firefighter* for *fireman*, are now commonly used instead.

manageress *see* -ESS.

mandatory is pronounced with the stress on the first syllable in BrE, **man**-duh-tuh-ri, and with the stress on the second in AmE, man-**day**-tuh-ri, which is also sometimes heard in BrE.

maneuver is an AmE variant of *manoeuvre.

mango, the fruit, has plural forms *mangoes* (preferred) or *mangos*.

mangy, meaning 'having mange' or 'squalid, shabby', is spelt this way in preference to *mangey*.

manic depression, manic depressive. Despite being terms with which many people are familiar, both are generally felt to be negative by people experiencing the condition and those working with them. A less loaded term increasingly used in medical and psychiatric circles is *bipolar disorder*, or *bipolar affective disorder*. People with the condition can be referred to simply as *bipolar*, or as *having bipolar disorder*.

manifesto has the plural form *manifestos*.

manikin, meaning 'an unusually short man', 'an artist's dummy', or 'an anatomical model', is generally spelt this way, but can also be spelt *mannikin*. A dressmaker's model is a *mannequin*, and people who model clothes are also *mannequins*. The *manikin* spelling is also used for these meanings.

Manila is the spelling for the capital of the Philippine Islands. The hemp and paper are both spelt *manila*, although *manilla* is sometimes found. A different word *manilla* (derived via Spanish from Latin *manicula* and related to our word *manacle*) denotes a metal bracelet traditionally used in West Africa as a medium of exchange.

manipulable. The derivative *manipulable* ('capable of being manipulated') is much more frequent than *manipulatable*, and always used instead of it when referring to people who can be easily influenced, e.g. *easily manipulable*.

mankind is pronounced with the stress on the second syllable when the meaning is 'the human species' and with the stress on the first syllable in the less usual sense 'male people, as distinct from female'. In the first meaning, *humankind* is now often used instead. *See* HUMANKIND; SEXIST LANGUAGE.

mannequin *see* MANIKIN.

manner. The phrase *to the manner born* is now commonly used to mean 'naturally at ease in a given situation'. This phrase is taken from Shakespeare, *Hamlet* I.iv.17 (*Though I am native here And to the manner born, it is a custom More honoured in the breach than the observance*), where it means 'destined by birth to follow a custom or way of life'. The phrase is also often spelt *to the manor born*, which some people will regard as a mistake.

manoeuvre has inflected forms *manoeuvred, manoeuvring*. The spelling in AmE is *maneuver*, with inflected forms *maneuvered, maneuvering*.

manpower *see* SEXIST LANGUAGE.

manqué. In the meaning 'having failed to become what one might have been', *manqué* is placed after the noun it refers to: *a poet manqué*. It should be printed in roman and should have the accent over the letter *e*, even if it is often left out in electronic media.

mantel, mantle. *Mantel* is originally a variant of *mantle*, both forms are derived from the Latin word *mantellum* meaning 'cloak', and both have meanings to do with covering. *Mantle* has several uses, including 'cloak' (usually as worn by women) and the figurative meaning 'responsibility or authority' (especially regarded as passing from one person to another). *Mantel* has one meaning, usually in the longer form *mantelpiece* or *mantelshelf*, 'a shelf over a fireplace'.

mantra, originally a term in Hinduism and Buddhism for a word or phrase repeated as an aid to meditation, is now used much more often in the extended sense 'a statement or slogan repeated frequently', with connotations of tedium or scepticism: *Doctors are not allowed to speak to the press directly: it's the managers who hold the line, learn the key-words, repeat the magical mantra 'No operations have been cancelled' and spin the agenda—Daily Telegraph*, 2007.

many. *Many*, like *much*, tends to sound more formal in positive contexts (*They have many friends*) than in negative ones (*They do not have many friends*). In conversation and less formal written English, *a lot of* (or, even more informally, *lots of*) is used instead in positive contexts.

Maori is pronounced as two syllables (**mow**-ri) and has the plural form *Maoris* in general usage, although Maoris themselves have been urging non-Maoris in

New Zealand and elsewhere to use their own pronunciation of the name with three syllables (**mah**-aw-ri) and to adopt their plural form *Maori*, the same as the singular. The plural form is more likely to succeed than the pronunciation, since the two-syllable form is more natural to most speakers of English.

marathon, the name of the long-distance race and, by extension, a word for any lengthy or difficult task or undertaking, is derived from the name of the famous battle fought between Greeks (mainly Athenians and Plataeans) and Persians on the east coast of Attica in 490 BC. The length of the race (26 miles 385 yards or 42 km 352 m) is based on a relatively late tradition that the Athenian Pheidippides ran from Marathon to Athens *after* the battle with news of the Greek victory, whereas the primary source for these events, the 5c BC historian Herodotus, records that Pheidippides ran to appeal for support *before* the battle from Athens to Sparta (in southern Greece), a distance that represents a much more remarkable achievement.

margarine. After a battle royal fought throughout the 20c between those who pronounce it with a 'soft' -j- sound (as in the shortened form *marge*) and those who favour a 'hard' -g- sound (as in *Margaret*), the first of these is now completely dominant, despite Fowler's objection (1926) that this was 'clearly wrong'. He based his view partly on the authority of the *OED* (which in its 2nd edition of 1989 still put the 'hard' form before the 'soft' but has since reversed them) and partly on the fact that the only other words in which g is 'soft' before a vowel other than e or i are *gaol* (and its derivatives) and *mortgagor*.

marginal, marginalize. To the editors of the *OED* around the turn of the 20c, *marginalize* meant no more than 'to write marginal notes [i.e. notes in the margin] upon', and they marked it 'rare'. Since then it has been so transformed that the 1991 edition of the *Oxford Dictionary of New Words* described it (or, more precisely, its derivative *marginalization*) as 'one of the main social buzz-words of the eighties'. Increased awareness of the rights of underprivileged groups and minorities has given the word its new lease of life in the meaning 'to treat (a person or group of people) as *marginal* and therefore unimportant'. The use of *marginal* reflected here is itself a 20c development, first in the sociological meaning 'isolated from or not conforming to the dominant society or culture; belonging to a minority group' and then in the more general meaning 'of minor importance, insignificant'. Examples: *Society, taking its lead from the media and its politicians, begins to reject a whole class and marginalizes them in the job market*—C. Phillips, 1987 / *Until recently, children's books were regarded as marginal, less than serious as literature*—J. Briggs, 1989 / *It is not yet clear that the church's long years of marginalisation in our national life have been ended*—Independent, 1990 / *You work with what are often called 'marginalized' people, such as African-Americans and people of color*—Bomb, 1992 / *Great love, great courage, great triumphs of the human spirit all have their opposites on the dark side. The best we can hope to do is to promote the one and marginalize the other*—Sunday Mirror, 2002.

markedly *see* -EDLY.

marriageable is spelt with an *e* in the middle.

marshal. The verb has inflected forms *marshalled, marshalling* in BrE, and usually *marshaled, marshaling* in AmE.

marten, martin. A *marten* is an animal like a weasel, whereas a *martin* is a bird of the swallow family.

marvel. The verb has inflected forms *marvelled, marvelling* in BrE, and usually *marveled, marveling* in AmE.

marvellous is the spelling in BrE, but *marvelous* is more usual in AmE.

Mary. The plural form is *Marys* (as in *the two Marys*).

masculine *see* MALE.

massacre (noun and verb) is spelt this way in BrE and AmE, and as a verb has inflected forms *massacres, massacred, massacring.*

massage is pronounced **mas**-ahzh or **mas**-ahj in BrE, and muh-**sahzh** in AmE. The agent nouns *masseur* (male) and *masseuse* (female) are pronounced with the stress on the second syllable in both BrE and AmE.

massive has become an overused word in contexts that have little to do with mass: *Yet another massive stage project, now previewing at the Aldwych, where it officially opens on June 19*—Times, 1980 / *It's a trend set to turn this year's festive season on its head—the up-side-down Christmas tree. The craze has been a massive hit in New York*—Daily Record, 2007. In many cases alternatives such as *immense, enormous, substantial, powerful, impressive,* or even *huge* or *large,* should be considered. In extended and figurative uses, *massive* is best reserved for contexts in which an image of vast size is appropriate: *Riot police looked on impassively . . . as a massive crowd of mourners . . . gave the clenched fist Marxist salute*—Times, 1977 / *The most important area on which to concentrate was the massive amount of water required by the production of textiles*—Daily Telegraph, 1992. But use

one of the alternative words when the image is unreal or forced: ✖ *Women have massive amounts of love invested in fathers, lovers and sons, and many of these women despise the systems their own men may be helping to sustain*—B. Cant et al., 1988. In 21c youth slang *massive* has acquired the meaning 'very popular', and from about 1990 the word has been used informally as a noun in the sense 'a group of young people from a particular area' (as in *the Bristol massive* or *the Scottish massive*).

mass noun denotes a smaller class of nouns such as *bread, wine, medicine,* which are usually uncountable nouns but can be countable nouns when they refer to types or amounts of something, e.g. *some bread / artisan breads, less wine / French wines.*

masterful, masterly. Although both words have at some time in their history shared the meanings involved here, they have settled down in more recent usage in such a way that *masterful* conveys meanings to do with dominance and power whereas *masterly* connotes skill and fine qualities: *'Oh, I do like the way you talk to the waiters, so masterful,' sighed Esther*—S. Mackay, 1984. / *The heart of the concert was some positively thrilling playing from the Grimethorpe Colliery and Black Dyke Bands, best of all when combined in Elgar's masterly Severn Suite*—Daily Telegraph, 2007. Fowler (1926) noted with regret that *masterful* was too often used for *masterly* (though not the other way round), and this is still the case. However, this use is widespread, and is also accepted in dictionaries. It is therefore a moot point whether the following examples should really be labelled incorrect: ✖ *There are just enough such slippages in this generally masterful book to suggest that Fish still has room for further self-revision*—Times Literary Supplement, 1990 / ✖ *This* *is the sort of television that deserves to win awards but very rarely does so—not just for the script and the acting but also for a sublime soundtrack and masterful camerawork—Observer, 2007.*

mat *see* MATT.

materialize is first recorded in 1710 and its first meanings were transitive (with an object): to *materialize* an idea was to realize it and to *materialize* a spirit was to make the spirit appear. Its intransitive use, now more familiar, dates from the late 19c, still in the context of spiritualism: *The . . . ghosts . . . gave dark séances and manifested and materialized—Harper's Magazine,* 1884. But in current use the sense has been generalized so much that it means little more than 'happen' or 'become available': *Plans do not always materialise in the anticipated way—Barbara Pym, 1982 / The alimony her ex-husband was supposed to pay never materialized—* R. Deacon, 1988 / *He denied the accusations and threatened legal action that has yet to materialize—Mirror,* 2007. This use is so common that objection to it is futile except perhaps in cases (such as the last example given) that are noticeably remote from material existence. Plans and payments can be envisaged in physical terms, whereas action cannot.

materiel meaning 'material and equipment used in warfare (as distinct from personnel)', has been naturalized in English and is printed in ordinary roman type without the accent on the first *e.*

matey, an informal, largely BrE and Australian adjective and noun, is spelt with an *e* in preference to *maty.*

mathematics is treated as a singular noun when it is the name of a subject (*Mathematics is not a requirement*) and as a plural noun when it means 'the

process of calculating' (*The mathematics of the problem are complex*).

maths is the BrE abbreviation for *mathematics*; in AmE it is *math.*

matinee literally means 'morning' in French, but it now invariably means 'in the afternoon' (in French and English) when used to distinguish an afternoon film or theatre performance from an evening performance. It is written and printed without the accent it has in French *matinée.*

matrix, meaning 'a mould in which something is shaped' (and other technical meanings), is pronounced **may**-triks and has the Latin plural form *matrices* (**may**-tri-seez) or, much less frequently, *matrixes.*

matt, meaning 'dull, without lustre', is spelt *matt* in BrE and either *mat* or (more usually) *matte* in AmE.

maty *see* MATEY.

mausoleum, meaning 'a grand tomb' (after that of the 4c BC king of Caria, Mausolus), most commonly has the plural form *mausoleums*, but occasionally *mausolea* is used, despite its sounding a little pretentious.

maven is an informal term (derived from Yiddish) that is familiar in North America in the sense of an expert or connoisseur; it is much less familiar in BrE but is making headway: *Hathaway plays Andy Sachs, a total novice who learns fast, changes from a sloppy dresser into a fashion maven and ends up winning the respect of her boss—Sunday Life,* 2006.

maximum. The plural in everyday language is *maximums*, and in formal and technical writing, where it is more often required and more frequent, *maxima.*

may, can *see* CAN.

may, might. 1 With reference to present or future possibility, *may* and *might* are both used, but with *may* the possibility is more open and with *might* it is more tentative or remote: (may) *The ACLU may have a strong case*—*Economist*, 1980 / *The cyclists may use up to 6,000 calories during a race*—*Times*, 1983 / (might) *The news that the Met season might have to be cancelled . . . is an annual threat*—*Listener*, 1980 / *Some players get a 'buzz' from the game [of Space Invaders] and that might explain why they become addicted*—*Times*, 1983 / *What is a little surprising is that even the programme's adult representatives claim they don't quite know what a bonk might be*—*Today*, 1986.

2 With reference to possibility in the past, *may have* leaves it open whether an event or circumstance was actually the case, whereas *might have* implies that it was not, and is explicit that it was not when the statement is part of an unfulfilled condition introduced by *if* or by inversion (as in the 1983 *Daily Telegraph* example below): (may have) *It may have been an awful night . . . but the meat and potato pies were brill*—*Guardian*, 1983 / *Police say they're anxious to trace a car and a van which may have been used by the gang*—television news broadcast, 1993 / (might have) *'You might have been killed yourself.' 'Not much chance; the raid had already gone past us.'*— A. Crawley, 1983 / *Had the Liberal Yellow Book been published in 1920 our history might have been different*—*Daily Telegraph*, 1983 / *Once he might have answered differently*—*might have said that the two things were different in kind*—*but now he was not so certain*—D. Wingrove, 1990. It is questionable to use *may have* when the possibility it expresses is not an open one, although this use is becoming increasingly common: *If some of the*

resources squandered this morning had been used more wisely, we may have been able to take steps to save his life— *Scotsman*, 1989 / *This advice may have stopped a fashion faux pas. . . . 'I wore my favourite hound's-tooth miniskirt on my first day. . . . What a mistake'*—*Times*, 2004 / *If Apple had licensed Windows for its computers instead of insisting on its own operating system, it may not have squandered the lead built up with the launch of the Macintosh in 1984*— *Independent*, 2006.

3 There are a few idiomatic uses of *might* and *might have* that are worth noting: *You might have said something!* (= you should have said something) / *Might I suggest . . . ?* (= a polite, now somewhat old-fashioned alternative for *May I . . . ?*). *Might have* is occasionally used with future reference, again with a suggestion of doubt about fulfilment: *The wind has dropped so it feels hotter and tomorrow might be a degree or two higher*—*Sunday Mirror*, 2007.

maybe, an adverb meaning 'perhaps', is such a familiar part of current standard English that it comes as a surprise to know that it fell out of use in the 19c to an extent that caused the *OED* to label it 'archaic and dialect'. It may still retain an ever so slightly informal air, admittedly, but it is used in a wide range of contexts, written and spoken, especially in AmE, and shares all the grammatical flexibility of *perhaps*: *Maybe a shotgun was all he had*—A. Munro, 1987 / *I think maybe that's what Setanta were trying to go for*—*Guardian*, 2007. Note that *may be* is spelt as two words when it is a combination of the modal verb *may* and the verb *be*: compare *Maybe that's no bad thing* and *That may be no bad thing*. Beware of mistakenly joining the words when they are used compositionally: ☒ *That maybe all we can do*. The same warning applies to the phrase *That's as may be*, meaning 'that may or may not be the case', which should not be written ⊠ *That's as maybe.*

me. 1 For idiomatic uses of *me, see* I. For constructions of the type *as good as I/me* and *better than I/me see* CASES 2B.

2 Informally, *me* commonly replaces *I* at the head of clauses when linked to a noun by *and*; *Me and the teacher are going to race tonight from the school to the store*—J. Crace, 1986. It would be awkward to say *I and the teacher*, and the alternative *the teacher and I*, though less awkward, has a formal sound that makes it less likely to occur in casual conversation. This use of *me* seems generally more acceptable than corresponding uses of *her, him, us,* and *them.*

meagre is spelt this way in BrE, and usually *meager* in AmE.

mean. 1 In the meaning 'to intend', *mean* can be followed by a *to*-infinitive (when the speaker intends to do something: *I meant to go*), by an object + *to*-infinitive (when the speaker intends someone else to do something: *I meant you to go*) and, more formally, by a *that*-clause with *should* (*I meant that you should go*). Use of *mean for* + object + *to*-infinitive (⊠ *I meant for you to go*) is non-standard.

2 *I mean* is legitimately used to introduce an explanation of what has just been said: *He was a marvellous butler. I mean, if you went there he'd welcome you in the most graceful and polite and proper way*—New Yorker, 1986. In conversation it is increasingly heard as a sentence-filler, rather like *you know* (*see* KNOW): *'Only ... very nice?' he asked woefully. 'Oh, it's great! I mean, it's fantastic!'*—Los Angeles Times, 1987. This use is informal only but, as so often, there are borderline uses that blur distinctions: *I wasn't interested in him. I mean, when you shoot juice, you lose the other thing*—H. C. Rae, 1972 / *I publish, I mean I have had published, a few what*

we used to call slim volumes of verse, um, poetry, you know—Christopher Hampton, 1974. It is all too easy to point to extremes that no one would consider standard (*You know, like, uh, hey, man, I mean, cool, huh?*—L. Woidwode, 1992); the real difficulties lie in the greyer areas of usage.

meaningful. The journalist and literary critic Philip Howard wrote in 1978 that 'ongoing situations and meaningful dialogues are two popular pieces of jargon ... at present', and they still are used, but probably less so than when he wrote. *Meaningful* is essentially the opposite of *meaningless*, i.e. 'having meaning', as in *meaningful elements in a language*. But *meaning* has other meanings, which are reflected in other uses of *meaningful*, especially 'important, significant, noteworthy', so that things such as discussions, tests, results, work, and even relationships can be called *meaningful*. There is some justification for using the word when the notion of something having meaning is present: *Chris and Jayne turned to each other with raised eyebrows and meaningful looks*—P. Hennessy, 1983. But alternatives such as *important, significant,* and *effective* should be considered when it is importance rather than meaning that is the issue: *It will take time for these changes in strategy to have a meaningful influence on financial performance*—Birmingham Post, 2007. And the phrase *meaningful dialogue* should generally be avoided outside the euphemisms of politics, as a reviled and ridiculed cliché.

means. 1 When the meaning is 'financial resources', *means* is treated as plural: *Their means are somewhat limited.* When the meaning is 'a way or method' it can operate as a singular noun (when preceded by a determiner such as *a, any,* or *every*) or as a plural noun (when preceded by a plural-marking word such as *all, many, several,* etc.): *Several means are available for indexing numbers not obtainable with standard plain indexing*—L. E. Doyle et al., 1961 / *They remained for her a means, and not an end, a bargaining power rather than a blessing*—Margaret Drabble, 1967 / *Derek and I drove down there and shut off the whole barn, preventing all means of getting in or out*—J. Hadwick, 1991 / *In those days gondolas were cheap and a perfectly normal means of transport*—Mail on Sunday, 2001. When *means* is preceded by *the*, the following verb can be either singular or plural, depending on whether one 'way or method' or several are intended: *Moreover, the means by which this end is achieved are remarkable*—Michael Foot, 1986 / *When I first travelled to England in 1960, the normal means was by boat*—Daily Telegraph, 2003.

2 The dual role of *means* in the 'way, method' sense is a survival of an earlier time, when both the singular *mean* and the plural *means* were used. The singular use has dropped out, but the construction, attached to the plural, has survived.

meantime, meanwhile. 1 Used on its own as an adverb, *meantime* has largely given way to *meanwhile*, but is still occasionally found: *Meantime, melt the remaining butter in a saucepan*—Delia Smith, 1978. It is most often used in the phrase *in the meantime*, which is now normally written as three words instead of four: *The telephone will ... redial the number you last called, even if you've hung up in the meantime*—Which?, 1987. Conversely, *meanwhile* is most often used by itself, and only occasionally in the variant phrase *in the meanwhile*: *The animals Mrs Murray cares for are always returned to the wild if possible. Meanwhile, they stay at her study centre*—Times, 1986 / *In the meanwhile, I'll just lie here, flat on my*

back, fingering my perfect bones—J. Shute, 1992.

2 In recent use, *meanwhile* is commonly used in journalism and especially broadcasting as a means of resuming a main theme after a digression or aside: *Meanwhile, as we say in the trade, Motherwell go bottom [of the League table]*—television broadcast, 1987 / *Meantime: food. We cannot live by bread alone, but it helps*—I. Maitland, 1993. The use may owe its origins to the catchphrase *Meanwhile, back at the ranch*, used originally in captions to silent Western films and later as a voice-over in films with sound. The complete phrase itself is used allusively in a wide range of contexts: *Meanwhile back in the Commons, Mrs Thatcher tried to resist questions by saying the issues were sub judice*—Today, 1987 / *Meanwhile, back at the ranch, the transport system is in chaos, there's a full-scale law and order crisis and the NHS is a basket case*—Sun, 2002.

measles is normally treated as a singular noun, although occasionally it is used as a plural, sometimes preceded by *the*: *A consultant said measles was on the increase / The measles have left him feeling weak.*

medal 1 Its derivative forms are *medalled, medalling, medallist* in BrE, and usually *medaled, medaling, medalist* in AmE.

2 Vociferous objections have been raised, particularly in Britain, against the intransitive use of *medal* in sporting circles, e.g. *Holland have only medalled three times at the world outdoor championships*. Objections are based on the perception that it is both an Americanism and an example of verbing. The *OED's* first citation for the verb is from none other than Thackeray in 1860, and the Cambridge University literary magazine *Granta* published this in 1890: *In* *that year it was decided that both crews should be medalled, the winners with silver, the losers with bronze.* Admittedly the meaning here is 'to be decorated with a medal' rather than to win one. That decried intransitive use is shown in the *OED* first in an isolated 1865 example, and then in a 1979 example from the *Washington Post*: *Our women are coming along beautifully—they've medaled well recently.* The verb is now as commonly used in BrE sports journalism as it is in AmE. Detested by some, it has become a fixture of sporting language.

media, in its modern meaning 'channels of mass communication such as newspapers and broadcasting regarded collectively', has long been treated as a plural noun: *When the media report events there must always be a line, an angle, a spin*—B. Morrison, 1998. It is increasingly used, especially by the media themselves, as a collective noun, followed by a singular verb. This use is disliked by some people: *The British media at its finest is the best in the world*—Tony Blair on BBC Radio, 1998. Similarly *a media* or *the medias* are viewed as non-standard by many people: *Often urged on by a mass media that magnified the public danger, politicians tried to answer the . . . call for protective action*—C. Townshend, 2002. The best advice is, if in doubt treat the word as a plural, and avoid *a media* and the plural *medias.*

medieval is now the recommended and much more common spelling, not *mediaeval.* It is pronounced me-di-**ee**-vuhl, with four syllables, although me-**dee**-vuhl or mi-**dee**-vuhl, with three syllables, is common in AmE.

Mediterranean is spelt with one *d*, one *t*, and two *r*s, as its derivation from the Latin words *medius* 'middle' and *terra* 'land' reminds us.

medium. In the spiritualist sense, the plural is *mediums*, and in the meaning 'means of mass communication' the plural is *media, which has its own pattern of behaviour. In all other meanings (e.g. 'an agency or means of doing something'), *mediums* and *media* are both used.

meet. There are two uses that deserve attention.

1 It is a transitive verb and so it is possible to meet someone, or simply meet. Idiomatically you meet with a circumstance rather than a person, typically something unpleasant or unwelcome; or you meet with a response or reaction, again often unfavourable (*This may not meet with the approval of the parents / Her appointment as chief vet met with sniffiness among some farmers*). Now *meet* is increasingly used with the link word *with* (or *up with*, based on *meet up*) when people are involved, typically in contexts involving prolonged discussion or dealings (*the people who will be meeting with the Secretary of State / A few weeks later I met up with them again*). This is not entirely a new use: it is recorded in the *OED* from the 13c in the sense both of a planned encounter, and of a casual or accidental one, as in the following examples: *An appointment to meet with the others of his company at the sign of the Griffin*—Scott, 1828 / *'Tis . . . rare to meet with persons, who can pardon another any opposition he makes to their interest*—David Hume, 1740. It is true to say however that *meet with* has become fashionable again in contexts of intentional or arranged meeting under the influence of AmE, and tends to be used in contexts where plain *meet* would be more usual.

2 *Meet* is used informally in a sense dating from the 1980s to refer to a mixture or blend of characteristics or attributes, the image being one of a dramatic or unexpected encounter.

The tense is always (indeterminate) present and the verb can be reduplicated: *A weird crew called Levellers 5, from Lancashire, give us Springtime Bob Dylan meets Half Man Half Biscuit meets Frank Zappa—Guardian*, 1990.

mega-, mega, a prefix meaning 'great', continues to be used in scientific and technical applications, often with the specific meaning 'denoting a factor of one million' (as in the statistical term *megadeath* denoting the deaths of a million people), or in computing language, a factor of 2^{20} (i.e. 1,048,576), as in *megabyte, megapixel*. In the 20c it took on a more informal role in words such as *megastar, megahit, megastore*, and *megabucks* (a huge amount of money). In all cases, words with this prefix are not hyphenated and are written as one unit. The prefix has also taken on a life of its own as an independent word in the form *mega*, meaning 'excellent' or (as an adverb) 'extremely': *It has never been my ambition to be mega famous or mega rich—I've just wanted to make a living—People*, 2007. This use still has an informal ring to it.

meiosis, pronounced miy-**oh**-sis, is a figure of speech involving an emphatic understatement made for effect, as when something outstanding is described as 'rather good'. A literary example occurs in Shakespeare's *Romeo and Juliet*, where Mercutio refers to his *mortal hurt* (at the hands of Tybalt) with the words *Ay, ay, a scratch, a scratch* (III.i.93). A special form of meiosis involving negatives is called **litotes*.

membership. *Her acceptance of this role has ... given enormous pleasure to the membership—B. Grant*, 1990. The use of *membership* to mean 'members collectively' (e.g. of a trade union) was noted by Gowers (1965) as 'now rife and corrupting other words'. Its use is normally restricted to official or reporting

contexts, and in general use *membership* most commonly retains its traditional meanings 'the status of being a member' (*I must renew my membership*) or 'the number of members in an organization' (*Membership is down by 15%*).

memento, meaning 'a souvenir', should not be converted into the dubious formation *momento*. The preferred plural form is *mementos*.

memo, a shortening of *memorandum* and now the more usual form in general use, has the plural form *memos*.

memorabilia, meaning 'souvenirs of memorable events, people, etc.', is a plural noun, and should not be treated as singular: ⊠ *We've got railway memorabilia and we're very proud of it—Best*, 1991.

memorandum has the plural form *memoranda* (recommended) or *memorandums*. In general business use in the meaning 'informal note or message', **memo* is more often used.

ménage, a somewhat literary word meaning 'the members of a household', is printed in roman type with the accent retained. The pronunciation is semi-naturalized, with the final consonant retaining its French form, so **may**-nahzh.

mendacity, mendicity. *Mendacity* (from Latin *mendax* 'lying') means 'habitual lying or deceiving', whereas *mendicity* (from Latin *mendicare* 'to beg') means 'the practice or habit of begging'. The words are ultimately related in having a common ancestor in the Latin word *mendum* meaning 'fault'.

-ment *see* -ION, -MENT, -NESS.

mental. The use of *mental* in expressions such as *mental hospital* and *mental patient*, recorded from the end of the

19c, has been replaced in modern use by *psychiatric*.

mentality, in its meaning 'mental character or disposition', is now nearly always used with unfavourable connotations, although this was not always so: *I hate the triviality of journalism, you know, the sort of fluttering mentality that fills up the page*—Humphrey Carpenter, 1978 / *A kind of unacknowledged underground mentality had permeated all kinds of places*—Arthur Miller, 1987 / *A self-centred bureaucracy more interested in itself than the businesses it is supposed to encourage, and with a tick box mentality to justifying an existence which actually doesn't deliver in a meaningful way*—Birmingham Post, 2007.

mentally handicapped. This term and *mental handicap*, though widely used a few decades ago, have fallen out of favour in recent years and have been largely replaced in official contexts and in ordinary use by less demeaning terms such as *learning difficulties.

merchandise as a noun can only ever be spelt -*ise*, and is normally pronounced -iyz, but can also be pronounced -iys. The verb is only rarely spelt with a final -*ize* in any variety of English.

merit as a verb has inflected forms *merited, meriting*.

Messrs., originally a contraction of French *Messieurs* 'gentlemen', was formerly common as a plural form of *Mr* in business and commercial use (e.g. *Messrs. Berkeley, Stratton & Co.*), but has now fallen into disuse in most parts of the English-speaking world, except in certain professions, notably law. There are certain technical limitations on its use that need to be guarded against; for example, it is not used with Limited Companies. If in doubt, consult *Debrett's Correct Form* or a similar manual on form.

meta-. In recent use this prefix has been borrowed from the term *metaphysics* and applied to other words with the meaning 'of a higher or second-order kind': a *metalanguage* is language used to describe language, *metafiction* is a form of fiction in which the author sets out to parody literary conventions, and *metadata* is data describing and giving information about other data.

metal, mettle. 1 Both are in origin the same word. In the 16c *mettle* began to move apart as a separate word used only in figurative meanings, of which the dominant one still current is 'ardent or spirited temperament; spirit, courage', as in the expressions *show one's mettle* and *be on one's mettle*.

2 The verb *metal* has inflected forms *metalled, metalling* in BrE, and usually *metaled, metaling* in AmE.

metallurgy, the science of metals, is pronounced with the stress on the second syllable in BrE, and with the stress on the first syllable in AmE.

metaphor and simile. 1 The difference between these two figures of speech, which together constitute a major element of English idiom, is largely one of form. A *simile* is a fanciful comparison couched in a form introduced by *as* or *like*, for example Byron's line *The Assyrian came down like the wolf on the fold*, whereas a *metaphor* directly equates the image with the person or thing it is compared to: *Achilles was a lion in the fight*. Many figurative uses of words (e.g. the *mouth* of a river, a *blanket* of fog, *music* to one's ears) and many idioms (e.g. *get the green light, have one foot in the grave, take the rough with the smooth, off the wall*) can be regarded as metaphors.

2 A type of metaphor that always arouses derision is the *mixed metaphor*, in which two incompatible images are combined: *He has been made a sacrificial* *lamb for taking the lid off a can of worms / In coal mines, mice are used as human guinea pigs* (both examples from letters pages of *The Times*) / *They are trying to shift the goalposts on one of their own flagship targets—Independent,* 2003 / *The grass roots are pretty cheesed off—* BBC Radio news, 1999 / *Europe's Central Bank should take its head out of the sand and call a spade a spade—Wall Street Journal,* 2001. A similar if less vivid kind of absurdity can be caused by combining figurative uses in which the corresponding physical senses merge to present an alternative picture, as in *taking concrete steps* (cited by Gowers) and *grass-roots consumers.* In the hurly-burly of rapid speech, such disasters are bound to occur, but they can be avoided in more considered or formal language use when there is time to reflect on what is being said.

metathesis, pronounced with the stress on the second syllable, is a term for the transposition of sounds or letters in a word, sometimes as a feature of a word's development (e.g *hasp* from Old English *hæpse*) and at other times as an erroneous process (e.g. *anenome* for *anemone*).

meter is the normal spelling in BrE and AmE for the measuring or recording instrument, and is the AmE spelling of the words in BrE spelt *metre* (unit of length and rhythm in poetry).

methodology. A *methodology* is not a mere method. It is either 'the branch of knowledge that deals with method generally' or it is 'a system of methods used in a particular area of study or activity'. In other words, it is scientific or scholarly: *A reconsideration of the problem [of] how the logical analysis of scientific procedure* (*methodology*) *is related to deductive logic—Methodology of Social Science,* 1944 / *Consumers must demand labelling and independent safety testing using methodology that consumers can trust—Co-op Connection,* 1993. A method is simply a 'procedure for accomplishing something' and, as the dictionary suggests, it is 'especially a systematic or established one'. The word *methodology* is unnecessary in contexts such as the following, where *method* or *methods* would suffice: *Given these principles of andragogy, experiential learning can be an effective methodology for teaching adults—NACTA Journal,* 2004 / *Some investors also question the methodology used by some analysts to make recommendations— BBC News,* 2004.

meticulous is derived from the Latin word *metus* 'fear', and in the 16c and 17c it had a corresponding meaning 'fearful, timid'. Then the word went out of use, only to reappear in the early 19c in a completely different sense, 'over-careful about details'. This was the meaning known to the Fowler brothers when they wrote *The King's English* at the turn of the century, and they did not care for it, classing it among the 'stiff, full-dress, literary, or out-of-the-way words'. Between then and now, it lost (almost completely, but not always quite) its connotations of excess, and settled down in the meaning it now has, 'careful, punctilious, precise'. If it differs at all from these synonyms, it is perhaps from a vestigial shadow of this strange past rather than any real distinction in meaning: *Utz has planned his own funeral with meticulous care—*Bruce Chatwin, 1988 / *Very many tedious hours were spent on the dull and routine tasks of listing, plotting on graphs, meticulously checking and classifying—* I. Young, 1990.

metonymy is a figure of speech in which an attribute or property is used to refer to the person or thing that has it, e.g. *the White House* for the American presidency and *the Crown* for the British monarchy. In the proverb *The pen is mightier than the sword*, *pen* and *sword*, by a process of metonymy, represent the written word and warfare respectively. *See also* SYNECDOCHE.

metope, a term in architecture for each of the square sections of a Doric frieze, is generally pronounced **met**-ohp (two syllables), or occasionally **met**-uhpee (three syllables).

metrosexual, a blend of *metropolitan* and *heterosexual*, is a word that sprang up in the 1990s for an urban heterosexual man who enjoys shopping, fashion, and similar interests traditionally associated with women or gay men. Once a talking point and a bit of a vogue word, it now seems to have settled down as an apt word to describe an ongoing social trend.

mettle *see* METAL.

mews, meaning 'a set of buildings around an open yard', is usually called *a mews* and is treated as a singular noun. (The word is originally the plural of *mew* meaning 'a cage for hawks'.) It is often used attributively (before a noun) to describe a building that is part of a mews, a favourite of estate agents' jargon: *It comes with a roof terrace, a self-contained two bedroom maisonette on the lower two floors, a landscaped town garden and a triple mews garage—Bath Chronicle*, 2002.

mezzanine, a low storey between two others (usually between the ground and first floors), is pronounced **mez**-suh-neen or **met**-suh-neen.

mic. According to the *OEC* evidence, this abbreviation for *microphone*, first recorded from 1961, now seems to be as frequent as, if not more frequent than, the older *mike*, first recorded in 1911.

Despite its appearance, it is pronounced like the name *Mike*.

mickle, muckle. These are merely variants of the same word meaning 'a large amount', and so the proverb *Many a mickle makes a muckle* is, in its usual form, strictly speaking a meaningless corruption. The correct form is *Many a little* (or occasionally *pickle* = 'small amount') *makes a mickle*, which is recorded from the 13c. The corrupted form is first attested in the works of George Washington (late 18c).

micro- has been and continues to be a highly productive prefix, with the following among many forms first recorded after 1900: *microclimate, microdot, microeconomics, micro-event, microfilm, microinstruction* (in computing), *microlight* (lightweight aircraft), *microprocessor, microsurgery, microsystem, microtechnology*, and *microwave*.

mid, meaning 'middle of', is normally joined by a hyphen to the following word, as in *mid-century* / *mid-fifteenth century*. Note that when the century is in attributive position (before a noun), two hyphens are needed: *a mid-fifteenth-century church*. Note also that *mid-air* is spelt with a hyphen whatever its position in the sentence, despite Fowler's preference (1926) for *mid air*.

midriff denotes the front of a man or woman's body between the chest and the waist, e.g. *Her friend . . . was wearing a sprayed-on dress that showed her pants and midriff—Bridget Jones's Diary*, 1996. It comes from Old English *midrhif,* = *mid* + *rhif* ('belly'). Folk etymology occasionally turns it into the entertaining *midrift*: ⊠ *However, the entire look is ruined by his refusal to unbutton the coat, which means it's gathered up in an aesthetically displeasing fashion around his midrift—Guardian*, 2005. Worse still is ⊠ *mid drift*.

midst is now most commonly used in the phrases *in the midst of* or *in our* (etc.) *midst*, meaning 'among, in the middle of'. Typical contexts can be either physical or abstract: *There was ... something sinister about this place, unhusbanded and yieldless in the midst of the abundant land all about*—R. Adams, 1974 / *The Swedes, who sometimes gave the impression of being embarrassed by this monumental figure in their midst, will be able to honour him without reservation*—*Independent*, 2007.

midwifery. The dominant pronunciation stresses the second syllable, regardless of how many syllables the word is given, i.e. mid-**wif**-ri (three syllables) or mid-**wif**-uh-ri (four syllables). In AmE **mid**-wiyf-uh-ri (with the second syllable as in *wife*), echoing the base noun *midwife*, is an alternative.

might *see* MAY, MIGHT.

migraine. The usual pronunciation in BrE is now **mee**-grayn, although now **miy**-grayn is also heard and is standard in AmE.

mil, a unit of measurement equal to one-thousandth of an inch (0.00254mm), is spelt without a full point.

mileage, with two *es*, is the recommended spelling, not *milage*.

milieu, a somewhat literary word for one's environment or social surroundings, is pronounced mil-**yur**. The plural form can be either *milieus* or, less commonly, *milieux* (both pronounced like the singular or as mil-**yurz**). *Milieus* is the more frequent form in AmE, *milieux* in BrE.

militate, mitigate. The two words are sometimes confused (usually *mitigate* is used for *militate*) because their forms and rhythm are close. *Mitigate* is transitive (i.e. it takes an object) and

means 'to make less intense or severe', whereas *militate* is intransitive and usually followed by *against*, and means 'to be a powerful factor in preventing'. The following examples show the correct use of *militate*, and then *mitigate*, followed by an incorrect use of *mitigate against* for *militate against*. It is also incorrect to use *mitigate against* in the straightforward meaning of *mitigate*, i.e. 'to make less intense or severe' as in the last example below: *The housing styles, narrowness of the streets and the location of the district vis-à-vis the rest of the city all militate against Neustadt becoming an environmentally attractive area overnight*—R. Rolley, 1990 / *A great yellow sun like a runaway balloon shone from a deep blue sky, and a cooling breeze from the lagoon mitigated the heat*—L. Wilkinson, 1992 / ☒ *Enforcement by quotas can mitigate against good police work and damage public confidence in the force*—*Western Mail*, 2007 / ☒ *The use of a highly specific test ... can mitigate against some of these effects*—*American Family Physician*, 2001. *Mitigate* is frequently used in the form *mitigating* with words such as *circumstance, effect, factor*, etc.: *We expect our athletes to compete in the trials unless there are mitigating circumstances, such as injury*—*Sunday Telegraph*, 2007.

millenarian *see* MILLENNIUM.

millenary, an adjective (and, less often, a noun) denoting a period of 1,000 years, is usually pronounced with the stress on the second syllable, although pronunciation with the stress on the first syllable is also heard and is the dominant form in AmE.

millennium, a period of 1,000 years, is spelt with two *ls* and two *ns*. The plural is generally the Latinate *millennia* and only rarely *millenniums*. For the problems of reckoning when a new millennium begins, *see* CENTURY. Whatever the arguments put forward on the basis of strict reckoning, the natural celebratory point for a new millennium is at the end of the year 1999, 2999, and so on, and not the year following. The adjective *millenarian*, meaning 'relating to the millennium' or 'believing in the millennium' (in the theological sense of Christ's second coming), is paradoxically spelt with only one *n*, being derived not from Latin *annus* 'year' but from *milleni*, the distributive form (meaning 'every thousand') of *mille* 'thousand'.

million. When preceded by a numeral or a quantifying word such as *many* or *several*, the plural is *million* (unchanged: *twenty million people*), but *millions* is used when it is followed by *of*, typically with imprecise reference (*have done it millions of times*). With *a few*, the plural is idiomatically *million*, not *millions*, even when followed by *of* (*a few million of them*).

mimic. The inflected forms of the verb are *mimics, mimicked, mimicking*.

mind *verb. Mind you, if you think she behaved strangely, you should have seen me*—Martin Amis, 1984. This absolute use of the verb *mind*, calling attention to or emphasizing what the speaker is saying, is recorded in the *OED* from the early 19c (Coleridge, Browning, etc.), along with the shorter form *mind* (without *you*): *Well, all right, but you aren't to do anything, mind*—Doris Lessing, 1988. This use is conversational or informal only.

mine, historically an alternative to *my* in uses such as *mine ease* and *O lady mine!* and still used occasionally in this way humorously (e.g. *mine host*), is in general use limited to its role as a pronoun, either after *of* (*a friend of mine*) or after a verb (*This one is not mine*).

mineralogy, the study of minerals, is spelt *-alogy*, not *-ology*. (Compare GENEALOGY.)

minimum. The plural, most often needed in formal and technical use, is *minima*, while *minimums* is much less common and is used in non-technical writing.

miniscule is fast establishing itself as an adjective in its own right with the meaning 'very small, minute', although as a corruption (influenced by the prefix *mini-*) of **minuscule* it is regarded by many people as non-standard, despite being accepted in some dictionaries: *Riborg showed her a photograph album, with herself by a fjord in a miniscule bikini*—J. Bow, 1991. There is a case to be made for allowing *miniscule* to have its way and leaving *minuscule* to its own more technical devices, but since this is not the accepted procedure at present the best advice is to avoid the word altogether in this meaning and use any of several available synonyms such as *minute, tiny, microscopic, diminutive*, etc.

minister. In its ecclesiastical sense, *minister* is the term to use for a member of the clergy, especially in the Presbyterian and Nonconformist Churches. It also has a more hierarchical meaning, reflecting the word's origin in Latin *minister* meaning 'servant' (from *minus* 'lesser'), denoting a church official who assists the higher orders (e.g. deacon or subdeacon) in discharging their duties. Care should be taken before using the term as a simple synonym for *priest*.

minority. 1 *Minority* has meanings at the other end of the scale of magnitude from **majority*. Like *majority* it can be treated as singular or plural, except when followed by *of* and a plural noun, in which case the verb is plural: *Only a minority of Germans* (*around a third of*

m

the population according to American surveys carried out in 1945) were prepared to concede that the war was lost—I. Kershaw, 1989. In one respect, however, *minority* has gone its own way, namely in its widespread current use referring to any relatively small group of people who differ from others in the society of which they are a part in race, ethnic origin, language, religion, political persuasion, sexual orientation, or other matters that give rise to questions of social treatment or discrimination: *Flaubert always sides with minorities, with 'the Bedouin, the Heretic, the philosopher, the hermit, the Poet'*—Julian Barnes, 1985 / *Among specific measures provided for in the convention were the launch of at least one radio station and a television network broadcasting in minority languages*—Keesings, 1990. In this meaning *minority* has acquired some flexibility of use, giving rise to apparently paradoxical collocations such as *growing* or *increasing minority* (i.e. increasing in numbers and therefore becoming less rather than more truly a minority): *Mixed race youngsters are the city's fastest-growing minority group*—Express, 2007.

2 Running parallel to this, but in an opposite direction as regards meaning, has been the use of *minority* as a quasi-adjective meaning 'of or for a minority', often with a favourable sense as in *minority interests* or *minority tastes* (generally = more exclusive or intellectual): *Drummond once told me that Radio 3 broadcasts to about 30 minority tastes, each of which is characterised by its intense dislike of the other 29*—Daily Telegraph, 1992. It is noteworthy that this use of *minority*, in relation to culture, implies an element of superiority or privilege, whereas the use described above, in relation to social position, implies one of inferiority or deprivation.

minus, in the meaning 'lacking, without', has been used since the mid-19c.

The Fowler brothers, doubtless affected by their experiences at the front in the First World War, illustrated this use in the first edition of the *Concise Oxford Dictionary* with the gruesome example *He came back minus an arm*; *arm* was changed to *dog* in a later edition.

minuscule is originally a technical term in palaeography for a type of small letter, and then the cursive script developed from it. In attributive use (before a noun) it denotes this type of writing, and in extended use it has acquired the general meaning 'very small': *The facilities here were minimal—a cracked washbasin, one minuscule bar of soap, and one off-white towel*—Colin Dexter, 1992. Not surprisingly, in this meaning the word has come under the influence of the prefix *mini-* to produce the altered (and not yet generally accepted) form **miniscule*.

minutiae 1 This plural noun means 'minor details or trivia'. Dictionaries recognize several pronunciations, so choice is a matter of taste. The first and last syllables vary. The *OED* gives preference to a Latin pronunciation for the last syllable, with variation of the first syllable, my-**nyoo**-shi-iy, mi-**nyoo**-shi-iy, and then gives the same variation in the first syllable but with the ending pronounced -shee. The singular form *minutia* is hardly ever used.

2 Two kinds of mistake occur with this word: (1) especially in AmE, *minutia* is treated as a plural (presumably as if it were the plural of a Latin second declension noun ending in *-um*), e.g. ✖ *The amount of care and consideration John Vanderslice puts into the minutia of his records is beyond impressive*—US website, 2004; (2) *minutiae* is used as a singular—✖ *Yet with every minutiae of the bid under scrutiny, the benefit of assurances from those politicians vying for* *power can do no harm—The Cherwell Mag.*, 2005.

mis- is a prefix with the meaning 'badly', 'wrongly'. Words formed with it do not need a hyphen, even when the stem begins with an *s*: *misbehave, miscarriage, miscount, mismanage, misshapen, misspelling, misspent*, etc. An exception is *mis-sell* (= to sell wrongly or inappropriately) and its inflections *mis-selling* and *mis-sold*, which might be misread without the hyphen.

misanthrope. A *misanthrope* is a hater of fellow human beings; a person who hates women is a *misogynist*. The corresponding nouns are *misanthropy* and *misogyny*; hatred of men is *misandry*. How significant it is that *misanthrope* dates from the 16c and *misogynist* from the early 17c, whereas *misandry* is first recorded in ordinary usage from the 1940s (and *misandrist* from thirty years later) must be left for others to determine.

mischievous. The incorrect pronunciation and spelling of this word as *mischievious* (four syllables) is one of the most commonly cited indications of poor use of language, and should be avoided.

misdemeanour is spelt *-our* in BrE and *misdemeanor* in AmE.

mislead has the form *misled* as its past tense and past participle.

misnomer is the misapplication of a name or term to something or someone inappropriate or undeserving, especially if it creates a misleading impression: *Morning sickness is a misnomer—it can strike at any time—The Guardian*, 2000 / *'Copy cat' is a misnomer because cats never copy anybody—*C. Van Vechten, 1996. It originated as a legal word meaning 'a mistake in naming a person or thing'.

Acts of Queen Victoria's reign were riddled with the proviso 'no misnomer or inaccurate description . . . shall hinder the full operation of this Act'. It was, characteristically, a lawyers' escape route. As often happens with underused words, usage put it to work among laypeople, who used it to mean 'the use of a wrong name' in any context, which is the meaning current today (as in the above examples).

Now *misnomer* is in danger of being watered down further in contexts that are not about the applicability of a name: *A Christianity without peace would be a misnomer—Catez Stevens, 2004.* [What is meant is 'contradiction in terms'] / *But there are also a lot of misnomers about this documentary, concepts that must be debunked and debased before really understanding what Blank and Gosling have fashioned—DVD Verdict, 2005.* [What is meant in this last example is 'misconception'.]

misogynist, misogyny *see* MISANTHROPE.

misquotations. *See box overleaf.*

misshapen, misspelling, misspent *see* MIS-.

mitigate *see* MILITATE.

mitre is spelt in this way in BrE, and usually *miter* in AmE.

mixed metaphor *see* METAPHOR AND SIMILE 2.

mixed race. When used attributively (in front of a noun), it should be hyphenated, e.g. *Mr Obama's appeal is partly his own mixed-race backstory—Guardian, 2008.* Contrast this with the following, which is not hyphenated. *This and other paintings portraying subjects of mixed race underscore the role of the artist in confirming and preserving their*

MISQUOTATIONS.

Many catchphrases and allusive expressions are based on altered forms of
literary quotations. The proverb *Every dog has his day* is based on a 16c adage
translated from the Dutch humanist Erasmus (1500) and was given currency by
a line spoken by Shakespeare's Hamlet: *Let Hercules himself do what he may,
The cat shall mew, and dog will have his day*—Shakespeare, *Hamlet*, v.i.286.
The idiom *to escape by the skin of one's teeth* is an altered form of the
Authorized Version of Job 19:20: *I am escaped with the skin of my teeth.* Idiom
and allusion go their own way in language; however, it is important to give the
correct form when the allusion is given as a quotation. The following table lists
the correct forms of some of the more common literary extracts, with the
popular versions alongside:

quotation	popular form	source
In the sweat of thy **face** *shalt thou eat bread*	by the sweat of one's **brow**	Bible, *Genesis* 3:19
I am escaped **with** *the skin of my teeth*	to escape **by** the skin of one's teeth	Bible, *Job* 19:20
To gild refined gold, to **paint** *the lily*	to **gild** the lily	Shakespeare, *King John*
A goodly apple rotten at the **heart**	rotten to *or* at the **core**	Shakespeare, *Merchant of Venice*
But yet I'll make assurance **double** *sure*	**doubly** sure	Shakespeare, *Macbeth*
Tomorrow to fresh **woods** *and pastures new*	fresh **fields** and pastures new	Milton, *Lycidas*
They kept the **noiseless** *tenor of their way*	the **even** tenor	Gray, *Elegy Written in a Country Church-Yard*
A little **learning** *is a dangerous thing*	a little **knowledge**	Pope, *Essay on Criticism*
The best laid **schemes** *o' mice an' men Gang aft a-gley*	the best-laid **plans**	Burns, 'To a Mouse'
Water, water, every where, **Nor any** *drop to drink*	**And not** a drop to drink	Coleridge, *The Rime of the Ancient Mariner*
I have nothing to offer but **blood, toil, tears and sweat**	**blood, sweat, and tears**	Winston Churchill, *Hansard*, 1940

m

identity and achievements—Art in America, 2005.

mnemonic, pronounced ni-**mon**-ik, is a device, usually a rhyme or sequence of words, used to help remember some fact or group of facts, e.g. the initial letters of the mnemonic *Richard Of York Gave Battle In Vain* give the order of the colours of the spectrum (red, orange, yellow, green, blue, indigo, violet).

mobile *see* MOVABLE.

moccasin, a name of a snake and a type of soft leather shoe, is the recommended spelling, with two *c*s and one *s*.

modal verbs. Modal (or, more fully, modal auxiliary) verbs are used in front of other verbs to express those verbs' moods, which, in the linguistic sense, distinguishes statements, commands, suppositions, questions, and so on. The principal modal verbs are *can, could, may, might, must, ought, shall, will*. They behave in special ways, of which the most important are (1) that they form questions and negatives without the use of *do* (*Can I go?* / *You may not leave*), and (2) their third-person singular forms do not add -*s* (*She will* / *It must*). A group of other verbs that share some of these features, such as *dare* and *need*, are sometimes called *semi-modal*. Note that *be, do,* and *have,* which behave somewhat differently, are not classed as modal verbs but as ordinary auxiliary verbs.

model as a verb has inflected forms *modelled, modelling* in BrE and usually *modeled, modeling* in AmE.

modus operandi, meaning 'a plan or method of working', is pronounced **moh**-duhs opuh-**ran**-diy or -dee and is printed in roman type. Its corresponding abbreviation is *MO*.

modus vivendi means 'a way of living or coping', most often (in law) an arrangement by which parties to a dispute can continue their activities while a settlement is reached. It is pronounced **moh**-duhs vi-**ven**-diy or -dee and is printed in roman type.

mogul is the spelling in the sense 'an important or influential person', e.g. *entertainment / media mogul*. In its historical meaning referring to the 16c–19c rulers of northern India, the form *Mughal* should be used.

Mohammed, Mohammedan. The preferred spellings are *Muhammad, *Muhammadan. Muslim* is preferred for the second of these.

mold *see* MOULD.

molt *see* MOULT.

moment. The phrase *at this moment in time* is a modern cliché (*see* CLICHÉS).

momentarily means 'for a moment, briefly' in BrE: *Ever the professional, Miss Turton flinched only momentarily and carried on with her report—Daily Mail*, 2007. In AmE it has this meaning and also the meaning 'at any moment, imminently': *Miss Loren had been delayed in traffic but would arrive momentarily—New Yorker*, 1970. For an analogous difference in usage, *see* PRESENTLY.

momento is an incorrect variant of *memento.

momentum. The plural, though not often needed, is *momenta* in any kind of serious scientific writing or *momentums* when the meaning is metaphorical.

Monday *see* FRIDAY.

monetarism, monetarist, monetary. These are pronounced with the first syllable as **mun**- in BrE and as **mon**- in AmE.

moneyed, meaning 'wealthy', is spelt -*eyed* in preference to *monied*.

moneys. The plural in the meaning 'sums of money' according to standard spelling rules is *moneys*, but *monies* took hold in 19c accounting circles and has become part of ordinary usage: *Certain monies had been put aside for them*—Anita Brookner, 1988. Nonetheless, *moneys* is preferable outside accounting circles.

mongol, mongoloid, mongolism, terms formerly used for people with what is now called *Down's syndrome*, and for the syndrome itself, are considered offensive and should be avoided.

Mongoloid, referring to peoples including those of east Asia and south-east Asia, is one of a set of terms used by 19c anthropologists to classify human races. Today they are recognized as having little validity as scientific categories. Although occasionally used when making broad generalizations about the world's populations, in most modern contexts they are potentially offensive, especially when used of individuals. The names of specific peoples or nationalities should normally be used instead.

mongoose, the small animal like a civet, has the plural form *mongooses*.

monk see FRIAR.

monkey. The noun has the plural form *monkeys*, and the verb has inflected forms *monkeys, monkeyed, monkeying*.

monologue, soliloquy. Both words (the first Greek and the second Latin in origin) denote a single person's action; *soliloquy* generally refers to speaking one's thoughts aloud regardless of any hearers, particularly in a play, whereas *monologue* primarily means speech that is meant to be heard and is used especially of the discourse of a talker who monopolizes conversation, or to describe a performance or recitation by a single actor or speaker.

month see DAY.

mood is a term in grammar that identifies utterances as being statements, expressions of wish, commands, questions, etc. It is a variant of the word *mode*, and has nothing to do with the more familiar word *mood*. In English, moods are expressed by means of an auxiliary verb (*can, may*, etc.) called a *modal verb, or by the *subjunctive mood.

moot. A *moot point* or *moot question* is a debatable or undecided one. The word is from Old English (from a verb *mōtian* meaning 'converse') and should not be confused with *mute* meaning 'silent'.

moral, morale. Fowler wrote at great length about the spelling of these words. This was because in the years following the First World War, *morale*, in the meaning 'mental attitude or bearing', was very much in people's minds, but they were unsure whether to choose *morale* (an early 19c respelling preserving the sound of the French word and distinguishing it from the other meanings of *moral*) or the spelling *moral*, reintroduced towards the end of the 19c for this meaning on the grounds that *morale* was artificial and not the form of the word in this meaning in French. Over time, *morale*, together with its French-like pronunciation, which Fowler recommended, has won the day, and few today will know that there was ever an issue. However, the story affords a colourful glimpse of the continuous interaction between two great languages.

moratorium, meaning 'a temporary suspension or prohibition', more often has the plural form *moratoriums* than *moratoria*, but both are correct.

more. 1 For *more* and *most* used in the comparison of adjectives, *see* ADJECTIVE 3–4. With adverbs, *more* and *most* are normally used when the adverb is formed with *-ly* from an adjective, e.g. *more richly, more happily*: *see* -ER AND -EST FORMS. The use of double comparatives, e.g. *They are more happier now*, though once a feature of English style (and used for example by Shakespeare), has fallen out of use and is considered non-standard.

2 more than one. This phrase, though plural in form and meaning, conventionally takes a singular verb: *More than one doctor attends each patient*. However, if the number following *than* is higher than one, or if the phrase is couched in the form *more* + plural noun + *than*, then the whole phrase moves into the plural: *More than two doctors attend each patient / More doctors than one attend each patient*. The same happens if *more than one* is followed by *of* and a plural noun or pronoun: *More than one of the doctors attend each patient*.

3 many more. Ambiguity can arise when *many more* is followed by an adjective. In the sentence *Many more important tasks had to be done*, it is unclear whether *more* belongs with *many* or with *important*, i.e. whether all the tasks referred to were important or only the additional ones. In speech, intonation usually clarifies the intended sense, but confusion can be caused when this kind of construction appears in written form.

4 For *more important* and *more importantly*, *see* IMPORTANT, IMPORTANTLY.

mores, meaning 'characteristic customs of a place or people', is the plural of the Latin word *mos* 'custom' and in BrE is generally pronounced **maw**-reez but also **maw**-rays, which is standard in AmE. It is treated as a plural noun in English: *It is in the context of specific family strategies and patterns that sexual mores developed and were transformed*— J. Weeks, 1992.

morphology is the study of the structure and form of words. It includes both inflection (how words change their forms according to grammatical function, e.g. *come, comes, came*, etc.) and derivation (how one word is formed from another, e.g. *unhelpful* from *helpful*, and *helpful* in its turn from *help*).

mortgage. Note the spelling with *-t-*. It sometimes confuses people that the lender in a mortgage contract (i.e. bank, building society, etc.) is called the *mortgagee*, and the borrower the *mortgager* (or in legal work, *mortgagor*).

Moslem. The preferred and more usual spelling is *Muslim*.

mosquito has the plural form *mosquitoes*.

most. 1 For *more* and *most* used in the comparison of adjectives, *see* ADJECTIVE 3–4. With adverbs, *more* and *most* are normally used when the adverb is formed with *-ly* from an adjective, e.g. *most richly, most happily*: *see* -ER AND -EST FORMS. The use of *most* with an already superlative form of adjective, e.g. *She is the most cleverest*, though once a feature of English style (occurring in Shakespeare and elsewhere), is considered non-standard in current usage. When the comparison is between two people or things, *more*, not *most*, should be used: *This is certainly the more interesting of your two proposals*.

2 As a noun, *most* + *of* is treated as singular or plural according to the number of the following noun or pronoun: *Most of his story is true / Most of them had nothing to say*.

3 The combination *most* + adjective often has an intensifying rather than superlative role: *She is a most remarkable woman.* When preceded by *the*, ambiguity can arise, which is normally clarified by intonation in speech but may call for rewording in writing: *This was the most wicked crime* [= utterly wicked in itself].

4 For *most important* and *most importantly*, see IMPORTANT, IMPORTANTLY.

5 *Dewey knew no fear, would just roar on into most any species of difficulty*—T. R. Pearson, 1991. In this meaning, in use since the 16c first in Scotland and now chiefly in British dialects and in AmE, *most* is a shortening of *almost* and therefore a distinct word, though often treated together with the main meanings of *most* in dictionaries.

mother-in-law has the plural *mothers-in-law*.

Mother's Day. In Britain, this is another name for *Mothering Sunday*, the fourth Sunday in Lent, traditionally a day for honouring mothers with gifts. In America, *Mother's Day* is on the second Sunday in May.

motivate, motivation. *Motivation* has a special meaning in psychology which the *OED* defines as 'the conscious or unconscious stimulus for action towards a desired goal especially as resulting from psychological or social factors; the factors giving purpose or direction to human or animal behaviour'. Both it and the corresponding verb *motivate* have entered the language of business and industrial personnel management to denote the factors that induce employees to work well: *The really crucial skills, to the headteacher charged with the responsibility of taking a school into this new territory, will be those of motivation, leadership and team-building*—T. Brighouse et al., 1991 / *Get to know the people you work with—by*

taking the time to do this you know exactly what motivates them—Irish News, 2007. From here it is a short step to over-generalized uses in which both words are little more than synonyms for *cause* (verb and noun) or *reason*: *The farming achievements of the eighteenth and early nineteenth centuries were also motivated by the need for more food*—J. Purseglove, 1989 / *There was no racial motivation for the attack*—Leicester Mercury, 2007.

motto has the plural form *mottoes*.

mould. There are three separate words spelt this way in BrE: a hollow container for making a shape, a fungous growth, and loose friable earth. All three have corresponding verbs. In AmE the spelling in all meanings is *mold*.

moult is the spelling in BrE for the verb meaning 'to shed feathers or hair etc.' and for the corresponding noun. In AmE the spelling is *molt*.

mouse. The plural in the traditional meaning is *mice*, but *mouses* is heard (in addition to *mice*) for the plural of the hand-held device which controls the movement of the cursor on a computer screen.

moustache (with stress on the second syllable) is the normal spelling in BrE, but *mustache* (with stress on the first syllable) is more usual in AmE.

mouthful has the plural form *mouthfuls*. See -FUL.

movable, mobile. *Movable* generally denotes that something can be moved by applying an external force to it, whereas *mobile* means that it has the ability to move or be moved as a special characteristic. A *mobile phone* is designed to be carried about, and a *mobile shop* is built into a vehicle so that it can be transported. *Mobile* is also used with special meanings as a noun (a decorative hanging structure, and = mobile phone). *Movable* has a special meaning in law to denote property that is regarded as personal to the owner rather than as a permanent fixture: in this sense it is typically used in the plural. Note that *movable* is normally spelt in this way, although *moveable* is the form often used in legal contexts.

mow. The past of the verb is *mowed*. The past participle is *mowed* or *mown* (*He has mowed / mown the grass*), but when used as an adjective *mown* is the only form used (*Mown grass*). In AmE, *mowed* is standard in all these uses, rather than *mown*.

MP (= Member of Parliament) is now normally used without full points. The plural is *MPs* (no apostrophe) and the possessive forms are *MP's* (singular) and *MPs'* (plural).

Mr, Mrs are now normally used without a full point in BrE (*Mr and Mrs J. Smith*), but with one (*Mr. and Mrs. J. Smith*) in AmE.

Ms, despite the derision from some quarters that greeted its early uses in the 1950s (at first in America and soon after in Britain), is now established as a useful and practical title applied to a woman irrespective of marital status (*Ms J. Smith*). It is normally used without a full point in BrE, but with one in AmE. Although it was originally devised out of concern for social equality and promoted especially by the feminist movement, it has proved a blessing to everyone, men and women alike, in avoiding the need to research into or divine the personal circumstances of female addressees. The plural abbreviation, if required, is *Mss(.)* or *Mses*.

much. For the complementary uses of *much* and *very*, *see* VERY.

muchly, once a serious adverb, is now used only humorously: *She stepped away from him as though evading her share in the pleasure. 'Thank you muchly,' he said.*—M. Keane, 1988 / *Much of it is muchly much of a muchness, but occasionally . . . there is a song which might just be played again if the rest of your collection is lost in a bizarre gardening accident*—Evening Standard, 1999.

much more, much less, still more, still less. *The principles, much more the practice, need a good deal of scrutiny. I didn't even see him, still less talk to him. Much more* (or *still more*) is used when the grammatical form of the sentence is positive, as in that first example, and *much less* (or *still less*) when it is negative. Uncertainty arises when the form is positive but the sense is negative, as with adjectives in *un-* and words like *difficult*. In the sentence *It is difficult to establish all the facts, much less to reach a conclusion, much more* is strictly needed, not *much less*, but the result is awkward and an alternative such as *let alone* is often preferable.

mucus, mucous. *Mucus* is the noun for a slimy substance secreted by a gland, and *mucous* is the corresponding adjective (as in *mucous cell / gland / membrane*).

Muhammad, Muhammadan. The name of the founder of Islam is now spelt *Muhammad* in English, not *Mohammed*. The word for a follower of Islam (and the corresponding adjective) is *Muslim*; *Muhammadan* (a term often used in the past) is now considered offensive by Muslims themselves in suggesting that Muhammad and not Allah is the object of worship.

mullah, meaning 'a Muslim learned in Islamic law', is spelt in this way.

multi- is used as a prefix in many words of different vintages, some directly from Latin, like *multifarious* (1593), others created from English elements, e.g. *multiculti* (1989). Hyphenation varies considerably, but generally the more established and more frequent a word is, the more likely it is to have no hyphen, e.g. *multimillionaire, multipurpose, multistorey.* Adjectives consisting of *multi-* prefixed to an adjective also tend to be written without a hyphen, e.g. *multicoloured, multidisciplinary, multi-faceted,* unless there would be an awkward combination of vowels, i.e. *multi-ethnic* rather than *multiethnic.* Adjectives consisting of *multi-* prefixed to a noun are also hyphenated, e.g. *multi-agency, multi-party,* etc. In other cases, it is advisable to use a single dictionary consistently as a style guide.

mumps, the illness, is usually treated as a singular noun (*Mumps is common in young children*), and is sometimes used informally or locally with *the* (*This morning I had a chat with one of the girls who has been off sick with the mumps—Evening Gazette,* 2005).

muscle, mussel. *Muscle* is the fibrous body tissue, *mussel* the bivalve mollusc.

Muslim is the preferred spelling for a follower of Islam (and for the corresponding adjective), not *Moslem* or other older forms. The *u* can be pronounced as in *muslin,* or as in *foot,* and the *s* can be pronounced like a *z.*

mussel *see* MUSCLE.

must. The use of *must* informally as a noun meaning 'something that must be done or had, or that should not be missed', dates from the 1890s in American use. In the earlier part of the 20c, it was often written in inverted commas as being not quite pukka in serious or

supposedly serious contexts, and this practice is still sometimes followed: *No. 1 on the list of 'musts' from the publishers surveyed was to find the right artist—Art Business News,* 2001. Now, the idiom has moved a stage further by being used attributively (before a noun: *This is a 'must' book*). Nowadays it is a rather overused combining form, creating nouns and adjectives such as *must-have, must-see,* etc. (in which *must* is a verb and not a noun): *The King George is, self-evidently, a royal occasion, one of the 'must-see' races—Observer,* 2007).

mute. For the mistaken phrasing *mute point see* MOOT.

mute e. *See box opposite.*

mutual. 1 *That done, our day of marriage shall be yours, One feast, one house, one mutual happiness*—Shakespeare, *Two Gentlemen of Verona,* v.iv.170–1. Until the 19c, *mutual* was used with little difficulty in two main meanings: (1) that reflected in Valentine's words just quoted from *Two Gentlemen,* i.e. 'common, shared by several', and (2) another, slightly older, meaning defined as 'experienced or done by each of two or more parties with reference to each other', i.e. more or less equivalent to the much more awkward word *reciprocal;* this meaning is also found in Shakespeare: *A contract of eternal bond of love, Confirmed by mutual joinder* [= joining] *of your hands—Twelfth Night,* v.i.154–5. Although the *OED* gives copious evidence for phrases of the type *our mutual friend* (first recorded in 1658, i.e. long before Dickens used it as a title), *our mutual acquaintance, our mutual opinion,* etc., the 19c grammarians decided on the basis largely of their Latin view of grammar and meaning that while 'the *mutual* love of husband and wife' is correct enough, 'a *mutual* friend of both husband and wife' is 'sheer nonsense' (Henry Alford, Dean of Canterbury,

MUTE E.

The letter *e* is mute or silent at the end of words such as *excite, move, sale,* and *rare.* Adding suffixes to words of this kind raises the question of whether the final *e* should be kept (as it is in *changeable*) or dropped (1) (as it is more usually, e.g. in *excitable* and *mauvish*). The choice is partly a matter of convention from word to word (2) and partly determined by principles, the most important of which are that final *-e* is retained (3) when it preserves the soft sound of a preceding *c* or *g* (as in *outrageous*), (4) when it distinguishes the root from another word (e.g. *dye -> dyeing / die -> dying*), (5) when the suffix begins with a consonant (as in *judge / judgement* (although *judgment* is also used) and *change / changeling*), and (6) optionally, in parallel with forms without the *-e*, as a visual reminder of the pronunciation of the vowel of the root word (as in *likeable / likable, lateish / latish*). The following table illustrates the major types, and some of the examples stand for others (in some cases many others) of the same category. The bracketed numbers show to which group listed above the words belong:

acknowledge	acknowledgement (5) (occasionally acknowledgment)
age	ageing (6) (also aging)
age	ageism (6) (also agism)
bloke	blokeish (6) (also blokish)
blue	bluey (2)
change	changeable (3)
change	changeling (5)
change	changing (1)
cleave	cleavage (1)
clique	cliquish (1)
conservative	conservatism (1)
dose	dosage (1)
due	duly (5)
dye	dyeing (4)
excite	excitable (1)
gauge	gaugeable (3)
hinge	hingeing (2) (also hinging)
hire	hireling (5)
judge	judgement (5) (occasionally judgment)
like	likeable (6) (also likable)
like	likely (5)
love	lovable (1)
love	loving (1)
mile	mileage (6) (also milage)
mouse	mousy (1)
move	movable (1)
notice	noticeable (3)
outrage	outrageous (3)
race	racist (1)
rate	rateable (6) (also ratable)
retrieve	retrieval (1)
sale	saleable (6) (also salable)
tiptoe	tiptoeing (2)
whole	wholly (5)

1864). (How 'sheer nonsense' can be used of something that is readily understood itself makes no sense.)

2 The state of affairs now, in the early part of the 21c, is that most usage guides warn against the use of *mutual* to mean 'common, shared' when there is no element of reciprocal action or feeling, i.e. not just shared but acting in both directions (and usually involving no more than two parties). But meaning is not that containable, and is not always obligingly resident in individual words. *Mutual* is the kind of word that draws its meaning from its surroundings: *On the whole even Marwan was pretty laissez-faire about a girl and a boy talking about subjects of mutual interest*—Nigel Williams, 1993 (the interest may not be two-way but the talking is). Furthermore, anyone who insists on using *common* instead of *mutual* is not living in the real world: *common* has acquired so much ancillary meaning from the other work it has to do that it will almost invariably change or weaken the sense. So the recommendation must be twofold: (1) use *common* or *joint* (or, often better, *in common* or *jointly*) if it fits without any of its other meanings getting in the way and has the force of meaning needed, especially in cases where it may be significant that the action is not two-way (*people facing common problems*), (2) otherwise use *mutual*, whether there is explicit reciprocal action or not: *Wilde and Yeats reviewed each other's work with mutual regard*—R. Ellmann, 1986 / *In the aftermath of their mutual suffering, a former British commando and a German opera singer's daughter found love, marriage and a joint desire to explain the significance of the events they experienced*—Independent, 2004.

3 The difference in usage between *mutual* and *reciprocal* was succinctly summed up by Fowler as follows: '*Mutual* regards the relation from both sides at once: *the mutual hatred of A and B*;

never from one side only: not *B's mutual hatred of A*. Where *mutual* is correct, *reciprocal* would be so too: *the reciprocal hatred of A and B*; but *mutual* is usually preferred when it is possible. *Reciprocal* can also be applied to the second party's share alone: *B's reciprocal hatred of A. Reciprocal* is therefore often useful to supply the deficiencies of *mutual*.'

Myanmar. The military authorities in Burma have promoted the name *Myanmar* as the official name for their state since 1989; *Burma* is often preferred by people who oppose the current government.

myriad, a somewhat literary word meaning 'an indefinitely great number' (from a Greek word meaning 'ten thousand'), is treated like *billion* and *million* in relation to a following noun, i.e. you can say either *a myriad stars* or *myriads of stars*. A third construction, *a myriad of stars*, is also found. Examples: (without *of*) *Acting as a walking/talking A-Z, directing traffic, dealing with accident victims and domestic disputes are several of the myriad activities that absorb police personnel*—M. Brogden, 1991 / *Tyres, brakes, state of alertness, and above all attitude towards risk are among the myriad relevant factors that bear on the outcome*—Times, 1998 / (with *of*) *Crystals are made of myriads of layers of atoms (or equivalent), and each layer builds upon the layer below*—Richard Dawkins, 1991 / *Three teleconferences about Sars sandwiched between a myriad of delayed patients waiting an hour in the office*—Guardian, 2003.

myself has two main roles: (1) as a reflexive pronoun in which the object of the action is the same as the speaker (*I managed to restrain myself / I was put in a room by myself*), (2) as an emphatic pronoun reinforcing the simple pronoun *I* (*I began to feel guilty myself*). It should not be used as the subject of a verb, although this is sometimes found especially in compound subjects joined by *and*: ☒ *It wasn't that Peter and myself* [read: *Peter and I*] *were being singled out*—Fay Weldon, 1988 / ☒ *My husband, son, and myself* [read: *my husband, my son, and I*] *went on our holiday as planned*—*Daily Mail*, 1998. Nor should it be used as the object of a verb when the action is not reflexive and *me* would do as well: ☒ *Palme Dutt's nervousness communicated itself to Isaac and myself* [read: *to Isaac and me*]—Nigel Williams, 1985.

naff. The phrasal verb *naff off*, a euphemistic substitute for *fuck off*, first appeared in print in Keith Waterhouse's novel *Billy Liar* (1959), and Waterhouse himself insists that it was originally conscript service slang as an acronym of '*nasty, awful, fuck it*'. The adjective *naff*, which has a range of meanings roughly corresponding to 'lacking taste or style, inept', is unrelated to the verb. Where the adjective originated is not known for certain.

naive, as an adjective meaning 'lacking experience or judgement', was originally the feminine of the French word *naïf* (which is now rarely used as an adjective, and rather more often as a noun). *Naive* is generally pronounced in a quasi-French way nah-**eev** or niy-**eev**, but it is now more often spelt without an accent on the *i* than with, and the unaccented spelling is accepted as correct. The corresponding noun to describe the quality of being *naive* most often used is *naivety* or, especially in AmE, *naivete*.

Nama. The *Nama* people are one of the Khoikhoi peoples of South Africa and SW Namibia. They have in the past been called *Hottentot* (actually a somewhat broader term), but that is now obsolete and *Nama* is the standard accepted term. *See* HOTTENTOT; KHOIKHOI.

name. 1 The elliptical construction *name of*, short for *by the name of*, is now common informally: *Keep your eyes peeled for a customer on his own, name of Sheldrake*—David Lodge, 1991.

2 The idiom *you name it*, used informally as a colourful equivalent of 'etc.', is first found in print in the 1960s, and is now well established: *Whatever they choose to say, Directors, DG, Higher Command, War Cabinet, Prime Minister, you name it, I'm not sending my units back into Europe*—Penelope Fitzgerald, 1980.

name(d) after, name(d) for. It is often assumed that the idiom *to name someone or something after* someone or something else is not used in AmE, and that *to name* someone or something *for* something only is used there. In fact, in all varieties of English both are used, but *name(d) after* is the preferred form by a very large margin, except in AmE, where it is nonetheless slightly more frequent than *name(d) for*: *Wellington, who, as we all know, has a boot named after him*—*Printing World*, BrE 1976 / *Each chapter is named for the element it recalls*—*New Yorker*, 1987. / *Which Canadian city is named for a Royal Navy captain and great explorer from Kings Lynn, Norfolk?*—*Liverpool Daily Post*, 2007 / *So they're named* [i.e. the Tea Party] *after a tax revolt, but they don't know anything about taxes*—CNN transcripts, AmE 2010.

napkin was preferred by Fowler (1926), Nancy Mitford, and others to *serviette*, which they judged to be a genteelism or 'non-U'.

nappy, a shortening of *napkin*, is the BrE term for what in AmE is called a *diaper* (pronounced **diy**-uh-puh).

narcissus. The plural form of the plant name is *narcissi*, pronounced nah-**sis**-iy, rather than the more awkward *narcissuses*.

nary. The colloquial or dialect expression *nary a* (= not a) was exclusively American until the 20c, when it began to appear in British works: *You can wander around the cavernous vaults of the Law Courts in the Strand these days and come across nary a person—New Society*, 1973.

nasal in phonetics denotes a sound produced with the breath passing through the nose, e.g. represented by *m*, *n*, *ng*, or French *en*, *un*.

native. In many of its meanings, *native* is uncontroversial: *native speaker, native of Liverpool, native oak* are typical examples of innocuous usage. The danger comes when the word is used as a noun to mean 'an original inhabitant of a country', because of the notions of cultural inferiority it conveys. A quotation from 1950 formerly in the *OED* catalogues the outdated and culturally offensive stereotypes often implied: *greedy for beads . . . and alcoholic drinks . . . Addicted to drumbeating and lewd dancing. More or less naked. Sporadically treacherous . . . Picturesque. Comic when trying to speak English or otherwise ape white ways*. In uses that are clearly humorous, there is less objection to *native*: *New York in the summer was too hot even for the natives*. Otherwise, it is better to use more neutral terms such as *original inhabitant*.

Native American. The indigenous peoples of North America have been called and referred to themselves as *Native Americans* since the 1950s, and the term is now generally preferred to *American Indians*.

natter, meaning 'to chatter idly', is largely confined to BrE. It seems to be an alteration of an earlier dialectal word *gnatter*, the origin of which is uncertain, but like *natter* meant 'grumble'.

nature. The phrase *of a . . . nature*, with an adjective before *nature*, should be used sparingly and only when the adjective by itself will not serve for some reason. For example, *allegations of a serious nature* could easily be rephrased as *serious allegations*. In other cases, *kind* or *type* could be used more effectively than *nature*: *These results, minor as they are, are of a nature that has not been achieved in any other use of the computer for style analysis in music—Computer & Humanities*, 1970. / *The men are accused of conspiring between January 1 and July 1 to cause explosions of a nature likely to endanger life or cause serious injury—Western Mail*, 2007.

naught, nought. *Naught* is an archaic or literary word meaning 'nothing' and it survives chiefly in phrases such as *come to naught* or *all for naught*. In BrE *nought* is the term for the digit 0 (*zero* in AmE). The game called *noughts and crosses* in BrE is known as *tick-tack-toe* in AmE.

nausea. In BrE the word can be pronounced with an *s* or a *z* sound, **naw**-si-uh or **naw**-zi-uh. In AmE the pronunciations -zhi-uh and -shi-uh are also frequent.

nauseated, nauseating, nauseous. 1 As participles of the verb *nauseate, nauseated* and *nauseating* have physical and metaphorical meanings, i.e. 'affected by/causing physical nausea' and 'disgusted/disgusting'. But while *nauseated* has a physical meaning rather more often than it has a literal one, *nauseating* is only rarely physical: (nauseated) *I got out of bed, but felt dreadfully giddy, nauseated and then panic stricken—Daily Telegraph*, 1990; *She had some brightly coloured blouses* and dresses hanging in the cupboard, and the mere sight of them made her feel shaky and nauseated—C. F. Roe, 1990 / The duo . . . await a wave of laughter from the crowd, but there is only a nauseated silence—See Magazine, CanE 2002 / (nauseating) He woke up to the nauseating smell of burning skin and a roaring sound—FlyPast, 1991 / What a nauseating little Miss Perfect you are—R. Goddard, 1993 / Most anecdotes associated with Diogenes consistently depict him as a nauseating and narcissistic sociopath—First Things (magazine), AmE 2004. Nauseous is used (1) most often to mean 'suffering from nausea' (She suddenly felt nauseous, and went to the sink and heaved uncontrollably—Q. Wilder, 1993), and (2) rather less often, metaphorically to describe things that cause physical revulsion or feelings of disgust (But that doesn't mean I have to be involved in this kind of nauseous business—R. Harrison, 1991).

2 In America, some usage guides insist that nauseous strictly means 'causing nausea', and cannot be used to mean 'suffering from nausea'. However, this artificial distinction is not adhered to, and nauseous is now commonly used in the same way as the physical meaning of nauseated: Was the President nauseous when he slumped to the floor, or was there any vomiting?—New York Times, 1992 / He felt slightly nauseous, and sore all over—fiction website, AmE 2005.

naval, navel. Naval is the adjective relating to navy, and navel is the rounded knotty depression in the centre of the belly (also in navel orange etc.). The two words are unrelated.

nay is still in use as a somewhat rhetorical (and often affected) way of expressing the meaning 'and more than that . . .': One could not but notice how theatrical, nay operatic, the whole adornment of the church was—Oxford Magazine, 1991. As a noun, nay means principally 'a no vote' in parliamentary divisions.

né see NÉE.

near, nearly. Near has almost fallen out of use as an adverb meaning 'almost', and nearly serves this purpose: He was nearly dead with fright. Exceptions include near-complete and near-perfect: Gunnell, captain of the British women's team, showed exactly how it should be done with what turned into a near-perfect performance—Daily Mirror, 1992 / Busch would surely be unwilling to take the job unless the bosses agreed to give her near-complete autonomy—cinema website, AmE 2001 / That performance was a near-perfect exhibition of his superb, effortless, but efficient technique—Caribbean Beat, 2004.

nearby, near by. When used as an adjective before a noun, it should be written as one word (at a nearby hotel), but as an adverb normally as two (at a hotel near by).

necessarily. The dominant pronunciation in BrE, which has been influenced by American practice, is with the stress on the third syllable; a first-syllable stress is often advocated by older speakers but whether they always use it themselves is questionable.

née, né. Née is the feminine form of the French adjective meaning 'born' and is traditionally used to identify the maiden name of a married woman: Mrs Ann Smith, née Jones. In other cases it is used to denote the original name of a woman who has changed her name; in this use it also appears in the masculine form né to refer to a man who has done this and even to non-human name changes: Diana Dors, née Diana Mary Fluck / Norman Charles, né Charles Norman

Diggs / The Morning Star, né Daily Worker.

need *verb*. **1** Like *dare*, *need* can behave in two ways: as an ordinary verb and as a modal auxiliary verb sharing some of the characteristics of the main modals such as *can* and *might*. As an ordinary verb, *need* is regular and can be followed by a simple object (*We need more bread*), a verbal noun (*The cupboard needs cleaning*), or a *to*-infinitive (*They need to see for themselves*). As a modal verb, it has certain grammatical restrictions: (1) it is only used with a so-called 'bare' infinitive without *to* (*I'm not sure you need answer*), (2) it is only used in the negative, or in phrases with a negative implication, and in questions without *do* (*You need not answer / Need I answer? / I need hardly add . . .*), (3) the third person singular form is *need* without addition of *s* (*He says she need not answer*). In many cases the modal meaning can equally be expressed by using *need* as an ordinary verb, e.g. *He says she does not need to answer.*

2 Some contextual examples follow: (modal use) *The Landlady need never know*—J. Frame, 1985 / *But need she lie? Was he just a boy?*—M. Leland, 1985 / *It need not only be children who can enjoy guessing games*—Spectator, 1988 / *Contemporaries do not conveniently die at the same time, nor need they all be dead before we write the history of their exploits*—M. Inwood, 2000 / (ordinary use) *The K2 tragedy shows that much more needs to be done to bring home the lesson*—Times, 1986 / *She acted as if Strawberry needed to be cuddled*—New Yorker, 1988 / *That's the area that one needs to be a little careful about*—CNN news transcripts, 2002 [*OEC*].

3 When used as an ordinary verb to mean 'stand in want of', *need* can be followed by either a verbal noun (which is more common in speech) or a passive *to*-infinitive (*The car needs washing / The car needs to be washed*). A third type, *The car needs washed*, is mainly Scottish or AmE regional dialect: *I walked round the cottage to see what needed done*—C. Burns, 1989.

needs, originally an adverb meaning 'of necessity, necessarily', survives in the somewhat literary phrases *needs must*: *He can kill a pig. Probably with his bare hands, if needs must*—Observer Food monthly, 2004. The phrase alludes to the old proverb *Needs must when the devil drives* (and its variants).

ne'er is a literary (chiefly poetical) shortening of *never*, in regular use since the 13c but now rarely used except in the compound *ne'er-do-well* meaning 'a good-for-nothing'.

negative, an emphatic form of *no* used for clarity, has been extended since about the 1950s from the language of radio communication into general use: *'Any result of my application for the return of my typist?' 'Negative,' said Mr Oates*—Evelyn Waugh, 1961.

negligee the preferred English spelling for the woman's light dressing gown, though the version with two acute accents, *négligée*, is also correct. The general pronunciation is **neg**-li-zhay, but AmE also stresses the last syllable neg-luh-**zhay**.

negligible is spelt *-ible*, not *negligeable*.

negotiate is one of Fowler's *lost causes. In 1926 he strongly attacked its use in what he called 'its improper sense' of 'tackle successfully' as in negotiating bends, obstacles, etc., a use that is now well established.

Negro, Negress. *Negro* and even more, *Negress*, have dropped out of favour (except with historical reference and among American Blacks themselves). The standard terms are now *black* (or *Black*) and (in America) *African-American*. The plural of *Negro* is *Negroes*.

Negroid, referring to the peoples of central and southern Africa, is one of a set of terms used by 19c anthropologists to classify human races. They are now outdated and potentially offensive, and the names of specific peoples or nationalities should normally be used.

neighbourhood. It is better to avoid the clumsy expression *in the neighbourhood of* as in *he wrote somewhere in the neighbourhood of a hundred novels*, when *roughly* or *about* would serve as well.

neither. 1 pronunciation. The two pronunciations, **nIy**-dhuh and **nee**-dhuh, are about equally common in British English. Both are correct, though many British people consider only **nIy**-dhuh right. American English dictionaries give **nee**-dhuh as the standard pronunciation, and **nIy**-dhuh as a variant.

2 parts of speech. *Neither* functions in two ways: as an adjective or pronoun, and as an adverb or conjunction.

a adjective and pronoun. *Neither* means 'not the one nor the other (of two things)': *Neither child knew the answer / Neither wanted to stay / Neither of them is right*. When more than two items are involved, *no* is preferable for the adjective and *none* for the pronoun, although *neither* tends to be used informally especially for the pronoun. Normally, *neither* governs a singular verb, as in the last example above, but with the type *neither of* (+ plural) a plural verb is sometimes used to emphasize the plurality of the statement as a whole: *Neither of them are suitable*.

b adverb and conjunction. *Neither* is regularly paired with *nor*, linking two subjects. If both subjects are singular

and in the third person, the verb should normally be singular: *Neither its chairman, Sir Frederick Dainton, nor its chief executive, Kenneth Cooper, is planning any dramatic gestures*—*Times*, 1985. But a plural verb is also attested historically and is still often found, especially when the essential plurality that is always present in *neither* comes to the fore: *Neither search nor labour are necessary*—Dr Johnson, 1759 / *But neither Baker nor Bush are needed for that*—*Newsweek*, 1991. As an adverb, *neither* can be used with *nor* to link more than two items: *Buildings made of some translucent and subtly incandescent material, neither glass nor stone nor steel*—Penelope Lively, 1991. *Neither* is used as a quasi-conjunction in constructions of the informal type *He's had no breakfast. Neither did he want any*, in which it is a substitute for *nor*.

3 change of number and person with *neither* . . . *nor* . . . Complications occur when the number (singular or plural) of the two subjects is different. If either of the subjects (especially the second) is plural, the verb is normally plural: *Neither the Conservative figures nor the evidence of Labour's recovery since 1983 produce any sense of inexorable movement in political fortunes*—*Times*, 1985. A mixture of persons is more difficult, and can normally only be resolved by rephrasing, so that (e.g.) *Neither you nor I am/are/is the right person* becomes *You are not the right person, and neither [or nor] am I*.

4 position of *neither* and *nor*. The position of *neither* and *nor* should be such that the grammatical structures are correctly balanced, as in *This suits neither one purpose nor the other* but not in ▣ *This neither suits one purpose nor the other*.

5 *neither* followed by *or*. Although the *OED* gives plenty of literary evidence for *neither* followed by *or* rather than *nor* (e.g. *I can neither tell how many we kill'd,* *or how many we wounded*—Daniel Defoe, 1719), in current usage this is considered incorrect and should be avoided.

6 *neither* replacing *nor*. When *nor* follows a negative statement (not necessarily one with *neither*) and introduces a different grammatical subject, it can be replaced by *neither*: *Becky is killed accidentally. The police don't care much; neither does Henry's wife*—Publishers Weekly, 1974.

nem. con., short for Latin *nemine contradicente*, means 'with no one dissenting' (from a vote or decision). It does not mean the same as *unanimously* since it can also include abstentions, which *unanimously* does not.

neologisms *see* NEW WORDS.

nerve-racking is the recommended spelling in BrE and AmE dictionaries, which also allow as a variant *nerve-wracking*.

-ness *see* -ION, -MENT, -NESS.

Net. As a shortening of *Internet*, in *the Net*, the word is spelt with a capital initial letter.

net. In the commercial meaning 'not subject to deduction', the preferred spelling is *net*, not *nett*.

Netherlands, Low Countries, Holland, Dutch. *The Netherlands* is the official name for the Kingdom of Holland; *Holland* (strictly only a part of the Netherlands) is used informally. The term *Low Countries* includes Belgium and Luxembourg as well as the Netherlands. *Dutch* is used as a noun and adjective for the language and people of the Netherlands, and in certain familiar phrases such as *Dutch courage* (= false courage got from alcohol) and *go Dutch* (= pay individually).

neurosis has the plural form *neuroses*, pronounced nyoo-**roh**-seez.

never. As a negative adverb, *never* refers primarily to repeated or continuous non-occurrence over a period of time: *They never answer letters* / *It never rained at all last month*. It should only be used informally to refer to one occasion, when a simple negative would be equally appropriate: *I phoned you but you never rang back* [better, *you didn't ring back*]; it is used with similar meaning in a number of fixed expressions such as *never fear* and *well I never*. It is also used idiomatically as an emphatic negative with reference to future time: *You'll never catch the train now*. The emphatic form *never ever* sometimes has a comma between the two words: *She continued, a little too vehemently, 'I've never, ever been bored'*—Maggie Gee, 1985 / *She was like a mother, but she could never ever be my mother*—fiction website, AmE 2001.

nevertheless, nonetheless. Both words mean 'in spite of that' and are interchangeable, although the first is more often used. They are both now normally written as one word.

news. *News is what a chap who doesn't care much about anything wants to read*—Evelyn Waugh, 1938. *News*, though earlier a singular or plural noun, has been treated since the early 19c as singular: *Here is* [not *are*] *the news* / *The news was* [not *were*] *not good*.

new words (technically called *neologisms*). It is always tempting, as much in the history of the language as in political and social history, to identify tendencies with centuries, but language change is a continuous process, and what is significant is the social and technological factors that have produced change. In the last twenty years or so, the most significant social and historical developments

n

that have given rise to new words and meanings are as follows (necessarily a selective list with fairly crude divisions in which some items belong in more than one category):

1 science and technology: *airglow, astrochemistry, cardphone, cash machine, cellphone, chaos theory, dark matter, digital compression, electronic banking* (and many other electronic phenomena), *genetic engineering, meme, smart card, voicemail.*

2 computing: *access* (verb, as in accessing data; this has spread into general use), *boot* (verb, noun), *browser, bulletin board, bundle, CD-ROM, chipset, cut and paste, cyberspace, dataglove, dialogue box, directory, download, email* (= electronic mail), *flaming, -friendly* (as a suffix as in *user-friendly*), *hacking, helpdesk, home page* (on the World Wide Web), *hypertext, information superhighway, Internet, laptop, log-on, millennium bug, motherboard, the Net, newsgroup, plug-and-play, scroll bar, search engine, shareware, software, spam, standalone, surfing, virtual reality, virus, World Wide Web, zip.* More recently a sinister terminology has arisen reflecting criminal uses of the Internet: *phreaking* and *phishing* (illegal 'hacking' of various kinds), *cyber-bullying,* and intrusive types of software planting called *adware, malware, spyware,* and so on. All this vocabulary is flexible enough, and sufficiently based on everyday words, to enable virtually limitless extension as activities, legal and illegal, develop.

3 environmental issues: *biodiversity, carbon footprint, carbon offsetting, CFC* (= chlorofluorocarbon), *climate change, eco-warrior, global warming, greenhouse effect, greenhouse gas, ozone depletion, ozone-friendly, zero-emission vehicle.*

4 popular culture: *babe* (= attractive young woman), *bad hair day* (= day when everything goes wrong), *body piercing, crack* (= cocaine), *Ecstasy, hoodie, lifestyle* (first recorded in the 1930s and adopted in marketing jargon in the 1980s), *massive* (= popular or trendy), *metrosexual, recreational drug, smart drug, supermodel.*

5 politics and society: *abuse* (as in *child abuse, narcotics abuse*), *acquaintance rape, cardboard city* (area of homeless people), *challenged* (PC term for a disability, as in *mentally challenged, physically challenged,* etc.), *change management, charisma, charm offensive, dependency culture, differently abled, double whammy, downshifting, downsizing, empowerment, Essex man, feelgood* (*factor*), *feng shui, fundholder, gap year* (between school and university), *gesture politics, glass ceiling* (barrier to personal advancement), *home shopping* (by means of a telecommunications link), *homophobia, human resources* (= personnel), *jobseeker, league table* (of schools' performance), *living will, loyalty card, mission statement* (= statement of a company's business principles), *nanny state, narcoterrorism, negative equity, outsourcing, pindown* (treatment of children in care), *pink pound, proactive, ram-raiding, reskilling, road rage, safe haven, serial monogamy, sexism* (and other words in *-ism*, e.g. *ableism, fattism, sizeism*), *sleaze, social chapter, speed bump, spin doctor, stakeholder economy, subsidiarity, surrogate mother, teleworking.*

6 international politics: *collateral damage, ethnic cleansing, Euroscepticism* (and other *Euro-* words), *fatwa, friendly fire, intifada, jihad, killing field* (= place of mass slaughter), *peace dividend, peace process, road map* (= a plan for peace), *safe haven, velvet revolution, weapons of mass destruction* (or *WMD*, made prominent by events in Iraq in 2003).

7 health and medicine: *Aids* (and *Aids-related*), *attention deficit disorder, BSE* (= bovine spongiform encephalitis),

CJD (= Creutzfeld–Jakob disease), *community care, dyspraxia, frozen embryo, functional food, interleukin* (proteins), *keyhole surgery, kinesiology, mad cow disease, ME* (= myalgic encephalomyelitis), *MMR* (= mumps, measles, and rubella [vaccine]), *MRSA* (= methicillin-resistant *Staphylococcus aureus*), *post-traumatic stress disorder, Prozac* (antidepressant drug), *RSI* (= repetitive strain injury), *SAD* (= seasonal affective disorder), *safe sex, sick building syndrome, trans-fatty acid, water birth.*

8 media and communications: *DAT* (= digital audio tape), *electronic publishing, infotainment, mini-series, multimedia, podcast, soundbite.*

9 food and drink: *alcopop* (= alcoholic soft drink), *ciabatta, decaf* (= decaffeinated coffee), *fajitas, foodie, functional food, nacho, tiramisu, tortilla.*

10 leisure: *adventure game, Aga saga* (= type of novel concerned with middle-class rural characters), *biopic, bungee jumping, edutainment, fantasy football, gangsta* (dancing), *golden goal, grunge* (rock music), *home cinema, jungle* (music), *karaoke, performance poetry, rap* (*music*), *quality time, rollover, scratch card, snowboarding.*

11 general slang and informal uses: *anorak, attitude* (= idiosyncratic attitude or outlook), *chav* (loud and tasteless young person), *dweeb, geek, gobsmacked, item* (= romantic relationship), *nerd, no-brainer, oick, saddo, spazz out, techie, wannabe* (= someone with an ambition). It will be noticed how many of these are terms of personal abuse addressed to or used of people.

12 catchphrases: *back to basics* (slogan for a return to honest principles in public life), *been there, done that* (assertion of experience), *economical with the truth, elephant in the room* (something obvious that no one dares to mention), *get a life, level playing field, move the goalposts, out of the box* (unusual or inventive), *you name it.*

next. As an adjective meaning 'immediately following', *next* normally precedes the noun it is governing (*next time / the next three*), but in denoting time it can follow the noun (*on Friday next / in July next*). Care needs to be taken in referring to a future day of the week, since usage differs. For some people, *next Friday* means the coming Friday of the same week one is in. For others, *next Friday* always means the Friday of the coming week, and to denote Friday of the same week *this Friday* would be used. If there is likely to be any doubt, it is better to be specific in some way, e.g. by adding the date or by saying, for example, *Friday of this week* or *Friday week* as appropriate.

nice. The word *nice* is the great *cause célèbre* of meaning change in English. In medieval and Renaissance literature, *nice* (derived from Latin *nescius* meaning 'ignorant') has a wide range of generally unfavourable meanings such as 'foolish, stupid' and 'wanton, loose-mannered', and in some cases it is not possible to be sure which meaning was intended. The meanings to do with precision and fine distinctions (as in *a nice point* or *distinction*) arose in the 16c, and are still in use, but they are now swamped by the generalized favourable use of nice to mean 'agreeable, pleasant': *All her furniture is second-hand and rather nice*—J. Rose, 1990 / *I have three children of my own now and I thought it would be nice to surprise them with the sugar mice on the tree, and also the chocolate cat*—Catherine Cookson, 1990. There is no doubt that *nice* is greatly overused in this meaning, and critics have some reason to call it a 'lazy word' (i.e. inducing laziness in its users). Many synonyms, often more apposite and stronger in meaning, are available (*good, pleasant, enjoyable, fine, agreeable, satisfying*, etc.) and it is often better to use them, but in conversation *nice* has established itself too well and too idiomatically for cautionary advice to have any real point: *I thought the shoulder of lamb would be much nicer and it looked nice and fresh!*—conversation recorded in the British National Corpus, 1992. *Nice* is used idiomatically followed by *and* in a quasi-adverbial role to introduce a positive adjective: *Talk to her in your best, professorial manner, make her think how nice and kind you are*—Nina Bawden, 1989 / *Pour the warm water from the teapot into the cup you're going to use, so that the cup gets nice and warm too*—weblog, AusE 2004 [*OEC*]. The *OED* traces this use back to the end of the 18c with a quotation from Fanny Burney: *Just read this little letter, do, Miss, do—it won't take you much time, you reads so nice and fast*—*Camilla*, 1796. It has always been largely restricted to conversational contexts, where it is deeply embedded in the language.

niche. The usual and preferred pronunciation is neesh, in the French manner, although the anglicized form nich is also heard. In business jargon, *niche* (always pronounced neesh, of course) means 'a special section of the market' to which the marketing effort for goods or services may be specifically directed. In this meaning the word has developed a range of attributive uses (i.e. before another noun) such as *niche market, niche product*, and *niche player* (= a firm which exploits a niche): *The move completes the group's strategy of becoming a niche player in the new securities market after the big bang*—*Times*, 1986.

niece is one of the most commonly misspelt words in English.

niggardly has no connection with the N-word, but because of the similarity of sound and its negative meaning of 'mean, ungenerous' many people are uncomfortable with using it for fear of causing offence, and in the US it is now widely avoided.

nigger. The word is highly offensive when used by a white person with reference to a black, and is nowadays the most taboo word in English. It is apparently sometimes used without offence (along with a respelt version *nigga*) by one black person referring to another, perhaps as a deliberate reclamation of the term by those who have suffered from it. Various phrases based on it, such as *nigger in the woodpile* and *work like a nigger*, have largely fallen out of use in ordinary language except in historical contexts.

nimby, an acronym for 'not in my back yard', was first used in the 1980s to refer to people who objected to the siting of something unpleasant or unwanted in their own neighbourhood, without being opposed to its introduction in principle (as long as it was located somewhere else). The word, unlike others of the same kind, has endured. It is most often spelt all in lower case.

nineties see EIGHTIES.

no. 1 *No* is used (1) as an adjective or (in the terminology of some linguists) negative determiner, with both singular and plural nouns, as in *no house* / *no children* / and *no food*, (2) as an adverb, as in *They were no wiser*, (3) as an interjection, as in '*Did you hear that?*' '*No, I didn't.*', and (4) as a noun (with plural *noes*), meaning 'a denial' or 'a vote of no', as in *We won't take no for an answer* and *The noes have it* (meaning a parliamentary motion has been defeated).
It is not often realized that there are two words involved here: the first meaning

comes from a Middle English word related to *none*, while the other meanings are of Old English origin.

2 In the first meaning, *no* can be used to form a negative statement instead of *not*, e.g. *There are no wasps at this time of year* instead of *There aren't any wasps at this time of year*. But note the difference in implication between *He is not a teacher* (= he is something other than a teacher) and *He is no teacher* (= he is not suited to be a teacher).

3 The idiom *whether or no* is an established though now somewhat dated alternative for *whether or not*, and tends to be found in the pages of romantic fiction: *For whether or no she had been instrumental in the making of that despicable will, it was her presence here that had caused it to be made*—E. Bailey, 1993.

nobody, no one. Like *anybody* and *anyone*, these are largely interchangeable, but *no one* is written as two words because *noone* would be too awkward. In a use such as *No one person was responsible*, *no* and *one* retain their separate meanings instead of jointly forming a pronoun. Note that a possessive word referring back to *no one* (pronoun) is often a plural one: *No one likes to have their word doubted*: *see* GENDER-NEUTRALITY.

no-brainer has been used since the 1970s as an informal term meaning 'an idea or choice that involves hardly any mental effort': *If this was the first Christmas it would be a no-brainer as to what the three kings would turn up with at the manger. Forget the gold, frankincense and myrrh. It would be iPods, Play Stations and MP3s, or similar technomiracles*—Irish News, 2006.

noisome means 'harmful, noxious' and has nothing to do with the word *noise*. It comes from a Middle English word *nay*, related to *annoy*: *The harm will persist long after Blair is no more than a noisome fish head in the dustbin of history*—Scotland on Sunday, 2005.

nom de plume, pseudonym. A *nom de plume* (also in translated form *pen name*) is a name assumed by an author to appear on the title page of a book; a *pseudonym* is a name assumed more generally although this too is normally applied in authorial contexts. The most widely used of all three to refer to authors' assumed names is *pen name* (unhyphenated).

nominative is a grammatical term denoting a noun or pronoun that is the subject of a verb or sentence, e.g. *house* in *The house stood on a hill*. See CASES.

non- is a prefix that makes negative forms (usually with a hyphen) of nouns and adjectives (mainly), e.g. *non-aggression*, *non-alcoholic*, *non-event*, *non-union*, and *non-violent*. In another more recent type *non-* is added to a verb to form a word meaning 'that does not—', e.g. *non-iron*, *non-skid*. *Non-* is regularly used to form adjectives that are neutral in meaning when a form in *un-* or *in-* also exists with a special (normally unfavourable) meaning, as with *non-professional* (= not professional in status) as distinct from *unprofessional* (= not conforming to professional standards); others of this type include *non-effective*, *non-essential*, *non-human*, *non-natural*, and *non-scientific*.

nonchalance, nonchalant. These are pronounced as English words, i.e. **non**-chuh-luhns and **non**-chuh-luhnt.

non-count nouns *see* COUNTABLE NOUNS.

none, which is not a shortening of *no one* but a descendant of an Old English pronoun, may be followed by a singular or a plural verb, depending on the sense. When individuality is being emphasized, or when *none* refers to something that cannot be plural, a singular form is used: *A fear which we cannot know, which we cannot face, which none understands*—T. S. Eliot, 1935 / *She is rather difficult to describe physically, for none of her features is particularly striking*—David Lodge, 1962 / *None of this was a matter of treachery*—P. Wright, 1987 / *It was afternoon, a quiet time—none of the other tables was occupied and he heard no sound from inside the bar*—B. Unsworth, 1996. When collectivity is the dominant notion, a plural form is used: *Though she had many affairs, none were lighthearted romances*—New Yorker, 1987 / *None of these situations exist here*—Independent, 2003.

nonetheless see NEVERTHELESS.

non-flammable see FLAMMABLE.

nonpareil, meaning 'something or someone unrivalled or unique', is pronounced non-puh-**rayl**, although other pronunciations are also heard.

nonplus, meaning 'to perplex', has inflected forms *nonplussed* and in AmE also *nonplused*. In a recent development, *nonplussed* has come to mean 'unperturbed' (*'Out of power?' asked McCoy, trying to appear nonplussed*—D. Kramer-Rolls, AmE 1990), the very opposite of the accepted meaning, probably by association with the prefix *non-*, which implies a negative meaning.

nonsense. Uses of *nonsense* as a countable noun (i.e. preceded by *a* or in the plural) have become common in current use, especially in BrE: *I knew you'd make a nonsense of it so I told Wallis to be ready to take over*—L. Cooper, 1960 / *I could only pray that the pathologist wouldn't come up with a time of death that made a nonsense of the alibi I was handing him*—V. McDermid, 1992.

non sequitur, meaning 'a conclusion that does not logically follow from the stated premise or argument', is now normally printed in roman type.

non-U see U AND NON-U.

non-white. Despite objections of cultural bias in assuming that 'white' is somehow normal and 'non-white' a departure from it, this is a standard term when general reference is needed.

no one see NOBODY.

no place, meaning 'nowhere', is still largely confined to AmE: *You're going no place until Herb gets here*—M. Pugh, 1969. It is sometimes written as one word.

no problem is recorded from the 1960s as an informal reply of assurance. The English playwright John Osborne missed the point (perhaps deliberately) when he wrote two years before his death: *Last week, on doctor's orders, I telephoned a pathology factory to organise a blood test. 'No problem.' How can they possibly know until I've had it? But I do hope they're right*—Spectator, 1992. It was the organization of the blood test, and not its outcome, that (at that stage at least) presented no problem, idiomatically if not actually. Many people object to its use instead of the more traditional *thank you*; it is best avoided in any kind of formal or business situation.

nor. 1 For the use of *nor* after *neither*, see NEITHER. Note that *nor* can be repeated to introduce a third or further item: *The comment that receives the heartiest agreement concerns neither the war, nor the earthquake, nor the crime rate*—Observer Magazine, 1992.

2 *Nor* is sometimes used when there is no negative present or implied in the preceding clause: *Horned head-dresses have been found but they belonged to an* *earlier period. Nor did Viking warriors have decorated shields*—*Independent*, 1998.

normality, normalcy. In BrE *normality* is the usual word, and *normalcy* is regarded with disfavour although both words date from about the same time (mid-19c): *The morning passed slowly, uneventfully, and with a beguiling normality*—Anita Brookner, 1989. In AmE and in some other varieties, both words are used with about equal frequency: *. . . partly in order to tidy up, tidy the room and return it to normalcy*—Anita Desai, IndE 1988.

north, northern, northerly *see* EAST.

northward, northwards. The only form for the adjective is *northward* (*in a northward direction*), but *northward* and *northwards* are both used for the adverb, with a preference for *northwards* in BrE: *The advancing Allied armies . . . forced themselves northwards from the toe of Italy*—R. Perry, 1979 / *Hope extended these wings northwards to meet his new gallery, an imposing space which was tripartite in plan*—*Apollo* (magazine), 2004.

nosy, meaning 'inquisitive', is spelt this way in preference to *nosey*.

not. 1 *Not* is used to form negative statements and questions, and is attached both to individual words and to whole clauses by means of their verbs, normally requiring the use of an auxiliary verb such as *do* or *have*: *We do not want to go* / *not usually* / *Not another one!* For the use of *not* with so-called 'modal' verbs such as *can, may*, and 'semi-modals' such as *dare* and *need*, see MODAL VERB.

2 *not* **with** *only*. Fowler (1926), in one of his more colourful images, wrote

that '*not only* out of its place is like a tintack loose on the floor; it might have been most serviceable somewhere else, and is capable of giving acute pain where it is'. It is important to keep *not only* attached to the item to which it relates, so that in the sentence *Katherine's marriage not only kept her away, but at least two of Mr. March's cousins* (C. P. Snow), a stress on *her* will clarify the meaning in speech, but in writing the sentence needs to be rewritten as *Katherine's marriage kept not only her away, but . . .* When *not only* is followed by *but also* (or sometimes just *but*), the placing of the two elements again needs to be correctly balanced: *Those who can not only read and count, but can operate data processing machines as well . . . are said to be 'computerate'*—*Times*, 1981 (the second *can* is strictly redundant) / *On January 25, 1959,* [Pope] *John announced not only the convening of the Council but also a synod for the diocese of Rome*—P. Hebblethwaite, 1984 / *I am beginning to come to the opinion that not only is Dylan the best DJ on the planet right now, but also that this might even be the crowning finale to his career*—*Independent on Sunday*, 2007 (better word order in the first part would be . . . *the opinion not only that Dylan is . . .*). In the following example, the positioning is so seriously awry as to be distracting: *At present, businessmen are allowed to pass along to customers not only their increases in costs, but also to tack on their standard profit margins*—*Time*, 1972 (the correct order is . . . *are allowed not only to pass along to customers . . .*).

3 *not* **with an infinitive.** The usual position of *not* when attached to a *to*-infinitive is before the *to*: *He promised not to do it again* / *She tried not to think about it any more*. Occasionally, and usually for a strong negative effect, *not* splits the infinitive, but this should be regarded as a literary device best avoided in normal writing and speech where the effect is more awkward: *My advice to any woman who earns the reputation of being capable, is to not demonstrate her ability too much*—Muriel Spark, 1988.

4 *not* in the type *not ungrateful, not unnoticed*, etc. This device, known as *meiosis, is very common in English and even Fowler (1926), although he disliked it, recognized that it was well established: *The presence of one of the . . . vans in the area had not passed unnoticed by the alert crew of a Berkshire County Police wireless prowl car*—N. Lucas, 1967. Note that this type, with the second word positive in form and only negative in implication, is not the same as an explicit double negative, such as *They didn't notice nothing*, which is regarded as non-standard.

5 *not* repeated in a subordinate clause. *I shouldn't wonder if it didn't turn to snow.* This type, in which *not* is wrongly placed in a subordinate clause as a mere echo of a negative in the main clause, should be avoided, although it is sometimes heard in informal speech. The correct form is *I shouldn't wonder if it turned to snow.* Sometimes the extra *not* results from the writer losing track of the grammar: *It is hard not to conclude that there was not a cynical and calculating element to the performance*—*Independent*, 2006 (read: *. . . that there was a cynical and calculating element . . .*).

noticeable is spelt with an *e* in the middle.

nought *see* NAUGHT. In expressing the figure nought out loud in a sequence of digits, BrE normally uses 'o' (as if it were the letter) whereas in AmE 'zero' is more usual.

noun. A noun is a word that names a person or thing. Common nouns name persons or things which are not peculiar to one example, i.e. are of a general nature (*bridge, girl, sugar, unhappiness*), whereas proper nouns name persons or things of which there is only one example (*Asia, Concorde, Dickens*). Concrete nouns refer to physical things (*bread, woman*), and abstract nouns to concepts (*greed, unhelpfulness*). Some nouns are concrete and abstract in different meanings, e.g. *cheek* is concrete when it refers to part of the face and abstract when it means 'impertinence'.

noun and verb differences. *See box opposite.*

no way. *He said he wouldn't start up a gang today—no way.*—*New Yorker*, 1975. This 20c Americanism (a shortening of *in no way* or *there is no way*) is now common in casual BrE speech, although its transatlantic origin is always near the surface: *I wrote back and said no way did I think that she ought to go into the unit*—D. Coulby et al., 1987 / *No way did I think he'd split the vote*—*Flak Magazine*, 2004. An intermediate stage can be seen in the fuller form *there is no way (that) . . .*: *The Doctor realises that there is no way the two teachers could have achieved all this*—J. Bentham, 1986.

nth. The popularized extension of the expression *to the nth degree* from the language of mathematics to general usage in the meaning 'to the utmost' has continued despite Fowler's disapproval of it (1926): *Leonard could be fastidious to the nth degree in completing his own work—he has always said that he works 'one word at a time'*—L. S. Dorman et al., 1990.

nubile. The original Latin meaning of *nubilis*, '(of females) of an age suitable for marriage', has given way in current usage to the meaning 'sexually attractive', making the earlier sense somewhat awkward to use, except with intentional ambiguity.

NOUN AND VERB DIFFERENCES.

The following table lists differences of stress, pronunciation, and spelling when
the same word is used as a noun and a verb, for example *compound, escort,
practice/practise, record*, and *use*. Differences are marked by the letters s
(= difference of stress, normally first syllable for the noun and second for the
verb), p (= pronunciation, e.g. between yoos and yooz for the noun and verb
use), and sp (= spelling, e.g. between *belief* and *believe*).

noun	verb	difference
abuse	abuse	p
accent	accent	s
advice	advise	sp
bath	bathe	sp
belief	believe	sp
breath	breathe	sp
calf	calve	sp
close	close	p
cloth	clothe	sp
commune	commune	s
compound	compound	s
concert	concert	s
conduct	conduct	s
conflict	conflict	s
conscript	conscript	s
consort	consort	s
contest	contest	s
contract	contract	s
contrast	contrast	s
convert	convert	s
convict	convict	s
decrease	decrease	s
defect	defect	s
dictate	dictate	s
digest	digest	s
discord	discord	s
discount	discount	s
discourse	discourse	s
escort	escort	s
excuse	excuse	p
export	export	s
extract	extract	s
ferment	ferment	s
grief	grieve	sp
half	halve	sp
house	house	p
import	import	s
imprint	imprint	s
incline	incline	s

increase	increase	s
indent	indent	s
inlay	inlay	s
insert	insert	s
insult	insult	s
licence	license	sp
life	live	sp
loss	lose	sp
misuse	misuse	p
mouth	mouth	p
practice	practise	sp
produce	produce	s
proof	prove	sp
record	record	s
reject	reject	s
relief	relieve	sp
sheath	sheathe	sp
shelf	shelve	sp
strife	strive	sp
suspect	suspect	s
teeth	teethe	sp
thief	thieve	sp
transfer	transfer	s
use	use	p
wreath	wreathe	sp

nuclear should be pronounced **nyook-li-uh**, and not as if it were spelt *nucular*, although this is occasionally heard, especially in AmE (famously by President Eisenhower in the 1950s, and more recently by George W. Bush).

nucleus has the plural form *nuclei*, pronounced **nyook**-li-iy.

number is a grammatical term denoting the status of words as singular or plural. *See* AGREEMENT.

number of. The expression *a number of* + plural noun, as in *a number of people*, normally takes a plural verb in both BrE and AmE, because the plural noun is regarded as the 'head' of the noun phrase and therefore as the real subject: *There have been a number of changes since the school went into special*

measures—Bolton Evening News, 2004. By contrast, the expression *the number of* + plural noun, in which the head of the phrase is *number* and not the noun, takes a singular verb: *As the number of people in the water rises, so do the odds that attacks will occur—Business Week Magazine*, 2001.

numeracy, a term denoting competence with basic mathematical concepts, was coined in 1959 on the analogy of *literacy* by a UK committee on education reporting in that year. The corresponding adjective is *numerate*.

numerals. In general, numerals are used in more factual or statistical contexts and words are used (especially with numbers under a hundred) in more descriptive material: *I have lived in the* *same house for twelve years / The survey covers a period of 12 years*. Words are used in idiomatic expressions such as *I must have told you a hundred times / Thousands of people swarmed through the gates*. Separate objects, animals, ships, persons, etc., are not units of measurement unless they are treated statistically: *The peasant had only four cows / A farm with 40 head of cattle*. With numerals consisting of four or more figures, commas should be used to divide off the thousands, e.g. *3,096 / 10,731*. In specifying ranges of numbers, use the least number of figures possible, e.g. *13-14 / 31-4 / 1923-6*. But dates BC should be written in full: *432-431* BC (since *432-31* BC and *432-1* BC *represent different ranges*). More detailed information will be found in *New Hart's Rules*.

nursling is the preferred spelling, not *nurseling*.

-o. See box opposite.

O, Oh. The recommended practice is to use *O* when a name being addressed or invoked follows (*O Death, where is thy sting?*) and *Oh* as an independent exclamation (*Oh, how do you know that?*).

oaf has the plural form *oafs*.

oasis, pronounced oh-**ay**-sis, has the plural form *oases*, pronounced oh-**ay**-seez.

obeisance means 'homage, submission', and is pronounced oh-**bay**-suhns.

object *verb*. The stress is on the second syllable (uhb-**jekt**), and the word is often followed by *to* + noun (which can also be a verbal noun): *Would the lady object to my lighting a pair of candles?*—Dickens, 1865 / *He also objected strongly to what he called your jack-boot methods when you interviewed Mrs Hurd*—R. Simons, 1968 / *I have never smoked and I object to being poisoned by other people's indulgence*—*Liverpool Echo*, 1993. The same construction is used with the noun *objection*: *We have no objection at all to helping in what she calls her 'psychological warfare'*—M. Babson, 1974.

objective genitive. An example of this is *the boy's murder*, in which the genitive form *boy's* denotes not possession (as in *the boy's dog*, which is the usual function of a genitive) but the object of the noun *murder*.

objector is the preferred spelling for 'someone who objects', not *objecter*.

oblique. The oblique stroke (/) in print or writing is used between alternatives (e.g. *and/or*), in fractions (e.g. *3/4*), in ratios (e.g. *miles/day*), in Internet addresses (http://public.oed.com/whats-new/), and to show the line breaks of the original when successive lines of poetry are run on as a single line ('Whose woods these are / I think I know, / His house is in the village, though.). *Oblique* is a BrE term for what is also called a *slash, forward slash*, or in editing and printing a *solidus*.

oblivious. The historical meaning of *oblivious* is 'forgetful, unmindful', followed by *of*: *Never before … has a great painter been completely oblivious of the style, or styles, of his time*—Kenneth Clark, 1949. This meaning survives, but another meaning, 'unaware of, unconscious of', which evolved during the 19c, is now more common, despite objections to it raised by Fowler (1926) and earlier by the *OED* editors, who labelled it 'erroneous'; this was changed to 'formerly regarded as erroneous', and the current online text reads 'now the usual sense'. In this meaning it is followed by *of* or (more often) *to*: *I stayed indoors all day for several days, oblivious to the damp heat of Falmouth*—C. Day Lewis, 1960.

oboe has the plural form *oboes*, and the player is an *oboist*, pronounced **oh**-boh-ist.

obscene. During the 20c repeated attempts were made to define the meaning

-o.

1 Plurals of nouns ending in -*o* cause difficulty in English because there are few convenient rules for choosing between -*os* (as in *ratios*) and -*oes* (as in *heroes*). What rules there are can be briefly summarized:

a When a vowel (usually *i* or *e*) precedes the final -*o*, the plural is normally -*os* (*trios*, *videos*), probably because of the bizarre look of -*ioes* etc.

b Names of animals and plants normally form plurals in -*oes* (*buffaloes*, *tomatoes*).

c Words that are shortenings of other words invariably form plurals in -*os* (*demos*, *hippos*). The same applies to fanciful extensions such as *saddo* (plural *saddos*).

d Alien-looking words and comparatively recent loanwords form plurals in -*os* (*boleros*, *placebos*).

e Multi-syllable words tend to form plurals in -*os* (*generalissimos*, *manifestos*).

f Proper names used allusively form plurals in -*os* (*Neros*, *Romeos*).

2 In other cases, practice varies from one house style to another, and the table below gives a consensus of informed usage.

singular	plural
alto	altos
banjo	banjos
buffalo	buffaloes
cargo	cargoes
casino	casinos
concerto	concertos *or* concerti
contralto	contraltos
do	dos *or* do's
dodo	dodos
domino	dominoes
dynamo	dynamos
echo	echoes
ego	egos
embargo	embargoes
fiasco	fiascos
flamingo	flamingos
fresco	frescos
gigolo	gigolos
go	goes
grotto	grottoes
hairdo	hairdos
halo	haloes
hero	heroes
hippo	hippos
innuendo	innuendoes
kilo	kilos
libretto	librettos

o

mango	mangoes
manifesto	manifestos
memento	mementoes
memo	memos
mosquito	mosquitoes
motto	mottoes
Negro	Negroes
no	noes
peccadillo	peccadilloes
photo	photos
piano	pianos
piccolo	piccolos
potato	potatoes
proviso	provisos
radio	radios
rhino	rhinos, or (collective) rhino
salvo (= firing of guns)	salvoes
silo	silos
solo	solos
soprano	sopranos
stiletto	stilettos
tiro	tiros
tobacco	tobaccos
tomato	tomatoes
torpedo	torpedoes
verso	versos
veto	vetoes
volcano	volcanoes
zero	zeros

and implications of obscenity in relation to literature, the performing arts, and (above all) the cinema. Meanwhile, the word *obscene* gathered strength in its other main meaning, 'highly offensive or repugnant', as a moral condemnation of social circumstances such as poverty and wealth, violence, human exploitation, etc. It was originally criticized—see the second example below—as an invalid new meaning (though Shakespeare first used it in its figurative sense), but has settled down as a standard, if somewhat journalistic, way of qualifying nouns to do with pay and salaries: *Something in the very robustness of*

Germany's economy seemed to the terrorists and their sympathizers profoundly obscene—Time, 1977 / *The idea of these old women being walled up and told what to do by a superstitious parson was* (Tibba allowed herself the modernism) *obscene*—A. N. Wilson, 1982 / *His pay was branded 'utterly obscene' amid calls for him to quit and drop his name from the company*—Daily Mirror, 1992.

observance, observation. These two words correspond to different branches in meaning of the verb *observe* ('to see or notice' and 'to follow or adhere to'). *Observance* is the word normally used in connection with respecting rules, carrying out duties and obligations, and performing formal customs and rituals, whereas *observation* is the equivalent in the more physical senses of seeing and perceiving, has the special countable meaning 'a remark or comment', and is used in special combinations such as *observation car* (on a train, chiefly AmE) and (military) *observation post*. Examples: *To act on or defy a socially established rule has effects on all who benefit or suffer by its observance*—A. C. Graham, 1985 / *Edinburgh can offer ethnically-based social facilities and opportunities for meetings for several forms of non-Christian religious observance*—undergraduate prospectus, 1993 / *I didn't try to go into details on the phone, but said that we were going to need some police observation*—J. R. L. Anderson, 1980 / *The playgroup leader will usually offer her observations as part of the parents' contribution to the Statement*—W. Swann et al., 1992.

obsess has been used since the 16c as a transitive verb, often in the passive with *obsessed* as a quasi-adjective: *Modern society is obsessed with romanticizing ancient societies*—*Times*, 1980. In the later part of the 20c a new intransitive use emerged, first in AmE and later in BrE, in which *obsess* means 'to be preoccupied or unduly worried (about something)' and is usually followed by *about* or *over*: *The only way to go about judging your work is not to obsess too much over it*—*Times*, 1998.

obsolete, obsolescent. Both words are derived from Latin *obsolescere* meaning 'to fall into disuse'. Something (either physical, such as a piece of machinery, or conceptual, such as a custom or idea) is *obsolete* when it is outdated and no longer used. It is *obsolescent* when it is falling out of use, i.e. is becoming obsolete but is not yet actually so.

obtain is a formal and often pretentious word, and no one should be afraid of using the perfectly respectable word *get* in most contexts.

occasion. When it means 'reason, grounds', the usual construction is with *for* + noun (or verbal noun) or, more rarely, with a *to*-infinitive: *Yesterday was Schubert's birthday ... suitable occasion for a Schubertiad*—*Times*, 1977 / *His demise was then made an occasion for executing the real earl of Warwick*—John Guy, 2000 / *The issue in this Court having been formulated and argued as it was, there is no occasion to consider any wider question about the construction and application of the proviso*—OEC, 2005. When the meaning is 'opportunity', often in the slightly formal phrases *to have / give / find occasion*, and in *take the occasion* it is followed by a *to*-infinitive: *I have had occasion recently to re-read Goethe's Theory of Colours*—*Nature*, 1971 / *These challenges kept us on the alert and gave occasion to educate a new generation of students and of young faculty*—*Academe*, 2000.

occur has inflected forms *occurred*, *occurring*, and the noun derivative is *occurrence* (with two *r*s, often misspelt).

occurrence. In BrE the stressed second syllable is pronounced like the first syllable of *current*. In AmE the stressed syllable is the same as that for *occur*, a pronunciation which is occasionally also heard in BrE.

octopus has the plural form *octopuses*. The pseudo-Latin form *octopi*, except when used jokingly, is misconceived, since the Greek stem is *octopod-* (which would produce in English the form *octopodes*, which has never established itself).

-odd. The hyphen is important in phrases such as *twenty-odd people* (= roughly twenty), to make it clear that we are talking about roughly twenty people, not a score of eccentrics.

odour, a slightly genteel word for 'smell', is spelt *-our* in BrE and *odor* in AmE. The corresponding adjective is *odorous* in both varieties.

oe-, e-. There is a tendency to simplify spellings with *-oe-* in BrE to *-e-* in AmE, e.g. *estrogen* for *oestrogen* and *ameba* for *amoeba*, but both types are used.

-oes (forming plurals of nouns) *see* -o.

of. 1 The preposition *of* is one of the key words in structuring phrases and sentences in English, and it is sometimes possible to make a slip in usage that can give the wrong meaning. Various problems associated with its use occur in extended sentences and consist of either adding an *of* where it is unnecessary (or where another preposition is called for) or leaving out an *of* that is needed to clarify the sense. This entry deals with these topics with examples taken from a wide range of sources.

2 Incorrect insertion of *of* usually happens at a point in a long sentence where it is meant to refer back to an earlier part but is the wrong choice, influenced by another *of* close by which has nothing to do with it: *He will be in the best possible position for getting the most out of the land and of using it to the best possible advantage* (the preposition wanted is *for* not *of*). In other cases, a repeated *of* is not incorrect but redundant: *A series of problem contracts and of bad debts does not explain the situation / On the one hand there are the conventional rules of good manners and of correct behaviour.*

3 The other principal mistake consists in leaving out an *of* when it is essential to convey the meaning intended: *The*

banning of meetings and the printing and distribution of leaflets stopped the agitation* (*of* should be put in before *the printing* to show that ban applies to everything that follows). Similarly, in *He has mapped the development of the animal's nervous system and of its behaviour*, the repeated *of* is necessary to show that *development* refers also to *behaviour*.

4 The word *of* should also be repeated in constructions with *both* when the position of the latter requires a balanced sequence: *There are teachers with low standards who think a mere pass at whatever grade is a feather in the cap both of themselves and of their pupils* (alternatively, one could put . . . *a feather in the cap of both themselves and their pupils*, but in this case the result would be awkward).

5 The informal type *of an evening, of a Sunday afternoon*, etc. (*All the intellect of the place assembled of an evening*— Carlyle, 1831), is beginning to sound literary or archaic, except in dialect use. In AmE, this type is often expressed in the form *evenings, Sunday afternoons*, etc., without any preposition (*She plays cards Thursdays*).

of course has a useful role as a term of insistence meaning 'as was to be expected', in which the hearer's or reader's prior knowledge or agreement can reasonably be assumed. Fowler (1926) rightly urged caution in the use of the phrase 'as the herald of an out-of-the-way fact that one has just unearthed', e.g. *Milton of course had the idea from Tacitus.* Some modern examples of *of course* signalling superior knowledge on the part of the writer or an unjustified assumption are: *Of course, there are a number of other phenomena, such as lightning and reflections of sunlight off tumbling satellites and orbiting debris, that can also give flashes in the sky*— Stephen Hawking, 1988 / *We were* *approached by Tom Lloyd, a young so-licitor from Carmarthen with a passion for historic buildings—particularly, of course, those of Wales*—M. Binney et al., 1991 / *He is a clear writer but not inspired enough to get away with generalisations like 'of course sublimation of sexual urges played a huge part in Ford's drive'*—Scotland on Sunday, 2003.

offence. This is spelt *-ence* in BrE, and *offense* in AmE.

offer. The verb has inflected forms *offered, offering*.

official, officious. The main meanings of *official* are 'in the nature of an office' (*Their official duties*) and 'authorized or confirmed by someone in authority' (*The official attendance was over 10,000*). By contrast, *officious* is a judgemental word meaning 'asserting authority aggressively or intrusively', and is most commonly used of a person or the actions of a person: *Officious meter maids checking overparked cars*—L. Egan, 1977 / *He plays the officious, incompetent manager of a dilapidated Irish railway station who comes up against gunrunners*—Guardian, 2005.

officialese. The term is first recorded in 1884 and was used by Sir Ernest Gowers (1965) as the heading of an article that explored the 'style of writing marked by peculiarities supposed to be characteristic of officials', i.e. pompous and opaque bureaucratic language. (Fowler had no entry on this topic in 1926.) An example given by Gowers concerned Anglo-American talks on the development of folding-wing aircraft, and was taken from a London evening newspaper: *The object of this visit is a pooling of knowledge to explore further the possibility of a joint research effort to discover the practicability of making use of this principle to meet a possible future NATO requirement, and should be viewed in the general context of interdependence*. It is laughably apparent at a glance that it has features typically found in official writing even today, particularly in EU writing, such as the use of verbal nouns (*a pooling*) instead of simple verbs, long-winded abstract nouns (*practicability*), and so on. Gowers condensed these 47 bloated words into a slimline phrase with a mere 16: *This visit is to find out whether we can, together, develop the folding wing for NATO*. He distinguished this kind of language, characterized by verbosity and circumlocution, from *legalese*, which though sometimes equally difficult to understand is characterized by concision and is dictated by the need to ensure that what is said will stand up to challenge and scrutiny in courts of law. *See further at* LEGALESE; PLAIN ENGLISH.

officious *see* OFFICIAL.

off of. This complex preposition is found in Shakespeare (*A* [*= I*] *fall off of a tree*—2 Henry VI II.i.98), and occurs in colloquial speech in AmE: *The night Wayne came at Randolph with a hammer to pull him off of Mary*—M. Golden, 1989. It is, however, non-standard in current British English.

offset. The verb means 'to counterbalance' or 'to compensate for' and apart from a couple of technical uses has had a limited range until recently. Now, with climate change in everyone's thoughts, it has taken on a new lease of life as the word that eases the conscience regarding carbon emissions caused by environmentally unfriendly activities: *Whitehall has adopted the fashionable habit of carbon offsetting—effectively paying penance for the contribution made by transatlantic flights, hotel air conditioning and cars to wrecking the ozone layer. Tree planting schemes are a particular favourite*—Observer, 2005.

The corresponding compound noun is *carbon offset*.

offspring, meaning 'a person's or animal's child or young', has the same form in the plural: *A person is a Jew if he or she is the offspring of a Jewish mother or has been converted to the Jewish faith*—J. R. Baker, 1974 / *So these offspring shared in the eventually growing prosperity . . . of the region*—E. Gellner, 1983. Although the form *offsprings* was used historically as a plural, it will nowadays be considered a mistake, as will hyphenated *off-spring*.

often. In current English this is more usually pronounced with the *t* silent, but pronunciation with the *t* is not uncommon. The comparative forms *oftener* and *oftenest* are permissible, although *more often* and *most often* are more commonly used.

OK. Despite the existence of many competing theories about the origins of this word, it has now been pretty conclusively established in 1839 by a journalist as a humorous rendering of the initial letters of the American dialect form *orl korrect* (= all correct). It rapidly acquired historical associations that gave it wider currency but do not constitute its true origin (e.g. as an election slogan of 'Old Kinderhook' (Martin Van Buren), the Democratic presidential candidate in 1840). No longer regarded as an Americanism, it is possibly the only English word that is universally recognized by speakers of other languages throughout the world. The alternative form *okay* is especially useful as a verb (= to say OK to, to authorize), allowing more comfortable inflected forms (*okays, okayed, okaying*) than *OK* does.

older, oldest *see* ELDER, ELDEST.

Olympiad, Olympian, Olympic. An *Olympiad* is an old term for a period of four years between Olympic Games (used principally in ancient dating), and a particular celebration of the modern (or ancient) Olympic Games. *Olympian* as an adjective generally refers to Mount Olympus and to the gods of Olympus, but as a noun it is now standard to refer to a contestant in the modern Olympic Games. *Olympic* is used principally of the games of ancient times and their modern revival; these are called *Olympic Games* or (for the modern games) *Olympics*.

omelette is the usual spelling in BrE, whereas *omelet* is more common in AmE.

omit has inflected forms *omitted*, *omitting*.

on. In AmE, *on* is idiomatic in two uses in which BrE traditionally uses a different preposition: *My father . . . had a dry-goods store on Gesia Street*—I. B. Singer, 1983 (BrE *in*) / *On weekends she would play disk jockey like that for hours*—*New Yorker*, 1987 (BrE *at*).

on account of *see* ACCOUNT.

onboard, on-board, on board. Which to use depends on the meaning. Talking about ship or plane passengers, you could write *on board*: *the plane crashed with twenty people on board*. You also write *on board* in non-literal phrases like *to take something on board* and *to bring someone on board*. In those examples, *on board* is an adverbial phrase. Dictionaries suggest writing *onboard* as a single word (or you can choose to write it with a hyphen, but you will be in the minority) when it is an adjective, for example referring to equipment or computers fitted into a car, boat, plane or other vehicle: *onboard DVD players for the kids*. It is worth noting, however, that, possibly as a result of *online* being generally written as one word, *onboard* is far more often written that way even in the cases where it is suggested above that it should be two. Perhaps dictionaries have some catching up to do, which would make *onboard* parallel with *online*. Examples: (adjectival) *He read in the onboard sensors that the ship was swinging back around for another pass* / *She just caught me by the collar as I was sinking along with the ship and she hauled me on board*; (adverbial, not recognized by dictionaries) *Some 220 passengers were onboard at the time* / *When a major brings him onboard and gives him room to work, watch out.*

-on-demand. *On demand* has been in use for many years to denote something that is available to those who want it when they want it, and in recent years has been used notably in the context of abortion (*He proved himself out of touch over the economy and by opposing abortion on demand*—Today, 1992). Its consolidation into a combining form has burgeoned in the context of the telecommunications industry, where we have *video-on-demand, listen-on-demand, news-on-demand*, etc.

one. 1 When the phrase *one of those who . . .* is used, it is normal to follow it with a plural verb (regarding *those* rather than *one* as the antecedent), except when particular emphasis is being placed on the individuality of *one*, in which case a singular verb is called for. The *OEC* data suggests that the singular construction is rather more often used: (plural verb) *She was one of those women who make an enchanted garden of their childhood memories*—Anita Brookner, 1990 / (singular verb) '*Don't you think,' said Bernard, 'that Hawaii is one of those places that was always better in the past?*'—David Lodge, 1991.

2 The use of *one* to mean 'any person', 'I', or 'me' is often regarded as an affectation, although English does not always have a ready alternative. It is probably true to say that the more *one* is associated with 'I' or 'me', the greater the affectation: *This performance commanded attention; at times . . . it brought one's blood to a boil*—Chicago Tribune, 1988. When it genuinely means 'any person' (including only incidentally the speaker), it seems a good deal more natural: *You must realize that there are risks that one doesn't take*—Nadine Gordimer, 1987. When *one* is used in this way there is a difference between BrE and AmE usage when the sentence is continued with a further pronoun having the same reference. In AmE *one* is followed either by another *one* (or *one's*) or by a third-person pronoun *he* or *she* (or, to avoid gender problems, occasionally *they*), or by *his* or *her* or *their*, whereas in BrE another *one* (or *one's*) always follows: (AmE) *I like to believe one can be honest and sincere and committed in what he's doing*—Chicago Sun-Times, 1988 / (BrE) *If one has no base on which to formulate probing questions, can one actually give informed consent?*—Dædalus, 1986.

one another *see* EACH 3.

ongoing. First recorded in 1877, this adjective gained such widespread currency in the 1950s and later that it quickly attracted criticism as a vogue word, and, especially in the phrase *ongoing situation*, as a cliché on a par with *at the end of the day* and *in this day and age*. Other combinations, such as *ongoing operation, ongoing process*, and *ongoing relationship*, are more acceptable: *He says he wouldn't have got anywhere without Move On, who helped him secure a flat and are now giving vital, ongoing support*—Big Issue, 1998.

online, on-line, on line. When referring to computing and the Internet, how should this be written? The simplest solution is to write it as one word whether it is an adjective (*online banking, community, game, service, shopping*, etc. / *the article is online*) or an adverb (*shoppers would rather pick up the phone than do business online* / *apply, chat, shop, vote*, etc. *online* / *available, popular, published*, etc. *online*). This is the style that *ODO* endorses. As an adjective, it should never be written as separate words. To complicate matters, as an adverb, however, there is justification for doing so, since it can be viewed as an adverbial phrase no different from e.g. *in line, on time, in full*, etc. Some people prefer to write it this way (e.g. *People who can't tell what the vegetables are in their box can look them up on line*), but most people write it as one word. Apart from uses in the digital sphere, the phrase also appears in collocations such as *bring / come / get on line*, meaning to come or be put into operation, e.g. *EKPC plans to get all the generators on line this summer*. *ODO* and some other dictionaries write this use also as a single word, but you are free to write it as two in order to keep it separate from the digital meaning. In any event, the hyphenated form *on-line* is to be discouraged for both parts of speech, in line with the trend to avoid hyphenation when not strictly necessary.

only. The position of *only* is one of the major unresolved topics of discussion in English usage. The upshot is that logical position, i.e. association with the word to which *only* most closely refers, is not always consistent with naturalness, which generally favours a position between the subject and the verb. Fowler (1926), in a long article on the subject, made a case for allowing 'illogical' positioning in a sentence such as *He only died a week ago*, which is a great deal more natural and stylistically satisfactory than *He died only a week ago*. Equally acceptable are the following examples of actual usage: *I was…made to attend a Catholic businessman's luncheon (where I only got wine by roaring for it)*—Evelyn Waugh, 1958 / *Those days, you only applied to one college*—New Yorker, 1986 / *He says he only took the job because the neon sign always cheered him up*—Julian Barnes, 1991 / *I only wanted to work with vocalists*—BBC Popular Music Reviews, 2004 [*OEC*]. In written English, the logical position of *only* should be respected when serious (rather than notional or theoretical) ambiguity would otherwise result, especially in contexts such as legal language in which precision is more important than a pleasing style: *The public interest is properly served only where companies pursue the traditional goal of profit maximization*—J. E. Parkinson, 1993. In general usage, the most natural position of *only* is where it always has been, between the subject and its verb, and invariable insistence on logical position sacrifices naturalness to pedantry.

on to, onto. *On to* is recorded in continuous use as a complex preposition from the late 16c, and the one-word form *onto* from the early 18c. In modern use both forms are found; *onto* has become more common in recent years but has still not achieved the dominance enjoyed by *into* (which goes back to Old English): *French windows opened from the breakfast-room on to the terrace and large walled garden*—Penelope Lively, 1981 / *The blue sky threw its light down onto the fields below*—L. Norfolk, 1991. Note that in some uses *on* is used as a full adverb and needs to be spelt separately: *They drove onto the beach* means 'they parked the car on the beach', whereas *They drove on to the beach* (with the sentence falling into two parts between *on* and *to*) means 'they continued their journey until they reached the beach'. Care also needs to be taken to write *on* separately when it forms part of the meaning of phrasal verbs and is followed by *to*: *It was some time before she* **cottoned on** *to what he meant / she* **clung on** *to life for 16 days.*

onward, onwards. The only form for the adjective is *onward* (*resuming their onward journey*), but *onward* and *onwards* are both used for the adverb, with a preference for *onwards* in BrE: *He'd subscribed to all sorts of causes, from the Spanish Civil War onwards*—A. Price, 1981.

op. cit. is a shortening of the Latin phrase *opere citato* meaning 'in the work already cited'. It is used in text to refer back to earlier references, normally preceded by the name of the author in the form 'Bloomfield, op. cit., pp. 54–5'.

operate has derivative forms *operable* ('able to be operated on', especially in medical contexts) and *operator*.

opportunity. The expressions *have* (or *take*, etc.) *the* (or *an, every*, etc.) *opportunity* are followed either by a *to*-infinitive or by *of* + verbal noun: *I was eager to snatch at every opportunity to get myself established as a writer, film-maker, what-have-you, in an effort to find a clearly defined career*—Chris Bonington, 1973 / *He takes the opportunity to castigate the creeping hypocrisy and social climbing which had always called forth his most bitter satire*—*Transactions of the Yorkshire Dialect Society*, 1978 / *The primary school kids have the opportunity of working with micros in their normal classroom activities*—*Listener*, 1983. *For* is normally used when an ordinary noun follows: *Happily there was no opportunity for soddishness about whom I should go with*—D. Craig, 1970.

opposite. As an adjective denoting position, *opposite* is followed by *to* (*Two people directly opposite to each other*); it is also used with the same meaning as a preposition without *to* (*Two people directly opposite each other*). As a noun, *opposite* is followed by *of* (*The effect was the opposite of what they intended*).

optimal, optimum. Both words entered the language in the late 19c and are used in the meaning 'best or most favourable (in given circumstances)' and therefore mean rather more than simply 'best': *He positioned himself so that he had optimum sight lines down the side street*—I. Melchior, 1975 / *Pursuing policies that would be optimal in a first-class world when one actually lives in a . . . third-best world can be highly inefficient*—*Dædalus*, 1979.

opus. When denoting a musical composition and in the phrase *magnum opus*, the recommended pronunciation is **oh**-puhs, with a long ō. The plural is either *opera* (**op**-uh-ruh) or *opuses* (**oh**-puh-siz).

or. 1 When *or* separates two singular nouns, the following verb should be in the singular: *A paint or steel company or a salt or coal mine was no place for the late Herr Baumgartner's widow*—Anita Desai, 1988. (When both nouns are plural the verb is of course also plural.) The following example is acceptable informally, but strictly *or* should be replaced by *and*, or the plural complement replaced by a singular one (. . . *is a typical method*): ✗ *A cassette recorder or disk system are typical methods*—*Choosing and using Your Home Computer*, 1984. When one of the nouns is singular and the other plural, the verb normally agrees with the one nearer to it, and the same applies to mixes of person as in *she or we, you or your brother*, etc.: *The child or its parents sign the form / Were you or your brother there?*

2 For *or* after *either, see* EITHER 2B, and after *neither, see* NEITHER 5.

oral *see* AURAL.

orator is spelt *-or*, not *orater*.

oratorio has the plural form *oratorios*.

orbit. The verb has inflected forms *orbited, orbiting*.

order *see* IN ORDER FOR; IN ORDER THAT; IN ORDER TO.

orderly is used only as an adjective (*They behaved in an orderly fashion*), not as an adverb. Since the notional adverb *orderlily* is too awkward to use, *in an orderly way* is the only alternative.

ordinance, ordnance, ordonnance. An *ordinance* is 'an authoritative order', *ordnance* is 'a branch of government service dealing with military stores and materials', and *ordonnance* is 'a plan or method of literary or artistic competition' or 'an order of architecture'. *Ordnance Survey* is an official UK survey organization, originally under the Master of Ordnance, that produces large-scale detailed maps of each region of the country.

orient, oriental. Both words now sound dated and have an exotic 18c or 19c aura more associated with the world of empire and romantic adventure than with factual description. In ordinary writing it is often better to use more neutral terms such as *eastern* or (*East*) *Asian* (or terms that specify particular countries). The noun *orient* is traditionally spelt *Orient* with a capital initial letter when referring geographically or politically to countries, whereas practice varies between *orient* and *Orient* when it is used in general (often literary) reference to the east. That is the rule normally stated, but it is often difficult to be sure of the distinction: *She was a blonde.*

They have a great time in the Orient, scarcity value—G. Black, 1972 / *Flaubert left Europe a Romantic, and returned from the Orient a Realist*—Julian Barnes, 1985 / *The need to give punters the opportunity to additionally sample delights from the orient hardly seems necessary*—*Guardian*, 1989 / *The orient has three species of tarsiers*—C. Willock, 1991. The adjective *oriental*, meaning 'eastern' with reference to a part of the world, is normally spelt with a small *o*.

orient, orientate, verbs. Both words are used (especially in the adjectival forms *oriented* and *orientated*) with the same meaning 'to place in a particular way in relation to the points of the compass' and 'to establish one's bearings': (orient) *Man needs relations with other people in order to orient himself*—R. May, 1953 / *In a youth-oriented society for a woman to grow old means to run the risk of being ignored*—A. Hutschnecker, 1981 / (orientate) *Kant's own philosophy was undeniably orientated towards problems that lay at the heart of the philosophical enterprise*—P. Gardiner, 1988 / *Many of the region's market towns have experienced difficult times brought on by changes to agriculture and rural life, as well as commercial pressures driven by the evolution of an ever more consumer-orientated society*—*Yorkshire Post*, 2007. These examples show how commonly the words are used in abstract or figurative contexts, and as the second element in combinations preceded by a noun (*youth-oriented, consumer orientated*). The shorter form *orient* is more frequent in every kind of English, including BrE, although in BrE *orientate* continues to be widely used. In AmE the longer form is practically unheard of, and many people will consider it a mistake.

originator is spelt *-or*, not *originater*.

ornament. The noun is pronounced **aw**-nuh-muhnt, whereas the verb has a more distinct -ment sound in the third syllable.

orthopaedic, denoting the branch of medicine concerned with treating deformities of the bones and muscles, is spelt -*paedic* in BrE and -*pedic* in AmE. The corresponding noun *orthopaedics* (AmE *orthopedics*) is normally treated as singular.

-os (forming plurals of nouns) *see* -o.

ostensible, ostensive. *Ostensible* means 'apparent but not necessarily real' or 'professed': *Despite their ostensible commitment to revolution, they played an ambivalent and ultimately counter-revolutionary role*—E. Acton, 1992. It is often used in the adverbial form *ostensibly*: *All such songs were ostensibly aimed at the respectable record-buyer, for whom seeing Frankie Vaughan in cabaret at the Talk of the Town was the acme of sophistication*—*Arts & Book Review*, 2007. *Ostensive*, a much rarer word, means 'directly demonstrative' and is normally used in technical contexts with words such as *definition* (meaning a definition that shows what it describes, e.g. a definition of the term *italics* printed in italics): *If one attempts to teach a dog by way of ostensive definition, it invariably responds by sniffing one's finger*—A. F. Chalmers, 1992. To complete the picture, *ostentatious*, which is less likely to be confused with the other two, means 'pretentious and showy'.

other. 1 For *each other, see* EACH 3.

2 *other than.* The use of *other* as a pronoun or adjective in the phrase *other than* is straightforward and causes no comment: *I'd never known anything other than hard times*—D. Dears, 1974. Objections are raised when *other* in this phrase is forced into the role of adverb (which it does not have in any other context), and Fowler (1926) regarded it as 'ungrammatical and needless' when a genuine adverb, *otherwise*, is available; so in the following example he would have argued that *otherwise than* should replace *other than*: *Other than at football matches or on coach journeys, people sing less spontaneously than in previous generations*—T. Portsmouth, 1992. However, the grammar of *other than* is not always so clear-cut, as the following example shows: *I married her . . . but it never even occurred to me that our marriage would be other than a marriage in name only*—A. Roudybush, 1972. Is *other* here an adjective linked to *marriage* or an adverb linked to *be*? (The answer is a bit of both.) In AmE, this use goes unnoticed; in BrE it is increasingly common and generally unremarkable. Moreover, it is often more idiomatic than the awkward alternative *otherwise than*, but readers should be aware of the caveat attached to it in more pedantic circles.

otherwise. *Professor Southern gave us some stimulating reflections about the aims, development, and achievements (or otherwise) of the Honour School of Modern History*—W. A. Pantin, 1972 / *It's the balance of foods you eat that is healthy or otherwise*—*Which?*, 1989. Fowler (1926) castigated this use of *or otherwise* to mean 'or the opposite (of a given noun, adjective, or adverb)' and urged rephrasing (e.g. *achievements or failures, healthy or unhealthy*), but these alternatives clearly do not convey the same sense of antithesis. In any case, the language has moved on, and the type condemned by Fowler is now in standard use.

ought. In current use the verb *ought* is followed by a *to*-infinitive: *You ought to have a cooked breakfast, these cold mornings*—David Lodge, 1988. Since it is a modal verb, it forms a negative directly with *not* and forms a question by plain inversion: *Things are being permitted that ought not to be permitted—Guardian*, 1972 / *If Canada should disintegrate . . . what ought the U.S. to do?—Wall Street Journal*, 1990. In the past, *ought* does not inflect, and the tense is expressed by the verb following it: *I remembered . . . that I ought to have put Sal out. . . . She barks rather a lot—*Edmund Crispin, 1977. See also DIDN'T OUGHT.

our, ours. 1 A difficulty arises when *our* is used in conjunction with another qualifying word as in *The American and our troops* or *Our and the American troops*. Here a better alternative is *The American troops and ours*, but not ✖ *Ours and the American troops.*

2 In clauses introduced by *which of us*, a following pronoun should normally be in the third person, relating to *which* rather than to *us*: *Which of us would wish to be ill in his kitchen, especially when it is also the family living-room?* If gender-neutrality is required, *his or her* (or informally *their*) has to be used.

ourself. The standard reflexive form of *we* and *us* is *ourselves* (as in *We are going to enjoy ourselves*), but a form *ourself* is recorded from the 14c onwards in uses corresponding to *we* used of a single person (*I loved your father, and we love ourself*—Shakespeare, *Hamlet*, IV.vii.40) and is occasionally found in modern English in contexts in which *we* stands for people in general or a group regarded collectively: *She tells us things about ourself*—Martin Amis, 1991 / *We see ourself as the biggest club in Britain, with a stadium to match—Today*, 1992. However, this use is not regarded as standard. See also THEMSELVES.

out. 1 In current use *out*, unlike *in*, is primarily an adverb (*We went out*), and to form a preposition it normally needs the addition of *of* (*We went out of the house*). Use of *out* as a direct preposition

without *of* is non-standard in BrE, although it is found in AmE and some other varieties: *Now he looked past Bacon, out the bay window behind him—*T. Wolfe, AmE 1987 / *I drove out the gates and left them open behind me, swinging in the wind—*S. Koea, NewZE 1994.

2 As a verb, *out* goes back to Old English in various meanings, 'to drive out or expel', 'to disable', '(of news or information) to become known', 'to disclose or speak out', and others. In the 1990s, the last meaning developed a new application in the context of the gay rights movement, namely 'to reveal the homosexuality of (a prominent or famous person)': *She 'outs' dozens as bi* [= bisexual]*— instead of exclusively straight or gay—The Face*, 1996. The process is called *outing*. The verb has now been further extended to mean to disclose private, often controversial or damaging information about a person, institution, etc.: *At his 80th birthday party, he officially 'outed' himself as a member of the Communist party for 50 years—Daily Telegraph*, 1991 / *Patients were brazenly stalked and 'outed'—their names emblazoned on picket signs—Rolling Stone*, 1993 / *She threatened to out him as father of her child—Total Film*, 2002.

outdoor, outdoors. *Outdoor* is an adjective (*outdoor games*), whereas *outdoors* is an adverb (*The concert was held outdoors*) or noun (*the great outdoors*).

outfit. The verb has inflected forms *outfitted, outfitting*, and a derivative form *outfitter*, in both BrE and AmE.

output. The past tense and past participle of the verb are either *output* (preferably) or *outputted* (occasionally). The present participle is *outputting*.

outside of. *Outside*, unlike *out*, functions equally well as an adverb and preposition. Nonetheless, *outside of* is used, especially in AmE, in two main

meanings: (1) 'exterior to, outside':
*People in show business refer to those
outside of it as 'civilians'*—Shirley
MacLaine, 1987, and (2) 'with the
exception of': *Outside of an unfortunate
sermon in which he confused the words
for charity and diarrhea . . . he never put a
foot wrong with his hosts*—W. Sheed,
1985 / *Not knowing if we'd ever be
together outside of dreams*—fiction
website, AmE 2003.

outstanding has two primary meanings which are open to ambiguity: (1)
'remarkable or conspicuous (among
others of its kind)' (*the outstanding performance of the evening*), and (2) 'not yet
settled or completed' (*three outstanding
matters to discuss*). In practice, however,
context and (in speech) intonation are
likely to render ambiguity theoretical
rather than actual.

outta is a representation of a slang
(especially Black AmE) use of *out of*, and
is found in non-standard language such
as descriptions of rock music: *Well-
formed soul—with added beats—straight
outta South London*—*New Musical
Express*, 1995 / *Hey, man, will you please
get outta my space*—*Daily Record*, 2004.

outward, outwards. The only form
for the adjective is *outward* (*the outward
journey*), but *outward* and *outwards* are
both used for the adverb, with a preference for *outwards* in BrE: *The small
circles of desert around waterholes and
settlements join up and spread outwards,
until a new desert has been created*—
Observer, 1977.

outwit has inflected forms *outwitted,
outwitting*.

outwith is a Scottish preposition
meaning 'outside, beyond', and along
with *wee* (for 'small') is often among the
first words that visitors to or new residents in Scotland notice: *Do you live
outwith the city? / We can discuss that
outwith the meeting*. It is a transposition
of *without*, corresponding to its physical
meanings (*see* WITHOUT 1).

over. *The national view is a graphic
composite of local reports across the
country from over 50 (Oops! Make that
'more than' 50) reporting stations*—
Chicago Sun-Times, 1989. In America,
editors of news and other information
often object to the use of *over* in the
sense 'more than' followed by a numeral
(other than in designations of age: an
American could say *I am over 50* without
fear of censure). In BrE all these uses
have gone unchallenged, and Garner's
Modern American Usage (2003) brushes
the objection aside as a 'baseless
crotchet'.

overall. 1 pronunciation. When the
word is a noun (singular *overall* or plural
overalls) the stress is on the first syllable;
when an adjective it normally falls on
the first syllable and when an adverb on
the third, but the stress is variable in
context.

2 parts of speech. As a noun, an
overall (in BrE) is a coat-like piece of
clothing worn over ordinary clothes to
protect them against stains etc., and
overalls (plural) are protective trousers
or dungarees or a combination suit worn
by people doing manual work. As an
adjective, *overall* is always used in
attributive position (i.e. before a noun),
as in *the overall effect*. As an adverb,
overall normally qualifies a whole
sentence, as in *Overall, the performance
was excellent*.

3 overall majority. An *overall majority* is the amount by which the largest
number of votes, parliamentary seats,
etc., exceeds all the others added
together, and also the fact of such a
majority (*failed to win an overall
majority*).

overestimate, underestimate.
Because these words are often used in negative or quasi-negative contexts, there is a danger of losing track of logic and using the wrong word, usually *underestimate* for *overestimate*. In a wallchart on the plays of Shakespeare published with the *Independent* newspaper in 2007, the text included the assertion *his contributions to the world of theatre and to language cannot be underestimated*. Faint praise indeed, if that were the case.

overflow, as a verb, has the past form and past participle *overflowed*.

overly. The use of *overly* in place of the prefix *over-*, e.g. *overly confident* instead of *overconfident*, is still regarded in some quarters in Britain as an Americanism although it is well established in British usage: *That same novel is now with Macmillan. I am not 'overly' hopeful*—Barbara Pym, 1977 / *Fitzpatrick's male adversary is an impassioned, overly emotional man*—*Times*, 1985 / *She is not overly cheerful about the future of British drama*—M. Geare, 1993. It is interesting to note how frequently *overly* is used in the context of feelings or emotions.

overseas is now the usual word for the adverb (*He was sent overseas*) and the adjective (*overseas postage rates*). *Oversea*, formerly used as an adjective, has largely fallen out of use.

oversight is potentially ambiguous since it has two almost diametrically opposed meanings, (1) 'supervision': *There must be a representative of Scotland in the United Kingdom Cabinet—with a general oversight over the economy and the framing of Scotland's budget*—Lord Home, 1976, and (2) 'a failure to notice or do something' (the more common meaning, corresponding to *overlook* rather than *oversee*): *'By a quite exceptional oversight,' said Rufus, 'I don't just*

happen to have any picture postcards of the Acropolis about me at present'—Barbara Vine, 1987 / *This procedure avoids possible oversight, and is a record that the answers have been considered*—R. M. Coates, 1991. In some cases the meaning may not be so clear, e.g. *Congressional oversight has proliferated*—*Time*, 1977. Normally, however, the context will clarify which meaning is intended.

overtone, undertone. Both words denote an extra layer of meaning or significance seen in a word or statement. An *overtone*, which is also commonly used in the plural *overtones*, suggests subtle additional meaning (and corresponds roughly to the meaning it has in music, i.e. 'a tone above the lowest in a harmonic scale'): *The prevailing tone of the book is highly satirical, with strong overtones of slapstick farce*—R. L. Wolff, 1977. An *undertone* is rather an unexpressed or underlying feeling (and again roughly matches the musical meaning 'a subdued tone of sound'): *Welsh's scabrous comedy of alcoholic manners is full of dark undertones*—*Sunday Times*, 2006.

ovum, meaning 'an egg cell', is pronounced oh-vuhm and has the plural form *ova*.

owing to see DUE TO 2.

ox has the plural form *oxen*. However, the plural of the idiom *dumb ox*, meaning a stupid person, is usually *dumb oxes*.

Oxford comma. 1 The so-called 'Oxford comma' is an optional comma that follows the last but one item in a list of three or more items and precedes the words 'and' and 'or': *We sell books, videos, and magazines.* It is called the 'Oxford comma' because it was traditionally used by printers, readers, and editors at Oxford University Press. However, the style is also used by other publishers, both in the UK and elsewhere. It is also known as the 'serial comma', as well as the 'Harvard comma'.

2 Further examples are: *mad, bad, and dangerous to know*; and a *thief, a liar, and a murderer*. The general rule is that it should be used consistently, or not at all. In the preceding examples the Oxford comma could easily be removed without affecting meaning (though it does serve the function of suggesting pauses in reading). However, it really can help to avoid ambiguity when any of the listed items are compound terms joined by *and*. In *These items are available in black and white, red and yellow, and blue and green*, leaving the comma out after *yellow* could suggest five different options, four of them being single colours, rather than the three options actually available. In *cider, real ales, meat and vegetable pies, and sandwiches*, the absence of a comma after *pies* would imply something unintended about the sandwiches, namely that they are meat and vegetable.

3 The omission of the Oxford comma can also provide unintended humour: the following suggests some unknown facets of Nelson Mandela: *'highlights of his global tour include encounters with Nelson Mandela, an 800-year-old demigod and an obsessive collector'*. But in any case, inserting the Oxford comma would not remove the ambiguity. As it currently reads, *encounters with Nelson Mandela, an 800-year-old demigod and an obsessive collector* is ambiguous because it is unclear if what follows the

comma is in apposition to Mandela, i.e. describes him, or whether those two nouns continue the list. However, inserting the comma to produce *encounters with Nelson Mandela, an 800-year-old demigod, and an obsessive collector* does not resolve the problem, since *an 800-year-old demigod* could still read as being in apposition. In the rare cases like this where ambiguity might be caused, rephrasing is the best option, e.g. *encounters with Nelson Mandela, with an 800-year-old demigod, and with an obsessive collector*.

oxymoron is derived from two Greek words opposed in meaning, *oxus* 'sharp' and *mōros* 'dull' or 'stupid'. It is a figure of speech in which two words of opposite meaning are brought together for special effect, e.g. *a cheerful pessimist* and *harmonious discord*. The name is properly used of a deliberate literary device, and should not be used to mean simply an accidental or casual contradiction in terms: ☒ *Robert proves why it's no oxymoron to be known as a creative producer—Take One* (magazine), 2003. ☒ *The divide is between man-centered worship (surely an oxymoron) and God-centered worship—*religious website, 2004 [OEC]. In neither of these sentences is there an oxymoron in the proper sense. The offence is even worse when the contradiction is not contained within a term at all: ☒ *It seems like an oxymoron, but rock has benefited enormously from singers who really shouldn't have been singing—Pitchfork Media album reviews*, 2004. The word wanted here is *paradox*.

pace, from the Latin word *pax* 'peace', means 'by the leave of' and is used in more formal (especially academic) writing to refer to someone whose opinion has been considered and rejected: *Tolstoy...is not, pace Albert Sorrel and Vogüé in any sense a mystic*—Isaiah Berlin, 1978. It is pronounced **pah**-chay or **pay**-si, and to avoid momentary confusion with the English word *pace*, is normally printed in italics.

pacifically. In spoken English, it is not uncommon for this adverb, from the adjective *pacific*, to replace *specifically*. Since the substitution is a feature of speech, written examples are not easy to find, while most instances of *pacifically* show it used correctly. Example: ☒ *Although Motorways are pacifically designed to deal with cars going quickly in a straight line the cops have decided to put cameras in on the M4*—dooyoo.co.uk (discussions), 2005.

package. The figurative meaning 'a set of proposals or arrangements considered as a whole', common in combinations such as *package deal* and *package holiday*, was a 20c development first in AmE and more recently in BrE: *The mass audience...is...merely given packages of passive entertainment*—Marshall McLuhan, 1967 / *Reassured, the package tourists sink into their seats*—Julian Symons, 1973.

paid *see* PAY.

pair. 1 When used to mean (1) a set of two persons or things regarded as a unit

(*a pair of eyes* / *a pair of gloves*), and (2) an article consisting of two equal parts which are joined together (*a pair of binoculars, clippers, jeans, pincers, pyjamas, scissors, shears, trousers*, etc.), the phrase is normally followed by a singular verb or pronoun (e.g. *pass me that pair of scissors* / *there's a pair of gloves in the drawer*). If *a pair of* is omitted a plural pronoun or verb is required: e.g. *those gloves, scissors*, etc., *need replacing*. Examples: *On the front of the radiator grille was mounted a pair of very large Cibie spotlights that dwarfed the standard headlamps*—M. Booth, 1980 / *To draw a heavy plough through wet clay soil, a pair of oxen yoked together was used*—M. Graham-Cameron et al., 1984 / *In addition to the various gripping wrenches, a pair of general-purpose pliers is always useful*—D. Holloway, 1992.

2 Used as a collective noun, *pair* takes a plural verb when the things or people that make up the *pair* are thought of as individuals, not as a unit. *A pair of bachelors, dogs, idiots, rock-climbers*, etc. (all taken from collocations occurring in *OED2*) would normally be plural. Examples: *The next pair of readings are concerned with what has perhaps been the single most salient political issue in British education in the twentieth century*—M. Flude et al., 1989 / *A pair of Pyracantha coccinea are placed strategically, one on either side of a cottage front door*—Gardener, 1992 In the next two examples, the idea of plurality overrides the rule given at **1** above: *When you've lived on subsistence for two years what do you do when your shoes wear out, when* *you get a £100 fuel bill, when the washing machine breaks down, when a pair of children's shoes cost you more than you'd spend on your own?*—B. Campbell, 1985 / *One pair of ruby earrings are especially important*—television news script, 1993. In referring back to a 'singular' *pair*, the plural is normally used because it refers not to *pair* but to the following (plural) noun: *She . . . handed me a pair of Japanese thongs. I slipped them on and felt the skin between my first two toes protest*—H. Engel, 1981. The standard plural form for more than one pair is (for example) *two pairs of shoes*, although *two pair of shoes* is used informally and in dialect.

3 The phrase *pair of twins* is generally understood to mean a single *set* (the more usual word in the context of twins), not two sets: *She gave birth to a pair of male twins, one of which was a stillborn with no malformations*—Lancet, 1977.

pajamas *see* PYJAMAS.

palaeo-. Words of the type *palaeography, palaeolithic*, etc., are normally spelt with -*ae*- in BrE, although the AmE form *paleo-* is beginning to influence British practice.

palindrome, from a Greek word meaning 'running back again', means a word or group of words that reads the same when the letters are reversed. *Noon, level*, and *radar* are all palindromes, as is the often quoted sentence *Able was I ere I saw Elba* (fancifully attributed to Napoleon). A word palindrome is a sentence which reads the same when the words in it are reversed, e.g. *Stout and bitter porter drinks porter, bitter, and stout.*

pallor, meaning 'paleness', is spelt -*or* in both BrE and AmE.

palpable. The literal meaning, 'that can be touched or felt', is encountered in medical contexts (*a palpable swelling*), and is familiar from Shakespeare's line in the duel scene at the end of *Hamlet*: *A hit, a very palpable hit.* The figurative use, conveying the idea of something so strongly present to the mind or senses that it can almost be physically felt, is the dominant one nowadays: *The tension—friendly tension—in the room was palpable*—Atlantic, 1991.

panacea, from Greek words meaning 'all-healing', denotes not just a remedy but a universal remedy and is therefore not appropriate in the context of particular illnesses, e.g. *a panacea for measles*. It is most commonly used in negative or ironic ways and in social rather than medical contexts: *Many in the academic sector remain sceptical about whether employer-led higher education is the panacea some believe it to be*—Times Higher Education Supplement, 2006.

panel has inflected forms *panelled, panelling*, and in AmE also *paneled, paneling*.

panic has inflected forms *panicked, panicking, panicky*.

panini in Italian is a plural form (just like *spaghetti*) as the -*i* ending shows. In English-speaking culture, the word usually refers to a small flat loaf, often served toasted. Although *panini* is plural in Italian, it has long been interpreted (since 1985 according to the *OED*) as singular in English, with its own plural *paninis*. By all means, use the precise Italian singular if you are an Italian scholar, but to ask for a *panino* may sound like pedantry, or worse still, a criticism of the provider's English.

pants. In BrE *pants* (plural noun) means 'underpants', whereas in AmE it means 'trousers or slacks'. The distinction can cause problems: *I heard an American student at Cambridge University telling some English friends how he climbed over a locked gate to get into his college and tore his pants, and one of them asked in confusion, 'But how could you tear your pants without tearing your trousers?'*—N. Moss, 1973. In attributive use (i.e. before another noun), *pants* tends to be used in general contexts in both BrE and AmE, and *pant* or *pants* in fixed combinations such as *pant suit*: *I took a jackknife out of my pants pocket*—R. B. Parker, 1974 / *Then we went downtown and bought pant suits*—L. Ellmann, 1988.

The use of *pants* to mean 'rubbish', especially in the phrase *a load* (or *pile*) *of pants*, is BrE: *A Liberal Democrat stunned his fellow peers when he dismissed a landmark report on the future of the historic environment as 'a load of pants'*—Independent, 2000.

paparazzi, the name for freelance photographers who pursue celebrities to get photographs of them, is spelt with one *p* and two *zs*. The singular (not often used, because they hunt in packs) is *paparazzo*, which is derived from the surname of a society photographer in Fellini's film *La Dolce Vita* (1960). The online *OED* has a separate entry for *paparazzi* treated as a singular form. This usage is likely to increase as long as the genuine singular form remains obscure, but it should not be imitated.

papier mâché, a kind of paper pulp, should be spelt with the two accents as shown, but is written in roman.

papyrus, is pronounced puh-**piy**-ruhs, and in the meaning 'a document written on papyrus' generally has the plural form *papyri*, pronounced puh-**piy**-riy.

paradigm. 1 *Paradigm* is pronounced with the last syllable as in *dime*. In technical use it denotes a model or pattern of

some kind; in linguistics, it means 'a representative set of inflections of a noun or verb', and so the paradigm of *come* is *come* (base form), *comes* (third person singular present), *came* (past tense), *come* (past participle), *coming* (present participle). In general use it has acquired the status of a vogue word in contexts where *example* or *model* or *pattern* would be more straightforward choices: *Perhaps, he suggests, Victorian scholars sanitised the past to create in the occupation of Britain a paradigm for the British Empire*—Times, 2007.

2 The corresponding adjective *paradigmatic* is pronounced -dig-**mat**-ik, with the g fully articulated.

paradise. Of the many adjective forms that have developed from this word, in current use the most common is *paradisiacal* followed by *paradisal*. Not surprisingly, *paradise* itself is often found to be less awkward in this role, and is used in certain fixed compounds such as *paradise crane* and *paradise duck*.

paraffin is spelt with one *r* and two *f*s. The equivalent term in AmE is *kerosene*.

parallel has inflected and derivative forms *paralleled, paralleling, parallelism, parallelogram*. The final -*l* is not doubled.

parameter. In technical use, a *parameter* is a measurable factor that contributes to determining a system or event. In the 20c it developed rapidly into the kind of word that Fowler (1926) described as a 'popularized technicality', many instances of which he deplored, especially when simpler alternatives are available. In popular use, a *parameter* is 'a constant element or factor, especially serving as a limit or boundary', and is best demonstrated by examples: *There are parameters to these recollections which may not be immediately apparent: the world of learning . . . and the* *war*—D. M. Davin, 1975 / *Lewis's refusal to accept her standards, her parameters, she regarded as threatening*—Anita Brookner, 1989 / *Given that they have been working together for only a month, and that Andrew's brief is so wide, the parameters of their respective roles have yet to be defined in practical terms*—*Times*, 2006. A wide choice of alternatives is available to those who feel uneasy about using *parameter* in this way: for example *criterion, factor, element, scope, boundary, limit, term, term of reference*.

paraphernalia originally denoted the personal property (Greek *parapherna* 'things set apart [from a dowry]') that a married woman was legally entitled to regard as her own. Over several centuries of use in English it has acquired the general meaning 'miscellaneous belongings or equipment'; it is still normally treated as a plural noun although occasional singular use is attested from the 18c (*a whole paraphernalia of plums*, 1845). Some modern examples follow: *Paraphernalia in his flat included Indian clubs and an adapted table to which boys were tied*—*Independent*, 1989 / *Exposed beams, road signs and horsey paraphernalia, it [a pub] had the perfect mix without being twee*—*Mirror*, 2007.

parasitic, parasitical. Both are in use as the adjectives from *parasite*. *Parasitic* is ten times more frequent and has both literal and figurative meanings, while *parasitical* is only ever figurative: *This parasitic castle life had left my funds comparatively intact*—Patrick Leigh Fermor, 1986 / *I am keen on police checks on people working with vulnerable adults. But who is doing the police checks? Yes—another hateful, skinflint, parasitical private agency*—*Guardian*, 2002.

paratroops, meaning 'troops equipped to be dropped by parachute', is a plural noun. The force is called a

paratroop regiment, and a member of this is a *paratrooper*.

parcel. The verb has inflected forms *parcelled, parcelling* in BrE, and in AmE usually *parceled, parceling*.

parenthesis. 1 *Parenthesis* is a term denoting an aside or extra remark that is added to a sentence; it is normally marked off by brackets, commas, or dashes, and the rest of the sentence is grammatically complete without it. Parentheses can be single words, phrases, or whole clauses: *In Italian, a language he had been told was the same as Rumanian, he asked to be directed to the British Legation*—Olivia Manning, 1960 / *He and Moira (then a milkman's pretty daughter) grovelled together long and effectively enough to cause the eventual birth of their son Rick*—Tim Winton, *Shallows*, 1985 / *On Thursday I come back from work to an empty house*—*Kate is spending the night at a girlfriend's house again*—*and the stillness and solitude calm me down*—Angela Lambert, 1989 / *Once, I told one of the men to do something, and he*—*my father, that is*—*asked me what it would be like if I couldn't order men around any more*—D. Leon, 2006.

2 *Parentheses* (plural) are, in printing terminology, round brackets. *See* BRACKETS.

pariah, meaning 'a social outcast', is pronounced puh-**riy**-uh to rhyme with *Isaiah*.

parking attendant has replaced *traffic warden* as the name of the street official in the UK. Since the primary function of the job remains punitive rather than supportive, this must be regarded as a euphemism.

parley, meaning 'a discussion of peace terms', has the plural form *parleys*, and as a verb has inflected forms *parleys, parleyed, parleying.*

parliament, parliamentary. The *-ia-* in both words is pronounced as a single syllable, i.e. **pah**-luh-muhnt, pah-luh-**men**-tuh-ri.

parlour is spelt *-our* in BrE and *parlor* in AmE.

parlous was described by Fowler (1926) as 'a word that wise men leave alone', and the current edition (2006) of the *Concise Oxford Dictionary* marks it as 'archaic or humorous'. This is a sad fate for a long-serving word, originally formed as a variant of *perilous* and for many centuries used side by side with it in the same range of meaning. It can be safely used in the expression *in a parlous state* (or *condition*) even in only moderately formal English: *He was altogether in a parlous state: the weather was bad, there was no water in the flat; he did not care to go out at nights and was seeing fewer people*—P. Ackroyd, 1988.

parricide, patricide. Both words come from the Latin word *pater* meaning 'father', but in current use *parricide* is the killing of a parent or other near relative whereas *patricide* is more specifically the killing of one's father. They are used to denote the crime or the person who commits it.

partake is followed by *in* or (especially with reference to food) *of*. Some conservative usage guides insist that the idea of sharing something in company should always be present, but uses which do not reflect a group activity have a long history and are well established. However, if you use *partake of* as a posh synonym for *eat* or *drink*, the result runs the danger of appearing slightly ludicrous or Mills and Boonish, as in Eric Partridge's example '*being alone, I consoled myself by partaking of a glass of stout*'.

part and parcel. This expression, meaning 'an essential part of something', retains an older meaning of *parcel* that has otherwise not survived, namely 'a constituent or component part' (as in Swinburne's *Till the soul of man be parcel of the sunlight*).

Occasionally it is misinterpreted as *part and partial*, e.g. ☒ *I mean this is part and partial of why things are so broken in Washington*—COCA, 2007.

Parthian shot. A *Parthian shot* is the same as a *parting shot*, i.e. a final remark or glance made on leaving. The allusion is to the supposed custom of the ancient Parthian horsemen of confusing their enemy by hurling spears into their ranks while in (real or feigned) flight. The earliest citation for *Parthian shot* in the *OED* is as late as 1902, although there is one from 1842 in a less developed sense (referring to an action rather than a remark) and another for *Parthian glance* from 1859, and the allusive use is dated back to the 17c in less fixed expressions. The first examples of *parting shot* are from the end of the 19c: *That was a parting shot he took at you, by jingo!*—J. Payn, 1888. This is now the standard form of the phrase, although Parthian shot is still occasionally used: *'Anyway,' he offered a Parthian shot, 'I don't know why you bother. You hate vegetarian food.'*—*Sunday Times*, 2005.

partially, partly. 1 The meanings of these two words overlap in ways that make it difficult to decide between them in any principled way, although certain patterns in their use can be identified. *Partially* (15c) is somewhat older than *partly* (16c) but their meanings have run in parallel except that for some of its history *partially* has meant 'in a partial or biased way', i.e. the opposite of *impartially*. In current English, according to the evidence of the *OEC*, *partly* is almost twice as common as *partially*.

2 Fowler (1926) attempted to make a distinction in principle between *partially* and *partly* by defining *partially* as contrasted with *completely* (i.e. = to a limited degree) and *partly* as contrasted with *wholly* (i.e. = as regards a part and not the whole). His illustrations based on this criterion were *It is partly wood* / *This was partly due to cowardice* and *a partially drunken sailor* / *his partially re-established health*, which in all cases show idiomatic uses that are not readily replaced by the alternative word. So if we say, for example, *The room is partly panelled*, we mean that only part of the room is meant to be panelled, whereas if we say *The room is partially panelled*, we mean that the panelling has still to be completed.

3 Fowler's rubric still works up to a point, but the meanings shade into each other and current usage reflects this: (partially) *I partially solved my money problems by being paid ten shillings to play regularly at the Black Horse*—Anthony Burgess, 1987 / *A partially built shopping centre, for instance, will adversely affect the tenant's business*—R. Walker, 1993 / *His new view was partially blocked by castle turrets and a gray stone drawbridge*—fiction website, AmE 2005 [OEC] / (partly) *Her untidy blonde fringe partly covered her eyes*—J. G. Ballard, 1988 / *The door to Suzy's bedroom was wide open and her partly clothed body was spreadeagled on the bed*—T. Barnes, 1991 / *The strategy was only partly successful*—Oxford Companion to Australian History, 2001.

4 Further observations can be made from a study of current usage:

a *Partly* is used when it is balanced by a further *partly* or is followed by some other link phrase such as *but also*, and many instances of its occurrence fall in this category: *She was shaking all over, partly because she was so angry with Oliver and partly because she was so afraid*—Nina Bawden, 1989 / *Maria jeered caustically, driven partly by masochism but also by a need to lash out*—J. Bauling, 1993 / *This move is partly about baseball and partly about ticket sales and all*—Sporting News, AmE 2002. But *partially* occurs occasionally in this role: *In practice there were innovations, partially because of the perceived need to reduce the influence of headmen, and partially because British officials naturally governed on the basis of their own training and inclinations* —J. D. Rogers, 1987.

b *Partly* is more often the choice when it qualifies an adjective or participial adjective that is also qualified in some other way: *Her dislike of him was of course . . . partly based upon a sense that he disliked her*—Iris Murdoch, 1980 / *This is partly attributable to the increased opportunity for away travel which has increased the contact between rival groups of supporters*—D. Waddington, 1992 / *His fear, partly based on intelligence he received, was if the two came together*—news website, BrE 2003 [OEC].

c Partly is also much preferred when it is followed by a reason or cause introduced by *because, due to, on account of, as a result of*, and so on (the OEC has over ten times as many examples of *partly because* as examples with *partially*), although *partially* can seem just as idiomatic: *I had chosen a homebirth partly for that reason*—Mothering Magazine, AmE 2002 / *The new class arose partly because almost all modern judges were educated in law schools staffed by professional law teachers as distinct from practitioners teaching part-time*—Quadrant (magazine), AusE 2003 / *Things quieted down, partially because no one could come up with a line to top it*—Eye Weekly, CanE 2005.

d *Partially*, rather than *partly*, is normally used to qualify words describing physical deficiencies such as *blind* and *deaf*: *Any generally available additional* *provision for deaf or partially blind or disturbed children, and others such as dyslexic children, was not special educational provision*—S. Johnstone et al., 1992.

e Both words are used to qualify judgemental and evaluating words such as *responsible, to blame, true*, etc.

5 In sum, Fowler's rule and the other observations will serve if a rule is needed; but usage is inconsistent and the alleged distinctions in meaning do not always work in practice.

participles. 1 There are two kinds of participle in English: the present participle ending in -*ing* as in *We are **going***, and the past participle ending in -*d* or -*ed* for many verbs and in -*t* or -*en* or some other form for others, as in *Have you **decided**? / New houses are being **built** / It's not **broken***.

2 Participles are often used to introduce subordinate clauses that are attached to other words in a sentence, e.g. *Her mother, **opening** the door quietly, came into the room / **Hearing** a noise I went out to look / **Born** in Rochdale, he spent most of his life in the area*. Participles in initial position, as in the last two examples, are acceptable grammatically but when overdone can produce a poor style, especially when the participial clause bears little relation to the main one: ***Being** blind from birth, she became a teacher and travelled widely*.

3 A worse stylistic flaw occurs with so-called 'unattached', 'misrelated', or 'dangling' participles, when the participle does not refer to the noun to which it is grammatically attached, normally the subject of the sentence: *Recently **converted** into apartments, I passed by the house where I grew up*. (No one will imagine that the speaker had been **converted** into apartments, but that is what the grammatical structure suggests, producing poor style.) Some examples of

unattached participles follow: ***Being** a vegan bisexual who's into Nicaraguan coffee picking and boiler suits, you could safely assume that I vote Labour*—Private Eye, 1988 / ***Driving** near home recently, a thick pall of smoke turned out to be a bungalow well alight*—Oxford Times, 1990. In sum, unattached participles seldom cause real ambiguity, but they jar and can distract the reader, and are to be avoided.

4 Certain participles, such as *considering, assuming, excepting, given, provided, seeing, speaking (of), having said that*, etc., have acquired the status of prepositions or conjunctions, and their use in a grammatically free role is well established: *'**Speaking** of money,' said Beryl, 'do you mind my asking what you did with yours?'*—A. Munro, 1987. *We're just one big happy family. **But having said that**, it's a family unlike your family because I don't pretend to be something I'm not*—X-Press Online, AusE 2004 [*OEC*]. *See* further at SAY 3.

particular. In its meaning 'considered as distinct from others', *particular* plays a useful identifying or emphasizing role: *For this particular show there is an audience ... and they arrive at 7.30 p.m.*—Guardian, 1970. In other cases, it can be superfluous: *It is entirely up to you to find these faults, if they exist, and to report them before the particular guarantee periods expire*—G. Collard, 1990.

particularly. It is particularly important to pronounce this as five syllables, and not as if it were spelt *par-tic-u-ly*.

partisan, meaning 'a zealous supporter of a cause' or 'a guerrilla in wartime', is normally pronounced in BrE with a -z-sound and with the stress on the last syllable, but in AmE a first-syllable stress is often preferred. It is also used as an adjective meaning 'loyal to a cause, biased'.

partly *see* PARTIALLY.

partner is an alteration of *parcener* 'partner, joint heir', from Anglo-Norman French *parcener*, based on Latin *partitio(n-)* 'partition', through association with *part*, and is first recorded c.1300. Its wide scope includes *bridge partners, tennis partners, partners in crime, business partners*, and *sexual partners*. As the *OED* puts it, it is 'Now increasingly used in legal and contractual contexts to refer to a member of a couple in a long-standing relationship of any kind, so as to give equal recognition to marriage, cohabitation, same-sex relationships, etc.' It is also increasingly used in general language. While many people find it useful precisely because it makes no comment about the legal status of the partnership or the sex of the person so described, others see it as the work of the thought police, forcing people to replace 'husband', 'wife', 'spouse' with what they view as a PC term. But there is no ban on using those words if one so wishes. In addition, *partner* seems a more dignified and neutral word in long-standing but unmarried mature relationships than *boyfriend, girlfriend*, or the tabloidish *fiancé(e)*. Nor is it purely a concoction of political correctness: Milton used *partner of my life*, and this phrase is found in later writers, though *partner* on its own in this modern meaning is a 20c development.

parts of speech. The traditional parts of speech (also called *wordclasses*) that have been in use for English since the 16c are *noun, verb, adjective, adverb, pronoun, preposition, conjunction*, and *interjection*. Some of these are subdivided; for example pronouns can be demonstrative (*this, those*, etc.), personal (*he, she, we*, etc.), possessive (*his, theirs*), or relative (*who, which*). These categories were taken over from those used to describe Latin grammar and often barely suit the word functions and sentence structure of English. The concept of 'adverb', for example, embraces words that are far apart in both function and meaning (*ever, fast, only, safely, thankfully, well*, etc). Other words are often described in special ways, such as *a* and *an* (indefinite article, determiner), *the* (definite article, determiner), *much* (quantifier). For general purposes, however, the traditional names remain in use despite their inadequacies, and they are used in this book rather than the more specialized terms that have been adopted in modern linguistics. The main parts of speech listed above have separate entries, to which the reader is referred for further information.

party occurs in informal and humorous contexts as a synonym for 'person': *June had taken Imogen from her—'what a stout little party'—and settled down for the interview with Imogen on her knee—*Joanna Trollope, 1990. This usage is an affectation derived from the legal use as in *the injured party / the party of the first part*, and so on.

passed, past. *Passed* is the past tense and past participle of the verb *pass*: *We passed a police car / The time has passed*. The related adjective, preposition, and adverb are all *past*: *for the past three hours / We drove past a police car / She hurried past*. The form *past* is also a noun: *living in the past*.

passer-by has the plural form *passers-by*.

passionate. As used in advertising and business, *passionate* long ago passed into the realm of cliché. The meaning 'ardent, extremely enthusiastic' dates to the 16c and was satirized by Kingsley Amis (*His wife . . . was frequently described as passionate without it being revealed what she was passionate about or at—I like it Here*, 1958). The collocation *be* + *passionate* + *about* is now widely used and abused by companies as a mantra of their professionalism, as the following quotes from websites illustrate: *At the new General Motors, we are passionate about designing, building and selling the world's best vehicles / We are passionate about helping you succeed*—Cox, Costello & Horne, UK accountants. Obviously it is more rewarding to do business with someone who is enthusiastic about what they do, and enthusiasm can be contagious; but ultimately one cannot avoid the suspicion that for many companies to say they are *passionate* about something amounts to nothing more than saying 'this is what we do'.

passive. 1 What is the passive?

France beat Brazil in the final is 'active' and *Brazil were beaten by France in the final* is its 'passive' equivalent. In the first, *France* performs the action of the verb, and its grammatical object *Brazil* is affected by the action. In the second, the grammatical object of the active sentence has become the subject of the passive verb *was beaten* and the subject of the active sentence is expressed as an 'agent' (the person or thing who does the action) introduced by the preposition *by*. Sentences containing an active form of the verb are in the 'active voice'; those containing a passive verb form are in the 'passive voice'.

2 Other forms of the passive include:

a impersonal constructions with *it.* *It is believed that no action should be taken / It is felt that your complaint arises from a misunderstanding.* Sir Ernest Gowers, who as a senior civil servant no doubt saw many such examples in correspondence that came his way, wrote (1965) that 'the impersonal passive . . . is a construction dear to those who write official and business letters'. 'It is reasonable enough in statements made at large,' he continued, giving the example *It is understood that the wanted man is wearing a raincoat and a cloth cap,* 'but when one person is addressing another it often amounts to a pusillanimous shrinking from responsibility' (as in the examples given at the beginning of this paragraph).

b double passive. This occurs with verbs such as *attempt, begin, desire, endeavour, propose, threaten,* and others involving constructions with a passive infinitive, as in *The order was attempted to be carried out / No greater thrill can be hoped to be enjoyed.* Clearly these types are often extremely awkward in not corresponding to a comparable active form (✖ *They attempted the order to be carried out* / ✖ *We hope no greater thrill to be enjoyed*), and a fully active construction should be used whenever possible: *They attempted to carry out the order / We can hope to enjoy no greater thrill;* in some cases the sentence can be rephrased, e.g. *There was an attempt to carry out the order.* Other verbs, such as *expect, intend,* and *order,* which are grammatically more versatile, will allow a double passive construction; we can say, for example, *They ordered the deserters to be shot,* and therefore the double passive form *The deserters were ordered to be shot* is acceptable.

3 Are passives always wrong?

Many people insist that any sentence in the passive voice should automatically be rephrased in the active. Such a view is exaggerated: there are many perfectly valid reasons for using a passive verb form.

a The agent is unknown, unimportant, or already mentioned: (unknown) *President Kennedy was assassinated in Dallas / Bring the pesticide material in for identification and disposal if the label has been removed from its container /* (unimportant) *Additionally, all* *penetrations, such as electrical outlets and light switches, should be carefully sealed* / (already mentioned) *They were shooting everybody. I felt a pain in my shoulder and a man told me I was hit.*

b It is obvious or easily deduced who or what the agent is: *He speaks of the case of a young student who is being treated for depression* / *Charged with sedition, Blake was tried and acquitted the following year.*

c People in general are the agents: *Adult beetles can be obtained from several sources* / *It has not been explained, however, why Swedish social democrats chose to do this.*

d It is tactful or politic not to mention the agent: *I don't oppose all wars. My grandfather signed up for a war the day after Pearl Harbor was bombed*—Barack Obama, as Senator, 2 October, 2002.

e You report an opinion or statement but wish to avoid saying whose opinion or statement it is. The passive is often used with verbs such as *accept, agree, allege, announce, claim*, etc., either in an 'impersonal passive', with 'it' as the subject, or with the person or thing referred to in the report as the subject of the verb: e.g. *It has been alleged that many officers in the Colorado City Police Department are practicing polygamists* / *Many officers in the . . . are alleged to be practicing polygamists.*

4 conclusions. a The passive voice supplies a useful means of achieving a different focus on an event than that provided by the active voice, as illustrated at **3**, and all such uses are legitimate. (Imagine how undramatic Churchill's 'Never in the field of human conflict was so much owed by so many to so few' would be in the active voice.) Additionally, in scientific writing the passive is seen as a crucial means of achieving objectivity.

b However, overuse of the passive in formal non-scientific writing often leads to wordiness, or worse, as the example below illustrates. If you find yourself writing a passive sentence which does not fit any of the patterns outlined at **3**, ask yourself whether you could just as easily express it in the active. The example from the *Oxford Guide to Plain English* (1995) provides a real-life example of how the passive in business or official letters can lead to inelegant, wordy, and unnecessarily pompous phrasing: *We have been asked by your home insurers to obtain your written confirmation that all their requirements have been completed by yourself* is clearer, friendlier, and more personal as *Your home insurers have asked us to obtain your written confirmation that all their requirements have been completed.*

c The double passive mentioned at **2b** is best avoided. As for the impersonal construction (**2a**), it is a double-edged sword. The use or avoidance of such passives depends on the level of formality being aimed at and often on the wisdom of accepting personal or group responsibility for the statement that follows. While it is undoubtedly true that the use of such structures sometimes amounts to a shirking of responsibility, they are also a useful tool for writers wishing or forced to distance themselves from the opinion expressed. The official who wrote Gowers' example *It is felt that your complaint arises from a misunderstanding* may have had good reason not to put himself (as it probably was) in the firing line for taking a wrong decision.

past master, meaning 'a person having special skill in an activity', is spelt with *past*, not (as formerly) with *passed*, although the allusion is to someone who has 'passed' the necessary training and qualification to achieve that status (originally in the context of free-masonry).

pastor is used, especially in AmE, as the term for or title of a member of the clergy in charge of a nonconformist church.

past tense. Three noteworthy special uses of the past tense of verbs are:

1 A continued action or state in indirect speech can be expressed either by the past or by the present: *Did you say you had [or have] a house to let? / How did you find out that I was [or am] the owner?*

2 A past tense is used in forms of enquiry about another's wish or attitude: *Did [or do] you want to come in?* (The time reference arguably differs here according to the tense: either 'Did you want to come in a moment ago, when you knocked?' or 'You knocked, so do you now want to come in?')

3 The hypothetical past tense is used in sentences of the type *It's time we left for the station*, and in unfulfilled conditions of the type *If you tried harder, you'd probably succeed.*

pâté, meaning 'a rich meat or fish paste', is pronounced **pat**-ay in BrE and pa-**tay** in AmE, and is spelt with the two accents to distinguish it from *pate* (pronounced payt, = head) and *pâte* (pronounced paht, = the paste of which porcelain is made).

patent. In the meaning 'a government authority giving a right or title', the standard pronunciation is **pat**-uhnt, although **pay**-tuhnt is often used in BrE. For the adjective meaning 'clear, obvious' (and in the corresponding adverb *patently*), and in the compound *patent leather*, **pay**-tuhnt is used in BrE. In AmE, **pat**-uhnt is more usual in these meanings.

pathetic, in its modern informal meaning 'inadequate, feeble', has compromised the primary (and by no means derogatory) meaning 'arousing pity or sadness' to the extent that a statement such as *The play opens with a pathetic speech* is likely to be understood the wrong way. Regard for context needs to be borne in mind when using or encountering this word.

patio, meaning 'a paved area adjoining a house', has the plural form *patios*.

patricide *see* PARRICIDE.

patriot. The pronunciations **pat**-ri-uht and **pay**-tri-uht are about equally common in BrE. In the derivative words *patriotic* and *patriotism*, **pat**- is more common. In AmE, **pay**- is the usual form for all these words.

patrol as a verb has inflected forms *patrolled*, *patrolling* in both BrE and AmE.

patron is pronounced **pay**-truhn, but the derivative words *patronage* and *patronize* both have initial **pat**-. In AmE, initial **pay**- is usual for all three words.

pavement means 'a paved way for pedestrians' in BrE (corresponding to AmE *sidewalk*) and in parts of the American east coast, and the hard surface of a paved road elsewhere in America.

pay. The past tense and past participle of the verb are both *paid*.

PC, pc is now as likely to stand for *political correctness* as *police constable*, *Privy Counsellor*, or *personal computer*.

peaceable, peaceful. In general, *peaceable* means 'disposed to peace, not quarrelsome' and refers primarily to people or activities: *The visitor from beyond the planets would obtain the*

p

impression that the Earth is a very peaceable place—New Scientist, 1991. The adverb *peaceably* occurs almost as often as the adjective: *On the whole they lived peaceably and had lots of fellowship together—*W. Green, 1988. The more common word *peaceful* means 'characterized by peace, tranquil' and the notion is more actual than potential: *The meal was peaceful, but when it was over the doors burst open and in surged a crowd of painters and models who hadn't been invited—*J. Rose, 1990. It can be used to describe a person as well as a situation: *Sometimes I felt plain scared. I am a peaceful man. I always felt we were a target—Guardian*, 2007. The meanings of *peaceable* and *peaceful* overlap rather more with the adverb *peacefully*: *The siege ended peacefully and Yacoub was later charged with taking hostages and with illegal possession of a firearm—Keesings*, 1990.

peak, peek, pique. Since all three words sound the same and function both as nouns and verbs, muddling them is perhaps inevitable. A *peak* is the highest point of something, and if something *peaks* it reaches its highest point. A *peek* means 'a quick or furtive look' and *to peek* means to 'look quickly or furtively'. *Pique* is irritation resulting from a slight; if something *piques* your curiosity, it arouses it, and if you feel *piqued* you feel resentful. The main rogue spelling seems to be *peak*, perhaps because it is the most common of the three. It often replaces *peek* (noun) in the collocations *have a peek, sneak a peek, take a peek*. With the verb such substitution seems less frequent, but does occasionally happen, e.g. ⌧ *I kept peaking at my watch—*weblog, 2007. *Peak* as a verb is also used where *pique* is correct, as in the last two examples below. Beware: spellcheckers cannot spot these confusions. Examples: (*peak* for *peek*) *Of those that do switch off* [i.e. their phones], *22*

per cent still can't resist having a peak at their work emails over the weekend—Daily Telegraph, 2010 / *The idea of sneaking a peak at a Web page before clicking on the link eventually came to fruition—PC World*, 2011 / (*peak* for *pique*) *It peaked my curiosity enough to buy the CD today during lunch* —weblog, 2005 / *Two aspects of Hox genes have peaked the interest of phylogeneticists—American Zoologist*, 2001.

peccadillo, meaning 'a relatively minor fault or sin', has the plural form *peccadilloes* rather more often than *peccadillos*, but both are correct.

pedagogy, meaning 'the science of teaching', is pronounced **ped**-uh-gog-i (with a hard second *g*) or **ped**-uh-goj-i (with a soft second *g*). The soft sound is used in the adjective *pedagogical*. In *pedagogue*, however (now mainly used disparagingly of a pedantic or dogmatic teacher), the *g* is hard, **ped**-uh-gog.

pedal as a verb has inflected forms *pedalled, pedalling* in BrE, but usually *pedaled, pedaling* in AmE.

pedantry. Fowler (1926) observed that the term 'is obviously a relative one; my pedantry is your scholarship, his reasonable accuracy, her irreducible minimum of education, and someone else's ignorance'. He referred to articles in his book and left the reader to decide where on the scale of pedantry his work belonged. Fowler was rarely pedantic but his readers often were, and read into his statements things that Fowler never intended. Some examples of pedantic attitudes to usage will be found in the following entries (not an exhaustive list, and the reader may be able to add others): **also* 2 (position of *also*), **barbarisms* (objections to mixed forms such as *television*), **circumstance* (objection to *under the circumstances*), **curriculum* (plural form *curricula vitarum*), **data*

(*data* as invariable plural), **ex-* (Fowler's objection to the type *ex-Prime Minister*), **fewer*, **less* (the type *12 items or fewer*), **fraction* (a *fraction* not necessarily a small quantity), **hoi polloi* (use of *the hoi polloi*), **only* (position of *only*), **other* 2 (use of *other than* for *otherwise than*), **per capita* (use of *per caput*), **target* (*doubled* targets are easier, not harder, to hit).

pedlar, peddler. The dominant BrE spelling has changed, along with a change in principal meaning, from *pedlar*, the traditional form for the itinerant seller of small items, to the AmE spelling *peddler*, associated especially with the selling of drugs and influenced by the verb *peddle* (itself a back-formation from *pedlar*). The development is somewhat circular but the result is that *pedlar* is falling out of use as the itinerant seller that the word used to denote disappears from the streets.

pee. Since the introduction of decimal currency in Britain in 1971 the spelling *pee* has come into use to represent the pronunciation of the initial letter of *penny*: *May I trouble you for forty-two pee?*—Ruth Rendell, 1974 / *Even the fundamental human need to spend a penny costs at least 20 pee at the mainline railway termini*—*Times*, 1999. Lack of precedent is the only argument available to those who condemn this pronunciation and insist on the traditional (but partly anachronistic) forms *penny* and *pence*.

peek *see* PEAK, PEEK, PIQUE.

peewit is the preferred spelling for the name of the bird, not *pewit*.

pence *see* PENNY.

penchant, meaning 'an inclination or liking', is pronounced **pã**-shã, in a French manner with nasalized vowels, or in an anglicized way in AmE, **pen**-shuhnt.

pencil as a verb has inflected forms *pencilled, pencilling* in BrE, and usually *penciled, penciling* in AmE.

pendant, pendent, pennant. The noun *pendant* means 'a hanging jewel or ornament' or in nautical use 'a short rope hanging from the head of a mast'; the adjective *pendent* means 'hanging or overhanging' and has a few technical uses. A *pennant* is a tapering flag, especially one flown at the masthead of a ship.

pending is used (1) as an adjective meaning 'awaiting a decision or completion' (*A new edition of the book is pending*), and (2) as a preposition meaning 'during, throughout the process of' (*A final decision cannot be taken pending his trial*).

peninsula is a noun meaning 'a piece of land almost surrounded by water' (*The Spanish peninsula*) and *peninsular* is the corresponding adjective (*The Peninsular War*).

pen name *see* NOM DE PLUME.

pennant *see* PENDANT, PENDENT, PENNANT.

penny. The plural for separate coins is *pennies* (*He had four pennies in his pocket*), although in Britain this usually means pre-decimal money, and for a sum of money is *pence* (*an increase of 50 pence*). *See also* PEE. In North America a one-cent coin is often called a *penny* (with plural *pennies*).

pension, meaning 'a French or European boarding house', is pronounced **pã**-syã, in a French manner with nasalized vowels, and is normally printed in italic type to distinguish it from the naturalized word *pension*.

people, persons. Both words have been in use for several centuries to denote the plural of *person*, the difference usually being explained in terms of *people* referring to a group of which the exact number cannot be determined or is irrelevant and *persons* to a number of individuals who are countable or regarded separately: *A great many people feel that a hug can make their day*—Chicago Tribune, 1991 / *It is morally certain that a number of persons signed confessions to crimes of which they were innocent*—K. Lindsay, 1980. However, this distinction is not watertight, as the following examples show: *Persons may squat in buildings by reason of inability to find other accommodation*—Oxford Companion to Law, 1980 / *It now numbers some 40 people, as well as the Jersey cows, the Aberdeen Angus bull, the horse, three ponies, and a handful of fecund goats and breeding sows*—Country Living, 1991. The supposed rule that *persons* must be used after a numeral, which thrived for some time in AmE, is now a dead letter, though many people think it still applies. To judge from the recent evidence, the distinction is based as much on context as on meaning, with *people* used as the general word and *persons* used in more formal contexts (e.g. law, on notices) and to emphasize individuality. The plural *persons* (and generally not *people*) also occurs in compound forms such as *barpersons*, *chairpersons*, *spokespersons*, and other gender-neutral forms. An exception is *sportspeople*, which is typically treated collectively in usage.

per. It is a sound general rule not to use this Latin word when an English equivalent exists and is idiomatic: it is better, for example, to say *The salary is £40,000 a year* rather than *The salary is £40,000 per year*, and *We will send the goods by parcel post* than *We will send the goods per parcel post*. *Per* is best reserved for use in official contexts, in Latin phrases such as *per annum*, and in formulaic

expressions such as *miles per hour* and *kilometres per gallon*. For *as per*, *see* AS 10.

per capita means 'by heads' and has largely replaced the more strictly correct form *per caput* ('for each head') as the normal way of saying 'for each person or head (of population)'. Fowler (1926) regarded this use of *per capita* as 'a modern blunder, encouraged in some recent dictionaries', but its use is now standard: *During the same period, per capita consumption rose 15 percent in terms of constant prices*—Dædalus, 1990. *Per caput* is also still found, but is much less common and often has a pedantic tone: *It may be argued that per-caput cigarette consumption is not a good measure of cigarette consumption in young women*—Lancet, 1976.

perceive is widely used somewhat pretentiously in the sense 'consider' or 'regard': *The economic, social, and psychological costs of becoming pregnant and having a child while on public assistance are perceived as clearly outweighing the benefits*—A. Bryman, 2004. Although this use is well established, and is recorded without comment in the *COD* (2006), it is often an unnecessary Latinate alternative for the perfectly good English word *see*, which could have been used in the example just given with no loss of meaning or effect. *Perceive* carries with it a substantial baggage of philosophical and psychological implications from which the simpler word *see* is free. If *see* won't do, *consider* and *regard* are also nearly always better choices.

per cent is normally written as two words in BrE but as one word (*percent*) in AmE. In attributive use (i.e. before a noun), it is normally written with a hyphen in BrE: *a 12 per-cent increase*. The type—*per cent of* is normally treated as singular if the noun is a collective or mass noun and as plural if the noun is an ordinary plural: *Fifteen per cent of the electorate* **has** *yet to make up its mind—Daily Telegraph*, 1987 / *50 per cent of children with nut allergies also* **react** *to egg—Observer*, 2007. In AmE, but not in BrE, *percent* is also used as a noun, an alternative to *percentage* (*a large percent of the population*).

percentage. Since a *percentage* can be a quantity of any size, and even (unlike *part*) more than the whole, it is best to qualify it with adjectives such as *small*, *tiny*, or *large*, or by the adverb *only*, as appropriate: *a large percentage of books published in the USA ... / all but a small percentage. ... See also* FRACTION.

peremptory means 'admitting no denial or refusal' and not (perhaps by confusion with *perfunctory*) 'abrupt, sudden'. A *peremptory decision* is not one that has been hastily reached but one that is definitive. The word is normally pronounced with the stress on the second syllable, although an older first-syllable stress survives in legal usage.

perennial, with reference to plants, means 'lasting several years' by contrast with *annual* which means 'lasting for one growing season'.

perfect. 1 In its primary meaning 'complete, not deficient', *perfect* is an absolute and cannot logically be qualified by words such as *more, most*, and *very*. (This is a philosophical point, not a matter of grammatical correctness.) As the *OED* notes, however, *perfect* is 'often used of a near approach to such a state [of complete excellence], and hence is capable of comparison'. Such uses are found in literature from the 14c onward, including Shakespeare's *Our men more perfect in the use of arms—2 Henry IV* IV.i.153. In modern use, *perfect* is used more often than not in weakened meanings and is therefore amenable to

qualification: *What figure is more perfect than the sphere*—William Golding, 1965 / *Maybe not purity but he seemed so perfect and so unreal, in a way*—Chinua Achebe, 1987. / *The almost-complete medieval town curls around the port and at one end ... is San Nicola Pellegrino, the most perfect of all cathedrals—Times*, 1995.

2 *Perfect* is pronounced with the stress on the first syllable as an adjective and with the stress on the second syllable as a verb.

perfectible is spelt *-ible*, not *-able. See* -ABLE, -IBLE.

perfect infinitive. This is the type *to have been, to have said*, etc., and occurs most commonly after the verbs *appear* and *seem*: *She appeared to have encouraged him / That seemed to have been an isolated incident*. In each case the reported event occurred before the time of the statement itself. If the event and the reporting occur at the same time, a present (or present continuous) infinitive is used instead: *She appeared to be encouraging him / That seemed to be an isolated incident*. For the type *would have liked* (or *preferred*) *to have been, see* HAVE 2; LIKE (*verb*).

perimeter, unlike *parameter*, is rarely used in figurative meanings, but occasional uses are found, usually in the context of broader metaphors: *The perimeter of her own life was shrinking*—J. Urquhart, CanE 1986.

period. For the meaning with reference to time, *see* EPOCH. For the punctuation mark, *see* FULL STOP.

periodic, periodical. *Periodic* is an adjective only, and although once largely restricted to technical and scientific contexts (e.g. *periodic decimal, periodic function*, and *periodic table*), it has become commoner in non-technical usage as well and has largely ousted *periodical* in the meaning 'appearing or occurring at regular intervals' (*Smoke detectors require periodic checks to ensure that they are working properly—British Medical Journal*, 2002). *Periodical* is very rarely used in this sense, but unlike *periodic* is used as a noun with the particular meaning 'a newspaper or magazine issued at regular intervals'.

permanence, permanency. The more usual choice in current use for the meaning 'a state of being permanent' is *permanence*, but *permanency* is also occasionally used in this meaning and more especially in the meaning 'something that is permanent': *A stranger is not a permanency. One can easily shed a stranger*—Graham Greene, 1988.

permit is pronounced with the stress on the first syllable as a noun and with the stress on the second syllable as a verb. The verb has inflected forms *permitted, permitting*.

pernickety, meaning 'fussy, fastidious', is a 19c word of Scottish origin which has spread to all English-speaking areas. In AmE, the form *persnickety* is also used.

perpetrate, perpetuate are verbs that are sometimes confused. *Perpetrate* means 'to commit (a harmful, illegal, or immoral action)', as in *a crime has been perpetrated against a sovereign state*, whereas *perpetuate* means 'to make continue indefinitely', as in *a monument to perpetuate the memory of those killed in the war*. Each is incorrectly used for the other in the following examples: ▣ *For example, violence perpetuated* (read *perpetrated*) *by adolescents is a major problem in our society—OEC*, 2004 / *Yet the Attorney General's prosecutors and the High Court judgment continue to perpetrate* (read *perpetuate*) *the myth that the massacre was spontaneous—OEC*, 2003.

per pro *see* P.P.

perquisite, prerequisite. A *perquisite* is an incidental benefit attached to a person's job or employment, and is almost always used in the shortened form *perk*. A *prerequisite* is something required as a condition before something else can be done: *Sponsorship is not a prerequisite for any of our courses but we are happy for students to arrange sponsorship if they wish to do so*—university prospectus, 1993.

persistence, persistency. Both words came into English in the 16c and they remain largely interchangeable, although in current use *persistency* is really rather unusual: *Agelessly silent, with a reptile's persistency*—D. H. Lawrence, 1921 / *By sheer persistence he'd achieved what at first seemed inaccessible*—E. North, 1987.

person. For the plural *persons*, *see* PEOPLE, PERSONS.

-person. *See box overleaf.*

persona. In current usage, *persona* (in origin the Latin word for an actor's mask) has acquired two special meanings and a generalized one that draws on both: (1) a character deliberately assumed by an author in his or her writing, (*Does he intend to stick with one character or will he develop another persona?—Bolton Evening News*, 2003), (2) in Jungian psychology, the set of attitudes adopted by an individual to fit himself or herself for an appropriate social role, (3) an aspect of the personality as shown to or perceived by others (*James Spicer, his military persona now well to the fore, ignored the question and picked up the phone*—M. Hamer, 1991). The psychological resonance of these uses makes *persona* a more powerful word than (say) *identity*, and

-PERSON.

1 The use of -*person* as a gender-neutral suffix denoting occupations instead of -*man* began in the 1970s with *chairperson* (*see* CHAIRMAN), and has spread rather more slowly than might have been expected, possibly because of a reluctance to adopt forms that are more socially acceptable but are linguistically more awkward or cumbersome. The table below lists some typical formations, some having an ephemeral appearance and others likely to achieve some permanence:

word	date
anchorperson	1976
barperson	1976
chairperson	1971
craftsperson	1976
draughtsperson	1976
Englishperson	1977
everyperson	1978
henchperson	1973
newspaper person	1976
salesperson	1971
spokesperson	1972
waitperson	1980

2 The substitution of *person* for *man* in other ways, e.g. in *personhandle* and *personpower*, and in *gingerbread person*, is showing no sign of gaining favour.

the development is a useful one. The plural is slightly more often the anglicized *personas* than the Latinate *personae*, but both are correct.

personally. The uses of *personally* illustrated by *The decision was made by the president personally* (= by the president and no one else) and *He took the criticism personally* (= in a personal manner) are unobjectionable. Doubts arise when *personally* is used to mean 'for myself, for my part', as in *Personally, I don't approve of such behaviour*. This use is best restricted to informal contexts. In many cases it can be simply omitted, or replaced by *for my part*.

personnel. The word is pronounced with the stress on the third syllable, and refers to the people belonging to an organization or institution, originally in the armed forces and later in the business world. It is often used attributively (i.e. before a noun), e.g. *personnel carrier* (in military contexts), *personnel officer* (in business contexts), or is qualified in some way, e.g. *military personnel* and *trained personnel*, and it is occasionally preceded by a numeral to denote a number of *personnel*: *one copy to every 25 personnel*. Used by itself it also means 'a personnel department' (*I'd better check with Personnel*), although this name has now given way, at least in professional parlance, to the more fashionable term *human resources*.

persons *see* PEOPLE, PERSONS.

perspective. 1 *Perspective* is well established in the meaning of 'point of view', as in: *from our perspective this is a sensible proposal*. Nowadays it is increasingly common to encounter phrases where *perspective* is wrongly replaced by *prospective*: ✖ *from our prospective this is a sensible proposal*. Though there are historical precedents for *prospective* being used in this way, it is best to avoid doing so, as many people, especially British speakers, will regard such a use as a mistake.

2 In its 17c meaning 'mental point of view or way of regarding something', *perspective* has developed a special use with *on* followed by the name of a subject or intellectual domain: *Perspectives on Thomas Hobbes* (book title, 1989).

perspicacious, perspicuous. Fowler (1926) snootily urged the use of simpler alternatives by 'those who are neither learned nor pretentious'. *Perspicacious* means 'having mental penetration or discernment, discerning', and its corresponding noun is *perspicacity*. *Perspicuous*, on the other hand, means 'clear to understand' (with reference to people and statements), and its noun is *perspicuity*. It is the nouns that are confused rather than the adjectives, and the following examples of correct uses may help to distinguish them in the reader's mind: *He went through the photographs. But it didn't take much perspicacity to tell that some . . . were missing*—Ruth Rendell, 1983 / *He [William Cobbett] wrote with perspicuity and vigour, in a prose style commended by Hazlitt as 'plain, broad, downright English'*—Margaret Drabble, 2000. Suitable alternative words are (for *perspicacity*) *perception, perceptiveness, acuteness*, and

shrewdness, and (for *perspicuity*) *clarity, lucidity*, and *lucidness*.

persuade *see* CONVINCE.

persuasion. The earlier, 19c. meaning 'belief or conviction', as in *a person of no particular persuasion*, has developed into a much weaker sense 'kind or sort', as in *no one of the male persuasion*. The *OED* used to label such uses as 'slang or burlesque' but has changed the label to 'colloquial and humorous', and in current use the intention is still usually humorous: *A sinister moustache of the tooth-brush persuasion*—R. Hichens, 1902 / *Today, I am pathetically grateful to be able to sit and type on the train. This is only possible because the poor sod jammed in beside me is a very slim young person of the female persuasion*—weblog, 2008.

peruse is a formal word. Many people insist that it means 'to read thoroughly', and that to use it to mean 'to read cursorily, to glance over', is a mistake. However, as the *OED* acknowledges, and as the examples show, in current use it covers the whole spectrum of reading, from skimming to going through with a fine-tooth comb; adverbs often specify the degree of thoroughness. On its own, it can be a straightforward, if somewhat precious, synonym for 'read'. But, since there is a widespread prejudice against using it to mean merely 'to read' or 'to skim', unless you are being literary or ironic, why not use those words if that is what you mean? *I am always incorrigibly interested in the behaviour of the 'human animal', and look forward to perusing divers effusions of your lively pen*—Kingsley Amis, 1946 / *For me, it had all the wearisome unfunniness of back numbers of Punch perused in the dentist's waiting-room*—Times Literary Supplement, 1980 / *Also take some time and carefully peruse the specification chart comparing the different models*—Guns (magazine), 2003 / *Perusing its promotional materials, you might get the idea the pharmaceutical industry is a non-profit research operation out to save the human race—The Nation*, 2003.

perverse, pervert, perverted.

1 *Perverse* and *perverted*, both derived from the Latin root *pervertere* 'to turn away' (from what is normal or correct), are easily confused. *Perverse* means 'stubbornly unreasonable' (usually of actions or circumstances but also of people): *Amazingly, perversely, and rather to her regret (a flat battery would have been a cast-iron excuse to abort the visit) the engine fired*—David Lodge, 1988 / *It would be perverse of him not to be pleased, but Matthiesson feels the plaudits are often misplaced*—Sunday Herald, 2002. *Perverted* means 'departing from right opinion or conduct' and is commonly used with reference to abnormal or deviant sexual behaviour: *I've seen blokes in hot countries go clean round the oojar because of the perverted practices of native women*—Brian Aldiss, 1971.

2 *Pervert* is pronounced with the stress on the first syllable as a noun (= a person who is sexually perverted) and with the stress on the second syllable as a verb (= to corrupt, lead astray).

petal has a derived form *petalled* in BrE, but *petaled* is also used in AmE.

petite, meaning 'attractively small' (usually with reference to a woman), is now usually printed in roman type as an anglicized word.

petitio principii means 'begging of a principle' and denotes a logical fallacy in which a conclusion is taken for granted in the premiss. For example, an essay entitled 'Against the excessive use of the apostrophe' poses a *petitio principii* because it assumes the use is excessive when that is the point at issue. *See* BEG THE QUESTION. It is printed in italic type.

pewit *see* PEEWIT.

ph-. These first two letters of the word *phone* have become a productive prefix or word-forming element, and have been used to create four 20c and 21c *portmanteau words, of which three are now very well known. It will be intriguing to see if more emerge in the near future. *Phishing*, first recorded in 1996, is a pun on *fishing*, and denotes the fraudulent practice of sending emails purporting to be from reputable companies in order to 'angle' online for the recipient's personal information, such as passwords and credit card numbers. *Phablet*, a blend of *ph(one)* + *(t)ablet* apparently first coined in 2010, was voted the word of 2012 'least likely to succeed' by the American Dialect Society. They seem to have misjudged, since the term is now used by the general public and by the manufacturers of these smartphones, which have a screen intermediate in size between that of a typical smartphone and a tablet computer. *Phubbing*, a blend of *(ph)one* and *(sn)ubbing*, refers to the discourtesy of ignoring someone in whose company you are because you are using your mobile phone or a similar device. It is unusual in that it was brainstormed into existence in May 2012 as part of a marketing campaign by an Australian dictionary publisher. It then went viral through social media, and, presumably, by the time you read this, will either have faded from view, or become completely established. Finally, a now largely forgotten term, *phreaking*, provided the model for the creation of *phishing*. First recorded centuries ago in technology terms (1971), it refers to the action of hacking into telecommunications systems, especially to obtain free calls, and is a blend of *phone* and *freak* in its sense 'a bizarrely abnormal person or thing';

there may also be a play on the words *free call*.

phablet *see* PH-.

phantasm, phantom. In current usage *phantom* primarily means 'a ghost' or 'a mental illusion', whereas *phantasm* means 'a visual illusion' or 'a vision of an absent person'.

phantasy *see* FANTASY, PHANTASY.

pharaoh, an ancient Egyptian king, is spelt *-aoh*, not *-oah*.

pharmacopoeia, meaning 'an official directory of drugs', is spelt *-poeia* in BrE and *-poeia* or *-peia* in AmE. The pronunciation in both cases is fah-muh-kuh-**pee**-uh.

phenomenal. The modern generalized meaning 'extraordinary, remarkable' (*Interest in the race has been phenomenal—York Press*, 2002 [*OEC*]) is now the dominant one, although it retains little of the notion of its meaning in technical (especially philosophical) contexts, in which the meaning is 'perceived by the senses'. (*Every event has a physical cause which is enough to bring it about—without holding that there can (even in principle) be an explanation of phenomenal consciousness in physical terms*—T. Crane, 2001).

phenomenon. The primary meaning now is 'an extraordinary or remarkable person or thing' rather than 'a fact or occurrence that is perceived', although this meaning runs it a close second. *Phenomena* is the plural form, but is often treated mistakenly as a singular noun: ☒ *Footsteps are heard all over the building causing surprise and apprehension and expectancy in those visitors who have heard about the phenomena but haven't experienced it* [correct to . . . *haven't experienced them*]—W. B. Herbert,

1992. Equally incorrect are the plurals *phenomenons* and *phenomenae*.

philharmonic is a loan translation, based on the Italian *filarmonico*, 'loving or practising music', and is a fusion of the Greek prefix *philo-* + *harmonic*. The standard pronunciation in BrE is generally with a silent *h*, but, possibly under the influence of AmE pronunciation, or of the speak-as-you-spell school of thought, the *h* is now quite often pronounced in BrE as well.

Philippines, the chain of islands in South East Asia, is spelt in this way, with one *l* and two *p*s. The inhabitants are called *Filipinos*.

Philistine. A *Philistine* (with a capital initial letter) is a member of an ancient Semitic people of Palestine. A *philistine* (with a small initial letter, usually) is a person who is hostile or indifferent to culture.

phishing *see* PH-.

phlegm, meaning 'a viscous substance discharged by coughing', is pronounced flem. The *g* is also silent in the adjective *phlegmy*, but is pronounced in *phlegmatic* (fleg-**mat**-ik), meaning 'stolidly calm and unemotional'.

phone, the shortening of *telephone*, is not written with an apostrophe before the *p-*.

phoney, an informal word meaning 'sham, fake' (adjective and noun), is of uncertain origin and not traced in print before 1900. Its currency was greatly boosted by the use of the term *phoney war* to refer to the relative inaction in the early months of the Second World War. *Phoney* is the preferred spelling, although *phony* is also used.

phosphorus, phosphorous. *Phosphorus* is the noun for the chemical

photo 482

element, and *phosphorous* is the adjective meaning 'containing phosphorus'.

photo is a well-established shortening of *photograph*, used chiefly in spoken English. Its plural form is *photos*, and it is commonly used in attributive position (i.e. before a noun), as in *photo call*, *photo finish*, and *photo opportunity*.

phrasal verbs. 1 A phrasal verb is a combination of a verb with an adverb or preposition (or both) such as *come about*, *draw up*, *put up with*, and *work out*. Phrasal verbs of all types have meanings that cannot be directly deduced from the individual words, and in some cases they have several meanings and grammatical patterns. For example, *run up* has three distinct meanings in the sentences *She ran up to meet them*, *She ran up debts*, and *She ran up the flag*. In these three examples *up* is an adverb, and in the last two the objects *debts* and *flag* are governed by the verb *ran*.

2 Phrasal verbs formed with adverbs can be either transitive (i.e. take an object, as in *He drew up a chair*) or intransitive (as in *A taxi drew up*). Phrasal verbs formed with prepositions are transitive (*I must go through some papers*). When the object of a phrasal verb is a pronoun, it normally comes between the verb and a following adverb, e.g. *He took up my references* but *He took them up*. This pattern can occur with noun objects as well, though not in all cases: *I'll put the shelf up* could be converted to *I'll put up the shelf* whereas *She heads up a team* cannot be converted to *She heads a team up*, although *down* and *up* are both being used as adverbs.

3 Phrasal verbs range from the informal to the neutral but are hardly ever formal in register. They form a highly productive area of current English, with recent new formations including *bottom out* (= reach the lowest point before stabilizing or improving), *chill out* (= relax),

dumb down (= make simpler), *factor in* (= include in an assessment or survey), *freak out* (= lose one's temper), and *talk up* (= stress or exaggerate the importance of), and the notorious *sex up* (= present in a more lively way). They tend to be informal in use (less so with the first and fourth). In some cases they can easily be translated into a single word, as for example *take off* (= mimic), or *work out* (= resolve), or into a phrase as in the case of *set off* (= begin a journey). Often, however, there is no simple one-to-one 'translation'. For example, the meaning and connotations of *dumb down* are not fully conveyed by 'simplify' or 'make simpler'.

4 Phrasal verbs produce noun derivatives of two types: (1) the verb precedes the adverb/preposition, e.g. *breakdown*, *copout*, *feedback*, and *lie-in*; (2) the adverb/preposition precedes the verb, e.g. *backdrop* and *outcome*. Some phrasal verbs produce both forms, e.g. *breakout* and *outbreak*. These also vary in register from the neutral (*breakdown*, *breakout*, *feedback*, *outbreak*) to the informal (*lie-in*). Nouns derived from phrasal verbs in which the verb comes first sometimes have a hyphen, e.g. *tie-in*, *lie-in*, *sleep-in*. Phrasal verbs themselves should never be hyphenated: ☒ *So we can't cover-up any imperfections—Sunday Times*.

5 For a fuller discussion of this topic, see *The Oxford Companion to the English Language* (1992), 772–6.

phreaking, phubbing see PH-.

physician, doctor, surgeon. The normal word for a medical practitioner in general contexts is *doctor* (abbreviated as a title to *Dr*). *Physician* is familiar from the proverb *Physician, heal thyself* (Luke 4:23) and has the same range of meaning as *doctor* but is not in general use. In current British use, a *doctor* in general practice is distinguished as a *general* *practitioner* (or *GP*). In AmE, *Doctor* is also used for a qualified dentist or veterinary surgeon; and in all English-speaking countries *Doctor* and *Dr* are used (as titles only) to refer to a person who has a doctorate in a non-medical subject (e.g. *Doctor of Philosophy*). A *surgeon* is a person who is qualified to practise surgery, and in Britain (except Scotland) is addressed as *Mr*, not *Dr*.

physiognomy, physiology. *Physiognomy* (pronounced with the *g* silent) is 'the cast or form of a person's features', whereas *physiology* is 'the science of the functions of living organisms and their parts'.

pianist is normally pronounced **pee**-uh-nist with the stress on the first syllable in BrE and pi-**ah**-nist with the stress on the second syllable in AmE.

piano. The plural form of the noun is *pianos*.

piazza, meaning 'an open square or market place', is normally pronounced in the Italian manner, pi-**at**-suh, and in English contexts has the plural form *piazzas*. In AmE the pronunciation is more often pi-**az**-uh, and it also has the special meaning 'the veranda of a house'.

picaresque is used to describe a type of fiction concerned with the adventures of a rogue (from Spanish *picaro* meaning 'rogue'). The type is represented in 18c English literature by Defoe's *Moll Flanders* (1722), Fielding's *Tom Jones* (1749), and other classic works, but the first record of the use of the term in an English context is by Sir Walter Scott in 1827.

piccolo, the smallest flute, has the plural form *piccolos*.

picket. The verb has inflected forms *picketed, picketing*.

picnic. The verb has inflected forms *picnicked, picnicking*.

pidgin. A *pidgin* is a simplified language containing vocabulary and grammatical elements from two or more languages, and is used mainly by traders who do not have a language in common. It differs from a Creole in being improvised for a special purpose as distinct from being the mother tongue of a speech community. The word *pidgin* is probably a Chinese corruption of the English word *business*, which is reflected also in the idiom *that's your pigeon* (= that's your affair or business).

piebald, skewbald. A *piebald* horse or other animal is one with irregular patches of two colours, especially black and white. A *skewbald* animal has irregular patches of white and another colour (other than black).

pièce de résistance, meaning 'the most important or remarkable item', is printed in italic type with the accents as shown. The plural (not often needed) is *pièces de résistance*, pronounced in the same way as the singular, pyess duh ray-zɪs-**tãs**.

pied-à-terre, meaning 'a small house or apartment kept for occasional use', is pronounced pyay-dah-**tair** and is now printed in roman type with the accent as shown. The plural form is *pieds-à-terre* (with the same pronunciation).

pietà, a representation of the dead Christ held by his mother, is pronounced pi-ay-**tah** and printed in roman type with an accent on the *a*.

pigmy *see* PYGMY.

pilau, a type of Middle Eastern or Indian spiced dish of rice, is normally spelt in this way in BrE, but *pilaf* or *pilaff* in AmE. These forms also occur, however, in BrE.

pilfer, meaning 'to steal (something trivial)', has inflected forms *pilfered*, *pilfering*.

pilot. The verb has inflected forms *piloted*, *piloting*.

pinch. The idiom *at a pinch*, meaning 'if absolutely necessary', is the BrE form; in AmE it is *in a pinch*.

piquant, meaning 'agreeably pungent' or 'pleasantly stimulating', is pronounced **pee**-kuhnt or **pee**-kont.

pique *see* PEAK, PEEK, PIQUE.

pis aller, meaning 'a course of action followed as a last resort', is pronounced peez **al**-ay and is printed in italic type. The literal French meaning is 'to go worse'.

pistachio, a type of nut, has the plural form *pistachios*.

piteous, pitiable, pitiful. All three words are recorded from Middle English and share the basic meaning 'arousing pity' and are to some extent interchangeable (as in *The abandoned children were a piteous sight*), although *pitiful* is the most versatile and *piteous* is the least common. *Piteous* and *pitiable* can both convey the meaning 'deserving pity', and *pitiable* and *pitiful* convey the meaning 'evoking mingled pity and contempt'. *Pitiful* alone is used in the meaning 'absurdly small or insignificant', as in *The state pension has been reduced to a pitiful sum.* Examples: *A pitiful tube squirts water to a height of a couple of feet*—J. D. R. McConnell, 1970 / *How she had suffered for him, for her poor pitiable ridiculous father*—Margaret Drabble, 1987 / *'What did I do this time?' Helen looked piteous*—Maeve Binchy, 1988 / *He had been a thorn in the Empire's side for many years, and he had eluded their pitiful armies again and again*—fiction website, BrE 2006 [*OEC*].

pixel(l)ated, pixil(l)ated. The adjective *pixilated* is a 19c AmE word derived from *pixie*, originally meaning 'bewildered or confused' (literally 'led astray by pixies'), and informally 'drunk'. Another word entirely is *pixellated*, a technical term for a digital image that has been distorted into component areas (*pixels*) in order to conceal the identity of the person being shown. However, as *ODO* acknowledges, the spelling *pixilated* is also used in that meaning. *Pixelated* is the more common spelling in AmE and *pixellated* in BrE, while *pixillated* with double *l* is not very common at all.

pizzazz, a slang term meaning 'verve, sparkle', has many variant spellings, of which the one given is the most common, with over five times as many examples as *pizazz* in the *OEC*. The more alliterative form *pzazz* occurs very rarely.

placebo, meaning 'a pill or medicine given for psychological effect', is pronounced pla-**see**-boh and has the plural form *placebos*.

plaid, pronounced plad, is a length of fabric worn over the shoulder as part of the ceremonial dress of members of the pipe bands of Scottish regiments. It should be distinguished from *tartan*, which is a woollen cloth with a pattern of different coloured stripes crossing at right angles, each pattern being associated with a particular clan. A *plaid* can be made from *tartan* cloth.

Plain English. 1 The expression *plain English*, meaning 'English that is clear and easy to understand', goes back to the 15c, and was the term often used in the titles of the first dictionaries that appeared during the 17c; Robert Cawdrey, for example, described the contents of his 1604 *Table Alphabeticall* as listing hard words 'with the interpretation thereof by plaine English words'. The current UK Plain English campaign was started in the 1970s and grew out of the consumer movement and the demand for fair dealing. It may be seen as belonging to the tradition of the work done by Sir Ernest Gowers in publications such as *Plain Words* (1948, later *The Complete Plain Words*, 1954 and later editions) and in the material he added to the second edition of Fowler's *Modern English Usage* (1965). A similar movement exists in the US, including the Plain English Forum set up in the 1980s.

2 Plain English insists on clarity as well as accuracy and wages war on convoluted, obfuscating language typified by the use of such words as *aforesaid, in the event of, incumbent on,* and *thereto.* It argues that inflated statements such as *Encashment of a foreign currency may incur a processing fee* may be stated more effectively as *We may charge you for changing your foreign money.* In some contexts, however, the need for precision can require the use of special terminology; this aspect is discussed in the entries for *legalese and *officialese. See also Martin Cutts, *The Oxford Guide to Plain English* (2nd edition, 2004).

plain sailing, meaning 'a straightforward situation or course of action', is an early 19c alteration of the original (late 17c) phrase *plane sailing*, which denoted a system of measuring short nautical distances by assuming that the earth's surface is a plane and not spherical.

plan. The verb is followed either by *to* or (especially in AmE) by *on*: *Do you plan on staying with Muriel forever?*—A. Tyler, 1985 / *Managers hope that an auction will drive the value of Europe's biggest coal-fired power station complex up towards the £2.5 billion that they plan to achieve if the company is floated on the stock market*—*Times*, 2005. As a noun *plan* typically collocates with *to* in expressing intention: *There are no plans to close the ambulance base in*

Kenmare—Killarney Kingdom, 2003 [OEC]. It is followed by *of* to introduce a defining word (*plan of action, plan of campaign,* etc.).

planet. In order to emphasize that something is superlative, the best, the most whatever it may be, it seems no longer enough merely to call it the best in the world: fashion dictates that it has to be the best *on the planet,* which, supposedly, conveys a stronger impression of its superlativeness, despite, in many contexts, sounding rhetorically inflated. Examples: *Still, he would have to be the most incompetent guy on the planet to mess up such jaw-dropping source material*—*Eye Weekly* (Toronto), 2005 / *Turturro is able to take Eddie Izzard—one of the funniest men on the planet— and put him in a purely serious role*—*Twitchfilm,* 2005 (BrE).

planetarium has the plural form *planetariums,* or occasionally *planetaria.*

plaster. The verb has inflected forms *plastered, plastering.*

plastic is now normally pronounced with a short first syllable as in *plan.* The adjectival form is *plasticky.*

plateau has the plural form *plateaux* (preferred to *plateaus*), pronounced in the same way as the singular.

plateful has the plural form *platefuls.*

platonic, referring to spiritual as distinct from erotic love, is spelt with a small initial *p.* When the reference is directly to Plato (as in *Platonic dialogue*), it is spelt *Platonic* with a capital initial letter.

platypus has the plural form *platypuses.*

player has extended its meaning from being a participant in a game of sport or fun to being a participant in a different type of game, namely commercial politics. This use originated in the US and has spread rapidly into BrE, although it is largely restricted to the domain of business journalism: *Other players include the Ford Motor company, which . . . has been talking about selling its mortgages through car showrooms*—*Economist*, 1986.

plc, PLC. Both forms are used for the abbreviation of *Public Limited Company*, a status introduced in the UK in 1980.

plead. The past tense and past participle in standard BrE are both *pleaded*, but *pled* and *plead* (pronounced pled) are used as well as *pleaded* in America, Scotland, and some dialects in the UK. In legal usage, an accused person can *plead guilty* or *not guilty*, but cannot *plead innocent*, which is a non-technical expression only.

please. The use of *please* by itself, as in *Will you come in, please?*, is a reduced form of *may it* (*so*) *please you*. It was first recorded in the 17c, but was not used by Shakespeare, whose shortest form is *please you*.

plebiscite, referendum. *Plebiscite* is pronounced **pleb**-i-siyt in AmE, as it often is also in BrE, where it alternates with **pleb**-i-sit. The term is most commonly used of a direct vote of a State's electors on a fundamental matter, and is not used with reference to the UK. A *referendum* is the referral of an important specific issue to the electorate for a general vote, and is used in the UK.

plectrum has the plural form *plectrums* when referring to guitar picks, and occasionally *plectra* in classical music or scientific contexts.

plenteous, plentiful. The normal word in current English is *plentiful*, but *plenteous* will be found especially in literary works of the 19c and earlier.

plenty is essentially a noun, and is used either by itself or with *of* + following noun (plural, or singular uncountable or mass nouns): *We have plenty / You will find plenty of books / There is plenty of time*. *Plenty* as an adjective without *of* is used in regional forms of English but is not standard: *Although there are plenty other ideals that I should prefer*—Robert Louis Stevenson / *Leopard Society in Sierra Leone. They kill plenty people*—Graham Greene, 1969. Use of *plenty* as an adverb meaning 'very, clearly, more than usually' is restricted to non-standard AmE: *He seems plenty dead to me*—R. Silverberg, 1985 / *I frowned at my mother plenty*—New Yorker, 1990.

pleonasm is a term meaning 'the use of more words than are necessary to give the sense'. An example in ordinary (as distinct from literary) usage is *please reply back* (the idea of 'back', i.e. in return, is inherent in *reply*).

plethora, meaning 'an oversupply, an excess', is pronounced **pleth**-uh-ruh and is a singular noun. When *plethora of* is followed by a plural noun, the relevant verb is singular if the noun phrase is thought of as a single unit and plural if it is thought of as a collection of separate entities: (plural concord) *And let's not forget the plethora of California organizations that consistently **honor** all that dairy has to offer*—Dairy Field (magazine), 2003; (singular concord) *Looking at the nonfiction category, a plethora of books **looks** at the current state of affairs*—weblog, 2004.

plough is the normal BrE spelling, but *plow* is used in AmE.

plunder as a verb has inflected forms *plundered, plundering*.

plurals of nouns. *See box opposite.*

PLURALS OF NOUNS.

English nouns normally form their plurals by adding -*s*, or -*es* if the singular
form ends in -*s*, -*x*, -*z*, -*sh*, or soft -*ch* (as in *church* but *not loch*). Words in -*y*
form plurals in -*ies* (*policies*) unless the ending is -*ey* in which case the plural
form is normally -*eys* (*monkeys*); but *see* MONEYS. Difficulties occur mainly
when the singular form is unusual and does not allow ready application of the
normal rules or when the word is of foreign origin (or both). Nouns in -*f*
and -*fe* are given in the entry *-fs, -ves, nouns of the type *cupful* at the entry
*-ful, and nouns in -*o* in the entry *-o; plurals of some Latin nouns in English
are given in the entry *Latin plurals. For plurals of abbreviated forms (such as
MP) *see* ABBREVIATIONS 3. The following table lists other plural forms that
cause difficulties of various kinds.

irregular plurals

child	children
foot	feet
goose	geese
louse	lice
man	men
mouse	mice
tooth	teeth
woman	women

animal names the same in the plural

bison	bison
cod	cod
deer	deer
grouse	grouse
salmon	salmon
sheep	sheep
squid	squid
swine	swine

nouns in plural form only: tools

bellows
binoculars
clippers
forceps
gallows
glasses
goggles
pincers
pliers
scissors
shears

p

spectacles (= glasses)
tongs
tweezers

---

nouns in plural form only: articles of clothing

braces
breeches
briefs
flannels
jeans
knickers
leggings
pants
pyjamas (US pajamas)
shorts
slacks
suspenders
tights
trousers

---

compound nouns

Attorney-General	Attorneys-General*
brother-in-law	brothers-in-law
commander-in-chief	commanders-in-chief
court martial	courts martial
daughter-in-law	daughters-in-law
father-in-law	fathers-in-law
Governor-General	Governors-General*
lay-by	lay-bys
man-of war	men-of-war
mother-in-law	mothers-in-law
passer-by	passers-by
Poet Laureate	Poets Laureate*
sister-in-law	sisters-in-law
son-in-law	sons-in-law
stand-by	stand-bys

*The forms Attorney-Generals, Governor-Generals,
and Poet Laureates are also used

---

p

plus is used primarily as the oral equivalent of the arithmetical sign + (*Three plus four is seven*). In the 20c it went from strength to strength as a quasi-preposition with the meaning 'with the addition of, and also' (e.g. *A cup of Epp's cocoa and a shakedown for the night plus the use of a rug and over-coat doubled into a pillow*—James Joyce, 1922). A more controversial use from the 1960s (first in America) makes *plus* a conjunction or adverb (with a comma following) meaning 'and furthermore, and in addition': (conjunction) *You can fly an aeroplane . . . and command a ship. Plus you ride horses*—New Yorker, 1987 / *'It's certainly a challenge. Plus it's a little overwhelming, but it's exciting,' says Nicole*—Daily Mail, 1998 / (adverb) *I'll quit romanticizing him. Plus, he never got to go on any road trips*—B. Ripley, 1987 / *It's a bad movie but at times it's the kind of bad movie worth watching. . . . Plus, there's an omnipresent horizontal flurry of ash in nearly every outdoor scene. Not snow, ash. At least it looks like ash*—film reviews, AmE 2005 [*OEC*]. These uses occur frequently in advertisements (e.g. *20% off everything—plus no deposit*) but should not be adopted in more formal writing.

p.m. As an abbreviation of Latin *post meridiem* 'after noon', *p.m.* is pronounced as two letters and written in the form 8.15 *p.m.* (or *pm*; in AmE 8:15 *p.m.*). The abbreviation is sometimes used informally as a noun: *We arrived here this p.m. See also* A.M.

pocket as a verb has inflected forms *pocketed, pocketing.*

pocketful has the plural form *pocketfuls. See* -FUL.

podcast, a digital audio file of speech, music, broadcast material, etc., made available on the Internet for downloading to a computer or portable media player. Like many 20c and 21c words, it is a portmanteau of the proprietary name *iPod*, a make of personal audio player, and *broadcast*. It has produced derivative forms *podcaster* and *podcasting*.

Though coined only in 2004, the word has quickly become an established part of English. When used as a verb, its past tense is sometimes written as *podcasted* rather than *podcast*. This alternation between forms is not unique: it occurs

also with *broadcast(ed)*, *forecast(ed)*, *input(ted)*, and *output(ted)*. Verbs consisting of a prefix and an irregular verb, like the four just mentioned and *podcast*, tend to inflect like regular verbs, rather than like the irregular verbs they contain. You are therefore free to choose whichever past form sounds better to you.

podium, meaning 'a raised platform or base (e.g. for a speaker or orchestral conductor)', has the plural form *podiums* or (occasionally) *podia*. In AmE podium also means the same as BrE 'lectern', i.e. a stand for holding a book (usually the Bible) in church, or a similar stand for a lecturer, etc.

poetess is now rarely used except with historical reference, as for example to the Greek lyricist Sappho (6c BC). Occasionally it is used when the sex of the poet is in some way significant and when the noun is already qualified by an adjective, making 'woman poet' unwieldy: *He paused in his writing only to listen to a rather attractive Finnish poetess reading a sequence about her marital problems*—D. M. Thomas, 1990. In general, *poet* is now regularly used of both female and male writers of poetry. *See* -ESS.

poetic, poetical. In general, *poetic* is much the more common word, but choice is often dependent on personal preference or on sentence rhythm. There are, however, a few fixed expressions, e.g. *the poetical works of, poetic justice, poetic licence.*

Poet Laureate. The plural is *Poets Laureate*, although *Poet Laureates* is often used.

pogrom, meaning 'an organized massacre', is pronounced **pog**-ruhm. It is of Russian origin, first applied to the massacre of Jews and later applied more generally.

point in time. The expression *at this point* (or *moment*) *in time*, meaning 'currently, now', is a modern cliché that is more often heard in speech, or in reported speech, than seen in print. *See* CLICHÉS.

point of view is largely interchangeable with *standpoint* and *viewpoint*. The reference of all three is general; when the use refers to an opinion on a specific matter *view* (alone) or *opinion* is often a better choice: *Their point of view is largely traditional* but *They take a largely traditional view on this question*.

polemic, polemical. *Polemic* is a noun meaning 'a controversial discussion' or 'a verbal or written political attack'; the corresponding adjective is usually) *polemical*, not *polemic*.

policeman, policewoman. Both terms are tending to be replaced by the gender-neutral term *police officer*. In the UK, an officer holding the rank of constable is a *police constable* (*PC*) or *woman police constable* (*WPC*).

policy. There are two separate words with this spelling: (1) meaning 'a course or principle of action' derived ultimately from the Greek word *polis* 'city', and (2) meaning 'a contract of insurance' derived ultimately, and by a very roundabout route, from the Classical Greek word *apodeixis* 'evidence, proof'.

politic, political. The normal adjective in general meanings is *political*. Apart from its use in the fixed expression *body politic*, *politic* means 'sensible' (referring to an action) and 'prudent' (referring to a person), and is normally used after a verb (such as *be*) rather than attributively (before a noun). The corresponding adverbs are *politicly* (from *politic*, but not often needed) and *politically* (from *political*). *Politic* is also found

as a verb meaning 'to engage in politics' (usually with disparaging overtones), and its inflected forms are *politicked*, *politicking*.

political correctness. The term *political correctness* (often abbreviated to *PC*) arose in the 1980s, first in America and soon afterwards elsewhere. It deals with many areas of social interaction; in language it is concerned with avoiding or replacing words and uses that can cause offence or can be seen as discriminating against certain sections of society, e.g. by being racist or sexist or in other ways, and extends to the avoidance of terms that may be regarded even coincidentally as offensive, such as *black* in *black economy* and *blind* (*to*) meaning 'unwilling to recognize (a fact)', and to other words that offend various groups, e.g. deaf people, gay people, racial groups, women, and old people. The political correctness movement is also devoted to promoting an alternative terminology that seeks to give a more positive aspect to negative or undesirable qualities, such as *deficiency achievement* for *failure*, *differently abled* for *disabled*, *non-waged* for *unemployed*, and many compounds formed with *-challenged* (*intellectually challenged*, *vertically challenged*, etc.: *see* CHALLENGED). Although the basic intentions of political correctness have attracted widespread sympathy, its more extreme forms have been met with scorn or even hostility. *See also* SEXIST LANGUAGE.

politics is treated as a singular noun when it means 'the art or science or business of government' (*Politics is a popular subject at many universities / one example of how Scottish politics has lost the faith of the people it is meant to serve*) and normally as a plural noun when it means 'a particular set of ideas, principles, etc.' (*His politics are plain enough*).

polytechnic, a term for an institution of further education, has largely fallen out of use in the UK since 1992, when polytechnics were legally entitled to call themselves *universities*.

pond is used humorously to mean the sea, especially the Atlantic as separating Britain and America: *Jackie Collins, born British, wrote . . . huge, earnest tomes which even started to feature safe-sex warnings when she took up residence across the pond*—J. Burchill, 1993.

poof, a largely BrE offensive term for a homosexual or effeminate man, is also written *poove* (and pronounced accordingly). The plural forms are *poofs* and *pooves*.

poorly is both an adverb (*They all performed poorly*) and, mainly in BrE, an adjective (= unwell, *Her husband had been poorly for months*). As in this example, the adjective is normally used after a verb (such as *be*), rather than in attributive position (before a noun).

popularized technicalities. *See box overleaf.*

popular music, pop music. The two terms are not interchangeable. *Popular* music is a generic term for music of all ages that appeals to popular tastes (e.g. one can refer to nineteenth-century popular music, the popular music of Greece, etc). *Pop music* is a more specific term for the commercialized popular music of the later half of the 20c, especially the 1950s and 1960s, and has in turn largely given way to the phenomenon of *rock music, rap music* and other special forms.

pore, pour. The verb *pore* means 'to think closely about (a subject)' and is chiefly used in the phrasal verb *to pore over* (a book etc.). It is sometimes mistakenly written as *pour*, perhaps by false analogy with 'pouring attention' over something.

porpoise is pronounced **paw**-puhs, in preference to a second syllable as in *poise*.

portfolio has the plural form *portfolios*.

portico has the plural form *porticoes* (preferred) or *porticos*.

portmanteau words are words formed by merging or blending two or more other words, e.g. *brunch* (*breakfast* + *lunch*), *ginormous* (*giant* + *enormous*), *motel* (*motor* + *hotel*), and *smog* (*smoke* + *fog*). Modern formations of this type are often used for items of social concern, popular culture, or technological consumer goods, e.g. *biopic* (*biography* + *picture*), *docudrama* (*documentary* + *drama*), *edutainment* (*education* + *entertainment*), podcast (*iPod* + *broadcast*), and *phablet* (*phone* + *tablet*). Some formations are more ephemeral or ad hoc, e.g. *sexcapade* (*sex* + *escapade*).

Portuguese (with two *us*) is the singular and plural form for the noun meaning a native or national of Portugal, and also the corresponding adjective.

position *verb. Uniformed constables had been positioned to re-direct traffic*—J. Wainwright, 1979. The use of *position* as a verb, meaning 'to place in position' has met with some criticism, usually from those who object to any verb made relatively recently from a noun (in this case early 19c). But *position* has a useful role (in physical and abstract contexts) that is not fulfilled by *place, put*, or *pose*.

position of adverbs see ADVERB 3.

possessive see APOSTROPHE.

possessive pronouns and determiners. For various points concerning

POPULARIZED TECHNICALITIES.

This was Fowler's term (1926) for technical terms that are adopted into general use, and the one he named as being then most in vogue was *acid test. Some popularizations (e.g. *leading question*) involve a change in meaning and are therefore usually more controversial. A range of examples from various domains, some known to Fowler and others more recent, are given in the table below.

word	technical domain	date of popularized use
allergy	medicine	mid-20c
asset	law	17c
chain reaction	chemistry	mid-20c
chronic	medicine	19c
clone	genetics	late 20c
complex	psychology	early 20c
devil's advocate	religion	19c
feedback	physics	mid-20c
fixation	psychology	early 20c
function	mathematics	18c
interface	physics and mathematics	mid-20c
leading question	law	20c
multitasking	computing	mid-20c
nth degree	mathematics	19c
parameter	mathematics	early 20c
persona	literary criticism	early 20c
protagonist	drama	mid-20c
quantum leap *or* jump	physics	mid-20c
syndrome	medicine	mid-20c

p

these, *see* GENDER-NEUTRALITY; HIS; OUR, OURS; THEY, THEM, THEIR.

possessive with gerund. For the type *She does not like my* (or *me*) *smoking in bed*, see VERBAL NOUN.

postdeterminer *see* DETERMINER.

post hoc, ergo propter hoc means 'after it and therefore because of it', and refers to the fallacy of assuming that if event A is followed by event B, event B is caused by event A. (On Sunday we prayed for rain, and on Monday it rained. Therefore our prayers were answered.) It is printed in italic type. *Post*

hoc by itself means 'after the event' (in Latin literally 'after this') and is printed in roman type.

posthumous, meaning 'occurring after death', is pronounced **pos**-tyuu-muhs, i.e. with the *h* silent.

postmodernism, the late-20c approach to the arts and architecture which generally distrusts existing ideologies and theories, is spelt as one word, as are the related words *postmodern* and *postmodernist*.

potato has the plural form *potatoes*.

potence, potency. For the meaning 'power, the quality or state of being potent', *potency* is the usual word, and this is also used in the context of the male ability to achieve sexual erection or orgasm. *Potence* is a rare word used only in technical applications and not in general contexts.

potter, meaning 'to occupy oneself in a desultory but pleasurable way', is normally used with *about* or *around*. Its inflected forms are *pottered, pottering*. In AmE the usual spelling is *putter*.

poverty, poorness. *Poverty* is the usual noun corresponding to *poor* in its meanings to do with lack of wealth and lack of things regarded like wealth (e.g. *poverty of inspiration*). *Poorness* is hardly ever used and is more usual in meanings to do with quality or evaluation (e.g. *the poorness of their performance*).

p.p. The formula traditionally stands for *per procurationem* meaning 'through the agency (of)', and is used in business correspondence when one person is signing on behalf of another: *A p.p. B.* In this case, A is the person writing the letter and B is the person signing it on behalf of A. However, *p.p.* is also understood to mean *per pro*, i.e. 'for and on behalf of', and in this case the formula is often used in reverse order, with A as the signatory and B the writer. American usage wisely avoids this ambiguous convention altogether, preferring a more explicit annotation such as 'signed by A in B's absence', and this practice is influencing British use.

-p-, -pp-. For the inflection of words such as *trap, gallop* and *kidnap, see* DOUBLING OF FINAL CONSONANTS IN INFLECTION.

practicable, practical. *Practical* usually has a general application, denoting what is possible in practice as distinct from theory, and can also describe a person ('inclined to action rather than speculation, able to make things work well'), whereas *practicable* means 'able to be carried out, feasible', is more usually applied to a particular instance under consideration, and occurs much less often in attributive position (before a noun): *I need to be practical but would like to look feminine as well*—Clothes Show, 1991 / *Woodblock has been used for a beautiful, yet practical, floor covering*—Ideal Home, 1991 / *As long as is practicable, therapy should be continued, even in patients with advanced disease*—American Family Physician, 2000. See also IMPRACTICABLE, IMPRACTICAL.

practically. The earlier (17c) meaning 'in a practical way' (*try to deal with the problem as practically as possible*) has been overwhelmed since the 18c by the meaning that is now the dominant one, 'virtually, almost': . . . *sitting through exams with practically nothing to show for them afterwards*—Rosemary Sutcliff, 1983. / *I've heard it so often I've practically memorized it*—S. Renee, 2005 [*OEC*].

practice, practise. In standard BrE, *practice* is used for the noun and *practise* for the verb, whereas in AmE *practice* is the dominant spelling of both noun and verb.

pre-. This prefix is often joined to the word it qualifies without a hyphen, e.g. *prearrange, predetermine, preoccupy*. But when the word begins with *e* or *i*, or when the word containing *pre-*coincides with another word from which it needs to be distinguished, it is usual to insert a hyphen, e.g. *pre-eminent, pre-ignition, pre-position* (to distinguish it from *preposition*).

precede, proceed. Note that *precede*, meaning 'to go before' is spelt -*cede*, whereas *proceed*, meaning 'to go ahead', is spelt *-ceed*.

precedence, precedent. In BrE, both words are pronounced with the stress on the first syllable, but in AmE the stress is sometimes put on the second, as it is in *precede*. *Precedence* means 'priority in time, order, or importance', whereas a *precedent* (countable) is 'a decision that may be taken as a model for future action'. The use of *precedent* as an adjective meaning 'preceding in time or order' is now rare.

preciosity, preciousness. *Preciosity* is now virtually restricted to the meaning 'over-refinement in art or language, especially in the choice of words', leaving *preciousness* as the noun corresponding to the general meanings of *precious*.

precipitate, precipitous. 1 The two words overlap in meaning and were used interchangeably from the 17c to the 19c. *Precipitous* has a physical meaning 'sheer like a precipice': *There was a precipitous wooden stair to the ground floor*—A. Craig, 1990. In its more frequent abstract sense it is concerned with the over-rapid progress of an action and often retains the notion of steep descent, and is therefore often found in the company of words such as *decline* (*A number of factors might be responsible for such a precipitous decline*—A. Wilentz, 1989), whereas *precipitate* is concerned rather with how an action is undertaken and means rather 'hasty, rash, inconsiderate' or 'headlong, violently hurried': *His precipitate action was clearly calculated to make life harder rather than easier for the PLO as he abandoned responsibility for civil servants in the West Bank.*— D. McDowell, 1990 / *One can't help wondering whether rumours of his precipitate departure might not be wishful thinking*—Sunday Herald, 2001. It is in this second set of meanings that the two words come closest, and *precipitous* has

in fact largely ousted *precipitate* in those meanings, despite the objections of purists. *There are important lessons from the outcome of the referendum and we need to consider them in the cold light of day rather than jumping overrapidly into any precipitous conclusions*—Daily Mail, 2004 / *And I'm concerned about any precipitous withdrawal of our troops that would jeopardize the success that we've made*—CNN (transcripts), 2011 / *Rather than drift along until a calamity galvanizes the world, and especially the United States, into precipitous action, the time to act is now*—New York Times, 2011.

2 Similarly, *precipitously* is more frequent than *precipitately*, especially in AmE: *I left precipitously because I didn't want to work there any longer*—A. Cross, AmE 1986 / *Angus had precipitately fled on learning that the king was loose and in vengeful mood*—J. Burke, 1990.

precis (= summary). The accent of the French original (*précis*) is no longer used in the English form of the word.

preciseness, precision. Both words have the same general meaning 'the condition of being precise, accuracy', but *precision* is the natural choice, as well as being used attributively (before other nouns), as in *precision bombing*, *precision timing*, etc. *Preciseness* is really rather a rare word.

predeterminer *see* DETERMINER.

predicate. *Predicate* and *predict* are distantly related but their meanings are distinct. The primary meaning of *predict* is 'to foretell', whereas the primary use of *predicate* is followed by *on* in the meaning 'to found or base (on a principle or assumption)': *That's a goal, and it's predicated on some things happening: having elections, having Iraqi security forces and police forces well trained, [etc.]*—CNN news transcripts, 2004 [OEC]. When *base* or *found* would do as well (as in the example given) it is better to use one of them: ☒ *The emotion was predicated on one particular hope: that one day the high purposes would be recognized, and the actors justified*—A. Wroe, 1991.

predominantly, predominately. *The huts are predominantly in valleys near rivers, and invariably the local area was swarming with mosquitoes*—R. Sale et al., 1991 /*The music was predominately '60s and '70s pop, but that didn't seem to bother the inimitable Mr Hurst*—*Bookseller*, 1993. Both words mean 'as the most important factor or element, mostly, largely' and both have long histories, although *predominately* was rare before the 19c and *predominantly* remains the more common of the two by an enormous margin.

preface *see* FOREWORD, PREFACE.

prefer. 1 The inflected forms of the verb are *preferred, preferring*, but other derivatives have a single -r- (*preferable, preferably, preference, preferential, preferment*).

2 When the subject of *prefer* is the same as that of a following subordinate verb, the normal construction is with a *to*-infinitive or with a verbal noun: *I prefer to stand* or *I prefer standing*. When the following verb is in the negative, the *to*-infinitive is the usual option: *I prefer not to live and work in the same room*—C. K. Stead, 1986. When a second person or thing intervenes as subject of the subordinate verb, the normal construction in BrE is with noun (or pronoun) + *to*-infinitive: *I'd prefer you to stay*. An alternative is *that* + clause, which is the more usual choice in AmE: *I'd prefer that you stay*. (A further, less formal, alternative is the type *I'd prefer it if you stayed*.)

3 When *prefer* is followed by a pair of alternatives, these are separated by *to*: *I prefer whisky to brandy / I prefer swimming to jogging*. Clearly in these cases a

construction with a *to*-infinitive would lead to a clash of *to*'s and is not possible: ☒ *I prefer to swim to to jog*, but an alternative is to use *rather than*: *I prefer to swim rather than to jog* (but not *I prefer to swim than to jog*).

preferable is pronounced with the stress on the first syllable. Because it is already a comparative form, it should not be preceded by *more*, although it may be followed by *far, greatly*, or *much*: *Since it was fed with steaks served in gold-plated bowls, the creature presumably regarded a dog's life in Romania as greatly preferable to its existence in Britain*—M. Almond, 1992.

prefix. In grammar, a *prefix* is a word or element added at the beginning of another word to adjust or qualify its meaning, such as *ex-* (*ex-husband*), *non-* (*non-smoking*), and *super-* (*supermodel*).

prejudice, in the meaning 'bias' or 'partiality', is followed by *against* or *in favour of*, but not (on the analogy of hostility, objection, etc.) *to*: *a prejudice against eating late*, not ☒ *a prejudice to eating late*. In its meaning 'irrational dislike', it can be followed by *towards*: *the hostility and prejudice that exists towards homosexuality*.

premature. In BrE this is pronounced **prem**-uh-tyoo-uh or prem-uh-**tyoo**-uh. In AmE the first syllable is often pronounced pree-.

premier. 1 In BrE the normal pronunciation is **prem**-i-uh, with the first syllable short. In AmE the dominant pronunciation is pruh-**mee**-uh, with the stress on the *i*.

2 The main meaning of the noun is 'a prime minister or other head of government'; in Canada it denotes the chief executive officer of a provincial government (with a capital initial letter when used as a title).

3 As an adjective *premier* is enjoying a period of great popularity on both sides of the Atlantic in the meaning 'first in order of importance, order, or time', as reflected in the title *Premier League* in football: *Hypersonic flight has become the premier area for aerospace research in the United States—Mechanical Engineering*, 1991.

premiere has long been established as a noun meaning 'the first performance or showing of a play or film', and as a verb meaning 'to give a premiere of' (*The film will be premiered next week*). The BrE pronunciation is **prem**-i-air, with the first syllable short, and in AmE it is normally pruh-**mee**-uh, with the stress on the *i*. The word is now so anglicized that the accent of the original French *première* is generally not printed.

premise, premiss. A *premiss* (usually pronounced **prem**-is) or *premise* is a previous statement from which another is inferred; the plural is *premisses* or *premises*. The spelling *premiss* is largely BrE and little used in AmE. In the plural, *premises* also means 'a house or building with its grounds'. As a verb, *premise* (pronounced like the noun or to rhyme with *surmise*) means either 'to say or write by way of introduction' or 'to assume from a premiss'.

prepared to. In its generalized meaning 'willing to', *prepared to* has gone the same way as *ready to*; in neither case is any element of preparedness or readiness necessarily involved, especially when it is used in the negative: *I am not prepared to wait any longer.* Sir Ernest Gowers, in *The Complete Plain Words*, warned that 'such phrases as these are no doubt dictated by politeness, and therefore deserve respect. But they must be used with discretion', and in the second edition of *Modern English Usage* (1965) condemned such examples as *I am prepared to overlook the mistake* as 'wantonly blurring the meaning of prepare'. But his argument that the expression should be reserved for cases in which there is some element of preparation, as in *I have read the papers and am prepared to hear you state your case*, was based on an unworkable distinction which ignored the role of idiom in such matters. Whatever influence Gowers may have had in Whitehall, it has not touched the rest of the world, where *prepared to* and *not prepared to* are regularly used in the simple meanings 'willing to' and 'unwilling to': e.g. *If non-executives are to carry out their duties properly, they must be prepared to blow the whistle—Independent*, 1991.

preposition. 1 A preposition is a word such as *after*, *in*, *to*, and *with*, which usually stands before a noun or pronoun and establishes its relation to what goes before (*the man **on** the platform / came **after** dinner / What did you do it **for**?*). The superstition that a preposition should always precede the word it governs and should not end a sentence (as in the last example given) seems to have developed from an observation of the 17c poet John Dryden, although Dryden himself did not always follow the rule in his own prose. It is not based on a real appreciation of the structure of English, which regularly separates words that are grammatically related.

2 There are cases when it is either impossible or not natural to organize the sentence in a way that avoids a final preposition:

a In relative clauses and questions featuring phrasal verbs: *What did Marion think she was up to?*—Julian Barnes, 1980 / *Budget cuts themselves are not damaging: the damage depends on where the cuts are coming from—Spectator*, 1993 / *The right to fail is one of the holy tenets of student drama, and it's a right that's taken full advantage of—Times* 2003.

b In passive constructions: *Even the dentist was paid for—New Yorker, 1987.*

c In short sentences with a *to*-infinitive or verbal noun: *There are a couple of things I want to talk to you about—F. Knebel, 1972 / Hand-turned treen are a joy to look at—Daily Telegraph, 1980.*

3 conclusion. In many cases, especially in more formal writing, it is preferable to avoid placing a preposition at the end of a sentence where it might look stranded. In many other cases, and in conversational English generally, it is impossible to contrive the sentence in such a way as to avoid a final preposition without producing awkwardness or unnaturalness, and it is inadvisable to try.

prerequisite *see* PERQUISITE, PREREQUISITE.

presage. The noun is pronounced **pres**-ij, with the stress on the first syllable, and means 'a portent or presentiment'. The verb can be pronounced the same or as pri-**sayj**, with the stress on the second syllable, and means 'portend' or 'give a warning of'.

prescience, prescient. In BrE the usual pronunciations are **pres**-i-uhns and **pres**-i-uhnt, with the first and second syllables both short.

prescribe, proscribe. A single letter distinguishes two words of very different meaning. A *prescribed* book (for example) is one that is chosen for a course of study, whereas a *proscribed* book is one that is forbidden or banned. *Prescribe* also has an important meaning used in medicine and more widely: 'to recommend or provide (a remedy or course of action)': *Your doctor may prescribe a change of air and a long rest.*

prescriptive. The term is fairly recent (1930s) with reference to language, and denotes a concept of grammar as laying down (or 'prescribing') rules rather than observing and describing the language in use (this latter concept being called *descriptive*).

present is pronounced with the stress on the first syllable as a noun, and with the stress on the second syllable as a verb.

presently. There are two meanings which serve well to illustrate the interactions of British and American English. The older meaning 'at the present time, now' dates from the 15c and is still the dominant meaning in AmE. In BrE it has been largely overtaken by the second sense 'in a while, soon', although the older meaning has begun to reappear under the American influence. The two meanings are shown by the examples that follow: (soon) *Her feet hurt and she was thirsty. Presently she set off to walk back to her lodgings—Hilary Mantel, 1986 / (now) According to the spokesperson, the study presently is under peer review—The New Farm, AmE 2003 [OEC].* The context normally makes clear which meaning is intended, but ambiguity can be avoided by using synonyms such as *at present, now,* or *currently* in the older meaning and *soon, shortly, in a while, imminently,* etc. in the other meaning. *See also* MOMENTARILY.

present tense. The natural and most frequent use of the present tense is in contexts of present time, whether actual (*The door is open*) or habitual (*The door is always open / Paris is the capital of France*). It is also used of past events in certain contexts, such as newspaper headlines (*Clinton says he is sorry*) and in narrative (*see* HISTORIC PRESENT).

prestige. 1 The word originally meant 'illusion, conjuring trick' and hence 'deception', and acquired its current favourable meaning 'reputation derived from status or achievements' in the 19c, the link being the element of magic common to both meanings. It is still pronounced pres-**teezh** in an only partly anglicized way; the *OED* (1909) recorded an anglicized form (**pres**-tij) but this has not survived.

2 *Prestige* occurs frequently in attributive position (i.e. before another noun) in such combinations as *prestige brand, prestige car, prestige product, prestige suite* (in a hotel), *prestige location,* etc., to denote something of superior quality, especially in marketing and advertising jargon.

prestigious. This older meaning 'deceptive, illusory', relating to the older sense of **prestige,* has given way to its current meaning 'having a great reputation or influence' so much that the earlier use has been largely forgotten. One of the earliest uses of the newer meaning occurs in a novel by Joseph Conrad: *'You have had all these immense sums . . . What have I had out of them?' It was perfectly true. He had had nothing out of them—nothing of the prestigious or the desirable things of the earth—Chance,* 1913.

presume *see* ASSUME, PRESUME.

presumptuous. The form *presumptious,* though formerly (15c–19c) valid, is now incorrect.

pretence. The usual AmE spelling is *pretense.*

pretty. 1 *Pretty* is used as an adverb with the meaning 'fairly, moderately', as in *The performance was pretty good / He did pretty much as he liked.* The adverb corresponding to the usual meaning of *pretty* is *prettily*: *She always dresses so prettily.*

2 It is also used ironically (i.e. with a meaning opposite to the normal) as an adjective in such uses as *A pretty mess you have made of it* and *Things have come to a pretty pass.*

prevaricate, procrastinate. Because their meanings, or at least the implications of their meanings, overlap, these two words are often confused. To *prevaricate* (derived from Latin *praevaricari* meaning literally 'to walk crookedly') is 'to speak or act evasively', whereas to *procrastinate* (derived from Latin *cras* meaning 'tomorrow') is 'to put off or delay'. But since you might *prevaricate* in order to *procrastinate, prevaricate* too now generally has implications of delaying. Indeed, the *OED* now declares that the meaning 'to behave evasively or indecisively so as to delay action; to procrastinate' is its usual sense. In practice, the two notions are so blended together in *prevaricate* that it is impossible to separate them, although purists insist that the distinction described above is absolute. Examples: *She prevaricated, wanting the story verified or denied before sharing it with him*—L. Grant-Adamson, 1989 / *Mr Mandelson . . . said European leaders would not listen to Britain while it prevaricates over whether to play a full role in the EU—Daily Telegraph,* 2003 / *Coleridge never arrived, and early in January the now beleaguered Southey decided that his endlessly procrastinating friend must be brought back from London*—T. Mayberry, 1992.

prevent. When *prevent* is followed by an object + verbal noun, the usual construction now is *prevent him going* or *prevent him from going,* rather than *prevent his going,* which (though considered formally more correct by some) is falling out of use. Examples of each type: *Two women climb up the iron bars, which are meant to prevent people or animals falling under the tram*—J. Berger, 1972 / *Cushla was only just quick enough to grab Colin's arms to prevent him from belting Restel across the head*—N. Virtue, 1990 / *His shoes were locked up to prevent his running away*—Penelope Fitzgerald, 1986. When *prevent* is used in the passive, the construction with *from* is the normal option: *Tanks are being prevented from entering the center of the city—New Yorker*, 1989.

preventable is the preferred spelling, not *-ible. See* -ABLE, -IBLE.

preventive, preventative. Both words are in use as adjectives meaning 'serving to prevent', especially in medicine, and also as nouns denoting a substance or procedure that does this. *Preventive* is the commoner (with nearly three times as many occurrences in the *OEC*), understandably in view of its more economical form: *Preventive medicine may be more effective if problem-based learning programmes are established in place of the traditional methods of education—Physiotherapy*, 1990 / *The most powerful preventives are on the shelves of your natural foods store—Better Nutrition*, AmE 2003 [*OEC*]. When *preventative* occurs it is more usually in generalized contexts qualifying words such as *action* and *measure* rather than (for example) *medicine: When we hear talk of a 'preventative strike' we must translate that term into what it really means: a surprise attack—V. Mollenkott*, AmE 1987.

priest. In its Christian context a *priest* is an ordained minister of the Roman Catholic or Orthodox Church, or of the Anglican Church (above a deacon and below a bishop), authorized to perform certain rites and administer certain sacraments. Women who are ordained ministers of the Anglican Church are also called *priests*. The term *priestess* is used only of a female priest in non-Christian religions.

prima donna, meaning 'chief female singer' of a company or 'a temperamentally self-important person', has the plural form *prima donnas*. The related adjective, meaning 'self-important and

temperamental' is best spelt with a hyphen as *prima donna-ish*.

prima facie, meaning 'based on a first impression' (as in *prima facie evidence*), is usually pronounced **priy**-muh **fay**-shi in BrE, although there are several alternative forms in AmE. It does not need a hyphen even when used attributively (before a noun), as in *prima facie evidence*.

primarily. In BrE, under American influence, the stress is increasingly heard on the second syllable, rather than (more awkwardly) on the first.

primeval is now far and away the more common spelling, not *primaeval*.

principal, principle. The spellings are occasionally confused even by the wariest users of English, the usual mistake being to use *principle* for the adjective *principal*, e.g. ✘ *the principle component. Principal* is an adjective and noun and essentially means 'chief' (*my principal objection / Meet the principal of my college*), whereas *principle* is a noun only and means 'a fundamental law or truth' (*Is there a principle behind your argument?*) or (in the plural) 'rules of conduct' (*They seem to have no moral principles*).

prioritize, meaning 'to establish priorities for (a list of items)', is first recorded in 1968, and is often cited as an example of unwelcome verb formations in *-ize*. It is nonetheless a generally useful word, despite its associations with the world of business and management jargon: *Butlins offered a comfortable exoticism, prioritizing pleasure for all—S. Ewen et al.*, 1991 / *It is dangerous to prioritize any one of these beliefs and proclaim it the elusive 'spirit of the age'—P. Langford*, 2002.

prior to is an alternative for *before* that is normally appropriate only in formal

p

contexts, where it conveys the extra meaning 'as a necessary preliminary to': *Candidates must deposit security prior to the ballot.* In general use it is often verbose and unnecessary.

prise, meaning 'to remove or open gently or with difficulty', is the normal form in BrE, but in AmE *pry* (a 19c shortening) and *prize* are more often found: *The hoard of money was prised out of Blue Rabbit and hidden at the back of his football-boot locker*—Joanna Trollope, 1990 / *The girl pried the lid from the showbox*—Tom Drury, AmE 1992.

pristine. 1 The usual pronunciation now is **pris**-teen, although the stress varies between the two syllables (and is often placed on the second in AmE).
2 The historical meaning of *pristine* is that present in Latin *pristinus* which meant 'ancient, original' in a favourable sense: *The translators . . . have happily preserved for us the pristine simplicity of our Saxon-English*—Disraeli, 1841. It is a short step from the notion of 'in its original newness' to 'new as if original' and hence simply 'pure or clean as new', the meaning acquired by the word in the 20c. Although objected to by language purists, the developed meaning is well established alongside the original meaning: *Thinking of the sour blackened brick of the place (scoured clean to a pristine rust once more)*—Penelope Lively, 1991 / *The pitch, as ever, looked in pristine condition at kick-off*—York Press, 2001.

privacy. In BrE, the pronunciation **priv**-uh-si, with a short first syllable, has largely replaced **priy**-vuh-si, although the second is still heard and is the usual one in AmE and in other parts of the English-speaking world.

privation *see* DEPRIVATION.

privilege. Note the spelling with two *i*s, not *privelege*.

prize *see* PRISE.

proactive is a vogue word, formed on the analogy of *reactive*, that came into prominence in the 1970s, and is used to mean 'creating or controlling a situation by taking the initiative', usually in the context of business administration: *a new kind of management able to take risks, . . . manage change, and be more proactive*—Financial Times, 1984. The back-formation (or parallel formation, perhaps) *pro-act* may cause raised eyebrows: *This versatility is allowing us to proact rather than react to changing market conditions*—Industry Week, 1986.

probe *noun*. The meaning that has come to the fore in recent usage, especially in the language of newspapers, is the one given first in the current (2006) edition of the *Concise Oxford Dictionary* as 'an investigation into a crime or other matter'. Its appeal to journalists lies largely in its brevity and consequent suitability for use in headlines. The earliest meaning historically is 'a blunt-ended surgical instrument used for exploring a wound or part of the body', and from this developed technical uses in aviation and space exploration.

problematic, problematical. Both forms are used in BrE and AmE with no discernible difference in meaning, but *problematic* is (understandably, being shorter) much more common (30 times more so in the *OEC*) than *problematical*.

proceed *see* PRECEDE, PROCEED. Note that *procedure* is spelt with only one *e* in its second syllable.

process. The familiar noun and verb are both pronounced **proh**-ses in BrE and **pro**-ses in AmE. The other verb *process*, meaning 'to walk in procession', is a back-formation from the noun *procession* and is pronounced pruh-**ses**.

procrastinate *see* PREVARICATE, PROCRASTINATE.

proffer, meaning 'to offer (a gift or service)', has inflected forms *proffered, proffering*.

program, programme. The standard spelling in BrE, except in computer language, is *programme*, and in AmE it is *program*. In the context of computing, *program* is used in both AmE and BrE, and as a verb has inflected forms *programmed, programming* in BrE (with the variants *programed, programing* also available in AmE). Historically, the spelling *program* is better established in BrE, but it was replaced in the 19c by the French form *programme*, which however did not establish itself in the US.

progress. In BrE the noun is pronounced **proh**-gres with the stress on the first syllable, and the verb (= make progress) with the stress on the second syllable, pruh-**gres**. In the transitive meaning 'to cause (work etc.) to make progress' is also generally pronounced in the same way, though **proh**-gres may occasionally be heard. In AmE the stresses are normally the same, but the word is pronounced with a shorter first syllable, pro- rather than proh-.

progressive tenses *see* CONTINUOUS TENSES.

prohibit. In current usage, *prohibit* in the active is followed either by a noun or pronoun denoting the thing prohibited (*The UN Declaration calls on all countries to prohibit all forms of human cloning*) or a noun or pronoun object denoting the person prohibited, followed by *from* + verbal noun (*The bill expressly prohibits the government from negotiating lower prices*). In the passive the noun or pronoun denoting the person prohibited is followed by the same construction (*Army officials are prohibited from discussing the case*). The older construction using a *to*-infinitive is unusual and is still occasionally found in both active and passive, but is not recommended: ⊠ *British law then prohibited skilled workers to leave the country.* ⊠ *Army officials are prohibited to discuss the case.*

project. In BrE the normal pattern is **proj**-ekt with the stress on the first syllable for the noun, and pruh-**jekt** with the stress on the second syllable for the verb. In other English-speaking countries (though not in AmE) a pronunciation with long first syllable (proh-) is also heard.

prolific is derived from the Latin word *proles* meaning 'offspring', and is properly applied to someone or something that produces either offspring or something compared to offspring such as writings, works of art, etc. Like many adjectives in English (e.g. *a generous gift, a thoughtful present*), it is often transferred from the producer to the thing produced (e.g. *a prolific output* as well as *a prolific writer*), and objections to this use that are sometimes made are hard to justify, although alternatives such as *abundant* and *numerous* are available to those who are inclined to be cautious in such matters: *McGonagall . . . had just had his prolific collection of bizarre poems translated into Russian, Chinese, Japanese and . . . Thai—Times*, 1977.

prone. 1 for *prone to* see APT.
  2 In its meaning 'lying face down', *prone* contrasts with *supine*, which means 'lying face up'.

pronounceable *See* UNPRONOUNCEABLE.

pronouns. 1 A pronoun is a word used to refer to (and instead of) a noun or noun phrase that has already been mentioned or is known, especially in order to avoid repetition, e.g. *We invited the Jones family to our party because we like* **them** and *When Jane saw what had happened* **she** *laughed.* Pronouns include the familiar forms *I, we, he, she, it, they, you* (plus their object forms *me, us, him, her, it, them, you*); the possessive pronouns (also now called possessive adjectives or possessive determiners) *my, your, his, her, its, our, their* (and the group *mine, yours, his, hers, its, ours, theirs,* which are normally used predicatively, i.e. after a verb as in *The responsibility is ours*); the reflexive pronouns *myself, yourself,* etc.; the demonstrative pronouns *this, that, these, those*; the relative pronouns *that, which, who, whom, whose*; the interrogative pronouns *what, which, who, whom, whose*; the indefinite pronouns *all, any, both, each, either, none, one, everybody, everyone, nobody, no one, somebody, someone*; and the so-called 'extended' pronouns *whatever, whichever, whoever, whosoever, each other, one another.*

2 When a pronoun refers back to a person or thing previously named, it is important that the gap is not so large that the reader (or hearer) might have difficulty relating the two, and that ambiguity is avoided when more than one person might be the antecedent, as in the following exchange in a play (where the ambiguity is deliberate): *Septimus: Geometry, Hobbes assures us in the Leviathan, is the only science God has been pleased to bestow on mankind. Lady Croom: And what does he mean by it? Septimus: Mr Hobbes or God?*—Tom Stoppard, 1993.

pronunciation. 1 Note that the correct spelling of this word is *pronunciation,* not *pronounciation,* and it is pronounced accordingly.

2 The British pronunciations given in this book follow the so-called 'received standard' based on the forms used by

educated speakers in southern England, although it is recognized that other forms of pronunciation are equally valid. American pronunciations, when given, follow the pattern identified as 'General American', i. e. 'the range of United States accents that have neither an eastern nor a southern colouring' (J. C. Wells, *Accents of English* (1982) Vol. I, p.10).

3 For disputed or controversial aspects of pronunciation (many to do with the placing of the main stress), *see* APARTHEID; CONTRIBUTE; CENTRIFUGAL, CENTRIPETAL; CONTROVERSY; DECADE; DESPICABLE; DISTRIBUTE; FOREHEAD; FORMIDABLE; HARASS; KILOMETER; PRIVACY; SUBSIDENCE. *See also* ACCENT; NOUN AND VERB DIFFERENCES.

4 Significant systematic changes in pronunciation that have occurred in the last fifty years or so include (under AmE influence) the placing of the stress in adverbs ending in *-arily* on the *-ar-* instead of earlier in the word (as in *necessarily, primarily,* etc.), the simplification of the final syllable of nouns in *-ein* and *-ies* (e.g. *protein, rabies, scabies*) to a single sound (-een and -eez instead of -ee-in and -i-eez as formerly), a tendency to first-syllable stress in words such as *research, dispute,* and *contribute,* and a change from **-ee**-i-ti to **-ay**-i-ti in words of the type *deity, homogeneity, spontaneity,* etc.

propaganda, meaning 'an organized programme of information in support of a cause or political policy', is not (despite its appearance) a Latin plural in origin but a singular noun taken from the modern Latin title *Congregatio de propaganda fide* 'congregation for propagating the faith' (originally a committee of Catholic cardinals), in which *propaganda* is a form of a verbal adjective. In current use, the sense is always derogatory.

propel has inflected forms *propelled, propelling.*

propellant, propellent. The noun *propellant*, meaning 'a thing that propels' (especially a rocket fuel or the agent in aerosol sprays), is the more familiar word. *Propellent* is an adjective meaning 'capable of driving or pushing forward'.

propeller is the usual spelling in BrE for the revolving set of blades on a ship or aeroplane; in AmE *propellor* is also used.

proper noun *see* NOUN.

proper terms. *See box overleaf.*

prophecy, prophesy. *Prophecy*, pronounced **profi**-si, is the noun, and *prophesy*, pronounced **prof**-i-siy, is the verb.

proportional, proportionate. Both words broadly mean 'corresponding in size or amount to something else', and as such are often used interchangeably, except in certain fixed expressions such as *proportional spacing* and *proportional representation*. *Proportional* is twice as frequent as *proportionate*, and both can modify similar nouns, e.g. *proportional* or *proportionate increase / reduction / decrease*. *Proportional* is the obvious choice in financial, numerical, scientific, etc., contexts, whereas *proportionate*, rather than expressing a numerical ratio, often suggests 'appropriateness in respect of quantity, extent, or degree', as is shown by collocations such as *necessary and proportionate, reasonable and proportionate*, etc. Examples: (proportional) *By 1979 all the beds and hospital places, which were provided up to the prescribed national levels proportional to the catchment population, had been opened*—D. Tomlinson, 1991 / *Some evidence exists in favor of a larger proportional reduction in juvenile, as compared to adult, survival in deteriorating conditions*— Ecology, 2000 / *equality is reached when a state's share of income is exactly proportional to its share of population*— Economic Geography, 2004 / (proportionate) *The United States does not have the vote that is proportionate to its funding*—CNN news transcripts, 2004 [OEC] / *The Tribunal could have adopted a much more proportionate response*—Spiked Online, 2004 / *The difficult but crucial central issue about the whole operation is whether it was proportionate to the threat posed*—Guardian (*Comment is Free*), 2010.

proposition. 1 The noun *proposition* has various well-established meanings arising from its basic sense of 'something proposed', e.g. a scheme or proposal, a statement in logic that is subject to proof or disproof, and a formal statement of a theorem or problem in mathematics. A more generalized meaning, 'an enterprise or undertaking', was regarded by Fowler (1926) as an intrusive Americanism which he wanted to see abandoned in favour of alternatives such as *proposal, task, undertaking, enterprise*, etc. Clearly this advice has not been heeded, and it would be difficult to sustain such an objection now in the face of the overwhelming evidence of usage. Note that *proposition* is normally used with reference to the viability or likely success of the thing in question: *'Call this a store?' he would say. 'Call this a paying proposition?'*—A. Tyler, 1980 / *Tinkering with the possibilities becomes an enticing proposition*—D. Shekerjian, 1990.

 2 The use of *proposition* as a verb arose in America in the 1920s in two main meanings: (1) to present (someone) with a proposition, and (2) to request sexual favours from. The second meaning is now usually the one that comes first to mind: *In Hyde Park, that black whore had propositioned him as he walked from work toward the Tube*— New Yorker, 1975.

PROPER TERMS.

This is the technical name for terms denoting groups of animals and birds, such as *flight* (of swallows) and *pride* (of lions), and occasionally people. Some, such as *herd*, have more general application (e.g. to cows, sheep, and elephants), while others are peculiar to one context and are largely fanciful inventions that have been passed from one antiquarian writer to another without any real authority in usage (e.g. a *siege* of herons and a *knob* of waterfowl). The table below lists these in alphabetical order of the animal or bird concerned. Those marked with an asterisk (*) are recorded in special lists of proper terms that were popular in the 15c, notably the *Book of St Albans* attributed to Juliana Barnes (1486).

item	term
apes	shrewdness
asses	herd *or* *pace
badgers	*cete
bears	*sloth *or* *sleuth
bees	hive, swarm, drift, *or* bike
birds	flock *or* flight
boar	sounder
boys	blush
buffalo	herd *or* gang
cats	*clowder *or* *glaring
cattle	herd *or* drove
chickens	brood *or* *peep
colts	*rag *or* *rake
cooks	*hastiness
coots	*covert
cranes	herd
curlew	herd
deer	herd *or* mob
dogs	pack *or* kennel
doves	flight, *dole, *or* *piteousness
ducks	(on water) raft, bunch, *or* paddling; (in flight) team
elephants	herd
elk	herd *or* (AmE) gang
ferrets	*business
finches	charm *or* *chirm
fish	shoal
flies	cloud
foresters	*stalk
foxes	*skulk
geese	gaggle *or* (in the air) skein, team, *or* wedge
giraffes	herd
goats	flock, herd, *or* (dialect) trip
grouse	pack *or* covey
hares	*husk *or* *down
hawks	cast
hermits	*observance
herons	*siege
horses	team; (breeding) stud *or* *haras

p

hounds	kennel, pack, cry, or *mute
insects	flight or swarm
kangaroos	mob or troop
kittens	kindle
ladies	bevy
lapwing	*desert
larks	*exaltation or bevy
leopards	*leap
lions	pride
magpies	*tiding
mallard	*sord or *sute (= suit)
martens	*richesse
merchants	*faith
moles	*labour
monkeys	troop
mules	*barren
nightingales	*watch
nuns	*superfluity
partridges	covey
peacocks	*muster
pedlars	malapertness (= impertinence)
penguins	rookery
pheasants	head or (dialect) nye
pigeons	kit (flying together)
pigs	herd
plovers	stand, wing, or *congregation
porpoises	herd, pod, or school
prisoners	*pity
pups	litter
quail	bevy or drift
racehorses	string
ravens	*unkindness
roes	bevy
rooks	parliament or *building
seals	herd or rockery; pod (= small herd)
sheep	flock or herd; (dialect) drift or trip
sheldrake	*dropping
snipe	wisp or *walk
sparrows	*host
starlings	*murmuration
swallows	flight
swans	game or herd; wedge (in the air)
swine	herd; *sounder (tame), *drift (wild)
waterfowl	bunch or knob
whales	school, herd, or gam; pod (= small school)
widgeon	company or trip
wildfowl	bunch, trip, or plump; knob (fewer than 30)
wolves	pack or *rout
women	gaggle (derisive)
woodcock	*fall
wrens	herd

p

proprietor is the standard spelling, not -*er*.

pros and cons, reasons or considerations for and against a proposition, etc., is written without apostrophes.

prosciutto. This Italian word for a type of cured ham is pronounced pruh-**shoo**-toh. The correct spelling is with the letter *i* before the *u*, not the other way round, as is often seen on menus. It may help to recollect which vowel comes first if you remember that in *fascist*, another Italian word, the same combination of letters -*sci*- is similarly pronounced as a *sh* sound.

proscribe *see* PRESCRIBE, PROSCRIBE.

prosecutor, a person who prosecutes, especially in a criminal court, is spelt -*or*, not -*er*.

prospect is pronounced with the stress on the first syllable as a noun, and with the stress on the second syllable as a verb (as in *prospecting* for gold, etc.).

prospective is an adjective describing a likely future event or situation, as in *prospective students*, and *prospective changes in the law*. For its use in phrases where *perspective* is the appropriate word, *see* PERSPECTIVE.

prospectus. The plural form is *prospectuses*. The form *prospecti* is not only pedantic but mistakenly pedantic, since in Latin *prospectus* is a fourth-declension noun with a plural form *prospectus* (which is not used in English).

prostate, prostrate. The *prostate* (or *prostate gland*) is a gland surrounding the neck of the bladder in male animals. *Prostrate* is an adjective and verb: the adjective is pronounced with the stress on the first syllable and means 'lying horizontally' (e.g. *they surged forward around the prostrate figure on the ground*) especially in the figurative sense of being overcome by grief or some other strong feeling (e.g. *his wife was prostrate with shock*). The verb is pronounced with the stress on the second syllable and means 'to throw (oneself) on the ground in submission' (e.g. *She prostrated herself on the bare floor of the church*).

protagonist. 1 This is a good example of what Fowler (1926) called a 'popularized technicality', i.e. a term used in a special domain (in this case, ancient Greek drama) and extended into general use with consequent and controversial shifts in meaning. In its literary use, *protagonist* meant 'first actor', i.e. the chief character in a play (often also the name by which the play is known, as with Sophocles' *Oedipus Rex* and Euripides' *Orestes*). The *protagonist* was accompanied by a *deuteragonist* and sometimes by a *tritagonist*, representing dramatic roles of second and third importance.

2 One consequence of all this for the use of *protagonist* in English is that there is strictly only one *protagonist* in any given situation. Another is that to speak of a *chief protagonist* or *leading protagonist* is tautological, since a protagonist is by definition the leading personage. The second point is cogent, but the first has little validity outside the context of ancient drama, beyond which the word had already progressed by the 19c:
If social equity is not a chimera, Marie Antoinette was the protagonist of the most . . . execrable of causes—J. Morley, 1877. The objection sometimes heard, that only one person can truly be 'first', belongs to the realm of philosophy, not language. We may therefore refer to the *protagonists*, the chief characters in a piece of literary fiction or the leading figures in various walks of life, as well as to the *protagonist*: *The two protagonists, the cuckoo and the nightingale, present a*

series of antithetical statements about the power of love, in which the cuckoo finally gains the edge—Dictionary of National Biography, 1993 / By then most of the original protagonists had gone their separate ways and the Salon itself was divided and no longer held in much esteem—Oxford Companion to Western Art, 2001.

3 A further development in meaning represents a more serious departure from the word's origins, and is illustrated by these examples: *There is a tendency of protagonists of the computational theory of mind to boast that they are restoring the Aristotelian emphasis on cognition and thought—R. Tallis et al., 1991 / These may be worthy views but they are not those of a true protagonist of the arts—Scotland on Sunday, 2003.* Here, *protagonist* (perhaps influenced by the coincidence of the word's form with the common prefix *pro-*) has come to mean 'advocate or proponent' rather than 'leading figure' (one may involve the other, but we are concerned here with meaning and not implication). In this meaning, alternatives such as *advocate*, *proponent*, or *supporter* are normally preferable, although it is true that they do not convey quite the same sense of innovation and personal involvement. Although this sense of *protagonist* is fast becoming established, a caveat should be entered that it is still regarded by many as a serious error.

protean, meaning 'able to change form, versatile' (after the ancient mythical figure Proteus), is normally pronounced with the stress on the first syllable, and is spelt with a small initial *p*.

protector is spelt *-or*, not *-er*.

protégé pronounced **prot**-i-zhay in BrE and **proh-** in AmE and meaning 'a person who is guided and supported by an older and more experienced or influential person' should be written and

printed with both its accents retained, but not in italic. There is a feminine form *protégée*, pronounced in the same way.

protest. 1 The noun is pronounced with the stress on the first syllable, and the verb with the stress on the second syllable.

2 *Anatoly Koryagin, who has been imprisoned for protesting the use of psychiatry for political purposes—New Yorker, 1987.* This transitive use of the verb, with the object of the protest as the grammatical object, is a relatively recent development that is widely accepted in AmE and is now widely used in World English and also in BrE, although it will sound odd to some British ears: *The ruin of Belfast's Black Mountain protested by the local community—Independent, 1991 / At the core really is the 'ownership' of cricketers, an issue which had emerged during a previous World Cup when the Indian players protested the use of their images by sponsors—sports website, BrE 2005.* In BrE the traditional construction is with a linking preposition *at* or *against*. Note however that *protest* is transitive in BrE in the sense 'to assert or maintain', typically with *innocence* as the object.

protester is spelt *-er*, not *-or*.

protractor, the instrument used in geometry, is spelt *-or*, not *-er*.

provable is spelt without an *e* in the middle.

proved, proven. The two forms relate to two different verbs derived from Old French *prover* (ultimately from Latin *probare*). In standard BrE, *proved* is the normal past tense and past participle of the verb prove (*They proved their point / Their point was proved*). *Proven* survived as a past participle in dialect use and is current in the Scottish legal term *not proven* (usually pronounced **proh**-vuhn)

p

and occasionally in general use in Britain generally (pronounced **proo**-vuhn), especially in attributive position (i.e. before a noun): *His love of precise dates and proven facts*—N. Shakespeare, 1989. Over the last few years, the frequency of *proven* in BrE has dramatically increased as a result of its repeated use in advertising both attributively and otherwise, e.g. *proven health benefits, scientifically proven to reduce wrinkles*. In AmE, *proven* is nearly as common as *proved* as the past participle, e.g. *the results have proven positive*.

provenance, provenience. *Provenance* (generally pronounced with the stress on the first syllable) is the standard word, and *provenience* (pronounced pro-**vee**-ni-uhns) a rare, especially AmE, equivalent, meaning 'place of origin of a manuscript, work of art, etc.' and in less specialized meanings.

provided that, providing that. The form *provided* is generally preferred, and *that* may be omitted in both cases: *In summer he will show visitors around the chapel provided he likes their faces and they are not wearing shorts*—Linguist, 1992 / *It works well enough providing I keep my blanket around me*—Jeanette Winterson, 1987.

proviso has the plural form *provisos*.

prowess. The standard pronunciation makes the first syllable rhyme with *now*, not with *dough*.

prox. is an abbreviation of Latin *proximo* (*mense*) meaning 'of the following month' and was once widely used in more formal commercial correspondence (e.g. *the 7th prox.*) to denote a date in the month following.

prudent, prudential. While *prudent* is a judgemental word meaning 'circumspect, judicious', *prudential* is merely descriptive in identifying actions and attitudes that have to do with prudence, e.g. *prudential motives* are motives determined by considerations of prudence.

pry *see* PRISE.

PS is an abbreviation of *postscript* and is used to add an additional point at the end of a letter, after the signature. Further additions are preceded by *PPS*, *PPPS*, and so on, although no one normally writes more than two except in jest.

pseudonym *see* NOM DE PLUME, PSEUDONYM.

psychic, psychical. Although *psychical* is the older word (attested in 1642 in the *OED*), *psychic* (1836) is now more common and has a wider range of meaning, most notably 'connected with or having occult powers'. In more neutral senses to do with the mind or the soul, *psychical* is sometimes used to avoid these occult associations, e.g. in the expression *psychical research*.

psychosis has the plural form *psychoses*.

publicly is the correct form of the adverb from *public*, not *publically*.

pucka *see* PUKKA.

pucker, meaning 'to gather into folds', has inflected forms *puckered, puckering*. *See also* PUKKA.

pudenda, pudendum. Both forms are used to refer to the female genitals; the first is plural and the second singular.

puisne is pronounced like *puny* and is derived from French *puis né* meaning 'born afterwards', hence 'inferior'. A *puisne judge* is a judge of a superior court inferior in rank to chief justices.

pukka, meaning 'genuine', is derived from a Hindi word *pakkā* meaning 'cooked, ripe, substantial'. This spelling is preferred to *pucka* and *pukkah*.

pulley. The noun has the plural form *pulleys*, and the verb (meaning 'to work with a pulley') has inflected forms *pulleys, pulleyed, pulleying*.

pun. Punning, 'the humorous use of words to suggest different meanings', has been a feature of language at least since the time of Aristotle, who approved of them in some kinds of writing. Some famous historical examples include the description by Pope Gregory I (6c) of English slaves as *Non Angli, sed angeli* ('not Angles, but angels') and, from a much later date (1843) the reputed message of Sir Charles Napier to the British War Office reporting his conquest of the Indian province of Sind with the single Latin word *Peccavi* ('I have sinned'). About 3,000 puns occur in the works of Shakespeare, among them Mercutio's dying words in *Romeo and Juliet* (III.i.98; modernized spelling): *Ask for me tomorrow, and you shall find me a grave man*. An intentionally dreadful pun can be found in a mock epitaph of Byron, dated 1807, for John Adams, a carrier of Southwell, who died of drunkenness: *For the liquor he drank, being too much for one, He could not carry off,—so he's now carri-on.* In modern usage, puns occur frequently in casual conversation and are much loved by writers of newspaper headlines: *see* JOURNALESE.

punctuation *see* APOSTROPHE; BRACKETS; COLON; COMMA; DASH; EXCLAMATION MARK; FULL STOP; HYPHEN; QUESTION MARK; QUOTATION MARKS; SEMICOLON.

pundit is a general term meaning 'a learned expert or teacher' (often slightly disparaging in tone and giving way to *guru* in more favourable contexts), but *Pandit* is the form used when prefixed to the name of a learned Hindu (e.g. *Pandit Nehru*). Both forms are derived from a Sanskrit word meaning 'a learned man'.

punter. *Our choice of venue is usually the Mermaid Restaurant, where punters can dine al fresco at white plastic tables, rain or shine, in season or out—Daily Telegraph*, 1992. This meaning of *punter*, 'a customer or client', developed in the 1960s from an older meaning 'a gambler; a backer of horses', i.e. a customer of a bookmaker, by way of several underworld slang meanings including 'an accomplice in a crime', 'a victim of a swindle', and then 'a client of a prostitute'. In the 1980s and 1990s it became a more salubrious vogue word, and even achieved enough respectability to be used in more highbrow contexts: *For the punters, it may not be all bad: alternative bookings* [at Covent Garden] *could include leading foreign dance and opera companies—BBC Music Magazine*, 1999. Despite continued use, however, it is already beginning to sound like yesterday's buzzword: *Its commitment to chuck around £10 million behind marketing broadband is also sure to help it pick up punters—Register*, 2002. The older meanings continue to be used, as do two other words having the form *punter*: 'someone who propels a punt on a river' and 'someone who punts a football'.

purchase, both as a noun and as a verb, is a formal word not normally used in general contexts (especially conversation). By contrast *buy* as a noun is somewhat informal (*a good buy*), and so English lacks a word of neutral register for the meaning 'the act of buying' or 'something bought', and has to resort either to rephrasing or to circumlocutions such as *acquisition* or *investment*.

purée, meaning 'a smooth cream of fruit or vegetables', is spelt with two *e*s and with an accent on the first *e*.

purple has a derived form *purplish*, with no *e*.

purport. 1 The word is pronounced with the stress on the first syllable as a noun and with the stress on the second syllable as a verb.

2 The verb is used to express an alleged claim or suggestion, typically with an element of scepticism or even falsehood implied. The most common construction in current English is with a *to*-infinitive, as in *Almost all the conditions and diseases that over-the-counter drugs of the past century were purported to relieve are still prevalent today—Addictive Diseases*, 1977 / *The Family Court of Australia held in contempt a layman who falsely purported to be a lawyer—D.* Pannick, 1992 / *The Seventh Letter contains what purports to be an autobiographical account by Plato of his early disillusionment with politics—J.* Annas, 2003. The use of *purport* followed by a *that*-clause, though recorded in the *OED*, has been largely superseded by a construction with an intervening verb, of the type *purport to show* (or *confirm*) *that*: *An utterly incredible 'poll' appeared on election day purporting to show that the Tories were the ones who were threatening to take the seat—Socialist Worker Online*, 2005 [*OEC*].

3 In the 1977 example above, *purport* is used in the passive, and in the 1992 example it is used with a person as the subject. Both these uses were frowned on by Fowler (1926), who regarded *suppose* (. . . *were supposed to relieve* . . .) as a more suitable choice in the first case and *claim* (. . . *falsely claimed to be* . . .) in the second; in other cases *allege* and *profess* are also possible. Despite Fowler's objections, these uses have

become established and cause little adverse comment today.

purposely, purposefully. *Purposely* is the older word (15c) and means 'on purpose, intentionally' (*We've purposely changed our programmes on Tuesday to fit in with the Royal timetable—BBC* Press Release, 2002 [*OEC*]), whereas the more recent word *purposefully* (19c) corresponds to the adjective *purposeful* and means 'with a strong purpose, resolutely': *He threw down a handful of sovereigns without even looking at Sam, then strode purposefully after the Squire—S.* Langley, 2006. A third word, *purposively* (20c), means 'for a particular purpose', and is more usual in technical contexts: *Socialism* . . . *would have to be built by active human beings working purposively and creatively—J.* Dignan et al., 1992. Occasionally *purposively* is used when *purposefully* would be the normal choice: *'Gerrart-of-it!' said the larger of the two, moving purposively towards me—Will Self*, 1993.

purveyor, meaning 'a supplier' (normally in commercial contexts), is spelt *-or*, not *purveyer*.

put, putt. *Put* (pronounced like the verb) is used in athletics (*shot-put*), whereas *putt* (pronounced like *gut*) is the term used in golf.

putrefy, meaning 'to go rotten', is spelt *-efy*, not *putrify*.

putsch. This word for a violent attempt to overthrow a government, comes via German from Swiss-German. It is a metaphorical extension of its meaning in that dialect of 'knock, thrust, blow'. It rhymes with *butch*, not with *Dutch*.

putter *see* POTTER.

pygmy is derived from a Greek word *pugmē* meaning 'the length of the forearm' and largely for this reason the spelling with *y* is preferable to the form *pigmy*.

pyjamas is the standard spelling in BrE, but in AmE it is *pajamas*. It is a plural noun in ordinary use (*Whose pyjamas are these?*), but takes a singular form when used attributively (i.e. before a noun, as in *pyjama jacket* and *pyjama suit*).

pyramidal, meaning 'having the form of a pyramid', is pronounced with the stress on the second syllable.

pyrrhic, used of a victory won at too great cost to be of use to the victor, is named after Pyrrhus, the king of Epirus who defeated a Roman army at Asculum in 279 BC but sustained heavy losses and was unable to exploit his success.

qua, pronounced kway or kwah, and printed in roman, is a somewhat formal word, with the air of philosophy and logic about it. It derives from the Latin relative pronoun *qui* (who) and in English means 'considered as' or 'in the capacity of' when a person or thing can be regarded in different ways or from different aspects, normally in the sequence 'A qua B', where B defines A more closely: *Dressed in an Armani suit . . . and espadrilles, he plays a cop qua existential hero—Literary Review,* 1989. In practice *qua* is used more flexibly, for example in the form 'A qua A' (with the same noun repeated) and in sentences lacking the first noun altogether, as the following examples show: *Look at the sky . . . What is there so extraordinary about it? Qua sky—Samuel* Beckett, 1956 / *I don't think that 'Hard Times' is a particularly good novel qua novel, whatever it may be as a social document—Broadcast,* 1977 / *'Beings qua being' are not a special class or kind of being; indeed, there are no such things as beings-qua-being at all—*J. Barnes, 2000.

quadrennium, meaning 'a period of four years', has the plural form *quadrenniums*. The Latin word from which it is derived is *quadriennium*, but the first *i* has been lost under the influence of other words of this type such as *decennium* and *millennium*.

qualm, meaning 'a misgiving or uneasy doubt', is pronounced kwahm, not any longer kwawm.

quantum leap, and the older form *quantum jump*, meaning 'a sudden large increase', are one of the more striking examples of modern *popularized technicalities.

quarrel. The verb has inflected forms *quarrelled, quarrelling* in BrE, and usually *quarreled, quarreling* in AmE.

quarter. 1 Practice varies in the hyphenation of *quarter* in compounds, and the following forms are recommended: *quarter day, quarter-deck, quarter-final, quarter-hour* (but *a quarter of an hour*), *quarter-light, quartermaster, quarter note, quarter sessions, quarter-tone.*

2 The BrE designation of time as *a quarter to ten* is normally expressed in AmE as *a quarter of ten*, and BrE *a quarter past ten* in AmE as *a quarter after ten.*

3 The word *of* is optional in expressions of the type *for a quarter* (*of*) *the price.*

4 The inflected forms of the verb are *quartered, quartering.*

quarto has the plural form *quartos.*

quasi- is used in combination with a following noun or adjective, often hyphenated, to denote things that are only seemingly or partly entitled to the name, e.g. *a quasi-conjunction, quasi-independent.* The recommended pronunciation is **kway**-ziy rather than **kwah**-zi.

quatercentenary, pronounced kwat-, means 'a four-hundredth anniversary' and is derived from the Latin word *quater* meaning 'four times'. It is a common error to treat the word as if it began with *quarter-*.

quattrocento, pronounced kwat-roh-**chen**-toh, denotes the style of Italian art of the 15c, i.e. 1400–99.

queer. The word was first used as an adjective and noun meaning 'homosexual' in the 1920s. Although it is still generally regarded as derogatory or offensive when used by heterosexual people, it has been adopted in recent years by some gay people referring to themselves, especially in terms such as *queer-bashing* and *queer rights. See* GAY.

question *see* BEG THE QUESTION; INDIRECT QUESTION.

question mark. 1 The principal use of the question mark (?) is to indicate a direct question: *Are they leaving tomorrow? / What time is it?* It is also used when the question is put in the form of a statement: *They told you that? / Surely it's the same one? / I wonder if you can help me?* It should not be used in indirect questions in which the question is reported rather than expressed (*He asked what time it was*), but should be used in tag questions of the kind *She's much taller now, isn't she?*.

2 A question that makes a formal or polite request does not always have a question mark: *Would passengers on platform 2 please proceed to platform 5.*

3 A question mark is conventionally placed before a word about which there is some doubt, e.g. uncertain locations on maps and uncertain dates (*Thomas Tallis, ?1505–85*).

questionnaire is spelt with two *ns* and is normally pronounced with an initial syllable kwest- rather than kest-.

queue. The verb has inflected forms *queues, queued, queuing.*

quiet, quieten. As a verb, *quiet* has been used transitively (with an object) since the 16c in the meaning 'to make (someone or something) quiet', and is still in use in this sense: *The unexpectedness of this departure from the routine at first disquieted but then quieted us all*—M. Lindvall, 1991. Since the 18c, and especially in North America, it has also been used intransitively (often in extended meanings to do more with disposition and temperament than actual sound): *When I switched to opiates at least I quieted down*—New Yorker, 1992. The alternative verb *quieten* appeared (often with *down*) in the 19c in both transitive and intransitive uses. Because *quiet* was available, *quieten* was regarded by Fowler (1926) as a 'superfluous word', but in more recent usage the stigma has mostly disappeared, leaving *quieten* now the more common choice than *quiet: The youth . . . revved the engine, then quietened it down to the soft ticking-over*—J. Wainwright, 1973 / *Arnica also helps to calm and quieten the upset child*—Health Shopper, 1990 / *It's not so much that I've quietened down, as that I've channelled my energies into things that are more productive than out-and-out hedonism*—Female First Online, BrE 2005 [OEC].

quiet, quietness, quietude. The most commonly used of these nouns is *quiet*, which denotes a state of silence or tranquillity (*the quiet that precedes a storm / a period of peace and quiet*). *Quietness* also has this meaning but tends to denote rather the condition of being quiet as applied in a particular instance (*I like to leave the noise of the discos and bars behind me and return to the quietness of my home for a good night's sleep*—Pattaya Mail, 2004), and *quietude* is a literary alternative for *quietness* (*Their two and one-half acres retain a bucolic quietude*—Angeles, AmE 1991).

q

quincentenary *see* ANNIVERSARIES.

quit has the past tense and past participle *quitted* or (especially in AmE) *quit*.

quite. 1 *Quite* is a highly mobile word with a wide range of uses qualifying adjectives and adverbs (*quite heavy / quite often*), singular nouns (*quite a lot*), and verbs (*We quite understand / I'd quite like to*). It causes difficulty because it has two branches of meaning which are not always distinguishable, especially in print which lacks the support of voice intonation. In idiomatic uses, the sense intended is not always clearly one or the other but varies on a scale between them. The two meanings are (1) the older 'stronger' meaning 'completely, entirely' (*You are a humourist . . . Quite a humourist*—Jane Austen, 1816), which remains the dominant sense in AmE but tends to be restricted to set expressions in BrE (e.g. *I quite agree*), and (2) the 'weaker' meaning 'rather, fairly' which emerged in the 19c and is now the dominant meaning in BrE (*The music was at times quite loud / We quite like what you have done*).

2 When *quite* qualifies adjectives and adverbs, there is a broad distinction in that the weaker meaning normally occurs with so-called 'gradable' adjectives (those that can be qualified by *more, very, somewhat*, etc.) such as *cheap, good, bad, heavy, interesting, large, small* (and where appropriate their corresponding adverbs *cheaply, well, badly, interestingly*, etc.), whereas the stronger meaning occurs with non-gradable or 'absolute' adjectives that denote all-or-nothing concepts such as *different, enough, excellent, impossible* (and their adverbs *differently, enough, excellently, impossibly*). So *quite good* normally means 'fairly good' whereas *quite different* normally means 'entirely different'. However, this distinction is not watertight, and examples can readily be found (especially with adverbs) which either leave the choice of meaning unclear or suggest a meaning somewhere between the two extremes (as more idiomatic uses often tend to): *The actual writing style of agony columns has changed quite noticeably over the years*—P. Makins, 1975 / *She has become, both figuratively and quite literally speaking, the absent subject*—Art Bulletin, 2001.

3 The use of *quite* with a verb is much more common in BrE than in AmE, and can have either the stronger meaning (*I quite agree* = I agree entirely / *We quite understand* = we understand completely) or the weaker meaning (*They'd quite like to come* = they'd rather like to come). The meaning entirely depends on the type of verb.

4 When preceded by a negative (*not, never*, etc.), *quite* has the stronger meaning: *A bona fide kook who is never quite able to get in gear till he finally dies paddling his canoe across the Atlantic*—Publishers Weekly, 1973 / *We should not be quite so narrow-minded, blinkered and xenophobic about the rest of the world*—Hansard, 1992 / *Bailey's production is very hot in the first half but crashes to a halt with a bit of design business that is as ludicrous as it is spectacular. It never quite recovers*—Guardian Unlimited, 2004 [OEC].

5 The combination *quite a* (or *an*) followed by a noun (without an adjective between) is an Americanism that has extended into BrE and can refer to quantity or quality (or both): *Occasionally he collects quite a crowd as he sits there cross-legged and expounds his philosophy*—Ruth Prawer Jhabvala, 1975 / *The killings do ensure that we understand Frank's desire for vengeance, but this is overdoing it by quite a margin*—Sofia Echo, 2004 [OEC]. When an adjective or adverb comes between *quite a* (or *an*) and the noun, *quite* tends more towards the weaker meaning: *The death of Wyatt's father in 1818 left him quite a* *wealthy man—Dictionary of National Biography*, 1993. But compare the following, in which the order *a quite +* adjective (or adverb) suggests a stronger, more positive meaning: *The items are programmed in a quite interesting way—Gramophone*, 1977.

6 The use of *quite* as a reply expressing agreement or confirmation is a characteristic of BrE: *'No takers,' I said. 'Quite. By the way, I'm sorry to say "quite" all the time but . . . my work lies amongst Americans and they expect Englishmen to say it.'*—K. Bonfiglioli, 1976.

7 It is clearly better to regard *quite* as operating in the realm of idiom rather than of distinct word sense, and as drawing on a range of meaning that varies subtly between the extremes of the traditionally distinguished 'stronger' and 'weaker' meanings.

quota has the plural form *quotas*.

quotation marks. 1 The main use of quotation marks (also called *inverted commas*) is to indicate direct speech and quotations. In writing it is common to use double quotation marks (" "), and in printing practice varies between the double and single style (''). Single marks are commonly associated with British practice (as in the Oxford and Cambridge styles) and double marks with American practice (as in the Chicago style), but the distinction in usage is not always so clear-cut.

2 The main rules of practice in BrE follow, with indications of any variant practice in AmE:

a In direct speech and quotations, the closing quotation mark normally comes after a final full stop: *She said, 'I have something to ask you.'* It should come after any other punctuation mark (such

as an exclamation mark) which is part of the matter being quoted: *They shouted, 'Watch out!'* (the final full stop is omitted after an exclamation mark in this position) / *Did I hear you say 'Go away!'?*

b When the quoted speech is interrupted by a reporting verb such as *say*, *shout*, etc., the punctuation that divides the sentence is put inside the quotation marks: *'Go away,' he said, 'and don't ever come back.'*

c If a quoted word or phrase comes at the end of a sentence or coincides with a comma, the punctuation that belongs to the sentence as a whole is placed outside the quotation marks: *What is a 'gigabyte'?* / *No one should 'follow a multitude to do evil', as the Scripture says*. In AmE, however, it is usual to place quotation marks outside the sentence punctuation (and note the more characteristic double quotation marks): *No one should "follow a multitude to do evil," as the Scripture says*.

d When a quotation occurs within a quotation, the inner quotation is put in double quotation marks if the main quotation is in single marks (or vice versa, especially in American practice): BrE *'Have you any idea,' he asked, 'what a "gigabyte" is?'* / AmE *"Have you any idea," he asked, "what a 'gigabyte' is?"*

quote has a derived form *quotable*, in the sense 'suitable or worth quoting'.

Qur'an is a transliterated Arabic spelling in English of *Koran.

q.v. is an abbreviation of the Latin phrase *quod vide* (= which see) and is used to indicate a reference incorporated into running text, e.g. *Events of the following year were dominated by the General Strike (q.v.)*.

rabbit. The verb (= hunt rabbits or, usually as *rabbit on* = talk excessively) has inflected forms *rabbited, rabbiting.*

racism, racialism. These two 20c words are used interchangeably in the meaning 'belief in the superiority of a particular race'; *racialism* is somewhat older, and is closer in form to *nationalism* (on which it was modelled), but in current usage *racism* is far more common.

rack in the phrase *rack and ruin* means 'destruction' and is normally spelt in this way in BrE, although it is originally a variant of the older form *wrack* (which is still sometimes used). *Rack* is one of nine nouns and seven verbs with this spelling, and has no historical connection with the more familiar forms, e.g. 'a framework for holding things'. The verb *rack* as used in *to rack one's brains* and *racked with guilt* is also sometimes spelt *wrack*.

radiator is spelt *-or*, not *-er*.

radio. The noun has the plural form *radios*, and the verb has inflected forms *radioes, radioed, radioing.*

radius. The recommended plural is *radii* (pronounced **ray**-di-iy), not *radiuses.*

rage. The word has been in use as a noun since the 14c, but it is perhaps a sign of the times that a special use has developed in the 1980s and 1990s relating to random violent behaviour by frustrated individuals, especially on public roads and motorways. Some of the reported incidents of *road rage* have led to severe injury and even death. In a disturbing development, we find references to rage in other contexts, above all *air rage* (violently irate behaviour by passengers in aircraft). Other contexts include *cycle rage, golf rage, lane rage* (in swimming pools), *phone rage* (annoyance at being disturbed by mobile phones), *spam rage* (vindictive anger provoked by unwanted emails), and *trolley rage* (by shoppers in supermarkets). It remains to be seen which of these achieve any kind of permanency along with the habits they describe.

railway, railroad. The usual word in BrE is *railway*, and in AmE *railroad*. *Railroad* is used in both varieties as a verb meaning 'to coerce into a premature decision'.

raise, rise *nouns*. An increase of salary is called a *rise* in BrE and a *raise* in AmE.

raison d'être means 'a purpose that accounts for or justifies or originally causes a thing's existence'. As a loanword (from French, literally 'reason for being') it is normally printed in italic type in English contexts. The plural form is *raisons d'être.*

rancour meaning 'malignant dislike', is spelt *-our* in BrE and *rancor* in AmE.

random. The long-established meaning of *random* familiar to everybody is 'done or happening without method or conscious decision': *here are some* *random thoughts*. The newer meaning, 'odd, unusual, or unexpected', can strike people above a certain age as novel and alien. Consequently, it is still informal in tone. First appearing in the 1970s, it is now well established among people below a certain age, especially in the US: *you are so incredibly random! / I find it impossible to not laugh at such a random guy*. In those examples, *random* functions as an adjective. People also use it as a noun, to mean someone who is somewhere by chance, or who is not part of a particular group: *randoms are a fundamental ingredient at any good party*.

rapport, meaning 'harmonious relationship', is still pronounced in a quasi-French way, that is, with the stress on the second syllable and the final *t* silent, despite having been a part of general vocabulary since the mid-20c.

rarefy, meaning 'to make or become less dense or solid', is spelt *-efy*, not *rarify*.

rarely, seldom. It is acceptable to say *rarely if ever* or *seldom if ever* but not (except informally) *rarely ever* or *seldom ever*: *We rarely if ever go out* / ⊠ *We rarely ever go out*. In the second example, *hardly ever* or *scarcely ever* could be substituted.

raring to do. The informal phrase *to be raring to* (*go*, etc.) 'to be extremely eager to (do something)' came into the standard language from AmE or from English dialects at the beginning of the 20c. The infinitive *to rare* from which *raring* derives is a variant of *rear*, as applied to a horse rising on its hind feet. Those who use the form *rearing to do*, which many will consider wrong, are, however, correct in making the horsey connection. Examples: *He's laid it on that the preacher makes some inflammatory remarks . . . so that the congregation . . . will be rarin' to go*—J. Tyndall, 1971 / *John Patten, the education secretary, was described by his aides as 'raring to go' after throwing off the viral infection that put him in hospital last month*—Times, 1993 / *First back on the pitch for the second half of this terrific game the boys in blue were rearing to go and the fans were as eager, waiting for the final score to dictate who would return for the final*—Laois Nationalist, 2003.

rateable is the preferred spelling, not *ratable*.

rather. 1 *Rather* is common in BrE as a so-called 'downtoner', i.e. an adverb that reduces the effect of the following adjective, adverb, or noun, as in *It is rather expensive, You were driving rather fast*, and *He's rather a fool*. With nouns, the sequence is *rather + a +* singular noun, and the construction is not possible in the plural, so instead of ⊠ *They're rather fools* you have to say *They're rather foolish*. When *rather* qualifies an adjective followed by a noun, two sequences are possible: *rather a large glass* or *a rather large glass*; the plural construction is *rather large glasses*.

2 The phrase *rather than* has two main meanings which shade into each other: (1) 'in preference to', and (2) 'instead of'. When a noun follows there is little difficulty: *I suggested beer rather than wine*. With other parts of speech certain difficulties arise:

a With pronouns, the case of the pronoun following *rather than* is normally the same as the word preceding *rather than*: *I wanted to see her rather than him / She, rather than he, decided to come*.

b With verbs, an *-ing* form is used after *rather than* when the meaning tends towards 'instead of': *When she voiced her grievances quietly and calmly, rather than screaming them, her family paid attention to her for the first time*—M. Herbert, 1989 / *Shareholders are* *greedy, that's why they buy shares rather than blowing their excess earnings on flashier cars or champagne*—weblog, BrE 2004. When the balance is between individual words and not phrases or clauses, the forms used before and after *rather than* tend to match: *This is the first time during a downturn in the economy when training by companies has increased rather than decreased*—Hansard, 1992 / *In the video Jones is, in the main, observing rather than advocating the ruthless antics of the hard men*—Daily Mirror, 1992 / *For decades afterwards, successive leaders attempted to utilise, rather than destroy, the Peronist bequest*—Spiked Online, 2004 [*OEC*] / *Mr Cameron admitted using the drug, but escaped the most serious punishment because he only smoked it, rather than traded in it*—Independent, 2007.

c When the meaning is more to do with preference and rejection than with parallel alternatives, and so especially after the verb *prefer* itself, an infinitive (with or without *to*) is more natural after *rather than*: *Better to part with what they must now, rather than lose more later*—M. Shadbolt, 1986 / *Many Vietnamese soldiers preferred to kill themselves rather than be captured*—Independent, 1989 / *Key executives will resign rather than face negative media attention*—Dollars and Sense (magazine), AmE 2003 [*OEC*]. (*See also* PREFER 3.)

d A mixed style, with an infinitive before and a verbal noun after *rather than*, is less natural in contexts based clearly on preference rather than alternatives: *I can't believe any sane parent would send their kids to a camp that actually advocates that their kids should kill themselves rather than being gay*—weblog, AusE 2005 [*OEC*].

3 After a comparative form such as *better*, *more*, etc., *than* and not *rather than* is the preferred construction, although *rather than* is sometimes more

natural when the two parts of the construction are far apart in the sentence: *It is better to give way and let them have what they want rather than standing up for the rule of law*—R. Muldoon, 1986.

4 The expression *would rather* (and its contracted form as in *I'd rather* etc.) is complemented by *than* + infinitive (without *to*): *A college would rather fall below its intake targets and lose revenue than take in sociology students*—R. Holland, 1977 / *I felt lucky to make it out of the country alive and would rather boil my testicles than risk returning*—Sunday Times, 2006. For *had rather*, *see* HAD 3.

ratio has the plural form *ratios*.

ravel. The verb has inflected forms *ravelled*, *ravelling* in BrE and usually *raveled*, *raveling* in AmE. The usual meaning is 'to entangle or become entangled', but *ravel out* has the opposite meaning, the same as *disentangle* or *unravel*.

raze is now the standard spelling for the verb meaning 'to destroy or tear down' (as in *The building was razed to the ground*), not *rase*.

re, meaning 'with regard to, concerning', is a piece of commercialese that is best suited to business language. In everyday writing it is a convenient abbreviation when it stands at the beginning of a statement, especially in the rapid-turnover world of faxes and emails, where it fits nicely: *Re your invitation, yes I'd like to come.*

re-. Words formed with the prefix *re-* are generally not hyphenated (*rearrange, regroup, reopen, reuse*, etc.) except when the second element begins with an *e* (*re-enter, re-evaluation*, etc.) or when the combination needs to be distinguished from another word with the same spelling, e.g. *re-collect* = collect again (*recollect* = to remember) and *re-sign* = sign again (*resign* = give up one's job). Other words in this last category include *re-count, re-cover, re-creation, re-form* (and *re-formation*), *re-serve, re-soluble, re-solve, re-sort.*

reaction. Since the later part of the 20c *reaction* has been used to mean little more than 'first impression' or 'initial response': *'I became more and more infatuated with that image as I grew older,'* *Rowan said and looked at me for some kind of reaction*—fiction website, AmE 2005 [*OEC*]. To do the word justice, it should involve some element of *reacting* to something that affects the person having (or asked to have) the reaction, rather than referring merely to passive hearing or reading of information. But the weakened meaning is well established, especially in the world of radio and television interviews: *What is your reaction to the extension of VAT to domestic fuel?*

readable *see* LEGIBLE.

real. 1 As an intensifying adverb *real* is a characteristic Americanism and even in AmE is informal: *You look real nice today, Carla*—New Yorker, 1987. The standard adverb in most contexts is *really.*

2 As an adjective *real* tends to be overused in an intensifying role equivalent to adjectives such as 'significant, important, strong': *It may be too late to halt the brain drain and decline in morale unless the Government shows a real commitment to research*—Daily Telegraph, 1992 / *There are real conflicts of interest and viewpoint*—Whole Earth, AmE 2000 [*OEC*]. In such contexts a more exact word, such as *strong* in the first example and *significant* in the second, can be more effective.

3 *For real* is an informal expression of AmE origin dating from the 1950s and used to emphasize the seriousness or genuineness of what is being said (*Global warming is for real*—farming website, AmE 2004 [*OEC*]).

reality is a word that has been around for centuries, denoting as it does one of the most basic (if elusive) concepts of human thought. Since the 1970s the broadcasters, first in America and then rapidly in Britain, have appropriated it as a modifying word to denote programming supposedly based on real-life material or subjects (*My obsession with reality television began when America's did*—Brill's Content, 2001) but with the aim of entertaining and not of informing. It is therefore one of the more laughable ironies of modern language.

-re and -er. 1 One of the great dividers separating the spelling of BrE and AmE is that many nouns are spelt with a final *-re* in BrE but with a final *-er* in AmE (in many cases preserving an earlier spelling from which BrE has since departed): *calibre / caliber, centre / center, fibre / fiber, litre / liter, louvre / louver, manoeuvre / maneuver, mitre / miter, ochre / ocher, reconnoitre / reconnoiter, spectre / specter, theatre / theater.* In BrE *metre* (= a metric measure) is distinguished from *meter* (= a measuring device) whereas in AmE both words are spelt *meter.*

2 In other cases, however, the AmE spellings are the same as the BrE, usually because an *-er* form might affect the pronunciation, e.g. *acre, lucre, massacre, mediocre, nacre,* and *ogre.*

rearing to do *see* RARING TO DO.

reason. 1 The construction after *the reason is* can be with *that* or *because*: *One reason was that the Kuwaitis wouldn't give anyone a visa, except female print journalists*—Photography, 1991 / *The reason I like the Beatles is because they remind me of Chuck*

Berry—*Q*, 1991. *See* the longer review of this question at BECAUSE 3.

2 The combination *reason why* followed by a clause is recorded from the 13c and is a standard construction: *Is there any good reason why we should have news bulletins, local and national, every hour on the hour, chat shows… and wall-to-wall discussion programmes?—Listener*, 1984. Objections occasionally heard are based on a spurious view of logic in language (i.e. *why* is already contained in *reason*) and cannot be regarded as sound. However, when *reason, why*, and *because* all occur in succession, the borderline into redundancy is crossed and the result is patently poor style: *The reason why everyone is doing it is because* [use *that*] *it's getting ratings—CNN news transcripts, 2000 [OEC]*.

rebel is pronounced with the stress on the first syllable as a noun and with the stress on the second syllable as a verb. The verb has inflected forms *rebelled, rebelling* in BrE and AmE.

rebound, redound. 1 *Rebound* is pronounced with the stress on the first syllable as a noun and with the stress on the second syllable as a verb.

2 The image with the verb *rebound* is of something bouncing back, and with *redound* it is of a tide or wave flooding back (from Latin *unda* 'wave'). When circumstances *rebound on* someone they have a harmful effect on the person or people responsible for them: *The allegation may rebound on the party making it—J. Kendall, 1992*. In some uses, however, the rebounding can be directed elsewhere: *The strategy of encouraging, supporting and protecting deliberate non-payers is deeply flawed, as it will rebound on the most vulnerable—Marxism Today, 1990*. When a circumstance *redounds to* someone's advantage or credit, it contributes to it: *Each piece of*

field research aims at achieving a 'scoop' which will redound to the anthropologist's credit—I. M. Lewis, 1992 / *Some of these [ideas] have implications for the growth of tourism, which will redound to the benefit of all states—Montserrat Reporter, 2004 [OEC]*. Contrary examples of both words occur occasionally (☒ *The moderate majority of Turks must realise it will rebound to their credit if they show magnanimity—Independent on Sunday, 2006*), but the distinction between the notions of harm (*rebound on*) and advantage (*redound to*) generally holds good and is worth observing.

rebut has inflected forms *rebutted, rebutting*.

receipt, recipe. In current English the meanings of these two words are distinct and cause no difficulty, but readers of Victorian or earlier literature should bear in mind that a *receipt* could then be what we now know as *recipe* ('a formula and method for preparing food'), while both a *receipt* and a *recipe* could mean what we now call a *prescription* (in the medical sense).

receive is a key word supporting the rule of spelling '*i* before *e* except after c'. *See* I BEFORE E.

received pronunciation (RP), received standard are names given to the form of speech associated with educated speakers in the southern counties of England and used as a model for teaching English to foreign learners. This system is the basis of the guidance given on pronunciation in this book, while it is recognized that other speech patterns and types apply elsewhere and are equally correct. The American equivalent is called *General American*. *See* PRONUNCIATION.

recess. The dominant pronunciation of both the noun and the verb is with the stress on the second syllable, but the noun is increasingly heard with the stress on the first syllable.

recherché, meaning 'rare or exotic', is normally printed in roman type but with the French accent over the letter *e* retained.

recipe *see* RECEIPT, RECIPE.

reciprocal *see* MUTUAL.

reciprocal pronouns. The reciprocal pronouns are *each other* and *one another*. *See* EACH 3.

reckon. 1 The inflected forms are *reckoned, reckoning*.
   2 The use of *reckon* without any element of calculation or consideration as in *I reckon it's time to go now* has a tinge of the American south about it, although it was a standard use in literary English as recently as the 19c (*I reckon, said Socrates, that no one . . . could accuse me of idle talking*—Jowett *translating Plato*, 1875). It is noteworthy that a word considered not so long ago as satisfactory for translating the conversation of Socrates should now be regarded as informal for normal use, which raises the question whether the fortunes of the word in this meaning will change again and for the better. *See also* CALCULATE.

recognize, recognition. Both words should be pronounced with the *g* fully articulated.

recommend. In addition to its familiar constructions with a direct object + *to*-infinitive (*The committee is being recommended to approve the proposals*) and with a *that*-clause (*We recommend that you stay at the local hotel*), *recommend* is one of a class of verbs, once dwindling but now showing signs of recovery, that allows the subjunctive to be used, the effect being one of formality rather than archaism: *One of the observers from the*

International Commission of Jurists . . . had recommended she be approached—Nadine Gordimer, 1990.

reconnaissance is now fully anglicized and is pronounced ri-**kon**-i-suhns.

reconnoitre is the BrE spelling, and *reconnoiter* the spelling in AmE.

record is pronounced with the stress on the first syllable as a noun and with the stress on the second syllable as a verb.

recount, re-count. The verb *recount* (with the stress on the second syllable) means 'to tell in detail, narrate'. *Re-count* (with hyphen) is both a verb (with the stress on the second syllable) meaning 'to count again' and a noun (with the stress on the first syllable) meaning 'a fresh count'.

recourse *see* RESOURCE, RESORT, RECOURSE.

recrudescence means in medical use 'the breaking out again of a disease', and in non-medical use tends to be restricted to contexts in which something harmful or unwelcome recurs: *Cohen's piece represents a recrudescence of the worst forms of cold war liberalism*—Dissent, 2002 [OEC]. Fowler (1926) noted that the word was becoming fashionable among journalists in his day as a simple synonym for 'revival' or 'reappearance'. He called this a 'disgusting use', but the word is occasionally used of something neutral or even positive in its effects. Since it is a rather literary word, it can sometimes sound a little bit overblown: *Both works, however, may be thought to share a secret, and a set of clues, which bear witness to the recrudescence of a hippy magic*—K. Miller, 1989.

recto, meaning 'the right-hand page of a book', has the plural form *rectos*. The left-hand page is called the *verso*.

r

rector. In the Church of England, the title is used of an incumbent of a parish where all tithes were formerly paid to the incumbent, as distinct from a parish with a *vicar* as incumbent, where the tithes formerly passed to a chapter or religious house. The word has a different meaning in some other churches, and is also used for the head of some schools (especially in Scotland), universities, and colleges.

recur has inflected forms *recurred*, *recurring*.

Red Indian, redskin. These terms are now considered offensive and have fallen out of use in favour of *American Indian* and (preferably) *Native American*.

reducible is spelt -*ible*, not -*able*. *See* -ABLE, -IBLE.

reductio ad absurdum is a method of proving the falsity of a premise by showing that the logical consequence is absurd. An example is that if eating less makes one healthier, the logical conclusion is to eat nothing. It is printed in italic type.

redundancy. *'She is lively and vital enough to be a member of a terrorist gang.' 'Lively and vital,' said Harvey, 'lively and vital—one of these words is redundant.'*—Muriel Spark, 1984. English idiom is characterized by redundancy, or apparent redundancy, that is, the presence of more words than strictly necessary to convey the intended meaning, and it is misguidedly pedantic to pick holes in discourse that includes it. Examples of idiomatic or functional repetition of words or ideas include *ATM machine* (the *M* in *ATM* already means 'machine'), *HIV virus* (the *V* in *HIV* already means 'virus'), *the hoi polloi* (*hoi* = 'the'), *LCD display* (the *D* in *LCD* already means 'display'), *PIN number* (the *N* in *PIN* already means 'number'),

safe haven (a *haven* is by definition safe), and *armed gunman* (a *gunman* is by definition armed).

refectory. The recommended pronunciation is with the stress on the second syllable, although in some religious houses the stress is placed on the first.

refer. The inflected forms are *referred*, *referring*. The derivative adjective is spelt either *referable* (one *r*; sometimes pronounced with the stress on the first syllable) or *referrable* (two *r*s; pronounced with the stress on the second syllable).

reference *verb*. To *reference* something has a precise technical meaning in bibliography, and a more general one. Technically, it means 'to provide a book or article with citations for the sources of information mentioned', e.g. *each chapter is referenced, citing literature up to 1990*. From this has developed a broader meaning of 'to mention or refer to': *one British Computer Society paper is referenced on page 35 of the White Paper.* Using the word in this broader way to mean that something is mentioned, often with a precise indication of where, is perfectly legitimate. But using it as a supposedly stylish replacement for the simpler *refer to* or *mention*, e.g. *the media referenced our association in almost 40 articles*, is merely modish and pretentious.

referendum. The recommended plural is *referendums*, although *referenda* is common.

refill is pronounced with the stress on the first syllable as a noun and with the stress on the second syllable as a verb.

reflection is now the standard form, although *reflexion* is the older.

reflector is spelt -*or*, not -*er*.

reflexive verbs are constructed with *myself, herself, ourselves*, etc., in which the subject of the verb and the object are the same person or thing, as in *We enjoyed ourselves* and *Make yourself at home.*

reform. The verb *reform* (with the stress on the second syllable) means 'to improve by removing faults'. *Re-form* (with hyphen) means 'to form again'.

refrigerator is spelt -*or* and without a *d* in the middle, although the standard shortening of the word is *fridge.*

refuse. The noun, meaning 'waste material', is pronounced with the stress on the first syllable, whereas the verb, meaning 'to withhold consent for', is pronounced with the stress on the second syllable.

refutable should according to some authorities be pronounced with the stress on the first syllable, but a second-syllable stress seems more frequent and natural.

refute means 'to prove (something) false by argument', and the element 'by argument' is important; it should not be used simply as an alternative for *deny* or *repudiate* (or in some cases *reject* or *dispute*) which imply straightforward rejection without argument. In the first of the following examples *refute* is used appropriately, whereas in the second it is not: *The criticisms . . . that Ruskin saw architecture only two-dimensionally, and that he never seems to have looked at a building structurally, are refuted with ample quotations—Journal of the Royal Society of Arts, 1979 / ☒ I refute Mr Bodey's allegation that it is our policy not to observe publication dates—Bookseller, 1980.* A following *that*-clause is a sure sign that *refute* is being used wrongly: ☒ *While economics professor Fred Gottheil admitted that the nation is experiencing an economic dip, he refuted that the economy is in a recession—Language Log, AmE 2004 [OEC].*

regalia, meaning 'the insignia of royalty' has become extended in use to non-royal contexts such as that of civic dignitaries. In both cases it is a plural noun.

regard. 1 *Regard* is used in a number of complex prepositions, *as regards, in regard to, with regard to,* as well as the form *regarding*; all have more or less the same meaning, although the first three are more common at the beginning of sentences.

2 In its meaning 'to consider, judge', *regard* is regularly followed by *as* + noun or adjective, with *regard* itself either active or passive: *We regard recording as an essential element in the actual teaching process—Language for Life, 1975 / Canon Watson was regarded by many as the leader of the charismatic movement in the Church—Daily Telegraph, 1984 / He regards his father as a hero, recounting his mother's first impression of him as 'tall, suntanned, lean as a wolf'—Sunday Times, 2006.* This construction differs from that for *consider*, which is normally followed by a direct complement without *as* or by the infinitive *to be: see* CONSIDER.

regime is fully anglicized in spelling, but is still pronounced in a French manner. *Regime change* is a pair of words that chance might throw together at any time (the earliest occurrence found by the *OED* editors happens to be from 1925), but events at the start of the 21c have brought it forcibly to our attention and have even given it a deep aura of euphemism, since what it means in practice is the violent overthrow of a foreign government by a power who regards that government as hostile. It therefore joins the stock of politically sanitized expressions alongside

r

collateral damage, ethnic cleansing, and others (see EUPHEMISM).

register office is the official form in the UK of the term for a State office for conducting civil ceremonies and recording births and deaths. *Registry office* is also widely used, but it is unofficial only, except in Scotland.

regress is pronounced with the stress on the first syllable as a noun and with the stress on the second syllable as a verb.

regret has inflected forms *regretted*, *regretting*, and a derivative form *regrettable*.

regretful, regrettable. *Regretful* means 'feeling regret' and applies to a person, whereas *regrettable* means 'causing regret' and applies to an action: *He did not crave recognition, but was understandably regretful about his lack of it*—E. Cashmore, 1982 / *Now let us come to the point: are you willing to overlook this—this regrettable incident and try again?*—M. Forster, 1990. The corresponding adverb *regretfully* (= in a regretful way) is commonly misused for *regrettably* (= as is to be regretted), especially as a *sentence adverb: ⊠ *Regretfully, the car parking problem at the Church Street end of Tullow seems to have been forgotten*—Carlow Nationalist, 2001 [OEC].

regularly should be pronounced with all four syllables articulated, not as if it were spelt *reguly*.

reign, rein. The simple nouns are not often confused, but the idiom *give free rein to* (= allow full scope to) is often incorrectly used in the form *give free reign to* (as if it meant 'give free rule to'), in both AmE and BrE: ⊠ *They say that if they are given free reign to invest and produce they will grow richer*—New Yorker, 1987 / ⊠ *The Machinist was such a*

good experience because I was given essentially free reign to make the movie that way—film website, BrE 2005.

reject is pronounced with the stress on the first syllable as a noun and with the stress on the second syllable as a verb.

rejoin, re-join. The verb *rejoin* (with the stress on the second syllable) means 'to say in answer'. *Re-join* (with hyphen) means 'to join again'. But when the verb conveys this meaning it too is generally spelt without a hyphen.

relate. The verb has a long history, being first recorded in Caxton. In the 20c it acquired a jargon-based meaning 'to have an attitude of personal sympathy towards': *Group formation such as takes place in the classroom tends to be adult-centred and dependent upon the varying ways children relate to the teacher*—Childhood Education, 1950 / *The best medicine was a person to relate to*—Big Issue, 1998.

relation, relationship, relative. As nouns, *relation* and *relative* both mean 'a person related by blood or by marriage', and both are idiomatic in the plural. (For some reason, however, *relation* is the normal choice in the explicit context of wealth: *He resented . . . the mother who had inconsiderately died and left him a poor relation*—Julian Symons, 1978.) The state of a person's connection with relations or relatives is his or her *relationship*, which is also used in the wider context of people's dealings with one another: *How difficult and un-natural are in-law relationships!*—Daily Telegraph, 1970 / *You need to consider the quality of the relationship which exists between your son and the teachers, your son and his peers, and between you and the teachers*—Where, 1972. In modern use, *relationship* has a sexual connotation which should always be borne in mind when using this word: *She can't* *forgive me for leaving and I've had to accept that our relationship's finally over*—Woman, 1991. *Relation* is often preferred to denote the way things (especially concepts and ideas) relate to each other (*It's now apparent that there's a positive relation between body mass index and the risk of acute coronary events in people with known coronary artery disease*—British Medical Journal, 2003), is the normal choice in meanings to do with activities and procedures, as in the expression *business relations*, and is the only choice in fixed expressions such as *in relation to* and *bear some* (or *no* etc.) *relation to*. The plural form *relations* typically has political connotations, as in *good relations, diplomatic relations, foreign relations*, etc.

relative clauses. 1 A relative clause is a clause that is connected to a main clause by means of a relative pronoun such as *who, which, whose,* or *that.* In the preceding sentence, the part from *that* to the end is a relative clause with the word *clause* as its antecedent. There are two types of relative clause, called 'restrictive' and 'non-restrictive'. A restrictive clause gives essential information about the noun or noun phrase that comes before, as in *She held out the hand that was hurt,* in which 'the hand' is defined or identified as 'the one that was hurt'. By contrast, in the sentence *She held out her hand, which I clasped in both of mine,* the information in the relative clause introduced by *which* is additional information that could be left out without affecting the core structure or meaning of the sentence, and this type is called a non-restrictive clause. Punctuation crucially distinguishes the two types: non-restrictive clauses are separated from the main clause by a comma.

2 The relative pronoun *that* or *which* can be omitted when it introduces a restrictive clause, especially when it is the

object of the verb in the relative clause and occasionally (but more informally) when it is the subject: *It reminded him of the Exhibition he was going back to*—Penelope Fitzgerald, 1977 / *It was your geography caused the doubt*—Tom Stoppard, 1993. For the choice between *that* and *which* in clauses of these types, *see* THAT 3.

relatively, like **comparatively,* is widely used as a 'downtoning' adverb meaning 'fairly, somewhat', without any real notion of relativity or comparison: *The natural question to pursue is whether the Chinese state has been able to maintain control in this relatively open geopolitical region*—Dædalus, 1993.

relevance, first recorded in the 18c, has almost completely ousted the alternative form *relevancy.*

reliable has, surprisingly, been in common use only since about 1850, and was once objected to on the ground that it ought to mean 'able to rely' and not, as it does, 'able to be relied *on*', since *rely* cannot by itself take an object, as most verbs forming passive adjectives in -*able* can (*bearable, believable, curable,* etc.; but note *dependable,* recorded from the 18c). *See also* UNACCOUNTABLE.

remit. The noun, meaning 'terms of reference', is pronounced with the stress on the first syllable or (less often) on the second, and the verb, meaning 'to send (money)', is pronounced with the stress on the second syllable. The inflected forms of the verb are *remitted, remitting.*

Renaissance is spelt with a capital initial letter when it refers to the period of revival in classical forms of art and literature in the 14c to 16c. In this meaning it is commonly used in attributive position (before another noun: *A whitestone Italian Renaissance mansion on Sixty-third Street*—R. Doliner, 1978).

In the general context of any 'revival', it is spelt with a small initial letter: *While the prospects for a true renaissance in neighbourhood shopping still look bleak, consumers will no doubt rejoice at the prospect of cheaper food—Sunday Herald*, 2000. The anglicized form *renascence* is an unnecessary affectation.

rendezvous. The plural is spelt the same, but is pronounced with the final syllable as -vooz. The verb has the inflections *rendezvouses* (-vooz), *rendezvousing* (-voo-ing), *rendezvoused* (-vood).

rendition. An early meaning of this word, 'the surrender of a place or person', has been revived in the sinister context of political euphemism. At the start of the 21c we have been made dramatically aware of *extraordinary rendition*, the practice of transporting terrorist suspects to places where they can be interrogated with fewer constraints than those applying by law in the transporting country. The term dates from the 1980s.

repairable, reparable. *Repairable* is the normal choice with reference to physical repair (*There is a reasonable chance that the tyre will be repairable—Police Review*, 1972), whereas *reparable* (pronounced with the stress on the first syllable), refers to abstract things, especially losses, and except in the negative form *irreparable* has an archaic flavour, as intentionally in the following example: *The loss is reparable, but your lives are greater worth—Ellis Peters*, 1993.

repeat, repetition. The modern use of *repeat* in broadcasting, meaning 'a radio or television programme that has been transmitted before', with its attributive use as in *repeat showing, repeat fee*, etc., has tended to put *repetition* in the shade even in the meaning 'the act of repeating' (as distinct from 'a thing repeated'), which is the meaning

historically more closely associated with *repetition* than with *repeat*: *Rare sturgeon valued at £670 were stolen from Syon Park last weekend, in a repeat of robberies committed last year—Croydon Guardian*, 2003. *Repeat* is also common in attributive position in medical contexts, with the meaning 'further or repeated': *Strangely, it was decided that a repeat investigation was not required and I was allowed to go on caring for the patient throughout her stay—A. Morton-Cooper*, 1990.

repel has inflected forms *repelled*, *repelling*.

repellent, repulsive. *Repulsive* is the stronger of the two words, implying physical recoiling rather than just a feeling of disgust: *I was given some repulsive food which, by the end of the second day, I trained myself to eat—Brian Aldiss*, 1991 / *It's hard to imagine a more repellent group of people—Sunday Herald*, 2000. For *repellent* the spelling -*ent* is preferable to -*ant* for both the adjective and the noun.

repertoire, repertory. These are in origin the same word, being the French and English equivalents of Latin *repertorium* meaning 'an inventory or catalogue'. A *repertoire* is a stock of dramatic or musical pieces which a player or company regularly performs; *repertory* also has this meaning, but is far less often used in that way. In the extended use, 'a stock of skills or types of behaviour that a person habitually uses', *repertoire* is far and away the more frequent and natural choice, e.g. *repertoire of moves / techniques /dishes /jokes /skills / anecdotes*, etc. In addition, *repertory* denotes a type of theatre involving regular changes in the choice of plays performed during a season. In this meaning it is often used attributively, as in *repertory theatre, repertory actor*, etc., and is common in the shortened form *rep*.

repetitive, repetitious. The meanings overlap, but *repetitive* is more than ten times as common as *repetitious*, and there is a difference of sense: *repetitive* is a more objective word and means 'occurring repeatedly': *A quiet but repetitive clicking noise caught his attention—Interesting Times*, 2003. When it is more judgemental, *repetitive* typically refers to tasks and duties that are unavoidably tedious, whereas *repetitious*, which originated in AmE but is now also common in BrE, is rather a judgement of the performer of the task and implies an avoidable tedium: *The story is both repetitious and predictable—New York Metro*, 2004.

replace, substitute. 1 The typical construction is to *replace* A *with* B (or, in the passive, B *is replaced by* A), or B can simply *replace* A, whereas with *substitute* it is to *substitute* B *for* A or to *substitute* B without any continuation (more usually in the passive: B *is substituted*). (In all cases, A is the person or thing 'going out' and B the one 'coming in'.) Examples: (replace). *It is nice to see 'stewardess' and 'steward' gradually being replaced by the general term 'flight attendant'—Scientific American*, 1982 / *Rugby nightmares replaced nightmares about witches, which had been the basis of my bad dreams for several years—*C. Jennings, 1990 / *Today, compost toilets are being replaced with Western-style flush systems, despite the fact that Ladakh has no sewers—Ecologist*, 2000 / (substitute) *Visibility on the course, however, was too poor to permit the senior relay and a three-mile race was substituted—Liverpool Echo*, 1976 / *Feel free to substitute your favorite whole-grain pasta for the ones I've recommended—Natural Health* (magazine), AmE 2002.

2 The use of *substitute* for *replace* is a more usual error than the reverse: ☒ *Some years ago I complimented a rabbi friend on the quality of the Kiddush wine.*

He confessed that he had substituted it with a decent Côtes du Rhône—Times, 2007. When a football commentator reports that a player is being *substituted*, he is referring to the outgoing player and means *replaced*, but the choice is determined by the dominant influence of the noun *substitute* by which the incoming player is known.

replaceable is spelt with an *e* in the middle to preserve the soft sound of the preceding *c*.

replete means 'filled or well supplied' either with food or with some other necessity, and denotes an abundance of the thing specified, which typically follows the preposition *with*: *This on-off deal was also replete with procrastination and posturing—Times*, 2006. It should not be used as an alternative for *complete*, which shares this grammatical pattern: ☒ *A two-storey retirement home, replete with pool, bar and stuccoed façade—Independent*, 2006. Attractive as these amenities doubtless are, we can safely assume that there is only one of each.

replicate. The modern use in the meaning 'to reproduce, imitate, or copy exactly', originally in technical contexts but spreading into general use, is an extension of a word that has been in use since the 16c in other meanings. It is best avoided when more straightforward alternatives are available, such as *duplicate, be modelled on, imitate*, etc.

reportage, pronounced rep-aw-**tahzh** in a semi-French way, now usually means 'the reporting of events for the press or broadcasting': *As a journalist, as well as a novelist, Dickens made Nicholas Nickleby into an example of reportage disguised as fiction—Yorkshire Post*, 2007. Its older meanings 'repute' and 'gossip' have fallen out of use.

reported speech, or *indirect speech*, is the reporting of what someone has said with a 'reporting' verb such as *said, replied, cried*, etc. In reported speech, the actual words spoken are usually changed with regard to the subject and tense of the verb to suit the viewpoint of the person now reporting, and quotation marks are not used, so that what appears in direct speech as (for example) *'They have a few points to add,' she remarked*, in reported or indirect speech becomes *She remarked that they had a few points to add*. See also INDIRECT QUESTION.

reprehensible, meaning 'deserving censure', is spelt *-ible*, not *-able*. See -ABLE, -IBLE.

reprieve, both verb and noun, is spelt *-ie-*, not *-ei-*.

reproducible is spelt *-ible*, not *-able*. See -ABLE, -IBLE.

reputable, meaning 'of good repute', is pronounced with the stress on the first syllable.

request. The noun is commonly followed by *for* (*a request for more time*). The verb, unlike *ask*, cannot be used in constructions of the type ✗ *We requested them for more time*; the correct sequence is either *We requested more time from them* or *We requested them to give us more time.*

require. The construction with a *to*-infinitive, as in *I require to know your names*, is not idiomatic in BrE but is known in other varieties of English. The type *Do you require tea?* is chiefly confined to BrE.

research. In BrE the noun and verb are both traditionally pronounced with the stress on the second syllable, but first-syllable stressing of the noun (**ree**-serch), influenced by American practice, is increasingly heard, especially on radio and television.

resistible is spelt *-ible*, not *-able*. See -ABLE, -IBLE.

resonate, which means literally 'to be resonant', i.e. to have a clear deep ringing sound, has acquired vogue status in the figurative sense 'to find agreement (with)' (typically of an emotional rather than intellectual kind). This meaning originated in the US and is now common in BrE, especially in journalism: *Lone travellers should have to pay no more than 50 per cent of the cost for two people on the same holiday. The demand will resonate with the rising number of Britons outside relationships, divorced or living on their own—Independent*, 2007.

resort, re-sort. The verb and noun *resort* (pronounced ri-**zawt**) has a wide range of meanings. *Re-sort* (with hyphen and pronounced ree-**sawt**) is a verb meaning 'to sort again or differently'.

resource is pronounced either ri-**zaws** or **ree**-saws, the first being more usual in BrE and both being used in AmE. The same patterns apply in the plural form.

resource, resort, recourse. *See box opposite.*

respect. As well as *respecting*, there are several complex prepositions all meaning 'regarding, as concerns': *in respect of, in respect to, with respect to*. The first two are more formal in character, and are normally found in business correspondence.

respective, respectively are useful words when two or more items need to be distinguished (in the order in which they occur, when they are named separately) in relation to what follows in the sentence: *MEPs are paid the same as national MPs in their respective countries—Which?*, 1984 / *Nicole*

RESOURCE, RESORT, RECOURSE.

1 The three words all have to do with finding help or support and are chiefly distinguished from one another by the typical phrase patterns in which they operate. These are given in the table below.

resource	*a valuable resource, at the end of one's resources, a person of many resources, to fall back on one's own resources*
resort	*as a last resort, in the last resort; (verb) to resort to, without resorting to*
recourse	*to have recourse to, without recourse to, one's usual recourse*

2 In general, *resource* denotes what one adopts for help or support whereas *recourse* denotes a process or avenue of finding support. There is an area of possible confusion in the overlap between *to resort to* (especially in the past, *to have resorted to*) and *to have recourse to*: *More than 100 governments had resorted to torture or the maltreatment of prisoners*—Keesings, 1990 / *Crazed individuals who wreak appalling acts of terror have recourse to the same self-justifying arguments*—Times, 2006. One normally *resorts* to things in extreme circumstances and has *recourse* to them more routinely.

Kidman and Ralph Fiennes, who starred for Minghella in Cold Mountain and The English Patient respectively, will head the cast—*Times*, 2007. In the first of these examples, the presence of *respective* shows that the national MPs are paid at different levels depending on their countries, and in the second the presence of *respectively* shows that the two actors starred separately, each in one film and not together in both. In other cases, *respective* (in particular) is redundant or replaceable by a simpler word such as *own* or *various*: *The parade dispersed, the Commandos returning to their respective units, and soon the village green was quiet*—B. Millin, 1991.

respite is pronounced either **res**-piyt or, less frequently, **res**-pit.

responsible is spelt *-ible*, not *-able*. See -ABLE, -IBLE.

restaurateur, meaning 'a restaurant owner', is spelt *-ateur* with no *n*.

restive, restless. Despite its form, *restive* is close in meaning to *restless*, but conveys a stronger implication of disruptive consequences: *It's no surprise, then, when she turns up a little late . . . , not tardy enough to be really rude but sufficient to put an already restive audience in a really bad mood*—Guardian, 2004. It is also used in the special context of a horse that refuses to move forwards.

result. The use of the noun to mean not just an outcome but a favourable outcome, familiar now in the language of sports commentators, seems to have its origin in plural uses going back to the 1920s: *Take some of those pamphlets with you to distribute aboard ship. They may bring results.*—Eugene O'Neill, 1922 / *They tried hard to get a result but rain stopped play and the game ended in a draw*—television news broadcast, 1993 /

r

And the shares paid me dividends along the way. Result!—www.motleyfool.co.uk, 2005.

résumé, pronounced **rez**-yuu-may, means 'a summary' in BrE, and in AmE (often with the first accent or both accents omitted) has the additional meaning 'a curriculum vitae'.

reticent followed by *about* + *-ing* verb form, or a *to*-infinitive has developed the meaning 'reluctant to act', in addition to its standard meaning of 'reserved, reluctant to speak': *At first, I was reticent about doing nudity*—film website, AmE 2003 / *And other than that I'm slightly reticent to talk about it*—weblog, 2005. This meaning has become so well established, that few are aware of any development in usage, but some may still object to it.

retiral, meaning 'retirement from office', is largely confined to Scottish use: *There is also a huge group of doctors who are on the verge of retiral or resignation, and are simply hanging on to see if this new contract will deliver improvements*—*Scotland on Sunday*, 2003.

retrieve is spelt *-ie-*, not *-ei-*.

rev *verb*. The inflected forms are *revved, revving*.

reveille, pronounced ri-**val**-i, is the current spelling for the word meaning 'a morning awakening' (especially in service life).

revel. The verb has inflected forms *revelled, revelling* in BrE and in AmE also *reveled, reveling*.

revenge *verb see* AVENGE.

reverend, reverent, reverential.
1 In its general meaning, *reverend* means 'deserving reverence', and is most often found in clerical contexts even when it is not a formal title,

whereas *reverent* means 'showing reverence' in wider contexts: *He also formed close links with the network of local Puritan ministers . . . whom he described in his will as 'my reverend and pious friends'*—*Dictionary of National Biography*, 1993 / *You can get away from the reverent hush of the concert hall*—*Times*, 2005. *Reverential* means 'characterized by reverence', and the main difference in meaning between it and *reverent* is that *reverent* describes a feeling or attitude and is judgemental whereas *reverential* denotes a connection with *reverence* and is informational: *When she walked into a village the Africans would often clap their hands in a reverential way*—W. Green, 1988.
2 *Reverend*, abbreviated *Revd* (no full stop) or *Rev.*, is most commonly found as a title applied to certain members of the clergy.

reversal, reversion. *Reversal* is the noun corresponding to the verb *reverse*, and means primarily 'the changing (of a decision)', whereas *reversion* corresponds to the verb *revert*, as in *The style represents a reversion to classical Japanese tradition*.

reversible is spelt *-ible*, not *-able*. See -ABLE, -IBLE.

review, revue. A *review* is 'a general survey or assessment of something' and has many special applications, including a published criticism of a book, play, etc. A *revue* is a theatrical entertainment consisting of a series of short acts or sketches. In this meaning the word is sometimes spelt *review*, but since this form coincides too closely with the meaning mentioned above and can cause confusion, this spelling is not recommended.

rhetorical question is an assertion put in the form of a question without expecting an answer, e.g. *Who do they think they are?*

rhino has the plural form *rhino* (collective) or *rhinos* (individual).

rhyming slang is a type of slang of cockney origin in which a word is replaced by words or phrases which rhyme with it, e.g. *apples and pears* (= stairs), *plates of meat* (= feet), and *trouble and strife* (= wife). The rhyming words are sometimes arbitrary (as in the first example) and sometimes significant (as in the other examples). Sometimes the rhyme is disguised by omission of the operative word: for example, *butcher's* (in *take a butcher's* = look) is a shortening of *butcher's hook*.

rhythmic, rhythmical. The two forms are virtually interchangeable, choice normally being determined by personal preference or the flow of the sentence, though the shorter form is many times more frequent than the longer. However, it is usually preferable to be consistent within a single piece of writing.

rick, meaning 'a sprain' or (as a verb) 'to sprain', is spelt *rick* rather than *wrick*. Both forms seem to have their origin in dialect.

rickety, meaning 'insecure or shaky', is spelt *-ety*, not *-etty*.

ricochet. The inflected forms of the verb are *ricocheted* (pronounced **rik**-uh-shayd) and *ricocheting* (pronounced **rik**-uh-shay-ing).

rid. The past tense and past participle are now normally *rid* rather than *ridded*, but *ridded* occurs occasionally in active constructions such as *He ridded the stable of flies. Rid* must be used in constructions of the type *I thought myself well rid of him.*

right, rightly. 1 *Right* is used as an adverb meaning 'in the right way, in a proper manner' with a number of verbs, notably *do right, go right* (as in *Nothing went right*), *guess right, spell something right, treat someone right.* In general, however, and especially when the adverb precedes the verb or qualifies an adjective, *rightly* is the more natural choice: *One of them was rightly furious as the escaper had whipped . . . his over-coat*—A. Miller, 1976 / *These practices were rightly banned generations ago*—weblog, BrE 2004. *Rightly* is commonly used with *so* to express approval for something described by a preceding word or clause: *She was angry, and rightly so.* It is also the more idiomatic choice, in BrE at least, in the phrase *if I remember rightly.*

2 *Right* is also idiomatic in the meanings 'directly, immediately' or 'completely' in phrases such as *right away* and *right now*, and in uses such as *I'll be right with you* and *Turn it right off.*

3 In an older use now considered archaic in BrE (but still in use in regional AmE), *right* means 'very, extremely' without any notion of rightness in the judgemental sense: *I was right glad . . . to see your writing again*—Coleridge, 1800 / *Miz Wilkes is right sensible, for a woman*—Margaret Mitchell, 1936 / *My husband reports from Iraq that he's right glad the Aussies aren't leaving*—weblog, AmE 2004. In BrE it remains in standard use only in certain titles and forms of address, such as *Right Honourable* and *Right Reverend.* But *right* has been used informally since the 1960s in BrE as an intensifying adjective in the sense 'utter, complete': *You look a right clown*—Iris Murdoch, 1978.

rightward, rightwards. The only form of the adjective is *rightward* (*a rightward glance*). For the adverb, *rightward* and *rightwards* are used both in BrE and in AmE (*turn rightward / rightwards*).

rigour is spelt *-our* in BrE and *rigor* in AmE. The corresponding adjective is *rigorous* in both varieties. Note also the spelling *rigor* in the medical sense ('a sudden feeling of cold and shivering') and in the Latin phrase *rigor mortis*, the stiffening of the body after death.

ring. There are two unrelated verbs with different inflections. The one to do with bells has a past form *rang* and past participle *rung*, whereas the one to do with circles and bands has *ringed* in both forms.

riot. The verb has inflected forms *rioted, rioting*.

rise *see* ARISE.

risky, risqué. *Risky* is the general word meaning 'involving risk', whereas the French loanword *risqué* means 'slightly indecent' (especially with reference to humour) and therefore risking shock.

rival. The verb has inflected forms *rivalled, rivalling*, and in AmE usually *rivaled, rivaling*.

rivet. The verb has inflected forms *riveted, riveting*.

road, street. 1 According to a law of Henry I of England (1100–35), a street was to be sufficiently broad for two loaded carts to meet and for sixteen armed knights to ride abreast. The history of *road* and *street* and of other terms such as *lane, avenue, crescent, gate, place, row, terrace, rise*, and *vale*, is extremely complicated, with fine distinctions between (for example) a wide lane and a narrow street. In current usage, a *street* is normally a paved way in a town or city, whereas a *road* is a way (paved or not) in a village or in open country. In certain fixed expressions there is

inconsistency of choice, since *one-way street* follows the distinction just given but *no through road* does not (necessarily).

2 Names attached to particular roads and streets are established by custom, although it is possible to refer to something called 'Street' generically as a *road* and something called 'Road' as a *street*. Note also that a division of the carriageway of a major road (especially a motorway) is called a lane, as the frequent instruction on road signs to 'keep in lane' reminds us.

roast, roasted. Meats and things associated with them are normally described as *roast*: *roast beef, roast lamb, roast meat, roast potatoes*, etc. (but *a roasted chicken* and *a well-roasted joint* are also possible), whereas nuts are normally called *roasted*: *roasted chestnuts, roasted peanuts*, etc. (*roast chestnuts* is also possible but less often *roast peanuts*). The past participle used as a verb is always *roasted*: *They had roasted a chicken for lunch / pork roasted in a lemon sauce*.

rob is used chiefly to mean 'to steal from'; its object is either a place (*rob a bank*) or a person, optionally with *of* followed by the thing stolen (*robbed her of her jewels*). An older use with the thing stolen as the object of *rob* (*He robbed money from the till*) is no longer standard.

robust has its stress on the second syllable, although first-syllable stress is creeping in, on the analogy of shifts in *dispute, romance*, and other words. There is a curious meaning given in the *COD*: 'not perturbed by or attending to subtleties', which is effectively a blend of the more general historical senses 'crude' and 'vigorous'. The following seem to be examples of this: *Chief constables are being urged to ... encourage officers to be more 'robust' in using their powers to take DNA samples—Scotland* *on Sunday*, 2002 / *Later I am meeting with [the] Chief Executive . . . for what may well become a 'robust' exchange of views*—weblog, BrE 2005. Alternatives are *rigorous, assertive, forthright, pragmatic, down-to-earth,* and *tough-minded,* although *robust* might be regarded as combining meanings from several of these.

rodeo has the plural form *rodeos*.

roguish, meaning 'like a rogue', is spelt this way.

role, meaning 'an actor's part' and related senses, is normally spelt without an accent, although *rôle* is also valid.

romance should be pronounced with the stress on the second syllable, although first-syllable stress is becoming increasingly common.

Romania is the official spelling of the country name. Other forms such as *Roumania* and *Rumania* will be found in older writing.

Roman numerals. *See box overleaf.*

rondo, a term in music, has the plural form *rondos*.

roof. The standard plural form is *roofs*, but *rooves* is often found, causing dismay in some circles (*Almost daily now I am troubled by the sound of 'rooves'. Is there no hope of a cure?*—letter in *Times*, 1986). *Rooves,* with its softer sound, may well win out in the end, but for now it is better to use *roofs*.

room is pronounced with either a long or a short vowel sound, but the longer is more common.

roomful has the plural form *roomfuls*. *See* -FUL.

root, rout. The *OED* records two verbs spelt *root* (and pronounced like *boot*), and no fewer than eleven verbs spelt *rout* (and pronounced like *bout*). An overlap

occurs in the meaning 'to poke about', which can be either *root about* or *rout about,* each pronounced in its own way. Choice depends largely on regional identity. Of the many other meanings of these words, *root for* (= encourage by applause) is mainly confined to American slang but is occasionally heard in Britain.

rosary, rosery. A *rosary* is a set of prayer beads, and is also used to mean a rose-garden alongside the newer (19c) form *rosery,* although *rose garden* is now the usual term.

rotary, rotatory. Both are 18c formations and each has a wide range of uses, but in current use *rotary* is much commoner.

rottenness is spelt with two *n*s.

rough, roughen. *Rough* is used as a verb chiefly in the expressions *to rough it* (= do without basic comforts), *to rough out* (= to make a sketch of), *to rough up* (= to attack). Otherwise the verb from *rough,* meaning 'to make or become rough' is *roughen*: *'Yes,' she agreed, her voice roughening*—E. Richmond, 1991 / *His face was roughened by days outdoors in the chill spring*—H. Rall, 2001.

round *see* AROUND.

roundabout, round about. The first as an adjective means 'indirect', e.g. *My chief of staff selected this roundabout route to throw the news media off our trail.* Written as two words, *round about* is an adverbial phrase meaning 'approximately' or 'close to in time', e.g. *round about 10,000 homes were affected / they arrived round about nine.* One spelling should not be used for the other: ☒ *This is a round about way of agreeing with what Jaq said about the failings of a limited amount of choice*—www.boris-johnson.com, 2005 / ☒ *Bibliographers woke up to this fact*

ROMAN NUMERALS.

Roman numerals are used less often than formerly, but still appear on older clock faces, on the preliminary pages of books, and to represent dates that follow the copyright symbol in the credits of cinema films and television productions. The main principle is that a sequence of letters having the same value or decreasing in value represents positive values, whereas a smaller value preceding a larger is subtracted from the larger, so that 1990 was written MCMXC (i.e. M = 1,000 + CM = 900 (1,000−100) + XC = 90 (100−10) = 1990). 1999 had to be written MCMXCIX, not MCMIC and still less MIM, as was also suggested, because a smaller value is followed by a higher value at the next available level; for those who reject the subtraction principle altogether as a late and inauthentic compromise, 1999 had to be written MDCCCCLXXXXVIIII. Since the turn of the millennium, the element of subtraction has been reduced and the problems have eased (at the time of writing we are in the year MMVIII). The table below gives the main values for each of the letters used (lower case and capitals).

units	i, ii, iii, iv, v, vi, vii, viii, ix	I, II, III, IV, V, VI, VII, VIII, IX
tens (up to 40)	x, xx, xxx, xl (occasionally xxxx)	X, XX, XXX, XL (occasionally XXXX)
50	l	L
tens (60 to 90)	lx, lxx, lxxx, xc (occasionally lxxxx)	LX, LXX, LXXX, XC (occasionally LXXXX)
hundreds (up to 400)	c, cc, ccc, cd (occasionally cccc)	C, CC, CCC, CD (occasionally CCCC)
500	d	D
hundreds (600 to 900)	dc, dcc, dccc, cm (occasionally dcccc)	DC, DCC, DCCC, CM (occasionally DCCCC)
1,000	m	M

r

roundabout the 1920s but this led to a fresh set of problems—*The Hindu*, 2003.

rout see ROOT, ROUT.

rout, route *verbs*. The *-ing* form of both these verbs, meaning respectively 'to put (an enemy force) to flight' and 'to send along a specified course', is *routing*, and context makes it clear which meaning applies. The spelling *routeing* is occasionally and correctly used for the second in BrE, but is far from being obligatory.

rowing boat is the normal term in BrE, and *rowboat* in AmE.

rowlock, meaning 'a device on a boat for holding an oar', is pronounced rol-uhk. The equivalent term in North America is *oarlock*.

royal we see WE 2B.

RP see RECEIVED PRONUNCIATION.

-r-, -rr-. Words of one syllable containing a single vowel *a, e, i, o,* or *u* double a final *r* when a suffix is added (*bar,* *barred, barring; fur, furry; stir, stirred, stirring;* but *pour, poured, pouring*). Words of more than one syllable double the *r* when the stress is on the final syllable (*confer, conferred, conferring; incur, incurred, incurring*) but retain a single *r* when the stress is earlier in the word (*enter, entered, entering; offer, offered, offering*). Verbs in *-fer* form adjectives in *-ferable* (with one *r*) with the stress on the first syllable (*preferable*; but *transferable* has the stress on the first or the second syllable) or in *-ferrable* (with two *r*s) with the stress on the second syllable (*conferrable*), or both (*referable, referrable*).

rubbish is used in BrE to mean 'household refuse'. The corresponding term in AmE, and in some other non-British varieties, is *garbage* or (in some contexts) *trash*, and a *dustbin* outside Britain is a *garbage can* or *trash can*.

rucksack, a pack for carrying on the back, should be pronounced **ruk**-sak, although its use is diminishing in favour of the more home-grown form *backpack*.

rule the roost, meaning 'to have full control or authority', is first recorded in about 1400 in the unexplained form *rule the roast*, which lasted until the 19c when *roast* was replaced by *roost*, thereby at least producing a clear image.

Rumania *see* ROMANIA.

rumbustious, a chiefly BrE word meaning 'lively or noisy', is spelt *-ious*, not *-uous*.

rumour is spelt *-our* in BrE and *rumor* in AmE.

runner-up has the plural form *runners-up*.

Russian. The 2006 edition of the *Concise Oxford Dictionary* gives the following options for the ethnic and political meanings of the noun: a native or national of Russia, or a person of Russian descent. (References in earlier editions to the Russian Federation and the former Soviet Union have been dropped.) When the term is used in print, the historical context is all-important.

r

's, s'. For the possessive forms *'s* and *s'*, *see* 'S AND S' AND 'OF' POSSESSIVES.

sabre is spelt this way in BrE, and *saber* in AmE.

sac, a French loanword, is used in English in medical and biological contexts to denote a bag-like cavity, enclosed by a membrane, in an animal or plant.

saccharin, saccharine. *Saccharin* is a noun denoting a sugar-substitute, and *saccharine* is an adjective meaning (literally) 'sugary' or (figuratively) 'unpleasantly over-polite or sentimental' (e.g. *The film is filled with humorous dialogue that is often sweet without being saccharine*). The last syllable in the noun tends to be pronounced -in, and -een in the adjective.

sack. The expressions *to sack* (someone) or *to give* (someone) *the sack*, meaning 'to dismiss' and *to get the sack*, meaning 'to be dismissed', are all still informal only despite a history of use since the 19c, possibly as a loan translation of the French phrase *donner son sac*.

sacrilegious, meaning 'violating what is regarded as sacred', is formed from the noun *sacrilege* and is spelt with the first *i* and the *e* in the order shown, not (by confusion with *religious*) the other way round.

sad has developed a new meaning 'pathetically inadequate or unfashionable' and is applied to people or their actions. It is easy to see how this arose from the traditional meanings of the word, but it is informal only, and the derivative form *saddo* for 'a pathetic person' is confined to BrE. The plural is *saddos*.

sadly is a somewhat overused alternative to the sentence adverb *unfortunately*, and has lost some of its force: *Sadly, his collection was sold and dispersed throughout the world after his death*—Lancashire Life, 1978 / *Sadly, standards of care and cleanliness are not a priority in British hospitals for many of us*—Express, 2007.

saga. The traditional use of the term *saga* to refer to medieval Norse narrative poems, especially those written in Iceland, dates from the early 18c and continues untroubled by more recent extensions of meaning, first to long novels or series of novels that recount family histories over several generations (for example, Galsworthy's *Forsyte Saga*) and then to any long or complicated sequence of events, real or imaginary: *'Found her! Where?' 'In Marseilles. Told me about it for two hours over dinner. It's a saga.'*—H. Wouk, 1978 / *The floods are already receding rapidly from our minds .... Given a few more weeks most of us will have forgotten the saga of Britain under water*—Times, 2007.

said. 1 *Said* is used as an adjective in legal contexts to refer to something mentioned earlier: *And you ceased to be the tenant and occupant of the said premises in the summer of 1915, did you not?*—P. Ling, 1993. Its extension into ordinary usage is often archly humorous and sometimes plain silly: *Marks are awarded for wiggling one's chiffon-clad bottom to the said music—Punch*, 1992 / *One stained, rubber swimming-hat, with teeny holes scattered on its surface; one hook; one sadist [hair] stylist who yanks your crowning glory in clumps through said holes with said hooks—Independent*, 2003.

2 Inversion of the normal order *he said, they said*, etc., is a standard stylistic device in reporting direct speech, especially when the speaker is identified by name rather than by a pronoun: *'I shall go directly,' said Judd. 'I should not like to be marked out in any way.'*—Hilary Mantel, 1989. More debatable, however, is the journalistic convention of using inversion as an eye-catching feature at the beginning of a sentence, e.g. *Said a Minister: 'American interests are not large enough in Morocco to induce us to . . .'. See* INVERSION 1.

sailor, sailer. The spelling is *sailor* when referring to a person, and *sailer* when referring to a ship in relation to its performance, e.g. *a slow sailer.*

Saint, when preceding a name, is spelt with a capital initial letter, and is shortened to *St* (no full stop in BrE though one is normal in AmE). The plural is *SS* or *Sts*, as in *SS* / *Sts Peter and Paul.*

sake. The standard forms are *for appearances' sake, for Christ's* (or *God's* etc.) *sake, for old times' sake*, with a singular or plural possessive form for the preceding noun. Practice varies in *for conscience'* (or *conscience's*) *sake* and *for goodness'* (or *goodness*) *sake*. In AmE, *sake* is sometimes used in the plural form *sakes: 'Shush, for God's sakes!' warned my mother*—L. S. Schwartz, 1989.

sale. In BrE *for sale* and *on sale* both mean 'available to buy'. In AmE *for sale*

has this meaning and *on sale* means 'on offer at a discounted price'. This difference is found occasionally in Britain as well.

saleable is the recommended form, although *salable* is used by some printers and publishers.

salubrious, salutary. Both words are derived from the Latin word *salus* meaning 'health'. *Salubrious* essentially means 'giving health' and hence also 'pleasant, agreeable' (*The Prince of Wales bestowed a polite eye upon her, then turned to the rather more salubrious prospect of his favourite savoury*—A. Myers, 1992), whereas *salutary* means 'producing healthy effects' and hence 'beneficial', usually in association with words such as *effect, lesson, reminder*, and *warning*: (*More generally comes a salutary warning that is well worth taking on board, that 'it is to the undying shame of the Scottish people that wild fish in Scotland are in a precarious state'*—*Scotland on Sunday*, 2006).

salvo, a simultaneous firing of guns, more often has the plural form *salvos* than *salvoes*.

same. **1** *Same* (or *the same*) was once commonly used as a pronoun in literary English (*But he that shall endure unto the end, the same shall be saved*—Matthew 24:13 (Authorized Version, 1611), but is now largely confined to legal and business contexts: *The cross motion for an order for renewal of plaintiff's motion for alimony pendente lite is denied, no sufficiently persuasive ground in support of same having been demonstrated*—*New York Law Journal*, 1973. In general use the effect is usually humorous or pseudo-legalistic, except in uses of the type *My wife ordered lemon sole and I had the same.*

2 When *same* is connected to a following word or phrase, the usual link

S

word is *as*: *Your car is the same make **as** mine*. When a clause follows, *as* may be replaced by *that*: *I've bought the same make of car **as** you have got* or *I've bought the same make of car **that** you have got*, and as a relative pronoun *that* may even be omitted in the normal way: *I've bought the same make of car you have got*. In more formal contexts, however, *as* should be used.

sanatorium is the customary word in BrE for an institution for treating invalids, but in AmE it alternates with *sanitarium* (but the variant *sanitorium* is a mistake).

sanction. 1 The main current meaning of the noun is 'a penalty for disobeying a law or rule', usually found in the plural, as in the phrase *economic sanctions*. This older meaning goes back to legal terminology of the 16c and 17c. A second, more recent (18c), meaning is 'approval or encouragement given to an action', and it sits happily beside the other one despite being virtually opposite in sense.

2 In the case of the verb, the historical order of senses is the other way round, with 'authorize, approve' as the earlier and 'impose sanctions on' as the later, although this second meaning is not often used: *Georgina Dufoix, the only politician so far sanctioned for allowing the Palestinian guerrilla chief... into France—Independent*, 1992.

's and s' and 'of' possessives.
1 The use of *'s* and *s'* to form respectively singular and plural possessive forms of nouns (*a woman's hat / their friends' house / the dog's dinner*) is a survival in an altered form of Anglo-Saxon inflections (normally *-es*) that have otherwise disappeared from English. (For rules *see* APOSTROPHE 1, 2.) Their use is commoner with nouns that represent humans or animals, as in the examples just given; in other cases the

alternative construction with *of* is more usual: *the petals of the flower / the windows of the house*. There are, however, notable exceptions to this general rule:

a nouns denoting time or space: *a day's journey / a stone's throw / at arm's length*.

b in a number of fixed expressions (in which the possessive noun is often in effect personified): *at death's door / out of harm's way / in his mind's eye / for heaven's sake*.

c nouns denoting vessels or vehicles: *the car's wheels / the ships' masts / the plane's engines*.

d names (or common nouns) for countries and large places: *Russia's tourist industry / London's homeless / the region's wildlife*. In all these cases there is probably an element of personification, making the nouns concerned 'honorary' living things.

2 Apparent exceptions also occur in uses that are not really possessives at all but denote a looser relationship: *the soil's productivity / the painting's disappearance*. (Compare uses in relation to people, such as *Napoleon's defeat / John's concentration*.)

3 Conversely, the type of construction with *of* known as a 'partitive genitive', e.g. *a glass of water / a dose of salts*, cannot be expressed with a form in *'s* (✘ *a water's glass* / ✘ *a salts' dose*).

4 It should be noted that some *'s* and *s'* forms with human or animal nouns cannot be converted into *of* forms, usually because the relationship is not simply possessive: *the man's reward / the writer's criticism / the boys' explanation / Sophie's revelation*.

5 For the type *a friend of my father's*, *see* DOUBLE POSSESSIVE.

sanguine, sanguinary. Both these somewhat recherché words are derived from the Latin word *sanguis* (stem *sanguin-*) meaning 'blood'. *Sanguine* originally meant 'blood-coloured' but now primarily means 'optimistic, confident' from an earlier association of blood (one of the four bodily 'humours') with this type of temperament. By contrast, *sanguinary* has retained its more physical meanings 'accompanied by blood' and 'bloodthirsty', the second of which is the more vivid and straightforward alternative.

sari is the dominant spelling for the traditional item of dress worn by Indian women, rather than *saree*. The plural form is *saris*.

sat, used for *sitting*, is largely associated with regional or dialect use, but it is becoming more widespread, especially in BrE: *I can't help thinking of that Tim sat there juddering his leg up and down—*Kingsley Amis, 1988 / *Now, I'm sat in a nice car, my husband at my side—*A. Duff, NewZE 1990 / *In no time at all, she was sat back on the bus going home—*fiction website, BrE 2005. This quasi-passive use remains for many people non-standard, nonetheless. *See also* STOOD.

Saturday *see* FRIDAY.

sauté, as an adjective meaning 'lightly fried', is better spelt with the accent, but is also correct without it. The verb has inflected forms *sautés*, *sautéed* (preferable to *sautéd*), *sautéing*.

savannah, a grazing plain in subtropical regions, is usually spelt this way in BrE but more often as *savanna* in AmE.

save as a conjunction (in combination with *that*) or preposition equivalent to *except* or *but* has a more formal or literary ring to it: *There was little chance of seeing her . . . save as a sari-shrouded figure on the occasion of her marriage—*M. M. Kaye, 1978 / *He had no answer—save that British scientists had been* *reorganised so often in recent years that it was time for stability—New Scientist,* 1991.

saw, meaning 'to cut with a saw', has the past form *sawed* and the past participle *sawn* or *sawed*; the first is the normal form in BrE; *sawed* is normal in AmE. This difference in use is reflected in AmE *sawed-off shotgun* and BrE *sawn-off shotgun*.

Saxonism is a semi-technical term for a word of Anglo-Saxon rather than Latin origin, e.g. *hundred* as distinct from *century*. Over the centuries since the Norman Conquest the Latinate stock of vocabulary has increased greatly, and recent years have seen a special recourse to words of Latin and Greek origin to give what is regarded as an appropriate importance to great new discoveries such as *television* (of mixed Latin and Greek origin) and *computers*. At various times there have been movements to encourage the use of Anglo-Saxon words, typified in the 19c by the efforts of the English poet William Barnes to promote words such as *bodeword* instead of *commandment* and *gleecraft* instead of *music*. Fowler, however, was not among these Saxonizers, noting (1926) that 'the wisdom of this nationalism in language—at least in so thoroughly composite a language as English—is very questionable'.

say. 1 In ordinary use *say* occurs as a noun only in the expression *have a say* (or variants of it such as *have a bigger say*).

2 The use of *say* as an imperative in uses such as *Let's meet soon—say next Friday* is an established idiom.

3 The participial phrase *having said that* has acquired a grammatically free status similar to phrases introduced by *considering*, *seeing*, etc. (*see* PARTICIPLES 4). The participle does not always agree with the (typically following) subject of the sentence, as it does in the first example but not in the second: *Having said that, I must say her depiction of what happened made me view Polanski with much more 'critical' eyes*—D. Poland, AmE 2003 / *There are times when the film . . . goes for the teen market with a lot of bad language and some silly, toilet humour. But having said that there are some clever in-jokes and many funny cameos*—film review website, BrE 2004 [*OEC*]. This grammatically loose structure is generally acceptable (especially in spoken English), but should be avoided in more formal or serious writing.

sc. is short for Latin *scilicet* (= *scire licet*, 'one may understand or know') and is used with the meaning 'that is to say' to introduce an explanation of a difficult or unclear term, e.g. *the policy of the NUT* (*sc. National Union of Teachers*).

scallop, pronounced **skol**-uhp, or **skal**-op, is the preferred spelling for the name of the mollusc, not *scollop*. The verb (meaning e.g. 'to decorate with scallop designs') has inflected forms *scalloped, scalloping.*

scallywag, a word of unknown origin, is normally spelt in this way in BrE, but in AmE other forms such as *scalawag* and *scallawag* are widely used.

scaly, meaning 'covered in scales', is spelt in this way, not *scaley*. The derived noun is *scaliness.*

scampi, meaning 'large prawns', is a plural noun (of Italian origin), but is sometimes treated as singular in the sense 'a dish of scampi'.

scant, scanty. Both words have meanings to do with smallness or insufficiency. *Scant* is of Norse origin and came into English as several parts of speech including the adjective. In current use it is only an adjective and appears quite frequently in a limited range of set combinations such as *scant attention* and *scant regard / evidence / consolation / information / respect / reward*. It is only used in attributive position (i.e. before a noun), whereas the related adjective *scanty* can also be used after a verb and has more general scope, although it tends to be used with reference to concrete rather than abstract nouns (e.g. *a scanty lunch / scanty clothing / affordable property in London is scanty*).

scarcely. 1 The standard construction is *scarcely . . . when . . .*: *Scarcely had he begun when Claverhouse ordered him to rise*—A. Boyle, 1990. The construction with *than*, though increasingly common and perhaps suggested by the analogy of *no sooner . . . than . . .*, is non-standard: ⊠ *But scarcely had he begun to investigate these new, if somewhat less adventurous, hunting-grounds, than the entire party was 'summoned back to Hobarton by Sir John'*—I. Tree, 1991. A construction with a comparative adjective or adverb following *than* is however acceptable: *There could scarcely be a less promising environment for an amphibian than the desert of central Australia*—David Attenborough, 1988 / *The difficulty of putting to rights two of the wrongs affecting children's education could scarcely be better illustrated than through the dilemma facing teachers over problem pupils*—Western Daily Press, 2000.

2 *Scarcely*, like *barely* and *hardly*, has a negative force without being grammatically negative, and another negative should be avoided in the same sentence unless it is in a following subordinate clause, as it is in this example: *There is scarcely an aspect of the race that is not rife with meaning*—New Yorker, 1989.

scarf. The word for a piece of outdoor clothing has the plural form *scarves*, whereas for the unrelated word meaning 'a joint or notch in timber, metal, etc.' it is *scarfs*.

scarify, pronounced with the first syllable as in *scab*, is a semi-technical word meaning 'to scratch or make incisions in', and has nothing to do with the verb *scare*. A verb *scarify*, pronounced like *scare* and formed on the analogy of *terrify*, meaning 'to scare or frighten', has been in existence since the 18c but is regarded as colloquial or even non-standard: *The use of macabre claymation models, which appear every now and again, to scarify sleepyheads*—film website, BrE 2001 [*OEC*].

scenario. 1 The pronunciation is normally si-**nah**-ri-oh in BrE and si-**nai**-ri-oh in AmE. The plural form is *scenarios*.

2 The word came into English from Italian in the late 19c as a term for the outline plot of a play, ballet, novel, etc., and was extended to the world of film in the early 20c. From the 1960s a new meaning exploded into use, and the word now commonly refers to any supposed or imagined series of events, or even to a static situation: *How then do we decide which class to assign a couple to where he is a builder and she is a secretary (not that uncommon a scenario)?*—R. Symonds, 1988 / *The entire education scenario is a joke*—*Liverpool Daily Echo*, 2007. This use of *scenario* is often regarded with suspicion, but it is hard to see why when so many other comparable figurative uses (such as *scene*) pass without comment. In its right place, when the imagined events or circumstances form a related sequence and are therefore comparable to the elements of a story-line, the word is a useful one.

scene, used figuratively in expressions such as *a scene of mayhem*, is part of the standard language. More informal are uses of the type *not my scene* and *the jazz scene*, originally associated with youth slang but now used more generally.

sceptic, sceptical. A *sceptic* (pronounced **skep**-tik) is someone who doubts accepted opinions or judgements and differs from a *cynic*, who believes that people are motivated purely by self-interest rather than acting for honourable or unselfish reasons. *Sceptic* is also an adjective, but the more common adjectival form is *sceptical*. In AmE the words are spelt *skeptic* and *skeptical*.

sceptre is spelt *-re* in BrE and *scepter* in AmE.

schedule. The dominant pronunciation in BrE is **shed**-yool, but the American form **sked**-yool is also used, especially among younger speakers.

schism, meaning 'the division of a group into opposing sections', is now commonly heard as skizm in place of the older form sizm recognized by the *OED* (1910).

schist, a term in geology for a type of layered rock, is pronounced shist.

schizoid, schizophrenia, schizo-phrenic. To use these words outside their medical context in a metaphorical way, e.g. *Gibraltar's schizophrenia continues to be fed by colonial pride*, is nowadays felt to be somewhat insensitive.

school, shoal. The two words are of the same Middle Dutch origin and are used with the same meaning of large numbers of fish and other sea animals swimming together. They are unrelated to the more familiar word *school*, which is derived from Latin *schola*.

scion, meaning 'a descendant of a (noble) family', is pronounced **siy**-uhn.

scissors is treated as a plural noun in its basic meaning (*The scissors are in the drawer*), but has a singular use in certain sports, where it is usually elliptical for a longer phrase such as *scissors movement* or *scissors pass* (*The ordinary scissors is the least effective of the four styles*).

scone is mostly pronounced skon in BrE, but skohn is also heard, especially in southern England, and is the dominant pronunciation in AmE. *Scone*, a village in central Scotland which was the site of a palace where the kings of Scotland were crowned, is pronounced skoon.

score = 20. *A score of* + plural noun is normally treated as a plural, the plural noun being regarded as the 'head' of the noun phrase: *A score of customers were waiting at the door.*

Scotch, Scots, Scottish. 1 The favoured terms are *a Scot* or *Scotsman* or *Scotswoman* for a person from Scotland, *Scottish* as the general adjective relating to Scotland, and *Scots* for any of the dialect forms of English spoken in (especially Lowland) Scotland (to be distinguished from *Scottish English* which is a variety of standard English). *Scots* is also used in certain expressions such as *Scots law* and the *Scots Guards* (*but Scottish Rifles*, another former regimental name).
2 The adjective and noun *Scotch*, though regularly used by Burns and Scott, fell out of favour in the 19c and is now confined to certain fixed expressions such as *Scotch broth, Scotch eggs, Scotch mist*, and *Scotch whisky*. Even among these there have been some adjustments: the dog formerly called *Scotch terrier*, for example, is now known as a *Scottish terrier*. Outside the UK, and especially in America, *Scotch* is likely to occur more often.

scrimmage, scrummage. *Scrimmage* is the more general word for 'a rough struggle or brawl' and is a technical term in American football, whereas

scrummage (more usually shortened to scrum) is the term used in rugby football.

seance, a term for a spiritualist meeting, is now rather more often spelt without an acute accent on the first *e* than with (*séance*).

seasonable, seasonal. *Seasonal* means 'occurring at or associated with a particular season' (*the farming year and its seasonal activities*), whereas *seasonable* is a more judgemental word meaning 'suitable for the season or time of year' (*All the married couples received seasonable gifts*).

second. The pronunciation is with the stress on the first syllable in all uses except the verb meaning 'to transfer to another use or employment', when the stress falls on the second syllable.

second hand is normally spelt as two words in uses such as *heard at second hand*, and is hyphened when used as an adjective (*a second-hand car*) or adverbial phrase (*They always buy second-hand*).

secretary should be pronounced as four syllables with the first *r* fully articulated, not as if it were spelt *seketerry* or *sekretry.*

sect is a word of Middle English origin denoting a party or faction holding views other than those of the majority (especially in a religious body). Historically it has been applied by Anglicans to various non-conformist groups (e.g. Methodists and Quakers) and it is now used of various groups, always with unfavourable connotations.

seeing is commonly used as a kind of conjunction, often followed by *that*, with the meaning 'because, considering that': *He was the kid-brother whom I helped as far as I could, seeing that we had no mother*—B. Cobb, 1971. The origin of the expression in actual observation is evident from continuing borderline uses: *Seeing that he was not about to change his attitude, I stood up and punched him in the nose*—fiction website, BrE 2001 [OEC]. The forms *seeing as* and *seeing as how* occur in informal contexts.

seem. For the type *seems to have been*, *see* PERFECT INFINITIVE.

seldom *see* RARELY.

self. Except in commercial contexts (*a cheque drawn to self*), *self* is now used as a substitute for *myself* or *oneself* only in humorous or informal contexts or in more casual styles of writing: *Memo to self: even if you don't think you're going to win, write a speech*—weblog, BrE 2002 [OEC].

self- is a highly productive prefix forming compounds of various types, in most of which *self* acts as the object on which the action or attribute signified by the second element operates, e.g. *self-betrayal* (= betrayal of oneself), *self-awareness* (= awareness of oneself), *self-addressed* (= addressed to oneself), etc. In other uses *self* is an agent, e.g. *self-educated* (= educated by oneself), *self-evident* (= evident in itself), and *self-service* (= service by oneself). Occasionally the second element is sufficient by itself and *self-* is arguably redundant, as in *self-assured*, *self-conceited*, and *self-confid-ent*, but the prefix serves a reinforcing role and most of this type are idiomatic.

selfie. Voted Oxford Dictionaries 'Word of the Year 2013', this term for a 'photograph taken of oneself, typically with a smartphone or webcam and uploaded to a social media website' goes at least as far back as 2002, but did not achieve prominence until 2013. The phenomenal growth words can enjoy thanks to the Internet and social media is illustrated by the 17,000% increase in the use of *selfie* between October 2012 and October 2013. The spelling in *-ie* is more frequent than that in *-y*, and highlights the word's Australian origin: the diminutive *-ie* ending appears also in *barbie* (barbecue), *firie* (firefighter), and *rellie* (relative).

semi- is the most active and versatile of the prefixes meaning 'half' (the other two being *demi-* and *hemi-*) in forming compounds, often with adjectives and verbal participles as the second element (*semi-automatic*, *semi-conscious*, *semi-detached*, *semi-skilled*, etc.) and occasionally nouns (*semicircle*, *semi-final*, *semi-invalid*, *semitone*). *Semi-* and *demi-* are Latin in origin, whereas *hemi-* is Greek.

semicolon. The semicolon is the least confidently used of the regular punctuation marks in ordinary writing, and the one least in evidence to anyone riffling through the pages of a modern novel. But it is extremely useful, used in moderation. Its main role is to mark a grammatical separation that is stronger in effect than a comma but less strong than a full stop. Normally the two parts of a sentence divided by a semicolon balance or complement each other as distinct from leading from one to the other (in which case a *colon is usually more suitable): *Most of his tools are old, handed down from his father and grandfather and uncles; here they are, handle upward, in tubs of oil and sand to stop them rusting*—Blake Morrison, 1993. It is also used as a stronger division in a sentence that already contains commas: *What has crippled me? Was it my grandmother, frowning on my childish affection and turning it to formality and cold courtesy; or my timid, fearful mother, in awe of everyone including, finally, me; or was it my wife's infidelities, or my own?*—Angela Lambert, 1989.

senator is spelt *-or*, not *-er*.

senior citizen. *She is a retired person, a senior citizen, you might say*—Barbara Pym, 1977. *Senior citizen* is a modern euphemism (first recorded in the 1930s) for an elderly person or old-age pensioner, and is an example of the use of more inclusive language because it refers positively to status rather than negatively to age. It is now widely used in official contexts. It is also shortened to *senior*, especially when used attributively, e.g. *senior centre, senior care*.

senior moment, first recorded in 1996, is a way of describing a short period of forgetfulness or confusion, such as might be experienced by an elderly person. It is best kept for informal contexts, since some people will consider it demeaning and ageist. Often, it is used by speakers of themselves, e.g. *I tell you, I had a bit of a senior moment yesterday! I only bloody left a bag of shopping outside!*—weblog, 2005 (UK).

sensational. The original meaning 'relating to sensation or the senses', first attested in the mid-19c, has been all but driven out by its extended meaning 'causing or intended to cause an exciting or startling effect' (i.e. causing a *sensation* in the corresponding sense): *The inquest was one of the most sensational legal dramas of the time*—BBC Press Release, 2004 [*OEC*].

sensible, sensitive. 1 The main meaning of *sensible* is 'having (common) sense', i.e. the opposite of *foolish*, and that of *sensitive* is 'easily offended or emotionally hurt'. In these uses they hardly get in each other's way. Where they overlap is in meanings to do with reactions involving the senses or feelings: you are *sensible of* something when you apprehend it with emotional consciousness and are *sensitive to* something when you react to it with strong emotional feeling, the words 'consciousness' and 'feeling' characterizing the difference between the two. However, *sensible of* now sounds old-fashioned, and a more likely choice of words might be *conscious of* or *aware of*, although these admittedly denote intellectual rather than emotional perceptions.

2 The nouns *sensibility* and *sensitivity* are harder to keep apart. *Sensibility* does not correspond to *sensible* (in its familiar meaning) at all and chiefly denotes (often in the plural) a person's delicate finer feelings: *Walter was a little hurt at this since he did most of the cooking at their place, but Zimmerman was too upset to worry about Walter's sensibilities*—Ben Elton, 1992. *Sensitivity* has a wider range of meanings concerned with physical or emotional reactions of various kinds, and can be paraphrased straightforwardly as meaning 'being sensitive': *My reference to it was simply a tease, and all the more tempting given Victor's known sensitivity on the point*—Climber and Hill Walker, 1991 / *This book's greatest strength is its sensitivity to Kissinger the man*—Scotland on Sunday, 2004.

sensitize, not the arguably more correct form *sensitivize*, is the standard word in meanings to do with making things sensitive, normally in physical senses (in photography, for example).

sensual, sensuous. 1 *Sensual* is the older word (15c), and originally described feelings that involved the senses as distinct from the intellect. As it became more closely associated with aspects of physical indulgence characterized by the expression *sensual pleasure* (principally sexual but also to do with food), *sensuous* came into use (first apparently by Milton in 1641) to take over the meanings that *sensual* had once had in relation to aesthetic rather than carnal sensations.

2 In current usage, this distinction holds good for those who want a rule:

(sensual) *Modigliani appreciated Kisling for what he was, a sweet-natured, high-spirited, sensual young man*—J. Rose, 1990 / *The Hindu god of love, Kama, is the husband of Rati, the goddess of sensual desire*—P. Allardice, 1990 / *A good slow, deep, seductive, sensual, sexual kiss can be the very thing that sends someone over the edge in my opinion*—weblog, BrE 2005 / (sensuous) *All the sensuous elements of the previous years have been banished; colour has been reduced to a severe combination of browns, dull greens and greys*—J. Golding, 1988 / *The passage exemplifies the distancing effect of simile, and the more sensuous effect of metaphor*—E. Black, 1993.

3 But in the hurly-burly of general usage the meanings are too close, and *sensuous* has gone the way of *sensual*, especially in modern popular fiction. In other words, it has developed a second meaning 'attractive or gratifying physically, especially sexually' in addition to its more neutral one, and it is most often used in that meaning: *He looked forward to this drink, the first of the day, with a sensuous desire*—Barbara Vine, 1987 / *There was something extremely sensuous about having a man dry her hair, especially this man*—A. Murray, 1993. Although the complex subtleties of sense perception cause meanings to merge into one another, it is prudent to remember the basic distinction when using these words, so that *sensuous* can retain its full force of meaning in uses that are primarily to do with aesthetics, for example in the context of music or poetry: *Cesti's great gift was for melody: sensuous and eminently singable*—G. Abraham, 1985.

sentence. 1 Many users of this book will have been taught that a sentence is a group of words that makes complete sense, contains a main verb, and when written begins with a capital letter and ends with a full stop (or a question mark if it is a question or an exclamation mark if it is an exclamation). This is a good working definition, and rather than pick holes in it we might more profitably add certain riders to it:

2 A sentence can contain ellipsis, i.e. a verb and other words can be understood or suppressed: *It had been a good party. An unforgettable party, actually. And still was.*—A. Huth, 1992. (Ellipsis of *it had been* in the second sentence and *it* in the third.) Grammarians may argue about whether these are all true sentences, but for practical purposes it is sensible to regard them all as qualifying for the term, if only to make straightforward discussion about language structure possible.

3 There are three basic kinds of sentence. A *simple sentence* normally contains one statement: *It had been a good party*. A *compound sentence* contains more than one statement, normally joined by a conjunction such as *and* or *but*: *It had been a good party and we had all enjoyed it* / *It had been a good party but I had known better*. A *complex sentence* contains a main clause and one or more subordinate clauses, such as a relative clause introduced by *which* or *who*: *It had been a good party, which we all enjoyed very much*.

sentence adverb. 1 Certain adverbs, such as *actually, basically, clearly, frankly, interestingly, normally, regrettably, strictly*, and *usually*, have the special role of qualifying entire statements rather than individual words. Some of these are adverbs of time and frequency and retain a closer connection with the verb despite being separated from it: *It is normally very difficult to get a new sport accepted for the Olympics*—New Yorker, 1984. The others have a more independent role in referring not to the content of the statement but to the opinion or attitude of the speaker to what is being said: *I'm sure you don't know every detail* *of her past either and, quite frankly, it's none of your business—Daily Star, 2007* (= to be frank, as I frankly believe) / *Clearly therefore, we suggest, this points to a 'mole' within British Telecom Prestel headquarters—Times,* 1984 (= as is clear). This phenomenon is commonly associated with 20c usage, but examples are recorded from an earlier date.

2 The examples given so far are mostly uncontentious, but controversy arises with *thankfully, regretfully,* and, above all, *hopefully: Hopefully, our experience will be of use to them—Independent,* 1989. This may be because, unlike the others, there is no phrasal basis corresponding to *it is clear that* (for *clearly*) or *to be frank* (for *frankly*), since 'it is to be hoped that' is passive whereas *hopeful* is 'active' (i.e. the person so described does the hoping). *See* HOPEFULLY.

separate. Note the spelling with two *a*s, unlike *desperate*. The verb is pronounced **sep**-uh-rayt, and the adjective **sep**-uh-ruht.

sepulchre is spelt *-re* in BrE and *sepulcher* in AmE.

sequence of tenses. This refers to the pattern of tenses in a sequence of verbs within a sentence. If a simple statement such as *I'm afraid I haven't finished* is put into indirect speech by means of a reporting verb such as *said, thought,* etc., the tense of the reported action changes in accordance with the time perspective of the speaker: *He said he was afraid he hadn't finished.* However, the tense of the reported verb can stay the same if the time relative to the speaker is the same as that relative to the person reported: *She likes beans* can be converted either to *She said she liked beans* or to *She said she likes beans,* and *I won't be here tomorrow* can be converted either to *He said he wouldn't be*

here tomorrow or to *He said he won't be here tomorrow.*

sergeant, serjeant. The normal spelling in the context of the police and the army is *sergeant; serjeant* is usually restricted to the titles of certain ceremonial offices, such as the *serjeant-at-arms* with reference to the British parliamentary or civic official.

serial comma *see* OXFORD COMMA.

series is spelt the same both as a singular and as a plural noun.

seriously. The use of *seriously* as an intensifier equivalent to 'very, extremely', e.g. *seriously good, bad, cool, rich,* etc. was originally AmE (1970), but is now widespread. In BrE it still sounds journalistic or somewhat exaggerated, and not quite part of everyday language: *Try the Gamekeeper's tea (venison, duck and pheasant pâté with toast) at this seriously good tea shop—Observer,* 2005 / *America's seriously wealthy step up the pressure on Obama—Independent,* 2010.

serviceable is spelt with an *e* in the middle, to preserve the soft sound of the *c.*

serviette *see* NAPKIN.

sesquicentenary *see* ANNIVERSARIES.

sett is still a common variant spelling of *set* in the meanings (1) a badger's burrow and (2) a paving-block.

seventies *see* EIGHTIES.

sew, sow *verbs. Sew* means 'to form stitches with a needle and thread' and has the past form *sewed* and the past participle *sewn* or *sewed. Sow* means 'to plant (seed)' and has the past form *sowed* and the past participle *sown* or *sowed.*

sewage, sewerage. *Sewage* is waste matter carried by sewers, and *sewerage* is a system of sewers.

sexcentenary *see* ANNIVERSARIES.

sexist language. Roughly since the 1970s, certain established uses of language have come to be regarded as discriminatory against women, either because they are based on male terminology or because women appear to be given a status that is linguistically and socially subsidiary. For specific aspects of this, *see* -ESS; GENDER-NEUTRALITY; -MAN; MS; -PERSON. Since the 1980s, many official style guides (including Judith Butcher's *Copy-editing*, third edition, Cambridge, 1992) have included advice on how to avoid sexist language. In 1989 the General Synod of the Church of England debated a report on the need to introduce non-sexist language into the liturgy, and in the same year a revised version of the Bible substituted *one* for *man* in such contexts as *Happy is the* **man** *who does not take the wicked for* **his** *guide*. It is in the realm of idiom that male-biased language will most likely persist, since it is difficult to reconstruct without awkwardness or affectation such compound words and phrases as *manpower, maiden voyage, every man for himself,* and *the man on the Clapham omnibus*.

sex up This colourful phrasal verb meaning 'to present (information) in a more interesting or lively way' dates from the 1940s, originally in AmE. It was given a substantial boost when the British Prime Minister was accused of misleading the country by publishing in 2002 tendentious information about the aggressive intentions of Saddam Hussein of Iraq. Even when sexual connotations are still present, these circumstances continue to influence all subsequent usage: *It should come as no surprise that this racy Nineties comedy comes from*

Andrew Davies, the man credited with 'sexing up' Jane Austen—Daily Mail, 2007.

shall and will. 1 The supposed rule is that to express a simple future tense *shall* is used after *I* and *we* (*In addition to my duties in the House, I shall be having further meetings later today—Hansard,* 1992) and *will* in other cases, whereas to express intention or wish the reverse applies (*We will give people a new right of access to open country, create new national parks and step up protection for special sites—It's time to get Britain working again* (Labour Party), 1992); but it is unlikely that this rule has ever had any consistent basis of authority in actual usage, and many examples of English in print disregard it. In general, the rule applies more strongly to *I* than to *we*.

2 Furthermore, the distinction is often difficult to establish, especially in the first person when the speaker is also the performer of the future action and intention is therefore implied at least partially. *Will* and (occasionally) *shall* are used as modal verbs to refer to future action or state, but other, more natural, ways of expressing this are commonly preferred, such as *am going to*: *I'm going to teach him people are more important than money—Maurice Gee, 1992.*

3 When *shall* and *will* are used in conversation, they are normally contracted to '*ll*, especially after pronouns, which makes the difference between the two words irrelevant: *They'll cook and clean for a week before a party—New York Times, 1976 / I'll remember this sodding day until the day I die—Dirk Bogarde, 1980.*

4 *Shall* has been largely driven out by *will* in all parts of the English-speaking world other than England. It survives mostly in first-person questions or suggestions (*Shall I help you to try again?—*B. Jagger, 1986 / '*Shall we take our drinks* to the bedroom?' she said softly—J. Francome, 1990), in legal language (*The landlord shall maintain the premises*), and in the contracted negative form *shan't* (*Have no fear . . . I shan't throw in the towel, I promise you*—M. Russell, 1979), but *shan't* is not used in American English. In the English of England (but *not* of Britain as a whole), *shall* half survives (albeit tending to sound old-fashioned and affected) in commands and assurances (*Yes, you shall take some eggs back to your aunt*—C. Harvey, 1992) and in questions seeking information rather than making a request) (*And where shall you be while I'm hobbling all over the castle?*—fiction website, BrE 2005 [*OEC*]), but *will* (or sometimes *can*) is just as common, especially in speech, and is more natural. In Scotland, *will* is used in the first person even in requests (*Will I help you with your bags?*).

5 There is not much doubt that *will* will win, and *shall* shall lose, in the end.

shambles. The word now most commonly used to mean 'a mess or muddle' has a colourful history. It started life in Old English in the singular form *shamble* meaning 'a stool or footstool', came to refer to a table or stall for the sale of meat, and was then applied (in the plural, *shambles*) to the slaughterhouse from which the meat came. From the 16c it meant any scene of blood and carnage. The modern meaning arose as recently as the 1920s, and is still disliked by some because it debases a powerful word. In these last two meanings *shambles* is normally treated as a singular noun, usually in the form *a shambles* (*The house was a shambles* or *The house was in a shambles*). The derived adjective *shambolic*, meaning 'disorganized, chaotic' is used mainly in BrE.

shamefaced, meaning 'showing shame', is a 16c alteration of an older word *shamefast*, meaning 'bashful', and

should be spelt as one word. The adverb *shamefacedly* should be pronounced as four syllables.

shampoo. The verb has inflected forms *shampoos, shampooed, shampooing*.

shanghai, meaning 'to kidnap for naval service', inflects awkwardly in English, but the recommended forms are *shanghais, shanghaied, shanghaiing*.

shan't *see* SHALL AND WILL 4.

sharp is used as an adverb only in expressions such as *at 10 o'clock sharp* (= exactly) and *He pulled up sharp* (= abruptly). In other meanings of *sharp*, the correct form of the adverb is *sharply* (*Prices dropped sharply / She spoke to them sharply*).

shave. The verb has a past form and past participle *shaved*, but the adjectival form is normally *shaven*, as in *clean-shaven*.

she. 1 For *she* or *her* after the verb *be*, *see* CASES 2A.

2 For the expression *he or she*, *see* GENDER-NEUTRALITY.

s/he. *A child's sexual orientation is determined before s/he enters school*—American Educator, 1978. This written representation of 'he or she' as a gender-neutral pronoun is generally limited to the written domain of reports and self-conscious English. Because it is unclear how it should be read out, namely is it 'he or she', which defeats the purpose, or 'he stroke she', ditto, or 'she stroke he', which many men will have difficulty with, it has failed to make inroads into the realms of standard usage. *See* GENDER-NEUTRALITY.

sheaf has the plural form *sheaves*. The verb meaning 'to make into sheaves' is *sheave*.

shear, sheer. *Shear* is a verb meaning 'to remove by cutting' or 'to cut the wool off (a sheep)', and has the past form *sheared* and the past participle *shorn* or (in the context of metal-cutting) *sheared*. *Sheer* is an adjective describing a steep cliff or ascent and is also used in expressions such as *sheer luck*.

sheath is pronounced sheeth (like *teeth*) in the singular and sheedhz (like *seethes*) in the plural.

sheep is the same in the singular and plural.

sheikh, pronounced shayk or sheek, is the most frequent spelling of the word for an Arab chief or leader.

shelf has the plural form *shelves*, and the corresponding verb is *shelve*. The compound form *shelf-ful* should be written with a hyphen for clarity, and its plural is *shelf-fuls*.

shew, show. The normal spelling is *show*. *Shew* is used in Scottish law and in citations from the Bible and Prayer Book. *See also* SHOW.

shibboleth. The primary meanings in current English are 'a moral formula held tenaciously and unreflectingly, especially a prohibitive one; a taboo' and 'an entrenched (political) belief or dogma': *You are a dinosaur—you're an old Marxist—if you challenge these new shibboleths of the neo-liberal age—Workers Online*, 2001 / *Instead, he spouted standard liberal shibboleths about solving our problems through federal programs and a higher minimum wage—New York Post*, 2006, and are extensions of the biblical meaning of a Hebrew word used by Jephthah as a test-word by which to distinguish the fleeing Ephraimites (who could not pronounce the *sh* sound) from his own men, the Gileadites.

shine. The normal past forms and past participle are *shone*, but *shined* is an alternative in AmE and in both varieties in the meaning 'to make (something) shine': *The car is a red Mercedes, newly shined*—S. North, BrE 1989 / *It occurred to me that this was not a reflection from his glasses or his crown, no matter how much they shined*—D. Pinckney, AmE 1992.

shingles, the disease, is normally treated as a singular noun (*Shingles sometimes follows a bad case of measles*), but it can be plural when the emphasis is on the resulting blisters rather than the illness itself (*The shingles were extremely painful*).

ship *see* BOAT.

shire. In England, the *shires* are traditionally the old foxhunting areas of Leicestershire, Northamptonshire, and the former county of Rutland. Since the reorganization of local government in 1972 and 1986 the term *shire county* has been applied to the 39 counties outside metropolitan areas which have county councils, as distinct from London and the six metropolitan counties.

shoe. The verb has inflected forms *shoes, shoeing*, and (past tense and past participle) *shod*.

shop *verb*. In BrE the verb is used intransitively (i.e. without an object) in its meaning 'to buy things at shops', whereas in AmE it is also used transitively with the meaning 'to examine or buy goods at (a store)': *One man who had shopped the entire store complained that he hadn't found what he was looking for*—S. Marcus, 1974. The informal transitive use 'to inform on (someone)' is chiefly BrE.

short, shortly *adverbs*. The roles of these two words are fairly clearly separated. *Short* usually means 'before the

S

expected time or place, abruptly' (*We cut short the celebration / They pulled up short*), whereas *shortly* is most often used to mean 'before long, soon' (*She is expected to arrive shortly*).

short-lived is pronounced shawt-**livd** in BrE and shawt-**liyvd** in AmE.

should and would. 1 As with *shall* and *will*, *should* has been largely driven out by *would* as a modal verb, but there is the added consideration that *should* also (in fact more often than not) denotes obligation or likelihood (*Now I think we should bring down the curtain on this little episode, and go to bed*—A. Browning, 1992 / *The letters, which should have arrived at patients' homes today, ask them to seek advice and counseling*—York Press, 2002 / *Patients with diabetes should have tighter limits placed on blood pressure*—British Medical Journal, 2003).

2 As a modal verb, *would* is more usual than *should* when stating a condition or proposition and is the only choice when asking a question (*They would like to stay / I would think so / Would you bring the children?*). *Should* is sometimes used in the first person (singular and plural) for statements and propositions, especially in the English of England ('*I should like one of these,*' *says Claudia*—Penelope Lively, 1987) and in tentative statements of opinion (*I should say that there is not only increasing public awareness of the problems of smoking and its long-term consequences to the health of smokers, but* [etc.]—Hansard, 1992), and is always used in inverted constructions expressing a condition: *You will find plenty of wood for a fire should you need one*—fishing website, BrE 2002 [OEC].

3 *Would* has to be used when referring to unfulfilled conditions and hypotheses (*Ordinarily, I would have chosen an empty table*—Brian Aldiss,

1991) and to habitual action in the past (*These he would produce with a flourish during our Wednesday- and Sunday-evening sessions*—Will Self, 1993), and to express the future in the past (*She realised they would have to come back at some point and face the music*—Yorkshire Post Today, 2001 [OEC]).

4 In conversational English, the contracted forms *I'd*, *you'd*, etc., are often used in simple statements instead of the full forms, so that the *should/would* distinction is not an issue (*I'd be delighted to join you*—Kingsley Amis, 1988 / *This particular one is limited to 400 so you'd better hurry if you want one*—BBC Popular Music Reviews, 2004 [OEC]), but in meanings to do with obligation or likelihood (*see* sense 1 above) the full form *should* has to be used.

should of. This incorrect form of *should have* arises in all English-speaking countries because the contracted form *should've* is indistinguishable from it in speech. It is often associated with the speech of children or poorly educated adults: *Well, you should of buyed some cigarettes for yourself so it's your own fault*—S. Mackay, 1984.

shovel. The verb has inflected forms *shovelled*, *shovelling* in BrE, and in AmE usually *shoveled*, *shoveling*.

show. The past tense is *showed* (*I showed it to them*), and the past participle is normally *shown* (*Have you shown it to them?*) but very occasionally *showed*: *I don't know what would have happened if they hadn't showed up*—Daily Mail, 2002.

shrink has a past tense *shrank* and a past participle *shrunk*, but *shrunken* is the normal adjective form in both physical and abstract senses: *She was a thin sickly child with a tremendous head of dark curly hair, a tiny shrunken face and enormous eyes*—S. Stewart, 1991 /

Eliot discussed the shrunken sense in which 'culture' was applied to the arts— R. Crawford, 1990.

shrivel has inflected forms *shrivelled, shrivelling*, and in AmE usually *shriveled, shriveling*.

shy. The adjective has comparative and superlative forms *shyer* and *shyest*, and derivative forms *shyly, shyness*.

Siamese twins *see* CONJOINED TWINS.

sibling is a kind of popularized technical term, a word reintroduced by anthropologists in the early 20c and useful now as a gender-neutral term for 'brother or sister': *Small groups drifted through the classroom: mothers and fathers, large numbers of children— Edward's pupils along with older and younger siblings—*Penelope Lively, 1990. The word is also common in the expression *sibling rivalry*: *Moses . . . shows more than a hint of sibling rivalry in his attitude to his brother Aaron—* C. Raphael, 1972.

sic, the Latin word for 'so, thus', is added in italic type, preferably in square brackets, but also in round, after a quoted word or phrase which might cause readers some puzzlement because of a misspelling (which the quoting writer does not want to correct) or some other mistake of use: *The Abbey PR office phoned to issue a statement: 'Abbey is committed to providing it's (sic) customers with good service, and we apologise if on this specific occasion we fell below our high standards'—Liverpool Daily Echo*, 2007, drawing attention to rather than silently correcting an erroneous apostrophe. (But if the Abbey office issued the statement by telephone the error must have been in the newspaper's own transcription in any case.) It should not be used as a supercilious comment on the quoted writer's style or

supposed looseness of grammar, as in the following example: *I probably have a different sense of morality to [sic] most people—Chicago Tribune*, 1994, quoting Alan Clark.

sick *see* ILL.

siege is spelt *-ie-*, as is *besiege*.

sienna, the pigment and its colour of yellowish-brown (*raw sienna*) or reddish-brown (*burnt sienna*) is spelt with two *n*s despite being derived from the name of *Siena* in northern Italy.

sieve, a device for separating solids from liquids, is spelt *-ie-*, and pronounced siv.

signal. The verb has inflected forms *signalled, signalling* in BrE, and in AmE usually *signaled, signaling*.

signatory is now the usual spelling (not *signatary*) for the noun meaning 'a party or state that has signed an agreement', and the corresponding adjective.

significant other is a somewhat coy term for a live-in partner and often occurs in journalistic, advertising, or facetious contexts. (*It is all about teasing the viewer—whether that is an audience of hundreds or simply your significant other—Plymouth Evening Herald*, 2007).

silken *see* -EN ADJECTIVES.

sillabub *see* SYLLABUB.

sillily, though formally correct, is too awkward for normal use and is usually replaced by the phrase *in a silly way* or by other one-word adverbs such as *foolishly* or *stupidly*.

silo has the plural form *silos*.

similar is followed by *to* not *as*: *It seemed to me that she was acknowledging an emotion similar to my own—* C. Rumens, 1987.

simile is a figure of speech consisting of a direct comparison using a construction with *as . . . as . . .* , or with the first *as* omitted: *Soft as rain slipping through rushes, the cattle came*—Edmund Blunden. Some similes belong to a stock type, e.g. *(as) drunk as a lord, (as) fit as a fiddle*, etc. *See also* METAPHOR AND SIMILE. Others are constructed with *like*, e.g. *Her skin is like honey*.

simplistic is first recorded in its modern meaning as recently as the late 19c. It differs from *simple* in implying a simplicity that is excessive or misleading rather than direct and useful: *She's quite right . . . It is simplistic to speak of malice*—Tom Stoppard, 1976. To preserve this useful distinction, care should be taken not to use *simplistic* when the sense is positive rather than judgemental and therefore *simple* itself is adequate. ☒ *We have got to take things back down to a more simplistic* [read: *simple* or *basic*] *level. Pensions . . . are essentially a life decision. Everything we do makes it more complicated*—Birmingham Post, 2007.

sincerely. For *Yours sincerely*, see LETTER FORMS.

sinecure, meaning 'a position that requires little or no work but provides profit or honour', is normally pronounced **siy**-ni-kyoo-uh, with the first syllable like *sign*, but the first syllable can also rhyme with *sin*.

sine qua non is normally pronounced **see**-nay kwah nohn, although other pronunciations are heard. It means 'an indispensable condition or qualification'. It is printed in italics.

sing. The past form is *sang* and the past participle is *sung*. The latter is found for the past tense in literature of the 18c and 19c, and occasionally also nowadays, especially in speech, but in writing is non-standard.

singeing, meaning 'burning lightly', is spelt like this to distinguish it from *singing* (formed from the verb *sing*).

Sinhalese is the recommended form of the noun and adjective associated with Sri Lanka, rather than *Singalese, Singhalese*, and other variants.

sink. The verb has the past tense *sank* (but formerly and occasionally still *sunk*) and the past participle *sunk*. The adjectival forms *sunk* and *sunken* are not readily distinguished: *sunken* is often used to mean 'submerged' (*a sunken ship*), 'fallen in, hollow' (*sunken cheeks, sunken eyes*), and often 'below the normal level' (*sunken garden*). *Sunk* is the form normally chosen for technical expressions such as *sunk fence, sunk key*, and *sunk panel*, although in these cases too *sunken* is sometimes used. In general use *sunken* is the more common choice for attributive uses (i.e. before nouns).

sinus has the plural form *sinuses*. In Latin the plural is *sinus*, not *sini*.

siphon is the recommended and much more often used form for the noun and the verb, not *syphon*.

sister, a senior female nurse, usually in charge of a hospital ward. The equivalent term in AmE is *head nurse*.

sister-in-law means (1) one's wife's or husband's sister, (2) one's brother's wife, (3) one's brother-in-law's wife. The plural is *sisters-in-law*.

sit *see* SAT.

site. Many people confuse *site* and *sight*. As a noun, *site* means 'a place where something is constructed or has occurred' (*the site of the battle /the concrete is mixed on site*), while *sight* chiefly means 'the faculty or power of seeing' (*he lost his sight as a baby*).

situation is a useful noun for expressing the meaning 'a set of circumstances, a state of affairs', especially when preceded by a defining adjective, e.g. *the financial situation, the political situation*, etc. It is less useful, indeed often redundant, when a noun precedes: *crisis situation* adds nothing to *crisis* and *emergency situation* adds nothing to *emergency* because both words implicitly denote situations in themselves. On the other hand, *hostage situation* is a convenient short way of saying 'a situation in which hostages have been taken' because *hostage* is not already a word equivalent in itself to a 'situation'.

sixties *see* EIGHTIES.

sizeable, sizable. The spelling with an *e* in the middle is the more frequent in World English and BrE, but *sizable* is preferred in AmE.

skeptic, skeptical *see* SCEPTIC, SCEPTICAL.

ski. The noun has the plural form *skis*, and the verb has inflections *skis, skied* (pronounced skeed), *skiing* (pronounced **skee**-ing). Words ending in *-i* (in this case from Norwegian) are always awkward in English, and some people prefer to use the forms *ski'd* and *ski-ing* rather than try to force the word into an uncomfortable English pattern, but these look if anything even more ungainly.

skier, skyer. A *skier* (pronounced **skee**-uh) is a person who skis, whereas a *skyer* (pronounced **skiy**-uh) is a high hit in cricket.

skilful, skilled. 1 *Skilful* is spelt in this way in BrE, and usually *skillful* in AmE.

2 *Skilled* is the word to use when referring to types of work (also *semi-skilled, unskilled*), and is classificatory in function, whereas *skilful* is evaluative and can refer to people and their

achievements (*a skilful painter / a skilful painting*).

skill-less should be spelt with a hyphen to avoid the awkward collision of three *ls*.

skyer *see* SKIER, SKYER.

slander *see* LIBEL.

slang. 1 The term *slang* is first recorded in the 1750s, but it was not used by Dr Johnson in his *Dictionary* of 1755 nor entered in it as a headword (he used the term *low word*, with implications of disapproval). Nonetheless, the notion of highly informal words or of words associated with a particular class or occupation is very old, and this type of vocabulary has been commented on, usually with disfavour, for centuries. More recently, the development of modern linguistic science has led to a more objective assessment in which slang is seen as having a useful purpose when used in the right context.

2 Drawing the line between informal language and slang is not always easy; slang is at the extreme end of informality and usually has the capacity to shock. In English slang often has associations of class or occupation, so that many slang words have their origins in cant (the jargon of a particular profession, e.g. *bogus, flog, prig, rogue*), criminal slang (*broad* = female companion, *drag* = inhalation of tobacco smoke, *nick* = to steal), racing slang (*dark horse, no-hoper, hot favourite*), military slang (*bonkers* = crazy, *clobber* = beat or defeat, *ginormous* = huge), and most recently computing slang (*hacking* = breaking into networks, *surfing* = browsing on the Internet). Other words stay largely within their original domain of usage, such as drugs slang (*flash* = pleasant sensation from a narcotic drug, *juice* = a drug or drugs) and youth slang (*blatantly* = definitely, *wicked* = excellent).

3 Slang words are formed by a variety of processes, of which the following are the main ones:

a established words used in extended or special meanings: *flash* and *juice* in the previous paragraph, *awesome* = excellent, *hooter* = nose, *take out* = kill.

b words made by abbreviation or shortening: *fab* from *fabulous*, *pro* from *professional*, *snafu* (= *situation normal: all fouled up*).

c rhyming slang: *Adam and Eve* = believe, *butcher's* (*hook*) = look.

d words formed by compounding: *airhead* = stupid person, *couch potato* = person who lazes around watching television, *snail mail* = ordinary mail as opposed to email.

e merging of two words: 'portmanteau' words such as *ditsy* = *dotty* + *dizzy*, *ginormous* = *gigantic* + *enormous*.

f backslang, in which the spelling or sound of other words are reversed: *yob* from *boy*, *slop* from *police*.

g reduplications and fanciful formations: *heebie-jeebies*, *okey-doke*.

h words based on phrases or idioms: *bad-mouth* = to abuse, *feel-good* as in *feel-good factor*, *in-your-face* = aggressive, *drop-dead* = extremely (beautiful etc.), *must-have* = essential, *one-night stand* = brief sexual encounter.

i loanwords from other languages: *gazump*, *nosh*, *shemozzle* from Yiddish, *kaput* from German, *bimbo* from Italian (= little child).

j words taken from dialect or regional varieties: *manky* = dirty, from Scottish; *dinkum* = genuine, right, Australian and New Zealand.

4 Slang uses are especially prevalent in areas in which direct language is regarded as taboo or unsocial, such as death (*to kick the bucket, to hand in one's nosebag, to snuff it*), sexual functions (*to have it off, to screw*), and excretion (*to dump, to sit on the throne*).

5 Slang is by its nature ephemeral, and relatively few words and uses pass into standard use. Examples of these include *bogus, clever, joke*, and *snob* (all classed by Dr Johnson as 'low words'). Conversely some words that were once standard have passed into slang (e.g. *arse, shit, tit*).

6 The first work to record English slang was published as B.E.'s *Dictionary of the Canting Crew* in 1699. Modern works include Eric Partridge's famous *Dictionary of Slang and Unconventional English* (1937; most recently edited by Paul Beale, 2002), *The Oxford Dictionary of Slang* (edited by John Ayto, 1998), *The Slang Thesaurus* (2nd edition, edited by Jonathon Green, 1999), and the *Cassell Dictionary of Slang* (also edited by Jonathon Green, 2000).

slash *noun see* OBLIQUE.

slate *verb*. There is an important difference between its meanings on the two sides of the Atlantic. In BrE it means 'to criticize severely', whereas in AmE it usually means 'to nominate' or 'to designate or schedule' (as in *slating* a meeting). The context will normally clarify which sense is meant, but care is needed in interpreting newspaper headlines such as *Summit meeting slated*.

slavish is spelt without an *e*.

slay, meaning 'to kill', has the past tense *slew* and the past participle *slain*. In BrE it has a literary flavour, but it is an ordinary word for violent killing in AmE, appearing in newspaper headlines such as *Serial killer slays seven*, which sometimes get carried over into British newspapers as well.

sled, sledge, sleigh. All three words are derived from Dutch and are used for vehicles that carry people or goods over snow. In BrE *sledge* is the normal word for vehicles of various sizes pulled by people or animals (*toboggan*, a native American word, is also used for the type used for sport on slopes). *Sled* is used mainly in North America for a large vehicle pulled by animals, and *sleigh* for the larger type of vehicle drawn by horses or reindeer.

sledgehammer is spelt as one word as noun and verb, not ✗ *sledge hammer* or ✗ *sledge-hammer*.

sleight, as in *sleight of hand*, is pronounced like *slight*. It is the noun equivalent of the adjective *sly*, as *height* is of *high*.

slew *noun* is the correct spelling, rather than *slue* for the mainly AmE informal word meaning a large group of things or people, e.g. *Fugitive Pieces was perhaps the decade's most celebrated novel about the Holocaust, winning a slew of awards including the Guardian and Orange prizes*—The Age, 2009. *See also* SLOUGH.

slimy is spelt without an *e*.

sling has the past tense and past participle *slung*.

slink has the past tense and past participle *slunk*.

slither, sliver The words are often confused, especially in newspapers. *Slither* is overwhelmingly a verb meaning 'to slip or slide unsteadily', whereas *sliver* is a noun meaning 'a thin narrow piece cut off a larger piece'. The more usual error is to put *slither* for *sliver*: ✗ *A shave here and a slither* [read: *sliver*] *of metal there can make all the difference to a bell*—Guardian, 1999.

sloe-worm *see* SLOW-WORM.

slogan was originally a Gaelic word for a warcry, but the dominant meaning now is the less specific one 'a watchword or motto' (*make poverty history, business as usual*) or 'a short catchy phrase used in advertising'.

slough. The noun meaning 'bog or swamp' is pronounced to rhyme with *now*. The separate word (noun and verb) to do with an animal's skin is pronounced to rhyme with *stuff*. In AmE, the first noun is often written *slew* and pronounced sloo.

slow, slowly. In current English the normal adverb for general purposes is *slowly* (*We drove slowly down the road / She slowly closed the door*). Literary uses of *slow* as an adverb died out in the 19c (*As the stately vessel glided slow beneath the shadow*—Byron, 1812), and in current usage it is confined to the expression *go slow*, to compounds such as *slow-acting* and *slow-moving*, and to occasional informal uses (*It was easy to drive slow and look into lighted uncurtained windows*—L. Ellmann, 1988). The comparative and superlative forms *slower* and *slowest* are however regularly used as well as *more slowly* and *most slowly*: *Neurotransmitters make the heart beat faster or slower*—Scientific American, 1974 / *In congested motorway traffic, I always appear to be in the lane moving the slowest*—Daily Mail, 2002.

slow-worm, a small legless lizard, is the dominant current spelling (formerly also *sloe-worm*). The word is unconnected with either *sloes* (the fruit) or the adjective *slow*.

slur. The verb has inflected forms *slurred, slurring*.

slush, sludge, slosh. *Sludge* is usually applied to something relatively thick and less liquid, e.g. to wet clinging mud or slimy deposits, whereas *slush* more typically describes thawing snow or melting ice. *Slosh* (in its related uses) is a verb meaning 'to move with a splashing sound' and *slush* as a verb is used in this way too, e.g. *there was water slushing around in the galley / water in the boat sloshed about under our feet*.

S

sly. The adjective has comparative and superlative forms *slyer* and *slyest*, and derivative forms *slyly, slyness*.

smart. Since the 1980s *smart* has taken on a smart new meaning in computing and information technology. It refers to a device or machine appearing to have a degree of intelligence and programmed to be able to provide information when read by an appropriate device. Originally most familiar in daily life in *smart card* (a plastic bank card or similar device with a built-in microprocessor), that role has now been taken over by *smartphones*, i.e. phones that perform many of the functions of a computer. Other machines that can unnerve us with their intelligence include *smart meters*.

smell *verb*. The form for the past tense and past participle in BrE is *smelled* or *smelt*; in AmE *smelled* is usually preferred. When the verb is used intransitively, the quality of the smell is normally expressed either by a phrase introduced by *of* or by an adjective, not by an adverb: *His jacket smelt of horses and tobacco and general maleness*—A. Fraser, 1975 / *As she stooped lower her breath, caught in all the black veils, smelled terrible*—Molly Keane, 1988. A comparative construction with *like* is also possible: *This smells like a poncey brothel*—L. Henderson, 1970 / *Whisky doesn't smell like whisky until it's been matured in oak barrels for a number of years*—Scotsman, 2007. When an adverb is used it is normally an intensifying adverb (*His jacket smelled strongly of horses . . . / . . . it smelled extremely putrid*), and adverbs are also used when *smell* is used absolutely with the meaning 'to smell badly, to stink': *The prison cell smelt abominably*.

smite has the past tense *smote* and a past participle *smitten*. In its physical meaning 'to hit', *smite* has fallen out of use outside literary contexts, but *to be*

smitten is still going strong in its figurative meaning 'to be infatuated or obsessed' (*He was smitten by her beauty*). When the object of the fascination is a person, *with* is much more often used than *by*; when the object is inanimate, the pattern is the opposite: *Roberts happens upon Grant's bookstore and is smitten with his English charm* / *a successful entrepreneur smitten by the film bug*.

smog, formed from *smoke* + *fog* and first recorded in 1905, is one of the most enduring portmanteau words from the 20c.

smoky is spelt without an *e*.

smoulder, meaning 'to burn slowly', is spelt in this way in BrE and usually *smolder* in AmE.

snail mail, an expressive term for the ordinary postal service, contrasted with the speed of email, is still somewhat slangy or informal in BrE and is best avoided in any kind of formal writing: *When I say cutting I mean just that, the piece cut from the paper! Not for her the wonders of email, her preference is snail mail*—weblog, BrE 2005 [OEC].

snaky, meaning 'winding or sinuous', is spelt without an *e*.

sneak *verb*. Its origins are shrouded in mystery (despite earlier similar forms in Old English and other Germanic languages) as it emerges fully clad in the works of English playwrights around 1600: *A poor unminded outlaw, sneaking home*—Shakespeare, *1 Henry IV*, IV.iii.58, 1596. In standard use it has the regular past tense and past participle *sneaked*. The form *snuck*, which has no precedent in other verbs in *-eak* and *-eek* (*creak, leak, peak, peek, reek, squeak*, etc.), has established itself in several varieties of English, including North American (*She must have snuck out in* *the night*), and is recognized in US dictionaries. It is beginning to be widely used also in BrE, but is generally considered informal.

snivel. The verb has inflected forms *snivelled, snivelling* in BrE, and in AmE usually *sniveled, sniveling*.

snuck *see* SNEAK.

so. 1 In modern slang, at first in AmE and now quite widely in British, use of *so* as an intensifier has been extended into roles that stretch standard grammar, e.g. modifying active verbs, non-gradable adjectives, and negatives: *Oh thank you, Josh, I so need lessons from you on how to be cool—Clueless*, 1994 / *We guess communism just got buried in the rubble there somewhere. And those Ceauşescus? So not missed—Salman Rushdie*, 1999 / *i so dont [sic] want to be here—weblog, AmE 2003 [OEC] / African models are so last year—Independent*, 2004. This usage is youthful and appealing, but it is nonstandard.

2 *So that* is well established as an alternative to *in order that*, but it is often used to denote result as much as intention: *Police . . . confiscated hundreds of pairs of laces from 'bovver boots' so that the youngsters wearing them could not kick anyone—Daily Telegraph*, 1980 / *She knew her father was waiting for her to leave so that he could talk to Michael alone—fiction website, AmE 2005*. In more recent usage, *so* is often used alone with the same meaning, leaving the causal connection even more tenuous: *My father had been a minor diplomat, so as a child I had lived in France, Turkey and Paraguay—Graham Greene*, 1980 (here *so* definitely denotes result rather than purpose).

3 For *do so*, see DO 3E.

sobriquets. *See box overleaf.*

so-called is traditionally used before a name or description to signal doubt about whether the thing or person so described is entitled to the description, as in *this so-called work of art*. In recent usage it has been applied in a way that simply calls attention to the description, or distances the user from it, without necessarily questioning it: *the so-called generation gap* (i.e. the phenomenon that people call the generation gap). In speech, intonation normally makes the meaning clear, and in print the context does the same. When used predicatively (after a verb) *so called* is normally explanatory rather than judgemental, and it is printed as two words: *Prayer plants are so called because the leaves fold upwards as if in prayer.*

sociable, social. These two words relate to different meanings of *society*, and should not normally get in each other's way. *Social* is a classifying word that relates to society in the broad sense of the relation of human beings to one another (*Man is a social animal / a social occasion*). A *social worker* is one who deals with those in society who need help, and *social security* is financial assistance given to them. *Sociable* is a judgemental word relating to the quality of human relations (corresponding to *society* in the sense 'companionship, good company'). A *sociable* person is one who is friendly and able to deal well with social occasions, and a *sociable* evening is one marked by friendliness and good humour.

social media. This noun denoting websites and applications that enable users to create and share content or to participate in social networking can be treated as singular or plural as regards its following verb: (singular) *As far as social media goes, it depends on what kind of business you have—StartUp Nation*, 2011 / *And that is the other area social media*

SOBRIQUETS.

A sobriquet (preferred spelling, not *soubriquet*) is a nickname that has become so firmly attached to a particular person, place, or thing, that it is understood independently of the real name and is often used in preference to it. The table below gives a selection.

name	stands for
Albion	England
alma mater	one's college or university
Athens of the North	Edinburgh
Auld Reekie	Edinburgh
Auntie	the BBC
Bard of Avon	Shakespeare
Beefeater	Yeoman of the Guard
Big Apple	New York
Black Country	the industrial west Midlands of England
Black Death	the 14c plague in England
Black Prince	the eldest son of Edward III
City of Dreaming Spires	Oxford
Emerald Isle	Ireland
Garden of England	Kent
Iron Duke	the Duke of Wellington
John Bull	an Englishman
Kiwi	a New Zealander
Left Bank	the artistic district of Paris
Maid of Orleans	Joan of Arc
Old Nick	the devil
Old Lady of Threadneedle Street	the Bank of England
The Pond	the Atlantic Ocean
sport of kings	horseracing
Stars and Stripes	the flag of the USA
Swan of Avon	Shakespeare
The Thunderer	*The Times* (newspaper)
Tinseltown	Hollywood
Tommy (Atkins)	a British soldier
Uncle Sam	USA
Union Flag (or Union Jack)	the British flag
Virgin Queen	Queen Elizabeth I of England
The Windy City	Chicago

works well: brand building—SEObook, 2009 / (plural) If we use the 'recreational' analogy, we may come up with better answers for education, in which social media play a role—Rough Type, 2012 / I attribute this to the transparency, *connectedness, and immediacy that social media offer—BusinessWeek, 2009.*

sociologese. The seemingly pretentious and opaque language found in some writing on sociology was an obvious target for Sir Ernest Gowers in his edition of Fowler's book (1965). Among several examples, all unattributed, the following was typical: *The technique here reported resulted from the authors' continuing interest in human variables associated with organizational effectiveness. Specifically, this technique was developed to identify and analyse several types of interpersonal activities and relations, and to provide a method for expressing the degree of congruence between two or more of these activities and relations in indices which might be associated with available criteria of organizational effectiveness.* But there is a difference between sociology written for sociologists (which this is) and sociology intended for a wider readership (if there is such a thing). For reservations about choosing linguistic targets from technical domains, *see more generally* GOBBLEDEGOOK; JARGON; PLAIN ENGLISH.

sojourn. *'You seem to have acquired a very utilitarian view of universities, from your sojourn in Rummidge,' said Professor Penrose, who was one of the very few people Robyn knew who used the word sojourn in casual conversation*—David Lodge, 1988. The word is normally pronounced **soj**-uhn.

solemnness is spelt with two *n*s, if needed instead of the more usual *solemnity*.

solidus *see* OBLIQUE.

soliloquy *see* MONOLOGUE.

solo has the plural form *solos*.

soluble, solvable. Substances are *soluble*, not *solvable*, but problems and difficulties are *soluble* or *solvable*. The opposites are *insoluble* and *unsolvable*.

sombre is spelt this way in BrE, and *somber* in AmE.

sombrero, a broad-brimmed Mexican hat, has the plural form *sombreros*.

some. 1 The use of *some* to mean 'very much' or 'notably such' in sentences of the type *This is some party* is still considered suitable mainly for informal contexts, and Churchill's famous line in a speech in 1941, *Some chicken! Some neck!* (in response to a warning that England would have her neck wrung like a chicken), does not seem to have affected popular perception of it. It is also used ironically with the opposite meaning in sentences such as *Some friend he is to treat you like that!*

2 In AmE *some* is used adverbially to mean 'to some extent', as in *She thought about it some*, in the same way that *any* is used to mean 'at all' (*You haven't aged any*), and is occasionally used with the meaning 'somewhat' to qualify an adjective *He's going to be some pissed off when he finds out about this*—M. Machlin, 1976. Adverbial *some* is not used in BrE.

3 When *some* is used before a number, the number should be an approximate or rounded one: *A row over the seating of the wives of a Gulf VIP held up a British Airways flight from Milan for almost three hours, resulting in some 50 fellow passengers missing connections*—Guardian, 2007.

4 The phrase *some of us* may be treated as a first-person or a third-person phrase depending on the degree of involvement by the speaker or writer: *Some of us want to change our plans* includes the speaker whereas *Some of us want to change their plans* excludes or at least distances the speaker from the intended change of plans. The choice only arises when a personal or possessive pronoun or adjective (here *our* and *their*) follows in the sentence.

somebody, someone. 1 Both words have been in use since the early

14c and are largely interchangeable. In phrases such as *Some one thousand eggs have been collected*, the words *some* and *one* retain their separate meanings and are therefore written separately. *Compare* ANY 4.

2 For the use of singular and plural in sentences of the type *I really resent it when I call **somebody who's** not home and **they don't have** an answering machine*, *see* AGREEMENT 4.

someday is now commonly spelt as one word in BrE as well as AmE when it is used as an indefinite adverb: *He likes writers and wants to be one someday*—J. McInerney, 1988 / *You can pay me back someday*—weblog, BrE 2005 [*OEC*]. When it is further qualified, and therefore more compositional in character, it is written as two words: *I'll go back some day soon.*

someplace is a common alternative for *somewhere* in AmE, but still sounds somewhat alien in British contexts: *She can get a good job herself someplace and they can get married*—Lee Smith, 1983.

somersault is now the standard spelling for the acrobatic movement, rather than *summersault*.

something. The practice, originating in AmE and now spreading to BrE, of adding *-something* to a multiple of ten to denote an age range (most often but not exclusively *thirty-something*) is a convenient informal device: *This comic strip collection chronicles the demands of a 'thirtysomething' career woman*—*Publishers Weekly*, 1989 / *Fifty-something baby boomers have poured their earnings into savings for their old age*—*Sunday Herald*, 2001.

sometime, some time. 1 *Sometime*, spelt as one word, is an indefinite adverb with two main meanings: (1) 'former', as in *their friend and sometime partner*, and (2) 'at some time in the future', as in *I'll tell you about it sometime*. When *some* and *time* both retain their separate meaning, they are spelt as two words: *We need some time to reflect / This has been known for some time.*

2 *Sometime* is also used to mean 'occasional', especially in the phrase *a sometime thing*, but this use is not standard: *The Federal bureaucracy has grown unwieldy and party discipline in Congress is a sometime thing*—*Newsweek*, 1980.

sometimes, some times. The common adverb *sometimes* is written as one word: *I sometimes like my coffee black*. *Some* and *times* are spelt as two words when they retain their separate meanings, normally as a noun phrase: *There are some times when you don't want to be surprised.*

somewhen would be a useful word if people took it seriously, but its use has always been rare and only in the company of a better established word such as *somewhere* or *somehow*: *I shall write out my thoughts more at length somewhere, and somewhen, probably soon*—John Stuart Mill, 1833 / *I cherished the belief that somehow and somewhen I should find my way to Oxford*—J. C. Masterman, 1975 / *He was looking forward to a leap into another life, somewhere and somewhen else*—fiction website, AmE 2004 [*OEC*].

son-in-law means someone's daughter's husband. The plural is *sons-in-law*.

soon. *No sooner*, being a comparative expression, is followed by *than*, not *when*: *No sooner had a vaccine for Marek's Disease been found than Fowl Pest swept through our poultry flocks*—*Country Life*, 1972.

soprano has the plural form *sopranos*.

sort of *see* KIND OF.

soufflé is spelt with an acute accent on the *e* and is pronounced **soo**-flay in BrE and soo-**flay** in AmE.

sound. 1 The primary meanings of the adjective, 'in good condition' and 'competent or reliable' have produced in informal British usage a generalized sense 'excellent' or 'okay': *'Okay', he said . . . 'Sound,' said Jimmy Sr.*—Roddy Doyle, 1991 / *We were rescued by two sound geezers who only drove us 20 miles, but they saved our lives*—Sunday Express, 1996. According to the *OED*, it originated among Irish Liverpudlians who used the expression *sound as a pound* from the 1980s.

2 The adverb is confined to expressions to do with sleeping: *sound asleep* (*How sound is she asleep! I must needs wake her*, declares the nurse with double irony in Shakespeare's *Romeo and Juliet* IV.iv.35, 1597) and *sleep (the) sounder* (as in *We can all sleep sounder in our beds tonight*).

sound bite, meaning 'a short pithy extract from a recorded interview', is a media word of the 1980s that is still going strong, along with *photo opportunity* and *spin doctor*. All three terms started in the US, and have spread rapidly to other parts of the English-speaking world.

south, southern, southerly *see* EAST.

southward, southwards. The only form for the adjective is *southward* (*in a southward direction*), but *southward* and *southwards* are both used for the adverb, with a preference for *southwards* in BrE: *Highway 61 Revisited, an exploration of the road running southwards from Dylan's home town*—Guardian, 2005.

sow *verb see* SEW, SOW.

spadeful has the plural form *spadefuls*. See -FUL.

spam, 'irrelevant or unsolicited messages sent over the Internet, typically to large numbers of users, for the purposes of advertising, phishing, spreading malware' etc., is probably named with reference to a 1971 sketch from the British TV series *Monty Python's Flying Circus*, set in a cafe where Spam was served as the main ingredient of every dish, and featuring a nonsense song whose lyrics consist chiefly of the repeated word 'Spam' interrupting or drowning out other conversation. The final letter *m* of *spam* is doubled in front of inflections and suffixes beginning with a vowel, e.g. *spamming, spammed, spammers.*

Spanglish, a blend of *Span*(*ish*) + (*En*)*glish*, first recorded from 1967 in English, is used to describe the hybrid language, combining words and idioms from both Spanish and English, used in certain Latin American countries and by some Hispanics in the US. It is one of many terms for hybrid languages mixing English with another language, in which -*glish* acts as a combining suffix: *Chinglish* (*Chinese* + *English*, 1957), *Hinglish* (*Hindi* + *English*, 1967). Predating all of these is the humorous *Yinglish* (*Yiddish* + *English*, 1951), a blend of English and Yiddish spoken in the United States or a form of English containing many Yiddishisms.

spastic has been used since the 18c to refer to victims of cerebral palsy and other afflictions causing spasmodic movements of the limbs. Its informal use in the generalized meaning 'inadequate, incompetent', to describe people, is deeply offensive and has compromised the normal use of the word to an extent that makes it too seem derogatory now. Consequently, a phrase such as 'suffering from cerebral palsy' is preferred for the adjective and 'person with cerebral palsy' for the noun.

-speak. George Orwell's term *New-speak*, used in his novel *Nineteen Eighty-Four* to describe a sinister language used for official communications, gave the English-speaking world a new suffix that could be used to form terms for any special mode of speaking or writing. Examples of its wide use include *Brit-speak, criticspeak, gutterspeak, netspeak* (the language of television networks), and *royalspeak*: *'I am most grateful and touched that you have decided to name a locomotive after me,' it* [a telegram] *said in classic royalspeak—Guardian*, 1981.

special, specially *see* ESPECIAL, ESPECIALLY.

speciality, specialty. In the primary meanings, 'a product, activity, or service in which a person or group specializes' and 'a special feature or skill', *speciality* is the word in BrE and *specialty* in AmE: *We had eaten nothing with the champagne except a small dish of potato crisps, a speciality from the island of Maui—* David Lodge, 1991 / *He also dabbles in real estate; selling murder houses is his specialty—*film website, AmE 2003 [OEC].

species is pronounced **spee**-sheez, and is unchanged in the plural. Note that *specie*, pronounced **spee**-shi, is a technical term for coin as opposed to paper money.

specifically. For the use of *pacifically* by mistake for this, *see* PACIFICALLY.

specious, spurious. *Specious*, like the Latin word *speciosus* from which it is derived, began its life meaning 'having a fine outward appearance' (from Latin *species* 'outward form'), but in the 17c acquired the unfavourable connotations 'plausible but in fact wrong' as in *a specious argument*. *Spurious*, which is sometimes confused with *specious*, is derived from the Latin adjective *spurius*

'false', and means 'not genuine, not being what it purports to be'. A *specious* claim is one that is attractive but insubstantial whereas a *spurious* claim is one based on a false premise.

spectator is spelt *-or*, not *-er*.

spectre is spelt this way in BrE, and *specter* in AmE.

spectrum has the plural form *spectra*.

speculator is spelt *-or*, not *-er*.

speed *verb*. The past tense and past participle are *sped* when the meaning is 'to go fast' (*The car sped onwards / By that time she had sped down the road*). It is *speeded* when the meaning is 'to break a speed limit' (*He speeded to get there in time*) and in the phrasal verb *to speed up* (*The reform process needs to be speeded up*). *Sped* is often preferred in AmE in the transitive use (*I sped my pace to catch up*) but is less idiomatic, even informally, in BrE.

spell *verb*. The form for the past tense and past participle is *spelt* or *spelled*. *Spelt* is more usual in BrE, especially in the primary meaning 'to write or name the letters of a word'; *spelled* is more common in AmE and in the phrasal verb *spell out* = to explain in detail.

spellchecker. Computer programs that attempt to check the spellings of words do this in an extremely limited and literal way. Generally they check each string of letters against a list of allowed words and reject or query any they find in the searched text that are not included in this list. At present their sense of grammar and context is crude, so that (for example) they are incapable of distinguishing *from* and *form* (words which are commonly miskeyed in word processing) because both words are formally allowable. Proper names are often rejected, although users are generally allowed to add their own stock of special words to the permitted lists. In more technical writing, the number of queries raised by the program is so great that the checking becomes not merely impractical but unsound because genuine errors are easily overlooked by the user in the maze of false errors reported. Also be aware that some programs are based on American word lists and therefore reject British spellings. Above all, do not assume that a text that has been spell-checked is therefore free of spelling errors.

spelling. *See box overleaf.*

spill. The form for the past tense and past participle is *spilled* or *spilt*: *He nearly spilled his drink*—John Updike, 1988 / *The lounge boy . . . left too much change on the table and a puddle where he'd spilt the Coke*—Roddy Doyle, 1990 / *Other multinationals doubtless polluted waterways or spilt their toxics*—*Guardian*, 1994. Although *spilt* was the more favoured form until the end of the 19c *spilled* is very much more common in current usage (especially in the past form), but *spilt* is secure in the expression (*crying over*) *spilt milk* in BrE (but often *spilled milk* in AmE)

spin 1 The form for the regular past tense and past participle of the verb is *spun*: *The other man spun towards the sound, gun extended, ready to fire*—A. Lejeune, 1986 / *I was spun round, and dragged back*—A. Billson, 1993. Before the 20c *span* was commonly used for the past tense but this is now a non-standard form.

 2 The noun, which formally means 'an act of spinning', has been appropriated by the language of politics to refer to what the *OED* describes as 'a bias or slant on information, intended to create a favourable impression when it is presented to the public; an interpretation or viewpoint'. If a single sense has to be

identified as the source, it is probably the cricketing sense of a twisting motion given to the ball when bowled or thrown, which can cause the ball to bounce away from a straight path. So now we have a new and seamy meaning that is as closely associated with the political life of the first years of the 21c as *back to basics* was with that of the 1990s. It has given rise to compound forms, including *spin machine* and—most notably—*spin doctor*, an evocative term for a political press agent or publicist employed to put the right spin on ideas and events for public consumption. This use of *spin* has also fed back to the verb, giving a new force to the sense of 'spinning a yarn': *The government stood accused of plotting to spin its way out of its failure to meet European targets on renewable energy on Monday*—*Morning Star*, 2007.

spinney, a BrE word for a small wood or copse, has the plural form *spinneys*.

spinster, meaning an unmarried woman, has overtones that vary from disapproving to offensive, unlike *bachelor* which still tends to have positive and even romantic associations. Both words have been replaced by single [person] in the official wording of recent Marriage and Civil Partnership Acts.

spiral. The verb has inflected forms *spiralled, spiralling* in BrE, but often *spiraled, spiraling* in AmE.

spirit. The verb has inflected forms *spirited, spiriting*.

spirt *see* SPURT.

spit *verb*. The form for the regular past tense and past participle in BrE is *spat*, but in AmE either *spat* or *spit* is used: *I was so mad I could have spit*—*New Yorker*, 1989.

spitting image, meaning 'an exact double', is an established phrase,

SPELLING.

1 Before the invention of printing in the 15c, English and other European languages lacked any regularity of spelling and how different people spelt was largely based on personal preference. Despite the development of rules, English remains notoriously beset by irregularities of spelling, and various proposals have been made over the years for reforms that would make spelling more straightforward for native speakers and foreign learners alike. These proposals have usually been based on phonetic principles, to make a reformed spelling conform more closely to pronunciation, but questions of whose pronunciation or which spelling is appropriate when more than one represents a particular sound (e.g. *ou* as in *count* or *ow* as in *cow*) have not been resolved. Another objection is that phonetic spelling would obscure word origins and connections, especially in groups of words in which the stress pattern changes, e.g. *adore / adoration* and *nation / national*. In any case, no machinery for reform exists, and significant change is unlikely to be achieved except by the weight of ordinary usage. (For a fuller discussion of this issue, see *The Oxford Companion to the English Language*, 1992, 973-6.)

2 A major cause of confusion is the way English allows variant spellings. This works in unpredictable ways, so that *accessary / accessory* and *judgement / judgment* are all permitted spellings whereas *accomodation* is not a permitted variant of *accommodation* nor *millenium* of *millennium*. In this book, preferred spellings are given when legitimate alternatives exist and correct spellings are identified when other occurring forms are not legitimate.

3 There are three broad categories of spelling difficulty: (1) systematic problems that occur in words belonging to a certain type (e.g. the formation of nouns from verbs in *-dge*, such as *acknowledgement* and *judgement*) and in the inflection of words (e.g. the plural of nouns in *-o* such as *potato* and *solo*, and the *-ed* and *-ing* forms of verbs such as *benefit* and *unravel*), (2) individual difficulties attached to particular words (e.g. *embarrass* with two *rs* but *harass* with one, and *millionaire* with one *n* but questionnaire with two), including words adopted with little change from other languages that cause problems of inflection in English (e.g. *shanghai* and *ski*), and (3) words with similar spellings that are confused, e.g. *complement / compliment*, *hoard / horde*, and *principal / principle*.

4 For guidance on the more important systematic features of spelling and inflection, see the following separate entries: ABBREVIATIONS; CO-; DE-; DIS-; DOUBLING OF FINAL CONSONANTS WITH SUFFIXES; -ER AND -EST FORMS; -ER AND -OR; -EY AND -Y IN ADJECTIVES; -FUL; HYBRID FORMATIONS; I BEFORE E; -IZE, -ISE IN VERBS; LATIN PLURALS; -LESS; -LIKE; -LY; MIS-; NON-; -O; PALINDROME; PRE-; -RE AND -ER; SELF-; SEMI-; -T AND -ED; -UM; UN-; -XION.

5 For differences in British and American spelling, *see* AMERICAN ENGLISH 3.

6 The table below lists words in common use that cause particular spelling difficulties. Some of these are also given as separate entries.

word	comment
accommodate, accommodation, etc.	two *c*s, two *m*s
acknowledgement	-*dge*- preferred form
acquaint, acquaintance, etc.	*acq*-
acquire	*acq*-
acquit	*acq*-
aggressive, aggression, etc.	two *g*s, two *s*'s
apostasy	ends -*asy*
appalling	two *p*s, two *l*s
artefact	*arte*- preferred to *arti*-; AmE *artifact*
asphalt	not *ash*-
bail / bale	see entry
baulk	see entry
beneficent	not -*ficient*
biased	preferred to *biassed*
billionaire	two *l*s, one *n*
breach / breech	see entry
changeable	-*eable*
chord / cord	see entry
commemorate	two *m*s followed by one *m*
committee	two *m*s, two *t*s
complement / compliment	see entry
connoisseur	two *n*s, two *s*'s
consensus	not *concensus*
cooperate, cooperation, etc.	no hyphen
desiccated	one *s*, two *c*s
desperate	two *e*s
diphthong	not *dipthong*
dispatch	preferred to *despatch*
dissect	two *s*'s
dissipate	two *s*'s, one *p*
draft / draught	see entry
ecstasy	ends -*asy*
eighth	two *h*s
embarrass, embarrassment, etc.	two *r*s, two *s*'s
enthral	one *l*; AmE *enthrall*
exhilarate	two *a*s
fulfil	one final *l*; AmE also *fulfill*
gauge	-*au*- not -*ua*-
guard, guardian, etc.	-*ua*- not -*au*-
harass, harassment, etc.	one *r*, two *s*'s
hoard / horde	see entry
idiosyncrasy	ends -*asy*
impostor	ends -*or*
install	two *l*s
instalment	one *l*; AmE *installment*
judgement	-*dge*- preferred form
liquefy	ends -*efy*
manoeuvre	-*oeu*-; AmE *maneuver*
mayonnaise	two *n*s, one *s*
medieval	-*e*- preferred to -*ae*-

S

mellifluous	two *l*s followed by *fl*
memento	*mem-* not *mom-*
millennium	two *l*s, two *n*s
millionaire	two *l*s, one *n*
minuscule	not *miniscule* (see entry)
mischievous	not *-ievious*
misspell	two *s*'s
moccasin	two *c*s, one *s*
necessary	one *c*, two *s*'s
niece	*-ie-* not *-ei-*
occurrence	two *c*s, two *r*s
Portuguese	*u* before and after *g*
practice / practise	see entry
principal / principle	see entry
questionnaire	two *n*s
rarefy	ends *-efy*
recommend	one *c*, two *m*s
restaurateur	no *n*
resuscitate	*-s-* followed by *-sc-*
Romanian	*Rom-* not *Rum-*
sacrilegious	*-i-* followed by *-e-*
seize	*-ei-* not *-ie-*
separate	two *a*s
siege	*-ie-* not *-ei-*
stationary / stationery	see entry
supersede	not *-cede*
threshold	one *h*
transsexual	two *s*'s (preferred)
twelfth	note the *f*
unwieldy	not *-wieldly*
veterinary	not *vetinary*
weird	*-ei-* not *-ie-*
wholly	preferred to *wholely*
withhold	two *h*s
yield	*-ie-* not *-ei-*

S

although it is in origin a misunderstanding of *spit and image* (*spit and picture* also occurred), which was itself an extension of the early 19c phrase *the (very) spit of*. A transitional form *spitten image* is first recorded in 1910. The older forms are also occasionally found: *Look at this, Father, appeared last Friday on Sister Philomena, the very spit and image of the nail marks in the palms of our Blessed Lord*—Hilary Mantel, 1989.

splendour is spelt *-our* in BrE and *splendor* in AmE.

split infinitive. 1 A split infinitive occurs when a word (usually an adverb) or phrase comes between the particle *to* and the verb of a so-called *to*-infinitive (*to really love* / *to really and truly love*). No other grammatical issue has so divided English speakers since the split infinitive was declared in the 19c to be incorrect: raise the subject of English usage in any conversation today and it is sure to be mentioned. The term itself is first recorded as recently as the 1890s, although the controversy is somewhat older and the practice very much so. Examples occur in Middle English (though only twice in Chaucer) but it went out of fashion from the 16c to the end of the 18c, and no examples have been found in Shakespeare (unless we count Sonnet 142: *Root pity in thy heart, that when it grows, Thy pity may deserve to pitied be*). During the 19c it came back into favour, with examples to be found in Fanny Burney, Mark Twain, Thomas Hardy, and most famously in a poem of Byron: *To sit on rocks to muse o'er flood and fell, To slowly trace the forest's shady scene—Childe Harold's Pilgrimage*, 1812.

2 Now, at the start of a new century the split infinitive is widely held to be an error on the grounds that the particle *to* and its verb belong together. The basis for this belief is highly questionable, because other separations occur, for example between a verb and its auxiliary verb (*I have never said so / We would always ask you first*). An altogether more compelling argument for avoiding split infinitives is that they can jar and sound ugly. This argument makes the issue one of style rather than grammar, and is especially valid when the adverb can be placed naturally in another position or when the split is a lengthy one: *We talked about how everything was going to suddenly change—Nigel Williams*, 1985 (defensible on grounds of emphasis, perhaps, but the normal order is *We talked about how everything was suddenly going to change*) / *You two shared a curious dry ability to without actually saying anything make me feel dirty—Philip Roth*, 1987 (split here for effect) / *Lectures . . . were introduced in the Middle Ages only because it was not possible to affordably type lecture notes for students—Independent*, 2006 (better to put the adverb at the end of the phrase: *not possible to type lecture notes for students affordably*).

3 On the other hand, the split infinitive avoided, usually by putting the adverb before or after the entire *to*-infinitive, can lead to results that are just as unnatural, often stylistically poor, and in some cases ambiguous or misleading: *Rhys considers it unwise to attempt radically to alter taxes on large cars, as proposed by Labour—Autocar and Motor*, 1990 / *It should be the Government's task quietly to advocate such a comprehensive strategy with our American allies—Times*, 1998 / *I know too that repeatedly to drink and drive is a profound and serious matter—Independent*, 2007. In these examples the natural position of the adverbs *radically, quietly*, and *repeatedly* is after the word *to*, and in the first case the important connection between *radically* and the verb it qualifies (*alter*) is compromised; in the second, there is a similar effect with *quietly* and *advocate*; and in the third, the sensible alternative is to recast the sentence and avoid the problem altogether (*I know too that repeated drink-driving is a profound and serious matter*). In some cases, the adverb becomes attached to the wrong verb: *It was in Paris that the wartime alliance began finally to break up—*television broadcast, 1998. It is arguable in these cases that the adverb, or adverb phrase, has a stronger claim to association with the verb than does the purely functional particle *to*. In writing it is often possible to rephrase so as to avoid the hazard altogether (as above), but in speech a sentence once begun has to be finished, and sometimes an infinitive is better split either because the rhythm of the sentence demands it or because ambiguity might otherwise result.

4 When an adverb, especially an intensifying adverb such as *actually, even, ever, further, just, quite, really*, belongs with a verb that happens to be an infinitive, it is usually better (and sometimes necessary) to place it between *to* and the verb: *I want to really study, I want to be a scholar*—Iris Murdoch, 1987 / *In face of all this Patrick managed to quite like him*—Kingsley Amis, 1988. In some cases, an adverbial phrase is also inseparable from its verb: *It allowed Fernanda Herford to slightly more than double her money*—Julian Barnes, 1993 (where *slightly more than double* is in effect a verb phrase).

5 recommendation. The prejudice against the split infinitive, though relatively recent in the broader context of the history of English, has a considerable weight of opinion behind it. The split infinitive is, therefore, best avoided, and especially when it is stylistically awkward. But it is not a major error or a grammatical blunder: and it is acceptable, even necessary when considerations of rhythm and clarity require it.

spoiled, spoilt. In BrE the more frequent form for the past tense and past participle is *spoiled*, although *spoilt* is also still widely used, whereas it almost never is in AmE. As an adjective in attributive position (i.e. before a noun, as in *a spoilt / spoiled child*) both spellings are used, and BrE prefers the first.

spokesperson *see* -PERSON.

sponge. *Sponge* has the derivative *spongeable* with an *e*, to keep the *g* soft, but *spongy* and the inflection *sponging* are very much more frequent than the forms with an *e*, though both types are correct.

spontaneity. The pronunciation spon-tuh-**nay**-i-ti has largely superseded the traditional spon-tuh-**nee**-i-ti.

spoonerism. The Revd W. A. Spooner (1844–1930), Dean and Warden of New College, Oxford, has given his name to this most endearing form of linguistic error involving the transposition of

letters, although those commonly attributed to him are likely to be spurious, e.g. *a well-boiled icicle* (for *a well-oiled bicycle*) and *a half-warmed fish* (for *a half-formed wish*). The word is generally written and printed without a capital first letter these days.

spoonful has the plural form *spoonfuls*.

spouse is a convenient gender-neutral term, less formal in tone than it once was, for a married man in relation to his wife and a married woman in relation to her husband.

spring *verb*. The past tense is *sprang* or occasionally (especially in AmE) *sprung*. The past participle is *sprung*.

spry. The inflected forms and derivatives are *spryer, spryest; spryly, spryness*.

spurt is the dominant spelling for the noun and verb to do with gushing and sudden increase of effort, not the archaic form *spirt*.

squalor is spelt -*or* in both BrE and AmE.

stadium. The plural forms are *stadia*, particularly referring to the ancient classical world, and *stadiums* otherwise, although in BrE *stadia* is quite often used for that meaning as well.

staff. The plural in the meanings 'pole' and 'body of employees' is *staffs*. In the music meaning it is *staffs* or *staves*.

stalactite, stalagmite. A *stalactite* hangs down from the roof of a cave, and is formed from dripping water containing rich minerals. A *stalagmite* rises up from the floor and is formed from deposits also caused by dripping. Both words are derived from the Greek word *stalassō* meaning 'to drip', and are pronounced with the stress on the first syllable in BrE but with the stress on the second syllable in AmE.

stanch *see* STAUNCH, STANCH.

stand *verb*. In BrE candidates *stand* for office, whereas in AmE they *run* for it.

standard English. The term has been variously defined and heavily politicized, but essentially it is the form of English that is most widely accepted and understood in an English-speaking country and tends to be based on the educated speech of a particular area, in England the south-east (although it can be spoken in a variety of accents). It is used in newspapers and broadcasting and is the form normally taught to learners of English. It is the kind of language one would be happy to write in a report or to put in CV or résumé. It contrasts with non-standard, rather than substandard; in this book anything described as non-standard falls outside standard English, but is not considered inferior, merely different. For a fuller treatment, see *The Oxford Companion to the English Language* (1992), 982–3.

standpoint *see* POINT OF VIEW.

state. It is usual to spell it with a capital initial letter when it refers to political entities, either nations (*The State of Israel / a State visit*), or parts of a federal nation (*the State of Virginia / crossing the State border*), and when it means 'civil government' (*Church and State / the Secretary of State*). This applies both to names and to general reference when necessary to avoid possible ambiguity with the general meanings of *state* (as in *the state* [= *condition*] *of Israel*). In other contexts a lower-case initial is used (*a police state / the welfare state*).

stationary, stationery. *Stationary* is an adjective and means 'not moving' whereas *stationery* is a noun and denotes paper and writing materials. Both words are derived from the Latin word *stare* 'to stand'. The relevance of this to *stationary* is obvious, and the connection with *stationery* (and *stationer*, a supplier of stationery) is through the medieval Latin word *stationarius* which meant 'a bookseller', who was a fixed (as distinct from itinerant) shopkeeper. To remember the difference in spelling, stationery includes paper.

statistics is treated as a singular noun as the name of the science (*Statistics is merely a form of knowledge*), and as a plural when referring to items of statistical information (*The statistics of suicide are striking*). The singular form *statistic*, denoting a single piece of information, is well established: *One startling statistic is that only 500 of the 18,000 work permits sought* [in Ireland] *last year were in the building trade—Sunday Business Post*, 2001.

status is pronounced **stay**-tuhs and has the plural form *statuses* (the Latin plural is *statūs* and is not used in English).

staunch, stanch. *Staunch* (pronounced stawnch) is used both for the verb meaning 'to restrain the flow of blood' (with the blood or the wound as its object) and for the adjective meaning 'trustworthy, loyal'. The variant form *stanch* (pronounced stahnch) is preferred in AmE for the verb.

stave *noun*. One of its meanings is the same as that of *staff*, a set of lines on which musical notes are written. The plural of both forms is *staves*.

stave *verb*. Both *staved* and *stove* are used for the past tense and past participle. *Staved off* is more usual in the meaning 'averted or deferred (danger or misfortune)' and *stove in* is more usual in the meaning 'crushed by forcing inwards'.

steep learning curve. If someone says that a particular skill or technique *has* or *is a steep learning curve*, they mean that it takes a lot of time and effort to master, e.g. *the latest software packages have a steep learning curve*. Statisticians object that such a situation should be described as a *shallow learning curve*, but the phrase is here to stay in the meaning of 'difficult'. Perhaps it is best avoided in the company of sticklers and statistically sophisticated people, and also because it is clichéd.

stencil as a verb has inflected forms *stencilled, stencilling* in BrE, and usually *stenciled, stenciling* in AmE.

stereo as a noun has the plural form *stereos*.

stewardess denotes a female steward, especially on a ship or aircraft. *Flight attendant* is now the preferred term with English-speaking airlines. *See* -ESS.

sticking place, sticking point. The phrase *sticking point* is first recorded in 1826, and in its common modern meaning 'the limit reached of progress, agreement, etc.' not until the 1960s. The allusion is to a line in Shakespeare's *Macbeth* (I.vii.60), where *place* is used: *But screw your courage to the sticking place, And we'll not fail*. The reference here seems to be to screwing up the peg of a musical instrument until it becomes tightly fixed in its hole.

stigma. The plural in its special meanings (e.g. 'the marks on Christ's hands and feet on the Cross', and in its medical meaning) is *stigmata*, with the stress either on the first or on the second syllable. In the figurative sense 'a mark of disgrace or discredit', the plural is *stigmas*.

stigmatize, meaning 'to describe as unworthy or disgraceful', behaves like *regard* in being followed by *as*:

Opponents were demonized and stigmatized as champions of anarchy and enemies of progress—Journal of Drug Issues, AmE 2005 [*OEC*].

stile, style. There are three words here, all derived from the Latin word *stilus* meaning 'a writing tool'. The two words spelt *stile* are (1) from Old English, meaning 'a set of steps for crossing a fence' and (2) probably from Dutch, meaning 'a vertical piece in the frame of a panelled door'. The word *style* in its familiar meanings is spelt with a *y* from a false association with the Greek word *stulos* meaning 'column'.

stiletto, the knife and the high-heeled shoe, has the plural form *stilettos*.

still life, the genre of painting, has the plural form *still lifes*.

stimulus has the plural form *stimuli* (pronounced **stim**-yoo-liy with the last syllable as in *lie*).

stimy, stimie *see* STYMIE.

sting. The verb has the past tense and past participle *stung*.

stink. The past tense of the verb is *stank* and the past participle is *stunk*. *Stunk* is occasionally used for the past tense, especially in North America and in figurative meanings (*A lot of it stunk of racism*—weblog, CanE 2004)

stoep pronounced like *stoop*, is a South African word for a terraced veranda in front of a house.

stoic, stoical. As an adjective, *stoic* is normally used attributively (i.e. before a noun, as in *stoic virtues* and *stoic indifference*), and preserves a more direct reference to the philosophy of the ancient Stoics from whom the word is derived. In predicative position (i.e. after a verb) *stoical* is more usual, and in all its uses conveys the more generalized allusive sense of personal restraint and self-control. A *stoic indifference* is the kind of indifference that the Stoics taught and practised, whereas a *stoical indifference* is indifference that is, on its own terms, concentrated and resolute. When the reference is to people rather than qualities, *stoical* has to be used: one can have *stoic* or *stoical* resolution but one can only be *stoical* oneself.

stone *adverb*. Combinations such as *stone cold* and *stone dead*, in which *stone* is used adverbially ('like a stone'), have been recorded for centuries. More recently, *stone* has developed a freer adverbial use as a mere intensive equivalent to *very* or *completely*, typically in the context of physical or mental impairment or loss of control (*stone crazy, drunk, mad*, etc). It is not easy to pinpoint the date of this development, (the *OED*'s earliest evidence is from the 1930s), but it is now more common, especially in AmE: *People . . . got stone drunk and cruised through red lights—*Garrison Keillor, 1989.

stood is used (in a quasi-passive role) for *standing* in non-standard uses comparable to *sat* for *sitting*, such as: *My husband was stood on the opposite side of the pits—Cycling Weekly*, 1993. The origins of this use are obscure and probably dialectal. It is now quite widespread in BrE, but it will still be considered incorrect by some people.

stop, stay. In 19c fiction people frequently *stopped* with friends (overnight in their house), *stopped* for dinner, or *stopped* at home. In modern English we would use *stay* instead of *stop* in all these cases. But the older use still survives: *'She's stopping with her daughter,' the woman said. 'She'll be back on Thursday.'—*Hilary Mantel, 1985. It is also to be seen in the phrasal verbs *stop off* and *stop over*, meaning 'to make a break in a journey' (especially a long journey), and in the noun equivalents *stop-off* and *stopover*.

storey, story. The plural form is *storeys*. In AmE *story* is the usual form and its plural is *stories*; and what in BrE is a *three-storeyed* house is in AmE a *three-storied* house.

straight, strait. 1 *Straight* is a Middle English past participle of the verb *stretch* and has many meanings in modern English, primarily 'extending uniformly in the same direction without a curve or bend'. *Strait*, which has the basic meaning 'tight, narrow', is used as a noun meaning 'a narrow passage of water connecting two seas', in the plural as in *dire straits*, and in combinations such as *strait-laced* and *straitjacket* (*straightjacket* is also used but the better spelling is *strait-*).

2 *Straight* is now the normal form in the phrase *the straight and narrow* ('the honest course of action'), it being understood in the sense 'honest, morally correct'; the older form *strait and narrow*, in which *strait* itself means 'narrow' (thereby producing a *hendiadys similar to *nice and easy*), has largely gone out of use.

3 *Straight* meaning 'heterosexual' was originally a US slang term, first recorded in 1941. Since then it has come to be widely used in this meaning, and, though marked 'informal' in *ODO*, is in many contexts the neutral term, the natural counterpart of *gay*, rather than the more formal *heterosexual*.

straight away, meaning 'immediately', is first recorded in the 17c. It continued to be used as two words until the beginning of the 20c, when (probably under the influence of the fast-fading adverb *straightway*) it began to be written as one word. Uses of this form are frequent, although in the *OEC* data the two-word form is several times more frequent. Both versions are correct: *He* couldn't decide whether to make for home straightaway—Steven Wall, 1991. In AmE, *straightaway* is also an adjective meaning 'direct' (of a course of action) and a noun meaning 'a straight section of a road or racetrack' (*roaring down a straightaway at top speed*).

strategy, tactics. In war, as in politics and business, *strategy* is used of an overall plan of action embodying certain principles and objectives, and *tactics* is used of the detailed means adopted to achieve them. *Tactics* is normally treated as a plural, with *tactic* available as a singular form with the meaning 'a tactical manoeuvre or device'.

stratum is normally pronounced **strah**-tuhm, and has the plural form *strata*. The use of *strata* as a singular noun (with a plural *stratas*) is incorrect: ☒ *The earth's crust contains stratas of hot, dry rock and natural aquifers—* C. Wheater et al., 1990.

street *see* ROAD.

strew has the past tense *strewed* and the past participle and adjectival form *strewn*, which is preferable to *strewed*, which is rarely used in that way.

stricken, as an alternative past participle of *strike*, survives in many compound adjectives such as *grief-stricken* and *panic-stricken*. It is also widely used, especially in journalism, as an adjectival past participle, e.g. *stricken with guilt, the stricken town*, and as a full passive in phrases such as *Goya was stricken with a mysterious illness*. It is distinguished from *struck* as a past participle because whatever someone is *stricken* with is always something unpleasant such as a disease or a distressing emotion, e.g. *cancer / fear / guilt / remorse*; *struck* is not used in the same way.

stride. The verb has the past tense *strode* and the past participle *stridden*.

The participle is not readily remembered, and *strode* is more often used instead, although technically incorrect: ☒ *Great strides are being strode in the cultivation of pre-teen female engineers—The Face*, 1987.

strike. The verb has the past tense *struck* and the past participle *struck* or, in certain contexts, **stricken*.

string. The normal form for the past tense and the past participle is *strung*. A musical instrument with strings is called a *stringed* instrument, but if the strings need renewing it is *restrung*.

strive. The past tense is often *strove* and the past participle *striven*, but *strived* is commonly used for both, especially in AmE: *We've strived to lead the way in offering you the tools you need—Money* 1993.

stubbornness is spelt with two *n*s.

stucco, a word of Italian origin for a type of plaster covering walls, has the plural form *stuccos*, and as a verb it has inflections *stuccoes, stuccoed, stuccoing*.

studio has the plural form *studios*.

stupefy, meaning 'to make insensible' or 'to astonish', is spelt *-efy* (like *liquefy* and *rarefy*), not *-ify* (like *dignify* and *modify*).

stupor, meaning 'a dazed state', is spelt *-or* in BrE and AmE.

sty. The word meaning 'a pen for pigs' has the plural form *sties*. The word for 'an inflamed swelling on the eyelid' should be spelt *sty*, not *stye*, and also has the plural form *sties*.

style *see* STILE.

stymie is now the regular spelling of the word used in golf and in the meaning 'to obstruct or thwart', rather than *stimy* or *stimie*. The verb has inflected forms *stymies, stymied, stymieing*.

subjunctive mood. 1 The subjunctive mood, one of the great survivors of an earlier state of English grammar, is a verbal form or mood expressing wish or hypothesis in contrast to fact, and usually denotes what is imagined, wished, demanded, proposed, and so on. In modern English it is distinguishable from the ordinary indicative mood only in the third person singular present tense, which omits the final *s* (*if he make* rather than *if he makes*) and in the forms *be* and *were* of the verb *to be*.

2 The subjunctive mood was common in Old English and until about 1600, then went into decline but became prevalent again in the 20c, first in AmE and then in other forms of English including BrE: *I was going to recommend that he be terminated*—New Yorker, 1987 / *It was as if Sally were disturbed in some way and was translating this disturbance into the habit of thought*—Anita Brookner, BrE 1986 (note the shift to indicative mood after *and*) / *She insisted Jane sit there*—Barbara Anderson, NewZE 1992 / *It was suggested he wait till the next morning*—Michael Ondaatje, CanE 1992 / *The Ministry of Defence demanded that a crash barrier be built around the 'central pool' where the submarines were dismantled*—Free India Media, IndE 2004 [*OEC*]. In many cases, an alternative construction with *should* can also be used: *It was important that he should be included in my photographs*—Dick Francis, 1980.

3 Typical subjunctive patterns are:

a After *if* (or *as if, as though, unless*) in hypothetical conditions: *Each was required to undertake that if it were chosen it would place work here*—Times, 1986 / *His voice strained as though he were walking on a wire above a pit of sharks*—fiction website, AmE 2003 [*OEC*]. In this type the indicative can also be used, i.e.

was instead of *were* in both the examples above, but the subjunctive conveys the hypothetical sense more forcefully.

b In *that*-clauses following a verb of suggesting, wishing, etc. (e.g. *demand, insist, pray, recommend, suggest, wish*): *Your situation demands that either Kooti be nobbled or Whitmore nullified*—M. Shadbolt, NewZE 1986 / *Fundamentalist Islam . . . decrees that men and women be strictly segregated*—Listener, 1988 / *He'd insisted his brother return home*—fiction website, AmE 2002 [*OEC*]. But note that when *insist* has the sense 'assert, state forcefully' (and not 'demand') the ordinary indicative mood is needed: *Collins insists he has no regrets about any aspect of his career*—Scotland on Sunday, 2002.

c *Be* or *were* placed at the head of a clause with the subject following in an inverted construction: *Statistically, afterworlds*—*be they Christian, Greek, Pharaonic*—*must be populated almost entirely by children*—Penelope Lively, 1987 / *There was a real risk of his suffering inhumane and degrading treatment were he to return to India*—London Review of Books, 2004.

d In negative constructions, *not* (or *never* etc.) is normally placed before the subjunctive verb (and this position identifies the subjunctive status of verbs in the first and second persons as well as the third): *One essential quality for a holiday novel is that it not be too light*—Frederic Raphael, 1988 / *Mr. Radley insisted that he not be sent to an asylum*—literature website, AmE 2002 [*OEC*]. In uses of this kind the negative form makes the subjunctive mood transparent in other persons than the third singular: *I recommend that we not approve this letter*—CNN news transcripts, 2005 [*OEC*].

e In certain fixed expressions and phrases, e.g. *as it were, be that as it may, come what may, far be it from me, God save the Queen, heaven forbid, long live the King, perish the thought, so be it.*

subpoena, a writ ordering a person to appear at a lawcourt, has the plural form *subpoenas*. In AmE it is sometimes spelt *subpena*, with the plural form *subpenas*. The verb has inflections *subpoenas, subpoenaed, subpoenaing*.

subscribe. *Ascribe* and *subscribe* are sometimes confused. If you *ascribe* a quality to a person or group of people, you think it is typical of them, as in *tough-mindedness is a quality commonly ascribed to top bosses*. If you *subscribe to* a belief, view, or idea, you agree with it: *we prefer to subscribe to an alternative explanation*. It is incorrect to give this meaning to *ascribe to*, as in ✱ *which theory do you ascribe to*?

subsidence. The traditional pronunciation is suhb-**siy**-duhns, with the stress on the second syllable, but the form **sub**-si-duhns, with the stress on the first syllable under the influence of *residence* and *subsidy*, is also common in standard speech.

subsidiarity. This is an awkward word that falls into place when you know that it is pronounced with the stress on the *-ar-*. It dates from the 1930s and has the special meaning 'the principle that a central authority should have a subsidiary function, performing only those tasks which cannot be performed effectively at a more immediate or local level' (*OED*). First uses referred to the organization of the Catholic Church, and the term was adopted in the 1980s (*The Times* calling it 'a meaningless or even misleading phrase in English') in the context of discussions about the role of member states in the European Union.

substantial, substantive. *Substantial* is pronounced with the stress on the second syllable and *substantive* with the stress on the first syllable or occasionally the second. Both words mean 'having substance', but *substantial* is the word in general use to denote people or things of size, importance, or value (*Scotland Yard said a 'substantial amount of firearms and explosives' had been recovered from the house—East Anglian Daily Times*, 1993), whereas *substantive* refers more to what something consists of (*This finding moves beyond rhetoric and provides substantive evidence that fathers have an important and measurable impact on the well-being of their adolescent children—Fathering*, AmE 2003). *Substantial* discussions are lengthy and wide-ranging ones, whereas *substantive* discussions deal with important topics. *Substantive* often occurs in technical contexts such as law and parliamentary procedure; for example, a *substantive motion* is one that deals specifically with a subject in due form.

substitute *see* REPLACE.

subtitles, supertitles, surtitles. *Subtitles*, printed captions that translate the dialogue in a foreign-language cinema or television film, appear at the bottom of the screen. *Supertitles* or *surtitles*, a more recent invention, translate the text of a play or opera as it is being said or sung, and are usually projected above the stage.

subtle has a corresponding adverb *subtly*, and the noun is *subtlety* (which is also countable with a plural form *subtleties*). The *b* is silent in all these forms.

succeed. When it means 'to be successful', *succeed* is followed by *in* + an *-ing* form, not (unlike *fail*) by *to*: *Some local preservation enthusiasts succeeded in getting the house listed as of architectural and historic interest*—E. Lemarchand, 1972.

succour, a rather formal word meaning 'aid or assistance, especially in time of need', with its related verb, is spelt *-our* in BrE and *succor* in AmE.

such. 1 *such* **as an emphasizer.** *How can the House express its indignant rejection of football hooliganism while setting* **such a persuasive** *example of undignified and daily indiscipline?—Guardian Weekly*, 1986. The construction with *such a* followed by an adjective is established and idiomatic in current English, despite occasional objections that *so* and not *such* should do the work of emphasizing here (. . . *while setting so persuasive an example*). (Compare the use of *such* qualifying a noun, to which nobody objects: *I can't believe I have made such an idiot of myself—*weblog, BrE 2004.) In some cases *such* appears to qualify the combination of adjective and noun: *He warns that now is not such a good time to be getting rid of pubs—Sunday Herald*, 2001.

2 *such as* **with following pronoun.** When an inflecting pronoun follows, it is more natural to regard *such as* as a preposition and to follow it with *me, her, him*, etc., rather than *I, she, he*, etc. (regarding *such as* as a conjunction with the continuation understood as *such as I am*, etc.) *They were not bad, for such as her—*Rose Macaulay, 1920.

3 *such as* **or** *like*. *Like* is common when a single instance follows (*a poet like Tennyson / take a girl like you*), but *such as* is preferable (and more idiomatic) when a list follows (*Members of the cat family, such as the lion, the tiger, and the leopard*). See LIKE 2.

4 *such...as...* **or** *such...that* .... *We are such stuff as dreams are made on.* The relative pronoun that follows *such* in sentences of this type is *as* and not *who, which*, or *that*. But *such* followed by *that* is legitimate in constructions of the following types, in which *that* is a conjunction: *Midge was such a dingbat . . . that she went to Hawaii for a vacation during World War II—*J. Irving, 1978 / *The scale of the influx of cheap drugs on to the market was such that a line of*

cocaine now costs less than a cappuccino—Scotland on Sunday, 2005.

suchlike. *He left the sea, having had what amounted to a nervous breakdown, 'always thinking of the other ships that went up, the bombings and suchlike'—Daily Telegraph*, 1971. Fowler's verdict in 1926 was that this use of *suchlike* 'is now usually left to the uneducated' and that *the like* should be used instead. In terms of current use this judgement is too severe, especially for everyday conversational usage.

suddenness is spelt with two *n*s.

suffice. In phrases of the kind *Suffice it to say he was not best pleased*, the verb and its subject *it* are technically in the subjunctive and mean 'let it suffice'. The verb form *suffice*, without the normal third-person *-s* clearly shows that the verb is subjunctive. However, nowadays it is just as common to hear and see *suffice to say*, with the *it* omitted. Nearly half the examples in the *OEC* are of that form. Although the form without *it* is attested historically, it seems likely that the truncated modern version is a reinterpretation of the syntax rather than a re-emergence of an older form. Subjunctives are rare outside certain fixed phrases, *suffice it* includes inversion, and most people have difficulty analysing the phrase, which is why they change it. The shorter form is now as correct as the longer one, though some will still prefer the longer.

suffix. In grammar, a *suffix* is a word or element added at the end of another word to adjust or qualify its meaning, such as *-ation* (*confirmation, privatization*), *-ing* (*driving, soldiering*), and *-itis* (*appendicitis*). Some suffixes are created artificially from the end part of words to form similar types of word with different reference, e.g. *-aholic* (from *alcoholic*, forming *workaholic* etc.)

S

suffixes added to proper names.

1 The suffix most commonly used to form nouns and adjectives relating to people's names (usually writers, artists, composers, etc., or founders of dynasties) is *-an* or *-ian*, and one of the oldest formations of this type is *Virgilian* (first recorded in 1513). Other formations include *Aristotelian* (1607), *Ovidian* (1617), and *Ciceronian* (1661), and it will be seen from this short list alone that some have survived more strongly than others. *Shakespearian* (with an occasional variant *Shakespearean*) is not recorded before 1755. Some words made in this way have multiple reference, e.g. *Alexandrian* (normally referring to the city of Alexandria or the literature or philosophy associated with it rather than to Alexander the Great). More recent formations include *Beethovenian* and *Shavian*, the latter derived from a Latinate form of the name of G. B. Shaw for reasons of euphony. Euphony often calls for use of other suffixes, such as *-esque* (from French, e.g. *Dantesque, Schumannesque, Turneresque*) and *-ic* (*Byronic, Platonic, Pindaric, Ptolemaic*), although in some cases the reason for a particular choice of suffix is less clear.

2 When *-ian* is added to an unaccented final syllable of a name, the syllable is normally lengthened to accommodate the addition, so that *Beethoven* makes *Beethovenian* (pronounced -vee-ni-uhn).

sugar has derivative forms *sugared* and *sugary*, each with one *r*.

suggest. 1 When followed by a *that*-clause (or one with that omitted) and proposing a course of action rather than hinting at a fact, *suggest* commonly generates a subjunctive verb, and the same is true of the noun *suggestion*: *Uncle doesn't suggest that she bring a lamp from the next room*—Saul Bellow, AmE 1987 / *The suggestion that all HIV-positive individuals be forcibly tattooed*—Dædalus, AmE 1989 / *He suggested she try her hand at adapting Beaumarchais's Eugénie*—M. Finberg, BrE 2001. Alternative constructions with *should* (*He suggested that they should find a scenic route*), and with an ordinary tense (*I suggest that he has another try*) are more common in BrE than in AmE, but in general this verb is one of the great mainstays of the subjunctive mood in modern English. *See* SUBJUNCTIVE MOOD.

2 Note that when *suggest* means 'state as a fact or hypothesis' rather than 'propose' an ordinary tense is used: *I cannot accept John Peel's suggestion that punk rockers are the only truly socialist representatives we have left*—Sounds, 1977.

suggestible means 'open to suggestion, easily swayed' and is used of a person: *highly suggestible individuals who have had paranormal experiences*. Less common is the sense 'able to be suggested' (used of an idea or proposal). In both meanings the word is spelt *-ible*, not *-able*. *See* -ABLE, -IBLE.

suit, suite. The two forms are in origin the same word, and differences of usage are the result of historical choices since the 17c. In modern English we speak of a *suit* of clothes, armour, and playing cards, as well as a *lawsuit* and paying *suit* to (i.e. courting) a woman; and a *suite* of rooms, furniture, musical pieces, etc., as well as people in attendance on a high-ranking person.

suitor, meaning 'a man seeking to marry a (particular) woman', is spelt *-or*, not *-er*.

sullenness is spelt with two *n*s.

sulphur. The traditional BrE spelling is *sulphur* and the AmE spelling is *sulfur*. In chemistry and other technical uses, however, the *-f-* spelling is now the standard form for this and related words in British as well as US contexts, and is increasingly used in general contexts as well.

summersault *see* SOMERSAULT.

summon, summons. *Summon* is a verb only, whereas *summons* is a noun and verb. A *summons* (plural *summonses*) is an order to appear before a judge or magistrate, and to *summons* someone is to issue them with a summons. *Summon* is the ordinary word meaning 'to call formally', as in *The ambassadors were summoned to the White House*, and (typically with *up*) in the figurative sense of evoking a reaction or feeling within oneself (*could not summon up the energy to reply*).

Sunday *see* FRIDAY.

super-. The prefix dates from the 15c and has been prolific ever since, taking on a new lease of life in modern formations such as *superhighway* (1925 in the physical sense in America, 1975 in computing and telecommunications), *superman* (1913), *supermarket* (1933), *supermodel* (1977), *superpower* (1921), *supersonic* (1919), *superstar* (1925), *superstore* (1965), and *supervirus* (1951 in the medical sense, 1990 in computing).

supercede is incorrect; the correct spelling is *supersede.

superior is not a true comparative (like *better* or *greater*, for example) and is followed by *to*, not *than*: *The taste of an open mushroom grilled with garlic, parsley and butter is so splendid, and superior to snails given the same treatment*—*Times*, 1980. In the language of advertising, *superior* has the depleted meaning 'above average in quality' (*a superior housing development / made of superior leather*).

superlatives *see* ADJECTIVE 3; -ER AND -EST FORMS.

supersede is the correct spelling for the verb meaning 'to take the place of'. It is derived from the Latin word *sedeo* 'sit', but the influence of *accede*, *intercede*, *precede*, and others (derived from Latin *cedo* 'go') often mistakenly causes this word to be spelt *supercede*.

superstitions. A superstition in language, like any superstition, is a widely held belief with no rational basis. In English these include the beliefs that sentences should not begin with *and* or *but*, that a sentence should not end with a preposition, that *none* should always take a singular verb, and that infinitives should not be split. *See also* FETISH 2.

supervise is spelt *-vise*, not *-vize*. *See* -IZE, -ISE IN VERBS.

supine *see* PRONE.

suppose, supposing. Both words function as conjunctions to introduce an assumption or hypothesis: *Suppose the guards were more alert, security measures more effective*—R. Ludlum, 1978 / *Supposing there's a change of venue*—CNN news transcripts, 2003 [*OEC*].

supposedly is pronounced as four syllables.

suppressible, meaning 'able to be suppressed', is spelt *-ible*, not *-able*. *See* -ABLE, -IBLE.

suppressor, a device for suppressing electrical interference, is spelt *-or*, not *-er*.

sure, surely. 1 In all parts of the English-speaking world, *surely* is the dominant form in the meaning 'in a sure or certain manner' (*slowly but surely*) and in the use inviting or presupposing agreement (*Surely that can't be right*). In BrE, *sure* is limited as an adverb to fixed expressions such as *sure as eggs is eggs* and *as sure as God made little apples*, and to use as a form of assent in replying to a question or proposition, although this is better established in AmE: *I asked if you could finish your lunch, and they said sure, no hurry*—Rex Stout, 1975 / *'Do you remember last night?' I asked calmly, slipping on the skirt. 'Sure I do.'*— fiction website, AmE 2003. (*Surely* is also used in this way.)

2 In other adverbial uses *sure* is most closely associated with AmE: *Parts of it were pretty, sure*—Alison Lurie, 1969 / *A chemical fire. You worry about those, sure, said Clerk*—New Yorker, 1988.

surmise, meaning 'to infer doubtfully' and (as a noun) 'a conjecture or suspicion', is spelt *-ise*, not *-ize*. *See* -IZE, -ISE IN VERBS.

surprise is spelt *-ise*, not *-ize*, as a noun and a verb. *See* -IZE, -ISE IN VERBS.

surveillance is pronounced suh-**vay**-luhns, with the *-ll-* articulated.

survey is pronounced with the stress on the first syllable as a noun and with the stress on the second syllable as a verb.

surveyor is spelt *-or*, not *-er*.

survivor is spelt *-or*, not *-er*.

susceptible has two principal meanings, each with its own construction. In the meaning 'likely to be affected by', it is followed by *to*: *The leopard frog . . . is particularly susceptible to a kidney carcinoma*—Scientific American, 1973 / *Stinnes had reached that dangerous age when a man was only susceptible to an innocent cutie or to an experienced floozy*—Len Deighton, 1984. When it means 'allowing, admitting of', it is followed by *of*: *In the late fourteenth century, one finds Wyclif using the word 'nation' (which was susceptible of a wide*

variety of usages), to denote men who had been bred in England—J. A. F. Thomson, 1992. It should not be used as a synonym of *liable to* or *prone to*: ✖ *Fast aircraft with swept-back wings are susceptible to dutch rolls*—B. Jackson, 1976.

suspect, suspicious. 1 *Suspect* is pronounced with the stress on the first syllable as a noun (*the chief suspect*) and adjective (*a suspect package*), and with the stress on the second syllable as a verb (*They suspect something*).

2 As an adjective, *suspect* is close in meaning to *suspicious*; both mean essentially 'causing suspicion'. The chief differences are (1) that *suspicious* can also be used to describe a person (= feeling suspicion, as in *They were suspicious of our intentions*), and (2) that *suspect* has additional connotations regarding worth or reliability (*suspect farm produce*).

3 The adverb *suspiciously* can mean either 'in a manner expressing suspicion' or 'in a manner causing suspicion', depending on the context: *She looked at us suspiciously* is an example of the first meaning and *She was behaving suspiciously* is an example of the second. An adverb *suspectly* is recorded but is hardly ever used in current English.

suspender. In BrE a *suspender* is a clip device holding up the top of a stocking or sock, whereas in AmE *suspenders* are what in BrE are called (men's) *braces*.

suspense, suspension. The two words used to be interchangeable in several meanings, but have since gone their separate ways. *Suspense* is used primarily to denote 'a state of anxious uncertainty or expectation', and is common attributively (i.e. before a noun, as in *suspense thriller or film*) to refer to a form of writing or drama. *Suspension* has more physical and technical meanings (as in a car's *suspension* and a *suspension bridge*) as well as the non-physical meaning 'the state of being suspended from an office or position'.

sustain. Fowler's view in 1926 was that '*sustain* as a synonym for *suffer* or *receive* or *get* belongs to the class of formal words, and is better avoided', and its use in the contexts of injuries, losses, hardship, etc., is still widely disliked. Fowler was anxious to confine it to circumstances that involved prolonged endurance (*Scarce one* [*of the cities*] *was now capable of sustaining a siege*—Macaulay, 1849), but there is a thin line dividing this kind of brave resistance from more temporary kinds. In its other meanings, 'to keep in being', 'to maintain in a certain state', 'to give support to', and others, *sustain* raises no usage issues.

swap, meaning 'exchange' (noun and verb) is the preferred spelling, not *swop*.

swat, swot. *Swat* is the spelling for the verb meaning 'to hit sharply' and the corresponding noun. *Swot* (originally a dialect variant of *sweat*) is a BrE colloquialism meaning 'to study hard' and 'someone who studies hard'.

swath, swathe. The word meaning 'a ridge of grass left after mowing' and 'a strip' is spelt *swath* (pronounced swawth; preferred) or *swathe* (pronounced swaydh). The noun and verb meaning 'a bandage or wrapping' and 'to wrap in bandages' is spelt *swathe* (pronounced swaydh).

sweat *see* GENTEELISM.

swell. The verb has the past tense *swelled* and the past participle *swollen*, although *swelled* is sometimes used for the past participle when the reference is to a specified increase in size or numbers rather than to an unwelcome or harmful expansion or swelling: *Unlike the dailies, the number of titles was not swelled by relaunches and changes of status*—C. Seymour-Ure, 1992.

swim. The past form of the verb is *swam* (*She swam to the shore*) and the past participle is *swum* (*Have you swum recently?*), but the reverse will be found in older writing: *Who, being shipwrecked, had swam naked to land*—Dr Johnson, 1750 / *As she sprang to meet it, with an eye that swum to thanks*—Tennyson, 1847.

swine is a normal word for *pig* in AmE, but in BrE is mostly used either as a collective plural or (more often) informally as a singular or plural to refer contemptuously to a person or thing one objects to.

swing. In current use the past tense and past participle of the verb are *swung* (*He swung his leg round* / *The street names were swung from signs on corners*), but *swang* will be found for the past tense in older writing: *His arms dangled rather than swang*—Hilaire Belloc, 1912.

swinging, swingeing. *Swinging* is the ordinary present participle of the verb *swing*, whereas *swingeing* means 'forcible, severe' (as in *swingeing tax increases*), and is part of an archaic verb *swinge* meaning 'to strike hard'.

swivel. The verb has inflected forms *swivelled, swivelling* in BrE, and in AmE usually *swiveled, swiveling*.

swop *see* SWAP.

swot *see* SWAT.

syllabub, a sweet dessert made of cream, is preferably spelt *syll-*, not *sillabub*.

syllabus has two plural forms *syllabuses*, and *syllabi*. BrE prefers the first, AmE the second.

syllepsis (from a Greek root meaning 'taking together') is a figure of speech in which a word, or a particular form or

S

inflection of a word, is made to fit two grammatical structures but is formally correct only for one, e.g. *She's a lovely, intelligent, sensitive woman who has and continues to turn around my life in a wonderfully positive way*—Woody Allen reported in *Times*, 1992 (*to turn* fits with *continues* but not with *has*). Constructions of this type are technically ungrammatical, but they occur from time to time in the more spontaneous world of conversational speech. The terms *syllepsis* and *zeugma* (from a Greek word for 'yoking') are both used for the type characterized by a meaning difference in the 'shared' word rather than a grammatical one: *Sir Geoffrey Howe, who had arrived in a limousine, the editor of the Daily Telegraph, who had arrived in a motor-boat, and Dave Nellist, who had arrived in an anorak*—Matthew Parris, 1991. There is much inconsistency in the way these two terms are applied.

sylvan is more common than *silvan* as the (chiefly poetic) word for 'wooded' or 'rural', despite its origin in the Latin word *silva* meaning 'wood'. It is nearly always used attributively *amid scenes of sylvan beauty*—A. Wainwright, 1990 / *He sits in a sylvan grove*—Art in America, 2002 [*OEC*].

symbolic, symbolical. Both words mean 'serving as a symbol' or 'involving the use of symbols', but *symbolic* is much more common (roughly 200 times more in the *OEC*): *On the day before Easter, there is a symbolic burning of a cloth-draped wooden statue of Judas*—C. Hammerschlag, 1988.

sympathetic, in the meaning 'eliciting sympathy' rather than 'feeling sympathy', dates from the beginning of the 20c. Despite Fowler's reservations (he wrote in 1926 when it was still a new meaning), it has become rapidly established in standard English: *Despite the sympathetic portrayal of his father in*

these anecdotes, Lawrence turned against him after the death of his mother—J. Meyers, 1990.

sympathy *see* EMPATHY.

symposium meaning 'a gathering for discussion', more often has the plural form *symposia* (preferred) or *symposiums*.

syndrome, pronounced **sin**-drohm, is originally a medical term for 'a set of symptoms'. Its use as a vogue word in general contexts meaning 'a characteristic combination of opinions, emotions, behaviour, etc.', is as recent as the 1950s; it is generally acceptable, but not when *syndrome* is simply a synonym for *factor* or *aspect*, i.e. a single circumstance rather than a set of circumstances coming together, which lies at the heart of its meaning: ✗ *Perhaps the improved performance at Boots is due to 'new broom syndrome'?*—business news website, BrE 2004 [*OEC*].

synecdoche, pronounced si-**nek**-duh-kee, is a figure of speech in which a more inclusive term is used for a less inclusive one or vice versa, as in *England came out to bat* (*England* more inclusive for 'the England team') and *a fleet of fifty sail* (*sail* less inclusive for 'ships'). *See also* METONYMY.

synonyms are words that have the same or a near meaning, such as the pair *close* and *shut*, or the trio *begin*, *start*, and *commence*. Some word sets of this kind arise because words coming into English from other languages failed to drive out those already in use; for example, *close* is a Middle English (13c) word derived from Old French, and joined the existing Old English word *shut*. Other pairs of words have different levels of appropriacy; for example, *kill* is a general word whereas *slay* is literary or rhetorical, and *little* carries connotations of affection that are not present in the more neutral word *small* (compare *my little house* and *my small house*). Many words are loosely described as synonyms although their meanings are close rather than identical (e.g. *danger* and *risk*, *entreat* and *implore*, *leave* and *depart*), and few synonyms are interchangeable in all contexts.

synopsis, meaning 'a summary or outline', has the plural form *synopses* (pronounced -seez).

synthesis, meaning 'a process of bringing together or connecting', has the plural form *syntheses* (pronounced -seez).

syphon *see* SIPHON.

systematic, systemic. The word in general use in the meaning 'done according to a plan or system' is *systematic*, and one can equally speak of *systematic learning* (i.e. following a system or set of principles) and *a systematic search* (i.e. one done methodically); the second is only a slight extension in meaning of the first. The less common word *systemic* means 'relating to or affecting a system as a whole (rather than to a part of it)', as in *systemic failures* in an organization, and has special technical meanings in medicine and linguistics.

S

T

table *verb*. In BrE to *table* a proposal means to place it on the agenda for discussion, whereas in AmE it means to put it aside for an indefinite period.

tableau, meaning 'a group of figures representing a scene', has the plural form *tableaux* (pronounced **tab**-lohz).

table d'hôte, meaning 'a meal consisting of a set menu at a fixed price', is printed in roman type with a circumflex accent on the *o*.

tablespoonful has the plural form *tablespoonfuls*, but in practice the type *three tablespoons of*—is more usual.

taboo is a noun, adjective, and verb, and is pronounced with the stress on the second syllable in all three. The noun has the plural form *taboos*, and the verb has inflected forms *taboos, tabooed, tabooing*. The variant form *tabu* is restricted to technical use in anthropology.

tacky. It is a little surprising that this current term meaning 'tawdry, in poor taste' (describing such things as decor, jewellery, nightclubs, souvenirs, wallpaper, and taste in general) has nothing to do with the word meaning 'slightly wet or sticky', but is of American origin and is an extension of a noun *tacky* (or *tackey*) that was used disparagingly to describe a weak horse or a poor white person from the southern States. It is first recorded in the newer meaning in the 1880s in uses that sound modern, e.g.: *Two little cards (with his name printed on them in gilt. Tackey? Ugh)*—I. M. Rittenhouse, 1883.

tactics *see* STRATEGY.

tag question. This is the grammarians' name for a question added at the end of a statement and acting as a reinforcer rather than seeking an answer, as in *You will do this for me, **won't you**? / She has been to America, **hasn't she**? / I don't need an umbrella, **do I**?* In each case the verb in the main statement has been changed into an equivalent question; if the statement is positive the tag is negative, and vice versa, although a positive tag can follow a positive statement in the type *You heard it too, did you?* The use of tag questions is subject to regional variation; for example, in some regions (including Wales in the UK and S. Asia outside it) *isn't it* is used as an all-purpose tag irrespective of the form of the statement: *You're going home now, **isn't it**?*—A. R. Thomas, 1994.

talisman, meaning 'an object supposedly endowed with magic powers', has nothing to do with the word *man* and the plural is therefore *talismans*. Its ultimate origin is an Arabic word connected with the Greek word *telesma* meaning 'consecrated object'.

talkative. This word is surprisingly early (15c). Fowler (1926) forbore to attack it despite its being a 'hybrid', i.e. the Latinate suffix -*ative* has been added to the English word *talk*. But he pointed out that this was the only example of its kind relating to this suffix, and did so 'with a view to discouraging imitation'. So far he has largely succeeded; imitation hybrids such as *writative*, *babblative*, and *scribblative* are recorded in the *OED*, and Shakespeare used *forgetive* (= inclined to forge, not really a hybrid), but these have not lasted.

-t and -ed. *See box overleaf.*

tangible. The primary meaning is 'perceptible by touch', but in practice figurative uses tend to be more common, in which the meaning becomes 'clearly intelligible, not imaginary or hypothetical', as in *tangible assets*, *tangible evidence*, *tangible improvement*, *tangible proof* and *a tangible sign*.

tantalize means more than just 'tease or torment', as is shown by the word's origins in the treatment meted out to the legendary Phrygian king Tantalus, who was forced to stand in water which receded when he tried to drink and under branches that drew back when he tried to pick the fruit. The word is therefore best used when it retains an element of torment caused by something offered and then withdrawn, although this cannot always be as explicit or obvious as it was for Tantalus. It occurs most often in the adjectival form *tantalizing* or the adverbial form *tantalizingly*: *Foremost among their key sources was a man whom the authors still tantalizingly refuse to name*—*Time*, 1974 / *There are tantalizing hints of a personal love story, but there is no development or continuity*—J. Culler, 2000.

Taoiseach, the title of the Prime Minister of the Irish Republic, is pronounced **tee**-shuhkh.

target. 1 The figurative use of *target* meaning 'an amount or objective to be achieved' arose during the Second World War and is now more common than the primary meaning. Sir Ernest Gowers, the senior Whitehall civil servant and writer on language, grew rapidly tired of the word: *We were offered a great variety of things that we might meritoriously do to our targets. We might reach them, achieve them, attain them or obtain them; we were to feel greatly encouraged if we came in sight of the target to which we were trying to do whatever we were trying to do, and correspondingly depressed if we found ourselves either a long way behind it or (what apparently amounts to the same thing) a long way short of it*—*ABC of Plain Words*, 1951. While care should be taken to avoid contexts that are jarringly incongruous (such as *keeping abreast of targets*, perhaps), the physical image is less strong than it is (for example) with *ceiling*, and Gowers' strictures now seem somewhat obsessive. To complain, as some do, that a *doubled target* is larger, and therefore necessarily easier to hit rather than harder, smacks strongly of pedantry. Used with care, *target* has a useful role alongside alternatives such as *aim*, *goal*, *object*, and *objective*.

 2 The verb, meaning 'to single out as an object of attack', has inflected forms *targeted*, *targeting*.

tarmac. The verb has inflected forms *tarmacked*, *tarmacking*.

tart *see* PIE.

tartan. 1 *see* PLAID.

 2 *Tartan* is used allusively in informal and normally affectionate compounds to denote people or things connected with Scotland; the *tartan army* is the body of Scottish supporters at football games abroad, and the *tartan tax* is a variation of income tax that the Scottish Parliament has had the power to apply since devolution.

tassel. The inflected forms are *tasselled*, *tasselling* in BrE and in AmE usually *tasseled*, *tasseling*.

-T AND -ED.

A number of irregular verbs have competing past forms and past participles in
-*t* and -*ed* (e.g. *leapt* and *leaped*); the most common of these are given in the
table below. In some cases the length of the vowel is shortened in the -*t*
forms (e.g. lept instead of leept for *leapt*). It is difficult to establish distinctions
based on region or meaning, but two tendencies are discernible: (1) the form
in -*ed* is more often preferred in AmE, and (2) in BrE there is a stronger
preference for the -*t* form when it is used as a participial adjective, as in *The
cakes are burnt* as distinct from *We burned the cakes.*

verb	-t form	-ed form
bereave	bereft	bereaved
beseech	besought	beseeched
burn	burnt	burned
cleave	cleft	cleaved
dream	dreamt	dreamed
dwell	dwelt	dwelled
earn	earnt*	earned
kneel	knelt	kneeled
lean	leant	leaned
leap	leapt	leaped
learn	learnt	learned
smell	smelt	smelled
spell	spelt	spelled
spill	spilt	spilled
spoil	spoilt	spoiled

*earnt is not standard, but is increasingly found

tasty, tasteful. *Tasty* is now restricted
to the context of food (and some transferred uses) and is not used in the
context of *good taste* (= aesthetic judgement), for which *tasteful* is the
appropriate adjective. The opposite
word *tasteless*, however, is used in all
meanings, physical and abstract.

tattoo. The verb has inflected form
tattoos, tattooed, tattooing. It can have as
its grammatical object either the design
that forms the tattoo (*A heart was tattooed on her left arm*) or the part of the
body on which the design is put (*Tattooed his cheek with a winged fist*).

tautology is the repetition of the
same idea or meaning in a phrase or

sentence, as in a *free gift* (all gifts are
free), a *new innovation*, and to *return
again*. Some tautologies are contained
within a small group of words such as
a noun phrase (e.g. *future prospects,
past history, no other alternative, the
general consensus*). Others occur in
the way sentences are put together (the
tautologous words are printed in bold):
*The activities of the club are not limited
only to golf* / *There is no need for
undue haste* / *The Cold War came to a
final close in Germany yesterday*. Except
when used as a literary or rhythmic device in which the effect is intentional,
this kind of tautology is normally
regarded as an error and should be
avoided.

taxi. The noun has the plural form *taxis*, and the verb has inflected forms *taxies, taxied, taxiing* (preferred to the variant *taxying*).

teaspoonful has the plural form *teaspoonfuls*. The phrase *three teaspoons of—* is also available.

techno-. The word *technology* and its main derivatives, *technological* etc., date from the 17c, but it was not until the 20c that the first element *techno-* became a formative element in such compounds as *technocracy* and *technocrat* (both first recorded in 1919), *technophobia* (1965, interestingly somewhat earlier than *technophile* of 1968 and *technomania* of 1969), *technofreak* (1973), and *technobabble* (1987), all associated with computing and other areas of advanced technology. Other formations refer to types of synthesized electronic music, e.g. *technopop* (1980) and *technorock* (1983), and have led to the independent word *techno*, used as an adjective and a noun: *This listener expected a jazz / techno hybrid*—*Milk Factory*, BrE 2004.

teem. It sometimes causes surprise that the two apparently close meanings involved here are of two distinct verbs. One, from an Old English word meaning 'to give birth to', means 'to be full of or swarming with' (as in *a sea teeming with fish*), and the other, from an Old Norse word meaning 'to empty', means 'to pour or flow copiously' (as in *teeming with rain*). Neither should be confused with the verb *team*, as used in the phrasal verb *team up with*.

teenager, meaning a person aged from 13 to 19, or sometimes loosely any adolescent person, is first recorded as recently as the 1940s (first in America), although *teenage* is somewhat older (1920s) and *teens* (as in *a person in his teens*) is much older (17c).

teetotaller is spelt with two *l*s in BrE, but in AmE often *teetotaler*.

tele-, derived from the Greek word *tēle* meaning 'at a distance', is one of the great formative elements of modern English and a genuine mirror of technological advance over several centuries. It occurred earliest in words such as *telescope* (first recorded in 1648), *telegraph* (1794), *telegram* (1852), *telephone* (1876 in its modern sense), *telepathy* (1882), and *television* (1907, a hybrid formed on the Latin element *vision*). In more recent formations *tele-* has been even freer of etymological constraints: *telecommunication* was formed first in French in 1932 at a conference in Madrid, *telecast* was modelled on *broadcast*, *telegenic* (meaning 'visually attractive on television') on *photogenic*, and *teleport* (a telecommunications centre involving the use of satellites, originally a back-formation from *teleportation*) on *transportation*; *telesales* (the selling of goods and services over the telephone) is chiefly BrE and dates from the 1960s, and words such as *teleprinter*, *teleprompter*, and *teletext* were formed simply by lumping *tele-* with an existing word of whatever origin.

televise is a back-formation from *television*, and is spelt -*ise*, not -*ize*, in both BrE and AmE.

temperature, meaning 'a high or abnormal temperature' (as in *Have you got a temperature?*) is idiomatic in modern English but mostly confined to spoken forms.

template. Now spelt as shown, though *templet* was the standard spelling 17-19c, and -*plate* is 'pseudo-etymological' on the basis of *plate*. The word is probably a derivative of *temple*, 'a device in a loom for keeping the cloth stretched'. The second syllable can be pronounced like *plate*, or simply as -plit.

tempo, a term in music for the speed at which a passage is played, has the plural form *tempos* or (often preferred in technical writing) *tempi*.

temporary, temporarily. *Temporary* is pronounced **tem**-puh-ruh-ri, as four syllables, with an additional stress on the -*ar*- in AmE. *Temporarily* has five syllables and until recently was pronounced in BrE with the stress on the first syllable, but the AmE pronunciation with the stress on the -*ar*- is now almost as common in BrE.

tend. There are two verbs here. One is a shortened form of *attend* and is used either with an object or intransitively with *to* in the meaning 'to take care of, look after' (*Shepherds tending their flocks / The thief was watching as she tended to her father*). The other is derived from Latin *tendere* 'to stretch' and is used with a *to*-infinitive to mean 'be inclined to' (*He tended to do what his parents advised*).

tenet, meaning 'a dogma or doctrine', is now normally pronounced **ten**-it.

tenor. The word has a strange range of meanings (a singing voice, a prevailing course or direction, a legal term, the subject of a metaphor), all relating in some way to the Latin word *tenēre* 'to hold'. The spelling is -*or* in all meanings in both BrE and AmE.

tense is the location in time of the state or action expressed by a verb. English verbs have only two simple tenses, the present (*I stay*) and past (*I stayed*). The future is formed by using *shall* or *will* (*I shall / will stay*: see SHALL AND WILL) or (to express intention or purpose) *be going to* (*I am going to stay*). Other forms of the past are formed with auxiliary verbs (*I have been staying/ I was staying / the emphatic form I did stay*), and the past perfect is formed with the past tense of *have* (*I had stayed*). Choice of tense mostly corresponds to actual time, but there are conventional uses of tenses other than this, e.g. the *historic present in narratives and the use of the future for present as in polite requests such as *Will that be all for now?* Choice of tense becomes more complex in reported speech (*He said it is/was a nuisance*): for this *see* SEQUENCE OF TENSES.

tenterhooks. The idiom *on tenterhooks*, 'in a state of suspense because of uncertainty about a future event', usually with the verb *to be* (*He was on tenterhooks waiting for his directors' decision*) is correctly spelt as shown, not ☒ *tenderhooks*. A *tenter* was a wooden framework on which cloth was stretched after being milled, so that it would set or dry evenly and without shrinking. *Tenterhooks* were hooks that held the cloth firmly and tautly in place on the tenters, whence the idiom. As the word is obsolete, *folk etymology has transformed it into ☒ *tenderhooks*, a form not accepted in dictionaries but quite often encountered.

terminal, terminus. 1 In BrE these words are to an extent interchangeable in meanings associated with transport, but *terminus* can be used to refer in the abstract for the final stop of any passenger journey, by train, bus, or aeroplane, as well as to physical buildings such as railway stations or bus stations. A *terminal* is more likely to be a complex of buildings at an airport (or in a city for connection with an airport), or the port buildings for ferry passengers. *Terminus* is not used in the airport sense but *terminal* is increasingly used in the bus and rail senses. In AmE *terminal* is used in all three senses, whereas *terminus* tends to refer to the location (town, city, etc.) at the end of a route.

2 The plural of *terminus* is usually *termini* (pronounced **ter**-mi-niy), especially in its scientific meanings, or occasionally *terminuses* in the meanings described above.

terminate is a formal word for 'stop or bring to an end', as in *terminating* a pregnancy, an agreement being *terminated*, and a train that *terminates* at Paris. In general contexts, a simpler word such as *stop* or *end* should normally be used.

terminus see TERMINAL, TERMINUS.

terrain is best reserved for contexts in which a geographical or military assessment is being made (*an uneven terrain / the peculiarities of the terrain*) rather than as a simple synonym for *area, ground, region*, or *tract*. Figurative uses however can be more effective than any of these alternatives (*the shifty terrain of modern politics / a film that explores the emotional terrain of its subject*).

terrible, terribly have gone the way of other words of this type, such as *awful / awfully, dreadful / dreadfully, frightful / frightfully*; that is, *terrible* intensifies something by definition bad (*a terrible mistake*) and *terribly* intensifies adjectives and other adverbs generally (*terribly important / not terribly good*). Colloquially, *terrible* is used disparagingly with neutral nouns (*a terrible speaker / What a terrible name to give a baby!*). However, the adjective and adverb retain their literal meanings 'horrifying, horrifyingly' in contexts such as *a terrible cry, terrible consequences*, and *terribly disfigured*. By contrast, *terrific* when used with neutral nouns is not disparaging but approving (*a terrific meal / a terrific speaker*).

tetchy, touchy. *Tetchy* means 'irritable, peevish', and is a near synonym of *testy*, whereas *touchy* means 'oversensitive, likely to take offence'.

tête-à-tête, meaning 'an intimate conversation between two people', is printed in roman type with the accents and hyphens as shown. The same spelling is used as an adjective or adverb (*dined tête-à-tête*), and the plural of the noun is either the same as the singular or (to avoid possible ambiguity) *tête-à-têtes*.

text *verb*. The meaning most familiar to people today, namely 'to send a text message' has revived this formerly obsolete verb, which in the late 16c meant 'to write in large or capital letters', and was used by Shakespeare, among others. If this verb conformed to the pattern of regular verbs in English, its past tense and past participle would be *texted*, and this is the form that dictionaries show or imply. However, at least in speech, the form *text* is often used, probably for phonetic reasons. This should be avoided in writing, since many people will consider it wrong.

text message. A *text message* (usually abbreviated to *text* for short) is a 'written message which is transmitted electronically, especially a short, keyed message sent from one mobile phone to another, or via the Internet'. The limitations of the screen format of earlier generations of mobile phone have given rise to ingenious conventions for abbreviating the written language and reducing the awkwardness of the miniature environment in which the message appears. Some of these use existing abbreviations such as the ampersand (&) and the 'at' sign (@). Others employ phonetic substitutions, such as 'l8' (= late), '2nite' (= tonight), 'thx'(= thanks), 'u' (= you), 'soz' (= sorry) and 'LOL' (= 'laughing out loud', but often mistakenly and notoriously interpreted as 'lots of love'). Concerns that this practice might corrupt use of language more generally are misconceived; such practices are as old as writing itself, and because they are a response to the restrictions of the

t

medium, they do not normally extend beyond it.

textual, textural. The contexts normally prevent these two words getting in each other's way: *textual* means 'relating to text' (*textual criticism*), whereas *textural* means 'relating to texture', often in figurative contexts such as art and music (*textural features / textural variation / textural and tonal modulations*).

than. 1 *Than* is normally used to introduce the second element in a comparison, and acts either as a conjunction (*He is older than I am*) or as a preposition (*He is older than me*). In uses such as *He is older than I*, *than* is normally regarded as a conjunction with the verb following *I* understood, but in spoken English at least the more usual choice is the type *He is older than me*. For this choice, *see* CASES 2B.

2 For other aspects of the use of *than*, *see* BARELY; DIFFERENT 3; HARDLY 1; INFERIOR; OTHER 2; PREFER 3; RATHER 2; SCARCELY 1; SUPERIOR.

thankfully has been used as an ordinary adverb of manner since Anglo-Saxon times, and is still current in this meaning: '*Until Friday,*' said Mrs Marsh, and shut the door thankfully behind her—Anita Brookner, 1992. Since the 1960s, it has developed the additional role of sentence adverb, in which it qualifies a whole statement and reflects the opinion of the speaker rather than modifying anything contained within the statement: *Thankfully, however, the old style has not entirely disappeared—Daily Telegraph*, 1982. Though frowned on from time to time, *thankfully* has not attracted the venom that *hopefully* has; this may well be to do with the meanings of the two words and the associations each has (*thankfully* expresses relief whereas *hopefully* raises doubts). For more on this issue in its context, *see* HOPEFULLY; SENTENCE ADVERBS.

thanks to. *Thanks to the rank stupidity of Steve Gillery's bride-to-be, he had to hold his stag night on Saturday morning and rush off to the ceremony during half-time in the afternoon*—M. Gist, 1993. This ironic use, in which *thanks to* is an equivalent of *because of* or *due to*, occurs in contexts where thanks are hardly appropriate, but it is attested from the 18c (and earlier in the form *no thanks to*), and its credentials are therefore sound. Meanwhile the straightforward use of *thanks to* continues in use: *Thanks to better budgeting, I haven't been overdrawn since early 2003*—finance website, BrE 2005 [*OEC*].

thank you. The standard written form of the expression of thanks is *thank you* (two words), although *thank-you* (with hyphen) and *thankyou* (one word) are sometimes found, especially in ephemera such as junk mail and restaurant bills, and *thank-you* is the correct form in attributive use (before a noun, e.g. *a thank-you letter*). *Thanks* is more informal and conversational than *thank you*, as are *many thanks* and *thanks a lot*.

that is a word with many roles, and plays a major part in English sentence structure. The following are its main grammatical functions:

demonstrative pronoun:
That was what I meant

demonstrative adjective:
*Why did you take **that** picture of me?*

demonstrative adverb:
*I was **that** angry / It didn't hurt **that** much*

relative pronoun:
*It was not the drug **that** had done it*

conjunction:
*He had assumed **that** we would want to see him*

1 As a demonstrative pronoun and adjective, *that* normally refers to something already mentioned or known: (pronoun) *She had not meant it so, but it*

could have been read like **that** / How the
hell did you manage **that**? / The witnesses, if they could be called **that**, continued to repeat that they knew nothing /
(adjective) If I were you, I would keep an
eye on **that** young man / It wasn't a
nature reserve, **that** Ark of yours. There
are also a number of familiar idiomatic
or formulaic uses: Something worth a lot
of money, **that**'s for sure / She had a
small, pretty face, I'll give you **that** / She
cleared her throat to speak but left it at
that / I just wanted to see her, **that**'s all.

2 Its use as a demonstrative adverb
equivalent to so or very (or so very) dates
from the 15c and has been slipping in
and out of standard usage ever since. In
current English it tends to be informal,
more so perhaps in positive contexts
(typically in questions and conditions)
than in negative contexts: 'Shut up,' says
Claudia . . . 'It's not **that** funny'—David
Lodge, 1988 / You and your brother,
you're not really **that** alike, are you?—
Encounter, 1989 / I promise that if I'm
that tired, I will pull over and take a
break—weblog, BrE 2003 [OEC] / Was he
really **that** angry with me?—fiction
website, BrE 2004 [OEC].

3 As a relative pronoun, that becomes
an alternative to which (and occasionally
who). Although they are often interchangeable, there are some uses that are
peculiar to each:

a When that is used it normally introduces a so-called 'restrictive' clause,
which defines or gives essential (rather
than additional) information about the
noun or noun phrase that comes before:
the pen that my father bought for me / the
pen that is over on the table / (in each
case the that-clause defines which pen is
meant). (See further at RELATIVE
CLAUSES). In these cases the that-clause
normally follows on without a comma.
Which can also be used in these examples, but in conversational English that is
more usual, and in some cases it is

possible to omit the relative pronoun
altogether and say the pen my father
bought for me. That can also replace who
(or whom), especially when the reference is non-specific, as in The person
that I saw was definitely a woman, and
when there are two antecedents, one
inanimate and the other human: It was
the drug and not her brother that had
upset her.

b That is also more idiomatic than
which in a number of cases: (1) when
which already occurs earlier in the sentence in another role (Which is the house
that you bought?), (2) after indefinite
pronouns such as anything, everything,
nothing, and something (There is something that I forgot to mention), and (3)
after a construction with the impersonal
it (It is the new one that we want). When
that is the object of the verb in its clause,
it is regularly omitted, especially in
speech (There is something I forgot to
mention).

c Which, not that, has to be used in
so-called non-restrictive clauses which
give additional rather than essential information: A new edition of the book,
which has taken ten years to write, will be
published this week. Which is also used
when a preposition precedes it (Is this
the book to which you are referring?); in a
corresponding construction with that,
the preposition has to come at the end
(Is this the book that you are referring to?
or Is this the book you are referring to?).

4 That is used as a conjunction to
introduce a subordinate clause, principally after verbs of saying, feeling,
believing, knowing, learning, etc.: The
President admitted that he had lied /
We would hate to think that they were
corrupting you / I understand that you
wanted to see me. A that-clause of this
type can also occur after the impersonal
it: It was natural that they should think
so. Normally the conjunction that can be
omitted, especially in speech: I

t

understand you wanted to see me / It was natural they should think so. In inverted constructions, however, in which the *that*-clause comes before the main clause, *that* is obligatory: *That they are guilty is assumed by everybody.*

the. 1 *The,* called the definite article, is the commonest word in English, occurring about once in every seven words of everyday language. It can therefore come as a surprise to know that it is pronounced in three ways, depending on its role and position. In normal use it is pronounced dhuh before a word beginning with a consonant (*the table / the green house*) and dhi before a word beginning with a vowel or a softly aspirated *h* sound (*the apples / the other leg / the hotel*). When emphasized, it is pronounced dhee (*You mean the Sharon Stone?*). These distinctions come naturally to most native speakers, but occasional divergences are heard, especially over-emphasis of *the* in cases where the weak form is called for.

2 When two nouns are joined by *and,* a second *the* is normally omitted: *the distortion and innuendo to which several of your correspondents have resorted.* But *the* must be repeated to avoid ambiguity: *the black and the white jerseys / the London and the Southampton trains.* When two nouns joined by *and* form the subject of a sentence, they are sometimes regarded as a single concept and treated as grammatically singular: *The innocence and purity of their singing comes entirely from their identification with the character*—Bernard Levin, 1985. See AGREEMENT 3.

3 In titles of books, plays, films, etc., *The* should be retained when it forms part of the recognized title, but can be omitted when it does not fit the structure of the sentence: *Look in The Times / a new edition of The Chicago Manual of Style* but *John is a Times reporter / J. R. R. Tolkien's Lord of the Rings.*

4 In BrE it is usual to add *the* when referring to a person by a title, as in *The Prime Minister, Gordon Brown, attended the meeting.* The style *Prime Minister Gordon Brown attended the meeting* is characteristic of AmE. After verbs such as *become, be appointed,* etc., the definite article can be omitted before titles or names of office that refer to a single person: *He became Prime Minister in 2007.*

theatre is spelt *-re* in BrE but usually *theater* in AmE.

their *see* THEY.

theirs. This possessive pronoun, as used in *The house is not mine but theirs,* is written without an apostrophe. In compound subjects connected by *and,* the correct form is (e.g.) *Our children and theirs went on holiday together,* not ☒ *Theirs and our children went on holiday together.*

theirselves. *They talked amongst theirselves until my mother stood there*—fiction website, BrE 2005 [OEC]. This is non-standard for *themselves,* and arises from the tendency to regard *self* as a noun needing a possessive pronoun to qualify it; this is legitimate only when an adjective intervenes, e.g. *their very selves.*

them. 1 *See* THEY.

2 Use of *them* as a demonstrative pronoun and adjective is non-standard or dialectal in current English: *Them's my sentiments*—E. M. Forster, 1924 / *I didn't know much about planes in them days*—P. McCabe, 1992.

themself. The standard reflexive form of *they* and *them* is *themselves* (as in *The children have hurt themselves*), but a form *themself* is recorded (with plural reference) from the 14c to the 16c, when it fell out of use. In the 1980s it was rediscovered in the search for gender-neutral pronouns, and it occurs from time to time (even in more formal contexts) referring back to singular nouns or pronouns (especially *anybody, everybody, somebody,* etc.) without yet being generally accepted: *I think somebody should immediately address themself to this problem*—A. T. Ellis, 1987 / *Pretender: a person who puts themself forward as having a rightful claim to someone else's throne*—A. Isaacs, 2000. The plural form *themselves* is also used in this way, but the effect is if anything more awkward: *It may be best, however, to confess to someone who will never meet her boyfriend, . . . just in case that third party got tremendously drunk at a party themselves, and blurted it out to someone else*—*Independent,* 1998. The final battle for a set of gender-free pronouns will probably be fought over *themself,* but for now beware of it.

then. Use of *then* as an adjective as in *the then President,* to mean 'at that time', has been continuous since the 16c and is useful despite occasional objections to it. It is also often used in front of an adjective or participial adjective: *In 1958 the Brussels Atomium optimistically heralded in the then emerging atomic industries*—*Architectural Review,* 2000. In neither use is a hyphen required: ⊠ *Caouette was helped enormously after he used an excerpt from the then-unfinished film as an audition tape*—*Scotland on Sunday,* 2005. In many cases of this type, *then* can be omitted without any significant loss of meaning.

thence is a formal or literary word meaning 'from a place or source previously mentioned' or 'as a consequence': *At first, bishops were regarded as equals of the people, but gradually they took upon themselves arbitrary powers. Thence arose the rigid distinction between clergy and laity*—Stephen Kreis, 2001 / *These boxes are shipped from Varna to Whitby and thence to Carfax*—

Margaret Drabble, 2000. Use of *from* before *thence,* despite its evident tautology, is established and idiomatic: *From thence he made his way to Egypt*—D. Ford et al., 2002. The word is no longer used in spoken English.

thereabouts meaning 'near that place' or 'near that amount' (*a hundred pounds or thereabouts*), is along with *thereby, therefore,* and *thereupon* one of the few medieval compounds formed with *there-* to survive in modern English without any hint of archaism. The variant form *thereabout* is now less common.

therefore. 1 This is the most resilient of the adverbs in *there-* and has been part of the core language since the 12c. It is always pronounced with the stress on the first syllable, and can be placed in various positions in a sentence, including the beginning. In short sentences and in constructions in which *therefore* is associated with a particular word or phrase, it is not necessary to separate it with commas: *Would I please therefore oblige her by using the musical notation provided*—*Guardian,* 1986 / *The relationship of patronage was therefore complex*—R. Greene, 1993. When commas are used, *therefore* becomes parenthetical and its force tends to be spread over the whole sentence in the same way as *however* (though with opposite meaning): *It's unsurprising, therefore, that the most expensive restaurant meal of all time—costing over £44,000—was served here last year*—*Observer Food Monthly,* 2002.

2 When *therefore* comes at the beginning of a sentence, a following comma is optional and depends on the flow of the sentence: *You're not here as a solicitor . . . Therefore, you're entitled to call some other solicitor*—J. Wainwright, 1972 / *Therefore I wear my 'power suit', I call it, if I have to go to a board in the* conference room on the top floor with senior officials—G. Kirkup et al., 1990. When it is immediately followed by a subordinate clause, it is more likely to be separated by a comma: *Therefore, when a battery shows signs of diminishing power and range effectiveness it makes sense to replace it*—B. Smithson, 1988.

there is, there are. This impersonal formula is used to indicate the existence of something or someone in a way that avoids the need to identify them more closely grammatically. *There is* (or *was*) is used when the following noun is singular, and *there are* (or *were*) when it is plural: *There is a spider in the bath / There were three biscuits a moment ago.* When the number of the following noun is more complex, choice is normally determined by what follows immediately; for example, *There **is** a pen and three sheets of paper on the desk* sounds more natural than *There **are** a pen and three sheets of paper on the desk*. Amounts regarded as a unit are also treated as singular: *There is £5000 in my account* (equivalent to 'the sum of £5000'). Use of *there is*, or more often *there's*, as an invariable formula regardless of number is often found but is only acceptable informally: *There's 35 branches throughout the country*.

there you are, there you go. *There you are* is used colloquially as a dismissive expression of regret: *I felt ridiculous of course, but there you are*—S. Wall, 1991. *There you go* is sometimes used in the same way, and is also a conversational formula used to draw a person's attention to something offered: *You haven't bought the great hardware yet? Well, there you go then*—Register, 2002.

thesaurus. A *thesaurus* (pronounced thuh-**saw**-ruhs) is a dictionary organized to supply alternative words rather than to offer analytical explanations of what words mean. Because synonymy is such

a complex phenomenon, most thesauruses can be, in their nature, as dangerous as they are useful. The plural is *thesauri* or *thesauruses*.

these kind of, these sort of *see* KIND OF, SORT OF.

thesis, meaning 'a dissertation', has the plural form *theses*, pronounced **thee**-seez.

they, them, their. These three pronouns have all been used since the 16c to refer back to a singular pronoun, especially an indefinite pronoun such as *anyone, everyone, nobody, someone*, etc.: *If someone walks across it, they interrupt the beam*—P. Niesewand, 1979 / *It could be you, your sister or your girlfriend who tries to abandon their child next*—Big Issue, 1998 / *Before you entrust your children to a babysitter, ask them into your home so that you can talk over what's involved in the job*—BUPA Factsheet, 2004 [*OEC*]. The value of this device has been enhanced in recent years by its validity as a gender-neutral option in place of more awkward conventions such as *he or she, his or her*, etc. For a fuller discussion of this issue *see* GENDER-NEUTRALITY.

they're is a contraction of *they are*, and should be distinguished from the like-sounding forms *their* and *there*.

thief has the plural form *thieves*.

thimbleful has the plural form *thimblefuls*. See -FUL.

thing. For *another thing coming*, *see* THINK 4.

think. 1 After *think*, *that* is usually omitted when a clause follows: *I think you are right. See* THAT 4.
　2 *Think* can be followed by a *to*-infinitive with the meaning 'to remember': *Did you think to lock the door?*

3 As a noun, *think* is relatively recent (early 19c) and is normally regarded as informal: *I'll have a think about it.*

4 *You have another think coming* means 'you are greatly mistaken'. This idiom in the form shown is the original, and always mirrors an expressed or implicit 'if you/he/etc. think(s)...', e.g. *If he thinks he will be blissfully free of directives and paperwork, he has another think coming—Independent, 2002.* Because the *k* sound at the end of *think* and the beginning of *coming* is identical, people have analysed the phrase as *another thing coming*. Many people will consider that a mistake, although it is nearly as old as the original.

thinkable, meaning 'imaginable, able to be grasped by the mind', is not recorded before the early 19c, some 450 years after its more common antonym *unthinkable*: *A crash is a moment of panic when events are out of control and outlandish predictions become think-able—Economist, 1991.*

thinness, meaning 'the quality of being thin', has two *n*s.

thirties *see* EIGHTIES.

this. 1 Though a less complex word than *that* (it is not a conjunction or a relative pronoun, to begin with), *this* has three distinct roles:

demonstrative pronoun:
This is what I mean

demonstrative adjective:
*Would you like a glass of **this** wine?*

demonstrative adverb:
*The show is not usually **this** good*

2 As a demonstrative pronoun and adjective, *this* normally refers to something or someone either present or being thought of at the time of speaking: *What had I done to deserve **this**? / Did you leave **this** book behind?* It can also refer back to an immediately preceding

statement when no single word can be identified as the antecedent: *Should governments do more, or ought this to be left to the private sector?* When contrasted with *that, this* refers to the one immediately in mind, whereas *that* refers to the one mentioned before or known previously.

3 In conversation, *this* is used informally to identify a person or thing even though they have not been previously mentioned: *He was this friendly guy, sorta cute, affable as the day is long—*weblog, BrE 2003 [*OEC*]. Although frowned on by some language purists, this use is idiomatic in more casual discourse.

4 When used informally as a demonstrative adverb, *this* has a more specific reference to immediate experience than does the corresponding use of *that*: *Keep in mind, however, that no existing property is this typical—Real Estate Review, 1972.*

thither *see* HITHER.

tho' is an informal or poetical shortening of *though*. The final apostrophe is omitted in special cases, notably in text messages.

though *see* ALTHOUGH. For *as though, see* AS 9.

thought shower *see* BRAINSTORM, BRAINSTORMING.

thrash, thresh. These words were once variants of the same word, but now have different spellings and pronunciations. To *thrash* is to beat (physically and metaphorically as in *thrashing* one's opponents), whereas to *thresh* is to separate grain.

three-quarter, three-quarters. The noun expressing a fraction is *three-quarters* (with hyphen). The adjectival form is *three-quarter* (e.g. *a three-quarter-length coat*), and this is also the form for the players in a rugby team.

threshold is spelt with one *h* (contrast *withhold*), but can be pronounced either with one *h*, i.e. as written, or as if it had two, **thresh**-hold.

thrice, an adverb meaning 'three times', was formerly in general use but is now limited to archaic or literary contexts.

thrive. The past and past participle of the verb are normally both *thrived*, although *throve* (past) and *thriven* (past participle) are used, albeit very infrequently, in BrE.

throes, as in *to be in the throes of*, is spelt in this way, and should be distinguished from *throws* as a part of the verb *throw*.

through. There are two important uses which are still regarded as Americanisms but are beginning to make an impression on BrE:

1 As a preposition meaning 'up to and including', as in *Monday through Friday*. British speakers are aware of this use but still regard it as non-British, useful though it is: *An eight-week summer program for disadvantaged children ages three through five—Dædalus*, 1993.

2 As an adverb meaning 'finished', as in *Are you through yet?* AmE might well say *Are you through with the phone?*, where BrE would prefer *Have you finished with the phone?* (Note that in BrE, in the context of telephones, *Are you through yet?* would normally be taken to mean 'have you got a connection yet?') In AmE this use of *through* is often followed by a verbal noun: *'I'm through eating,' said my father, pushing his plate away*—L. S. Schwartz, 1989.

thru is an informal variant of *through* in AmE and in varieties influenced by it: *When she was little, and had stuttered*

thru a sentence—Black World, 1971 / *Luckily he let me thru and we continued out*—weblog, AusE 2005 [*OEC*]. It is used more formally in the term *thruway*, meaning 'an expressway'.

Thursday *see* FRIDAY.

thus, thusly. *Thus* is a word with an awkward role in modern English. Used sparingly and appropriately, it is highly effective, whereas when overused it can seem stilted and affected. However it is used, it brings an air of formality with it. It has two basic meanings, (1) 'in this way', and (2) 'accordingly, therefore'. In the first meaning, it is placed in the same position as 'in this way' would be, but sits more comfortably before a verb or participle: *He persistently declines to extend to the Press that assistance (such as circulating in advance scripts of major speeches, or sticking to the text of speeches thus pre-released) which so greatly facilitates newspaper production—Church Times*, 1976. In the second meaning, it can follow the word order used with *therefore*, except that initial position in a sentence often seems clumsy: *Thus the parents, in conversation at home, are able to identify themselves with the place and people under discussion—Where*, 1972. In some uses, *thus* combines the two meanings: *He attempts to defamiliarize and deconstruct the text and thus account for its persuasive power—Review of English Studies*, 1984. *Thusly* seems an unnecessary form, since *thus* is already an adverb, but it is used in AmE both in jocular and in formal contexts: *On his way home George mused thusly—Boston Journal*, 1889 / *The division of responsibilities evolved thusly, with the help of a business consultant who enabled them to focus on specific areas—Art Business News*, AmE 2002 [*OEC*].

tidal, along with *coastal*, belongs to the list of Fowler's *lost causes. His objection was that a Latinate suffix (-al corresponding to Latin *-alis*) is attached to a word of English origin (*tide*). Such objections seem absurdly puristic today.

tidbit *see* TITBIT, TIDBIT.

tight, tightly. *Tight* is used as an adverb in combination with a number of verbs, primarily in commands or instructions: *hold tight, sit tight, sleep tight*. It also occurs as the first element in a few compound adjectives, e.g. *tight-fisted, tight-fitting, tight-knit, tight-lipped*. In general use, *tightly* is the normal adverb.

tilde is a mark (~) put over a letter to modify its pronunciation; e.g. *ñ* in Spanish (as in the second *n* in *niño*) is pronounced -ny-.

till *see* UNTIL.

time. For words denoting lengths of time, *see* EPOCH.

times. When followed by an adjective or adverb in the comparative degree, *times* normally denotes an increase and not a decrease, e.g. *five times bigger*, not *five times smaller*. There are occasional exceptions for special effect, but the rule should be followed in everyday language.

timpani, tympanum. *Timpani* is a plural noun meaning 'orchestral kettle-drums' (informally shortened to *timps*). *Tympanum* is the technical term for 'eardrum', and has the plural form *tympana*.

tin *see* CAN.

tinker, meaning 'to play about', is now normally followed by *with* rather than (as formerly) by *at*: *Whatever moral doubts there may be about tinkering with nature, the biotechnology revolution will not be stopped in its tracks—Oxfam News*, 1990.

tiptoe. The verb has inflected forms *tiptoes, tiptoed, tiptoeing*. The noun is confined to the expression *on tiptoe(s)*, where it can be singular or plural.

tirade is normally pronounced tiy-**rayd**, with the stress on the second syllable, in BrE, and **tiy**-rayd, with the stress on the first syllable, in AmE.

tiramisu, a rich chocolate dessert, is Italian and is derived from the words *tira mi sù* meaning 'pick me up' (which it certainly does). It is mainly used as a mass noun and not in the plural, so the question of inflection does not arise.

tire (of a wheel) *see* TYRE.

tiro *see* TYRO.

tissue should be pronounced **tish**-oo rather than **tis**-yoo.

titbit, tidbit. *Titbit* is the usual spelling in BrE and *tidbit* in AmE. The first element is probably derived from an English dialect word *tid* meaning 'tender, nice, special'.

titillate, titivate. *Titillate* means 'to excite' (*Some interesting titles to titillate your literary tastebuds*), and often has sexual overtones (especially in the noun derivative *titillation*), whereas *titivate* is a now rather dated word meaning 'to adorn or smarten' (*Striking abstract paintings titivate the otherwise bare walls*). *Titivate* is occasionally used by mistake for *titillate* (although the reverse mistake does not occur): ☒ *Even now twelve heartfelt pages are titivating the senses of a Dead Letter superintendent—*Dylan Thomas, 1933.

titles *see* CAPITALS 2A; THE 3.

to. 1 For the type *to really love*, *see* SPLIT INFINITIVE.

2 In AmE, *to* is beginning to be used as an alternative for *of* to denote possession or (in particular) human relationship: *He's married and the father to a son*—Chicago Tribune, 1989 / *Maya plays surrogate mother to her three sullen siblings*—film website, AmE 2004 [*OEC*].

tobacco has the plural form *tobaccos*.

toboggan. The verb has inflected forms *tobogganed*, *tobogganing*, and derivative forms *tobogganer*, *tobogganist*.

today, tomorrow, tonight are still occasionally seen in their hyphenated forms *to-day, to-night*, and *to-morrow*, but the regular spellings are now as whole words.

to die for *see* DIE.

together *see* ALL TOGETHER.

toilet. *Toilet* is the most frequently used word in BrE for what used to be called *water closet* (or *WC*) and is still sometimes called *lavatory*. It is the word normally used on signs and notices when more specific reference to *ladies / women* and *gentlemen* (or *gents*) / *men* is not given. In middle-class British conversation *loo* (of uncertain origin: see the note in the *COD*) has become a regularly used alternative; *toilet* is regarded as non-U, and *lavatory* is now out of favour almost as much. In AmE, the regular terms are *restroom, bathroom*, and *washroom*, with *john* as a more informal alternative. Many slang terms and euphemisms exist in both varieties (in BrE, *bog, khazi*, etc., and in AmE *can, comfort station, powder room*).

token. The phrase *by the same token* is used to connect a statement to something said previously, and means roughly 'for the same reason' or 'in the same way'. Although it is used less precisely than these definitions imply, there should always be some causal or consequential connection of this kind: *I've dined out on a few stories about her. But not ones that matter. By the same token,*

she could have made quite a good thing about telling how she saw you . . . that night—D. Halliday, 1970. It is less appropriate when introducing a parallel or additional circumstance rather than a causally related one: *Style is a heady compound of instinct, experience and context: what cuts a dash in the Masai Mara won't necessarily do the trick in Mayfair. By the same token* [read: *At the same time*], *while style is nailing a kind of timelessness, it has to look modern*—Times, 2006.

tomato has the plural form *tomatoes*.

tome. A *tome* is a large heavy book, not a synonym for a book of any size.

tomorrow *see* TODAY, TOMORROW, TONIGHT.

ton. A *ton* is a unit of weight, and a *tun* is a cask or wine-measure. Both are pronounced tun and were once the same word, but they became differentiated in the 17c. A *tonne*, also pronounced tun, is a metric ton equivalent to 1,000 kilograms.

tonight *see* TODAY, TOMORROW, TONIGHT.

tonsil. The derivative forms are *tonsillectomy, tonsillitis*, and *tonsillotomy*, all with two *l*s.

tonsorial has nothing to do with tonsils, but is an adjective derived from the Latin word *tonsor* meaning 'barber' and is used facetiously to refer to a hairdresser or hairdressing (*The reason why he was called Ginger may now be more of historical document than tonsorial fact*—Sunday Herald, 2002).

too. 1 *Too* is the normal word used to qualify an adjective or adverb to denote excess: *The house is too large / I spoke too soon*. It should not be used to qualify a participial adjective when this could not idiomatically be qualified by *very*: *She was too tired* is acceptable because *tired* has acquired the role of an ordinary adjective, but *She was too affected by their criticisms* is less satisfactory because *affected* is still regarded as part of a verb. In this case a better alternative is *She was too much affected by their criticisms* or *She was excessively affected by their criticisms*.

2 When *too* qualifies an adjective followed by a noun, the usual order is (for example) *too large a house* rather than *a too large house*. In more complex sentences it is often preferable to rephrase in order to avoid a clumsy sequence of words with *too*; for example, *The incident arose from a too sudden reaction to the danger* would be better expressed as *The incident arose because they reacted too suddenly to the danger*.

toothcomb. The expression *toothcomb* or (*fine toothcomb*) arose from a misreading of the compound noun *fine-tooth comb* (i.e. a comb with fine teeth). Purists will insist on the original form, but the altered form follows the familiar pattern of idioms that lose direct association with their origins, and is acceptable: *A novel which has been picked over with toothcombs, in search of clues to 'The Mystery'*—*Times Literary Supplement*, 1972.

tormentor is spelt *-or*, not *-er*.

tornado has the plural form *tornadoes* rather more often than *tornados*, and both are correct. The plural form of the military aircraft, however, is *Tornados* only.

torpedo has the plural form *torpedoes*, and the verb has inflected forms *torpedoes, torpedoed, torpedoing*.

torpor is spelt *-or* in both BrE and AmE.

torso has the plural form *torsos*.

tortoise should be pronounced **taw**-tuhs. The form **taw**-toyz, with the second syllable like *poise*, is non-standard.

tortuous, torturous. Both words are derived from Latin *torquēre* meaning 'to twist', but their literal meanings are different. The less common word *torturous* is a derivative of the English word *torture*, whereas *tortuous* has no such related noun. A *tortuous* route is one that is twisting and winding, and a *torturous* illness or anxiety is one that is extremely painful. It is in their figurative uses, in which both words mean 'difficult or complex', that the overlap is most noticeable. A *tortuous* judgement is one that has many complicating features, and a *torturous* judgement is one that is painfully difficult to make; these are two aspects of a similar outcome. *Tortuous* is more common in this range of meanings and is usually the better choice.

total. The verb has inflected forms *totalled, totalling* in BrE, and usually *totaled, totaling* in AmE. The derivative words are *totally* (adverb) and *totality* (noun).

tother, originally a Middle English form (*the tother*) derived from wrong division of *that other*, is still used in humorous contexts and to produce a lightened effect in BrE: *One solution would be for tother participants in the cross-channel rail industry . . . to take a stake in a larger Eurotunnel*—*The Business*, 2004. The phrase *tell tother from which* (= tell one from the other) now sounds dated and has largely fallen out of use.

toupee, a kind of wig covering a bald spot, is spelt in this way without any accents.

toward, towards. In BrE *towards* is much the more common form for the preposition, and is more frequent in World English, whereas in AmE *toward* is more usual: *We walked toward / towards the house.*

towel has inflected forms *towelled*, *towelling* in BrE, and usually *toweled*, *toweling* in AmE.

trade marks, also called proprietary terms, such as *Bovril, Google, Hoover,* and *Xerox,* should normally be spelt with a capital initial in writing or print, but when they are used as verbs it is customary to use a small initial letter since the term has then become fully lexicalized (*I found it by googling / I'll xerox the article*). When trade marks are entered as headwords in dictionaries they normally appear with an explicit statement of their status; nonetheless, the trade mark owners are often hostile to their inclusion, since this can be taken to imply (although linguistically it does not) that the term has become generic and can accordingly threaten the status of the trade mark. It is an interesting area, difficult to resolve, in which actual things, the names for them, and their legal status all demand different priorities from those who use them.

trade union is the correct form, not *trades union.* The plural form is *trade unions.* But *TUC* is short for *Trades Union Congress.*

trade wind is written as two words.

traffic. The verb has inflected forms *traffics, trafficked, trafficking.* The derivative noun meaning 'someone who traffics' is *trafficker.*

tragedy was originally a term for a kind of drama which involves the downfall of the principal character or characters, brought about by significant events which are often the actions of the protagonists themselves. It has been developed in use to refer to major misfortunes in real life (*The government . . . had been captured by the extreme right and its* budget measures were 'a tragedy for many good New Zealanders'—*Keesings,* 1990). This is a typical and well-established example of semantic weakening; nevertheless, the word still ought to retain some overtones of seriousness, and should not be used for more trivial or ephemeral setbacks, such as defeat in a sports event: it is best reserved for describing serious misfortune. The same applies to the adjective *tragic,* which describes meaningful events that have disastrous consequences. Strictly speaking, a *tragic accident* is a contradiction in terms, since an accident by definition lacks the import involved in the notion of tragedy; but the combination is so well established that objection to it is futile. Both *tragedy* and *tragic* are much used by journalists to add flavour to their accounts: *Exactly a decade to the day that Diana was killed in a tragic car crash—Coventry Evening Telegraph,* 2007.

train station, first recorded in the *OED* as recently as 1955, seems in BrE to be taking over from *railway station* in contexts where something more specific is needed than just *station: I was with my friend at Forest Gate train station, east London, when we were stopped and searched—Socialist Worker Online,* 2003 [OEC].

trait, meaning 'a person's distinguishing characteristic', is now usually pronounced trayt rather than tray in both BrE and in AmE.

trammel has inflected forms *trammelled, trammelling* in BrE, and usually *trameled, trameling* in AmE.

tranche, meaning 'a portion of something, especially money', is spelt with a final letter *e,* as shown, not ✖ *tranch.* It can be pronounced in a semi-anglicized way to rhyme with *branch,* or nasalized in a French manner, but should not be pronounced like *haunch*.

tranquillity, tranquillize, tran-quillizer are spelt with two *l*s in BrE, but usually with one *l* in AmE. The adverb is *tranquilly* in both varieties.

transcendent, transcendental.
1 The word used in general contexts to mean 'excelling, surpassing normal human experience' is *transcendent*, which typically collocates with words for grand notions such as *beauty, good*, and *truth*. It is wasted in mundane and trivial contexts such as descriptions of sports events (*Wales and South Africa derived almost equal pleasure from a transcendent test match*—*Express*, 2004).
2 *Transcendental* has the basic meaning 'outside experience' and is used mainly in technical contexts: (1) in theology, to refer to God as being outside the universe, the opposite of *immanent* (*see at* IMMINENT), (2) in philosophy to denote the teaching of the 19c American philosopher Ralph Waldo Emerson, and (3) in the term *transcendental meditation*, a form of meditation derived from Hinduism.

transexual *see* TRANSSEXUAL.

transfer is pronounced with the stress on the first syllable as a noun, and with the stress on the second syllable as a verb. The verb has inflected forms *transferred, transferring*; the derivative words are *transferable, transference, transferor* (used chiefly in legal contexts), and *transferee* (all with one *r*) but *transferral* (with two *r*s).

transgressor, meaning 'someone who violates a rule or law', is spelt *-or*, not *-er*.

tranship, transhipment *see* TRANS-SHIP, TRANS-SHIPMENT.

transient, transitory. Both words mean 'brief, fleeting', with *transient* conveying rather more strongly the notion of people or things 'passing through' while *transitory* denotes temporary situations that are more static: *The highly transient nature of the casual labour force in hotels and catering, and the low attachment to work of many casuals ... mean that the unions' task will scarcely be an easy one*—B. Casey, 1988 / *In traditional critical study, questions about politics were rarely felt important since politics engaged with transitory activities*—T. Healy, 1992. *Transient* has special meanings in music, philosophy, electricity, and nuclear physics, and *transitory* has a special meaning in law. The noun *transience* is generally preferable to the more cumbersome word *transitoriness*.

transistor is spelt *-or*, not *-er*.

transitive verbs *see* INTRANSITIVE AND TRANSITIVE VERBS.

translator is spelt *-or*, not *-er*.

transliterate means 'to replace the letters or characters of a word with the corresponding letters in another alphabet'. Words may be transliterated into the Roman alphabet from their originals in Greek, Chinese, Japanese, and so on. The result is a *transliteration*, which preserves the form of the original, as distinct from a *translation*, which gives the equivalent word (often unrelated in form) in another language. For example, *pteron* is a transliteration from Greek, and *wing* is its translation.

translucent *see* TRANSPARENT.

transmit has inflected forms *transmitted, transmitting*, and derivative forms *transmitter, transmittal* (but more commonly *transmission*). The adjectival forms *transmittable* and *transmissible* are both in use.

transparent is the general word used to describe anything through which light can pass, so that what is on the other side is visible, as distinct from *translucent*, which denotes passage of light but not necessarily visibility (as with frosted glass, for example). *Transparent* also has figurative senses relating to mental comprehension rather than physical vision (e.g. *Their intentions were transparent*) and to political openness and accessibility to public scrutiny. The derivative noun is *transparency*.

transpire. The origin of the word is in the Latin verb *spirare* 'to breathe', and in its primary physical sense meant 'to give off vapour' or 'to perspire' (a meaning still used in the physical sciences). In the 18c it developed two abstract meanings, both looked on with suspicion: (1) 'to leak out, to become known', usually with an impersonal *it* as subject (*It transpired later that the social workers were all under instruction to have identification*—R. Black, 1992 / *The couple, it transpires, have quietly been buying art for a decade*—Arts & Book Review, 2007), and (2) 'to happen, to occur' (*What actually transpired upon the outbreak of the Civil War is lost in the mists of time*—E. G. Holland, 1986 / *It is imperative now … that Tony Blair comes clean with the British public as to what transpired during the course of those 10 days*—Guardian Unlimited, 2005 [*OEC*]), a sense that probably arose from a misunderstanding of the previous one. In the course of time the first of these meanings has become accepted, but the second, despite its closeness in some contexts, is still widely disliked (in the 19c the American writer Richard Grant White went so far as to describe it as a 'monstrous perversion') and it should not be used except informally.

transport, transportation. *Transport* is used both for the conveying of passengers and goods and for the vehicles used in this. *Transportation*, which is primarily an American word, is also used in BrE in the first of these meanings: *Its chief original purpose was to facilitate transportation by road of the products of the Coalbrookdale iron works, which had previously been conveyed by river and canal transport*—B. Bailey, 1985. The word is also used historically with reference to prisoners sent to penal colonies overseas.

transsexual is the preferred form, not *transexual*.

trans-ship, trans-shipment are the preferred forms, not *tranship*, *transhipment*.

trauma, from the Greek word meaning 'wound', originated as a term used in medicine for a serious physical injury, but it is more widely used to refer to emotional shock following a stressful event or, more generally, to an experience that is deeply distressing. The word is both countable and uncountable: one can experience *trauma* or *a trauma*; the plural form is *traumas*. It is constantly weakened or trivialized in newspaper reports: *Blair crashed on with his schedule, side-stepping the trauma of a strike by South African Airline's ground crew*—Observer, 1996 (*inconvenience* or *discomfort*, the words wanted here, make less journalistic impact). The preferred pronunciation is **traw**-muh, but **trow**-muh is more common in AmE.

travel. The verb has inflected forms *travelled*, *travelling*, *traveller* in BrE, and usually *traveled*, *traveling*, *traveler* in AmE.

treble *see* TRIPLE, TREBLE.

trek. The verb has inflected forms *trekked*, *trekking*. The word implies a strong element of difficulty or arduousness, and as a synonym of *go* is used in hyperbole or for jocular effect.

trellis has inflected forms *trellised*, *trellising*.

tremor is spelt *-or* in BrE and AmE.

tribe. 1 *Tribe* is used without difficulty when the reference is historical (*Balbindor was a coastal Malay of the Iban tribe*—Brian Aldiss, 1993), and some ancient societies had constitutional divisions normally translated by the term *tribe* (e.g. Athens and Rome). In modern contexts, however, the associations of empire and implications of cultural superiority make it a controversial term when applied to communities living within traditional societies. When these are not technically or traditionally known by the term *tribe*, alternative terms such as *community* and *people* are usually preferable.

2 For several centuries, *tribe* has been used disparagingly to mean 'social circle' or 'set of associates', but in recent usage this meaning has become more neutral in tone: *Nick and she, they were proportioned to each other, they seemed to belong to the same tribe*—Ruth Rendell, 1988. On the whole, since its boundaries are clear, this use is unexceptionable.

tricolour, meaning 'a flag of three colours', especially the French flag of blue, white, and red, is spelt *-our* in BrE and pronounced **trik**-uh-luh. In AmE it is spelt *tricolor* and pronounced **triy**-kul-uh.

trigger. The verb has inflected forms *triggered, triggering*.

trillion. Now that **billion* means 'a thousand million' in both BrE and AmE, *trillion* has taken over the earlier BrE meaning of *billion*, i.e. 'a million million' (1,000,000,000,000 or 10^{12}). Previously *trillion* had the rarely needed meaning 'a million million

million' (1,000,000,000,000,000,000 or 10^{18}).

trio has the plural form *trios*.

triple, treble. In general contexts (outside music, betting, etc.) the two words are largely interchangeable as noun, verb, and adjective, but *triple* is more common for the verb (especially in intransitive uses, in the sense 'to become three times as many': *The editorial staff had tripled and was producing issues 250 pages thick*—Columbia Journalism Review, 2003) and the adjective (*I was starting to get triple vision and wondering how you did that with only two eyes*— Iain Banks, 1990). Both words are used in the meaning 'three times as many', as in *treble / triple the number* and *treble / triple the size*.

triptych, meaning 'a painting or carving on three panels', is pronounced **trip**-tik. The second element is derived from the Greek word *ptukhē* meaning 'fold'.

triumphal, triumphant. *Triumphal* is a classifying word denoting things connected with victory, such as a *triumphal arch* or a *triumphal procession*. *Triumphant* is more descriptive and means 'exulting in a victory or success' with a wide range of applications: *'I thought so,' said Gray, with a small triumphant laugh*—Sebastian Faulks, 1993 / *Whatever the result, this is a triumphant election*—Sunday Times, 2005. The two words can occasionally occur in the same context: a *triumphal* entry into a captured city is one in which victory is celebrated with appropriate pomp and circumstance, while a *triumphant* entry can refer to the same event, but emphasizing the jubilation.

trivia, like *trivial*, has an interesting history. Both words are derived in roundabout ways from the Latin word *trivium* meaning 'a place where three roads meet', and come via the medieval sense of a three-part education in grammar, rhetoric, and logic as a division of the liberal arts. *Trivia* is treated as both a plural noun and a singular mass noun: *Besides, trivia has its importance, too. Or, to put it another way, trivia have their importance too*—Sunday Times, 1978.

trolley is spelt *-ey* and has the plural form *trolleys*.

troop, troupe. A *troop* is an armoured unit of soldiers or a group of Scouts, whereas a *troupe* is a company of actors or performers. Correspondingly, a *trooper* is a soldier in an armoured unit (and, in America and Australia, a mounted police officer) and a *trouper* is a member of a group of actors or performers and (figuratively) 'a staunch colleague' (usually with a favourable qualifying word: *I don't think you're selfish at all. In fact, Maisie, I think you're a proper trouper*—Dick Francis, 1976).

trouble. *As a comedian he had trouble finding a persona*—New York Times, 1974 /*He'll have a lot of trouble finding his paintbrushes*—fiction website, BrE 2004 [*OEC*]. This use, in which *trouble* is followed immediately by a verbal noun, is acceptable informally, but in more formal contexts it should include the preposition *in*: *Once you have spoken to the potential recipients you should have no trouble in getting addresses*—J. Ridgway, 1984.

trousers is a plural noun in ordinary use (*Where are my trousers?*), but takes the form *trouser* when used attributively (i.e. before a noun, as in *trouser leg* and *trouser suit*).

trousseau, meaning 'clothes collected by a bride in preparation for her marriage', has the plural form *trousseaux* (preferred) or *trousseaus*, both pronounced **troo**-sohz in BrE and troo-**sohz** in AmE.

trout is the same in the plural, except that *old trout* (a derogatory informal term for an old woman) has the plural form *old trouts*.

truly. For *Yours truly*, *see* LETTER FORMS.

trumpet. The verb has inflected forms *trumpeted, trumpeting*.

trunkful has the plural form *trunkfuls*. See -FUL.

truths. The recommended pronunciation for the plural form is troodhz, although troothz is also heard.

try and, try to. 1 *Try*, like *come* and *go*, can be followed by *and* + verb instead of by a *to*-infinitive: *Try and survive, try and live with the system*—Gerald Seymour, 1983. This use is somewhat more informal than the construction with *to*, and also has the effect of placing the weight of meaning less on *try* and more on the following verb (compare the balance of meaning in *Try to survive...*). It is most common in the present and future tenses, and especially in the imperative (giving an order or instruction), and there are occasions when *and* is the more likely or natural choice: (1) when *try* is already preceded by *to* (*Jack didn't stop to try and work it out*—A. Masters, 1991), (2) in casual or formulaic commands and invitations (*Turn yer light out and try and get some sleep*—Hammond Innes, 1991 / *Seoul promised yesterday that it would continue to seek a diplomatic solution to the crisis and that it would be holding talks with both Russia and China to try and find a means of resolving the dispute*—Scotland on Sunday, 2002), and (3) in expressions of challenge or defiance (*Just you try and stop me*—Julian Barnes, 1992). But these are tendencies only, and many contrary examples can be found: *That girl was* *going to try to put the blame on her, she could tell*—S. Shepherd, 1988 / *They had to try to find out for themselves what went on inside the secretive home*—online essays, AmE 2005 [*OEC*].

2 When *try* is in the negative, *to* and *and* occur more interchangeably in the same types of construction (for example, in commands), but *and* is noticeably more informal: *Don't try and change the subject!*—M. Dibdin, 1989 / *Don't try to deny it*—S. Howard, 1993 / *So Herbie didn't try and jump in the car before I could lift him*—conversation recorded in British National Corpus, 1991 / *They should not try to be fair to other countries*—*New Scientist*, 1991.

3 The construction with *and* is not available after any other form of *try*, i.e. not after *tries, tried*, or *trying* (*They tried to warn us / What were you trying to tell me? / What if she tries to ring you? / I . . . paced around and tried to absorb all the details*—Anita Brookner, 1986), but it is available to tenses formed by auxiliary verbs + the simple form of *try* (*So let's not try and be too funny, eh?*—T. Lewis, 1992 / *I could try and make my own films*—film website, AmE 2003 [*OEC*] / *We might try and get back later today*—weblog, BrE 2004 [*OEC*]). A construction with *to* is also obligatory when *try* is followed by a negative proposition: *Try not to hang things too close, too high, or too far apart*—M. Gilliatt, 1992 (not ✖ *Try and not hang things too close . . .*).

4 conclusion. From all this evidence we must conclude that choice between *try to* and *try and* is largely a matter of spontaneity, rhythm, and emphasis, especially in spoken forms. Generally speaking, *try and* is somewhat more casual in effect, and is especially idiomatic in speech, whereas there are often good reasons for preferring *try to* in more formal contexts. But

usage is unstable, and is likely to remain so.

tsar, czar. Both spellings are in use for the title of the Russian emperors before 1917, but *tsar* (which is closer to the Russian form) is more common in BrE and *czar* in AmE. In the extended meaning of an official with special powers in some designated domain, such as a *drugs tsar / czar* or a *cancer tsar /czar*, the spelling used depends on the preference in the variety of English concerned.

-t-, -tt-. For the inflection of words such as *ballot* and *target*, *see* DOUBLING OF FINAL CONSONANTS IN INFLECTION.

Tuesday *see* FRIDAY.

tumour is spelt *-our* in BrE and *tumor* in AmE.

tun *see* TON.

tunnel. The verb has inflected forms *tunnelled, tunnelling* in BrE and *tunneled, tunneling* in AmE.

turban has an adjectival form *turbaned* (one *n*).

turbid, turgid. The two words are unrelated but both can describe the flowing of water in their literal meanings (*turbid* means 'opaque and cloudy' and *turgid* means 'swollen and overflowing'), and both refer to styles of writing in their figurative meanings. *Turgid*, meaning 'inflated, bombastic' (as in *turgid prose*), is the more commonly used, whereas *turbid* means 'confused, muddled'.

Turco- is the normal combining form of *Turkish* (as in *Turcocentric, Turco-Russian*, etc.), not *Turko-*.

turf. The noun in its countable meaning ('a single piece of turf') has the plural form *turves* (preferred) or *turfs*.

turkey has the plural form *turkeys*.

turquoise. The recommended pronunciation in BrE is **tur**-kwoiz, but a more French-like form **tur**-kwahz is sometimes heard.

turret has an adjectival form *turreted* (one *t*).

tweet. A *tweet* is, of course, a posting made on the social networking service *Twitter*. Each posting is in the form of a text-based message of up to 140 characters. *To tweet* is to create such a posting. Noun and verb both date to 2006. The verb has rapidly acquired its own syntax: (intransitive) *She talks about her own life, but she's just as likely to tweet about budget cuts and Keynesian economics* / (transitive) *She tweeted a picture of them smiling at the camera / email us, tweet us, go to our blog, and find us on Facebook* / (introducing a clause) *He tweeted that he would be willing to take a lie detector test* / (with direct speech) *The president tweeted: 'After you vote, tell your Facebook friends "I voted"'* / (ditransitive) *The Communications Director tweeted us the following.*

twenties *see* EIGHTIES.

Twitter. The social media website is written with a capital first letter. The verb, meaning 'to talk rapidly in a trivial way', is not. In the early days of *Twitter* there was some uncertainty about whether the verb to denote making a posting on *Twitter* was *twitter* (lower case) or *tweet*. *Tweet* is now standard, while *twitter* is likely to sound odd, or even disparaging.

-ty and -ness. Most English adjectives can form nouns by adding the active (originally Old English) suffix *-ness*, and these nouns denote either a state or quality (*cleverness, happiness*) or an instance of a state or quality (*a kindness*). The suffix *-ty* (often in the form *-ity*) represents via Old French a Latin noun

ending *-tas* or *-itas*, and is very common in English (e.g. *honesty, notoriety, prosperity, sanity, stupidity*); some forms also denote an instance of the quality in the way that some *-ness* nouns do (*an ability, an ambiguity, a curiosity, a fatality, a subtlety, a variety*). In most cases parallel nouns in *-ness* (*ableness, curiousness, honestness*, etc.) are not normally used, but in other cases a form in *-ty* has developed a special meaning or a sense of remoteness from the adjective that leaves room for an alternative in *-ness*, e.g. *casualty / casualness, clarity / clearness, crudity / crudeness, enormity / enormousness, ingenuity* (from *ingenious*) */ ingenuousness* (from *ingenuous*), *nicety / niceness, purity* (with sexual overtones) */ pureness, preciosity* (used of literary or artistic style) */ preciousness, speciality / specialness*. Some adjectives of Latinate origin that might have been expected to have forms in *-ty* in fact do not, and *-ness* forms are used instead, e.g. *facetiousness, massiveness, naturalness, seriousness, tediousness*. Conversely there are nouns in *-ty* for which no corresponding adjectives exist in English, e.g. *celerity, fidelity, integrity, utility*. For other noun forms *see* -ION, -MENT, -NESS.

tympanum *see* TIMPANI.

type of *see* KIND OF, SORT OF.

typo, meaning a typographical error, has the plural form *typos*.

tyrannize, meaning 'to behave like a tyrant (towards)' is used both transitively (i.e. with an object) and intransitively followed by *over*. Fowler (1926) rejected the transitive use but it is now the more common pattern: (transitive) *We can use it to tyrannize ourselves, to live in the future instead of the present*— M. Williamson, 1992 / (intransitive) *Since whites will always be the majority in America, they will, he thinks, have* *some inclination to tyrannize over minority populations*—C. White, 2001.

tyrant. In modern use the word denotes the manner in which authority is exercised, i.e. oppressively and cruelly. In its ancient Greek context, it refers to the manner in which authority was achieved, i.e. by unconstitutional means. Once in power, a Greek tyrant might be a benevolent ruler. The adjectival derivatives *tyrannical* (with stress on the second syllable) and *tyrannous* (with stress on the first syllable) cover the same range of allusive meaning; the first is now much more common than the second although the second is the older word (15c).

tyre, tire. The standard spelling for a wheel's rubber covering is *tyre* in BrE and *tire* in AmE. *Tire* is the older spelling, and may be related to the word *attire*, a tyre being regarded as a form of 'clothing' for the wheel.

tyro meaning 'a novice', is generally spelt in this way rather than as *tiro*. The plural form is *-os*.

U and non-U. *See box opposite.*

ult. is an abbreviation of Latin *ultimo* (*mense*) meaning 'of the previous month' and is still used occasionally in more formal commercial correspondence following a day (e.g. *the 7th ult.*) to denote a date in the month preceding.

ultimatum has the plural form *ultimatums*. The form *ultimata* is unusual and pretentious.

ultra vires, meaning 'beyond one's legal power or authority', is pronounced **ult**-ruh **viy**-reez and is printed in roman type.

-um. For plural forms of Latin nouns ending in *-um* that have been adopted into English (e.g. *addendum, compendium*) *see* LATIN PLURALS.

umbilical is pronounced um-**bil**-i-kuhl (preferred) or um-bi-**liy**-kuhl.

un-. The prefix *un-* is used to form negatives of words with two types of meaning: (1) denoting the opposite of an adjective or its derivative (*uneducated, unhappiness*), and (2) denoting a reversal of the action implied by a verb (*undress, unlock*). Some adjectival forms in *un-* have a special and usually unfavourable sense (*unprofessional, unscientific*) and when a neutral classificatory form is needed *non-* is used instead (*non-professional, non-scientific; see* NON-). For the choice between *in-* and *un-* forms, *see* IN- AND UN-.

unaccountable. *Unaccountable* means (1) 'that cannot be accounted *for*', i.e. 'inexplicable' (*The unaccountable and secret reasons of disaffection between man and wife*—Milton, 1643), which remains the dominant sense, and (2) 'not liable to be called to account', i.e. 'irresponsible' (in the technical sense: *sinister laws imposed on us by distant, unaccountable bureaucrats*). Like *reliable* and a few other adjectives in *-able*, it is formed somewhat controversially from an intransitive verb (one that does not take an object), the linking prepositions *for* and *on* (*account* + *for*, *rely* + *on*) being suppressed in the *-able* forms. *See also* RELIABLE.

unartistic is sometimes used as a more neutral classificatory term (i.e. 'not concerned with or relating to art') instead of the more usual (and more judgemental) *inartistic*, e.g. *artists have to do unartistic things to put food on the table.*

unashamedly is pronounced as five syllables.

unattached participles *see* PARTICIPLES 3.

unaware, unawares. 1 The adjective *unaware* is used predicatively (i.e. after a verb) and is followed either by *of* or by a *that*-clause: *She still seemed unaware of the peril that she was in*—M. Lide, 1991 / *Quite unaware that he had a month's redundancy money coming, Cornelius finished his breakfast*—R. Rankin, 1993. It is occasionally used without any further complementation:

U AND NON-U.

The term was not known to Fowler (1926) but the idea of language use as a distinguishing feature of class most certainly was, as his article on 'genteelisms' (*paying guest* for *lodger*, *serviette* for *napkin*, etc.) shows. The term U, denoting the language of the upper class, was coined by the linguist A. S. C. Ross in 1954, and was turned into a kind of cult by Nancy Mitford in her book of essays entitled *Noblesse Oblige*, which explored a theme already present in her earlier writing, notably in her largely autobiographical novel *The Pursuit of Love* (1945) where Uncle Matthew (representing her father) explodes with indignation at words such as *handbag* and *notepaper*. The table below lists words considered U and non-U taken from Nancy Mitford's book, plus some pairs that have come to be distinguished in the same way since she wrote. (*See also* GENTEELISM.)

U	non-U
bag	handbag
bike	cycle
drawing-room	lounge
enough	ample, sufficient
false teeth	dentures
house	home
lavatory	toilet
looking-glass	mirror
luncheon	dinner
napkin	serviette
pudding	sweet, dessert
rich	wealthy
scent	perfume
be sick	be ill
sofa	settee
sorry	pardon
vegetables	greens
writing-paper	notepaper

Forms of pronunciation as well as choice of words are also a feature of U and non-U; for example, the pronunciation of *scone* to rhyme with *stone* is often regarded as non-U, as distinct from the U (originally northern) form that rhymes with *gone*, and for *either* iy-dhuh is U and ee-dhuh is non-U.

Social exclusiveness of a potentially sinister kind lies behind what can easily be taken for a language game. Nonetheless, the spirit of fun is hard to resist, as the poet John Betjeman found in his gently satirical poem 'How to Get on in Society' (1954):

Phone for the fish-knives, Norman,
  As cook is a little unnerved;
You kiddies have crumpled the serviettes
  And I must have things daintily served

(four more verses follow)

Once having looked, he could never again be unaware—Edith Pargeter, 1989.

2 *Unawares* is an adverb, used especially in the phrase *to catch* someone (or *be caught*) *unawares*: *However, everyone comes unstuck once in a while, especially when caught unawares*—S. Romain, 1989.

unbeknown, unbeknownst. These entered the language in the 17c and 19c respectively. They are typically used in the form *unbeknown to* or *unbeknownst to* (someone), and in current use *unbeknownst* is more common: . . . *whose real father, unbeknownst to her, is her mother's one-time Jewish lover*—*New York Review of Books*, 1990. Both have a rhetorical tone but cannot now be said to be 'out of use except in dialect or uneducated speech or in imitations of these' (Fowler, 1926).

unbiased, unbiassed. The preferred form is *unbiased*, although *-ss-* is also correct.

uncharted, unchartered. In its literal use, *uncharted* denotes an area of land, sea, space, etc., not mapped or surveyed: *the plane landed on a previously uncharted islet* / *an uncharted region of space*. From this comes its metaphorical use, especially with *territory* and *waters*, e.g. *The stakes are terribly high as operators enter uncharted territory in the broadband world*. In both literal and figurative meanings, *unchartered* is wrongly used in examples such as ✖ *In that sense, the Lisbon agenda is sailing into unchartered waters*—*BBC News*, 2004.

uncooperative, uncoordinated. Both words are now spelt as shown, without a hyphen and without a diaeresis over the second *o*.

uncountable nouns *see* COUNTABLE NOUNS.

under *see* BELOW, BENEATH, UNDER.

underestimate *see* OVERESTIMATE, UNDERESTIMATE.

underlay, underlie. 1 The past tense and past participle of *underlay* are *underlaid*, whereas the past tense of *underlie* is *underlay* and its past participle *underlain*. The primary meaning of *underlay* is 'to lay one thing under (another) to support it' as in *underlaying* a floor covering with another layer of material (e.g. *a beautiful collection of songs featuring soaring string work underlaid by metal drumming*), whereas the more common verb *underlie* means 'to lie under (something)', and more often has a metaphorical meaning 'to form the basis of' (*These motives underlie all they do* / *the policy considerations that have underlain the courts' attitudes to certain types of claimant*).

2 *Underlay* (with stress on the first syllable) is also a noun, meaning 'material laid under a carpet', whereas *underlie* is only a verb.

underneath has from earliest times been in competition with *below*, *beneath*, and *under*, and in current use tends to be used mainly in a physical sense, e.g. (adverb) *a building with a garage underneath*, and (preposition) *underneath the arches of the bridge*. Unlike the other words, *underneath* is also a noun (*the underneath of the vehicle*).

undertone *see* OVERTONE, UNDERTONE.

under way. There is a choice between *under way* and *underway*, with the two-word form still marginally preferable although the other is equally well attested: *I started up the bagpipes and was soon under way, marching up and down the church hall*—B. Millin, 1991 / *The foot-and-mouth outbreak led to the suspension of the testing programme that was* *underway to try to monitor and contain TB*—farming website, BrE 2002 [*OEC*]. The reworking of the phrase as *under weigh*, which arose from associations of ships weighing anchor and setting sail, was common in 19c writers (including Byron, Marryat, and Thackeray) but has largely disappeared since the nautical connection is irrelevant to most contexts.

underwhelm. *He was … fluent in speech and crashingly dull. If there was an opportunity to be underwhelming, he unfailingly seized it—Observer*, 1984. This fanciful variation on *overwhelming* means 'unimpressive' (*underwhelmed* and occasionally the simple verb *underwhelm* are also used); it dates from the 1950s but seems much more recent. The tone is generally jokey and this should be remembered in more formal contexts.

undeservedly is pronounced as five syllables.

undoubtedly *see* DOUBTLESS, NO DOUBT, UNDOUBTEDLY, DOUBTLESSLY.

uneatable *see* INEDIBLE, UNEATABLE.

uneconomic, uneconomical. These two words correspond to the meanings of the positive forms *economic* and *economical*. *Uneconomic* means 'not economic, not capable of being operated profitably', whereas *uneconomical* means 'not economical, wasteful'.

unequal. In its meaning 'inadequate in ability or resources', *unequal* is used with *to* followed by a noun or verbal noun (*They were unequal to the task / They were unequal to completing the task*).

unequalled is spelt in this way in BrE and usually *unequaled* in AmE.

unexceptionable, unexceptional. These two words are the precise opposites of their positive forms *exceptionable* and *exceptional*. *Unexceptionable* means 'with which no fault can be found, entirely satisfactory' (*The idea is unexceptionable, indeed worthy of applause*), whereas *unexceptional* means 'not out of the ordinary, run-of-the-mill' (*The food was unexceptional plain pub fare*). *Unexceptionable* is much more common than its positive form *exceptionable*.

unfollow means 'to stop tracking (a person, group, or organization) on a social media website or application' e.g. *never unfollow someone just because they unfollowed you!*

unfriend as a transitive verb, meaning 'to remove (someone) from a list of friends or contacts on a social networking website' is, of course, a thoroughly modern meaning first noted from 2003. However, the verb itself is of venerable antiquity, being first recorded in a letter written by the 17c cleric and writer Thomas Fuller: *I Hope, Sir, that we are not mutually Un-friended by this Difference which hath happened betwixt us.* Fuller would doubtless have been perplexed by the transient, trivial nature of 'friendships' that can be terminated with a keystroke: *I wrote 'your' instead of 'you're' on a post and she corrected that so I unfriended her—Sunday Times*, 2012. The alternative *defriend* is also used, but less frequently.

uninterest *see* DISINTEREST.

uninterested *see* DISINTERESTED.

unique. 1 This is one of a handful of words that give rise to strong feelings. Its primary meaning is 'having no like or equal, peculiar to an individual': *Throughout these fluctuations of fortune, Edith's unique teaching style was getting more finely honed—Medau News*, 1986. In this meaning it is regarded (like *perfect*) as absolute in sense, i.e. something or someone is either unique or not unique; they cannot be described as *very* unique or *more* unique or *rather* unique. (On the other hand, it is possible to be *nearly* or *almost* or *perhaps* unique just as it is to be *nearly* or *almost* or *perhaps* perfect.) This objection is philosophical rather than linguistic, and grammar caters for the logically impossible as readily as it does for the patently true. And is it not at least arguable that a person with three heads is *more* unique than a person with only two? Or than a person with twelve fingers?

2 The word is derived via French from the Latin word *unicus* meaning 'single, sole' and retained close links with its roots down to the 19c, when it broke loose and became conceptually an English word, marking its independence with a developed meaning that is now the controversial one, i.e 'unusual, remarkable'. This sense is regarded as 'gradable' and is regularly qualified by *very* and other intensifying adverbs: *Some design choices become so unique that they border on the eccentric and make a property difficult to sell—Chicago Tribune*, 1995 / *I imagine that would be a fairly unique experience for you—*film review website, BrE 2004.

3 Its adoption in unconvincing contexts by the world of advertising and marketing, which offers *unique advantages, challenges, features, flavours, insights, opportunities*, and so on, and spins meaningless slogans such as *Hollywood's unique night life* and *a unique blend of Scottish heather honey and rare old malt whisky*, has done much to discredit this meaning, which is a natural one. Indeed, as so often with this type of sense development, meanings that are conventionally distinguished often shade into one another, and it is difficult to apply rules in the border areas of usage: *All these diverse atmospheres merge together beautifully to create a most delightful and unique East Lindsey*

*market town—*P. Furlong, 1989 / *Gavrilov was the outright winner of Moscow's Tchaikovsky Competition where jury and audience alike were bowled over by his flame-throwing technique, by the unique drive and physicality of his playing—Gramophone*, 1992.

4 Meanwhile *unique* continues to be used in its primary meaning, often followed by the preposition *to* which identifies the object of uniqueness; an achievement or feat can be unique, so can an identifying number (which often has to be), and so can a method or technique: *Tuck stitch is one of those fabrics that almost all machine knitters recognise at once, it is so unique in its formation—Machine Knitting Monthly*, 1992 / *Few dishes are unique to Jordan; one unique dish is mansaf, chunks of stewed lamb in a yogurt-based sauce served with rice—World Cultures*, AmE 2004 [*OEC*].

5 Because *unique* is itself 'unique' in its primary meaning this will continue to be used, and it is more common than the strength of opposition to the weakened meaning might lead us to believe. But precise meanings are always vulnerable to drift, and in this case we are seeing a weakening of strength (as has happened to analogous words such as *peculiar* and *similar*), rather than the emergence of a distinct new meaning. If a rule is needed, prudence suggests that the weakened meaning should be used sparingly, and that it is best to avoid modifying the word with intensifiers such as *very, extremely*, and so forth.

United Kingdom *see* BRITAIN, GREAT BRITAIN, THE BRITISH ISLES, ENGLAND, ETC.

unlawful *see* ILLEGAL, ILLEGITIMATE, ILLICIT, UNLAWFUL.

unless and until is an established expression which, like *as and when*, serves to intensify doubt about the outcome. It occurs in alternative forms such as *unless or until, until or unless,* and so on: *Until and unless he discovered who he was, everything was without meaning*—D. Potter, 1986 / *Membership of the House of Commons is still the only legitimate qualification for real power in Great Britain and likely to remain so unless or until our national identity is totally submerged in Europe*—Spectator, 1991.

unlike is an adjective (*animals as unlike as the bear and the lion*), and a preposition meaning 'dissimilar to' (*a journey unlike any other*). Informally it is used as a quasi-adverb in constructions involving a following preposition: *Unlike with fax messages you can edit and re-use the text of e-mails once they arrive on your computer*—Times, 1998. In more formal contexts, combinations such as this can usually be replaced by alternatives such as *in contrast to* or *as distinct from*, or *unlike* without *with*. The form *unalike*, in the same way as *alike*, is an adjective only and is always used predicatively, i.e. with a linking verb (*realized how unalike we were*).

unparalleled is spelt in this way in BrE and AmE.

unpractical means 'not practical', whereas *impractical* has a wider range of meaning: *see* IMPRACTICABLE, IMPRACTICAL.

unprecedented is pronounced with its second syllable -pres- not -prees-.

unpronounceable is spelt -nceable, to keep the soft sound of the letter *c* in *pronounce*; the same applies to *pronounceable*.

unravel has inflected forms *unravelled, unravelling* in BrE and usually *unraveled, unraveling* in AmE. In current English it is likely to have a figurative meaning, either (1) 'to solve (a mystery or puzzle)' or (2) in intransitive use, 'to fail or collapse', the image being of a scheme or enterprise that begins to come apart in the manner of a piece of woollen clothing: *No other army could have done better. If it all unravels it won't be their fault*—Mirror, 2007.

unreadable *see* ILLEGIBLE, UNREADABLE.

unrepairable *see* IRREPARABLE, IRREPAIRABLE.

unreservedly is pronounced as five syllables.

unrivalled is spelt with two *l*s in BrE and usually as *unrivaled* in AmE.

unsanitary *see* INSANITARY, UNSANITARY.

unseasonable, unseasonal. The difference in meaning between **seasonable, seasonal* does not apply to these two words. Both are used to describe circumstances (especially weather conditions) that are not appropriate to the season in which they occur: *Younger people, because of the unseasonal heat, were wearing sweaters tied round the hips*—James Kirkup, 1991 / *The weather looked heavy and thundery, as if the unseasonable warmth would soon break*—K. McCallum, 1993. *Unseasonable* occasionally means 'not opportune, untimely' more generally: *According to BBC News, 'North Korea's unseasonable gift to the world was to unleash a new nuclear crisis'*—Spiked Online, BrE 2004 [OEC].

unsociable, unsocial. Like the positive forms (*see* SOCIABLE, SOCIAL), *unsocial* is a classifying word that essentially means 'not suitable for society' (and in BrE has the special meaning denoting hours outside the normal working day), whereas *unsociable* is a more judgemental word referring to people (primarily) who dislike the company of others, although it too is used to refer to hours outside the normal working day.

u

To complete the picture, *antisocial* is sometimes used in the same way as *unsociable*, but properly means 'contrary to or harmful to the social order' (with reference to people and activities) and is therefore a much stronger word with more sinister implications.

unsolvable *see* INSOLUBLE, UNSOLVABLE.

unstable is the standard negative form of *stable*, but the corresponding noun is *instability*, not *un-*. *See* IN- AND UN-.

unthinkable is still used in its original meaning 'unable to be imagined or grasped in the mind': *You wander . . . in cool glades of unthinkable beauty*—*Westminster Gazette*, 1897. But far more common now is the extended and more evaluative meaning 'too unlikely or absurd to be considered', comparable to similar shifts that have occurred with *unimaginable* and *inconceivable*: *In these circumstances the removal of British troops was unthinkable*—C. Allen, 1990 / *What is known about the clergyman's honesty and integrity would have made such an act unthinkable*—*Contemporary Review*, 2003. Despite Fowler's objections to this use in a lengthy and ultimately futile tirade (1926), it is a natural development that retains the essence of the original meaning and applies it in a more realistic way, since nothing that is postulated can be literally 'unthinkable'. Fowler knew this and saw in it the word's appeal, but common usage has taken a more practical course. To *think the unthinkable* means to consider ideas or possibilities usually regarded as too disturbing or undesirable to be contemplated. It originated in the 1960s as the title of a book (*Thinking about the Unthinkable*) by Herman Kahn about the prospect of a nuclear war.

until, till. 1 *Till* is not a shortened form of *until* but is the older word; the *un-* of *until* adds the element 'up to, as far as'. The two words can both be used as prepositions (e.g. *until/till tomorrow*) or conjunctions (e.g. *until/till we reach home*). They are largely interchangeable, except that *until* is more usual at the beginning of a sentence and can sound somewhat more formal, especially in speech: *He didn't ask any more questions but he kept himself awake till Noreen came home*—Ann Pilling, 1987 / *Until he got Jackson's note he had been convinced that the man was suffering from some sort of regular illness*—C. Horrie et al., 1988 / *They say they don't trust him, until he looks them in the eye*—*Scotland on Sunday*, 2004.

2 *Up until* and *up till* are needless variants in which the word *up* is usually redundant and (especially with *until*) awkward: *The fast-growing food-supplement market, in particular that for vitamins, which up till now* [read: *till now* or *up to now*] *has largely remained in the hands of smaller companies*—*Ecologist*, 2001 / *My dad had a stammer up until he was 18* [read: *until he was 18* or *up to the age of 18*]—*London Review of Books*, 2003.

3 *See also* UNLESS AND UNTIL.

4 *Until such time as* can be effective in emphasizing uncertainty about an outcome, but it should not be made to serve as a more verbose alternative to the simple word *until*: *Such noisy groups of youngsters . . . need to be broken down into smaller groups each controlled by a responsible competent leader or instructor until such time as they become mature canoeists*—*Canoeist*, 1991.

unto is generally archaic as an alternative for *to*, and in current use it is normally restricted to fixed expressions such as *do unto others* and *faithful unto death*.

untouchable. In meanings relating to the traditional Hindu caste system, the noun *untouchable* and the social restrictions accompanying it were declared illegal in the constitution of India in 1949 and of Pakistan in 1953. The official term for 'untouchables' today is *the Scheduled Castes*. The word is, however, often used metaphorically, e.g. *You will also be attacked ad hominem. The aim will be to make you a leper, an untouchable—Butterflies and Wheels*, 2004.

up. As well as its familiar uses as an adverb and preposition denoting a high place or position (*jump up in the air / walk up the hill*), *up* has an extraordinarily prolific existence in a role that can go unnoticed: as a particle forming a host of phrasal verbs such as *come up, eat up, get up, look up, sit up, start up, take up*, etc. In some of these, *up* is merely an intensifier that does not affect the basic meaning of the verb it is attached to: there is little difference in reality between *eating* your greens and *eating up* your greens except that the second is more positive. In other cases, the presence of *up* determines or affects the meaning in important ways: something *comes up* when it happens or occurs but the ordinary senses of *come* have no such connection; you can only *look at* something (i.e. *look* is intransitive) but you can *look* something *up* (i.e. *look* is transitive); and *sitting up* is almost but not quite the opposite action to *sitting down*. Most of these uses are based on native English words, and many of them have Latinate equivalents that sound more formal and often less idiomatic (*arise* or *occur* for *come up, consult* or *refer to* for *look up, initiate* or *inaugurate* for *start up, accept* or *assume* for *take up*, etc.). These uses of *up* cause amusement or amazement when people stop to think about them, but they lie at the heart of idiom and help define the Englishness of English. We should not be afraid to use them.

up, down. In geographical terms, *down* means south and *up* means north, and so you go *up* to Scotland from London and *down* to Atlanta (Georgia) from Chicago. A conventional exception to this straightforward logic occurs with capital or major cities; for example it used to be customary to speak of going *up* to London from whatever direction. In the context of railways, the *up* line (or *up* train) is the one that goes into London, and the *down* line (or *down* train) is the one that goes out of London. This rule is not, however, absolute, and has changed over time; from York, Manchester, Newcastle, for example, and all other places in the north of England it is more usual to talk of going (or driving or flying) *down* to London than *up* to it because distance makes the geographical orientation again the primary consideration.

upcoming, as an alternative to *forthcoming*, is recorded in AmE from the 1950s and is now quite widespread in British, especially journalistic, usage, although *forthcoming* is still much more frequent in *OEC* data: *He told last week of the spectator who telephoned Selhurst Park to enquire about Wimbledon's upcoming game—Spectator*, 1996.

upgradeable, 'capable of being upgraded or improved', is spelt preferably with an *e* in the middle, but the alternative spelling without is also correct. The related noun is *upgrad(e)ability*.

upmarket, upscale. the originally BrE adjective and adverb *upmarket* to describe the superior end of the market is used throughout the English-speaking world, but rather infrequently in AmE, where the synonyms *high-end* and *upscale* are preferred. In BrE too, *high-end* is used nearly as often as *upmarket*, while *upscale* has made only limited inroads, mainly in journalism. Presumably *upmarket* is now felt to be too **downmarket* a word.

u

upmost *see* UTMOST, UTTERMOST.

upon tends to sound more formal and emphatic than *on* when the two are used interchangeably: to look *upon* someone as a friend is a somewhat more imposing proposition than to look *on* them as a friend. *Upon* is the only choice in certain fixed expressions, such as *once upon a time* and *upon my word,* and in uses such as *row upon row of seats* and *the holiday season is nearly upon us.*

upstairs, upstair. *Upstairs* is the normal form for both the adjective (*the upstairs rooms*) and the adverb (*go upstairs*). *Upstair* (formerly used occasionally as an adjective) is now virtually obsolete.

up to *see* DOWN TO, UP TO.

upward, upwards. 1 The only form for the adjective is *upward* (*in an upward direction*), but *upward* and *upwards* are both used for the adverb, with a preference for *upwards* in BrE: *The launcher consists of a small nozzle that directs a jet of water upward at an angle of approximately 45 degrees*—Scientific American, 1973 / *James had rounded off sums downwards rather than upwards*—writing £900 for an actual £975 for example—K. M. E. Murray, 1977.

2 *Upwards of* (or occasionally *upward of*) is first recorded in the early 18c in the meaning 'rather more than' and remains in standard use: *British Gas boiler installations cost upwards of £2,000, but you can get them much cheaper elsewhere*—Sunday Times, 2007.

3 The adverb *upwardly* occurs mainly in the expression *upwardly mobile,* meaning 'aspiring to social and professional advancement'.

us. 1 *Us* is used informally to mean 'me' in invitations such as *Give us a kiss* and *Let's have a look.*

2 *Us* should not be used as the subject of a clause in standard English, although it is so used in informal English, e.g. *Us country boys should stick together,* which in standard English would read *We country boys* . . .

-us. For plural forms of Latin nouns ending in -*us* that have been adopted into English (e.g. *focus, nucleus*) *see* LATIN PLURALS.

usable, useable can be spelt with or without an *e* in the middle, but the spelling without *e* is very much more frequent.

use. 1 The transitive verb meaning 'to make use of' is pronounced yooz and the past form is *used* (yoozd). The corresponding noun *use* is pronounced yoos.

2 *Used* is pronounced yoost and followed by *to* in a number of special constructions:

a *Be* or *become* or *get used to* + noun or verbal noun means 'be (etc.) accustomed to or familiar with': *She had got used to the sissy . . . thin-blooded climate of Auckland*—D. M. Davin, 1986 / *He still isn't used to her being old enough to drive*—New Yorker, 1987 / *He . . . became used to collectors visiting the family home in the early 1950s to record his mother's folk songs*—Independent, 2007.

b *Used to* (or *had used to*) + infinitive refers to what happened or existed in the past but no longer does at the time of speaking or writing: *She had used to squat with old Mataka on the ground*—Muriel Spark, 1969 / *I know what you're thinking, Patrick, and I used to think it too*—Kingsley Amis, 1988. In affirmative statements of this kind *use to* is often wrongly written, e.g. rephrasing the last example, ☒ *and I use to think it too.*

c Difficulties can also arise with negatives and questions. There are two options. (1) The first and more usual one is to treat *used* like any ordinary verb, namely one that has *did* as an auxiliary: *What time did she use to return?*—L. Thomas, 1972 / *I didn't use to curse or swear at them*—M. Brogden, 1991. Note that the final *-d* of *used* is dropped in these cases (in the same way that *I liked* / *I wanted*, etc., become *I didn't like* / *want*, etc.). It is therefore grammatically wrong to write *used* in sentences such as ✖ *I didn't used to eat bananas.* (2) The second option with negatives and questions is to treat *used to* in the same way as *dare* and *need*, technically as a 'semi-modal' verb. This is markedly more formal or literary than using *do*. For negatives, *not* directly follows *used* used as a separate word, or is shortened and joined to it: *I used not to dream*—Nina Bawden, 1987 / *She used not to be so censorious of others' behaviour*—T. Barnes, 1991 / *You usen't to be like that*—A. Christie, 1964. In questions, inversion of subject and verb takes place: *Used she to come here?* This would now sound very formal in speech, and is unusual even in writing.

utilize. This 19c loanword has led a precarious life for a century and a half beside the much older word *use* (13c). In many contexts *use* is adequate and preferable, but a case can be made out for *utilize* when the emphasis is on practicality and effective exploitation: *Fewer victims meant fewer death sentences and so executioners in the provinces retired and, utilizing their professionally acquired anatomical skills, became surgeons' assistants or animal doctors*—G. Abbott, 1991.

utmost, uttermost. Both are used to mean 'most extreme, greatest', e.g. of the *ut(ter)most importance*, but *utmost* is much more commonly used in this meaning. *Upmost* is a somewhat rare adjective and a variant of *uppermost*. It refers to the position of something, as in *the upmost layer.* Through a process of *folk etymology it is sometimes incorrectly used instead of *utmost*: e.g. ✖ *with the upmost care*, instead of *with the utmost care* / ✖ *to do your upmost,* instead of *to do your utmost.*

u

vacation is in North America the ordinary word for BrE *holiday*. In Britain it is only used in the context of universities and the law courts. The corresponding word for Parliament is *recess*.

vacuum has the plural form *vacuums* in general use, but *vacua* is sometimes used in scientific contexts.

vade-mecum, meaning 'a handbook or guidebook' (from modern Latin meaning 'go with me'), is pronounced **vah**-di **may**-kuhm and has the plural form *vade-mecums*.

vagary, meaning 'an eccentric idea or action', is pronounced **vay**-guh-ri.

vainness is spelt with two *n*s.

valance, valence, valency. A *valance*, pronounced **val**-uhns, is a short curtain round the edge of a canopy or bed. *Valence* and *valency* (both pronounced **vayl**-, the first more common in AmE and the second in BrE) are terms in chemistry relating to the power of atoms.

valet. The noun is pronounced **val**-ay or **val**-it in BrE, and also vuh-**lay**, with second-syllable stress, in AmE. The verb meaning 'to clean the inside of (a motor vehicle)' has inflected forms *valeted, valeting*, pronounced **val**-ayd and **val**-ay-ing in BrE, vuh-**layd** and vuh-**lay**-ing in AmE.

valley has the plural form *valleys*.

valour is spelt *-our* in BrE and as *valor* in AmE. The corresponding adjective is spelt *valorous* in both varieties.

vapour is spelt *-our* in BrE and *vapor* in AmE. Derivatives such as *vapourless* and *vapourish* follow the spellings of the root forms, but *vaporous* (adjective) *vaporize* (verb), and *vaporizer* (noun) are spelt *-or-* in both BrE and AmE.

variance. The phrase *at variance* should be followed by *with*, not *from*: *The pace at which strategy was being implemented was at variance with the quick decision-making this business requires—Guardian*, 2006.

variant. In language, a variant is a legitimate form or spelling of a word that differs from the main one. For example, *judgment* is a variant of *judgement*.

variegated, meaning 'marked by irregular patches of colour', is pronounced **vair**-i-gay-tid as four syllables in BrE but in AmE more often as five syllables (with the middle *e* articulated).

various, like *many* and *several*, is used as a pronoun (followed by *of*) in both BrE and (more commonly) in AmE: *Various of his colleagues . . . offer to go with him if he is dismissed—American Spectator*, 1994 / *Various of his essays and lectures have been published—*Margaret Drabble, 2000. Although disapproved of by some language purists, this usage is well established.

vase. The standard pronunciation in BrE is vahz, and in AmE vays or vayz.

've. This contraction of the verb *have* is normally added to pronouns or to modal verbs such as *might* and *would*: *I've had my eye on both of you*—D. Raymond, 1985 / *You would've thought at least she could've cut the bubbles off*—Margaret Foster, 1986. Double or multiple contraction is a feature of some writing that seeks to reproduce conversational language: *Can't've been a nightmare then, can it?*—Pat Barker, 1991.

velvet has derivative forms *velveted*, *velvety*.

venal, venial. These two unrelated words are sometimes confused, chiefly because they are close in form but perhaps also because their meanings both have to do with forms of transgression. *Venal* means 'able to be bribed, corrupt' (from Latin *venum* 'thing for sale') and is used of people and their actions; *venial* means 'pardonable' (from Latin *venia* 'pardon') and refers in Roman Catholic teaching to minor or pardonable sins as distinct from mortal sins which bring eternal damnation.

vendor, vender. The usual spelling for this formal and legal word meaning 'seller' is *vendor*. In AmE, *vender* is also used.

venue is derived from a French word meaning 'a coming', which underlies all its English uses. It has several obsolete meanings to do with coming forward in attack (e.g. in fencing) and from the 16c referred to the place where a jury was appointed to come together for a law trial. Its primary modern sense relates to coming together more generally, denoting the place where a meeting, sports event, concert, or other organized occasion takes place. A miniature social history can be made to unfold from this interesting little word.

veranda is now the more common spelling than *verandah*, but both are correct.

verbal has four meanings, all close enough to cause possible confusion: (1) 'having the nature of a verb' (*verbal noun*), (2) involving words rather than actual things (*Opposition between these two modes of speaking is rather verbal than real*—B. Jowett, 1875), (3) consisting of words (*verbal wit*), and (4) involving speech as distinct from writing (*a verbal agreement*). The most likely confusion is between the third and fourth of these meanings, and it is often advisable to use *oral* instead of *verbal* to preclude any doubt when the intended meaning is the 'involving speech' one (as in *oral examination*), restricting *verbal* to a few fixed phrases such as *verbal agreement*, *verbal contract*, and *verbal evidence* in which the meaning is established. Note also that *oral* occurs in several fixed expressions, such as *oral tradition* (the transmission of ancient poetry and stories by word of mouth before they were written down).

verbal noun. 1 A verbal noun (also called a *gerund*) is a form of a verb ending in -*ing* that acts as a noun, for example *smoking* in the phrase *no **smoking*** and in the sentence ***Smoking** damages your health*. It should be distinguished from (identically formed) participial adjectives (*a **smoking** chimney*) and participles used to form continuous tenses (*The chimney is **smoking***).
  2 Because a verbal noun is a part of a verb as well as being a noun, it can retain some of the characteristics of verbs in its grammatical behaviour; for example the constructions *They do not like us smoking in the house* (non-possessive) and *They do not like our smoking in the house*

(possessive) are both established in ordinary usage, although the second, in which *smoking* is treated as a full noun, is often preferred in more formal writing. Fowler (1906, 1926) rejected the first type as 'grammatically indefensible', since the words defy grammatical analysis (an example he gave was *We need fear nothing from China* [change to *China's*] *developing her resources*), but the basis of his argument lay in Latin rather than English grammar and has rightly been questioned since (notably by the Danish linguist Otto Jespersen, 1860–1943). In current use, certain patterns are discernible:

a The possessive is the more normal choice when the word preceding the -*ing* form is a personal name or a noun denoting a person, but less so when the name is of an organization: *One cannot say that Kafka's marvelling at mundane accomplishments was not genuine*—London Review of Books, 1987 / *I was now counting on my father's being able to make some provision somehow*—Ved Mehta, 1987 / *There is no question of Gazprom cutting off supplies in Russia*—Independent, 2007.

b When the noun is non-personal, is part of a phrase, or is in the plural, the possessive is not normally used: *They turned a blind eye to toffee apples going missing*—Jeanette Winterson, 1985 / *Then we had our old conversation about the house being haunted*—C. Rumens, 1987 / *I'm not averse to others making good money or big profits*—Western Morning News, 2007.

c With personal pronouns, usage varies between the possessive and non-possessive, the possessive being more usual at the start of a sentence: *Fancy his minding that you went to the Summer Exhibition*—A. N. Wilson, 1978 / *His being so capable was the only pleasant thing about the whole dreadful day*—E.

Jolley, AusE 1985 / *There can be no question of you disturbing the clerks*—Peter Carey, AusE 1988 / *Their Aunt Martha had been remarkably circumspect on the subject of their leaving her house so soon after arriving*—fiction website, AmE 2005 [*OEC*].

d With indefinite pronouns the non-possessive form is more usual, and the possessive sounds less natural: *He didn't think for a time of anyone clawing at his back*—D. A. Richards, CanE 1981 / *There are many sound reasons, then, for everyone's wanting to join in this new Gold Rush*—Encounter, 1988 / *There is nothing wrong with everyone knowing your public key, but they should verify that it is yours*—Linux Journal, 2005 [*OEC*].

e To sum up, the possessive is on the retreat, but its use with proper names and personal pronouns and pronouns persists.

3 The *to*-infinitive also acts as a verbal noun (***To err** is human, **to forgive** divine*), and choice between this and an -*ing* form is largely a matter of idiom. For example, one *hopes to do* something but one *thinks of doing* something, has a *fondness for doing* something, and has *an aversion to doing* something. Care needs to be taken not to confuse these patterns, especially when more than one is used in the same sentence.

verbatim, meaning 'word for word', is pronounced ver-**bay**-tim.

verbs. 1 A verb is traditionally regarded as a word that describes the action or state which the sentence seeks to convey and is normally an essential element in a clause or sentence: *She **locked** the door / She **was** angry*. Verbs are either transitive (i.e. take an object, as in *She **locked** the door*) or intransitive (as in *She **smiled***); for a fuller description of these functions, *see* INTRANSITIVE AND TRANSITIVE VERBS.

2 Verbs are occasionally omitted from sentences, for example in radio and television announcements (*This report from our Washington correspondent*) or as stylistic devices, afterthoughts, ways of avoiding repetition, etc.: *Friday morning. By tube to a lecture at the London School of Economics—Encounter*, 1981 (in diary style) / *That way, they can work out their aggressions. Once a year—New Yorker*, 1987.

3 For other aspects of verbs and their behaviour, *see* AUXILIARY VERBS; MODAL VERBS; PHRASAL VERBS; REFLEXIVE VERBS; VERBS FROM NOUNS.

verbs ending in vowels and -ay etc. *See box overleaf.*

verbs from nouns. By a process called technically 'conversion', and informally 'verbing', verbs have for several centuries been formed from nouns (and occasionally adjectives), by using the same word (e.g. *to question, to knife, to quiz, to service, to access, to premiere,* and *to text* [= send a text message to, a modern revival of an obsolete verb]), by adding a suffix such as *-ize* (*to customize, to prioritize, to randomize*), or by back-formation in which the noun form is shortened (*to diagnose, to televise*). Although objections are raised to some of these formations (especially the longer ones in *-ize,* such as *hospitalize* and *privatize*), it is an established process and generally a useful one.

veritable featured prominently in English from the 15c to the 17c, and then fell out of use until it was revived as a Gallicism in the 19c with the intensive meaning 'deserving its name' (*a veritable feast*). In modern use it has a somewhat rhetorical or affected tone: *So tough, you'd like us all to think, but inside you're a veritable marshmallow—M. Yorke,* 1973 / *Despite its close proximity to the airport, it's a peaceful place and*

a veritable oasis away from city life—Bristol Evening Post, 2007.

vermin is normally treated as a plural in both its meanings ('mammals and birds that are harmful to other life' and 'vile or despicable people'), although it can refer to a single person or animal: *Suddenly the older of the two little girls said, 'Why is a squirrel called vermin, Dad?'—M. Bowring,* 1993. There is no plural form *vermins.*

vermouth, the drink, is normally pronounced with the stress on the first syllable in BrE, and with the stress on the second syllable (to rhyme with *tooth*) in AmE.

verse can mean (1) poetical composition in general (*She writes verse as well as prose*), (2) a line of poetry, (3) a section of a poem also called a *stanza*, and (4) each of the short numbered divisions of a chapter in the Bible.

verso, meaning 'the left-hand page of a book', has the plural form *versos.* The right-hand page is called the *recto.*

vertebra means 'a segment of the backbone'; in the plural *vertebrae* (pronounced **ver**-ti-bray or -bree) it refers to the backbone as a whole.

vertex, meaning 'the highest point', most often has the plural form *vertices* (pronounced **ver**-ti-seez) and very occasionally *vertexes.*

very, much. 1 The uses of *very* and *much* as intensifying adverbs are for the most part complementary. *Very* qualifies adjectives and adverbs (*very large / very slowly*), whereas *much* qualifies past participles that are used as adjectives (*a much enlarged edition / They were much criticized*). There is a grey area including words that are strictly speaking past participles but have come to be treated

VERBS ENDING IN VOWELS AND -AY ETC.

The following table lists routine inflections of representative verbs having certain awkward vowel endings in their base forms, and shows any exceptions:

verbs in -ay

allay	allays	allayed	allaying	
play	plays	played	playing	playable
exceptions				
lay	lays	laid	laying	layable
pay	pays	paid	paying	payable
say	says	said	saying	sayable

verbs in -ey

convey	conveys	conveyed	conveying	conveyable

verbs in -i

ski	skis	skied	skiing
taxi	taxis	taxied	taxiing

verbs in -ie

die	dies	died	dying

verbs in -o

veto	vetoes	vetoed	vetoing
video	videoes	videoed	videoing

verbs in -oy

enjoy	enjoys	enjoyed	enjoying	enjoyable
cloy	cloys	cloyed	cloying	

verbs in -uy

buy	buys	bought	buying	buyable
guy	guys	guyed	guying	

verbs in -y after a consonant

copy	copies	copied	copying	copiable
deny	denies	denied	denying	deniable
specify	specifies	specified	specifying	specifiable
try	tries	tried	trying	triable

verbs in -ye

dye	dyes	dyed	dyeing*	dyable

to avoid confusion with **dying** *from* **die**.

as full adjectives, notably words of feeling such as *annoyed, pleased, tired, worried*, etc., and words with a strong adjectival element such as *sheltered* (*a very sheltered upbringing*) and *involved* (*He is very involved in charitable work*). These are now more naturally qualified by *very* than by *much*. When the verb element is uppermost, *much* is preferred; we would for example speak of a *much honoured* dignitary rather than a *very honoured* one, and we would say that reforms are *much needed* rather than *very needed*. At the heart of this grey area lie words such as *respected*, in which the adjective and verb emphasis is infinitely variable: if we say *a much respected politician* we stress the process, whereas if we say *a very respected politician* we assess the effect.

2 It is worth adding that *much* can itself be qualified by *very*; consequently any of the words we have been reviewing that can be intensified by *much* can be more strongly intensified by *very much* (e.g. *very much criticized / very much enlarged*).

3 Some types of participial adjective are conventionally qualified by intensifying words other than *much* and *very*, e.g. *injured* (and similar words such as *burnt, scarred*, etc.) is qualified by *badly* or *seriously, bungled* by *badly* or *severely*, and *outnumbered, outvoted*, etc., by *heavily*.

4 In a recent development, *very* is used to qualify nouns that have assumed the role of adjectives: for example, a song might be called *very sixties* (characteristic of the 1960s), and a building might be called *very art deco* (built in that style).

-ves. For plurals such as *calves, see* -FS, -VES.

vest. In BrE, a *vest* is an undergarment for the top part of the body and also a garment worn by athletes. In AmE the first of these is called an *undershirt*, and *vest* is a term for what in BrE is a man's *waistcoat* and also for a short sleeveless jacket worn by women.

vet is a standard shortening of *veterinary surgeon* and the normal word in BrE. In AmE *vet* and *veterinarian* are used in this sense, and *vet* also means 'a veteran'. The verb, meaning (1) to treat (a sick animal) and (2) to examine or check critically, has inflected forms *vetted, vetting*.

veto. The noun has the plural form *vetoes*, and the verb has inflected forms *vetoes, vetoed, vetoing*.

via, meaning 'by way of' (*Paris to Athens via Venice*) is originally the ablative of Latin *via* meaning 'way, road', and is now fully naturalized in English. It is increasingly used to indicate a form of transport or a mode of transmission rather than the route, in place of the more obvious preposition *by* (*via airmail / via satellite / via email / the Internet/Twitter*, etc.).

viable is a 19c loanword from French, and was first used to describe a fetus or newborn child that was capable of maintaining life. Metaphorical uses developed in the 19c, but it was not until the 1940s that it became a vogue word applied to a whole range of ideas, plans, propositions, etc., regarded in terms of their practicability. Sometimes the metaphor is justified, but often alternatives such as *feasible, practicable, sustainable, tenable, valid, workable* will do just as well.

vibrator is spelt *-or*, not *-er*.

vice, a formal term meaning 'in place of' (*appointed Secretary vice Mr Jones deceased*), is pronounced **viy**-si and is originally a form of a Latin word meaning 'in place of, in the stead of'. It is the same word used as a combining form in *vice chancellor, vice president*, etc.

V

vicegerent. A *vicegerent* (pronounced viys-**jer**-uhnt) is a person appointed to carry out the office of another, for example the Pope regarded as God's representative on earth.

vice versa, meaning 'the other way round', is more correctly pronounced **viy**-si **ver**-suh, but the first word is also pronounced as a single syllable viys. It is derived from a Latin phrase meaning 'the position being reversed', and is fully naturalized in English.

victuals, pronounced **vit**-uhlz, is a rather old-fashioned or regional (plural) noun meaning 'food or provisions', and like all such words is sometimes used in humorous or affected contexts.

vie, meaning 'to compete for superiority', has inflected forms *vies, vied, vying*.

view is used in two common idioms, *in view of* and *with a view to*. *In view of* is used as an equivalent of *because of* or *considering* followed by a noun (or verbal noun) to introduce a known or expected circumstance: *He was especially anxious to court the Kremlin in view of the rapid cooling of the U.S.'s interest in Ethiopia*—Time, 1977. *With a view to* is a more formal expression, is usually followed by a verbal noun, and means 'in order to achieve': *We should pledge to hold a referendum to seek a mandate for fundamental renegotiation of our position in Europe, with a view to recreating a European partnership of sovereign nations*—Daily Telegraph, 2007. In ordinary language a construction with *in order to* (+ infinitive) is often preferable.

viewpoint *see* POINT OF VIEW.

vigour is spelt *-our* in BrE and *vigor* in AmE. The adjective *vigorous* is spelt *-or-* in both varieties.

villain, villein. The two spellings are forms of a single word with two branches, originally meaning either 'a low-born rustic' or 'a serf in the feudal system' and derived from the Latin word *villa* meaning 'country house or farm'. The spelling *villain* was associated from the 17c with the worsened meaning 'an unprincipled scoundrel', while the other form *villein* slipped into historical use as the feudal system was replaced by capitalism. The distinction is preserved in current usage.

viola. The musical instrument is pronounced vi-**oh**-luh, and the flower **viy**-uh-luh. The plural form in both cases is *violas*.

violable, not *violatable*, is the derivative form of *violate*.

violoncello is the correct spelling, not *violin-*. It is an Italian word, a diminutive of *violone* which is a double-bass viol. The plural form is *violoncellos*. Normally, however, the shortened form *cello* is used.

virago, meaning 'a fierce or abusive woman', is pronounced vi-**rah**-goh and has the plural form *viragos* or *viragoes*.

viral. *Viral marketing* is a term describing marketing that relies on the rapid spread of information amongst customers and potential customers by word of mouth, email, social media, etc. If something, not necessarily commercial, *goes viral*, it is massively copied and forwarded on the Internet especially in social media. Examples: *Many of the new games are viral, meaning that they permit players to spread the games by e-mail to friends*—New York Times, 2001 / *Their petition also went viral, gathering half a million signatures in a few weeks*—A. Boyd, 2004.

virement, meaning 'a process of transferring public funds from one account to another', was taken from French in the early 20c. An anglicized pronunciation with the first syllable as in *fire* is now usual.

Virgil is the preferred spelling of the name of the Roman poet, not *Vergil* (despite the Latin form *Publius Vergilius Maro*).

virile is pronounced **vi**-riyl in BrE, and also **vi**-ruhl in AmE.

virtual, used in English since the 14c, has taken on a brand new meaning in the computer age which is now its most frequent one. Beginning in the late 1950s with the sense 'not physically existing but made by software to appear to do so', as in *virtual memory*, this use then extended to computerized simulations of something, particularly in *virtual reality*, 'a computer-generated simulation of a lifelike environment that can be interacted with in a seemingly real or physical way'. That sense also applies to things such as *virtual images* and *virtual world*. In a further expansion of meaning, *virtual* also denotes activities carried out, or data accessed or stored, by means of a computer, especially over a network, instead of by more traditional methods, such as *virtual business / community / tour / learning / library*. Examples: *Internet connectivity promises to reduce knowledge workers to independent telecommuters, interacting in a virtual corporate environment*—Business Economics, 2000 / *The idea is to scale this up and bind virtual corporations that coalesce very quickly in internet time for a project*—Bombay Times, 2000 / *Writing open-source code that becomes widely used and accepted serves as a virtual business card*—First Monday Journal, 2000.

virtuoso, an Italian loanword meaning 'a person highly skilled in musical technique', more often has the anglicized

plural *virtuosos*, although the Italianate *virtuosi*, pronounced -si or -zi, is also used.

virus has the plural form *viruses*. In computing, a virus is a self-replicating program that harms other systems. It is malicious in intention, unlike a *bug*, which is an unintentional flaw in a program.

visage, a literary word meaning 'face, countenance', is pronounced **viz**-ij.

vis-à-vis (also printed without the accent) is pronounced vee-zah-**vee** and is now mostly used as a preposition meaning 'in relation to': *The state has a duty to protect its citizens from external enemies, and this can best be achieved by maximizing its power vis-a-vis other states*—P. Gill et al., 1984

viscount is a British nobleman ranking between an earl and a baron. The rank is called a *viscountcy*.

visible, visual. *Visible* means 'able to be seen', whereas *visual* is a classifying adjective denoting anything to do with sight or vision. The *visual arts* are those forms of art that are appreciated by the eye, and a *visual display unit* (*VDU*) is a computer screen.

vision. '*How do you find Weedin?*' '*Totally,*' Dougal said, '*lacking in vision. It is his fatal flaw. Otherwise quite sane.*'— Muriel Spark, 1960. This meaning, 'statesmanlike foresight', grew out of a much older set of meanings to do with intellectual perception as a metaphor based on physical seeing. Fowler dubbed it a 'vogue word', a status that to some extent it still has.

visit. To *visit with* someone, i.e. pay them a brief call, is now regarded as an Americanism although it was current in Britain in the 19c, occurring for example

V

in writings of Ruskin and George Eliot (*Middlemarch*, 1872).

visitation, once a formal word for *visit*, is now largely confined to special meanings such as official visits of inspection and an affliction attributed to some supernatural agency or other. In AmE *visitation* also refers to the right granted by a court to a divorced parent to visit a child that is in the custody of the other parent. It should not be used as a simple synonym for *visit*.

visitor is spelt *-or*, not *-er*.

visor is the preferred spelling for the various kinds of covering for the face, not *vizor*.

vitamin is pronounced **vit**-uh-min in BrE and **viy**-tuh-min in AmE and in some other parts of the English-speaking world.

viva voce, meaning 'an oral examination', is pronounced **viy**-vuh **voh**-chi. It is usually shortened to *viva* (plural *vivas*) and this is also used as a verb (with inflected forms *vivaes, vivaed, vivaing*).

viz. is a shortened form of *videlicet*, a Middle English word based on Latin words meaning 'it is permissible to see'; the final *z* is explained as a medieval symbol standing for the ending *-et*. The abbreviation is used to mean 'namely' in introducing a specific mention of what has been only vaguely or indirectly referred to (*my only means of income, viz. my fiddle*), and is often articulated as 'namely', although informally the more direct pronunciation viz is also used. Note that it differs from *i.e.* (= *id est*) in identifying rather than explaining.

vocal chords, vocal cords *see* CHORD, CORD.

vogue words. In its meaning 'popular use or currency', *vogue* dates from the 17c, but the expression *vogue word* (or *term*) did not come into general use until the 20c. Fowler, who was one of the first to use the term, defined it as a word that 'emerges from obscurity . . . into sudden popularity'; he was generally open-minded about their usefulness, and it has been later critics who have tended to pour scorn on the practice of words coming into and going out of fashion. Some vogue uses arise because they are associated with events of particular public interest (such as *yomping* = marching over heavy terrain, used by Royal Marines in the Falklands war of 1982, and hardly used since). Others fall in the category of 'popularized technicalities' (such as *chain reaction, parameter,* and *persona*). When Fowler wrote (1926), the vogue words to which he drew attention included *acid test, asset, distinctly* (as in *distinctly colder*), *far-flung* (which he liked, in the right place), *frock* (= woman's dress), *intensive, mentality, unthinkable,* and *vision* (= political foresight). Gowers, writing in 1965, retained *acid test* and *unthinkable* (!) and added, among others, *coexistence, overtones, psychological moment,* and *target.* More recent vogue uses include *crafted* (instead of *produced* or *performed,* in non-physical contexts), *designer* (as in *designer clothes*), *icon* and *iconic, interface, meaningful, must-see* (or *-have* etc., of consumer products), *off-message* (not following a party line), *ongoing, paradigm, parameter, resonate, spin doctor, syndrome,* and *unravel. See also* POPULARIZED TECHNICALITIES. The term *buzzword,* meaning much the same as *vogue word,* is first recorded in the 1940s in America.

voicemail, an electronic system of storing messages from telephone callers, has achieved such rapid familiarity that it is normally spelt as one word.

volcano has the plural form *volcanoes*.

volley. The noun has the plural form *volleys*, and the verb has inflected forms *volleys, volleyed, volleying*.

volte-face, meaning 'a sudden change of opinion or reversal of policy', is pronounced volt-**fays** or -**fahs** and is printed in roman type as an anglicized word.

voluntarily is traditionally pronounced in BrE with the stress on the first syllable, but the awkwardness of this pattern has led, under American influence, to the stress being placed often on the third syllable (-*ar*-).

vomit. The verb has inflected forms *vomited, vomiting*.

vortex has the plural form *vortexes* in general use, but *vortices* (pronounced **vaw**-ti-seez) in technical contexts.

wage, wages. *Wages* is normally used in the plural (*Their wages are still too low*); an older singular construction survives only in the biblical line *For the wages of sinne is death* (Romans 6:23). But *wage* is also used (*What sort of wage are you paid?*), and is the obligatory form in certain fixed expressions (*wage-earner, minimum wage*).

wagon, waggon. The form with one g is recommended, although the house style of some printing houses in Britain is the *-gg-* form.

wainscot, meaning 'panelling on the lower part of a wall near the floor', has derivative forms *wainscoted, wainscoting* (one *t* in each).

wait see AWAIT, WAIT.

waitress, waitperson. *Waitress*, a female waiter in a restaurant or cafe, is one of the few remaining gender-specific terms that is still going strong, despite occasional objections to it. *Waitperson* has found no currency in BrE and very little in AmE.

waive means 'to give up (a right or claim) voluntarily', as in *waiving* an immunity or *waiving* formalities. It is not formally confused with the more familiar verb *wave* except in phrasal verbs such as *waive aside* and *waive away* (= to put aside as if with the wave of the hand), which are incorrect (✖ *I cannot waive away all the teaching of history*).

wake, waken see AWAKE, AWAKEN.

wallop. The verb has inflected forms *walloped, walloping*.

want *verb*. **1** *Want* is of Norse origin and came into English in the 13c. The dominant meaning in current usage is 'to desire or wish for' (*Tom wants a computer for Christmas / What do you want to do now?*), and a range of earlier meanings equivalent to 'to lack or need' has been reduced to a few uses as in *The house wants painting* and *The standard is sadly wanting* (= inadequate), in the expression *to want for nothing* (or *not want for anything*), in advertisements (*bar staff wanted*), and in the non-standard types *You want to pull yourself together* and *You want to go straight on and turn right at the lights* (= need to, should). Occasionally the two branches of meaning (i.e. 'lack' and 'wish for') merge (*The organization badly wants better leadership*), and it is easy to see how the 'needing' branch led to the 'wishing' branch.

2 Some special and modern uses of *want* are:

a Forms in *-ed* and *-ing* in constructions of the type *We want our car washed* and *The roof wants mending* are sometimes reversed as *We want our car washing* and *The roof wants mended*. These uses are mostly regional or literary in BrE and are non-standard.

b *Want* is followed by a *that*-clause: *You want that I should lose both my lieutenants together?*—A. Lejeune, 1986. This is a rare, mainly AmE, use that is not much found in everyday language.

c *Want* is followed by *for* + object + *to*-infinitive, most often in cases in which *want* is followed by an intensifying word or phrase such as *very much* or *so much*: *My mother wanted so much for my sister to have the best animals*—New Yorker, 1989.

d *Want* is used for *want to*, especially in the form *if you* (etc.) *want*: *Stay home if you want*—Fay Weldon, 1988 / *Let us not kid ourselves that the solution is to let people drive wherever and whenever they want*—York Press, 2004 [*OEC*].

e There is ellipsis of a following verb (*come, go,* etc.) in the expressions *to want in* (= to be included) and *to want out* (= to be excluded): *The message here is once again clearly stated: They want in. She wants out*—arts website, BrE 2002 [*OEC*].

wantonness is spelt with two *n*s.

warn *verb* is traditionally a transitive verb with a grammatical object corresponding to the person or people receiving the warning: *She warned them of the danger* / *She warned them that it was unsafe*. In the 20c an intransitive use with a following *that*-clause came into common use, with the intended recipient of the warning left unspecified: *Arafat also warned that any Palestinian group that rejected the idea. . . . must read itself out of the P.L.O.*—Time, 1976 / *Farmers warned that delays in agreeing rules could lead to next year's Italian harvests being unintentionally 'contaminated'*—Guardian Unlimited, 2004 [*OEC*].

wash up in BrE means 'to wash crockery and cutlery after use', whereas in AmE it means 'to wash one's hands and face'.

wastage should not be used as a synonym of the noun *waste*, but has special (often technical and always non-judgemental) meanings: (1) loss by natural means, e.g. wear or erosion, (2) an amount wasted, (3) in the phrase *natural wastage*, reduction in staffing by resignations and retirement rather than enforced redundancies. *Waste* has connotations of disapproval in its meaning 'a bad use of resources or assets' (as in *go to waste, a waste of time*, etc.), but is neutral when it means 'refuse, unwanted material or food'.

waste-paper basket is the BrE term; in AmE it is *wastebasket*.

-watch. The noun *watch*, meaning 'a state of alert', first produced a suffix (or combining form) in the 1950s, and is known earlier in verbs such as *firewatch* (a term from the Second World War), but it is essentially a creation of the 70s (*doomwatch*) and 80s in combinations to do with animal welfare such as *badger-watch, birdwatch,* and *whale-watch,* and in other uses such as *crimewatch* (the name of a UK television programme), *hacker-watch* (precaution against computer hackers), and *stormwatch*. Other ad hoc uses occur, establishing *-watch* as a productive element within fairly narrow limits: *Family-sized platters contain an entire chicken or spaghetti for eight. . . . No reservations, so prepare to people-watch while you wait*—Minnesota Monthly, 1994 / *Are there no dog watch organisations to make sure that dog prices don't shoot up too high?*—Bolton Evening News, 2005.

Watergate see -GATE.

watershed, originally a term in geology referring to the flow and division of river currents, has been used since the late 19c in the figurative meaning 'a turning-point in affairs': *In the social history of twentieth-century Britain the Second World War stands out as a watershed*—H. Smith, 1986. It is often used attributively (i.e. before a noun: *Ade became one of the more astute*

w

chroniclers of the daily preoccupations of ordinary people who were living through the 'watershed period'—T. Tobin, 1973). In the UK *watershed* has a special meaning in broadcasting, denoting the time in the evening after which programmes are no longer guaranteed as suitable for viewing by children.

wave see WAIVE.

wax *verb*. In the meaning 'to assume a specified tone or state', *wax* is followed by an adjective, not an adverb: *to wax lyrical, to wax enthusiastic*, etc.: *When the Roman soldiers were asked to take part in the Claudian invasion of 43, they waxed indignant*—Antonia Fraser, 1988. This use is primarily rhetorical.

way see NO WAY; UNDER WAY.

waylay has inflected forms *waylays, waylaid, waylaying*.

ways. *I was standing out in the street a little ways*, wrote the American novelist Tom Wolfe in his *Bonfire of the Vanities* (1987). This use of the plural *ways*, meaning 'at some indeterminate distance (in time or place)' is related to a use (with a qualifying word) that was once standard in BrE (*Falmouth . . . is no great ways from the sea*—Byron, 1809) but is now confined to dialect and regional use (*We have traveled a ways down the road to achieving gender integration*—*Parameters* (magazine), AmE 2000 [*OEC*]).

we. 1 The personal pronoun *we* has a wide range of reference, so that care is often needed to avoid misunderstanding. In its primary meanings it can denote any of the following: (1) you (singular or plural) and I, (2) you and I and some others, or (3) I and some others (but not you: *We are going now, but don't you hurry*). Informally, it can also mean just 'you', as in the

condescending form of enquiry *How are we today?*

2 *We* is also used with indefinite reference in the following conventional uses:

a When a writer or speaker includes his or her readers or hearers and other unnamed people in a statement or proposition: *As we saw in the last chapter . . . / What do we, as a nation, care about books? / We have to tackle the problem of inflation.*

b When a monarch is using the first person (the so-called *royal we*). This practice is dying out, however. Queen Victoria is credited with the remark *We are not amused*, but Queen Elizabeth II is noted for *My husband and I* and generally uses the singular form when referring to herself. (Margaret Thatcher's pronouncement *We have become a grandmother*, quoted in *The Times* of 4 March 1989, was blatant affectation.)

3 *We* is sometimes used mistakenly for *us*, possibly as a kind of hypercorrection, in sentences such as: *Perhaps this product is best suited to we cloth-capped northerners.* For the wrong use of *us* for *we, see* US 2.

wear, gear. *Wear* is normally used as the second element in compounds denoting forms of clothing, such as *footwear* and *underwear*, but *gear* is used in *headgear*. Used by itself, *gear* (= clothing, attire) is now considered informal, although it was once used as a regular word in this meaning.

weave *verb*. Historically, there are two words involved here, although their meanings overlap in figurative applications. The one meaning 'to form fabric by interlacing threads' is from Old English, and the other, meaning 'to take a winding course', is a form of a later (13c) word taken from Old Norse. The two verbs have different inflection: the 'form fabric' word has a past form *wove* and a past participle *woven,* and the later word has *weaved* for both. Care needs to be taken to distinguish the figurative use of the 'fabric' meaning from the 'movement' meaning: *She returned to Sierra Leone and wove a love story in and around the twin horrors of civil war and the scars left on its survivors*—OEC, 2013 / *Then they got on to the little scooter and weaved down the lane*—Jeanette Winterson, 1987.

Web is normally spelt with a capital *W* when it refers to the *World Wide Web,* the information system on the Internet. (This is often abbreviated to *WWW,* which is usually printed in small letters at the start of domain names.) In combinations such as *web page* and *website,* however, it tends to be spelt with a small initial letter. Other additions to Web vocabulary include *webcam* (a video camera connected to the Internet), *weblog* (usually shortened to *blog*), *webcast* (a live video broadcast on the Internet), *webmaster* (a person in charge of a particular site on the Web), and *webspace* (the amount of disk space allowed on an Internet server).

wed (= marry). The form of the past tense and past participle is either *wedded* or *wed.* Its shortness makes it a popular word with headline-writers and journalists (*Nicole said of meeting Urban, whom she wed in June last year: 'I think we were two lonely people a mixture of frightened and brave'*—Mirror, 2007), but otherwise its use has become increasingly restricted to special contexts (e.g. *in a state of wedded bliss* / *With this ring I thee wed*) and to figurative uses (*This power plant is wed to a double-pivot spring strut suspension*—Transpacific AmE, 1992). To *be wedded to* an idea, activity, etc., is to be entirely or even obsessively devoted to it (*Effie became*

almost wedded to her duties—J. Sutherland, 2000).

Wednesday *see* FRIDAY.

week *see* DAY, MONTH, WEEK, YEAR.

weird, meaning 'strange, unnatural', is spelt *-ei-,* not *-ie.*

well *see* AS WELL AS.

well, well-. People are unsure whether forms such as *well(-)made* and *well(-)received* should contain a hyphen or be spelt as two words. The normal rule is that the combination is hyphenated when it occurs in attributive position (i.e. before a noun, as in *a well-made cupboard* and *a well-received suggestion*), but not when it occurs after a verb (as in *The cupboard looks well made* and *The suggestion was well received*).

well-nigh, meaning 'nearly, almost wholly or entirely', has been in continuous use since the Old English period and is still regularly used, particularly with adjectives with a negative meaning, despite being slightly literary or archaic in tone: *If your country is the size of a postage stamp, your population is unsophisticated and your borders are well-nigh indefensible, you need luck*—Economist, 1992.

welsh. The expression *welsh on,* meaning 'to evade (an obligation)' or 'to fail to carry out (a promise)', dates from the 1930s, although the verb (of unknown origin) was used transitively (with a person as object) in the 19c. To avoid a direct and possibly offensive association with the Welsh people, it is often spelt *welch.*

Welsh rabbit, the dish of cheese on toast, has no obvious connection with the Welsh or with rabbits, but has been known in this form since the early 18c (and is the name used in Mrs Glasse's

w

The Art of Cookery in 1747). Its origin is obscure, as is the emergence of the alternative form with *rarebit*, a word otherwise unrecorded. In modern use, *OEC* data, other corpora, and Google searches show that the spelling *rarebit* is now considerably more frequent.

were. For its use in *if I were, as it were*, etc. *see* IF 1; SUBJUNCTIVE MOOD 3C, 3E.

werewolf should be spelt in this way rather than as *werwolf* and the recommended pronunciation is with the first syllable as in *ware*. The Old English form was *werewulf* and the first element is thought to be based on *wer* meaning 'man'. The modern plural form is *werewolves*.

west, western, westerly *see* EAST, EASTERN, EASTERLY.

westward, westwards. The only form for the adjective is *westward* (*in a westward direction*), but *westward* and *westwards* are both used for the adverb, with a preference for *westwards* in BrE: *He climbed the lower slopes of Big Allen and stood, looking westwards*—Ruth Rendell, 1988.

wet *verb*. The form of the past tense and past participle is *wet* or *wetted*. *Wet* is used in certain familiar contexts (*He wet the bed / After they had wet their whistles* [= had a drink]), but in general use *wetted* seems now to be more common, especially for the participle to distinguish the action of being made wet from the resulting state indicated by the simple adjective: *Two weeks ago a heavy rain had leaked through the ceiling and wetted the box*—New York Review of Books, 1987 / *With her clothes wetted and her pockets full of big round stones*—A. S. Byatt, 1990.

wh-. Words beginning with *wh-* (*what, where, wherever, white*, etc.) are normally pronounced with the *h* unaspirated in Received Pronunciation in

England and Wales. In general American, in Canadian, and in Scottish and Irish English they are commonly aspirated as hw-. Variation occurs in all these varieties.

wharf has the plural form *wharves* (preferred) or *wharfs*.

what. 1 general. As a relative pronoun, *what* is an especially complex word because it can be either singular or plural and can refer both to words that have gone before and to words that come later in the sentence. In general it stands for a group of two or more words such as *that which, those which, the thing* (or *things*) *that, anything* (or *everything*) *that*, etc.: *What you need. . . . is some outside interest*—Ruth Rendell, 1974 / *They contribute what they can, if they are lucky enough to find work*—Contemporary Review, 2000. It must not be used as equivalent to the simple relative pronouns *that, which*, or *who*, a use characteristic of highly informal or uneducated speech: *I was the only boy in our school what had asthma*—William Golding, 1954.

2 singular *what*. A problem of singular or plural verb agreement arises when *what* is singular but looks forward to a plural noun or pronoun later in the sentence: *What we need is/are clear guidelines*. Fowler had a useful rule that if the sentence begins in the singular (i.e. if the initial *what* is singular), the continuation should also be singular; so the example just given would be expressed in the form *What we need is clear guidelines*. In current use this rule is often respected, as the following examples show: *What really worries me is the numbers*—Nina Bawden, 1987 / *What bothered him was drivers who switched lanes without signalling*—New Yorker, 1989. In these cases, it is arguable that a noun phrase such as *the circumstance of* or *the fact of* should be understood after the main verb; it is not the numbers as such that cause the worry in the first example or the drivers as such that cause the bother in the second, but the fact of what they represented or were doing. There are, however, counter-examples to be found: *What concerns me are the number of construction projects that are delayed—York Press*, 2004 [OEC].

3 plural *what*. A different situation arises when *what* is plural: *I have few books, and what there are do not help me.* In this sentence, *what* refers back to *books*, and so its plural status is clear. When *what* refers forward, the choice is less obvious: *We seem to have abandoned what seem/seems to us to be the most valuable parts of our Constitution.* Fowler (whose example this is) had another useful rule in these cases: if *what* can be resolved into *the —s that*, with —*s* standing for the plural noun later in the sentence to which *what* refers forward, the verb governed by *what* should be plural. In the example just given, *what....* can be resolved into *the parts of our Constitution that....*, and the verb should therefore be *seem* (plural), not *seems*. If the relative clause introduced by *what* comes at the head of the sentence, the same rule can be followed if *what* can be resolved into *that which*: *What [= that which] is required is faith and confidence, and willingness to work.* This principle is much less secure, however, since *what* in the example given (Fowler's again) can as easily be resolved as *the things which* (plural): *What [= the things which] are required are faith and confidence, and willingness to work.* Here there is clearly a choice, and naturalness and rhythm will often be decisive; the important point is that the choice between singular and plural should be consistent throughout the sentence, and that a singular verb after *what* should not be followed by a plural verb: ☒ *What is required are faith and confidence, and willingness to work.*

4 sentences containing *what....and which...* When a relative clause introduced by *what* is followed by further relative clauses joined by a conjunction such as *and* or *but*, the *what* should be repeated when it refers to something other than at its first occurrence: *There is a definite mis-match between what universities are producing and what industry is wanting—Daily Telegraph*, 1971. In this example, the first *what* refers to one thing and the second *what* to another, and both are needed. But the temptation to use a further *what* (or worse, a relative *which*) should be resisted when this would have the same grammatical status (as subject or object in its clause) and reference, since the first *what* is adequate to sustain the sense: ☒ *Nobody is going to object to what is a popular measure and which will help those most in need* should be rewritten as *Nobody is going to object to what is a popular measure and will help those most in need* (or as *Nobody is going to object to what is a popular measure which will help those most in need*, where *a popular measure* becomes the antecedent of *which*).

5 *what* after *as* and *than*. *What* should not be used after the conjunctions *as* and *than* in comparative constructions of the following type: ☒ *People who have difficulty in 'hearing' intonation patterns are generally only having difficulty in relating what they hear (which is the same as **what** everyone else hears) to this 'pseudo-spatial' representation—P. Roach*, 1983 (read: *the same as everyone else hears*) / ☒ *She sometimes comes out with more than **what** she went in with—R. Hamilton*, 1993 (read: *more than she went in with*). But *what* should be used when it is essential to the structure of the sentence: *It was always easier to say what such a school should not be, rather than what it should be—H. Judge*, 1984.

whatever, what ever. 1 *Whatever* is written as one word when it is an indefinite relative pronoun or adjective used in statements or commands: *Whatever you're up to during the snowy season, a wonderful warm woolly makes the perfect winter wear*—Hair Flair, 1992 / *They make it harder to discuss differences openly, and to take a stand against racism whenever and in whatever form it arises*—Times, 2007. It is also used with concessive force equivalent to 'regardless of what' (*Whatever Ned Kelly was really like. . . . he can scarcely have been like Mr Jagger*—New Statesman, 1970), and elliptically (with the continuation omitted) in informal uses such as: *People want a kind of more adult conversation instead of just talking about a policy, be it tuition fees or foundation hospitals or whatever*—Scotland on Sunday, 2003.

2 A comma is sometimes needed to clarify the meaning when a sentence begins with a *whatever*-clause, especially when the verb of the main clause can be understood either intransitively or as referring back to *whatever*: *Whatever they have done, they are now leaving* means 'they are leaving (intransitive), regardless of what they have done', whereas *Whatever they have done they are now leaving* means 'they are leaving (transitive) whatever it is they have done'.

3 *Whatever* is also the correct form when used as an adverb to strengthen negative statements: *There is no reason whatever not to seize this opportunity and practice with greater and greater exertion*—Buddhist website, *BrE* 2000.

4 *What ever* is written as two words when *ever* is used as an intensifying word and the expression as a whole is equivalent to *what on earth*, usually in direct questions: *'Pardon me asking, sir, but what ever happened to your pilot's licence?'*—J. Neale, 1993. *See* EVER 1.

whence, whither. Both words have centuries of history behind them and were once routine in their respective meanings 'from which place' and 'to

which place', but in current use they are regarded as archaic or at least highly formal, although they occur occasionally in modern literature: *He has also, of course, a passport which nails him for who he is and whence he comes*—Penelope Lively, 1987 / *I write, now, from my bed, whither Dr Felton has banished me*—M. Roberts, 1990. Though strictly redundant, *from* can idiomatically precede *whence*, a usage with impeccable credentials (*I will lift up mine eyes unto the hills, from whence cometh my help*—Psalm 121, Authorized Version, 1611).

whenever, when ever. *Whenever* is written as one word when it is a conjunction (*Whenever possible he liked to make a point of talking to drug users on their own ground*—Times, 1970) or a quasi-adverb used informally (*I'll do it at the weekend or whenever*). *When ever* is written as two words when *ever* is used as an intensifying word, usually in direct questions: *When ever did they arrive? See* EVER 1.

where-. Words still in general currency that are formed with the prefix *where*- include, in addition to those listed here as separate entries, *whereas* (used in contrasts), *wherefore* (only in *the whys and wherefores*), *wherein* (supposedly formal but common), and *whereupon* (in narration). Many others have fallen out of use or are regarded as archaic, but will be met in older writing, e.g. *whereat, wherefrom, wheresoever, wherethrough, whereto, wherewith.*

whereabouts *noun.* The plural form ousted the singular form *whereabout* in the 19c; when a verb follows it is more often in the plural than in the singular, but both constructions occur regardless of the number of people or things in question: (plural) *They have since 'gone to ground' and their precise whereabouts are not known to the authorities*—Times,

w

1998 / (singular) *The current whereabouts of the prisoners remains a mystery—Morning Star*, 2007.

whereby, meaning 'by what or which means', is one of a dwindling number of *where-* forms still in common use. It is especially useful in attaching an explanatory statement to a noun or noun phrase: *The 'ratchet effect' in politics, whereby the right seems to have acquiesced in the changes the left brings about—Listener*, 1977 / *Schemes whereby such patients can quickly get such medicines direct from the pharmacist. . . . will be promoted and extended—British Medical Journal*, 2003.

wherever, where ever. *Wherever* is written as one word when it is a conjunction (*One knows the type. . . . They're complete poison, wherever they go—R. Barnard*, 1977) or a quasi-adverb used informally (*The traffic wardens will effectively end up lying in wait for people outside schools or wherever—Bolton Evening News*, 2003). *Where ever* is written as two words when *ever* is used as an intensifying word, usually in direct questions: *Where ever have they gone? See* EVER 1.

wherewithal, meaning 'the means or resources for something', is always used with *the*: *You don't need the intellectual wherewithal to function in society—Steven Pinker*, 1994.

whether. 1 For the choice between *if* and *whether, see* IF 2.

2 When the alternative to the *whether* clause is a simple negative, this can take several forms, but *whether or not* is now more usual than *whether or no*: *I brooded all the way whether or not I had hit the right note—Jane Gardam*, 1985 / *In many of Shakespeare's other plays, we see the tragic consequences of acting on hearsay or prima facie evidence without seeking to establish whether it is true or*

not—J. Baginni, 2002. For *whether or no, see* NO 3.

3 *Whether* is often repeated as a clearer marker than a bare *or* of an alternative that forms a separate sentence, especially when the gap between *whether* and *or* is a long one: *You must decide yourself whether each new Beaver* [= junior Scout] *should be asked to pay for his scarf and woggle, or whether these should be provided by the Colony—J. Deft*, 1983.

4 When a clause introduced by *whether* relates to a preceding word such as *matter, issue, problem,* or *question, whether* can follow directly or be separated by *of*: *Senator Ervin said the issue of whether the subpoenas were continuing was 'a difference in a teapot'—Times*, 1973 / *The whole question whether women actually are more pacific by nature is not the subject of the present book—Antonia Fraser*, 1988 / *This. . . . goes some way to answering the problem of whether there is free will in heaven—Christis* (magazine), 2004 [*OEC*].

which. 1 For the choice between *that* and *which, see* THAT 3. It is especially important that *which*, not *that*, should be used in so-called non-restrictive clauses giving additional rather than essential information: *A new edition of the book, which has taken ten years to write, will be published this week.* (Note that in this role, *which* is usually preceded by a comma.)

2 The use of *which* to introduce a clause that is grammatically a relative one but in fact adds new information or leads on to a new point has been recorded for several centuries but has become especially common in the last fifty years or so: *He does Mr Rabinowitz's teeth which is super—Nigel Williams*, 1985 / *Head office may look at the figures and decide to close again, which defeats the whole point—tourist website, BrE* 2003 [*OEC*] / (starting a new sentence) *It* *was as though Hungary was not another place but another time, and therefore inaccessible. Which of course was not so*—Penelope Lively, 1987.

3 Use of *which* with a personal antecedent is now archaic only, and is familiar mainly from the Prayer Book: *O God, which art author of peace, and lover of concord*—Book of Common Prayer, 1548-9 (modern spelling).

4 When a *which*-clause is followed by another *which*-clause joined by *and* or *but*, the second *which* must have the same grammatical status as the first. In the following example the first *which* is the subject of its clause, whereas the second is the object of the verb (*found*): *In contrast Peake's use of elevated language has a childlike quality, which is appropriate given that the protagonist, Titus, is a boy, and which I found endearing.*

while, whilst. 1 Both forms are used in BrE, but *whilst* is not much used in AmE. There is no distinction in usage as regards meaning, although varying grammatical patterns are noted below.

2 The word is a conjunction, and its primary sense is temporal, meaning 'during the time that' (*They had begun drinking while he prepared to cook*) or 'at the same time as' (*She enjoyed drawing while she was being read to*). Since the time of Shakespeare, however, other uses have emerged in which *while* (or *whilst*) means 'although' or 'whereas', with concessive or contrastive rather than temporal force (*While I enjoy his company, I couldn't live with him / I live in London, while my sister lives in New York*). The concessive use (in particular) has been disapproved of by some (including Eric Partridge in *Usage and Abusage*, 1942 and later), but it is so well established that criticism is futile. Instances of possible ambiguity between the temporal and concessive–contrastive

types of meaning are sometimes adduced, but they are usually contrived and unlikely to arise in practice (such as the old chestnut *The Curate read the First Lesson while the Rector read the Second*). Examples: (temporal) *Here father and daughter sat side by side on the window seat while he coached her each evening in the school holidays*—C. Brayfield, 1990 / (concessive) *While domestic happiness is an admirable ideal, it is not easy to come by*—T. Tanner, 1986 / *While this division does not correspond exactly to Kant's division of chapters . . . , it is sufficiently close not to be misleading*—R. Scruton, 2001 / (contrastive) *Whilst Mackenzie carried on and ended up editing the Sun, Sutton began to question what he was doing*—C. Horrie et al., 1988 / *They practise in the town, with Champion cycling the streets to the peep of Gran's whistle, while Bruno spends the evenings climbing up and down stairs to bark at the trains*—film website, BrE 2002 [OEC].

3 *While* and *whilst* are used elliptically, with the omission of a subject and main verb such as *they were* (in the first example following) or *he was* (in the second): *Dinner ladies helping with playground supervision have been jostled and abused while trying to tackle unruly pupils*—Daily Telegraph, 1983 / *While still working for the restaurant in 1956, he began his franchising career*—Money, 1985. In this type of construction *while* (or *whilst*) is usually temporal (as in both of these examples) or concessive (as in the following example), and when concessive it tends to come before the main clause: *More recent evidence, whilst not addressing this issue directly, tends to suggest that this desired relationship is still important*—J. Finch, 1989.

4 A sentence such as the following is incorrect: ⊠ *While being in agreement on most issues, I would like to challenge one in particular.* The omission is misconceived since the full form is *while I* *am* and not *while I am being*; correct *while being* to *while I am in agreement* or *while in agreement*.

whinge, meaning 'to grumble peevishly', is BrE. Its *-ing* form is *whingeing*, with an *e* to preserve the soft sound of the *g*.

whirr, meaning 'to make a continuous buzzing sound', is spelt with two *r*s in BrE and usually with one *r* in AmE, and the corresponding noun follows suit. The verb has inflected forms *whirred*, *whirring* in both varieties.

whisky, whiskey. *Whisky* is the usual spelling in BrE (especially with reference to *Scotch whisky*) and Canada, and *whiskey* is used of the spirit made in Ireland and the USA and is the usual spelling generally in AmE.

Whit. *Whit Sunday* (or *Pentecost*) is the seventh Sunday after Easter, and *Whit Monday* is the day following Whit Sunday. *Whitsun* and *Whit* are regularly used as informal shortenings of *Whitsuntide*, the weekend including Whit Sunday. *Whit* is related in form to *white*, and the name is probably derived from the white robes of those newly baptized at Whitsuntide.

whit, a 16c word derived ultimately from an Old English form meaning 'a thing or creature of unknown origin', is commonly used in both BrE and AmE in the phrase *not a whit* or *no whit* (= not at all, by no means): *This much ballyhooed Andrew Lloyd Webber musical is fun—if you're not bothered by theatre that cares not a whit for words and contains not one ghost of an idea—New Yorker*, 1991 / *I, like many other parents I suspect, do not care one whit if someone perceives such actions as immoral—BBC Education News*, 2004 [*OEC*]. Fowler (1926) and Gowers (1965) classed it among the so-called 'Wardour Street words' (i.e. old-sounding words

affectedly adopted like old-looking furniture), but it has lost most of these associations in the meantime.

white. For a time it was thought appropriate to spell *white* with a capital initial when it was used as a racial term with reference to light-skinned people, but the normal preference now is for a small initial. Unlike *black*, *white* in this sense does not have any derogatory overtones, but various sensitivities have led to a growing preference for terms based on geography rather than skin colour, in this case *European* (if appropriate) instead of *white*.

whiten is the usual form of the verb in current usage in the meanings 'to make white' and 'to become white', but *white* is used in the expression *whited sepulchre* (meaning 'a hypocrite', in allusion to Matthew 23:27) and in the phrasal verb *white out* meaning 'to correct (a mistake) with white correction fluid'.

whither *see* WHENCE, WHITHER.

whitish, meaning 'somewhat white', is spelt without an *e* in the middle.

whizz is the recommended spelling for the noun and verb (and also in *whizz-kid*), not *whiz*, although this too occurs.

who and whom. 1 *Who* is used as a relative pronoun (*The woman who saw you*) and as an interrogative (*Who is there?*), and *whom* is, formally, its objective form (*The woman whom you saw / Whom did you see?*). In all these uses *who* (or *whom*) refers to a person or to several people, but as a relative pronoun *who* can informally refer to an animal or to an organization regarded in terms of its members (*The committee, who meet on Friday, . . .*).

2 In practice, *whom* is in decline and is increasingly replaced by *who* (or *that*), especially in conversational English.

(This is not a new development; examples can be found from Shakespeare onward.) In the examples given in the preceding paragraph, it would be more natural to say *Who did you see?*, and in the one before it *The woman who you saw* or *The woman that you saw* or *The woman you saw* (for the omission of the pronoun, *see* RELATIVE CLAUSES 2).

3 When the relative pronoun is governed by a preposition, a construction with *whom* now seems formal, or even over-formal, and an alternative construction with *who* and the preposition at the end is the usual option in everyday language: (formal) *They. . . . argue about a man called Simpkins of whom the poet is jealous*—Encounter, 1987 / *Lord Jenkins likened this stance to countries. . . . 'who in the two world wars have waited to see which side was winning before deciding with whom to ally themselves'*—Times, 1999 / (informal) *What did she know of his life, who he went to bed with?*—Iris Murdoch, 1993 / *Mentzer didn't name any of these companies specifically, but it's clear who he was thinking of when we asked him about such developments*—Register, 2003 [OEC]. (A mixed style sometimes occurs, but is not ideal: *There were other people whom I would have liked to speak to*—G. Butler, 1983.)

4 The same distinction of formality applies in the choice between *who* and *whom* used as an interrogative pronoun in questions: (formal) *Whom should we support in the present fluid situation?*—Bulletin of the American Academy, 1990 / *To whom have you complained?*—V. Finkelstein et al., 1993 / (informal) *Who do you think you're speaking to?*—W. McIlvanney, 1985.

5 Opinions about the diminishing use of *whom* vary widely from complete tolerance ('We have got rid of *ye* as the subjective form of *you*, so why not *whom* as the objective form of *who*?') to strong regret or outright disapproval. Most

severely criticized now are uses in which *who* replaces *whom* in grammatically straightforward contexts which traditionally call for *whom*: *Christ, who went for who first?*—V. O'Sullivan, 1985 / *The stuff which was kept under wraps most of the time came flooding out in elections: who had fought on what side, who had killed who, who had really represented the will of the Irish people*—Independent, 1999. Then there are those who regard the use of *whom* as a sign of education and reliability: *'I don't know whom else to ask.' The elder of the two policemen, Butterworth, noticed that she had said 'whom' and decided that she was a credible witness*—Anita Brookner, 1992.

6 There are occasions when *whom* is used incorrectly (or hypercorrectly) when *who* is needed: ☒ *The baronet whom Golitsin claimed had been the target for homosexual blackmail*—P. Wright, 1987. In this sentence, *whom* should be *who*, because it is the subject of *had been* (. . . *who had been the target* . . .) and not the object of *claimed*. This type, with the insertion of a word such as *claim, say, think*, etc., is extremely common: *He is demanding £5,000 from the elderly woman whom* [read: *who*] *he says ruined his life*—Sunday Times, 1990. Note also constructions in which a whole clause introduced by *who* is the object of a verb or preposition; in these cases also, *who* is correct: *The staff have noisy arguments about who should siesta on the cold stone floor*—Len Deighton, 1976 / *She wanted him to love her for who she really was*—Times, 1998.

whoever, who ever, whomever.

1 The same distinction applies here as to *whatever* and *what ever*, *whoever* being written as one word when it is an indefinite relative pronoun equivalent to 'whatever person' used in statements or commands (*Whoever wants it can have it*) and when the meaning is 'regardless of whom' (*Whoever it is, I don't want to see them*). *Who ever* is written as two words when *ever* is used as an intensifying word and the expression as a whole is equivalent to *who on earth*, usually in direct questions: *Who ever are those people? See* EVER 1.

   2 The objective form *whomever* still occurs but it can sound formal or affected in general contexts: *To impose his will on whomever he sees comfortably settled*—Max Beerbohm, 1920. In some cases it is wrongly used: ⊠ ... *ready at once to relax with whomever came to hand*—Anita Brookner, 1992 / ⊠ *Accepting the poverty it entailed, he* [Socrates] *appears to have spent all his time in unpaid discussion with whomever would join with him*—E. Craig, 2002 (in each case *with* governs the whole following clause, *came to hand* and *would join with him*; the pronoun is the subject of the clause and should therefore be *whoever*).

whole range is a fudge expression used by politicians to give the impression that what they are doing or discussing is far-reaching, whereas the limits are nowhere defined and the notion of completeness is therefore at best an illusion and at worst a deception: *We believe a whole range of benefits can and should be created*—Rochdale *Observer*, 2002. Usually, *wide range* is more honest and makes better sense: *Supermarkets in the United States have a wide range of fresh fruit and vegetable choices*—Agricultural Research (magazine), 2003. But *whole range* is more acceptable when preceded by *the* and used in contexts where the limits are known or have been identified: *Pulau Langkawi offers the whole range of accommodation to suit every budget and taste*—Asian Diver (magazine), 2004.

wholly, meaning 'entirely, completely', is spelt this way, not *wholely*.

whom *see* WHO AND WHOM.

who's is a contracted form of *who is* (*Who's going to the party?*) or *who has* (*The person who's got my pen*). It is occasionally used in error for *whose*: ⊠ '*Conor*,' *called Vaun, humping a churn of milk.* '*Who's turn to deliver?*'— J. Leland, 1987.

whose. 1 Despite a long-established folk-belief (which Fowler deplored) that *whose*, when used as a relative, should only mean *of whom* and not *of which*, usage over several centuries from the time of Shakespeare and Milton supports its use with reference to inanimate things as well as to people. Fowler, quoting the opening lines of *Paradise Lost* (*Of man's first disobedience, and the fruit Of that forbidden tree, whose mortal taste Brought death into the world*), insisted that 'good writing is surely difficult enough without the forbidding of things that have historical grammar, and present intelligibility, and obvious convenience, on their side', a verdict that still has the ring of good sense. The following modern examples show how awkward it can be to replace *whose* with a construction involving *of which*, especially when an adjective comes between *whose* and the following noun (as in the first example): *He looked up again at the tank whose huge cannon seemed to be pointing at him*—P. P. Read, 1986 / *Biala was born in Biala, Poland* (*a town whose name she took as her own*)—Art in America, 2000 [*OEC*].

   2 This does not mean that *of which* cannot be used; when it fits comfortably in the sentence structure, it is a legitimate and often preferable alternative: *The greater crime, the truth of which is emerging on a piecemeal basis, was committed before a shot was even fired*—Scotland on Sunday, 2004. It has to be used, of course, in contexts where there is no possessive or similar relation: *The* *independent production sector in Britain includes over 1,000 companies, most of which are located in London and the South-East*—J. Tunstall, 2001.

why. 1 For *reason why, see* REASON 2.

2 The plural form of the noun is *whys* (used in *whys and wherefores*).

wide rather than *widely* is used in a number of fixed expressions such as *wide apart, wide awake*, and *wide open*, as an element in the word *widespread*, and in the phrases *hit* (or *shoot*) *wide* and *open one's eyes wide*.

wife has the plural form *wives*.

Wi-Fi *see* WIRELESS.

wilfing is the name for the habit, or addiction, of being diverted from the Internet search one originally undertook to all manner of other sites, with no particular purpose in mind. It is a verb acronym derived from the question 'What was *I* looking *for*?', and usefully describes the trance-like state of point-less website-hopping the Internet so easily induces. Though most common as the verbal noun shown, it exists in other forms: *Shopping is the online activity most likely to make users wilf / Men are more likely to admit to being wilfers than women*—Daily Telegraph, 2007.

wilful is spelt in this way in BrE, but *willful* is also used in AmE.

will *see* SHALL AND WILL.

wimmin, a phonetic spelling of *women*, is recorded in facetious contexts from the early part of the 20c. It was adopted by feminists in the 1980s because it dispensed with the element *-men*, and has achieved a limited currency in contexts where female status is being underlined or highlighted in some (often ironic) way: *Why are these* (*ignorant*) *gay men* (*and sadly sometimes*

wimmin) *stereotyping gayness?*—Pink Paper, 1990 / *Anyone, Roisin. That includes adolescent boys, wimmin, transgender hang gliders, and people of all ethnic, religious, social, political backgrounds and persuasions*—Sunday Business Post, IrishE 2004 [OEC]. *See also* WOMYN.

wind *verbs.* There are two verbs here. The verb meaning 'to twist, coil, etc.' is pronounced wiynd and has the past tense and past participle *wound* (pronounced wownd). The unconnected verb meaning 'to exhaust the breath' is pronounced wind and has the past tense and past participle *winded*.

windward, referring to the side from which the wind is blowing, is spelt *-ward* as adjective, adverb, and noun. The form *windwards* is no longer used.

wireless. Known for many years as a word for a radio set and radio broad-casting that dates its user to an older age, *wireless* has been given a new lease of electronic life in a more literal adjectival sense 'not involving the use of wires', i.e. using radio or microwaves to trans-mit signals (as in a *wireless connection* of components). A *wireless application protocol* (abbreviated to *WAP*) is a 'spec-ification for the transfer of data to and from a handheld wireless device, espe-cially a mobile phone' (OED), and *Wi-Fi* (an extension of the start of the word based on *hi-fi*) has become familiar as the method by which people use the Internet without tripping over cables. It is a trade mark in the US but not in Britain.

-wise, -ways. Both suffixes were active in forming adverbs (*always, sideways / crosswise, edgewise*) up to the 19c, and tended to overlap (e.g. *edgeways / edge-wise, crossways / crosswise*), but in current use only *-wise* is now productive in the special meaning 'in the manner of —' in ad hoc formations: *Her mass of chestnut hair parted Rossetti-wise in the middle*—Rose Macaulay, 1923 / ... *dangling his arms beside his hips and rolling his head idiotwise*—J. McInerney, 1985. From the 1940s, the suffix developed a further meaning 'as regards —'; 'in respect of —': *Plotwise, it offers little more or less* [etc.]—*Saturday Review*, 1948 / *They all keep up with me, drinkingwise*—*New Yorker*, 1993 / *Many of us know that sometimes that's the way it crumbles, cookie-wise*—weblog, AmE 2005 [*OEC*].

wish *verb*. The use with a simple direct object (*Would you wish a little more hot water, ma'am*—Dickens, 1854) has been replaced in BrE by *like*, but is still said to be current in AmE.

wisteria is the usual form for the climbing plant, not *wistaria*. It is named after the 18c American anatomist Casper Wistar (or Wister).

wit *verb*. This old native word for *know* barely survives in the phrase *to wit* (= that is to say, namely), in the derived forms *wittingly* and *unwittingly*, and in the first and third person singular archaic form *wot* (especially in T. E. Brown's often quoted remark (1892), *A garden is a lovesome thing, God wot!*).

withhold is spelt with two *h*s.

without. 1 Unlike the corresponding physical meaning of *within* (= inside), the original meaning of *without*, 'outside' (preposition and adverb), is no longer much used, although it will be familiar from literary contexts (*There is a green hill far away, Without a city wall*—Cecil Frances Alexander, 1848 / *The throng without was ... becoming more numerous and more savage*—Macaulay, 1849). The primary current uses are in the sense 'lacking, not having' (*I came without an umbrella*) and governing verbal nouns (*She left without saying anything*).

2 Also defunct is the use of *without* as a conjunction meaning 'unless', 'except when', although it still occurs in regional or dialect use and will be found occasionally in modern fiction: *I can truthfully say he never sat an exam without he was bad with his asthma*—Pat Barker, 1991.

3 *How'd you like to make yourself a passel* [= parcel] *of money without hardly havin' to do any work?*—D. Westheimer, 1973. The use of *without* + *hardly*, which is a combination of a negative and an implied negative, is non-standard. The standard expression is *almost without* (or in some contexts, *with hardly*: *His eyes flickered to left and right, with hardly a turn of the head*—T. Barnes, 1991).

wizened, meaning 'thin and shrivelled', is a Scottish word derived from Old English that has now become a general English word.

woman *see* LADY, WOMAN.

-woman. This suffix denoting female occupations is in decline as the search for *gender-neutrality gathers pace. *Policewoman* has been largely replaced by *police officer* (or *woman police constable*, *WPC*), *chairwoman*, *spokeswoman*, and others by forms in -*person*, and so on. Other compounds that remain in use generally have a cultural or historical reference, e.g. *needlewoman*, *servicewoman*. *See* FEMININE DESIGNATIONS.

womanly, womanish. *Womanly* is a complimentary word applied to women and meaning 'having the good qualities of women', whereas *womanish* is applied to men and is usually derogatory in the sense 'effeminate, unmanly'. *See also* FEMALE, FEMININE.

womyn is a non-standard spelling of *women*, invented by feminists to replace the element -*men*. It is used occasionally in North America but has little currency in Britain. *See also* WIMMIN.

wonder is followed by *whether* or *if*, and in more formal writing can take a subjunctive verb in the past: *Hilliard wondered whether Barton were not right after all*—Susan Hill, 1971 / *They had never had a serious conversation, and she wondered if that were wrong*—Anita Brookner, 1992. In general contexts, however, an ordinary verb is normal: *She wondered if I was free to have dinner at her house*—C. McCarry, 1977. For the type *I shouldn't wonder if . . . see* NOT 5.

wont, the surviving past participle of an obsolete verb *won* meaning 'to accustom oneself to', is pronounced *wohnt* and should be distinguished from *won't*, the contracted form of *will not*. It is used in two principal ways: followed by a *to*-infinitive as in *They were wont to say*, and as a noun in the type *as is their wont*. The form *wonted*, meaning 'accustomed, habitual', is used before a noun, as in *He showed his wonted skill*.

won't, the contracted form of *will not*, is the only survivor of several forms derived from *woll* (= *will*) *not*.

woodenness is spelt with two *n*s in the middle.

woollen, woolly are the spellings in BrE, and in AmE *woolen, wooly*.

word order *see* INVERSION.

workaday, workday. *Workaday* is now used only as an adjective in the meaning 'ordinary, everyday'. The usual nouns for a day on which work is done are *workday* and *working day*. In AmE, *workday* also means 'the part of the day used for work' (as in *an 8-hour workday*).

worldly, meaning 'temporal or earthly', has two *l*s.

World Wide Web *see* WEB.

worsen *see* -EN VERBS FROM ADJECTIVES.

worser. *Changed to a worser shape thou canst not be*—Shakespeare, *1 Henry VI* v.iv, 1591 / *Woke up the next morning with a worser headache*—CNN news transcripts, AmE 2002 [*OEC*]. This so-called 'double comparative' has good literary credentials, but is not standard in current English.

worship has inflected forms *worshipped, worshipping*, and a derivative form *worshipper* in BrE, and often *worshiped, worshiping, worshiper* in AmE.

worst. The idiom *if the worst comes to the worst* has been standard in BrE since the late 16c. In AmE it usually occurs in the form *if worst comes to worst*.

worth while, worthwhile. The traditional distinction is to use the two-word form predicatively (i.e. after a verb, as in *The experiment was worth while*) and the one-word form attributively (i.e. before a noun, as in *a worthwhile experiment*). However, the one-word form is increasingly used in all contexts. Note that the correct use with a following verbal noun is *worth*, not *worth while* (*It was worth doing* / ☒ *It was worth while doing*).

would *see* SHOULD AND WOULD.

wrack *see* RACK.

wrath, wrathful, wroth. *Wrath* is an archaic or literary noun meaning 'anger', and is pronounced *rawth* or *roth*, or in AmE *rath*. *Wrathful* is the corresponding adjective meaning 'angry'. *Wroth* is also an adjective, and is always used predicatively, i.e. after a verb, especially in the expression *wax* *wroth* meaning 'to become angry'. As these words move further back into the remoteness of archaism, their distinctions are becoming blurred, with *wroth* in particular being used where *wrath* is needed.

wreak is used in the expression *wreak havoc* (*on*). It is derived from an Old English verb meaning 'to avenge'. The unrelated verb *work* is also used in this connection, with its archaic participial form *wrought* occasionally coming into service: *Moko, the banana disease, has already wreaked havoc on the trade—Times*, 1983 / *A series of worms and viruses has wrought havoc on Windows PCs—Business Pundit*, AmE 2004.

wreath has the plural form *wreaths*, pronounced reedhz or reeths. The verb, meaning 'to encircle with a wreath', is spelt *wreathe* and is pronounced reedh.

write. *I had written my mother about all this—New Yorker*, 1987. The transitive use with the recipient as the object is well known in AmE, but has disappeared in BrE, except occasionally in old-fashioned commercial correspondence (*Please write us at your convenience*).

writ large. *Every project has success writ large over it—Author*, 1994. This still-popular phrase is first recorded in the 17c, and is based on a participial form of *write* that is otherwise obsolete.

wrong, like *right*, exists as an adverb alongside *wrongly*. It is used with a limited number of words and means roughly 'incorrectly', or 'astray', as in *We guessed wrong* and *I said it wrong*. In these cases *wrongly* can also be used, but the effect can be somewhat ponderous. *Wrongly* is appropriate in the more general meaning 'in error' or 'in the wrong way', especially when coming before rather than after an adjective or participle (= in error) *It arrived at Heathrow as mishandled luggage, having been wrongly off-loaded in Rome from a flight from Australia to London—Daily Telegraph*, 1972 / (= in the wrong way) *The court was told the machine had been wrongly calibrated at the police station—*news website, BrE 2003 [OEC]. Note that in the expression *go wrong, wrong* is probably not an adverb but still an adjective (agreeing with the subject as with *become* and other verbs).

wroth see WRATH, WRATHFUL, WROTH.

wrought is an old past form and past participle of the verb *work*, surviving only in the term *wrought iron*, in the occasional variant *wrought up* (= worked up, i.e. agitated, nervous), and as a form of the expression *work havoc* (*see* WREAK).

wry has inflected forms *wryer, wryest*, and derivative forms *wryly, wryness*.

wych is the usual spelling in the name of the tree *wych elm*. It is apparently derived from a Germanic form meaning 'to bend'.

w

-x is used to form the plural of a number of loanwords from French that are not fully naturalized, for example *chateau* (= a castle or large house) and *plateau*. Other words tend to be treated in a more native way and form plurals in *-s*, for example *gateau*. Usage is unstable in this regard.

Xerox, a proprietary term for a make of photocopier, should be spelt with a capital *X*. As a verb, however, it is spelt *xerox*.

-xion. A small number of nouns derived from Latin words ending in *-io*, *-ionis* have been spelt either *-ction* or *-xion* in English. Where there is a choice, current usage tends to prefer *-ction* (e.g.

deflection, inflection), but in other cases *-xion* is the only ending in use (the main cases are *complexion, crucifixion,* and *transfixion*).

Xmas. In this abbreviated form of the name *Christmas*, first recorded in the 18c, the initial *X* represents a Greek *chi* (= ch), the first letter of the name *Christ*. It is a convenient shortening commonly used in newspaper headlines, on cards, and in personal letters, but it is better to pronounce it as 'Christmas' than as 'ex-mass' which some people consider tasteless.

X-ray is spelt in this way as a noun and verb.

y and i. For problems of spelling involving *y* and *i* in words, *see* CIPHER; GYPSY, GIPSY; LYCHGATE; PYGMY; SIPHON; STYMIE; TYRE, TIRE; TYRO; WYCH.

Yankee. A *Yankee* is properly an inhabitant of New England or of the northern states of the USA, and the name was used with this meaning during the American Civil War. On the other hand the shortened form *Yank* is commonly applied to Americans generally. Both words are informal only, and their origin, though widely discussed, remains unclear.

ye, a pseudo-archaic form of the definite article *the*, is used commercially in names such as *ye olde tea-shoppe*. Though pronounced yee, its first letter represents an old runic letter called 'thorn' (pronounced dh as in modern *this*), which in written form had come to resemble the letter *y*.

yeah is the conventional spelling of the informal shortened form of *yes*. In print it is used only to represent a spoken form, commonly used in the phrase *Oh yeah?* expressing doubt or disbelief.

year *see* DAY, MONTH, WEEK, YEAR. A possessive apostrophe is needed in expressions of the type (singular) *a year's imprisonment* and (plural) *two years' imprisonment*.

yes, used as a noun (*refused to give a definite yes*), has the plural form *yeses*.

yet and still. 1 These two adverbs used to be more interchangeable than they are now. A sentence such as *Mrs. Throckmorton was shot in her apartment last night, and the bullet is in her yet*, in which *yet* denotes continuity of action up to the time in question, would be acceptable, especially informally, in America (the source of this extract) and Scotland, but in the English of England *still* would be used instead of *yet* and the word order would usually be different: *. . . and the bullet is still in her*. In England, *yet* is used to mean 'up to this time' or 'up to then' (1) in a question or after a negative (*Is she 21 yet?* / *She wasn't yet 18* / *Have they arrived yet?* / *They haven't arrived yet* [or *haven't yet arrived*] / *I hadn't yet decided what to do*). Note the position of *yet* in these examples. In the negative examples, *still* can also be used, e.g. *They still haven't arrived*. Note that with action verbs the perfect tense (formed with *have*) or past perfect tense (formed with *had*) is used, but in AmE a past tense formed with *do* is also used informally: *Did they arrive yet?*

2 It is worth pointing out that in Scottish English a question such as *Is it raining yet?* would be ambiguous, equivalent to the English English questions 'Has it started to rain yet?' and 'Is it still raining?'. In conversation, intonation would normally clarify, but this might need to be accentuated south of the border.

3 In affirmative contexts, *yet* is used as a more formal alternative to *still* in the following types of phrase, normally with *be*, *have to*, or a modal verb such as *can*: *We'd better do it while there is yet time / I have yet to receive a reply / I can hear her yet.*

4 See also ALREADY 2.

Yiddish words in English. *See box opposite.*

yodel. The verb has inflected forms *yodelled*, *yodelling* in BrE, and usually *yodeled*, *yodeling* in AmE.

yogurt is the preferred spelling, although *yoghurt* (with an *h*) is also common. It is pronounced **yog**-uht in BrE, and **yoh**-guht in AmE and in Australia and New Zealand.

yoke, yolk. A *yoke* is a wooden crosspiece of the kind fixed over the necks of work animals. A *yolk* is the yellow part of an egg (and is related to the word *yellow*).

you and I. For *between you and I*, see BETWEEN 5.

you name it is a cliché of the 1960s, still much in vogue. It means 'and so on, and other familiar things of the same kind' and often has a continuation: *'I've picked up rocks, glass, parts of beer cans—you name it,' she said—New Yorker*, 1988 / *Viruses, Trojans, scripts, malware packages you name it, you'll end up with it—Register*, BrE 2004 [OEC].

you're is an informal contracted form of *you are* (*You're sure, are you?*). It needs to be distinguished from the identical-sounding possessive word *your*.

yours. This possessive pronoun, as used in *The blame is not mine but yours*, is written without an apostrophe. In compound subjects connected by *and*,

the correct form is (e.g.) *Our children and yours should have a joint party*, not ⊠ *Yours and our children should have a joint party*.

yourself, yourselves. *Yourself* (singular) and *yourselves* (plural) have two primary roles, (1) as reflexives (*Are you talking about yourself? / Help yourselves to biscuits*), and (2) as emphatic words in apposition to the pronoun *you* (*You yourself told me so*).

Staff who deal with customers in restaurants, call centres, etc., sometimes use *yourself* as a substitute for you, e.g. *is this soup for yourself? is the appliance for yourself, sir*? Though best avoided in writing, *yourself* sounds more formal and less direct than *you*, and is thus perceived as more polite by those who use it.

yous, youse are regional and dialectal forms of *you* (plural). In Britain they are associated especially with the speech of Glasgow and Liverpool, and they occur in American, Australian, and New Zealand literature reproducing non-standard speech: *It's the least I can do for youse—*E. Jolley, AusE 1985 / *By time youse all get here, youse big thirsty—New Zealand Ezine*, 2004.

youth has the plural form *youths*, pronounced yoodhz. As well as meaning 'a young person' (in BrE usually a boy but in other varieties a boy or girl) and 'a young time of life' (*in their youth*), it has a collective sense 'young people', normally preceded by *the*: *The youth of Australia have been saved once more from the dreaded lurgy, marijuana—It*, 1971. In this meaning it is commonly used in attributive position (i.e. before a noun, e.g. *youth centre*, *youth movement*). When used in newspaper reports with reference to a person, it tends to be disapproving in tone: *Police arrested a*

YIDDISH WORDS IN ENGLISH.

Yiddish is a vernacular language used by European Jews, based chiefly on High German with Hebrew and Slavonic borrowings, and written in Hebrew characters. English, especially AmE, has adopted many words and phrases from Yiddish in the last two hundred years or so, and some of these are given in the table below.

item	meaning
bagel	hard ring-shaped ring of bread
chutzpah	shameless audacity
klutz	clumsy or inept person
kvell	to boast or gloat
mazuma	money
need it like a hole in the head	can well do without it
nosh	food
schlemiel	clumsy person, fool
schlep	to haul or drag
schmuck	abusive term for a person
shtoom	silent
What's with you?	What's the matter?

15-year-old youth (in the singular this generally means *boy* unless otherwise specified, but *boy* in place of *youth* in this statement would reduce the sinister import).

-yse, -yze. The BrE English form of the suffix is *-yse* (*analyse, catalyse, dialyse, paralyse*). In AmE the normal forms are *analyze*, etc.

y

zap *verb* is a vogue word from the last part of the 20c meaning 'to liven or revitalize', and commonly occurs as a phrasal verb with *up*: *A whole head of garlic is olive-oiled, oven-baked, blobbed with brie, then zapped up with a sprig of fresh thyme on top*—Western Living, 1991. An earlier meaning, 'to kill', familiar from comic strips and the world of electronic games, is still in use, as is a more recent meaning, 'to switch casually from one television channel to another'. The inflected forms are *zapped, zapping*.

zenith is pronounced **zen**-ith in BrE and **zee**-nith in AmE.

zero. The noun can have the plural *zeros* or *zeroes*, but the first is rather more frequent; and the verb (normally used in the form *zero in*) has inflected forms *zeroes, zeroed, zeroing*.

zeugma *see* SYLLEPSIS.

zigzag. The verb has inflected forms *zigzagged, zigzagging*.

zinc. The adjectival form meaning 'coated in zinc' is *zinced*.

zoology. The older pronunciation zoh-**ol**-uh-ji, favoured by *OED* editors and supposedly by zoologists themselves, has largely given way in general use to zoo-**ol**-uhji (influenced by the common shortening *zoo*). Despite occasional complaints this form is likely to prevail.